# Teacher Preparation Classroom

See a demo at
**www.prenhall.com/teacherprep/demo**

## Your Class. Their Careers. Our Future. Will your students be prepared?

We invite you to explore our new, innovative and engaging website and all that it has to offer you, your course, and tomorrow's educators! Preview this site today at www.prenhall.com/teacherprep/demo. Just click on "go" on the login page to begin your exploration.

Organized around the major courses pre-service teachers take, the Teacher Preparation site provides media, student/teacher artifacts, strategies, research articles, and other resources to equip your students with the quality tools needed to excel in their courses and prepare them for their first classroom.

This ultimate on-line education resource will provide you and your students access to:

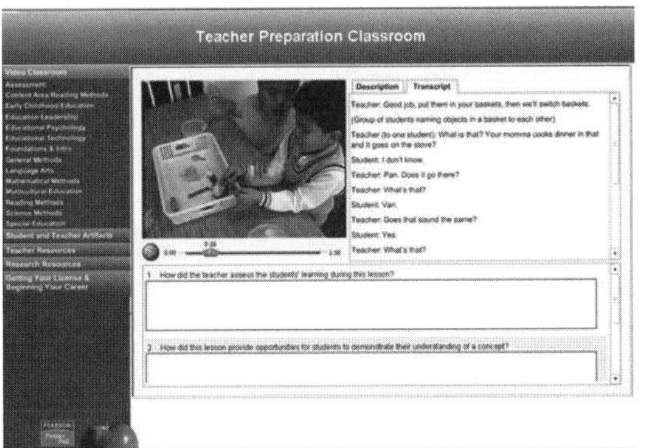


**Online Video Library.** More than 250 video clips—each tied to a course topic and framed by learning goals and Praxis-type questions—capture real teachers and students working in real classrooms.

**Student and Teacher Artifacts.** More than 200 student and teacher classroom artifacts—each tied to a course topic and framed by learning goals and application questions—provide a wealth of materials and experiences to help your students observe children's developmental learning.

**Lesson Plan Builder.** Step-by-step guidelines and lesson plan examples to support students as they learn to build high-quality lesson plans.

**Articles and Readings** Over 500 articles from ASCD's renowned journal *Educational Leadership* are available. The site also includes Research Navigator, a searchable database of additional educational journals.

**Strategies and Lessons** Over 500 research-supported instructional strategies appropriate for a wide range of grade levels and content areas.

**Licensure and Career Tools** Resources devoted to helping your students pass their licensure exam, learn standards, law, and public policies, plan a teaching portfolio, and succeed in their first year of teaching.

### How to ORDER *Teacher Prep* for you and your students:

For students to receive a *Teacher Prep* Access Code with this text, instructor **must** provide a special value pack ISBN number on their textbook order form. To receive this special ISBN, please email: **Merrill.marketing@pearsoned.com** and provide the following information:

- Name and Affiliation
- Author/Title/Edition of Merrill text

Upon ordering *Teacher Prep* for their students, instructors will be given a lifetime *Teacher Prep* Access Code.

NINTH EDITION

# *Strategies for Teaching Learners with Special Needs*

EDWARD A. POLLOWAY
Lynchburg College

JAMES R. PATTON
University of Texas

LORETTA SERNA
University of New Mexico

Upper Saddle River, New Jersey
Columbus, Ohio

**Library of Congress Cataloging-in-Publication Data**

Polloway, Edward A.
Strategies for teaching learners with special needs/Edward A. Polloway, James R. Patton, Loretta Serna.—9th ed.
p. cm.
Includes bibliographical references and index.
ISBN-13: 978-0-13-179155-8
ISBN-10: 0-13-179155-9
1. Children with mental disabilities—Education—United States. 2. Children with mental disabilites—Education—United States—Curricula. 3. Learning disabled children—Education—United States. 4. Individualized instruction—United States. 5. Remedial teaching—United States. I. Patton, James R. II. Serna, Loretta. III. Title.
LC4631.P65 2007
371.92—dc22

2007024217

**Vice President and Executive Publisher:** Jeffery W. Johnston
**Executive Editor:** Ann Castel Davis
**Development Editor:** Heather Doyle Fraser
**Editorial Assistant:** Penny Burleson
**Production Editor:** Sheryl Glicker Langner
**Production Coordination:** Rebecca K. Giusti, GGS Book Services
**Design Coordinator:** Diane C. Lorenzo
**Photo Coordinator:** Valerie Schultz
**Cover Designer:** Ali Mohrman
**Cover Image:** Super Stock
**Production Manager:** Laura Messerly
**Director of Marketing:** David Gesell
**Marketing Manager:** Autumn Purdy
**Marketing Coordinator:** Brian Mounts

This book was set in Garamond Book by GGS Book Services. It was printed and bound by Edwards Brothers. The cover was printed by Phoenix Color Corp.

**Photo Credits:** Patrick White/Merrill, pp. 2, 196, 453; Lori Whitley/Merrill, p. 22; Valerie Schultz/Merrill, p. 53; Maria B. Vonada/Merrill, p. 87; Scott Cunningham/Merrill, pp. 120, 310, 347; David Mager/Pearson Learning Photo Studio, p. 163; Cynthia Cassidy/Merrill, p. 227; Barbara Schwartz/Merrill, p. 263; Anne Vega/Merrill, p. 372; Liz Moore/Merrill, p. 398; Todd Yarrington/Merrill, p. 424.

---



Pearson Education Ltd.
Pearson Education Singapore Pte. Ltd.
Pearson Education Canada, Ltd.
Pearson Education—Japan
Pearson Education Australia Pty. Limited
Pearson Education North Asia Ltd.
Pearson Educación de Mexico, S.A. de C.V.
Pearson Education Malaysia Pte. Ltd.

10 9 8 7 6 5 4 3 2 1
ISBN-13: 978-0-13-179155-8
ISBN-10: 0-13-179155-9

*Ed Polloway:*
*In Memory of Edward J. Polloway*

*Jim Patton:*
*In Memory of Dorothy K. Patton*

*Loretta Serna:*
*In Memory of Irene G. Serna*

# Preface

*Strategies for Teaching Learners with Special Needs* is now in its ninth edition. We are pleased to share this book with preservice and inservice professional educators and hope that the information contained herein will complement your knowledge and skills for working with students with disabilities and other learning challenges.

*Strategies for Teaching Learners with Special Needs* was published on a four-year cycle from 1977 to 2005. Covering a series of years that sound like prime numbers, the text has thus come out subsequent to every election year since the election of Jimmy Carter and has served as, one might say, an inauguration gift for Presidents Carter, Reagan, Bush, Clinton, and Bush. This edition follows the 2005 edition as a third-year revision. We thank Heather Fraser and Allyson Sharp at Merrill for convincing us that we needed to change our revision schedule to reflect the significant changes that have impacted special education in recent years and the implications for teachers, in particular, of the reauthorization of IDEA in 2004 and the widespread application of the standards and regulations associated with the No Child Left Behind Act.

When a textbook goes through multiple revisions, it develops its own stories and those stories necessarily reflect the lives of the individuals who have been involved in its development. In 1975, Dr. Jim Payne, teacher extraordinaire, magician, and mentor, casually mentioned to James (Smitty) Smith and me at lunch at a Hardee's that he had an offer from Merrill Publishing to develop a methods book in special education but was too busy at that time to do so. Smitty and I stopped Jim in mid-cherry pie and demanded that he reconsider, assuring him that the two of us would gladly share the burden of getting the book written (in spite of the fact that our experience was almost nonexistent in textbook development at that time). In order to be allowed to finish his pie, he consented and the first edition, with fourth author Ruth Ann Payne as the practitioner authority and dispenser of good sense for the project, moved forward.

Several years later, we lost Smitty, a wonderful colleague and most special friend who is still missed by all of those who had the good fortune to know him. The book moved on into its third edition, nevertheless, with the addition of our close friend, Jim Patton, as the fourth author. In addition, the book took on a more generic special education focus and broadened its emphasis beyond that of mental retardation. The fourth edition continued under the authorship of Jim and Ruth Ann Payne, Jim Patton, and myself, and became truly a generic book in terms of methods for students with high-incidence disabilities.

Jim Payne saw *Strategies for Teaching Learners with Special Needs* as an opportunity both for us to take on increased responsibilities and also to mentor new persons in the field, thus he removed himself from the text after the fourth edition. For the fifth and sixth edition, Jim Patton and I served as co-authors of the text. We also mourned the loss of Ruth Ann Payne, a person who had taught us so much about special education and who served as a surrogate mother for us.

In keeping with Jim Payne's legacy, Jim Patton invited Loretta Serna to join us as co-author of first one and then several chapters. Loretta brought to the book expertise that Jim and I could only dream of having, and we were pleased to have her join us as third author on the seventh edition. Her work continues to make the ninth edition what we believe to be a unique contribution to the special education literature, particularly because of the breadth of coverage that is presented within the book.

## ORGANIZATION OF THE TEXT

Although much of the core content remains true to that of previous editions, we have made some significant organizational and content changes in the ninth edition. As in previous editions, the chapters in Part I, Teaching Learners with Special Needs, serve as a foundation for the later chapters in the text. In Part I we discuss:

- Special Education in an Era of Inclusion and Standards (Chapter 1)
- Strategies for Collaboration (Chapter 2)
- Strategies for Curriculum Development, Effective Instruction, and Classroom Adaptations (Chapter 3)
- Strategies for Classroom Management and Behavioral Supports (Chapter 4)

In Part II, Content Areas, we discuss how to put the information from Part I into action with strategies for specific content areas:

- Spoken Language (Chapter 5)
- Reading: Introduction and Word Recognition (Chapter 6)
- Reading Comprehension (Chapter 7)
- Written Language (Chapter 8)
- Mathematics (Chapter 9)
- Science and Social Studies (Chapter 10)
- Creative Arts: Visual Arts, Music, Dance, and Drama (Chapter 11)

In Part III, Critical Skills, we thoroughly discuss additional strategies that cross all content areas:

- Study Skills (Chapter 12)
- Social Competence and Self-Determination (Chapter 13)
- Functional Academics and Career Development (Chapter 14)
- Transitions Across the School Years (Chapter 15)

## SPECIAL FEATURES OF THE NINTH EDITION

The focus for the ninth edition of *Strategies for Teaching Learners with Special Needs* is on effective teaching strategies for students being taught in any setting. This increased emphasis on successful strategies—in the text and in your teaching—will enable students with special needs to be successful in inclusive classrooms. Additionally, we have added or enhanced the following features in our attempt to create a more balanced and useful text.

- **Teaching Tips:** There are two Teaching Tips features in all of the content area chapters—one that relates to an elementary classroom and one that relates to a middle/secondary school classroom.
- **Focus on Grade Level:** In addition to the Teaching Tips features in the content area chapters, there are sections within each of these chapters that discuss strategies and activities specific to elementary students and also those strategies that work best with students in middle and secondary school.
- **Technology in the Classroom:** All of the content area chapters contain a section on technology in the classroom to help facilitate a better understanding of how technology can be used with all students in this era of inclusion and standards.
- **Diversity in the Classroom:** Throughout the text we have included diversity features that relate specifically to chapter content and give readers a broader understanding of today's classroom.
- **Making It Work:** This section summarizes key validated approaches within a given subject area.

### Instructor Supplements

- Online Instructor's Manual with Test Items: Each chapter of the Online Instructor's Manual with Test Items contains the following: chapter outline, chapter objectives, key themes, instructor activities, student activities (separated by elementary and middle/ secondary level), author recommended readings/journal articles, resources, and a test bank with answer key (multiple choice, true/false, short answer, and essay).
- Online PowerPoint Lecture Presentation: Every lecture presentation (in PowerPoint) highlights the key concepts and content for each chapter.

Both the Online Instructor's Manual with Test Items and the Online PowerPoint Lecture Presentations are available online. To access these resources, go to www.prenhall.com and click on the Instructor Support button and then go to the Download Supplements section. Here you will be able to log in or complete a one-time registration for a user name and password. The Instructor Resource Center opens the door to a variety of print and media resources in downloadable, digital format. As a registered faculty member, you can log in directly to premium online products and download resource files directly to your computer.

## ACKNOWLEDGMENTS

After nine editions and the stories briefly noted above, we also recognize the contributions of many other persons to the development of this text. Of particular note are the multiple edition contributions of chapters by Rosel Schewel, Glenn Buck, Lynda Miller, John Hoover, and Ginger Blalock. For those persons who have used previous editions of the book, we know that the respective chapters related to reading, creative arts, language development, study skills, and collaboration have all been of high quality because of the contributions of these experts in the field.

In addition, a number of other persons helped with the book or with individual chapters; we have recognized their contributions throughout previous editions and regret that they are too numerous to note here. One colleague that I need to mention is Betty Shelton, who has supported our efforts over eight editions of this book and has made it possible for me to work with Jim, Loretta, and the Merrill staff in keeping the books updated and relevant for generations of special educators. For this particular edition, we also are most appreciative of the support given by Shelly Pearce, Amy Smith-Thomas, Aaron Johnstone, and Julie Beyer, whose efforts in helping us research specific topics, track down elusive references, and secure valued permissions have made it possible for us to approximate the ambitious production schedule that Heather Fraser has set for us. The fact that the book was completed is a further credit to Heather's gentle yet insistent guidance.

Finally, we give special thanks to those individuals who provided recommendations for the development of the ninth edition: Ellen Brantlinger, Indiana University, Bloomington; Melissa Jones, Eastern Illinois University; Robert F. Moore, University of Miami; and Diane Torres-Velasquez, University of New Mexico.

Our hope is that this book will enhance your skills as you take on the world's most important work, that of teacher and particularly that of teacher of individuals with special needs.

Edward A. Polloway

# *Brief Contents*

# Contents

*NOTE:* Every effort has been made to provide accurate and current information in this book. However, the Internet and information on it are constantly changing, so it is inevitable that some f the Internet addresses listed in this textbook will change.

P A R T   O N E

# Teaching Learners with Special Needs

CHAPTER

# 1

# *Special Education in an Era of Inclusion and Standards*

Few careers can promise the opportunities for service to others and for personal growth that teaching can. Teaching can bring rewards and personal fulfillment to confident, well-prepared teachers. Students learning from these teachers can acquire the knowledge and skills they will need to pursue academic and life dreams. Moreover, they will develop the ability to apply what they have learned to the everyday challenges of life.

This text provides strategies and methods for teaching students with academic, social, and behavioral difficulties. The book emphasizes practical, relevant teaching approaches derived from theory, research, and practical experience. The teaching strategies presented are intended to enable beginning teachers to achieve classroom success as soon as possible and also to provide experienced teachers with an opportunity to extend and refine their repertoire of knowledge and skills. Overall, the text has two broad objectives. The first is to direct attention to the necessity for effective teaching methods that will result in the learning of specific skills. Second, the text presents appropriate curricula and instructional materials to ensure that learning proves to be both *meaningful* today and *relevant* for the future.

This chapter introduces a number of key concepts that are the foundation of subsequent chapters. To achieve this objective, the chapter begins with a discussion of changes that have occurred in schools in recent years. The next section identifies the target populations for whom the topics addressed in the book are most appropriate and raises select concerns about teaching these target groups. Next, a preliminary discussion of federal legislation provides a backdrop for the delivery of educational services to students who have special learning needs. Following this discussion, attention is directed to current key elements that define special education today. The next section introduces a model of effective instruction on which much of the instructional content of the book is based. The subsequent section focuses on a consideration of teachers' roles in an ever-changing world of education. The final section provides a brief overview to the structure and organization of the book.

## A NEW WORLD ORDER

Special education is different today in many dramatic ways than it was in the not-too-distant past. Today, standards-based education drives what schools do, how teachers function, and how students respond. One of the dominant themes in special education is inclusion. The desire to create a system where students with special needs receive their education in the general education classroom and for these students to have access to the general education curriculum is clearly evident from recent federal initiatives.

Special educators need new knowledge bases and skill sets to function effectively in the multitiered system that now exists to address the needs of students with learning-related needs or who are placed at risk for other reasons (e.g., homeless). The role of the special education professional has changed in recent years, and dramatically so in some cases—a point that will be discussed later in the chapter. With these changes, students in general have been the beneficiaries when programs are successful. For example, as a prominent special educator notes, "we have developed instructional programs that fit also in regular classes such as classwide peer tutoring, cognitive strategies, and direct instruction. A large handful of instructional models have been researched and developed and are working with large numbers of children" (Polloway, 2002, p. 110).[1] A similar observation is as follows: "The field has developed advanced methods for the prevention of problems for students in general [e.g., self-regulation, curriculum-based measures, peer tutoring, memory strategies]. Their development has led to their use in general education. The tools are there, even if they are not being used. Thus

[1]This quote is taken from interview protocols with distinguished special education professionals as reported by Polloway (2002).

they do not have as great an impact as a consequence" (Polloway, 2002, p. 106).[2]

Teachers are encouraged to carefully consider their role in facilitating the inclusion of students with disabilities in general education and in evaluating the efficacy of these efforts. We encourage the use of the term **supported education** (Hamre-Nietupski, McDonald, & Nietupski, 1992; T. Smith, Polloway, Patton, & Dowdy, 2008) for inclusion to emphasize that successful inclusion hinges on the provision of appropriate supports in the general education classroom as a basis for establishing a successful learning environment for students.

## TARGET POPULATIONS AND ASSOCIATED CONCERNS

The primary focus of this text is on strategies for teaching students who experience learning difficulties. Included in this generic category are subgroups of students who may have been identified by schools in a variety of ways, such as learning disabled, dyslexic, attention deficit hyperactivity disordered (ADHD), developmentally delayed, developmentally disabled, mild mentally retarded, emotionally disturbed, and behaviorally disordered. The particular terms vary on a state-by-state basis (and often regionally) but taken collectively represent individuals who have often been referred to as constituting high-incidence disabilities. We prefer the term **high incidence** to **mild disabilities** because the latter term understates the significant learning needs of these students and thus inadvertently can be used to question their need for specialized instruction. Based on data from the U.S. Department of Education, four key groups of students (those with learning disabilities, speech or language impairments, mental retardation, or emotional disturbance) make up nearly 93% of the school-age students served under the Individuals with Disabilities Education Act (U.S. Department of Education, 2002).

Although we have begun our discussion of populations of students with disabilities from a categorical perspective, teachers are encouraged to consider three caveats (presented in order of ascending importance) when attempting to match curriculum design and instructional methods to students' needs. First, the populations associated with specific categorical groups is continually influenced by public policy decisions and both research-informed and nonresearch-based professional decisions. Additionally, efforts to revise definitions and terminology regularly bring about regulatory changes that may further alter the populations served under the labels of learning disabilities, emotional or behavioral disorders, mental retardation, or other health impaired (see, for example, Luckasson et al., 2002; Polloway, 2002). As an example of key policy issues, variance in identification patterns across cultural groups must be considered for its implications.

Second, and more significantly, categorical labels convey little about curriculum design and specific teaching strategies that should be used. Such labels at face value indicate only that a student has met a set of arbitrary criteria established by a state for a specific disability. Furthermore, these categorical labels often indicate only that students so classified have experienced difficulty learning through traditional means or within traditionally organized general education classroom environments to such an extent that schools recognize and identify them. Ultimately, these students are likely to require more directive, intensive, extensive, innovative, and/or highly individualized instruction to reach their learning potential or require specific accommodations to existing curricular and instructional structures.

Thus, the strategies highlighted in this text may have applicability for individuals with a variety of learning problems, regardless of whether they have been labeled as disabled (e.g., learning disabled, mentally retarded, attention deficit hyperactivity disordered) or merely set apart from others in the classroom (e.g., "at-risk," remedial, or slow learners). A large number of students who can be considered "placed at risk" for having academic, social, or behavioral difficulties will not meet eligibility criteria for special education, yet may benefit greatly from the ideas contained in this book. Ultimately, an analysis of an individual's learning needs is necessary to determine the relevance of any particular curricular orientation or any specific instructional procedure.

The third and most critical concern is to ensure an appropriate curriculum for students with high-incidence disabilities. Consequently, emphasis must be directed toward achieving the balance among students' academic, social, and functional needs. For example, some students with ADHD, emotional/behavioral disorders, or learning disabilities may require differentiation in curriculum based on whether or not they are candidates for academic postsecondary education and need to satiate the course requirements for entry into postsecondary

[2]Ibid.

education. On the other hand, a more functional curriculum may be needed to prepare other students for successful community living immediately following secondary education. At the same time, these emphases must be balanced with the concern for **access to the general curriculum** as consistent with federal law (Wehmeyer, Lance, & Bashinski, 2002).

One overriding concern across categories of exceptionality and programs, services, and supports is that individual children and youth should not be focused on only in terms of their needs at the present time. Rather, an attitude typified by concurrent concern for students' success in the future must be adopted. Regardless of the population being served or the setting in which services are being delivered, all teachers must be cognizant of how their programmatic efforts ultimately will affect students' transitions into school and community environments that lie ahead; such outcomes-focused and results-oriented thinking should be at the core of educational efforts. A focus on **subsequent environments** provides a strategic direction that should be central to all instructional planning. Professional attention has been increasingly directed toward certain significant transitions: those from early intervention (Part C of IDEA) to early childhood programs, from preschool to kindergarten, from elementary to secondary school, from school to postschool settings, and from one stage of adult development to another. All such transitions are crucial for a positive quality of life.

The specific transition that has received the most attention has been that from school to postschool settings. Over the years teachers and researchers have devoted much time and energy to the task of preparing students with disabilities for life after high school. Nevertheless, adults with disabilities are proportionately underrepresented in the nation's workforce as well as in many educational, training, and employment programs and coincidentally are overrepresented in the ranks of school dropouts. The transition process is complex, involving the efforts of students, their families, school personnel, and an array of adult service providers (e.g., vocational rehabilitation counselors, postsecondary educators, and various community agency staff). Cultural issues must be considered and culturally responsive transition planning must be implemented (Trainor & Patton, in press). Because students are guaranteed the right to an appropriate education, they should also be assisted in benefiting from it—both during their school years and in experiencing personal fulfillment as adults. This commitment has always been a major tenet of this book and underlies the focus of this edition.

## CRITICAL LEGISLATIVE AND FEDERAL INITIATIVES

Special education owes much of its structure, and to some extent its very existence, to federal and state legislation. The legislative contributions (both positive and negative) have been so profound on special education programs that a prominent professional in the field indicated that "[federal] legislation is the greatest achievement [in the field]. We did not have to provide services before and now we have mandates. Though problems remain, at least the law supports what we are doing in providing special education" (Polloway, 2002, p. 108).[3] At the same time, another observation was that such legislation was "good to ensure the rights of kids to an appropriate education [but it] has not played out as intended. Some elements destined out failure as procedural foci became primary" (Polloway, 2002, p. 108).[4]

A concise survey of key legislation thus sets the foundation for this text's attention to curriculum and instruction.

### No Child Left Behind Act

Although a standards-based movement has been in existence for a number of years, this movement was solidified by the passage of the No Child Left Behind (NCLB) Act of 2001 (PL 107-110)—the reauthorization of the Elementary and Secondary Education Act (ESEA). With a major intent to better serve the "neediest" of students in our schools and to hold schools more accountable, NCLB includes a number of key provisions.

- **Increased accountability:** implementation of statewide accountability systems that are based on state standards in reading and mathematics; annual testing for all students in grades 3–8; annual statewide progress objectives that all students must reach by 2013; adequate yearly progress (AYP) evaluation of school districts and individual schools.
- **Parent and student choice:** funds available to allow parents (a) to move their children who attend "failing" Title I schools to attend a "better" public school within the school district and/or (b) to obtain supplemental educational services

[3]This quote is taken from interview protocols with distinguished education professionals as reported by Polloway (2002).
[4]Ibid.

(e.g., tutoring) from a public- or private-sector provider.
- **Greater flexibility to states, school districts, and schools:** unprecedented flexibility in the use of federal education funds.
- **Putting reading first:** goal (and funding) to ensure that every child can read by the end of third grade; emphasis on the use of scientifically based reading instruction.
- **Highly qualified teachers:** stresses the need to have "highly qualified" teachers in schools; sets a goal of having all teachers fully qualified by 2006 (Note: not yet achieved).

The NCLB Act clearly underscores the heavy reliance on standards and the high-stakes testing that accompanies them as key components of the accountability process. The focal question is *not* whether students with special needs will participate in a standard-based system but more appropriately concerns how well students with special needs will do in this new system. Almost all students with disabilities must now meet a challenging set of standards and participate in the testing process.

Those who favor the philosophy of the NCLB Act strongly support the idea that students with disabilities are now included in the accountability process where comparable results are available. As a result, a true picture of how students are doing should now be provided. Furthermore, supporters of the NCLB Act are encouraged by the fact that parents, teachers, and students themselves should develop higher expectations, resulting ultimately in higher achievement.

Opponents of the law are concerned that, as Turnbull, Turnbull, Shank, and Smith (2004) note, "the same-standards approach can conflict with the individualized needs of students as set out in their IEPs" (p. 47). Moreover, concern exists that these students will encounter significant amounts of failure in trying to meet the state-identified standards and participate in the high-stakes testing, resulting in a host of pejorative outcomes. Bottge and Yehle (1999) highlight this latter point: "Caught in a web of new standards and assessment are students who have disabilities, many of whom were not successful in school before the push for higher standards and graduation tests" (p. 23).

The NCLB Act provides great promise for students with special needs as well as some key concerns that will have to be monitored over the years. Adjustments have been made (e.g., changes in the ceiling for the number of students who are exempt from the high-stakes testing) and other changes will likely occur. The bottom line is that overall provisions of this law are now in place and will not disappear anytime soon. So, parents, teachers, and students must operate within the new system.

## Individuals with Disabilities Education Act of 2004

Over 30 years have passed since the initial passage of the Education for All Handicapped Children Act (EHA, Public Law 94–142), now referred to as the **Individuals with Disabilities Education Act (IDEA).** In spite of various efforts to restrict its interpretation, its influence on special education delivery has been profound, bolstered by significant amendments over the years that have strengthened and expanded various provisions and have extended coverage to a more broadly defined population.

This major piece of federal legislation had been amended/reauthorized three times (1983, 1990, 1997) prior to the most recent reauthorization that occurred in 2004 (PL 108–446). Although some changes were made to the law, as expected, the major provisions of IDEA remained intact. The original law (PL 94–142) initially authorized funding to the states to assist in the development, expansion, and improvement of special education programs. The spirit of the law was to provide an appropriate education to students who, in many instances, had not received such in the past. Moreover, the law also ensured the rights of all children with disabilities. Access to the funds to address these rights was dependent on adherence to mandated provisions.

The 2004 reauthorization of IDEA is noteworthy because an articulation between this law and the NCLB Act can be seen. For example, IDEA 2004 put a major emphasis on access to the general education curriculum for all students identified under the law. Some of the major components of IDEA 2004 are listed and briefly described in Table 1–1. Six key provisions of IDEA, as articulated in the original legislation, that remain the framework for IDEA 2004 are reviewed below due to their importance to the content of this book.

**Free, Appropriate Public Education.** A **free, appropriate public education (FAPE)** indicates that school districts must provide special education and related services necessary to meet the needs of students with special learning requirements. If school programs cannot meet a student's specific needs, other agencies must provide necessary services at public

**TABLE 1–1** Key components of reauthorizations of PL 94–142/IDEA

| *Reauthorization* | *Key components* |
|---|---|
| 1983 (PL 98–199) | 1. Provided incentives for states to serve preschool children with disabilities.<br>2. Required states to collect information and address issues related to students transitioning from school to postschool. |
| (PL 101–457) | 1. Mandated services for children ages three to five, lowering all of the requirements of PL 94–142 to include three- to five-year-old children.<br>2. Provided for attorney's fees in due process or court cases where parents prevailed. |
| (PL 101—476) | 1. Added autism and traumatic brain injury to the list disabilities covered under IDEA.<br>2. Charged the name of the act from the Education for All Handicapped Children Act to the individuals with Disabilities Education Act.<br>3. Required schools to initiate transition services no later than age sixteen. |
| 1997 (PL 105–17) | 1. Required schools to initiate transition planning no later than age fourteen.<br>2. Required schools to include behavior intervention plans for students with behavior problems. |

*Source:* From "IDEA 2004: Another Round of Re-Authorization Process" by T. E. C. Smith, 2005, *Remedial and Special Education, 26,* p. 316. Copyright 2005 by PRO-ED, Inc. Reprinted with permission.

expense. The schools must also furnish transportation and related services (e.g., counseling, physical therapy) when deemed necessary to ensure an appropriate education.

The 2004 IDEA reauthorization underscores the original intent of this provision of IDEA and highlights the importance of this concept to students who are suspended, expelled, or in prison (if they are under 18 years of age). Though seemingly a simple concept, the determination of appropriate education remains the subject of legal scrutiny (Bateman & Linden, 1998).

**Appropriate Evaluation.** IDEA requires that prior to a student receiving special education and related services for the first time, a full and individual initial evaluation must be conducted. The law also requires parental consent, evaluation by a team, use of more than one procedure, testing in the student's native language, and reevaluations conducted when necessary. A key element is the requirement of nondiscriminatory evaluation, a significant concern especially in the light of cultural variance in prevalence rates (i.e., overrepresentation). The language of the law states clearly that a parent must be part of the team that determines eligibility. In addition, as discussed previously, the law mandates that students with disabilities be included in general and districtwide assessments. The advent of the standards-based involvement often did not bring with it a commitment to including students with disabilities in related high-stakes assessment; IDEA 2004 now makes it official.

**Individualized Education Program.** An **individualized education program (IEP)** is a written document summarizing a student's learning program and is required for every student who qualifies for services. The major purposes of an IEP are to establish learning goals for an individual student, to determine the services the school district must provide to meet those learning goals, and to enhance communication among parents and other professionals about a student's program. Both the stated goals and the services to be delivered should depend on an analysis of a student's *present levels of performance*. New changes to the law have eliminated the mandate to have short-term objectives (STOs) as part of the IEP; nevertheless, most teachers are likely to continue to use STOs, as they provide a useful structure for addressing the goals in a student's IEP.

Attention in the IEP (according to IDEA) must be given to "how a child's disability affects the child's involvement and progress in the general curriculum." The IEP should explain the extent, if any, to which the student will not participate with students who are nondisabled. Statements related to the student's participation or lack of participation in statewide and districtwide assessments must also be included in the IEP. The increased focus on inclusion also results in the need for increased efforts to reflect access to the general curriculum for all students (Hoover & Patton, 2004a; Wehmeyer et al., 2002).

IDEA also reflects a commitment to **transition planning** for students. Transition planning and services must begin prior to a student reaching age 16.

Transition services are defined as a coordinated set of activities for a student, designed within a *results*-oriented process, which promotes movement from school to postschool activities including postsecondary education, vocational training, integrated employment, continuing and adult education, adult services, independent living, and/or community participation. The coordinated activities should be based on the individual student's needs, taking into account the student's preferences and interests, and should include instruction, community experiences, the development of employment and other postschool adult living objectives, and when appropriate, acquisition of daily living skills and functional vocational evaluation.

A critical area of consideration is assistive technology. Golden (1999) provides the following guidelines for IEP teams to consider:

- Assistive technology may be specified in any part of the IEP.
- IEP teams must consider assistive technology for each student with disabilities.
- Schools must assume maintenance or replacement responsibilities for family-owned assistive technology that is written in the IEP.
- A try-out period for the use of assistive technology in the school environment is the best assessment of how a device will work for an individual student.

**Least Restrictive Environment.** IDEA 2004 specifies that schools must educate children with disabilities—to as great an extent as possible—in general education settings with their peers who are nondisabled. The least restrictive environment (LRE) principle provides an opportunity for students to attend school in the most inclusive setting possible, which is most often defined as the general education setting (i.e., in a regular classroom). This element of IDEA has certainly fueled the trend toward inclusive classrooms as the most common setting for educating students with disabilities (U.S. Department of Education, 2002).

**Parent and Student Participation in Decision Making.** Parents have always been encouraged to participate in the special education process. However, the amount and quality of this participation has varied greatly since IDEA was first enacted. Some parents engage the process fully whereas others choose not to participate for a variety of reasons. Parental consent must accompany every decision that affects a child with a disability. Further, parents must consent to the evaluation of a student's educational abilities and needs, the determination of necessary services, and the actual placement of a child in any type of special program. Parents have the right to obtain an independent educational evaluation (IEE) of their child. Parents are considered participants in the development of their child's IEP. In addition, parents have the right to challenge or appeal any decision related to any aspect of the special education process.

**Procedural Safeguards.** Safeguards were included within IDEA to protect the rights of both parents and their children. Parents have the right to educational records, the right to obtain an IEE, the right to request a due process hearing, the right to appeal decisions, and the right to initiate civil action when appealing a final hearing decision. In addition, disciplinary language (particularly in relation to change of placement due to violation of school rules or code of conduct, weapons policy, or drug policy), the need for a functional behavioral assessment, and the development of behavioral intervention plans are also included in the recent reauthorization. Finally, IDEA also encourages efforts to increase student involvement in the decision-making processes related to their education, especially as related to transition planning.

## Section 504

Section 504 of the Rehabilitation Act has had profound effects on access for students with characteristics that have a limiting effect on their ability to learn. Any student who has a physical or mental impairment that *substantially limits* one or more *major life activities* can qualify for special services under Section 504.

Perhaps of greatest recent importance has been the use of this law to provide services to students who may not be categorized under IDEA (i.e., those who may not require special education services per se) but who nevertheless need certain accommodations and are entitled to protection under law (T. Smith, 2006). Detailed analyses of Section 504 and its implications for the schools are is discussed elsewhere (Miller & Newbill, 2006; Smith & Patton, 2000).

## Americans with Disabilities Act

Although the Americans with Disabilities Act (ADA) definitions of disability and its implications for educational programs are virtually the same as those under Section 504, this 1990 landmark legislation is critical because it represents broad civil rights coverage for individuals who are disabled. Although the specific elements of the legislation are too numerous to list, teachers who serve as advocates for persons with disabilities should be aware that this law establishes guidelines for employment, public accommodations, transportation, state and local governmental operations, and telecommunications systems. A key element is to protect individuals with disabilities who are "otherwise qualified" from discrimination (e.g., in employment; T. Smith, 2001). In the light of the Supreme Court decision in *Sutton v. United Air Lines*, this issue and related concerns under ADA will continue to receive scrutiny in the coming years (Turnbull & Stowe, 2001).

## KEY ELEMENTS OF SPECIAL EDUCATION IN SCHOOLS TODAY

Although public education has experienced a long history of criticism, professionals, business leaders, politicians, parents, and other laypersons increasingly have called for literate graduates, offering varying directions for change. The common factor is that these requests have been consistent in their demand for accountability and system reform.

Surprisingly absent from the early calls for reform in the 1980s and 1990s was direct attention to students with disabilities and to the role of special education (Thurlow, 2000). This lack of attention was particularly inopportune because this time period corresponded chronologically with increasingly urgent calls for the inclusion of students with disabilities in general education classrooms.

With the advent of the No Child Left Behind Act (2001), students with disabilities are now recognized as an important component of the school population and thus subject to the opportunities and accountability inherent in this act. These are further reflected in the work of the *President's Commission on Excellence in Special Education* (2002). The Commission stressed results rather than process, prevention and early intervention, and the importance of general and special education sharing responsibility for students with disabilities. Key recommendations as adapted from the summary provided by the President's Commission (2002) include:

1. Reduce the regulatory burden and increase flexibility (i.e., reduce paperwork and simplify regulations so that they are easily understood).
2. Simplify the process used to identify children with disabilities and implement identification practices that are based on a student's response to interventions.
3. Implement research-based early identification and intervention programs for young children with learning and behavioral difficulties.
4. Set high expectations for special education and hold local school districts accountable for results.
5. Increase parental empowerment and school choice.
6. Prevent disputes and improve dispute resolution.
7. Simplify IDEA's federal student transition requirements.
8. Invite all children and youth with disabilities to attend every IEP meeting.
9. Recruit and train highly qualified general and special education teachers.
10. Require rigorous training in the teaching of reading.

The following sections focus on a number of key elements of special education as implemented in schools today: standards-based education, inclusion, multitiered education system, access to the general education curriculum, universal design, differentiated instruction, evidenced-based practice, diversity considerations, and empowerment.

### Standards-Based Education

**Standards-based education** means that what is taught must be tied to the state-derived content and performance standards that now exist in almost all states in the core subject areas of language arts/English, mathematics, social studies, and science. The intent of developing standards is to have a common set of goals and mileposts. As Hogan (2000) suggests, standards have been developed "with the purpose of ensuring that all students can demonstrate the knowledge and skills necessary to read, write, compute, problem solve, think critically, apply technology, and communicate across subject areas" (p. 55).

In addition to these core subject areas, many states have also developed standards for other subject areas. For instance, Texas has identified standards for foundation subjects (i.e., core subjects) as well as for enrichment subjects such as foreign languages, health, and fine arts, among others.

**Key Features of Standards.** Two particular features of standards warrant some discussion: types of standards and critical elements of standards. Turnbull and colleagues (2004) offer clear explanations of the components of both of these features. Although a number of ways exist for classifying standards, the most common distinction is between content and performance standards:

- *Content standard:* knowledge, skills, and understanding that students should attain in academic subjects.
- *Performance standard:* levels of achievement that students must meet to demonstrate their proficiency in the subjects. (p. 45)

The other dimension of standards is the distinction among the terms *standards, benchmarks*, and *indicators*. A brief description of each term, as used in Kansas, is as follows:

- *Standard:* "a general statement of what a student should know and be able to do in academic subjects."
- *Benchmark:* "a specific statement of what a student should be able to do."
- *Indicator:* "a statement of knowledge or skills that a student has demonstrated in order to meet a benchmark." (p. 50)

**Curricular and Instructional Implications for Students with Special Needs.** A curricular dilemma facing professionals in special education is finding the balance between addressing the content and performance standards (general curriculum) that most students with disabilities must show progress in and ensuring that the current and future needs of students with disabilities (comprehensive curriculum) are addressed appropriately. In their informal assessment of state standards, Patton and Trainor (2002) concluded that most standards aligned well with the functional needs of students. However, making curriculum and instruction more real-life relevant requires some knowledge, skills, and effort. Most important, it requires the right attitude so that in so doing the needs of students are addressed in meaningful ways.

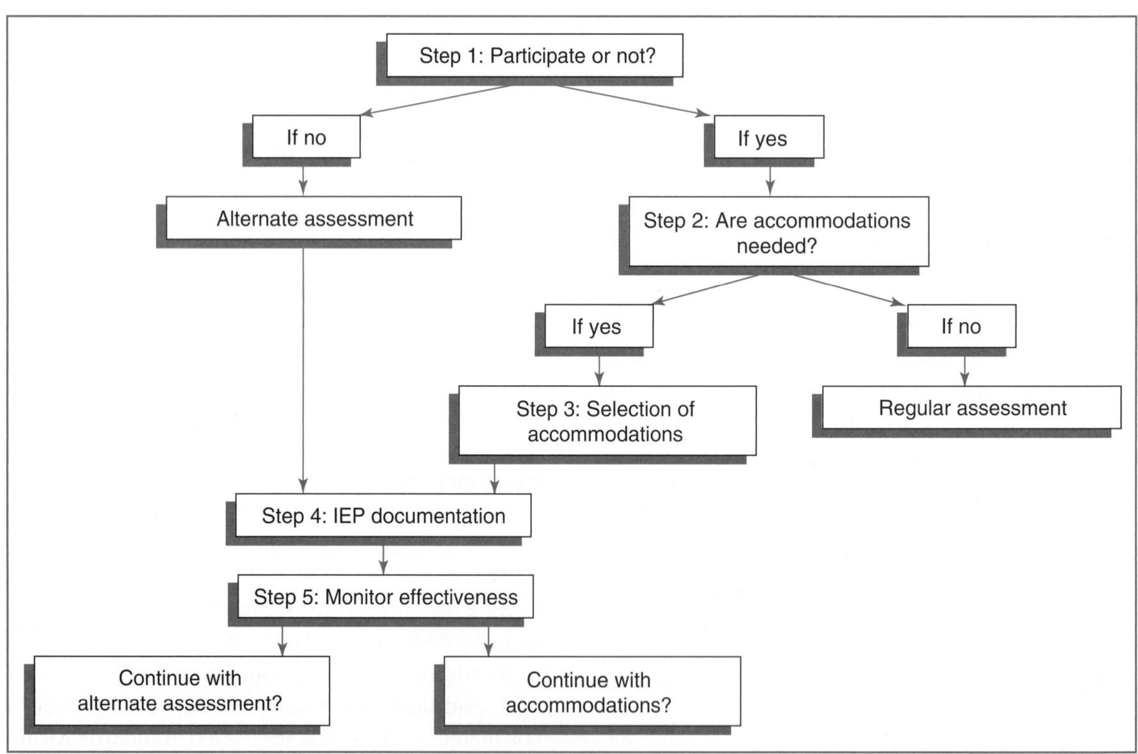


**FIGURE 1–1** High-stakes test decision-making process

*Source:* From *Step-by-Step Guide for Including Students with Disabilities in State and District-Wide Assessments,* by D. F. Bryant, J. R. Patton, and S. Vaughn, 2000, Austin, TX: PRO-ED.

**Student Accountability.** As discussed previously, the NCLB Act and standards-based reform underscore the need for accountability through student evaluation—typically by means of high-stakes standards-based testing. The NCLB Act now requires testing on an annual basis for all students in grades 3–8 in the areas of reading and mathematics.

Most students with disabilities can and will take the regular districtwide or statewide tests that nondisabled students take. A certain percentage of students with disabilities will take these tests using some type of accommodation. Some students with more significant needs will be exempt from taking a regular standards-based test and will be administered an alternative assessment. The way in which a student will take these high-stakes tests must be documented in the IEP. If and how a student will participate in this process is determined by the IEP team. The sequence of decision making for this process is depicted in Figure 1–1.

## Inclusion

The most constant theme in special education has been the commitment to providing persons with disabilities the opportunity to have a place in society. Figure 1–2 (adapted from an original concept of Polloway, Smith, Patton, & Smith, 1996) schematically outlines this trend. According to the 24th Annual Report to Congress (U.S. Department of Education, 2002), 47.32% of all students with disabilities (ages 6–21) were served in regular classes for at least 80% of the day and 28.32% in resource rooms (defined as outside regular class for 21–60% of the time) during the academic year of 1999–2000.

Voltz, Brazil, and Ford (2001) provide an important perspective on inclusion:

> [T]he physical placement of students in general education classes is not an end in and of itself but rather a means to an end. *Inclusion* does not refer to a physical space; it refers to a condition or state of being.

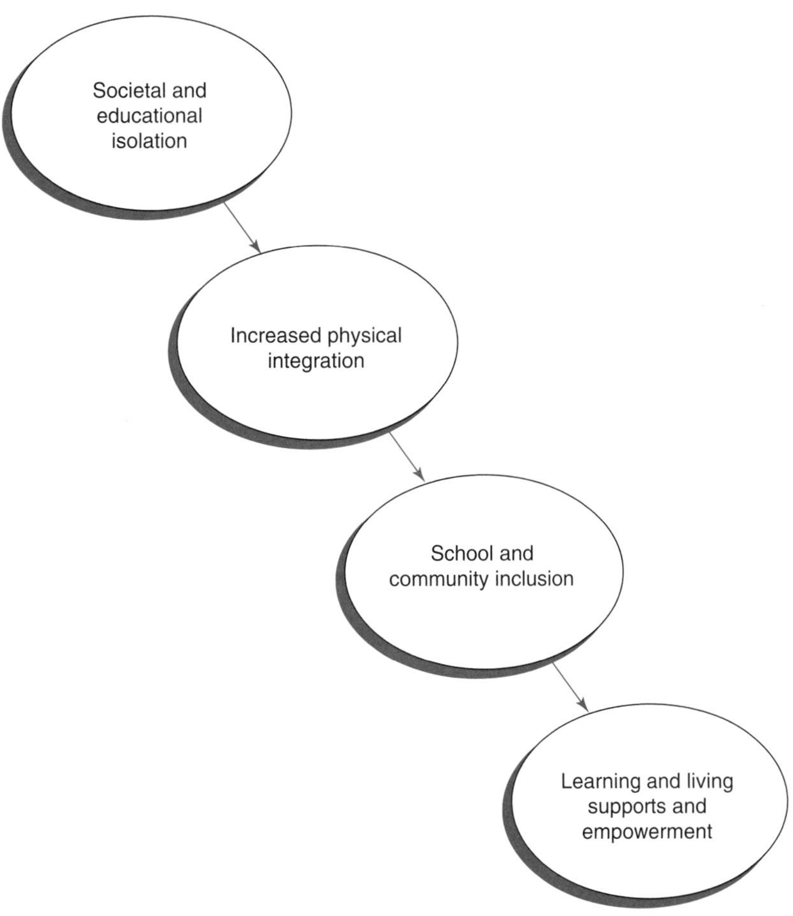


**FIGURE 1–2** Historic changes for individuals with disabilities

> The concept of inclusion implies a sense of belonging and acceptance. Hence, inclusion has more to do with how educators respond to individual differences than it has to do with specific instructional configurations. The physical placement of students with disabilities in general education classes is often overemphasized, while other aspects of developing inclusive environments are neglected ... [such as] the creation of instructional environments that promote educational success and a sense of belonging for all students. (p. 24)

## Multitiered System of Addressing the Needs of Special Learners

With the passage of the NCLB Act, multitiered instructional models have emerged for at-risk and special learners in most schools throughout the country. Other terms such as multilevel, tri-level, three-tiered, and even four-tiered instructional models may be used to describe this system. In general, tiered instruction provides layers of intervention to meet student needs, increasing in intensity as a student progresses through different tiers over time (Vaughn, 2003). Figure 1-3 highlights the three major levels of multitiered intervention.

As shown in Figure 1-3, Hoover and Patton (in press) define the different tiers in the following way:

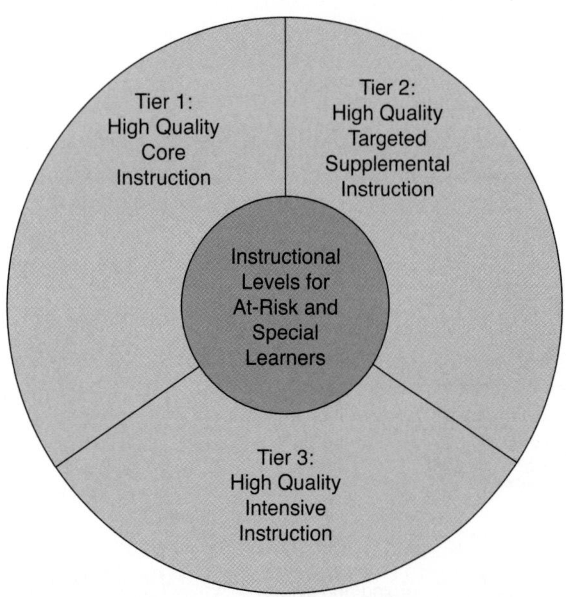


**FIGURE 1–3** Three-tier instruction for at-risk and special learners

*Source:* From "Three-Tier Instruction for At-Risk and Special Learners," in J. J. Hoover and J. R. Patton (2007), *Study Skills for Students with Learning Problems: A Teacher's Guide Meeting Diverse Needs,* 2e. Austin, TX: PRO-ED, Inc. Reprinted with permission.

- **Tier 1:** High-Quality Core Instruction: High-quality, research-based, and systematic instruction in a challenging curriculum in general education.

  **Outcome:** Students initially receive quality instruction and achieve expected academic and behavioral goals in the general education setting.

- **Tier 2:** High-Quality Targeted Supplemental Instruction: Targeted and focused interventions to supplement core instruction.

  **Outcome:** Students who do not meet general class expectations and exhibit need for supplemental support receive more targeted instruction. Learners may receive targeted, tier 2 instruction in the general education classroom or in other settings in the school such as a pull-out situation; however, students receive various types of assistance in terms of differentiations, modifications, more specialized equipment and technology in order to target instructional related needs. Critical within tier 2 is the documentation of student's responses to the interventions used, which serves as important prereferral data should more formal special education assessment be determined necessary. Students who make insufficient progress in tier 2 are considered for formal special education assessment.

- **Tier 3:** High-Quality Intensive Intervention: Specialized interventions to meet significant disabilities.

  **Outcome:** If found eligible for special education services, tier 3 provides students with more significant disabilities and more intensive, evidence-based interventions within a range of possible special educations settings.

As Hoover and Patton (in press) suggest, "Within three-tiered instructional programming, students initially are provided *high quality core instruction* in the general education setting. As 'reasonable and targeted' differentiated instruction is implemented within the core instruction, some students emerge as requiring additional *high quality targeted supplemental instruction.*" This supplemental instruction:

- may occur in the general education setting or other settings within the school,
- is targeted to specific areas of need, and
- directly complements the core instruction.

Evidence-based intervention should be provided to the student along with systematic documentation and evaluation of the targeted supplemental instruction. For those students who continue to experience significant academic and/or socioemotional problems, *high-quality intensive intervention* will then be considered. In the three-tiered model, formal referral for special education consideration is a latter-stage, tier 2 event and would only be initiated if supplemental support has been demonstrated to be unsuccessful at meeting student needs, but prior to formal placement in tier 3. Hoover and Patton (in press) provide an example of how a multitiered system works in the area of reading:

> Estimates in the area of reading are that approximately 80% of all learners are successful with high quality core instruction, 15-20% are estimated to need targeted supplemental instruction, and 5-10% will require intensive or special services through high quality intensive intervention (Yell, 2004; Hasbrouk, 2002). Students within a three-tier educational programming system are not provided formal special education services until: (1) they are unsuccessful with the core instruction [Tier 1], (2) make insufficient progress with targeted supplemental instruction [Tier 2], and (3) receive formal special education assessment and placement, including implementation and documentation of appropriate prereferral activities and interventions.

## Access to the General Education Curriculum

Introduced in the 1997 amendments to the Individuals with Disabilities Education Act (IDEA) and reinforced in IDEA 2004, access to the general education curriculum has become an overriding theme of special education service delivery. This emphasis is reflected in the many instances on the IEP where reference to the general curriculum arises:

- statement of the child's present levels of educational performance
- statement of measurable annual goals
- statement of the special education and related services and supplementary aids and services to be provided
- statement of the program modifications or supports for school personnel that will be provided to the child
- an explanation of the extent, if any, to which the child will not participate with the children without disabilities in general education classes and activities

IDEA 2004 considers the general curriculum as the same curriculum as that afforded to students without disabilities. The general curriculum is the explicit curriculum (i.e., clearly identified by the district or state) for the majority of students in the school, as defined by

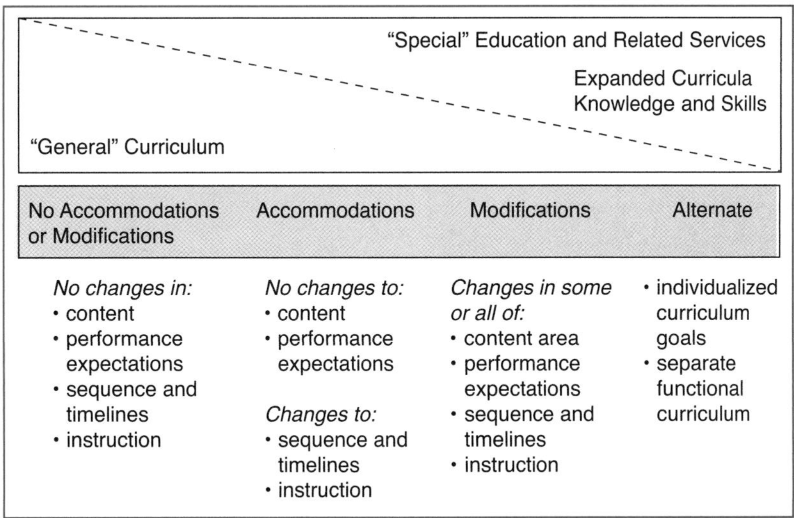


**FIGURE 1–4** Special education and general curriculum

*Source: Accessing the General Curriculum: Including Students with Disabilities in Standards-Based Reform,* by V. Nolet and M. J. McLaughln, 2000, Thousand Oaks, CA: Corwin Press. Reprinted by permission.

the content and performance standards that states have identified. Thus, a critical subgoal of special education intervention, in addition to the general purposes of special education, is to ensure that students gain those skills and acquire the knowledge that will allow them to gain access to the curriculum afforded to general education students.

The major challenge is to determine appropriate ways for students with diverse needs to access the general curriculum. One way to approach this task is to consider "levels of access." Nolet and McLaughlin (2000) developed a model that depicts this type of system (see Figure 1-4). Integral to this model is the notion of a continuum of options for accessing the general curriculum. The overriding assumption, however, is that most students with disabilities can be presented with the same curriculum as their nondisabled peers. The system shown in Figure 1-4 allows for individual needs; however, many of the suggested changes could be addressed proactively in a system that incorporates a perspective where curriculum and instruction are designed with everyone in mind, as discussed in the next section.

## Universal Design for Learning

The concept of universal design emerged out of the field of architecture and has been more recently applied to education. The general meaning of *universal design,* from an architectural perspective, is "the design of products and environments to be usable by all people, to the greatest extent possible, without the need for adaptation or specialized design" (Mace, 1997, p. 2). Applying this concept to education, Pisha and Coyne (2001) describe universal design as "the development of educational curricula and materials that include potent supports for access and learning from the start, rendering them effective for a far wider range of students than traditional materials" (p. 197). The term that has emerged to describe the application of these principles to educational situations is **universal design for learning (UDL).**

The main attractions of UDL include the following:

- It attends to individual needs in a general fashion that does not draw attention to any one individual.
- This approach is *proactive* rather than reactive—that is, it avoids "retrofitted changes and accommodations to classroom instruction" (Scott, McGuire, & Shaw, 2003).
- Developing curricula and materials that attend to the needs of students with special needs "increases usability for everyone" (Meyer & Rose, 2000).
- UDL capitalizes on new technologies and electronic resources.
- UDL provides a new way of looking at students with disabilities—along a continuum of students with learning-related differences (Meyer & Rose, 2000).

Much of the professional discussion of a framework on which to organize UDL techniques has been based on Vygotsky's three systems that must be active for learning to occur: *recognition system* (reception and interpretation of sensory input); *strategic system* (ability to plan and take action); and *affective system* (an individual's motivation to engage in an activity). Curricula and materials that adhere to the principles of UDL contain features that allow for a range of differences in these three areas.

The emerging focus in terms of inclusion (or supported education) is therefore not placement but access to successful learning opportunities within the general education curriculum. This principle emphasizes curriculum design for all learners. According to Hitchcock, Meyer, Rose, and Jackson (2002), a curriculum that incorporates a UDL orientation features the following:

- Goals provide an appropriate challenge for all students.
- Materials have a flexible format, supporting transformation between media and multiple representations of content to support all students' learning.
- Methods are flexible and diverse enough to provide appropriate learning experiences, challenges, and support for all students.
- Assessment is sufficiently flexible to provide accurate, ongoing information that helps teachers adjust instruction and maximize learning. (p. 8)

## Differentiated Instruction

Closely related to UDL is **differentiated instruction,** as advocated by Tomlinson (2001) and others (Bender, 2002; Heacox, 2002). To a certain extent the term is a reformulation of the basic idea of "individualizing instruction" that has been espoused for many years within special education; however, the current term borrows from gifted education and has been applied consistently to general education settings. The essence of this concept is that a wide range of student needs can be accommodated within general education classrooms, as expressed by Hall (2003):

> Differentiated instruction is a process to approach teaching and learning for students of differing abilities in the same class. The intent of differentiating instruction is to maximize each student's growth and individual success by meeting each student where he or she is, and assisting in the learning process. (p. 2)

The integration of the principles of UDL and differentiated instruction provide a potentially powerful way to address the individual needs of a range of students within the general education classroom. This point is particularly noteworthy, as more students who are at risk, who have special needs, and/or who have debilitating learning-related disabilities are in these settings.

## Evidence-Based Practice

The principles of good science, at long last, have made their way to general education (via NCLB) and special education (via IDEA 2004) by way of requiring teachers to use interventions that have evidence that they work with the populations with whom they are being used. The rationale for requiring such action is not new; however, the strong emphasis in recent legislation requiring evidence-based practice is. The overriding tenet of accountability is now how teachers instruct students.

Historically, translating research into practice in education has lagged significantly. As a result, difficulty exists in separating validated from nonvalidated interventions (Gersten & Dimino, 2001). The challenge of closing the gap between research and practice is described well by Abbott, Walton, and Greenwood (2002):

> Both researchers and teachers survive and thrive and are rewarded within different realms of the educational world. Teachers must juggle students' varying academic, social, and cultural needs every day throughout the school year. Researchers observe, intervene, analyze, and then write about a specific aspect of instructional intervention. Teachers enjoy the day-to-day student successes within the classroom community. Researchers relish positive changes in academic performance, competent research design, publication, and successful grant funding. . . .
>
> Because of these differing reward systems, teachers and researchers ask different questions about instruction and speak different languages. Teachers speak the understandable language of the general population, whereas researchers speak the technical language of research design and statistics. Special educators, as well as general education teachers, are concerned with strategies that will work for each student. Researchers want to know how, why, and under what conditions instructional strategies work so that this information can be generalized to populations of students. Consequently, before teachers can successfully implement research-validated instructional strategies in the classroom, researchers must "translate" this knowledge into teacher-friendly instructional forms. (p. 21)

In a field traditionally beset with new and often unproven ideas, teachers must be cautious in adopting treatments which, at a minimum, threaten the availability of precious instructional time and/or financial resources. For example, in discussing health fraud Worrall (1990) provides a series of helpful suggestions that have utility beyond the areas of medical and health treatments:

> 1. If it sounds too good to be true, it probably is.
> 2. Be suspicious of any product or therapy that claims to treat a large number of illnesses.
> 3. Be wary of any treatment or product offering a "cure." In legitimate medicine, cures are actually few and far between.
> 4. Don't rely only on testimonials from satisfied users. They rarely can be confirmed.
> 5. Be cautious when "complete," "immediate," "effortless," "safe," or "guaranteed" results are promised.
> 6. Legitimate . . . researchers do not use words such as "amazing," "secret," "exclusive," "miracle," and "special" in describing treatments. (p. 212)

Kauffman (2002) describes this important problem in an educational context:

> Education has a long history of scams, sham instructional programs, and programs implemented on a large scale but based on little or nothing more than assertions or theories that are never tested. For example, reading or math curricula may be adopted for an entire school system or even a state without evidence that they are effective in helping students learn what is desired. (p. 230)

A new era now exists where instructional practices should have a research base if they are to be used with students with special needs. Such a time is long overdue.

## Diversity Considerations

The student population in most schools reflect significant diversity. Diversity, in this sense, implies that many students do not represent the stereotypic image of the typical student. However, the norm of what is typical has changed dramatically in recent years. Figure 1–5 highlights most of the key features on which diversity can be recognized.

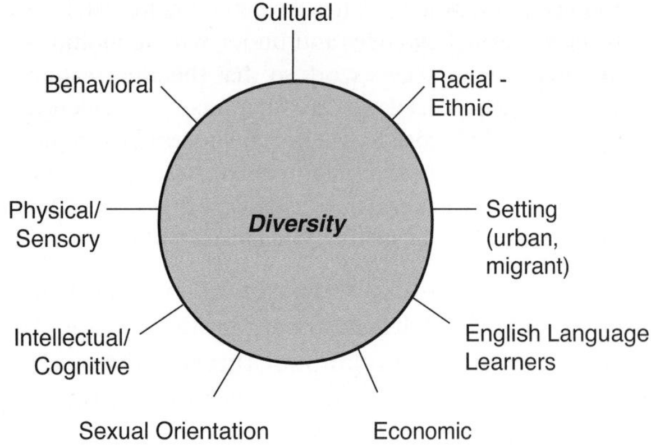


**FIGURE 1–5** Dimensions of diversity

Of the dimensions of diversity noted in Figure 1-5, only three of them (behavioral, physical/sensory, intellectual/cognitive) align with the typical notions of disability. Most of the dimensions suggest that diversity is definitely more than just disability. A multitiered system of intervention, as introduced earlier in the chapter, should be designed to address the needs of a range of learners with diverse needs. Such a system would be beneficial not only to the students but also to the teachers who teach them. The bottom line is that teachers in schools today *must* develop a sensitivity to the needs of a diverse group of students. Moreover, teachers *must also* acquire specific knowledge about diverse students and develop skills to address the needs that these students present in classrooms.

### Empowerment

An outgrowth of the movement toward inclusion has been the focus on the **empowerment** and the related self-determination of individuals with disabilities. Moreover, the emphasis on the rights of students transferring to individuals when they reach the age of majority, as mandated by IDEA, underscore the importance of empowering students with disabilities. Empowerment is a multifaceted concept that embraces many essential aspects of what it truly means to be respected and given dignity.

For teachers, a commitment to empowerment as a goal involves the need to give more attention to assessing how well students are developing the ability to make choices, to become advocates for themselves, and to exercise control over their lives. The central feature is **self-determination.** As Wehmeyer (1992) notes:

> Self-determination refers to the attitudes and abilities necessary to act as the primary causal agent in one's life, and to make choices and decisions regarding one's quality of life free from undue external influence or interference. (p. 16)

Browder, Wood, Test, Karvonen, and Algozzine (2001) summarized Wehmeyer et al.'s (1998) teachable components within the domain of self-determination as follows:

- Decision making
- Choice making
- Problem solving
- Independent living (risk taking and safety skills)
- Goal setting and attainment
- Self-observation, evaluation, and reinforcement
- Self-instruction
- Self-understanding
- Self-advocacy and leadership
- Positive self-efficacy and outcome expectancy
- Internal locus of control
- Self-awareness

The abilities required to achieve self-determination most significantly relate to decision making and problem solving. These concerns need to be part of the responsibilities of teachers and such foci should be included within the curriculum and presented in the early grades. With the increased likelihood of education being provided in inclusive classes, there should be a similar increase in commitment to a focus on self-determination in such settings (Zhang, 2001).

## EFFECTIVE TEACHING

Teacher effectiveness is a function of two dimensions: the learning the child masters and the teaching behaviors associated with this learning (e.g., time and effort). Obviously, the more a student learns, the more effective is the teacher and/or the learning climate. If students learn more quickly from one teacher than from another, the more efficient teacher logically also will be judged as the more effective.

Over 20 years ago, Rosenshine and Stevens (1986) developed a general model of effective instruction highlighting six specific teaching activities validated from research as associated with student achievement that continue to have bearing today.

- a review or check of the previous day's work (reteaching, if necessary)
- presentation of new content/skills

- guided student practice (with verification for understanding)
- feedback and correction (reteaching, if necessary)
- independent student practice
- weekly and monthly reviews

Englert (1983) contributed to the thinking on effective instruction by identifying four teacher behaviors that are associated with direct instruction and are linked to achievement: maintaining a high level of content coverage, providing successful practice activities for students, providing feedback to signal the beginning and the conclusion of individual learning trials, and maintaining a high level of student task involvement.

Englert, Tarrant, and Mariage (1992, 1998) identified four complementary elements that derive from a **constructivist approach** to teaching: embedding instruction in meaningful activities, promoting dialogue for self-regulated learning, demonstrating instructional responsiveness, and establishing classroom learning communities.

A substantial database exists indicating what elements of teaching constitute effective instructional practice. Figure 1–6 represents our model of effective

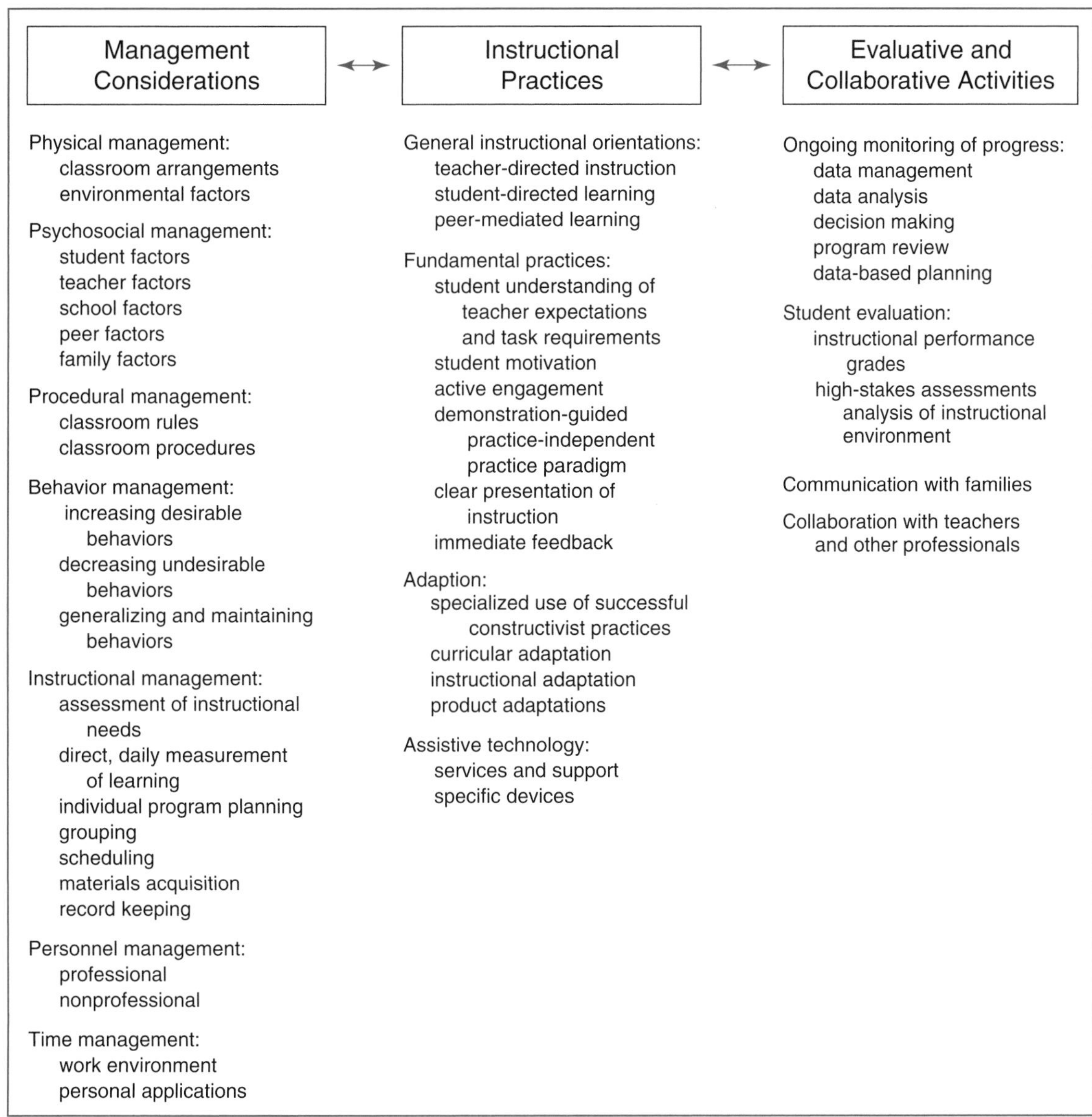


**FIGURE 1–6** Dimensions of effective educational practice

educational practice. The model is predicated on a division of the phases of the instructional process into a focus on three major time-related aspects: (a) activities and events that precede teaching, (b) various activities associated with the actual instructional process, and (c) actions that are performed subsequent to instruction. Furthermore, the model reflects interactivity across the three areas. For instance, various evaluative activities will have an effect on management dimensions or instructional practices. The comprehensive nature of delivering effective instruction is evident from examination of the entries in the model.

Consistent with the purposes of this book, the elements of this model will be explicated throughout the book. The first column of the model (Management Considerations) and the second column (Instructional Practices) are covered more thoroughly in Chapters 3 and 4, respectively. The topics highlighted in the last column (Evaluative and Collaborative Activities) are discussed in Chapter 2. This graphic representation of the key elements of effective practice serves as a reference for the discussions that follow in subsequent chapters.

## SPECIAL EDUCATION TEACHER AS PROFESSIONAL

Beyond the instructional demands of a teacher's role, effective special educators also must display a high degree of personal determination to positively influence the education and acceptance of persons with special needs. Bateman's (1971) historical challenge still has merit; she indicates that teachers must have a personal philosophy of education, have a willingness to be agents of social change, be accountable for services provided, possess and continue to develop personal competencies and knowledge base, and care deeply about all human beings, including themselves. These professional attributes serve as the foundation for advocacy crucial to the welfare of students. However, they may also present special challenges to the professional.

### Teacher as Advocate

Although teachers, particularly beginning teachers, probably would not be well advised to upset the structure of education, the role of special educators as change agents requires them to question whether their own and others' actions best benefit students. Accepting minimal levels of professional conduct or acquiescing to administrative practices contrary to students' and parents' basic interests threatens those aspects of special education that originally attracted committed individuals.

To illustrate potential dilemmas, Bateman (1982) discusses several situations in which teachers must decide between what is best for the child and what is consistent with local policy. She notes the following dilemmas that teachers may face: informing parents of their legal rights, knowing that such information will give parents a basis for demanding more extensive services for their child; testifying at due process hearings when the employer is believed to be at fault; and instructing in controversial topics, such as sex education, which the teacher deems crucial to the curriculum but which often conflict with parental concerns or administrative guidelines. Assuming a professional role thus requires the commitment of an advocate as much as it demands effectiveness in instruction.

### Ethical Decisions

A related concern for teachers within the domain of ethics concerns the continuing dilemma of making decisions about the value of specific educational interventions. What may be one person's belief system vis-à-vis an intervention or treatment may be perceived by others as poor practice, quackery, or even fraud. As noted by Kauffman (2002):

> The fact that nothing works every time and everything appears to work sometimes shouldn't keep us from choosing what's most likely to work most of the time. And when we encounter a nonresponder to our best bet, our tactic should be to go to the *next best* bet, not abandon reason or try things at random. We expect physicians, pilots, mechanics, and every other group of practitioners to try the best-tested, most likely-to-work things first and to have backup plans if the best bet doesn't work. We expect that they will not try things at random, and we interpret random selection of tools or strategies as incompetence or panic. (p. 231)

### The Role of the Special Educator in Today's Schools

As has been noted throughout this chapter, schools are different today than they were in recent years. Special educators needs to function within a multitiered instructional system that demands attention to standards and high-stakes testing. In addition to the realities of teaching in schools today and the competencies that are needed, NCLB now requires that teachers be "highly qualified."

Hoover and Patton (in press) stress that teachers today need a more extensive set of skills ("contemporary sets of skills") than they did in the past ("traditional sets of skills"). Skills such as task analysis, individualizing instruction, and making adaptations/modifications were the mainstay of special education, whereas today, new more diverse and challenging sets of skills are needed to function in a multitiered system. Hoover and Patton (in press) identified five contemporary skill sets required of special education teachers: collaboration, differentiation, evidence-based instruction, socioemotional supports, and data-driven decision making. A listing of these skill sets and associated subskills is provided in Table 1-2.

## Professional Development

To provide the best possible education for students who are at risk or who have special needs in an ever-changing and more demanding workplace, teachers must commit to continuing professional development (e.g., credit and noncredit workshops, conferences, and regular reviews of professional journals). Unlike some professions (e.g., speech and language pathology) that have comprehensive and regulated requirements for

**TABLE 1-2** Special Education Multilevel Skill Sets and Associated Subskills

| |
|---|
| **Data-Driven Decision Making** |
| Curriculum-based assessment/measurement |
| Strategies for effective decision making |
| Data analysis |
| Multiple monitoring strategies |
| Basic skills assessment |
| Functional skills assessment |
| Special education eligibility process/criteria |
| **Evidence-Based Instruction** |
| Knowledge of core disciplines |
| Higher-order thinking skills |
| Evidence-based instructional strategies |
| Task analysis |
| Direct instruction |
| Programmed instruction |
| Impact of culture and language on learning |
| Determining difference vs disability |
| Compensatory strategies for specific disabilities |
| Functional living and transition skills |
| Mastery learning |
| **Socioemotional and Behavioral Supports** |
| Classroom management |
| Behavior management |
| Applied behavioral analysis |
| Targeted behavioral supports |
| Social skills instruction |
| Self-management skills instruction |
| Impact of culture & language on behavior |
| Socioemotional development |
| Functional behavioral assessment |
| Positive behavioral supports/behavioral plans |

*(continued)*

**TABLE 1–2** (continued)

| |
|---|
| **Differentiation** |
| Accommodations & modifications |
| Differentiation strategies |
| Second language acquisition |
| Culturally relevant instruction |
| Sheltered instruction |
| Study skills & learning strategies |
| Student peer tutoring models |
| Targeted academic learning time (time, task focus, intensity) |
| Scheduling strategies |
| Alternative curriculum and materials |
| Adapting to address functional living abilities |
| **Collaboration** |
| Communication skills |
| Co-teaching/team processes |
| Consulting/coaching |
| Change strategies |
| Parent-school-community partnerships |
| Cultural/linguistic diversity and collaboration |
| Working with parents on IEP and disability-related issues |
| Knowledge/understanding of IDEA |
| Knowledge of district special education referral and assessment proceed |

continuing education, teaching is much looser about this important area. Teachers who work in special education *must* keep current of new developments and practices in the field. We strongly suggest that teachers do the following activities as a part of their professional development activities:

- Maintain membership in professional organizations such as the Council for Exceptional Children.
- Attend inservice trainings that are sponsored by one's school, district, or regional service centers.
- Read professional journals. Some of the ones that we recommend include:
    - *Teaching Exceptional Children*
    - *Intervention in School and Clinic*
    - *Focus on Exceptional Children*
    - *Exceptional Children*
    - *Remedial and Special Education*
- Reacquaint oneself with textbooks in key areas of professional activity.
- Read professional books that are published and that relate to areas of professional focus.

## ORGANIZATION OF THE BOOK

The chapters in this book address the broad range of management issues, instructional practices, and curricular concerns associated with teaching students with high-incidence disabilities.

Chapter 2 focuses on collaboration with general education teachers and paraeducators. This element is crucial to providing appropriate education to students with learning and behavioral difficulties who are placed in inclusive settings.

Chapters 3 and 4 cover topics associated with the entries in the first column of Figure 1–6. Chapter 3 includes an overview of curriculum development and program design. Attention to the curriculum precedes an analysis of various curricular orientations found in schools and a discussion of program design. The chapter also provides a discussion of effective instructional practices consistent with the second column of Figure 1–6. The chapter is fundamental to understanding how to deliver and adapt the content discussed in the curricular chapters (i.e., Chapters 5–11).

The organization and management of a classroom is initially discussed in Chapter 4. Topics include various classroom arrangements, grouping, scheduling, homework materials selection, grading, and record keeping. Chapter 4 includes further management strategies to facilitate behavior change. General goals, prerequisites to successful management, and specific techniques for promoting appropriate and discouraging inappropriate behavior are discussed.

Chapters 5 to 11 present strategies for instruction within six important curricular areas: spoken language, reading, written language, mathematics, science and social studies, and the creative arts. Each chapter includes information on assessing learners within a particular curricular area, general and specific approaches to instruction, and suggested teaching activities.

Additional topical areas for students with special learning needs are covered in Chapters 12 to 15. Chapter 12 discusses study skills. Chapter 13 covers the areas of social competence and self-determination. Chapter 14 discusses functional academics and career development. Chapter 15 provides information about transition, transition planning, and life skills instruction.

This text provides concepts and information with which to develop good teaching techniques. Good teachers are, above all, effective; they nurture learning and their students, are confident, constantly evaluate their teaching programs, and make learning enjoyable. Most teachers gain additional skill with experience; in time they accumulate a variety of motivating methods and materials. A teacher who remains energetic, enthusiastic, and positive (see Busch, Pederson, Espin, & Weissenberger, 2001 for a discussion of first-year teacher attributes) and who continues to work hard, masters good teaching competencies, and develops a broad repertoire of skills, ideas, and instructional activities can achieve teaching excellence. We are hopeful that this text will assist in this process.

CHAPTER

# 2

# Strategies for Collaboration

Education has changed significantly in recent years. Special education, in particular, has witnessed significant changes since the 1975 passage of Public Law 94–142 and its reauthorizations as the Individuals with Disabilities Education Act (IDEA) in 1990, 1997, and 2004. One important change for special educators has occurred in the redefining of professional and partner roles in response to federal, state, and local legislative and regulatory action. As Hoover and Patton (2007) point out, "as expectations associated with full inclusion, the No Child Left Behind Act of 2001 (NCLB), response to intervention, and standards-based education continue, the need for collaboration in instruction also increases" (p. 147).

The special education arena now places a variety of demands on educators. Teachers are expected to be competent not only in instruction and management, but also in their interactions with many partners serving diverse roles and often from backgrounds different than their own. This latter expectation is pointedly evident in interviews for educators' positions as well as in applications for professional preparation programs, where teamwork is considered a major component.

Today each special educator must operate as part of a team in many aspects of his or her role, including screening, making assessments, planning individual programs, developing placement options, providing direct or indirect support, and monitoring success. Being a member of a collaborative effort is not an option, as various components of IDEA directly or indirectly expect such participation, as highlighted in Figure 2–1. In addition, teachers regularly feel the effects of external forces (standards-based reform efforts, the inclusive education movement, site-based restructuring, state-mandated assessments, board-mandated curricula), whether or not they have had a part in influencing those forces. They must work with many others to operationalize the required aspects of all initiatives or changes in effect within the instructional program.

Although teaming skills are recognized as learned behaviors that typically require at least some explicit instruction, many personnel preparation programs for teachers fail to adequately prepare their participants to collaborate with the full range of likely partners (O'Shea, Williams, & Sattler, 1999; Villa, Thousand, Nevin, & Malgeri, 1996). At the inservice level, the continually evolving roles of teachers—both general and special education—have presented problems, especially in developing collaborative relationships. A number of factors and barriers that retard change can be found in schools across the nation. Hourcade and Bawens (2003) identify "retraining forces" (focus on the present, not future; resistance to change; lack of administrative support; failure to stay current with professional developments; lack of knowledge and skills; and lack of perseverance) along with critical barriers (attitudinal, structural, and competency) as often inhibiting this process.

This chapter focuses on issues and strategies for developing partnerships with the five key groups of significant stakeholders with whom special educators should and must work: (a) students (consumers), (b) families (consumers), (c) general educators, (d) paraeducators, and (e) related services personnel. Because many of the central principles of collaboration apply across all types of partnerships, the general features of consultation and collaboration are presented first as a foundation for the subsequent, more specialized sections.

*The authors acknowledge that earlier versions of this chapter were written by Ginger Blalock, University of New Mexico, and thank her for her contributions.*

**FIGURE 2–1** Collaboration expectations within IDEA

- **General education teachers**

  At least one general education teacher must participate on the IEP team if the student has any general education involvement. This provision makes general education teachers integral to the team of professionals who design and implement special services.

- **Least restrictive environment**

  The law presumes that students should receive education in a general education setting, and it requires justification for any placement that is not general education. This presumption strongly suggests that classroom teachers and special educators will need to work together on behalf of students.

- **Assessment process**

  Parent roles in the assessment process have been clarified; initial parent permission for assessment does not constitute permission for possible special education placement. This process requires ongoing communication between school professionals and parents. Even more communication responsibility occurs when students are reevaluated: Since a decision may be made in some cases to omit standardized testing, parent involvement in decision making is even more critical.

- **Transition**

  Because transition must be addressed for students beginning at age 14, strong collaboration is necessary and should involve students as well as parents. Further, transition plans often require the involvement of professionals from other agencies, and so interprofessional collaboration may be required.

- **Discipline and behavior support plans**

  For any student with behavior problems, a functional assessment and behavior support plan is required. The process of gathering data, identifying the problem, designing alternative interventions, implementing them, and evaluating the outcomes typically will include participation by several professionals, paraprofessionals, and parents/family members.

- **Paraprofessionals**

  Paraprofessionals, teaching assistants, and other individuals in similar roles should receive appropriate training for their jobs and supervision of their work. Although not all interactions with paraprofessionals may be collaborative, the specific expectation for teacher paraprofessional interactions can foster collaboration.

- **Mediation**

  Unless declined by parents, states must make no-cost mediation available to parents as a strategy for resolving disagreements concerning their children with special needs. The implication is that a strong bias exists toward all parties, working together on behalf of students, to design the most appropriate education rather than escalating conflicts.

*Source:* From Friend, M., and Cook, L. *Collaboration Skills for School Professionals*, 4e. Published by Allyn & Bacon, Boston, MA. Copyright © 2002 by Pearson Education. Reprinted by permission of the publisher.

## CONSULTATION AND COLLABORATION: MODELS AND SKILLS

This section discusses six key aspects of the collaboration process: definitions of collaboration, principles of collaborative consultation, key players in the collaborative process in schools, stages of collaborative consultation, skills required for collaboration, and personnel preparation strategies.

### Definitions of Collaboration

At the heart of working with essential partners are consultation and collaboration. According to Idol, Nevin, and Paolucci-Whitcomb (1994), **consultation** generally involves an expert who works with one or more consultees to create a positive change for the target learner or issue. Thus, consultation implies expertise, which may inadvertently lead to unequal status of partnering professionals.

The consultant–consultee relationship places the consultant (often the special educator) in a position of authority (whether warranted or not) on a variety of learning, behavioral, or even legal and administrative matters. This stance propels the myth that special educators have the "secrets" to working with students with exceptionalities, perpetuates the mystique the field has acquired, and relegates "ownership" of this group of students to special education personnel.

A more equitable arrangement might be to have each participant serve as consultant in her or his particular area of expertise (the concept of a multidisciplinary or interdisciplinary team), so that all key parties (general educator, special educator, student, parent or caregiver, therapist, medical professional, adult provider, and employer, among others) have the opportunity to share their specialized knowledge and skills. Thus, the term **collaborative consultation** is defined as "an interactive process that enables groups of people with diverse expertise to generate creative solutions to mutually defined problems" (Idol et al., 1994, p. 1).

Five basic elements make up collaborative consultation, according to Nevin, Thousand, Paolucci-Whitcomb, and Villa (1990) cited in Idol et al. (1994): (a) an agreement by all group or team members to view all partners (including novices) as having unique and needed expertise, (b) frequent face-to-face interactions, (c) shared leadership responsibilities and accountability for one's commitments, (d) orientations that acknowledge reciprocity's role and that weigh task or relationship actions in terms of their contribution to the group goal, and (e) a commitment to use consensus-building in a conscious effort to improve interaction and/or task achievement abilities. In this configuration, collaborative consultation essentially equals collaboration, which better conveys the cooperative role required for education's challenges, such as successful inclusion of diverse learners in general education.

## Principles of Collaboration

Friend (2000) highlighted four myths and misinterpretations regarding collaboration that can contribute to the ineffective implementation of this process. The implications and the realities of these myths are explored below.

- **Myth 1:** Everyone Is Doing It. *Implication*: All schools are using collaborative processes. *Reality*: Few schools have developed truly comprehensive collaborative systems.
- **Myth 2:** More Is Better. *Implication*: If collaboration is such a good idea, then more of it should be done. *Reality*: If true collaborative efforts have not been implemented, then more might be better; however, if collaboration is ongoing, there are realistic limits to the amount of time available for such efforts.
- **Myth 3:** It's About Feeling Good and Liking Others. *Implication*: Ideal collaborative arrangements may indeed be characterized by the establishment of new, rich personal relationships, but this is not the goal. *Reality*: The goal of collaboration is to establish systems that have benefit to students. If this cannot be achieved through collaborative processes, then their continuation cannot be substantiated.
- **Myth 4:** It Comes Naturally. *Implication*: Experience and personality should be enough to ensure that quality collaboration occurs. *Reality*: Skills are needed to engage in effective collaboration; these skills are not the same as being social and gregarious.

Idol (2002) discussed the importance of certain activities that "may enhance the collaborative process" (p. 13). She articulated 13 principles that should be heeded in the development of collaborative systems. These principles are listed in Table 2–1.

**TABLE 2–1** Principles of collaborative consultation

1. Establish informal relationships among team members prior to beginning professional work.
2. Treat all team members with respect.
3. Use situational leadership to guide the group, adjusting the leadership style to the needs of the group.
4. Learn to manage conflict and confrontation effectively.
5. Be willing to share information and create a trustworthy relationship so others feel safe to share.
6. Listen actively when others are speaking.
7. Engage in nonjudgmental responding when sharing ideas.
8. Use appropriate interviewing skills for gaining and sharing information; expressing and discovering feelings; planning for action; problem solving.
9. Use appropriate and jargon-free language for both oral and written communication.
10. Gather practical and useful data and information to aid in decision making.
11. Be willing to both give and receive feedback from team members.
12. Always remember to give others credit for their ideas and accomplishments.
13. Be aware of nonverbal messages, so that positive signals are given.

*Source:* Adapted from *Collaborative Consultation* (2nd ed.), by L. Idol, P. Paolucci-Whitcomb, and A. Nevin, 1994, Austin, TX PRO-ED.

## Key Players in the Collaboration Process in Schools

At the school level, collaborative consultation is useful in various situations, including *student assistance teams* (Lenz, Deshler, & Kissam, 2004; O'Shea, O'Shea, Algozzine, & Hammitte, 2001), *teaching teams* (T. Smith, Polloway, Patton, & Dowdy, 2008; Vaughn, Bos, & Schumm, 2003), *consulting teacher programs* (Idol, 1993), and *self-governance procedures* such as curriculum or school restructuring committees (Lenz et al., 2004; Turnbull & Turnbull, 1997). Collaboration is also manifest in various direct and indirect services to students, as will be discussed in the next section.

What becomes obvious is that a number of different school staff members as well as family members will be involved in collaborative efforts depending on the need. Table 2–2 lists some of the key school personnel who will play a significant role in different collaborative activities. The table also highlights one of many significant roles that this member might serve.

**TABLE 2–2** Collaboration team members

| *Member* | *Role significance in collaboration* |
|---|---|
| School principal | Provides support, motivation, and overall leadership |
| Inclusive educator | Planning, implementation, monitoring of classroom-based program |
| Special educator | Differentiated strategies and accommodations |
| School counselor | Value-added support beyond the classroom |
| Paraprofessionals | Individualized instructional support |
| Parents | Home-based support of classroom program |
| Community | Community resources/programs to assist in educational programs |

*Source:* From *Teaching Study Skills to Students with Learning Problems: A Teacher's Guide for Meeting Diverse Needs* (2nd ed.), J. R. Patton, 2007, p. 144. Austin, TX: PRO-ED. Copyright by PRO-ED. Adapted by permission.

## Stages of Collaborative Consultation

According to Idol and colleagues (1994), the collaborative consultation progresses through six stages. (Readers are encouraged to consult Idol and colleague's work for a comprehensive background on this sequence and for specific implementation strategies.) The six problem-solving stages are listed in Table 2–3.

The problem-solving worksheet by Knackendoffel, Robinson, Deshler, and Schumaker (1992) is a useful tool for carrying out these six stages (see Figure 2–2). Any configuration of partners can use the worksheet to specify problems, sort through potential solutions, and poise for action and monitoring.

Collaborative consultation and collaboration imply that both parties are in parallel positions to share ideas, talents, professional development experiences, materials, and energy as the team or partnership evolves. To take advantage of these opportunities, partners need certain qualifications or abilities.

## Skills Required for Collaboration

Idol et al. (1994) assert that use of the collaborative consultation process requires that group members have three areas of expertise: "(a) an appropriate

**TABLE 2–3** Problem-solving stages

| *Stage* | *Description* |
|---|---|
| 1. *Entry and establishment of team goals* | The consultant and consultee(s) work together to identify the broad problem and plan accordingly. |
| 2. *Problem identification* | Both parties gather data as needed, identify the specific problem(s), and set specific goal(s) to address identified challenges. |
| 3. *Intervention recommendations* | Both parties suggest ideas for activities to address the challenges. |
| 4. *Implementation of recommendations* | The consultee(s) and consultant may each implement recommended interventions. |
| 5. *Evaluation* | Both parties may be involved in selecting an evaluation model and in monitoring success. |
| 6. *Follow-up* | Both parties are continuously engaged in ongoing follow-up or follow-along so that interventions can be changed as needed. |

**FIGURE 2–2** Problem-solving worksheet

## PROBLEM-SOLVING WORKSHEET

Team Members: ______________________ Role: ______________________

______________________ ______________________

______________________ ______________________

______________________ ______________________

Student: ______________________ Date: ______________________

Problem:

Details: ______________________

______________________

______________________

Alternative Solutions Brainstormed: Ratings:

______________________ __ __ __

______________________ __ __ __

______________________ __ __ __

______________________ __ __ __

______________________ __ __ __

Solution(s) to Be Tried First:

______________________

______________________

Implementation Steps: When? Who?

______________________ ________ ________

______________________ ________ ________

______________________ ________ ________

______________________ ________ ________

______________________ ________ ________

______________________ ________ ________

How Will the Plan Be Monitored?

______________________

______________________

What Are the Criteria for Success?

______________________

______________________

Date and Time of Next Appointment: ______________________

*Source:* From *Collaborative Problem Solving: A Step-by-Step Guide to Creating Educational Solutions* (pp. 71–72), by E. A. Knackendoffel, S. M. Robinson, D. D. Deshier, and J. B. Schumaker, 1992, Lawerence, KS: Edge Enterprises. 

underlying knowledge base, (b) interpersonal communicative, interactive, problem-solving skills, and (c) intrapersonal attitudes" (p. 2).

**Underlying Knowledge Base.** The *underlying knowledge base* incorporates all that the professional now knows and strives to know about what works and what does not in serving diverse learners within the range of service delivery models. A systems orientation that aims at strategic learning environments and a problem-solving perspective drives the professional's approach to the most effective use of the knowledge base.

**Interpersonal Skills for Collaboration.** Bos and Vaughn (1998) and Idol et al. (1994) have outlined several major areas of interpersonal skills, which Idol and colleagues refer to as "generic principles of collaborative consultation." These areas incorporate attitudes or perspectives, summarized in Table 2–4, in addition to behaviors or skills. A tool that may help individuals proactively orient themselves toward the collaborative experience, through self-assessment, is found in Figure 2–3.

**Intrapersonal Attitudes Related to Collaboration.** Idol et al. (1994) delineate a set of intrapersonal beliefs, values, and experiences that significantly shape one's approach to the collaborative consultation process. The "attitudes" are actually practices that can enhance one's personal and professional growth and greatly promote the group's interactions and task accomplishments.

- Face fear.
- Share a sense of humor.
- Behave with integrity.

## DIVERSITY IN THE CLASSROOM *Tips*

**Isaura Barrera, Ph.D.**, is currently an associate professor in special education at the University of New Mexico. She has conducted research on *Skilled Dialogue* and conducts training on its application to working with diverse children and families.

Skilled Dialogue provides an evidence-based framework for communicating and interacting respectfully, reciprocally, and responsively with practitioners, families, and children from diverse backgrounds. Six principles are particularly relevant.

1. **Acknowledge the range and validity of diverse perspectives.** Always assume that there are at least three equally valid ways of responding to any particular situation. Never take a "This is the (only) right way" position that implicitly or explicitly places the other person(s) in the wrong. Be respectful of diverse behaviors and values even when they seem counterproductive from your perspective. All behaviors have roots in particular beliefs and values; seek to understand what these are.

2. **Stay with the tension of differing perspectives.** Never rush to resolve or "fix" a problem. Stay with the tension until there is sufficient understanding. The fact that someone else's behavior or values trigger discomfort is not necessarily a sign that they are any less useful or valid. Such "culture bumps" (Barrera & Kramer, 1997) may only be a signal that we need to more closely examine what is happening by asking ourselves "What values and meanings are we attaching to others' behaviors?" "Are these appropriate or do they only reflect my own biases?"

3. **Establish interactions that allow equal voice for all participants.** Take an additive rather than a subtractive approach; that is, assume that two perspectives are always stronger than one. Allow ample opportunity for those perspectives to emerge before deciding for or against them. Ask. Learn. Listen. Decisions will be all the more appropriate as a result of the added knowledge.

4. **Seek complementarity between apparent contradictions.** Heads and tails are, for example, only two sides of the same coin. Ask "How does this apparently contradictory perspective actually contribute to my own?" Does a practitioner, for example, practice certain teaching strategies that are unfamiliar or not valued by the students (e.g., direct questioning)? How can the student's preferred strategies (e.g., apparently random conversation) contribute to the overall goal of competent teaching?

5. **Communicate your respect for and understanding of the other's perspective.**

6. **Create options that integrate and provide access to the strengths of diverse perspectives.** This last principle requires that we place differences into a context within which they can, when integrated, form a larger picture; for example, shifting the English-only or bilingual debate to a discussion of language development, within which both monolingual and bilingual approaches can become maximally meaningful. To address this principle is to remember to ask: What is the "larger container" that can integrate the strengths of apparently contradictory perspectives?

**TABLE 2–4** Major areas of interpersonal skills

| *Collaborative Skill* | *Description* |
|---|---|
| *Team ownership of the identified problem* | Equitable access to information, participation in decision making, and interactions across multiple disciplines—a working alliance |
| *Recognition of individual differences in the effort's developmental progress* | Understanding and acceptance of where one is and where the group is along the continuum of team stages and changes |
| *Situational leadership to guide the practice of collaborative consultation* | Strategically employing skills such as flexible presentation, flexible implementation, and leadership styles (e.g., telling, selling or encouragement, participating, and delegating) to accomplish tasks |
| *Cooperative conflict resolution processes* | Moving from categorizing, organizing, and concluding to presenting opposing viewpoints, to seeking new information and experiences, to reasoning to revised conclusions |
| *Appropriate interviewing skills* | Assuming responsibility for, adapting for diversity within, and directing the progress of the conversation so that data required to enhance the learner's outcomes are obtained |
| *Active listening behaviors* | Receiving information without judgment, questioning to clarify messages, restating, paraphrasing, summarizing, and using responsive body language |
| *Oral and written communication using common (nonjargon) terms, and positive nonverbal language* | Assumption of "mutually interdependent roles as senders and receivers," including ongoing feedback and positive use of the elements of nonverbal language to improve one's perceptions about messages |

- Live with joy.
- Take risks.
- Use self-determination.
- Think longitudinally.
- Create new norms.
- Respond proactively.
- Adapt upward (don't regress to poorer functioning).
- Use self-differentiation (separate self from surrounding systems and pressures, as well as take responsibility for one's own outcomes and well-being) (Idol et al., 1994, pp. 33–37).

These practices are useful as guides to all professional endeavors, due to their orientation toward positive outcomes and responsible decision making.

## Personnel Preparation Strategies

Kochhar and West (1996) describe the roles of all parties involved in developing and enhancing partnerships for inclusive education and other programs, with emphasis on universities' preparation of teachers to embrace those roles.

**Preservice Teacher Preparation.** The implications for teacher preparation are clear. General education majors must learn methods and curricular modifications that respond to the diverse learning needs of all students in the classroom. A single course in exceptionalities and/or mainstreaming is insufficient to create the attitude change, mindset, and skills needed to individualize for each learner. Innovative colleges of education are integrating diversity training throughout their teacher preparation programs to address all learners' challenges, and in the process are modeling collaboration across disciplines for their students and colleagues. T. Smith et al. (2004) propose that three important activities toward such preparation include (a) opportunities to observe good examples; (b) information about models, students, and proven practices as well as skills training to meet student needs; and (c) time for planning with team members.

**Induction Support.** School districts, and teacher preparations programs, have learned how important mentoring, professional development, and other forms of support are for teachers in their first few years of teaching, just to keep them in the profession. Most school districts have established some form of mentoring process for new teachers.

**Advanced Professional Development.** Experienced teachers require regular opportunities to acquire new competencies, as demanded by changing needs within

**FIGURE 2–3** Collaboration self-assessment questionnaire

NAME ______________________________ SETTING/SITUATION______________________

GOAL FOR COLLABORATION (if applicable): ______________________________

## PERSONAL PERSPECTIVES:

1. What are two important perceptions I hold about the other team members?

______________________________

______________________________

2. What are two important perceptions I hold about the target students?

______________________________

______________________________

3. What are two important perceptions I hold about the organization that potentially impact the team's collaboration and productivity?

______________________________

______________________________

4. How willing am I to collaborate in this effort? Very much X X X X X Very little

**MY SKILLS AND KNOWLEDGE:**

Check the skill/knowledge areas listed below which you have learned from work, leisure, and general life activities. List a specific competency (or two) that you have in every possible area. Then star **(*)** the five competencies that you feel would contribute most to the collaborative process.

| Compentency Area and Examples | Specific Competency(s) | Help Team Process? |
|---|---|---|
| 5. *Detail/follow-through skills* (expediting, resource expertize, detailed, ordered) | | |
| 6. *Financial/money management skills* (inventorying, budgeting, economical, using numbers for reasoning) | | |
| 7. *Influencing/persuading skills* (building rapport/trust, promoting, recruiting, arbitrating, selling) | | |
| 8. *Performing skills* (leading groups, acting, showmanship) | | |
| 9. *Leadership skills* (initiating, organizing, problem solving, leading others, directing talent) | | |

10. *Developing/planning/organizing skills* (prioritizing, designing, scheduling, organizing)

11. *Executing/supervising/management skills* (directing others, managing others, producing, reviewing)

12. *Instructing/interpreting/guiding skills* (informing, explaining, coaching, facilitating)

13. *Helping/human relations skills* (relating, serving, sensitive support, social skills, strong teamwork, nurturing)

14. *Intuitive/innovative skills* (imagining, innovating, synthesizing, intuitive perceiving)

15. *Observational/learning skills* (observing, reading, detecting, assessing, discovering)

16. *Research/investigative skills* (anticipating, surveying, examining)

17. *Analysis/evaluation skills* (dissecting, diagnosing, classifying, judging, evaluating)

**COMMUNICATION SKILLS:**

18. Listening skills

19. Public speaking or assertiveness skills

20. Reading skills

21. Writing skills

**OTHER SKILLS:**

schools such as inclusion and new forms of collaboration. The following paragraphs describe strategies for ensuring the relevance and capacity-building impact of a school, district, or agency professional development program.

***Needs Assessment.*** Professional development activities, whether formal training or technical assistance, should always be based on the results of a formal or informal needs assessment, that is, linked to a real need. *Needs assessment* is the collecting and analyzing of information that will assist in decision making. Given the job and life demands faced by many adults, this assessment process needs to be precise, timely, and relevant.

Often, needs assessments can best be conducted while simultaneously developing skills in formal training sessions. The steps that follow are intended for cross-training sessions that simultaneously assess the status of participants as well as needs for further support. Thus, at every point through the experience, information about professional development needs becomes available to aid in planning for follow-up.

- Anonymously share perceptions about the other discipline to "vent" frustrations developed over time and help all share humor about stereotypes.
- Self-assess one's attitudes and goals about the collaborative process.
- Self-assess one's feelings about the other professional(s) or parent(s), the student(s), and the organization(s), and describe how those perceptions might impact the collaborative process.
- Self-report the most important skills learned throughout one's life that would support collaboration (e.g., goal planning, organization, communication).
- Small group problem solve a case situation, drawing on each other's strengths and backgrounds.
- Brainstorm ways to support collaboration immediately, 6 months in the future, and 2 years in the future.

***Inservice Training Workshops.*** Three broad formats can be identified for inservice workshops and related training activities in general: (a) awareness, (b) instructional or procedural information, and (c) hands-on learning (skill building).

- *Awareness workshops* simply seek to expose participants to a body of information or to foster a particular attitude (often so that additional, more in-depth instruction or development is welcome). This format is probably most common for numerous one-shot in-school workshops, such as presentations during orientation sessions at the start of a year.
- The *instructional* or *procedural information* format aims to share useful guidelines for developing instruction or other interventions. Even though the presentation may at least partially appear like an awareness workshop (i.e., lecture type, large-group arrangement), the goal is quite different.
- Both the awareness and the instructional format are typically isolated events without opportunity for active involvement or follow-up, so generalization to the classroom may be questionable. Two alternatives are the *active training format* and the *technical assistance, individualized problem-solving format*, both of which emphasize much more learner participation.

**Reflective Question 2.1:** ***How has recent federal legislation influenced the trend toward collaboration? What forms does such collaboration take?***

## COLLABORATION WITH STUDENTS

The most essential partners in the educational process, of course, are those most affected: the individuals with special needs themselves and their family members. Our educational institutions, as a whole, are currently poised to keep that belief foremost in their thinking and actions. Recent emergence of self-determination curricula, peer-mediated learning models, self-regulation approaches for learning and behavior, conflict mediation training, and other forms of student leadership and self-advocacy have demonstrated that student-directed decision making carries enormous merits.

IDEA 2004 continues to include specific requirements that promote student participation and voice in educational planning. Two examples illustrate this fact. First, the student should be a member of the IEP team, whenever this is possible. This implies that the student be considered an equal member of this team, that the student be empowered to participate as a fully contributing member, and that collaborative exchanges occur. Second, transition planning that must occur by age 16 must be based on students' preferences, interests, and postschool goals, addressing all major future life domains (e.g., education, employment, adult living, community participation, recreation/leisure, etc.).

In addition to IDEA's requirements related to the IEP, educators have access to numerous other formal and informal approaches for collaborating with students. Chapter 13 describes *self-determination instruction* for learners with exceptionalities, which helps to build the foundational skills needed for students to actively engage in their educational programs. Furthermore, Holub, Lamb, and Bang's (1998) portrayal of varied high schools' experiences with self-determination instruction in special and general education provides helpful insights, as well as implementation suggestions for teachers and administrators.

Additional opportunities for collaborative activities include cooperative learning, peer tutoring, and conflict resolution training. Murray (1994) lists the most researched **cooperative learning** practices—learning together—student teams-achievement divisions (STAD); team assisted individualization (TAI); teams-games-tournaments (TGT), and jigsaw—in describing the power of mutual dependence in motivating many students to work harder to achieve. **Partner learning** or **peer tutoring,** such as peer-assisted learning (Fuchs, Fuchs, & Burish, 2000), has demonstrated numerous benefits over the past 20 years (McNeil, 1994). **Conflict resolution training** has successfully prepared students of all ages to take charge of and resolve interpersonal conflicts at school (Schrumpf, 1994). Finally, when given opportunity and support, many students will *assess and direct their own learning* in positive, productive ways (Moore, 2003), such as taking charge of parent conferences, even at the elementary level (Austin, 1994; Bassett & Lehman, 2002).

One area where teachers can establish a collaborative arrangement with students is preparing them to be in inclusive classrooms. Often students, especially older students, may have concerns about being placed in such a setting. Teachers should identify the concerns that students have and then discuss ways to address these concerns. A simple checklist for inducing such a discussion is provided in Figure 2-4.

**Reflective Question 2.2:** ***What strategies can be used to promote the involvement of students in their own educational programs?***

**FIGURE 2–4** Inclusion concerns guide for the student

Educator: ____________________ Students: ____________________ Subject: ____________________

Check each item perceived by you to be of concern to the mainstreamed student relative to the identified subject area.

- ☐ Completing assignments on time
- ☐ Having too many assignments
- ☐ Understanding the material and assignments
- ☐ Remembering times to go to special education classroom
- ☐ Keeping track of daily assignments and responsibilities
- ☐ Keeping track of books and supplies
- ☐ Knowing where the special education classroom is located and how to get there
- ☐ Missing activities of interest as a result of attending different classes (general or special education)
- ☐ Being on time when changing classes
- ☐ Different expectations by teachers in general and special education classrooms
- ☐ Difficulty level of class assignments
- ☐ Receiving necessary assistance to complete assignments in the general education classroom
- ☐ Dealing with problems associated with changing classrooms throughout the day
- ☐ Sufficient time to complete in-class assignments
- ☐ Sufficient time to complete classroom tests
- ☐ Homework from general education classroom
- ☐ Having to make up large amounts of work when returning to the general education classroom from the special education classroom
- ☐ Feelings about being mainstreamed
- ☐ Feelings toward own abilities
- ☐ Other:

*Source:* From *Curriculum Adaptations for Students with Learning and Behavior Problems,* 3e (p. 38), by J. J. Hoover and J. R. Patton, 2005, Austin, TX: PRO-ED, Inc. Copyright 2005 by PRO-ED, Inc. Reprinted with permission.

## COLLABORATION WITH FAMILIES

Families of students with exceptionalities are not only faced with the typical challenges of child rearing but also must deal with additional demands associated with a family member with special needs (Turnbull, Turnbull, Erwin, & Soodak, 2005). Additionally, the extent of the family's involvement in their child's program may depend on events affecting the family at a given time. For instance, families who receive services when their child is an infant or toddler (Part C of IDEA) will engage the system much differently than they will later when their child is of preschool or school age. Nevertheless, parents are part of the IEP team and are equal members of this team.

Wehmeyer, Morningstar, and Husted (1999) summarize the changing characteristics of families that present new sets of challenges: family composition, employment patterns, widening income gaps, and ethnic/cultural identities. Teachers must be sensitive to these issues along with the fact that parents will interact with schools in a variety of ways, ranging from very involved to little or no involvement at all.

The concerns of families are particularly noteworthy in a time of change in service delivery, when their needs for communication and support are likely to be significantly increased. This section offers several suggestions for inviting and supporting *families* to be real partners in the home-school collaborative effort.

### Types of Collaborative Arrangements

Teachers and families can create a number of different types of collaborative relationships. Epstein (1995) discussed six types of partnerships between home and school. The following list of important home-school collaborations incorporates some of Epstein's partnerships with other key situations that arise as a result of IDEA.

- communication about school programs
- communication about the student's progress in school
- involvement of family members with their children in learning activities at home (i.e., homework)
- involvement of families as part of the IEP process (i.e., members of the IEP team)
- provision of information and skills about various aspects of parenting (e.g., managing behavior)
- empowerment of families as their child prepares to transition from school to dealing with the challenges of young adulthood by providing key information about postschool options
- involvement of families as volunteers at school

### Changing Paradigms to More Family-Centeredness

Increasingly, the fields of special education and rehabilitation view families as "systems" with their own style of family dynamics, their own unique cultures, and their status as a "system" to be regarded with respect equal to that given to agencies. Schoeller (1995, p. 5) asserts that to "walk the walk" and "find the story in the stranger" (i.e., to listen well to what they have to say) are the best ways to identify what youth and families want and need.

One major role of professionals in this relationship is to inform families and individuals with exceptionalities, based on experience, of what their options are, as well as to inform them of what the likely outcomes will be, and then to empower the family and individual to make the decisions about best options. Some parental needs that teachers can help to meet include (a) clear and accurate information concerning their child, (b) the opportunity for frequent communication, (c) assistance with academic and behavioral supports strategies, and (d) help with linking with other parents for mutual support.

Families' overriding need from teachers and other school professionals is twofold (Overton, 2005): (1) conveyance that teachers are committed to their child; and (2) recognition that teachers have respect for the family. In addition, families need to feel that a partnership really does exists, that is, that meeting the student's needs is truly a shared concern and that input from family members will be genuinely sought and respected (Overton, 2005; Springate & Stegelin, 1999).

School-based personnel also need to develop a cultural competence so that they can work effectively with families who come from backgrounds different from their own. Friend and Cook (2003) discuss four steps that can contribute to attaining such competence:

1. Determine one's cultural self-awareness.
2. Learn as much as one can about other cultures.
3. Develop an awareness of features that cut across cultures.
4. Acquire information about cultural practices related to students with whom you work.

Granting families agency status helps bureaucratic systems (which schools are) to more systematically treat families with the respect they merit. Systems deal with each other by giving sufficient advance notice of joint meetings so that attendance by all desired parties is maximized, holding meetings at times and locations agreeable to other parties, monitoring meeting exchanges to support all voices being heard, and ensuring that copies of all pertinent information are distributed in a timely fashion. Families should (and with this paradigm, will) receive equal consideration. A number of specific indicators of a collaborative partnership were summarized by Wehmeyer et al. (1999), including:

- prompt, honest, open sharing of information, impressions, and judgments
- two-way sharing of information without fear of being negatively judged
- mutual respect for each other's expertise and sensitivity to new areas of learning
- shared goals, planning, and decision making

Teachers must accept and impress upon parents their critical role in the assessment, IEP planning, and instructional process. The impact of parent participation on struggling students' academic performance has been clearly documented (Callahan, Rademacher, & Hildreth, 1998). To achieve parental cooperation, sharing with parents the variety of ways in which they can be involved will be beneficial. Table 2-5 summarizes possible roles that parents can play.

## Strategies to Promote Family Partnerships

**Conferences.** We all know communication is the key to positive, productive relationships. A key element of home-school communication is the meeting or conference, whether formal or informal. Some specific suggestions for teachers can be helpful with family conferences and program planning meetings:

- Be honest and direct with families.
- Avoid technical terms.
- Be clear and concise.
- Do not speculate about issues for which you have no information. Discuss only what you know and

**TABLE 2–5** Parents' role in the assessment process to identify disabilities

**Before the evaluation, parents:**

- May initiate the evaluation process by requesting that the school system evaluate their child.
- May be notified by the school, and give their consent, before any initial evaluation of the child may be conducted.
- May wish to talk with the person responsible for conducting the evaluation.
- May find it useful to become informed about assessment issues in general and any specific issues relevant to their child.
- May need to advocate for a comprehensive evaluation.
- May suggest specific questions they would like to see addressed through the evaluation.
- Should inform the school of any accommodations the student will need.
- Should inform the school if they need an interpreter, translator, or other accommodations during their discussions with the school.
- May prepare their child for the evaluation process, explaining what will happen and, where necessary, reducing the child's anxiety.

**During the evaluation process, parents:**

- Need to share with the school their insights into the child's background and past and present school performance.
- May wish to share with the school any prior school records, reports, tests, or evaluation information on their child.
- May need to share information about cultural differences that can illuminate the educational teams understanding of the student.
- Need to make every effort to attend interviews the school may set up with them and provide information about their child.

**After the evaluation, parents:**

- Need to carefully consider the results that emerge from their child's evaluation, in light of their own observations and knowledge of the child.
- May share their insights and concerns about the evaluation results with the school and suggest areas where additional information may be needed. Schools may or may not act upon parents' suggestions, and parents have certain resources under law, should they feel strongly about pursuing the matter.
- Participate fully in the development of their child's Individualized Education Program (IEP).

*Source:* From "Assessing Children for the Presence of Disability," by B. B. Waterman, 1994, *NICHCY News Digest, 4*(1), p. 12. Copyright 1994 by NICHCY. Adapted with permission.

about which you have data (i.e., what you can document).

- Prepare for the meeting by discussing the meeting with parents well in advance, agreeing mutually on a time and location for the meeting, organizing your notes, reviewing pertinent information, and planning an agenda—with input from the family and student when possible.
- Create a positive atmosphere, agree on the purpose of the meeting, employ good communication skills, take notes of what is being discussed, and end the meeting with a positive statement and appreciation to the family members for coming.
- After the meeting, organize your notes for future reference, initiate action on any items requiring attention, determine when a follow-up meeting is needed, and send out a summary of the meeting.
- If you are scheduling a conference that may be a hostile one, have someone else sit in to help verify what transpires and to assist with redirecting awkward interactions. Encourage family members to do the same.

**Informal Communication.** Other forms of communication may be less formal than conferences but equally important and productive. These include telephone contacts (often a key way of monitoring positive communication lines) and written communication. Telephone conversations provide an excellent vehicle for sharing information, usually of a more immediate nature. Some teachers encourage families to call them at home, whereas others discourage this practice. A teacher's job can be enriched by establishing open lines of communication with families, which often requires availability beyond the school day. Teachers should take notes of every phone conversation with families that relates to a student, school, or home issue. Research indicates definite benefits from telephone communication, even if primarily through voicemail (Jayanthi, Nelson, Sawyer, Bursuck, & Epstein, 1994).

Written communication is another ongoing vehicle for home-school collaboration. The most common form of written communication is the note, intended to convey information in a variety of formats, although e-mail is rapidly replacing handwritten notes. However, teachers must first investigate to determine if this mode will work for each family and in what language(s). Teachers with written language or spelling challenges should have someone else proofread their notes. Progress reports to parents are also common. Although they typically occur only at the end of a grading period, more regular correspondence about progress is encouraged—daily for some students, less often for others.

Whatever the schedule, teachers need to develop systems for sharing progress information with parents in a form they can use. One approach uses student assignment books with space for homework assignments and for teacher and parent comments as well. This type of interchange can easily occur on a daily basis. In research on home communication, general educators at elementary and middle school levels indicated that assignments sheets and parent signatures on assignments were helpful (Polloway, Epstein, Bursuck, Jayanthi, & Cumblad, 1994). Some districts are moving to grades being posted weekly on district websites.

Some teachers find that newsletters are an interesting way to convey to families what occurs in their classrooms. Obviously, this technique does not address individual student concerns, but it helps to share overall program information, upcoming events, and general topics. Even though the quality of newsletters varies greatly according to the equipment and technical expertise available, we believe that newsletters should look attractive and be error-free. Teachers who want to produce newsletters should be alert to what may be the most difficult obstacle—keeping to a regular schedule.

Teachers and families may be creative in identifying other methods, such as web pages, for ongoing communication and regular planning. It is the educators' responsibility to search for a mutually agreeable set of means by which to accomplish that collaborative work, so that students have the opportunity to do their best work. To help toward that end, Dietz (1997) has delineated a comprehensive set of practical methods for promoting school-family partnerships, embodied in the following components:

- Ways to increase family involvement
- Measures to assess partnership success
- Needs assessments/partnering status surveys
- Sample district policies that promote school-family partnerships
- Parent survey guidelines for input regarding curriculum
- Partnering checklist
- Partners in learning agreement (for student, parent, teacher, and administrator)

**Reflective Question 2.3:** ***How can special educators most effectively convey to families the nature of the home-school partnership necessary for the success of students with special needs?***

## COLLABORATION WITH GENERAL EDUCATORS

General education personnel at all K–12 levels are important partners in many different types of collaboration. The particular configuration of the special and general education interaction may vary, depending on which student and/or program situations exist. This section describes the barriers to effective partnership, the various possible collaborative arrangements that exist in schools, and ways to make the process work.

### Barriers to Collaboration

Several issues may impede the success of students with exceptionalities who are partially or fully included in general education settings, as well as of the teachers attempting to serve them. This latter point relates directly to certain barriers or challenges to establishing effective collaboration between special and general education teachers. Some of the ideas listed below were introduced earlier in the chapter and have been compiled from a variety of sources (Elliott & McKenney, 1998; Friend & Cook, 2003; Hourcade & Bauwens, 2003; Jones & Carlier, 1995).

- lack of administrative support and encouragement of collaborative activities
- attitudinal issues
- teacher's focus on the class as a whole rather than on individual learning needs
- required coverage of content standards overlaid with needs for curricular accommodations
- insufficient preparation or confidence to differentiate instruction for diverse learners, especially those with extreme behavioral events
- lack of funds needed to directly support all students needing individualized help (e.g., adaptive equipment, personnel)
- insufficient time allocated for real collaborative efforts to work
- intensification of teachers' daily challenges when students with exceptionalities are included on top of a full class load
- lack of real assistance due to the caseloads among special educators and delays with referrals
- absence of an efficient and effective prereferral system that would assist general education teachers with students prior to an official referral and eligibility determination
- students' lack of self-determination/self-advocacy and other collaborative skills

### Changing Relations, Changing Options

The ongoing relationship between general and special education has transformed regularly since the original passage of Public Law 94–142 in 1975, as systems have adapted to the sociopolitical dynamics of a given time and to federal/state mandates that have been issued by statute or regulatory action. A number of resources (see Lewis & Doorlag, 2003; Smith et al., 2008; Vaughn, Bos, & Schumm; 2003) provide rationales and strategies for unifying learners with a broad range of diverse learning needs, including those linked to cultural and language differences as well as specific exceptionality categories.

As a result of changes in IDEA, requirements of NCLB, and the emergence of a multitiered system of intervention for students with special needs, the role of special educators has significantly changed in recent years. The emphasis is clearly on providing these students access to the general education curriculum and doing so within the general education classroom whenever possible. As Table 1–2 illustrated, the skill sets that special education personnel now must possess are broader than before and have a decided feel of collaboration with other school-based personnel.

**Inclusive education,** however, must be approached with careful planning, an individualized learner perspective, and recognition that certain factors have to be in place for it to be considered "responsible inclusion" (Smith et al., 2008; Webber, 1997). Table 2–6 lists the five dimensions and associated features identified by Smith and colleagues (2008). Failing to plan, recognize individual needs, and address the five dimensions of responsible inclusion will inevitably lead to unsuccessful outcomes.

Many advocacy and professional organizations (e.g., Council for Learning Disabilities, Learning Disabilities Association of America, Children and Adults with Attention-Deficit/Hyperactivity Disorder, Council for Exceptional Children, and the National Education Association) have issued position statements or papers that (a) affirm inclusion as an important goal *when appropriate*, and (b) caution against wholesale placement policies that ignore specific learners' special support needs. A number of philosophical and practical issues about inclusive education, the widely differing models of implementing it, and conflicting research findings all have helped sustain widespread and often emotional debate about this concept.

**TABLE 2–6** Critical dimensions of inclusive classrooms

| *Dimension* | *Features* |
|---|---|
| **Sense of community and social acceptance** | • Every student is valued and nurtured.<br>• All class members are viewed as equal.<br>• All students have the opportunity to contribute.<br>• All contributions are respected.<br>• Basic needs of children and youth are met within the context of the learning environment.<br>• Teachers have a positive attitude about students.<br>• Teachers hold high expectations for students with special needs.<br>• Students with special needs enjoy high levels of interaction with all students in the classroom.<br>• Friendships are developed and facilitated by the teacher. |
| **Appreciation of student diversity** | • Teachers make effort to get to know all students.<br>• With the teacher's lead, the teacher and students demonstrate a sensitivity to cultural, linguistic, community, and family differences.<br>• Diversity is promoted as a valuable opportunity to learn from and about others.<br>• Teachers create an atmosphere where diversity is celebrated. |
| **Attention to curricular needs** | • The specific curricular needs of students are not compromised by placement.<br>• Access to the general education curriculum should be an operating goal.<br>• A student's learning and life needs should be the driving force that directs program planning.<br>• Specific knowledge and skills acquisition is recognized and addressed within the context of the general education setting.<br>• Content must be meaningful to students in a current and future sense.<br>• Curricular adaptations are likely to be needed.<br>• The concept of university design for learning should become the operant principle guiding future curriculum development. |
| **Effective management and instruction** | • Students thrive in a setting where learning is encouraged and nurtured.<br>• Classrooms that are managed well allow for students to experience educational benefit from the experience.<br>• Classroom management includes the following dimensions: psychosocial, physical, procedural, behavioral, instructional, and organisational (Smith, Polloway, Patton, & Dowdy, 2004).<br>• Teachers must be aware of and demonstrate appropriate and instruction use of effective instructional practices, as students with special needs will benefit from empirically based instruction.<br>• Teachers need to be able to make necessary accommodations (i.e., instructional supports) to lesson planning, instructional delivery, and student responses to account for a wide range of individual differences.<br>• Consideration of assistive technology is warranted. |
| **Personnel support and collaboration** | • General education teachers will need the support of others to adequately address the needs of a range of students who are experiencing learning and behavioral difficulties.<br>• Special education personnel should work closely with general education teachers—a variety of models for doing so are possible: collaborative consultation, teacher assistance teams, co-teaching.<br>• Paraeducators can provide valuable support to students in inclusive settings; however, specific methods for supervising and working with this group must be understood (Pickett & Gerlach, 2003).<br>• Related service personnel such as speech-language pathologists, occupational therapists, and physical therapists will also need to be available to the general education teacher. |

*Source:* From *Curriculum Adaptation for Students with Learning and Behavior Problems,* 3e (pp. 30–31), by J. J. Hoover and J. R. Patton, 2005, Austin, TX: PRO-ED, Inc. 

## Collaboration Models Linking General and Special Education

Since the inception of special education programs, the relationship between general and special educators has been essential for a number of reasons. Since the inception of IDEA, the need to collaborate has existed. However, in recent times, as noted above, an emphasis on collaboration has emerged. This section describes a range of collaborative arrangements that involve both general education and special education teachers and is based, in part, on the organizational schema introduced by Idol (2002). The arrangements discussed below include prereferral collaboration, consulting teacher services, cooperative teaching, supportive resource programs, and collaborative efforts between school and community.

**Prereferral Collaboration.** The need to address learning, social, and behavioral issues that are likely to arise in the general education classroom due to the diversity of these classes is a foremost concern. In addition, eliminating any misdiagnoses (false positives) is the ultimate aim of any assessment program within general and special education. Several collaborative models have been found effective in accomplishing this purpose, including the original mainstreamed assistance team (MAT) project, which used a multidisciplinary, preventative, prereferral, and intervention process to serve large numbers of students with mild disability levels as well as nondisabled at-risk students (Fuchs & Fuchs, 1987).

The student assistance team (SAT) described by McKay and Sullivan (1990) involved collaboration within a team of general and special educators to serve both mainstreamed and unidentified at-risk students in the general program. The five-step process led to interventions that could be aimed at the entire class or individual students. Use of the SAT approach was found to decrease the referrals for special education services as well as the number of "no exceptionality" classifications.

Similar to the MAT and SAT is the **teacher assistance team (TAT)** model (Chalfant & Pysh, 1989), defined by Bos and Vaughn (1998) as "a within-building problem-solving model designed to provide a teacher support system for classroom teachers" (p. 472). The TAT model is built around a set of assumptions that recognize the knowledge, experience, and power that teachers bring to the learning experience and that encourage teachers to rely on each other to seek their own solutions (Chalfant & Pysh, 1989). TATs follow a basic set of procedures. A core team of three members is elected by their peers (most should not be specialists), with those who are asking for help joining the team for their respective concerns. Others are asked to join as needed. Referring teachers complete a request for help that includes the following information:

- What do you want the student to be able to do differently?
- What are the student's strengths and weaknesses?
- What strategies have been used to help the student resolve the issues?
- What other background information and/or test data are relevant?

The team member assigned to coordinate the referral examines the case information, gathers additional data if needed, creates (and shares) a visual representation of the problem, and arranges a problem-solving meeting. At the meeting, recommendations for the teacher(s) to use in the classroom are generated, or referral to another program might be suggested. Finally, the team's success in resolving issues brought to them is evaluated. This approach's numerous benefits for students, families, and professionals have been documented (Bos & Vaughn, 1998).

A structured way of identifying and clarifying the needs of students at a prereferral stage is the use of instruments that gather information systematically from general education teachers. This informaton is then used by the team to determine the type and quantity of intervention needed. Two resources have been developed to assist with this process. The first resource is a manual for establishing and implementing an effective prereferral process (Buck, Polloway, Patton, & Williams, in press). The second resource is a formal instrument for collecting data on a student, *Prereferral Assessment Inventories*, that includes both a normative component (if needed for determining need for services) and an informal component obtaining detailed information about skill competence in four areas (reading, writing, math, and social) (Hoover, Patton, Hresko, & Hammill, 2007).

**Collaborative Consulting Teacher Services.** This collaborative option involves the special education teacher working outside of the classroom with the general education teacher. This arrangement is subject to the potential problem of the special education teacher being perceived as an "expert" consultant and thus vulnerable to establishing a relationship that is not based on equal status. Moreover, new special education teachers lack the experience that is associated with credibility by many general education teachers.

Even though the above cautions must be noted, this arrangement can be designed and executed to provide benefit to general education teachers and the students with special needs whom they have in their classes. Idol (2002) generated a list of services that special education personnel can provide in this model (see Table 2-7).

**Cooperative Teaching.** Cooperative teaching, sometimes referred to as co-teaching, is a type of direct collaboration whereby "two or more professionals jointly deliver substantive instruction to a diverse, or blended, group of students in a single physical space" (Cook & Friend, 1995, p. 1). Hourcade and Bauwens (2003) further explain the meaning of this collaborative option by indicating that the personnel involved

- voluntarily agree to work together in a coactive and coordinated fashion
- possess distinct and complementary sets of skills
- share roles, resources, and responsibilities in a sustained effort
- work toward the common goal of school success for all students (p. 41)

Cooperative teaching can involve a variety of strategies including those used by the general education and special education teacher to promote learning. These roles are outlined in the Teacher Tips on page 41.

Friend and Cook (2000) share a helpful set of questions for creating a collaborative interaction in co-teaching situations (see Table 2-8).

**Supportive Resource Programs.** Many students with special needs receive part of their education outside of the general education classroom. Although not thought of as a very collaborative setting due to the lack of interaction between the special and general education teachers, the resource room can, if designed properly, function as a support to the ongoing activities of the general education classroom. If set up correctly, a collaborative dynamic can be achieved.

An example of a supportive resource room concept is the *content mastery center* that is used in some states. This arrangement is completely supportive of

**TABLE 2–7** Sample role description for a consulting teacher

Consulting teachers work indirectly with classroom teachers as a means of facilitating the progress of special education students who are included in the general education program or who are mainstreamed for part of the school day. Special education consultation is a process for providing special education services to students with special needs who are enrolled in general education. Consultation is (a) indirect, in that the special education consultant does not provide the instructional service to the student(s), (b) collaborative in that all individuals involved in the consultative process are assumed to have expertise to contribute and responsibility to share for instructional outcomes, (c) voluntary, in that all parties are willing participants in the consultative process, and (d) problem-solving-oriented, in that the goal of consultation is to prevent or resolve student problems.

The types of services provided by the consulting teacher include the following:

1. collaborative involvement in the development of all IEPs for students receiving consulting teacher services;
2. monitoring of all IEPs for students receiving consulting teacher services;
3. provision of consultation services to classroom teachers;
4. help in solving student-related problems pertaining to academic problems, study skill problems, and behavior and discipline problems;
5. help in solving classroom-related problems pertaining to curricular modifications, instructional adaptations, and teaching arrangements;
6. help in facilitating successful transitions of students with disabilities who were previously in more restrictive special education placements and are now enrolled in either inclusive or mainstream classrooms;
7. provision of demonstration teaching and modeling of newly developed teaching innovations;
8. participation in collaborative problem solving with classroom teachers of inclusive or mainstream classrooms;
9. facilitation of involvement of parents of special education students to accommodate parental involvement in program development;
10. provision of classroom-based assessments using curriculum-based assessments, portfolio assessments, and classroom observations;
11. monitoring of student progress of all special education students assigned to consulting teacher services.

*Source:* Adapted Creating Collaborative and Inclusive Schools (p. 36), by Idol, 2002, Austin, TX: PRO-ED, Inc. Copyright 2002 by PRO-ED, Inc. Adapted with permission.

TEACHER *Tips*

## Cooperative Teaching

A variety of cooperative teaching arrangements can be used to enhance classroom collaboration. These include:

- **One teaching, one assisting:** One teacher takes the instructional lead, and the other teacher simultaneously observes, monitors, or tutors individual students.
- **Station teaching:** The teachers divide the physical arrangement of the room into three sections, two that support teacher-directed instruction and one for independent seatwork. Course content and classwork are also divided into three distinct lessons. One lesson is taught by each of the two teachers, and the third lesson consists of a seatwork assignment that students will complete independently or with minimal supervision. The students in the class are assigned to three separate groups, and each group rotates through each of the three teaching stations.
- **Parallel teaching:** The class of students is divided into two heterogeneous groups of equal size (both groups containing students with disabilities). After jointly planning a lesson, each teacher teaches the same content, at the same time, to half of the students in the class. Each teacher is free to design practice assignments and explanations that uniquely suit his/her teaching style and his/her students' learning needs and capabilities.
- **Alternative teaching:** The class of students is divided into two unequal groups, a larger group that can be engaged in a review or extension activity and a smaller group that needs to have concepts retaught, a lesson previewed, or a particular skill reemphasized.
- **Team teaching:** Both teachers are actively engaged in instruction to the entire class of students. Though one teacher may take the instructional lead at one point in the lesson and the other teacher may assume the lead in another part of the lesson, both teachers are providing instruction together—finishing each other's sentences, clarifying each other's comments, or answering student questions.

*Source:* Adapted from "A Focus on Co-Teaching," by N. Zigmond and K. Magiera, 2001, *Current Practice Alerts;* 6, pp. 1–2.

**TABLE 2–8** Questions for creating a collaborative work relationship in co-teaching

| *Topic* | *Questions* |
|---|---|
| Philosophy and Beliefs | What are our overriding philosophies about the roles of teachers and teaching and about students and learning?<br>How do our instructional beliefs affect our instructional practice? |
| Parity Signals | How will we convey to students and others (e.g., teachers, parents) that we are equals in the classroom?<br>How can we ensure a sense of parity during instruction? |
| Classroom Routines | What are the instructional routines for the classroom?<br>What are the organizational routines for the classroom? |
| Discipline | What is acceptable and unacceptable student behavior?<br>Who is to intervene at what point in students' behavior?<br>What are the rewards and consequences used in the classroom? |
| Feedback | What is the best way to give each other feedback?<br>How will we ensure that both positive and negative issues are raised? |
| Noise | What noise level are we comfortable with in the classroom? |
| Pet Peeves | What aspects of teaching and classroom life does each of us feel strongly about?<br>How can we identify our pet peeves so as to avoid them? |

*Source: From Interactions: Collaboration Skills for School Professionals* (3rd ed., p. 64), by M. Friend and L. Cook, 2000, Published by Allyn & Bacon, Boston: MA. Copyright © 2000 by Pearson Education. Reprinted by Permission of the publisher.

the instruction and curricular goals of the general education classroom. Students who need some additional, temporary assistance can go to this setting when needed for a variety of reasons (e.g., accommodations to testing). What is essential to this process is that collaboration between teachers is operative.

**Collaboration Between School and Community.** Collaborative efforts with persons outside of school are regularly needed and should be cultivated, as with other collaborative efforts. Outside contacts and services might be needed for students with significant mental health issues or in the process of acting on the goals in a transition plan.

## Establishing Collaborative Programs

The essential elements for establishing collaborative programming seem similar to those employed for specific problem solving. Nowacek (1991) gleaned several stages in the process from her extensive interviews with teachers about their teaming. These stages are summarized in Table 2-9.

**Taking the First Steps: Deciding to and Selecting Who.** Deciding to collaborate and selecting the collaborators were the first steps experienced by Nowacek's (1991) interviewees. The choices were made by the teachers, although having a supportive administration was helpful. In one case, the speech-language therapist approached a special educator and general educator about co-teaching and introduced them to a program that gave them a focus with which to begin working together. In another case, professional development on a collaborative model inspired a group of special educators to implement the model. They carefully reviewed and planned students' schedules and caseloads before identifying content-area teachers with whom they needed (and secondarily also wanted) to collaborate. In the third situation, the high school principal introduced the special educators to successful team teaching through a visit to another city; then he recruited general

**TABLE 2–9** Stages, features, and examples of the process to establish collaborative programs

| *Steps* | *Features* | *Examples* |
|---|---|---|
| 1. Deciding to collaborate and selecting the collaborators | Teachers have choices. Supportive administration is very helpful. Many varied role groups are potential partners. Needs assessments can help direct decisions. | Professional development activity inspired a group of special educators to try it, and they selected potential partners based on students' needs. |
| 2. Planning roles and responsibilities | Often staff find they need new or modified skills and activities, including how to collaborate. They may need to self-teach or learn formally how to do that. Partners may need to define just what roles they are willing to play. Those roles will change each year as kids' needs change and teachers' growth evolves. | "I did a lot of grading the first year. . . . I just felt it was really important that I understood the kids' work."<br><br>"You have to be willing to look and see what the needs are and then fit yourself into those." |
| 3. Discussing implementation problems | Structured processes help teams tackle barriers to student or collaboration success. A problem-centered, team-oriented approach is required due to ongoing systemic challenges. Students are part of the solution. | Problem-solving worksheet, teacher work groups, and circles of friends help generate good solutions to barriers. |
| 4. Planning the curriculum | Options for participation and team support exist all along the spectrum. Systematic processes for planning allow strategic up-front curricular development that can build in easy access/participation for all. | Students may do the same things, totally different things, or anywhere in between. Curricula can be designed flexibly to allow varied modes for getting into, responding, and engaging. |
| 5. Differentiating Instruction | Teams plan specific changes in content, delivery, materials, and so on that students require to succeed. Strategic organization and delivery of content can enhance all learners' achievement. | Adding or highlighting pictures for nonreaders during oral reading time. Graphic organizers can "unlock" stories, chapters, lessons, units, and courses. |

educators to participate. In all situations, educators' choice and empowerment to act were key.

**Planning Roles and Responsibilities.** General and special educators often find that new or modified skills and activities are needed as a next step to make inclusive programming successful for individual students and for themselves, as can be seen from examining Table 1-2. Each group may need to self-teach or formally learn better ways to work collaboratively. Langone (1998) describes the competencies needed for inclusive settings, including management of personnel; management of time, materials, technology, and environment; and management of communication needs and conflict.

*Shared decision making* at some point is critical (in this case, during or prior to the IEP process, given the expanded role of general educators in that activity). Preparing all parties for the inclusion of the target student(s) is essential.

**Discussing Implementation Issues.** Logistical issues become important in this collaborative process for inclusive schooling. First and foremost, the *schedules* of students and teachers become paramount in making it work. Specialists may be the only one of their kind in the group, grade level, or "family" with whom they are teaching and thus must spread themselves rather thinly. For instance, at the middle school level, they may be teaming in the core classes (language arts, mathematics, social studies), have one or two pull-out sections for study skills instruction and extra support for staying caught up in content classes, and have a shared planning period with their teammates. The shared planning period is difficult to make time for but is critical for successful teaming and problem solving.

Another logistical issue pertains to the particular grade level of the student(s). Elementary programs generally tend to be geared more to addressing diverse learning needs. As a result, scheduling, adaptations, teaming, and other arrangements are likely to be flexible and focused on student success.

High school programs have a tendency to be more content oriented than learner oriented, with the focus on having students acquire large amounts of information in target areas rather than on learning about learning. Thus, the focus on acquiring academic credits (toward graduation) often generates a resistance to creative scheduling, content arrangement, and teaming options. Exceptions exist, of course, as in the specialized, team-oriented academies around which many high schools now pattern their curricula, or the block scheduling that many high schools now offer. Middle school programs tend to share characteristics of both, and many middle school personnel are rethinking their roles and approaches due to their recognition of that stage as such a critical turning point for youth.

*Problem-solving sessions* become an integral part of initial and ongoing planning for all parties involved. Bishop and Jubala (1994) describe how a special educator and general educator met regularly at the beginning of a student's sixth-grade year to identify his needs and adapt his program as necessary. They examined the sixth-grade schedule, addressing times when the student required more support or curricular adaptations and ways to meet those needs. Knackendoffel et al. (1992) find that a worksheet format is particularly useful for resolving a range of dilemmas. Figure 2-2 introduced at the beginning of this chapter is an example of this type of worksheet.

***Student-Driven Solutions.*** Numerous examples exist of creative answers to inclusive education issues that peers readily work out. Person-centered planning procedures (e.g., personal futures planning) necessarily include the target student's friends in brainstorming activities and have proven very helpful in solving problems (Bassett & Lehmann, 2002). Bishop and Jubala (1994) describe how a meeting of one student's circle of friends addressed the student's refusal to wear his hearing aids. The friends' demonstration of orthodontic retainers, glasses, and protective sports equipment helped the student see that everybody uses special equipment, and he began wearing his aids.

***Teacher-Generated Solutions.*** Teacher workgroups or study groups are "simply two or more teachers who get together on a regular basis to help each other understand and solve the problems they encounter as they try to improve educational outcomes for students" (Ferguson, 1994, p. 43). The original groups began in Oregon from a need to identify or develop innovative interventions for students with severe disabilities, resulting in the Elementary/Secondary System (ESS) used in several states.

Teacher work/study groups often collaborate with area universities to support themselves in proactively addressing the changes and problems that occur systemically. Three critical features drive the groups: (a) teacher directedness, (b) outcomes orientation, and

(c) a focus on continuous evaluation and improvement. Ferguson describes three common rules (be positive, be fair, and keep focused), gives a series of "tricks" and guidelines (e.g., do not interrupt), and lists the most effective teacher workgroups. In many schools or districts, solutions are collaboratively created by curriculum committees, school restructuring councils, site-based management teams, grade-level families, or other ongoing teams.

**Planning the Curriculum.** York, Doyle, and Kronberg (1992) present a curriculum development process for inclusive classrooms that incorporates four "rounds":

1. Teams initially plan and prepare for a smooth transition to the new arrangement. This stage may include initiating dialogues about inclusion, identifying potential barriers, and planning strategies to maximize a sense of community.
2. During the first weeks, team members encourage cohesiveness and identify the needs and performance of the target student(s).
3. Later, the entire class collectively envisions their desired future of inclusiveness. (What do they want to happen in their classroom among learners with special needs? among all learners?)
4. Given what they now know, the team decides how to optimize current options; individual student priorities are carried out within the schedule and attention is given to specific learning outcomes.

IDEA 2004 makes it clear that students with disabilities must have access to the same curriculum to which students without disabilities are exposed. Giancreco, Cloninger, and Iverson (1993) specify four major levels for students' participation in the general curriculum. Determining the appropriate level for each student is a critical prerequisite to planning the content and delivery of the curriculum. The levels are:

- **same as others:** same activities, same curricular focus and objectives—and what should be used to ensure access to the general education curriculum
- **multilevel:** same activities but different level (e.g., fewer items, lower grade-level demands of items)—basically differentiated instruction.
- **curriculum overlapping:** same activities but different objectives (e.g., a health objective within a science class or a functional math objective within a vocational class)—this represents a modification and is appropriate for students with more significant challenges who are in inclusive settings
- **alternative:** different activities, different objectives

Fad and Ryser (1993) found that emphasis on social/behavioral factors was just as important as academic competencies when supporting students' success in general education.

The nearby Teacher Tip provides a list of survival skills that will often be critical to success in the curriculum. They reflect the need for both academic and social survival skills.

**TEACHER *Tips*** — **Secondary Level**

### Teaching Survival Skills

Currently more instruction for students with disabilities is taking place through co-teaching arrangements in general education settings. Often school survival skills are best taught to everyone at once since all students can benefit from them. These include:

| For *Academic Survival*, teach skills like: | For *Social Survival*, teach skills like: |
|---|---|
| note taking<br>time management | giving and accepting compliments |
| test taking | working together in a group |
| outlining | giving and accepting criticism |
| reading for meaning | empathizing with others |
| skimming, scanning | expressing appreciation |
| listening | dealing with frustration |
| paraphrasing | initiating and ending conversations |
| organization | compromising |
| | expressing appreciation |

***Differentiated Instruction.*** Students with exceptionalities will invariably require some personalized package of adaptations of instructional content, delivery, materials, environment, response options, and/or evaluation methods within the general setting. Smith et al. (2008) offer specific curricular adaptations distinguished by elementary and secondary levels. Increasing resources in ready-to-use formats (e.g., workbooks, notebooks, CD-ROMs) are available, including items such as graphic organizers, test adaptation recommendations, alternative assessment strategies, communication tools, organizational strategies, and other supports.

The key point is that differentiated instruction must be tailored to individual students' needs, such as adding or highlighting pictures to allow a nonreader to follow along in a novel the class is reading, or providing speech therapy within a student's small science group (where they are learning technical vocabulary) rather than pulling the student out of class (Bishop & Jubala, 1994). Many adaptations are simple and beneficial to all learners, whereas some require more effort and specialization.

> Reflective Question 2.4: ***What specific roles can special and general educators respectively play in successful classroom collaboration?***

## COLLABORATION WITH PARAEDUCATORS

**Paraeducators** comprise a significant portion of the workforce serving individuals with exceptionalities, and their roles continue to evolve as those of teachers and other staff change as well, including becoming an important part of the collaborative process as students are increasingly served in the general classroom (Pickett, Gerlach, Morgan, Likins, & Wallace, 2007). Their strategic participation can make or break a program, or a single student's success. Unfortunately, few teacher and administrator preparation programs work on how to select, train, lead, and collaborate on a long-term basis with these staff members (Pickett et al., 2007).

### Definitions

Various terms are used to describe paraeducators in school settings. Some of the more common terms include teacher's aide, educational assistant, instructional assistant, and paraprofessional. The common feature is that this individual works under the supervision of a teacher. Other paraprofessionals such as therapy assistants or job coaches may be in school settings as well.

Pickett, Faison, and Formanek (1993) define paraeducators as

> employees: (1) whose positions are either instructional in nature or who deliver other direct services to students and/or their parents; (2) who work under the supervision of teachers or other professional staff who have the ultimate responsibility for the design, implementation and evaluation of instructional programs and student progress. (p. 11)

This definition clearly refers to those whose job titles include teacher or educational assistants, human service technicians, therapy assistants, job coaches, and many others. These personnel work in settings that range from preschool to adult services and from total integration to almost total segregation.

### Rationales and Framework

Reasons to include paraeducators as team members, and for preparing to fully utilize their services, are apparent. Even model programs may be damaged if interpersonal or values conflicts between two or more adults, or failure to embrace job responsibilities, interfere with students' learning. Students or consumers ultimately pay the price. These problems typically result from inadequate communication and lack of planning. This section provides suggestions for improving and monitoring collaboration between professionals and paraeducators in educational or related services programs. The ideas offered are based on the notion that effective teamwork is the desired outcome; the ultimate goal, of course, is high quality of life for persons with exceptionalities (resulting from effective, efficient instructional and support programs).

Teamwork in the classroom or center involves distinct, complementary roles that sometimes overlap but that serve separate, unique purposes. The professional who wants to fully utilize the paraeducator's potential contributions should use a democratic style of leadership, with most responsibilities shared. Because the only real justification for hiring another adult in a program is to improve teaching and learning (broadly), paraeducators should actively participate in almost every aspect of the teaching process and classroom management. The teacher should be asking, "Is this a task that I would readily do, but because of time or student factors I cannot or should not do it right now?" If the answer is "yes," and the paraeducator understands that perspective, most problems of role expectations can be dispelled. The ideas that follow are based on this flexible team approach and are designed to fully integrate the paraeducator into the program as a true partner.

## Definition of Roles and Responsibilities

The instructional team model begins with a definition of roles and responsibilities for each team member. The biggest area of frustration between educators and paraeducators appears to be their (spoken or, more often, unspoken) expectations about respective roles and duties. Professionals have ultimate responsibility for their students' assessment and intervention programs and therefore are closely engaged with the preparation of IEPs or other individualized plans. Development and implementation of a beneficial program for a student, however, necessarily involves many other personnel, such as ancillary or related services providers, the paraeducator, parents, the student, and possibly others.

The paraeducator role is one of support and assistance, whether in general or specialized settings, teaming with various people, supervising small groups, tutoring students, supporting socioemotional adjustment, or coordinating with other professionals and parents (Blalock, 1991). The National Resource Center for Paraeducators has developed a multilevel system that describes the responsibilities of paraeducators. The three levels along with specific responsibilities are listed in Table 2-10. As Wallace (2007) notes, this list is not exhaustive and other knowledge and skill competencies are required to carry out the duties of being a paraeducator in school settings.

Figure 2-5 shows a breakdown of some major responsibilities delegated to both the teacher and the paraeducators, as a way to ensure that both are clear on role expectations. More detail about tasks frequently found in special education or related programs should be developed into lengthier checklists for discussion and possible demonstration, because numerous influences complicate the actual roles and responsibilities assumed by paraeducators in schools.

Paraeducators' support of students included in general education has been widespread and seriously appreciated for at least 20 years, but few have been prepared and truly supported in that role. "The inclusion team should establish that the instructional assistants are a significant part of the educational team, with the stipulation that they must not take independent action and make decisions without the teachers' knowledge" (Langone, 1998, p. 9). Langone also cautions that the team needs to protect paraeducators from being assigned inappropriately or being overused, by specifying their roles.

Paraeducators have been increasingly hired to implement community-based instruction (CBI), work/study, transition, and supported employment programs in schools, colleges, adult agencies, and the community. A growing number of programs for students 18–22 years of age to learn adult life skills in the community exist across the United States, employing paraeducators as community support assistants. Though these paraeducators work under the ultimate supervision of professionals (e.g., transition teachers), they typically are independent in the community (once trained), providing critical instruction or support in natural settings to individuals or small groups so that students with moderate or significant support needs can apply classroom learning in meaningful ways.

## Identification of Strengths, Weaknesses, and Work Styles

During interviews and initial employment, the supervising professional has the opportunity to assess (at least informally) the applicant's experiences, abilities, interests, educational philosophy, and goals in an effort to effectively match the position and the person. Brizzi (1982) suggests a variety of questions that could provide insights into the assignment of academic and general responsibilities:

- Why do you want to work with students?
- Tell me what you think makes the best learning environment.
- What do you think you can offer the students in this class?
- What are your talents? skills? What do you do in your leisure time?
- Do you type? speak another language? participate in sports, recreation, games? like math? do artistic activities?
- Are you comfortable communicating with students? staff? parents?
- What work have you done before? What did you like and dislike about your previous job(s)?
- What is your goal beyond this job?
- What subjects did you like and dislike in school?
- Who was your favorite teacher and why? What kind of teacher did you dislike and why?
- What could students learn from you that would help them develop independence? What do you think an independent person is? (p. 4)

**TABLE 2–10** Responsibilities for Paraeducators

**Level I Responsibilities for Paraeducators**

- Escorting students to buses and different learning environments
- Monitoring playgrounds, lunchrooms, hallways, and study halls
- Preparing learning materials and maintaining learning centers
- Assisting students with personal and hygienic care
- Assisting teachers in maintaining supportive learning environments that protect the safety, health, and well-being of students and staff
- Reinforcing learning experiences planned and introduced by teachers
- Practicing standards of professional and ethical conduct that are within the scope of paraeducator responsibilities

**Level II Responsibilities for Paraeducators (The responsibilities for Level II paraeducators include those in Level I as well as the following.)**

- Instructing individual or small groups of students following lesson plans developed by the teacher
- Assisting individual students with supplementary or independent study projects, as assigned by the teacher
- Assisting teachers with documenting student performance using assessment activities
- Sharing with teachers information that facilitates the planning process
- Implementing teacher-developed behavior management plans for students
- Preparing learning and instructional materials and maintaining adaptive equipment
- Assisting teachers in providing supportive learning environments that facilitate inclusion of students with diverse learning needs and in protecting the safety, health, and well-being of students and staff
- Participating in regularly scheduled teacher and paraeducator meetings that may also include other team members

**Level III Responsibilities for Paraeducators (The responsibilities for Level III paraeducators include those in Levels I and II as well as the following.)**

- Consulting with teachers during regularly scheduled meetings to share information that will facilitate the planning of learning experiences for individual or groups of students with disabilities, English language limitations, or other learning needs that may place learners at risk
- Implementing lesson and other plans developed by teachers to increase academic skills and the development of social and communication skills, self-esteem, and self-reliance
- Modifying curriculum and instructional activities for individual students, under the direction of teachers
- Assisting teachers to engage families in their children's learning experiences
- Supporting students in community-based learning environments to prepare them to make the transition from school to work and to participate in adult work (as appropriate)
- Familiarizing employers and other members of the community with the needs of individual students (as appropriate)
- Assisting teachers to maintain the student records required by the state or district
- Participating in Individualized Education Program (IEP), Individual Transition Plan (ITP), and Individual Family Service Plan (IFSP) planning team meetings, as required by the student's needs

*Source:* From Para in the schools (pp. 124–125), by A. L. Pickett, K. Gerlach, R. Morgan, M. Likins, and T. Wallace, 2007, Author, TX: PRO-ED, Inc. Copyright 2007 by PRO-ED, Inc. Reprented with permission.

The supervising professional can enhance the paraeducator's willingness to respond by sharing some personal experiences in some of the areas mentioned. Patience and a little coaxing are recommended because few paraeducators (especially potential ones) are used to discussing their strengths and talents.

Individual work styles are also important to understand for a teamwork relationship. They are best explored when team members first begin to work together, to avoid or minimize mistaken assumptions and disappointments. Houk and McKenzie (1985) developed two scales—one for the teacher and one for the paraeducator—that delineate a limited number of work style behaviors for both supervisors and paraeducators. The parallel structure of the two forms aids discussion about areas in which the pair's ratings significantly

**FIGURE 2–5** Complementary duties of teachers and paraeducators

| Teacher | Paraeducator |
|---|---|
| *Program/Classroom Management* | |
| Plans weekly schedule with team, if applicable | Helps with planning and carrying out of lessons/activities |
| Plans lessons/activities for class and individuals, with team | Makes teaching aids, helps gather or copy teaching materials |
| Plans learning centers | |
| Is responsible for all students at all times | Provides emergency classroom supervision |
| Participates in teacher's duty schedule | Participates in paras' duty schedule |
| Arranges schedules for each student's related services | Accompanies students to other locations in the school |
| *Assessment* | |
| Assesses all students as needed on an ongoing basis | Assists with giving, monitoring, and scoring tests, other assignments |
| Administers formal tests | Helps with observing/charting student behaviors/progress |
| Is responsible for collection and recording of all student data | Assists in grading assignments or tests and recording grades |
| *Teaching* | |
| Introduces new material | Assists with follow-up instruction for small groups or individuals |
| Teaches entire class, small groups, or individuals | Helps support large-group instruction as needed |
| *Behavior Management* | |
| Plans strategies for behavioral supports program for entire class or individuals | Assists in implementing the teacher's behavioral supports program, using same emphasis/techniques |
| *Parent Collaboration* | |
| Meets with parents | Helps with parent contacts, such as phone calls or notes |
| Initiates conferences<br>Schedules IEP meetings | Contributes to parent conferences and IEP meetings when appropriate and feasible |

differ, so that solutions can be planned before potential problems arise.

## Team Planning Strategies

If teachers and paraeducators want a successful program operation, they need to seek mutually satisfying ways to accommodate their differences in work styles. Differences in most of life's major indices (e.g., education, income, religion, culture, or language) are practically guaranteed between teachers and paraeducators (Blalock, 1991).

For example, if a supervisor values a paraeducator's instructional and management abilities but the paraeducator's need to stick to the duty-day hours prevents planning time, numerous options may be possible (depending on agency policies about flex time). For example, if some flexibility exists, the paraeducator might stay longer than 1 day per week to participate in planning and take that time off within the week; the teacher and paraeducator might plan independent activities for the students for one period twice weekly so that they could do some planning; or another teacher or paraeducator in the grade-level team may be able to fill in to allow planning once weekly.

Supervisors can significantly enhance the confidence and sense of belonging of paraeducators by consistently including them, when appropriate, in decision making regarding students' programs, unit plans, activities, and collaboration with other professionals and parents. IEP and annual review meetings are another important arena in which experienced paraeducators contribute critical information about students with whom they work. Even if they do not attend IEP meetings, paraeducators should be familiar with each student's IEP goals and objectives.

In addition, they may be key members of some parent conferences, providing valuable information, language translation, or clarification of school policies or cultural practices. Such meetings, as well as events throughout the year, provide the opportunity to highlight important contributions of the paraeducators. Administrators and supervising teachers often have to set the stage for recognition of the role of paraeducators in instructional programs; their advocacy efforts communicate that the paraeducators' participation as team members is truly valued.

### Paraeducator Professional Development Activities

Paraeducator positions often require only a high school diploma or equivalency, and the supervisor necessarily becomes the primary trainer for the paraeducator. Initial discussions of expected duties (described earlier) are an important means of identifying training needs.

After areas of needed training are determined, the most feasible scheduling and vehicles to achieve the training must be explored and arranged—for example, scheduling specific demonstrations of procedures when they are actually needed by students, to maximize relevance. Options for securing specific training vary from location to location, potentially involving specialists in clerical, media, technologies, administrative, ancillary, therapeutic, community resources, and content areas.

Langone (1998) describes a series of activities that could support the paraeducator in effective support of inclusively served students: presenting brief training programs, providing periodic review sessions (e.g., on observation and recording techniques), developing a training manual (possibly with photos of methods in progress), and including them in regular planning.

Several important considerations relate to teaching adults in general that differ from teaching children. Because adults' needs for learning are based on actual life demands, their learning activities should target tasks perceived as part of their lives. Adults are also more task oriented than theory based, preferring to do rather than to listen. Thus, role-playing and problem-based learning are important strategies. In addition, training personnel need to validate the adults' lives and work experiences and use them as foundations on which to build new learning—for example, by using commonly shared situations as examples (a local sports event, the opening of a new mall, growing up in the same town). Adults must be involved in any decisions about desired learning outcomes (i.e., goal setting), as well as assessment strategies and the steps to achieving those goals.

### Monitoring and Feedback Techniques

Regularly scheduled meetings provide a forum for supervisors to give ongoing feedback (especially positive) about paraeducators' performance. Many performance rating instruments have been developed for paraeducators in special education and related fields (Pickett, 1989; Vasa, Steckelberg, & Sundermeier, 1989). However, the most important guideline is that feedback should be based directly on the current job description(s) provided to the paraeducator. To carry meaning, performance feedback also should relate to future goals for both student and paraeducator growth.

Finally, career ladders provide a *long-term incentive* for improving competence and exhibiting professionalism that short-term supports cannot sustain for very long (e.g., time off for courses, payment for training costs). Career ladders typically involve a sequence of three to four levels, each distinct from the other in terms of required competencies and salary levels, and are usually implemented by an employing agency and/or the state education department, sometimes in partnership with area colleges or universities. Professionals who extend themselves to improve paraeducators' working conditions and expertise through avenues such as a career ladder will experience enhanced teamwork and watch their students reap the rewards many times over.

> Reflective Question 2.5: ***What are processes and strategies that new teachers can employ to effect strong partnerships with veteran paraeducators?***

## COLLABORATION WITH OTHER PERSONNEL

A whole spectrum of other partners, beyond the general and special education teachers, is critical to ensure that school, center, and community programs accomplish their missions well. Some of these potential team members include administrators and related therapists in the schools or centers, community and state agency personnel, community members such as employers and government officials, and many others.

## Related Service Personnel

Traditionally, related services personnel have included IDEA-identified professionals in this category—those who provide the related services required by students to benefit from their educational programs and who are identified in their IEPs. The primary partners in this category include assistive technology specialists, speech/language therapists, occupational therapists, and physical therapists. IDEA's reauthorizations also included rehabilitation services specialists if needed.

## Administrators

Working with administrators is essential to implementing innovative programs and also can open doors for better programming for students with exceptionalities. However, administrators often must be convinced of the benefits of new directions and are constantly besieged with competing requests to exhaust their school's limited resources. One strategy is to go in numbers (as a team) with your requests for planning and consulting time, reconfigured student assistance teams, or other priorities, and to be prepared for rejection the first time. Often one's initiative in developing a request is acknowledged without being rewarded, but repeated requests by a team, based on data and student-centered goals, can often achieve the desired ends.

**FIGURE 2–6** Qualities of an exemplary collaboration

Qualities of an exemplary collaboration

- Unconditional support: Based on a shared goal, team members may agree to disagree.
- High morale: Positive attitudes pervade interactions, strengthened by team members' respect for each other.
- Shared responsibility: Leadership crosses membership of the team.
- Removal of barriers: Working together to solve problems tends to wreak havoc on barriers.
- Team spirit: Equity about who each is underlies the group's mentality.
- Team member development: Support for each other's growth and effectiveness is pervasive.
- Community support: Ongoing favorable interactions with the community generate, in turn, community support for the team's work.

*Source:* From "What Does It Take?" by P. Hunt, 1995, in *What's Working: Transitions in Minnesota* (p. 1), Minneapolis, MN: University of Minnesota Institute on Community Integration. Copyright 1995 by the University of Minnesota Institute on Community Integration. Reprinted and adapted with permission.

## Personnel Outside of the School

Hunt (1995) details the qualities of exemplary collaborations that would characterize the best joint efforts of multidisciplinary teams or community teams. Hunt's list is adapted in Figure 2–6. At the community level, Goetz, Lee, Johnston, and Gaylord-Ross (1991) offer several strategies for collaborating with employers and co-workers to promote job-site inclusion of persons with disabilities, including emphasizing the natural supports that can be instrumental in their success (e.g., co-workers' prompts, supervisors' praise).

**FIGURE 2–7** Suggestions for ending and assessing team meetings

____ Ask members to describe how they felt surprised by, delighted with, displeased with, or confused by today's meeting or the team meetings over time.

____ Ask members to name one thing they will take with them to use in their daily lives.

____ Ask members to describe what they need to do to prepare for the next session or for future teams.

____ Ask members to describe what worked for them and what did not work for them in the team meeting.

____ Ask members to talk about any appreciation or regret they feel now that the team's work is ending.

____ Ask each member to say or write, "Something I did (today/_________ date) that helped the team operate was . . ."

____ Ask an outside observer to watch and report the team's interactions and actions.

____ Ask each member to comment on how frequently and well the team used the specified collaboration or teamwork skills.

____ Ask each member to say or write, "Something I plan to do differently next time to help the team work together better is . . ."

____ Ask each member to say or write, "I learned . . . " or "I relearned . . ." in the context of teamwork and collaboration.

*Source:* Taken partially from *Making Task Groups Work in Your World,* by D. Hulse-Killacky, J. Killacky, and J. Donigian, 2001. Upper Saddie River, NJ: Merrill/Prentice Hall.

## EVALUATION OF THE COLLABORATIVE EXPERIENCE

Participants, and perhaps overseers, of the collaborative activities need regular opportunities to step back, check on the progress of both team and target students, and change the interventions as needed to enhance students' performance and to give the process a chance for sustainability. Evaluation serves as the final component of a collaborative program so that feedback on current efforts can influence future activities.

Within a school, evaluation may be handled in an informal fashion, such as partners asking each other about their perceptions of the process and its outcomes (e.g., see Figure 2–7). Knackendoffel et al. (1992) created a self-evaluation checklist (see Figure 2–8) for team

**FIGURE 2–8** Self-evaluation checklist

### Self-Evaluation Checklist

| *Did you use the following skills:* | *Yes* | *No* |
|---|---|---|
| **Assume a posture of involvement?** | | |
| Lean torso slightly forward | ☐ | ☐ |
| Directly face the other person | ☐ | ☐ |
| Maintain eye contact | ☐ | ☐ |
| Use appropriate facial expressions | ☐ | ☐ |
| Minimize distractions | ☐ | ☐ |
| **Use nonverbal encouragers?** | | |
| Nod your head | ☐ | ☐ |
| Smile | ☐ | ☐ |
| Take notes | ☐ | ☐ |
| **Provide brief verbal encouragers?** | ☐ | ☐ |
| **Make reflecting statements?** | | |
| Paraphrase | ☐ | ☐ |
| Reflect emotions | ☐ | ☐ |
| Pause after making the statement | ☐ | ☐ |
| **Ask good questions?** | | |
| Open-ended questions | ☐ | ☐ |
| Close-ended questions | ☐ | ☐ |
| Indirect questions | ☐ | ☐ |
| Clarifying questions | ☐ | ☐ |
| **Summarize information periodically?** | ☐ | ☐ |
| **Use partnership-building skills?** | | |
| Accepting statements | ☐ | ☐ |
| Compliments or appreciation statements | ☐ | ☐ |
| Empathic statements | ☐ | ☐ |
| Focusing statements | ☐ | ☐ |
| Agreement statements | ☐ | ☐ |
| Productive solution statements | ☐ | ☐ |

| *Did you complete all the problem-solving steps:* | *Yes* | *No* |
|---|---|---|
| **Define the problem?** | ☐ | ☐ |
| **Gather specific information about the problem?** | ☐ | ☐ |
| **Explain the problem-solving process?** | ☐ | ☐ |
| **Identify alternative solutions?** | | |
| Ask other person to suggest ideas first | ☐ | ☐ |
| Introduce your ideas in an open-minded manner | ☐ | ☐ |
| **Summarize solutions mentioned?** | ☐ | ☐ |
| **Analyze consequences of each solution?** | ☐ | ☐ |
| **Rate each solution?** | ☐ | ☐ |
| **Select the best solution?** | ☐ | ☐ |
| **Determine satisfaction with chosen solution?** | ☐ | ☐ |
| **State your support for the decision?** | ☐ | ☐ |
| **Develop a plan of action?** | | |
| Specify implementation steps | ☐ | ☐ |
| Indicate who is responsible for each step | ☐ | ☐ |
| Indicate when each step will be completed | ☐ | ☐ |
| **Develop a monitoring system?** | ☐ | ☐ |
| **Specify criteria for success?** | ☐ | ☐ |
| **Schedule the next appointment?** | ☐ | ☐ |

**Notes and comments about use of skills:**

**Notes and comments about use of problem-solving steps:**

*Source:* From *Collaborative Problem Solving: A Step-by-Step Guide to Creating Educational Solutions* (pp. 69–70), by E. A. Knackendoffel, S. M. Robinson, D. D. Deshier, and J. B. Schumaker, 1992, Lawrence, KS: Edge Enterprises. Copyright 1992 by Edge Enterprises, Inc. Reprinted with permission.

members to reflect on their own use of good communication skills and problem-solving steps. However, in some instances a more structured approach is beneficial, particularly if districtwide or schoolwide collaborative training has been implemented.

**Reflective Question 2.6:** ***How do multidisciplinary partnerships contribute to effective programs for students with special needs?***

## SUMMARY

This chapter first lays the foundational concepts and skills needed for collaboration with any individuals or groups. Various models of collaborative efforts in schools were discussed. Attention was then directed at five key stakeholder groups with whom special educators need to collaborate: students, families, general educators, paraeducators, and associated personnel both within and outside the school. Finally, suggestions for evaluating collaborative efforts were presented.

The imperative to connect with the full range of partners becomes increasingly evident as we pay greater attention to the assets and needs of the whole person in our educational systems with increasingly diminished resources. Only by such stakeholders sharing ideas, emotional and physical energy, and resources can students have access to the high-quality level and full range of educational services that they require and deserve.

CHAPTER

# 3

# Strategies for Curriculum Development, Effective Instruction, and Classroom Adaptations

The two critical questions in education are the question of curriculum (what?) and instruction (how?). Effective school programs obviously begin with considerations of what is the information that students need to learn and how best can they learn that information. The primary purpose of this chapter is to address these two concerns.

In addition to the overriding questions of curriculum content and instructional methodology, a third critical, related topic is the use of adaptations, both to curriculum and to instruction. Included within this area, for example, are key variables that are too often overlooked but frequently represent the difference between successful and unsuccessful educational programs, particularly in inclusive settings (e.g., homework, classroom assessment and testing, and grading). The chapter concludes with a discussion of technology applications.

## CURRICULUM DEVELOPMENT

The core components of educational programs for individuals with disabilities is the curriculum. Regardless of teaching effectiveness and efficiency, questions related to the value of education must properly address the issue of what is taught.

Events in the early 1990s in education, such as changes made to IDEA, the promulgation of standards-based education, and the No Child Left Behind (NCLB) legislation, are having a profound effect on the programs of students with special needs. These students are now being given more access to the general education curriculum. Nearly all states have instituted standards to ensure that students develop a common set of knowledge and skills during their school experience. With such changes come a host of issues that have to be recognized and addressed.

It is helpful to begin by considering the various applications of the term *curriculum*. It can refer strictly to the courses taught in school or to a document that includes a design that others have developed and that teachers implement in the classroom. Hoover and Patton (2004a) refer to curriculum as planned and guided learning experiences under the direction of the school with intended educational outcomes.

One of the primary concerns of the curriculum is its "functionality" in meeting the needs of the individual student. For our purposes, curriculum functionality is defined as the degree to which the curriculum prepares students for the environments in which they will live, work, and learn. At the same time, careful attention must be given to how a student's needs can be met within the context of the general education curriculum and while placed in inclusive settings.

Three general concerns for curriculum include the various types of curricula that exist in schools, the need for providing curricula that are comprehensive, and the organizing principles associated with a contemporary multitiered model of curriculum development.

### Curriculum Types

Hoover and Patton (2004a) point out that curriculum needs to be conceptualized on the basis of what is taught and what is not taught but should be. The three types of curricula that are frequently mentioned are explicit, hidden, and absent (Eisner, 1985; Schubert, 1993). These are defined as follows:

- **Explicit curriculum:** the formal and stated curriculum that teachers and students are expected to follow.
- **Hidden curriculum:** the actual curriculum implemented in the classroom.
- **Absent curriculum:** the curriculum that, for whatever reason, is not included in school.

Other terminology is also used to describe types of curricula (see Table 3-1). In general, the various perspectives highlight the same points; however, some subtle differences exist (Platton & Trainor, 2003).

The explicit curriculum (intended curriculum) can be found in a state's standards and thus is typically reflected in a school district's curriculum guides. This type of curriculum includes the specific goals and

**TABLE 3–1** Types of curricula

| | Terminology | | |
|---|---|---|---|
| *Curricular Outcome* | *Nolet & McLaughilin (2000)* | *Hoover & Patton (1997)* | *Patton (2001)* |
| Official/adopted | Intended curriculum | Explicit curriculum | |
| Curriculum that is actually covered | Taught curriculum | Hidden curriculum | |
| Curriculum that students actually learn | Learned curriculum | | |
| Curriculum that is not covered | | Absent curriculum | |
| Curriculum that is added to the official/adopted curriculum | | | Enrichment curriculum |

*Source:* From "Using Applied Academics to Enhance Curricular Reform in Secondary Education," by J. R. Patton and A. Trainor, in C. Kochhar-Bryant and D. S. Basselt (Eds.), *Aligning Transition and Standards-Based Education: Issues and Strategies* (2003, p. 67). Arlington. VA: The Council for Exceptional Children.

objectives for subject areas across grade levels. With the increased attention to and pressure of state content and performance standards and school accountability, a heightened interest in ensuring that this content is covered pervades instruction today.

The hidden curriculum (taught curriculum) is what students are exposed to on a daily basis. It is likely to include much of the explicit curriculum as well as lessons on topics other than those stated in curriculum guides. The hidden curriculum includes interpretations of the explicit curricula related to implementation procedures and the emphasis different explicit curriculum aspects receive. It also includes the insertion of content that the teacher chooses to cover, either by necessity based on student needs (e.g., study skills instructions) or by personal interest (enrichment).

The absent curriculum represents content that is not covered. Sometimes this is because certain content is not part of the explicit curriculum. Other times, it is a choice made by teachers. An example of subjects often absent from the curriculum are social skills instruction and the development of self-determination skills (see Chapter 13).

As Hoover and Patton (2004a) stress, elements from all three types of curricula operate continually in classrooms, sometimes in complementary ways and other times in a conflicting fashion.

## Comprehensive Curriculum

When educational programs are designed for students who are disabled, the importance of a **comprehensive curriculum** should be apparent because the primary goal is to develop an outcomes focus consistent with their diverse needs. A comprehensive curriculum refers to a program of study guided by the reality that each student is in school on a time-limited basis. Moreover, the real test of the value of the curriculum is how students fare once they exit the program (i.e., how what was taught affects adult outcomes). Thus educators must consider what lies ahead for their students; this requires a perspective that is sensitive to the environments in which students will need to adapt and function in the future. Hence, curriculum design should be influenced not only by the stated standards and individual needs of the students, but also by a "subsequent environments" perspective (Polloway, Patton, Smith, & Roderique, 1992). A subsequent environment perspective requires school personnel to consider the demands of the likely settings to which an individual will be moving in the near and more distant future. The central attributes of a comprehensive curriculum include:

- responding to the needs of an individual at the current time
- accommodating the concurrent needs for maximum interaction with peers, the realities associated with access to the general education curriculum, the demands of meeting state standards, and attention to crucial needs that are absent from the general education curriculum
- developing curriculum from a realistic appraisal of potential adult outcomes of individuals
- ensuring consistency with each individual's transitional needs across levels of schooling and life span
- remaining sensitive to graduation goals and specific diploma track requirements

The importance of comprehensive curriculum at the secondary level relates closely to the basic elements of the transition process that will be covered later in Chapter 15. The value of a comprehensive curriculum for students with special needs is further warranted based on the following realities:

- Many individuals are not being prepared for the complex demands of adulthood that they face on a daily basis.
- A significant percentage of the students who have special needs do not find the school experience valuable and drop out.
- The educational programs of many students with special needs do not meet their academic, social, and emotional needs.
- The opportunities for continuing educational options for adults with special needs upon their exiting of high school are limited but nonetheless critical.

The recurring need is for relevant curricula that address these concerns and features. However, although a careful analysis of secondary programs is essential, consideration of curricular design must begin at the elementary level in order to overcome the problems that otherwise may be recognized at the secondary or postsecondary level.

## Multitiered Model

As noted in Chapter 1, multitiered models are commonly advocated now for providing guidance particularly in curriculum development. Such an approach to curriculum development is central to the discussion of curriculum alternatives. Hoover and Patton (in press) define the three tiers in this fashion:

- **Tier 1: High-quality core instruction.** This tier refers to empirically validated and systematic instruction embedded in challenging, academically rigorous curriculum in the general education classroom. Universal design for learning and differentiated instruction (see Chapter 1), for example, provide guidelines for vehicles to successfully implement tier 1 interventions.
- **Tier 2: High-quality targeted supplemental instruction.** The focus of the second tier is to provide supplemental supports in addition to the core instructional program. Such instruction could be provided in the general education classroom or through a variety of pull-out programs such as resource rooms. Specific examples of such programs are those that are identified as general education supports programs.
- **Tier 3: High-quality intensive intervention.** The third tier is more consistent with the traditional concept of special education as modified to reflect scientifically validated instructional programs to teach relevant curricular content. Such programs typically are offered to students with more significant disabilities and may more often be delivered in specialized settings. Examples include certain remedial and adult outcomes-oriented programs. However, depending on the instructional programs in general education, many of these curricular goals can be achieved in such settings as well.

The discussion that follows related to curriculum development is based on this model. Examples of curriculum approaches are embedded within this model in the subsequent subsections of this portion of the chapter.

**Tier 1: High-quality Core Instruction.** In Chapter 1, we surveyed key features of concern regarding curriculum within this tier. Such an approach reflects an orientation to the curriculum that all students, with and without specific learning needs, experience. The focus thus is essentially the explicit curriculum, as determined by state standards. It will be the option of choice for students who exit special education or, though still eligible for special education and related services, do not need highly specialized supports or adaptations while in general education settings.

Two overriding concerns are foundational. First, state standards, consistent with federal guidelines, govern the design of core curriculum for all learners. The core of the standards-based reform movement in recent years has been the focus on content and performance standards. As Pemberton, Rademacher, Tyler-Wood, and Cereijo (2006) noted in their summary, "content standards define the knowledge and skills of students or what students should know and be able to accomplish as a result of their educational experiences. Performance standards define how well students should demonstrate the knowledge and skills" (pp. 283–284).

Providing further clarification, Wehmeyer (2006) referenced the work of the Committee on Goals 2000 and the Inclusion of Students with Disabilities (1997) in noting that standards could be made defensible in several ways for use with students with disabilities. Wehmeyer noted that content standards must reflect those skills that are critical to the success of students after leaving school, that these standards should be appropriate based on the age of the students, and that the standards-based curriculum should be taught to students with special needs while not effectively impacting their opportunity to be taught, and acquire, functional behaviors and skills that are critical for community success.

To provide a more detailed analysis of the elements of standards-based education and their relevance for the curriculum, Hoover and Patton (2005) identified key elements and provide a description of how this approach to education is reflected in curriculum development (see Table 3-2).

Second, students with special needs must be provided access to the core, standards-based curriculum, such as through the use of differentiated instruction (see Hall, Strangman, & Mayer, n.d.).

To have access to, and experience success in, the general education curriculum, we briefly noted in Chapter 1 the value of programs based on a universal design for learning (see also McGuire, Scott, & Shaw, 2006).

Hitchcock et al. (2002) defined universal design for learning as including these considerations:

- Curricular goals that provide an appropriate challenge for all students.
- Instructional and curricular materials that have flexible format and that support the transformation between media and multiple representations of content to support all students' learning.
- Instructional methods that are flexible and diverse enough to provide appropriate learning experiences, challenges, and supports for all students.
- Ongoing assessment that is sufficiently flexible to provide accurate, ongoing information that helps teachers adjust instruction and maximize learning.

To meet the needs of all students, including those with special needs, a curriculum based on universal design principles should be open-ended rather than close-ended. As Wehmeyer (2006) noted: "Close-ended standards are specific and require narrowly defined outcomes or performance indicators. Open-ended standards do not restrict the ways in which students exhibit knowledge with skills and focus more on the expectations that students will interact with the content, ask questions, manipulate materials, make observations, and then communicate their knowledge in a variety of ways" (pp. 226–227).

Hoover and Patton (2005) analyzed standards according to four curricular elements (i.e., content, instructional strategies, instructional settings, and student behaviors) and then identified specific considerations related to differentiating instruction and educational programs. The model that they developed is reflected in Table 3-3.

A common concern is that with the trend toward increased inclusion certain instructional supports might be needed but may not be available for students.

**TABLE 3–2** Elements of standards-based education and curriculum

| *Element* | *Description* |
|---|---|
| Assessment closely linked to the curriculum | A significant alignment exits between the curriculum being taught and the skills and knowledge being assessed. |
| Comparison to standards, not other students | Standard-based curriculum emphasizes the development of standards, and the assessment reflects the level of proficiency for each student. Thus, the assessment compare students' proficiency levels with established standards and not with other students. |
| Alternative assessments used | Assessment of standards-based curriculum may include a variety of assessment strategies such as constructed response, writing essays, authentic and real-life problem solving, or rubrics. |
| Achieving proficiency | NCLB requires that states and school systems annually monitor progress toward helping all students achieve proficiency of the standards, rather than simply reporting grouped, grade-level scores. |
| Application of results | Standards-based assessment results can be used to determine graduation requirements, hold educators accountable, and adapt curriculum. Results are no longer simply reported; rather, they are used for program improvement and documentation of progress toward full proficiency. |
| Inclusion of all students | Standards-based curriculum is designed to challenge all students to increase their expectations and proficiency levels. This includes English language learners and students with disabilities. |

*Source:* Hoover, J. J., & Patton, J. R. (2005). *Curriculum adaptations for students with learning and behavior problems* (3rd ed.). Austin, TX: PRO-ED (p. 21).

**TABLE 3–3** Adapting standards with curriculum elements

| *Curricular Element* | *Standards* | *Differentiation Considerations* |
|---|---|---|
| Content | Content standards<br>Performance standards<br>Opportunity to learn | Review specific benchmarks and adapt as necessary.<br>Identify optimum levels of proficiency necessary to master content.<br>Ensure that adequate materials, hands-on activities exist to support content. |
| Instructional strategies | Content standards<br>Performance standards<br>Opportunity to learn | Identify strategies that facilitate mastery and generalization of content.<br>Consider compatibility between teaching and learning styles used.<br>Ensure that strategies used facilitate effective use of materials/resources. |
| Instructional settings | Content standards<br>Performance standards<br>Opportunity to learn | Determine which setting(s) best facilitate mastery of content.<br>Ensure that the setting(s) facilitate mastery and generalization of skills.<br>Setting(s) must allow for high-quality and effective learning to occur. |
| Student behaviors | Content standards<br>Performance standards<br>Opportunity to learn | Student behaviors must assist learners to acquire and master content.<br>Acceptable levels of self-management should be identified and monitored.<br>Overall class management must facilitate safe/effective learning environment. |

*Source:* Hoover, J. J., & Patton, J. R. (2005). *Curriculum adaptations for students with learning and behavior problems* (3rd ed.). Austin, TX: PRO-ED (p. 25).

As a consequence, students may flounder, receive poor grades, and be at risk of dropping out. However, the potential problems that students may face in class situations where no specialized supports are provided can be alleviated when the principles of universal design are incorporated into the development of the education curriculum.

**Tier II: High-Quality Instruction with Supports.** This second tier suggests that students with special needs are in general education classrooms where various adaptations are made and/or certain supports are provided (i.e., supported education). In reference to the former point, Bigge and Stump (1999) note that "attention is given to adapting or modifying the curriculum in ways that allow certain students with disabilities and special education needs to gain knowledge, skills, and understandings from it" (p. 57). The topic of adaptations is such a significant one that it is discussed later within its own major section of the chapter. Within this section of the chapter, we focus on several general education supports models.

The concept of **supported education** is based on Hamre-Nietupski, McDonald, and Nietupski's (1992) classic suggestion that embedded in the concept of inclusion is the assumption that appropriate supports are being provided in the general education classroom. This same point is reinforced by T. Smith, Polloway, Patton, and Dowdy (2008) in their discussion of critical dimensions of inclusive classrooms.

Edgar and Polloway (1994) highlighted how the general education supports model could be effective for students with special needs whose goal is to pursue higher education:

> These are the students who have the interest and aptitude necessary for success at that level. . . . Development of an appropriate preparatory curriculum for these students should become a primary focus during high school. Curricular foci should include maximum participation in regular high school programs, not only for generation of units toward a regular diploma, but also for attention to content necessary for college success. . . . For success in academic postsecondary programs, attention should also be given to transitional needs relevant to these settings, including intensive writing instruction, study, and college survival skills training skills (e.g., time management, organizational skills, and selection of major). (pp. 445–446)

However, this program orientation is appropriate not just for students whose likely subsequent environment after high school is higher education, but also for the vast majority of students with disabilities, including those who have more significant challenges and require ongoing supports.

Support models presume that students will profit most from the core curriculum offered in the general education classroom. Their goal is thus to enhance success in such classes. Whereas tutorial instruction has often been the most common means of providing support to students who experience difficulties in the same education classroom, other program orientations offer more attractive alternatives to this challenge.

***Cooperative Teaching.*** **Cooperative or collaborative teaching** (or co-teaching) represents a viable system of general education class support for students with disabilities as well as for other students who experience learning difficulties. Hourcade and Bauwens (2003) describe cooperative teaching as occurring when "two educators combine their complementary sets of professional knowledge and skills and work simultaneously in general education classrooms" (p. xiii).

The principles of teacher collaboration on which cooperative teaching is based were discussed in Chapter 2. It is sufficient to note here that cooperative teaching involves a team approach to supporting students within the general education classroom, combining the content expertise of the classroom teacher with the pedagogical skills of the special education teacher (T. Smith et al., 2008). It is a logical outgrowth of collaboration between teachers that includes consultative arrangements, additional help given by special educators to children not identified as eligible for special services, and the sharing of teaching assistants, especially to accompany students who are disabled in the general education classroom.

Weise and Lloyd (2002) developed a model for analyzing the roles of special educators teaching in both inclusive and special education settings. The model of roles in these two respective settings is outlined in Figure 3–1. To provide further guidance, a model for the construction of daily lesson plans for use in a cooperative teaching situation is presented in Figure 3–2.

Hourcade and Bauwens (2003) note that the essential philosophy of cooperative teaching is a simple one: *sharing*, especially of responsibilities and accountability. They suggest that true cooperative teaching emerges when five key elements are appropriately addressed:

- **Cooperative presence:** initial stage related to mere proximity
- **Cooperative planning:** regular meetings occur where various planning-related activities are done collaboratively
- **Cooperative presenting:** teachers present simultaneously and are actively involved for a sustained period of time
- **Cooperative processing:** determination of how monitoring and evaluation will occur
- **Cooperative problem solving:** devoting time to solving inevitable problems that arise when implementing a cooperative teaching arrangement

The trend toward co-teaching warrants careful attention. Murawski and Swanson (2001) used a meta-analysis to research cooperative teaching and found limited research on this intervention. The existing studies reflected a moderate level of success for co-teaching. Mastropieri et al. (2005) reported that success was influenced in particular by the compatibility of the two teachers based on mutual trust and respect and on shared commitment to effective teaching behaviors (i.e., "structure, clarity, enthusiasm, maximizing student engagement, and motivational strategies," p. 269).

Zigmond and Magiera (2001) concluded their review with this assessment:

> Despite the current and growing popularity of co-teaching, research on student outcomes in this service delivery model is very limited. Only four studies could be found. In the three elementary studies, co-teaching was just as effective in producing academic gains as resource room instruction or consultation with the general education teacher; in the high school study, students' quiz and exam grades actually worsened during the co-teaching experiment. If the goal of co-teaching is to allow students with high-incidence disabilities to access the general education curriculum and to "do no harm" to them in terms of academic achievement, then the three elementary studies provide modest support for a co-teaching model in elementary schools. If the goal, however, is to achieve greater academic gains than have been traditionally achieved in a resource program, then co-teaching has not yet proved itself useful.
>
> Furthermore, the research suggests that the prevailing assumptions about the effectiveness and usefulness of co-teaching for students with disabilities in inclusive classrooms need to be reexamined. (pp. 3–4)

***Tutorial Assistance.*** Traditionally, tutoring has been one of the most popular models in special education for several apparent reasons. Foremost is the motivational aspect tied to such an approach. Quite simply, students are interested in the supportive services that come with this model and that enable them to be more successful in the general classroom. Perhaps, as a byproduct, some general education teachers and parents may also be frequent supporters. To the extent that such an orientation is effective, tutoring may have positive implications for grades and for meeting diploma requirements.

In spite of the possible benefits of such an approach and although all special education teachers engage in some tutoring, this orientation has a short-term emphasis and may be of little lasting value. In addition, there are valid concerns about whether the material taught and learned is relevant to and powerful enough

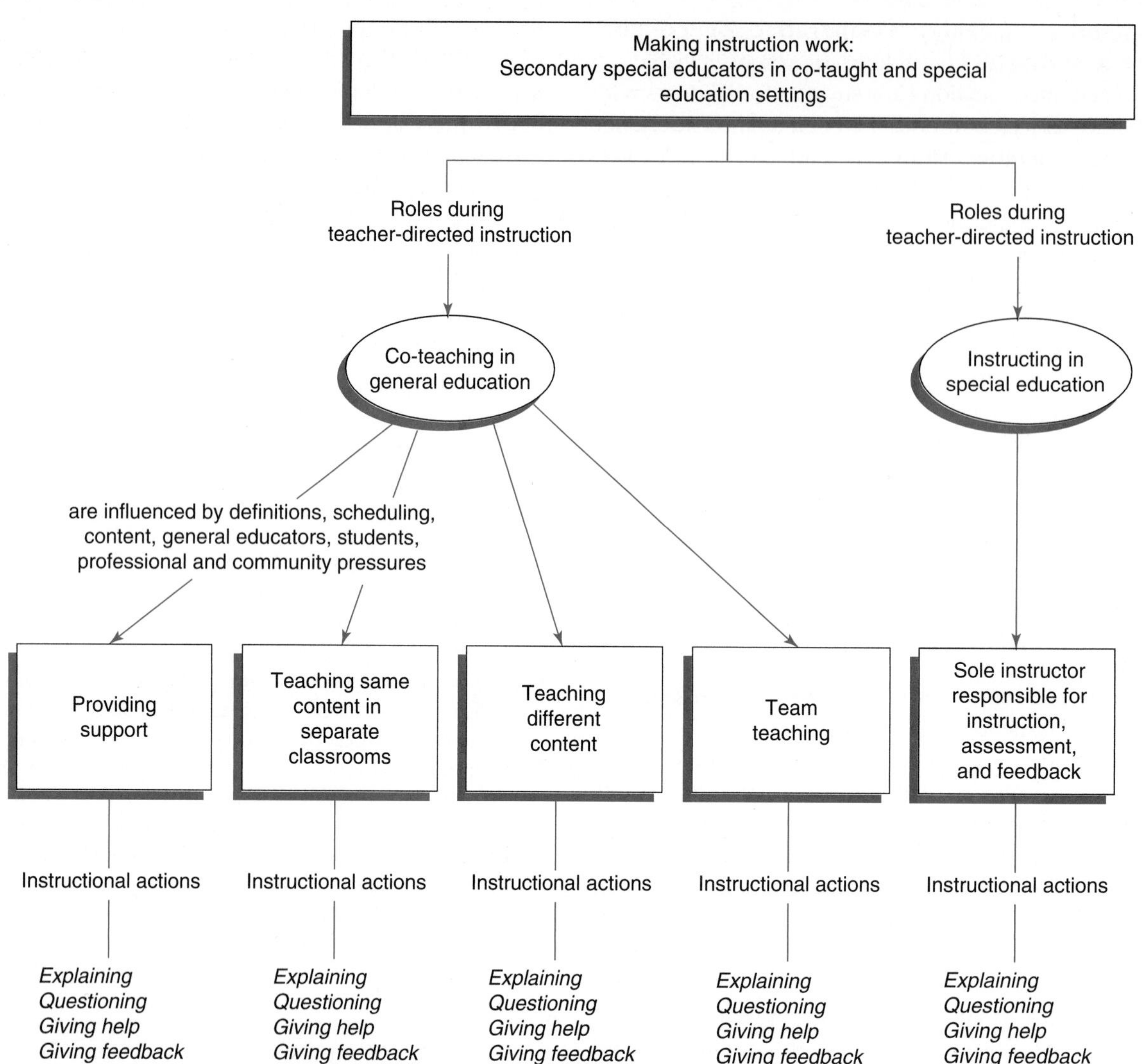


**FIGURE 3–1** Description of special educator's roles in cooperative teaching

*Source:* Adapted from "Congruence Between Roles and Actions of Secondary Special Educators in Co-Taught and Special Education Settings," by M. P. Weiss and J. W. Lloyd, 2002. *The Journal of Special Education, 36,* p. 64. Copyright 2002 by PRO-ED, Inc. Reprinted with permission.

for the learning needs of the students. Further, tutoring may be problematic because of the possible undertraining (e.g., being asked to provide tutorial assistance across a wide range of subjects) or possible overtraining of special educators (e.g., tutoring frequently requires little advanced training and can be handled by paraeducators).

Deshler (2005) offered cautions concerning tutorial programs. He noted that this "can be an extremely costly and fatal error because it is generally done at the expense of teaching valuable strategies that will enable students to function independently in the content classroom. Thus, in the absence of this type of instruction, students with LD will not change as learners. Although they may 'get by' and even be promoted socially they will leave the educational system grossly underprepared to face the harsh realities of the postsecondary world" (p. 123).

The tutorial orientation's heavy emphasis on short-term outcomes is responsible for its major advantages as well as its numerous disadvantages. Teachers working with students who require tutorial support should

**FIGURE 3–2** Co-teaching daily lesson plans

General Educator ______________________ Special Educator ______________________

| Date | What are you going to teach? | Which co-teaching technique will you use? | What are the specific tasks of both teachers? | What materials are needed? | How will you evaluate learning? | Information about students who need follow-up work |
|---|---|---|---|---|---|---|
| | | | | | | |
| | | | | | | |
| | | | | | | |
| | | | | | | |
| | | | | | | |

*Source:* Adapted from "A Passion for Action Research," by N. L. Langerock, 2000. *Teaching Exceptional Children, 33*(2) p. 30. Reprinted with permission.

investigate the possibilities of involving peers, paraeducators, and classroom volunteers in the process.

***Learning Strategies.*** **Learning strategies** are extremely valuable to students. Learning strategies are "task-specific techniques that students use in responding to classroom tasks" (Archer & Gleason, 1995, p. 236). Utilizing a cognitive orientation to learning ("learning to learn"), learning strategies provide students with a method for using their own abilities and knowledge to acquire, organize, and integrate new information. Ultimately, successful demonstration of learning strategy competence leads to more self-regulated, independent learning as these strategies are generalizable to other situations where a specific task is required. Table 3-4 illustrates types of learning strategies according to the function each strategy serves.

In Table 3-5, a summary of the steps included in teaching a learning strategy are provided. Inherent within this sequence of teaching learning strategies are several basic principles, as highlighted by Swanson and Deshler (2003). First, extensive, explicit practice is necessary and provides the foundation for successful learning of strategies. In the absence of explicit practice, students are unlikely to learn the strategy correctly and consequently will not be able to use it independently. Further, for this reason, it is important to teach a limited number of strategies well rather than attempt to teach students more strategies than they are able to successfully use.

**TABLE 3–4** Types of learning strategies as a function of primary operation

| Acquiring Information | Organizing Information | Demonstrating Competence |
|---|---|---|
| **1. Deshler et al. (1996)** | | |
| • word identification | • first-letter mnemonic | • sentence writing |
| • paraphrasing | • paired associates | • paragraph writing |
| • self-questioning | • listening and note taking | • error monitoring |
| • visual imagery | | • theme writing |
| • interpreting visuals | | • assignment completion |
| • multipass | | • test taking |
| **2. Archer & Gleason (1989)** | | |
| • reading expository material | • gaining information from verbal presentations (lectures, demonstrations) | • completing daily assignments |
| • reading narrative material | | • answering written questions |
| | | • writing narrative and expository products |
| **3. Hoover & Patton (1995, 2006)** | | |
| • active processing | | • preparing for and taking tests |
| • analogy | | |
| • coping | • organization | • rehearsal |
| • evaluation | | |

*Sources:* Developed from *Teaching Students with Learning Problems to Use Study Skills: A Teacher's Guide,* by J. J. Hoover and J. R. Patton, 1995 and 2006, Austin, TX: PRO-ED; *Skills for School Success,* by A. Archer and M. Gleason, 1989, North Billerica, MA: Curriculum Associates; and *Teaching Adolescents with Learning Disabilities: Strategies and Methods,* by D. D. Deshler, E. S. Ellis, & B. K. Lenz, 1996, Denver, CO: Love Publishing.

**TABLE 3–5** Eight stages of the strategies intervention model: Purpose statements

1. Students make a commitment to learning strategies that can help them do better in content-area class.
2. Teacher presents the new strategy to students so that they can learn the processes involved in using it.
3. Teachers model the strategy primarily by thinking aloud and working through the strategy.
4. Students describe the learning strategy in their own words.
5. Students apply the strategy in the context of carefully selected materials and situations.
6. Students apply the strategy in the context of real-classroom demands.
7. Students learn how the strategy can be applied in other settings.
8. Students apply and adapt the strategy in other settings.

*Source:* From "Procedural Facilitators and Cognitive Strategies: Tools for Unraveling the Mysteries of Comprehension and the Writing Process, and for Providing Meaningful Access to the General Curriculum," by S. Baker, R. Gersten, and D. Scanlon, 2002 *Learning Disabilities Research and Practice, 17,* p. 66. Copyright 2002 by Blackwell Publishing UK. Reprinted with permission.

Most learning strategies also are accompanied by a "remembering device" (Archer & Gleason, 1995). Such devices typically consist of a word or acronym that relates to the steps one must follow to implement the strategy.

A learning strategies approach is particularly appropriate when a major instructional objective for a given student is generalization of skills within, or to, the general classroom or to a postsecondary environment. Within the schools, a major focus of the approach is thus necessarily the importance of cooperation between special and general education teachers.

Lenz (2006) highlighted the critical characteristics of a learning strategies approach. These principles provide core guidelines for the successful implementation of a program that can be beneficial beyond the individual classroom and can permeate a school curriculum. This schoolwide approach has been implemented in a number of school divisions and, for example, served as a basis for training school administrators in the Commonwealth of Virginia to implement broad-based programs. The following characteristics are identified by Lenz (2006):

1. Instruction is provided to all students, with more explicit, intensive instruction given to students who have difficulty. . . .
2. Strategy content includes teaching students how to use cognitive (thinking) and metacognitive (how to think about thinking) processes.
3. Strategies contain elements that ensure generalization.
4. In both instruction and practice, students are able to see how using these strategies creates success.
5. Learning strategy instruction is guided by ongoing assessment and feedback.
6. Strategies are taught and used in all subject areas.
7. Teachers have different expectations regarding content mastery, based on the content's importance for helping students meet standards, and students are mastering critical content.
8. The school supports and promotes widespread use of instruction in learning strategies. (p. 262)

The learning strategies approach is an effective way for students to use strategic behaviors in inclusive settings, especially for middle and high school students. However, certain considerations need to be made when evaluating the possible adoption of such an approach as a major part of the curriculum. Careful attention should be given to the appeal of the particular strategy being taught. Motivating some students to learn a strategy that affords long-term benefits may be difficult. This approach's emphasis on transfer of learning, self-instruction, and independence recommends its use with students beyond the specific target population. Further, the efficacy of various learning strategies must be judged in part by how well they can be generalized because a prime objective of this model is to foster transfer across content subjects and to postsecondary and community environments.

Deshler (in Chamberlain, 2006) provided an apt summary in noting: "teaching a student a given learning strategy doesn't necessarily make that student a strategic learner. In other words, you can teach him the steps of a strategy; he can go through it and mechanically apply it, but it's not really changing the way he thinks about processing information and learning. To do that, we as teachers must do those reflective things, engage the students in [metacognition], and so forth" (p. 306). Further discussion of learning strategies and related study skills instruction is provided in Chapter 12.

***Content Enhancement.*** Another important focus related to curriculum development is the use of content enhancement strategies. Although the general concept of enhancing curricular content has been a staple of education in general, and special education in particular, for some time, the focus received increased emphasis through the work of Deshler and colleagues from the University of Kansas. The core emphasis of such an approach is that if the information is truly worthy of being learned, then it also warrants being intentionally taught.

To enhance content, teachers can analyze the curriculum for a particular academic subject and identify those key concepts that must be learned in order for students to benefit from instruction on that topic. Once identified, instructional units and lesson plans can be developed that highlight the essential elements of the content, and specific strategies such as advance organizers, and more particularly graphic organizers (discussed later in the chapter), can be used to highlight these concepts and promote learning. If the lessons are designed in a way to promote active engagement by students, then benefits are far more likely to accrue.

Given the fact that there is significant underachievement in American schools, particularly at the secondary level, efforts to enhance content to promote learning have broad appeal. Further, they become more significant when they are used with students who experience attention deficits, have problems focusing on relevant concepts, have difficulty recalling and/or retrieving key information, and have problems expressing what they have learned. Further, and perhaps more importantly, an effort to systematically teach content to enhance learning also has the potential benefit of increasing the likelihood of generalization so that students can use the information in subsequent settings both within and beyond a particular academic course (Haight, 2003; KU-CRL, 2006b). A content enhancement focus thus underscores the fact that the content taught within standards-based curricula has been determined to have merit beyond the too often narrow focus on scores achieved on standards-based assessments.

Although a number of strategies have been used to promote content enhancement, the most comprehensive

**DIVERSITY IN THE CLASSROOM** *Tips*

**Jean Schumaker, Ph. D.**, is associate director of the University of Kansas Center for Research on Learning and a professor in the Departments of Special Education and Applied Behavioral Science. She and her colleagues have developed the *Strategic Instruction Model*, a comprehensive program for students with learning disabilities.

Adapting curricula for diverse groups of secondary students in required courses can be difficult since teachers are responsible for covering more and more content each year at higher and higher levels of complexity. When students with disabilities and other at-risk students are enrolled in content courses, the teacher's role becomes even more complex. Thus, in classrooms where such diverse groups of students are being educated, effective teaching routines that correspond to a variety of these students' needs must be used. Since 1983, a series of research studies have demonstrated the positive effects of specially designed teaching routines on the learning of diverse groups of students. These routines are called Content Enhancement Routines because they enable teachers to enhance the learning of content by all the students in their classes. In general, through the use of Content Enhancement Routines, teachers review the information that students need to learn, organize that information in a way that makes it "learner friendly," and present it to students in a way that keeps them active in the learning process and enhances their retention of the content. Built into the routines are teaching procedures that enable a teacher to (a) ensure that students' background knowledge is activated, (b) make the students active participants in the learning process, (c) highlight the meaning of key vocabulary, (d) draw connections between pieces of information, (e) present abstract information in a two-dimensional, concrete form, and (f) tie information to the students' lives and current events. Through use of the Content Enhancement Routines teachers can create a learning apprenticeship in their classrooms whereby they show students how to learn information through modeling the processes involved in manipulating and transforming it.

Fifteen Content Enhancement Routines have been designed corresponding to different teaching tasks. Some routines were designed for introducing a course, or each unit in a course, or particularly difficult lessons. Others have been designed for teaching complex concepts such as "democracy" or "sound energy." Still others were designed for teaching the main ideas and the details of a course. Some routines were created for helping students master key vocabulary terms and other important information.

Regardless of the type of routine, the Content Enhancement Routines have been shown, through a series of research studies, to be effective in enhancing student learning. Moreover, the research has shown that the performance of a wide variety of learners, including high achievers, normal achievers, low achievers, students with disabilities, and students representing a variety of cultural and ethnic backgrounds, improves as a result of teacher use of the routines. Research has also shown that teachers can learn to use each routine with fidelity in a relatively short period of time (i.e., about 3 hours of professional development time). In addition, research has shown that teachers can learn to use the routines through interactive hypermedia instruction at levels that are equal to levels achieved with live instruction.

program for students with learning difficulties is that developed at the University of Kansas. The list below summarizes their specific routines available for enhancing course content (KU-CRL, 2006b).

- Routines for planning and leading learning
  - Course Organizer Routine
  - Unit Organizer Routine
  - Lesson Organizer Routine
- Routines for exploring text, topics, and details
  - Clarifying Routine
  - Framing Routine
  - Survey Routine
  - Vocabulary LINCing Routine
- Routines for teaching concepts
  - Concept Mastery Routine
  - Concept Anchoring Routine
  - Concept Comparison Routine
- Routines for increasing student performance
  - Recall Enhancement Routine
  - Question Exploration Routine
  - Quality Assignment Routine
  - ORDER Routine

**Tier III: High-Quality Intensive Instruction.** The third tier focuses on curricular approaches that can be viewed as more consistent with specialized education. These emphases can be delivered in either general education classrooms or in pull-out programs within the schools. They are discussed here because they may reflect alternatives to the typical, core curriculum within general education. For many students with special needs, their inclusion within a comprehensive curriculum will be the key to school—and postschool—success.

The focus below is on academic remediation and adult outcomes curricular approaches. A third area, social and self-determination skills development is addressed in depth in Chapter 13.

***Academic Remediation.*** The most common, historical model for special education curricula has been the academic remedial, basic skills orientation. Such a model presumes that the major attention of instruction should focus on developing academic skills. A **basic skills** model is typically the focus of most elementary curricula for students with disabilities. This orientation has both a long- and short-term outlook based on the assumption that direct instruction of academic skills will ultimately increase academic performance, allow students to reach acceptable levels of literacy, and more immediately provide students with the skills needed to access the general curriculum.

The particular advantages of a remedial model are that it focuses on students' specific deficits, offers an intensive option to general class programs, and can assist in increasing literacy, thus potentially benefiting the individual in both school and extra-school learning tasks.

However, such an orientation may neglect the specific strengths of students and may reinforce their sense of failure by continuing to focus on areas of difficulty. In addition, although the special education setting may be able to provide intensive interventions (i.e., consistency of program, appropriate direction of the program, monitoring of success, student feedback), such as using a powerful program such as the Wilson Reading Program, far too often the interventions that are implemented are not intensive, comprehensive, or scientifically based. Further, such an approach may fail to address issues of transfer, whether to the general-class setting or to postsecondary environments.

***Adult Outcomes Curriculum.*** Two adult outcomes models are introduced in this section. These options are interrelated but have been separated because some of their features are discrete. The models are introduced briefly here and then discussed in greater detail in Chapter 15.

A **life skills** orientation emphasizes a comprehensive life-demands view of the postschool adjustment process. Although such curricula tend to include occupational and employment considerations, they focus less intensively on vocational training. These types of curricula are typically more responsive to varied concerns with the demands of adulthood (Cronin, Patton, & Wood, 2004). Although life skills instruction may become the major curricular focus primarily for some students with disabilities, Clark, Field, Patton, Brolin, and Sitlington (1994) argue for its importance for all students:

> Students with disabilities are especially in need of life skills instruction in light of the predominance of evidence that indicates . . . a large percentage of them find adult living demands outside their skill range. The fact remains, there are other students within the educational system who find adult demands just as difficult when they leave school and have similar problems of adjustment—socially, vocationally, and in independent living. A life skills instruction approach should be a part of (i.e., included within existing coursework) or a recognized and approved option to (i.e., alternative coursework) every school curriculum for all students at all grade levels. Only then can all students and their families have the opportunity to make life-related decisions with regard to individual educational outcomes they view as important. (p. 126)

Clark et al. (1994) further discussed this issue:

> [T]he potential benefits of inclusive education are the stripping away of stigma, the building of self-esteem, and the developing of social skills and interpersonal relationships within an inclusive environment. Given this, the first consideration for where life skills should be taught should be general education settings and the community. Like any other instructional content area, it should be assumed that unless the student is unable to learn the needed life skills within an inclusive, general education setting, even with every provision of support and reasonable accommodations, no move to separate the student from his or her peers should be made. (pp. 128–129)

A life skills emphasis implies a top-down orientation to curricular development, that is, a focus looking down from the demands of adulthood. Bigge and Stump (1999) suggest that the major components of life skills curricula include functional academics (e.g., money management); daily and community living skills (e.g., health, civic and social responsibilities, leisure skills, social skills, self-determination); and transition-related skills. Such a program is intended to be indexed against the realities of the community in which an individual will be living and thus clearly focuses on key transitional areas (Patton & Dunn, 1998).

Students who have been experiencing chronic difficulty in school may be inherently interested in a curriculum that radically shifts attention away from academic deficits and toward future learning and skill needs. Thus, an approach emphasizing life skills is frequently more attractive to adolescents and may have positive motivational consequences. For individuals with more significant cognitive disabilities, the importance of such a focus becomes even clearer.

A related focus is on **vocational training,** whether delivered through general or special vocational classes, which has traditionally been associated with secondary programming for students with mild retardation (e.g., see the classic work of Kolstoe & Frey, 1965). However, a vocational emphasis also should be considered for students identified as learning disabled or behaviorally disordered.

The obvious advantage of vocational training programs is that they are related to transitional efforts undertaken to prepare adolescents for postsecondary environments. Their relevance to adult settings is a major factor in motivation. Enrollment in a vocational program may keep many students from dropping out of school.

Two observations are worthy of note. First, there is a significant need for community-based learning opportunities as an alternative to, or complement of, simulated vocational opportunities within a school setting. Community-based instruction moves education beyond the school so that specific skills can be taught *in situ.* The implications for generalization and realistic job training are obvious. Second, vocational training can be enhanced through the use of workplace supports. Basically a job-coach approach, this orientation places individuals on the job and provides them with assistance that is gradually faded out over time. For example, an individual may be placed at a fast-food outlet for a work opportunity, with support provided as necessary on the job.

A vocational orientation provides specific training in skills for life beyond the school setting and adds relevance and motivation to the curriculum. The model emphasizes training in skills relevant to adult outcomes, and participation is associated with a significant decrease in school dropout rates.

Several possible concerns with vocational training also must be considered, however. In some school settings, a limited number of vocational training options are available. Some vocational training programs focus on job skill development in areas that have limited community validity. Far too often, there is an absence of congruence between vocational assessment and instructional planning and instruction. Although these possible concerns can be overcome, they nevertheless present significant issues to be addressed.

Reflective Question 3.1: ***Curriculum has changed with the advent of the national and state commitment to standards-based programs delivered primarily in the general education classroom. Evaluate the relative benefit of this trend for students with special needs.***

## EFFECTIVE INSTRUCTION

Twenty-first century classrooms are diverse and thus the challenges for teaching are significant. Students represent diverse cultural backgrounds or are bilingual. In inclusive classrooms, special education supports are provided to an increased number of students. Students at varying academic levels are being served by one teacher. Consequently, there has not been a time when the use of effective instructional methodologies has been of greater significance. Consistent with IDEA (2004) and NCLB (2002), effective instruction has now been defined as those practices that are research based and empirically validated (Boardman, Arguelles, Vaughan, Hughes, & Clingmer, 2005; Stanovich & Stanovich, 2003).

Special education brings to the challenge of inclusion a wealth of instructional strategies that will be discussed throughout this text. As Lloyd and Hallahan (2005) noted, the field of learning disabilities in particular has been one of the "foremost sources for empirically founded practices—practices that are proven valuable for a wide spectrum of students, not just those with learning disabilities. Reasonably informed people interested in learning disabilities . . . argue strongly for explicit, systematic instruction that focuses on teaching students strategies for completing academic tasks and that includes monitoring of progress so instruction can be adjusted to maximize progress" (p. 135).

In an important article focused on effectiveness in special education, Heward (2003a) identified six dimensions of practice that characterize positive features of instruction. In Table 3-6, these dimensions and features are provided. They provide a strong foundation for the focus of effective teaching of students with special needs.

This section describes teaching approaches consistent with both the effective instruction model presented in Chapter 1 and the list of teacher effectiveness variables in Figure 3-3. An overview and description of the following effective teaching practices is presented: teacher-directed instruction, grouping for instruction,

**TABLE 3–6** Dimensions and defining features of special education

| *Dimension* | *Defining Features* |
|---|---|
| Individually planned | • Learning goals and objectives based on assessments and input from parents and student<br>• Teaching methods and instructional materials selected and/or adapted for each student<br>• Setting(s) where instruction will occur determined relative to opportunities for student to learn and use targeted skills |
| Specialized | • Sometimes involves unique or adapted teaching procedures seldom used in general education<br>• Incorporates variety of instructional materials and supports to help students acquire and use targeted learning objectives<br>• Related services (e.g., audiology, physical therapy)<br>• Assistive technology |
| Intensive | • Instruction presented with attention to detail, precision, structure, clarity, and repeated practice<br>• "Relentless, urgent" instruction<br>• Efforts to provide students with incidental, naturalistic opportunities to use targeted knowledge and skill |
| Goal directed | • Purposeful instruction to help individual students achieve personal self-sufficiency and success in present and future environments<br>• Value of instruction determined by student attainment of outcomes |
| Research-based methods | • Recognizes that all teaching approaches are not equally effective<br>• Instructional programs and teaching procedures selected on basis of research |
| Guided by student performance | • Careful, ongoing monitoring of progress<br>• Frequent and direct measures/assessment of learning that inform modifications of instruction |

*Source:* Adapted from Heward, William L., *Exceptional Children: An Introduction to Special Education* (7th ed.) © 2003, pp. 40–41. Reprinted by permission of Pearson Education, Inc., Upper Saddle River, NJ.

scaffolding, self-regulated learning, and peer-mediated learning.

## Teacher-Directed Instruction

With **teacher-directed instruction,** the teacher plays an active role in the teaching process. This role varies depending on the objectives of the lesson or subject area. Students with learning problems often require special services and instructional supports because they are not dealing well with traditional methods and materials. These students must be provided with lessons in which teachers proceed systematically, sequence within and between lessons, pace instruction briskly, question students appropriately, and involve them actively.

A key aspect of successful instruction is the intensity of the instruction provided. As Deshler (2005) noted, it must be highly intensive:

> Intensive instruction involves helping students maintain a high degree of attention and response during instructional sessions that are scheduled as frequently and consistently as possible. In other words, a key factor affecting learning is both the amount of time and instruction and how effectively each instructional moment is used to engage students in activities that contribute to their learning. Intensity during instruction is achieved by progressive pacing, frequent question-answer interactions, and frequent activities that require a physical response (e.g., pointing, writing, raising hands, repeating). Intensity can also be achieved through reflective or open-ended questions if the activities are focused on a process that engages interest and maintains the student's attention. For adolescents who are far behind, all of these elements must define the instructional dynamic. (pp. 123–124)

One of the most widely used instructional methods is the use of **direct instruction.** Although there are many versions of direct instruction, it typically includes the essential elements of explaining the skill, teaching the skill, modeling the skill, practicing the skill, and giving feedback on the skill performance.

Teachers who engage in direct instruction present lessons that provide students with opportunities to respond and receive feedback on what they think about

**FIGURE 3–3** General teacher effectiveness variables

| Examples of General Effective Teaching Behaviors | Resulting Desired Student Behaviors |
|---|---|
| 1. Classroom management skills<br>a. Rules established and enforced<br>b. Clear instructions given<br>c. Consistent reinforcement of desired behavior<br>d. Environment structured so children can predict consequences of behavior<br>e. Transition periods structured | 1. Students demonstrate appropriate classroom behaviors (e.g., on-task behavior without disruptions). |
| 2. Systematic instruction<br>a. Introduction of content<br>b. Explanation of procedures/materials<br>c. Questioning student understanding<br>d. Modeling and demonstrating<br>e. Guided practice<br>f. Descriptive feedback<br>g. Independent practice<br>h. Pacing | 2. Students demonstrate mastery over skills and content and meet learning goals and objectives. |
| 3. Assessment of learner progress | 3. Students understand goals and objectives and are able to monitor their own progress. |
| 4. Modification of content when children are having difficulties. | 4. Student frustration is diminished. |
| 5. Self-reflection/evaluation of teaching and student–teacher interactions | 5. Students learn respect, self-evaluation skills, and problem solving. |

the lesson being presented. They are shown how a skill is performed and are then given ample time to perform the new skill in a guided practice situation. Teachers engage all students by providing positive as well as constructive feedback while they are practicing, the ultimate goal being mastery over the skill. Typically, such lessons follow a pattern so that students can predict the structure of the lesson and the learning environment.

Kauffmann (2002) stressed the importance of direct instruction when he stated:

> Nothing is gained by keeping students guessing about what it is they are supposed to learn. In all or nearly all of the education programs in which the majority of students can be demonstrated to be highly successful in learning the facts and skills they need, these . . . are taught directly rather than indirectly. That is, the teacher is in control of instruction, not the student, and information is given to students. Giving information doesn't mean that the instruction is dull, and it doesn't mean that students don't learn to apply their knowledge and skills to everyday problems. Neither does it mean that students have nothing to say about their education. But it does mean that students don't waste time and effort trying to figure out what they're to learn. It also means that students aren't allowed to learn misrules—learn the wrong thing or a faulty application so that their learning can be described as false, misleading, or useless. (p. 236)

The following description provides an example of a systematic instructional approach to provide teachers with a way to remember direct-instruction procedures as well as to employ generalization procedures so that students can perform the skill outside the classroom environment. The procedure is divided into seven steps (Figure 3–4). The discussion describes how the **PURPOSE** teaching format can be implemented during instructional periods.

**FIGURE 3–4** Learning with PURPOSE: Structured teaching model

**Did the instructor:**

_________ **P**repare the student to learn the skill?
- _________ Define the skill?
- _________ Discuss different situations where the skill could be used?

_________ Have the student **U**nderstand and learn the skill steps?
- _________ Define each skill step?
- _________ Give rationales for each skill step?
- _________ Give examples of how each skill step should be performed?

_________ Have the students **R**ehearse the skill correctly?
- _________ Model the skill for the students?
- _________ Have the students rehearse the skill?

_________ Have students **P**erform a self-check of the skill?
- _________ Have each partner check to see if the skill user performed all steps and rehearsed the skill until each student reached criterion?
- _________ Have the students perform a self-check of their performance?

_________ Help the students **O**vercome any skill performance problems?

_________ Have the students **S**elect other situations where the skill can be used?

_________ Have the students **E**valuate any skill performance areas outside the teaching setting?

**Prepare the Student to Learn the Skill.** This step requires that the teacher prepare the students to learn the skill and know why it is important to learn. The teacher asks the students to (a) define the skill to be learned, (b) state why it is an important skill, and (c) explain where they can use this skill once learned. It is important that the teacher incorporate an interactive dialogue with the students and listen to their answers.

**Understand the Skill Steps.** The second step requires the teacher to help the student understand the skill components to be learned. The teacher reviews each component of the skill's task analysis by presenting each skill component individually, asking students to state what it is and why it is needed to execute the skill. If the students are unable to do this, the teacher should explain the skill component, give an example of it, and state why it is an essential component of the skill. Again, the teacher should involve the students in the discussion.

This step also builds on task analysis of the skill so that each step is easy to grasp. Task analysis allows the teacher to determine whether the skill is too difficult for a student and at what point the student is having trouble. By analyzing the steps associated with each skill, teachers are able to modify the skill to best meet the needs of the students.

**Rehearse the Skill.** After the students have a clear understanding of each skill component, teachers rehearse the skill for and with the students. The teacher begins by modeling the skill as it should be performed. If the skill is interactive, the teacher can model the skill through a role-play situation and the students then perform the skill exactly as the teacher modeled it.

If the skill is cognitive, the teacher can model it by "talking through" each step of the skill. The importance of having the students hear and see what the teacher is thinking is also underscored. Students will see and hear how a person thinks through a cognitive problem and can perform the skill.

After the modeling, the teacher should seek feedback by asking the students about each skill step and requiring them to provide some details about the skill component that was just modeled. The teacher should praise the students for their correct answers and refresh their memories when they cannot remember what happened during the performance of a skill step.

The teacher then should require the students to learn each of the skill components before they are asked to perform the skill. This task can be accomplished through strategies dependent on the age and cognitive ability of the student, such as (a) memorization of the skill steps through verbal rehearsal, (b) development and utilization of a mnemonic, and/or (c) use of flash cards or pictures. When the students are able to verbally state each step of the skill, they should try to perform the skill under guided practice. Mastery of the skill should be achieved during this step.

Rehearsal focuses on the importance of developing proficiency in a particular skill and then maintaining it once mastered. To provide further elaboration on concepts related to rehearsal and practice, Hardman and Drew (2005) identified the following types of practice that result in enhanced learning: massed practice (e.g., cramming before an examination), distributed practice (daily practice sessions that may be shorter in duration but regularly occurring and may reflect varied context), and naturally distributed practice (e.g., practicing the skills in the context of where that skill will be most importantly used; naturally distributed practice relates directly to the importance of generalization, which is discussed below).

**Perform a Self-Check.** After a mastery rehearsal, the teacher and student perform a self-check of the skill performance. It involves an evaluation of each skill component. When the student thinks that mastery of the skill has been accomplished, he or she should ask the teacher to evaluate the performance for accuracy. This outside check will confirm the students' perceptions of their own performance.

**Overcome Any Performance Barrier.** As with the acquisition of any skill, there may be difficulties in obtaining performance at targeted levels and thus teachers will need to help students overcome any performance problems.

When these situations occur, the teacher must pinpoint where the problem lies in order to help the student overcome the problem, and in order to develop and appropriate instructional intervention. The teacher may need to develop supplemental materials, or provide extra practice, to accomplish the desired goal of learning the skill to mastery.

**Select Other Situations Where the Skill Can Be Performed.** As the student achieves mastery over the skill, the teacher and student must select other situations where the skill can be used. During this step, the teacher focuses on generalizing a skill mastered in the classroom to other situations. This emphasis on generalization provides a foundation for showing students how they can apply knowledge or skills to new tasks, problems, or situations and acquire a set of rules to solve problems of a similar nature in the future (T. Smith et al., 2008).

Together, the student and teacher decide where or with whom the skill can be used and determine when the student will use the skill. They might talk about how the skill will be performed and the importance of using the skill in the selected situation. Once a specific situation is selected, the student and teacher agree that the student will perform the skill as soon as the occasion arises and that the student will report the outcome of the performance as soon as possible. This generalization step requires students to use the skill where it is most meaningful to them. Further, generalization can be promoted by teaching the skill in multiple contexts, providing reinforcement for the successful generalization of the skill behavior, and reminding students when it is appropriate to apply the skill that they have learned in a new situation (Smith et al., 2008).

**Evaluate Skill Performance.** The last component is to evaluate the skill performance in the generalized situation. Once the situation has occurred, students must assess the effectiveness of their performance and determine the outcome. If possible, students should be encouraged to use a checklist to evaluate how well each skill component was executed. If all the skill components were executed successfully, the student must then determine whether the performance of the skill accomplished the desired goal. If the student did not perform the skill correctly, the teacher and the student should determine why it was not performed correctly and develop a procedure that would help the student the next time the performance of the skill is necessary. If problems persist, the teacher engages in additional practice of the skill with the student or problem solves with the child to ensure that a similar situation outside the classroom might be met with more favorable results in the future.

## Grouping for Instruction

A key consideration that is integral to planning for instruction is grouping. Vaughn and Schumm (1997) provided a detailed analysis of the grouping practices of general and special education teachers, respectively. For the former, the most commonly used strategy was whole-class grouping with students of mixed ability combined within the group. The most common finding was that general educators use smaller groups for practice and reinforcement activities but not for teacher-led instruction and, when the groups are used for that purpose, the students are of mixed ability.

On the other hand, special educators reported that they were much more likely to use groups of similar ability. Further, they reported that they had greater autonomy in making decisions about how students were grouped. Consequently, the traditional pattern of homogeneously set up groupings appeared more common with this group of teachers. To the extent that students need work on specific skills, large-group instruction with mixed-ability groups would likely not be an effective instructional practice.

Although there is much benefit in the use of skills-based grouping for students with special needs, too often such groups have remained static; achievement level has been the primary determinant of group placement. Instead, teachers should consider options that periodically introduce change and flexibility into grouping procedures. Interest and skill groups should be incorporated into the program at regular intervals.

Interest groups can be formed around a common theme (e.g., marine biology, baseball) regardless of achievement level. The teacher can assign trade book material at levels appropriate for each student, with questions and activities suitable for the group. In skill groups, students periodically meet with the teacher to work on a specific skill deficit. Here again, students of varying levels of achievement work together on a common problem. With planning assistance from the teacher, this peer tutoring approach can be as motivating and instructional for the tutor as it is for the tutee.

## Scaffolding

The concept of scaffolding describes interactions between teachers and students that facilitate the learning process. Stone (1998) describes the scaffolding metaphor as follows:

> In providing temporary assistance to children as they strive to accomplish a task just out of their competency, adults are said to be providing a scaffold, much like that used by builders in erecting a building. [Scaffolding] connotes a custom-made support for the "construction" of new skills, a support that can be easily disassembled when no longer needed. It also connotes a structure that allows for accomplishment of some goal that would otherwise be either unattainable or quite cumbersome to complete. (p. 344)

In scaffolding instruction, teachers think aloud or talk through the steps they follow to reach a specific conclusion. As students begin to understand the process, they gradually take over this talking-through procedure and the teacher acts as a coach, providing prompts when needed.

An example of a scaffolding procedure is seen in this exercise, which focuses student attention on story grammar. The teacher begins by modeling the scaffolding steps, thinking aloud by saying to the students after they have read to a designated point in the story, "I see a problem." The teacher states the problem and writes it on a notesheet for students. The teacher then describes the attempts in the story to solve the problem or conflict and gives an analysis of the events that led to the solution of the problem. After the teacher models these steps, the students begin to talk themselves through a story following the same steps (Gersten & Dimino, 1990). This strategy leads students into being active participants in the reading process, and when used, students' responses to both lower- and higher-level questions are likely to improve.

## Self-Regulated Learning

Ultimately, students must become independent learners, able to direct their own behavior in ways that assist in maximizing the amount of time engaged in learning (i.e., **student-directed learning**). Many students with special needs have significant difficulty in this area, which can limit their success in general education where self-regulated behaviors are expected (but often not directly taught). Teachers have the responsibility for assisting students to become independent learners and to structure the classroom environment to help them achieve this goal. Self-directed learners typically demonstrate a variety of **metacognitive skills** as well as self-regulation skills resulting in motivation, skills needed to navigate their learning environment, and the social interaction skills needed to support their self-directed behaviors. The learning strategies approach discussed earlier is based on students taking responsibility for directing their own learning.

The following discussion consists of two types of teaching that will foster self-direction skill in students with disabilities: skill building and problem-based learning.

**Skill Building.** The first type of teaching focuses on skill building through direct instructional procedures. Four self-direction skills illustrate this process.

**Action planning** is a procedure used to develop a long-term strategy to identify goals and tasks that might be needed to accomplish a desired life achievement (e.g., going to college, getting a job, moving to a different state, attaining financial stability). This long-term strategy includes identifying steps that will lead to attaining the life achievement and analyzing each step and breaking it down into tasks/goals (Serna & Lau-Smith, 1995).

Action planning gives an individual a purpose for engaging in certain activities. Through the use of direct instruction, students are able to develop their own action plans and determine a strategy that will allow them to accomplish their goals. Seeing each step that is required to accomplish that goal can give purpose to the many tasks that must be completed.

**Goal setting** can be defined as a skill that enables the learner to determine the necessary tasks or events needed to be accomplished for certain outcomes to be obtained. Teachers might introduce this skill to a student by stating that many people complain about not having or getting the things they want. Often, they do not know specifically what they want so they have a difficult time working toward getting something.

A student might set a goal by identifying what is wanted or what needs to be accomplished (e.g., getting a good grade in math class). Then the student must put this task into a proactive "I will" statement (e.g., "I will get a good grade in math"). Clarification of the goal statement can occur by determining what exactly the task is, with whom it will be accomplished, where it will be accomplished, and by when it will be accomplished.

**Goal planning** allows an individual to develop the steps needed to achieve a particular goal. A student could begin the goal-planning process by reviewing the goal statement just outlined. Next, the student would think of activities or steps (behaviors) that would help in the accomplishment of the goal.

**Self-management** to accomplish goals is a complex set of procedures used to regulate or guide a person's behavior so that a goal can be accomplished. The first subskill in the skill of self-management is *developing a reward system*. This requires that the teacher and students identify the items, activities, or people that are rewarding to them. The teacher will need to do some preliminary work to develop a list of possible rewards to choose from.

The second subskill involves *developing a self-monitoring system*. Using the rewards (identified in the subskill on developing a reward system) and the goal steps (developed in the goal planning step), the students can fill out a self-contract by (a) deciding when it will begin, end, or be reviewed; (b) specifying the goal steps to be accomplished; (c) determining the reward to be received upon the completion of the goal steps; (d) stating what penalty will be enforced if the goal steps are not performed; and (e) scheduling a review of the contract to determine if it is working or if it needs to be changed. After these terms are delineated, students can create a system to monitor their progress, as this will assist them in their self-management process.

The final subskill within self-management is *monitoring the desired behavior*. Students begin this skill by locating their self-contract and reviewing the goal steps, rewards, penalties, and signature commitment. The subskill then begins by developing rules or criteria that must be followed for each goal step. The rules should be specific actions or behaviors that the students must do in order to accomplish the goal step. After the students begin to perform their goal steps, they monitor their behaviors by using a self-monitoring sheet (created in the subskill on developing a monitoring system). Following the completion of the each goal step and according to the criterion established, the students reward themselves.

**Problem-Based Learning.** Problem-based learning consists of activities in which the students become investigators of a real problem or topic. First, students are guided, through different activities, to *explore many topics*, issues, and areas into which they may delve more deeply. Teachers must assess the interests of the student and explore several avenues, as students may not know what they would like to learn about.

The second activity is *choosing a topic* and determining certain goals and objectives that are to be accomplished in order to develop the content into an interesting project. Teachers can help students determine these goals and objectives by working with them to decide what is to be accomplished.

The third activity is *developing a management plan*. This plan includes creating timelines, getting started, and finalizing product ideas. After the plan is outlined, the student begins to research the ideas and produce the products based on research and guidance from the teacher. The final step of this process is guiding students through the process of independent or small-group study to help them evaluate what they have accomplished. Students and teachers can develop evaluation plans that best suit their needs.

## Peer-Mediated Learning

The main purpose for using **peer-mediated strategies** is to promote learning as a function of collaborative interactions among students. Although the focus is often placed on making students *independent* learners, they also need to be *interdependent* learners. Students benefit not only from being able to direct their own learning activities, but also from knowing how to seek assistance when needed. The focus is on activities in which students with learning-related problems engage along with their fellow students. The discussion in this section focuses on peer tutoring and collaborative learning.

**Peer Tutoring.** **Peer tutoring** typically, but not always, involves the pairing of a competent student with a student who is less competent in a particular behavioral or academic area. Peer tutoring procedures have been used to teach academic skills and develop social behaviors with regard to classroom discipline, peer relations, and appropriate interaction behaviors. The effectiveness of peer tutoring has been demonstrated across ages, settings, and types of students.

Cooke, Heron, and Heward (1983) summarized the advantages of peer tutoring as follows: (a) children can effectively teach each other skills when tutors emphasize repetition, mastery, and a review system; (b) tutors are able to learn from teaching others; (c) tutors can individualize content material to meet the needs of each student; (d) students can engage in one-to-one instruction without requiring a full class lesson; (e) one-to-one teaching greatly increases the opportunity for correct responses by the tutee; and (f) tutors and tutees gain in self-esteem, self-respect, and ability to interact with each other on a constructive and appropriate basis.

When selecting tutors, teachers must consider that the students should be individuals who can help in the teaching process. These students should be enthusiastic about being peer tutors and willing to learn the procedures necessary to work with another student. Figure 3–5 outlines a direct instructional procedure, using the PURPOSE format described earlier (see Figure 3–5), that a teacher can use when preparing students to become peer tutors.

An example of a successful peer tutoring approach is **Peer-Assisted Learning Strategies (PALS).** With PALS, groups as varied as beginning readers or middle school math students (Kroeger & Kouche, 2006) are assisted in learning through paired instruction. Each member of the pair takes turns serving as a coach and a reader with the first coach being the reader at a higher achievement level who listens to, comments on, and reinforces the other student before the roles are reversed. Mathes and Torgesen (1998) reported that PALS enhanced students' learning by promoting careful attention to saying and hearing sounds, sounding out words, and reading stories. They recommended using the approach three times a week for approximately 16 weeks with each session lasting 35 minutes. In addition, Fuchs, Fuchs, Mathes, and Martinez (2002) reported that participation in PALS resulted in enhanced social acceptance for students with learning disabilities and that these students had similar social standing when compared to their peers who were not disabled. Further applications in reading instruction are described in Chapters 6 and 7.

Kroeger and Couche (2006) similarly provided an example of a successful application of PALS to middle school students in math. As they noted, the benefits reflected in "a world of students discussing and talking through math problems, regardless of ability levels or past experiences in math classes. . . . PALS is an effective intervention to increase engagement and opportunities to respond for all students" (p. 12).

Another research-based approach for using students as instructors is classwide peer tutoring (CWPT). Maheady, Harper, and Mallette (2003) identified the four primary components of CWPT as follows: "competing teams; a highly structured tutoring procedure; daily point earning and public posting of people performance; and direct practice in the implementation of instructional activities. In using CWPT, the teacher's role changes from primary 'deliverer' of instruction to facilitator and monitor of peer-teaching activities" (p. 1).

CWPT is intended to be a reciprocal tutoring approach. That is, students assume roles as both tutors and tutees during individual instructional sessions. Further, the sessions are highly structured by the teacher to ensure that students are on task and focused on key instructional content.

To enhance the impact of any peer tutoring program, students can be taught to enlist the help of their peers by teaching them strategies to get assistance. Wolford, Heward, and Alber (2001) demonstrated that teaching simple phrases (e.g., "Can you help me?" or

**FIGURE 3–5** Teaching peers how to be tutors

**A Systematic Procedure for Teaching Peers to Be Tutors**

- **P**repare the students to learn about peer tutoring:
  ____ Ask the students if they know the *definition* of a "tutor."
  ____ Ask the students why it is *important* to be a tutor.
  ____ Ask the students for *examples* of what subjects they might tutor.

- Help the student to **U**nderstand and learn the steps to being a tutor.
  ____ *Outline* the steps tutors must exhibit in order to tutor a peer in a designated subject area.
  ____ *Explain* each step to the tutors and ask them to tell you why that step is important.

- **R**ehearse the skill by watching a model and then practicing the lesson with someone else.
  ____ *Show or model* how you would like the tutors to execute the lesson when tutoring another student in a particular subject area.
  ____ Have the students *rehearse* the lesson with you role-playing the tutee.
  ____ *Give feedback* to the tutors after each role-play situation.

- **P**erform a self-check to ensure that the lesson was performed correctly.
  ____ Once the tutors have role-played the lesson, have them *evaluate* whether they performed each step needed to teach the lesson.

- **O**vercome any performance problems to produce the desired outcomes.
  ____ If a tutor is not exhibiting all of the steps needed to correctly teach the lesson, *work with the tutor* until he/she is able to execute it appropriately.

- **S**elect or recognize other situations where the skill can be performed.
  ____ Pair the tutors with other students and have them *begin tutoring* the students.

- **E**valuate the performances of the tutor and the tutee during the lesson.
  ____ Evaluate whether the tutor executed the lesson appropriately and if the tutee's skill level improved.

"How am I doing so far?") had a positive impact on the rate at which feedback was received, and/or students' accuracy and productivity on classroom tasks.

**Cooperative Learning. Cooperative learning (CL)** also can be employed to enlist the support of students while simultaneously promoting the learning of academic and behavioral skills. According to Schniedewind and Salend (1987), teachers can structure their class lessons so that students work together to achieve a shared academic goal. They state: "cooperative learning is especially worthwhile for a heterogeneous student population, because it encourages liking and learning among students of various academic abilities, [disabilities], and racial and ethnic backgrounds" (p. 22).

When planning a CL lesson, teachers should consider four elements: (a) positive interdependence, (b) individual accountability, (c) collaborative skills, and (d) processing. Within a lesson, *positive interdependence* is structured by having each student group agree on the answer to the task and the process for solving each problem.

*Individual accountability* is determined if group members have mastered the process of solving the problem or demonstrate the skills necessary for accomplishing the task. The element of individual accountability is structured by having the teacher randomly score a group's work and determine whether the correct answer has been written on their answer sheet. If the answer is correct, the teacher then asks a student to explain how to solve each problem.

*Collaborative skills* emphasize student support for one another (e.g., praising and offering help), enthusiasm for group work, and contributions to the group's

**FIGURE 3–6** Guidelines for cooperative learning groups for students with disabilities

- Each *group* will produce one product.
- Each *group member* will assist other group members to understand the materials.
- Each *group member* will seek assistance from his or her peers.
- No *group member* will change his or her ideas unless logically persuaded to do so.
- Each *group member* will indicate acceptance of the group's product by signing his or her name.

*Source:* Adapted from "Cooperative Learning Works," by N. Schniedewind and S. Salend, 1987, *Teaching Exceptional Children, 19*(2), 22–25. Reprinted with permission.

efforts. These collaborative skills are necessary for the appropriate behaviors to occur within a group.

Finally, *problem-solving processing* requires that the group evaluate how well they worked together and what they could do in the future to be an even more effective group member or group. This type of evaluation requires that the group function as a whole as well as that individual group members engage in self-evaluation for personal improvement in the classwork. Figure 3-6 presents guidelines for implementing CL.

McMaster and Fuchs (2002) reviewed cooperative learning research from 1990 to 2000. They concluded that the effectiveness of the approach continues to need further research but that strategies that incorporate individual accountability and group rewards are particularly promising. They note that

> in light of inconclusive findings in the literature regarding the efficacy of using CL with students with LD, teachers may wish to use caution in deciding whether to use CL to improve these students' academic performance. Research that reveals which features are most essential to CL's effectiveness, when and where it is most successful, and whether it results in sufficient academic gains for students with LD should help to better inform teachers of its utility in the classroom. Teachers who choose to implement CL might also systematically evaluate whether it is indeed benefiting their students, and explore the use of other empirically validated teaching methods when CL does not elicit desired academic gains. (p. 116)

Reflective Question 3.2: ***Effective instruction is defined as strategies that are consistent with research on enhancing student achievement. Discuss the key teacher-directed, student-regulated, and peer-mediated strategies that are most applicable for use in a given academic subject (e.g., reading) and/or at a given grade level (e.g., 8th grade).***

**TEACHER *Tips*** **Elementary Level**

Cooperative learning (CL) can be challenging if students have not mastered critical social skills or have little experience working with others. It may be best to begin CL with pairs, so that they can learn to work together in less complicated and demanding situations. Fad and Gilliam (1996) suggest ways to structure CL with groups of two:

- Study Buddies: one student reads, the other follows along and asks questions; then they switch roles.
- Partners: students are assigned to a two-person team; one partner will repeat the teacher's directions, the other will ask questions and clarify; before asking the teacher for help, they ask each other.
- Reading Pairs: two students read the same material; both write answers to the comprehension questions; then they compare and produce their best responses.
- Math Pairs: pairs of students work the problems independently; they check each other's work, compare, and decide on the correct answer.
- Radio Readers: students choose a selection, then read together orally; this allows them to build their fluency and rhythm, as well as model accurate reading for each other.
- Spell-Checkers: pairs of students check each other's writing for correct spelling.
- Peer Editors: students edit each other's writing, checking punctuation, grammar, usage, and organization; students sign off after completing their editing.
- Lab Partners: in the science lab, students work together to complete the laboratory assignment, handing in one completed lab with both students' names.

*Source*: Adapted from *Putting It All Together for Student Success*, by K. M. Fad and J. E. Gilliam, 1996, Longmont, CO: Sopris West.

## CURRICULAR AND INSTRUCTIONAL ADAPTATIONS

Teachers seeking to educate all of their students are faced with the challenge of meeting the curricular needs of these children to prepare them for a competitive world. Much of the information instructors must teach is complex and abstract. New vocabulary is necessary and the applicability of new information to everyday life must be understood.

Unfortunately, many students have limited interest in learning things that they do not understand or that seem irrelevant to their immediate future. This lack of motivation among students is a formidable barrier. If teachers are unable to introduce new information in an understandable manner, students will become frustrated and will not persist on their own to learn the material. If teachers are unable to teach students how to acquire new concepts and to have them relate these concepts in a meaningful way, the students will not pursue the new content areas presented to them in their classes.

An additional challenge is the expectation for improving on high-stakes exams that places more pressure on increasing the scores of children. When students are unable to score well on these exams, the schools and the academic curricula are pressured to improve performances.

Teachers therefore must focus on strategies that enable students to succeed in the general education curriculum. Central to this success are classroom **adaptations.** Such efforts are critical to the success of students with disabilities in terms of their access to the general curriculum (Hedeen & Ayers, 2002). Further, "the need to adapt curricula increases as the variability of student abilities and learner characteristics increases" (Hoover & Patton, 2005, p. 43).

Within this chapter, we use *adaptations* as a generic term to include both accommodations and modifications:

- **Accommodations** refer to changes in input and output processes in teaching and learning; they do not change the test items or task content itself.
- **Modifications** refer to changes in content or standards; they change the task or test itself (Polloway, Epstein, & Bursuck, 2003).

Examples in a college-level course in foreign language might include the following:

- **Accommodations:** extended testing time, distraction-free testing site.
- **Modifications:** the substitution of the study of culture for the language instruction requirement.

As shown in Table 3-7, Jitendra, Edwards, Choutka, and Treadway (2002) provide a more comprehensive set of examples of these concepts.

To promote successful inclusion in general education programs for students with special needs, adaptations in both curriculum and instruction will frequently be needed. Wehmeyer 2006 noted that curriculum adaptations include "efforts to modify the representation of the curriculum content or to modify the student's engagement with the curriculum to enhance and progress" (p. 229). The complementary concept of instructional adaptation refers to ways in which teachers can design and deliver instruction and seek student responses to reflect learning in varied ways that enhance success for students with special needs. The discussion below addresses both curriculum and instructional adaptations.

An important context for the use of adaptations is teacher acceptability, which includes the following concepts (Polloway et al., 2003):

- Will a given practice be *helpful* to students with disabilities?
- Is it currently being *used* with their peers who are not disabled?
- Is it *feasible* to implement it in the inclusive classroom?
- What *resources* and *time requirements* are related to the intervention?
- Is it a *desirable* intervention?
- Is the intervention *fair* to peers who are not disabled?

The following discussion summarizes a variety of curricular and instructional adaptations that will assist learners with special needs in being successful in the general education classroom. Each of these adaptations can be beneficial to students. The important point is that none of these adaptations should be made if they are not needed and, if they are needed, the least amount of change as is necessary should be made.

### Material Adaptations

A wide variety of materials are used in school settings, including print materials as well as nonprint materials such as maps, globes, models, photographs, videos, and computer-based images.

**TABLE 3–7** Classroom adaptations

| |
|---|
| **What Are Accommodations?**<br>The student is expected to learn substantially the same information as the rest of the class.<br>Accommodations can include:<br>• Alternative acquisition modes (e.g., videotape, audiotape, computer, readers, Braille)<br>• Content enhancements (e.g., advance organizers, visual displays, study guides, mnemonic devices)<br>• Alternative response modes (e.g., oral responding, untimed responding, computer/word processing) |
| **What Are Modifications?**<br>The student is expected to learn something different than the rest of the class (e.g., different content, different quantity).<br>Modifications can include:<br>• Less material (e.g., fewer objectives, shorter units/part of a unit, fewer pages, problems, shorter lessons)<br>• Different products (e.g., selection rather than production responses, different type of problems, alternative products such as oral instead of written, word processed instead of handwritten)<br>• Different material (e.g., alternative objectives based on prior knowledge and long-term goals, alternative unit according to specific needs of student, alternative curricula such as high interest-low demand, alternative instruction that is less but more explicit)<br>• Different expectations (i.e., information to be taught is divided into what all, some, and a few students learn) and differential content expectations (i.e., analyze information to be taught according to knowledge form [facts, concepts, rules, strategies], make decisions about who learns what on the basis of the content analysis). |

*Source:* From "A Collaborative Approach to Planning in the Content Areas for Students with Learning Disabilities: Accessing the General Curriculum," by A. K. Jitendra, L. L. Edwards, C. M. Choutka, and P. S. Treadway, 2002, *Learning Disabilities Research and Practice, 17*, p. 259. Copyright 2002 by Blackwell Publishing UK. Reprinted with permission.

The key concerns that precipitate the need to make adaptations to instructional materials for the most part cut across the different types of materials. These concerns include:

- The student does not display the skills necessary to handle the material.
- The conceptual complexity of the material exceeds the level at which the student understands (i.e., insufficient background knowledge and/or experience).
- The linguistic complexity of the material is such that the student is unable to extract meaning from it. Primary sources of problems are vocabulary and syntactic factors.
- The amount of information presented to students is overwhelming. Typically emphasis has been placed on breadth of, rather than depth of, coverage.
- The design/format features of materials (e.g., advanced organizers, layout, organization, graphics, cueing, clarity, use of examples, practice opportunities) are lacking or insufficient, thus making them difficult to use.

**Textual materials** refer to any type of material that requires reading as the primary means of obtaining information. Text-based materials typically used in classrooms include basal textbooks, workbooks, worksheets, literature, weekly periodicals, and handouts.

Two general approaches can be implemented to address problems that arise with text-based materials: (1) substitution of an alternative material in place of the existing textual material; and (2) content enhancement techniques (as discussed earlier in the chapter), which include strategies to increase comprehension and tactics for retaining information over time. The first technique aims to avoid the problems associated with existing textual material. The other option primarily supports the student in using existing material, particularly when the student is in a general education setting.

One type of material adaptation warrants particular attention. *Graphic organizers*, advance organizers that provide visual models for presenting curricular content, have been widely promoted as a particularly efficacious approach to content learning by students with special needs (Wehmeyer, 2008). As such, the widespread use of graphic organizers has become an important aspect of the application of universal design for learning, which was discussed earlier in the chapter.

Graphic organizers can be developed for content in any instructional area. For example, graphic organizers can provide outlines for note taking from lectures, a template for organizing reports and speeches for oral presentation in class, a format for deriving key content information from reading assigned as homework, and a prompt to assist students in monitoring their own errors in writing as part of a proofreading strategy. The chapters in Part II of the text provide a wealth of examples of graphic organizers. For example, semantic maps in reading (Chapter 7) and paragraph development models for writing (Chapter 8) are particularly good examples.

The following discussion of various other techniques for adapting instructional materials with textual material is based in part on the recommendations of Schumm and Strickler (1991).

- **Audiotape textual material:** Ideally, the material being used is already available through Recordings for the Blind and Dyslexic and the student can qualify for this service. Otherwise, unless volunteers or other students are available to do the taping, taping may be difficult to do.
- **Read the material aloud:** This suggestion has the same advantages and limitations as taping.
- **Pair students to master textual material:** This technique has short-term and targeted usefulness and requires the availability of such supports whenever the textual material is being used.
- **Use other ways to deliver the material (e.g., direct experiences, media):** Other vehicles for delivering information are useful for presenting content-laden topics.
- **Work with students individually or in small groups:** This works when students can understand the textual material to some extent and time is available on a regular basis for this activity.
- **Simplify existing textual material:** Vocabulary, terminology, and expressions that are difficult for students to understand can be simplified by the teacher. In place of rewriting complete textual passages, one can place a transparency over a page of written material and, with a marker, cross out the more difficult words and write a more understandable equivalent in the margin (Hoover & Patton, 1997).

A variety of ways exist for enhancing content so that students are better able to understand what they read. The following recommendations focus on tactics for improving comprehension of textual, particularly grade-level, material:

- Preview the reading assignment to prepare the student for the specifics they will encounter. This prereading activity should introduce the student to new vocabulary and concepts that may pose problems. The use of a diagram or story frame may be helpful (see Chapter 7).
- Teach students how to use format features including the ability to use headings, boldface type, visual aids, opening sections, and summaries of textual material to gain an organization and additional meaning from the textual material.
- Use a study to guide the student through the reading material by having them respond to questions or statements related to the passages they are reading or have read.
- Modify the reading assignment to reduce the length of the assigned reading or to slow the pace at which content is being covered.
- Adapt text-based activities such as reorganizing and rewriting the "end-of-chapter" questions that are often included with textbooks. For students experiencing reading problems, these types of questions can be frustrating.

In addition to textual material, other types of curricular materials may pose problems for learners with special needs. For example, often adaptations may need to be made with the math materials that are used in most schools. Key factors that teachers must consider focus on both student materials as well as the teacher's guide. If the challenges associated with using this approach to teaching math are recognized, solutions can be implemented.

A particularly useful approach was developed by Rotter (2006). To highlight material presented to students, Rotter identified a checklist for materials based on the four elements of Contrast, Orientation, Lettering, and Artwork (COLA) (see Figure 3–7).

Attention also needs to be given to any type of learning aid (e.g., outside readings, games, in-class projects) that might be part of the ongoing instructional program. Caution must be exercised to ensure that students know how to use these materials. If textual material (e.g., lab manuals) is part of the learning aid, the preceding specific suggestions may need to be implemented. In regard to the use of instructional games, students need to possess appropriate game-playing skills and behaviors—this is crucial if students play games in cooperative situations without teacher involvement or supervision.

**FIGURE 3–7** Checklist for COLA review of materials

| | | |
|---|---|---|
| **C** | Contrast | There is plenty of white space around important information and answer spaces. |
| | | Color of the text is in clear contrast from background (this includes avoiding the use of pencil or lightly printed dittos). |
| | | Color, underlining, dark borders, and/or highlights are used to point out critical information, such as directions. |
| | | Bold font is used infrequently, for highlighting important information only. |
| **O** | Orientation | Important information, such as directions, is in the top-left position. |
| | | All information reads from left to right, top to bottom. |
| | | Material is aligned to the left. |
| | | There is a clear visual path created by the organization of the material. |
| **L** | Lettering | Material is printed, not handwritten. |
| | | The same clear font is used throughout. |
| | | The font is big enough to read easily at the typical viewing distance. |
| | | The material uses upper- and lowercase letters as they would typically appear in print. (No use of all caps or small caps fonts.) |
| | | Italicized fonts are not used. |
| **A** | Artwork | Artwork is used only to support information and not to make the paper "pretty." |
| | | The page is not too "busy," and pictures are not distracting. |
| | | Students will easily recognize the picture(s). |
| | | Artwork is recognizable to the pupils, not dated (e.g., rotary phones). |
| | | Artwork is culturally sensitive. |

*Source*: From "Creating Instructional Material for All Pupils: Try COLA," by K. Rotter, 2006, *Intervention in School and Clinic, 41*, pp. 273–282. Copyright 2006 by PRO-ED, Inc. Reprinted with permission.

## Instructional Delivery Adaptations

- **Capitalize on location:** Proximity to students who are experiencing learning-related problems can assist students to attend to the important dimensions of what is occurring in the classroom, give them easier access to support, and minimize behavioral problems that might arise.
- **Use multisensory experiences:** Multisensory activities can have a positive impact and thus can be instructionally useful.
- **Use lecture-related adaptations:** Teacher-controlled adaptations include scheduling the session so more breaks are possible, organizing the lecture so that a variety of instructional methods (e.g., discussion, media) are utilized, moving around the room, being responsive to the audience and to specific students, highlighting important points, and providing advanced organizers. In addition, note-taking skills and listening strategies may need to be taught. If the lecture format allows for discussion, then the student may also need to develop question-asking skills.

## Product and Assignment Adaptations

A key consideration is using a variety of *work product options*. To provide some choice about options is desirable practice (Morgan, 2006) and is supported by the emerging emphasis on self-determination (see Chapter 13). Too often teachers tend to make the same assignments. For students with special needs who have strengths in areas in which they are seldom allowed to show their ability, having alternative products might be just what they need. The notion of having different outcomes for students fits with the previously discussed suggestion of varying input and output modes.

Another key area relates to the need to adapt in-class and out-of-class (see homework discussion below) assignments given to learners with special needs. Teachers can alter assignments in the following ways: shorten assignments (i.e., break them into smaller versions), change the criterion that has been established that designates successful completion of the assignment, allow more time to complete the assignment, reduce the difficulty of the content, and change the output mode.

## Homework and Adaptations

A staple of the education diet is homework. The research literature generally supports the value of homework to achievement and learning good work habits. When this conclusion is combined with the reform literature supporting increased use to enhance quality, it is apparent that students with special needs must be able to respond effectively, especially as they spend more time in inclusive settings. Prior to the early 1990s, less than a dozen articles and only a handful of papers were published on the topic; within less than a decade at least four special journal issues, one book, and over 60 manuscripts were published (Polloway, Bursuck, & Epstein, 1999).

Although homework presents special problems for students with disabilities and their families, intervention efforts can result in beneficial outcomes. The following suggestions (adapted from Patton, 1994) provide direction for developing and implementing homework practices, including making adaptations for learners with special needs.

1. **Assign homework from the beginning of the year.** Getting students accustomed to the routine of having homework is best accomplished by assigning it early and continuing with it on a regular basis.

2. **Establish a class routine for homework.** If the homework process is to run efficiently, adequate time must be allocated to assign, collect, and evaluate homework. Teachers need to have a reasonable amount of time to inform students of their assignment.

3. **Communicate consequences.** Students need to know the procedures that are expected of them as well as the consequences of violating these procedures. Logical consequences for noncompletion of assignments should be determined beforehand.

4. **Minimize demands on teacher time.** Homework is only one of many duties that teachers must manage. Therefore, any mechanism created to handle homework must demonstrate efficiency. If individualized assignments are indicated, they can be provided by adapting the general assignment rather than developing completely different activities.

5. **Present instructions clearly.** A thorough explanation of a homework assignment should include (a) the purpose, (b) directions for completing the assignment, (c) an estimate of how long the assignment should take, (d) a note when due, (e) the format to be used, (f) the materials needed to complete the assignment, and (g) how it will be evaluated. Teachers also should query students to determine whether they understand what is assigned and/or let them begin working on it in class.

6. **Use assignment books.** Homework assignment books can help compensate for organizational difficulties. Typically, the students will write their assignments in these books and the teachers can initial the books before the students leave the class, confirming that the correct assignment has been recorded. Folders also can be used to provide a quick and simple way for the teacher to evaluate completion of the assignment, thus underscoring the importance of turning in assignments on time.

7. **Evaluate assignments.** Homework that is collected, evaluated, and used to determine a grade is more meaningful to students and has a positive effect on achievement. The challenge is to find ways to manage this aspect of the homework process efficiently such as through the use of assignments that can be evaluated through peer grading or self-correction techniques or by paraeducators.

8. **Help students recognize the purpose and relevance of the assignment.** The major reasons for homework are practice opportunities, completion of unfinished work, preparation for future course activities or upcoming tests, and extension. Homework is best used for proficiency, generalization, or maintenance types of learning activities. Guided by a clear purpose for giving homework, teachers should also identify specific objectives for each assignment and inform students of these objectives when an assignment is introduced. Further teachers should show students how a particular assignment relates to their scholastic or nonacademic lives.

9. **Adapt assignments.** As more students face the challenges of completing homework assignments in general education, practical ways to adapt assignments must be identified. Options to be considered include shorter assignments, extended timeline, alternative evaluation techniques (i.e., based on effort, not accuracy), fewer assignments, extra-credit opportunities, alternative response formats, and group assignments.

**TABLE 3–8** Strategies for home–school collaboration on homework

- Provide computer-generated progress reports on homework performance to parents with descriptive comments about performance.
- Communicate using written modes of communication (e.g., progress reports, letters). Use brightly colored paper to grab attention and prevent misplacement.
- At the beginning of the year, give information regarding assignments, homework adaptations available, and policies on missed assignments and extra credit.
- Communicate with other teachers to avoid overloading the student with homework (and to) prevent completion problems.
- Be sensitive that homework may be a lower priority for families when compared with other issues (e.g., school attendance, family illness) and respond accordingly.
- Help students in completing homework on time (e.g., remind students of assignment due dates periodically, assign homework in small units, write assignments on board).

*Source:* Adapted from "Strategies for Successful Homework," by M. Jayanthi, W. Bursuck, M. H. Epstein, and E. A. Polloway, *Teaching Exceptional Children, 30*(1), 1997, pp. 4–7. Copyright 1997 by the Council for Exceptional Children. Adapted with permission.

10. **Develop self-management skills.** A significant outcome of a successful homework system is the students' taking responsibility for outside class aspects of their own learning. Teachers should help students understand that the effort they put forth can lead to academic success.

11. **Consider student preferences.** It is beneficial to consider students' views on homework practices. A number of studies address the issue of student preferences (see, for example, Nelson, Epstein, Bursuck, Jayanthi, & Sawyer, 1998).

12. **Communicate with parents.** If a smooth school–home communication system is operating, this suggestion is moot because many ongoing opportunities to share views on homework exist. Nevertheless, parents should be contacted regarding homework to request their views and to be informed of their child's school-based performance. Table 3-8 lists some specific strategies that can assist in enhancing home-school collaboration.

## Testing Adaptations

Another area of critical importance is classroom testing. Adaptation options include the following:

- Test preparation (study guides)
- Test construction (space, number of questions)
- Test administration time
- Form of response (oral, written)
- Site of testing (distraction-free)
- Forms of feedback
- Curriculum modification
- Use of portfolios
- Use of checklists
- Development of shared grading approaches between general and special educators

Polloway, Bursuck, Jayanthi, Epstein, and Nelson (1996) identified the testing adaptations that teachers indicated were most helpful to students. This ranking, presented in Table 3-9, is a useful resource for making testing adaptations.

## Classroom Grading Adaptations

Along with testing and homework, grading is one of the most discussed topics related to students with special needs who are in a general education classroom. Grading is a required form of student evaluation and record keeping and an integral part of our educational system.

Grading issues have become more significant for students with disabilities, given increased school inclusion. Salend (2005) stressed the role of communication in the grading process, particularly as related to the usage of differentiated instructional strategies in inclusive settings. The special education teacher generally needs to provide a clear description of an individual student's strengths, weaknesses, capabilities, and needs, thus giving the classroom teacher additional data on which to base a letter grade evaluation. The solution that emphasizes cooperative efforts is the one most likely to succeed.

To facilitate this process, teachers should jointly consider possible adaptations that will be effective and also be deemed acceptable by general education teachers (Polloway, Bursuck et al., 1996). Grading adaptations may include:

- Altering grading criteria (e.g., variant weights for assignments, individualized contracts).

**TABLE 3–9** Teachers' ratings of helpfulness of testing adaptations[1]

| Rank | Adaptation |
|---|---|
| 1 | Give individual help with directions during tests |
| 2 | Read test questions to students |
| 3 | Simplify wording of test questions |
| 4 | Give practice questions as study guide |
| 5 | Give extra help preparing for tests |
| 6 | Give extended time to finish tests |
| 7 | Use black-and-white copies |
| 8 | Give feedback to individual students during test |
| 9 | Highlight key words in questions |
| 10 | Allow use of learning aids during tests (e.g., calculators) |
| 11 | Give frequent quizzes rather than only exams |
| 12 | Allow students to answer fewer questions |
| 13 | Allow oral instead of written answers (e.g., via tape recorders) |
| 14 | Give the actual test as a study guide |
| 15 | Change question type (e.g., essay to multiple choice) |
| 16 | Teach students test-taking skills |
| 17 | Use tests with enlarged print |
| 18 | Test individuals on less content than rest of class |
| 19 | Provide extra space on tests for answering |
| 20 | Give tests in small groups |
| 21 | Give open-book/open-notes tests |
| 22 | Allow word processors |
| 23 | Allow answers in outline format |
| 24 | Give take-home tests |

[1]Ranked from most helpful to least helpful by general education teachers.

*Sources:* Adapted from "Treatment Acceptability: Determining Appropriate Interventions Within Inclusive Classrooms," by E. A. Polloway, W. D. Bursuck, M. Jayanthi, M. H. Epstein, and J. Nelson, 1996, *Intervention in School and Clinic, 31,* p. 140; and from "A National Survey of General Education Teachers' Perceptions of Testing Adaptations" by M. Jayanthi, M. H. Epstein, E. Polloway, and W. D. Bursuck, 1996, *The Journal of Special Education, 30,* 99–115. Copyright 1996 by PRO-ED, Inc. Reprinted with permission.

- Supplementing letter and number grades with additional information (e.g., comments, portfolio).
- Providing alternatives to number or letter grades (e.g., checklists) (Munk & Bursuck, 2001).

More comprehensive lists of grading adaptations are presented in Table 3–10 and by Munk and Bursuck (2004).

An interesting perspective was provided in research by Nelson, Jayanthi, Epstein, and Bursuck (2000). They noted that middle school students preferred these adaptations:

- Open notes
- Multiple choice over short answer/essay
- Simplify words in questions
- Open-book tests
- Practice questions

On the other hand, middle school students least preferred the following practices:

- Teacher reading questions aloud
- Tests with fewer items than others
- Tests covering less material for some than other students
- Teaching them test-taking strategies

To implement an effective grading intervention, teachers may wish to use the concept of **personalized grading plans (PGP)** (Munk & Bursuck, 2001, 2004). Munk and Bursuck (2001) describe the implementation of the PGP model as follows:

> During Stage 1, the student, parents, and teachers identify . . . what purpose they believe the grade should meet. During the second stage, the student, parents, and teachers review their school's grading policy and a menu of possible grading adaptations. During the third stage . . . the student, parents, and the teachers meet together to review their perceived purposes for a report card grade, and identify one or more mutually agreed upon purposes that will be used to steer selection of a specific adaptation. In Stage 4, the team collaborates to implement the PGP. Stage 5 involves evaluating the effects of the PGP on the student's grade(s), the student's and parent's satisfaction with the accuracy and meaning of the grade, and the teachers' perceptions of the accuracy and usefulness of the PGP. (p. 212)

The following summative recommendations on grading are adapted from T. Smith et al. (2008) and Polloway, Bursuck, and Epstein (2001):

- Plan for general and special education teachers to meet regularly to discuss individual student progress.
- Use cooperative grading agreements (e.g., grades for language arts might reflect performance both in the general education classroom and resource room).
- Emphasize the acquisition of new skills as a basis for grades assigned to provide a perspective on the student's relative academic gains.

**TABLE 3–10** Common grading adaptations

| *Adaptation* | *Description* | *Example* |
|---|---|---|
| **1. Changing criteria** | | |
| A. Vary grading weights. | A. Vary how much certain criteria count toward grade. | A. Increase credit for in-class group activities and decrease credit for essay exams. |
| B. Modify curricular expectations. | B. Identify individualized curriculum upon which to base grade. | B. Write on IEP that student will be graded on work on addition while rest of class works on fractions. |
| C. Use contracts and modified syllabi. | C. Teacher and student agree on quality, quantity, and timelines for work. | C. Written contract states that student will receive an A for completing all assignments at 85% accuracy, attending all classes, and completing one extra-credit report. |
| D. Grade on basis of improvement. | D. Assign extra points for improvement over previous performance. | D. Change C to B if student's points were significantly higher than in previous marking period. |
| **2. Changes to types of grades** | | |
| E. Add written comments. | E. Clarify criteria used to determine the letter grade. | E. Write on report card that grade reflects performance on IEP objectives and not on regular curriculum. |
| F. Add information from student activity log. | F. Keep written anecdotal notes indicating student performance in specific areas over time. | F. State on report card that although grade was same this quarter, daily records indicate student completed math assignments with less assistance. |
| G. Add information from portfolios and/or performance-based assessment. | G. Collect work that measures effort, progress, and achievement. | G. State on report card that written language showed increase in word variety and sentence length. |
| H. Use pass/fail grades. | H. Give student a "pass" if she meets minimum requirements for class. | H. Give student pass for completing 80% of daily work with at least 70% accuracy. |
| I. Use competency checklists. | I. Construct list of goals and objectives for quarter. | I. Attach checklist to report card indicating that during period student mastered addition facts, two-digit addition with regrouping, and counting change. |

*Sources:* Adapted from "Can Grades Be Helpful and Fair?" by D. Munk and W. Bursuck, 1998, *Educational Leadership, 55*(4), Figure 1, p. 46. Used with permission. The Association for Supervision and Curriculum Development is a worldwide community of educators advocating sound policies and sharing best practices to achieve the success of each learner; and "Report Card Grading Adaptations for Students with Disabilities: Types and Acceptability," by D. D. Munk and W. D. Bursuck, *Intervention in School and Clinic, 33*, p. 307.

- Investigate alternatives for assessing what has been learned (e.g., oral examinations for poor readers in a science class)
- Use narrative reports as a portion of, or adjunct to, report card grades. Such reports can include comments on specific objectives within the student's IEP.

Reflective Question 3.3: ***Curricular and instructional adaptations are critical to the success of students with special needs. For example, homework, grading, and classroom testing are often key reasons why students with special needs fail to achieve in general education. What are key strategies that teachers can employ to transform these areas from barriers to vehicles for success?***

## TECHNOLOGY

The revolution in technology for persons with disabilities received significant support with the Technology-Related Assistance for Individuals with Disabilities Act of 1988 (Beirne-Smith, Patton, & Kim, 2006). Although subsequent legislation has reinforced educational programs, this act provided a foundation for assisting persons with disabilities to exercise greater control over their own personal lives, increase participation and contribution to activities in their communities (including home, school, and workplace), increase interaction with individuals who were nondisabled, and take advantage of opportunities that exist, and are taken for granted, by individuals who are not disabled.

**Assistive technology (AT)** provides an important vehicle for instruction and a complementary source of learning adaptations for learners. "Assistive technology devices include any item, piece of equipment or product system, whether acquired commercially, modified, or customized, that is used to increase, maintain, or improve the functional capabilities of individuals with disabilities" (Beirne-Smith et al., 2006, p. 436).

The potential outcomes of the use of AT devices include the following:

- Helping students meet the challenges of daily life
- Providing vehicles to help overcome impediments to inclusion and independence
- Compensating for an individual's functional limitations
- Fostering social interactions with peers (Beirne-Smith et al., 2006).

AT options range from low-tech applications (e.g., tape players) to high-tech ones (e.g., interactive multimedia, voice synthesizers). Without question, the use of AT with students with special learning needs may make a substantial difference in their academic progress. In addition, there are numerous devices to enable people with disabilities to access computers (e.g., Web Tutorials, Dragon Dictate, Microsoft Access Pack, Word Prediction Software, switches, eye gaze, screen readers, refreshable Braille screen, and Touch Windows). It is essential that teachers know what devices are available, how students can be evaluated, and, if AT devices are used, how they work. The nearby Teacher Tip provides additional ideas.

**TEACHER *Tips*** — **Secondary Level**

Maccini, Gagnon, and Hughes (2002) identify a set of promising practices for technology usage for secondary students. These include the following:

#### Hypertext and Hypermedia Programs

- Hypertext software is software that allows users to "interact with information in a non-linear fashion." Similarly, hypermedia study guides are nonlinear in that they allow students to access other forms of computer-based information to enhance lessons.
- Unlike hypertext software, hypermedia contains a number of variations including graphics, sound enhancements, and digital videos.
- Hypertext and hypermedia programs are particularly useful for social studies instruction, primarily because the software tends to significantly enhance the interactions between learner and text in this subject area.

#### Videodisc Instruction

- Effective instruction utilizing a videodisc can involve allowing students to view the videodisc, answer questions related to the video in written or verbal form, and then complete workbook exercises.
- Videodisc instruction is best implemented in instruction involving problem solving that occurs in the real world. The use of this technology tends to lead to generalization.
- Students receiving videodisc instruction in mathematics, specifically in the area of fraction computation, received significantly higher scores than students who did not receive such instruction.

#### Multimedia Software

- Computer-based assessment instruments as well as computer-assisted adaptations are additional instruments that have proven useful for secondary students with learning disabilities.
- Computer tutorials, such as mapping tutorials developed in the area of social studies, have proven effective in the course of teaching geography.
- Students with learning disabilities who have used computer-based study guides to assist in note taking and reading comprehension have also demonstrated gains in these areas.
- Assessments administered via computer that include fact-based questions have also yielded higher scores for high school students with learning disabilities.

*Source:* Adapted from "Technology-Based Practices for Secondary Students with Learning Disabilities," by P. Maccini, P. Gagnon, and C. A. Hughes, 2002, *Learning Disability Quarterly, 25*, 247–261.

*Note:* We acknowledge the work of Amy Smith-Thomas in the development of this tip.

## Internet Usage

The Internet has become the most common research tool for students in classrooms (e.g., to access many libraries, museums, websites, and research articles). The use of this technology can be expanded to serve students with disabilities in breaking down hurdles they encounter.

Use of the Internet also can complement efforts to implement universal design for learning by effecting their challenges:

1. **Reduce barriers to full participation in society.** Peters-Walters (1999–2000) notes that students with disabilities can use the Web to complete a course in desktop publishing. The use of telecommunication and electronic mail can help students communicate with various people regardless of their disability.
2. **Reduce communication barriers.** Technology can help students with hearing impairments access information that may not have been accessible to them in the past. They can access electronic mail and communicate with other people on a regular basis without relying on an interpreter.
3. **Reduce barriers to the "basics" in an information society.** For students with disabilities, the use of the computer and the Internet to access information can be a door to learning about the world around them by enabling them to access basic information that may not have been easily available to them in other forms.

Smedley and Higgins (2005) advocate the use of virtual technology to bring the world to students with disabilities. One of their examples is through the use of "virtual field trips." Through this approach, teachers can take advantage of the various benefits of such trips without concerns for preparation time, scheduling, funding, transportation, and liability. Examples include their list of online virtual field trips to selected locations (see nearby Technology Tip).

Reflective Question 3.4: ***How can assistive technology applications and the use of resources such as the Internet provide teachers with an opportunity to apply the principles of universal design for learning to their classrooms?***

**TECHNOLOGY *Tip***

### Creating a Virtual Field Trip

1. Locate an appropriate venue—a site that the teacher feels will enrich a unit of study being taught in the classroom.
2. Research the site to determine whether or not photography and/or videotaping are permitted.
3. Decide what type of media to use. This decision should be made based on available equipment and personal expertise.
   a. Use a digital camera to take photos and download them. . . . A photography program can be used to edit the photos and add captions. The completed field trip can be printed out, saved to post on a website, or recorded to a compact disc.
   b. Use a digital camcorder. Visit the site and record both video and an audio narrative. After downloading the resulting video to a computer, edit both audio and video using a movie editing program. The finished product can be saved to a compact disc, VHS tape, or a website.
4. Use the finished product . . . in several ways:
   a. As a stand-alone product. Students experience the virtual field trip as they would a regular field trip. They prepare before the trip by doing research on the site and are given a list of questions they must answer while experiencing the trip. . . .
   b. As a preactivity to an actual field trip. Some students gain more from a field trip if they are familiar with the environment and have some background knowledge about it.
5. Other suggestions:
   a. Make sure the field trip has relevance. . . . Students will gain more meaning from a field trip if they can use it to enrich learning that is already taking place.
   b. Network with educators in other areas and exchange your virtual field trips and ideas.
   c. Develop a library of virtual field trips.

*Source:* From "Virtual Technology: Bringing the World into the Special Education Classroom," by T. Smedley and K. Higgins, 2005, *Intervention in School and Clinic, 41*, 2, p. 119. 

## MAKING IT WORK

The list of items that follows represents a summary of key instructional components related to student achievement. Although these concepts are developed to a greater extent elsewhere in this chapter and throughout the text, they are summarized briefly here.

1. **Group instruction:** To promote effectiveness in learning while at the same time being efficient, small-group instruction is most effective for student learning.
2. **Individualization:** Within the context of group instruction, individualized instruction should be provided to students to promote learning, with differentiation based on student learning needs. The result should be active participation and learner accountability.
3. **Direct instruction:** Teacher responsibility for teaching critical academic content is best reflected in the systematic procedures associated with direct instruction.
4. **Academic engaged time:** The best predictor of achievement is the amount of time in which students are engaged in academic learning. The various challenges to sufficient time for learning (e.g., classroom transition, nonacademic periods) often limit opportunities for academic progress. Further, with appropriate instructional intensity and pacing, students remain more actively involved and thus engaged in the learning process.
5. **Stages of learning:** Instructional focus should vary based on whether the goal is, for example, acquisition (learning something new), proficiency (developing accuracy and fluency), maintenance (recalling information learned for future use), and generalization and application (transferring learned information to another skill or another setting).
6. **Making learning meaningful:** When instructional tasks are related to content that is meaningful to the students, the information is far more likely to be learned, retained, and used.
7. **Instructional responsiveness:** Achievement is enhanced when teachers are responsive to students such as by providing instructional challenges that are ahead of, but within reach of, the instructional and developmental level of students and when opportunities are grabbed to capitalize on "teachable moments." The former reflects the appropriate use of scaffolding. The latter includes both planned teachable moments (such as with life skills infusion) as well as spontaneous moments when a classroom event provides an unique opportunity for learning.
8. **Learning communities:** The opportunities for students to learn from each other, such as through group peer-mediated strategies, complements what can be achieved through teacher-directed instruction.
9. **Student-centered strategies:** The emphasis on having students take responsibility for their own learning through self-regulation strategies is critical for student success and ultimately independence.
10. **Curriculum-based assessment:** The use of classroom data to frame instruction is supported by numerous research studies showing that effective teachers derive instructionally relevant learning targets from the curriculum and from students' progress through it.

## SUMMARY

The focus of this chapter is on the three key areas of curriculum development, effective instruction, and classroom adaptations.

The first section focused on curriculum. Key considerations are the types of curriculum, the need that students with special needs have for a comprehensive curriculum, and the central focus at this time of curricula built on state standards. The subsequent discussion provides examples of how to develop curriculum within a multitiered model.

The key to student learning is the implementation of empirically based instructional procedures. Teacher-directed, student-directed, and peer-mediated learning provide vehicles for addressing the instructional needs of students. Teaching students how to think for themselves and work with others will enhance their ability to succeed in their world and should be one of the primary foci of any student's educational program.

A third concern is for the implementation of a variety of adaptations that are based on student needs and immediate instructional demands. Operating with the philosophy of only making adaptations when absolutely necessary helps students become more capable of dealing with a real world that is not always accommodating. Key areas for adaptations include homework, classroom testing, and grading.

CHAPTER

# 4

# Strategies for Classroom Management and Behavioral Support

One of the most important issues for teachers is managing their classroom and providing interventions for students who need particular support for appropriate behavior. These issues have been compounded by 20 years of public concern as teachers and school administrators have had to confront the threats regarding school safety and effectiveness. Coupled with the growing diversity of learners and the complexity of working toward meeting the demands of federal legislation, teachers and educational leaders are challenged with the task of thinking about school behavior and classroom management in different ways (Kerr & Nelson, 2006).

To meet this challenge Marzano (2003) and others have initiated a model that uses research-based approaches to guide teachers and administrators toward effective schools and classrooms. Marzano contends that three factors are essential for behaviorally and academically successful students. These factors comprise three distinct (but related) levels: school, teacher, and student. Marzano and other researchers (e.g., Sprague & Walker, 2005) recognize that as we consider each factor, evidenced-based strategies are available at all levels and can be implemented through schoolwide interventions, classroom interventions, and student-centered practices.

Using each of these factors, as they relate to classroom management and behavioral support systems, will be the basis for the organization of this chapter. Specifically, within the first *factor of school*, teachers and administrators must address school safety, an orderly environment, and the culture or climate of the school before teachers can address classroom issues. Therefore, the first section of this chapter will include Schoolwide Positive Behavioral Support (SWPBS) as the research-based initiative that will address this factor.

Addressing the second *factor of teachers*, the next section of the chapter involves how teachers organize and manage their classrooms. This section will contain (a) prerequisite strategies for setting up and organizing the classroom; (b) behavioral principles to produce a positive climate; and (c) research-based interventions. The final section of the chapter considers the *factor of students* and will discuss benefits for considering cultural background and classroom diversity that may interact with school and teacher factors. Included in this section is the topic of individualized education programs (IEPs).

## SCHOOL FACTORS RELATED TO SUCCESSFUL SCHOOLS, CLASSROOMS, AND STUDENTS

For the past 30 years, research has supported the notion that school and other child-oriented environments must establish positive communities (sometimes called cultures or climates) for children to learn and flourish. Sprague and Walker (2005) support the concept that school climate is a powerful variable when considering the safety and well-being of students. They continue by advocating that "whole-school interventions . . . clearly communicate and enforce consistent behavioral expectations for all students and . . . create a climate of competence and mutual respect within the school setting" (p. 8). Furthermore, a climate of competence and mutual respect fosters a sense of community or belonging to something that is worth the effort of participation. This established attitude begins at the school level with teachers and administrators and then translates into the classroom with teachers–student and peer relationships.

This section emphasizes Schoolwide Positive Behavioral Support (SWPBS) systems as well as focusing on the cornerstones of positive behavioral support mechanisms: (a) functional behavioral assessments (FBAs) and (b) positive behavioral intervention planning (BIP). We will highlight an evidenced-based SWPBS that is a stellar example of how to implement a schoolwide program (a universal or primary intervention): the Best Behavior program (Sprague & Golly, 2004).

## Schoolwide Positive Behavioral Support

In general, **positive behavioral support** focuses on the prevention of academic and school failure and the enhancement of positive behavior through a three-tiered system (see Chapter 1 for a full explanation of the three-tiered system). This three-tiered system begins with primary/universal interventions that enhance protective factors within the environment and can occur at the school level or the classroom level. At the classroom level, approximately 90% of the student population responds to the intervention. This student response-to-intervention data makes a universal intervention most cost effective.

At the school level, SWPBS systems have been investigated extensively by the University of Oregon researchers (e.g., Sprague, Sugai, & Walker, 1998; Sugai & Horner, 1994). The goal for the support system is to improve discipline at the school level so that each student feels respected as an individual in the community. Sprague and Walker (2005) outline the key practices of SWPBS:

1. Clear definitions of expected behaviors (i.e., appropriate, positive) are provided to students and staff members.
2. Clear definitions of problem behaviors and their consequences are defined for students and staff members.
3. Regularly scheduled instruction and assistance regarding desired positive social behaviors is provided to enable students to acquire the necessary skills to effect the needed behavior change.
4. Effective incentives and motivational systems are provided that encourage students to behave differently.
5. Staff commit to implementing the intervention over the long term and to monitoring, supporting, coaching, debriefing, and providing booster lessons for students, as necessary, to maintain the achieved gains.
6. Staff receive training, feedback, and coaching in the effective implementation of the system.
7. Systems for measuring and monitoring the intervention's effectiveness are established. (p. 63)

**Best Behavior Program.** Although several approaches to SWPBS have been documented over the years (e.g., Embry & Flannery, 1994; Knoff & Batsche, 1995; Taylor-Green et al., 1997), this chapter will feature only one program. The Best Behavior program highlights general school behaviors that indicate positive outcomes with regard to discipline referrals and staff satisfaction with their work (Sprague & Golly, 2004). Additionally, the program is based on 30 years of experience and research in education and related fields. The importance of this program is that the authors have provided a standardized staff development process for improving school and classroom discipline. The primary goal of the program is to facilitate the academic achievement and healthy social development of children and youth.

The Best Behavior program follows the above-listed key elements of SWPBS and packages the information so that it is user friendly. The program begins by having school and staff delegate a group of individuals to be a representative school team to be trained to develop and implement the school rules (e.g., be respectful, be responsible, be safe). The team is involved in teaching the rules and establishes positive reinforcement systems for the rule-governed behavior. Specific and effective classroom management methods and curriculum adaptations (some covered in the second section of this chapter) are outlined. Finally, the cornerstones of SWPBS, functional behavioral assessment and behavioral intervention plans, are outlined in the Best Behavior program.

## Functional Behavioral Assessment

Because universal interventions, such as SWPBS, may not be effective for all students, secondary and tertiary prevention interventions (see three-tiered system in Chapter 1) must be considered. As part of a behavioral support system, a functional-based approach to determine environmental events that trigger and maintain problem behavior is appropriate.

The **functional behavioral assessment (FBA)** provides a contextual view of specific behaviors and behavioral patterns (McConnell, Patton, & Polloway, 2006). In doing so, teachers can determine the cause(s) of a given behavior and thus provide a basis for intervention (McConnell, Hilvitz, & Cox, 1998). Using an FBA approach requires professionals to understand and evaluate a behavior within the broad context of the student's home and school environment. A typical FBA format provides a structured way to analyze the contextual aspects of a behavior by asking for an exact description of the specific behavior in question along with information regarding precipitating conditions, consequences that follow the behavior, and hypotheses about the purpose the behavior serves. A sample completed FBA is shown in Figure 4–1. It provides a link to specific assessment techniques that can be used to analyze behaviors. This form also allows professionals to add other qualitative information (e.g., academic,

Student's Name: **Mike Harris**

## Background Information

The following sources of background information were considered for this FBA.

☑ Parent information/interview (see Parent Contact form) Attached? ☑Yes ☐No
Summary of parent information: **Mike's parents have had problems with him at home. They think positive approaches work best.**

☐ Behavior checklist or rating scale Attached? ☐Yes ☐No
Summary of checklist or rating scale:

☑ Recent observation data (see data collection forms) Attached? ☑Yes ☐No
Summary of observations: **Frequency data from math observation indicated that Mike follows only about half of teacher directions.**

☑ Discipline records Attached? ☑Yes ☐No
Summary of discipline records: **Five referrals this semester.**

☑ Assessment information Attached? ☑Yes ☐No
Summary of assessment information. **Mike is learning disabled (LD) in math and emotionally disturbed (ED).**

☐ Information from other agencies or service providers Attached? ☐Yes ☐No
Summary of other information.

☑ Review of prior BIP (see Reasons and Review form, Section Three) Attached? ☑Yes ☐No
Summary: **Music is a motivator. Detention not working.**

☐ Student interview/conference Attached? ☐Yes ☐No
Summary:

☐ Video- or audiotape Attached? ☐Yes ☐No
Summary:

☐ Teacher/administrator interview(s) Attached? ☐Yes ☐No
Summary:

SECTION **ONE**

**FIGURE 4–1** Sample functional behavioral assessment

*Source:* McConnell, K., Patton, J. R., & Polloway, E. A. (2006). *Behavioral Intervention Planning* (3rd ed.). Austin, TX: PRO-ED (pp. 32–34).

Student's Name: **Mike Harris**

## Analysis of Behavior

Prioritized Behavior # **1** **Following directions**

### Antecedents
(Events or conditions occurring before or triggering the behavior)

- ☐ Setting, subject, or class:
- ☐ Time of day:
- ☐ Person(s):
- ☐ Interruption in routine
- ☑ Directive or request to: **begin an assignments**
- ☐ Consequences imposed:
- ☐ Lack of social attention
- ☑ Difficulty or frustration: **with assignments**
- ☐ Other(s):

### Behavior
(Exactly what the student does or does not do)

Behavior in observable, measurable terms:

**Refuses to follow directions, Ignores, says "no," argues**

**Baseline measures of behavior**

Frequency of behavior: **50% of requests**

per

Duration of behavior:

per incident

Intensity of behavior:

### Consequences
(Actions or events occurring after the behavior)

- ☐ Behavior is ignored
  - ☐ Planned
  - ☐ Unplanned
- ☑ Peer attention
- ☑ Adult attention
  - ☑ Reminder(s)
  - ☑ Repeated directive or request
  - ☑ Private meeting or conference
  - ☑ Reprimand or warning
  - ☐ Change in directive or request
  - ☐ Loss of privilege:
  - ☐ Time out in classroom
  - ☑ Administrative consequence:
  - ☐ Parent contact
  - ☐ Other(s):

### Function of Behavior
(Hypothesized purpose of the behavior)

- ☑ Avoidance or escape
  - ☑ Avoide a directive or request
  - ☑ Avoide an assignment
  - ☐ Escape a situation of a person
- ☐ Attention
  - ☐ Gain peer attention
  - ☐ Gain adult attention
- ☐ Self-control issue
  - ☐ Express frustration
  - ☐ Express anger
  - ☐ Vengeance
  - ☐ Power of control
  - ☐ Intimidation
- ☐ Sensory or emotional reaction
  - ☐ Fear or anxiety
  - ☐ Sensory relief or stimulation
- ☐ Other(s):

(continued)

Student's Name: Mike Harris

## Analysis of Behavior

Prioritized Behavior # 2 Verbal aggression

| Antecedents (Events or conditions occurring before or triggering the behavior) | Behavior (Exactly what the student does or does not do) | Consequences (Actions or events occurring after the behavior) | Function of Behavior (Hypothesized purpose of the behavior) |
|---|---|---|---|
| ☑ Setting, subject, or class: math class | Behavior in observable, measurable terms: Threatens, yells, and curses at teacher | ☐ Behavior is ignored<br>☐ Planned<br>☐ Unplanned | ☑ Avoidance or escape<br>☑ Avoide a directive or request<br>☑ Avoide an assignment<br>☐ Escape a situation of a person |
| ☐ Time of day: | | ☐ Peer attention | |
| ☐ Person(s): | Baseline measures of behavior | ☑ Adult attention<br>☐ Reminder(s)<br>☐ Repeated directive or request<br>☑ Private meeting or conference | ☐ Attention<br>☐ Gain peer attention<br>☐ Gain adult attention |
| ☐ interruption in routine: | Frequency of behavior:<br>2 times per class | ☑ Reprimand or warning<br>☑ Change in directive or request | ☑ Self-control issue<br>☐ Express frustration<br>☑ Express anger<br>☐ Vengeance<br>☑ Power of control<br>☑ Intimidation |
| ☐ Directive or request to: | Duration of behavior:<br>per incident | ☐ Loss of privilege: | |
| ☐ Consequences imposed: | Intensity of behavior:<br>Escalates to loud yelling, moves too close to teacher | | ☑ Sensory or emotional reaction<br>☑ Fear or anxiety<br>☐ Sensory relief or stimulation |
| ☐ Lack of social attention | | ☑ Time out in classroom | |
| ☑ Difficulty or frustration: math assignments | | ☑ Administrative consequences: Removal from class Detention | ☐ Other(s): |
| ☐ Other(s): | | ☑ Parent contact | |
| | | ☐ Other(s): | |

SECTION TWO

FIGURE 4–1 (continued)

social/peer, family) that might play a factor in the demonstration of a behavior.

A functional behavioral assessment provides a valuable approach to more fully understanding a behavioral pattern as a basis for selecting intervention strategies. Further, it provides a basis for developing a behavioral intervention plan. The information obtained from the FBA can then be used as a critical aspect of the steps of successful behavioral change programs (i.e., definition and measurement of a target behavior, identification of behavioral occurrences, identification of factors causing the behavior, and determination of appropriate procedures for intervention; Simpson, 1998). It also is an essential element in developing positive behavioral supports in which interventions are focused on changing the system or setting within which a behavior occurs and/or the skills of an individual as a basis for changing challenging behaviors (Ruef, Higgins, Glaeser, & Patrode, 1998).

**Functional Behavioral Assessment Technology.** Perhaps the most useful technological tool in behavioral assessment is an interactive training module developed by Liaupsin, Scott, and Nelson (2004). This self-paced interactive CD-ROM is used to instruct teachers in observing behavior, plotting events, conducting FBA interviews, and reviewing archival records of students. It comprises over 70 PowerPoint slides that help a facilitator (or an individual) guide participants toward conducting accurate assessments and thus creating effective behavioral intervention plans.

**Behavioral Intervention Plans.** Under the Individuals with Disabilities Education Act (IDEA), students with disabilities are protected from arbitrary suspension or expulsion from school in instances in which their behavioral difficulty was determined to be related to their disability. This provision clearly has decreased the likelihood that such students could be denied a free, appropriate public education. The unforeseen result was that the protection of the rights of an individual became perceived as a potential threat to school discipline in general and to the safety and security of other students, teachers, and staff (McConnell et al., 2006). Teachers—both general and special education—are concerned with the problem of balancing individual rights with equitable school discipline policies (Butera, Klein, McMullen, & Wilson, 1998). This need for balance led to the development of the 1997 IDEA discipline amendments (Zurkowski, Kelly, & Griswold, 1998).

The extent of serious behavioral problems associated with students with disabilities has been controversial. Nevertheless, clearly a distinct minority of such students does present troublesome behaviors that challenge a school's ability to educate all students effectively. As a result, when regulations for the amendments to the IDEA were developed in 1999, a key issue was determining the appropriate balance between the rights of students with disabilities and the need for an orderly learning environment (McConnell et al., 2006).

The legal resolution of this debate was the incorporation of a requirement for specific practices in the 1997 amendments to IDEA. Foremost among these were the establishment of clearer guidelines for the removal of students with disabilities from the regular school setting, the need for functional behavioral assessment, and the establishment of a requirement for the development of a **behavioral intervention plan (BIP)** for individual students who present challenging behaviors within the school setting (McConnell et al., 2006).

Given the latitude in IDEA, appropriate practice suggests that BIPs should include the following components: the overall goals to be achieved, attention to planned activities, the persons responsible for implementing the proposed activities, timelines to be followed, and plans for intervention. Figure 4–2 illustrates a sample BIP completed in case study format.

> Reflective Question 4.1: ***What is the climate of your school? Are students and teachers happy to be there? Are they respectful, responsible, and safe?***

## TEACHER FACTORS RELATED TO CLASSROOM ORGANIZATION AND MANAGEMENT

Marzano (2003) lists the second factor that contributes to successful schools as *the teacher*. Specifically, he speaks of how teachers manage the classroom as well as initiate the intervention strategies used to ensure that behavior is supported (Marzano & Marzano, 2006). This section of the chapter is divided into three areas. The first two areas are universal interventions that occur in the classroom: (1) classroom organization and prerequisite elements of classroom management that must be present for effective classroom behavior

Student's Name: **Mike Harris**

Behavior # **1** Behavior to Be Decreased: **Refuse to follow directions**

Replacement Behavior: **Say "okay" and begin**

| Specific Behavioral Objective | Interventions* | Person(s) Responsible | Evaluation Method(s)/Timeline |
|---|---|---|---|
| **Mike**<br>will:<br>**Say "okay" and begin assignment within 2 minutes** | Positive environmental supports:<br>**Contract**<br>**Visual cues**<br>**Partner for assignments** | **Teachers**<br>will:<br>**Use contract, provide visual cues, assign partners** | Method(s):<br>**Check grades for zeroes**<br>**Review contract with Mike**<br>**Contact parents** |
| Under these conditions:<br>**When given a verbal direction** | Instructional strategies:<br>**Repeat directions**<br>**Provide an extra example** | **Principal**<br>will:<br>**Administer detention** | Timeline:<br>**2 weeks, 4 weeks, 6 weeks** |
| To meet these criteria:<br>**Improve from 50% to 80% of time** | Positive reinforcement:<br>**Points for music time or early lunch, home reward—car races** | **Mr. Harris**<br>will:<br>**Reward Mike with a trip to the car races** | |
| | Reductive consequences:**<br>**Make up work before school**<br>**Lunch detention** | | |

Additional Information: **Mike has a secondary diagnosis of emotional disturbance.**

**FIGURE 4–2** Sample behavioral intervention plan

*Source:* McConnell, K., Patton, J. R., and Polloway, E. A. (2006). *Behavioral Intervention Planning* (3rd ed.). Austin, TX: PRO-ED (pp. 35–36).

and academic instruction to occur; and (2) behavioral principles and behavioral support strategies to increase successful behavior in the classroom. The third area consists of strategies to decrease behaviors and still be supportive of the PBS framework.

The first area begins with the prerequisite elements of physical and instructional dimensions of management that are intrinsically associated with effective teaching. Three topics are included as considerations and activities that teachers need to perform so that

Student's Name: **Mike Harris**

Behavior # **2** | Behavior to Be Decreased: **Verbal aggression**

Replacement Behavior: **Express feelings without threatening**

| Specific Behavioral Objective | Interventions* | Person(s) Responsible | Evaluation Method(s)/Timeline |
|---|---|---|---|
| **Mike**<br>will:<br>**Express a complaint or frustration without verbal threats** | Positive environmental supports:<br>**Visual cue to calm down**<br>**Bonus points on contract** | **Math Teacher**<br>will:<br>**Cue Mike**<br>**Use contract**<br>**Call parents** | Method(s):<br>**Check discipline referrals**<br>**Review contract**<br>**Conference with Mike** |
| Under these conditions:<br>**In math class** | Instructional strategies:<br>**Anger management class** | **Counselor**<br>will:<br>**Provide anger Management class** | Timeline:<br>**2 weeks, 4 weeks, 6 weeks** |
| To meet these criteria:<br>**100% of time** | Positive reinforcement:<br>**Music time**<br>**Early lunch**<br>**Call parents** | **Mike**<br>will:<br>**Attend anger management class, practice new ways to express fellings** | |
| | Reductive consequences:**<br>**Lunch detention**<br>**In-school suspension** | | |

Additional Information:

*Interventions must include positive behavior supports (positive environmental supports and positive reinforcement). The BIP may not contain only reductive consequences.

**All students are subject to the student code of conduct (SCC). Short-term disciplinary consequences that do not involve a change of placement may be imposed for any SCC violation.

their classrooms function efficiently: (a) functions of the physical arrangement of the classroom, (b) successful classroom management, and (c) organizing and planning for instruction.

As this area begins, we recognize that a strong case can be made for the value of flexibility in instruction and thus in classroom organization. However, students with special needs profit from classrooms and instructional programs that are well-organized, orderly, and predictable (Abrams & Segal, 1998; Montague & Warger, 1997). The discussions that follow in this chapter should provide a basis for developing classrooms and programs that promote learning through structure, organization, and behavior support and yet promote interest and involvement through flexibility, variety, and responsiveness.

## Managing the Physical Environment

The classroom environment is a crucial determinant of successful teaching and learning, yet discussions of teacher competencies frequently overlook it. In a classic review of critical instructional factors, Christenson, Ysseldyke, and Thurlow (1989) note the importance of a positive climate in the classroom, partly related to an orderly school environment. The issue of environmental planning takes on new meaning with the inclusive education movement. Needed accommodations might include (a) seating arrangements that stimulate responding and discourage distractibility, (b) technology that assists in highlighting important points, (c) charts that provide reminders of specific rules, and (d) classroom areas that encourage cooperative interaction and sharing. Although a prosthetic environment, that is, a classroom designated to facilitate learning (Lindsley, 1964), is physically separate from the teacher–student dyad, conceptually it is an extension of the teaching–learning paradigm. Antecedents and consequences emerge from any environment. The effectiveness and efficiency with which they are managed are enhanced in a well-planned environment. The discussion of various environmental aspects in this chapter should assist teachers in planning an effective environment and should provoke further thinking about environmental options.

**Environmental Design.** Historically, U.S. education has recorded dramatic changes with regard to what the school environment should be and how it should appear. The one-room school of the turn of the 20th century eventually led to graded, self-contained classes. Later, the emphasis shifted to open classrooms, which were aesthetically pleasing with carpeted floors, nondistracting illumination, brightly colored walls and furnishings, and ample space in which to create. However, many schools became disenchanted with this concept and returned to more traditional, structured situations. Today, emphasis is being given to the advantages of cooperative learning situations and more cooperative teaching arrangements between special and general education (Bauwens & Hourcade, 1995). Currently multigrade classrooms are again being considered in many schools.

Though significant numbers of students with special needs still receive special education in resource or self-contained settings, the trend to place these students in more inclusive settings will continue to build. However, two basic points must be considered: (1) most students with special needs will need supports to ensure that their experiences in general education settings are successful, and (2) not all students benefit from the same type of educational setting. For these reasons, educators must remain vigilant about how students with special needs are progressing regardless of setting.

Students who are disabled may initially require more structure and guidance than their nondisabled peers. However, one of a teacher's major goals must be to help students learn how to handle and control their own behavior in less structured situations. This fact is particularly significant in light of the movement toward inclusion. Therefore, classroom arrangements should provide structure, organization, and regimentation when needed as well as freedom, exploration, and choice. To achieve these seemingly conflicting goals, teachers should conceptualize the degree of structure along a continuum from highly structured to less structured arrangements and determine which best suits the needs of particular learning tasks. Educational environments must be flexible and adaptable to individual needs, must allow for differing levels of need within a given group of students, and must change as students grow.

Several noteworthy considerations related to designing and organizing an educational environment (adapted in part from Reeves, 1989) include:

- **Sense of community:** Students need to feel welcome in a classroom as an important member of this community—this is especially important in inclusive settings. The teacher plays a crucial role in creating an accepting and nurturing classroom environment.
- **Personal territory:** Students and teachers alike need a sense of their own turf. This may include a place to keep personal possessions as well as a place to be alone to think and to be separate from the group.
- **Authentic motivation:** A classroom setting in which students are motivated to participate in the learning process has three fundamental factors: collaboration (learning together in teams), content (relevant and meaningful), and choice (opportunities to make a decision about what is learned) (Kohn, 1993).
- **Classroom flexibility:** Patterns of use within a classroom need not be fixed or predetermined. The

environment must allow itself to be manipulated by its users so that spaces can be changed.

- **Environmental acknowledgment:** A school facility must allow its occupants to stamp their presence on it. It must be ready to accept the graphic presentation of student activities and interests so that the building reflects who the students are and how they are doing.
- **Flexible seating and work areas:** Classrooms should acknowledge that people work in a variety of natural postures (e.g., sitting up straight, lounging, leaning, and standing). It should offer a variety of seating and work-surface heights to accommodate individual styles.
- **Work aesthetic:** The look of learning in action is a busy one, with things out and in use. An engaging, relevant environment becomes attractive to its users.
- **Barrier-free:** The environment must be able to accommodate students whose disabilities demand special attention (e.g., physical or vision needs).

**Classroom Arrangement.** Each classroom teacher must operate within certain administrative guidelines and physical limitations. Nevertheless, the teacher must provide for large- and small-group instruction, individual work, and a nonseated area where students can become involved in interesting independent activities. Whether the room is a small resource room or a large general education setting, these dimensions are essential for developing a prosthetic, effective environment.

The starting point for classroom arrangement is the same as that for all other instructional strategies: the assessment of students' strengths and needs in core curricular areas and in their response to various environmental demands. After this initial assessment, teachers may begin to develop a prosthetic environment. As more is learned about the students and as they learn and develop, the classroom should be adaptable and flexible.

When students are in inclusive settings, their needs will be addressed as a result of the collaborative efforts of the general and special educators. Even though special educators do not have sole responsibility for the inclusive classroom design, they can make reasonable suggestions for accommodating specific students. In general, recommendations for special settings are frequently applicable for the general education classroom as well.

There are multiple strategies available for desk arrangements in the classroom. Dowdy, Patton, Smith, and Polloway (1998) describe the advantages and disadvantages of three approaches: vertical rows, group circles, and small clusters. Advantages of vertical rows are that they create an orderly environment and create opportunities for students to physically interact with each other. A disadvantage is that vertical rows make it difficult for students in the back to see or hear the teacher. A large group circle allows the teacher and students to see each other easily, facilitates discussion, and provides an alternative to traditional row-by-row seating, but it also limits opportunities for physical interaction among students. Small clusters facilitate student interactions and provide an alternative to traditional row-by-row seating, but they require teachers to move about the room, make it difficult for teachers to see all of the students at all times, and can restrict total group discussion.

***Study Carrels.*** Classrooms can benefit from having at least one study carrel for use with students who have learning-related difficulties. Carrels or cubicles have the two main purposes of limiting outside stimuli and providing a specific place for concentrated study.

A study carrel should be designed to minimize the distraction of various other classroom activities and thus it should be placed in a quiet area. Cubicles come in many shapes and forms. Some are commercially produced, while others are little more than a small table and chair placed in the back corner of the classroom. The carrel becomes a work area for the student who uses it as a special place for concentrated study. Use of carrels should emphasize the positive features they afford (i.e., a quiet place to work) rather than their association as a location where one is sent for inappropriate behavior.

***Interest Centers.*** Interest centers are attempts to add variety to classroom instruction and to enrich the curriculum. Interest centers can be used for instruction in which a student works at the center to review something previously learned or apply something learned in a new way, the promotion of social interaction for two or more students who are working together, and the development of independent work skills and self-direction.

Teachers should consider several key components of interest centers: (a) characteristics of the user, (b) objectives that the activities are designed to meet, (c) interest value to students, (d) procedures and directions, and (e) materials or equipment needed. Because centers are intended for students, the user is the most important element. In developing ideas for effective interest centers, teachers should keep in mind the user's characteristics (e.g., behavior, language). In effect, an interest center becomes a well-planned lesson presented primarily without the teacher's direct assistance with a particular learning objective.

For centers to be effective, they must be engaging. Students must find the activities as well as the materials used in the centers stimulating. Additionally, procedures and directions go hand in hand in promoting effective use. Procedures are general guidelines telling students how to use the center; directions tell them how to perform the specific activities.

The last concern in developing a center is securing the materials and equipment that promote independent study habits and on-task behavior. Keeping component parts of an interest center to the minimum increases the probability of the students working efficiently.

## Prerequisites to Successful Behavior Management

**Classroom Procedures.** In keeping with the initiative of positive behavioral support systems, the classroom culture/climate has a tremendous impact on a positive learning environment. It is an effective preventative method that will help teachers and students be successful (see Table 4-1). Classroom procedures are the key to this success. Antecedents to learning can be traced back to teachers' initial planning in setting up their instructional days. As Christenson et al. (1989) conclude in their review of critical instructional factors, proactive management—structuring the classroom as a basis for management—is the key element in avoiding disruptions and increasing instructional time. In addition to concern for the physical and temporal environment, a number of procedural aspects of teaching are important. Evertson, Emmer, Clements, Sanford, and Worsham (1984) focus on the five specific elements involved in planning classroom procedures that "form the mosaic of the management system" (p. 24). These elements include (a) room use, (b) seatwork and teacher-led instruction, (c) transition in and out of the classroom, (d) procedures during group work, and (e) general procedures (see Table 4-2 for a secondary school example of a breakdown of subjects under each of the five elements).

**TABLE 4-1** Elements of positive classroom climate

- Order, structure, and consistency.
- Well-organized and predictable environment.
- Clear and realistic expectations.
- Students experience success, academically and socially.
- Curriculum stresses student interests and talents.
- Teacher able to interpret communicative intent of students.
- Students given choices and input into classroom decisions.
- Students encouraged to express feelings.
- Students able to socially interact with others.
- Students' psychological needs (belonging, safety, competence, and self-esteem) met.
- Positive teacher–student relationship.

*Source:* Adapted from "How to Prevent Aggressive Behavior," by B. J. Abrams and A. Segal, *Teaching Exceptional Children, 30*(4), 1998, p. 12. Copyright 1998 by the Council for Exceptional Children. Reprinted with permission.

**Classroom Rules.** Most children and adolescents function best when they know what is expected of them. Students need to be aware of what a teacher expects and will accept. Explaining classroom rules and then posting them are sound practices to aid in preventing problem behaviors; students should not have to test the limits if the teacher has clearly explained the distinction between acceptable and unacceptable behaviors. Classroom rules should be few in number, clearly defined, and linked to specific consequences when violated. Teachers should encourage students to discuss the rules and assist in their formulation and development. Students benefit from learning the give-and-take process of developing and modifying classroom rules.

Establishing rules is a crucial aspect of the prevention of specific management problems. Thereafter, regular review, immediate notification of infractions, and frequent praise for compliance facilitate adherence.

**Group Management.** A classic contribution to classroom management is Kounin's (1970) research on which teacher variables predict compliance and appropriate behavior in students. Berliner (1988) notes that Kounin's work is "enormously influential . . . and has given us a set of concepts that help us understand the process of monitoring a workplace free from deviance and in which students attend to their assignments" (p. 32). As Kounin reports, previous efforts to determine the efficacy of "desists"—that is, traditional statements that teachers make so that students will desist from inappropriate behaviors—had proven less than fruitful. According to Kounin, the following

**TABLE 4–2** Planning classroom procedures at the secondary level

| *Subject* | *Procedures or Expectations* |
|---|---|
| **1. General procedures** | |
| a. Beginning-of-period procedures | (Note: To be filled in for an individual classroom). |
| 1. Attendance check | |
| 2. Students absent the previous day | |
| 3. Tardy students | |
| 4. Behavior expected of all students | |
| 5. Leaving the room | |
| b. Use of materials and equipment | |
| 1. Equipment and materials for students | |
| 2. Teacher materials and equipment | |
| c. Ending the period | |
| 1. Readiness for leaving | |
| 2. Dismissal | |
| **2. Procedures during seatwork and teacher-led Instruction** | |
| a. Student attention during presentations | |
| b. Student participation | |
| c. Procedures for seatwork | |
| 1. Talk among students | |
| 2. Obtaining help | |
| 3. Out-of-seat procedures | |
| 4. When seatwork has been completed | |
| **3. Procedure for student group work** | |
| a. Use of materials and supplies | |
| b. Assignment of students to groups | |
| c. Students' goals and participation | |
| **4. Miscellaneous procedures** | |
| a. Signals | |
| b. Public address (PA) announcements and other interruptions | |
| c. Special equipment and materials | |
| d. Fire and disaster drills | |
| e. Split lunch period | |

*Source:* From *Classroom Management for Elementary Teachers* (p. 34), by C. M. Evertson, E. T. Emmer, B. S. Clements, J. P. Sanford, and M. E. Worsham 1984, Upper Saddle River, NJ: Prentice Hall. Copyright 1984 by Prentice Hall, Inc. Adapted with permission.

variables are among those related to successful classroom management:

1. *"With-it-ness,"* essentially awareness, refers to the teacher's ability to follow classroom action, be aware of possible deviance, communicate awareness to the class, and intervene at the initiation of the problem. Christenson et al. (1989) refer to a similar concept of having an "ongoing surveillance system" (p. 22).
2. *Overlapping* indicates an ability to deal with two events simultaneously and thus to respond to target behaviors promptly.
3. *Movement management* refers to smooth transition between activities. When the teacher can maintain momentum between instructional periods, the degree of behavioral compliance is likely to increase. Table 4–3 illustrates transition cues to facilitate this process.
4. *Group alerting* consists of specific skills for maintaining attention throughout various teaching lessons, as with a specific signal or procedure that involves all students.
5. *Accountability and format* include the methods that teachers develop to ensure a group focus by actively involving all students in appropriate activities.
6. *Avoiding satiation* on instructional activities refers to the ability to vary activities to prevent inappropriate behaviors.

These principles will minimize the time needed for problem management, thus leading to an increase in the time available for individualized instruction. They

**TABLE 4–3** Varieties of transition cues: Elementary level

1. Teacher gives verbal cues to group or individuals.
2. An appointed child gives verbal cues to group or individuals.
3. Teacher touches children to dismiss.
4. Lights blink, a bell rings, a piano sounds, or a buzzer buzzes to signal dismissal.
5. Teacher begins a song that routinely tells children to move.
6. Teacher makes a routine gesture or stands in a routine place to signal dismissal.
7. Teacher distributes cards with symbols for the students' intended destination printed on them.
8. Teacher gives each child an object that will be needed in the next activity.
9. Teacher tells children to go and find their names at the destination.
10. Teacher dismisses children by gender or physical characteristics (e.g., brown eyes, red hair).
11. Teacher dismisses students by letters in name.
12. Teacher shows a letter, number, or word and asks for volunteers to identify it; correct answers earn dismissal.
13. Teacher dismisses students by tables or rows.
14. Children look at a picture list on the chalkboard or cue card to learn where to go next after finishing an assigned activity.

*Source:* Adapted from "Teaching Mainstreamed Children to Manage Daily Transitions," by S. E. Rosenkoetter and S.A. Fowler, 1986, *Teaching Exceptional Children, 19* (1), p. 22.

provide for classroom management that is based on prevention.

**Grouping for Instruction.** A major organizational concern is instructional grouping. A discussion of how best to group for instruction must first address a concern for individualization. Among the foremost principles on which special education was founded is the importance of individualization in instruction. In many cases the primary justification for the provision of special services has been the assumption that instruction must be geared to the individual's specific needs.

Nonetheless, a distinction should be made between individualization and one-to-one instruction. Individualization refers to instruction appropriate to the individual, whether or not it is accomplished on a one-to-one basis. By this definition, individualization can be accomplished through one-to-one or one-to-two ratios, in small groups, or even occasionally in large groups. Even though individualization presumes that instruction is geared to the needs of the individual student, it does not mean that it is provided on a one-to-one basis. The following discussion focuses on one-to-one versus group instruction.

***Instructional Concerns.*** Three predominant concerns—instructional effectiveness, efficiency, and social benefits—are important in the context of inclusive education.

*Effectiveness* is a measure of whether the skills taught have been learned by students. Research on the effectiveness of grouping alternatives has been equivocal, with advantages cited for one-to-one instruction. More commonly, comparable results have been reported.

In particular, direct instruction programs, characterized by small-group work, have demonstrated effectiveness for students identified as learning disabled, intellectually disabled or mentally retarded, disadvantaged, and slow learners (e.g., T. Smith et al., 2008).

*Efficiency* refers to the amount of time required for something to be learned. Most research in this area has favored the use of group instruction because an undeniable benefit of group instruction is an increase in the number of students who can be served. Even more urgent is the reality that more students receive their education in general education settings where group instruction is very much the core of the instructional routine.

A third consideration relative to the efficacy of group or one-to-one instruction is that of *social outcomes*—whether there are benefits or detriments. A key social benefit of group instruction is simply the opportunity for learning to participate with others. On the other hand, a predominant focus on one-to-one instruction can result in greater difficulty for students who are included in general education classrooms where the student-teacher ratio is much higher than in special education.

A potential solution to the problem of isolation or rejection and one that further enhances learning is peer instruction as it relates to socialization and learning (see also Chapter 3). A variety of peer instructional strategies can be used to Smith, Polloway, Patton, and Dowdy (1999) summarize them as follows:

- **Peer tutoring:** An opportunity for peer instruction that benefits both the tutor and the student being tutored. Examples include reviewing directions, drill and practice activities, recording material dictated by a peer, and providing pre-test practice (e.g., spelling).
- **Classwide peer tutoring:** This approach divides classes into two teams for competition of several weeks' duration. Students work in pairs and are tutored and provide tutoring on the same material. Students accumulate points for their team by giving correct answers and using correct procedures, and individual scores on master tests are then added to the team's total.
- **Group projects:** This cooperative learning alternative allows students to pool their skills and knowledge in order to complete a specific assignment. Group projects are uniquely appropriate for inclusive settings where the talents of high, average, and low achievers can be blended together into specific aspects of the task.

***Implications.*** Research on grouping arrangements encourages the consideration of group experiences for students who are disabled. A variety of positive benefits can accrue from the use of group methodology, including the promotion of observational learning, facilitation of overlearning and generalization, the teaching of turn-taking, increased and better use of instructional time, more efficient student management, and increased peer interaction. What seems to be the most critical variable favoring group instruction is increased contact with the teacher. In Stevens and Rosenshine's (1981) classic review of best practices, the importance of "academic engaged time" and its relationship to higher achievement levels was clearly demonstrated. The opportunities for teacher demonstration and corrective feedback are strong arguments in favor of group instruction.

***Grouping for Acquisition.*** Meeting students' diverse needs across different stages of learning requires organization. The teacher's goal is to maximize teaching to ensure optimal **acquisition** of skills and abilities. For the teacher to work daily with each child, the problem becomes one of ensuring the highest degree of learning efficiency.

An initial option is to work with each student on a one-to-one basis. This approach has the advantage of providing the learners with instruction specifically tailored to their needs and abilities. Individual teaching appears to be ideal for the acquisition stage of learning. However, as noted earlier, a one-to-one arrangement has a number of drawbacks (e.g., inefficiency).

Teaching lessons to the entire class provides another alternative, which can increase instructional time for each child. Teachers can thus supervise each student throughout entire periods and can provide constant instruction of a large-group nature. However, because large groups may not properly accommodate individual needs, such instruction may drastically reduce the acquisition of skills, knowledge, and concepts.

The obvious alternative to one-to-one and large-group models is to provide instruction in small groups. Unfortunately, grouping evokes images of educational or recreational rank ordering (e.g., reading groups of sparrows, redbirds, and crows). However, use of grouping should not dictate rigid adherence to a standardized grouping arrangement across all subjects. To assist students in acquisition learning, the group can organize around a specific skill the members need to acquire. Groups should be flexible and fluid; they should neither restrict a student's improvement beyond the group mean nor force the child to work too fast.

Bickel and Bickel (1986) note that grouping for instructional purposes has positive benefits under the following conditions:

1. Number and size of groups are dependent on student characteristics and content taught.
2. Different groupings are used for different subjects.
3. Frequent shifts among groups occur during the school year as well as between years.
4. Groups are based on current levels of skills.
5. Groups are established as a result of instruction.
6. There is a combination of small group and whole class instruction.
7. Groupings are responsive to instruction. (p. 494)

How do large-group and one-to-one models fit into this grouping picture? Large-group instruction never quite accommodates the acquisition stage of learning, but it can provide the class with general introductions, serve as a forum for classwide discussions, and allow more advanced students a chance to review what other students are seeing for the first time. On the other hand, individual attention will continue to demand some class time. It may be essential for students who are unable to learn in the small-group setting, who are working on a skill different from the focus of the rest of the class, or who are receiving assistance with specific aspects of work assignments. One-to-one instruction suggests the need for supports such as a paraeducator, cooperative teaching, or resource services.

Ideally, grouping can afford the teacher some organizational flexibility while providing a vehicle to give individuals what they need. For example, a class divided into three groups during a 1-hour academic period could provide several advantages: each child would receive 15 or 20 minutes of teacher-directed, small-group instruction; the teacher would need to plan for only a limited number of children outside the group at any one time; and the teacher could still supervise individual students occasionally and briefly. Thus, this flexible system would allow maximum efficiency at each learning stage.

If acquisition of a skill or concept is important, then its learning cannot be left to chance. Instruction through flexible grouping arrangements is essential to sound teaching that maximizes the probability of learning.

***Grouping for Proficiency and Maintenance.*** A system for ensuring **proficiency** and **maintenance** must accompany acquisition learning strategies. Small-group instruction provides a regular opportunity for students who are not working directly with the teacher to pursue educational activities that further develop and maintain what was acquired through teacher-directed instruction. Some simple techniques and activities to assist in fluency building and overlearning of skills previously taught include the following:

- being tutored by a peer
- doing board work
- participating in group projects
- preparing individual seatwork folders
- using instructional games
- using software programs
- working cooperatively with partners
- writing a short composition
- reading assignments silently
- tutoring other students

In addition, several guidelines may help teachers keep these activities going smoothly:

1. Ensure that students display acceptable independent working and interpersonal relationship skills.
2. Choose assignments that can be accomplished independently to avoid constant interruptions by students.
3. Be sure directions for completing each task are clear.
4. Build in self-correction methods so that students will receive immediate feedback.
5. Vary the activities, allowing each student to experience several different activities during a period.
6. Allow students some freedom to choose their activities.
7. Allow time to provide feedback or reinforcement for independent work.

Finally, after acquisition, proficiency, and maintenance, the fourth component of learning that should be planned for is generalization. Instruction in the classroom should provide the basis, for example, for generalizing from the resource room to the inclusive setting, from learning in the school to learning from in the community, learning new content by building on previously learned material, and through working with different instructors.

**Lesson Planning.** Lesson plans should focus directly on the teaching objectives for each student. Thus, plans should be consistent with prior assessment of students' specific learning needs.

Lesson plans force teachers to identify what they will teach and how. The important aspect for the teacher is not the format of the lesson plan but rather the careful consideration of what will be taught and how. In fact, a survey of over 200 special educators indicated that more than half (58.5%) reported that they did not write out plans for each lesson they taught, although the teachers did indicate the key role of conscious (i.e., mental) planning for preparation (Searcy & Maroney, 1996). The essential concern is whether the system used by the teacher results in sufficient preparation for teaching.

Figure 4-3 illustrates a typical lesson plan format. Because teachers present varied types of material to many students, experienced teachers may not regularly write such detailed lesson plans; however, many do and they are particularly valuable to beginning teachers (Maroney & Searcy, 1996) because constructing detailed plans assists in focusing precisely on the instructional process.

Regardless of format and specificity, all plans should attend to the questions of why, what, and how. An assessment of needs determines *why*. The *what* is

**FIGURE 4–3** Sample lesson plan

**Sample Lesson Plan**

Instructional Objective:

---

Materials–Equipment–Supplies:

Teacher-Directed Activities:

- Anticipatory Set:
- Input & Modeling:

Guided Practice:

Independent Practice:

Closure:

Evaluation:

---

Special Considerations:

- Early Finishers:
- Anticipated Problems:
- Special Accommodations:

expressed as objectives stated in terms of observable student performance, which can be evaluated to determine whether the student has attained the objective. For illustration purposes, Table 4–4 provides data on the patterns of special education teachers using five planning methods for each of 14 potential lesson plan components.

The *how* of the lesson plan is the method of presentation; it describes the teaching process and any materials or programs to be used. All plans should also provide for evaluation of teaching efficiency and effectiveness.

Some specific suggestions on developing lesson plans include:

1. Create interest in and clarify the purpose of lessons. This is particularly important for students with special needs.
2. Provide direct instruction on key topics to help students acquire an initial grasp of new material.
3. Assign independent practice, some of which can be accomplished in class and some of which should be done as homework.
4. Plan activities for students who finish early.
5. Anticipate problems that might arise during the course of the lesson and identify techniques for dealing with them (T. Smith et al., 2008).

**Reflective Question 4.2:** ***What are my beliefs about managing a classroom? How much structure do I need? How much structure do my students need?***

## Positive Behavioral Support Strategies

A major factor in successful teaching is the ability to implement educational strategies that increase a student's motivation to perform while assisting in the development of appropriate classroom behavior. The teacher's role is as a change agent whose primary goal is designing and implementing effective interventions. Given that research consistently indicates "high marks" for the effectiveness of behavioral techniques for promoting learning in students with special needs (see Lloyd, Forness, & Kavale, 1998), such interventions should be key components of a teacher's repertoire. Therefore, this section focuses on strategies for changing behavior with an emphasis on those approaches that have been found particularly effective with students who have special needs.

In considering the various techniques to assist in behavior change, the primary focus is on effectiveness. To facilitate effectiveness, the teacher should reflect on two key concerns. The first is the need to be systematic. Haphazard modification is misleading in the interpretation of results. It can also be confusing and possibly detrimental to the student who needs structure and predictability. The need for a systematic policy of record keeping to accompany teaching techniques cannot be overstated, particularly for children with more serious learning difficulties.

The majority of intervention efforts undertaken to produce behavior change are oriented toward increasing appropriate, desirable behaviors. For students with special needs, this orientation includes a variety of adaptive behaviors, most notably academic, social, and daily living skills. The most pedagogically sound method of providing consequences to increase appropriate behavior is through **positive reinforcement.**

**TABLE 4–4** Lesson planning methods used by special educators

| | Planning Method | | | | | | | | | |
|---|---|---|---|---|---|---|---|---|---|---|
| | *Written Out* | | *Habit or Instinct* | | *Conscious Planning* | | *Student Choice* | | *Other* | |
| ***Lesson Plan Component*** | *%* | *n* | *%* | *n* | *%* | *n* | *%* | *n* | *%* | *n* |
| Student objectives | 26.6 | 55 | 4.8 | 10 | 55.1 | 114 | — | 0 | 13.5 | 28 |
| Materials required | 37.7 | 78 | 15.9 | 33 | 35.3 | 73 | 1.0 | 2 | 10.1 | 21 |
| Time required | 14.5 | 30 | 23.7 | 49 | 40.6 | 84 | 7.2 | 15 | 14.0 | 29 |
| Prerequisite skills | 2.9 | 6 | 29.0 | 60 | 57.0 | 118 | 0.5 | 1 | 10.6 | 22 |
| Seating arrangement | 9.2 | 19 | 24.6 | 51 | 16.4 | 34 | 30.9 | 64 | 18.9 | 39 |
| Anticipatory set | 9.7 | 20 | 33.3 | 69 | 42.5 | 88 | 1.0 | 2 | 13.5 | 28 |
| Instructional steps | 28.0 | 58 | 24.2 | 50 | 35.3 | 73 | — | 0 | 12.5 | 26 |
| Check understanding | 15.5 | 32 | 34.8 | 72 | 38.2 | 79 | 1.0 | 2 | 10.6 | 22 |
| Guided practice | 28.5 | 59 | 28.0 | 58 | 32.9 | 68 | 1.0 | 2 | 9.6 | 20 |
| Independent practice | 41.1 | 85 | 16.4 | 34 | 27.5 | 57 | 4.3 | 9 | 10.6 | 22 |
| Closing | 7.2 | 15 | 42.5 | 88 | 37.7 | 78 | 0.5 | 1 | 12.1 | 25 |
| Evaluation | 34.8 | 72 | 17.9 | 37 | 32.9 | 68 | 1.0 | 11 | 14.5 | 19 |
| Follow-up activity | 23.2 | 48 | 22.7 | 47 | 36.2 | 75 | 3.9 | 8 | 14.0 | 29 |
| Self-evaluation | 1.9 | 4 | 47.8 | 99 | 31.4 | 65 | 1.4 | 3 | 17.4 | 36 |

*Note:* All percentages were calculated based on $N = 207$.
*Source:* From "Lesson Planning Practices of Special Education Teachers," by S. Searcy and S.A. Maroney, 1996, *Exceptionality, 6,* p. 179.

**Principles of Positive Reinforcement** Reduced to its simplest terms, positive reinforcement refers to the supplying of a desirable consequence after appropriate behavior. In more precise terms, it refers to those consequent environmental events that increase a specific desired behavior by presenting a positive reinforcer. Positive reinforcement can be simply a smile or a wave extended to a courteous driver, a weekly paycheck, or a thank you from someone receiving a gift. The classroom presents constant opportunities for the use of positive reinforcers. The key is to select the "least intrusive" reinforcer that will produce the desired results.

Positive tools can be used in three basic ways. First and most common, reinforcement can be made contingent on appropriate target responses selected to be increased. This approach provides motivation for building new skills. Second, positive events can be used to reinforce a behavior incompatible with one to be decreased. An example might be reinforcing on-task time to decrease out-of-seat behavior. Third, teachers can positively reinforce peers to demonstrate to a given student that certain actions will receive reinforcement.

Successful use of positive reinforcement initially involves determining reinforcer preferences. With a wide variety of alternatives available, a teacher can establish a menu of reinforcers most effective for an individual student. A menu could include a list inclusive of free time, use of a software game, or some tangible prize.

The following techniques can be used to develop a menu:

- direct questioning of the student
- indirect questioning of parents, friends, or past teachers
- observation of the student within the natural environment
- structured observation (i.e., arranging specific reinforcement alternatives for selection)
- trial and error of a variety of reinforcers (i.e., reinforcer sampling)

Generally, teachers can construct a reinforcement menu by selecting from a pool of three types of reinforcers: social (most commonly, praise), tangible, or activity reinforcers. The latter two are discussed further below.

**Tangible Reinforcers.** The addition of tangible reinforcement to an instructional program may enhance the value of the social reinforcers with which they should be paired. Tangible reinforcers can be a powerful component of the reinforcer hierarchy for many students.

The tangible item with primary reinforcing value is usually food because it is desired instinctively. For some students, food can be very effective. However, because highly desirable edible items, such as sweets, are often nutritionally unsound, the volume of food intake should be considered. One efficient method of using food as a consequence is to break it down into small pieces that can be earned for specific steps in an instructional task. For adolescents, obtaining a soft drink at the end of the day may become the focus of points earned throughout earlier instructional periods.

Other paired reinforcers might be considered to promote delaying gratification. Pairing allows certain items to serve as symbols of reinforcers and to be exchanged later for other reinforcers. In our society money serves this purpose; in the classroom this same principle can be applied through the use of points or tokens. Both represent items that learners desire; they will work to earn those tokens because they have learned that they are paired with the actual reinforcers. On a basic level tokens can be used in an individual instructional session to reinforce appropriate behavior and then can be exchanged immediately upon task completion. On a grander scale tokens can become the exchange medium for a classroom-based economy, which is discussed later.

***Activity Reinforcers.*** Activities can also be highly reinforcing positive consequences. As an incentive, an activity should be an event in which a child earns the right to participate because of appropriate behavior. The teacher must distinguish between positive activities that the child normally has been accustomed to, such as lunch and recess, and those that are contingent on certain behavior. This concept requires that the activity be desirable for the student as well as extra.

In addition to activities like recess, many other alternatives are available to the teacher. Depending on the student, free time, being first in line, taking the lunch money to the office, or assisting with school maintenance can become positive consequences. Table 4-5 contains other activities that might be reinforcing to individual students.

**TABLE 4–5** Activity reinforcers

| |
|---|
| Selecting topic for group discussion |
| Selecting a game or activity for recess |
| Reading to a friend |
| Tutoring a classmate |
| Using the tape recorder |
| Listening to a CD player with earplugs |
| Having extra time in a favorite subject |
| Going out first to recess |
| Taking attendance |
| Handing out papers |
| Helping to correct papers |
| Being team captain |
| Helping put up a bulletin board |
| Getting an extra recess |
| Reading comics, magazines |
| Playing games |
| Doing arts and crafts |
| Keeping behavioral point records |

***Reinforcement Schedules.*** An important consideration after the selection of a particular consequence is the schedule according to which it is presented to the learner. In general, schedules can be defined as either continuous or intermittent. A **continuous schedule** indicates that reinforcement is given with each occurrence of a given behavior; it is most useful for teaching and learning at the acquisition stage.

**Intermittent schedules** provide reinforcement less frequently and are more advantageous for maintenance/proficiency and generalization learning. Six intermittent schedules are fixed ratio, fixed interval, fixed response duration, variable ratio, variable interval, and variable response duration. A fixed ratio schedule specifies a particular relationship between occurrences and reinforcement (e.g., 5:1) and can be illustrated by piecework (e.g., stacking bricks) or rewards given according to the number of worksheets completed (e.g., a token given for every worksheet completed with 90% accuracy). Fixed interval reinforcement specifies the amount of time that will elapse before reinforcement—for example, using classroom timers and awarding points to all students working when the buzzer sounds at regular 5-minute intervals. A fixed duration schedule differs from a fixed interval schedule in that the target behavior must have occurred for the duration of the entire interval in order for the individual to earn the reinforcement. Variable ratio, variable interval, and variable duration schedules allow planned alterations in the frequency, elapsed time, or duration of time, respectively, between reinforcers.

Reinforcement schedules should be selected according to specific instructional objectives. For certain goals, such as completing worksheets or establishing quiet time during reading, fixed schedules may be most appropriate. In many situations, however, variable schedules are more effective because students are unable to predict receipt of reinforcement as precisely; thus, programming tends to produce behaviors most resistant to extinction. The variable ratio schedules inherent in slot machines illustrate how effective these contingencies can be in maintaining desired responses. Variable interval or duration schedules are most appropriate for nondiscrete behaviors such as on-task or in-seat behaviors.

***Gradual Change Processes.*** The basic principles of positive reinforcement can create a false picture that learning, as defined by behavior change, is simply a matter of selecting the correct reinforcer and scheduling it effectively. For most educational objectives, learning is best characterized as a gradual process of behavior change. The purpose of **shaping** is to reach an academic or behavioral goal through the gradual achievement and mastery of subgoals. The process involves establishing a shifting performance criterion to reinforce gradual increments in performance. As it is most precisely defined, it refers to the gradual change in performance that is tied to a single behavior, to distinguish it from **chaining**, which generally refers to multiple, related behaviors such as those involved in getting dressed.

A shaping program includes four steps (Martin & Pear, 2006): specification of a final desired behavior, selection of the starting behavior, choosing of the specific shaping steps, and movement through the steps at an appropriate pace, with reinforcement provided accordingly. Because shaping is based on a series of small, more easily achieved subgoals, it provides the teacher with a valuable strategy for building responses that are well beyond a child's present functioning.

Shaping behavior through successive approximations to the desired goal is one of the basic uses of reinforcement. When combined with both task analysis and prompting, it can be the basis for teaching precise, manageable skills to students. Such an approach provides the foundation for chaining, the linking of skills to complete a complex behavioral task. Forward chaining can be used to teach sequential steps in consecutive order, as with self-help skills such as shaving; backward chaining can effectively teach skills such as dressing by beginning just short of the completed task and gradually requiring the student to complete more steps within the task hierarchy.

**Positive Reinforcement Programs.** Effective teaching often requires the use of systems for implementing reinforcement strategies. This section describes several reinforcement programs that have been successfully used in classroom situations, as well as the Premack principle, which conceptually underlies the various programs.

***Premack Principle.*** The most basic concept for dealing with consequences is the **Premack principle** (Premack, 1959). It is often called "grandma's law" because it is reminiscent of the traditional dinner table remark, "If you eat your vegetables, then you can have your dessert." The principle asserts that a low-probability activity can be increased in frequency when paired with a high-probability activity. For example, a student who finishes a spelling lesson (a low-probability behavior) will be allowed to go out and play volleyball for 5 minutes (a high-probability behavior). Because volleyball is a desirable activity, the student has increased incentive to finish the lesson.

***Contingency Contracting.*** Contracting represents a potentially effective, versatile management system. Contracts can be oral or written; they state the work assignment that the learner has contracted to complete and the consequences that the instructor will provide upon completion. Contracts should be perceived as binding agreements between student and teacher; signatures on written contracts emphasize this perception. In his classic work, Homme (1969) identifies 10 fundamental rules of contracting:

1. The contract reward should be immediate.
2. Initial contracts should call for and reward small approximations.
3. Small rewards should be given frequently.

4. The contract should call for and reward accomplishment rather than obedience.
5. The performance should be rewarded after it occurs.
6. The contract must be fair.
7. The terms of the contract must be clear.
8. The contract must be honest.
9. The contract must be positive.
10. Contracting as a method must be used systematically.

Although contracts are usually associated with individuals, contingency contracting can also be handled efficiently and effectively within a large-class setting. For example, a teacher responsible for a 1-hour arithmetic period can make assignments that a student will need approximately 50 minutes to complete.

The remaining 10 minutes can then be given to students to play games, explore the Internet, or work at an interest center, contingent on the completion of specific academic tasks. Although the instructional time has been decreased by one-sixth, the students' motivation to complete their work and gain their free-choice time will probably compensate for the reduced time.

Figure 4–4 illustrates a simple form for an individual contract. Changes and elaborations depend on the instructional goals of the specific situation. Contracts can be an extremely useful technique in a classroom situation. They can be age appropriate, can provide initial training in understanding formal contracts, can facilitate home–school coordination, and can serve as an appropriate step toward self-management.

***Group Contingencies.*** Group contingencies are another possible source of effective intervention strategies. They represent peer-mediated interventions and can include independent contingencies (i.e., all members of the group work individually toward reinforcement provided on an individual basis), dependent contingencies (i.e., reinforcement is contingent on performance of a designated student), and interdependent contingencies (i.e., reinforcement is contingent on the performance of a group of students).

***Token Economies.*** Another systematic method for programming reinforcement is through the establishment of a **token economy**. In general, a token system is based on items symbolizing actual reinforcers, much like the use of monetary rewards. Just as adults receive money for their performance, students can earn tokens for appropriate behavior and completion of tasks. Just as adults can exchange their money for food, clothes, shelter, and entertainment, students can redeem their tokens for items they desire.

Token systems afford the teacher a number of distinct advantages over other forms of contingency management. Tokens can help bridge the gap between a specific behavior and the actual reinforcer with a minimal disruption in instruction. In addition, the interest generated by obtaining tokens may actually increase the value of the reinforcer for which they are exchanged. Tokens can be constructed to ensure portability and availability and can allow for a flexible reinforcement menu without incorporating a variety of reinforcers

**Contract**

I will do twenty multiplication problems every day for a week during my math period.

Jerry Jeff Walker

After successfully doing this, I may play basketball outside for fifteen minutes.

Date signed January 6, 2004 Ms. L Brook (signed)

Date completed January 13, 2004

**FIGURE 4–4** Sample contingency contract

into the instructional class activities. Finally, token economies can have positive effects on teachers by emphasizing the need to reinforce students frequently and consistently.

Tokens can also be beneficial in enhancing skill training and academic learning. Amounts to be paid when work is completed can be established for specific assignments. For example, a math sheet might be worth 10 tokens when completed with 90% accuracy. With this added incentive for work completion, teachers frequently find that a student's quantity of work and rate of learning improve dramatically.

Token systems can be used in a variety of ways. Outgrowths may include banking and checking, stores, and classroom governments. Tokens can also become integral parts of inclusion efforts and home-school relations. Token economies can have direct educational benefits beyond providing an organized program of consequences. Such a system's ultimate goal of reducing a learner's reliance on external reinforcers also has direct implications for the possible success of self-regulatory forms of behavioral intervention (discussed later).

## The First Step to Success Program

This chapter covers a variety of interventions based on reinforcement principles to increase appropriate behavior. What is of particular interest is the ability of teachers to take these interventions and integrate them into their classroom as an early, universal, or secondary intervention. By doing this, teachers are able to address unwanted behaviors from occurring or give support to children who need additional interventions for difficult behaviors.

The First Step to Success program, developed over a period of 20 years by Hill Walker and his colleagues (e.g., Walker, Kavanagh, Stiller, Golly, Severson, & Feil, 1997), is one of the most comprehensive behavior-change programs that can be found for young children (preK–third grade) today. The program targets the behavior of young children who exhibit emerging antisocial behavior patterns (e.g., oppositional behaviors, aggression toward others, tantrums, conflicts and confrontations with peers and teachers, and rule infractions). The program consists of three components that exemplify the use of behavioral assessment, consultant- and teacher-based intervention, and parent involvement/reinforcement. The following summary presents these three components (Walker, Stiller, Golly, Kavanagh, Severson, & Feil, 1997).

***The Screening Component.*** The first component of the program was developed to evaluate each child with regard to behavioral indicators that would help teachers identify children most appropriate for the program. For young children, the Early Screening

**TEACHER *Tips*** **Elementary Level**

Many special education teachers may be required to use several types of behavior management programs with students who are confrontational in a verbally or physically aggressive manner. To do so they may consider the use of three basic approaches to this type of behavior: prevention, defusion, and follow-up. The prevention stage of the behavior management approach is a period of time when a teacher places a strong focus on teaching desirable behaviors. These behaviors include proactive behaviors such as social skills, rule following, self-management skills, and problem-solving skills. During this period, rules are established and consequences for rule infractions are enforced.

In many scenarios, teachers react to confrontational or inappropriate behaviors by presenting an ultimatum. The student usually reacts by not complying and may display additional oppositional behavior. When this situation arises, the teacher will find it best to use methods found in the defusion stage of a behavior management program. During the defusion period, teachers use strategies designed to address the confrontational behaviors after the behavior has begun. The goal here is to stop the behavior before it escalates into a dangerous situation. Some of these strategies include:

1. Focus on the task and ignore the noncompliant behavior. Redirect the student and if necessary present a small negative consequence for the behavior.
2. Present options privately. A teacher should state the rule of desired behavior, request that the student "take care of the problem," and present options for the student on how to take care of the problem.
3. Disengage and delay responding in the presence of serious threatening behavior.

*Source:* From "How to Defuse Confrontation," by G. Colvin, D. Ainge, and R. Nelson, *Teaching Exceptional Children, 29*, pp. 47–51. Copyright 1997 by the Council for Exceptional Children. Reprinted with permission.

Project (Feil, Walker, & Severson, 1995) may be used. Older children might be assessed through the Social Skills Rating Scale (Gresham & Elliott, 1990) and the Systematic Screening for Behavior Disorders (Walker & Severson, 1992). The children who seem to show problem areas are then designated to participate in the program.

**The School Component.** The second component of the First Step to Success program is the school intervention component. This component comprises three phases: consultant, teacher, and maintenance phase.

During the consultant phase of the program, an outside responsible person (e.g., school counselor, resource teacher, behavioral specialist, teacher assistant, volunteer parent, or college student) is trained to implement several tasks. These tasks include (a) explaining the program to the teacher, parents, child, and peers; (b) ascertaining a consent to participate from all participants; (c) initiating the program in the classroom for the first 5 program days (20–30 minutes per day); (d) developing a negotiated list (among the teacher, child, and parent) of school rewards and home privileges to be earned by the child; (e) implementing the first 5 days of the program and training the teacher in the application of all aspects of the program; and (f) turning the program over to the teacher, supervising its operation, and beginning the HomeBase program with the parents (Walker, 2006).

As soon as the teacher is trained, the teacher phase of the component begins. Annemieke Golly, the First Step to Success trainer (personal communication), describes the mechanics of the actual component.

> The First Step program is based on five research-based principles: (1) develop clear expectations, (2) directly teach expectations through examples and nonexamples, (3) provide lots of feedback when students are doing well, (4) minimize a lot of attention for minor misbehavior, and (5) have very clear consequences for unacceptable behavior. These principles are effective strategies when working with all students, including students with special needs and/or students with a diverse cultural background. Students are taught school skills through one-on-one role-play situations to (a) follow directions, (b) get along with others, and (c) stay on task.
>
> During the first few days of the program, the coach provides feedback to the child in the classroom using a card that is green on one side and red on the other side. The child earns points on the green side of the card. When enough points have been earned during a small period of time, the child gets to pick a fun activity for the entire class. The strategy works extremely effective to elicit positive interaction from peers who might have rejected the child before. In fact, teachers report that the First Step to Success program significantly increased positive peer interactions as well as their own teaching behavior and classroom atmosphere.

(See Diversity in the Classroom for further tips by Annemieke Golly.)

The maintenance phase of the school component extends the program for up to 10 days. During this time, the students' dependence on the program is slowly reduced. The feedback and points are substituted by giving occasional rewards contingent on exemplary performances. Additionally, the teacher at school and the parents at home verbally reinforce the students' behavior, primarily with praise and expressions of approval.

After the maintenance phase is completed, the HomeBase component is the final piece of this program. It is designed to teach the parents/caregivers six lessons to build child competencies and skills in school adjustment and performance. These lessons consist of (1) communication and sharing, (2) cooperation, (3) limits setting, (4) problem solving, (5) friendship making, and (6) development of confidence. The goal of this component is to build a strong, positive relationship between the home and the school. Parents and caregivers are recruited to be partners with the school to work cooperatively to help the student be successful in school.

Reflective Question 4.3: ***How often do I use positive reinforcement? Is it part of my everyday routine? Do I believe in the value of reinforcing a student's behavior?***

## Behavior Reduction Techniques

Successful teaching requires the ability to resolve problem behaviors successfully. The use of reductive strategies requires an initial consideration of the techniques most natural to the classroom and school environment. The following list provides a sequence of selected strategies from least to most restrictive alternatives:

1. natural and logical consequences
2. differential reinforcement
3. extinction
4. verbal reprimand
5. response cost
6. time out from positive reinforcement

## DIVERSITY IN THE CLASSROOM *Tips*

**Annemieke Golly, Ph.D.**, is a researcher and trainer of the First Step to Success program at Oregon Research Institute. She has written numerous books in the area of *Positive Behavior Support Systems* for young children.

First Step to Success is an early intervention program for young students with challenging behaviors. First Step has three components: (a) screening, (b) a classroom, and (c) a home intervention. First Step to Success is considered a selected intervention for some children who do not respond to positive, proactive universal interventions in the school and/or classroom. First Step to Success is not intended to be used as the primary or only strategy for the few students who need targeted interventions. It has been implemented with students of many diverse backgrounds across the country. At least half of the children who completed the program have significantly changed their behavior in a positive way.

As one of the co-authors of the First Step to Success program, I have trained and provide ongoing technical assistance to numerous teachers in North America (including teachers working on Indian Reservations and those from many Hispanic and African American communities) for the past decade. If the classroom is a positive and predictable environment, First Step candidates have a better chance to change and maintain their behavior in a positive way. Therefore, proactive and preventive classroom strategies that are beneficial to all children but especially to children with challenging behaviors are essential. Some of the strategies include (a) developing, teaching, and reinforcing clear expectations; (b) modeling and role-playing; (c) providing an attention signal; (d) giving short and clear directions; (e) minimizing a lot of attention for minor inappropriate behaviors; (f) using a neutral tone; and (g) most importantly, always treating the child with respect.

When children misbehave, they usually are trying to communicate that a need must be met (e.g., attention, escape/avoidance). Children typically don't misbehave because they intentionally want to aggravate adults. The following is an example of adults figuring out the function of inappropriate behavior and providing the child with opportunities to get this need met when positive behavior is displayed.

Some years ago, an extremely organized and positive kindergarten teacher in a rural school district asked me to be a First Step coach for her student, Corey. After numerous interventions, Corey still ended up in the principal's office daily for throwing rocks, hitting, and being noncompliant. Corey's mom reported that Corey was the youngest of five children. Dad was in jail for burning down the house with everyone in it. Mom worked from noon until nine. Grandma took care of the kids after school. Mom realized that Corey had problems and was willing to do whatever was necessary. Corey was usually in bed by the time mom got home and she only saw him in the morning. Mom followed through with the request to reinforce Corey for doing well during the First Step program by reading him a story after she got home each day. Corey's need was to get a few minutes of his mother's undivided attention. Mom appreciated the structure provided by the program. Corey has since developed into a successful high school student.

**Natural and Logical Consequences.** Before teachers consider high-powered consequences for inappropriate behavior—and before punishment strategies are implemented—attention should be given to consequences that are natural and/or logical relative to a given behavior. Although in some instances these may be behaviorally defined as punishment, their cognitive relationship to the behavior itself makes them more attractive alternatives. As West (1986) notes, the use of natural and logical consequences can result in children and adolescents learning responsibility.

**Natural consequences** occur when a parent or a teacher "does not intervene in a situation but allows the situation to teach the child. The technique is based on this adage: "Every generation must learn that the stove is hot" (West, 1986, p. 121). Two examples illustrate how this process can operate in a classroom setting. A student may refuse to do classwork or homework. The natural consequence is that he receives no credit for the work. The teacher need not say or do anything. In another situation a child may habitually forget her permission slip to attend a class function away from school. The natural consequence is that she has to stay behind when the class goes on a trip. Natural consequences are an effective means to teach common sense and responsibility (West, 1994).

With certain behaviors, natural consequences could result in severe eventualities, such as injury. For example, depending on the natural consequences of walking into the street without looking would clearly be inappropriate. In these instances consideration should be given to alternatives that are **logical consequences** of the behavior. Logical consequences attempt to tie the disciplinary response directly to the inappropriate behavior (West, 1994). For example, when a student pushes another child in the hall, the teacher may give the child the choice of not pushing or of going back to the classroom, waiting until the group has reached its destination, and then starting out alone. In considering the use of behavior reduction strategies, the teacher is encouraged to continuously evaluate how natural and logical consequences can enhance a management program.

**Differential Reinforcement Strategies.** A number of strategies are available to reduce inappropriate behaviors through positive reinforcement strategies. As outlined by Webber and Scheuerman (1991), these include **differential reinforcement** of a low rate of responding (DRL), differential reinforcement of the omission of behavior (or of other behavior) (DRO), and differential reinforcement of incompatible (DRI) or alternative behaviors (DRA).

A DRL strategy employs reinforcement based on the successive reduction of behavioral occurrences; it can thus be used, for example, to gradually decrease talking out of turn during an instructional period. DRL is an underused yet effective tool for changing behavior.

As a classroom example, consider a program for students in sixth grade. An initial average problem level of 10 examples of profanity per day is determined. An initial criterion standard of 5 is set. Reinforcement (e.g., an agreed-upon group activity) is then based on staying below this level in a given period. Subsequently, the standard can be lowered to 3, to 1, and to 0, thus essentially shaping down the behavior as the rate of behavior is successively reduced.

DRO procedures call for reinforcement based on the omission of a given behavior or the occurrence of other behavior. Kazdin (2001) describes two types of DRO schedules. With momentary DRO, reinforcement is delivered if the target behavior is not occurring at the end of an interval (e.g., when the bell rings). It is best used to "catch" students who are or are not behaving appropriately. For example, it could be used to decrease the occurrence of out-of-seat behavior. With whole interval DRO, students are reinforced if the target behavior does not occur for the entire time period. To return to the previous example, reinforcement in this case could be tied to a student's remaining seated for a period of 10 minutes. Subsequently, with a DRO schedule sequence, the time could be increased to the entire instructional period; the inappropriate behavior is effectively omitted during these successively longer periods.

DRI/DRA approaches can be used to strengthen behaviors that are not compatible with or that represent an alternative to the targeted inappropriate behavior. Thus, the reinforcement of hand raising could be used to decrease the occurrence of calling out in class. When using a DRI approach, teachers should select an incompatible behavior that requires "doing something" so that the student is not reinforced for simply "sitting quietly" (Kerr & Nelson, 2006). A traditional measure of whether the behavior selected is appropriate is to ask, "Can a dead person do it?" The following example underscores the importance of this consideration.

Positive methods, via differential reinforcement, represent a valuable option and should be considered before more restrictive means are selected. Thus, they offer an attractive alternative to reliance on aversive techniques.

**Good-Behavior Game.** One example of the use of differential reinforcement (especially DRL) is the good-behavior game. This technique, originally reported by Barrish, Saunders, and Wolf (1969), divides a class into teams or groups. Each person has specific standards for meriting free time. Teams that remain below the maximum number of occurrences of inappropriate behavior receive the designated reinforcement. The technique, which relies on an interdependent group contingency (defined earlier), is easy to implement and has been used successfully in general education as well as in special education settings.

Although group contingencies such as those in the good-behavior game may seem unfair to individual students who are penalized for the actions of others, any technique that effectively enhances classroom management ultimately serves their best interests. Naturally, the teacher must modify the structure of the game if one student consistently misbehaves for attention-seeking purposes and thus penalizes the team.

**Extinction Procedures.** As behaviorally defined, **extinction** refers to the withholding of reinforcement that previously maintained a specific behavior or behaviors. Analysis of antecedents, behaviors, and consequences relative to a particular situation may indicate that change can be affected by removing the reinforcer maintaining the behavior, thus extinguishing the response. The most typical use of extinction in the classroom occurs when teacher attention has inadvertently been tied to students' inappropriate behavior. For example, the teacher may originally have spoken to students only when they were disruptive. An extinction procedure would then involve withholding attention at these times so that only appropriate behavior elicits reinforcement. For other behaviors, peers may need to be involved in the intervention plan if their attention has been maintaining the inappropriate behavior. For example, if a child is using infantile language to receive others' attention (e.g., laughter), then peers will need to be trained to withhold their laughter in response to this behavior.

Several cautions are needed concerning the use of extinction. First, extinction should be used only for a behavior for which it is apt to be effective. Thus, for example, its utility is likely to be greater for talking out in class than for self-stimulatory behavior (e.g., twirling a pencil). Second, the initial withholding of attention or other forms of reinforcement may prompt a dramatic rise in the target behavior as students increase their efforts to receive attention. The efficacy of the procedure thus cannot be truly evaluated until several hours or perhaps days have passed. Third, extinction occasionally produces an initial aggressive response. A fourth concern is consistency of application. Without a commitment to consistency, the teacher may accidentally reinforce the undesirable behavior on an irregular basis and thus inadvertently maintain it at a higher rate of occurrence. Finally, other students may begin to imitate the behavior being ignored, thus exacerbating the situation. Alberto and Troutman (2006) aptly comment on the use of extinction:

> "Just ignore it and it will go away. He's only doing it for attention." This statement is one of the most common suggestions given to teachers. In truth, extinction is much easier to discuss than to implement. It will go away, all right, but not necessarily rapidly or smoothly. (p. 308)

**Time Out.** Punishment through withdrawal of positive reinforcement is best typified by **time out,** which generally entails preventing a student from receiving the positive reinforcement that otherwise would be available (hence its full name, "time out from positive reinforcement"). Time out can include planned ignoring, contingent observation (i.e., the student is removed from but can still observe the group), exclusion from the time-in environment, and seclusion in an isolated room or cubicle (Kerr & Nelson, 2006). The discussion here focuses primarily on the last of these forms.

Teachers should observe several cautions in using time out. First, the effectiveness of time out depends on the presence of positive reinforcement in the classroom and its absence in the time-out area. Without both of these elements, the procedure can be of only limited assistance to the teacher. For example, if Susan dislikes the classroom situation (e.g., there is a substantial amount of yelling by the teacher and difficult work assignments) and she is sent to the hall for time out, where friends wander by and chat, she has been rewarded for her behavior, not punished. This approach in the long run could increase her misbehavior.

A second caution about time out pertains to the other end of the spectrum. The time-out area should be bland and unstimulating but not a dungeon. Time out may occur in a corner of the room or in a small room adjacent to the classroom. It should be used sparingly for short periods (i.e., 5 to 10 minutes). If it needs to be used frequently for a particular child, the teacher should consider alternatives.

Use of time out naturally varies according to the space available, the type of students, and the teacher. Regardless of the circumstances, however, time out should be (Gast & Nelson, 1977):

- selected only after trying alternative solutions
- preceded by an explicit statement about when it will be used
- accompanied by a brief explanation of why it is being used
- kept brief
- documented through record-keeping procedures
- terminated contingent on appropriate behavior
- combined with reinforcement for incompatible behavior

Time out must be used carefully. The student must know in advance that the teacher will not accept a particular behavior. Classroom rules must clearly indicate which specific behaviors merit time out, and the teacher must enforce the rules consistently. The teacher should also consider any legal aspects that may apply in a given school district.

**Response Cost.** A second example of punishment based on withdrawing positive reinforcement is the use of **response cost (RC)**. Such procedures include, in particular, subtracting points or tokens within established reinforcement systems. Response cost procedures can be used concurrently with positive reinforcement in the classroom, producing a reasonably rapid decrease in behavior, and they can be combined with other procedures to yield a comprehensive behavior program (Heron, 1987).

Walker (1983) noted that response cost is likely to have maximum effect when the teacher has clearly explained the system to the students, has closely tied it to a reinforcement system, and has developed an appropriate feedback and delivery system. In addition, he suggests seven rules for implementation:

1. RC should be implemented immediately after the target response or behavior occurs.
2. RC should be applied each time a target behavior occurs.
3. The student should never be allowed to accumulate negative points.
4. The ratio of points earned to those lost should be controlled.
5. The teacher should never be intimidated by the target child using RC.
6. Subtraction of points should never be punitive or personalized.
7. A student's positive, appropriate behavior should be praised as frequently as opportunities permit.

## Behavioral Strategies for Adolescents: Extra Attention

Although many of the tools previously discussed in this chapter have been used effectively with older students, special circumstances should be considered in selecting a strategy to implement with adolescents. In light of the inherent difficulties in motivating students with long histories of school failure and chronic patterns of inappropriate behavior, intervention programs must be carefully evaluated to determine their likely outcome. First, natural and logical consequences relative to the outcome of the behavior should be emphasized (e.g., being late results in detention). Second, careful attention should be given to the reinforcers controlled by a student's peer group. The use of peer-mediated strategies should be carefully considered as possible interventions. As noted earlier these strategies can be dependent (e.g., students are reinforced based on the behavior of the child), interdependent (e.g., reinforcement is given to a group working together), and independent (e.g., all students work on similar tasks for similar reinforcement but the reinforcement is contingent on only the individual's performance).

For use with adolescents, reinforcers that require a minimum of teacher intervention should be sought; this concern is particularly important with response cost procedures that can be associated with confrontational outcomes. A point system, for instance, would be easier to use than a token system if something must be removed from a student's total.

Most important, teachers must carefully choose strategies based on their anticipated reception by adolescents. In the case of positive reinforcement programs, the system must be designed in an age-appropriate fashion; for example, token programs using Daffy Dollars or the like are obviously high-risk approaches at the secondary level. Furthermore, backup reinforcers for any systematic positive reinforcement program must reflect students' interests and must be varied. For behavior reduction strategies, teachers should obviously avoid interventions with potential for exacerbating current situations.

## Self-Management

Student-regulated strategies, including self-management, can be defined as interventions which, though initially taught by the teacher, are intended to be implemented independently by the student.

The goal of self-management programs is to "try and make children more consciously aware of their other thinking processes and task approach strategies, and to give them responsibility for their own reinforcement" (Reeve, 1990, p. 76). Self-management thus represents a shift from extrinsic to intrinsic control. This transition can be facilitated by considering these procedures: (a) gradually reducing the frequency and amount of extrinsic reinforcement provided, (b) gradually delaying access to extrinsic reinforcement through the use of feedback to students, (c) gradually fading from the application of artificial reinforcers to reliance on naturally occurring reinforcing events, and (d) teaching self-control through an emphasis on the cognitive aspects of behavior change (Wallace & Kauffman, 1986).

A number of specific aspects of self-management can be utilized. Self-instruction includes a cognitive approach to management, using self-cuing to inhibit certain inappropriate behaviors and to direct appropriate ones. It typically involves instruction in a specific verbal strategy that students perform to complete a task or control a behavior.

Self-determination of reinforcement places on the student the primary responsibility for selecting reinforcers so that they can be self-administered, contingent on performance of the specified appropriate behavior (Dowdy et al., 1998). Self-evaluation or self-assessment involves the learner in determining the need for change in behavior and then measuring (in some form) the change. Young, West, Li, and Peterson (1997) highlight components of self-evaluation, done in consultation with the teacher:

- determining the expectations or standards for acceptable behavior for each of the settings in which behavior is monitored

**TEACHER *Tips*** — **Secondary Level**

In his book, *Your First Year of Teaching: Guidelines for Success*, Richard Kellough (2005) outlines 50 errors that new teachers should avoid. Kellough contends that it is easier to avoid these errors than try to remediate the behaviors that are caused by the teacher's inexperience. Although all 50 errors cannot be outlined here, following are 5 of the errors Kellough describes. These errors were selected because they are some of the errors that new teachers (and old) fall into quite easily.

1. **Inadequately attending to long-range and daily planning.** Because teachers are so busy, they may fall into the trap of working from a day-to-day philosophy. This lack of planning ahead is heading for teaching failure for the teacher and learning failure for the student.
2. **Emphasizing the negative.** Teachers can easily fall into a negative mode by emphasizing what students are doing wrong. Remind students of the correct procedures with rationales why these procedures benefit them.
3. **Not requiring students to raise their hands or allowing students' hands to be raised too long.** How teachers manage their classroom can have an impact on students. By allowing students to communicate their need by raising their hands gives them assurance that they will have the teacher's attention. Once raised, however, the teacher must recognize the student in a timely fashion. Off-task behavior will result if appropriate behavior is not recognized.
4. **Being too serious and no fun.** Students (especially adolescents) enjoy teachers who are willing to work with them and help make learning fun. Although teaching is a serious business, young people love to use humor to communicate.
5. **Relying too much on teacher talk.** Teachers may continue to lecture or talk to students when they want to give them a lot of information. Too much talking, however, can create confusion and boredom. If students are not able to detect what is the information that is most important, they will tune the teacher out.

*Source:* Kellough, R. D. *Your First Year of Teaching: Guidelines for Success* (3rd ed.) © 2005, pp. 18–21. Reprinted by permission of Pearson Education, Inc., Upper Saddle River, NJ.

- comparing the counts or ratings of behavior (based on self-monitoring) to the standards
- determining whether the behavior is acceptable or should be changed in either quantity or quality

The most researched self-management strategy is the technique of self-monitoring, or recording, of behavior (Harris et al., 1994). Self-monitoring, particularly of on-task behavior, is a relatively simple technique that has been validated with children of diverse abilities.

One common approach to self-monitoring involves an easily implemented series of techniques that can be used in both general and special education classrooms (Hallahan, Lloyd, & Stoller, 1982). It consists of the use of a tape-recorded tone that sounds at random intervals, averaging every 45 seconds, and a self-recording sheet. Children are instructed to ask themselves, each time the tone sounds, whether they were paying attention and then to mark the yes or no box on the self-recording sheet. Although this strategy has been used with accompanying reinforcement for correct use of the self-recording sheet, in most instances it has been successful simply with appropriate training in the techniques.

Dunlap et al. (1991) outline the key steps in a successful self-monitoring program as follows: define target behavior, identify functional reinforcers, design the self-monitoring method or device, teach the child to use the device, and fade the use of the device. Figure 4–5 illustrates a sample self-monitoring device.

**Reflective Question 4.4:** ***How can I make self-monitoring procedures effective in inclusive classrooms?***

## STUDENT FACTORS RELATED TO CLASSROOM MANAGEMENT AND BEHAVIORAL SUPPORT

The third component of Marzano's (2003) model includes the consideration of the individual child in the school. The schools and classrooms of today are experiencing more diversity in the student population. The diversity we speak of includes both cultural diversity as well as diverse learners in the classroom. The final section of this chapter discusses the topic of the individual child and the sensitivity that teachers and administrators need to exhibit when working with

## Katy's Self-Monitoring Checklist

| Step | Problem Number 1 | 2 | 3 | 4 | 5 | 6 | 7 | 8 | 9 | 10 |
|---|---|---|---|---|---|---|---|---|---|---|
| 1. I copied the problem correctly. | | | | | | | | | | |
| 2. I regrouped when I needed to. | | | | | | | | | | |
| 3. I borrowed correctly. (The number crossed out is 1 bigger.) | | | | | | | | | | |
| 4. I subtracted all of the number. | | | | | | | | | | |
| 5. I subtracted correctly. | | | | | | | | | | |

**FIGURE 4–5** Self-monitoring device

*Source:* From "Using Self-Monitoring to Increase Independence," by L. K. Dunlap, G. Dunlap, L. K. Koegel, and R. L. Koegel, 1991, *Teaching Exceptional Children, 23*(3), p. 21. Copyright 1991 by The Council for Exceptional Children. Reprinted with permission.

each child (as well as his/her family). In keeping with the uniqueness of every child, the chapter concludes with the individualized education program designed for every student who has diverse learning needs, regardless of his/her culture.

## Considering Diversity in Classroom Management

As we consider diversity in the classroom, key terms should be defined. According to Barrera, Corso, and MacPherson (2003), *cultural diversity* may be defined as "behavioral, value, linguistic and other differences ascribed to peoples' cultural backgrounds." *Cultural competence*, however, may be considered as "the ability to skillfully address communication and learning across diverse cultural parameters. It is more specifically defined . . . as the ability to craft respectful, reciprocal, and responsive interactions across diverse cultural and linguistic parameters" (p. xx). It is precisely these definitions that outline the acknowledgement of students as being considered unique and contributing members in any school.

By attending to a student's cultural diversity and how it relates to classroom management, classroom climate, and classroom instruction, teachers become culturally competent to address the needs of each individual child in their classrooms. Barrera et al. (2003) outline three benefits of recognizing and attending to the challenges of the culturally diverse student. First, teachers have a *professional responsibility to address the needs of shifting demographics* in the schools of today. Children from diverse backgrounds are becoming a significant population in schools in the United States. Many teachers will come into contact with at least one child from a diverse background. Attending to the individuality of that child may make the difference in him or her becoming a successful student.

A second benefit for addressing the challenge of culturally diverse students in the classroom is the *professional responsibility of supporting a student's developmental, social, and academic growth*. Barrera et al. (2003) state that "one of the core needs of all children is to have their behaviors and beliefs mirrored and valued by adults around them" (p. 18). Learning the values, beliefs, and customs of an individual can greatly contribute to understanding the student's classroom behavior. This knowledge can greatly influence how a teacher interacts with students as well as how behavioral assessments are conducted and interpreted.

Finally, the *professional responsibility of developing appropriate and responsive curriculum* can be a benefit for every student, including the culturally diverse student. By understanding the expectations and experiences of individual children (including children with disabilities) and how they are associated with specific cultures can influence how teachers determine a student's status in relation to goals of the classroom management procedures and interventions that are implemented.

In this chapter, Golly talks about behavior as a child's means of communication (see Diversity in the Classroom, p. 110). If we apply the above three benefits with Golly's advice, we can further see how students of different backgrounds may behave differently. Understanding these differences and responding to them accordingly can enhance any classroom management system.

Vaughn, Bos, and Schumm (2006) offer five suggestions to enhance classroom management when responding to diversity in the classroom. First, teachers must remember that students are children/adolescents first. That is, teachers should respond first to accepting, recognizing, and valuing students as members of the community—respecting their common needs and goals. Second, teachers should focus on abilities and expertise of all members of the classroom. Third, teachers should celebrate diversity in student learning and behavior as well as cultural backgrounds and languages. Fourth, teachers should demonstrate a high regard for all students. Finally, teachers should provide opportunities for students to work in mixed-ability groups. In keeping with the child as an individual with specific needs, we conclude this chapter with the need for developing individual programs for students with disabilities.

## Designing Individualized Education Programs

Over 30 years ago, the passage of PL 94–142 incorporated the individualized education program into routine pedagogical practice. Reauthorization of this law brought forth changes to initiate IDEA in 1990 (PL 101-476), which added the requirement that plans for transition services be part of the IEP for all students no later than age 16. Seven years later, the 1997 changes to IDEA (PL 105–17) as well as the 2004 amendments to IDEA (now IDEIA) added other features to this document. Some of the most recent amendments require FBAs (mentioned earlier in this chapter) and behavior intervention plans. Furthermore, disciplinary regulations were clearly outlined.

The IEP is the primary document that outlines specific plans for services, placement, transitional planning, and now other assurances. Ideally, data gathered for the eligibility process and any further information collected by multidisciplinary specialists and by both special and regular teachers can assist with the development of the IEP. Realistically, special education teachers will have to conduct further curriculum-related assessments to gather the type of instructionally useful data to be able to develop appropriate goals and objectives and to know where to begin instruction.

Although IEPs can be used for a number of purposes, three stand out from the rest. First, IEPs should provide instructional direction. Effective written goal setting can help to remedy the "cookbook approach" (i.e., pulling together isolated or marginally related instructional exercises in the name of good teaching). Second, IEPs function as the basis for evaluation. Formally established learning objectives for students help determine the effectiveness and efficiency of instruction, although this form of accountability is not intended to become the basis for evaluating teacher effectiveness per se. A third use of IEPs is improved communication. Individualized education programs can facilitate contact among staff members, teachers, and parents, and ideally between teachers and students. Parental involvement, in particular, has resulted in increased mutual support and cooperation between home and school.

**IEP Team.** The identified members of the IEP team, as specified in the most recent reauthorization of IDEA, reflect key emphases of the new law: parent involvement, coordination with the general education curriculum, and involvement in the general education settings. The members include parents of the student; special education teacher; regular education teacher; local education agency representative (i.e., a person with authority to commit necessary resources); person who can interpret the evaluation results; the student, when appropriate; and other knowledgeable persons whom the parents or school may choose to invite.

**IEP Components.** Individualized education programs are intended to serve as the guiding document for the provision of an appropriate education. Moreover, IEPs function as an integral link between assessment and instruction; thus, the development of the IEP follows the collection of assessment data. The IEP then details the least restrictive, most appropriate placement and outlines the instructional program. The IEP must be evaluated and then rewritten annually as long as services are still necessary.

The major components of the IEP include the following key features. The general content of an IEP is:

- statement of the child's present level of educational performance
- statement of measurable annual goals, including benchmarks, or short-term objectives when applicable
- statement of the special education and related services and supplementary aids and services to be provided to the child
- statement of the program modifications or supports for school personnel that will be provided to the child

- explanation of the extent, if any, to which the child will not participate with nondisabled children in the regular class
- statement of any individual modifications in the administration of statewide or districtwide assessments of student achievement
- projected date for the beginning of the services and modifications
- anticipated frequency, location, and duration of those services and modifications
- statement of how the child's progress toward the annual goals will be measured
- statement of how the child's parents will be regularly informed of their child's progress toward the annual goals

Two other components of the IEP will be necessary for older students.

- **Transition services:** By age 14, a statement of transition service needs must be in place (focus on student's course of study) and, by age 16, a statement of needed transition services is required.
- **Transfer of rights:** Beginning at least 1 year before a student reaches the age of majority under state law, the IEP must include a statement that the student has been informed of his or her rights that will transfer upon reaching the age of majority.

The remainder of this section focuses primarily on the first two general components previously listed: present levels of performance and measurable annual goals.

**Present Levels of Educational Performance.** A summary of a student's current functioning provides a basis for subsequent goal setting. **Performance levels** should be determined for all areas needing special instruction. Depending on the individual, relevant information could be gathered for academic skills, behavioral patterns, self-help skills, vocational talents, or communication abilities.

Performance levels should be viewed as summaries of an individual's strengths and weaknesses. We suggest that these statements emphasize the positive aspects of the student (i.e., what the student can do), while clearly indicating what needs to be addressed.

Although performance statements can take a variety of forms, including formal test scores, informal test results, behavioral descriptions, a listing of specific abilities relative to a sequence of skills in a given area, and self-report data obtained from the student, descriptions that are instructionally relevant are warranted. Gibb and Dyches (2000) recommend that present levels of educational performance include the following three elements:

- Statement of how the disability affects the student's involvement and progress in the general curriculum
- Description of the student's performance levels in the skill areas affected by the disability
- Logical cues for writing the accompanying goals for improvement

**Annual Goals.** The next key component of an IEP is listing measurable annual goals. As the name implies, these goals predict long-term gains that can be evaluated clearly during the school year. The annual goals should reflect the educator's (and the parents') best guess of what the student can reasonably achieve within the school year. The following features can help determine realistic expectations: (a) chronological age, (b) past learning profile, and (c) recent learning history and response to instruction. Teachers can conceptualize annual goals, which may range from outcomes that might be considered the most optimistic to the most pessimistic. Against these parameters, reasonable estimates can be derived.

Annual goals should include four major elements. The IDEA of 1997 lists four characteristics of an annual goal:

- It must be measurable.
- It must tell what the student can reasonably accomplish in a year.
- It must relate to helping the student be successful in the general education curriculum and/or address other educational needs resulting from the disability.
- It must be accompanied by benchmarks or short-term objectives. (Gibb & Dyches, 2000)

Measurable goals provide a basis for evaluation. Statements should use precise behavioral terms that denote action and can therefore be operationally defined (e.g., *pronounce, write*, or *identify* motorically) rather than vague, general language that confounds evaluation and observer agreement (e.g., *know, understand*, or *appreciate*). For example, "will correctly identify all initial consonant sounds" is more appropriate than the unmeasurable "will learn to read."

Positive goals provide an appropriate direction for instruction. Avoiding negative goals creates an atmosphere that is helpful in communication with parents as well as in charting student progress. The goal "will learn to respond at appropriate times" gives the student something to strive for, as opposed to "will learn to keep mouth closed," which negatively emphasizes something to avoid.

Goals should also be oriented to the student. Developing students' skills is the intent, and the only measure of effectiveness should be what is learned, not what is taught. Thus, "will verbally respond to questions with two-word phrases" is preferable to "will be given oral language readiness materials."

Finally, goals must be relevant to the individual student's current and future needs across a range of academic, personal/social, and daily living domains. Unfortunately, research indicates that IEPs frequently do not meet this criterion.

## SUMMARY

The implementation of successful strategies for classroom organization and management can clearly differentiate between effective and ineffective educational programs. The various topics addressed within this chapter represent important concerns that should be addressed as precursors or follow-ups to the process of teaching. The chapter addresses schoolwide, classroom, and individual student factors.

An effective environment facilitates student learning. To be aesthetically pleasant, a classroom should look lived in, show graceful wear, and contain signs of renewal. Environmental designs should include areas in which to conduct a variety of instructional activities as well as a place for social interaction and reinforcement.

An important consideration for teachers is the grouping of students. Particular concerns relate to the effectiveness and efficiency of small-group, large-group, and one-to-one arrangements. Effective practices for acquisition and proficiency/maintenance learning also have implications for grouping.

Behavior change strategies afford teachers a wide variety of options for motivating and managing students with disabilities. The techniques discussed in this chapter focus first on schoolwide considerations for behavioral support and then on the importance of understanding behavior and on antecedent and consequent events in successful teaching and learning.

Systematic use of positive reinforcement can increase appropriate behavior. Teachers can program positive consequences to shape desired behaviors through contingency contracting and token economies, both of which are based on the Premack principle.

Behavior reduction strategies can include the use of a variety of differential reinforcement strategies. Although teachers should emphasize positive intervention, they may need to select techniques from among the various forms of punishment to successfully decrease targeted inappropriate behaviors.

The techniques discussed in this chapter can be powerful tools. Teachers should use them carefully, constantly evaluating whether the changes sought and achieved are in their students' best interests. Teachers should engage in continuous reflection concerning the needs of the individual child and how student behavior can be supported so that social and academic success is achieved.

PART TWO

# Content Areas

CHAPTER

# 5

# Spoken Language

Lynda Miller

Spoken language, also called oral communication or oral language, allows humans to communicate with each other using a series of oral-motor movements—**speech**—to express an abstract and rule-governed set of symbols—**language.** Although **communication** also occurs through other means (e.g., music, dance, Morse code, sign language, written language), spoken language is used by the majority of people to convey to others their ideas, feelings, emotions, beliefs, and thoughts. Oral communication is considered by corporate and professional experts to be one of the most important skills an employee can bring to the job (Roman, 2001).

Spoken language underlies most school-based learning in the early grades, and it predicts children's success with reading, spelling, written language, and literacy in general (Polloway, Miller, & Smith, 2004). Many children diagnosed with learning disabilities have spoken language difficulties that interfere with their ability to succeed in reading, writing, and spelling, without which they cannot make the transition from learning language to using language to learn (Polloway et al., 2004).

The chapter is organized into eight sections:

- a description of how spoken language is related to communication, speech, language, and literacy
- an overview of the relationship between culture and language literacy
- a model of language and its basic processes
- a discussion of language development across five stages
- a discussion of language disorders and how they differ from language differences
- a description of how to assess students' language with standardized and nonstandardized instruments and procedures
- a description of language-based teaching strategies that can be used with students in the classroom
- teaching with technology

## COMMUNICATION, LANGUAGE, SPEECH, AND LANGUAGE LITERACY

**Communication** is the interchange of ideas, beliefs, thoughts, feelings, and emotions. Communication can occur through various means, both verbal and nonverbal, including:

- speaking
- signing
- alternative augmentative communication systems
- reading
- writing
- music
- dance
- mathematics
- codes
- games
- runes (a character from one of the alphabets used by Germanic people between the 3rd and 13th centuries)
- glyphs (a symbol that conveys information nonverbally, such as a road sign)

Most verbal forms of communication involve the use of **language,** which is an arbitrary set of abstract symbols governed by a set of rules that determine how sounds, words and word parts, and phrases can be combined to make meaning. Because the rules governing languages are arbitrary, they can be used to describe almost anything. That is, virtually any combination of sounds, words, or phrases can be used to describe things, ideas, beliefs, and so on. Because there is no inherent reason why a horse, for instance, is called a horse, or justice is called justice, the rules of language remain independent of the way the world works. This arbitrariness can be difficult for children to grasp and often poses special difficulties for students, as will be shown later in the chapter.

**Speech** refers to the actual sounds of any given language, described by Polloway et al. (2004) as "the conventionally established combinations of speech sounds

[used] to produce meaningful units of language" (p. 2). Although language can be expressed in various ways, the majority of people use speech, or spoken language, as their primary means of communicating.

The National Communication Association (2006) defines speaking as the uniquely human ability to communicate information, ideas, and emotions to others using oral language. Small children should be able to:

- ask and answer simple questions
- retell a simple story
- express feelings verbally
- imagine and express how someone else might feel

Speech occurs in every human culture and, even within a given language, can exist in multiple dialects. The speaking conventions associated with dialectal variations can also vary widely and can result in communication breakdowns or misunderstandings. The American Speech-Language-Hearing Association (2003a) provides a discussion of the historical, social, and cultural aspects of American dialects and their relationship to each other, arguing that each is a legitimate example of a rule-governed system of language.

One of the primary emphases in education today is on **literacy,** or how well children read, write, speak, compute, and solve problems. The National Literacy Act of 1991, PL 102-73 (U.S. Congress, 1991), defines language literacy in the context of the proficiencies necessary to function on the job and in society, as well as to achieve one's goals and to develop one's knowledge and potential. More specifically, the National Communication Association (2006) emphasizes media literacy, which they describe as "understanding and assigning value, worth, and meaning to media and their messages. Small children should:

- begin to understand what media are
- be able to identify several forms of media that they use

In this chapter, we focus on language literacy as a set of competencies necessary for children to succeed in school, as well as their lives outside the classroom. Thus, we emphasize the abilities and skills requisite to speaking, reading, writing, and listening in interactions presented by teachers, textbooks, peers, families, and the media.

**Reflective Question 5.1:** ***What is the relationship between the concepts of communication, language, speech, and literacy?***

## CULTURE AND LANGUAGE LITERACY

Schooling in the United States emphasizes the development of language literacy, particularly speaking, listening, reading, and writing. In some states, children are expected to arrive in kindergarten with skills already developed in **metalinguistic ability,** alphabet knowledge, and print and word concepts (Roseberry-McKibbon, 2003). In addition, they are expected to know how to understand and tell stories, how to tell about their experiences in a narrative form, and how to respond to adult questions that are designed to stimulate children to display their knowledge. As children progress through the elementary grades, they are expected to make the shift from primarily oral narrative forms associated with stories to the more literate expository forms found in textbooks, and they are expected to learn to read well enough that, by third grade, they can begin using their reading ability as a means for further learning.

Peña, Summers, and Resendiz (2006, in press) report that, in a typical school district in the United States, "[t]hirty-seven percent of the students are from racial minorities (5% Asian, 15% Hispanic, and 17% African American" (p. 1). Further, "[u]p to 12% of the total population will be bilingual or in the process of becoming bilingual as they learn English as a second language" (p. 1).

Children from cultures outside middle-class America can arrive at school with few of the language abilities necessary for successful participation in the classroom. Some of the factors that can affect speech, language, and literacy development include the following (Roseberry-McKibbon, 2003):

1. Access to health care may be limited or absent. Consequently, children may be frequently sick or absent from school. When they are in attendance, they may experience difficulties attending or focusing on schoolwork. In addition, many may suffer from middle ear infections, which can affect their abilities in auditory discrimination and processing, as well as their speech and language development.
2. Nutrition may be a problem. Growing up malnourished is now being linked to disrupted cognitive performance. Roseberry-McKibbon (2003) stated, "Childhood malnutrition produces permanent, structural damage to the brain. Between birth and 2 years of age, the brain grows to approximately 80% of its adult size; malnutrition during this period is especially devastating to cognitive growth" (p. 9).

3. Parents may have a lowered educational level with resulting lowered language stimulation. Roseberry-McKibbon (2003) indicated that the strongest predictor of children's academic success is the mother's educational level rather than ethnic background of language abilities. In addition, lowered rates of literacy are associated with families receiving welfare. In part, this can be related to the lack of early language stimulation.

Roseberry-McKibbon (2003) indicated that some parents do not believe it is important or necessary to talk to babies or to provide early language stimulation. Even when they do talk to their children, they may use directive forms rather than inquiries that tend to foster further interaction. In addition, many families may not have the funds necessary to expose their children to the experiences and cultural events that children from other cultural groups routinely experience, nor are they able to provide the types of language stimulation associated with readiness for reading and successfully participating in classroom discourse. As a result, their children may not perform as well initially on formal schooling tasks and may even experience their early school interactions as a culture shock.

However, many children who enter school from diverse backgrounds, including impoverished circumstances, learn and adapt quickly to the school environment and go on to perform as well as or better than their peers. Some who display differences in their language abilities may require individualized modifications in the classroom, whereas others may need intervention aimed specifically at a language disorder. Differentiating between language differences and language disorders is a topic we return to later in the chapter.

**Reflective Question 5.2:** ***Why are cultural and environmental differences significant in all considerations of language and literacy?***

# A MODEL OF LANGUAGE

To understand spoken language, it is useful to see how language is typically discussed and described. A variety of models of language have been proposed over the centuries during which humans have shown an interest in language. Models of language, as with descriptions of other human processes, have been proposed along the nature-nurture continuum shown in Figure 5–1.

At one extreme, proponents of the "nature" model argue that the human brain is "hardwired" to learn language and that language acquisition is primarily the result of biological factors. On the other end of the continuum, proponents of the "nurture" model hold that language arises out of the interactions between the brain and its environment, with the child seen as a passive accumulator of the external stimuli that shape her or his behaviors into language.

The model we use incorporates both nature and nurture, holding that children are primed to learn language at birth and need opportunities to interact with and practice using language with proficient language users. This model is termed the **social-interactionist** model because it emphasizes the interaction between biological abilities and environmental influences as they acquire the aspects of language necessary for successful communication.

## Describing Language

Language is most often described in terms of its basic modalities and levels (Bloom & Lahey, 1978; Polloway et al., 2004):

- language use, including pragmatics, narrative discourse, classroom discourse, and expository discourse
- language form
- language content
- literal language compared with figurative language

**FIGURE 5–1** Continuum of language models

| *Nature Model* | *Social-interactionist Model* | *Nature Model* |
|---|---|---|
| • Child is hardwired to learn language | • Child is affected by both nature and nurture | • Child is a passive reactor |
| • Language emerges from biological factors | • Brain is primed to learn language | • External factors shape the child's verbal behaviors into language |
| • Child is active constructor of her/his reality | • Child must have opportunities to practice with language | • Biological factors operate in response to environmental processes |

**Language Use.** Within the social-interactionist model of language, the use of language in social interactions with significant others is seen as the context within which children develop the conventional content and forms of language necessary for successful communication. Language use is most typically discussed under the categories of pragmatics and discourse.

**Pragmatics** describes how people use language and the ways in which they alter their language forms and content to match the conversational requirements of differing social circumstances. It explains the functions of language, or what people are trying to make happen through their language, especially in social situations. In general, pragmatics describes how people get things done through their language through an informal conversational "code" of conduct (first described by Bates, 1976) that includes the following:

- Tell the truth when you're communicating.
- Cooperate with your conversational partner.
- Offer only information you believe to be new and relevant.
- Only ask for information you truly want to have.
- Give your listener neither too much nor too little background information to make your point.
- Be unambiguous.
- Alter your language to fit each social setting.

Of course, no one actually adheres strictly to these rules. In fact, violations of the rules are themselves conventionalized and carry separate meanings. For instance, the use of satire or irony in storytelling or journalism is, strictly speaking, a violation of the truth principle. Similarly, idioms violate the truth principle because, though they say one thing, they actually mean something different.

Learning the conventions for violating the rules comprises an important aspect of children's language acquisition and frequently appears as one aspect of some language disorders. In addition, because cultural and dialectal variations of these rules exist, students communicating across dialects or from culturally different communities can suffer communication breakdowns or misunderstandings.

**Discourse** is defined as a linguistic unit (as a conversation or a story) larger than a sentence. Humans use a variety of discourses, among them:

- conversational
- classroom
- narrative
- poetic (including songs)
- dramatic
- expository (descriptive, explanatory, argumentative/persuasive)

In almost all cultures, children are exposed first to **conversational discourse,** which, though it varies in form and content across cultures, functions primarily as a way to communicate within social-interactive contexts. Almost all cultures utilize narrative discourse in the telling of stories. As a consequence, children hear narrative discourse in the stories told within their cultural group. In many cultures, children are routinely included in oral storytelling activities and are expected to become proficient storytellers as soon as their language skills allow. In cultures with a strong tradition of oral storytelling, narrative discourse often includes poetic and dramatic discourse, which function to highlight certain aspects of the story, create dramatic tension, or complicate the action.

According to Cazden (2001), **classroom discourse** comprises the content, forms, and functions of the language used in teaching and learning. Classroom discourse includes:

- students talking to each other during classroom discussions
- students responding to teachers' directions or queries
- teachers directing students' learning
- teachers scaffolding students' language and/or learning
- teachers revoicing students' comments as a way to facilitate peer-to-peer discussion

Adults in **language literate households** frequently converse with their children using one or more forms of classroom discourse, particularly in their efforts to teach their children about the world and how to display their knowledge about it to adults. However, children from homes that are less language literate may not be exposed to classroom discourse until they enter school and, therefore, have little experience demonstrating their knowledge in ways that are expected in the classroom.

Miller, Gillam, and Peña (2001) offer a model of **narrative discourse** (Table 5–1) that can be used for both assessment and instruction. Their model shows the key elements of narrative discourse in developmental order across and within types. Children's stories first exhibit one or more of the Story Components, followed by Story Ideas and Language, and then by Episode Elements and Structure.

**TABLE 5–1** Aspects of narrative discourse

| *Story Components* | *Story Ideas and Language* | *Episode Elements and Structure* |
|---|---|---|
| Setting: Time and Place | Complexity of Ideas | Basic Episode: |
| Character Information | Complexity of Vocabulary | Initiating Event |
| Temporal Order of Events | Grammatical Complexity | Action |
| Causal Relationships | Knowledge of Dialogue | Consequence |
| | Creativity | |
| | | Complete Episode: |
| | | Initiating Event |
| | | Internal Response |
| | | Attempt |
| | | Plan |
| | | Consequence |
| | | Reaction/Ending |
| | | Multiple Episodes: |
| | | Story Contains |
| | | Embedded Episodes |

**Dramatic discourse** is used whenever a scene, story, or play is portrayed by actors and conveyed to an audience either live or through radio, film, television, or the Internet. Children acting out scenarios or play-acting stories utilize dramatic discourse, which consists of:

- the set, or scene(s)
- the lighting
- the timing of the action
- the physical appearance of the actors
- turn-taking (keeping the "floor") among the characters, including interruptions, silence, ignoring the speaker, and simultaneous speaking

**Poetic discourse** utilizes language "chosen and arranged to create a specific emotional response through meaning, sound, and rhythm" (Merriam-Webster.com, 2003). Children are exposed to poetic discourse when they hear song lyrics and play rhyming games, or when adults read (or sing) poetry or songs aloud to them.

**Expository discourse** includes the nonnarrative discourses common to textbooks, treatises, articles, essays, and editorials. The most common types of expository discourse are:

- descriptive (describes a thing, process, event, or idea)
- explanatory (explains how something works or how to do something)
- argumentative/persuasive (attempts to convince or persuade the audience/reader of something)

Although some children are exposed to expository text (either orally or in print) before they enter school, they are not expected to understand the structure or function of print-based expository discourses until they have learned to read.

**Language Form.** Language form is typically described using three basic categories: phonology (or in sign language, **cherology**), morphology, and syntax.

***Phonology.*** Phonology comprises the set of rules governing which sounds are pronounceable and used to make meaning, as well as how they can be combined to make meaning. Different languages have varying rules for how this works. For instance, although in English, /t/ and /l/ cannot be combined at the beginning of a word to make meaning, in Tlinglt (a native Alaskan language), /t/ and /l/ at the beginning of a word are pronounced "kl." The San and Kwhe people, who live in southern Africa, use a set of four or five different click sounds that were known to appear in only one other language, Damin, an extinct aboriginal language in Australia (Wade, 2003).

**FIGURE 5–2** Five English words represented in phonetic notation (IPA)

| *English Spelling* | *IPA Notation* |
|---|---|
| alter | /ɔltə/ |
| church | /ʈʃɝʈʃ/ |
| remember | /rimɛmbɚ/ |
| clinging | /klɪŋɪŋ/ |
| opportunity | /ɔpɚʈunɪʈi/ |

The smallest linguistic units to carry meaning are *phonemes*, which are the pronounceable sounds in any given language. Thus, in each language, some sounds carry meaning, and some do not. In English, how one pronounces /t/ makes no difference in meaning, though in other languages, adding a puff of air, for instance, indicates a shift in meaning and is considered a separate phoneme.

Phonemes are typically represented by a notational system, the International Phonetic Alphabet (IPA). Figure 5-2 shows the phonemes associated with five common English words.

English consists of a set of 44 phonemes that are further categorized into vowels and consonants, the latter including voiced, voiceless, oral, nasal, and place and manner of articulation.

***Morphology.*** Morphology is the set of rules governing how phonemes can be combined into larger units (syllables and words) in order to convey meaning. Morphemes are the smallest grammatical units that carry meaning. Morphological rules govern the specific phonemic combinations that can be used by any given language to indicate, for example, past tense (e.g., "The three girls *swam* across the pond"), plural number (e.g., "The *dogs* were barking at the intruder"), pronoun differentiation (e.g., "*My* brother's sons gave *him* a puppy for his birthday"), or possession ("The truck *driver's* brakes failed, but he managed to get *his* rig stopped without incident").

***Syntax.*** Syntax is the set of rules governing how phrases and sentences must be constructed in order to convey meaning. For instance, syntactic rules include those governing word order ("The dog ate the bone" and not "The bone the dog ate" or "The bone ate the dog") and those governing active or passive voice ("The chairperson counted the votes" [active], "The votes were counted by the chairperson" [passive]). Syntactic rules allow people to construct unique utterances in order to perform these functions, among others:

- comment
- seek attention
- greet
- request information, acknowledge others, and respond to others
- negate, refuse, reject, protest, indicate absence, and assert falsity
- direct others to carry out instructions
- tell stories
- teach
- make indirect requests
- describe or explain things
- bargain and negotiate
- repair conversations
- persuade others

**Language Content.** Language content is usually discussed in terms of semantics, described by Polloway et al. (2004) as "the linguistic representations of ideas, feelings, events, relationships, processes, and things" (p. 8). In children, semantics is described through analysis of their oral vocabulary development (preschool and early elementary), their reading vocabulary (elementary), and their written vocabulary (upper elementary and beyond). Learning the semantic aspects of language involves learning:

- how words relate to their referents (the actual thing, idea, concept, feeling, event, or process a particular word stands for), and
- that the relationships between words and referents are **arbitrary** and **symbolic.**

Children learn these two aspects of semantics gradually. Their earliest words are more **iconic** than symbolic, and meaning is often closely tied to the word (e.g., "moo," "choo-choo," "bowwow").

**Literal and Figurative Language.** Language users employ language on different levels of abstraction, ranging from the literal and concrete to the abstract and figurative. At the literal level, language, although still operating in an arbitrary relationship with what it is referring to, functions to convey the concrete, primary meaning of a word or phrase, as in, "The man slept deeply." In the earliest stages of language development, children use concrete, literal language to get things done in a direct and efficient way.

At the figurative level, language conveys a more abstract and secondary meaning through expressing one thing but being understood as meaning something different, as in, "The man was sawing logs all night." In the figurative meaning, the man slept deeply, even though the sentence says otherwise on the literal level. As children's language abilities grow, they see that they can use language in a less direct way to alter how (and how efficiently) they can get things to happen.

Examples of figurative language use include:

- polite forms (e.g., "May I please have more juice," or "Would you mind closing the door?")
- idioms (as in the "sawing logs" example above)
- simile (e.g., "She swam like a porpoise" or "It was as bright as daylight under the lights")
- metaphor (e.g., "She was a jackrabbit once the race began")
- satire (e.g., an essay, story, poem, play, or novel that ridicules or scorns human vices)
- irony (e.g., the expression of something other than the literal meaning, as in "You look fantastic," meaning the opposite)
- adage (a metaphorical saying embodying a common observation, e.g., "What is essential is invisible to the eye" [Saint-Exupery, 1968])
- proverb (a short maxim, e.g., "You can't teach an old dog new tricks")
- allegory (fiction using symbolic characters and actions to express a truth regarding human existence, e.g., "Jack and the Beanstalk," or "The Matrix")
- alliteration (e.g., "She sold sea shells on the sea shore")
- personification (e.g., "The sun smiled down on us that day")

Many types of humor rely on figurative expressions or words or phrases with double meanings. Puns use double meanings to convey humor, as in these two examples:

- "We saw an old beater," which could mean either an egg beater or a car
- "When we took 12 rabbits and put 6 in one pen and 6 in another, we were splitting hares," which plays on the pronunciation of "hare" to evoke its homonym in the expression "splitting hairs"

Riddles also use double meanings as a way to express humor, as in:

- "Why didn't the skeleton cross the road? Because it didn't have the guts," which refers to both the "courage" and "innards"
- "What is the smartest insect? A spelling bee," which refers to both the insect and the classroom spelling game

To be able to understand and use figurative language, children must develop the ability to reflect on language, talk about it, and manipulate it. This ability is called metalinguistic ability and begins to emerge when children first grasp the idea that different people can have the same name. As children become more proficient with language, they learn how to use it to better get what they want (e.g., through using indirect language to request a wanted object or food, "I *need* to have this cookie" vs. "Give me a cookie!"). Gradually, most children discover that idiomatic expressions say one thing but mean another, that polite forms are required in certain social situations, and that language has parts that can be rearranged. At the higher levels of language development, people use their metalinguistic abilities to understand and express ideas in graceful and artistic ways.

One of the most important aspects of metalinguistic ability is **phonological awareness,** the understanding that speech consists of sounds and syllables. Phonological awareness is a basic prerequisite for learning to correlate speech sounds with printed letters in order to decode the written word and evolves out of the child's awareness that language has parts that can be talked about and analyzed.

**Reflective Question 5.3:** ***Language competence derives from abilities related to use, form, and content. How do these considerations interact in the development of children with special needs?***

## LANGUAGE DEVELOPMENT

Language development is typically described as occurring in stages. One of the most thorough stage models of language was developed by Paul (2001) and includes the following stages:

1. Prelinguistic
2. Emerging language
3. Developing language
4. Language for learning
5. Adolescent/advanced language

### Prelinguistic Stage

In most families, children are surrounded by language from the time they are born. Adults in these families include their babies in social interactions that are based on the routines of everyday life and punctuated by language. During infancy, normally developing children develop the ability to engage in what Bruner (1975) called **joint attending** and **joint referencing,** both of which lead directly to the use of words for communicating.

**Emerging Language Stage.** The emerging language stage begins sometime between 12 and 18 months of age when children begin using singe-word utterances and ends somewhere around 26 months when they regularly use utterances of two or more words. During this stage, children make significant progress in semantics, syntax, phonology, discourse, and pragmatics.

**Semantics.** During this stage, children's vocabulary increases from approximately 20 different words at the end of their first year to about 200 words by the time they are 2 years old (Gillam & Bedore, 2000). Most of these words serve a particular communicative purpose, described below.

**Syntax.** According to Gillam and Bedore (2000), by the end of this stage, children are using two-word utterances to convey a small number of semantic relationships between agents (whatever initiates an action), actions (what occurs), objects (things that are acted upon), and locations (places). For instance, typical two-word utterances at this stage are: "Daddy eat" (meaning "Daddy is eating"), "Doll chair" (meaning "The doll is in the chair"), "Go Nonny's" (meaning "Go to Grandma's"), and "Mommy car" (meaning "It's Mommy's car").

In addition, toward the end of this stage, children develop two-word utterances to express both negation and interrogatives, for instance, "No milk" (meaning "I don't want any more milk"), or "More juice?" (meaning, "May I have some more juice?").

**Phonology.** Gillam and Bedore (2000) reported that the first set of phonemes acquired by children by age 3 is /m/, /b/, /n/, /w/, /d/, /p/, and /h/, although children in this stage exhibit a wide variety of phonological abilities. Most children develop a set of words that, although different from the adult forms, are recognized by their adult conversational partners as having a particular meaning.

**Pragmatics and Discourse.** Children during the emerging language stage are learning the pragmatics of conversational discourse, or how to use conversation to get things done. Increasingly throughout this stage, children use verbal communication rather than nonverbal means, and their communicative intentions become increasingly sophisticated as they experiment with using language to participate in conversations.

Some of the most common intentions children exhibit during this stage include (Paul, 2001):

- requesting information through asking what things (and events, processes, actions, etc.) are called, or, later, through using rising intonation or a *wh-* word
- acknowledging that the conversational partner's utterance was received through nodding or imitating the partner's intonation pattern
- answering, or responding appropriately to, the conversational partner's request for information

Part of learning the pragmatics of conversational discourse involves figuring out what the conversational partner already knows so one needn't say too much or too little to make the conversation work. For children in the emerging language stage, these **presuppositions,** or assumptions about the what the partner already knows, are not apparent. At first, these children act as if their conversational partners know exactly what they, themselves, know, providing little or no background information, and using pronouns without saying whom they refer to. They also have difficulty taking the listener's perspective or providing clarification when someone asks. By the end of this stage, children can usually respond to *wh-* questions, provide clarification with support, and give more information when asked.

A second critical aspect of conversational discourse is **turn-taking.** Most children during the emerging language stage exhibit turn-taking, especially during the routines developed with their caregivers. However, over extended conversations, children in this stage have difficulty taking turns or sharing turns with more than one or two conversational partners. Although children at the end of this stage are clearly more adept with conversation than they were at the beginning, they remain relative beginners with conversational discourse, especially with people who are not familiar with their lives and routines.

The American Speech-Language-Hearing Association (ASHA) (2003b) offers an online overview of the speech and language characteristics of preschool children, including tips for parents about how to communicate with their preschool children. In addition, ASHA (2003c) hosts a public page describing language and literacy development in preschoolers.

## Developing Language Stage

The developing language stage begins at approximately 27 months, when children routinely use utterances of two or more words, and ends somewhere around 46 months of age. During this stage, children acquire most of the basic structures of language, develop considerable facility with the pragmatics of conversational and narrative discourse, and begin showing awareness that language functions on the figurative level as well as the literal.

**Semantics.** Children's semantic development during this stage is tremendous. At the beginning of the stage, their expressive vocabulary is somewhere around 200 words, whereas by age 4, it has expanded to somewhere around 1,800 different words (Gillam & Bedore, 2000). The semantic forms used by children in this stage expand beyond nouns and verbs to include:

- prepositions (e.g., *behind, on top of*)
- adjectives (e.g., *pretty, sunny*)
- temporal words (e.g., *after, last*)
- pronouns (e.g., *she, him, it*)
- inflections (e.g., *cats*)
- tense markers (e.g., *running*)
- regular and irregular verb forms (e.g., *move/moved, sit/sat*)
- word contraction (e.g., *I'm, she's*)
- pronouns (e.g., *me, my, mine, he, she, it, her, their, our*)

**Syntax and Morphology.** At the beginning of this stage of language development, children are typically using two-word utterances. According to Gillam and Bedore (2000), at the end of this stage, they are using sentences containing up to 10 words. As they enter this stage, children increase complexity by adding modifiers or auxiliary verbs. As they leave the stage, their sentences include phrases within clauses or combine two or more clauses into one, a process called **embedding.** According to Hulit and Howard (1998), the most common types of embedding early in this stage are (listed in developmental order):

- prepositional phrases (e.g., *He's sitting on the sofa*)
- participial phrases (e.g., *The spinning clown was funny*)
- infinitive phrases (e.g., *I want to go play*)
- gerunds (e.g., *Driving is hard*)

Later in the stage, children begin combining clauses into one sentence to produce compound sentences, (e.g., *I'm drawing and he's cooking*), or embedding clauses within clauses to produce complex sentences (e.g., *think he's hurt*).

Gillam and Bedore (2000) reported that the earliest morphemes used by children in this stage are the plural (e.g., *The dogs play*), the possessive (e.g., *The doll's dress*), and the progressive (e.g., *Daddy sleeping*). Later, they use the copula (e.g., *Daddy is happy*) and the auxiliary (e.g., *Daddy is sleeping*). Notable during this language stage is that children tend to generalize the syntactic and morphological rules they learn, producing such words as *mouses, eated, drived, childs*, and so on. Gradually, they learn to specify the rules and reduce the overgeneralizations, although some of this learning continues into the next stage of development.

**Phonology.** During this stage of development, children acquire most phonemes. According to Gillam and Bedore (2000), children between 3 and 5 acquire these phonemes: /k/, /g/, /f/, /v/, /tS/ (ch), /dZ/ (dg). Between 4 and 8, children acquire these phonemes: /S/(sh), /T/ (voiceless th), /s/, /z/, /D/ (voiced th) /l/, /r/, /Z/ (azure). In addition, after age 3, children are usually able to begin stringing consonants together into consonant clusters such as *spin* and *string*.

**Pragmatics and Discourse.** During this stage of language development, children's abilities as conversational partners grow considerably. They become able to maintain a topic over several conversational turns, they develop the ability to take turns and understand what signals a turn change, and they become more proficient in understanding their listeners' needs for background information. Early in this developmental stage, children acquire the knowledge needed to repair conversations that may need clarification, revision, or repeating in order for the listener to understand what is being said. Initially their revisions or clarifications may not be sophisticated or effective, but as their skills increase, they become more adept.

Another pragmatic development that occurs in this stage is that children shift from using direct requests when they need something to using indirect means for the same purposes. At the beginning of this stage, children use straightforward requests for what they want, and there is no question about their intent. For instance, the child might say, "I want more juice." Later in the stage, as they learn about polite forms, they shift to more indirect statements, such as "I *need* more juice," or "I'd really like more juice." By the end of the stage, their requests can be quite indirect, as in, "I'm thirsty" rather than "I need more juice."

At the same time that children in this stage are developing more proficiency with conversational discourse, they are also learning about stories and narrative structure. Especially in literate families, children hear stories and narratives in the course of their everyday routines so that by the time they are nearing the end of this stage, they are telling stories with fictional elements and they are constructing retellings of their personal experiences. By the time these children reach kindergarten age, they are usually able to tell a story that contains a basic episode, which includes (Miller et al., 2001):

- an initiating event (a problem that begins the action)
- an attempt by a character to solve the problem
- a consequence, or resolution, of the problem

During the developing language stage, children also begin incorporating dramatic discourse into their play. Developmental guidelines from the Cedar Rapids, Iowa, Area Education Agency 7 (2003) indicate that children at ages 3–4 begin to use dramatic play that includes acting out whole scenes such as traveling, playing house, and pretending to be animals. By ages 4–5, children's dramatic play becomes more realistic as they attend to detail, time, and space. Children of this age like to play dress up and use stage props for acting out scenes such as playing store, doctor, or firefighter.

**Figurative Language.** The language used by children entering the developing language stage reflects the literal level rather than the figurative. They are unable to understand that words are anything different from the things they refer to, nor can they understand that language can be talked about, analyzed, or parsed. Gradually, they discover that certain things can have the same name (people, for instance) or that words can sound the same but carry different meanings (e.g., *pear, pare*, and *pair*). Too, children in this stage come to understand that they can talk about talking, saying things like, "My mother told me I can't say *ain't*," or "That's not how you say it. You say it this way."

During the developing language stage, children's awareness of idiomatic expressions and humor increases as their understanding of the metaphoric expands. By the end of this period, children may be using a set of idiomatic expressions common in their families, though they may not know exactly what the figurative meaning is. Similarly, they may begin using some forms of humor, especially riddles, by the end of the period, but they may not yet understand exactly why these forms of humor are, indeed, funny.

## Language for Learning Stage

Once children enter school, their language development is increasingly influenced by their educational experiences. Their language development, focused in earlier stages on learning the basics of use, content, and form, shifts into the more literate aspects of reading, writing, figurative language, and more abstract discourse forms.

According to Hulit and Howard (1998), when children enter school, they most likely exhibit these language characteristics:

- Their vocabulary includes almost all the basic words of their language or dialect.
- Their phonological system is almost equivalent to that of adults.
- Their syntactic skills are developed enough to use the most direct forms, as well as some transformations of direct forms such as negatives and interrogatives.
- Their conversational abilities include the ability to make indirect requests, take turns appropriately, and know when their listeners need more information.

In addition to these abilities, children who come to school from literate homes also know how stories work; how to talk about language; and how to demonstrate to adults, through specific conversational routines, what they know and have experienced. They have also experienced the various "artifacts" associated with print (pens, pencils, computers, paper, magazines, and books), and they know that language is a powerful tool for producing results.

**Semantic Development.** In the language for learning stage, children continue to add new words to their vocabularies, but they also learn to refine how they use words. They develop proficiency in:

- choosing among words to select the most precise meaning to fit what they are trying to express
- using the same words to mean different things (e.g., *cool wind* compared with *cool shoes*)
- distinguishing among words with similar meanings (e.g., *sword* compared with *saber*)

- classifying words into categories and hierarchical subcategories (e.g., animal > mammal > hooved > herbivore)

Children in this stage complete their elaboration of the English pronoun system, shown in Table 5–2.

In addition, children figure out that pronouns have antecedents that can appear in previous sentences or even in previous conversations.

**Syntax and Morphology.** Children's syntactic development in this stage is both an expansion of the forms they have already acquired and the acquisition of some of the more difficult syntactic forms. They learn how to:

- expand noun and verb phrases (e.g., ordering adjectives such as *big blue truck* and not *blue big truck*)
- use some passive sentences (e.g., *The cabinet was made by a craftsman* and not *The craftsman was made by a cabinet*)
- make exceptions to the rules (e.g., *ate, swam, drove, children, mice)*
- embed more complicated structures (e.g., *I have a CD I know you'll like*);
- conjoin sentences with conjunctions other than *and* (e.g., *The dog was hungry, so we gave him a sandwich; If it doesn't rain, we get to go to the park*)

Morphological development in this stage is characterized by their acquisition of the ability to make nouns from verbs using *-ing* (e.g., *eat* > *eating*), add *-er* to verbs to make agents (e.g., *play* > *player*), and to produce adjectives by adding *-ly* to adjectives (e.g., *sincere* > *sincerely*).

**Phonology.** Children's phonological systems contain most of the phonemes of the adult system on entry to school. However, some children are 8 or sometimes even older before they finish acquiring all the phonemes, and some children may exhibit inconsistency in their use throughout this stage of language development. Gillam and Bedore (2000) reported that the phonemes acquired last by most children are /S/ (sh), /T/ (voiceless th), /s/, /z/, /D/ (voiced th), /l/, /r/, and /Z/ (azure).

**Pragmatics and Discourse.** Although most children enter school as decent conversationalists, they continue to develop proficiency with conversational discourse during the language for learning stage. They become better able to maintain topics, clarify an utterance or repair a conversational breakdown, and use indirect requests to get what they want. During the language for learning stage, these conversational skills become increasingly important in their interactions with peers.

**TABLE 5–2** English personal pronouns

| | *Singular* | | | *Plural* | | |
|---|---|---|---|---|---|---|
| | *1st* | *2nd* | *3rd* | *1st* | *2nd* | *3rd* |
| **Subjective** | | | | | | |
| **Female** | she | you | | | you | |
| **Male** | he | you | | | you | |
| **Neutral** | 1* | | it, one | we* | | they |
| **Possessive** | | | | | | |
| **Female** | her, hers | your, yours | | | your | |
| **Male** | his | your, yours | | | your | |
| **Neutral** | my, mine* | | its, one's | our* | | their, theirs |
| **Objective** | | | | | | |
| **Female** | her | you | | | you | |
| **Male** | him | you | | | you | |
| **Neutral** | | | it, one | us* | | |
| **Reflexives** | | | | | | |
| **Female** | herself | yourself | | | yourselves | |
| **Male** | himself | yourself | | | yourselves | |
| **Neutral** | myself* | | itself, oneself | themselves* | | themselves |

*Self-referring pronouns are assumed to carry the gender of the person using them.

Equally important, children in this stage make the transition from being primarily oral to being increasingly literate, which requires proficiency with narrative, classroom, and various expository discourses.

***Narrative Discourse.*** Children at the beginning of this stage typically tell stories that, although containing most aspects of a narrative, cannot be considered true narratives. Sometime after about age 8, most children begin to tell stories that can be considered true narratives, which Miller et al. (2001) describe as stories that contain a central theme, character(s), a plot, a setting, and a complete episode. A complete episode includes:

- an initiating event (the "problem" that begins the story)
- an internal response, the character's feelings or intentions resulting from the problem
- a plan, what the main character intends to do and why
- an attempt, what the character does to try to solve the problem
- a consequence, what happens when the character is trying to solve the problem
- a reaction or ending, the character's reaction to the consequence

***Classroom Discourse.*** Cazden (2001) calls classroom discourse the language of teaching and learning. When children enter school, they are expected to engage in the unique conversations characteristic of the classroom, which typically involve the teacher initiating a topic, followed by a student response, and the teacher's evaluation of that response. Classroom discourse differs from conversational discourse because the teacher chooses most of the topics and takes most of the turns. In addition, the teacher determines whether, when, and how long students talk, when students relinquish turns, and whether their responses are correct or acceptable. Because adults in literate families often use this form of discourse with their preschool children, these children come to school with ample experience in how it works as a teaching and learning process.

***Expository Discourse.*** As described earlier, during the language for learning stage, children are expected to acquire the more literate aspects of language, among them various expository discourse styles. The most prevalent types of expository discourse children encounter during the elementary school years are explanation and description. Both these forms of discourse differ from conversational and narrative discourse in that they are decontextualized. That is, rather than referring to shared experiences, events, or settings, they function to state facts or hypotheses; to ask questions and draw conclusions; and to interpret, classify, synthesize, and summarize.

In addition, expository discourses typically use a hierarchical organization scheme, in contrast to conversation and narrative, which both use either an event-driven structure (conversation) or a plot-driven story grammar (narrative). The format of expository discourse depends on the paragraph, with a topic sentence that states the main idea, the body of the paragraph elaborating on the main idea, and a summary sentence.

The information conveyed by expository discourse is often unfamiliar to the student because it uses abstract, enumerative, and logical means to convey information. In contrast, conversation and narrative both convey information that is familiar to the student in a more concrete and not necessarily purely logical manner.

**Figurative Language.** During the language for learning stage, children develop considerable ability with figurative language, metalinguistic knowledge, metapragmatic ability, and metacognitive strategies. Their figurative language knowledge expands to include various forms of humor (described above in the language model section), including riddles, puns, witticisms, metaphors, similes, idioms, proverbs, adages, and maxims.

Children in the language for learning stage develop considerable metalinguistic proficiency, especially as they meet the challenges of learning about defining words; identifying homonyms, synonyms, and antonyms; resolving semantic ambiguities (e.g., *Visiting relatives can be a nuisance*); identifying sounds in words and learning their corresponding letters in print; and identifying the various syntactic and morphological characteristics of both oral and printed language.

One of the most critical metalinguistic abilities for children is **phonological awareness,** the ability to recognize individual phonemes in spoken language. S. B. Smith, Simmons, and Kame'enui (2003) described phonological awareness as "sensitivity to the sound structure of language and a conscious ability to detect, combine, and manipulate different sizes of sound units" (p. 4).

To make the correspondence between sounds and letters—i.e., to decode words—children rely on their phonological awareness to identify the sounds in the first place. By the time children leave second grade, most decode well enough to comprehend what they are reading, and by the end of fourth grade, most will be able to decode fluently enough to use reading as a vehicle for learning.

Children in this stage of language development also acquire a more elaborate understanding and ability with the **metapragmatic** aspects of manipulating conversation, narrative, classroom, and expository discourse. That is, they become able to evaluate the specific requirements of each type of setting (e.g., conversing with a peer, demonstrating their knowledge to a teacher, disagreeing with a classmate) and how to manage the pragmatic aspects of each. These aspects include learning:

- how to identify who has more or less authority
- the degree of formality required
- the role of cultural differences among participants
- how to manage conversational breakdowns
- how to interrupt
- how to manage other people's interruptions

Children in the language for learning stage of language development also develop **metacognitive ability,** which allows them to reflect on and manage their own thinking and learning processes. The two metacognitive processes that have been described most thoroughly are **comprehension monitoring** and **organizational and learning strategies** (Paul, 2001). Comprehension monitoring involves recognizing when one does or does not understand something, such as a teacher's instruction or something being read), an ability most children acquire between the ages of 5 and 8 (see Chapter 7). After age 8, most children also begin to exhibit compensatory strategies, including:

- asking for help
- analyzing context for clues
- reasoning through
- checking to see if there is additional information somewhere (e.g., overhead, chalkboard)

A related development occurs when children begin to exhibit the ability to organize themselves to process new information through such means as analyzing what they already know or inferring from what they already know (Wallach & Miller, 1988).

## Adolescent/Advanced Language Stage

By the time students reach adolescence, most have achieved considerable proficiency with the language required for the intense social interactions they engage in with peers, for manipulating literate forms, and for engaging in critical thinking (Paul, 2001).

**Semantics.** Adolescents continue to add to their vocabularies. In addition, they further refine the meanings and usages of the words they already know, such as discovering how words are related through language family (i.e., Greek and Latin), derivation (e.g., poor, impoverish), meaning (e.g., antonyms, synonyms), and sound (e.g., homonyms). By the time most students reach late adolescence, they have learned how to define words using more sophisticated structures than they used in earlier stages of development. For instance, where previously they might define a word using simple, one-word descriptions, during adolescence they become able to provide definitions such as, "An edict is a proclamation (superordinate term) carrying the force of law (description of characteristics)."

**Syntax.** Most syntactic growth during adolescence occurs across sentences rather than within sentences. Adolescents begin using more coordinate and coordinate clauses, as well as sentence structures more typical of literate (i.e., printed) language.

**Pragmatics and Discourse.** Most adolescents can be skilled conversationalists, especially with their peers. They understand that different listeners require different amounts and types of background information, and they know how to efficiently and effectively repair conversational breakdowns and how to request and provide clarification when needed. They maintain topics appropriately; take, maintain, and yield turns; and interrupt according to the politeness rules of their culture. In short, they have generally mastered conversational discourse.

By adolescence, most students will also have mastered the art of negotiating classroom discourse, and they will have learned how to apply their knowledge to different teachers and teaching styles. They will have written numerous narrative pieces, giving them additional experience and practice with narrative discourse, and they will have been exposed to a wide variety of types of expository discourse. Nonetheless, during adolescence, they continue to develop their skill within discourse types, and they begin developing proficiency with an additional expository discourse type: argumentative/persuasive.

Argumentative/persuasive discourse differs from the other expository discourse types in that it puts forward a fact or proposition as a thesis, then uses a set of logically ordered statements to support the thesis. Although they use the same format, they differ slightly in their basis. Argumentative discourse expresses a statement or proposition, along with a set of supports for the proposition. A typical example of argumentative discourse is an essay in which the speaker or writer proposes an idea (the proposition), provides several supporting supports for the idea (the argument), and gives a summary iteration of why the arguments support the proposition.

Persuasive discourse offers a statement of belief, along with reasons why the belief is "true." Advertisements commonly use persuasive discourse in an attempt to convince the listener or reader of the validity, superiority, or truthfulness of a particular product. Both argumentative and persuasive discourse can express disagreement with facts, beliefs, or interpretation of events.

**Figurative Language.** Most adolescents develop considerable skill with figurative language, particularly in spoken conversation. The most obvious example is slang, which changes generationally and is influenced by movies, television, music groups, music videos, and Internet chat rooms. Because conversation with peers is vitally important during adolescence, a proficiency with slang is a basic prerequisite for belonging to a peer group.

In addition, through reading, most adolescent students have considerable experience with reading print containing metaphors, similes, allegories, irony, and

## DIVERSITY IN THE CLASSROOM *Tips*

**Kristine Noel, M.S., CCC-SLP,** is a speech-language pathologist and a doctoral candidate at the University of New Mexico. She has 20 years of experience with high-risk children and youth, and 11 years experience in juvenile justice.

Deficits in oral language abilities in juvenile delinquents have been documented for over 30 years. Nonetheless, juvenile delinquent adolescents are a group of school-age youth with language deficits that are often overlooked and, as a result, are underserved. These students have trouble attending to, understanding, and remembering what they hear. Their spoken language may be limited, excessive, vague, or just confusing to their listeners. They may have trouble using language as a tool to reason, plan, and make decisions. This often contributes to their failure to experience success in school and the world beyond school.

Difficulties in oral language may limit a young person's ability to negotiate our complex legal system, access and move forward in academic and behavioral health programs, and ultimately successfully transition back to families and communities to achieve positive adult outcomes. Delinquent adolescents have more difficulty than their peers in literacy acquisition. They, therefore, have escalating problems with academic achievement, as the demands for literacy increase with advancing grade levels.

Although it is not surprising to see language and learning deficits in this population, it is surprising that language assessment and intervention are not always seen as a critical component in the prevention and treatment of delinquency. Delinquent youth often present with multiple and complex issues, making diagnosis and intervention planning challenging. Many students come from bicultural and/or bilingual backgrounds. Other students have significant mental health challenges or substance abuse issues. Others have not consistently attended school for several years. The behavior and learning problems presented by many delinquent youth may be so significant that we treat those areas intensively, while the underlying communication problems may go unrecognized and, therefore, untreated.

What do classroom teachers look for to help them identify these young people, not only as they exist in our facilities, but also as they exist in all of our high schools? These students may:

- not describe events in a logical, sequential manner
- not turn in assignments as they cannot understand classroom conversations and textbooks, or formulate written work
- show major, chronic behavior issues
- not be able to actively problem solve with an adult

Language intervention can help these students learn knowledge, skills, and strategies that will increase their success. Although language intervention is important for delinquent and adjudicated youth, prevention is even more important. General and special education teachers can support early intervention and prevention programs by recognizing that challenges in communication may be a source of great frustration and a key component underlying these students' failure and anger. Working with multidisciplinary teams to facilitate early referral of students showing behavioral, language, and/or academic difficulties is paramount to adequately addressing the needs of these young people.

satire. If they attend schools in which writing is stressed, they may also have experienced opportunities to practice using these figurative forms in their own writing.

By adolescence, much of the schooling process rests solidly on metalinguistic abilities to analyze, manipulate, and synthesize both oral and printed language. Writing is particularly demanding because it demands of us focusing or reflecting on and manipulating language forms, content, and usages. Students with more experience in writing tend to develop more skill with the metalinguistic skills necessary to succeed in the secondary curriculum, particularly note taking, paraphrasing, summarizing, recognizing and using figurative language forms, and understanding and using diverse literate styles in their own oral and written language.

Adolescents typically develop strong metapragmatic abilities through their interactions with different discourse types. In fact, using different types of discourse is itself a metapragmatic function. Deciding ahead of time what to say (either orally or in print), how to say it, the discourse type to use, and how to use humor appropriately in discourse all demand metapragmatic proficiency.

Reflecting on one's understanding in the classroom and organizing oneself to most effectively and efficiently learn what is expected both depend on metacognitive ability. Adolescents are expected to independently devise learning strategies that work best for them and to modify them when they encounter new, more demanding learning tasks. To do so, they use their metacognitive skills, first, to analyze what they know, what they're expected to learn and how, and how best to accomplish that learning, and, second, to apply the results of their analysis.

The secondary curriculum carries special metapragmatic and metacognitive demands because students

**TEACHER *Tips*** — **Secondary Level**

Knowing the differences between oral and literate language is crucial for students to be able to interact with and compose literature and nonnarrative text. First, prepare a handout for your students using the characteristics shown in the table below. Have your students use the handout as a checklist each time they prepare an oral presentation or written expository text. Most of their checks should be in the Literate Language rows. When they are writing fiction, their checks may fall equally in both rows.

**Differences Between Oral and Literate Language**

| | Function | Topic | Structure |
|---|---|---|---|
| Oral Language Style | To regulate social interactions<br>To request objects and actions<br>To communicate face-to-face with few people<br>To share information about concrete events and objects | Everyday objects and events<br>Here and now<br>Topics flow according to participants' desires<br>Meaning is contextually grounded. | High-frequency words<br>Repetitive, predictable, redundant syntax and content<br>Pronouns, slang, jargon, shared meaings<br>Cohesion based on intonation patterns |
| Literate Language Style | To regulate thinking<br>To reflect and request information<br>To communicate over time and distance<br>To transmit information to large numbers of people<br>To build abstract theories and discuss abstract ideas | Abstract or unfamiliar objects and events<br>There and then<br>Discourse is centered around a preselected topic<br>Meaning arises from inferences and from textually defined information | Low-frequency words<br>Concise syntax and content<br>Specific, abstract vocabulary<br>Cohesion based on vocabulary and linguistic devices |

*Source:* Adapted from Westby, C. (1991). "Learning to Talk—Talking to Learn: Oral-Literate Language Differences". In C.S. Simon (Ed.). *Communication Skills and Classroom Success: Assessment and Therapy Methodologies for Language and Learing-Disabled Children* (p. 337). Eau Claire, WI: Thinking Publications. Reprinted with permission.

must deal with multiple teaching styles and communication rules, decontextualized language forms, increasing amounts of work requiring increased length of time focusing (including increased demand for self-organizational skills), independent work, and use of logical and critical thinking (Paul, 2001).

**Reflective Question 5.4:** ***What are the key implications of the specific language stage at which the students you are teaching, or planning to teach, function?***

## LANGUAGE DISORDERS

The National Information Center for Children and Youth with Disabilities (2003) defines a language disorder as "an impairment in the ability to understand and/or use words in context, both verbally and nonverbally." Shames, Wiig, and Secord (1998) describe a specific language impairment (SLI) as a significant deficit in linguistic functioning that does not appear to be accompanied by deficits in hearing, intelligence, or motor functioning. The American Speech-Language-Hearing Association (2003d) indicates that SLI can occur after a period of normal development through infection, tumor, stroke, epilepsy, or brain injury, and commonly causes poor academic performance and frustration. Frequently, the cause for a language disorder is unknown.

Approximately 8% to 12% of preschool children have some form of language impairment, approximately 5% of preschool children have SLI, and approximately 8% of kindergarten boys and 6% of kindergarten girls have SLI (American Speech-Language-Hearing Association, 2003d).

### Language Difference Versus Language Disorder

Language disorders should not be confused with language differences arising from differences in dialect, culture, ethnicity, or influence of a foreign language. Children from culturally and linguistically diverse (CLD) backgrounds can exhibit characteristics that may be confused with a language disorder. However, the learning processes of these children differ significantly from children with learning disorders. Although children with language disorders often have difficulty acquiring new language content, forms, or usages, children from CLD backgrounds usually show no such difficulty when given appropriate instruction, a topic we address later in this chapter.

Nonetheless, determining whether a child has a language disorder or is simply a "late bloomer" can be a difficult process, particularly in young children. The American Speech-Language-Hearing Association (2003e) reports four factors differentiating slow language development from a language disorder:

1. Late bloomers tend to have age-appropriate receptive language abilities.
2. Children using a large number of gestures associated with different communicative intentions are more likely to catch up to their peers in language development.
3. Older children who are still behind their peers are more likely to develop language disorders, especially if they exhibit slow growth when their age peers are in a period of rapid progress.
4. Children showing little progress in language development are more likely to develop language disorders than slow talkers who continue to make noticeable changes in their language.

Children who are non-native English speakers can also exhibit characteristics that can be mistaken for language disorders. Roseberry-McKibbon and Brice (2003) described a common situation for children who are learning English at the same time they are learning academically. These children can struggle academically, go through periods in which they appear silent, and intermingle words and phrases from both languages.

According to Roseberry-McKibbon and Brice (2003), children learning a second language require 2 years to acquire the basic interpersonal language abilities involved in context-sensitive conversational speech. In addition, it takes the same children 5 to 7 years to acquire the decontextualized language of academics at a level commensurate with their peers.

Compared with their peers during these years, the language abilities of these children can be mistakenly thought to represent language disorders. Peña and Bedore (2006, in press) argue that most CLD children are sequential bilinguals, learning first the language spoken at home and beginning to learn a second language when they begin formal schooling. Until recently, little was known about the language development of sequentially bilingual children, how to properly assess their language abilities, and how to design appropriate instruction and/or intervention. However, Peña et al. (2006, in press), using information about language development in bilingual children with and without language impairments, describe methods that distinguish between language difference and language disorders and intervention/instructional techniques that work well with CLD children. These methods and techniques are described in later sections on assessing language and teaching spoken language.

**Language-Based Learning Disabilities.** According to Polloway et al. (2004), language-based learning disabilities (LLD) are the most common type of learning disability, primarily because most learning disabilities involve deficits in reading, writing, or spelling, which are based on oral language abilities. Language-based learning disabilities are believed to include the child's phonological, semantic, syntactic, pragmatic, and discourse systems.

School-age children diagnosed with LLD often have a history of delayed speech and language development during preschool. The American Speech-Language-Hearing Association (2003f) describes the risk factors associated with LLD, as well as some of the problems typically exhibited by children with LLD:

- learning the alphabet
- retrieving specific words
- learning new vocabulary
- understanding questions and directions
- recalling spoken or printed letters and numbers
- understanding and recalling stories or classroom lectures
- discriminating left from right
- learning sound-letter correspondences
- mixing up letters in words when writing
- spelling
- memorizing multiplication tables
- telling time

Reflective Question 5.5: ***Language difficulties represent the most common secondary disability of students who have problems in other areas as well. How do language challenges influence school learning and place children at risk for academic difficulties?***

## ASSESSING LANGUAGE

How children's language abilities are assessed depends primarily on the purpose and goals for instruction, and, if necessary, intervention. With students of any age, the overall purpose of assessing language skills is to learn what the student's needs are in order to design appropriate teaching strategies, classroom modifications, and accommodations to help the student succeed. For young children, the primary goal of language assessment is to determine their level of development to assist them in moving to the next developmental stage.

Once children reach school, however, the goal of language assessment shifts to determining whether their language abilities are developed well enough for them to make the shift from orality to literacy in order to succeed in the academic environment. For elementary students, language assessment focuses on discovering how (and how well) they use language to:

- participate successfully in the classroom
- talk about language and its parts
- understand and tell stories
- learn to read, write, and spell
- comprehend the various types of expository text

For adolescents, language assessment is aimed at discovering:

- how adept they are with the social discourse used by their peers
- how they interact with literate language forms, including the various discourse genres characteristic of the secondary grades
- the extent of their metalinguistic, metacognitive, and metapragmatic abilities and how successful they are in exercising them appropriately for learning

### Culturally and Linguistically Diverse Backgrounds

As discussed above, students from culturally and linguistically diverse backgrounds sometimes exhibit language characteristics similar to those shown by students with language disorders. Sometimes these characteristics represent an actual language disorder or delay, and assessment is recommended. Owens (2004) developed recommendations for assessing the language of students learning English as a second language based on their degree of proficiency with English, shown in Figure 5-3.

Damico, Smith, and Augustine (1996) devised an assessment strategy specifically for students from

**FIGURE 5–3** Guidelines for assessment of students from culturally and linguistically diverse backgrounds

| *Bilingual English Proficient* | *Limited English Proficient (LEP)* | *Limited in English and Native Langauge* |
|---|---|---|
| • proficient in both their native language and in English<br>• conduct assessment in English | • proficient in their native language but not in English<br>• conduct assessment in student's native language (mandated by federal law) | • experiences difficulties in both their native language and in English<br>• conduct assessment in whichever language is dominant and most appropriate for assessment, intervention, and instruction |

*Source:* Adapted from Owens, Robert R.E. Jr. *Language Disorders: A Functional Approach to Assessment and Intervention* (4th ed.). Published by Allyn & Bacon, Boston, MA. Copyright © 2004 by Pearson Education. Adapted by Permission of the publisher.

culturally and linguistically diverse backgrounds. Their strategy entails five aspects:

1. Build a collaborative team, including the student and her or his parent(s), to include members who bring:
   - knowledge of language and assessment instruments and procedures (speech-language pathologist)
   - knowledge of the student's culture (cultural informant)
   - knowledge of the academic curriculum (teacher)
   - knowledge of the student's strengths and needs in the classroom (teacher)
   - knowledge of bilingualism (bilingual teacher)
2. Utilize the teacher assistance team before referring the student for special education testing to analyze:
   - design modifications for the student that provide time and learning supports to the student
   - how the student is assimilating after the modifications have been in place for a period of time

   Students with typical language/learning will assimilate more quickly and easily than students with language disorders.
3. Design a diversity framework into the assessment process:
   - determine which difficulties the student exhibits are attributable to the CLD background
     - use functional assessment procedures to describe the student's communication and academic performance in various contexts
     - if the evaluator observes difficulties, then determine whether features of classroom instruction or the student's cognitive and linguistic abilities account for the difficulties
   - use the collected data to decide whether the student's difficulties are most likely attributable to cultural and linguistic differences, disorders, or a combination
4. Focus on functionality:
   - observe the student within the context of how successful the student is as a communicator in a variety of school contexts, focusing on:
     - how effectively the student communicates meaning
     - how fluently the student communicates meaning
     - how appropriately the student communicates meaning
   - use a rating scale, protocol, or checklist to guide observation
   - use structured probes such as question-answer, role-playing, interactive computer probes
   - use behavioral sampling such as a video or audio recording of the student performing a required task
5. Use all collected data to determine student's communicative and linguistic competence.

Peña and Bedore (2006, in press) report that identifying language disorders in bilingual children and designing appropriate language instruction is challenging for two reasons. First, the tests available for assessing children's language do not accurately discriminate between bilingual children with and without a language impairment. Second, although there are many models for planning language intervention and instruction for CLD children, there is little evidence-based research that describes what actually works. Further, determining the most effective language of instruction for bilingual children is fraught with political and cultural differences of viewpoint and power. We describe some evidence-based strategies and instruments in assessing CLD students on page 141.

## Types of Assessment

Two types of assessment are typically used to evaluate students' language: standardized and nonstandardized. Standardized assessments compare students' language development with other children of the same chronological age.

Standardized tests are designed to be administered and scored the same way each time, usually in a quiet room with no one present except the student and the examiner. As a result, standardized tests do not reflect a student's ability to use language in contexts other than the testing situation. In addition, standardized tests tend to underestimate the language abilities of children for whom English is not their native language. Consequently, assessment also includes the use of nonstandardized approaches. Table 5–3 shows some of the more commonly used standardized instruments used for assessing language.

Nonstandardized assessment procedures include criterion-referenced procedures, curriculum-based language assessment, developmental scales, interviews, questionnaires, observational checklists, language sampling, and dynamic assessment.

Criterion-referenced procedures assess the child's ability to attain a certain level of performance. They are used (1) to establish what the child knows about a specific language function, form, or content, and (2) to design instructional targets based on the results. Criterion-referenced approaches are usually used with school-age children and adolescents.

Curriculum-based language assessment evaluates the student's use of language in attempting to learn the curriculum (Nelson, 1998). Nelson recommends using three types of data collection as part of curriculum-based language assessment, as shown in Table 5–4.

Developmental scales are used more often with children in the emerging and developing stages of language development. These scales provide developmental milestones against which the child is compared to determine where along the scale a particular aspect of language development lies. Interviews, observational checklists, and questionnaires are used to collect information about a child's use of language in specific situations. Evaluators use interviews, observational checklists, and/or questionnaires with parents, caregivers, teachers, and students of all ages.

Language sampling is a technique aimed at discovering detailed information about the child's use of the structural aspects of language, specifically, syntactic and morphological forms. Examples include the number of morphemes per sentence, number and type of embedded clauses, number and type of conjunction, complex sentence usage, proportion of simple to complex sentences, type of complex sentences used, and number of disruptions.

**TABLE 5–3** Commonly used standardized language tests

| |
|---|
| *Clinical Evaluation of Language Fundamentals—Preschool* (Sernel, Wiig, & Secord, 1998) |
| *Detroit Test of Learning Aptitude—Primary 4* (Hammill & Bryant, 1999) |
| *Expressive One-Word Picture Vocabulary Test—Revised* (Gardner, 2000) |
| *Illinois Test of Psycholinguistic Abilities* (Hammill, Mather, & Roberts, 2001) |
| *Peabody Picture Vocabulary Test—3rd Ed.* (Dunn & Dunn, 1997) |
| *Sequenced inventory of Communication Development—Revised* (Hedrick, Prather, & Tobin, 1995) |
| *Test for Adolescent Language—3* (Hammill, Brown, Larsen, & Wiederholt, 1994) |
| *Test for Auditory Comprehension of Language—3rd Ed.* (Carrow-Woolfolk, 1999) |
| *Test of Early Language Development—3rd Ed.* (Hresko, Reid, & Hammill, 1999) |
| *Test of Early Written Language—2* (Hresko, 1996) |
| *Test of Language Competence—Expanded* (Secord & Wiig, 1993) |
| *Test of Language Development—Intermediate* (Newcomer & Hammill, 1997a) |
| *Test of Language Development—3: Primary* (Newcomer & Hammill, 1997b) |
| *Test of Phonological Awareness Skills* (Newcomer & Barenbaum, 2003) |
| *Test of Pragmatic Language* (Phelps-Terasaki & Phelps-Gunn, 1992) |
| *Test of Problem Solving—Revised-Elementary* (Bowers, Barrett, Huisingh, Orman, & LoGiudice, 1994) |

**TABLE 5–4** Types of data used in curriculum-based language assessment

| *Artifact[1] Analysis* | *Onlooker Observation* | *Participant Observation* |
|---|---|---|
| • lecture notes<br>• written assignments<br>• class notes<br>• homework<br>• portfolios<br>• exams | • classroom observation of attention, listening, communicative expression, language usage<br>• videotapes of student in classroom | • observer utilizes dynamic assessment as the student attempts a curricular task (e.g., reading a passage and answering questions)<br>• observer addresses four questions:<br>  • Which external contextual demands influence how the student processes the information?<br>  • What linguistic abilities does the student bring to the task?<br>  • What new linguistic abilities or strategies would help the student improve in this situation?<br>  • What contextual modifications would help the student achieve success? |

[1]Artifacts are produced created by students as they engage in regular curricular activities.

*Source:* Adapted from *Childhood Language Disorders: Infancy Through Adolescence* (2nd ed.), by N.W. Nelson, 1998. Boston: Allyn & Bacon. Published by Allyn & Bacon, Boston, MA. Copyright © 1998 by Pearson Educaion. Adapted by permission of the publisher.

Dynamic assessment is a method used to observe how a child changes a language behavior when given structured help. First, the evaluator determines what the child knows about a specific language behavior (e.g., including setting in a story). Then, in a series of sessions called mediated teaching, the evaluator provides information and supports that the child uses to begin incorporating the language behavior. Miller et al.'s (2001) description of using dynamic assessment with children's narrative is an example of how dynamic assessment is used to evaluate a particular aspect of language.

## Assessing CLD Students

Peña et al. (2008) advocate using a greater number of informal measures than standardized tests in assessing the needs of CLD children, primarily because most standardized instruments have been designed for and normed using children for whom English is the primary language. Figure 5–4 shows some of the procedures these authors use in assessment that leads to designing appropriate instruction for CLD children.

Figure 5–5 describes the process used to assess the language abilities of an 8-year-old African American girl in the second grade. The process uses mediated instruction as a means for discovering the student's responsivity to learning how to include character descriptions in stories.

The information gleaned during the mediated lesson(s) will be used to guide planning for instruction aimed at teaching the student to include all the necessary components of a "good" story. Figure 5–6 shows the teacher's notes regarding what she did to support the student, as well as the student's responses.

## Assessing Students Who Might Need Augmentative or Alternative Communication

Students with certain disabilities often need to use augmentative or alternate communication (AAC) systems to communicate. Augmentative and alternate communication refers to methods people use to communicate when speech may be difficult. The most common of these methods involve facial expressions, gestures, and writing. According to the American Speech-Language-Hearing Association, special augmentative techniques designed specifically for an individual communicator include:

- specialized gestures
- sign language
- Morse code
- communication aids (e.g., charts, bracelets, and language boards)
- electronic devices (e.g., computers)

Communication aids and electronic devices can include representations of objects, events, and people using pictures, photographs, drawings, letters, words, sentences, special symbols, or any combination. Assessment

**FIGURE 5–4** Questions to guide assessment of CLD children

1. Which language or dialect should be used to assess and ultimately intervene with the child?
   - Ask parents and teachers to record hour-by-hour the language(s) the child uses and hears.
   - Which language(s) are used by the child's primary conversational partners?
   - What is the percentage of time the child is exposed to each language?
   - What is the percentage of time each language is used at home?
   - What is the percentage of time each language is used at school?
   - Based on this information, which language is the child's stronger language?
2. How can the child's language performance needs at home and in the classroom be determined?
   - Do you and others understand the child when she or he speaks English and *second language* (e.g., Spanish)?
   - Is the child able to follow directions at home in her or his first language (e.g., Spanish)?
   - Where do you see the child communicate and perform the best?
   - Which contexts are the hardest for the child? What language is used in these contexts?
   - What strategies help the child succeed in communicating?
   - What strategies have you tried that do not result in the child's communication improving?
   - Which language suffers the most communicative breakdowns?
3. Is it appropriate to translate tests from English to *second language* (e.g., Spanish) to assess the child?
   - Translating tests can render individual items more or less difficult in the second language, thus invalidating the normative process.
   - What is considered a language impairment in one language may not be in the second, so the test may not target appropriate language targets.
4. If the child speaks a dialect:
   - Is the child familiar with taking tests? If not, standardized testing may result in artificially lowered scores.
   - Use a standardized test that has been designed specifically for the child's dialect.[1]
   - Use informal assessments such as dynamic assessment or provide contextual support during the testing.
5. What other measures can be used to help determine whether the child has a language impairment?
   - Nonword repetition tasks[2] differentiate between children with and without language impairment.
   - Language sampling[3] can be done in conversation, dialogue, and answering questions in varying contexts, including on the playground, in the lunchroom, and before/after school.
   - Analysis of the child's narrative abilities.[4]
   - Analysis of the child's ability to learn new skills when instruction includes dynamic assessment.[5]

**[1]Tests designed for children who speak dialects or are Spanish-English bilingual**

*Diagnostic Evaluation of Language Variance*—designed for children who speak African American English (Seymour, Roper, & de Villiers, 2003)

*Expressive One Word Picture Vocabulary Test—2000* (Brownell, 2000)

*Preschool Language Scales—4 Spanish* (Zimmerman, Steiner, & Pond, 2002)

*Test of Narrative Language*—bias analysis shows limited item bias for targeted groups of English-speaking children (Gillam & Pearson, 2004)

**[2]Nonword repetition tasks**

*Diagnostic Evaluation of Language Variance* (Seymour, Roper, & de Villiers, 2003)

*Comprehensive Test of Phonological Processing (CTOPP)* (Wagner, Torgeson, & Rashotte, 1999)

**[3]Language sampling**

Language sampling is the process of collecting a representative set of the child's utterances in a variety of contexts. Usually performed by a speech-language clinician, the sample is transcribed and analyzed to determine such things as the mean length and complexity of each utterance, the level of vocabulary, the syntactic and semantic characteristics, and the pragmatic complexity and success of the utterances. Analysis of the language of children with language impairments shows shorter and less complex utterances, fewer vocabulary words, simpler syntactic structures, and less pragmatic complexity and success.

**[4]Analysis of the child's narrative abilities**

Narratives can be analyzed by examining the ability to take the listener's perspective into account, the complexity of the episode structure of the story, the number and complexity of the elements of a story, and the sophistication of the language used. The stories of children with language impairments are less developed and shorter, use less sophisticated language and truncated episode structure, and usually fail to take the listener's perspective into account.

**[5]Dynamic assessment**

Dynamic assessment is the process of obtaining a baseline measure (formal or informal) of the behavior of interest, teaching the student the behavior—or one aspect of it—through one or two sessions of mediated teaching, followed by a retesting phase used to determine how much change the child makes as a result of the mediated teaching (Miller, Gillam, & Peña, 2001). Children with language impairments typically have significant problems understanding and generalizing the strategies they learned during the mediated teaching sessions and are less responsive during the teaching sessions (i.e., they exhibit problems attending to the task, lack persistence and motivation, have difficulties with solving problems, and are relatively inflexible) (Peña, Summers, & Resendiz, 2006, in press).

**FIGURE 5–5** Language assessment for an 8-year-old speaking AAE

Amarisa, an 8-year-old African American girl, is in the second grade. Her teacher, Ms. Rodriguez, indicated in her weekly team meeting that she has been concerned about Amarisa's ability to understand classroom instructions and to answer questions in the classroom. She also indicated that Amarisa uses African American English dialect, and she wanted to make certain her language development was progressing appropriately. The speech-language clinician recommended the following assessment procedures:

1. Administer the Comprehension Subtest of the *Stanford-Binet Test of Intelligence Scale* (Thorndike, Hagen, & Sattler, 1986), which has been shown to be unbiased toward CLD children.
2. Observe Amarisa in the classroom and interview a family member to determine how well she communicates in the classroom and outside it.
3. Analyze a language sample to determine whether Amarisa produces complex sentences and uses various conjunctions, articles, and modal auxiliaries.
4. Administer the *Diagnostic Evaluation of Language Variation Screening Test* (a nonword repetition task) because it has been shown to be nonbiased toward CLD students.

**Results of the Assessment Procedures**

| *Test/Procedure* | *Score/Result* | *Significance* |
|---|---|---|
| Comprehension Subtest of the *Stanford-Binet Test of Intelligence Scale* | standard score = 59 | mean score = 50 |
| *Diagnostic Evaluation of Language Variation Screening Test* | *Language Variation Status:* Strong variation from mainstream American English<br>Diagnostic Risk Status: Developing language normally | *No further testing* |
| Observations in the classroom and outside | Amarsia converses easily with family and friends and interacts easily with peers outside the classroom. Her mother reports that Amarisa is shy about talking in the classroom. | |
| Language Sample | Amarisa's use of AAE indicates that her language development is typical for children her age speaking AAE. | |

Given these results, the team designed a mediated instruction lesson for Ms. Rodriguez to use with Amarisa to see how she responded to this type of instruction. Because Amarisa enjoys books and stories, the lesson centers on including appropriate episode structures in a story.

**Mediated Instruction Lesson—Providing Character Information in a Story**
**Point of the Lesson:** To teach Amarisa that stories should contain information about the characters.
**Teaching Sequence: 1.** Show Amarisa *The Ugly Duckling* and have her retell the story. Remind her before she begins to describe the characters. **2.** Tell Amarisa what you're going to do in this lesson and why it is important. **3.** Using the story, help Amarisa describe the main characters. **4.** If Amarisa describes the characters without much help from you, help her extend the concept to another story. If she has difficulty, help her evaluate why it is important to describe the characters in a story. **5.** Help Amarisa plan how to describe the characters when she tells another story. **6.** Help Amarisa respond to the questions throughout. Use prompts, cues, and models as needed to support her. **7.** Help Amarisa figure out how she can remember to describe the characters next time she tells a story.

| *Strategy* | *Examples of Instruction* | *What You Did to Support Amarisa* | *How Amarisa Responded* |
|---|---|---|---|
| What you're going to do | "Today we're going to talk about telling stories. When we tell stories, we usually describe the characters." | | |
| Why that's important | "Telling about the characters is important because it tells your listener who they are and what they are like." | | |
| Help Amarisa describe the main characters | "Let's look at *The Ugly Duckling* again. Let's see if we can describe the mother duck, the duckling, and the old woman." Help Amarisa describe who they are and what they look like. "What does the mother duck look like?" "What does the baby duck look like?" "What can you tell me about the baby duck?" Help Amarisa use descriptive words and phrases. | | |
| Help Amarisa extend the concept to another story | "How would you change the story if there were a dog and a cat instead of ducks and a swan? What would you say about the dog and the cat?" "Would the dog and cat do the same things as the duck and the swan?" "Have you ever read or heard another story that described things about the characters?" If not, present a familiar story and help her discover the character information. | | |
| Help Amarisa plan | "The next time you tell a story, what are you going to remember to put in it?" | | |
| Help Amarisa generalize her learning | "We've been talking about describing the characters in your stories. How are you going to remember to describe characters when you make up your own stories?" | | |

**FIGURE 5–6** Results of a mediated lesson on including character description in a story

**Mediated Instruction Lesson—Providing Character Information in a Story**

**Point of the Lesson:** To teach Amarisa that stories should contain information about the characters.
**Teaching Sequence: 1.** Show Amarisa *The Ugly Duckling* and have her retell the story. Remind her before she begins to describe the characters. **2.** Tell Amarisa what you're going to do in this lesson and why it is important. **3.** Using the story, help Amarisa describe the main characters. **4.** If Amarisa describes the characters without much help from you, help her extend the concept to another story. If she has difficulty, help her evaluate why it is important to describe the characters in a story. **5.** Help Amarisa plan how to describe the characters when she tells another story. **6.** Help Amarisa respond to the questions throughout. Use prompts, cues, and models as needed to support her. **7.** Help Amarisa figure out how she can remember to describe the characters next time she tells a story.

| *Strategy Responded* | *Examples of Instruction* | *What You Did to Support Amarisa* | *How Amarisa Responded* |
|---|---|---|---|
| What you're going to do | "Today we're going to talk about telling stories. When we tell stories, we usually describe the characters." | Pointed to each character as I talked. | Looked carefully at the characters. |
| Why that's important | "Telling about the characters is important because it tells your listener who they are and what they are like." | Asked Amarisa how she would describe who she is and what she's like. | "I'm tall and my eyes are brown. I'm like a ice cream cone." |
| Help Amarisa describe the main characters | "Let's look at *The Ugly Duckling* again. Let's see if we can describe the mother duck, the duckling, and the old woman." Help Amarisa describe who they are and what they look like. "What does the mother duck look like?" "What does the baby duck look like?" "What can you tell me about the baby duck?" Help Amarisa use descriptive words and phrases. | Asked Amarisa what made the mother duck look different from the others. Ditto-re the baby. | "She pretty! She green and shiny." . . . "The baby bigger than the others, and kinda brown. He feel bad because the others tease him." |
| Help Amarisa extend the concept to another story | "How would you change the story if there were a dog and a cat instead of ducks and a swan? What would you say about the dog and the cat?" "Would the dog and cat do the same things as the duck and the swan?" "Have you ever read or heard another story that described things about the characters?" If not, present a familiar story and help her discover the character information. | | "In the Ugly Duckling, they in a lake." |
| Help Amarisa plan | "The next time you tell a story, what are you going to remember to put in it?" | | "What the characters look like and feel." |
| Help Amarisa generalize her learning | "We've been talking azbout describing the characters in your stories. How are you going to remember to describe characters when you make up your own stories?" | | "How the baby duck look when he see his self in the water! He beautiful!" |

for students using AAC systems or devices should focus on whether the student would benefit from a low-tech device such as pointing with a headstick or laser light, or from a high-tech device such as a computer that produces synthesized speech. In addition, assessment should include attention to the suitability of the symbol system used (iconic symbols are easier for younger children, whereas more abstract symbols may work for older students); whether the system or device is easy for the child, family, and teachers to use; the social effectiveness of the system; and its suitability for promoting language development (Polloway et al., 2004).

Polloway et al. (2004) argue that adolescents who enter secondary school using an AAC system or device will benefit from an assessment addressing several issues. Specifically, they recommend that the assessment should ask whether the current AAC system/device:

- is adequate for the communication demands of the secondary curriculum
- is equal to the student's cognitive abilities
- can expand to meet the student's developing communication and cognitive growth
- is appropriate for nonacademic communication needs
- can be maintained independently by the student in vocational, recreational, domestic, and academic settings (If not, how will maintenance be provided?)

## TEACHING SPOKEN LANGUAGE

One of the most effective ways to teach spoken language is within the context of academic learning standards. For students who qualify for special education services, IDEA 1997 mandates that their IEPs be linked with their state learning standards (Miller & Hoffman, 2002) so that their IEP goals, objectives, and benchmarks reflect the learning standards deemed most appropriate for them by the school-based team. The linking process involves (1) identifying the state standards applicable to the student's age or grade level and (2) generating annual goals and benchmarks geared to help the student achieve the applicable standard or standards.

Every state publishes a list of standards using a variety of categories and subcategories to specify what its citizens have agreed are the critical aspects of learning they want their children to achieve as a consequence of public schooling. Though this will vary, the academic standards most likely to be used on IEPs for students with language disorders include:

- communication
- listening
- receptive language
- expressive language
- speaking
- reading
- writing
- mathematics
- science
- spelling
- literacy

Figure 5-7 shows the specific details of one of the English Language Arts performance descriptors from Illinois ("Students who meet the standard can apply word analysis and vocabulary skills to comprehend selections") for grades 1 and 2. A second-grade student would be expected to meet the standards in all three columns, presumably by making progress from Stage A to Stage B to Stage C throughout the school year.

For a first-grade student with a language disorder, the team might decide that the standards in Stage A represent the most appropriate standards for this particular student. The student's annual goal might be the same as the performance descriptor (e.g., "The student will apply word analysis and vocabulary skills to comprehend selections"). However, instead of expecting the student to meet all the standards listed in Stage A, the team might conclude that, for this student, a more realistic objective would be for him to meet four of the eight standards by the end of the school year. The IEP would specify these components (Miller & Hoffman, 2002):

- present levels of education performance, the student's learning strengths, and how the student's disability affects his progress in the general curriculum
- which people and/or programs are going to be involved in assisting this student meet these objectives (including personnel, frequency, location, and duration of services)
- goals and objectives (the four aspects of Stage A), including how they will be evaluated and by what objective criteria, and expected date of accomplishment

For those students who do not qualify for special education services, instruction linked to state learning standards can be designed using a Section 504 plan, which provides a way to specify the accommodations and modifications necessary to ensure the student's success (Miller & Newbill, 1998). (See Chapter 1 for a discussion of Section 504.)

Using the same process described above for linking an IEP to learning standards, the team can link the 504 plan to standards and specify a learning plan for the student. An example is a fourth-grade student whose psychoeducational report shows slow processing speed and some language delays, neither of which interferes enough with academic functioning to be considered a disability under IDEA. The school-based

**FIGURE 5–7** English language arts standard and corresponding stages

**1A** Students who meet the standard can apply word analysis and vocabulary skills to comprehend selections.

| Stage A | Stage B | Stage C |
|---|---|---|
| 1. Use phonics to decode simple words in age-appropriate material. | 1. Use phonics to decode new words in age-appropriate material. | 1. Use phonics to decode new words in age-appropriate material. |
| 2. Demonstrate phonological awareness (e.g., counting syllables, hearing rhyme, alliteration, onset and rime) of sounds in words. | 2. Use phonemic awareness knowledge (e.g., isolate, blend, substitute, manipulate letter sounds) to identify phonetically regular one- and two-syllable words. | 2. Use word analysis (root words, inflections, affixes) to identify words. |
| 3. Demonstrate phonemic awareness by blending or segmenting phonemes in a one-syllable word. | 3. Recognize 300 high-frequency sight words. | 3. Discuss the meanings of new words encountered in independent and group activities. |
| 4. Recognize 100 high-frequency sight words including environmental print (but not including words the child can read using phonics). | 4. Use a variety of decoding strategies (e.g., phonics, word patterns, structural analysis, context clues) to recognize new words when reading age-appropriate material. | 4. Use synonyms and antonyms to define words. |
| 5. Use appropriate strategies of decoding (e.g., illustrations, phonics, word patterns, context clues) to recognize unknown words when reading material. | 5. Use letter-sound knowledge and sight vocabulary to read orally and silently/whisper read age-appropriate material. | 5. Use a variety of decoding strategies (e.g., phonics, word patterns, structural analysis, context clues) to recognize new words when reading age-appropriate material. |
| 6. Use knowledge of letter-sound correspondences and high-frequency words to orally read age-appropriate material. | 6. Self-monitor reading and use decoding strategies to self-correct miscues. | 6. Self-monitor reading and use decoding strategies to self-correct miscues. |
| 7. Begin to recognize miscues that interfere with meaning and use self-correcting strategies. | 7. Use a variety of resources (e.g., context, previous experiences, dictionaries, glossaries, computer resources, ask others) to determine and clarify meanings of unfamiliar words. | 7. Use context and previous experience to determine the meanings of unfamiliar words in text. |
| 8. Use a variety of resources (e.g., age-appropriate dictionaries, pictures, illustrations, photos, ask others context, previous experience) to determine and clarify meanings of unfamiliar words. | | 8. Use a variety of resources (e.g., dictionaries, thesauruses, indices, glossaries, Internet, interviews, available technology) to clarify meanings of unfamiliar words. |

Grade 1 (A-B) Grade 2 (A-B-C) Grade 3 (B-C-D) Grade 4 (C-D-E) Grade 5 (D-E-F)

*Source:* From *English Language Arts Performance Descriptors*, by the Illinois State Board of Education, 2004, retrieved June 7, 2004, from *http://www.isbe.state.il.us/ils.* Used by permission.

team members designed a Section 504 plan using the standards shown in Figure 5–8. The team concluded that, with appropriate classroom modifications, all of the standards listed in Stages C, D, and E were appropriate for this student. The modifications they generated, based on Newbill and Miller (2006), are shown in Table 5–5.

Children entering elementary school face formidable challenges if they have language disorders, particularly when they are expected to make the transition from the world of oral language into the literate world of print. These children have particular difficulties when the curriculum shifts from teaching them to read to using reading as a way to learn. Perhaps the most important aspect of language instruction for elementary age children with language disorders is literate language forms and metalinguistic, metapragmatic, and metacognitive ability.

**FIGURE 5–8** English language arts standard and corresponding stages

**1A** Students who meet the standard can apply word analysis and vocabulary skills to comprehend selections.

| Stage C | Stage D | Stage E |
|---|---|---|
| 1. Use phonics to decode new words in age-appropriate material.<br>2. Use word analysis (root words, inflections, affixes) to identify words.<br>3. Discuss the meanings of new words encountered in independent and group activities.<br>4. Use synonyms and antonyms to define words.<br>5. Use a variety of decoding strategies (e.g., phonics, word patterns, structural analysis, context clues) to recognize new words when reading age-appropriate material.<br>6. Self-monitor reading and use decoding strategies to self-correct miscues.<br>7. Use context and previous experience to determine the meanings of unfamiliar words in text.<br>8. Use a variety of resources (e.g., dictionaries, thesauruses, indices, glossaries, Internet, interviews, available technology) to clarify meanings of unfamiliar words. | 1. Use a combination of word analysis and vocabulary strategies (e.g., phonics, word patterns, structural analyses) to identify words.<br>2. Learn and use high-frequency root words, prefixes, and suffixes to understand word meaning.<br>3. Use synonyms and antonyms to define words.<br>4. Use word origins to construct the meanings of new words.<br>5. Apply word analysis and vocabulary strategies across the curriculum and in independent reading to self-correct miscues that interfere with meaning.<br>6. Recognize the difference between denotative and connotative meanings of words.<br>7. Determine the meaning of a word in context when the word has multiple meanings.<br>8. Use additional resources (e.g., newspapers, interviews, technological resources) as applicable to clarify meanings of unfamiliar words. | 1. Use a combination of word analysis and vocabulary strategies (e.g., word patterns, structural analyses) within context to identify unknown words.<br>2. Learn and use root words, prefixes, and suffixes to understand word meanings.<br>3. Use synonyms and antonyms to define words.<br>4. Use word origins to construct the meanings of new words.<br>5. Use root words and context to determine the denotative and connotative meanings of unknown words.<br>6. Determine the meaning of a word in context when the word has multiple meanings.<br>7. Identify and interpret common idioms, similes, analogies, and metaphors.<br>8. Use additional resources (e.g., newspapers, interviews, technological resources) as applicable to clarify meanings of material. |

Grade 1 (A-B) Grade 2 (A-B-C) Grade 3 (B-C-D) Grade 4 (C-D-E) Grade 5 (D-E-F)

*Source*: From *English Language Arts Performance Descriptors*, by the Illinois State Board of Education, 2004, retrieved June 7, 2004, from *http://www.isbe.state.il.us/ils.* Used by permission.

## Literate Language Forms

The most pertinent literate language forms elementary age children encounter are the discourse genres (narrative, classroom, and expository discourse) and figurative language.

**Narrative Discourse.** Miller et al. (2001) advocate teaching students about narrative discourse through the use of dynamic assessment and mediated teaching. Their approach involves having the student first look through a wordless picture book (they use *Two Friends,* [Miller, 1999] and *Bird and His Ring* [Miller, 1999]) and then tell the story the pictures show.

Using a protocol they developed, teachers can analyze these aspects of the story as a baseline measure for comparison with a second story the child tells following two mediated teaching sessions:

- Story components:
  - setting: time and place
  - character information
  - temporal order of events
  - causal relationships
- Story ideas and language:
  - complexity of ideas
  - complexity of vocabulary
  - grammatical complexity

**TABLE 5–5** Section 504 classroom modifications

1. Target = Work completion and loss of motivation

**Modifications**

- Allow more time to complete assignments when practical. However, long extensions for projects often encourage procrastination. Break big assignments into smaller parts and give small amounts of extra time for specific parts when needed.
- Reduce assignment length and amount wherever possible. If the student has been working diligently for the whole time period allotted for a specific assignment, give full credit for that assignment and move on.
- Allow the student to demonstrate mastery in different ways (orally, on tape, etc.)
- Limit homework time. Agree with the student and his parents on a reasonable and developmentally appropriate amount of time for homework each day and accept what can be completed in that amount of time. Prioritize assignments so essential work can be completed first.
- Who is responsible?
- Classroom teacher, students, parents, and support staff. Support staff, such as the SLP, might need to provide a supervised place for untimed tests to be taken.

2. Target = Low test scores.

**Modifications**

- Allow for unlimited tests, which have been shown to best support students with slow processing speed. Although students with weak attention controls will waste extra time, students with slow processing speed and adequate attention controls often see significant gains in test scores when tests are untimed. Frequently they don't need a lot of extra time, but knowing they have as much time as they need lowers anxiety and actually improves processing speed.
- Who is responsible?
- Classroom teacher, student, parents, and support staff. Support staff (again, the SLP) might need to provide a supervised place for untimed tests to be taken.

*Source: From Section 504: What Is It and How Do I Use It?* online course by C. Newbill and L. Miller, 2006, Austin, TX: PRO-ED.

- knowledge of dialogue
- creativity

After the first story has been analyzed, the teacher can conduct two mediated teaching sessions in which this set of mediation strategies is used to support the student's learning about stories:

1. Intention to teach—The teacher explains what the goal is for the session.
2. Meaning—The teacher explains why the goal they're addressing is important in telling good stories.
3. Example—The teacher shows the student specific examples of the targeted story structure or element.
4. Planning—The teacher helps the student think about what new skill(s) he or she has learned and how he or she will use it (them) the next time he or she tells a story.
5. Transfer—The teacher summarizes the session to help the student think about using her or his new narration skill in related situations (story time, show-and-tell, etc.).
6. Hypothesizing/transcendence—By asking a series of "what if" questions, the teacher helps the student develop some metacognitive awareness of alternative strategies or responses in telling the story.
7. Self-evaluation—the teacher helps the student become aware of her or his own learning. The mediation sessions are designed to be fluid and dynamic interactions, rather than static lessons. The idea is to provide the student with support, explanation, examples, and opportunities to try things out, all the while focusing on what makes a story good, that is, worth listening to.

Following the mediation sessions, the teacher has the student tell a second story, using a different wordless picture book, which the teacher analyzes using the same criteria used to analyze the first story. By comparing the student's performance on each aspect of narration, the teacher can determine which areas need to be targeted for instruction and which are likely to develop on their own given adequate opportunities to interact with stories.

Polloway et al. (2004) devised an approach for teaching narrative discourse that can be used with students whose language skills are developed well enough that they can use printed worksheets as a guide, shown in Figure 5-9. The worksheets provide a guide for students to follow as they analyze a story they've heard or read in order to determine its story ideas and language, story components, and episode structure.

According to Scott (1999), the narrative abilities adolescents are expected to understand and manipulate include:

- understanding the characters' motivations, feelings, and plans
- drawing inferences
- summarizing a story
- providing listeners (or readers) with enough **cohesive markers** (e.g., pronouns, conjunctions, ellipsis, definite articles) that they know how things in the story hang together

In the secondary grades, students encounter a variety of forms of narrative discourse, each of which, although obviously exhibiting the primary aspects of narrative discourse, exhibits a unique set of characteristics. According to Polloway et al. (2004), some of the most common are:

- novel
- comic book
- folktale
- myth
- tall tale
- personal essay
- autobiographical narrative
- oral history
- creative nonfiction

Novels, regarded almost as prototypical narratives, utilize numerous linguistic and organizational devices to convey their intent. For instance, Nestvold (2002) posits three possible voices in a novel: the narrator, the author, and the implied author. Nestvold describes the implied author as "a presence inferred by the reader as the guiding personality behind the work" (not necessarily synonymous with the actual author). She sees the author as the actual person who wrote the book (and who may have written other books with a different "voice"). Voice, according to Nestvold, refers to the authorial voice (also called the implied author) behind the characters, narrators, and personae characteristic of novels. The method of expression used by the actual author determines how the reader perceives the authorial voice; these methods include irony, lyricism, and specific language usages.

Further complicating narration is the fact that narrators tell their stories using a particular point of view, usually third-person or first-person narration. According to Nestvold, in third-person narration, the narrator stands outside the story itself, whereas in first-person narration, the narrator participates in the story. Third-person narration uses third-person pronouns ("she," "her," "them"), whereas first-person narration uses the first person ("I," "my," "we").

These guidelines, based on a set of questions devised by Nestvold, can be used to guide students' learning about the finer points of narrative discourse (these can be modified only slightly for students to use in writing their own narratives):

- Who is communicating with the reader in the story?
- Which voice did the author use to communicate: a character's voice, the author's "own" voice, or a relatively "objective" voice?
- From what position or angle regarding the story did he or she tell it? Where was the "camera" (above, periphery, center, front, or shifting)?
- What channels of information did the narrator use to convey the story to the reader (author's words, thoughts, perceptions, feelings; character's words and actions; or character's thoughts, perceptions, and feelings)?
- How much of the story was "telling" (describing action) and how much "showing" (i.e., having the characters engage in a scenario that "shows" an idea)?

Comic books offer two advantages to students struggling with narrative: they usually exhibit a less complex narrative structure than novels, and they use visual images to convey a significant portion of the meaning. Specifically, the visual images convey setting and character information that, because it is present visually, does not need to be described linguistically.

Using comic books is a good way to introduce students to the idea that printed forms of narration encompass various components. Teachers can target setting, character information, temporal order, and causal relationships.

Using a particular comic book (carefully screened), the teacher can have students identify and orally describe the settings, which are usually provided visually

**FIGURE 5–9** Narrative outlines of stories

**Story Components**

This story takes place ______________________ and ______________________.
(where) (when)

The main characer ______________________.
(describe what he or she looked like, said, did, thought, felt)

Events in the story happened in this order ______________________.
(first, next, then, and then, last)

Events in this story happened because ______________________.

**Story Ideas and Language**

The literal events that occured in this story were ______________________.

Some things that happened that weren't described in words are ______________________.

Some things this story could mean that weren't described in words are ______________.

Some words that were used that mean more than one thing are ______________.

Some examples of figurative words (simile, metaphor, irony, satiric) used in this story are ______________________.

Some examples of grammatically complex sentences used in this story are ______________________

______________________.
(compound, complex, compound/complex)

An example of dialogue I particularly liked and why: ______________________.

Here's what made this story interesting: ______________________.

**Episode Structure**

Here's what happened to start the story (the problem): ______________________.

Here's what the main character did in response to the problem: ______________________.

Here's how the main character felt about the problem: ______________________.

Here's what the main character intended to do (and why) about the problem: ______________________.

Here's how the problem was solved: ______________________.

Here's how the main characer reacted to the solution: ______________________.

If there were another episode in this story, here is what happened to start it: ______________________.

Here's how the main character of this episode responded to this problem: ______________________.

Here's how the main character felt about this problem: ______________________.

This is what the main character intended to do (and why) about the problem: ______________________.

Here's how this problem was solved: ______________________.

If there were more than one episode, this is how the episodes were related to each other: ______________________.

This is how the overall story ended: ______________________.

Here's how the main character(s) felt about how the problems were solved: ______________________.

*Source*: From *Language Instruction for Students with Disabilities* (3rd ed., pp. 228–229), by E. A. Polloway, L. Miller, and T. E. C. Smith, 2004, Denver, CO: Love Publishing. Used by permission.

in the comic. Next, students can write their descriptions of the setting as a way of practicing the inclusion of setting in their written narratives. They can experiment with different ways to describe the same setting, trying out different adjectives, for example.

The same approach can be used to help students learn to include information about the characters. At first, the students can identify and orally describe the characteristics of each character, focusing on aspects such as clothing, physical features, body type, etc. Then, students can write descriptions of the characters, again experimenting with the effects produced by using different adjectives or shifting focus from describing physical appearance to state of mind or mood and the language required to successfully describe these character attributes.

The comics can be cut into individual panels so that students can see how temporal order works, and, by rearranging the panels, students can play with how meaning is altered when temporal sequence is changed. At first, they can orally describe what is happening and use appropriate linguistic markers such as "First," "then," "and then," and "finally." After they've had some practice with orally describing temporal order, they can begin writing a description of the unfolding of events, again practicing the use of appropriate linguistic markers.

Causal relationships can be targeted by having the students focus on which events seem to result in which consequences. With the comics cut into individual panels, students can experiment with rearranging the causes and the effects to see if events still make sense. All the while, they can be orally describing their perceptions of why things in the panels are happening the way they are. After experimenting with rearranging the panels and orally describing the resulting causal relationships, the students can write out two or three scenarios depicting the different causal relationships emanating from their experiments. Emphasis in each scenario should be on describing which event(s) resulted in which consequences. For more advanced students, the teacher can have them write their assessment of the degree to which each set of causal relationships in their experiments seemed most likely to be considered realistic or probable.

Steele (2003) compiled a comprehensive set of rubrics and lesson plans teachers can use to teach secondary students about incorporating the various aspects of narrative discourse into their writing. Her approach is organized around the Six Trait Analytic Writing Model (Web English Teacher, 2003), which addresses ideas and content, organization, voice, word choice, sentence fluency, and writing conventions.

**Classroom Discourse.** For some elementary students, classroom, or instructional, discourse is an extension of one of the types of discourse they've already experienced at home. For other students, particularly those from CLD backgrounds, classroom discourse may pose some difficulties, particularly because some of its rules are never verbalized by the teacher. In effect, classroom discourse that is not explicated constitutes what Cazden (2001) calls the "hidden curriculum," which follows what she describes as the *initiation-response-evaluation* (IRE) format. The initiation occurs when the teacher initiates a topic, a student responds, and the teacher evaluates the student's response. An example is:

T. *Who knows what day this is?*

S. *Armistice Day?*

T. *Yes, that's right.*

Nelson (1998) has described the language of the classroom in terms of its four primary functions:

1. instruction from the teacher in how to read and write language
2. the teacher talking about and expecting students to talk about language (requiring metalinguistic ability)
3. the teacher using language to convey procedure and expecting students to use language to learn how to do other things
4. the teacher using language to convey content and expecting students to use language to learn about other things

To teach students about instructional discourse, Nelson suggests that teachers modify their language expectations, for instance, by adding redundancy or slowing speaking rate, and focus on helping students develop skill in the metalinguistic, metapragmatic, and metacognitive areas, a topic addressed later in this section.

Results from a survey Simon (1998) conducted with secondary classroom teachers regarding the student classroom behavior they judge to be most desirable show eight aspects:

1. following directions
2. showing respect to fellow students and to teachers
3. working cooperatively with fellow students
4. appearing interested in class
5. taking notes

6. successfully skimming texts and reference sources for information
7. participating in class discussions
8. giving oral reports

Although these results were collected from secondary teachers, the behaviors they listed can be used to guide instruction regarding classroom discourse at both the elementary and the secondary level. The behaviors can be used as standards, with students progressing toward them at varying rates, depending on their language abilities. Each of the eight behaviors, or standards, can be fine-tuned into a set of steps progressing from the least linguistically demanding through increasing levels of linguistic load.

**Expository Discourse.** By the time students in elementary school reach third or fourth grade, they are expected to begin using their reading skills to read texts that teach them new information. Those texts typically use one or more forms of expository discourse, which, as discussed above, differ significantly from the narrative discourse of stories. In the middle elementary grades and later, the most common types of expository discourse students encounter are descriptive and explanatory.

Most typically developing children begin producing oral descriptions before they begin school, and, once they enter school, their verbal descriptions become tied to academic content. In addition, much of classroom discourse contains elements of description and explanation. By third or fourth grade, students are expected to read, understand, and write descriptive and explanatory discourse, and by the time they enter the secondary grades, to read and understand argumentative/persuasive texts. By the time they leave secondary school, most students will also be expected to produce their own written argumentative/persuasive discourse.

Students usually encounter expository discourse first in oral forms such as lecture, oral reports, laboratory reports, and research reports. Later, they interact with printed forms of expository discourse such as essays, descriptions, letters, explanations, and argument/persuasion. To begin teaching students about expository discourse, Nelson (1998) recommends teaching them to differentiate narrative from nonnarrative genres, which requires students to understand what constitutes a good narrative, or story. Once students can discriminate the narrative from nonnarrative, they can begin to learn the characteristics of the nonnarrative discourse genres. Nelson's summary of the salient characteristics of nonnarrative discourse is shown in Figure 5–10.

Westby (1991) described a set of keys teachers can use to teach students about expository discourse in terms of what it does, some key words associated with three types of expository discourse, and its underlying organizational structure. Westby's keys for these three types of expository text can be used to design a template for students to use in identifying and understanding how to access these three types of expository text. For instance, descriptive text tells what things are (what it does); uses such key words as *is called, is defined as, is explained as, refers to*; and is organized around defining, describing, listing the

**TEACHER *Tips*** — **Elementary Level**

You can use the following strategy to help students identify components of expository text. This particular example focuses on explanatory text, but color coding can be used for other types of expository text as well. Write a sample paragraph on an overhead. Ask the students which sentence is the beginning of the paragraph. Circle or highlight it in green. Have the students identify the middle sentences of the paragraph. Circle or highlight them in yellow. Have the students identify the ending or closing statement. Circle or highlight it in red. Have each students choose three colored markers or crayons, a green one to mark the beginning of the paragraph, a yellow one to mark the middle, and a red one to mark the ending or closing statement.

You can also provide these starter sentences and have the students write an explanatory paragraph and then color the beginning, middle, and ending sentences:

- Baseball is my favorite sport.
- Fall is a beautiful season.
- My favorite music is _____.
- My favorite book is _____.
- The president of the United States has a hard job.
- My family likes to celebrate _____.

**FIGURE 5–10** Non-narrative discourse types

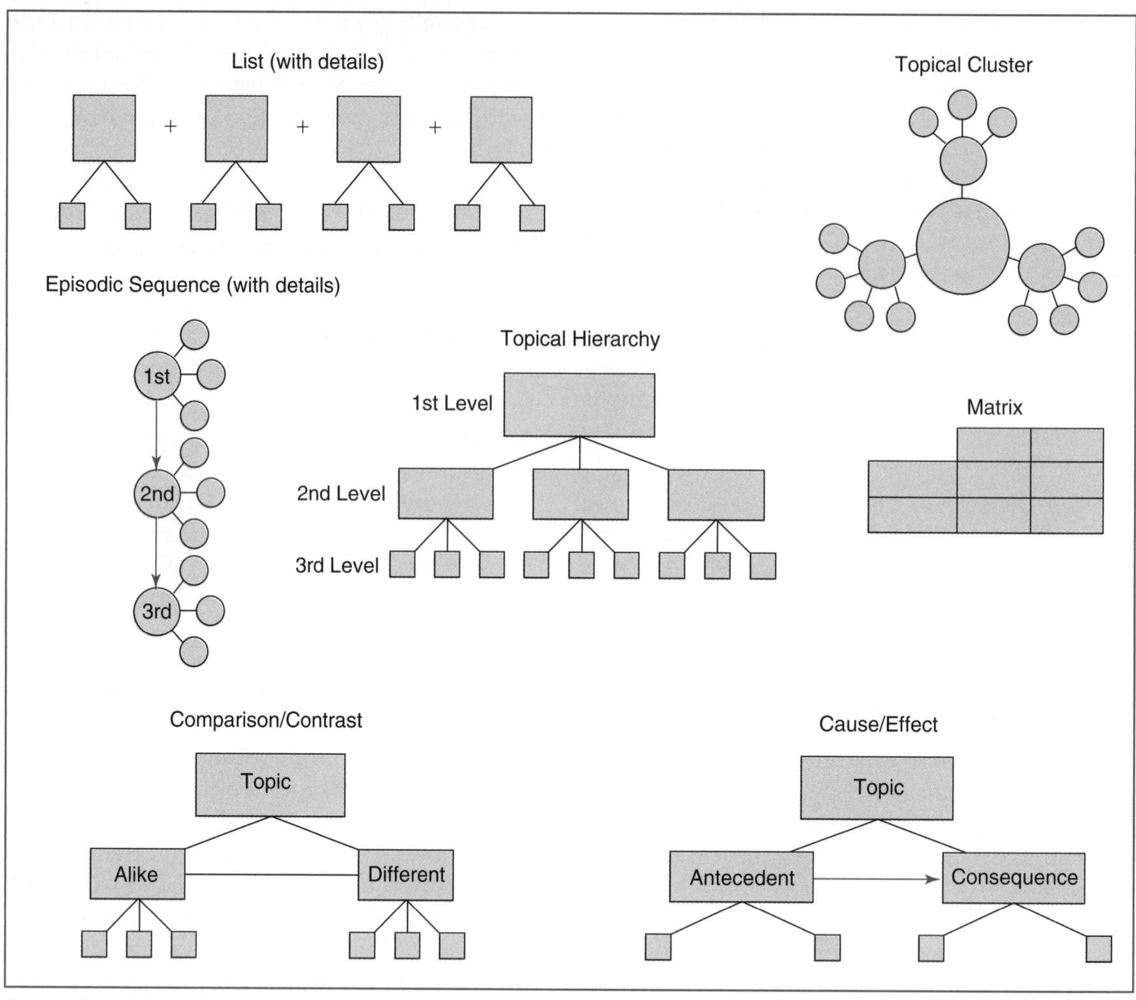


*Source:* From *Childhood Language Disorders in Context: Infancy Through Adolescence* (2nd ed., p. 419), by N. W. Nelson, 1998, Boston, MA: Allyn & Bacon. Used by permission.

features of, or answering the questions "What is . . . ?" and "Who is . . . ?"

Cause-effect explanatory text gives reasons why something happened; uses such key words as *because, since, then, therefore, thus, is a function of*; and is organized around explaining, predicting, and identifying causes.

Comparison/contrast text shows how things are alike and different; uses such key words as *same, different, alike, similar, although, however, yet, still, but*; and is organized around comparing and contrasting things in terms of their similarities and differences.

Once students have learned how to recognize the various types of expository text, they can begin focusing on the structural aspects. Wallach and Miller (1988) suggested teaching students about the macrostructure, or overall text structure, used in expository discourse to organize content. According to Wallach and Miller, the most typical macrostructure for expository discourse is:

- the title
- chapter headings (or, for articles, first-level headings)
- first-level chapter headings (or, for articles, second-level headings)
- second-level chapter headings (or, for articles, third-level headings)

The teacher can use this macrostructure to create a checklist or outline for students to follow as they begin learning how to comprehend and orally describe the organizational characteristics of the expository text they interact with.

Paul (2001) developed a six-point rubric students can use to increase their skill with expository discourse. The scoring system on the rubric ranges from 1 (beginner) to 6 (most sophisticated) and addresses five aspects of expository writing:

1. the organization and structure of the text
2. how the content is presented and developed through the use of cohesive features
3. the developmental levels of syntax, vocabulary, and cohesion strategies
4. writing mechanics
5. the sense of audience

Polloway et al. (2004) described a set of sample prompt cards for six types of expository discourse structure that shows students how to introduce the topic, how to expand and/or explain the main point or idea, and how to conclude. The Secondary School Educators (2001) website offers a set of rubrics for students and teachers showing how to evaluate compare/contrast, expository, debate, and persuasive essays. Their rubric for expository discourse emphasizes focus, organization, conventions, and understanding and support, each rated along a six-point scale. In addition to the rubrics, the site also provides a tutorial on how to write rubrics for any assignment.

Sponsored by thirteen ed online (WNET New York), Friedman (2003) offers a lesson plan for 10th, 11th, and 12th graders on how media shapes perception of events through analyzing the subtexts present in the audio, language, and visual aspects of media coverage of tragic events. Students have opportunities to explore how the media shapes their opinions and emotional reactions to tragic events. After looking at various news organizations' homepages, students convey their own opinions and emotions by creating their own homepage designs.

**Figurative Language.** Learning that language exists on more than one level is a delight for some children, a mysterious and troubling task to others. The ability to use nonliteral forms of language is necessary to participate fully in social interactions, which often rely on idioms, slang, and shortcuts, and to access written language, particularly poetry, drama, and fiction. Websites oriented toward teaching English as a second language are rich source of ideas about teaching figurative language types. An example is ESL.com (2003), which offers textbook recommendations, teaching tips, lesson plans, and related links.

The earliest types of figurative language elementary students learn about are homonyms, synonyms, and antonyms. Numerous lesson plans for teaching homonyms are available online. J. Smith (2003) devised a homonym game for middle school students, and Florida Tech Net (2003) has posted a comprehensive lesson plan to teach homonyms, as well as a list of the most common homonyms. Although the Florida Tech Net site was designed for adolescents and adults, it can be easily modified for use with younger students. Garosshen's (2003) Ask Eric lesson plan for second and third graders uses jokes and riddles as a vehicle for teaching students about homonyms. The Internet TESL Project (2003a) has compiled a set of self-study homonym quizzes students can use to learn about the most common English homonyms, ranging in difficulty from easy to medium-difficult.

Teacher's Desk.org uses the game Hinky Pinky with both younger and older students as a way to teach synonyms (as well as rhyming and syllable manipulation). Florida Tech Net (2003) provides a detailed lesson plan focused on antonyms and synonyms, and Teacher Net.com (2003a) provides a lesson plan for middle school students using sports headlines to teach synonyms and antonyms. And, in an interesting application, Cyber Smart (2003) has designed a lesson plan teaching students how using synonyms facilitates searching on the Internet. Sass (2003) has compiled a list of online lesson plans, elementary through secondary, to teach homonyms, synonyms, and antonyms.

Most children are exposed to idioms and idiomatic phrases well before they enter school. However, because idioms vary by geographic region, cultural influences, and education level, children entering school do not necessarily know the exact idioms commonly used by their schoolmates. Also, children from families that are less oriented toward literate uses of language may not recognize that idioms are figurative expressions. J. C. Miller (2003) designed a lesson plan for third- through fifth-grade students that also includes a list of common idioms. The ESL.com (2003) website includes an entire section devoted to teaching idioms. They recommend textbooks and dictionaries in four areas: general idioms, phrasal verbs, slang expressions, and cliches. Rizzo (2003) used *Amelia Bedilia* (Parish,

1992) to devise a lesson plan for teaching idioms to fourth though sixth graders.

**Reflective Question 5.6:** ***What do you consider to be the basic principles that should govern appropriate assessment procedures in the area of spoken language?***

Sanders (2003b) defines slang as "a kind of informal language that generally follows the grammatical patterns of the language from which it stems but that reflects an alternate lexicon with connotations of informality." In other words, slang is a set of specialized idioms and idiomatic expressions that change frequently. Because slang is a variant of idioms, teaching students about slang is virtually the same process as teaching them about idioms. Teachers can find the most recent slang expressions online at a site hosted by Sanders (2003a), who directs a project to collect college slang from around the world. The site includes a slang dictionary, frequently asked questions about slang, and links to other websites collecting college slang.

## Metapragmatic, Metalinguistic, and Metacognitive Abilities

Learning to reflect on and talk about communication, language, speech, and one's own learning is one of the most critical skills students learn in elementary school. As discussed earlier, the ability to reflect on and talk about how people communicate is called **metapragmatic ability;** the ability to reflect on and talk about language and speech is described as **metalinguistic ability;** and the ability to reflect on and talk about one's own learning is termed **metacognitive ability.**

Teaching students metapragmatic skills focuses on helping them recognize that the "rules" governing how

**TECHNOLOGY *Tip***

### Figurative Language

A number of excellent Internet sources are available to teach figurative language. For example, a comprehensive collection of English idioms and quizzes is available from the Idiom Connection (2003). Idioms are grouped by category, such as animal, heart, food, fish, clothes, business, body, money, and number. The multiple-choice quizzes provide immediate feedback in an easy-to-use format, making them ideal for students to use online. The Internet TESL Journal (2003a) has collected a set of idiom quizzes, organized into three categories (idioms, phrasal verbs, and slang) by level of difficulty (beginner, more difficult). A4esl.org (2006) offers a web page devoted to idioms and slang that allows the student to select an idiom, from an alphabetical list, in a sentence and then click to see what it means in plain English. The idioms are categorized from medium to high difficulty so students can choose the appropriate level.

LessonPlanz.com (2006) provides numerous links to lesson plans and rubrics for teaching various types and aspects of figurative language, including alliteration, simile, metaphor, forms of poetry, imagery, onomatopoeia, personification, proverbs, and puns. Rekate (2003) has designed a lesson plan using Martin Luther King, Jr.'s "I Have a Dream" speech to teach fifth- through ninth-grade students about analogy, symbolism, personification, the use of repetition, chronology, metaphor, and figurative language. Tolerance.org (2006) offers a downloadable lesson plan for grades 9 through 12, "Political Allegory in the Harry Potter Series," with four goals:

- students will identify archetypes and symbols (supernatural helpers, the hero, death, a curse)
- students will understand the concept of a sociopolitical allegory
- students will apply the concept to the Harry Potter series
- students will consider how stereotypes, group dynamics, and social power relations in the Harry Potter series might reflect real life (p. 2)

The Family Education Network has a lesson plan that can be used with students in grades 3 through 12 addressing both simile and metaphor. The Harris Middle School has developed a lesson plan for 5th- through 12th-grade students to learn to interpret and write similes and metaphors through studying poetry. The Shelbyville Middle School (2003) has a lesson plan for teaching upper elementary school students about puns through using poetry and valentine verse.

language is used in different situations can be talked about and analyzed (Polloway et al., 2004). According to Polloway et al., metapragmatic instruction for elementary students emphasizes showing students how to:

- decide when to violate the "tell the truth" principle
- identify the unspoken rules governing classroom discourse
- participate in classroom discourse
- demonstrate knowledge appropriately in the classroom
- talk about different types of discourse (e.g., slang, school talk, home talk, church talk)
- participate successfully in different types of discourse
- talk about discourse rules
- use different discourse genres in their writing

For secondary students, Polloway et al. (2004) recommend organizing instruction for metapragmatic ability around teaching students how to:

- communicate successfully in class discussions
- decide what to say in different situations
- fine-tune their conversations
- put themselves in another's place (take someone else's perspective)
- solve problems that arise during communication

For elementary students, one of the most important metalinguistic abilities they must acquire is **phonological awareness,** which plays a major role in learning to read and write. Teaching phonological awareness, however, has become entangled in a controversy about whether to teach students using a whole language or a phonics instruction approach (also called phonemic awareness; see also Chapter 6).

What follows here is a discussion of approaches to assist children in developing an awareness of the phonetic and phonemic aspects of spoken language.

A rich resource for teachers is Chard and Dickson's (1999) online discussion of instructional and assessment guidelines for phonological awareness. Chard and Dickson provide a brief history of phonological awareness and describe both historic and contemporary research into the relationship between phonological awareness and early reading. The bulk of their discussion is devoted to evidence-based guidelines for teaching phonological awareness and phonemic awareness, including students with learning disabilities or difficulties with early reading. Their instructional guidelines include specific activities that can easily be integrated into any curriculum.

Edelen-Smith (2003) has developed a comprehensive set of phoneme awareness activities for use in collaborative kindergarten and first-grade classrooms. Arranged developmentally, the activities are based on research demonstrating that explicitly teaching phonemic awareness to children reduces their risk of early reading failure. She recommends beginning with word play involving rhyming, followed by simple phoneme awareness through activities focused on:

- recognizing isolated sounds
- counting words, syllables, and phonemes
- synthesizing sounds
- matching sound-to-word
- identifying sound positions
- segmenting sounds
- associating letter with sounds
- matching word-to-word
- deleting sound

The metacognitive strategies students need to succeed in school involve learning how they learn, how to manage their learning, and how to manage learning problems or breakdowns. Bowen, Hawkins, and King (1997) developed an approach that focuses on helping students discover how they naturally attend and learn. Using Bloom's taxonomy of educational objectives and multiple intelligences as the vehicle, these authors devised seven steps for students:

1. recognizing and recalling information to gain knowledge
2. translating and summarizing/paraphrasing to gain comprehension
3. interpreting through generalizing, defining, and making connections between facts
4. solving problems through identifying them and the skills necessary for solving them
5. analyzing all the parts of a problem to discover what is similar and dissimilar
6. synthesizing or solving a problem through original, creative thinking
7. evaluating or comparing and discriminating between ideas

Bowen et al. (1997) designed teacher resource sheets, showing academic strategies across content areas, to use to teach students general learning strategies as well as some tailored specifically to communicating, focusing and attending, staying organized, and solving problems.

LD Online (2003a) published an essay by Joan Sedita describing how parents can help their children with organizational and study skills. The article can be used in two ways: it can be accessed by parents (or printed out and given to them), and it can be used as a model for teaching organization and study skills in the classroom. Specifically, the article describes a three-part study skills model:

- organization strategies for notebooks, materials, and assignments; study space; and time
- three foundation study skills:
  - reading and listening for main ideas
  - applying two-column note-taking skills
  - summarizing
- combining the foundation skills for building skills in:
  - accessing and understanding textbooks
  - engaging in research
  - writing reports

### Teaching Culturally and Linguistically Different Students

According to the North Central Regional Education Laboratory (NCREL, 2000), a critical aspect of instruction for students who are CLD is to build on students' prior knowledge and skills and provide appropriate **scaffolding,** or first providing a model for learning a particular behavior or skill and gradually shifting responsibility for learning to the student. NCREL points out that building instruction around these elements not only provides students with opportunities for authentic learning but also improves student engagement. Following this teaching strategy requires that teachers acquire an understanding not only of their subject matter, but also of their students. That is, teachers must continually develop their knowledge of literacy instruction at the same time that they increase their awareness and understanding of "their students' cultures, experiences, and backgrounds" (NCREL, 2000, p. 3).

**Specific Language Instruction for CLD Students.** Peña et al. (2006, in press) propose designing instruction for CLD children based on two fundamental principles. First, mediated instruction that focuses on their underlying skills that can be used to support language learning, regardless of the language or dialect the children speak, has been shown to increase children's ability to learn specific language structures. The authors conclude that an important aspect of mediated instruction aimed at underlying cognitive skills helps children develop behaviors for learning in general. Second, mediated instruction that focuses on skills that are specific to the language, dialect, and circumstances in which the children need language to communicate effectively and interact successfully has been shown to help them understand their language goals, why those goals are important, and how they can use their new skills to enhance their own learning.

Figure 5-11 shows a sample mediated instruction lesson for the same second-grade student described on pages 142-143. Figure 5-5 and 5-6 in the assessment section. The lesson was built from information gleaned during a mediated instruction session that measured the student's responsivity to learning how to include character descriptions in her stories. During the mediated instruction session, the student responded quickly and eagerly to learning how to include character information in a story. She was able to generalize her learning to different characters, and she was able to tell her teacher how she planned to remember to include character information next time she told a story. As a result of the student's high responsivity, her teacher designed a mediated instruction lesson for the student's reading and writing group, who were each telling the group their favorite story in preparation for completing a story guide that would act as a template for them to use in writing a story over a 5-day period. Although the teacher addressed each of the five students and elicited their responses, she recorded only the questions, supports, and responses related to the specific student. The lesson focused on including setting information in the story, which the student learned relatively quickly.

> Reflective Question 5.7: ***What strategies and procedures can be pursued to enable classroom teachers to complement the work of speech/language pathologists in designing and implementing a comprehensive language instruction program for students with disabilities?***

## TEACHING WITH TECHNOLOGY

As access to technology has increased over the last decade, students increasingly use a variety of technologies on a daily basis. Today's children are surrounded by

**FIGURE 5–11** Mediated instruction focused on including setting information in a story

**Mediated Instruction Lesson—Providing Setting Information in a Story**
**Point of the Lesson:** To teach Amarisa that stories should contain information about time and place.
**Teaching Sequence: 1.** Show Amarisa *Two Friends* and have her retell the story. Remind her before she begins to include information about when and where the events in the story take place. **2.** Tell Amarisa what you're going to do in the lesson and why it is important. **3.** Using the story, help Amarisa describe time and place. **4.** If Amarisa describes the setting without much help from you, help her extend the concept to another story. If she has difficulty, help her evaluate why it is important to describe time and place in a story. **5.** Help Amarisa plan how to describe the setting when she tells another story. **6.** Help Amarisa respond to the questions throughout. Use prompts, cues, and models as needed to support her. **7.** Help Amarisa figure out how she can remember to describe time and place next time she tells a story.

| Strategy | Examples of Instruction | What You Did to Support Amarisa | How Amarisa Responded |
|---|---|---|---|
| What you're going to do | "Today we're going to talk about telling stories. When we tell stories, we tell when and where the events happen." | Reminded her what she learned about including character information | "Oh, yeah. The baby was big and kinda brown" |
| Why that's important | "Telling about when and where things happen is important because it tells your listener about the world the characters live in." | Asked Amarisa to describe her 7th birthday and how it was different from her 8th. | "My mom have a party this year. Last year we go to my granmommy's." |
| Help Amarisa describe the setting | "Let's look at *Two Friends* again. Let's see if we can see where and when things are happening." Help Amarisa describe where the dog and cat are at the beginning of the story. "When do you think this story happened? Was it yesterday? Ten years ago? A hundred?" Help Amarisa use time/place words and phrases. | Pointed out the pictures in the story that showed where and when | "Oh, he sleeping. It night there." "He swimming in a river." |
| Help Amarisa extend the concept to another story | "How would you change the story if the dog and cat lived on a different planet? How would you change the story if it happened in the year 3000?" And, "Can you think of another story that tells where the characters are and when things are happening?" If not, present a familiar story and help Amarisa discover the setting. | | "It cold on the moon And dark on one side." "In 3000 they ride in a spaceship." "I'd say the dog was big and fluffy and the cat was orange and rounds." |
| Help Amarisa plan | "We've been talking about telling about time and place. The next time you tell a story, what are you going to remember to put in it?" | | "Tell the place and the time, like now or the future." |
| Help Amarisa generalize her learning | "We've been talking about putting time and place in your stories. How are you going to remember to include time and place when you make up your own stories?" | | "I think about the dog swimming in the river. Or him sleeping at home at the end." |

digital technology from infancy. In 2005, 87% of teenagers (21 million teens between 12 and 17 reported using the Internet; of those, 78% (16 million) say they use the Internet at school; NCREL, 2006). NCREL further reported that 57% of all children in school ages 7–17 use a computer at home for schoolwork and 75% of online teens (approximately 16 million) use instant messaging, 75% of them to talk about schoolwork, homework, or tests (NCREL, 2006).

Increasingly, business, policy, and nonprofit organizations are developing descriptions and definitions of the higher-level, technology-related skills (termed Information and Communication Technology, or ICT, Literacy skills) students will need in the workplace. According to NCREL (2006) these skills include the ability to:

- communicate effectively in various media, including print, video, animation, and design across multiple environments that include books, e-mail, websites, streaming media, web logs, podcasts, and message boards

- analyze and interpret data available in electronic formats (including the Internet)
- understand computational modeling used across a wide range of disciplines
- manage and prioritize tasks while multitasking across technology applications while working individually and in teams
- solve problems by applying what they know to new situations

Until recently, students with special needs often had limited access to and interaction with a variety of technologies. However, with rapidly evolving communication technologies more readily available in an increasing number of classrooms, these students now have more opportunities to use technology in a number of ways. The Center for Applied Special Technology (CAST), a nonprofit organization devoted to expanding learning opportunities for all learners, has adopted universal design for learning (UDL) to research and develop ways to support all learners (CAST, 2006a). According to CAST, the three basic principles of UDL are:

> - Multiple means of representation, to give learners various ways of acquiring information and knowledge,
> - Multiple means of expression, to provide learners alternatives for demonstrating what they know,
> - Multiple means of engagement, to tap into learners' interests, offer appropriate challenges, and increase motivation. (CAST, 2006b, p. 4)

One of CAST's web pages offers a rich set of resources to support teachers who want to learn about and practice UDL (2006c). The page includes information, opportunities to connect with other educators who are learning about and using UDL, tools and activities that utilize UDL, and model lessons across content areas and grades. The page also provides the following UDL toolkits:

- Planning for All Learners (PAL)
- Digital Content in the Classroom
- UDL Training Guide
- Internet Inquiry
- Guide for a One-day Workshop—the UDL Way

Each toolkit contains procedures, examples, resources, and an opportunity to share with others engaged in related work. For instance, the Example section of the Digital Content in the Classroom contains an extensive set of lesson plans that use digital content (among others) to teach plot and vocabulary in grades 9 and 10 (CAST, 2006d).

One of the richest technology resources available is the Internet, which contains an almost unimaginable scope of information for virtually any subject or content area. As a resource, the Internet is invaluable precisely because it is so vast. That same vastness, however, can be intimidating and confusing without forethought and planning. As a means of teaching students with special needs, the Internet offers a wide range of resources related to specific aspects of language instruction, many of them noted throughout this chapter. Many of the online resources related to teaching language arts can be used and/or modified for students needing specific language instruction. Figure 5–12 lists some of the best online resources for language instruction.

The North Central Regional Educational Laboratory (2006) hosts an online library of resources related to literacy and technology. The site includes discussions on the following topics:

- literacy and hypermedia in the future
- literacy and the Internet
- fostering literacy
- multiliteracies
- hypermedia and persons with special needs
- literacy and educational equity
- strategies for using hypermedia for literacy instruction
- tools to evaluate literacy programs
- smart guides on literacy and technology

In addition, the site includes answers to these questions:

- How can hypermedia resources be designed to help at-risk readers?
- How is literacy related to issues of educational equity?
- What are some concrete ways of incorporating hypermedia resources into classroom teaching?
- What characteristics of hypertext reading programs most affect the ways that people read hypertexts?
- What does research say about the effectiveness of computer-based resources for increasing reading comprehension?
- What literacy standards have been developed at the end of the 20th century?

**FIGURE 5–12** Online resources for language instruction

About.com. http://7-12educators.about.com/msublplneng.htm. *Secondary school educators: Language arts lesson plans.* Links to numerous secondary language arts lesson plan sites.

Cape Breton-Victoria Regional School Board. http://www.cbv.ns.ca/sstudies/english/eng.html. A large database of language arts lessons (mostly for middle and high school) collected from teachers throughout Nova Scotia.

Columbia Education Center. http://www.col-ed.org/cur/lang.html. Language arts lesson plans for primary, intermediate, and high school.

Education World. http://www.education-world.com/a_tsl/archives/00-1/lesson0004.shtml. A lesson plan for grades 3–8 (adaptable for all grades) on using a thesaurus.

Educator's Reference Desk. http://www.eduref.org/cgi-bin/lessons.cgi/Language_Arts. Dozens of links to language lesson plans and resources.

Educator's Reference Desk. http://www.eduref.org/cgi-bin/printlessons.cgi/Virtual/Lessons/Language_Arts/Vocabulary/VOC0003.html. Lesson plans designed to teach students to choose appropriate synonyms for both speaking and writing.

Educator's Reference Desk. http://www.eduref.org/cgi-bin/printlessons.cgi/Virtual/Lessons/Language_Arts/Writing/WCP0020.html. A sixth-grade lesson plan for learning synonyms and antonyms in pairs.

Educator's Reference Desk. http://www.eduref.org/cgi-bin/lessons.cgi/Language_Arts/Vocabulary. Vocabulary lesson plans for all grades.

Educator's Reference Desk. http://www.eduref.org/cgi-bin/printlessons.cgi/Virtual/Lessons/Language_Arts/Vocabulary/VOC0201.html. A lesson plan for third and fourth grade on homophones.

Mid-Continent Research for Education and Learning Lab. http://www.mcrel.org/lesson-plans/lang/index.asp. Language arts lesson plans.

Gibson Associates. http://www.netcore.ca/%7Egibsonjs/c1001-lt.htm. Lesson plan using word families to build vocabulary and rules of phonics.

Lesson Plan Page. http://www.lessonplanspage.com/LAMatchingWithSynonymsAntonyms4.htm. A fourth-grade lesson in matching with synonyms and antonyms.

Outta Ray's Head. http://home.cogeco.ca/%7Erayser3/. A collection of lesson plans and handouts, collected by Ray Saitz and fellow teachers in Ontario, Canada.

Read, Write, Think. http://www.readwritethink.org/. Lesson plans, standards, web resources, and student materials from the International Reading Association, the National Council for Teachers of English, and marcopolo.

Saskatchewan Teachers' Federation. http://www.stf.sk.ca/teaching_res/library/teach_mat_centre/teach_mat_units/eng_lang_arts.htm. Online units for elementary, middle, and secondary levels.

- What research shows that hypermedia resources can help at-risk readers?

The Education Podcast Network (2006) provides access to hundreds of podcasts of various sorts, including:

- education and ICT
- student and class podcasts from elementary, middle, and secondary schools
- subject-specific podcasts:
  - computer/technology skills
  - dance education
  - English language arts
  - healthful living
  - information skills
  - mathematics
  - music education
  - science
  - second languages
  - theatre arts education
  - visual arts education
  - career development
  - current events
  - miscellaneous

One of the English language arts links is to the blog from the Colorado State University Writing Project, which includes poetry, photos, and reports on a writing camp for young storytellers and teachers from the St. Vrain Valley School District. One of the podcasts in the English language arts sections is of the original Sherlock Holmes books, presented in 15- to 20-minute episodes. Another is a podcast about children's literature from the viewpoint of a school library/media specialist from Auburn, Washington; most of the episodes include book news, reviews of books, and interviews with students and authors. A third offers short bedtime stories, a fourth provides a link to podcasts of English idioms and slang, which can be previewed in text before playing the podcast. The idioms and slang site also includes review questions to help students remember what they've learned.

## Teaching Students with AAC Systems

Although most students with special needs benefit from using and interacting with a variety of technologies, some students with limited expressive language abilities function best through using a specific AAC system (the types of AAC systems were described in the section on Assessing Language). Students who can access print rather than pictures are at an advantage over those who are limited to pictures or symbols. This is the case because print-based systems offer at least two opportunities that nonprint systems cannot: the opportunity to develop the literacy skills needed to communicate through print, and the possibility of a greater range of conversational partners (Polloway et al., 2004).

However, Paul (2001) has pointed out that AAC devices that use voice output (i.e., computers that produce synthesized voice) bring a different sort of benefit to the students using them. First, they help students match words and sentences to their intended meanings, thus improving phonological awareness. Second, children using voice output devices show greater speech and language growth than children using different sorts of systems. And, third, voice AAC devices have been shown to increase children's language literacy development.

In recent years, speech recognition software design has progressed so that it can be used to help students who have difficulty with reading and writing. Higgins and Raskind (2000) reported that students with learning disabilities involving writing improved significantly in writing productivity, content, and ideas when using speech recognition software rather than dictating to someone or attempting to write themselves.

LD Online (2003b) has compiled numerous resources for teachers wishing to learn more about using assistive technology (AT) of all sorts, including AAC devices, multimedia software, and reading software. Their site also includes links to the following sorts of information:

- what assistive technology is and how it's useful (for students and families)
- how to provide classroom support to students with AT (for teachers)
- how to ensure that AT works (for parents and teachers)
- answers to frequently asked questions about AT (for parents and educators)
- an overview of how AT can help students with learning disabilities

Another useful resource is provided by LD Online's (2003c) frequently asked question and corresponding answer guide to assistive technology. The questions address issues ranging from how to find assistive technology products to recommendations for resources or computer programs to assist teachers with math disabilities.

Family Village (2006), described as a global community of disability-related resources and funded in part by the Waisman Center at the University of Wisconsin, hosts an ever-changing web page devoted to assistive technology for students with disabilities. The page includes links to numerous articles and websites, each annotated with a succinct, accurate summary to aid the user in finding relevant information.

The Alliance for Technology Access (2006) hosts a web page devoted to assistive technology (AT) in K–12 schools, including (in both English and Spanish):

- an introduction to assistive technology and an overview of assistive technology issues for schools; ideas, tools, and resources from around the United States; best practice and stories about classroom success; a summary of access tools built into Macintosh and Windows computers
- a comprehensive description of what assistive technology is in relation to the reauthorization of IDEA; examples of AT in the classroom; connections to AT vendors and state community AT centers; a discussion of when AT is required under IDEA; a description of who pays for AT; and

a list of questions (a mini-assessment rubric) for sites and/or districts to rate themselves on the seven essential qualities for high-quality AT services
- a tutorial in selecting software for young learners, including a two-page downloadable checklist that can be used in evaluating a software title for purchase
- a list of assessment resources that includes quality indicators for AT services; links to descriptions of the Education Tech Points Framework, which covers referral, evaluation, extended assessment, plan development, implementation, and periodic review; a link to an AT policy checklist that can be used to address conceptual, legal, empirical, theoretical, normative, political, cultural, and historical issues surrounding the use of AT
- a best practices section that includes 10 components
- success stories from many areas
- a comprehensive summary of operating system software access features for Macintosh and Windows computers
- description of a teacher training program in AT in a large, suburban school district
- a description of AT training resources, including links to different guidelines related to different training outcomes and an annotated list of links to training resources

The Georgia Department of Education, on their Teacher Resource Center web page, offers an annotated list of links to web resources in assistive technologies. The links include:

- ABLEDATA, a searchable database
- descriptions of how assistive technology helps students with physical and/or mental challenges
- explanations of assistive technology for parents
- assistive technologies for students with mild disabilities
- an assistive technology guide published by the Schwab Foundation for Learning
- a checklist for using assistive technology across instructional areas
- suggestions for using assistive technology in the classroom
- technical support services for local school system personnel and their students
- an activity exchange for users of Intellitools—by teachers for teachers
- a searchable, online sign language dictionary (MySignLink)
- a portal for teachers, school personnel, administrators, families, policy makers, and students with disabilities—current research findings regarding the use of assistive technology in education
- an organization that connects people with disabilities to technology tools
- information on the legal rights regarding obtaining assistive technology in the United States

Amdor (2006) has developed a lesson plan using assistive technology with secondary students in language arts, specifically in the writing process. The purpose of Amdor's plan is for her students to use AT software to research, organize, write, and edit essays. The unit plan may take several days to several weeks to complete. She describes the process in detail, including:

- the preparation required, the procedures the students engage in (linked to Iowa's language arts standards)
- tools and resources
- hardware
- timeline and course outline
- the final assessment
- technology resources
- background information about her school and community
- detailed information about her students, their learning needs, and their progress through the unit
- how the activity has evolved over the school year

The lesson plan is downloadable, as are copies of the probe questions Amdor used throughout the unit.

**Reflective Question 5.8:** ***Consider an individual student with a particular disability and assume a given age. What forms of assistive technology may be particularly beneficial to this student in enhancing their learning?***

## MAKING IT WORK

Integral to any type of language instruction, regardless of age or developmental abilities, is a learning environment that is geared toward maximizing students' continuing development and learning. McCombs and Miller (2007) describe these evidence-based principles, the results of McCombs's longitudinal research into what makes successful learners.

McCombs's research shows that learners learn best when:

- their individual strengths, capabilities, and preferences for learning are taken into account;
- they can combine their own experience and knowledge with new information;
- they can create patterns of knowledge that are personally meaningful;
- they construct their own knowledge and apply it to new situation;
- they become able to think about how they think and learn;
- instructional practices provide a nurturing context for learning;
- instructional practices account for the individual's emotional states, beliefs, interests and goals, and habits of thinking;
- instructional practices include optimal novelty and difficulty, relevant to the individual's personal interests, reflecting real-world situations, and providing for personal choice and control;
- the individual has opportunities to engage in interactive and collaborative instructional experiences;
- their linguistic, cultural, and social backgrounds are taken into account;
- they are challenged to work toward high goals and ongoing assessment is used to provide valuable feedback about their understanding, knowledge, and skills.

## SUMMARY

Increasingly, language instruction takes place in the classroom through collaborative efforts between the classroom teacher and other members of the building support team (e.g., the speech-language pathologist, learning disabilities specialist, psychologist, reading teacher). Because of the tremendous heterogeneity of students, including students from culturally and linguistically diverse backgrounds, teachers require a thorough understanding of communication, language, and speech. To provide the most effective language instruction, teachers must have knowledge about how children develop oral language, make the transition from orality to literacy, and become able to monitor and modify their language learning processes.

Assessment of children's language usually focuses on language form (phonology, morphology, and syntax), language content (semantics), and language use (pragmatics, discourse, and figurative language). Teachers have access to both standardized (norm-referenced instruments) and nonstandardized measures and approaches (e.g., dynamic assessment, questionnaires, developmental scales, criterion-referenced procedures). The primary purpose of language assessment for early elementary students is to evaluate their progress in using their oral language to succeed in learning to read, write, and spell. For upper elementary students, the primary purpose is to determine whether they are making the shift into the world of print and expository texts. Language assessment for adolescents focuses on how well they engage with literary language forms, as well as their success using their metalinguistic, metapragmatic, and metacognitive skills to successfully engage the secondary curriculum.

Teaching spoken language within the context of academic learning standards offers teachers a rich template for designing instruction, particularly given the current developments in the various technologies available in classrooms. Once the teacher's state standards have been identified, student goals can be linked directly to specific standards representing the areas of spoken language targeted for instruction. For teachers of early elementary students, the focus of language instruction is on vocabulary (semantics), metalinguistic ability (phonological awareness, homonym/antonym/synonym knowledge, humor, multiple-meaning words), pragmatic ability (narrative and classroom discourse), and early metacognitive ability (developing students' awareness of how they think and learn).

The emphasis of language instruction for teachers of upper elementary students is on discourse (understanding and learning from classroom lectures, accessing descriptive and explanatory text) and fine-tuning metalinguistic, metapragmatic, and metacognitive abilities. Language instruction for secondary students focuses on increasing their understanding and use of persuasive/argumentative discourse, expanding their knowledge of written narrative discourse, increasing their figurative language use, and extending their metacognitive abilities.

CHAPTER

6

# Reading: Introduction and Word Recognition[1]

The ability to read is essential for living in today's world; personal independence requires at least functional literacy. Failure to read restricts academic progress because proficiency in math, English, science, or social studies depends on an ability to read. Most careers require at least minimal reading skills. Reading is also a key to personal and social adjustment and to successful involvement in community activities. As a consequence, this text includes two chapters on reading, with an introduction and a focus on word recognition in this chapter and comprehension as the emphasis of Chapter 7.

Reading, reading failure, and ways to teach reading are dominant issues for teachers working with students with special needs. This concern—and appropriate preoccupation by teachers—is underscored by Lyon (1995) in his observations about students with learning disabilities, a concern that can be generalized to other students with special needs as well. He states:

> At least 80 to 85 percent of children and adults diagnosed with LD have their most severe difficulties in learning to read. This is unfortunate since the major task in the early school grades is to learn to read, and most activities in the early and later grades, as well as in adulthood, involve and rely upon the ability to read. For example, consider being a child in elementary school, who, at the tender age of seven, cannot read—who cannot do what most others are able to do effortlessly—and knows it. Consider the humiliation and embarrassment that this youngster feels when called upon to read aloud in class and can only respond in a labored and inaccurate fashion. Think ahead to the fourth grade and beyond, where the ability to learn about history, the English language, mathematics, current events, and the rich tapestries of literature and science are inaccessible because all of this learning requires the ability to read rapidly, fluently, and accurately. . . . The eager third graders experiencing reading difficulties become, in turn, the frustrated ninth graders who drop out of school, the barely literate 25-year-olds who read at the fourth-grade level, the members of the thirty-something generation who are unemployed, and the defeated adults struggling to raise families and needing to go on public assistance.

[1]The authors acknowledge the assistance of Amy Smith-Thomas, Shelly Pearce, and Alexandra Barnett in the development of this chapter.

## READING PROBLEMS AND CHALLENGES

The acquisition of reading skills is a challenging task for children. As opposed to oral language acquisition, reading acquisition has been characterized as an "unnatural" process (Shaywitz, 2003) that creates difficulties for students at the emergent literacy, beginning reading, and fluent reading levels. Thus before considering the problems that children may experience, it is helpful to first conceptualize what children achieve at these three levels. Table 6-1 provides an overview.

Media reports underscore the problems that students experience in reading. Common estimates of the scope of reading problems include:

- Up to 20% of the total school population
- Up to 50% of the students in some inner-city schools
- 75% of individuals identified as juvenile delinquents
- 85% of students with disabilities

A critical focus for problem readers is the gap between grade placement and achievement and, consequently, the gap between students with reading difficulties and those who are progressing in a typical fashion. This gap has been referred to as the *Matthew effect* based on the biblical verse from Matthew 25:29, "for everyone who has will be given more and he will have an abundance. Whoever does not have, even what he has will be taken from him" (as reported by Mattox, 2004). As Stanovich (1986) explained:

> [O]ne mechanism leading to Matthew effects is the facilitation of further learning by a previously existing knowledge base that is rich and elaborated . . . The

**TABLE 6–1** Literacy development stages

| | |
|---|---|
| Emergent | • Notice environment print<br>• Show interest in books<br>• Pretend to read<br>• Use picture cues and predictable patterns in books to retell the story<br>• Identify some letter names<br>• Recognize 5–20 familiar or high-frequency words |
| Beginning | • Identify letter names and sounds<br>• Match spoken words to written words<br>• Recognize 20–100 high-frequency words<br>• Use the beginning, middle, and ending sounds to decode words<br>• Apply knowledge of cueing systems to monitor reading<br>• Self-correct while reading<br>• Read slowly, word by word<br>• Read orally<br>• Point to words when reading<br>• Make reasonable predictions |
| Fluent | • Identify most words automatically<br>• Read with expression<br>• Read at a rate of 100 words per minute or more<br>• Prefer to read silently<br>• Identify unfamiliar words using cueing systems<br>• Recognize 100–300 high-frequency words<br>• Use a variety of strategies effectively<br>• Often read independently<br>• Use knowledge of text structure and genre to support comprehension<br>• Make inferences |

*Source:* Adapted from Tompkins, Gail E. (2006). *Literacy for the 21st Century: A Balanced Approach,* 4th Edition, © 2006, p. 91. Reprinted by permission of Pearson Education, Inc., Upper Saddle River, N. J.

> very children who are reading well and who have good vocabulary for reading more, learn more word meanings, and hence read even better. On the other hand, those who experience reading difficulties will often develop a failure set about reading, have diminished motivation for success, and will have compounding difficulties over time, thus increasing the potential gap related to their reading ability. (p. 381)

A number of hypotheses have been offered as to the source of reading problems. For example, one common problem cited often is the complexity of the English language (e.g., 1,120 ways to spell 44 phonemes). (See Table 6–2 for a listing of English language phonemes.)

A broader view was espoused by Mathes and Torgesen (1998), who identify three stumbling blocks to successful reading:

- Understanding and using the **alphabetic principle** that written spellings represent spoken words, words are made up letters, the letter system has a purpose and letters correspond to specific sounds, and ultimately that 26 letters (graphemes) are used to map 44 sounds (phonemes).
- Transferring spoken language comprehension skills to reading and learning new strategies.
- Lacking the motivation to read or failing to develop an appreciation of its rewards.

Although the majority of contemporary special education research on reading problems has focused on students with learning disabilities, attention to the reading instruction of students with mental retardation has been more sparse in recent years (Joseph & Seery, 2004; Katims, 2000). Because reading challenges are significant for these students, their need to reach a level of minimum literacy (including the ability to develop a sight vocabulary, decode, and comprehend) remains clear and is consistent with many of the students' capabilities (Katims, 2001).

In addition, students with emotional disturbance also typically have significant problems. Nelson, Benner, and Gonzalez (2005) noted:

> Unfortunately children with or at risk of emotional disturbance (ED) face enormous challenges learning to read. Many of these children have reading problems. . . . Further compounding the reading problems of children with or at risk of ED is a growing body of evidence that suggests that they are likely to respond poorly to generally effective prereading and reading intervention. (p. 3)

Regardless of the inherent reasons for reading problems, the critical element is our educational response (e.g., intensity of instruction, time spent on instruction). Illustrative of this perspective, Schumm, Moody, and Vaughn (2000) report that in their studies of grouping patterns in inclusive classes, instruction was characterized by a "one size fits all" approach (e.g., whole-class instruction, similar materials) rather than intensive and explicit instruction. The consequence was limited achievement gains for students with learning disabilities.

**TABLE 6–2** English language phonemes

| *Consonant Phonemes* | | *Vowel Phonemes* | |
|---|---|---|---|
| ***Phonetic Symbol*** | ***Spelling Example[a] (common graphemes)*** | ***Phonetic Symbol*** | ***Spelling Example[a] (common graphemes)*** |
| /p/ | pie | /ei/ | cake, rain, day, eight |
| /b/ | bag | /i/ | tree, eat, key, happy |
| /t/ | tap | /ai/ | my, tie, fine |
| /d/ | dog | /ou/ | go, toe, coat, snow |
| /m/ | mat | /u/ | boot, true, blew |
| /n/ | nail, know | /æ/ | cat |
| /k/ | cat, duck, key | /e/ | wet |
| /g/ | go | /t/ | sit |
| /ŋ/ | ring | /o/ | box |
| /f/ | fit, phone, cuff | /^/ | cup |
| /v/ | van | /ɔ/ | BOOK |
| /s/ | sun, miss, science, city | /s/ | sir, her, fur |
| /z/ | zoo, buzz | /ɔ/ | for, saw, Paul |
| /θ/ | teeth | /a/ | car |
| /ö/ | the, breathe | /ɔi/ | coin, boy |
| /ʃ/ | sheep, brush | /au/ | cow, out |
| /ʒ/ | measure | | |
| /dʒ/ | jump, bridge | | |
| /l/ | lake, bell | | |
| /r/ | rain, write | | |
| /j/ | yes | | |
| /w/ | wet | | |
| /m/ | where | | |
| /h/ | hat | | |

[a]Examples children may encounter in the early school years are provided. Further examples and an in-depth discussion of English phonemes are provided by Moats (2000).

*Source:* From *Phonological Awareness: From Research to Practice*, by G. Gillon, 2004, New York: Guildford Press: Reprinted with permission.

Vaughn, Levy, Coleman, and Bos (2002) reported on a series of classroom observational studies and noted that, though there was substantial time allocated for reading instruction, the quality of instruction was generally low. They noted that there was:

- more individual and group instruction in special education
- considerable time waiting in both settings
- excessive time allocated to seatwork and independent activities (over 50% of the time)
- limited time for actual text reading or direct instruction

Moody, Vaughn, Hughes, and Fischer (2000) indicate that practices too often provide a basis for failure. They state that "[in our study] the opportunity to receive specialized, intensive instruction is not available to students who are serviced in large resource room classes. . . . We must reinvent special education so that we can provide intensive, direct, and special instruction" (p. 315).

According to Kauffman (2002), the problem is often one of pedagogical emphasis:

> Nothing is gained by keeping students guessing about what it is they are supposed to learn. In all or nearly all of the education programs in which the majority of

students can be demonstrated to be highly successful in learning the facts and skills they need, these facts and skills are taught directly rather than indirectly. Giving information doesn't mean that the instruction is dull, and it doesn't mean that students don't learn to apply their knowledge and skills to everyday problems. . . . [I]t does mean that students don't waste time and effort trying to figure out what they're supposed to learn. It also means that students aren't allowed to learn misrules—the wrong thing or a faulty application—so that their learning can be described as false, misleading, or useless. (p. 236)

Against this backdrop of reading problems, teachers are faced with several key instructional goals. In their classic book on teaching reading, Kirk and Monroe (1940) outline three such goals for readers who are disabled. A minimal goal is the ability to read for protection. Implicit in this goal is reading for survival. Though an important objective, it is by definition self-limiting and teachers of students with high-incidence disabilities should strive for much greater achievement (Katims, 2001). A second goal, reading for information and instruction, includes functional reading that allows the individual to deal with job applications, newspaper advertisements, job instruction manuals, telephone books, and countless other sources of information and assistance. The third goal, reading for benefit and pleasure, should be realistic for most adolescents.

Finally, the importance of reading to all students dictates a broad-based response by schools. Denton, Foorman, and Mathes (2003) note these common threads from effective schools:

- Climate with a sense of urgency and commitment to learning
- Strong instructional leadership and accountability
- Professional development and coaching
- Regular assessment and monitoring of student progress
- Targeted instruction and intervention
- A "no excuses" approach with high expectations for every child (pp. 260–261)

**Reflective Question 6–1:** ***Students with disabilities commonly experience problems in reading. One model that has been used to describe these problems that increase over time is the "Matthew effect." Discuss this concept and identify specific reading experiences that may exacerbate the problems that students have as they move through their school career.***

## READING IN THE CURRICULUM

The importance of reading for all students is universally accepted. Reading must be a significant part of the school day, and teachers should seek ways to integrate reading instruction into other area of the curriculum. Given the frequency of difficulties among students with disabilities, additional practice to maintain and refine skills is essential. In addition, such opportunities provide a place for students to generalize their reading ability. Thus, adolescents can improve their comprehension skills while acquiring basic vocational competencies from trade books; younger students can benefit from vocabulary development while learning basic science concepts.

Regardless of the specific reading approach used, a key issue in reading instruction is grouping strategies. Table 6–3 provides an overview of strategies that can enhance reading achievement.

Agreement on how best to teach reading (particularly beginning reading) has been debated throughout the 20th century and into the 21st century. The key emphases in the reading debate have been decoding-based emphases (e.g., phonetic analysis approaches that teach sound–symbol correspondences) and holistic approaches (e.g., placing primacy on meaning). The following discussion briefly highlights these concerns.

**Decoding-based programs** typically emphasize a skills-based, "bottom-up" approach to reading. Usually focused on teaching sound–symbol correspondences in language (e.g., c-a-t→cat), they are characterized by the direct teaching of a sequence of skills that begins with an emphasis on the phonological basis of language and thus provides a foundation for the subsequent transfer of skills to reading comprehension. This general approach is consistent with research on phonological awareness difficulties in students with special needs. As Fletcher, Foorman, Francis, and Schatschneider (1998) summarize:

> Success in beginning reading reflects the development of fast, efficient decoding skills. Although the primary goal of reading is to comprehend what is read, comprehension is compromised if decoding is not accurate, fluent, and automatic. Underlying both success and failure in word recognition skills is the development of phonological awareness skills. . . . the ability to deal with sound units in speech smaller than the syllable. Children learn to crack what is essentially an alphabetic code by relating language to print. When children learn how print represents the internal structure of words, they become accurate at word recognition; when they learn to recognize words quickly and

**TABLE 6–3** Grouping strategies: Implications for reading instruction

**Whole-Class Instruction**

1. Teachers can involve all students during whole-class instruction by asking questions and then asking students to partner to discuss the answer. . . .
2. Teachers can use informal member checks to determine whether students agree, disagree, or have a question about a point made.
3. Teachers can ask students to provide summaries of the main points of a presentation. . . .
4. Because many students with LD are reluctant to ask questions in large groups, teachers can provide cues to encourage and support students in taking risks. For example, teachers can encourage students to ask a "who," "what," or "where" question.
5. At the conclusion of a reading lesson, the teacher can distribute lesson reminder sheets, which all the students complete. These can be used by teachers to determine (a) what students have learned from the lesson, (b) what students liked about what they learned, and (c) what else students know about the topic.

**Small-Group Instruction**

1. Flexible grouping has also been suggested as a procedure for implementing small-group instruction that addresses the specific needs of students. . . . [In] this way teachers can use a variety of grouping formats at different times, determined by such criteria as students' skills, prior knowledge, or interest.
2. Student-led small groups have become increasingly popular based on the effective implementation of *reciprocal teaching* . . . [which] allows students to take turns assuming the role of the leader and guiding reading instruction through question direction and answer facilitation.

**Peer Pairing and Tutoring**

1. *Classwide peer tutoring* (CWPT) is an instructional practice . . . [in which] tutees begin by reading a brief passage from their book to their tutor, who in turn provides immediate error correction as well as points for correctly reading the sentences. When CWPT is used for reading comprehension, the tutee responds to "who, what, when, where, and why" questions provided by the tutor concerning the reading passage. . . .
2. *Peer-assisted learning strategies* (PALS) borrows the basic structure of the original CWPT but expands the procedures to engage students in. . . . three strategic reading activities . . . partner reading with retell, paragraph summary, and prediction relay.
3. *Think-pair-share* . . . [is] a procedure for enhancing student engagement and learning by providing students with opportunities to work individually and then to share their thinking or work with a partner. First, students are asked to think individually about a topic for several minutes. Then they are asked to work with a partner to discuss their thinking or ideas and to form a joint response. Pairs of students then share their responses with the class as a whole.

*Source:* Adapted from "Instructional Grouping for Reading with Students with LD: Implications for Practice," by S. Vaughn, M. T. Hughes, S. W. Moody, and B. Elbaum, 2001, *Intervention in School and Clinic, 36*, pp. 133–135. 

> automatically, they become fluent. . . . For some children, however, learning these skills is not straightforward. . . . In the absence of explicit instruction in word recognition and phonological awareness skills, our research suggests that many children will not develop proficiency in word recognition ability, and consequently, are destined to a life of reading failure. (pp. 3–4)

The **holistic approach,** most often considered within a **whole language** emphasis, focuses on the meaningfulness of language, stresses the importance of the child's language as a bridge to literacy, and includes speaking, listening, and expressive writing as integral parts of literacy development. This approach builds on the diversity of literary experiences that children are exposed to prior to entering school. For example, as a result of having been read to by parents, young children often develop an awareness of the structure of texts and understand the implicit relationship between speech and print.

When a whole language approach is used, students are provided more time to read "real" books and write their own stories. Basic to the program is an environment rich in reading choices, with easy access to many resources, as well as an opportunity for students to respond to what they have read in a variety of active and creative ways.

As Mather (1992) asserts, no single reading methodology exists that can meet all the needs of all students. Some students learn to read quite easily, requiring little or no direct instruction. Thus, a meaning-based whole language program is likely to provide appropriate experiences for these students. On the other hand, students with disabilities often require intensive, direct instruction that is not available in classrooms that have adopted a purely whole language philosophy. Mather concludes that whole language programs that incorporate various instructional techniques tailored to individuals' needs (i.e., decoding) are a viable option for students with reading disabilities.

Pressley and Fingeret (2005) reviewed relevant research and provided an interesting perspective on decoding and meaning orientations in teaching. They noted that those young students who have difficulties and are struggling are the ones who benefit most significantly from decoding skills instruction at the primary grades. At the same time, those who are of high ability, may benefit more from emphases that are inclusive to a greater extent of holistic instruction and tied more directly to, for example, language experiences.

Although often presented as opposing viewpoints, the holistic and the decoding-based approaches can be successfully combined to guide balanced literacy instruction. Upon analysis of data from their survey of outstanding literacy teachers, Pressley and Rankin (1994; see also Pressley, Rankin, & Yokai, 1996) noted that teachers' classroom practices generally are eclectic. Even those who referred to themselves as whole language teachers reported using direct instructional approaches in addition to meaning-based methodologies in their classrooms. Direct teaching of decoding skills, auditory and visual discrimination skills, and letter–sound relationships were listed as techniques used with students with reading difficulties. Pressley and Rankin (1994) support the assertion that students with reading disabilities need reading instruction that goes beyond the scope of whole language programs.

**TEACHER *Tips*** — **Elementary Level**

## Balanced Literacy Instruction

Pressley and colleagues (2002) identify the following elements of balanced instruction based on their observations of teachers nominated as most effective within their district:

- *Phonemic Awareness*—Instruction in phonemic awareness is a significant component of a balanced program. The methods for increasing phonemic awareness include word games that involve identifying words that rhyme as well as pronouncing words when sounds are added and removed. Students who acquire phonemic awareness skills in the primary grades generally experience fewer long-term reading difficulties.
- *Word Recognition Instruction*—The synthetic phonics approach and related instructional techniques have generally proved more successful in balanced programs than whole word recognition (learning words as wholes), especially with struggling readers.
- *Vocabulary Teaching*—Children often learn vocabulary words incidentally through their experiences in the world, but the meanings learned from these various contexts are sometimes inaccurate. Therefore, vocabulary instruction has been found most effective when the meanings of words are taught directly. Explicit vocabulary instruction has been shown to improve reading comprehension abilities and consequently to produce better readers.
- *Comprehension Strategies*—Some effective techniques for improving comprehension include modeling and explaining strategies (e.g., predicting, questioning, and gaining clarification). Once these strategies have been adequately explained by the teacher, students should demonstrate and continually practice these skills independently (see Chapter 7).
- *Self-Monitoring*—Students in a balanced program learn to self-monitor while reading. Instruction in self-monitoring involves teaching students to reread words and passages to facilitate accurate decoding and comprehension.
- *Extensive Reading*—Students who read a large number of quality books and articles exhibit gains in word recognition, vocabulary, comprehension, and general knowledge.
- *Teaching Students to Relate Prior Knowledge While They Read*—The ability to relate the content of a text to prior knowledge is not automatic skill. Students can increase their ability to make these connections through "why-questioning." The use of *why* questions encourages the reader to utilize previously acquired information in order to better understand content.
- *Motivating Reading*—An essential strategy for literacy instruction involves motivational techniques for struggling readers who may feel they lack the capacity for literacy. The following techniques have proven beneficial:
  - Teach students to believe that they can improve their skills with effort.
  - Provide a variety of enriching reading opportunities.
  - Relate literacy instruction to content areas.
  - Encourage cooperative learning and avoid competition.

*Source:* Adapted from "Balanced Literacy Instruction," by M. Pressley, A. Roehrig, K. Bogner, L. M. Raphael, and S. Dolezal, 2002, *Focus on Exceptional Children, 34*(5), 1–14.

Both approaches can offer benefits for students with disabilities. Whole language reminds us that the goal of instruction is comprehension and that good literature is the best way to attract students to books (Chapter 7 provides further information). Decoding approaches provide a foundation for recognizing words that is essential for ultimately deriving meaning from reading opportunities discussed in this chapter. With careful planning, a teacher can develop a successful reading program that includes direct instruction of phonetic and structural analysis skills that complements a meaning emphasis in teaching reading.

As Polloway, Miller, and Smith (2004) conclude, the key consideration is to develop comprehensive programs (e.g., decoding and comprehension emphases; teacher- and student-directed instructional experiences) derived from validated approaches to instruction. Based on his review of studies of outcomes, Swanson (1999) indicates that successful, comprehensive instructional programs reflect a combination of direct instruction by teachers along with comprehension strategy instruction that enhances the ability of students to work independently.

Comprehensive school programs with multiple facets include, for example, the Success for All program that was used initially with students at risk for reading difficulties in grade 1 and extended through grade 6 (see Slavin, Madden, Dolan, & Wasik, 1996). As Unrau (2004) notes in his review, the program embraced systematic instruction in phonics, individual tutoring, explicit comprehension strategy instruction, program of family support, and professional training for teachers.

No validated reading approach is universally effective for all students. Consequently, as Fuchs and Fuchs (2005) note: "professional pedagogy demands ongoing monitoring of student progress, irrespective of instructional program, so that non-responders can be identified promptly for more tailored attention" (p. 42).

In spite of the volume of research on reading instruction, teachers of students with special needs therefore must be prepared to focus on teaching word recognition and analysis skills as well as on the promotion of meaning through well-designed reading comprehension programs. This chapter examines assessment in reading in general and instruction of skills related to word recognition in particular. Chapter 7 then focuses on reading comprehension. The approaches discussed here provide a foundation for the development and implementation of comprehensive reading programs.

Reflective Question 6–2: ***For years, the "reading wars" have pitted advocates of decoding against those focused on meaning as the primary emphasis for beginning readers. Discuss these two positions and analyze your own views as to the most effective ways to initiate reading programs for young children.***

## ASSESSMENT

Reading presents the reader with many challenges and consists of many essential components. The teacher must understand the many facets of the reading task and know how to determine which skills each student does or does not possess. The teacher also needs to determine each student's reading level before implementing any program. The primary purpose of reading assessment is instructional planning.

Informal and formal assessment instruments can assist the teacher in determining an individual's level of reading competency. Instruments of both types can help determine an approximate reading level for determining where to begin instruction and how to begin to analyze specific strengths and weaknesses.

### Teacher-Oriented Assessment

**Informal Reading Inventories.** An **informal reading inventory (IRI)** is a common instrument to assess reading skills. Several IRIs are commercially available; they typically contain a word-recognition inventory, oral reading passages, silent reading passages, and comprehension questions to accompany the passages.

Word-recognition inventories are lists compiled from the vocabularies used in instructional materials. Administration of the test continues with increasingly more difficult word lists until the student misses 25% of the words. The number of words per grade list usually ranges from 20 to 30.

Three classifications of reading ability can be determined from these inventories. The independent reading level refers to vocabulary that a student can read without teacher assistance and content that can be comprehended at a high level while still identifying approximately 95% of the words correctly. Library books and seatwork instructions should be at the student's independent level. The instructional level refers to vocabulary and content that the student can read with some outside assistance. Students should be 85%

to 95% accurate at this level. The frustration level is that at which the student cannot read with any degree of independence, accurately identifying fewer than 80% of the words. These ranges are included for illustration purposes; views vary on precisely what percentage of accuracy is associated with any given level.

An IRI can also provide for an analysis of errors, which can give added information on specific word analysis difficulties; for this reason mispronounced words should be recorded phonetically. The errors can be classified in common areas, such as incorrect sounds, full reversals, partial reversals, or incorrect beginning, medial, or final consonants. A typical scoring sheet is shown in Figure 6–1.

An oral reading inventory samples a student's oral reading and comprehension capabilities at various levels. The format, administrative procedures, and scoring practices may vary. However, it is advantageous to record the student's reading so that the teacher can listen critically and analyze errors as a basis for instruction. IRIs can also assess silent reading. Achievement and skill difficulties can be determined by students' responses to comprehension questions.

**Curriculum-Based Measurement.** Curriculum-based measurement (CBM) assesses a student's academic progress by sampling his or her mastery of the actual curriculum. For example, to assess reading progress, 1- to 3-minute oral reading samples can be taken under the assumption that as the decoding process becomes more automatic, more attention can be allocated to comprehension. CBM is a valid, efficient, easily understood, and repeatable assessment procedure (Potter & Wamre, 1990) that can enable teachers to, for example, select text material at appropriate levels, monitor fluency, track oral reading miscues, and provide a basis for student self-monitoring of skill, acquisition, and reading progress (Unrau, 2004). CBM procedures are criterion-referenced assessments that measure specific mastery of individual skills. They do not assess a student's performance in relation to a standardized sample but focus on the ability to perform the specific skill stated in the accompanying behavioral objective. An example of the use of the CBM process in reading is provided in Table 6–4.

Checklists developed from a summary of competencies are also an effective informal procedure. The

**FIGURE 6–1** Oral reading scoring system

1. Mispronunciations: Write the child's pronunciation above the word.

   (E.g., They bought the bread at the store.) [handwritten above "bought": brought]

2. Assistance: Write the letter A above each word pronounced for the child after allowing five seconds to elapse.

   (E.g., Hawkeye performed the delicate operation.) [handwritten above "delicate": A]

3. Omissions: Circle each word or portion of word that the student omits.

   (E.g., After the race, the runner was winded.) [circled: "ed."]

4. Letter or Word Inversions: Use the traditional typographical mark to indicate this type of error.

   (E.g., The ball seemed to fly forever—it was a homerun!) [inversion mark between "home" and "run"]

5. Self-correction: Write the letter C above the word if the student corrects an error on his/her own.

   (E.g., They were late but they arrived just in time to ride the train.) [handwritten above "arrived": C, arose]

6. Insertions: Use a caret to indicate additions inserted by the reader.

   (E.g., She was afraid to go into the haunted house.) [caret before "haunted", handwritten: old]

7. Hesitations and Repetitions: Though not errors, these can be noted by a check mark and a wavy line, respectively.

   (E.g., The dog scratched and itched until they put on his flea collar.) [check mark above "scratched"; wavy line under "put on his"]

*Source:* From *Language Instruction for Students with Disabilities* (3rd ed., rev.), by E. A. Polloway, L. Miller, and T. E. C. Smith, 1999, Denver, CO: Love Publishing (p. 280).

**TABLE 6–4** Step-by-step: Curriculum-based measurement (CBM)

**Step 1:** Select a passage of about 600 words from . . . text designed for the grade level the students are currently in or are about to enter. Make sure the passage has a reasonable starting point with respect to content and does not include a large number of specialized words. . . .

**Step 2:** For the student copy, type the text in approximately the same font and size as the original.

**Step 3:** For the teacher's copy, produce the same text as you did for the student copy; however, on the right hand side of the page, make a column for line-by-line cumulative word counts. . . . On the bottom of the page, create a rate box with space for the following information: Words Read in Two Minutes, Total Number of Scored Miscues, Total Number of Words Correctly Read in Two Minutes, and Average Number of Words Correctly Read in One Minute (or Correctly Read Words/2).

**Step 4:** Using the student copy of the text, the student reads aloud for two minutes. When exactly two minutes are up, put a slash mark after the last word read.

**Step 5:** As the student reads, the teacher marks miscues on the teacher's copy by putting a line through miscued words or writing in an inserted word. Miscues are responses to texts that differ from expected responses. . . . Miscues include use of nonsense words, substitutions (e.g., ran for rain), omissions, reversals (words not read in the correct order . . . ), inserted words, and no attempt to say a word. However, self-corrected words, repeated words, hesitations, words read with an accent or dialect, and improper intonation resulting from ignored punctuation makes are all scored as correct. . . .

**Step 6:** Observing a reader's problem-solving strategies while reading a text is quite instructive. Teachers should observe carefully what readers do when they encounter a difficult word. Do they try to sound it out, use context cues, ask for help, give up? Do some of the mistakes make sense? . . . How are errors corrected? . . .

**Step 7:** After a student reads the text for two minutes, the teacher calculates the student's oral fluency rate or number of words correctly read in one minute. This is done by dividing the total number of words read correctly in two minutes by 2. . . .

**Step 8:** Oral fluency rates should be kept for each . . . student. The same text can be used at three points over the traditional academic year to measure oral fluency development: September, January, and May.

*Source:* Adapted from Unrau, Norman, *Content Area Reading and Writing*: Fostering Literacies in Middle and High School Cultures, 1st Edition, © 2004, pp. 102–103. Reprinted by permission of Pearson Education Inc., Upper Saddle River, NJ.

**FIGURE 6–2** Checklist of comprehension skills

| Student Names | Main Idea | Sequence | Details | Cause and Effect | Fact v. Opinion |
|---|---|---|---|---|---|
| Martha | X | X | X | X | X |
| Raul | | X | X | X | |
| Lucinda | X | X | X | | |
| Harry | | X | X | | |

teacher selects a particular area to assess and, during a classroom lesson, observes and records a student's skills on the checklist. For example, in observing comprehension skills during a small-group reading lesson, the teacher might focus on the specific skills reflected in Figure 6–2.

## Formal Instruments

Formal tests provide specific guidelines or tools for screening and other administrative purposes (e.g., eligibility). The instruments typically provide teachers with standard score and grade level information and may provide data on specific skills.

Some formal instruments can be used to analyze skills in the same way as informal inventories are used. If word lists or paragraphs are read orally by a student, the teacher phonetically records the errors at the time of the reading or later from a tape recording. Once categorized, the errors provide a picture of the student's needs.

The purposes of formal instruments are on a continuum ranging from surveying global reading performances to pinpointing specific strengths and weaknesses. Diagnostic tests are used primarily to identify specific problems and to highlight skills needing remediation.

**Wide Range Achievement Test-4 (WRAT-4).** The WRAT-3 (Wilkinson & Robertson, 2006) is an individual achievement test that covers arithmetic, spelling, and reading, including sentence comprehension. The student's test performance determines a grade level, standard score, and percentile rank. The word reading subtest can be administered in approximately 10 to 15 minutes. It is composed of a group of words that the student reads orally. Words pronounced incorrectly are marked phonetically to aid in determining the need for remedial instruction. Because the WRAT-3 assesses only word recognition and sentence comprehension, no judgments can be made about total reading ability.

**Peabody Individual Achievement Test—Revised—Normative Update (PIAT-R-NU).** The PIAT-R-NU (Markwardt, 1998) tests mathematics, reading recognition, reading comprehension, spelling, and general knowledge. The reading recognition subtest measures word-attack skills. As with the WRAT-3, errors can be analyzed to determine skills that need to be taught. The comprehension subtest presents paragraphs to be read silently, after which the student is shown four pictures and is instructed to pick the one that best fits the paragraph. The PIAT-R-NU yields grade and age equivalents, percentiles, and a standard score.

**Slosson Oral Reading Test—Revised (SORT-R).** The SORT-R (Slosson & Nicholson, 1990) is an individualized test of a student's reading level using lists of sight words. Word lists progress in difficulty from primer to high school levels, and the test can be repeated to measure the student's achievement annually. It consists of one page of word lists and is easy to administer and score. Results must be used with caution because the total assessment is derived from isolated sight words.

**Gray Oral Reading Test-4 (GORT-4).** The GORT-4 (Wiederholt & Bryant, 2001) measures oral reading fluency and diagnoses oral reading problems. The test is available in two forms; each contains 14 developmentally sequenced reading passages ranging in difficulty from pre-primer to college level. Each passage is accompanied by five comprehension questions that orally measure literal comprehension. Error analysis gives performance levels for meaning similarity, function similarity, graphic/phonemic similarity, and self-correction.

**Woodcock Reading Mastery Test—Revised—Normative Update (WRMT-R-NU).** The WRMT-R-NU (Woodcock, 1998) is appropriate for students from grades 1 through 12. It is an individual test that measures reading achievement and provides specific diagnostic information. The test is available in two forms with subtests for visual-auditory learning, letter and word identification, word attack, word comprehension, and passage comprehension. The test takes approximately 30 minutes to administer.

**Lindamood Auditory Conceptualization Test-Third Edition (LAC–3).** The LAC (Lindamood, P. C. & Lindamood, P., 1998a) is a criterion-referenced assessment instrument that is individually administered. It is focused on the discrimination of one speech sound or phoneme from another and the segmentation of the spoken word into its component phonemic units. It is intended to identify students who will be at risk for reading and spelling problems because of poor phoneme-grapheme correspondence ability. Its primary intent is to measure the ability to distinguish and manipulate sounds as a basis for success in reading and spelling.

**Test of Phonological Awareness (TOPA-2t) Second Edition.** The TOPA-2t (Torgesen & Bryant, 2004) is intended to measure young children's awareness of beginning and ending sounds in specific words. The assumption is that children who are not sensitive to the phonological structure of words will have more difficulty learning to read. The TOPA-2t is intended for kindergarteners who can benefit from phonological awareness activities as a basis for reading instruction. An early-elementary version of the test is intended to assess difficulties in reading that may be present in first and second graders.

## Use of Assessment Data

Efficient assessment can begin with survey tests that identify major areas of difficulty. Diagnostic tests then pinpoint specific strengths and weaknesses, which are described as precise tasks through informal assessment. Goals and objectives for individualized programs are derived from this information. Teachers then

**FIGURE 6–3** Reading assessment summary

Student's name: ______________ Age: ______________
Class placement: ______________ Teacher: ______________

Key: N = Not acquired P = Needs practice M = Mastered

Reading levels: Independent ______ Tests used: IRI ______________
Instructional ______ Survey ______________
Frustration ______ Diagnostic ______________
Other ______________

Sight word vocabulary: SORT _____ Dolch list_____ Other_____

Phonics:
Consonants

| b | c | d | f | g | h | j | k | l | m | n | p | q | r | s | t | v | w | x | y | z |
|---|---|---|---|---|---|---|---|---|---|---|---|---|---|---|---|---|---|---|---|---|
| | | | | | | | | | | | | | | | | | | | | |

| Vowels | a | e | i | o | u | y |
|---|---|---|---|---|---|---|
| Long sound | | | | | | |
| Short sound | | | | | | |

| Digraphs | ch | sh | th | wh |
|---|---|---|---|---|
| | | | | |
| | | | | |

| Variant vowels | ar | er | ir | or | ur | au | al | on | ow | oi | oy |
|---|---|---|---|---|---|---|---|---|---|---|---|
| | | | | | | | | | | | |

| Blends | bl | cl | fl | gl | pl | sl | br | cr | dr | fr | gr | pr | tr | wn | ap | st |
|---|---|---|---|---|---|---|---|---|---|---|---|---|---|---|---|---|
| | | | | | | | | | | | | | | | | |

Comprehension: Factual questions ______ Main idea ______
Inferential questions ______ Sequence of events ______
Application questions ______ Cause and effect ______

Reading interests: ______________
Comments: ______________

prepare instructional lessons to teach the specific skills indicated by the diagnosis, using teaching approaches that capitalize on students' strengths. The teachers evaluate the lessons through the use of CBM when they are completed and try alternative methods if necessary. Assessment should be considered a continuous process.

Tailoring reading lessons to meet each student's needs can be facilitated by efficient, simple record-keeping procedures. Figure 6-3 represents a form to use to analyze a student's strengths and weaknesses in various reading areas. To use this form, teachers should establish criteria for the evaluation of which skills require practice or have been mastered. Figure 6–4 is a sample class profile of word analysis skills in a format that is appropriate for other reading skill areas as well. Figure 6-5 presents some specific questions that teachers can then use to translate assessment information into individualized teaching plans.

Once information about each student is organized and easily accessible, a teacher can individualize group instruction. Within a reading group, for example, a few students might be assigned a literal-level purpose in reading a selection whereas other students might be required to make inferences. The group can discuss the story together with teacher guidance.

**Reflective Question 6–3:** ***Numerous assessment strategies are available in the curricular area of reading. Discuss ways in which information obtained from formal assessments can be***

**FIGURE 6–4** Class profile of word analysis skills

| Skills | | Lyndsay P. | Karen C. | Mike E. | Sharon G. | Jason T. | Marcus W. | Tony S. |
|---|---|---|---|---|---|---|---|---|
| Reading levels | Independent | | | | | | | |
| | Instructional | | | | | | | |
| Consonants | Initial consonants | | | | | | | |
| | Final consonants | | | | | | | |
| | Consonant blends | | | | | | | |
| Vowels | Long sound | | | | | | | |
| | Short sound | | | | | | | |
| | Variant | | | | | | | |
| | Prefixes | | | | | | | |
| | Suffixes | | | | | | | |
| Comments | | | | | | | | |

Key: N = Not acquired
P = Needs practice
M = Mastered

***blended with curriculum-based measures and other informal assessments to enable teachers to develop an effective and responsive reading program.***

## WORD-RECOGNITION INSTRUCTION: ELEMENTARY LEVEL

The remainder of this chapter is devoted to instructional strategies related to enhanced word-recognition skills. The majority of students with special needs will experience problems in decoding because of difficulties related to phonological awareness and to using sound-symbol correspondences to phonetically analyze words and thus will profit from direct instruction in those areas as well as from instruction in sight-word acquisition, structural analysis, and contextual analysis.

### Phonological Basis for Reading Success

A crucial foundation to reading is the ability of young students to learn and use the productive relationships between the sounds and symbols of their language system. Teachers must attend to this area if problems are to be prevented in children who are at risk for reading failure and if remediation is to be achieved for these young readers who fail to make satisfactory progress.

Research by Shaywitz and Shaywitz (1997) indicates that the difficulties of many children with reading disabilities are related to the limited neurological linkages between the written word and its phonological

**FIGURE 6–5** Assessment considerations to assist in instructional planning

1. What are the student's specific strengths?
   a. What specific phonetic knowledge is mastered: letter names? letter sounds? blending?
   b. What specific knowledge of structural analysis is mastered: plural endings? prefixes? suffixes? compound words?
   c. What sight-word categories are mastered: Dolch list? content-area words?
   d. What specific comprehension skills are mastered: vocabulary? getting the main idea? summarizing? making inferences? recognizing cause and effect?
   e. Does the student comprehend best when reading orally or silently?
   f. What is the student's reading level?
2. What skills are priority concerns (based on the state standards)?
3. What is the next needed skill in each area that can be taught to the student at this time?
4. What is the student's attitude toward reading and reading instruction?
5. What reading program is most appropriate for the student?
6. What independent practice and reinforcement activities can the student engage in successfully?
7. What serves as a reinforcer for the student?

elements. The implication is that these linkages must be taught to give these children an opportunity to improve their skills.

Coyne, Kame'enui, and Simmons (2001) posit that beginning reading instruction should have as its foundation a focus on three "big ideas" which govern instruction: phonological awareness, alphabetic understanding (i.e., the linkage between speech sounds and print), and automaticity with the phonological/alphabetical code. These big ideas can then be complemented with rich, meaningful literary experiences to promote vocabulary development and comprehension.

**Phonological Awareness.** The importance of facility with phonology is best understood by first considering the importance of **phonological awareness,** that is, the awareness of the phonological structure of words (i.e., syllable awareness, onset-rhyme awareness, phoneme awareness; Gillon, 2004). Because the phonological system is the primary problem area for students with reading disabilities, it requires explicit instruction for those who do not learn to read independently.

Phonological awareness includes concern for *discriminating* between words and between sounds, *identifying* certain sounds within words, *manipulating* the sounds in words, *identifying* phonemes (e.g., ax = a/k/s, bake = b/a/k, thing = th/i/ng), and *isolating* sounds in words, such as in the initial, medial, and final positions.

Instruction based on these considerations promotes the ability to be aware of phonemes in words and serves as a foundation for the use and application of sound–symbol correspondences in reading as a component of phonetic analysis. Consistent with this transitional focus, Simmons, Gunn, Smith, and Kame'enui (1994) thus propose that appropriate prereading instruction should include an emphasis on direct teaching of auditory segmenting (breaking words into component parts) and auditory blending (recombining words from smaller parts), as well as letter–sound correspondences. Simmons et al. also recommend that teachers follow these steps in phonological awareness instruction: (a) focus on the auditory components of words initially; (b) introduce the concept of segmenting by starting with sentences and moving to words, then syllables, and finally, phonemes; (c) control task complexity by beginning with words containing fewer phonemes; (d) model and reinforce segmenting and blending skills; and (e) integrate segmenting and blending skills into meaningful contexts of reading, writing, and spelling activities.

Torgesen and Mathes (2000) summarize the following instructional principles for phonological awareness:

> 1. Instruction should begin with easier tasks and move toward more difficult tasks. . . . Many programs begin with general listening activities designed to help children attend to sequences of individual sounds, and then move to activities that

**Laura Smolkin** is a professor of elementary education in the University of Virginia's Curry School of Education, where she coordinates the *Reading Education* program. Her published papers appear in journals such as *Reading Research Quarterly* and *Research in the Teaching of English*.

With the release of *Developing Literacy in Second-Language Learners: Report of the National Literacy Panel on Language-Minority Children and Youth* (August & Shanahan, 2006), the field of reading instruction has begun assembling a synthesized understanding of English language learners and instruction in phonemic awareness and word recognition. The panel suggests that the same principles of instruction for English speakers can be applied to English learners, with certain adaptations. Before considering these principles, it is important to note that English language learners can be very different from one another in terms of their literacy backgrounds. Children who begin learning English after they are already literate in their first language have already developed certain word level skills and may not need the same types of instruction as a native English speaker first learning to read.

#### Phonemic Awareness

One important finding of the panel is that teachers do not have to wait for English learners to acquire English proficiency before beginning phonemic awareness instruction. However, teachers need to keep in mind certain differences between their native English speakers and their English learners as well as certain instructional caveats.

- The sounds of English are likely different in some way from the sounds of the student's first language. This means that children may have difficulty hearing and/or producing certain English sounds.
- After learning about sound differences between the child's first language and English, teachers will need to help children to both hear these differences and to account for these differences in writing. Bear et al. (2007) highlight beginning this work with obvious contrasts between sounds, using the examples of *s* and *m*, for example, which both look and sound very different from one another. Teachers should not overemphasize standard English pronunciations. Students who have repeated exposures to the sounds and pronunciations of English through planned oral activities and wide reading will steadily improve in their pronunciations.
- Finally, if English language learners have developed high levels of phonological awareness in their first language, it is likely that they will also have high levels of phonological awareness in English, particularly if their first language used an alphabetic writing system as opposed to a logographic system such as Chinese.

#### Word Recognition

One challenge in word-recognition instruction with English language learners is that these children, unlike their English-speaking peers, are much more frequently attempting to decode or recognize words for which they have no spoken counterpart. When an English-speaking student tries to decode the word *moon*, successful decoding efforts lead to a known word and its accompanying denotations and connotations. For the English language learner, decoding the word *moon* may be the same as decoding the nonsense word *poom*: the end goal of attaching decoded word to meaning is not achieved. Teachers can address meaning through approaches such as picture support and simple explanations and/or definitions.

This same attention to meaning can be achieved by presenting function words in commonly used English phrases. Rasinski (2003) suggests using phrases such as *What did they say?* or *Where are you?* to provide support for words that cannot easily be conveyed through pictorial representations.

Finally, teachers should keep in mind the good news that studies have shown that effective instructional practices, such as those described above, have enabled English language learners who have initially lagged behind their English-speaking peers to perform as well as, and sometimes even better than, those same peers in a full range of literacy tasks. The key to these improvements is the systematic nature of instruction.

help children become aware of individual words in sentences, and then syllables in words. . . . It may be easiest for children to move next to activities that involve comparing words on the basis of first, last, and middle sounds. . . . Once children have some beginning proficiency with sound comparison tasks, they can be moved to training activities that involve segmenting beginning sounds and blending of onset-rhyme patterns (i.e., c-at, d-og). The final series of tasks should be those that involve completely segmenting the sounds in simple words, or blending all the sounds, or manipulating the sounds in words (e.g., "What word do we have if we say *cat*, but don't say the /k/sound?").

2. Instruction . . . should take place for 15 to 20 minutes every day throughout the entire kindergarten year. . . . For children who require more intensive instruction, small group or individual tutoring should be provided daily. . . .
3. Instruction should involve both *analytic* and *synthetic* activities. Analytic activities require children to identify individual sounds within whole words (e.g., "Tell me some words that begin with the same sound as *dog,*"). . . . In contrast, synthetic activities involve blending together separately presented phonemes (e.g., "What word do these sounds make: /f/a/t/?"). (pp. 45–48)

Varied exercises can promote the development of phonological awareness. Some examples include:

- Expose children to nursery rhymes to highlight how sounds are stripped from words and replaced with other sounds to make new words.
- Teach phoneme segmentation: "What sounds do you hear in the word *hot*?"
- Play oddity games: "Which last sound is different in *doll*, *hop*, and *top*? Which middle sound is different in *pin*, *gun*, and *bun*?"
- Play sound to word matching: "Is there a /k/in *bike*?"
- Work on sound isolation: "What is the first sound in *rose*?"
- Teach blending skills: "What word do the sounds /m/, /a/, /t/ make?"
- Teach children to tap out the number of syllables in a word such as *backyard* or the number of sounds in single-syllable words such as *mat, pin, big,* and so on. (*CEC Today*, 1995, p. 9)

In their review of studies on phonological awareness, the National Reading Panel (2000) concluded that:

- Instruction in phonological awareness is effective in enhancing the ability of children to attend to and manipulate speech sounds in words.
- Instruction in the manipulation of the sounds of language subsequently assists students in learning how to read.
- The value of instruction is more significant for word reading than for comprehension.
- Instruction is most effective when the focus of instruction is on the manipulation of phonemes with letters and when children are taught within small instructional groups.
- Phonological awareness is always a means and not an end, and consequently the inclusion of letters is important so that the phonemic skills can be transferred to reading and writing tasks.
- The provision of early instruction of phonological awareness is not a guarantee of later success in literacy.

Troia (2004), in his review, indicated that phonological awareness (PA) training was effective, but he added these caveats:

- Spontaneous transfer from a trained skill such as segmentation to an untrained one such as blending is rare.
- Segmentation training, either in isolation or along with instruction in blending, yields the most positive effects on reading achievement.
- Some students do not respond favorably to explicit instruction in segmentation and blending and thus continue to experience deficits in phonological awareness, reading, and/or spelling.
- Even when gains are realized, these gains often diminish within 18 months unless the initial training is followed by additional instruction in phonics.
- Sufficient phonological sensitivity may be conferred to children through intensive, systematic phonics instruction in the absence of a special focus on phonological awareness.

Hammill (2004) evaluated the extant literature on phonological awareness and offered cautions related to instruction in this area. He noted that such instruction is most effective if inclusive of training in letters and letter sound associations. Hammill (2004) further concluded: "professionals . . . should focus on actual reading (e.g., decoding, comprehension) and other print activities because they correlate [most significantly] with reading performance. . . . The current interest in using non-print abilities for screening instruction might be overemphasized" (p. 465–466).

**Phonetic Analysis.** Teaching **phonetic analysis,** traditionally called phonics, builds on phonological awareness as students learn how to apply their knowledge of the phonology to the written word.

Instruction in phonetic analysis can build directly on that of phonological awareness. While the latter provides an explicit awareness of a word's sound structure such as through phoneme blending (e.g., /c/ /a/ /t/=cat) and through phoneme segmentation (e.g., bat=/b/ /a/ /t/), the former provides instruction in critical sound-letter (phoneme-grapheme) correspondences (Gillon, 2004).

Phonetic analysis provides a strategy to attack unknown words via verbal mediation; that is, it offers the student a way to decode the unknown by applying a learned rule. Morgan (1995) notes that students who need and would profit from instruction in phonetic analysis need to be placed in those general education classes where explicit instruction is provided.

The National Reading Panel (2000) evaluated research on phonetic analysis instruction and reported that:

- Programs that involve the use of systematic phonics instruction make larger contributions to achievement than do programs that provide no such instruction or unsystematic phonics instruction.
- Systematic phonics instruction can be effective through a variety of delivery modes including tutorial approaches, small-group instruction, and class instruction.
- Instruction is most effective when taught to younger children (i.e., grades K–1). It should begin with basic foundational knowledge, which includes instruction on letters and phonemic awareness.
- Systematic phonics instruction results in significant improvement in the reading performance of young children at risk for developing further problems and also for readers with disabilities. However, in general, low achieving readers nevertheless make less progress.
- Rather than interfering with students' ability to read and comprehend textual material, systematic phonics instruction has a positive effect on their growth in this area as well.

The National Reading Panel (2000) concluded with this caution: "phonics teaching is a means to an end. . . . Students need to be able to blend sounds together to decode words, and they need to break spoken words into the constituent sounds to write words. Programs that focus too much on the teaching of letter-sound relationships and not enough on putting them to use are unlikely to be very effective" (section 2, p. 96).

Coyne, Kame' enui, Simmons, and Hart (2004) discuss two hypotheses concerning early, phonologically based reading interventions. They identify a hypothesized *inoculation* or *vaccination effect*, suggesting that intensive and strategic early intervention programs that are effective are likely to prevent further difficulties. On the other hand, the hypothesized *insulin effect* would suggest that the positive benefits of such early intervention programs in the short term would only be maintained if there was a commitment to continue intensive support for young readers. Their research indicated, on the one hand, the importance of explicit and systematic instruction in phonological skills and the alphabetic system in kindergarten. However, the results were not clear as to whether the maintenance of these skills subsequently was due to a true inoculation effect or whether it was sustained because a continued emphasis on code-based instruction in grade 1 sustains the skills.

Phonics instruction has also been evaluated for its impact on reading fluency. Fluency is defined as reading effectively, as reflected in speed, word recognition, and *prosody* (i.e., "the ability to orally read sentences expressively, with appropriate phasing and intonation," Tompkins, 2006, p. 174). Although research supports the fact that word-recognition skills benefit from intensive and systematic instruction in phonics, it will not always result in the development of fluent readers (Pressley & Fingeret, 2005).

As is often the case in special education research on instruction, the primary population is students with learning disabilities. However, phonics-based approaches also have been found effective with students with mental retardation and such focus should be part of programs for these students as well. Joseph and Seery (2004) noted:

> The findings . . . suggest individuals with mental retardation have capabilities to grasp and generalize phonetic analysis skills from one context to another context. . . . Teachers . . . might want to consider incorporating explicit teaching of sound-symbol correspondences, as well as prerequisite skills like phonemic awareness, in their literacy program. (pp. 93–94)

Phonetic analysis can be used as an initial step in a developmental program with young students just beginning to learn to read, or it can be used as a remedial technique with students who have developed a strong sight vocabulary but lack the skills needed to analyze unfamiliar words. The teacher's goal is to produce fluent readers with the necessary skills to decode unknown words. Once decoded, the words should become part of the students' sight-word vocabularies so that they can be read without analysis when next encountered.

The sequence for learning phonetic skills described below is adapted from the classic work of Orton (1964):

1. /b/, /s/, /f/, /m/, /t/ in initial and final positions
2. short /a/
3. all consonants except the five already learned

4. short vowels: /o/, /i/, /u/, /e/
5. consonant digraphs (/sh/, /ch/, /th/, /wh/)
6. initial consonant blends (/bl/, /br/, /st/)
7. final consonant blends (/nd/, /nk/)
8. long vowels (final /e/, double vowels)
9. r-influenced vowels (/er/, /ir/, /ur/, /ar/)
10. suffixes (*-s*, *-ing*, *-ed*)
11. vowel teams (/ai/, /ea/, /ow/, /ea/)
12. vowel diphthongs (/oy/, /au/)
13. prefixes (*e-*, *pre-*, *un-*)

This sequence introduces five consonants, then short /a/. It allows the formation of short words quickly (e.g., *bat, fat, tab*) to provide immediate decoding experience.

The Center for the Future of Teaching and Learning (1996) emphasizes that explicit instruction should be provided on the sound-spelling correspondences that are observed most frequently in the English language. Successful ability to decode based on these sound-spelling relationships is necessary for learning to read and to eliminate the need for the virtually infinite number of potential relationships that could be incorporated within an instructional program (see Table 6–5).

**Teaching Phonetic Analysis Skills.** A variety of strategies and numerous commercial programs are available for teaching phonetic analysis. Grossen and Carnine (1993) outline four general steps for successful phonics instruction:

1. **Introduce letter–sound correspondence in isolation.** Letter-sound correspondences should be taught directly, instead of through implicit

**TABLE 6–5** The 48 most regular sound–letter relationships

| | | | | | |
|---|---|---|---|---|---|
| a | as in fat | g | as in goat | v | |
| m | | l | | e | |
| t | | h | | u-e | as in use |
| s | | u | | p | |
| i | as in sit | c | as in cat | w | "woo" as in well |
| f | | b | | j | |
| a-e | as in cake | n | | i-e | as in pipe |
| d | | k | | y | "yee" as in yuk |
| r | | o-e | as in pole | z | |
| ch | as in chip | ou | as in cloud | kn | as in know |
| ea | beat | oy | toy | oa | boat |
| ee | need | ph | phone | oi | boil |
| er | fern | qu | quick | ai | maid |
| ay | hay | sh | shop | ar | car |
| Igh | high | th | thank | au | haul |
| ew | shrewd | ir | first | aw | lawn |

*Source:* From "Thirty Years of NICHD Research; What We Now Know About How Children Learn to Read," by the Center for the Future of Teaching and Learning, 1996. *Effective School Practices, 15*(3), p. 40.

approaches in which individual letters are never pronounced in isolation. For example, instead of introducing /s/ by its inclusion in *sun* or *soap*, it should be written in isolation and pronounced /sss/. Some instructors would like to see sounds in isolation used carefully and tied as quickly as possible to usage in words.

2. **Teach students to blend sounds to read words.** Students should be taught to blend sounds after they have learned two sounds that can be blended, such as */a/* and */m/*. Breaks in words can be dealt with by instructing students to say the word faster.
3. **Provide immediate feedback on oral reading errors.** Oral reading provides a mechanism by which teachers can identify and correct students' reading errors.
4. **Provide extensive practice.** New sounds should be practiced in isolation daily over several days, then incorporated in reading activities.

Polloway et al. (2004) note that a sequential program emphasizing the most critical phonetic elements is essential. The instructional sequence they present includes:

1. Initial and final consonants
2. Consonant digraphs (e.g., /ch/, /sh/, /th/)
3. Short vowels (/vc/, /cvc/ stems)
4. Consonant blends (e.g., /bl/, /st/, /tr/)
5. Long vowels (final /e/, double vowel patterns)
6. *R*-influenced vowels
7. Diphthongs and other vowel sounds (e.g., /aw/, /ou/, /ow/, /eu/, /ew/, /oi/) (p. 323)

In this approach, consonant sounds are taught initially because they are easier than vowels to learn, are most consistently associated with only one sound, and are the first sound in most words. Teachers first must ensure that students can discriminate between the sound being taught and different consonant sounds at the beginning of a word. Consonant sounds can be taught with keywords and pictures. Individual consonants and digraphs should be introduced one at a time and then reviewed along with the sounds previously taught. Before moving to vowel sounds, students should have mastered common consonant sounds in the initial and final positions and should be able to blend teacher-pronounced sounds into words. Once vowel sound instruction is initiated, this sequence is effective to integrate vowel and consonant instruction:

1. Provide the child with auditory experiences to discriminate between similar vowel sounds. A student must be able to hear how a sound is different and unique before he or she can reproduce it in a new word or identify it in a word to be spelled.
2. Teach students to blend a vowel sound to final consonants and blends, and to spell these stems (e.g., *-ack*).
3. Teach students to use onset-rhyme to blend initial consonant sounds to these stems (*b* + *ack* = *back*) (see Table 6–6 for a list of common rhymes).
4. Present words containing the vowel sound being taught and have the student rehearse: find the vowel, cover all the letters that come before it, pronounce the vowel stem, add the initial consonant or blend, pronounce the whole word.
5. When the child can analyze words (which in isolation contain the sound in question), provide guided opportunities that allow the child to use the new sound to decode unknown words in context.

## Phonological Awareness and Elementary Decoding Programs

**Lindamood Phoneme Sequence Program.** The Lindamood Program for Reading, Spelling, and Speech (Lindamood & Lindamood, 1998b) focuses on the development of phonemic awareness by enabling learners to identify and sequence individual sounds in their order within words to promote competence in reading, spelling, and speech. The key element is learning consonant and vowel sounds through feedback from articulating the sounds. It includes a training manual, a research booklet, videotapes, photos of correct formation for phoneme pronunciation, and a variety of instructional materials. A comprehensive review of related research by Truch (1998) focuses on the effectiveness of the Lindamood program within the context of an analysis of the role of phonological processing in reading and spelling.

**Phonological Awareness Training for Reading.** The Phonological Awareness Training for Reading program was developed by Torgesen and Bryant (1994) and is designed to increase phonological awareness in young children with particular emphasis on kindergarten children at risk for failure and first- and second-grade children who have already begun to experience difficulty in learning to read.

**TABLE 6–6** Common rhymes

| | |
|---|---|
| **-ack**<br>black, pack, quack, stack | **-ide**<br>bride, hide, ride, side |
| **-ail**<br>mail, nail, sail, tail | **-ight**<br>bright, fight, light, might |
| **-ain**<br>brain, chain, plain, rain | **-ill**<br>fill, hill, kill, will |
| **-ake**<br>cake, shake, take, wake | **-in**<br>chin, grin, pin, win |
| **-ale**<br>male, sale, tale, whale | **-ine**<br>fine, line, mine, nine |
| **-ame**<br>came, flame, game, name | **-ing**<br>king, sing, thing, wing |
| **-an**<br>can, man, pan, than | **-ink**<br>pink, sink, think, wink |
| **-ank**<br>bank, drank, sank, thank | **-ip**<br>drip, hip, lip, ship |
| **-ap**<br>cap, clap, map, slap | **-ir**<br>fir, sir, stir |
| **-ash**<br>cash, dash, flash, trash | **-ock**<br>block, clock, knock, sock |
| **-at**<br>bat, cat, rat, that | **-oke**<br>choke, joke, poke, woke |
| **-ate**<br>gate, hate, late, plate | **-op**<br>chop, drop, hop, shop |
| **-aw**<br>claw, draw, jaw, saw | **-or**<br>for, or |
| **-ay**<br>day, play, say, way | **-ore**<br>chore, more, shore, store |
| **-eat**<br>beat, heat, meat, wheat | **-uck**<br>duck, luck, suck, truck |
| **-eil**<br>bell, sell, shell, well | **-ug**<br>bug, drug, hug, rug |
| **-est**<br>best, chest, nest, west | **-ump**<br>bump, dump, hump, lump |
| **-ice**<br>ice, mice, nice, rice | **-unk**<br>bunk, dunk, junk, sunk |
| **-ick**<br>brick, pick, sick, thick | |

*Source:* Tompkins, Gail E., *Language Arts: Patterns of Practice*, 6th Edition, © 2005, p. 176. Reprinted by permission of Pearson Education, Inc., Upper Saddle River, NJ.

It is an approximately 12-week-long program that teaches sensitivity to phonological structures. The program includes a training manual, picture word cards, rhyming picture cards, and a variety of other instructional materials. It is based on validation studies conducted by the senior author under the auspices of the National Institute of Mental Health. Wanzek, Dickson, Bursuck, and White (2000) report that the program includes a number of key features: is consistent with preferred curriculum design principles, requires limited adaptations for at-risk learners, is user friendly, and provides teachers with an explicit script to follow for instructions.

**Direct Instruction Programs.** Several direct instruction programs can provide approaches to reading instruction in general, with a focus on decoding. The original DISTAR (originally the Direct Instruction System for Teaching and Remediation) program initially was based on the instructional procedures developed by Carl Bereiter and Siegfried Engelmann in the 1960s for use with young, culturally disadvantaged children. These programs are highly structured, sequence each step of learning, and contain criterion objectives for each learning task as a developmental program in beginning reading instruction for any student, but these programs are more commonly used for remedial purposes. Two programs are noteworthy, Reading Mastery and Corrective Reading (discussed later in this chapter).

**Reading Mastery Program.** The Reading Mastery Program (Engelmann, 2003) relies on auditory and sound-blending skills. The program presents a phonetic alphabet of 40 symbols taught in a highly sequential manner before introducing letter names. In each lesson, the teacher reads the material to a small group of students and asks individuals to respond orally when given certain designated symbols. Student behavior and responses are monitored during exercises. The program contains reading materials using specialized symbols and seatwork activities focused on both word analysis and comprehension. Other materials in this series are teacher's guides, lesson plans, reading books, workbooks, spelling books, and take-home readers.

**Spalding Method.** The Spalding method (Spalding Implementation, 2000; Spalding Method, 2002) for literacy instruction is a total language approach that involves explicit, multisensory instruction in spelling, writing, and listening/reading comprehension. Specifically, the essential components for this method include phonics instruction, writing, comprehension instruction, literacy appreciation, and a philosophy centered on the development of critical thinking skills for children. The program is commonly used with both general and special education students in grades K–12.

The Spalding program utilizes a variety of techniques in the course of literacy instruction. For instance, during phonemic awareness training students are taught explicitly to segment spoken words and syllables as well as blend sounds into spoken words. Students also learn to speak and write 70 common sound-symbol relationships. Both of these techniques are reinforced through daily phonogram and spelling reviews. In addition, the program incorporates extensive fluency training, vocabulary instruction, and comprehension strategies through which teachers may provide modeling and immediate feedback. Another essential component of the Spalding program is providing students with quality literature and then encouraging independent reading to complement the other elements of the program.

## Sight-Word Vocabulary

For learners who are disabled, a key component is learning **sight words.** Through a whole-word approach students learn to recognize important, high-frequency words without analysis. Students must achieve **automaticity** with the sight words they have learned—they must recognize them immediately and automatically—to be able to move continuously through a written passage. Fluent readers use their sight vocabulary consistently, applying phonetic analysis only to new words.

To be remembered, sight words must already be in the learner's speaking and comprehension vocabulary. The most common source of sight words is from high-frequency word lists (see Table 6–7). As can be noted in the list, a substantial number of these words are phonetically irregular, do not lend themselves to decoding, and thus are best learned as sight, or whole words. Sight words also can be selected from a variety of sources. Language experience stories (see Chapter 7) include words that are inherently important to the student and are therefore an excellent source of initial words. Survival words (e.g., *exit* and *poison*) and survival phrases (e.g., *keep out*) are also important (see page 191). If a basal series is used, words from the particular program become a focus of sight-word instruction.

With all students, but especially with those experiencing reading difficulty, a variety of strategies should be used to teach sight words and success is often a function of multiple exposures to achieve automaticity. Thus the challenge of sight-word instruction is to provide students with multiple exposures to words through varied means. Several strategies are described below.

**Fernald Method.** The Fernald method (Fernald, 1943) is a classic multisensory approach combining language experience with visual, kinesthetic, and tactile (VAKT) instructional techniques. The program consists of four steps: eliciting a word from the student, writing it large enough for the student to trace, saying the word as the student traces the word, and having the student write the word from memory. These steps are intended to provide ways to develop a sight vocabulary by offering the students multiple ways of experiencing the word. Words can then be alphabetically filed in a word bank. When several words have been learned, the student uses them to dictate a story to the teacher. As the student progresses, the procedure can be modified in various ways. For example, tracing can be done with letters made of sandpaper, smooth paper laid on sandpaper, or sand sprinkled on glue. Teachers should focus on the potential benefits of teaching new words through multiple means. Rather than rigid adherence to the sequence outlined by Fernald, teachers are encouraged to investigate multisensory strategies that are effective for individual students and enhance their recognition of sight words.

**Repeated Readings.** Sometimes referred to as multiple oral readings (MOR), this approach is based on the assumption that limiting the number of possible responses results in an increased probability of accuracy; the greater the problems the child experiences in word recognition, the greater the benefit of redundancy through **repeated readings.** Although this discussion of MOR is included within the sight-word vocabulary section, the technique has far greater utility (e.g., fluency, comprehension). For example, Mercer, Campbell, Miller, Mercer, and Lane (2000) indicate that they found the use of repeated readings beneficial to middle school students in terms of building fluency and reinforcing instruction in sound-symbol correspondences.

Moyer (1982) outlines the following steps for MOR:

1. Choose materials at a level that results in limited difficulty in word recognition.
2. Read initially at a comfortable pace.
3. Reread three to four times, increasing the speed with each reading.
4. Use passages of approximately three to four paragraphs on the average; vary according to the student's needs.

A derivative of multiple oral readings is timed-repeated readings (Sample, 2005). With this approach,

**TABLE 6–7** 300 high-frequency words

| | | | | | |
|---|---|---|---|---|---|
| a | children | great | looking | ran | through |
| about | city | green | made | read | time |
| after | come | grow | make | red | to |
| again | could | had | man | ride | toad |
| all | couldn't | hand | many | right | together |
| along | cried | happy | may | road | told |
| always | dad | has | maybe | room | too |
| am | dark | hat | me | run | took |
| an | day | have | mom | said | top |
| and | did | he | more | sat | tree |
| animals | didn't | head | morning | saw | truck |
| another | do | hear | mother | say | try |
| any | does | heard | mouse | school | two |
| are | dog | help | Mr. | sea | under |
| around | don't | hen | Mrs. | see | until |
| as | door | her | much | she | up |
| asked | down | here | must | show | us |
| at | each | hill | my | sister | very |
| ate | eat | him | name | sky | wait |
| away | end | his | need | sleep | walk |
| baby | even | home | never | small | walked |
| back | ever | house | new | so | want |
| bad | every | how | next | some | wanted |
| ball | everyone | I | nice | something | was |
| be | eyes | I'll | night | soon | water |
| bear | far | I'm | no | started | way |
| because | fast | if | not | stay | we |
| bed | father | in | nothing | still | well |
| been | find | inside | now | stop | went |
| before | fine | into | of | stories | were |
| began | first | is | off | story | what |
| behind | fish | it | oh | sun | when |
| best | fly | it's | old | take | where |
| better | for | its | on | tell | while |
| big | found | jump | once | than | who |
| bird | fox | jumped | one | that | why |
| birds | friend | just | only | that's | will |
| blue | friends | keep | or | the | wind |
| book | frog | king | other | their | witch |
| books | from | know | our | them | with |
| box | fun | last | out | then | wizard |
| boy | garden | left | over | there | woman |
| brown | gave | let | people | these | words |
| but | get | let's | picture | they | work |
| by | girl | like | pig | thing | would |
| called | give | little | place | things | write |
| came | go | live | play | think | yes |
| can | going | long | pulled | this | you |
| can't | good | look | put | thought | you're |
| cat | got | looked | rabbit | three | your |

*Source:* Adapted from Tompkins, Gail E., *Literacy for the 21st Century: A Balanced Approach*, 4th Edition, © 2006, p. 201. Reprinted by permission of Pearson Education, Inc., Upper Saddle River, NJ.

teachers can (1) select a passage of approximately 100 words, (2) have students reread the passage until they reach a predetermined rate of fluency with regard to words per minute and also word recognition accuracy, (3) engage in self-assessment by graphing the results to show continued improvement, and (4) use self- or peer-mediated strategies to enhance further performance.

The National Reading Panel (2000) concludes that repeated reading can positively affect students' reading:

> In the early stage of reading instruction, the beginning reader may be accurate in word recognition but the process is likely to be slow and effortful. With increased practice and repeated exposure to the words in a text that the student reads, word recognition continues to be accurate [and improvements are] evident in the speed and ease of word recognition as well. Continued reading practice helps make the word recognition process increasingly automatic. (p. 3–8)

Based on their review of research since the publication of the National Reading Panel's report, Pressley and Fingeret (2005) concluded that multiple readings is an effective approach to enhance fluency. Further they indicated that teacher guidance was the critical component and resulted in more significant gains in both fluency and in reading comprehension than occurred when the student was assigned to reread passages on his or her own.

**Unison Reading.** Several approaches represent forms of *unison reading.* With the neurological impress method (NIM), the students and the teacher read aloud in unison or echo fashion. The instructor sits behind the student and reads slightly faster and louder, pointing to the words as they are read (Ekwall & Shanker, 1988). This method is recommended for use for 10 minutes daily. Progress usually occurs quickly, so this strategy should be terminated if no improvement is noted in a reasonable period of time. Because research on this technique has been mixed, teachers should evaluate its effectiveness when using it.

Teachers may also want to use *imitative reading*, which is a similar procedure for improving the fluency of students with reading difficulties. The teacher reads very simple, short segments aloud as the student follows silently. The student then tries to read the same phrase or sentence aloud. The procedure is repeated until the student reads the material with fluency. Gradually the teacher increases the length of the sections being read to the student (Henk, Helfeldt, & Platt, 1986).

In *paired reading*, two students who work well together and who have similar instructional reading levels read aloud in unison (Henk et al., 1986). Material familiar to both students is used in the initial stages of paired reading. After the two develop a sense of trust and cooperation, less familiar text can be introduced. As they work together, one student can assist when the other hesitates or makes an error. Tape recording of these oral reading sessions can help both students evaluate their reading fluency.

**Edmark Reading Program.[2]** The Edmark Program consists of two levels designed to teach basic sight vocabulary. The program was originally designed to instruct students with mental retardation through a systematic approach that would encourage motivation and cooperative behaviors (Bijou, Birnbrauer, Kidder, & Tague, 1966), but it has been used successfully with other students, primarily to help them acquire a basic sight vocabulary. Print and software editions are available.

For each lesson, students are asked to follow a systematic method of learning, with emphasis on errorless discrimination. Following each lesson, the student participates in a set of various activities including stories, direction cards, and picture/phrase cards. Both levels introduce words in groups of 10. There are posttests given at the end of each group for review. The stories and activities that follow each lesson have story ideas that relate to real-life situations to capture student interest. The stories increase to storybooks in Level 2.

Level 1 includes lessons for 150 basic sight vocabulary words. This level also introduces simple endings (-ed, -ing, -s). The goal of Level 1 is to have the nonreader at a first-grade level. Level 2 introduces 200 new words. This level includes more complex words, including compound words. The goal of Level 2 is to have the student reading at a third-grade level.

**Vocabulary Instruction.** Sight-word development often focuses on the recognition and rapid recall of words in text. However, a critical aspect is the development of vocabulary. Because of its clear ties to comprehension, we consider it briefly here and then focus further on the topic in Chapter 7.

Pressley and Fingeret (2005) note the following research-validated approaches to vocabulary development:

> - Expose students to a variety of new vocabulary
> - Repeat new words over a number of days
> - Provide word definitions but also highlight nuances not obvious from a short dictionary definition
> - Give students the chance to practice new words and use them in a variety of ways. (p. 49)

[2]The authors thank Valerie Casto for developing this section describing the Edmark Reading Program.

**TABLE 6–8** Common words with more than five meanings

| | | | | | |
|---|---|---|---|---|---|
| act | drive | lay | place | set | strike |
| air | dry | leave | plant | sharp | stroke |
| away | dull | line | plate | shine | strong |
| bad | eye | low | play | shoot | stuff |
| bar | face | make | point | short | sweep |
| base | fail | man | post | side | sweet |
| black | fair | mark | print | sight | swing |
| blow | fall | mind | quiet | sign | take |
| boat | fast | mine | rain | sing | thick |
| break | fire | natural | raise | sink | thing |
| carry | fly | new | range | slip | think |
| case | good | nose | rear | small | throw |
| catch | green | note | rest | sound | tie |
| change | hand | now | return | spin | tight |
| charge | have | off | rich | spread | time |
| check | head | open | ride | spring | touch |
| clear | heel | out | right | square | tough |
| color | high | paper | ring | stamp | train |
| count | hold | part | rise | star | trip |
| cover | hot | pass | roll | stay | turn |
| crack | house | pay | rule | step | under |
| cross | keep | pick | run | stick | up |
| crown | key | picture | scale | stiff | watch |
| cut | knock | piece | score | stock | way |
| draw | know | pitch | serve | stop | wear |

*Source:* Tompkins, Gail E., (2006). *Literacy for the 21st Century: A Balanced Approach*, 4th Edition, © 2006, p.201. Reprinted by permission of Pearson Education, Inc., Upper Saddle River, NJ.

Students with reading difficulties are often challenged by the complexity of vocabulary. For example, particular problems can include confusion with homophones (i.e., words that sound the same but are spelled differently) and words with multiple meanings. Table 6–8 presents a list of the latter.

## Structural Analysis

**Structural analysis** skills enable students to use larger segments of words for decoding cues. Recognition of root words, compound words, prefixes, suffixes, contractions, and plurals allows students to use clusters of letters to assist in reading a new word. Structural analysis is an essential word-recognition strategy that directly influences fluency; continued letter-by-letter phonetic analysis slows the reading process and will inhibit comprehension. The strategies suggested for teaching phonics also apply to teaching the structural elements related to meaning units, that is, morphemes in words (e.g., prefixes, suffixes).

One key area of structural analysis is syllabication. The method described herein was developed to teach students to recognize and count syllables, to apply two rules to words with two or more syllables, and to rely on vocabulary to correct any distortions in pronunciations. Without a multitude of rules to memorize, students can read longer words using the phonetic generalizations learned previously.

The first rule, dividing syllables between two consonants, can be illustrated by the word *rabbit*. Instruction emphasizes that *rabbit* should have two syllables (two sounded vowels), should be divided between *b* and *b* (two consonants together), and then read as two small words and blended.

The second rule, dividing syllables between a vowel and a consonant, can be illustrated by the word *favor*. Division would fall between *a* and *v* (because of the vowel-consonant-vowel combination), and the word would be read and blended. These two rules can extend to words with more syllables (e.g., *discussion* and *tomato*, respectively) and with both combinations present (e.g., *envelope, remainder*). The steps (as adapted from Polloway et al., 2004) include:

1. Student identifies how many syllables are heard in known words. Student will divide a known word orally.

a. Teacher orally explains concept and demonstrates on known words.
b. Student is given words to divide orally.

**Sample Word List:**

*tomato, sunshine, toe, cucumber*

2. Student recognizes that a word has as many syllables as vowels heard.
   a. Teacher writes known words and student tells how many syllables are heard and how many vowels are seen and heard.
   b. Process continues until student learns that the number of vowels heard equals the number of syllables.

   **Sample Word List:** *tomato, sunshine, toe, cucumber*

3. Student determines how many syllables an unknown word will have.
   a. Review the two rules of the silent *e* and when two vowels come together, one sound results.
   b. Teacher writes unknown word; student determines which vowels will be silent and predicts number of syllables.

   **Sample Word List:** *domino, barbecue, stagnate, mouse*

4. Student syllabicates words that follow the *vc/cv* (vowel consonant/consonant vowel) pattern.
   a. Teacher writes and student divides two-syllable words.
   b. Student practices dividing and pronouncing two-syllable *vc/cv* words.
   c. Teacher demonstrates process of dividing longer known words:
      1. Determine number of syllables.
      2. Establish first division by starting with first vowel and look for *vc/cv* pattern, then divide.
      3. Establish second division by starting with second vowel and look for *vc/cv* pattern, then divide.
      4. Continue procedure until all syllables are determined.
      5. Pronounce word.
   d. Student practices dividing and pronouncing unknown words that contain *vc/cv* pattern.

   **Sample Word List:**

   - *Teaching: rabbit, bitter, pepper, mixture*
   - *Practice: Volpone, Vermeer, Bellew, Aspic* (*Note:* Names are recommended to serve as unknown words.)

5. Student syllabicates words that contain the *v/cv* (vowel/consonant vowel) pattern.
   a. Follow instructions for Step 4, substituting the *v/cv* pattern.

   **Sample Word List:**

   - *Teaching: labor, favor, basic, demand*
   - *Practice: Cahill, Zuzo, Theimer, Tatum*

6. Student syllabicates words that contain both *vc/cv* and *v/cv* patterns.
   a. Teacher writes and student divides known words that contain both patterns.
   b. Student practices dividing and pronouncing unknown words with both patterns.

   **Sample Word List:**

   - *Teaching: envelope, cucumber, remainder, resulting*
   - *Practice: Provenzano, Tedesco, Dannewitz, Oberlin*

7. Student syllabicates words that have a *vcccv* (vowel consonant consonant consonant vowel) or *vccccv* pattern.
   a. Teacher writes and student divides known words containing *vcccv* or *vccccv* patterns until student recognizes that the division is based on consonant blends and digraphs.
   b. Student practices dividing and pronouncing unknown words containing both patterns.

   **Sample Word List:**

   - *Teaching: concrete, pitcher, contract, merchant*
   - *Practice: Omohundro, Armentrout, Marshall, Ostrander*

8. Student syllabicates words ending with *-cle* (i.e., consonant *-le*).
   a. Teacher writes and student divides known words ending with *-cle* until student generalizes that when preceded by *cl*, the final *e* is not silent but produces a syllable that contains *-cle* and the preceding consonant.
   b. Student practices dividing and pronouncing unknown words containing the *-cle* ending.

   **Sample Word List:**

   - *Teaching: candle, rattle, dribble, staple*
   - *Practice: whipple, biddle, noble, radle*

9. Student recognizes the *y* in the medial or final position as a vowel.
   a. Teacher tells student that *y* will be a vowel in the medial or final position.

b. Teacher writes and student divides known words containing *y* in both positions.
c. Student practices dividing and pronouncing unknown words that contain *y* in the medial or final position.

**Sample Word List:**

- *Teaching: funny, my, cranky, style*
- *Practice: Snydor, Murtry, Tyson, Gentry*

10. Student divides and pronounces unknown words containing mixed patterns.

**Sample Word List:**

*Hirshoren, Shirly, Ruckle, Espenshade*

11. Student syllabicates and pronounces unknown words in context.

This sequence builds on the student's existing sound–symbol skills to analyze longer words beyond the student's current reading vocabulary. To the degree that such a task can be done automatically, it can be incorporated within the process of reading a passage without significant interference with comprehension.

### Contextual Analysis

**Contextual analysis** involves the identification of an unknown word based on its use in a sentence or passage. It functions as a system of syntactic and semantic cueing. Context clues potentially may help readers identify words and derive word meanings, particularly in content-area subjects (Roe, Stoodt, & Burns, 1995).

At the early elementary school level, students' listening vocabulary and comprehension may supercede their decoding skills and thus their ability to use context may be relatively effective. They can use structural and meaning cues to follow the sentences to anticipate forthcoming words and make a guess about one that they might not be able to recognize on sight (e.g., "Susie liked to watch the funny shows on the _____ (television)." "John had a little red _____ (wagon)" (Greene, 1998). Thus context clues may appear to be a useful strategy for young children, particularly for its impact on comprehension. Its use with older students, however, is more problematic and is discussed later in the chapter (see p. 192).

### Peer-Mediated Strategies

With reading instruction being critical to student success, students must be provided the maximum amount of instruction time within the school day. However, meeting students' needs when their ability levels are significantly at variance is difficult. One approach is to use peer-mediated strategies, as discussed in Chapter 3.

In the area of reading, the best-researched intervention using peers at the elementary level is the Peer-Assisted Learning Strategies (PALS) approach (see Fuchs & Fuchs, 2005). The PALS program matches a student with a peer and includes a higher and lower performer within the class. Although the roles of tutors are reciprocal, the program has the student who is higher performing reading first for each of the activities as a way to model the goal performance.

Fuchs and Fuchs (2005) summarized their findings across multiple studies as follows:

- Some instructional content reserved for older and more sophisticated learners can and should be directed to younger children. This content includes decoding and word recognition in kindergarten and fluency building in first grade.
- PALS is a means of transforming knowledge about reading instruction, developed and highly controlled in artificial context, into routines and programs that real teachers in the real schools can implement.
- In spite of our treatments' general effectiveness and robustness, they did not help all individual children. There was always 10% to 20% who did not respond to either of our most successful treatments.
- Teaching of some higher order reading skills, including those that may appear developmentally appropriate, may be unproductive: first graders who received instruction in word-reading skills outperformed those participating in both word-reading and comprehension activities because, we believe, the activities designed to strengthen comprehension inadvertently interrupted reading practice. (p. 42)

**Reflective Question 6–4:** ***Phonological skills have been identified as a key predictor of successful reading achievement, and instruction in this area is validated by research, particularly for beginning and struggling readers. What are the key elements of a program to build phonological skills in readers? How can these emphases be balanced by a focus on other word-recognition instructional strategies?***

## WORD-RECOGNITION INSTRUCTION: MIDDLE AND SECONDARY STUDENTS

The Alliance for Excellent Education (2005) provides a clear context for the reading challenges for struggling readers who are adolescents:

- The number of students who lack literacy skills is not negligible: there are eight million struggling readers in grades 4–12 in schools across the nation.
- If partial mastery is interpreted as performing below grade level, then almost 70 percent of students entering ninth grade and 60 percent of twelfth graders can be considered as reading below grade level. (p. 1)

As the Alliance (2005) further noted:

> Students are less motivated to read in later grades. While these problems may coexist with any of the difficulties cited above, a lack of incentive and engagement also explains why even skilled readers and writers often do not progress in reading and academic achievement in middle and high schools. The proportion of students who are not engaged or motivated by their school experiences grows at every grade level and reaches epidemic proportions in high school. (p. 3)

The critical focus in education on intensive beginning reading instruction for young children must be complemented by a comparable emphasis on reading instruction for older students. As McCray, Vaughn, and Neal (2001) note:

> [I]ntensive and highly structured reading programs can make a qualitative difference in students' reading performance, even for students with a history of reading failure. Our knowledge about what middle school students need to know and how that needs to be taught has improved. What appears to be missing is sweeping agreement that high-quality and effective intervention programs in reading need to be in place for struggling middle school readers. (p. 29)

The discussion below complements the earlier part of the chapter by addressing unique emphases for older students. Topics addressed include decoding instruction, functional reading, contextual analysis, and the use of multiple word-recognition strategies.

## Decoding and Adolescents

Lewkowicz (2002) highlighted a series of *incorrect* assumptions, and provided responses, for *not* teaching decoding skills to adolescents.

1. *"If a student has not mastered decoding skills by grade 8, he/she never will."* The spelling of English polysyllables [is] a lot more regular and predictable than most people think. If students can't decode these words, they need to be given a more effective set of rules and techniques.
2. *"Besides the relatively few students with decoding difficulties, remedial classes are full of students who can sound out words effectively but can't comprehend. . . . Remediating word-attack problems will merely move students from the former group into the later group."* Improving comprehension and improving decoding skills should not be regarded as competing approaches. Decoding . . . helps students to recognize words that are in their oral vocabulary, and this recognition can be critical to understanding. . . . [It] also plays an important role in gradually elevating words to sight word status, thus speeding up comprehension.
3. *"Decoding ability is no longer very important after the middle grades because there is an increasing load of unfamiliar vocabulary, especially in content area reading. Thus it is better to emphasize getting meaning from the context."* [Context] . . . should not be regarded as a substitute for decoding ability. . . . Frequently the context is of limited value, especially if it contains other words that the student doesn't recognize. But it is important to realize that decoding skills also work in tandem with context use to make valuable contributions to vocabulary growth.
4. *"Focusing on the isolated skill of decoding, or any other isolated skills, is pedagogically unsound."* [A] good candidate for teaching as an isolated skill would be a skill that has a fairly complex internal structure, uses information from only a small segment of text, and is regarded by students as an important route to meaning. Decoding meets all of these criteria.
5. *"Older students dislike word-attack training."* [T]he key is to use a more effective approach that results in actual word recognition. Success can be enormously motivating. (p. 29)

**Corrective Reading Program (CRP).** The CRP (Engelmann, 1999) is a direct instruction program for upper elementary, middle, and high school students who have not mastered decoding and/or comprehension skills. The program is divided into two strands, decoding and comprehension, each with three levels of skill development. The comprehension strand presents a variety of formats involving real-life survival situations that are excellent for the adolescent learner.

CRP promotes academic engaged time by providing group lesson plans using teaching strategies that require students to answer aloud and in unison. Each lesson is fast-paced, keeping students thinking and providing less opportunity for students to become distracted. Because CRP uses the direct

TEACHER *Tips* Secondary Level

### Word-Identification Instruction

1. The goal of word-identification instruction for secondary struggling readers is to help them develop and apply strategies for tackling unfamiliar or difficult words accurately, effortlessly, and rapidly.
2. Instructional guidelines for teaching word-identification skills include:
   - Provide explicit, systematic instruction.
   - Directly teach words from the content-area materials that students have difficulty reading.
   - Help students develop basic word-identification skills, including the following:
     - sound–symbol correspondence
     - recognition of phonetically regular consonant-vowel-consonant words
     - recognition of some sight or high-frequency words
3. Research-based interventions for teaching word-identification skills to secondary readers include:
   - *Word-identification strategy:* Students learn how to break words into parts to facilitate decoding. It is helpful if students know prefixes and suffixes and have some knowledge of phonics.
   - *Overt word parts strategy:* Students circle word parts at the beginning and end of the word and underline letters representing the vowel sounds in the remaining part of the word. Students pronounce the parts fast to say the word.
   - *Making long words:* Students use their knowledge of sound–letter correspondences, orthographic patterns, structural analysis, and content-specific vocabulary to form words.

*Source:* Adapted from "Secondary Students with Learning Disabilities in Reading: Developing Word Identification Skills," by D. P. Bryant, J. Engelhand, & L. Reetz, 2002, *CLD Infosheets,* retrieved November 3, 2002, from http://www.cldinternational.org/c/@aH47Gt6iaSFzg/Pages/wordID.htm

instruction approach, it provides a script for teachers to follow. Special motivation for adolescent students is provided in a group reinforcement component, with each student receiving additional points based on the group's performance. Some research (e.g., Polloway, Epstein, Polloway, Patton, & Ball, 1986) indicates that students with learning disabilities as well as those who were mildly retarded increased decoding and comprehension skills after participating in the Corrective Reading Program for an academic year. Further, when implemented with 11th- and 12th-grade peer instructors, CRP was effective in increasing achievement test scores and oral fluency (R. E. Harris, Marchand-Martella, & Martella, 2000). Comprehensive reviews are available from the publisher on the effectiveness of the program (Grossen, n.d.; McGraw-Hill, n.d.).

## Functional Reading

**Functional reading** refers to a level of literacy necessary for information and protection. An understanding of this concept is particularly important for teachers of secondary students who must decide how to teach reading. Instruction at this level raises a number of difficult questions: Which reading program should the current teacher select? Is it best in the limited time remaining to teach functional reading so that students will know some words for their own protection and safety? Or is there still time to teach students decoding strategies, aiming toward an acceptable level of literacy?

Teachers of adolescents continually encounter this dilemma. Choosing the most appropriate approach for each student must depend on a number of critical factors.

- the student's participation, or nonparticipation, in standards-based assessment
- the student's motivation for learning to read
- the teacher's assessment of the previously used instructional approaches
- the assessment information that points to the reasons for the student's inability to read
- the identification of the type of program that will provide a successful experience for the student

After weighing these factors, the teacher can decide to concentrate efforts on functional reading, exert a final effort toward teaching remedial skills, or focus primarily on one option but include the other in a less intensive form. Students need to understand clearly what the goal is and how it will be measured at specific intervals. When goals are organized into small steps, adolescent students are motivated by their progress, which suggests that the

**TABLE 6–9** Fifty most essential survival words[a]

| *Word* | *Mean* | *Word* | *Mean* |
|---|---|---|---|
| 1. Poison | 4.90 | 26. Ambulance | 4.02 |
| 2. Danger | 4.87 | 27. Girls | 4.00 |
| 3. Police | 4.79 | 28. Open | 3.98 |
| 4. Emergency | 4.70 | 29. Out | 3.98 |
| 5. Stop | 4.66 | 30. Combustible | 3.94 |
| 6. Not | 4.53 | 31. Closed | 3.90 |
| 7. Walk | 4.49 | 32. Condemned | 3.90 |
| 8. Caution | 4.46 | 33. Up | 3.89 |
| 9. Exit | 4.40 | 34. Blasting | 3.87 |
| 10. Men | 4.39 | 35. Gentlemen | 3.86 |
| 11. Women | 4.32 | 36. Pull | 3.73 |
| 12. Warning | 4.32 | 37. Down | 3.72 |
| 13. Entrance | 4.30 | 38. Detour | 3.71 |
| 14. Help | 4.26 | 39. Gasoline | 3.70 |
| 15. Off | 4.23 | 40. Inflammable | 3.70 |
| 16. On | 4.21 | 41. In | 3.68 |
| 17. Explosives | 4.21 | 42. Push | 3.68 |
| 18. Flammable | 4.21 | 43. Nurse | 3.58 |
| 19. Doctor | 4.15 | 44. Information | 3.57 |
| 20. Go | 4.13 | 45. Lifeguard | 3.52 |
| 21. Telephone | 4.11 | 46. Listen | 3.52 |
| 22. Boys | 4.11 | 47. Private | 3.51 |
| 23. Contaminated | 4.09 | 48. Quiet | 3.51 |
| 24. Ladies | 4.06 | 49. Look | 3.49 |
| 25. Dynamite | 4.04 | 50. Wanted | 3.46 |

[a]Maximum rating of an item was 5; minimum was 1.

*Source:* From "Survival Words for Disabled Readers," by E. A. Polloway and C. H. Polloway, 1981, March, *Academic Therapy, 16*, p. 446. Copyright 1981 by Academic Therapy Publications. Reprinted with permission.

problems they have faced unsuccessfully throughout their school careers may have solutions.

Reading for protection requires minimal but practical competence. Generally, this is the level of reading achievement that enables minimal survival in today's word-dependent world. Survival words should be taught as sight words, consistent with the strategies described earlier in the chapter. The teacher should provide actual experiences that demonstrate the word's meaning, produce a concrete object, or identify a special characteristic of the concept. A list of survival words is provided in Table 6–9. A parallel set of survival phrases is available from the same source.

Fortunately, most students with disabilities learn to read well beyond the level of survival words. The next stage of functional reading addresses what the world of work requires and thus focuses on sufficient skills to fill out applications and related forms, pass a driver's test, follow simple factor check-in directions, order from a restaurant menu, and handle similar life tasks.

Teachers can use a combination of strategies to teach this level of functional reading. Using a sight-word approach, the specific vocabulary of applications and forms can be taught. The most important step is teaching students to generalize this knowledge by providing practice with the variety of formats and situations that they are likely to encounter. Many workbooks contain samples of forms and applications.

## Contextual Analysis for Older Students

The discussion earlier in the chapter alluded to the difficulty in the use of context that becomes evident as students move to middle school. As Greene (1998) notes:

- New content-area vocabulary words do not preexist in their listening vocabularies. They can guess wagon. But they can't guess circumnavigation or chlorophyll based on context. . . . these words are not in their listening vocabularies.
- When all of the words readers never learned to decode in grades one to four are added to all the textbook vocabulary words that don't preexist in readers' listening vocabularies, the percentage of unknown words teeters over the brink; the text now contains so many unknown words that there's no way to get the sense of the sentence.
- Text becomes more syntactically embedded, and comprehension disintegrates. Simple English sentences can be stuffed full of prepositional phrases, dependent clauses, and compoundings. Eventually, there's so much language woven into a sentence that readers lose meaning. When syntactically embedded sentences crop up in science and social studies texts, many can't comprehend. (p. 76)

Therefore, the challenge for teachers is to find a way to encourage the use of context primarily when it assists in enhancing comprehension of text (e.g., through vocabulary development) and figuring out the occasional word but not to overemphasize it to the point where it becomes a primary strategy used by students.

Stanovich and Stanovich (1995) spoke directly to this issue in noting that "research has consistently indicated that the word recognition of better readers is *not* characterized by more reliance on contextual information. . . . There *is* considerable evidence that better readers are better able to use contextual information to facilitate their *comprehension* processes. . . . However, research . . . has shown that hypotheses about context use in comprehension were inappropriately generalized to the *word recognition* level. . . . In summary, contextual information is simply no substitute for the ability to decode the words on the page" (pp. 90, 92).

The Center for the Future of Teaching and Learning (1996) posits that an overemphasis on prediction from context can have a negative effect on reading and delay successful acquisition. Drawing on the work of Stanovich and Stanovich (1995), the Center indicates that it is incorrect to assume that predicting forthcoming words in sentences is a relatively easy activity and one that results in a high level of accuracy. Rather, it appears that the use of semantic and syntactic cues is a minor aspect of the way that mature readers attack the reading task. Consequently, poor readers are more likely to rely on context to a significant degree when their ability to decode is too weak to assist them in the task.

## Applying Multiple Word Strategies Independently

The use of contextual analysis is a step in the use of CRUSCH, a word-recognition strategy for identifying unknown, polysyllabic words (Polloway et al., 2004). CRUSCH refers to the following:

- **C**onsonant: Focus on the initial consonant sound.
- **R**apid: Rapidly focus on initial consonant, vowel sounds, and prefixes and suffixes while reviewing whole words.
- **U**nimportant: Skip over unimportant words that do not require precise pronunciation (e.g., names).
- **S**yllabicate: Apply syllabication strategies if word pronunciation is essential.
- **C**ontext: Use contextual analysis for periodic (i.e., infrequent) determination of meaning for new vocabulary words.
- **H**elp: Seek help (e.g., from teacher, peer, dictionary).

CRUSCH can assist students in thinking about how they will respond when confronted with unknown words. Although research indicates that mature readers are most successful when they respond to the inherent sound–symbol correspondences in their reading, the steps as outlined will give those who experience difficulty ways to generate meaning for new vocabulary words, focus on the most efficient sound–symbol correspondences that provide key graphophonemic cues, ignore the need for pronunciation of words that do not affect meaning, and utilize more complex syllabication strategies when they are necessary to determine the pronunciation of a particular word and/or an understanding of its meaning.

**Reflective Question 6–5:** ***Although much of the emphasis in reading instruction has focused on elementary-aged students, the struggles in reading continue for too many students at the middle and secondary school level. Consider the instructional emphases that should be pursued for older students and develop a plan to differentiate appropriate approaches for students who can***

***continue to profit from word-recognition instruction and/or students who need a shift toward a more functional emphasis in reading instruction.***

## TECHNOLOGY IN THE CLASSROOM

As with other curricular areas, there has been a significant influence of technology-based interventions in the area of reading. Specifically in terms of reading recognition, computer-based programs provide teachers with opportunities for self-guided lessons that can promote, for example, practice toward proficiency and maintenance learning on vocabulary, an opportunity to match sound-symbol correspondences for specific phonemes in isolation or within a word, and opportunities to drill on structural features of words in order to enhance one's ability to use, for example, prefixes, suffixes, and root words in the decoding process.

Much of the development of assistive technology related to reading recognition has been focused on the challenges faced by students with learning (i.e., reading) disabilities. For this population, the tools available typically represent ways to provide reading remediation assistance and to complement the direct instruction provided by the teacher. For students with mental retardation or intellectual disabilities, there has been far greater emphasis on the use of technology as related to functional skills acquisition (such as related to lifelong skills and community inclusion). However, as the emphasis continues to increase for classrooms to be developed in ways that are consistent with the concept of universal design for learning (see Chapters 1 and 3), technology will continue to afford unique opportunities for providing individualized instructional strategies for students who are being taught in general education classrooms.

As Jeffs, Morrison, Messenheimer, Rizza, and Banister (2003) noted, there are a number of technology-based approaches that can enhance instruction and thus learning, an example of a particularly beneficial approach is the use of multi media—"a combination of graphics, video, animations, pictures, and sound [which] provides diverse learning instruction [and] provides the learner with ample opportunities to become interactive in the learning process. . . . Multimedia learning materials engage the learner in multiple representations of content to be learned" (p. 133). In an area such as reading, multi-media presentations can be extremely helpful adjuncts to instruction by enhancing the likelihood of actively engaging the learner in the reading process.

Another important technological resource for reading instruction is the use of web-based resources. As teachers continue to work toward creating more inclusive classrooms that promote the success of students with special needs, website resources assist in helping teachers develop responsive classroom lessons that provide guidance in instruction, integration of thematic units and specific topics, adaptations for learners with specific reading difficulties, and opportunities to align plans with state curriculum standards (Polloway, Miller, & Smith, 2004).

**Reflective Question 6–6:** ***Considering the content throughout this chapter, identify ways in which assistive technology can be used to accomplish various instructional goals. Pay particular attention to enhancements related to phonological awareness, letter–sound correspondence, and the development of a stronger sight vocabulary.***

## MAKING IT WORK

According to Moats (2003), validated approaches to reading instruction have been identified through research and include these listed below. The discussion in Chapter 7 will build on these principles further.

- Direct teaching of decoding and comprehension skills
- Phonemic awareness instruction
- Systematic, explicit instruction in decoding
- Exposure to varied texts
- Vocabulary instruction on word meanings, structure, origins
- Comprehension strategies for prediction, summarizing, clarification, questioning, visualization.

## SUMMARY

This chapter focuses on assessment and instruction in reading with special emphasis on decoding. Specific suggestions are made for formal and teacher-oriented assessments that assist in instructional planning. Instructional strategies and programs for promoting word analysis and recognition are presented. Special emphasis is placed on phonological awareness and phonetic analysis for students with reading disabilities.

## ACTIVITIES

### ELEMENTARY LEVEL

The activities listed serve as a basis for reinforcing skills in word recognition. The activities are grouped according to activities for word analysis and sight vocabulary.

#### Word Analysis

1. Initial consonant sounds can be practiced by gluing pictures of simple objects on small cards. Have students place the cards on a grid on which each square has a consonant letter corresponding to the beginning sound of an object on the cards. Consonant blends and final consonant sounds can be drilled in the same manner.
2. Make word wheels of word families, changing only the initial consonants. These devices not only give practice in consonant sounds but also are excellent for sound blending. Word wheels are two circles made of oaktag, one smaller than the other and fastened together in the center with a brass fastener so that they can rotate. The different word bases (e.g., *-ag*, *-ad*, *-at*) are written on the exposed edge of the larger circle, and the different initial consonants are written on the edge of the smaller circle. As students rotate the top circle, different words are formed, which students can read aloud to a friend.
3. Make two-part puzzles with an initial sound on one part and a word family on the other. Have students put the puzzles together and pronounce the words. Animal shapes are popular and can be cut between the head and body or body and tail. Use the same idea for contractions, compound words, and root words with endings. Character combinations are popular also: Snoopy and his doghouse, Woodstock and his nest, and Batman and his cape. Three-part puzzles can be made to accommodate adding prefixes and suffixes to root words (e.g., unfolded).
4. Have students make notebooks for sounds. As sounds are presented, students can cut out pictures of objects that begin with each specific sound and glue them into the book. Later, students can write words that they have learned to recognize or spell that begin with each specific sound.
5. List on the board the letters for the vowels, blends, or consonants that have been studied. Have students stand in a large circle with one student in the center. The student in the center tosses a ball to a student in the circle and calls out one of the letters from the board. The student who catches the ball has to say a word that contains the sound that was called. That student then goes to the center and throws the ball.
6. An excellent source providing multiple examples of motivational phonics activities is Morgan and Moni (2005).

#### Sight Vocabulary

1. List words on the chalkboard. Have two students stand with their backs to the lists. As you call out a word, the students turn; the first to find the word receives a point.
2. Make a game board of oaktag with a path of squares. Mark "start" and "finish" squares and various outer squares with directions like "move ahead three squares," "move back three squares," or "shortcut" with a path to another square. Write words that are to become sight vocabulary words in the open squares with a grease pencil. Students then throw dice to determine how far they are to move. They must pronounce the word they land on to remain in the game. The game can be varied by changing the words, and several boards can be made to fit the season of the year.
3. Put pictures of words like *ball* or *car* on one side of a card, and write the word on the other side. Make a game board similar to a bingo card, with each sight word written on it for each child. Place cards with the word-side-up in a pile. Students take turns drawing cards. They must be able to say the word correctly before placing it on their boards. The picture on the back makes the game self-correcting. If the student cannot recognize the word, the card is placed at the bottom of the pile. The first student to get four words in a row in any direction wins the game.
4. A form of "Concentration" can be played by making two sets of identical cards with sight words. Begin with five pairs of cards. Place the cards spread out in two areas, face down on a flat surface. The child turns up a card in one set and then tries to find the card that matches in the other set. When a match is made, the student pronounces the word and gets to keep the cards.

5. Use a chart-size pegboard and attach hooks on which index cards can be hung. Write vocabulary words on index cards, punch a hole in each card, and hang the cards from the hooks on the pegboard. Give students a rubber jar-ring to toss at a hook on the board. When a ring lands on a hook, that card is removed from the hook, and the student pronounces the word to earn a point. The one with the most points wins. The game can be varied by using bean bags to throw at a card on a board or at cards hung from a miniature clothesline with pins.

### MIDDLE AND SECONDARY LEVEL

1. Recognition of prefixes and suffixes can be practiced by listing words on the chalkboard or on a worksheet and having students underline the prefix, suffix, or both. You may also call out words while students write the prefix or suffix they hear in the word, or they may find and write different words containing the same prefix or suffix.
2. Write multisyllabic words on small cards, one word per card. Place the cards in an envelope and clip it to a manila folder. Inside the folder draw several columns, numbered 2, 3, 4, and so on as room permits. The student counts the number of syllables in the word on the card and writes in the proper column. The cards have the correct number of syllables written on the back, or an answer sheet can be provided for immediate feedback.
3. For compound words, develop exercises such as:
   - Matching drills using two lists of words with pairs that can be combined.
   - Adapting the cloze procedures in which one half of each compound word is left blank (e.g., When the winter blows, we huddle around the _____ place).
   - Giving students ridiculous pictures to label (e.g., a stick of flying butter for butterfly).
   - Providing a list of invented words or colloquialisms to be defined (e.g., *slamdunk, skyhook*).
4. To enhance an ability to use prefixes and suffixes, consider activities such as:
   - Color coding of the designated affix being taught.
   - Word wheels with root words in the center surrounded by prefixes, or a suffix in the center surrounded by root words.
   - Speed listing of all the words that begin with a prefix (e.g., *un-*: *undress, untie, uncover, undo*).
5. To assist with vocabulary development, establish a word retirement area on a bulletin board. During the week have students list words that they and their peers overuse. Once a week have the class review the words and choose one or two to focus on. Have students look the word(s) up and agree on the intended meaning(s). Then have them use a thesaurus to find synonyms for the overused word(s). Students should keep a record of their use of the chosen synonym(s) for the next week. At the end of the time period the student using the new vocabulary word(s) the most becomes the manager of the word retirement "home" and is in charge of recording the next week's words (Pearson, 1987).

CHAPTER

# 7

# *Reading Comprehension*

Although word analysis and word recognition are clearly important basic skills, they are not the primary goal of an instructional reading program. The goal of reading is comprehension—obtaining meaning from printed material.

Mastropieri and Scruggs (1997) define comprehension as "a process of constructing meaning from written texts, based on a complex coordination of a number of interrelated sources of information" (p. 197). The authors of the RAND Reading Study Group (2002) define reading comprehension as "the process of simultaneously extracting and constructing meaning through interaction and involvement with written language" (p. 11). Both definitions convey the complexity of this skill and also suggest the complexities associated with effective instruction.

A strong argument can be made that comprehension is the most important academic skill that is taught in school. Shaywitz (2003) estimates that students who are good readers read 1.8 million words per year, whereas these who are poor readers read only 8,000 words per year. Reading is required throughout the school experience and to deal effectively with the demands of adult living (i.e., lifelong learning). Furthermore, it must be applied to a variety of types of textual material (e.g., narrative and expository materials).

The ability to understand written material involves two facets of comprehension: word knowledge and text comprehension. The first facet relates to the development of an adequate and functional vocabulary. The second facet relates to the ability to acquire meaning—understanding, figuring out, and remembering what is read (Shanahan, 2003)—from interacting with a variety of textual materials. Although vocabulary also was discussed briefly in Chapter 6, both areas are emphases within this chapter.

Reading comprehension is certainly an area that is problematic for many students. A combination of key factors associated with the student, the textual material, and the reading comprehension process contribute to the difficulties that some students have. Therefore, their reading programs must emphasize and explicitly teach comprehension skills. Unfortunately, reading comprehension has been an area to which inadequate amounts of instructional time and attention have too often been dedicated (Carnine, Silbert, Kame'enui, & Tarver, 2004).

Students with special needs commonly encounter problems in understanding, figuring out, and remembering what they read for many different reasons, ranging from decoding words to monitoring their understanding of what is read (Vaughn & Edmonds, 2006). Often they lack the background and experiences that contribute to making sense out of text. Dealing with abstract constructs and complex concepts poses significant challenges to some students. The nature of the textual material itself (e.g., the way it is organized, the type of textual material) further contributes to the problems of some students. When engaging printed text, strategic behaviors are needed and many students with special needs do not produce these strategies naturally.

Comparing good readers with poor readers provides a way to conceptualize the problems that poor readers present within classrooms. Bryant, Ugel, Thompson, and Hamff (1999) highlight the characteristics of both types of readers (see Figure 7–1). It is those features of poor readers that require educational attention through well-planned and explicit instruction.

How can reading comprehension be promoted and advanced in learners with special needs? Shanahan (2003), in referring to the National Reading Panel Report (2000), points out that teaching does matter.

> Children can figure out lots of things on their own, of course, and practice can be as helpful in reading as in anything. But the greatest success is . . . accomplished when teachers offer explicit instruction and guidance in several different reading skills and strategies simultaneously. (p. 648)

**FIGURE 7–1** Characteristics of good and poor readers

| Good Readers | Poor Readers |
|---|---|
| **Before Reading** | |
| ■ Consider what they already know about the topic<br>■ Use text features (e.g., boldface, headings, illustrations) to get a sense of what they will read. | ■ Begin reading without a purpose for reading<br>■ Do not consider their background knowledge about the topic<br>■ Lack motivation or interest |
| **During Reading** | |
| ■ Monitor their reading by recognizing comprehension programs and using fix-up strategies<br>■ Use context clues to figure out the meaning of vocabulary and concepts<br>■ Identify the main idea and important details<br>■ Read fluently<br>■ Use word identification strategies to decode unfamiliar words<br>■ Recognize and use text structures to gain meaning from reading | ■ Move through the text, even if they do not understand what they have read<br>■ Do not read fluently<br>■ Do not recognize text structures<br>■ Lack strategies to figure out new words<br>■ Lack strategies to repair comprehension problems |
| **After Reading** | |
| ■ Summarize reading<br>■ Reflect on content<br>■ Draw inferences | ■ Cannot summarize important points<br>■ Do not use strategies to reflect on reading |

*Source*: From "Instructional Strategies for Content-Area Reading Instruction," by D. P. Bryant, N. Ugel, S. Thompson, and A. Hanff, 1999, *Intervention in School and Clinic, 34*, pp. 293–302. Copyright 1999 by PRO-ED, Inc. Reprinted with permission.

## THE NATURE OF READING COMPREHENSION

The definitions of comprehension presented at the beginning of this chapter indicate that this complex skill involves more than being able to answer questions after one has read some type of printed material. The importance of comprehension is evident not only in most school contexts but also in most life contexts, as the demand of being able to comprehend oral and written information on a daily basis is clearly apparent.

A number of key concepts associated with comprehension need to be addressed prior to the subsequent discussions of assessment and intervention. These topics include the principal components of comprehension (inclusion of work and text comprehension skills); types of text structure; specific phases of the reading process; and the instructional implications of contemporary research.

### Principal Components

Comprehension can involve either oral or written input. Understanding information presented orally is a complex process as well and can also be characterized as interactive, strategic, and adaptable. The educational implications of understanding orally presented information were covered in Chapter 5. This chapter is focused on making sense of textual material.

The National Reading Panel (NRP) (2000) identifies five essential areas of reading instruction:

- Phonemic awareness instruction
- Phonics instruction
- Fluency instruction
- Vocabulary instruction
- Text comprehension instruction

The last two areas noted by the NRP relate directly to the understanding of textual material.

The two main components of comprehension are word knowledge (vocabulary) and text comprehension. Word knowledge simply means that students understand the meaning of words and word variations such as figurative language. Clearly a difference exists between word identification (see Chapter 6) and word knowledge. Text comprehension means that students are able to make sense out of passages of varying length and to use this information in other ways.

Specific skills in comprehension do not fit into a clear scope and sequence to the degree that is often seen with word recognition, but there are clearly areas of emphasis that teachers need to assess and address as part of a systematic instructional program.

Lerner (2000) divided comprehension skills into four semidistinct levels: literal, inferential, critical, and creative. Students need to become proficient in each of these areas. State standards in English/language arts require it. For instance, examining the performance standards for a typical standard such as "Read with understanding and fluency" indicates that students must be able to demonstrate competence in these areas. Lerner's four levels of comprehension are as follows:

- **Literal comprehension:** refers to information as printed in text. Attention to literal recall includes comprehension for details, sequence of events, and major characters in the story. Most reading programs have traditionally addressed literal comprehension as their primary concern.
- **Inferential comprehension:** requires the reader to move beyond the literal information to infer the meaning of text. Although it is often mistakenly referred to as a lower-level skill, deriving the main idea from text is a good example of inferential comprehension. In this case, students are required to consider what they have read and infer the primary focus of the author.
- **Critical comprehension:** requires the reader to analyze and evaluate the information that has been read, typically to develop new perspectives relative to the content. All comprehension draws on prior knowledge, but critical comprehension in particular asks the reader to use new information, for example, to compare and contrast it with other information learned at a prior time or to make judgments related to what was read.
- **Creative comprehension:** refers to refining what was read to a level where the student produces new insights and thoughts that spin off the content read.

To complement this model of four levels of comprehension just described, Idol (1997) provides an alternative way to look at text comprehension, as follows:

- *Text explicit:* This type of comprehension is text dependent in that the answer is explicitly stated in the text (passage or picture).
- *Text implicit:* This type of comprehension is implied within the text (or pictures). The derivation of this type of information is based upon two or more nonexplicitly connected details of the passage or picture.
- *Script implicit:* This type of comprehension requires integration of prior knowledge about the subject being read with one or more details from the passage or picture. (p. 112)

## Types of Text Structure

To fully recognize the complexities of reading comprehension, it is necessary to recognize that different types of textual material exist. This is important because these different types of textual material present different demands and, as a result, the need arises to teach students to recognize the differences in text structure and to use appropriate strategies for the type of material they are reading. The two major forms of text structure are narrative and expository.

**Narrative text** is related to storytelling. It is manifest in material such as short stories, legends, science fiction, and other types of fiction. According to the Texas Reading Initiative (2000), narrative structure most often features a beginning, a middle, and an ending. It also typically includes clear story elements, or *story grammar*, including characters, setting, themes, a central problem or conflict, a sequence of events that forms the story line, and a resolution to the conflict.

**Expository text** relates to material that is factual. Examples of expository text include textbooks, biographies, newspapers, magazines, catalogs, and other nonfiction materials. Much of the material that is encountered on the Internet is expository in nature. Expository text will not have the story grammar elements associated with narrative text but is likely to have other types of structures that students must be able to master (e.g., cause-and-effect or compare/contrast features). In addition, expository text (such as illustrated with this textbook) typically will incorporate headings and graphics into the textual material.

## Phases of the Reading Process

The key elements of reading comprehension can be examined across three phases of the reading process: before, during, and after reading. Features that contribute to proficiency and that the student needs to display are listed for each of these phases.

### Before Reading

- Adequate and dependable reading vocabulary in place
- Purpose and motivation for reading established
- Awareness of text structure

### During Reading

- Awareness of one's reading by monitoring comprehension
- Words, phrases, sentences read accurately and quickly
- Connections made between/among sentences/statements
- Questions generated about what is being read
- Background experiences called upon to make predictions and establish relevance to content encountered
- Selectivity applied to what is and is not read
- Content that is of central importance, that is supportive or supplemental, and that is not important can be identified
- Visualizations (e.g., character, setting) can be created to help understand what is being read
- Inferences made in regard to topics presented

### After Reading

- Reflections made on what has been read
- Summarization of what was read
- Main idea and key points identified
- Connections made from what was read to new situations

## Implications for Instruction

The literature on reading comprehension instruction has been consistent in recommending that instruction be characterized as being explicit, intensive, and persistent (Texas Reading Initiative, 2000). In addition, it needs to be well-organized and systematic.

*Explicit instruction* implies that the skills and strategies needed by students are taught to them using some form of direct instruction. The elements of effective instruction, as introduced in Chapter 3, apply here. The modeling/guided practice/independent practice paradigm should be implemented.

*Intensive instruction* suggests that sufficient time is allocated to comprehension. Moreover, intensive instruction includes a broad scope and sequence, incorporating the active participation of the student in the lessons. Lessons should include many opportunities for the students to try out what they have learned and should include ample feedback to the students.

*Persistent instruction* refers to the idea that instruction must be planned in such a way that a systematic set of lessons are developed and presented over time. What we want to avoid is the "quick hit" type of lesson that does not provide enough opportunities for the students to master the skills being taught before moving on to other skill development.

Recently, much attention has been given to the use of *science-based* or *empirically validated* approaches to teaching reading. This emphasis gained national attention as part of the No Child Left Behind Act. A number of efforts were initiated to identify which reading practices had empirical support. One of these efforts was the creation of the National Reading Panel (NRP).

Key examples of effective practices identified by the NRP will be discussed throughout the chapter. In addition, the reader is referred to Pressley and Fingeret (2005) for an analysis of research findings since the work of the NRP. The reader is referred to the section entitled "Making It Work" (p. 224) for a summary of NRP recommendations.

**Instructional Orientations.** We suggest two general ways that teachers can address reading comprehension. First, teachers can select and refine a general teaching approach that has as its focus the enhanced ability to derive meaning from the printed word. Second, teachers can rely on strategies that develop specific skills in comprehension and fluency. After a discussion of assessments, these two considerations frame the outline for the remainder of this chapter, which concludes with a discussion of special considerations relative to implementing a successful reading program.

**Reflective Question 7–1: *Reading comprehension is the most critical academic domain in the school curriculum. What are the key components of reading and why are they problematic for learners with special needs?***

## ASSESSING READING COMPREHENSION

This section focuses on other procedures specifically assessing comprehension. The assessment of reading skills in general was covered in Chapter 6. Many of the techniques discussed in the previous chapter included subtests or methods for obtaining information about proficiency in certain aspects of reading comprehension. The main point of this section is reflected in Blachowicz and Ogle's (2001) summary of the purposes for assessing comprehension:

> Assessment helps us to make informed decisions regarding the level of materials our students can handle. But knowing *what* they can read is only the first step. We also need to know how they read, so we can build on strong strategies and introduce new ones. Assessment thus both alerts us to the ways in which our students are capable comprehenders and strategy users, and helps us to see their instructional needs. (p. 62)

The assessment of reading comprehension must go beyond merely asking questions to determine whether the examinee was able to obtain literal meaning from what he or she has read. Assessment must look at word knowledge as well as some of the more complex areas of comprehension (e.g., inferential and critical aspects). Furthermore, assessment must include analysis of the strategic behaviors that are required during the reading process as well.

### Formal Instruments

Formal measures provide results that allow for comparisons with other students of similar age or grade level. Typically, the results are reported as percentiles, grade or age equivalents, or standard scores. The diagnostic value of the results from formal tests varies depending on the test and how responses can be analyzed. Three types of formal instruments are briefly discussed in this section: individual general achievement tests, general reading tests, and tests specifically designed to measure reading comprehension.

**Individual General Achievement Tests.** As noted previously, many general achievement tests include subtests that measure both word knowledge and text comprehension. Some of the more commonly used tests that include subtests on reading comprehension are the Woodcock-Johnson III Tests of Achievement (Woodcock, McGrew, & Mather, 2001) and the Peabody Individual Achievement Test—Revised—Normative Update (PIAT-R-NU; Markwardt, 1998). The PIAT-R-NU illustrates the way reading comprehension is typically measured. The instrument includes a subtest on reading comprehension where the examinee reads a passage and then responds to multiple-choice questions that are based on the reading and that tap literal and interpretive comprehension.

**General Reading Tests.** A number of tests have been developed that focus solely on reading skills (see also Chapter 6). The Gray reading test battery includes three instruments, all of which include comprehension measures. The Gray Oral Reading Tests—Fourth Edition (GORT-4) (Wiederholt & Bryant, 2001) taps comprehension by asking the examinee to answer five questions after he or she has read a short passage orally. The Gray Diagnostic Reading Tests—Second Edition (GDRT-2) (Bryant, Wiederholt, & Bryant, 2004) includes two subtests that provide information related to comprehension: Reading Vocabulary and Meaningful Reading. The Gray Silent Reading Tests (GSRT) (Bryant & Blalock, 2000) is designed like the GORT-4 in that examinees read developmentally sequenced reading passages. It differs from the GORT-4 in that the passages are read silently and the five comprehension questions that follow each passage use a multiple-choice format.

One of the most popular general reading tests in schools is the Woodcock Reading Mastery Tests—Revised—Normative Update (WRMT-R-NU) (Woodcock, 1998). The WRMT includes six tests, two of which provide comprehension information: Word Comprehension and Passage Comprehension. Word Comprehension measures reading vocabulary at several different levels of cognitive processing and consists of three subtests (antonyms, synonyms, and analogies). Passage Comprehension measures the ability to identify a keyword that as been omitted from a text passage.

**Reading Comprehension Tests.** Very few instruments have been developed that focus only on reading comprehension. The most popular such instrument is the Test of Reading Comprehension—Third Edition (TORC-3) (Brown, Hammill, & Wiederholt, 1995). The TORC-3 includes eight subtests—all of which require the examinee to respond to multiple-choice items. Four of the subtests (General Vocabulary, Syntactic Similarities, Paragraph Reading, and Sentence Sequencing) are combined to determine a General Reading Comprehension Core, which is expressed as a Reading Comprehension Quotient. The other four subtests form the Diagnostic Supplements section of the test. Three of these subtests measure an examinee's ability to read the vocabulary of math, science, and social studies. The other subtest, Reading the Directions of Schoolwork, is designed for young and remedial readers and measures their understanding of written directions.

## Informal Measures

A wide range of informal techniques can be used to obtain information on how well a student comprehends words and text. Assessment techniques can be incorporated in ongoing reading materials or can be accomplished through the use of related, but different, materials. The majority of these measures would be classified as curriculum-based measures.

Vail (1999) suggests that the proficiency and comprehension of students who are reading at lower grade levels can be assessed informally using the following procedure, which encompasses the key elements of informal reading inventories, described in Chapter 6.

1. Find two short, grade-normed passages in a basal reader, a reading test, or other reliable source.
2. Photocopy them and put one on a card marked "Oral," and the other on a card marked "Silent."
3. Devise 10 questions for each, two apiece in the following five categories:
   a. Fact retrieval
   b. Sequence
   c. Vocabulary
   d. Main idea
   e. Inference (p. 26)

An example of the procedure recommended by Vail (1999) is provided in Figure 7-2. One could easily add other types of questions to the recommended list.

**FIGURE 7–2** Teacher-generated text comprehension questions

For example, if the passage is about a boy going for a walk in the woods with his dog, the questions might be:

(Fact) What was the name of the dog?
(Fact) How old was the boy?
(Sequence) What was the first thing the dog tried to chase in the woods?
(Sequence) What did the boy do after the dog retrieved the stick?
(Vocabulary) What does the word *scamper* mean?
(Vocabulary) When the story talks about *brush*, does it mean something that goes with a comb?
(Main Idea) Why do you think the title *A Surprise in the Woods* is a good one for this story?
(Main Idea) How would the story have been different if the boy had taken a cat or a friend for the walk in the woods?
(Inference) Does the boy have brothers and sisters, or is he an only child?
(Inference) What part of the story makes you think that?

*Source:* From *Reading Comprehension: Students' Needs and Teacher Tools*, by P. L. Vail, 1999, Rosemont, NJ: Modern Learning Press.

Many other informal techniques can generate useful information on present levels of performance in the comprehension area and on which IEP goals can be developed and appropriate instruction implemented. Table 7-1 describes the most frequently used informal techniques for assessing reading comprehension. For many struggling readers, the techniques highlighted in Table 7-1 must be used to determine the nature of their reading difficulties and thus lead to powerful and explicit instruction.

A final type of informal technique represents various types of instruments that are part of commercially available materials. An example of this assessment option is the rating scale included within *Practical Ideas That Really Work for Students with Dyslexia and Other Reading Disorders* (Higgins, McConnell, Patton, & Ryser, 2003). The instrument includes 23 items and rates student competence in three areas: vocabulary, text comprehension, and content areas reading skills. A portion of the instrument is depicted in Figure 7-3. A key feature is that it is tied to intervention, based on the results derived from completing the scale. For those items for which a student "frequently" or "almost always" displays difficulties, a number of specific intervention ideas from the manual can be identified using the "Idea Matrix."

**Reflective Question 7–2: *Which assessment strategies are most appropriate for grade level placement, specific skills identification, student evaluation, and program evaluation?***

# GENERAL INSTRUCTIONAL APPROACHES: ELEMENTARY FOCUS

The selection of a general approach or approaches to teach word knowledge and text comprehension provides a basis for a program to enhance learning to read. The following examples illustrate some options that teachers have and that, as needed, can be blended in with decoding programs as discussed in the previous chapter. The focus here is primarily on elementary level learners; in a subsequent section, special

**TABLE 7–1** Informal assessment techniques

| *Technique* | *Key Features* |
|---|---|
| Classroom Fluency Snapshot | • Allows for a quick "snapshot" of how well students can deal with the word level of the grade level material and the fluency demands of the text<br>• Should be considered a supplemental technique to other assessment procedures |
| Running Record | • Requires the student to read from text of a known readability level<br>• Used to determine reading instructional level<br>• Criteria are applied to oral reading performance |
| Informal Reading Inventories | • Sets of graded word lists and oral and silent reading passages with questions<br>• Used to determine independent, instructional, and frustrational reading levels |
| Cloze Passages | • Used to match students with appropriate materials<br>• Students read passage and use context cues to supply a missing word<br>• System for developing materials and scoring performance are utilized |
| Selection Map | • System for generating good questions to ask during instruction |
| Retellings | • Procedure involves allowing students to freely recall what they have read<br>• Teacher asks students to retell the selection they have read<br>• Use of a retelling checklist enables data to be collected |
| Think-Alouds | • Technique provides information on both what students understand and how they understand the material they read<br>• Students share their thoughts before, during, and after reading a selection—thus, allowing insight to the process of understanding text |
| Comprehension Rubrics | • More general formats for looking at how well students are comprehending text<br>• Rubrics can include holistic-oriented approaches or more skill-oriented systems |

*Source:* Based on *Reading Comprehension: Strategies for Independent Learners,* by C. Blachowicz & D. Ogle, 2001, New York: Guilford Press.

considerations for middle and secondary school students are addressed.

## Basal Reading Approach

Basal reading programs are used in the vast majority of elementary schools; consequently, such materials are readily available. They usually contain a series of books or stories written at different difficulty levels, with most beginning at preprimer and primer levels and progressing through upper elementary levels. Most readers also have workbooks that allow students to practice specific skills.

Comprehensive, highly structured teacher manuals that completely outline each lesson typically accompany most basal readers. They provide skill objectives, new vocabulary, suggested motivational activities, verbatim questions to check comprehension on each page of text, and lesson activities. The lessons follow a hierarchy of specific reading skills. Although some teachers think basal manuals limit creativity, others find their structure and guidance valuable.

A basal program exposes students to a basic vocabulary that provides for repetition. Although structured in format, basal programs can be modified to meet individual needs while following a sequential developmental pattern of skill building. They have often been used to assess a student's reading level and subsequent placement in an appropriate reading group. As long as the basal meets students' needs and falls within their interests and abilities, such placement may be temporarily adequate. Basal programs will not meet all needs, however, so the teacher must be prepared to revise and supplement the program.

Several methods can be used to supplement basal reading programs when students begin to have difficulty with the vocabulary or text comprehension demanded at increasingly higher levels. Teachers should avoid recycling students through the same stories, which can lower students' motivation to read. One alternative is to place students in another basal series at approximately the same level, thus giving them different reading experiences at approximately the same level and allowing for overlearning, which is important to students who have learning problems.

A second option is to follow the series' outline of skills as the manual presents them, supplementing

## Rating Scale

DIRECTIONS

- In your opinion, to what degree do the behaviors listed interfere with the student's success in school? Use the following scale to circle the appropriate number:

0 = Not at all like the student so it never interferes with success in school.
1 = Somewhat like the student so it sometimes interferes with success in school.
2 = Very much like the student so it frequently interferes with success in school.
3 = Exactly like the student so it almost always interferes with success in school.

- Put a check in the appropriate box for items with a score of 2 or 3.
- For items with a score of 2 or 3, select up to three intervention ideas from the ideas matrix on page 4. Write the idea numbers in the blanks provided in the last column.

| BEHAVIOR | RATING (Never / Sometimes / Regularly / Almost Always) | SCORE OF 2 | SCORE OF 3 | IDEA NUMBERS |
|---|---|---|---|---|
| **Vocabulary/Word Recognition** | | | | |
| 1. Has limited sight word vocabulary | 0 1 2 3 | ❑ | ❑ | ____ ____ ____ |
| 2. Has limited oral vocabulary | 0 1 2 3 | ❑ | ❑ | ____ ____ ____ |
| 3. Is slow/hesitant, and makes frequent errors when reading orally | 0 1 2 3 | ❑ | ❑ | ____ ____ ____ |
| 4. Learns to recognize word during one instructional period, but cannot recall word at a later time | 0 1 2 3 | ❑ | ❑ | ____ ____ ____ |
| 5. Lacks specialized vocabulary necessary for understanding grade level material | 0 1 2 3 | ❑ | ❑ | ____ ____ ____ |
| 6. Lacks specialized vocabulary necessary for understanding content area material | 0 1 2 3 | ❑ | ❑ | ____ ____ ____ |
| 7. Has limited vocabulary due to lack of experience or prior exposure | 0 1 2 3 | ❑ | ❑ | ____ ____ ____ |
| **Comprehension** | | | | |
| 1. Has difficulty answering factual questions about a reading passage | 0 1 2 3 | ❑ | ❑ | ____ ____ ____ |
| 2. Has difficulty making predictions about what might occur next in a passage | 0 1 2 3 | ❑ | ❑ | ____ ____ ____ |
| 3. Is unable to identify main idea of reading passage | 0 1 2 3 | ❑ | ❑ | ____ ____ ____ |
| 4. Is unable to summarize or retell information read in passage | 0 1 2 3 | ❑ | ❑ | ____ ____ ____ |

**FIGURE 7–3** Example of an informal rating scale

*Source:* From *Practical Ideas That Really Work for Students with Dyslexia and Other Reading Disorders*, by J. Higgins, K. McConnell, J. Patton, and G. Ryser, 2003, Austin, TX: PRO-ED.

them with other commercial reading materials. Many low-vocabulary supplemental materials cover interesting topics.

A third option is to require students to write their own stories, as in the language experience approach discussed in a subsequent section of this chapter. Such an experience can provide practice on reading skills that need reinforcement, and the students' stories can provide reading material.

A final option is to discontinue basals in favor of an alternative approach. Teachers should realize that many students cannot learn effectively through basal programs and should not force such students to fit into a program that is inappropriate for them.

## Language Experience Approach (LEA)

While LEA was mentioned briefly above as an alternative to use with a basal series, it need not be used only with other approaches. In their classic work, Allen and Halvorsen (1961) described the basis for LEA:

> What I can think about, I can talk about.
> What I can say, I can write.
> What I can write, I can read. (p. 33)

LEA encourages students to verbalize their thoughts and experiences, which are then written down by the teacher or the student and can be read. These stories are reread by the student and by other students as the program progresses. Word lists are made from the words used in the stories to develop word-recognition skills and a working vocabulary. Phonetic and structural analysis skills can be taught when the teacher observes the student's readiness for such instruction. However because LEA lacks the developmental structure of the basal approach, most teachers choose to follow the outline of a basal or another sequential program to guide students successfully through an LEA program.

The formal stages for using LEA are straightforward. Tompkins (2005) outlines them as follows:

> 1. *Provide an experience.* A meaningful experience is identified to serve as the stimulus for writing. . . .
> 2. *Talk about the experience.* Students and teacher discuss the experience prior to writing. The purpose of the talk is to generate words and review the experience so that the children's dictation will be more interesting and complete. . . .
> 3. *Record the dictation.* Teachers write down the child's dictation. Texts for individual children are written on sheets of writing paper or in small booklets, and group texts are written on chart paper. . . .
> 4. *Read the text.* After the text has been dictated, the teacher reads it aloud, pointing to each word. This reading reminds children of the content of the text and demonstrates how to read it aloud with appropriate intonation. Then children join in the reading. (p. 187)

Beginning readers may be introduced to LEA as a class. The teacher should establish a common interest, such as a class animal, field trip, or television program. As students tell about their experiences, the teacher needs to assist them in transcribing the words on paper. Students then receive copies of the stories for their books. Word lists and seatwork activities are made from the stories. Independent reading books are also made available and should be encouraged. The transition from student-written material must be made at some point. Commercial materials should be presented early in the program, but it must be well within the student's independent level to ensure success.

Because of LEA's versatility and valuable motivational qualities, it is recommended as a supplementary program for students of any age. It is most appropriately used for students with special needs when it accompanies systematic instruction in word-attack skills.

## Whole Language and Literature-Based Approaches

Whole language is a reading instructional method that represents a logical expansion of the philosophy of the LEA. As Engelhard (1991) notes:

> Whole language is conceptualized as a philosophy in which children learn naturally and holistically through the integration of reading and writing with good literature, emphasizing meaning and the use of real texts such as familiar stories and content area texts instead of basal readers. Further, all aspects of language (oral and written) are integrated and taught across content areas. (p. 3)

Polloway, Miller, and Smith (2004), basing their summary on Reid and Kuykendall (1996), provide the following summary of the concepts underlining the whole language approach:

> - Language, including speaking, listening, reading, and writing, develops interdependently as well as in a social context.
> - Students learn to read using authentic books, not basals.
> - Students learn to write by engaging in the writing process.
> - Students are allowed to learn at their own pace.
> - Teachers serve as mediators, providing support but not interfering with the learning process.
> - Students become involved in reading and writing that is connected to their own lives.
> - Students should be immersed in an environment that is filled with language materials and activities, including high-interest reading materials, and print that they have helped produce.
> - Students must be encouraged and motivated to share their experiences through literature. (p. 317)

Core instructional activities that characterize this approach include (a) teacher-led discussions of stories; (b) shared book experiences through material such as Big Books; (c) sustained silent reading (SSR) (i.e., a regular time when students have an opportunity to practice reading using self-selected stories and content silently (Gartland, 1994); (d) silent reading time segments in which students write responses to what they are reading and share these with other students or with the teacher in individual conferences; (e) language experience activities in which children write stories in a group or individually to be used for future reading experiences; (f) time set aside for large-group writing instruction, followed by students' writing, revising, editing, and sharing their own writing; and finally (g) reading and writing activities that involve a content-area theme such as science or social studies (Chiang & Ford, 1990).

Brand (1989) suggests theoretical reasons why such activities may be useful in addressing some of the difficulties students with disabilities experience. Organizing teaching around themes or topics may be easier for students with memory or cognitive difficulties than learning isolated skills or changing from one topic to another. Anxieties may be lessened and self-esteem enhanced because whole language provides more opportunities for students to feel personal success when telling or writing an original story or experience.

A program based on whole language has much to offer in the area of reading instruction. It provides an emphasis on reading authentic texts rather than the contrived stories that may often appear in basal readers, it provides a way to blend reading with instruction in the other language arts, and it emphasizes students' active involvement in constructing meaning.

At the same time, documentation of its success with students with special needs has been limited. In part this is likely because whole language advocates have primarily emphasized the use of qualitative (vs. quantitative) research that relies more heavily on case studies than group achievement test data. As Mastropieri and Scruggs (1997) note, such research has typically been more helpful in the description of educational interventions but less helpful in providing documentation of the effectiveness of the interventions. Although teachers are encouraged to draw from the tenets of whole language, there also is clear merit in the teaching of decoding skills (see Chapter 6), and comprehension skills and strategies, as presented later in this chapter.

A key aspect of whole language programs is the reliance on *literature* (including novels, stories, magazines, and trade books) as the source of content for reading opportunities. As Mandlebaum, Lightbourne, and VandenBrock (1994) noted, literature has the advantages of being authentic, varied, on the market faster, and thus current. It can meet diverse student needs and interests and offers alternative points of views on topics and issues as well as the opportunity to study topics in depth.

O'Neil (1994) highlighted the use of literature in the elementary classroom. As he notes:

> Dick and Jane, it seems, are on the way out, and classrooms are filling up with dog-eared versions of children's classics and fiction and nonfiction on every conceivable topic. . . . In general, literature-based programs differ from traditional approaches by surrounding students with rich, authentic, whole pieces of literature from the earliest grades; by teaching reading skills in the context of real literature; and by using literature throughout the curriculum. . . . The books, moreover, are diverse—in topics, culture of the characters and the authors, and difficulty. Students and teachers are talking to each other about their reading. Pupils are using books for information to help them in subjects other than reading or language arts. (p. 2)

Units based on literature selections are often used as key elements in comprehension programs. When such a focus becomes the core of the program, a number of key features emerge including:

- Teachers develop units using the reading process.
- Teachers choose picture-book and chapter-book stories or informational books for units.
- Teachers scaffold reading instruction as they read with the whole class or small groups.
- Teachers teach minilessons on reading skills and strategies.
- Students explore vocabulary and literary language.
- Students develop projects to extend their reading (Tompkins, 2006, p. 32).

The challenges for such an approach with students with special needs include, in particular, the difficulty of the reading material and the less explicit focus on teaching strategies for comprehension.

To complement a literature-based approach to comprehension instruction, teachers can avail themselves of texts and supplemental books that promote diversity. Curriculum can be designed to reflect cultural, religious, ethnic, social class, and gender variance (T. S. Jones, 2005).

One attractive option is the use of *predictable books*, children's books or stories that use repetition, as in *Brown Bear, Brown Bear, What Do You See?* (B. Martin, 1983); a cumulative pattern, as demonstrated in the familiar story of the gingerbread man; or familiar day, month, or time sequences, as found in Maurice Sendak's (1962) *Chicken Soup with Rice*. These three types of predictable stories—through the use of rhythm, rhyme, and redundancy—give semantic and syntactic language cues that stimulate fluent reading for children with disabilities and that can enhance sight-word recognition.

To use predictable books as a strategy for promoting reading, the teacher first reads the story aloud to children, using an enlarged version or distributing multiple copies of the material so that children can read along for most of the story. After this, group and individual activities are developed by the teacher to teach and reinforce the sight words and phonics generalizations that are used in the predictable book (McClure, 1985).

Another source of reading materials consistent with a whole language approach is the use of *big books.* Tompkins (2006) described the practice as follows: "big books are greatly enlarged picture books that teachers use in shared reading, most commonly with primary-grade students. In this technique, teachers place an enlarged picture book on an easel or chart stand where all children can see it. Then they read it with small groups of children or the whole class" (p. 96).

> **Reflective Question 7–3:** ***Evaluate the use of basals, LEA, and whole language approaches. What features make their advantages as well as disadvantages for use with learners with special needs?***

## COMPREHENSION STRATEGIES

### Word Knowledge Strategies

Much of what happens in classrooms on a daily basis is associated with vocabulary acquisition. Blachowicz and Ogle (2001) remark that "vocabulary is a reflection of our knowledge and experience and of our social interactions" (p. 164). As Carnine et al. (2004) note, most vocabulary is learned indirectly from everyday encounters.

McKeown and Beck (1988) suggest that words can be understood at different levels. One way to think about this notion is to consider three levels of word knowledge: unknown, acquainted, and established (Beck, McKeown, & Omanson, 1987). This conceptualization has implications for instruction, as different levels of word understanding can be programmed into lessons.

The following key points related to vocabulary acquisition serve as a guide for designing instruction.

- Vocabulary acquisition is enhanced by time spent in reading.
- Vocabulary knowledge is fundamental to comprehending text (Nagy, 1998).
- Expressive vocabulary usage is much more difficult than receptive vocabulary usage (Carnine et al., 2004).
- Approximately 300 new words can be learned each year as a result of direct vocabulary instruction (Carnine et al., 2004).
- Approximately 8 to 10 new words can be taught each week (Partnership for Reading, 2001).
- It is important to identify and provide instruction for new words that are *important* (i.e., critical to understanding); *useful* (i.e., useful in a variety of contexts); and *difficult* for the students (Carnine et al., 2004). Key considerations to help plan vocabulary instruction (based on the work of Allen, 1999) are presented in Figure 7–4.

The report of the National Reading Panel (2000) contains the following findings related to vocabulary instruction:

- Vocabulary instruction leads to gains in comprehension.
- Computers can be effective in vocabulary development.
- Learning words prior to reading textual material is helpful.
- Certain techniques such as task restructuring and repeated exposure enhance vocabulary development.
- Substituting easy words for more difficult ones can be helpful to low-achieving readers.

In their review of the literature, Pressley and Fingeret (2005) concluded that "students acquire vocabulary

**FIGURE 7–4** Considerations to guide vocabulary instruction

- importance of the words to text understanding
- frequency of the word's appearance in text
- possible multiple meanings
- grouping words to facilitate conceptual understanding
- repeated exposure to specific words to promote fluency
- use of words in multiple contexts
- linkage to prior reading, experiential opportunities
- similarity of meaning to other known words
- opposite in meaning to other known words

from exposure to vocabulary, for example, in texts that they read, with repeated encounters with vocabulary increasing learning. Even so, learning vocabulary words from text context is never certain, nor is it certain that vocabulary will be learned well even if students are provided the definitions for newly encountered vocabulary words. A promising form of instruction involves long-term use of new vocabulary, with students thinking about the meanings of the new words as they do challenging activities with them . . . ; this approach is known as rich vocabulary instruction" (p. 20). These researchers further recommend that teachers "flood" students with vocabulary exposure by making sure that new lessons are replete with opportunities for students to be immersed in an environment with new words.

## DIVERSITY IN THE CLASSROOM *Tips*

Laura Smolkin is a professor of elementary education in the University of Virginia's Curry School of Education, where she also coordinates the *Reading Education* program. Her published papers appear in journals such as *Reading Research Quarterly* and *Research in the Teaching of English*.

Whereas research on English language learners suggests that teachers do not need to wait to begin phonemic awareness and phonics instruction until the student has achieved proficiency in English, proficiency in English does make a large difference in students' reading comprehension abilities (August & Shanahan, 2006). Children's English vocabulary knowledge and English oral language proficiency are directly related to their success in English reading comprehension.

### Vocabulary Knowledge Is Critical to Students' Reading Success

Research has long shown that vocabulary knowledge is highly correlated with reading comprehension. Given that an average English-speaking kindergarten child comes to school knowing between 5,000 and 7,000 words, the challenge for English language learners is great indeed. Therefore, intensive efforts at enhancing children's vocabulary knowledge must begin as soon as the English language learner arrives at school.

In the primary grades, teachers can use various approaches to preteach vocabulary prior to working with students' own reading materials or in preparation for read alouds. Teachers can take sentences from the text that contain new vocabulary and paraphrase those sentences with simpler vocabulary. They can also provide quick demonstrations of a word's meaning.

Effective support of students' comprehension does not end with an introduction to new words prior to the reading event. Teachers' questioning during the reading event must reflect an awareness of words that have multiple meanings. If a geographical text says, "A river runs through that valley," teachers must, through questioning, assist students in determining the meaning of *runs* in that particular sentence.

Multiple exposures to a word are essential for a child's developing knowledge of that word. In addition to supporting understanding through the visual modes mentioned above, teachers of upper elementary, middle, and high school students can encourage English language learners to supply definitions in their own words. Teachers can additionally make use of peer teaching for new vocabulary.

One area of particular importance to text comprehension is the vocabulary that provides cohesion to a text. Words such as *whereas* or *while* are difficult to present through pictures or demonstrations, but they are critical in determining the meaning of a sentence and can impact a student's understanding of a text.

Teachers should create opportunities for students to talk as well as to listen. Opportunities for discussion and use of new vocabulary can be found in small-group work in content studies such as math, science, and social studies, where new vocabulary is linked and reinforced thematically.

### Comprehension

In the area of comprehension, there are two issues critical to work with English language learners. First is the nature of the material; the second concerns how students are taught to approach a text.

Background knowledge is critical to text comprehension; therefore, it makes sense that there can be cultural influences on comprehension. As an example, children newly arrived from Spanish-speaking countries where *El Dia de los Muertos* (the Day of the Dead) is regularly celebrated will have a greater ability to understand text written about this holiday than they will for a text that describes as yet unknown practices for the Fourth of July.

Finally, even though a recent review of the literature (Shanahan & Beck, 2006) suggests there have been insufficient numbers of studies to make a definitive recommendation, teachers of English language learners can make use of comprehension strategy instruction typically recommended as part of a balanced literacy program. When using cognitive strategies such as predicting or summarizing, teachers should keep in mind that continuing work on English language learners' oral English abilities cannot be neglected.

**TABLE 7–2** Instructional suggestions for vocabulary development

| *Primary Goal* | *Instructional Strategies* |
|---|---|
| Developing word awareness | • Classroom labeling<br>• Opportunities to read<br>• Using technology<br>• Using humor and word play<br>• Using riddles, jokes, and puns<br>• Using word games (e.g., card games) |
| Developing general vocabulary knowledge | • Using logs<br>• Peer teaching<br>• Sharing of personal words |
| Developing content vocabulary | • Learning new words for known concepts<br>• Learning new words for new concepts<br>• Building and retaining content specific vocabularies (e.g., personal dictionaries)<br>• Learning textbook vocabulary (e.g., semantic mapping) |
| Developing independent Strategies | • Understanding word parts and generative word parts (prefixes and suffixes)<br>• Dictionary use—print and electronic<br>• Figuring out new words from context (e.g., context instruction, cloze procedure) |

*Source:* Based on *Reading Comprehension: Strategies for Independent Learners,* by C. Blachowicz and D. Ogle, 2001, New York: Guilford Press.

Blachowicz and Ogle (2001) provide suggested strategies for developing word knowledge. They organize instructional strategies around four major goals of vocabulary instruction: developing word awareness, developing general vocabulary knowledge, developing content vocabulary, and developing independent strategies. We have used this framework and many of Blachowicz and Ogle's suggestions to create Table 7–2, which presents a variety of instructional ideas accompanied by a brief description of how each technique works.

Ultimately, students need to be able to understand not only the basic meaning of words quickly but also "how words can be used across different contexts" (Bryant et al., 1999, p. 296). Attending to the development of word knowledge through both indirect and direct means is essential to enhancing a student's ability to comprehend textual material. Assessment and instruction in this area should not be neglected.

## Text Comprehension Strategies

The general approaches to instruction described earlier in the chapter provide a foundation for comprehension, but teachers will need to include explicit instruction on strategies that allow students to better engage textual material. The strategies that are discussed in this section provide several ways to enhance comprehension that can be adapted for varied purposes. Pressley and Fingeret (2005) caution that teachers are well-advised to use a small repertoire of strategies (e.g., to promote prediction, summarizing, questioning). Further, teachers should monitor the effectiveness of these strategies in enabling students to achieve success on identified comprehension skills.

The teacher's task is to ensure that appropriate attention is given to different levels of comprehension based on the learning needs of individual students. Through effective teaching, instructors can work with groups of students and incorporate a concurrent focus on literal, inferential, critical, and creative comprehension questions within the same lesson. Such an approach enhances inclusion efforts for students with special needs when they are participating in larger group instruction with other students whose cognitive abilities may be significantly greater.

Traditionally, many teachers have taught comprehension solely by asking students questions after they have read a specific passage. Thus, instructional lessons might typically include questions such as the following after a reading sample:

- What is the main idea?
- What are the sequential events that took place in the story?
- Who are the main characters?
- What do you conclude about the story?

General questions such as these provide a basis for evaluating whether students have understood the passage they have completed.

However, such an approach continually tests students' comprehension without necessarily directing or instructing them in comprehension strategies, and thus may fail to provide students with what Coyne, Zipoli, and Ruby (2006) refer to as *conspicuous instruction*—that is, teaching in a direct and explicit fashion. The following strategies focus on comprehension in a more multifaceted fashion. The discussion focuses first on some specific strategies and then concludes with more broad-based strategies that can be used for variant purposes.

The strategies discussed in this section are organized into five areas: **teacher-directed questioning** strategies; student-directed questioning strategies; peer-mediated strategies; graphic-aid strategies; and fluency strategies. Figure 7–5 graphically illustrates these major topical areas. The section concludes with a discussion of oral reading.

**Teacher-Directed Questioning Strategies.** Questioning by teachers is the instructional strategy used most often in teaching comprehension. As a general approach, this has frequently been found to be effective, particularly when students are taught to ask themselves questions before, during, and after the reading process.

Questioning permeates the reading process. Factual, inferential, and analytical questions are all essential for comprehension development.

F. Smith (1979) emphasizes that as people read, listen to speakers, and study, they constantly ask questions. Comprehension occurs when people perceive answers to their own questions or find their predictions validated or refuted. Knowledge and experience directly influence predictions and thus comprehension.

However, frequently the majority of questions that teachers ask are factual, and the answers are directly stated in the text, requiring no higher-level thinking by students. Teachers can stimulate students to begin inferential and critical thinking through higher-level questioning. Students who can decode the material adequately can, with guidance and practice, become critical readers. If properly guided and questioned, slow learners as well as gifted students can learn to make inferences from the material they have read. Questions that stimulate thought and motivate students to higher levels of comprehension can be asked on material at any readability level. Evaluative and interpretive questions also apply to every level of readability.

Comprehension requires connecting what is read with prior knowledge of the topic. The printed material provides new information; to understand it, readers use various information sources within their own memories. Thus, each reader's background of concepts directly influences the comprehension of passages read. Most instruction therefore should be initiated prior to reading

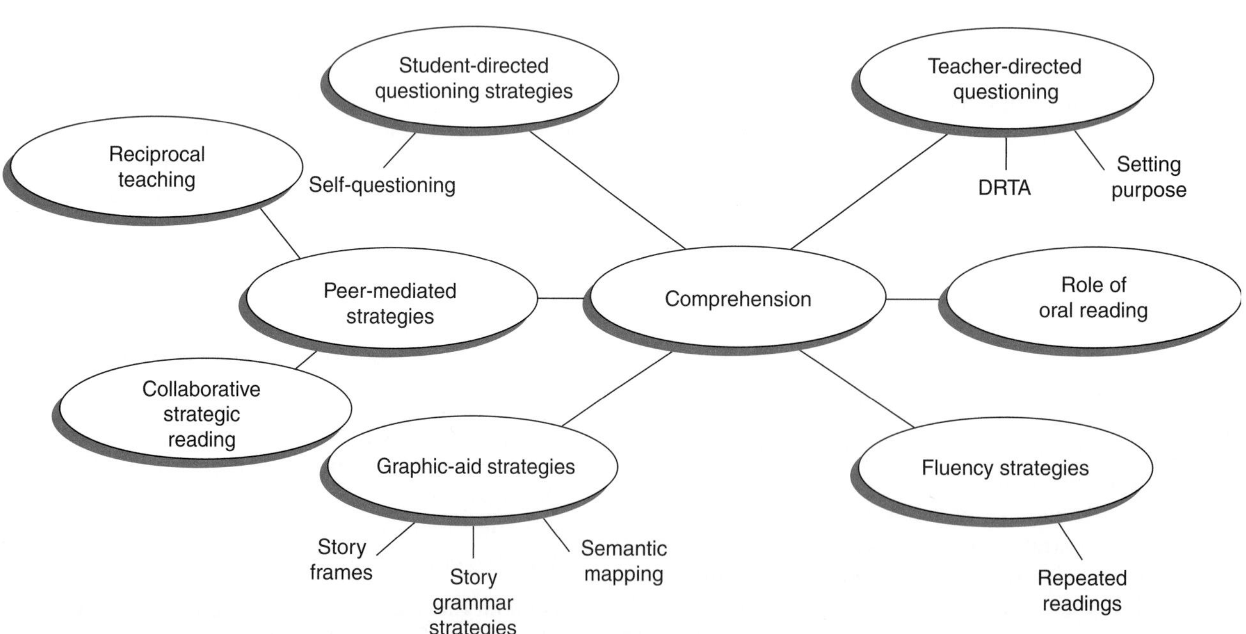


**FIGURE 7–5** Graphic overview of text comprehension strategies

the material. The teacher must stimulate students' thinking about the topic before oral or silent reading begins. Strategies include setting the purpose for reading to arouse students' prior knowledge and the use of the directed reading/thinking activity.

*Setting the purpose* in advance of reading is one way to stimulate students' prior knowledge. A teacher can introduce a selection by saying, "As you read, think about what you would do if you were caught in a flood as Van is in this story." Immediately, students' prior knowledge (or lack of it) concerning floods comes to mind and thus helps prepare them for the passage to be read. Wilson (1983) stresses the importance of teaching students to assume responsibility for their own comprehension. She advocates instructing students to self-monitor by having the students ask themselves periodically, "Is this making sense to me?" Students who realize that they are not comprehending can try a variety of strategies: rereading the material, trying to rephrase it, reading ahead, or, if necessary, asking for help.

One of the most useful questioning techniques to teach comprehension of content or expository material is the **directed reading/thinking activity (DRTA).** Although originally developed in the 1960s, DRTA remains an effective teacher-directed strategy to develop metacognition and enhance comprehension (Unrau, 2004). In this activity students are taught to make predictions about what they are going to read before they begin reading the text. While reading, the students test and refine the predictions they made in advance. These predictions generate divergent questions and stimulate expanded thinking. DRTA teaches students to verify and defend their predictions and gives them guidelines for reading to learn. The following procedures comprise the DRTA technique.

1. Students examine the story title, pictures, and subheadings.
2. Individually or in a group, students list information they anticipate finding in the selection.
3. Students read the selection.
4. Students then look at each prediction on their list and decide whether it was correct or incorrect.
5. When uncertainty or disagreement occurs, students defend their positions by locating validating information in the text.

DRTA stimulates students to generate their own questions. Their predictions become questions when they search the text for supportive information.

**Student-Directed Questioning Strategies.** Although teacher questioning is the staple of much that has been done in the area of reading comprehension instruction, students must learn to ask themselves questions in order to become more effective and independent readers and develop self-efficacy as readers (see nearby Teacher Tip). Several strategies can accomplish this goal. These include the direct teaching of self-monitoring strategies (referred to as metacomprehension) as well as instructional programs that involve students working reciprocally with teachers and their peers. These are discussed next.

A key focus must be the use of self-monitoring of the reading process such as through the development

**TEACHER *Tips*** — **Elementary Level**

### Development of Self-Efficacy

Ferrara (2005) promotes the importance of self-efficacy in young readers. She identified 20 ways to achieve this; those of particular significance are presented below:

- Provide appropriate-level reading materials
- Give students a choice of reading materials
- Activate prior knowledge
- Introduce new vocabulary
- Encourage learners to set a purpose for reading
- Teach students to select their own books for independent reading
- Encourage use of imagery to remember details
- Model how to find the answers to literal and inferential questions
- Anticipate author's questions and answers in a passage
- Increase reading speed and focus on comprehension
- Help students develop relatively high but accurate self-efficacy beliefs
- Maintain and communicate high expectations for success
- Help students set goals

of *self-generated questions*. Classic research in the field has indicated that one major influence on students' inability to read is that they do not take an active role in their own learning (Brown & Palinscar, 1982; Torgesen, 1982). The lack of metacognitive skills or, in other words, inability to monitor their comprehension (e.g., self-monitoring, predicting, and controlling one's own attempts to study and learn) limits students' success in learning to read (Wong, 1982). Self-questioning is one way to stimulate development of the poor reader's metacognitive skills and to improve comprehension monitoring that has proved to be effective for enhancing achievement (Swanson & de la Paz, 1998). As Bryant (2001) noted, a key goal is to "teach them when and how to use effective comprehension monitoring strategies before, during, and after reading so they can 'repair' comprehension problems and understand text" (p. 1).

To facilitate a strategy of using self-generated questions, students can first be trained in question phrasing or writing. This orientation includes identification of good and poor questions, discrimination between questions and statements, and awareness of question words. Students are then instructed to read the story, describe what it is about, and generate two questions. Finally, students answer their own questions or exchange questions with peers. Teachers can further enhance students' metacognitive skills by directly teaching and modeling comprehension processing. Students can be instructed to perform the following self-questioning tasks (Schewel & Waddell, 1986):

1. Identify the main idea of a paragraph and underline it.
2. Develop questions related to the main idea and write them where they can be referred to easily.
3. Check those questions with the teacher's models to be certain that they are correctly stated.
4. Read the passage, answer the questions, and learn the answers.
5. Continually look back over the questions and answers to note the accumulation of information.

Jitendra, Hoppes, and Xin (2000) recommended the use of a prompt card to help students find the main idea. Students can be given a series of printed prompts to consider to help them determine the main idea:

- Who (or what) is the subject?
- What is the action?
- Why (or where, when) did something occur?
- How was something done (or how did it look)?

Several learning (or study) strategies can also be used to help with thinking while reading. A key one to use for paraphrasing and summarizing is RAP (Schumaker, Deshler, & Denton, 1984, cited in Ellis & Sabornie, 1986):

- **R**ead a passage.
- **A**sk yourself: who/what it is about? what is happening?
- **P**ut the main ideas in your own words.

In emphasizing the use of self-monitoring approaches, Mastropieri and Scruggs (1997) report that several common features are characteristic of research on strategies that promote enhanced reading comprehension:

> - clear, explicit instruction in a strategy associated with enhancing reading comprehension
> - detailed self-monitoring procedures containing cards that require students to mark off steps as they proceed
> - informing students about the purpose of the strategy instruction
> - attributing success to controllable factors (e.g., reminding students that the use of a strategy would be beneficial to them and would influence success) (p. 205)

Table 7–3 presents a series of steps that facilitate student use of a variety of comprehension strategies.

**Peer-Mediated Strategies.** Peer-mediated strategies involve the participation of other students in the reading comprehension process. An example of a successful peer-mediated technique is the Collaborative Strategic Reading (CSR) process developed by Vaughn and Klingner (1999, 2004; Vaughn & Edmonds, 2006). This technique includes four specific strategies: Preview, Click and Clunk, Get the Gist, and Wrap-Up. These strategies are taught to the whole class using expository texts and then cooperative groups implement their roles (Leader, Clunk Expert, Gist Expert, Announcer) and the techniques. Specific procedures for the four strategies are highlighted in Figure 7–6.

A strategy that involves questioning and additional activities to activate comprehension and that commonly includes both student-generated questions and peer-mediation, is **reciprocal teaching.** This approach is based on the assumption that comprehension is enhanced when students read a text and then take turns leading small-group discussions to help their peers also understand what was read (Reid, Baker, Lasell, & Easton, 1993; Schulz, 1994).

**TABLE 7–3** Developing self-regulated comprehension strategies

1. *Describe the comprehension strategy.* Explicitly describe the strategy steps, and discuss *why* it should be used, *what* it accomplishes, and *when* and *where* it may be used.
2. *Activate background knowledge.* Review information students may have learned previously that is necessary for learning the strategy.
3. *Review current performance level.* Provide feedback to students regarding their current level of functioning and reiterate potential benefits of the strategy.
4. *Modeling of the strategy and self-instructions.* Demonstrate how to use the strategy in a meaningful context, and use relevant self-regulatory behaviors by thinking out loud. Self-statements include ideas such as "What should I do first?" "I am using this strategy so that I can understand what I am reading better . . . "; or "I need to take my time," which show students the purpose of the procedures and how to manage their performance.
5. *Collaborative practice.* Provide opportunities for practice using the strategy and self-statements as a whole class, in small groups, or in pairs. Monitor students' progress in following the strategy steps. Facilitate students' success in using the strategies by prompting them to complete steps if they are omitted or by providing assistance in completing strategy steps accurately.
6. *Independent practice and mastery.* After determining that the students know and understand the steps of the strategy, each student practices using the strategy and self-statements without help. Continue to give guidance, reinforcement, and feedback. Gradually fade assistance until each student is capable of using the strategy without any help.
7. *Generalization.* Discuss with students whenever situations arise where it is appropriate for students to apply the strategies. In addition, provide students with different types of materials (e.g., lookbacks are useful with narratives, expository text such as science book chapters, and learning rules to play a game) so that students learn to use the strategies flexibly.

*Source:* Adapted from "Teaching Effective Comprehension Strategies to Students with Learning and Reading Disabilities," by P. N. Swanson and S. de la Paz, 1998, *Intervention in School and Clinic, 33,* p. 211. Copyright 1998 by PRO-ED, Inc. Reprinted with permission.

Reciprocal teaching includes four specific strategies: *questioning* about the content read, *summarizing* the most important information, *clarifying* concepts that are unclear, and *predicting* what is occurring. An example from the work of Ann Brown illustrates the process:

> A group of second-grade students . . . are beginning a new book on a topic they have been researching. Tyrone, the designated teacher for this session, begins by reading aloud the book's title. Next, Tyrone asks if anyone has questions. The teacher's aide prompts the quiet group by asking, "What are shells?" Katie responds that shells provide coverings for soft-bodied animals and names snails as an example. Tyrone then asks the group to predict what information might be found in the book. After the students list possible topics, Tyrone begins reading. Katie and Kendra assist him with difficult words. Next, Tyrone asks if any words need to be clarified. Katie asks, "What are exoskeletons?" Several incorrect guesses are ventured. The teacher's aide suggests that the group think about the topic in order to answer the question. Katie summarizes their reading and announces, "Oh! I think it means skeletons on the outside!" (Schulz, 1994, pp. 21, 24)

Reciprocal teaching was developed by Palinscar and Brown (1984) and was originally used with middle school readers who were struggling to achieve (Unrau, 2004). A step-by-step procedure is provided within the Secondary Level Teacher Tip.

The key to the effectiveness of reciprocal teaching is that the approach enables students to learn specific strategies that foster their comprehension rather than simply asking them questions about what they have read. By using this approach, a variety of questions can be modeled, practiced, and used in an active fashion. The planned outcome is that students can then generate appropriate questions themselves while reading.

**Graphic-Aid Strategies.** These strategies use visual formats to assist students in organizing information for better comprehension. Several graphic aids apply well to teaching students who struggle with reading comprehension. The use of graphic aids provides a way to enhance the teacher-directed and student-directed questioning strategies that are being used to build comprehension skills. Graphic aids provide systems where students can organize their thoughts and make notes on what they are going to read or have read; they also recall and provide a basis for further study.

Kim, Vaughn, Wanzek, and Wei (2004) summarized research on the effects of graphic organizers on the reading comprehension of students with learning disabilities. As they noted, "our findings support the use of semantic organizers, cognitive maps with and without mnemonics, and framed outlines to promote

**FIGURE 7–6** Strategies and steps in collaborative strategic reading

**Preview**

We preview before reading. Previewing has two steps:

- Brainstorming. Think about what you already know about the topic.
- Predicting. Find clues in the title, subheadings, or pictures about what you will learn. Skim the text for keywords that might give you hints.

**Click and Clunk**

We find clicks and clunks while we are reading. When we understand what we read, everything "clicks" along smoothly. But when we don't understand, "clunk," we stop. When we get a clunk, we use the following fix-up strategies to figure out what the clunk means:

- Reread the sentence with the clunk and the sentences before or after the clunk, looking for clues.
- Reread the sentence without the word. Think about what would make sense.
- Look for a prefix or suffix in the word.
- Break the word apart and look for smaller words.
- Use a picture.
- Ask for help.

**Get the Gist**

We get the gist after reading each paragraph or section of a passage. To get the gist means to summarize or restate the most important idea. Do not include the supporting details. State the gist in your own words using the following cues:

- Decide who or what the paragraph is mostly about (the topic).
- Name the most important idea about the topic.

**Wrap-Up**

We wrap up after finishing the day's reading assignment. Wrap-up includes:

- Asking (teacher-like) questions about the passage.
- Reviewing by thinking about what was important that you learned from the day's reading assignment.

*Source:* From *Strategies for Teaching Students with Learning and Behavior Problems* (p. 214, Figure 5.16), by C. S. Bos and S. Vaughn, 1998. Boston: Allyn & Bacon. Copyright © 1998 by Allyn & Bacon. Reprinted with permission.

[comprehension]. . . . when students were taught to use graphic organizers, large effect sizes were demonstrated on reading comprehension. Thus, visual displays of information . . . enhance reading comprehension, by helping them organize the verbal information and thereby improving their recall" (p. 116).

Graphic strategies frequently serve as advanced organizers that provide an introduction to or an overview of the passage to be read. One example of this is an outline containing major headings with space for students to fill in the supporting details (Graham & Johnson, 1989). Students with learning disabilities using and discussing the outline before attempting content-area textbook reading scored higher on comprehension measures than those in the control group. The comprehension of students with learning disabilities also improved after they were given prompts to be used with basal reader stories prior to reading. Prompts included looking for, saying, and discussing new or difficult words; skimming for the story setting; and asking "Does the title give a clue to the story?" (Graham & Johnson, 1989).

Several graphic-aid strategies are discussed below. Collectively they represent effective strategies to enable students to develop "maps" of stories and are associated with enhanced comprehension (Swanson & de la Paz, 1998).

**Story frames** constructed by the teacher help students organize and summarize information. This strategy guides comprehension by helping students to sort out the important concepts and ideas of the material. Fowler and Davis (1986) describe the five steps necessary for constructing a story frame:

1. Identify the problem on which you want students to focus.
2. Write a paragraph about that problem.
3. Delete words, phrases, and sentences that are not necessary to guide one through the paragraph.
4. Under selected spaces, place a clue to ensure that students can follow the frame.
5. Modify the frame for subsequent selections.

Story frames are useful with narrative texts because they can focus attention on character comparison or analysis, plot, or setting. When first introducing story frames, the teacher should read a story to the students, and together they should discuss and fill in the blanks on the frame. Following this instruction, students should be able to complete the frames successfully and with minimal assistance and begin working through frames independently.

**Semantic mapping** is based on schema theory, which postulates that new information is learned and understood when it is integrated with prior knowledge. When a student is introduced to new information through reading or other experiences, the new knowledge is learned as it is stored in the brain with similar schemata.

The teacher's role is twofold: to continually work on building students' knowledge background through experiences, discussion, and literature and to teach students to stimulate their own schemata about a topic before beginning to read a passage. The teacher might instruct students in the use of self-questioning (e.g., "What do I already know about the Civil War?") or prediction strategies. Students with disabilities often have limited experiential backgrounds and need additional guidance in gaining knowledge from the experiences they encounter.

Brainstorming is an essential element in the mapping process. The student's active participation in this activity stimulates prior knowledge and encourages students to associate new information with what is already part of their schemata (Schewel, 1989).

Semantic mapping is a method of promoting comprehension that stimulates prior knowledge of the topic. Semantic maps are diagrams developed by students and teacher before students read an assigned selection. The maps can be reused after reading to further stimulate comprehension. The procedure is as follows:

1. The teacher presents a stimulus word or a core question related to the story to be read.
2. Students generate words related to the stimulus word or predict answers to the question, all of which the teacher lists on the board.
3. With the teacher's help, students then put related words or answers in groups, drawing connecting lines between the topics to form a semantic map.
4. After reading the selection, students and the teacher discuss the categories and rearrange or add to the map.

Semantic mapping can appear in various forms. Figure 7–7 presents an example of a semantic map.

When using semantic mapping, students are actively engaged in a strategy that stimulates retrieval and organization of prior knowledge. It is also useful as a postreading exercise to enhance comprehension and as a study skill technique (Heimlich & Pittelman, 1986).

**Story grammar strategies** also can enhance the reading and writing skills of students with special needs; the concept builds on many of the aforementioned strategies. Story grammar strategies are included

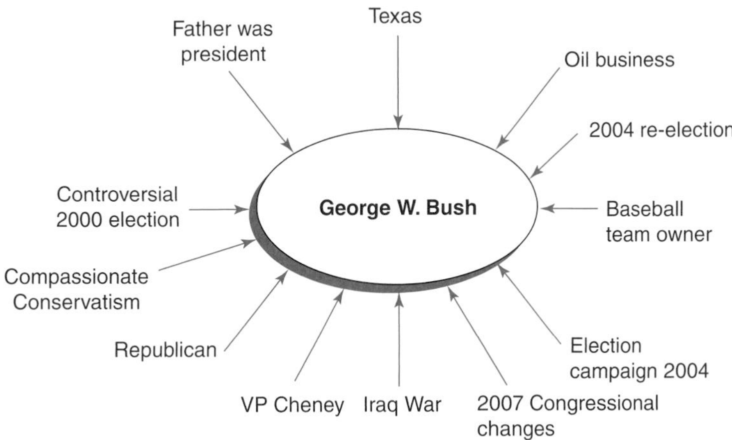


**FIGURE 7–7** Example of a semantic map (wheel)

here although they can complement a variety of graphic and nongraphic approaches to promoting comprehension. Hagood (1997) outlines a series of strategies that provide ways to enhance learning for students:

- Teach students to use self-questioning techniques to increase their comprehension of a narrative text (see Figure 7–8 for a list of sample questions).
- Teach students to use story maps to organize a story's components (i.e., use visual organizers to enable students to enhance their understanding; see Figure 7–9).
- Develop group narrative dramatizations through the use of visual, auditory, and kinesthetic learning channels.
- Teach students to analyze and critically compare the elements of two similar stories (e.g., use graphic organizers to discuss similarities and differences between stories).
- Teach students to manipulate and analyze the components of story grammar (e.g., rewrite stories by changing the setting of a story and modifying other elements that necessarily change when the setting does).

**Fluency Strategies.** Fluency refers to the ability to read effectively as reflected in the three components of *speed* (i.e., rate with a goal of 100 words per minute (wpm) by grade 3 and 300 wpm for adults], *word recognition* (i.e., automatic recognition of most words read), and *prosody* (i.e., expressive reading, in terms of phrasing, intonation, and rhythm) (Tompkins, 2006). Although the development of fluency is a complement to, rather than a direct approach to, comprehension, the process of reading through passages continuously and smoothly can enhance comprehension. For this reason, fluency is discussed here as well as primarily in Chapter 6, where it was related to word recognition.

With **repeated readings** or *multiple oral readings*, students receive a selection approximately 200 words in length with instructions to practice reading it orally while listening to a tape of the same material (see also Chapter 6). When students decide that they are ready, their time and errors are recorded. After further oral practice, another time/error check is made. This procedure continues until the student reads 85 words per minute, at which time the process begins again with new material. Samuels (1979) reports that after practice with this technique, students require fewer readings with each new selection and comprehension continuously improves. He concludes that comprehension improves because the attention required for decoding is minimized and automaticity is enhanced.

In their review of research, Mastropieri and Scruggs (1997) conclude that reading the same passage three or four times does have a positive effect on fluency and also on passage comprehension. However, they

**FIGURE 7–8** Sample story map questions

1. Where did this story take place?
2. When did the story take place?
3. Who were the main characters in the story?
4. Were there any other important characters in the story? Who?
5. What was the problem in the story?
6. How did the character(s) try to solve the problem?
7. Was it hard to solve the problem? Explain.
8. Was the problem solved? Explain.
9. What did you learn from reading this story? Explain.
10. Can you think of a different ending?

*Source:* From *Reading Success: A Specialized Literacy Program for Learners with Challenging Reading Needs* (p. 61), by L. Idol, 1997, Austin, TX: PRO-ED.

**STORY MAP** TITLE Cinderella (Perraut/Jeffers)

**CHARACTERS:**

Cinderella
Stepmother, father
2 Stepsisters
Fairy Godmother, Prince

**SETTING:**

Time: Long ago

Place: Kingdom

**PROBLEM:**

Father dies, Cinderella mistreated and not allowed to go to the King's ball.

**GOAL:**

To go to the ball and meet the handsome Prince.

**EVENTS TO REACH SOLUTION**

1. Fairy Godmother comes.
2. She makes a pumpkin into a coach
3. and rags into a gown for the ball.
4. Cinderella dances with the prince until almost midnight.
5. She runs away and loses one of her glass slippers.
6. The prince searches until he finds the girl who can wear the glass slipper.

**SOLUTION:**

Cinderella can wear the slipper. When she puts on the matching one, she turns back into the way she looked at the ball. She leaves with the prince to be married and live happily ever after.

**FIGURE 7–9** Sample story map

*Source:* From "Constructing Meaning: An Integrated Approach to Teaching Reading," by K. D. Barclay, 1990. *Intervention in School and Clinic, 26,* p. 88. Copyright 1990 by PRO-ED. Inc. Reprinted with permission.

caution that additional readings would yield diminishing returns and that repeated readings of a given text may have a positive effect on other texts only to the extent that there are significant overlaps in words.

Therrien, Gormley, and Kubina (2006) present a systematic approach to fluency instruction tied to comprehension, referred to as the Reread-Adapt and Answer-Comprehend (RAAC) intervention. It is summarized in Figure 7-10. For additional strategies to promote fluency in general, the reader is referred to the recommendations provided by Welsch (2006) and to Therrien and Kubina's (2006) a model for teaching repeated readings.

**Oral Reading.** Oral reading is an important component of a total program. It is particularly necessary in the early stages of instruction because it gives the teacher insight into the beginning reader's knowledge of sight words and decoding skills. Oral reading has three core purposes: diagnosis, conveying directions or instruction, and personal pleasure. For learners with special needs, oral reading has four additional purposes: articulation and vocabulary practice, memory reinforcement, rereading for better comprehension, and group participation.

Oral reading can assist the development of correct word pronunciation by providing the reader with disabilities who seldom verbalizes with a structured opportunity to speak. When reading aloud, the student takes in information both auditorily and visually, adding an additional pathway to learning that is often necessary for memory. Rereading a passage orally after it has been read silently assists comprehension, particularly when the teacher designates a purpose for each reading.

**FIGURE 7–10** Reread-adapt and answer-comprehend (RAAC) intervention sequence

**Step 1: Prompt Student.** "Read this story the best you can and as quickly as you can. Pay attention to what you are reading, as you will need to answer a few questions."

**Step 2: Read Prompts.** Ask student to read question-generation prompts ("who, what, where, when, how" questions, such as "Who is the main character?" "Where does the story take place?").

**Step 3: Reread.** Ask student to reread passage aloud until reaching goal—

- No less than 2 times.
- No more than 4 times.

**Step 4: Correct Errors.**

- If student pauses during reading, correct word and have student repeat.
- Correct all other errors after passage read and ask students to repeat them.

**Step 5: Praise.** Provide feedback to student on improvements in speed and accuracy.

**Step 6: Adapt and Answer.** Ask student to adapt and answer questions you have placed on cue cards.

Error correction process:

a. If no answer or incorrect answer first time, prompt student to look for information in the passage: "See if you can find the answer in the passage."
b. If no or incorrect answer second time, point to sentence(s) where answer can be found and prompt: "See if you can find the answer in this sentence."
c. If no or incorrect answer third time, provide answer and point to where you found the answer.

**Step 7: End and Adjust.** When session ends, adjust the reading material for next time.

Adjust the difficulty of the reading material for use in the subsequent session using the following guidelines:

- If for three sessions in a row, the student was unable to reach the fluency goal in four readings, lower the reading material to be used in the subsequent session by one grade level.
- If, for three sessions in a row, the student reached the fluency goal in two readings or less, raise the reading material to be used in the next session by one grade level.

*Source*: Therrien, W. J., Gormley, S., & Kubina, R. M. (2006). "Boosting fluency and comprehension to improve reading achievement." *Teaching Exceptional Children, 38,* p. 25.

Continuing oral reading for students with special needs longer than for children without disabilities is often beneficial. However, the students also clearly need practice and guidance in the transition from oral to silent reading (directed and encouraged by the teacher), because silent reading is the critical skill to develop. The previous discussion on self-questioning illustrates ways in which students can be taught to monitor their own reading to ensure that the silent reading process promotes comprehension.

**Reflective Question 7–4:** ***Compare and contrast the key features of instruction that are primarily classified as teacher-directed, student-directed, and peer-mediated strategies.***

## INSTRUCTIONAL CONSIDERATIONS: MIDDLE AND SECONDARY LEVEL

It is not surprising that the most significant problem faced by adolescent learners is their ability to read effectively. The challenge for teachers is that students' specific problems vary greatly and are likely to reflect years of failure experiences in schools. As the Alliance for Excellent Education (2005) observed:

> Some young people still have difficulty simply reading words accurately, but these students make up the minority of older struggling readers. Most older struggling readers can read words accurately, but they do not comprehend what they read, for a variety of reasons. For some, the problem is that they do not yet read words with enough fluency to facilitate comprehension. Others can read accurately and quickly enough for comprehension to take place, but they lack the strategies to help them comprehend what they read. Such strategies include the ability to grasp the gist of a text, to notice and repair misinterpretations, and to change tactics based on the purposes of reading. Other struggling readers may have learned these strategies but have difficulty using them because they have only practiced using them with a limited range of texts and in a limited range of circumstances. (p. 2)

In Chapter 6, the concept of the Matthew effect in reading achievement was discussed. The graph in

Figure 7-11 illustrates this concept. Schumaker et al. (2006) explain the graph, and concept, as follows:

> The area between the solid line (representing normal achievement) and the dotted lines (representing underachievement) depicts the "performance gap" for each group of students. This represents the gap between what students are expected to achieve and perform in their classes and what they can actually do. Over time, this gap grows larger and larger, and it is especially exacerbated in the later grades when the academic growth of students with disabilities plateaus. As a result of this performance gap, these students are unable to "access the general education curriculum" and meet the demands of required courses for graduation from high school. Their resulting failure leads to discouragement and disengagement from school, and, for too many, this disengagement manifests itself in dropping out of school altogether. (p. 64)

The adolescent who struggles with reading is likely to have experienced considerable frustration and failure in past efforts to learn or improve reading skills. Thus, the teacher must overcome not only skill deficits, but also problems in attitude, motivation, and fear related to failure expectancy. A positive, reinforcing manner and realistic expectations should underlie any approach to reading instruction with older students.

In responding to these challenges, the Alliance for Excellent Education (2005) identified 15 core elements in a comprehension reading program for secondary school students.

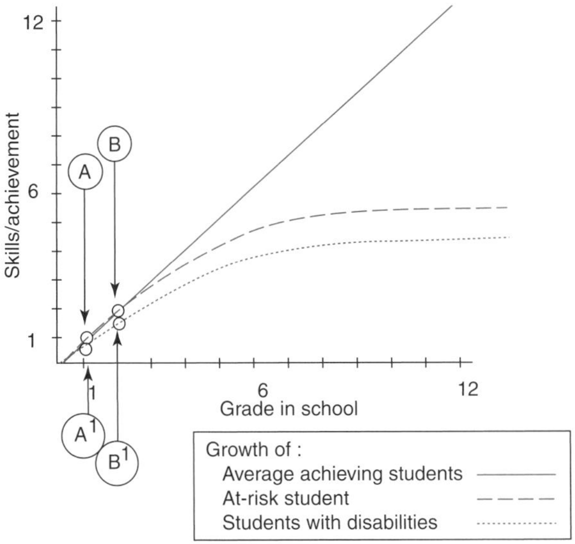


**FIGURE 7–11** The performance gap

Source: Adapted from "Reading Strategy Interventions: Can Literacy Outcomes Be Enforced for At-Risk Adolescents?" by J. Schumaker et al. *Teaching Exceptional Children, 38,* 2006, p. 65. Copyright 2006 by the Council for Exceptional children. Reprinted with permission.

Those particularly apt to this chapter include the following:

- Direct, explicit comprehension instruction
- Effective instructional principles embedded in context
- Motivation and self-directed learning
- Text-based collaborative learning
- Strategic tutoring
- Diverse texts
- Intensive writing
- Technology component
- Ongoing formative and summative assessment of students
- Extended time for literacy
- Teacher teams
- Comprehensive and coordinated literacy program (pp. 1-10)

The discussion of strategies earlier in the chapter's elementary level included approaches that are also often useful with older students; this section provides further attention to their applicability to older students. Discussion includes the use of diverse texts, such as high-interest, low-vocabulary books, literature-based instruction, strategy training, and reciprocal teaching.

A key consideration is the use of diverse texts as core elements in adolescent literacy programs. The Alliance for Excellent Education (2005) noted:

> Whether teaching reading and writing or a subject area, teachers need to find texts at a wide range of difficulty levels. Too often students become frustrated because they are forced to read books that are simply too difficult for them to decode and comprehend simultaneously. . . . Texts must be below students' frustration level, but must also be interesting; that is, they should be high interest and low readability. Given the wide range of reading and writing abilities present in almost any middle or high school classroom, this means having books available from a wide range of levels on the same topic. The term "diverse texts" is also used to indicate that the material should represent a wide range of topics. . . . The range of topics should include a wide variety of cultural, linguistic, and demographic groups. Students should be able to find representatives of themselves in the available books, but they should also be able to find representatives of others about whom they wish to learn. High-interest, low-difficulty texts play a significant role in an adolescent literacy program and are critical for fostering the reading skills of struggling readers and the engagement of all students.

An important consideration is the use of ***high-interest, low-difficulty (HILD) books***. These books (see Table 7-4) are designed for students who read at

**TABLE 7–4** High-interest, low-difficulty (HILD) books

| *Publisher* | *Title/Topic* | *Reading Level* | *Interest Level* |
|---|---|---|---|
| STORY HOUSE CORP.<br>Bindery Lane<br>Charlottesville, NY 12036<br>1-800-847-2105 | *Walt Morey Adventure Library*<br>Fast-paced adventure in the world of Walt Morey (focus on bears, eagles, cougars, and rugged men and women). | 5 | 10 to adult |
| HIGH NOON BOOKS<br>A Division of Academic Therapy Publications | *Tom & Ricky Mystery Series*<br>Two 14-year-old boys set out to solve strange happenings in their hometown. | 1 | 9 to 14 |
| 20 Commercial Blvd. Novato, CA 94949<br>1-800-422-7249 | *Meg Parker Mysteries*<br>Meg and Kate solve a variety of exciting mysteries, ranging from a bank robbery to counterfeiting. | 1 to 2 | 11 to 15 |
| | *High School Highways*<br>Exciting novels about Black and Hispanic students in inner-city settings. | 2 to 3 | 12 to 16 |
| | *Prospectives*<br>Bike rides through the desert, space exploration, and white-water rafting are examples of the encounters of the characters. | 3 to 4 | 12 to 18 |
| | *Romance Series*<br>Love, romance, growing up, and disappointment are some of the topics. | 4.5 to 5.0 | 12 to 18 |
| | *Spy Series*<br>Adventures of the FBI, foreign agents, American diplomats, and spies are included. | 4.5 to 5.0 | 12 to 18 |
| | *Science Fiction Series*<br>Life in the 23rd century, robots, UFOs, and invaders are examples. | 4.5 to 5.0 | 12 to 18 |
| JAMESTOWN PUBLISHERS<br>P.O. Box 9168<br>Providence, RI 02940<br>1-800-872-7323 | *Jamestown Handbooks*<br>Information about sports is used to motivate reluctant readers. Each book focuses on how to play a sport. | 5 | 11 to 18 |
| | *Attention Span Stories*<br>Each of these books contains a single cliff-hanger story told in one-page episodes (e.g., a safari, a trip to outer space, and sports stories). | 2 to 3 | 11 to 14 |
| FEARON/JANUS<br>500 Harbor Blvd.<br>Belmont, CA 94002<br>1-800-877-4283 | *An American Family*<br>Eight 80-page stories tell tales through 200 years, ranging from the settlement of the colonies through the 20th century. | 4.5 | 12 to 18 |
| | *Hopes and Dreams*<br>Ten novels, each 80 pages, dramatize experiences of immigrant groups. | 4.5 to 5.0 | 12 to 18 |
| LITERACY VOLUNTEERS OF NEW YORK CITY<br>Publishing Department<br>121 Ave. of Americas<br>New York, NY 10013<br>219-925-3001 | *Writers' Voices*<br>A series containing works by contemporary writers. It includes true stories, short stories, and poetry on a variety of topics. Examples include *Elvis and Me, The Godfather, The Right Stuff*, and *Jaws*. | 1 to 6 | 15 to adult |

**TABLE 7–5** Most popular books in secondary schools

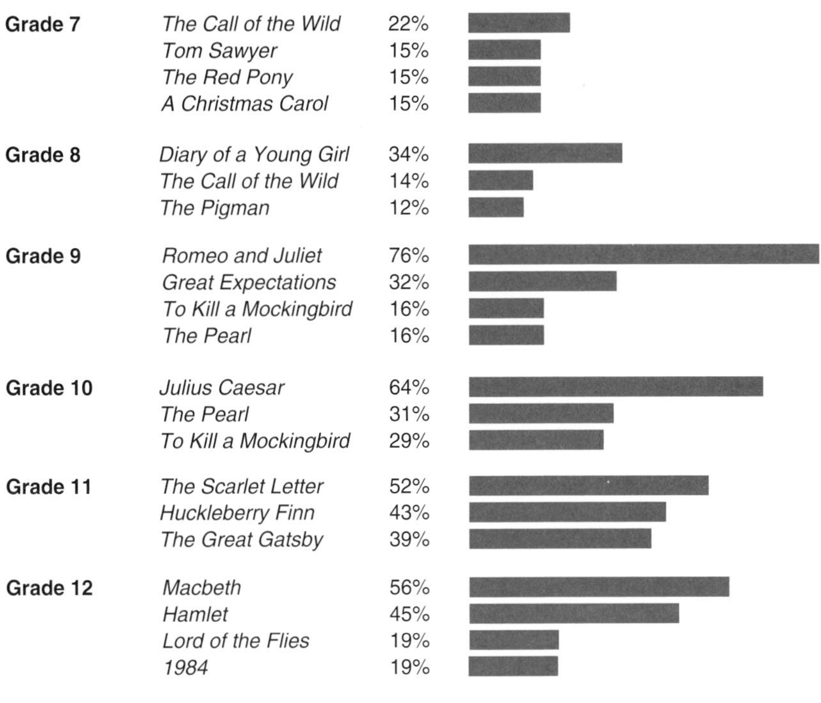

**The Most Popular Works**

The most popular book-length works assigned in public schools, by grade and the percentage of schools requiring them, are:

|  |  |  |
|---|---|---|
| Grade 7 | *The Call of the Wild* | 22% |
| | *Tom Sawyer* | 15% |
| | *The Red Pony* | 15% |
| | *A Christmas Carol* | 15% |
| Grade 8 | *Diary of a Young Girl* | 34% |
| | *The Call of the Wild* | 14% |
| | *The Pigman* | 12% |
| Grade 9 | *Romeo and Juliet* | 76% |
| | *Great Expectations* | 32% |
| | *To Kill a Mockingbird* | 16% |
| | *The Pearl* | 16% |
| Grade 10 | *Julius Caesar* | 64% |
| | *The Pearl* | 31% |
| | *To Kill a Mockingbird* | 29% |
| Grade 11 | *The Scarlet Letter* | 52% |
| | *Huckleberry Finn* | 43% |
| | *The Great Gatsby* | 39% |
| Grade 12 | *Macbeth* | 56% |
| | *Hamlet* | 45% |
| | *Lord of the Flies* | 19% |
| | *1984* | 19% |

*Source:* From "Rewriting the Book on Literature," adapted by J. O'Neil, 1994. *Curriculum Update*, p. 5. Copyright 1994 by Association for Supervision and Curriculum Design. Adapted with permission.

reading levels well below their interest level. For example, a teacher might recommend the book *Specter* (published by Globe Fearon), which is about weird events and psychic phenomena, to a 15-year-old interested in such topics, but who reads at a much lower level.

A related consideration has to do with the use of *literature* in reading programs. Particularly for special educators who may be working with English teachers in a cooperative teaching venture, the list in Table 7-5 of the most popular works of literature taught in schools may be of interest. To use textual material, teachers should assess the content to be assigned. In Table 7-6, Sperling (2006) presents a useful checklist for this purpose.

Earlier in the chapter, principles for using such a literature-based approach were presented. In Figure 7-12, a graphic organizer to facilitate this process for older learners is provided; it can complement efforts for students to work independently with peers in identifying and studying key textural information.

*Strategy instruction* is another critical element of instruction. Strategies for comprehension provide vehicles for students to monitor their comprehension as they are learning new words and concepts presented in texts (Vaughn & Edmonds, 2006).

For older students who are struggling readers, reading an entire text chapter can be time consuming and often does not lead to high levels of comprehension. One option is to have students attack the chapter through a series of structured stages that can familiarize them with the context and enhance focus on key information. Numerous strategies are available; the approaches discussed earlier in the chapter under

**TABLE 7–6** Evaluating a text source for learners in the content areas

1. Is the text source appropriate for your objectives?
2. Are objectives stated, or are students clearly told what they are to learn from the text?
3. Does students' prior knowledge support comprehension of the content?
4. Is the readability of the text appropriate for the learners?
5. Is the vocabulary level appropriate for the students? Consider both domain-specific vocabulary and domain-general vocabulary.
6. Is information that is provided only from this text source something that the learners will need to independently comprehend?
7. Are there appropriate text-based activities?
8. Are text supplements redundant or independent of the text content?
9. Is this text source commensurate with other sources that might be provided to either more- or less-able learners?
10. Is this text source interesting or motivating for the learners?

*Source:* From *"Assessing Reading Materials for Students Who Are Learning Disabled,"* by R. A. Sperling, 2005, *Intervention in School and Clinic, 41,* p. 139. Copyright 2005 by PRO-ED, Inc., Reprinted with permission.

**Literature Chart**

_______________________
Name of Work

| Setting | Main Characters | Conflict or Action | Theme, Lesson, or Meral |
|---|---|---|---|
| | | | |
| | | | |
| | | | |

**FIGURE 7–12** Literature chart

*Source*: Higgins, J., McConnell, K., Patton, J. R., and Ryser, G. (2003). *Practical Ideas That Really Work for Students with Dyslexia and Other Reading Disorders* (p. 133). Austin, TX: PRO-ED. Reprinted with permission.

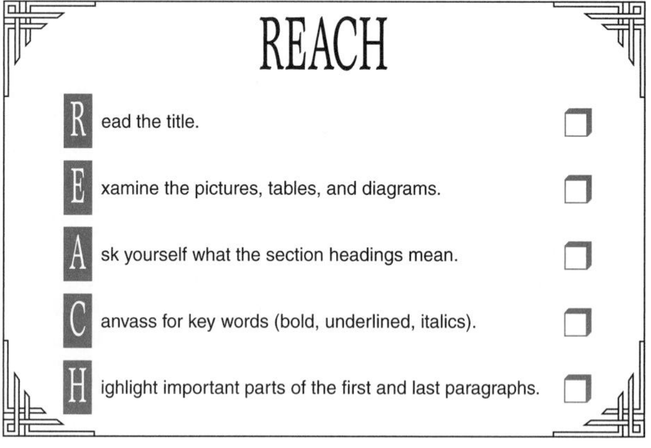


**FIGURE 7–13** REACH comprehension strategy

*Source*: Higgins, J., McConnell, K., Patton, J. R., and Ryser, G. (2003). *Practical Ideas That Really Work for Students with Dyslexia and Other Reading Disorders* (p. 46). Austin, TX: PRO-ED. Reprinted with permission.

self-directed questioning and graphic strategies are also appropriate for older students. In addition, Figure 7-13 presents one such example for use with older students (i.e., REACH).

Another important approach for older students is *reciprocal teaching*. The nearby Teacher Tip focuses on the use of this approach, which was introduced earlier in the chapter. When used with older students, this approach can be expanded to enable students to develop advanced reading skills.

Unrau (2004), basing his work on that of Lenners and Smith (1999), illustrated how students could develop literal skills (or *on-the-surface* reading through retelling and summarizing) as well as inferential and comprehension skills (or *under-the-surface* reading, focused on the meaning of passage and its connections to the reader's experience and inclusive of clarifying, evaluating, and making predictions). Figure 7-14 provides an example of a chart for reading partners to complete according to these levels.

**Reflective Question 7–5:** ***Identify the primary challenges associated with teaching adolescents who are struggling readers and determine which strategies offer the best promise for addressing these problems.***

**FIGURE 7–14** Reciprocal teaching question log

1. Reader reads section aloud to partner. Reader asks an on-the-surface question. Partner repeats the question and then answers. Partner records question on log.
2. Partner asks an under-the-surface question. Reader repeats the question and answer. Reader records question on log. Switch roles and go on.

| *On-the-Surface Question* (When, Where, What, Who) | *Under-the-Surface Question* (Why, How, Would, Should, Could) |
|---|---|
| 1. | 1. |
| 2. | 2. |
| 3. | 3. |

*Source*: Unrau, N. *Content Area Reading and Writing: Fostering Literacies in Middle and High School Cultures*, 1st Edition, © 2004, p. 232. Reprinted by permission of Pearson Education Inc., Upper Saddle River, NJ.

TEACHER *Tips* Secondary Level

## Reciprocal Teaching

Reciprocal teaching is a scaffolded procedure that was introduced earlier in this chapter. As noted, it was originally intended for middle school readers experiencing difficulty. Tompkins (2006) outlined the stages as follows:

1. **Teach with comprehension strategies.** Teachers teach students to predict, question, clarify, and summarize as they read stories and informational books. They model how to use each strategy, and they think aloud to show students their thinking. . . .
2. **Introduce reciprocal teaching.** Teachers explain reciprocal teaching is a way to get more involved in the reading experience and to understand the big ideas better. They use shared reading to model how to use the four strategies as they read aloud a short text, stopping often to share their thinking. While thinking aloud, teachers make predictions, ask questions, clarify confusing words and ideas, and summarize what they have read. Afterward, they discuss what they have read and how each strategy enhanced their comprehension of the text.
3. **Practice in teacher-led small groups.** Students practice reciprocal teaching in guided reading groups or other small groups. Teachers scaffold students as they read short sections of text and use the four comprehension strategies. Students often begin by making predictions and then reading silently. They pause partway through the text to modify the predictions they made earlier, ask questions and clarify the meanings of unfamiliar words and other confusions. . . . After they finish reading, they summarize, ask additional questions, and clarify any confusions. The order in which students use strategies varies depending on the students and the text they are reading. . . .
4. **Practice in student-led small groups.** Students form literature circles or other small groups to use the procedure to read novels, chapters in content-area textbooks, or other texts. Students . . . use self-stick notes to track their strategy use, or they can make strategy charts by dividing a sheet of paper or a page in their reading logs into four sections where they record their predictions in one section, and their questions, clarifications, and summaries in the other sections. After reading, students discuss their strategy use and share the notes they made or charts they created.
5. **Continue to use reciprocal teaching with longer texts.** After students become proficient at reading and comprehending short sections of text, teachers have them use reciprocal teaching to read increasingly longer sections of text. (pp. 495–496).

**TABLE 7–7** Materials for fluency practice

| *Program* | *Website* | *Material Provided* |
|---|---|---|
| Great Leaps | http://www.greatleaps.com | Provides words in lists, phrases, and passages from kindergarten to adult |
| Quick Reads | http://www.pearsonlearning.com/mcp.quickreads.cfm | Provides passages on social studies and science themes with reading levels from second to fifth grades |
| Read Naturally | http://www.readnaturally.com | Provides passages from kindergarten through adult reading levels; also a good source of multicultural passages in Spanish |

*Source:* From "Individualizing Guided Oral Reading Fluency Instruction For Students with Emotional and Learning Disorders," by S. Al Otaiba and M. O. Rivera, 2006, *Intervention in School and Clinic, 41,* p. 146. Copyright 2006 by PRO-ED, Inc., Reprinted with permission.

## TECHNOLOGY IN THE CLASSROOM

As noted earlier in the chapter, new learning situations have further emphasized the need of students to be proficient in comprehension. At the same time, new technologies that present textual material electronically will only become more prevalent and more widely used. In addition, the use of the Internet presents a number of reading comprehension challenges for students. Students must engage a medium that taps what could be considered typical comprehension demands as well as new challenges such as using search engines (Coiro, 2003).

The problems that students will face are a result of Web-based textual material being nonlinear, interactive, and inclusive of multiple media forms (Coiro, 2003). Although some of these features are quite beneficial because they are engaging and because they reflect a universal design for learning, they nonetheless put new demands on students to be able to understand the content that is contained in this format. For some students, there may be simply too many options and too many distractions. To facilitate fluency in reading challenging text, the websites listed by Al Otaiba and Rivera (2006) are provided in Table 7-7.

Blachowicz and Ogle (2001) encouraged professionals in the field of reading to be sensitive to what and how students will read in the future. They note that "we have often depended on enjoyment of literature and practice with narratives to become good readers . . . now there are so many different varieties of reading, and so many everyday demands, that we must go beyond narratives" (p. 13). They further pointed out that studies of adult reading habits suggest that less than 25% of reading involves narrative material. The fact that more reading in life involves expository material, or perhaps the emerging type of text presented on a computer screen, suggests that reading instruction in comprehension take these facts into account. The nearby technology tip provides guidance to help students become critical users of online textual material.

> **Reflective Question 7–6:** ***How can technology be used to help promote achievement in reading comprehension?***

## MAKING IT WORK

The National Reading Panel (2000), after reviewing 203 text comprehension studies, identified eight evidence-supported successful instructional techniques for classroom use. The eight areas were:

- Comprehension monitoring
- Cooperative learning
- Graphic and semantic organizers
- Story structure
- Question answering
- Question generation
- Summarization
- Multiple strategy teaching

Building on, and extending from, the NRP report, Pressley and Fingeret (2005), recommended that teachers:

- Teach a small battery of strategies: prediction, summary, questioning, imagery
- Explain and model these strategies
- Encourage students to use them until they begin to self-regulate (p. 50)

**TECHNOLOGY *Tips***

For many students, their primary resource for information is the Internet. Given this reality, Burke (2001) provides guidelines (as adapted below) to consider when using information from a given website source.

**Sources**

- Where does the author get the evidence . . . to support his claims?
- What other sources—experts, publications, institutions—does the author cite? . . .
- Who is responsible for the content of the site?
- Is the source of all information clearly identified and properly cited?

**Timelines**

- When was this written? Updated?
- Is this information consistent with our current understanding?. . .

**Authority**

- On what basis is this person or organization qualified to inform people about this subject? . . .
- How current is the author's knowledge of this subject?
- Does the author or institution clearly establish or provide links to its credentials, affiliations, and sponsors? . . .
- Does this person or institution have a reputation for thorough, accurate, objective work?

**Audience**

- Does the author clearly identify his intended audience? . . .
- Does the site suggest any bias in favor of its audience's perspective?
- What do the Web site's links tell you about its audience?
- Does the site offer an "About Us" section or an introduction that describes the site's purpose and intended audience?

**Quality Control**

- Are articles published by respected, peer-reviewed journals, newspapers, or reputable magazines prior to or in addition to being published on this site?
- Is the information within the site consistent in terms of point of view, tone, and content? . . .
- If the site offers a biased perspective on a subject, does it provide an opposing view or an opportunity for readers to respond with other perspectives?
- Is information offered as fact or opinion? Is this clearly stated for the reader?
- Are the authors of all content clearly identified? Are any articles anonymously written? (pp. 25–26)

## SUMMARY

This chapter focuses on enhancing reading comprehension in students. It begins with the identification of the problems that students who are struggling in reading typically present in classroom situations. Next the chapter focuses on reading comprehension and the major components associated with this skill area. The text then examines three general approaches to reading instruction: the use of basal readers, language experience, and whole language. Strategies for developing vocabulary and word knowledge are discussed. The chapter then provides information on a variety of specific strategies related to teacher-directed questioning, student-directed questioning, peers-mediated strategies, graphic-aid strategies, and fluency strategies. The chapter concludes with attention to several special considerations for adolescent learners and technology usage.

## ACTIVITIES

The following activities relate to specific aspects of enhanced reading comprehension.

### ELEMENTARY LEVEL

1. Have students read to remember instead of reading to find out and answer questions. Tell them to read to remember something they can share with their peers. When they finish, have them volunteer information to the class and write their statements on the board. At first begin with three pieces of information from each student. Write these statements on the board and have the students place them in the sequence in which they occurred in the story. As students improve, more statements can be required and/or the remembered information can be written (Harden, 1987).
2. To encourage the use of the library and promote independent reading, have students help rate books. With the librarian's assistance, ask students to help the teachers and the rest of the students at the school by reading the books in the library that fall within their reading ability. As a group, have them establish a system for evaluating and recommending books to others (Jamison & Shevitz, 1985).

3. Have students complete follow-up activities.
   - Write a letter to a main character in the book suggesting other ways the character might have solved the problem or acted in the situation.
   - Write sentences from the story that show that someone was excited, sad, happy, or ashamed.
   - Draw a picture of something in the story that indicates the setting is past, present, or future.
   - Find three pictures in magazines that remind you of the main characters in the story. Under each picture write your reasons for selection.
   - Draw a picture of one of the memorable scenes from the story, showing as many details as possible.
   - Make a poster advertising your book.
4. Students can motivate others to read by sharing a book they have enjoyed. Some creative ways for them to share are listed here.
   - Publish a book review column for the school paper with short reviews and reactions to books read.
   - After reading a biography or book of fiction, describe the main characters and their common problems. Tell how these problems were or were not solved.
   - Prepare a collection of something the class has read about (e.g., rocks, coins, stamps), with appropriate information for an exhibit.
   - Make a poster (either flat or three-dimensional) showing a scene or stimulating interest in a book.
   - Make and decorate a book jacket; write an advertisement to accompany the book.
   - Write a letter to a friend or a librarian recommending a book you especially liked.
   - Dress as one of the characters in a book and tell about yourself.
5. T. S. Jones (2005) encourages the use of the Internet and print magazines (e.g., National Geographic) that can provide an intentional perspective by focusing, for example, on variations in housing.
   - Students comprehend and retain information better if they are active readers.
   - Always give students a purpose for reading and gradually train them to set their own purposes.
   - Teach them to make predictions about content before beginning to read.
   - After reading, have students defend or reject their predictions.
   - Encourage students to ask themselves after each paragraph, "What is the main idea?"

### MIDDLE AND SECONDARY LEVEL

1. Journal writing can be used to enhance comprehension. In character journals, students can comment on a story they have read in the voice of one of the characters. In this way, they may think more about what they are reading. Further, when students do not agree with a character's actions or attitudes, they may come away with an improved sense of their own identity (Gartland, 1994).
2. In groups, have students write and produce a videotaped commercial advertising a novel they have read. Each student will serve on their group's "ad committee," which will determine the type of commercial to be produced (e.g., public service announcement, testimonials) and how the information will be presented. The goal of each group should be to create an informative, entertaining commercial about their book, which will convince "viewers" to read that book. Commercials may also be shared with other classes and teachers.
3. After reading a selected story or novel, ask the students to paraphrase the story and develop a script for a class play. The students make props, costumes, and puppets if desired. For a shorter version, students role-play parts of the story without verbalizing the information. The remainder of the class guesses the part of the story that is being dramatized. This activity reinforces the events of the story and improves comprehension.
4. Gartland (1994) encourages students to consider K-W-L as a technique to focus attention, with *K* representing what is known, *W* what the student wants to know, and *L* what has been learned.
5. An activity that includes reading for information, survival, and amusement uses menus from the community's restaurants, fast-food chains, or food counters. Give students specific assignments to compare prices, develop lists of meals, or identify the top 10 places to go on a special date. Students might also construct a composite menu to be printed in the graphics department and used for personal review. This menu can provide a basis for a variety of exercises to develop vocabulary, attack skills, and word recognition.

CHAPTER

# 8

# Written Language

Written language subsumes the three areas of handwriting, spelling, and written expression and demands that the individual draw from a variety of mechanical, memory, conceptual, and organizational skills in order to communicate successfully. Therefore it is not surprising that writing can present significant challenges to students with special needs, who may have existing linguistic deficits in oral language and/or reading, low societal expectations for success, inconsistent encouragement and reinforcement for appropriate usage, and limited motivation and/or expectation for success.

The importance of writing to all students is apparent because it opens a critical avenue for communication. At initial levels, students must develop the capability to write their names and other personally identifying information and write short stories. At more advanced levels they need to take notes, respond to test questions, develop elaborate compositions and essays, and write letters of inquiry and complete job applications as they transition into adult life. Further, they need to develop the ability to communicate through functional and/or creative writing such as in compositions, reports, and research papers. As Graham (1992) aptly states, "Writing has increasingly become a critical occupational skill. Successful performance in a variety of occupations requires the ability to write in a clear . . . manner" (p. 137).

Since the 1990s, written language has received increased attention in educational programs for students with special needs, particularly as students are challenged to be successful in inclusive classrooms. It is important to contextualize the writing difficulties of children and adolescents who have disabilities, however, by noting that such problems are also experienced by large numbers of students who are not identified as disabled. Troia (2005) summarized a recent report of the National Assessment of Educational Progress as follows:

**In grade 4 . . .**

- 66% of students report that they like to write. 32% consider writing a favorite activity.
- 67% of students believe they are good writers.
- 27% of students performed at or above the proficiency level.

**In grade 8 . . .**

- 52% of students report that they like to write. 38% consider writing a favorite activity.
- 51% of students believe they are good writers.
- 23% of students performed at or above the proficiency level.

This chapter initially provides an orientation to the importance of written language in the school curriculum. Subsequent major sections then focus on the three instructional areas of handwriting, spelling, and written expression.

## WRITTEN LANGUAGE IN THE CURRICULUM

The writing process requires the translation of thoughts into the written word. It involves two distinct processes. **Text generation** involves the transfer of ideas into representations in language; this is commonly referred to as written expression. **Transcription** involves the translation of such language representations into the format of written language, most commonly through handwriting (or keyboarding) and spelling (Maki, Vauras, & Vainio, 2002). The model presented by Polloway, Miller, and Smith (2004) provides an overview of written language and illustrates the role of handwriting and spelling as supportive skills to written expression (see Figure 8–1).

A number of specific facets of writing serve as general programming considerations. First, writers must draw on *previous linguistic experiences*. Thus, prior problems in listening, speaking, or reading may be

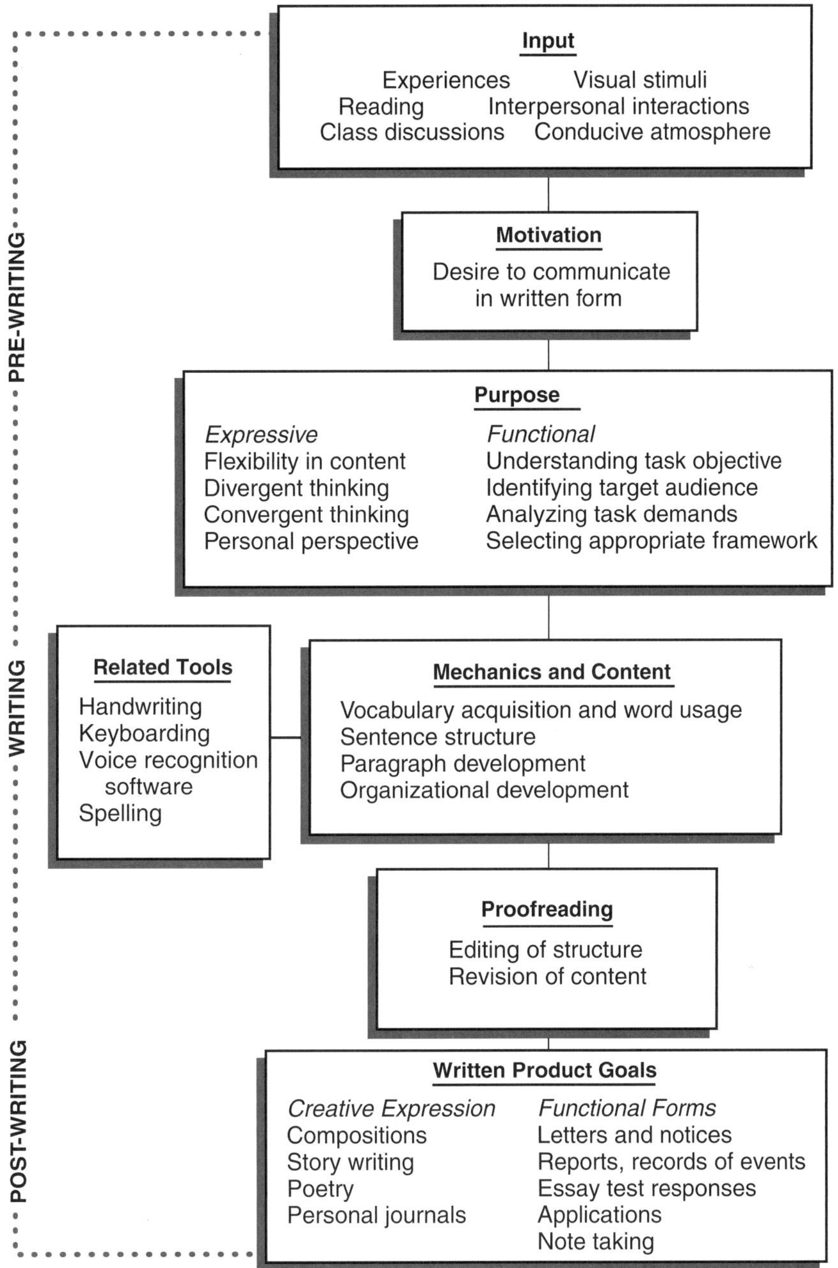


**FIGURE 8–1** Model for written language

*Source:* From *Language Instruction for Learners with Special Needs*, by E. A. Polloway, L. Miller, and T. E. C. Smith, 2004, Denver, CO: Love Publishing.

reflected and perhaps magnified in the area of writing. To write in a coherent, understandable manner, one must be able to think, read, and comprehend in a logical way.

Second, writing involves a complex blend of *ideation as content and technical skills as craft*. Particularly when teaching the more mechanical aspects of writing (e.g., handwriting, spelling, grammar), teachers should remember that the goal is to use craft to enhance the expression of content. Thus, work on technical skills is more effective if the skills taught offer a high rate of return because of their relative importance and usage, and if the skills are directly used in subsequent writing assignments (Graham, 1999).

Third, writing must be viewed as both *process* and *product*. Products often have served as the primary educational goal. However, educators need to ensure that students learn how to reach that goal. For example, some students may have the mistaken impression that the textbooks used in various subject areas were written by an obscure scholar who simply transcribed thoughts directly to the finished product. These children need to understand the process behind the product, which provides an opportunity to emphasize the concept of the working draft.

Fourth, writing also provides a communication link for *personal expression*. In this sense, writing is not simply a goal but also a vehicle. Writing can provide opportunities for the expression of feelings and attitudes. A comprehensive program thus provides for the development of both *creative and functional uses of written language*. The creative emphasis stresses individual expression and can promote personal and social adjustment, whereas the functional serves a more utilitarian purpose, stressing skills that are directly applicable to independent living. Teachers, particularly at the secondary school level, should carefully evaluate standards for learning along with both current writing ability and expected future needs in order to determine which skills will benefit each student most.

Fifth, writing instruction provides another opportunity for *demonstrating cultural sensitivity* (e.g., through the use of students' and parents' native language in written form, through the use of words and phrases to affirm the importance of their native language, and through a broad level of respect for linguistic differences; Bae & Clark, 2005).

Finally, teachers of writing should consider their *own roots as writers*. Graves (1994) encourages teachers to consider their own experiences with writing and writing instruction in order to take a fresh look at writing themselves as a basis for their work with their students.

## HANDWRITING

Handwriting instruction traditionally has been a core focus of the curriculum for all students at the elementary level. For example, primary grade teachers have reported that they spend an average of 72 minutes a week on instruction (Graham & Harris, 2005). They further indicated that 12% of those students experienced difficulties. Instruction was seen as important because failure to master skills would have a negative impact on how much they write, writing quality, writing grades, and time taken to complete assignments (Graham & Harris, 2005).

Though handwriting has been a staple of the school curriculum for years, technological advances have caused some educators to question its relevance as an important skill to be taught. Nevertheless, as Polloway et al. (2004) note:

> Although the advances made in technology have clearly impacted on the everyday use of handwriting for some people, competencies in this skill definitely remain important. . . . Without the ability to communicate with handwriting, individuals will be unable to make notes, take down information quickly, and communicate with others. (p. 366)

Greenland and Polloway (1995) highlight issues related to a number of the key first impressions that may be associated with handwriting: Does an employer disregard sloppy and/or illegible applications? Does a teacher initially regard a student with poor handwriting as academically inferior? Are poorly written credit applications reviewed from a less favorable perspective? Graves (1994) acknowledges that even though meaning in writing is clearly paramount, it should not result in handwriting being ignored.

Many children are delayed or disabled for reasons that also may impact their handwriting skills. For example, they may have deficits in attention or visual memory, or they may have physiological problems that inhibit the development of fine motor skills. In addition, they may be more susceptible to the effects of poor teaching in the primary grades. Because writing combines fine motor skills, sequencing, language, memory, attention, thinking skills, and visual-spatial abilities, it may be quite difficult, especially for those students with disabilities.

All students, but especially those with disabilities, are disadvantaged when handwriting is not taught correctly and frequently (Polloway et al., 2004). As Bertin and Perlman (2000) note, "handwriting is a basic skill that needs to be systematically taught so that children can learn to use written language to communicate their knowledge and express their ideas" (p. 1). In addition, the speed and fluency with which students use handwriting can affect academic success (Mlyniec, 2001). Further, research has shown a relationship between handwriting skills and the overall writing process (Graham, Harris, & Fink, 2000).

In instructing learners with special needs, teachers should remember that the ultimate goal is legibility. Efforts to achieve perfect reproduction are most often doomed to fail; even when reasonably successful, they are frequently short-lived triumphs because most students eventually develop their own personal style. Therefore, instructional programs should avoid stressing the perfection associated with some recognized standards and instead encourage a legible yet unique style (Wallace, Cohen, & Polloway, 1987).

## Assessment of Handwriting Skills

The assessment of handwriting is dominated by informal areas of assessment. Speaking to writing assessment, inclusive of handwriting, Gregg and Mather (2002) note:

> A comprehensive assessment requires the use of informal measures of writing. Informal measures help identify the many factors that affect writing performance as well as the many skills and abilities involved in the successful orchestration of the writing process. . . . Performance across writing components (e.g., handwriting, spelling, syntax) and across different types of task formats (i.e., copy, dictation, spontaneous) can help clarify a student's writing competence. Careful investigation of error patterns leads to an understanding of educational needs and the identification of instructional goals. (p. 21)

If a student has not formally started to write or is experiencing difficulty in acquiring a certain writing skill, the teacher must be able to assess his or her potential to develop this skill. Though informal areas of assessment are essential, several formal tests provide additional, initial guidance in the process. The Test of Written Language-3 (TOWL-3) (Hammill & Larsen, 1996) evaluates handwriting according to graded scales; it is discussed later in this chapter.

Given the limited diagnostic options available, the most common assessment tools are teacher observations and related informal techniques. Thus, once screening has been accomplished, a close visual examination should give the teacher information on which to build a program to help a student develop or improve specific handwriting skills.

## Elementary Considerations

**Prerequisites.** The development of prewriting skills builds on visual acuity and its coordination with motor movements. Therefore, when students who are disabled enter formal schooling they must engage in the same type of visual and motor activities that average children may have mastered by that time. Two objectives—developing visual-motor integration and establishing handedness (i.e., preferred hand for writing)—are central concerns at this stage. To achieve these goals, numerous activities have typically been suggested: manipulation of objects, tracing of objects with the index finger in sand, manipulation of scissors for cutting paper, and crayon and finger painting. Visual-motor activities adjusted for differences in chronological age also may be helpful for older students. For example, fine motor skills can be developed in shop classes and in vocational training.

Nevertheless, several important concerns arise about such activities. First, some activities (e.g., cutting with scissors) are clearly important for their own worth, regardless of their relationship to writing. However, there is no empirical support confirming that these types of exercises directly assist in refining existing writing skills. Instead, some argue, the focus on nonwriting fine motor activities simply takes time away from direct instruction in writing. Another caution concerns the use of visual-motor activities with the vast majority of children with limited writing skills. The handwriting process itself provides fine motor practice and thus can accomplish both linguistically relevant goals (i.e., objectives that promote language development) and motoric goals. As Hammill (1986) notes, so-called prerequisites often can be naturally developed by directing students to write letters and words rather than giving extensive readiness instruction. For the limited number of students with significant motoric difficulties, occupational therapists often can provide assistance to both teachers and students.

**Manuscript Writing.** Because manuscript writing is the initial instructional focus for most students, the teacher's first planning tasks are to determine an instructional sequence of letters and to select instructional methodology; often this decision may be governed by the curriculum followed in the general education classroom. There is no correct letter to start with in teaching manuscript writing; however, certain letters lend themselves to that function. For example, the letters of a child's first name have high utility value and thus can have a positive effect on motivation to learn.

To ensure an appropriate instructional sequence, the teacher can group different letters by their shapes (see Figures 8-2 and 8-3) or can follow the letter sequence in one of many commercial manuscript workbooks available. Another alternative is to follow the order in which letters are introduced for reading. Attention should be given to the relative similarity of strokes required for the letters.

For students who experience difficulty at the beginning stages of writing, modifications of the writing

o a d g q / b p / c e /
t l i k / r n m h / v w
x y / f j / u / z / s

**FIGURE 8–2** A sequential grouping of lowercase manuscript letters according to common features

L H T E F I / J U /
P R B D K / A M N
V W X Y Z / S /
O Q C G

**FIGURE 8–3** A sequential grouping of uppercase manuscript letters according to common features

implement can be considered; the greatest problem often encountered is the child's use of the correct grip on the utensil. A variety of aids have been used to facilitate appropriate grip, including the larger primary-sized pencils, tape wrapped around the pencil, use of a multisided large pencil, and the adaptation of a standard pencil with a **Hoyle gripper** (a three-sided plastic device that requires the child to place two fingers and the thumb in the proper position).

Although research on handwriting instruction has not demonstrated the benefits of modifying writing utensils (Tompkins, 2002), modifications nevertheless have been reported to be useful by some primary teachers (Polloway et al., 2004). It seems prudent to assess the grip of individual students who are experiencing difficulties in order to determine whether an adaptation is warranted.

The most effective approach to teaching specific letters and words is one in which teacher presentation is consistent. Most programs assume that these forms are best taught in isolation but that opportunities must be provided for their use in actual writing exercises. In their classic paper on handwriting, Graham and Miller (1980) provide an excellent review of effective instructional techniques and sequences to facilitate letter formation. The procedures that follow are based on the specific steps they outlined for instruction.

The first step is for the teacher to demonstrate the formation of individual letters while students observe the specific strokes involved. Students' attention should be directed to the distinctive features of these letters and their comparison with letters previously learned. As the children begin to transcribe letters, the teacher should use prompting (e.g., manual guidance during writing, directional arrows) and tracing to facilitate the task. When there is no longer a need for this more intrusive type of prompt, instruction becomes a function of copying—typically, from near-point (i.e., from a paper on the student's desk) and then from the chalkboard). While students are copying and then writing from memory, they should be encouraged to engage in self-instruction by verbalizing to themselves the writing procedures being followed. After a letter can be written from memory, repetition of the form is needed to ensure learning and enhance proficiency. Finally, corrective feedback from the teacher, extrinsic reinforcement, and/or self-correction can be used so that the letter will be retained and increased legibility will be achieved.

Once the student has made appropriate progress acquiring competence in the formation of manuscript letters, the transition to cursive should begin. This usually occurs in the third grade in most school divisions. Criteria for the transition include manuscript proficiency, ability to write all letters from memory, and self-initiated imitation of cursive forms.

**Cursive Writing.** The set of skills acquired while learning manuscript writing is helpful to students when they begin to learn how to write in cursive form. The movement to cursive should stress the key features of that style: paper positioning, the pencil remaining on the paper throughout the writing of individual words, all letters starting at the baseline, a left-to-right rhythm, an appropriate slant to the right, connection of letters, and spacing between words. Students should be encouraged to begin with manuscript letters that directly evolve into cursive forms.

Instruction in cursive writing can follow the same format used with manuscript form: (a) start with letters that students are presently working with while following a predetermined sequence (see Figures 8–4 and 8–5) based on common features, or follow the sequence found in the commercial cursive writing workbook that is being used in the general education classroom; (b) consistently use the terms *uppercase* and *lowercase* to describe a letter; and (c) work with previously written words at the beginning of students'

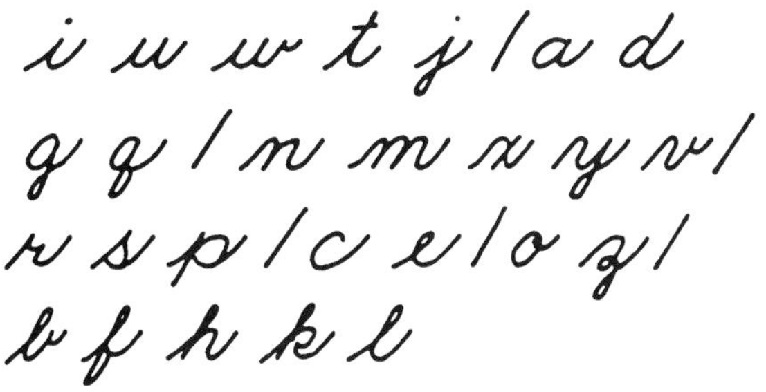

FIGURE 8–4 A sequential grouping of lowercase cursive letters according to common features

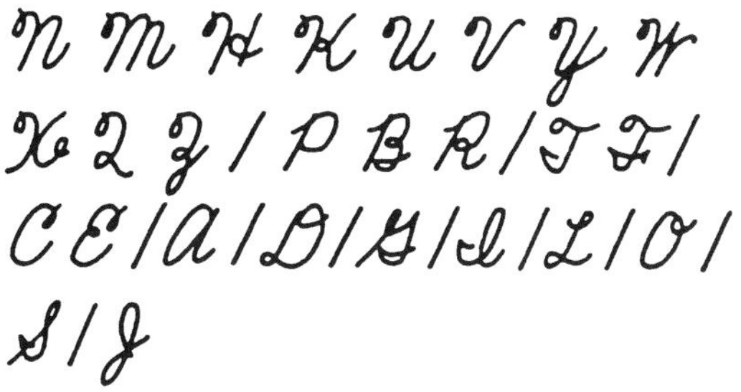

FIGURE 8–5 A sequential grouping of uppercase cursive letters according to common features

cursive writing experiences to promote transfer and overlearning. In addition, teachers must always tell students whether they should be writing in cursive or manuscript. When students begin to use cursive writing, they will also be using more complex language forms and will be able to record them in sentence and paragraph form.

**Perspective: Manuscript and Cursive Writing.** The question of teaching manuscript versus cursive handwriting has been debated for many years. Rationales for teaching only manuscript traditionally include its similarity to book print, the relative ease of letter formation, and its benefit in not confusing students with a second writing form. Rationales for cursive have included its natural rhythm, amelioration of problems with spacing and reversals, social status, and speed.

Despite the various claims and disclaimers about the merits of these forms, the question is often moot: most students with high-incidence disabilities have already been taught according to the traditional sequence in the general education classroom (i.e., manuscript followed by cursive in the second or third grade), and students with more significant disabilities must be taught first in manuscript because it makes fewer motoric demands and is consistent with (and thus reinforces) the printed words in reading. Because most students ultimately will learn both forms, they can then use the form of handwriting with which they feel most comfortable and at which they are most proficient. No empirical data establish that one form of handwriting is clearly and inherently better than the other for a given population of students.

### Middle and Secondary Level

Handwriting is a common key feature of the elementary classroom but should not be completely overlooked at the secondary level. For example, a key consideration would include preparing adolescents for the world of work and for the forms and applications that so frequently specify "please print," teachers should continue to provide practical opportunities for using manuscript writing at the secondary level.

Because most adults write in a form of cursive, some support can be generated for having persons with special needs write in this way to foster inclusion. However, only in personal signatures does cursive writing take clear precedence over manuscript. An analysis of the writing of many adolescents and adults typically will reveal reliance on a **mixed script** with elements of manuscripts and cursive merged (see p. 234).

**Proficiency and Maintenance.** Although these concerns are important at the elementary level as well, we discuss them here because these are the key considerations in handwriting instruction for older students. Both manuscript and cursive writing call for instructional procedures that promote proficiency and maintenance, although attention is not often given to such follow-up to initial instruction. Teachers may assume that handwriting was taught in elementary grades and that the students will independently maintain good handwriting skills just by doing the writing required for daily assignments. However, the value of guided practice should not be overlooked. As Alston and Taylor (1987) note, "practice does not make perfect, it only makes permanent" (p. 127).

The goal of **proficiency** and **maintenance** learning activities is to enhance and retain both accuracy and fluency. Consequently, the teacher must periodically evaluate retention and use direct instruction to maintain both accuracy and speed. Penmanship tends to deteriorate with time, and the importance of repetition to enhance retention is relatively infrequently stated in reference to handwriting.

The first concern in developing a maintenance program is to evaluate the handwriting of each student. In an inclusive setting, it is likely that some students who are not disabled will need such attention while some students with disabilities will not. Thus it represents an apt opportunity for collaborative teaching. To facilitate this process, teachers can maintain checklists of specific letters and skills for individual students with the student's involvement.

Alston and Taylor (1987) suggest a four-step approach to maintenance. First, the whole school should become involved. Teachers are to monitor, praise, and instruct. Second, each class should have periodic writing sessions to practice handwriting. Work should be displayed to encourage and motivate the students. Third, modifications should be made for those with chronic or severe handwriting problems. These students should be instructed on the basics (e.g., grip, posture, paper position) as well as on letter formation (e.g., size, shape, reversals, spacing). They should also be taught a style that lends itself to speed. Finally, group lessons should be included.

A key need is for student self-evaluation and correction. The greatest improvement occurs when students are taught to evaluate their own handwriting and are encouraged to improve, such as by self-monitoring letter forms and by self-grading, finding their own mistakes and making corrections.

A useful technique to promote proficiency is selective checking (Lovitt, 1975). A teacher using this technique selects a specific letter to be evaluated at the end of a given daily assignment. A model is provided for the student, with an established criterion for acceptable legibility. After reviewing the specific examples of the letter-of-the-day within the particular task, the teacher uses illegibility as the basis for assigning additional practice exercises and correct letter formation as the basis for reinforcement.

Research by Weintraub and Graham (1998) provides further guidance for issues related to proficiency in handwriting. Based on their study of students with learning disabilities and those who were normally achieving, they found that students with disabilities were able to make adjustments in their handwriting in order to write more quickly and neatly. They indicated:

> [T]eachers can typically expect that students with [learning disabilities] are capable of improving the legibility of their writing when requested to do so. Thus, it is not unreasonable to ask these students to make the final drafts of their papers more legible or encourage them to try to make single draft material, such as a written message, neater and easier to read. It is important to realize, however, that they will require more time to do this. . . . On the basis of handwriting alone, it will generally take 50 minutes [for them] to do what normally achieving students do in 30 minutes. Consequently, we encourage teachers to provide these students with additional time when taking tests or completing writing assignments, and teachers may want to consider how their writing assignments can be modified so that they are responsive to individual differences in text production skills. (p. 151)

## Handwriting Alternatives

The traditional approach to instructional sequences is still commonly followed by the majority of general education classrooms and schools. Thus a common program used is the classic Zaner-Bloser approach, which identifies both manuscript and cursive handwriting forms (see Hackney, 1993, or Tompkins, 2005, for examples of these model letters).

Although most classrooms follow a traditional handwriting curriculum, two potential options are worth noting:

- **D'Nealian Handwriting Program:** The purpose of the D'Nealian program (Thurber, 1987) is to reduce teaching/learning time by initially establishing the letter formations, rhythm, size, slant, and spacing that will be used for cursive writing. The program stresses continuous skill progression with transition from manuscript to cursive. Materials are available for readiness through eighth grade. The teacher's edition suggests ways to modify instruction for those experiencing motor coordination and other handwriting problems. The instructional sequence provides an alternative to traditional instruction. Graham (1999) encourages caution in its adoption because the bases of the program have not been substantiated. Most importantly, the program's merit would likely be governed by whether it has been adopted in the general education classroom.
- **Mixed script:** Mixed script programs (e.g., Mullins, Joseph, Turner, Zawadski, & Saltzman, 1972) use a simplified script that combines elements of both manuscript and cursive writing, thus simplifying the task of learning letter forms and eliminating the need for transition from manuscript

to cursive. Whether such a mixed script is formally taught or not may be moot; many writers naturally gravitate to it. Graham and Harris (2005) report some limited data that suggest such writers may be faster and also may have higher levels of legibility.

Finally, it is worth considering handwriting in terms of *cultural variance*. A study of handwriting can provide students with an awareness of diverse practices, including those of historical value. For example, T. S. Jones (2005) recommended the exploration of styles such as calligraphy, hieroglyphics, and Braille.

### Left-Handedness

Left-handed students (approximately 10% of the U. S. population or perhaps two or three students in each general education classroom) often encounter special problems in writing that may accentuate the other problems already present in students with learning difficulties. Left-handed students cannot see letters adequately as they form them because the left hand blocks out a letter shortly after it is written.

As Polloway et al. (2004) note, the primary difference between right- and left-handed writers is in their physical orientation. "Right-handed students pull their arms toward their bodies as they write, whereas left-handed students push away. As left-handed students write, they move their left hand across what they have just written, often covering it" (Tompkins, 2005, p. 615).

One simple strategy is for left-handed students to grasp the writing utensil farther away from the tip while maintaining the same grip on the pencil or pen. They should not be encouraged to hook their hands to see better; this practice is tiring and may cause more problems. However, students who are already successfully writing in a hooked fashion should not be reeducated. The left-handed student's paper should also be slightly angled to the right side of the desk. If possible, students should be provided with a model. Alternative positioning strategies for left-handed persons are illustrated in Figure 8–6.

**Reflective Question 8–1:** ***How can handwriting instructional programs best be designed to enable students to produce legible letters and words and thus communicate effectively?***

## SPELLING

Although limited efforts have been made to ascertain the prevalence of spelling disorders, it is generally assumed that such problems are widespread, with primary teachers in a recent survey indicating that 26% of their students experienced difficulty (Graham & Harris, 2005). The challenge is exacerbated because the English language has 26 letters, 300 different letter combinations, and 17 vowel and 27 consonant phonemes, and thus over 500 spellings to represent phonemes.

Individuals experiencing difficulty in spelling are typically classified as demonstrating isolated deficits in

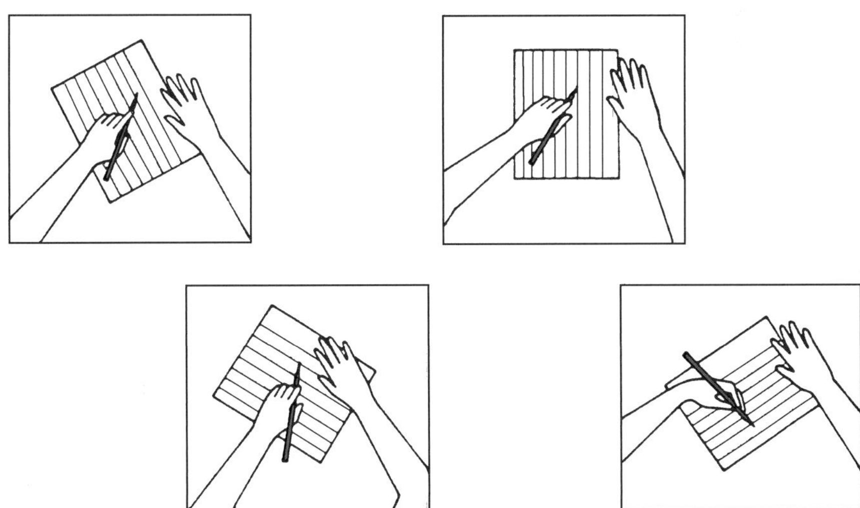

**FIGURE 8–6** Alternative positioning for left-handed writers

*Source:* From "Handwriting Research and Practice: A Unified Approach," by S. Graham and L. Miller, 1980, *Focus on Exceptional Children, 13*(2), p. 12. Copyright 1980 by Love Publishing Company. Reprinted with permission.

specific spelling skills or as exhibiting a general pattern of academic and language-learning disabilities, of which spelling is just one symptom (Beirne-Smith & Riley, 2004). In either case, spelling represents an important area of curricular concern for students with disabilities. Further, it is a unique area of concern because it is "one curriculum area in which neither creativity nor divergent thinking is encouraged. Only one pattern or arrangement of letters can be accepted as correct; no compromise is possible" (Lerner, 1996, p. 468).

Beirne-Smith and Riley (2004) summarize research on proficient and less proficient spellers as follows:

> Proficient spellers . . . typically depend on sensitivity of patterns of letters, have visual ability to distinguish when words look correct, and have strong phonemic awareness and knowledge of spelling patterns. . . . When faced with unknown or unfamiliar words, proficient spellers access, devise, or apply strategies to determine the correct spelling of the word. They use their knowledge of phonemic and morphemic rules to spell the word phonetically, generate several alternative spellings of the word, and then use revisualization to determine the correct spelling, or they consult an outside source such as the teacher, a peer, or the dictionary. . . . Less fluent spellers, in contrast, seem to lack skills essential to producing correctly spelled words. [They] experience word confusions, recall failures, and have unexpected problems remembering certain words. (pp. 397–398)

An interesting case is the recent domination of national spelling bees by immigrants from India. As Berger (2005) concluded:

> Unlike many American children who are schooled in sometimes amorphous whole-language approaches to reading and writing, Indians are comfortable with the rote-learning methods of their homeland, the kind needed to master lists of obscure words that easily stump spell-checker programs. They do not regard champion spellers as nerds.

Though the emphasis on spelling has waned somewhat in light of, for example, spell-checkers on computers, it remains an important skill. Graves (1994) notes that good spelling retains a degree of social status because it reflects an educated person. Further, because writing is communication, spelling must be accurate enough for the reader to respond.

## Assessment

Although many achievement tests contain sections devoted to spelling, these tools generally can provide a global estimate (e.g., grade-level scores) of a student's achievement. The teacher must then analyze and evaluate the responses to determine exactly what the problem is. One available instrument is the Test of Written Spelling—4 (TWS-4) (Larsen, Hammill, & Moats, 1999), which measures a student's ability to spell both phonetically regular and irregular words. As Beirne-Smith and Riley (2004) note, "the TWS-4 reflects the authors' theories that mastery of a certain number of spelling rules is necessary for independence in spelling and that words that do not conform to standard generalizations must be learned by rote memorization" (p. 401). The TWS-4 uses a dictation format and includes two tests of 50 words each. These words were selected because of their frequent occurrence in six basal spelling series. A modified form of the TWS is also included in the Test of Written Language—3 (Hammill & Larsen, 1996).

Informal approaches to assessment are of particular value to the teacher in planning instructional programs. One way to conceptualize the assessment process is to consider the learner's progression through stages of spelling proficiency with attention to identifying developmental errors. Beirne-Smith and Riley (2004) summarize Gentry's (2000) five-stage system as follows:

1. **Precommunicative spelling.** Spellers randomly string together letters of the alphabet without regard to letter–sound correspondence (examples: *opsop* = eagle; *rtat* = eighty).
2. **Semiphonetic spelling.** Letters represent sound, but only some of the letters are represented (examples: *e* = eagle; *a* = eighty).
3. **Phonetic spelling.** Words are spelled like they sound. The speller represents all of the phonemes in a word, although the spelling may be unconventional (examples: *egl* = eagle; *ate* = eighty).
4. **Transitional spelling.** A visual memory of spelling patterns is apparent. Spellings exhibit conventions of English orthography: vowels in every syllable, e-marker (i.e., silent *e* at end of words) and vowel digraph patterns, correctly spelled inflectional endings, and frequent English letter sequences (examples: *egul* = eagle; *eightee* = eighty).
5. Words are spelled correctly. (p. 399)

*Error analysis* also can provide specific information to develop an instructional program; it should be based on careful scrutiny of patterns in a student's misspellings. Areas of specific attention (with sample words) include:

- additions of unneeded letters (*neccessary*)
- omissions of needed letters (*togehr*)
- reversals of letters (*bog* for *dog*)

- reversals of whole words (*was* for *saw*)
- letter-order confusion (*recieve*)
- final consonant changes (*trys* for *tries*)

Another approach is to develop a simple diagnostic survey of words containing some of the most common spelling errors and administer it to students as an informal test. For example, an assessment could emphasize letter changes at the end of words:

- *y* to *i* when a suffix is added (*happiness*)
- *y* to *i* in plurals and tense (*flies*)
- final *-e* that makes preceding vowel long (*rate, cane*)
- final *-e* dropped when suffix is added (*liking, using*)
- final consonant doubled when suffix is added (*stopped*)

C. J. Jones (2001) provides an informal spelling inventory based on phonetic elements (see Table 8–1). The skills evaluated include a variety of vowel and consonant sounds. This approach could also be used for morphological considerations (e.g., root words, affixes, compound words).

## Elementary Instruction

Spelling instruction should begin soon after young students have started to learn to read because they will be attempting to write certain words that they can read. The close ties among spelling, reading, and writing should lead to integrated language instruction. Graham and Harris (2005) noted that primary teachers

**TABLE 8–1** Informal spelling inventory

| *Words* | *Skills* | *Words in Sentences* |
|---|---|---|
| 1. pass | Short vowel /a/ | Please pass the potatoes. |
| 2. held | Short vowel /e/ | He held the football tightly. |
| 3. spill | Short vowel /i/ | Be careful not to spill the milk. |
| 4. crust | Short vowel /u/ | The cherry pie has a nice crust. |
| 5. drove | Long vowel v-c-e | They drove to the beach. |
| 6. remain | Long /a/ spelled /ai/ | Remain in your seats until called. |
| 7. field | Long /e/ spelled /ie/ | The field was full of flowers. |
| 8. flight | Long /i/ spelled /igh/ | Watch the flight of the hawks. |
| 9. boast | Long /a/ spelled /oa/ | Would you boast about your fish? |
| 10. view | Long /o/ sound /yoo/ | The view of the lake was lovely. |
| 11. moist | Diphthong /oi/ | The cake was moist and sweet. |
| 12. mouth | Diphthong /ou/ | The dentist examined his mouth. |
| 13. forest | *R*-controlled /or/ | The forest was green and still. |
| 14. bought | aw /o/ sound spelled /ough/ | She bought a new sweater. |
| 15. thirst | *R*-controlled /ir/ | Her thirst for juice was great. |
| 16. spark | *R*-controlled /ar/ | She saw a spark of light. |
| 17. spread | More vowels than vowel sounds | He spread the jam on his bread. |
| 18. knife | More consonants than sounds | The knife was very sharp. |
| 19. quarrel | Digraph /qu/ | The quarrel was over candy. |
| 20. dodge | /j/ spelled /dge/ | Sally liked to play dodge ball. |
| 21. bubble | Final /le/ | She loved a bubble bath. |
| 22. moisten | Final /en/ | She decided to moisten the sponge. |
| 23. tractor | Schwa-r spelled /or/ | The farmer had a new red tractor. |
| 24. kindest | Suffix /est/ | She was the kindest lady he knew. |
| 25. brake | Homophones | The man quickly stepped on his brake. |
| 26. they'll | Contractions | They'll go to the beach next weekend. |

*Source:* From "Teacher-Friendly Curriculum-Based Assessment in Spelling," by C. Jones, *Teaching Exceptional Children, 34*(2), 2001, p. 35. Copyright 2001 by the Council for Exceptional Children. Reprinted with permission.

reported spending an average of 87 minutes per week in instruction.

**Word Selection.** The first words that students write are often meaningful to them, not just because they are new, but because they are usually the names of people, places, and things with which the students are familiar. Teachers should make other new words as meaningful as possible, perhaps by using new words to make up stories about students' immediate environment, thus facilitating a transition from the old to the new, or by placing new words in colorful sequence on a bulletin board, thereby causing students to be interested in finding out what the words are and how to spell them.

Word selections can be made from a variety of sources. Based on a student's ability and interest level, a teacher can select from frequency-of-use-in-writing lists (e.g., see Table 8–2), linguistic word families (e.g., fan/tan/pan), words used regularly within a student's oral expressive vocabulary, lists from specific basal and/or remedial programs, commonly misspelled words, and words taken from the student's list of mastered reading words.

**General Teaching Strategies.** A variety of instructional strategies can assist young (and older) students who are having difficulty with spelling. Teachers should plan a program allowing for regular, systematic instruction while drawing from a variety of word-study techniques that are effective for particular students. The most successful word-study techniques use multisensory approaches, promote revisualization of words, assist students in formulating specific rules for accurate spelling, or promote self-correction. Some selected techniques as adapted from Graham and Miller (1979) and by Beirne-Smith and Riley (2004) are presented in Table 8–3.

The classic example of a word-study technique is the **Fernald** (1943) **multisensory approach.** The following specific procedures for teaching spelling are based on Fernald's directions for children learning new words and provide an example of the multisensory nature of the approach.

1. Look at the word very carefully and say it over to yourself.
2. See if the word can be written just the way you say it.

**TABLE 8–2** High-frequency words: "Spelling for writing" list

**Grade 1 Word List**

| | | | |
|---|---|---|---|
| A | day | into | play |
| all | did | is | ran |
| am | do | it | red |
| and | dog | its | ride |
| at | for | let | run |
| ball | fun | like | see |
| be | get | look | she |
| bed | go | man | so |
| big | good | may | stop |
| book | got | me | the |
| box | had | my | this |
| boy | he | no | to |
| but | her | not | two |
| came | him | of | up |
| can | his | oh | us |
| car | home | old | was |
| cat | I | on | we |
| come | if | one | will |
| dad | in | out | yes |
| | | | you |

**Grade 2 Word List**

| | | | | | |
|---|---|---|---|---|---|
| about | boat | fast | give | know | most |
| after | both | father | going | land | mother |
| an | brother | feet | happy | last | much |
| any | buy | fell | hard | left | must |
| are | by | find | has | little | myself |
| as | call | fire | have | live | name |
| ask | candy | first | help | long | new |
| away | city | fish | here | looking | next |
| baby | coming | five | hit | lot | nice |
| back | could | food | hope | love | night |
| bad | doing | four | horse | mad | now |
| been | door | from | house | made | off |
| before | down | funny | how | make | only |
| being | each | game | just | many | open |
| best | eat | gave | keep | men | or |
| black | end | girl | kid | more | other |
| our | say | stay | there | try | what |
| outside | school | still | they | used | when |
| over | sea | store | thing | very | while |
| park | ship | story | think | walk | white |
| playing | show | take | three | want | who |
| put | sleep | talk | time | way | why |
| read | small | tell | today | week | wish |
| room | snow | than | told | well | with |
| said | some | that | too | went | work |
| same | soon | them | took | were | your |
| saw | start | then | tree | | |

*Source:* From "The Spelling for Writing List," by S. Graham, K. R. Harris, and C. Loynachin, 1994, *Journal of Learning Disabilities, 27,* 213–214. Copyright 1994 by PRO-ED, Inc. Reprinted with permission.

**TABLE 8–3** Word-study techniques

| Fitzgerald Method (Fitzgerald, 1951) |
|---|
| 1. Look at word carefully. |
| 2. Say word. |
| 3. With eyes closed, visualize word. |
| 4. Cover word; then write it |
| 5. Check spelling. |
| 6. If word is misspelled, repeat Steps 1–5. |
| **Horn Method (Horn, 1954)** |
| 1. Pronounce word carefully. |
| 2. Look carefully at each part of word as you pronounce it. |
| 3. Say letters in sequence. |
| 4. Attempt to recall how word looks; then spell it. |
| 5. Check this attempt to recall. |
| 6. Write word. |
| 7. Check this spelling attempt. |
| 8. Repeat steps 1–7 if necessary. |
| **Simultaneous Oral Spelling (Gillingham & Stillman, 1960)** |
| 1. Select regular word and pronounce it. |
| 2. Repeat word after teacher. |
| 3. Say sounds in words. |
| 4. Name the letters used to represent the sounds. |
| 5. Write word, naming letters while writing them. |
| **Cover-and-Write Method** |
| 1. Look at word; say it |
| 2. Write word two times |
| 3. Cover and write it one time. |
| 4. Check work. |
| 5. Write word two times. |
| 6. Cover and write it one time. |
| 7. Check work. |
| 8. Write word three times. |
| 9. Cover and write it one time. |
| 10. Check work. |

3. Shut your eyes and see if you can get a picture of the word in your mind. If you cannot, remember the parts that are written the way you say them. Pronounce the word to yourself or feel your hand make the movements of writing the word.
4. When you are sure of every part of the word, shut your book or cover the word and write it, saying each syllable as you write.
5. If you cannot write the word correctly after you have looked at it and said it, ask the teacher to write it for you. Trace the word with your fingers. Say each part as you trace it. Trace the word carefully until you can write it correctly. Say each part of the word as you write it.
6. If the word is difficult, turn the paper over and write it again.
7. Later in the day, try writing it from memory.
8. Make your own dictionary.

An emphasis on *rules* can also be beneficial within a spelling program. Because within English there is a productive relationship between sounds and symbols, such an emphasis can be important as a mediating influence. The classic instructional sequence provided by Brueckner and Bond (1967) can be helpful in teaching generalizations.

1. Select a particular rule to be taught.
2. Secure a list of words exemplifying the rule. Develop an understanding of the rule through a study of words that it covers.
3. Lead pupils to discover the underlying generalization by discussing the characteristics of the words in the list. If possible, have pupils formulate the rule; help them to sharpen and clarify it.
4. Have pupils use and apply the rule immediately.
5. If necessary, show that the rule does not apply in some cases, but stress its positive value.
6. Review the rule systematically on succeeding days. Emphasize its use, but do not require pupils to memorize a formalized statement. (p. 374)

Another effective word-study approach is the corrected-test method. Under a teacher's direction, students correct specific spelling errors immediately after being tested. This strategy enables students to observe which words are particularly difficult, identify the part of the words creating the difficulty, and correct the errors under supervision (Graham & Miller, 1979).

Goddard and Heron (1998) provide examples of two **self-correction strategies.** Of particular note is letter-by-letter proofreading in which students are taught proofreading marks to check and correct their spelling. Figure 8–7 shows a five-column practice sheet that students use to practice new words. To proceed, Column 1 is completed by the teacher with the lesson's stimulus words; this column is folded back. Students then write the word from dictation in Column 2 and compare it to

| COLUMN 1 | COLUMN 2 | COLUMN 3 | COLUMN 4 | COLUMN 5 |
|---|---|---|---|---|
| horse | ho[u→r]se | horse | horse | √ |
| better | bet(t)ter | better | better | √ |
| passage | pass(ga)e | passage | pass[^a]ge | passage |
| brain | br(ia)n | brain | brain | √ |
| forget | forg[o→e]t | forget | forg[^e]t | forget |
| measure | me[e→a]sure | measure | me[^a]sure | measure |
| target | target | √ | target | √ |
| activate | activate | √ | activate | √ |
| forty | fo[^r]ty | forty | fort[i→y] | forty |
| pinnacle | pin[^na][e]c(c)al[^e] | pinnacle | pin[^n]ac(a)l[^e] | pinnacle |

**FIGURE 8–7** Letter-by-letter proofreading

*Source:* From "Please, Teacher, Help Me Learn to Spell Better," by Y. L. Goddard and T. E. Heron, 1998, *Teaching Exceptional Children, 30*, 41. Reprinted by permission.

Column 1, making corrections where needed (as noted in Figure 8–7). In Column 3, they write the corrected form or make a check if they were correct. Then Columns 4 and 5 are used for additional practice. This approach provides an apt transition to the use of strategy training in spelling.

## Middle and Secondary Instruction

Spelling is less often a key focus beyond the elementary level. However, there are several key considerations that are particularly relevant for older students; while these also can be relevant at elementary level, they become the primary foci of instruction for adolescents.

One key concern is to make spelling functional. Thus students should have as many functional words in their spelling vocabularies as possible. Functional words help young students communicate more effectively and help older individuals gain and maintain employment, adjust to environmental and social demands, and thus achieve social independence. Teachers are in the best position to draw up a list of community-relevant, functional words for students to learn. Functional word lists can be integrated into the reading program and can help students develop skills not only for spelling but for life in general.

**Mnemonic Strategies.** Accurate spelling of difficult words can also be facilitated through the use of *mnemonic strategies* such as have been found useful in teaching students memory tasks in reading and recalling information to be learned in content areas. As Greene (1994) notes, mnemonics are effective when they associate several items together, are unique, add concreteness to abstractions, have multisensory appeal, and provide rhythm or repetition. The task of learning a series of mnemonic devices, however, can place as much strain on the student's memory as the memory task itself. Therefore, the use of mnemonic techniques in spelling should be limited to examples that students can retain and use regularly (e.g., "a princi**pal** is your **pal**").

To facilitate retention, having students generate their own mnemonics is a plus; the following strategies were developed by middle school students (Burns, 1988).

- fowl—foul: An owl is a fowl.
- dessert—desert: Which would you like to have two of?
- hangar—hanger: An airplane is stored in a hangar.
- niece: Ellen is my nice niece.
- courtesy—curtsy: You have to show a lot of courtesy when you're in court.

**Strategy Training.** Another key strategic approach to success for older students is the development of a word-study method that can be used by the student on an independent basis after interaction and support by the teacher. One useful approach is the method referred to as *copy-cover-compare*. Students study the word, copy it, cover it, develop an image of it, write the word, and then compare it with the original. The precise steps can be modified for a particular student and/or situation. The strategy is a simple one to use in spelling and provides for a straightforward approach to word study. Figure 8-8 provides a sample word list worksheet format for this approach.

This approach is consistent with the procedure referred to as **look, cover, write, check (LCWC)** (Greene, 1994). This strategy is as follows:

> Students begin . . . by looking at a word they are learning to spell and saying the letters out loud (*verbal rehearsal*). This is followed by the student closing his/her eyes and attempting to visualize . . . the letters in the word (*visual imagery*). The student then looks at the spelling word again to verify the accuracy of the visual image and covers the word with his/her hand and writes it from memory. Following this step, the student checks for spelling accuracy once again and either repeats the procedure for the next word in the spelling list or starts over with the steps of LCWC on the present word until mastery is achieved. (p. 35)

## Program Design

A number of specific considerations can assist in designing an effective spelling program regardless of classroom settings. These considerations (adapted from Beirne-Smith & Riley, 2004; Gordon, Vaughn, & Schumm,

**FIGURE 8–8** Copy-cover-compare

Name ___________________

Spelling Worksheet

| 1. Word to practice | 2. Spelling | 3. Copy Word | 4. Cover/Compare | 5. Spelling |
|---|---|---|---|---|
| about | | | | |
| after | | | | |
| again | | | | |
| all | | | | |
| also | | | | |
| always | | | | |
| am | | | | |
| an | | | | |
| and | | | | |
| another | | | | |
| any | | | | |
| are | | | | |
| around | | | | |
| as | | | | |
| asked | | | | |
| at | | | | |
| away | | | | |
| back | | | | |
| be | | | | |
| bear | | | | |
| because | | | | |

*Source*: From "Improving Academic Performance Through Self-Management: Cover, Copy and Compare," by T. F. McLaughlin and C. H. Skinner, 1996, *Intervention in School and Clinic, 32*, 114. Copyright 1996 by PRO-ED, Inc. Reprinted with permission.

1993; Graham 1999; Graham & Voth, 1990; Graham et al., 2000; McNaughton, Hughes, & Clark, 1994) include:

1. Instruction should focus initially on high-frequency words and misspelled words from the student's own writing efforts.
2. Words should be organized into small units (6 to 12 words) that emphasize a common structural element.
3. Students should be directed to name letters and words during practice to enhance attention and retention.
4. Students should be taught how to recognize and retain the patterns of words by focusing on morphemic analysis (e.g., suffixes, root words).
5. Students should be provided with immediate error-correction procedures.
6. Students should be taught strategies for word study to help them with their spelling and should use a systematic study procedure for words missed on a pretest.
7. Students should practice missed words on succeeding days using games and other activities to improve fluency and accuracy.
8. Maintenance of correct spelling of words should be ensured through periodic review activities.
9. The teacher should establish links between instruction in spelling and the students' writing. Written products should be examined to determine if learned spellings are being generalized.
10. Reinforcement strategies related to spelling should be considered to ensure that motivation is sufficient.

## Research-Validated Strategies

In addition to the general procedures noted above, Graham (1999) and Graham et al. (2000) presented the following specific research-based procedures for teaching vocabulary:

1. Before studying new spelling words, the student takes a pretest to identify the words that need to be studied.
2. After studying new spelling words, the student takes a posttest to determine the words that were mastered.
3. Immediately after taking a spelling test, the student corrects any misspellings.
4. The student is taught a systematic and effective strategy for studying new spelling words.
5. Study and testing of new spelling words occurs daily.
6. Students work together, using cooperative arrangements such as classwide peer tutoring to learn new spelling words.
7. The number of words to be mastered each week is reduced to 6 to 12 new unknown words, depending on the capabilities of the student.
8. While studying, the student monitors on-task behavior or the number of times words were practiced successfully.
9. Spelling words previously taught are reviewed to ensure retention.

Regardless of the word list selected or the approach utilized, spelling instruction can be effective only if students have opportunities to use the target words in written assignments and to proofread their work for possible errors. Although learning words in isolation is recommended to facilitate acquisition, maintenance and generalization are achieved only when students are encouraged to make regular use of the words they have learned. However, because students risk an interruption in the conceptual task of writing when they ponder the correct form of a difficult word, they can be encouraged to write an approximation of the word initially and then review it and correct it as necessary during the postwriting phase.

## Invented Spellings

A frequent component of whole language instructional programs is **invented spellings.** Typically students' creations of spellings reflect a direct application of phonology to words [e.g., *mi* (my), *lade* (lady), *nit* (night)] (Tompkins, 2005). It is based on the assumption that students should be able to express themselves initially in writing without having to be concerned with spelling accuracy. Without question, when students invent their own spellings, teachers are naturally provided with helpful assessment data. Further, it is logical to assume that the use of invented spellings may have a positive effect on writing fluency and creativity by not interfering with the writing (i.e., conceptual) process.

The efficacy of invented spellings used with students with special needs, however, is largely unexplored territory (Graham, 2000) and has not been validated empirically. There remains disagreement as to whether acceptance or encouragement to create new spellings ultimately will have a positive effect on the writing of students. Teachers therefore should consider invented spelling only as an experimental method and should evaluate its effectiveness and continue its use only if it is having positive results. With students with special needs, the use (or nonuse) of this approach often will be determined by how spelling is taught within the inclusive setting in which students spend a portion or all of their instructional day. Teachers are advised to consider its use only on an experimental basis and, if used, to commit to careful classroom research to monitor effectiveness.

Reflective Question 8–2: ***Spelling is often undervalued in our society but nevertheless is an important tool for communication. What are the key principles of effective instruction?***

## WRITTEN EXPRESSION

Written expression builds on the other language domains. The National Assessment of Education Progress (NAEP, 2003) noted the varied purposes of writing, identifying them as follows:

- **Narrative:** writing stories and personal essays
- **Informative:** sharing knowledge and communicating instructions, ideas, and messages
- **Persuasive:** influencing the reader's action and bringing about change

Success in writing thus derives from the coordination of numerous language-based skills. Montague and Leavell (1994) noted that writing requires "coordination and integration of multiple processes, including planning, production, editing, and revision. Composing requires prior knowledge of topic, genre, conventions, and rules as well as the ability to access, use and organize that knowledge when writing" (p. 21).

Based on their review of research, Butler, Elaschuk, and Poole (2000) note that effective writers analyze requirements of the task and plan accordingly, identify goals, use strategies to achieve their goals, adjust goals as needed, and monitor the success of their endeavors. On the other hand, Troia (2002) characterized the writing of students with special needs as "shorter, less linguistically sophisticated, more poorly organized, more mechanical errors, poorer in overall quality . . . [and reflective of] difficulties in executing and regulating the cognitive and meta-cognitive processes underlying proficient writing" (p. 251).

In response to these challenges, Troia (2005) indicated that exemplary writing teachers use a balanced approach to instruction, emphasizing the explicit teaching of skills and strategies. In addition, they provide a higher degree of assistance to struggling writers. At the same time, however, less than half of teachers in general make more than limited adaptations for struggling writers.

The process of writing can best be conceptualized by a multicomponent model, a series of sequential stages that not only define the process but also guide the necessary instruction. Writing models typically divide the process into the three stages: prewriting, inclusive of planning and organizing; writing, or drafting of ideas into sentences and paragraphs; and postwriting, or revision and editing (see Figure 8-1).

**Prewriting** consists of what the writer considers prior to the act itself. Input includes the various forms of stimulation that assist in forming a basic intent to write, such as environmental experience, reading, listening, and media exposure. Motivation includes the effects of various stimulating activities, as well as the external factors that reinforce writing. In addition, the purpose for writing must be established to assist in organization.

The **writing or drafting stage** encompasses handwriting and spelling as previously discussed, as well as the other craft aspects and content of written language. Considerations include vocabulary usage, sentence form, paragraph sense, the overall sequence of ideas, consistency, clarity, and relevance.

The **postwriting stage** includes the editing of the craft aspects of writing and the revision of content, with both emphases having the goal of improving the written product. The term *proofreading* has been used to refer to postwriting concerns. It also includes *publishing*—sharing the written work with an audience (e.g., reading, displaying, submitting for publication) (Unrau, 2004).

Viewing these three stages of writing as distinct and significant enables instruction to focus on the specific tasks facing the would-be writer. However, in practice, these phases are not perfectly discrete and linear (Isaacson, 1987; Scarmadalia & Bereiter, 1986; Unrau, 2004). For example, planning and rethinking continues to take place during the postwriting stage, and revising may take place during the drafting stage. Nevertheless, an initial focus on distinct stages of writing can promote a process orientation that will assist students in thinking about what they are writing.

### Assessment

Even though writing produces a permanent product to aid teachers in assessment, a number of problems have typically complicated such evaluation. Some of

## DIVERSITY IN THE CLASSROOM *Tips*

**Deoksoon Kim,** assistant professor of Secondary Education, teaches foreign language/ESOL at the University of South Florida. Her foci include second language acquisition and literacy, bilingual education, and multicultural pedagogy.

Cultural diversity and diverse learners are distinguished by race, ethnicity, gender, socioeconomic status, ability, language, and culture. My dialogue began with myself as an English language learner nurtured by Asian culture.

Literacy is a complex phenomenon, and writing in literacy is a process as well as a product. In teaching culturally diverse learners, educators address the nature and uses of language, interpersonal and intrapersonal relations, sociocultural differences, the cultural nature of human development, and second language literacy learning.

*Understanding English language learners from diverse cultural backgrounds* is fundamental. Significant factors to consider are first and second language proficiency, cognitive development and style, and cultural orientation—past experiences and cultural knowledge. Teachers need different strategies for learners from different backgrounds, different learning stages, and different social contexts.

Literacy practices are culture-specific ways of knowing. Socioculturally, learning to read and write are acts of knowing, reflected as values within a given cultural and social context, recognizing the student's own experiences values, and aspirations for improvement. Increasing students' knowledge, awareness, and understanding of language and culture are important objectives in helping empower them. The teacher facilitates connections among students' community, national, and global identities. Being literate is not only being able to manipulate symbols, but doing so in a culturally appropriate manner, supporting critical thinking skills, the next level of literacy learning.

Reading and writing processes enhance each other. As students read in a specific genre, they understand it and link it to their writing process through the dialogue between the text and themselves. Using effective diverse reading materials and instructions for English language learners, the teacher conveys strategies and background knowledge from reading to writing, following a cycle of prewriting, drafting, revising, editing, and publishing. Writing is a thinking, communicating, discovering, and creating process. Writing is a practice of inviting thoughtful responses through engaging conversations. I recommend the author's chair and dialogue journaling as sample authentic activities.

*The author's chair* allows learners to take ownership of the writing process. One approach is to connect reading and writing processes as students explore and visit the genre of memoir and how it differs from autobiography. Students can begin by writing "predrafts" of memories; then they can write the draft, revise it through conferencing, edit their writing, and publish it.

*The dialogue journal* provides a unique picture of the second language learning developmental process, explored as craft and art woven together. Recent research discusses methods of discourse within the constructivist framework for viewing the acquisition and use of language. Journals also develop mutuality between teacher and student, increase shared understanding of experience, and maintain common values of respect, trust, and cooperation. Dialogue journaling allows for feedback without correction, modeling in written language, and deeper dialogue. Learners make meaning through authentic written conversation while the teacher learns the learner's culture and background knowledge though ongoing conversation.

these are the relative paucity of formal tools and the emphasis of existing tests on contrived formats (e.g., multiple-choice items) that assess only the mechanical aspects of writing; this latter problem is particularly common in achievement-oriented tests with written language subtests.

A contemporary concern is the increased emphasis on school standards in the assessment of writing. Isaacson (2004) noted that the benefits of this trend include an increased emphasis on writing, more consistent curricular goals leading to clearer expectations, and a greater focus on explicit instruction and purposeful activities. On the other hand, negative consequences may include anxiety, overlooking individualized goals, and possible adherence to rigid criteria.

One diagnostic tool that can provide a more comprehensive analysis of written language abilities is the Test of Written Language–3 (TOWL-3) (Hammill & Larsen, 1996), which was developed to assess the adequacy of abilities in handwriting, spelling, and the various other components of written expression. The test includes scales for vocabulary, thematic maturity, word usage, and style. Both spontaneous and contrived formats provide a basis for assessment, with primary emphasis on evaluating an actual writing sample. The TOWL-3 is the best-designed, most useful formal tool available for analyzing the writing of students with disabilities.

Because formal tools cannot fully evaluate the total scope of written expression, informal assessment approaches should receive primary attention. Effective assessment strategies in writing are comprehensive in scope, derived from the curriculum, and reliant on data from a variety of sources. According to the Association for Supervision and Curriculum Development (ASCD) (1997), qualities that should be assessed in writing are as follows:

- *Ideas and Content*—Is the message clear? Does the paper hold the reader's attention?
- *Organization*—Does the paper have an inviting introduction? Are supporting details placed in a logical order? Can the reader move easily through the text?
- *Word Choice*—Are the words chosen specific and accurate? Do lively verbs energize the writing?
- *Fluency*—Does the writing have a cadence and easy flow? Do sentences vary in length as well as structure?
- *Conventions*—Does the writer demonstrate a good grasp of standard writing conventions, such as grammar, punctuation, and paragraphing? Is punctuation accurate? Is spelling generally correct? (p. 5)

The techniques described in Table 8-4 facilitate informal analysis of a number of aspects of writing. The key to using any of the procedures listed in this table is to analyze students' writing samples. Frequent opportunities to communicate must be part of the weekly experiences of all students possessing basic skills in the area. Teachers should plan a sequence of skills that will be evaluated on an ongoing basis and should resist the temptation to provide corrective feedback for all types of errors simultaneously. Error analysis should thus focus on an individual skill deficit as a basis for remediation. Though this set of assessment procedures focuses on a variety of specific writing skills that emphasize craft in particular, most important is the successful communication of ideas (i.e., the content). Content is often best assessed via more holistic writing measures.

**Portfolios** are particularly appropriate for writing assessment. Portfolios enable teachers to involve the students in the evaluation of their own writing samples, particularly by selecting samples to be kept and then working with them to compare changes in writing over time. Three types of portfolios that are likely to be used in inclusive classes are:

- *Sampling of Works*—This type of portfolio is often used in primary grades to compare early writing samples with later writing samples. . . . These portfolios are often sent on to the student's next teacher.
- *Selected Works*—In these portfolios, students collect samples of their writing in response to a teacher prompt.
- *Longitudinal*—These portfolios are oriented toward district goals for student achievement and [essentially yield pre- and post-test measures] to provide an accurate assessment. (ASCD, 1997, p. 51)

## Instruction

To discuss the broad array of writing instructional strategies, this section focuses on general principles of instruction; later in the chapter specific considerations for middle and secondary level students are addressed. Given the challenges that students with special needs face in writing, the most important consideration in instruction is sufficient opportunity for students to develop their writing ability. Thus, they need a substantial amount of time to write. Graham (1992) notes the following suggestions for providing frequent and meaningful writing opportunities:

1. Encourage students to decide for themselves what they will write about.
2. Ask students to establish goals for what they hope to achieve.
3. Arrange the writing environment so that the teacher is not the sole audience for students' writing.
4. Provide opportunities for students to work on the same writing project across days or even weeks if necessary.
5. Incorporate writing as part of a larger, interesting activity.
6. Select writing activities that are designed to serve very specific and real purposes. (p. 137)

A primary focus of instruction should be the three stages. Although the lines between these stages can blur, they are presented here separately for ease in presentation. Table 8-5 provides an overview for working with students as they develop their inner voices to use self-instruction across the three stages.

**Prewriting.** Instruction taking place during this stage should reflect the reality of the way students present themselves for instruction. In particular, assumptions should not be made that students have had the necessary experiential prerequisites to develop ideation, that they have a desire to communicate via written means, or that they understand their purpose in writing and their intended audience. As a consequence, teachers need to focus on providing rich experiences and assisting students in getting ideas, structuring content, setting

**TABLE 8–4** Informal written language assessment procedures

| *Technique* | *Description* | *Methodology* | *Example* | *Comment* |
|---|---|---|---|---|
| Type ratio token | Variety of words ratio used (types) in relation to overall number of words (tokens) | $\frac{\text{Different words used}}{\text{Total words used}}$ | type = 28<br>token = 50<br>ratio = $\frac{28}{50}$ = .56 | Greater diversity of usage implies more mature writing. |
| Index of diversification | Measure of diversity of word usage | $\frac{\text{Total number of words used}}{\text{Number of occurrences of the most frequently used word}}$ | total words = 72<br># of times word *the* appeared = 12<br>index = 6 | An increase in index value implies broader vocabulary. |
| Average sentence length | Words per sentence (WPS) | $\frac{\text{Total number of words used}}{\text{Total number of sentences}}$ | TW = 54<br>TS = 9<br>WPS = 6 | Longer length implies more mature writing ability. |
| Error analysis | Measure of word and sentence usage | Compare errors found in sample with list of common errors. | | Determine error patterns and prioritize instruction. |
| Correct word sequences (CWS) (Walker et al., 2005) | Writing fluency | Walker et al. (2005) define CWS as (1) adjacent, correctly spelled, capitalized, and punctuated words; (2) capitalized and correctly spelled beginning of sentences; or (3) correctly spelled and punctuated ending of sentences. All phrases must be in standard English usage. | "That yung boy has many friends. We all him." = 8 CWS "has that butifl girl developed any friends She seems nise" = 6 CWS | Provides a measure of writing growth. |
| T-unit length (Hunt, 1965) | Measure of writing maturity | 1. Determine the number of discrete thought units (T-units)<br>2. Determine average length of T-unit:<br>$\frac{\text{Total words}}{\text{Total number of T-units}}$<br>3. Analyze quantitative variables:<br>a. no. of sentences used<br>b. no. of T-units<br>c. no. of words per T-unit<br>4. Analyze qualitative nature of sentences | "The summer was almost over and the children were ready to go back to school."<br>*Quantitative*: (1; 2; 5–10)<br>*Qualitative*:<br>1. compound sentence<br>2. adverbs: of degree—"almost" of place—"back"<br>3. adjective—"ready"<br>4. infinitive—"to go"<br>5. prepositional phrase adverbial of place—"to school" | Provides information on productivity and maturity of writing. |

*Source:* Adapted from "Written Language for Mildly Handicapped Students," by E. A. Polloway, J. R. Patton, & S. B. Cohen, in E. L. Meyen, G. A. Vergason, & R. J. Whelan (Eds.), *Promising Practices for Exceptional Children: Curriculum Implications* (pp. 300–301), Denver: Love Publishing. Copyright 1983 by Love Publishing Company. Reprinted with permission.

**TABLE 8–5** Strategies for writing subprocesses

| *Subprocesses* | *Strategies* | *Self-Talk* |
|---|---|---|
| **Prewriting: Planning** | Identify audience.<br>Identify purpose.<br>Activate background knowledge; brainstorm. | Whom am I writing for?<br>Why am I writing?<br>What do I know? What does my reader need to know? |
| **Prewriting: Organizing** | Identify categories of related items.<br>Label related ideas.<br>Identify new categories and details.<br>Order ideas. What comes first? | How can I group my ideas?<br>What can I call each set of ideas?<br>Am I missing any key details?<br>How can I order my ideas? |
| **Writing: Drafting** | Translate plan into text.<br>Check text against plan.<br>Add signals to aid comprehensibility and organization. | When I write this up, I can say . . .<br>Did I include all my categories?<br>What signal word will tell my reader what this idea has to do with other ideas? |
| **Postwriting** | Monitor for comprehensibility.<br>Check against plan.<br>Revise as necessary.<br>Monitor from audience's perspective. | Does everything make sense?<br>Did I include all the ideas in my plan?<br>Do I need to insert, delete, or move ideas?<br>Did I answer all my readers' questions?<br>Is my paper interesting? |

*Source:* Adapted from "Making Writing Strategies Work," by D. D. Stevens and C. S. Englert, *Teaching Exceptional Children, 26*(1), 1993, 36. Copyright 1993 by The Council for Exceptional Children. Adapted with permission.

purpose, determining audience, and building vocabulary (Scott & Vitale, 2003).

The first concern at this stage is *stimulation*. Teachers should strive to provide opportunities to expose students to varied experiences through listening and reading; provide them with a chance to discuss and clarify ideas on a given topic, thus encouraging active thinking about the task at hand; promote brainstorming with peers; develop story pictures, outlines, and webs with students to organize ideas; and establish a conducive, supportive classroom atmosphere. Concerned teachers working with learners with special needs must stimulate students before giving them a chance to write. Though stimulation is clearly insufficient for the achievement of competence in writing, it can help to start writers thinking clearly.

When provided with an opportunity for creative writing, students can be stimulated by topics of personal interest. Teachers should generate a collection of possible themes to use as general assignments. For example, at the elementary level, these might include:

I knew something was wrong when I heard that sound . . .

When I was a baby . . .

The day I became a . . . (name an animal)

The day at the circus . . .

My favorite movie

My favorite sports hero

If I could be anybody in the world for one day, I would most like to be . . .

Why colors remind me of moods

The second concern at this stage is *motivation*, which is particularly important for adolescents with disabilities. A substantial amount of research focused on the writing of students without disabilities argues that motivation must come from within; teachers can stimulate students, but they cannot actually motivate them. According to this logic, if students have something meaningful and/or interesting to think about, their writing will reflect it. This premise, however, presents some difficulty because writing does not just happen much of the time. Teachers of students with special needs should consider ways to promote motivation, such as using external reward systems to complement the internal motivation of reluctant writers.

The third aspect of prewriting is *setting the purpose*. The writer must have a clear understanding of who the audience is and thus what the purpose is. Expressive and functional writing have different intents and thus require different formats. For students with special needs—and for many other students in inclusive settings as well—planning is an area given insufficient

**TABLE 8–6** Expository writing planning strategy

| *Planning Strategy: STOP* | *Instructions for Each Planning Step* |
|---|---|
| 1. ***S**uspend judgment* | Read the prompt and do TAP (identify *t*ask, *a*udience, & *p*urpose). Brainstorm ideas about purpose. Use webbing, lists, or other ways to jot down ideas. |
| 2. ***T**ell your thesis statement* | Read your ideas. Write your thesis statement on your planning sheet. Decide whether you will put your thesis statement first or "start with an attention getter." |
| 3. ***O**rganize ideas* | Choose strong ideas and decide how to organize them for writing. Put a star by *major points* and some other mark by *elaborations* of the main points. Number major points in the order you will use them. |
| 4. ***P**lan more as you write* | Use the essay sheet, cue cards, and **DARE:**<br>***D**ifferent kinds of sentences*<br>***A**void first-person pronouns if you can*<br>***R**emember to use good grammar*<br>***E**xciting, interesting, $100,000 words* |

*Source:* Adapted from "Strategy Instruction in Planning: Teaching Students with Learning and Writing Disabilities to Compose Persuasive and Expository Essays," by S. de la Paz, 1997, *Learning Disability Quarterly, 20,* 244. Reprinted with permission.

attention. Table 8–6 depicts a planning strategy. Intended for expository writing, the strategy promotes a series of steps to follow in preparing to write.

**Writing.** The writing or drafting stage is the broadest of the three components. Consequently, it is of little surprise that problems and deficits in this phase are common in many students. The educator's key concern is to determine how skills are most effectively taught and learned. With this focus, it is useful to consider the distinctions between the two roles inherent in the writing process: the author and the secretary (Isaacson, 1987, 1989). Whereas the *author* role is concerned with the formulation and organization of ideas and the selection of words and phrases to express those ideas, the *secretarial* role emphasizes the physical and mechanical concerns of writing, such as legibility, spelling, punctuation, and grammatical rules. Obviously, both roles are critical to a writer's success, and both have influenced instructional practice.

The roles of author and secretary can be applied in the two instructional emphases of *teach-write* and *write-teach* (Sink, 1975). The former emphasizes formal grammar instruction, structure, skills exercises, and often a reliance on worksheets. Another traditional emphasis was diagramming sentences (see Schuster, 2005, for a historical review of this nonvalidated practice). Even though the teach-write approach is common, it lacks validation for learners without disabilities as well as those with special needs. A major concern is that these instructional activities can be completed without opportunity for actual writing. At the same time such activities can damage motivation to write and may usurp a major block of time, something that writing programs often have in limited supply. Thus, although skills are important, they may not be truly learned—that is, applied—in this fashion.

The alternative is the process approach of a write-teach focus, with initial stress on the primacy of the author role, on ideation over form, with structure emphasized later. The write-teach approach is process-oriented and capitalizes on the desire to write without stifling that effort. Structure is then taught within the context of actual writing opportunities.

Graves (1985) states the case for such a **process approach to writing:**

> Most teaching of writing is pointed toward the eradication of error, the mastery of minute, meaningless components that make little sense to the child. . . . Most [programs have been] directed toward the "easy" control of components that will show more specific growth. Although some growth may be evident on components, rarely does it result in the child's use of writing as a tool for learning and enjoyment. Make no mistake, component skills are important; if children do not learn to spell or use a pencil to get words on paper, they won't use writing for learning any more than the other children drilled on component skills. The writing-processing approach simply stresses meaning first, and then skills in the context of meaning. (p. 43)

As noted by Troia and Graham (2002), the process approach to writing typically includes these emphases:

> 1. frequent opportunities for writing using a predictable routine;
> 2. mini-lessons in which instruction in critical writing skills and strategies takes place when the need for such instruction becomes evident;
> 3. the formation of a community of writers writing for authentic purposes and audiences;
> 4. teacher and peer conferencing activities during which students receive individualized feedback about the substance and form of their compositions; and
> 5. regular occasions for sharing and publishing written work. (p. 292)

The process approach leads to a number of clear implications for instruction. Most significant is that for writing to improve, students need to write regularly. Rankin-Erikson and Pressley (2000) report that effective teachers had students write from 4 days per week to several times per day. Daily journal writing is an approach that has been used effectively for this purpose.

However, once the opportunity to write is confirmed, the development of structural or mechanical skills still needs attention because writing opportunities alone will not yield competence. Troia and Graham (2002) caution that a process approach may be overreliant on informal or incidental methods of instruction and that explicit instruction in skills and strategies is still needed for learners with special needs. The process approach combined with explicit instruction remains most fruitful.

Unrau (2004) spoke to the importance of explicit instruction in reference to teaching students in multicultural urban classrooms when he noted the following from his research review:

> One of the general findings that emerged from these inquiries was that, if teachers wanted to achieve high standards for writing while empowering their students, they would need to teach explicitly the conventions of standard edited English. That guideline applied to both non-native speakers of English and those speaking a nonstandard dialect. Teachers should also provide explicit instruction in other writing skills and knowledge, including composition structures and writing styles. The script for the process approach to teaching writing, as some teachers saw it, got modified in urban classrooms to meet the specific learning needs of diverse students. (pp. 277–278)

The challenge therefore is to enhance the acquisition of skills without interfering with the writing process. Graham (1992) offers three well-reasoned tenets to assist with instructional decision making: (a) maintain a balanced perspective between the extremes of decontextualized teaching of mechanics (including handwriting and spelling) and complete deemphasis on skills information to the extent to which acquisition becomes incidental; (b) focus on teaching skills that are likely to benefit the student rather than unlikely to produce generalizable benefits (e.g., learning to spell high-frequency words versus learning to diagram sentences); and (c) tie instruction on skills to the context of real writing opportunities. Students should be shown that these skills reflect conventions followed to enhance communication.

Rankin-Erickson and Pressley (2000) provide perspective on the balance between a process approach and the mechanics of writing. Based on their survey of effective teachers, they report that teachers indicated that:

> their writing instruction consisted of elements of process writing (i.e., planning, drafting, and editing) . . . being taught in tandem with direct strategies for carrying out the processes as well as instruction in the mechanical aspects of writing such as punctuation and spelling. These writing skills were not taught in isolation, however, but rather as part of an act of purposeful communication. Teachers saw getting ideas down on paper as being different from the editing process. . . . These instructional practices are consistent with practices shown to be effective with students with writing and learning difficulties. (p. 223)

One approach consistent with these concerns is selective feedback (Lovitt, 1975), which focuses on a limited number of skills at a given time. Selective feedback is a preferred alternative to both inordinate corrections or nonspecific comments (e.g., "good work").

One way to accomplish selective feedback and provide support to writers is through teacher conferencing. The teacher reads written assignments and provides feedback directly to students, most often in an oral conference. Such an approach provides an opportunity to introduce and reinforce specific skills and writing conventions. As students enhance their skills, teachers must ensure that they have many chances to develop and use these skills.

**Vocabulary Development.** A key focus of the writing stage is building vocabulary. Selected instructional practices to promote vocabulary development are presented below.

Because students' oral vocabulary typically is much larger than their written vocabulary, teachers should look for ways to facilitate transition from oral vocabulary to writing. This can be accomplished by introducing them to objects and experiences outside their daily lives and assisting them in writing about these events. The **language experience approach (LEA)** offers such a natural approach by combining attention to listening, speaking, reading, and writing (see Chapter 7). With LEA, students dictate stories that teachers transcribe for subsequent reading. Students then revise the stories, establishing the link between oral and written expression.

Within the context of specific writing tasks, several strategies may promote vocabulary development. Students can generate specific words that might be needed in a writing assignment, and the teacher can write them on the board for illustration and later reference. A list of words can also be kept on a bulletin board for students to copy and place in a notebook for later use. This is especially helpful with high-frequency words (e.g., Dolch words) that may also be spelling demons in order to minimize interruptions in the conceptualization process.

Instructional activities should also focus on the development of descriptive language. Students can brainstorm alternative words to use in a specific instance and then systematically substitute them in their own written compositions. This exercise can target synonyms as well as adjectives and adverbs to increase the descriptiveness of writing. However, for older students who may still have very limited writing abilities, the most appropriate goal is the acquisition and correct use of a limited number of functional words.

Vocabulary building can also be facilitated by reinforcement strategies. A variety of contingency arrangements has been reported; collectively, they indicate that reinforcement for specific targets, such as use of unusual words, not only produces gains in that area but often produces generalization to related skills (Polloway et al., 2004).

**Sentence Development.** Another significant aspect of writing instruction is sentence development. The sentence is the nucleus of structural work with students and the basis for teaching about appropriate syntax. Often, the poor writer's efforts are characterized by sentence fragments, safe and repetitive short sentences, and/or rambling prose without any structure. It is important to balance an emphasis on "real writing" with focused instruction on patterned sentence guides and structures (Isaacson, 1987). With such guides, students can enhance their efforts to communicate effectively. The simplest form of patterned guide presents a picture for which students must write a sentence, following a set pattern (e.g., "The [dog] is [running]").

Several other instructional alternatives are also available. The first is to use a **sentence extension** approach. A program developed by Phelps-Terasaki and Phelps-Gunn (1988, 2000) analyzes sentences into a series of *Wh*-questions (who, what, when, and where) instead of initially labeling nouns, verbs, adjectives, adverbs, and prepositions. This alternative is beneficial because it avoids the density of instruction in parts of speech, and keeps instruction meaningful and relevant. The program contains four units focused on beginning sentence writing, expanding sentence writing to paragraph development, paragraph writing for a purpose, and theme writing.

A sentence extension model can be used in two ways. One approach is to take a sentence and analyze it according to specific word categories, thus outlining the specific parts of a sentence. The second option is to have students generate a series of words or phrases to fit in each of these columns; at that point a sentence or series of sentences can be synthesized. Both exercises emphasize a direct relationship between words and sentences and facilitate sentence sense. Either approach enables students to appreciate how lexical items can vary sentence usage, sentence sense, and sentence generation.

A further step is **sentence combining,** an effective way to increase syntactic maturity and improve the overall quality of writing (Scarmadalia & Bereiter, 1986). A sample set of clusters from Strong's (1983) program is shown here:

1. Most of us remember Groper.
2. We remember him from our high school days.
3. He was angular.
4. He was muscled.
5. He had huge hands.
6. The quarterback would send him down.
7. The quarterback would send him out into the flat.
8. And then the football would come.
9. It looped in an arc.
10. The arc spiraled.
11. Groper would go up.
12. He would scramble with the defense.
13. The defense clawed at his jersey.

14. He was always in the right place.
15. He was always there at the right time. (p. 38)

Even though Strong's program does not begin with true writing, it encourages students to expand and develop their own creation. Individual tasks finish with an invitation to finish the story. Teachers can develop their own sentence clusters to provide practice and enhance mastery. A more detailed program for teaching sentence combining is presented by Schuster (2002).

**Paragraph Development.** Just as sentences are the transition from words to organized thoughts, paragraphs represent the transition from sentences to a unified composition. Instruction in paragraphing thus provides training in organization. Students learn that paragraphs are a matter of making assertions and elaborating on those assertions.

To begin, teachers can identify a topic sentence and students can provide elaboration. Then students can generate the first sentence and the teacher can monitor their efforts. Later, teachers can have students support their topic sentences with two to three follow-up sentences and, as appropriate, one clincher (as transition) sentence (see Figure 8–9 for an example).

A helpful technique to assist in building paragraphs as well as a useful skill for writing in general is paraphrasing. One example of a paraphrasing strategy is **RAP** (Schumaker, Deshler, & Denton, 1984, cited in Ellis & Sabornie, 1986). The acronym comes from **R**ead a paragraph, **A**sk yourself what the main ideas and details in the paragraph were, and **P**ut the main idea and details into your own words.

**Composition Writing.** Composition writing is the key goal in written language. Included within this area are initial considerations of story writing and then extensions of skills into further opportunities for expository writing.

| Indent → | Topic sentence |
|---|---|
| Detail sentence | |
| Detail sentence | |
| Detail sentence | |
| Final or Transition sentence | |

**FIGURE 8–9** Graphic organizer for paragraphs

*Source:* Brice, R. G. (2004). Connecting oral and written language through applied writing strategies. *Intervention in School and Clinic, 40*(1), p. 44.

Several general considerations that can enhance students' composition writing in both areas are worthy of note. Teachers should provide students with models that exhibit the desired behavior. For example, the teacher can model the desired behavior by writing short stories, paragraphs, or essays that students copy, or students who have reached the desired outcome can exhibit their work for others to view.

Hallenbeck (2002) identifies specific implications for students eventually taking responsibility for their own writing. He notes the following considerations:

1. Students must be willing to make a commitment of time and energy to improve their writing. It is helpful for them to see other students' pretest and posttest papers in order to realize the kind of progress that is possible.
2. Students must recognize the importance of gaining greater control over their own learning and must be willing to make this a personal priority. It is important in this regard for the teacher to spend considerable time modeling and scaffolding during the first paper, while explaining that students would be expected to be much more independent with subsequent papers.
3. Students must develop the ability to "walk in somebody else's shoes." This is especially important when anticipating the needs of their readers and when serving as a peer collaborator on a partner's paper. They often require role-playing simulations and teacher guidance in order to engage in productive behaviors during collaborations.
4. Students must learn to recognize opportunities to employ what they are learning about the writing process in other settings. They also should practice applying this process to additional expository text structures (e.g., explanation paper, comparison/contrast paper, persuasive essay). (p. 245)

Two key areas of concern are story writing and expository writing. To facilitate *story writing*, Graves and Hauge (1993) recommend the use of a **story grammar** cueing system. Students learn to focus on the setting of the story to be written, the main and supporting characters, the problem in the story and the plan to solve it, and the ending or resolution. With a cueing system, students check off each of these five elements as they plan and write it. The checklist should then be practiced and maintenance and generalization should be emphasized.

Harris and Graham (1992) provide a useful strategy approach to assist students in writing stories. It includes a series of story grammar elements that are summarized in the mnemonic *W-W-W, What-2, How-2*:

- Who? (is main character)
- When? (does it take place)
- Where? (does it take place)
- What? (does main character want to do)
- What? (happens when she does it)
- How? (does it end)
- How? (does the character feel)

This mnemonic is then embedded within a self-instructional strategy training procedure that includes the following steps:

1. Provide pretraining (prerequisite skills).
2. Review current strategies/motivation.
3. Describe the strategy.
   a. Look at the picture.
   b. Let your mind be free.
   c. Write down the story reminder: *W-W-W, What-2, How-2*.
   d. Write down story ideas for each part.
   e. Write your own story, use good parts, and make sense.
4. Model the strategy.
5. Promote mastery (repeat necessary steps).
6. Provide controlled practice.
7. Encourage independence and generalization.

To support students' ability to understand the specific story grammar elements discussed, have them discuss each of them and derive specific concepts. One important area is understanding problems and plans within the story. Montague and Leavell (1994) note that the problems put the story in motion, whereas plans indicate how characters will solve these problems. Sample problems can be generated by students in response to a topic to be written about and summarized on a poster. Sample problems may include money, work, heartbreak, insanity, family, friends, sickness, war, business, love, death, and being trapped.

Another important component of story writing is the development of characters. Leavell and Ioannides (1993) encourage teachers to provide explicit instruction in character development by focusing students' attention on the attributes of physical appearance, speech and actions, and thought and emotions. Table 8-7 provides a list of thought and emotion words to assist students in character development.

In addition to story writing, students also need to be taught *expository writing* skills. For many students with disabilities, this is a daunting challenge. Assisting these students to understand the various structures inherent in such writing requires a significant commitment.

**TABLE 8–7** Thoughts and emotions chart

| **Thought Words** | | | |
|---|---|---|---|
| wanted | realized | thought | wished |
| noticed | reasoned | hoped | felt |
| knew | needed | wondered | believed |
| understood | remembered | pondered | |
| **Emotion Words** | | | |
| happiness | hate | sadness | anxiety |
| satisfaction | nervousness | boredom | worry |
| amazement | tension | jealousy | fear |
| excitement | surprise | panic | loneliness |
| depression | envy | love | compassion |
| joy | agony | frustration | sympathy |

*Source:* From "Using Character Development to Improve Story Writing," by A. Leavell and A. Ioannides, 1993, *Teaching Exceptional Children, 27,* 43. Copyright 1993 by The Council for Exceptional Children. Reprinted with permission.

One helpful way to teach expository text structures is to teach students to use advanced organizers as vehicles for enhancing their planning and writing. Figure 8–10 presents a framework that highlights specific questions associated with the task of explanation.

Another useful strategy that can be adapted for use in both expository writing and story writing is Rooney's (1989) *Wheels for Writing*. This approach includes a focus on the use of circles or wheels to provide a graphic organizer for planning and writing. With this approach, the student is taught to begin with five wheels: the first for the "start" of the paper, the next three for the three main ideas within the composition, and the fifth a "therefore" or conclusion. These five wheels then become circles around which specific ideas in the form of details can subsequently be developed (see Figure 8–11).

This approach can be complemented with the strategy highlighted in Figure 8–12. De la Paz (1999) developed a series of cue cards that will assist students in writing a five-paragraph essay answer.

Writing strategies provide vehicles for enabling students to enhance their writing across all stages of the writing process. The key element is to encourage students to think about, and talk to themselves, their teachers, and their peers about, the writing process.

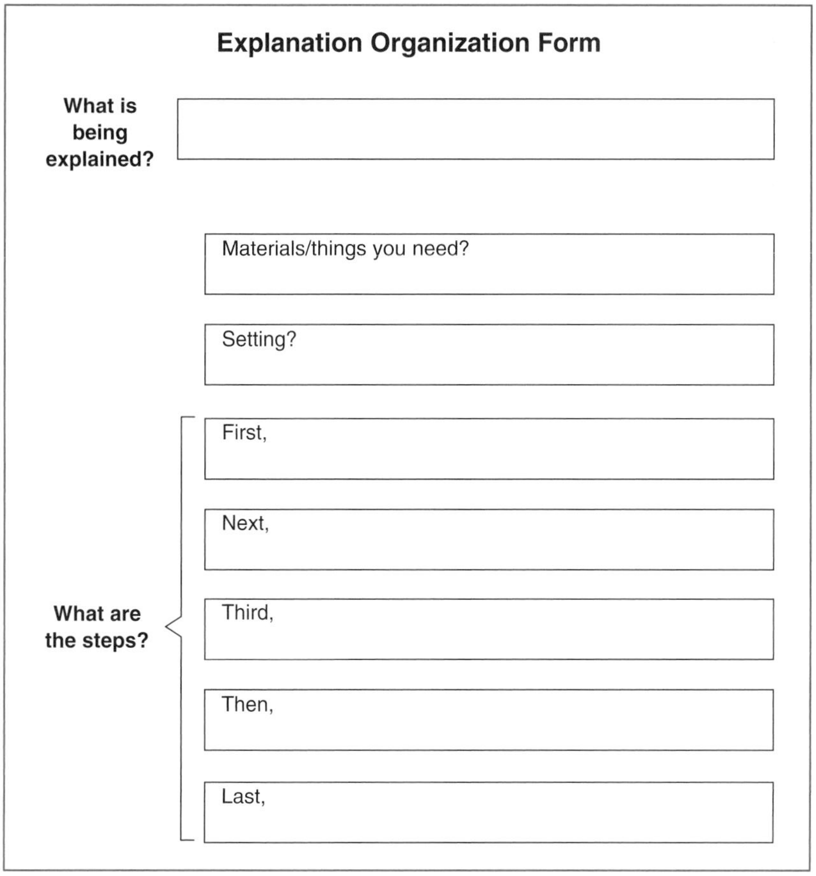

**Explanation Organization Form**

**What is being explained?** [ ]

Materials/things you need?

Setting?

**What are the steps?**

First,

Next,

Third,

Then,

Last,

**FIGURE 8–10** Explanation organization form

*Source:* From "Shared Understandings: Structuring the Writing Experience Through Dialogue," by C. S. Englert and T. V. Mariage, 1991, *Journal of Learning Disabilities, 24*, 334. Copyright 1991 by PRO-ED, Inc. Reprinted with permission.

Baker, Gersten, and Scanlon (2002) refer to these strategies as **procedural facilitators** and **elaborated dialogue.** They note that:

- Procedural facilitators help bridge the gap between oral and written language, think sheets, graphic organizers, and story maps.
- Elaborated, interactive dialogue provides explicit modeling of strategies, critical evaluation of responses, questioning of students, and elaborated responses by students.
- The use of these interventions facilitates achievement of the goal of structured writing through think aloud/procedural facilitators complemented by elaborated dialogue with teachers.

**Postwriting.** The general goal of writing instruction is to enable students to communicate effectively with others while achieving personal satisfaction in the process. To achieve this goal, the postwriting stage must become a routine and integral part of the writing process. Students must be sold on the concept of the "working draft" as the initial effort to get the information to be shared on paper. Postwriting must acquire a positive association, removed from any connection with punitive action. Students should be assisted in deriving personal satisfaction from writing that comes from looking at it as a process rather than as a polished product.

Postwriting requires the active involvement of the writer in the careful editing and revision of what has been previously written. Initially, students must have the opportunity to establish the concept of editing and revision. Training can begin with anonymous papers and direct instruction to, for example, identify correct and incorrect sentences, find three spelling errors,

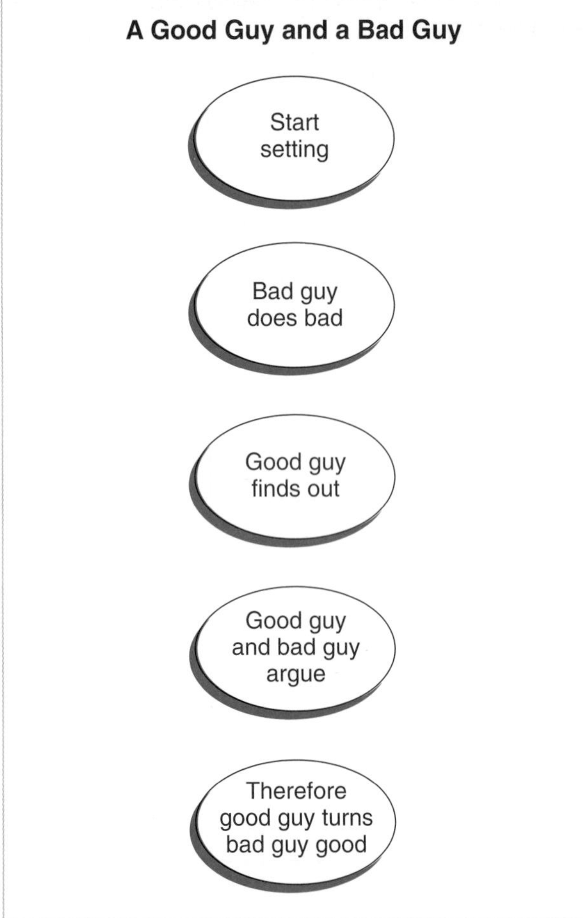


**FIGURE 8–11** Wheels for writing (overview)

*Source*: From *Independent Strategies for Effective Study* (p. 74), by K. Rooney, 1989, Richmond, VA: Educational Enterprises. Copyright 1989 by Educational Enterprises, Inc. Reprinted with permission.

and/or correct all punctuation errors on a given page. After reaching an acceptable criterion, students can shift to their own work.

Focusing on the full spectrum of editing and revision is an overwhelming task for any student who has difficulties with writing. Therefore, only one or two skills should be stressed at any time. A helpful approach for the initiation of editing activities is the error-monitoring strategy indicated by the acronym **COPS** (Schumaker et al., 1981):

- **C**apitalization: Have I capitalized first word and proper nouns?
- **O**verall appearance: Have I made handwriting, margin, messy, or spacing errors?
- **P**unctuation: Have I used end punctuation, commas, and semicolons correctly?
- **S**pelling: Do the words appear to be spelled correctly?

The COPS process is intended to be introduced one step at a time. Students should first learn a particular skill and then learn to edit for that skill. After they have been trained to proofread for each of the four components separately, they can be directed to use all four at the same time. The procedure has been validated for use with students who are at or above the middle school level (Shannon & Polloway, 1993) though it may be successfully used at the upper elementary level as well.

There is of course far more to the postwriting stage than checking for capitalization, overall appearance, punctuation, and spelling. If students acquire these skills, instruction should then focus on the higher levels of editing, with special attention to content and organization.

Postwriting should focus on the revision of the content in writing as well as the craft. Isaacson (2004) presented edit sheets that can be used by the author and a peer editor, respectively. These are presented in Figure 8–13. Another useful peer editing guide was developed by Marchisan and Alber (2001). It is presented in Figure 8–14. The nearby Teacher Tip provides recommended procedures for the use of writing groups.

One strategy for use by the writer or by a peer editor in the revision process is REVISE:

- **R**eread your paper to confirm overall goal reached
- **E**dit using COPS
- **V**ocabulary selected to be appropriate for purposes
- **I**nteresting and lively topic developed
- **S**entences complete and varied
- **E**vidence provided to support your points

## Special Considerations: Middle and Secondary Level

Chalk, Hagan-Burke, and Burke (2005) aptly summarized the importance of writing instruction for older students:

> Written expression is a fundamental skill for today's high school students. Those who lack the ability to adequately demonstrate conceptual knowledge and communicate their thoughts and beliefs in writing are at grave disadvantage. Being facile with written language and writing is required to pass state and district exams, advance from grade to grade, and to graduate from high school. An alarming number of students with learning disabilities struggle to develop writing skills sufficient to satisfy these crucial benchmarking. (p. 85)

**FIGURE 8–12** Cue cards for writing five-paragraph essays. Italicized cards were provided for students who wished to attempt more sophisticated introductory paragraphs.

| Introductory paragraph: Thesis statement first<br>• Answer the prompt in your first sentence.<br>• Write your first main idea in 2nd sentence.<br>• Write your second main idea as the 3rd sentence.<br>• Write your third main idea as the last sentence.<br>(1) | Introductory paragraph: Thesis statement last<br>• "Start with an attention getter" and lead up to the thesis statement.<br>• Answer the prompt in your last sentence. Include your 1st, second, and 3rd main idea in a series.<br>(2) |
|---|---|
| How to "start with attention getter"<br>• Use a series of questions<br>• Use a series of statements<br>• Use a brief or funny story<br>• Use a mean or angry statement<br>• Start with the opposite opinion from what you believe<br>(3) | First body paragraph: Use transition words to introduce ideas<br>• First of all...<br>• (The/My) first (reason/example) is...<br>• One (reason why/example is)...<br>• To begin with...<br>• In the first step...<br>• To explain...<br>(4) |
| 2nd and 3rd body paragraphs: Use transition words to connect or add ideas, or give examples<br>• Second...Third...<br>• My second (reason/example) is...<br>• Furthermore...<br>• Another (reason) to support this is...<br>• What is more...<br>• The next step...<br>(5) | Concluding paragraph: Use transition words to summarize ideas<br>• In conclusion/To conclude...<br>• In summary/To sum up...<br>• As one can see.../As a result...<br>• In short/All in all...<br>• It follows that...<br>• For these reasons...<br>(6) |

*Source:* From "Self-Regulated Strategy Instruction in Regular Education Settings: Improving Outcomes for Students with and Without Learning Disabilities," by S. de la Paz, 1999. *Learning Disabilities Research and Practice, 14*, p. 99.

**FIGURE 8–13** Personal narrative edit sheet

| *Author:* __________ | | | *Editor:* __________ | | |
|---|---|---|---|---|---|
| 1. Does my story tell what happened to me? | Yes | Fix | 1. Does the story tell what happened to *the author*? | Yes | Fix |
| 2. Does it focus on *one* interesting event? | Yes | Fix | 2. Does it focus on *one* interesting event? | Yes | Fix |
| 3. Do I tell everything in the order that it happened? | Yes | Fix | 3. Does the author tell everything in the order that it happened? | Yes | Fix |
| 4. Do I use details that help the reader "see" the action? | Yes | Fix | 4. Does the author use details that help you "see" the action? | Yes | Fix |
| 5. Do I tell why I remember it or what I learned? | Yes | Fix | 5. Does the author tell why he/she remembers it or what was learned? | Yes | Fix |
| One thing the reader will like about the story: | | | One thing you like about the story: | | |
| One thing I could do to make it better: | | | One thing the author could do to make it better: | | |

*Source:* From "Instruction That Helps Students Meet Standards in Writing," by S. Isaacson, 2004, *Exceptionality, 12*, p. 46. Copyright 2004 by Lawrence Erlbaum Associates, Inc. Journals. Reproduced with permission of Lawrence Erlbaum Associates, Inc. Journals in the format Textbook via Copyright Clearance Center.

**FIGURE 8–14** Revision guide for fiction and nonfiction writing

Title ______
Author ______
Date ______
Peer Editor ______

_____ Is the beginning interesting?
_____ Does the story make sense?
_____ Are the characters believable? Do they act like real people?
_____ Do the characters use conversation?
_____ Are the characters' personalities developed?
_____ Does the story have a problem that needs to be solved?
_____ Are the descriptions of the scenes clear?
_____ Does each scene build toward the high point (climax) of the story?
_____ Is there an exciting or high point of the story?
_____ Is the conclusion logical? Does it wrap up all the loose ends?
_____ Was the conflict or problem resolved?
_____ Was there a moral or theme?

Title ______
Author ______
Date ______
Peer Editor ______

_____ Has the author written for a particular audience?
_____ Has the author written for a specific purpose?
_____ Does the introduction to the piece get the reader involved right away?
_____ Are the ideas developed in a logical sequence?
_____ Does the author stay on topic?
_____ Are the ideas clear?
_____ Are there details to support the main ideas?
_____ Is correct grammar used?
_____ Are words spelled correctly?
_____ Is there a surprise ending or strong conclusion?

*Source:* From "The Write Way: Tips for Teaching the Writing Process to Resistant Writers," by M. L. Marchisan and S. R. Alber, 2001. *Intervention in School and Clinic, 36*, p. 158. Copyright 2001 by PRO-ED, Inc. Reprinted with permission.

Writing instruction presents significant challenges for teachers who are working with students who have experienced limited prior success. A first key focus is *motivation*. Alley and Deshler (1979), in their classic text on teaching adolescents with special needs, provide several apt observations on motivation. Identifying attitude toward writing as a key concern, they suggest the following strategies: encourage students to focus initially on ideation rather than mechanical skills so that they feel comfortable with writing before trying to achieve perfection (thus sensing failure); expose students to a variety of experiences to build their knowledge base for writing; use tape recorders as a way to record thoughts, followed by subsequent efforts to transcribe and revise these thoughts; and have students write daily or weekly journals without corrective feedback.

A second key focus for adolescents must be on the acquisition of *strategies* for writing as described earlier. As Chalk et al. (2005) noted in their study, students benefit from writing instruction that helped students develop specific strategies for brainstorming, semantic mapping or webbing, goal setting, and composition revision.

The discussion earlier in the chapter focused on specific strategies that can be used effectively with both elementary and secondary students. For older students, however, it is particularly noteworthy to consider the challenge of developing competence in strategy usage. Toward this end, Troia (2002) identified the following concerns:

- Training often occurs for only several weeks while students need prolonged intervention.
- Students have functional limitations in memory and the execution of cognitive tasks.
- Motivational problems are common and students often attribute success and/or failure to factors not under self-control.
- Students need to develop the will and effort to execute the process in a systematic fashion.

These challenges also provide a framework for instructional emphases. Troia (2002) thus provided the following recommendations to promote strategy use,

**TEACHER Tips** — **Elementary Level**

## Writing Groups

Tompkins (2005) provides the following recommendations for a step-by-step implementation of writing groups focused on content:

1. **The writer reads.** Students take turns reading their compositions aloud to the group. All students listen politely, thinking about compliments and suggestions they will make after the writer finishes reading. Only the writer looks at the composition, because . . . listening to the writing read aloud keeps the focus on content.
2. **Listeners offer compliments.** Writing-group members say what they linked about the writing. These positive comments should be specific, focusing on strengths, rather than the often heard "I liked it" or "It was good." Comments may focus on organization, leads, word choice, voice, sequence, dialogue, theme, and so on.
3. **The writer asks questions.** After a round of positive comments, writers ask for assistance with trouble spots they identified earlier when rereading their writing, or they may ask questions that reflect more general concerns about how well they are communicating.
4. **Listeners offer suggestions.** Members of the writing group ask questions about things that were unclear to them, and they make suggestions about how to revise the compositions. . . . It is important to teach students what kinds of comments and suggestions are acceptable so that they will word what they say in helpful rather than hurtful ways.
5. **The process is repeated.** The first four steps are repeated for each student's compositions. This is the appropriate time for teachers to provide input as well. . . .
6. **Writers plan for revision.** At the end of the writing-group session, all students make a commitment to revise their writing based on the comments and suggestions of the group members. The final decisions on what to revise always rest with the writers themselves, but with the understanding that their rough drafts are not perfect comes the realization that some revision will be necessary. When students verbalize their planned revisions, they are more likely to complete the revision stage. Some students also make notes for themselves about their revision plans. (p. 137)

maintenance, and generalization. He indicated that teachers should:

1. Model strategy use and provide opportunities for student practice.
2. Teach students both self-regulatory behaviors as well as the strategies that are task-specific.
3. Communicate to students expectations for use and transfer and then reinforce these applications.
4. Promote "mindfulness" and help students think about generalization of strategies on similar as well as dissimilar tasks.

A special writing challenge for learners with disabilities at the middle and secondary school level is *note taking* from class lectures. Because the lecture format is often used at these levels (as well as in postsecondary education), students need to develop strategies for making notes for later review and study.

Though a variety of strategies are available to enhance note taking, a full review is beyond the scope of this chapter. In Figure 8–15 one representative strategy is presented. *CALL UP* was developed for middle school students in inclusive classes. The full process of teaching and learning to proficiency and generalization took 6 months according to Czarnecki, Rosko, and Fine (1998). In addition, Czarnecki et al. also present a parallel lecture notes revision strategy ("A" NOTES) intended for secondary school students. Further information on related aspects of note taking will also be presented in Chapter 12, which focuses on study skills and strategies.

Finally, consider these summative concerns. Vaughn, Gersten, and Chard (2000) reported on contemporary research on written expression. They concluded that three core elements were present in effective instructional practices:

- *Explicit teaching of the critical steps in the writing process:* This was often supported by a "think sheet," prompt card, or mnemonic. However, the teacher invariably modeled how to use these steps by writing several samples.
- *Explicit teaching of the conventions of a writing genre:* These "text structures" provided a guide for undertaking the writing task at hand, whether it is a persuasive essay, a personal narrative, or an essay comparing and contrasting two concepts.

**FIGURE 8–15** A note-taking strategy: CALL UP

| Memory Device | Intended Associations (What each step cues the student to do) |
|---|---|
| **C**opy from board or transparency | 1. Be aware that teachers usually write the main ideas on the board or on a transparency—copy these.<br>2. Listen and look for cue words or phrases that will identify the main idea and copy them down next to the margin and underline them. |
| **A**dd details | 3. Listen and look for details and add them to your notes. Write them one inch from the margin with a line (-) in front of the detail. |
| **L**isten and write the question | 4. Listen to the question that the teacher asks and that students ask and write it down if it helps your understanding. Put a "Q" in front of the question to signal that it is a question. Indent this, just like the details, under the main idea. |
| **L**isten and write the answer | 5. Listen to the answer to the question and write it down. Put an "A" in front of the answer to signal that it is an answer. Indent this just like the details, under the main idea.<br>6. Continue adding details and questions and answers to the main idea. If the teacher discusses another main idea, skip six lines before writing the next main idea. |
| **U**tilize the text | 7. At home, utilize your textbook to help you review and understand the information. Read about the main idea in your textbook. |
| **P**ut it in your own words | 8. Put the information in your own words and write these statements in your notes. Write your statements under the main idea on the six lines that you skipped in #6. Write the page number where you found the information in the book in the margin so you can go back later if needed. |

*Linking Device to the Strategy*

1. Use the CALL UP note taking strategy to help you CALL UP your memory.
2. This strategy also helps you to CALL UP your attention by helping you to be more focused on what is being said in class.

*Source:* From "How to Call up Notetaking Skills," by S. Czarnecki, D. Rosko, and E. Fine, *Teaching Exceptional Children, 30*(6), 1998, 14. Copyright 1998 by the Council for Exceptional Children. Reprinted with permission.

- *Guided feedback:* Teachers or peers provided frequent feedback to students on the quality of their work, elements missing from their work, and the strengths of their work. (p. 103)

**Reflective Question 8–3:** ***How can teachers develop effective instructional programs that balance concerns for the craft and content aspects of writing?***

## TECHNOLOGY IN THE CLASSROOM

The teaching of writing, and learning to write, can benefit from the use of assistive technology. Several examples illustrate uses related to handwriting, spelling, and written expression.

*Keyboarding* instruction represents an alternative to handwriting instruction that may be particularly beneficial for students who have significant problems with fine motor coordination. Tompkins (2005) notes that it is important that students receive instruction in elementary grades so that they can learn touch typing, learning to look at the screen rather than their fingers in the process. Several training programs (e.g., Kid Keys, Mavis Beacon Teaches Typing) can assist with this process. In addition to teaching typing and computer skills, the advantages of keyboarding include faster speed, higher degree of legibility, and inherent motivational advantages. With greater classroom access to computers, including laptops, the benefits of this shift will become more pronounced.

**TEACHER** *Tips* **Secondary Level**

## Writing Opportunities

Improving and maintaining skills requires practice. Writing skills are especially difficult for many students to master, so they should be provided with frequent opportunities to practice. Provide them with a wide variety of writing opportunities such as:

- job or college applications
- letters requesting freebies
- written math problems
- thank-you letters
- want ads
- imaginary obituaries
- advice columns
- descriptions of items for magazine advertisements
- critiques of TV shows or movies
- book reviews
- travel brochures
- jokes or riddles
- business letters

Another key alternative approach is through *voice recognition software*. The promise of this technology is particularly significant for students who have motoric difficulties with handwriting and keyboarding (e.g., some students with cerebral palsy). Programs such as Naturally Speaking are reasonable in cost and sufficiently accurate in recognition.

Technology also affords a useful approach for word study in spelling practice. While computers are not necessarily substitutes for "pencil and paper tasks," Graham (1999) recommends that a key issue is determining whether the motoric demands are a confounding variable. Teachers can observe students using the different approaches to evaluate their relative effectiveness and thus determine if computer practice enhances spelling performance.

Technological support also can be used on a regular basis to enhance writing and support the skills associated with postwriting. Word-processing opportunities have been validated for two decades on their positive effect on the length and quality of writing efforts and, importantly, on the way that the revision and editing process is viewed (e.g., Morocco & Neuman, 1987; Vallecorsa & deBettencourt, 1992).

In a recent review, Englert, Wu, and Zhao (2005) provided an apt summary of the benefits of technology for advanced writing:

> First, technology can be used *to offload some of the cognitive work* from the inexperienced writer onto the computer, just as a calculator might be used to offload some of the cognitive demands on students in mathematics. . . . In the case of text structures, for example, technology can be used to make visible the text structures of written language in ways that make them accessible, thereby furthering their use as conscious objects by students. . . . Second, technology offers the potential to mediate students' performance through the provision of prompts or scaffolds to elicit cognitive processes or information that might not be employed by writers with disabilities. . . . The concept of scaffolding is based on the notion that with assistance, students can accomplish tasks or apply strategies that they could not perform independently. . . . Third, technologies can offer basic tools that support writing performance. By making text-to-speech or spelling functions accessible, for example, students might find it easier to read, write, and edit their texts in order to clarify potential confusions. Through the use of such skill-enabling tools. . . , students with disabilities can bolster their performance and exhibit conventional writing practices that are in advantage of what they could produce in unassisted situations. (pp. 185–186)

Reflective Questions 8–4: ***With the advent of increased use of technology, what are the potential positive and negative impacts on handwriting, spelling, and written expression?***

## MAKING IT WORK

The key considerations for writing instruction is to develop individuals who can communicate effectively. Although handwriting and spelling are important ultimately, it is written expression that will be critical for student success. A successful writing instructional program involves a comprehensive commitment to the

**TECHNOLOGY *Tip***

Castellani and Jeffs (2001) outlined a program for enhancing writing, and reading, with the use of the Internet. Their approach is summarized as follows across three time frames.

| | Reading | Writing | Using Internet |
|---|---|---|---|
| **Before** | | | |
| | • Recognize reading level | • Recognize writing level | • Complete interest inventory |
| | • Identify vocabulary and begin creating word list for new or difficult words, prepare prediction questions or questions specific to text you have found on Internet | • Use visual concept organization software, such as Inspiration, graphing software (Flowchart) | • Scan for pictures<br>• Preview links ahead of time, bookmarks<br>• Search for information, locating text sites on grade level |
| | • Use fundamental skills software | • Use fundamental skills software | • Find materials for grade level<br>• Find information on Internet, based on student preferences or individualized student searches |
| **During** | | | |
| | • Use text readers, grammar, abbreviation expansion | • Answer questions to expand on story and provide detail | • Make decisions about interest and authenticity of materials and student motivation |
| | • Reread text, have computer reader, take turns reading with student | • Use writing templates, word-prediction software | • Transfer pictures and text to word processor for further work with information |
| | • Use an available electronic dictionary, thesaurus | • Use graphic-based writing software<br>• Turn questions and answers into sentences | |
| **After** | | | |
| | • Provide comprehension activities with extended activities through different modalities | • Publish and share work with others on Internet<br>• Create literacy portfolio for each student | • Create booklets on Internet sites and have students rate story site<br>• Search for related future reading activities and extensions |
| | • Look at suggested readings on similar topics by same author | | |

*Source:* From "Emerging Reading and Writing Strategies Using Technology," by J. Castellani and T. Jeffs, *Teaching Exceptional Children, 33*(5), 2001, p. 66. 

success of the individual learners. Graham, Harris, and Larsen (2001) identify these exemplary practices:

- A literate classroom environment where students' written work is prominently displayed, the room is packed with writing and reading material, and word lists adorn the walls.
- Daily writing with students working on a wide range of writing tasks for multiple audiences, including writing at home.
- Extensive efforts to make writing motivating by setting an exciting mood, creating a risk-free environment and promoting an "I can" attitude.
- Regular teacher–student conferences concerning the writing topic the student is currently working on, including the establishment of goals or criteria to guide the child's writing and revising efforts.
- A predictable writing routine where students are encouraged to think, reflect, and revise.
- Overt teacher modeling of the process of writing as well as positive attitudes toward writing.

- Cooperative arrangements where students help each other plan, draft, revise, edit, or publish their written work.
- Group or individual sharing where students present work in progress or completed papers to their peers for feedback.
- Follow-up instruction to ensure mastery of targeted writing skills, knowledge, and strategies.
- Integration of writing activities across the curriculum and the use of reading to support writing development.
- Frequent opportunities for students to self-regulate their behavior during writing, including working independently, arranging their own space, and seeking help from others. (p. 77)

Finally, in reference to the basic skills of spelling and handwriting, Troia (2005) noted the following in his review of contemporary research:

- Spelling and handwriting instruction have demonstrable impact on measures associated with those skills as well as writing fluency.
- Students with and without problems benefit from basic skills instruction.
- Treatment effects may diminish over time.
- Spelling instruction improves decoding performance.
- Composing strategies should be taught alongside basic skills to influence the development of both.

## SUMMARY

This chapter addresses assessment and instructional concerns across the three areas of written language. The discussion of handwriting focuses on the relative value of skill development in this area and the importance of initial instruction and maintenance and proficiency. In spelling, particular attention is given to common problems and teacher- and student-directed strategies. For written expression, emphases are placed on the three stages of prewriting, writing or drafting, and postwriting.

## ACTIVITIES

### ELEMENTARY LEVEL

#### Manuscript Writing

1. Make name tags for all students, and have them copy their names.
2. Write students' names at the top of a sheet of primary writing paper, and have them copy their names.
3. Make dot letters and have pupils form the letters by connecting the dots.
4. After a series or group of letters has been learned, have the children write the letters on primary writing paper.
5. Have the class dictate several sentences about some event that has previously occurred, and then have students copy the sentences that you have written on the board or chart paper.

#### Cursive Writing

1. Make dot cursive letters and have students form the letters by connecting the dots.
2. Play "Concentration" using cards with manuscript or cursive letters copied on them. Ask students to match the cursive and manuscript forms of a letter.
3. Let students collect samples of cursive writing to share and compare. Signatures from staff members, parents, or other community members can be interesting.
4. A classroom mailbox encourages students to write notes to their friends during specified times of the day or at home. Notes must be legible in order to be read and answered. The students especially want to use their best handwriting when they are writing to someone special outside the classroom (e.g., principal, last year's teacher).

#### Spelling

1. Have pupils keep words that they can spell in a box to be reviewed periodically. They can also be used for spelling games, alphabetizing, homework assignments, or creative writing.
2. The Dolch and other word lists can be grouped into different sets of words (e.g., nouns, adjectives). Have pupils pick out words that they do not know how to spell.
3. Show the children that there is some linguistic regularity to English by giving them a word or stem and having them form and spell other words (e.g., *-ad*: had, dad, mad; *-amp*: damp, lamp, stamp; *-oe*: hoe, foe, toe).
4. Divide the class into two teams and list spelling words on the board in short columns. While students from each team stand with their backs to the board, pronounce a word. The students then turn and find the word on the board; the first person to find the word gets a point for the team.
5. Play bingo. Give each student a playing card. Instruct students to write a word from a current

spelling list on each square of their cards. Collect and redistribute the cards. The game proceeds until the first student to cover the appropriate squares says "Bingo!"

### Written Expression

1. At the beginning of the day, set aside a silent writing time to write in journals. The aim of this activity is to foster enjoyment; therefore, entries should not be evaluated.
2. Develop visual imagery as a prerequisite to writing. Students can imagine making an angel in the snow, flying a kite in March winds, eating ice cream on a hot summer day, or burying a friend in a pile of leaves. Initially, have students relax and think at their desks. Later, have students list adjectives associated with their images. Finally, direct students to write sentences or paragraphs.
3. Use progressive writing exercises. The object is to pick up where a classmate has left off and write for 2 or 3 minutes. The final writer should write a conclusion. One student can read the finished product.
4. A class newspaper can help students improve written expression. Assignments can be made according to ability and interest. Class, school, community, national, or international topics can be reported.
5. Use photos to teach students topic sentence development. Start by describing the photograph, and then write sentences and paragraphs.

## MIDDLE AND SECONDARY LEVEL

1. As students get older, a handwriting goal is to increase speed without loss of legibility. The students write an assignment for a certain amount of time. When time is up, each letter is evaluated against preset criteria. One point is given for each correctly formed letter. The writing assignment can be content material, classmates' names, ABCs, or sentences that contain all the letters of the alphabet (Alston & Taylor, 1987).
2. Students may enjoy opportunities to make, as well as solve, spelling puzzles. Students can make word searches by placing spelling words in different spaces on graph paper (diagonally, horizontally, vertically) and then filling in the other blocks with random letters. The puzzles can then be exchanged and solved by classmates.
3. Direct students to write responsible letters to elected officials. Help students express their opinions on various political or social issues.
4. A motivating activity is "Contest Week." Many contests merely require students to place their name and address on a postcard and mail it to a company or radio station. Others require them to express ideas or opinions.
5. Cut pictures out of the newspaper and remove the captions. Students write a title and caption based on what is happening in the picture, read their ideas to the class, and then write a short article about what they believe is going on.
6. Have students obtain a copy of, or transcribe the lyrics of, a favorite song. Then have them rewrite the words in standard English.
7. To help students expand their sentences while reinforcing the concepts of subject and predicate, have them write a simple sentence on the board, dividing it into subject and predicate (e.g., "The dog barks"). Working in pairs, have students add details to both parts. Then have them share their expanded sentences. Discuss the differences between the simpler and expanded versions.

CHAPTER

# 9

# *Mathematics Instruction*

Mathematics is an important part of everyday life. Although not always obvious, mathematics pervades much of what we do at home, on the job, and in our communities. Often, we give little thought that it is an integral part of the business, science, and technology sectors of our country. It is not surprising, therefore, that researchers (e.g., Marchand-Martello, Slocum, & Martella, 2004) address the need for effective mathematics instruction so students are able to attain life goals such as college and competitive jobs. Because of the integral nature of mathematics in today's society, the instruction of mathematics (along with reading) has come to the forefront of the educational community.

The fact that mathematics instruction has taken such an important position in today's educational arena is not by accident. America has been concerned with the mathematical competence of our youth for decades (Klein, 2003). For example, the last 50 years of mathematics instructional history began when Russia launched the first satellite into space in 1957. This advancement was recognized as a national security issue, and in 1958, Congress responded by initiating the National Defense Act to support the math and science education of America's children (Coyne, Kame'enui, & Carnine, 2007). Just a few years later, President Lyndon B. Johnson responded to the educational needs of our youth by signing into law the Elementary and Secondary Education Act (ESEA) in 1965. This law was intended to address the poverty of children in America. That is, if children from poverty stricken communities could attend academically effective schools, then they could work their way out of their social condition. The law was intended to provide resources to elementary and secondary schools so they would become better providers for these educational goals. Unfortunately, much debate has taken place with regard to the effectiveness of this law and how the allocation of money without accountability has produced less than satisfying results (Baker & Gulley, 2004).

Some 15 years after the ESEA was put into law, Klein (2003) chronicles two major reports regarding the lack of educational progress made by our children. These reports were *An Agenda for Action* (National Council of Teachers of Mathematics, 1980) and *A Nation at Risk* (National Commission of Excellence in Education, 1983). The National Council of Teachers of Mathematics (NCTM) put forth, in *An Agenda for Action*, a strong statement with regard to problem solving and the use of technology (e.g., computers) to increase the mathematic skills of our students. The National Commission of Excellence in Education, reported the failure of the educational reform laws that had dominated the 1960s and 1970s. The commission documented the disparity between the mathematics and science scores of U.S. students and students of other nations and emphasized that America did not have a comprehensive education system that would prepare students for the workplace of the future. Furthermore, the commission recommended the need for preparing students with well-developed cognitive skills as well as producing remedial mathematics courses at the college level and improving the quality and quantity of mathematics teachers. In combination, these reports sensitized the educational community to the need for research and improved mathematics instruction. The response resulted in a number of national initiatives and research efforts that have influenced the teaching of mathematics and, ultimately, the instruction of students with disabilities.

The purpose of this chapter, therefore, is threefold. The first purpose is to inform teachers of the initiatives that have taken place in the last 30 years and how they impact the teaching of mathematics to students with disabilities. The second purpose is to introduce assessment procedures that reflect the progress students are achieving. Finally, the third purpose is to introduce evidence-based instructional procedures and strategies in mathematics for students with special needs.

## NATIONAL INITIATIVES

### The NCSM Initiative

In 1977 the National Council of Supervisors of Mathematics (NCSM) paralleled the concerns of low mathematics scores by identifying 10 basic skill areas that need to be included in the math curriculum: (a) problem solving; (b) applying mathematics to everyday situations; (c) alertness to the reasonableness of results; (d) estimation and approximation; (e) appropriate computational skills; (f) geometry; (g) measurement; (h) reading, interpreting, and constructing tables, charts, and graphs; (i) using mathematics to predict; and (j) computer literacy. Although these areas are postulated for general mathematics education, they are appropriate for special populations too. In fact, the first two items, which embody many of the other skills, are critically important.

### The NCTM Initiatives

The National Council of Teachers of Mathematics (1980) next presented a list of eight recommendations related to the future direction of mathematics education. Five of the eight recommendations have direct relevance to students with special needs:

> 1. Problem solving must be the focus of school mathematics.
> 2. The concept of basic skills in mathematics must encompass more than computational facility.
> 3. Mathematics programs must take full advantage of the power of calculators and computers at all grade levels.
> 4. The success of mathematics programs and student learning must be evaluated by a wider range of measures than conventional testing.
> 5. More mathematics study must be required of all students, and a flexible curriculum with a greater range of options should be designed to accommodate the diverse needs of the student population. (p. 1)

These recommendations are important because they helped spell out the needed changes in mathematics education and shaped reform efforts.

The NCTM initiated its first updated position on mathematics education in 1989 by publishing the *Curriculum and Evaluation Standards for School Mathematics*. The standards of that version were developed to judge mathematics curricula and to provide a basis for reform. The major goals promoted in this document encourage students to do the following:

learn to value mathematics
learn to reason mathematically
learn to communicate mathematically
become confident of their mathematical abilities
become mathematical problem solvers

By the year 2000, the NCTM had produced a second, updated version of the standards: *Principles and Standards for School Mathematics* (NCTM, 2000), or "Standards 2000."

The standards presented in the 2000 document are divided into Content Standards (Number and Operations, Algebra, Geometry, Measurement, and Data Analysis) and Process Standards (Problem Solving, Reasoning and Proof, Communication, Connections, and Representation). The Content Standards describe what knowledge and skills the students should learn, and the Process Standards highlight the ways of acquiring and using content knowledge. Table 9-1 represents examples of the Content Standards for children in grades 3–5, with descriptions of what mathematics instruction should enable students to know and do.

Along with these changes, the Standards 2000 document presents six principles for school mathematics. Interestingly, these principles have undertones for working with and accommodating the needs of students with disabilities or of diverse backgrounds. The six principles address the following themes:

> 1. *Equity.* Excellence in mathematics education requires equity—high expectations and strong support for all students.
> 2. *Curriculum.* A curriculum is more than a collection of activities: it must be coherent, focused on important mathematics, and well articulated across the grades.
> 3. *Teaching.* Effective mathematics teaching requires understanding what students know and need to learn and then challenging and supporting them to learn it well.
> 4. *Learning.* Students must learn mathematics with understanding, actively building new knowledge from experience and prior knowledge.
> 5. *Assessment.* Assessment should support the learning of important mathematics and furnish useful information to both teachers and students.
> 6. *Technology.* Technology is essential in teaching and learning mathematics; it influences the mathematics that is taught and enhances student learning. (p. 11)

Furthermore, the principle regarding equity specifies that "some students may need further assistance in meeting high mathematics expectations" (p. 13). The document continues to state that students who are not native English speakers should receive the extra help

**TABLE 9–1** Example of the Standards 2000, grades 3–5

| *Example of Content Knowledge* | *Standard* | *Example of Required Expectation* |
|---|---|---|
| Number and Operations | Understanding numbers, ways of representing numbers, relationships among numbers, and number systems<br>Understand meaning of operations and how they relate to one another<br>Compute fluently and make reasonable estimates | • Understand the place-value structure of base-10 numbers and be able to compare whole numbers with decimals<br>• Recognize and generate equivalent forms of commonly used fractions, decimals, and percents<br>• Understand the effects of multiplying and dividing whole numbers |
| Algebra | Understand patterns, relations, and functions<br>Represent and analyze mathematical situations and structures using algebraic symbols<br>Use mathematical models to represent and understand quantitative relationships<br>Analyze change in various contexts | • Develop fluency with basic number combinations for multiplication and division and use these combinations to mentally compute related problems such as $30 \times 50$<br>• Describe, extend, and make generalizations about geometric and numeric patterns<br>• Represent and analyze patterns and functions, using words, tables, and graphs<br>• Identify such properties as commutativity, associativity, and distributivity and use them to compute with whole numbers<br>• Represent the idea of a variable as an unknown quantity using a letter or a symbol<br>• Express mathematical relationships using equations<br>• Model problem situations with objects and use representations such as graphs, tables, and equations to draw conclusions<br>• Identify and describe situations with constant or varying rates of change and compare them |

they need to participate fully in classroom activities and discussions. As evidenced by Kitchen's reflections on mathematics instruction (see Diversity in the Classroom), this principle is of great importance to mathematics educators.

Additional attention was given to students with disabilities in that the NCTM recognized that these students may need increased time to complete assignments and could benefit from modified assessments and additional resources. The NCTM strongly urged schools and school districts to make accommodations for these students. Suggestions such as after-school programs, peer mentoring, or cross-age tutoring were given as examples of possible accommodations.

Although the equity principle does recommend accommodations for students with disabilities, special educators and researchers have voiced some concern for this issue since the 1989 standards. Cawley, Baker-Kroczynski, and Urban (1992) remark that "both the standards and the extent to which they are ultimately implemented in the schools have deep implications for professionals involved with the education of children with disabilities. No comparable statement of goals and outcomes for mathematics exists within the special education community" (p. 40). Furthermore, Maccini and Gagnon (2000) comment that the recommendations are challenging for teachers of students with disabilities, especially at the secondary level. At the secondary level, students with disabilities will be required to engage in high-level mathematical reasoning and problem solving. For students who already have trouble with a wide range of mathematical tasks, the challenge will be great for all teachers servicing students with special needs.

To meet the current challenges, teachers must reflect on the purpose of mathematics instruction. If the ultimate goal in mathematics instruction of learners with special needs is to help them prepare for using mathematics at a later point in their lives, programs must include content that is based on the type of mathematics that will be needed. For instance, the math programs appropriate for students going on to higher education must be different from programs designed for students who will be entering the workforce immediately after leaving school.

## DIVERSITY IN THE CLASSROOM *Tips*

**Richard Kitchen** is an associate professor of mathematics education at the University of New Mexico. His primary research interests are in mathematics education in the areas of teacher education, equity, and assessment.

In my classes for prospective P-12 teachers, my primary goal is to engage in dialogue with and model equitable instructional strategies that they can use when they start teaching. These strategies are intended to promote the academic learning and achievement of all learners, particularly diverse students from populations that are historically underrepresented in mathematics and the sciences (e.g., Hispanics and American Indians). In general, these strategies can be encapsulated as both preparing prospective teachers to implement mathematics curriculum and instruction consistent with reform visions put forth by the National Council of Teachers of Mathematics and others, and challenging prospective teachers to continually reflect upon how to value and integrate their students' backgrounds and life experiences in their teaching.

Mathematics education reforms stress the need for a problem-solving curriculum and instructional strategies that foster students' understanding of mathematical ideas. Pedagogy inspired by this view engages students in posing and solving problems, making and proving conjectures, exploring puzzles, sharing and debating ideas, and contemplating the beauty of ideas in an academic discipline. In mathematics courses I teach for prospective teachers, students are frequently solving problems and verbally sharing their problem solving strategies with their peers. Additionally, they are asked questions that clarify and extend their solutions rather than simply showing them how to solve problems.

I try to actively demonstrate how to value equity, diversity, and multiculturalism. For instance, I model and discuss the importance of holding high academic expectations for all students. Though we may not always be aware of it, many of us grow up unconsciously believing that only some students are really meant to be successful in school. To have high expectations for all students does not mean that all students will necessarily learn and achieve at the same levels. However, it does entail believing that we as teachers can help *all* students learn at high levels to develop their unique human potential. Furthermore, I believe that in addition to having high expectations, successful teachers affirm and actively value the diverse cultural backgrounds of their students. Before this can happen, though, I am convinced that prospective mathematics teachers must personally identify with individual students different from themselves. This is important so students feel included in mathematics. I try to make transparent in my classes the contributions of women and peoples of all nations to the development of mathematics.

In summary, my goal for prospective teachers of mathematics is to help them create a vision for their mathematics classrooms that contrasts strongly with traditional instruction. I want them to challenge themselves to hold high expectations for all their students and to value the uniqueness of each of their students. One last thing—I encourage all new teachers to collaborate with their colleagues to learn how to teach mathematics in dynamic, equitable, and culturally affirming ways. This work is challenging and extremely rewarding, especially when done with others committed to ensuring your school becomes an exceptional place for the teaching and learning of mathematics for all.

Because the special education community has not developed its own set of standards or goals for math, one must consider how each school and school system will address the implementation of Standards 2000. Perhaps a fundamental goal of all programs should be to teach consistent methods for solving number-related problems encountered in everyday situations. In essence, this goal is not inconsistent with Standards 2000. If this is so, then teachers must be aware of the major life demands of adulthood that require math proficiency. Furthermore, students must receive systematic, direct instruction so that they will acquire a range of mathematical skills extending beyond computational competence. Concepts of money management, time, estimation, and geometry are likely to play greater roles in a person's life than computational skills (Patton, Cronin, Bassett, & Koppel, 1997). Implicit within the goals of mathematics education for students with learning problems is the idea that these students must receive opportunities, encouragement, and instruction on using fundamental math skills to solve everyday problems.

## The National and International Achievement Studies

In 1994–1995, the Third International Mathematics and Science Study (TIMSS) was published (National Science Board, 1998). This cross-national comparative study of student achievement in mathematics and science compared test scores and educational systems across 42 countries (Schmidt, Houang, & Cogan, 2002). The results of this study indicated that 4th-grade students in the United States ranked high. Unfortunately, by 8th-grade U.S. students scored below average when compared to peers across several nations. More concerning, however, was that 12th-grade U.S. students demonstrated the poorest achievement as they scored near the bottom of the list of nations. Again, the results of the TIMSS placed educators on alert as no other country's scores showed such a deterioration of progress in mathematical knowledge (Loveless & Diperna, 2000).

The Programme for International Student Achievement (PISA) study echoed the results of the TIMSS in that the U.S. students scored below the international average (Organization for Economics Co-Operation and Development, 2004). Similarly, the U.S. National Assessment of Educational Progress (NAEP) conducted their own studies (National Center for Educational Statistics, 2000, 2003). In their report, called "Nation's Report Card," they indicated that 4th-grade students had made the greatest improvement over a 30-year period. Unfortunately, 12th-grade students had shown no significant gains since 1990.

The results of these international studies prompted many educators and researchers to reexamine the mathematics curricula in the United States. The consensus was that the U.S. mathematics curricula (as well as the science curricula) were described as "a mile wide and an inch deep (United States National Research Center for TIMSS, 1996). Researchers (e.g., Coyne et al., 2007; Lenz & Deshler, 2004; Marchand-Martello et al., 2004; Stein, Kinder, Silbert, & Carnine, 2006) have indicated that the spiraling curricula in the United States is unfocused and covers many more topics than the countries that produced high mathematics scores on international achievement tests.

## Need for a Focused Curricula

Underscoring the consensus concerning the broad scope of the U.S. mathematics curricula, the National Council of Teachers of Mathematics acknowledged that our country's mathematics curricula has resulted in a lack of clear, consistent priorities and focus. In their September 2006 publication entitled *Curriculum Focal Points for Prekindergarten through Grade 8 Mathematics: A Quest for Coherence*, the NCTM further acknowledged that teachers are stretched "to find the time to present important mathematical topics effectively in depth" (p. vii). This document was written as an initial step toward providing a more coherent and focused curriculum (preK–8) and begins a collaborative dialogue regarding what students should know and be able to do in mathematics.

The NCTM regards the curriculum focal points as "mathematical topics for each of grade level." These topics are designed to organize or structure the curriculum and instruction of mathematics for children. They are meant to be goals and desirable learning expectations that organize content and connect concepts that are to be taught. Because of this clearer focus, the NCTM (2006) also recognizes that the focal points can be much more important when it comes to diverse learners and students with disabilities. They state:

> The decision to organize instruction around focal points assumes that the learning of mathematics is cumulative, with work in the later grades building on and deepening what students have learned in the earlier grades, without repetitious and inefficient reteaching. A curriculum built on focal points also has the potential to offer opportunities for the diagnosis of difficulties and immediate intervention, thus helping students who are struggling with important mathematics content. (p. 5)

Examples of the focal points, by grades level, will be presented later in this chapter. The intent of the examples is to give teachers a perspective of the goals needed when organizing their mathematic curriculum.

## No Child Left Behind

One of the most recent national initiatives regarding educational reform took place in 2002 with the No Child Left Behind (NCLB) Act. This Act had two major purposes: (a) to raise student achievement so that all students have access to our competitive society with changing job requirements and advances in technology; and (b) to eliminate the achievement gaps among students of diverse populations (this includes students with disabilities) (see Chapter 1). The NCLB requirements reinforce the standards-based educational reform. The goals, therefore, are to raise standards as well as close achievement gaps. These goals and requirements impact mathematics education as well. What is important to consider, however, is the difficulty educators will have in fulfilling these goals. Lenz and Deshler (2004) have written extensively in this area and their concern regarding how this educational reform movement affects our diverse populations must be noted. With regard to students with disabilities, students from ethnically and linguistically diverse populations, as well as students from low SES families, Lenz and Deshler (2004) state:

> Discrepancies in achievement between groups should prompt us to set instructional goals to close gaps. However, that is not simple in an educational, social, and political system as complex as ours. Various groups with different access to power compete for finite educational resources. Moreover, educational research and practice lag behind the needs of many learners, and no one is quite sure exactly how to reach our national goals, no matter how lofty the rhetoric and well-intentioned the effort. (p. 26)

Lenz and Deshler go on to address the needs of these students. How we approach the unique instructional aspects of these children can greatly reflect on the conditions that are prerequisites for learning. The authors outline the variables that might impact student learning, equity, and barriers to the reforms being presented. These variables, or prerequisites, can be examined by the following questions:

1. Do all students have access to reasonable supplies of learning materials and decent facilities?
2. Do all students have qualified teachers who know the subjects that they are asked to teach?
3. Have the teachers had extensive professional development experiences aligned with the new standards? Do they understand the standards sufficiently well to develop or adopt appropriate curricula and teaching practices?
4. Is the school management team making decisions consistent with reform goals and analyzing troubling patterns of achievement among groups in order to reprioritize resources? (Lenz & Deshler, 2004, p. 38)

In essence, the questions outlined by Lenz and Deshler make a case for good instruction of teachers as well as good instruction for children. These questions are directly applicable to the instruction of mathematics and the special education teachers of mathematics. This chapter addresses good instruction by presenting evidence-based practices in assessment of mathematics as well as its instruction for elementary, middle, and secondary students.

**Reflective Question 9–1:** ***How is your school addressing the many aspects of systemic reform in mathematics instruction?***

## ASSESSMENT

Let us assume that Ashley responds to the following algorithm as indicated: $13 - 7 = \partial$. Is the response right or wrong? The teacher's decision may depend on any number of factors, such as knowledge of the student and/or the objectives that have been established for this activity. For instance, if Ashley frequently writes the numeral 6 this way, the teacher may accept her response as correct arithmetically. The important point is that teachers sometimes need to dig a little deeper to understand fully how a student is performing, and they need to remember what information they are evaluating.

Educational assessment is the systematic process whereby information about students is collected and used to make decisions about them. One of the more educationally relevant questions that should be asked and answered is, What are the student's strengths and weaknesses? In other words, a major instructional reason for assessing students is to obtain diagnostic information. Other motivations for assessing students may stem from a need to determine eligibility for services, to choose the most suitable placement option, or to evaluate student progress or program effectiveness. All these reasons for assessing students occur daily in educational settings and are inexorably entwined with providing appropriate education. Nevertheless, the problems inherent in this process demand caution.

Typically, assessment is equated with testing. Although testing is one way to answer some educationally relevant questions, it is not the only way. Information about students can and should be obtained through other techniques as well: direct observation of students' behaviors; interviews, checklists, and rating scales; and examination of students' work. Assessment in mathematics should utilize all of these techniques but should not be limited solely to a demonstration of arithmetic skills. Affective dimensions (e.g., how students feel about math) as well as communication and process evaluation (e.g., how students are able to communicate their math knowledge as well as their critical thinking skills) are worth investigating, too.

### Standardized Measures of General Achievement

General achievement instruments are formal devices that usually assess a range of skill domains (e.g., reading, mathematics, written language) and result in a variety of derived scores (e.g., percentiles, standard scores, grade equivalents). These norm-referenced tests are designed to show how a student's score compares with the scores of other students on whom the test was standardized. From an instructional perspective, such tests do provide some general indication of the skill/subject areas in which students are strong or are having difficulty. However, these instruments are not intended to be diagnostic and therefore offer little information and guidance about student needs or where to start teaching.

There are two major types of achievement tests: individual and group. Individual tests have enjoyed a great deal of popularity in special education. Some of the more commonly used include tests such as the Wide Range Achievement Test—III (Wilkinson & Robertson, 2006) and the Diagnostic Achievement Battery—3 (Newcomer, 2001). Most individual achievement tests are developed for school-age populations. If one requires standardized data related to math performance for adult populations, then one is referred to tests that extend coverage to this age range (e.g., Wide Range Achievement Test—III [WRAT-III]) or to tests that are developed specifically for adult groups (e.g., Scholastic Abilities Test for Adults).

Both types of achievement tests are limited from an instructional perspective, as they give only one or two different samples of any major skill area. As a result, they may not tap certain skills at all and do not provide enough examples to establish error patterns.

## Standardized Diagnostic Measures

Instruments that assess specific academic areas in more detail than the general achievement measures help teachers determine particular problems and strengths of students. For the most part, instruments in this category are attractive because of their potential diagnostic usefulness; they usually contain a number of mathematically related subtests. Some of the more frequently used instruments are featured in Table 9–2.

Some of these tests may not be as diagnostic as teachers would like them to be. There are a limited number of behavioral samples for specific subskills within each subtest and, if derived scores are the only items used, diagnostic usefulness decreases. Thus, to obtain the information necessary to plan instructional interventions, teachers must augment these tests with informal, teacher-constructed measures. For example, if a student has difficulty with two items on an addition subtest (66 + 4 and 86 + 29), then it is advisable to explore this skill with additional problems (16 + 8 + 15, 37 + 20, 66 + 44, 145 + 159, 390 + 148, 524 + 386). Such an analysis provides a more detailed assessment of the pupil's ability to do two- and three-digit addition problems that require regrouping and handling a zero.

## Diagnostic Test of Arithmetic Strategies (DTAS)

The DTAS (Ginsburg & Mathews, 1984) is an individually administered diagnostic instrument designed to analyze the strategies that students use to perform arithmetic calculations in addition, subtraction, multiplication, and division. It is useful to teachers who work with students who are having difficulty in these computational areas. Each subtest is divided into four parts:

1. **Setting up the problem:** setup only, no calculations are performed.
2. **Number facts:** students respond to basic problems presented to them visually.
3. **Written calculation:** students work problems while verbalizing what they are doing.
4. **Informal skills:** students work problems using pencil and paper while verbalizing what they are doing.

The stimulus items for the "Written Calculations" part of the DTAS are presented in Figure 9–1. Each problem that the student is asked to perform and verbalize is analyzed with the help of the checklist shown in Figure 9–2. If used appropriately, this form can assist teachers in pinpointing where a student is having basic factual or procedural problems.

## Curriculum-Based Measures

The most instructionally useful methods of assessing mathematical performance and diagnosing math difficulties are measures based on the curriculum being used. This approach allows an in-depth probe of specific skills based on the types of problems encountered in everyday instructional situations and instructional goals set for students.

A procedure that can be followed in collecting curriculum-based data is to ask students to complete a sheet containing multiple samples of math skills that are being taught (Figure 9–3). Students are given 2 minutes to solve as many of these items as they can. This sheet and alternative forms of it are administered on a regular basis. The results of each data collection can be graphed; decisions can be made as to whether students are progressing toward the intended goal.

**TABLE 9–2** Formal, standardized diagnostic tests

| *Test* | *Grade Appropriateness* | *Subtests* | *Results* | *Remarks* |
|---|---|---|---|---|
| KeyMath—Revised: A Diagnostic Inventory of Essential Mathematics (KeyMath-R) (Connolly, Nachtman, & Pritchett, 2007) | Grades K–8 | 3 areas/13 subtests/43 domains:<br>Basic concepts<br>Numeration<br>Rational numbers<br>Geometry<br>Operations<br>Addition<br>Subtraction<br>Multiplication<br>Division<br>Mental computation<br>Applications<br>Measurement<br>Time and money<br>Estimation<br>Interpreting data<br>Problem solving | Derived scores for total test and area composites:<br>Standard scores (mean = 100, S.D. = 15)<br>Grade equivalents<br>Age equivalents<br>Percentile ranks<br>Stanine<br>Normal curve equivalents<br>Derived scores for individual subtests:<br>Standard scores (mean = 10, S.D. = 3)<br>Percentile ranks<br>Domain performance scores | Individually administered<br>Two Forms—A and B<br>Two easels<br>Each subtest composed of 3–4 domains<br>Written responses required on subtests in operations<br>Software available for converting scores and developing profiles |
| Stanford Diagnostic Mathematics Test (SDMT) (Beatty, Gardner, Madden, & Karlsen, 1985) | Grade 2–12 | 3 subtests: Number system and numeration<br>Computation<br>Applications | Center-referenced scores<br>Norm-referenced scores<br>Percentile<br>Stanines<br>Norm curve equivalents<br>Scaled scores | Group administered<br>Four overlapping levels:<br>Red: Grades 2–4<br>Green: Grades 4–6<br>Brown: Grades 6–8<br>Blue: Grades 8–12 |
| Test of Mathematical Abilities (TOMA—2) (Brown, Cronin, & McEntire, 1994) | Grades 3–12 | 5 subtests:<br>Vocabulary<br>Computation<br>General information<br>Story problems<br>Attitude toward math | Derived scores for total test and composites:<br>Standard scores (mean = 100, S.D. = 15)<br>Percentiles<br>Age equivalents<br>Grade equivalents | All subtests except general information can be group administered |

Advantages of **curriculum-based measurement** approaches are many. For example, (a) items or problems assess a specific skill; (b) tests include enough problems to ensure knowledge or lack of knowledge regarding a specific skill; (c) if the teacher has any doubts about the test results, similar problems can be constructed and given to the pupil, and those results can be checked against previous results; and (d) student-specific data can guide instructionally meaningful decisions.

## Informal Diagnostic Techniques

One way to obtain diagnostically useful information is to expand on and/or subdivide concepts and skills found in formal instruments. For instance, a student might miss items on the WRAT-III designed to assess the concepts of "more" and "less" because of an inability to identify or recognize the numerals (or their value) or because of a lack of understanding of the concepts of more and less. (The specific WRAT-III assessment items are "Which is more: 9 or 6?" and "Which is more: 42 or 28?"). In this case, to determine numerical identification and recognition, the teacher might present index cards to the student with one numeral on each card and have the student respond by naming each numeral. If the student hesitates or misses a particular numeral, the card should be presented again later to assess consistency. Another approach would be to present a group of numerals on a sheet of paper, pronounce a number, and ask the student to respond by pointing to that numeral. To determine whether numerical values are understood, the teacher might present an index card with a

| 5 | 6 | 7 | 8 |
|---|---|---|---|
| 32<br>× 3 | 24<br>× 2 | 43<br>× 21 | 32<br>× 23 |
| 9 | 10 | 11 | 12 |
| 93<br>× 6 | 46<br>× 7 | 438<br>× 40 | 613<br>× 30 |
| 13 | 14 | 15 | 16 |
| 67<br>× 74 | 76<br>× 35 | 459<br>×243 | 864<br>×154 |

**FIGURE 9–1** Written calculations part of DTAS

*Source:* From *Diagnostic Test of Arithmetic Strategies*, by H. P. Ginsburg and S. C. Mathews, 1984, Austin, TX: PRO-ED. Copyright 1984 by PRO-ED. Reprinted with permission.

numeral on it and instruct the student to give the teacher the corresponding number of checkers. The task can be varied by instructing the student to select two checkers, five checkers, nine checkers, and so on.

By subdividing and expanding the concepts and skills assessed by informal tests, teachers can begin to pinpoint the difficulties students have in acquiring specific arithmetic understanding, comprehension, and skills. Some effort is required here, as most standardized instruments do not provide guidance or assistance in analyzing individual responses. The following diagnostic techniques may be used to analyze individual student responses.

**Error Patterns.** Carefully examining the work samples of students often provides clues to patterns in the types of errors they are making. Upon close examination, a teacher can determine the error pattern a student is demonstrating, and reteach to correct the problem (Ashlock, 2006).

Computational errors can be classified into different categories. One possible system is outlined as follows:

- Random responding (RR): Student errors are without any recognizable reason.
- Basic fact error (BF): Student performs the operation correctly, but makes a simple error (addition, etc.).
- Wrong operation (WO): Student performs the wrong operation (e.g., adds instead of subtracts).
- Defective algorithm (DA): Student does not perform the operation appropriately; the steps involved are out of sequence or are performed improperly.

**FIGURE 9–2** Checklist for written calculations

| | Problems | | | | | | | | | | | |
|---|---|---|---|---|---|---|---|---|---|---|---|---|
| | 5 | 6 | 7 | 8 | 9 | 10 | 11 | 12 | 13 | 14 | 15 | 16 |
| 1. Answer | | | | | | | | | | | | |
| Correct (circle) | 96 | 48 | 903 | 736 | 558 | 322 | 17,520 | 18,390 | 4,958 | 2,660 | 111,537 | 133,056 |
| Incorrect (write in) | ___ | ___ | ___ | ___ | ___ | ___ | ___ | ___ | ___ | ___ | ___ | ___ |
| 2. Standard school method | ___ | ___ | ___ | ___ | ___ | ___ | ___ | ___ | ___ | ___ | ___ | ___ |
| 3. Informal method | ___ | ___ | ___ | ___ | ___ | ___ | ___ | ___ | ___ | ___ | ___ | ___ |
| 4. Number fact error | ___ | ___ | ___ | ___ | ___ | ___ | ___ | ___ | ___ | ___ | ___ | ___ |
| 5. Bugs | | | | | | | | | | | | |
| A. Units by units, tens by tens | ___ | ___ | ___ | ___ | ___ | ___ | ___ | ___ | ___ | ___ | ___ | ___ |
| B. Partial product problems | | | ___ | ___ | | | | | ___ | ___ | ___ | ___ |
| C. Addition errors | | | | | ___ | ___ | ___ | | ___ | ___ | ___ | ___ |
| D. Crutch difficulties | | | | | ___ | ___ | ___ | | ___ | ___ | ___ | ___ |
| E. Zero makes no difference | | | | | | | ___ | ___ | | | | |
| F. No need to write zero | | | | | | | ___ | ___ | | | | |
| G. Left to right | ___ | ___ | ___ | ___ | ___ | ___ | ___ | ___ | ___ | ___ | ___ | ___ |
| H. Other | ___ | ___ | ___ | ___ | ___ | ___ | ___ | ___ | ___ | ___ | ___ | ___ |
| 6. Slips | | | | | | | | | | | | |
| A. Skips numbers | ___ | ___ | ___ | ___ | ___ | ___ | ___ | ___ | ___ | ___ | ___ | ___ |
| B. Multiplies or adds twice; uses wrong number | ___ | ___ | ___ | ___ | ___ | ___ | ___ | ___ | ___ | ___ | ___ | ___ |
| C. Other | ___ | ___ | ___ | ___ | ___ | ___ | ___ | ___ | ___ | ___ | ___ | ___ |

*Notes:* ______________________________

*Source:* From *Diagnostic Test of Arithmetic Strategies*, by H. P. Ginsburg and S. C. Mathews, 1984, Austin, TX: PRO-ED. Copyright 1984 by PRO-ED. Reprinted with permission.

- Place value problems (PV): To some extent this category is a subset of the previous category. The student knows the facts and the beginning stages of an operation but is deficient in some aspect of place value.

Whether teachers use this or another system, recognizing students' systematic errors is a diagnostic skill that has great bearing on determining the focus of instruction.

**Task Analysis.** The process of **task analysis** can be utilized to determine a hierarchical sequence. Diagnostic information may be obtained from checklists corresponding to thorough task analyses of specific computational operations. These lists can be found in commercial instruments or they can be developed by teachers based on their understanding of different arithmetic procedures. Table 9-3 is an example of one such task analysis. Knowledge of the steps involved in solving this particular subtraction problem can be used to help isolate specific problems.

**Student Verbalizations.** An extremely useful practice for determining the nature of the problems that students are experiencing in math is to have them verbalize the procedure they are employing in solving a given task. After such an analysis, teaching strategies

| 12 | 33 | 43 | 26 | 55 |
|---|---|---|---|---|
| + 23 | + 26 | + 44 | + 51 | + 23 |
| 56 | 42 | 52 | 66 | 71 |
| + 11 | + 20 | + 32 | + 33 | + 24 |
| 55 | 68 | 16 | 79 | 30 |
| + 44 | + 21 | + 52 | + 10 | + 56 |
| 37 | 17 | 76 | 62 | 45 |
| + 12 | + 72 | + 22 | + 36 | + 41 |

**FIGURE 9–3** Sample curriculum-based assessment sheet

can be developed to address the specific problems. This is not a difficult procedure to use, but it does require teachers to structure their class periods such that they have an opportunity to work individually with students. The benefits of scheduling time for this activity far outweigh the hassles of scheduling the time.

**Interviews.** Researchers such as D. Clark, Stephens, and Waywood (1992) have investigated the advantages of evaluating students' communication and learning of mathematics through interviewing techniques. The hypothesis that students can learn through guided self-questioning and suggested self-management of learning (Briggs, 1988) is tested by asking questions that reflect the students' ability to communicate their mathematics knowledge as well as give the instructors insight into their problem-solving ability. Generic questions such as (a) "What was the best thing to happen in mathematics?" (b) "What is the biggest worry affecting your work in mathematics?" (c) "How do you feel in mathematics class?" and (d) "How could we improve mathematics classes?" are found to show students' conceptions of mathematics as well as their increased use of technical mathematical terms (D. J. Clark, 1987). Other, more specific questions or directives such as (a) "What would you most like more help with?" (b) "Write down one particular problem that you found difficult." (c) "Write down one new problem that you can now do," and (d) "How could we improve mathematics classes?" are beneficial in that students report attitudes and say whether procedures are useful to them. In response to these questions, teachers seem to take a proactive approach to teaching by engaging in more organization, instruction, individual assistance, and counseling. D. J. Clark (1985) also reports that several instances were documented in which teacher reaction to interview questions led to positive changes in student attitude and achievement.

**Journal Writing.** Journal writing is an opportunity to introduce self-evaluation skills to students in connection with mathematics learning. Through journal writing, teachers may be able to identify whether students are choosing to use mathematical procedures, principles, and facts without being cued or questioned on tests. Journal writing may be able to identify when students are distinguishing strategies within the problem-solving process. Additionally, students may be able to report in their journals a systematic approach of reviewing what

**TABLE 9–3** Task analysis of a subtraction problem

*Computational Task:* $\begin{array}{r} 400 \\ -\ 175 \\ \hline \end{array}$

**Prerequisite Skills Required**

1. Visually discriminate numbers
2. Write numerals
3. Follow written or oral directions
4. Name numerals
5. Match numerals
6. Identify the minus sign
7. Given the minus sign, state the concept of take-away
8. Compare basic subtraction facts
9. State the concept of regrouping for computing problems that require regrouping

**Math Procedures Required**

1. Identify the problem as subtraction
2. Identify the starting point
3. Recognize state, refuse to compute 0 minus 5
4. Move to the tens column to regroup
5. Recognize, state, refuse to group 0 tens
6. Move to the hundreds column
7. Identify 4 hundreds as a number than can be regrouped
8. Regroup the hundreds
   a. Cross out 4
   b. Write 3 above 4
   c. Place 1 on tens column
9. Regroup tens
   a. Cross out 10
   b. Write 9 above 10 in tens column
   c. Place 1 on ones column
10. Subtract 10 minus 5
11. Write 5
12. Subtract 9 minus 7
13. Write 2
14. Subtract 3 minus 1
15. Write 2
16. Read the answer correctly (225)

they know. Such approaches may include the discussion of planning, decision making, verifying, and evaluating their solutions. Finally, journal writing can show teachers whether students are motivated in the mathematics classes, whether they are developing appropriate work habits, and their concepts of the purpose of mathematical activities (Clark et al., 1992). When students are asked to write in their journals after every mathematics class, a continuous dialogue between students and teacher can result.

Clark et al. (1992) note that despite the benefits of journal writing, students may find it a challenging experience, demanding of their time and concentration. Teachers who use journal writing do, however, report that improvement in students' journal writing is seen over the year and particularly across several years.

**Reflective Question 9–2:** ***Which assessment procedures best complement your teaching approach to mathematics instruction?***

## MATHEMATICS INSTRUCTIONAL CONSIDERATIONS

A variety of general factors should guide programming in mathematics. Many of these issues are closely related and are as applicable to other subject areas as they are to mathematics. Nevertheless, they are of particular importance when teaching mathematical skills.

Every school system has a scope and sequence for math skill development. Most mathematics programs are developed in compliance with the organization suggested by such systems. Some argue that the scope of mathematics programs for students with special needs should be reexamined in light of what they will need as adults. Others (e.g., Cawley, 2002) have raised questions about the sequencing (i.e., when math topics are covered) of math programs. Cawley and his colleagues suggest that we do not have to adhere to the traditional sequence of teaching addition and subtraction before multiplication and division.

Many learners with special needs require that their programs reflect a realistic examination of their subsequent environments. If postsecondary education is not likely, then the curriculum should reflect a strong orientation toward the life skills and knowledge needed to survive in the community and on the job; that is, an adult outcomes mathematics curriculum (Cronin & Patton, 2007). Students for whom higher education is likely should be in programs that will prepare them for these settings. School systems must remain sensitive to a range of student needs, individual personal goals, and probable subsequent environments when developing programs.

### Concept and Skill Development

Within mathematics education in general there is some debate over two different instructional approaches: didactic and discovery. The didactic approach stresses initial instruction in basic skills development, followed by the application of these skills to problem solving. The discovery approach allows students to establish an individual understanding of the process needed to solve a problem prior to formal instruction in the basic skills. Advocates of a discovery approach believe that such an orientation enhances concept and skill development.

Teachers of students with disabilities must confront this dilemma as well. Recognizing that a discovery approach implies minimizing various prompts and teacher direction, Bartel (1990) warns that such an approach may not be warranted for those students who need various degrees of prompting.

Cawley and his colleagues (Cawley, 2002; Cawley, Fitzmaurice-Hayes, & Shaw, 1988) have stressed the importance of teaching students to understand mathematical concepts rather than forcing them to memorize rote responses to basic facts or algorithms:

> Many concepts are understood by young children long before they can perform skills. For example, young children deal quite effectively with the division of a whole number by a fraction in real situations, such as cutting an apple into halves or near-halves, even though these children have no idea of the computational algorithm. (Cawley et al., 1989, p. 1)

Any discussion of skill development needs to address the question of generalization. Opportunities for applying basic skills to new situations must be programmed systematically. Teachers should give students many chances to apply their acquired skills in new contexts and settings. One way to do this is to integrate math into other subject areas. This can be done easily in a subject like science but it can also be done in other subjects.

## Adaptations and Differentiated Mathematics Instruction

Even though drill and practice are essential to mastering certain math skills, the learning process need not be as tedious as it sometimes becomes. Variety in instructional techniques continues to be suggested (Bartel, 1990), yet it is often absent in classrooms.

Many students with learning problems need more practice than other students require. Teachers must ensure fluency and mastery of specific math skills by developing novel practice activities (Bott, 1988). Many good teachers incorporate variety into their instruction as a matter of course, and these teachers serve as good resources for ideas and assistance.

Another source of ideas for programming variety is the **interactive unit** model originally developed by Cawley et al. (1976) as part of Project math. This model

**TEACHER *Tips*** — **Elementary Level**

### Concrete, Semi-Concrete, Abstract (CSA), Learning Tactic

One method of teaching students to master mathematics concepts beyond the number sense level is to employ a three-level strategy called the Concrete, Semi-Concrete (or representational), and Abstract Strategy (e.g., Bender, 2005). This research-based instructional tool is particularly used to help children problem solve at the elementary years. The strategy involves the use of tangible objects/manipulatives that facilitate the learning of the mathematic concept (level one: Concrete). Once the students are able to grasp the concrete example of the concept, the semi-concrete level is introduced. This second level may be a representation of the concrete example (e.g., pencil/paper) so the students can move away from the manipulative. While introducing the concrete and the semi-concrete level, teachers will pair the abstract instruction so students will understand the concept once levels one and two are no longer represented.

Bender (2005) presents an example of using the Concrete level to teach the concept of basic multiplication tables using Popsicle sticks. Notice from the example that students are looking, feeling, and verbally describing the multiplication table. Bender's example of teaching the three's times tables is as follows:

> Students may use three sticks to make a triangle on their desk. Then they count the sides (which equal three). They should then say, "One triangle with three sides equals three Popsicle sticks" and then shorten that to "One times three equals three."
>
> Next, they add another triangle and count all of the sides (which equal six). They would say, "Two triangles with three sides each equal six sticks" or "Two times three equals six." They continue this process until they have ten triangles on their desks, representing the entire times table.
>
> The same activity can be repeated using squares to represent multiples of four and stars to represent fives and sixes. (p. 58)

focuses on the interaction of teacher, students, and skill area while allowing a great deal of instructional variation. The teacher can provide instruction by:

- manipulating something (e.g., physical action)
- displaying something to the students (e.g., materials or pictures)
- saying something (e.g., verbal instructions or directions)
- writing something (e.g., on worksheet or chalkboard)

The student can respond in four ways:

- by manipulating something (e.g., working with physical materials)
- by identifying something (e.g., pointing to or circling)
- by saying something (e.g., responding verbally)
- by writing something (i.e., using some form of graphic symbols—numerals or words)

The various combinations of teacher action and student response allow 16 ways to vary instruction. The virtue of this model is that it allows the teacher great flexibility when planning instruction for a variety of student needs; moreover, it allows the teacher to program instructional variation into math lessons. Figure 9–4 illustrates how this interactive idea can be used with three groups of students working on distinctly different skills: addition, geometry, and fractions. It also shows how the teacher–student interaction can be scheduled to provide direct teacher contact for all groups.

Many students will need certain modifications to their curriculum, instructional materials, and/or teaching procedures. Table 9–4 provides a list of suggestions that may be appropriate for accommodating specific needs. Close inspection of the table shows that the ideas contained in the interactive unit model can serve as a resource for making needed modifications.

## General Instructional Approaches

Currently, mathematics instruction recognizes two major approaches to teaching mathematics. One approach is frequently connected to the constructivist approach that is linked to the work of Piaget and Vygotsky. This approach focuses on student-centered and discovery-oriented instruction. The second approach is explicit instruction or an approach that encompasses "direct instruction and is derived from the research literature on teacher effectiveness" (Stein et al., 2006). Because of the differences in these two approaches, many individuals regard the two approaches to be in conflict with one another.

In an interview (Tilly, 2006), Fuchs was asked about the math war that is occurring. Her response indicated that although the constructivist approach clearly dominates general education mathematics instruction today, both approaches are needed. Some children respond well to the constructivist approach, but other children are in clear need of explicit instruction. Clear assessment as to student progress should be the variable in determining the decision as to which approach to use.

Since this is an era of accountability, where teachers are required to use evidenced-based instruction and interventions, teachers are urged to seek out those instructional methods and curricula that are researched and produce effective results for students with disabilities. Stein and her colleagues (2006) note how teachers conduct specific instruction, and design instructional strategies could have an impact on student performances in mathematics. These findings indicate that commercial programs must consider the instruction of teachers; how they teach and what they teach are primary factors in student performance. The approach teachers adopt for their instruction is crucial to the success of their students. With increasing attention being given to mathematics, new programs and materials appear on a regular basis. Some of the most recent instructionally useful materials are microcomputer software programs and other multimedia programs. This section presents major approaches to mathematics instruction that can be used with students who have problems in this area.

**Basal Textbook Approach.** The most frequently employed approach to teaching math is the use of basal textbooks, which all major publishers produce. These textbooks are written primarily for students in general education math classes; however, most teacher's editions included in these series offer suggestions for addressing the needs of students with learning-related problems. Nevertheless, teachers of students who are experiencing difficulties in math must be prepared to augment and/or adapt these texts as necessary.

Although there are many commonalties across basal series, there are notable differences as well. Before selecting a specific series, teachers should evaluate the instructional features of each thoroughly. In particular, attention should be directed to the teacher's edition,

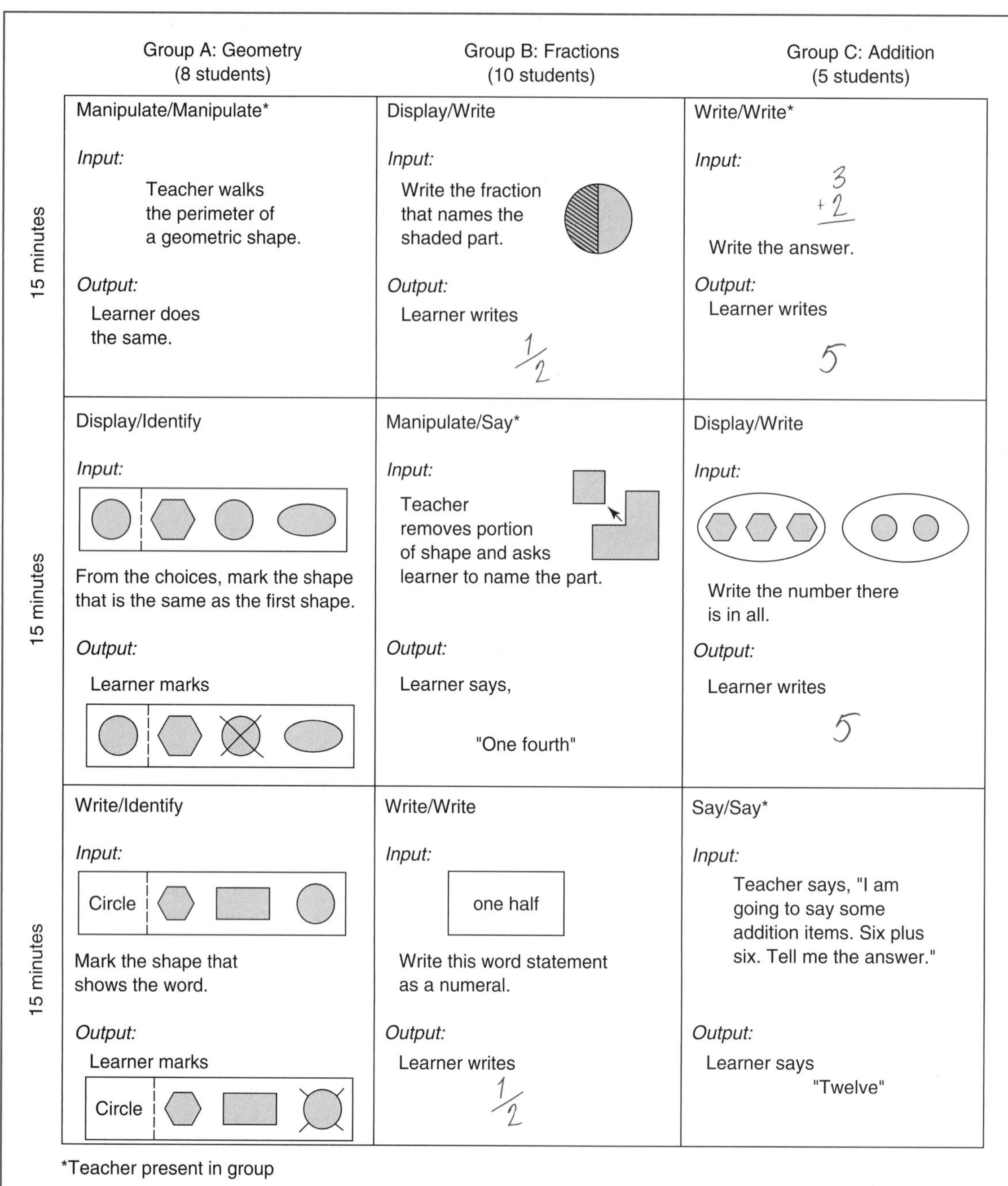


**FIGURE 9–4** Interactive unit model

*Source:* From *Developmental Teaching of Mathematics for the Learning Disabled* (p. 246), by J. F. Cawley (Ed.), 1984, Austin, TX: PRO-ED. Copyright 1984 by PRO-ED, Inc. Reprinted with permission.

the student textbook/workbook, and any supporting materials that accompany the series.

The more attractive series include specific suggestions for dealing with diverse needs and offer ways to augment lessons. A key variable to consider is the amount of practice included to achieve mastery of the skill(s) being taught. Many commercially available textbooks now come with sets of supplementary hands-on materials as well, which must be evaluated in terms of students' needs.

**TABLE 9–4** Modification of instruction in mathematics for students with learning disabilities

| *Instructional Modification (Stage of Learning)* | *Description* | *Examples* |
| --- | --- | --- |
| Modify the content (acquisition). | Alter the type or amount of information presented to a student; substitute content. | A unit on rate-time-distance algebraic problems is not taught to a seventh-grade student; instead, the student is given extra practice learning how to balance a checkbook. A third-grade student is provided with the correct answers to a set of story problems—the student's task is only to describe how the correct answer was obtained. |
| Modify the nature of teacher input (acquisition and generalization). | Alter the input from the teacher (e.g., manipulate, display, say, write); repeat or simplify instructions; read the questions to the student (rather than telling the student to read). | Before having a second-grade student begin work on a page of subtraction and addition problems, the teacher requires the student to point to the operation sign of each problem and orally state whether the problem requires addition or subtraction. |
| Adjust the instructional pace or sequence (acquisition, proficiency, maintenance, and generalization). | Alter the length or frequency of instructional periods; slow down the rate of presentation; defer the introduction of certain content; provide more frequent reviews. | The teacher plans two 15-minute math periods each day rather than one 30-minute period. Worksheets are kept to a maximum of six problems each. |
| Use alternative teaching techniques (all stages). | Change some aspect of verbal instruction, demonstration, modeling, rehearsal, drill and practice, prompts and cues, feedback, reinforcement, or error contingencies. | The teacher provides step-by-step direct supervision for each of three long division questions during the acquisition stage of instruction; feedback is given on each step of the process. |
| Alter the demands of the task (all stages). | Allow use of a calculator; allow the student to make pointing rather than oral responses or oral rather than written responses. | The teacher allows a third-grade student to use counting beads as an adjunct to completing a worksheet. The teacher works orally for a few minutes each day with a first-grade student who has difficulty writing. |
| Change the instructional delivery system (all stages). | Change the *primary instructional personnel* (use peer tutors, classroom aides, or itinerant or consultant teachers); change the *instructional format* (use computer-assisted instruction, or programmed instruction); change the *instructional context* (use small-group instruction or one-to-one instruction). | The teacher assigns a peer to play a number game and to use multiplication flashcards with a student for 3 days before any independent written work is required. For a review of making change with money, a small group of third-grade students are permitted to "play store." As a reward for completing an assignment, a student is permitted to use the computer for a game-format drill and practice on division facts. |

*Source:* From *Teaching Students with Learning and Behavior Problems* (5th ed.), by D. D. Hammill and N. R. Bartel, 1990, Austin, TX: PRO-ED. Copyright © 1990 by Allyn & Bacon. Reprinted with permission.

Textbook usage with students who have learning problems has distinct advantages as well as some disadvantages that may be characteristic of some books. Some of the advantages are:

1. Skill development is laid out in a comprehensive and sequential fashion.
2. A number of primary and supplemental materials are provided: text, teacher's edition, student workbook, ditto masters, quizzes and placement tests, and record-keeping procedures.
3. Some series are oriented to real-life situations and use student-relevant examples.

4. Some series provide a hands-on, activity-oriented approach.

Some of the disadvantages are:

1. Teacher's editions do not provide specific teaching strategies for acquisition-stage learning (e.g., scripted instructions for teachers).
2. Enough practice may not be provided (proficiency stage).
3. Movement from one skill/topic to another may be too rapid.
4. Sometimes there is not enough review of previously acquired skills and knowledge (maintenance stage).
5. Linguistic and conceptual complexity may inhibit student understanding.
6. Types of activities may have limited variety.
7. The activities may lack relevance to students.
8. Problem-solving applications are often too contrived.

**Direct Instruction.** A direct instruction approach to teaching mathematics is teacher directed, structured, and demonstrative of the components of effective instruction presented in previous chapters (Stein, Kinder, Silbert, & Carnine, 2006). According to Silbert, Cornine, and Stein (1990, p. 1), "Direct instruction provides a comprehensive set of prescriptions for organizing instruction so that students acquire, retain, and generalize new learning in as humane, efficient, and effective a manner as possible." Direct instruction (DI) is predicated on careful consideration of three major elements: (a) instructional design, (b) presentation techniques, and (c) organization of instruction. The attitude that almost all students can learn mathematics is inherent in formal DI.

Silbert et al. (1990) provide techniques for constructing effective lessons and developing specific instructional procedures. They suggest an eight-step sequence:

1. Specify objectives that are observable and measurable.
2. Devise problem-solving strategies that can be useful across situations.
3. Determine necessary preskills and teach those first.
4. Sequence skills in an appropriate order.
5. Select a teaching procedure related to the three types of tasks required of students (motor, labeling, and strategy).
6. Design instructional formats, including the specifics of what the teacher does and says, correction procedures, and anticipated student responses. (See Figure 9–5 for a sample instructional format.)
7. Select examples based on what students are learning and what they have been taught previously.
8. Provide practice and review, including guided and independent practice.

Additional instructional suggestions address maintaining student attention, teaching to criterion, selecting various instructional materials, augmenting commercial materials, assessing students, and grouping for instruction.

**Cooperative Learning.** Cooperative learning approaches involve the grouping of students so that a particular goal is accomplished by the group members. In the past, researchers (D. W. Johnson & Johnson, 1989a, 1989b; Slavin, 1989) have applied the cooperative learning method to mathematics instruction and have reported effective instructional results in primary grades.

Implementing a cooperative learning program in mathematics requires that teachers structure the group work to promote a group effort toward meeting the academic goal. Slavin (1989) states that cooperative learning is most effective when group goals and individual accountability are incorporated in the cooperative learning lesson.

One cooperative learning model is the Think-Pair-Share model (McTighe & Lyman, 1988). Using this model, students are required to follow three steps: (a) think, (b) pair, and (c) share. During the "think" step, students listen to a question or presentation about a mathematic situation and then think about how they might solve the problem.

After the children are able to think about a solution, they are grouped together to undertake the "pair" step of this model. Within their groups of pairs, students must share their ideas and solutions with their partners; this allows the students to communicate in mathematical language with one another and to practice their skills in a safe, manageable, small-group atmosphere.

The final step, the "share" step of the model, requires the teacher to place the students in larger groups. The students are then encouraged to share their paired discussions within a larger group framework. In this way different ideas are shared and students realize that there is more than one way to solve a problem.

**FIGURE 9–5** Sample instructional format for reducing fractions in Direct Instruction Math

| Day | Part A Structured Board Problems | Part B Structured Worksheet Problems | Part C Less Structured Worksheet Problems | Part D Supervised Practice Problems | Part E Independent Practice Problems |
|---|---|---|---|---|---|
| 1-2 | 4 | | | | |
| 3-4 | 2 | 6 | | | |
| 5-6 | | 2 | 6 | | |
| 7-8 | | | 2 | 6 | |
| 9-Until accurate | | | | 8 | |
| Until fluent | | | | | 8-12 |

PART A: Structured Board Presentation

| TEACHER | STUDENTS |
|---|---|
| Write on board: $\frac{8}{12} = \left(\ \right)\frac{}{}$ | |
| 1. "WE'RE GOING TO REDUCE THIS FRACTION. WE REDUCE BY PULLING OUT THE GREATEST COMMON FACTOR OF THE NUMERATOR AND DENOMINATOR. HOW DO WE REDUCE A FRACTION?" | "Pull out the greatest common factor of the numerator and denominator." |
| 2. "WE WANT TO REDUCE 8/12. WHAT IS THE GREATEST COMMON FACTOR OF 8 AND 12?" Pause. | "4" |
| TO CORRECT: Tell correct answer. Explain why student's anwer is incorrect. | |
| 3. "SO WE PULL OUT THE FRACTION 4/4. WHAT FRACTION DO WE PULL OUT OF 8/12?" | "4/4" |
| Write on board: $\frac{8}{12} = \left(\frac{4}{4}\right)\frac{}{}$ | |
| 4. "LET'S FIGURE OUT THE TOP NUMBER OF THE REDUCED FRACTION." Point to symbols as you read. "EIGHT EQUALS FOUR TIMES WHAT NUMBER?" | "2" |
| Pause. | |
| Write on board: $\frac{8}{12} = \left(\frac{4}{4}\right)\frac{2}{}$ | |
| 5. "LET'S FIGURE OUT THE BOTTOM NUMBER OF THE REDUCED FRACTION." Point to symbols as you read. "TWELVE EQUALS FOUR TIMES WHAT NUMBER?" Pause, signal. | "3" |
| Write on board: $\frac{8}{12} = \left(\frac{4}{4}\right)\frac{2}{3}$ | |
| 6. "THE FRACTION IN PARENTHESES EQUALS 1. WE DON'T CHANGE THE VALUE OF A FRACTION WHEN WE MULTIPLY BY 1. SO WE CAN CROSS OUT 4/4." Cross out. "WHEN WE PULL OUT THE FRACTION OF 1, THE REDUCED FRACTION IS 2/3. WHAT IS THE REDUCED FRACTION?" | "2/3" |

*Source:* From *Direct Instruction Mathematics* (2nd ed., p. 338), by J. Silbert, D. Carnine, and M. Stein, 1990, New York: Merrill/Prentice Hall. 

Unfortunately, caution must be taken in recommending this approach. Some research has indicated that the learning gains made, when using cooperative learning as an intervention, are minimal for students with high-incidence disabilities. Further research must be done to resolve confusion regarding these findings.

**Cognitively Demanding Instructional Approach.** The Cognitively Demanding Instructional Model (Sosniak & Ethington, 1994) is based on studies that looked at the successful student scores related to problem solving in the Second International Mathematics Study (SIMS). Sosniak and Ethington wanted to isolate what teaching variables could be accounting for the more successful student scores at the end of a particular academic period; they identified the following four components.

The first component of a successful problem-solving program is to emphasize the most difficult mathematics concepts and skills rather than focusing on the basic or easier concepts of problem solving. Sosniak and Ethington believe that teachers should emphasize the students' opportunity to learn more difficult mathematics ideas and skills. They emphasize different problem-solving activities or word problems in this area.

The second component of a successful problem-solving program relates to the type of materials the teachers use in their teaching. These authors found that successful teachers rely on teacher-created sets of materials rather than district mandates or school-selected materials. These teachers seem to personalize their teaching of problem-solving skills through carefully prepared lessons and materials that they themselves conceptualize.

The third component of a successful program focuses on the teacher behaviors of getting other students involved in the process of learning. Successful teachers call on students who do not volunteer answers as well as on students who do volunteer answers. These teachers promote an atmosphere of participation regardless of whether the students' answers are right or wrong. It is more important to know how students are conceptualizing mathematics and that they are able to communicate their thoughts than to establish whether a student has a right or wrong answer. Thus, an atmosphere of openness and acceptance of students as well as the notion of help with mathematics seems to prevail.

The fourth component looks at the teachers' beliefs about mathematics itself. Successful teachers think that mathematics is principally an intellectual matter or subject; unsuccessful teachers believe that mathematics is a procedural matter or a rule-oriented subject. The two beliefs seem to account for the different emphasis on mathematical teaching by the two groups of teachers. The more successful teachers may focus on problem-solving strategies whereas the unsuccessful teachers focus on rule-oriented strategies.

Sosniak and Ethington (1994) conclude by stating that "demanding teaching requires that teachers ask questions about content and method, examine their means for realizing them, and strive for fit activities" (p. 53). These authors state that the teacher behaviors just described accounted for approximately one fourth of the differences in student achievement between successful and unsuccessful teachers of mathematics. They note that demanding teaching is stressful and requires work, but that students benefit most by these approaches to problem solving in mathematics.

## Mathematics Instruction for Elementary Students (K–5)

Mathematics instruction for children (5–8 years of age) is very important as these young students are beginning to learn and understand arithmetic and mathematics and how they relate to the world around them. This section of the chapter will introduce the NCTM Curriculum Focal Points for children (grades K–5) and how accommodations might be made for children who begin to have trouble with learning specific mathematics skills during these early years of school.

**NCTM Curriculum Focal Points.** According to the NCTM (2006), the *Curriculum Focal Points for Mathematics* should be "considered as major instructional goals and desirable learning expectations" for children in grades prekindergarten through eighth grade. These focal points are designed to help teachers focus on specific goals in (a) number and operations and algebra, (b) geometry, and (c) measurement. Table 9–5 exhibits a sample of the elementary grade level Curriculum Focal Points and Connections to the Focal Points that are recommended by the NCTM.

**Number Sense and Number Knowledge.** When considering the learning of mathematics skills in young children, Bender (2005) discusses the concept of **number sense.** In his book on differentiated mathematics, Bender describes number sense as "a student's

**TABLE 9–5** Curriculum focal points and connections for grade 3

The set of three curriculum focal points and related connections for mathematics in grade 3 follow. These topics are the recommended content emphases for this grade level. It is essential that these focal points be addressed in contexts that promote problem solving, reasoning, communication, making connections, and designing and analyzing representations.

| *Grade 3 Curriculum Focal Points* | *Connections to the Focal Points* |
|---|---|
| ***Number and Operations and Algebra:* Developing understandings of multiplication and division and strategies for basic multiplication facts and related division facts**<br><br>Students understand the meanings of multiplication and division of whole numbers through the use of representations (e.g., equal-sized groups, arrays, area models, and equal "jumps" on number lines for multiplication, and successive subtraction, partitioning, and sharing for division). They use properties of addition and multiplication (e.g., commutativity, associativity, and the distributive property) to multiply whole numbers and apply increasingly sophisticated strategies based on these properties to solve multiplication and division problems involving basic facts. By comparing a variety of solution strategies, students relate multiplication and division as inverse operations.<br><br>***Number and Operations:* Developing an understanding of fractions and fraction equivalence**<br><br>Students develop an understanding of the meanings and uses of fractions to represent parts of a whole, parts of a set, or points or distances on a number line. They understand that the size of a fractional part is relative to the size of the whole, and they use fractions to represent numbers that are equal to, less than, or greater than 1. They solve problems that involve comparing and ordering fractions by using models, benchmark fractions, or common numerators or denominators. They understand and use models, including the number line, to identify equivalent fractions.<br><br>***Geometry:* Describing and analyzing properties of two-dimensional shapes**<br><br>Students describe, analyze, compare, and classify two-dimensional shapes by their sides and angles and connect these attributes to definitions of shapes. Students investigate, describe, and reason about decomposing, combining, and transforming polygons to make other polygons. Through building, drawing, and analyzing two-dimensional shapes, students understand attributes and properties of two-dimensional space and the use of those attributes and properties in solving problems, including applications involving congruence and symmetry. | ***Algebra:*** Understanding properties of multiplication and the relationship between multiplication and division is a part of algebra readiness that develops at grade 3. The creation and analysis of patterns and relationships involving multiplication and division should occur at this grade level. Students build a foundation for later understanding of functional relationships by describing relationships in context with such statements as, "The number of legs is 4 times the number of chairs."<br><br>***Measurement:*** Students in grade 3 strengthen their understanding of fractions as they confront problems in linear measurement that call for more precision than the whole unit allowed them in their work in grade 2. They develop their facility in measuring with fractional parts of linear units. Students develop measurement concepts and skills through experiences in analyzing attributes and properties of two-dimensional objects. They form an understanding of perimeter as a measurable attribute and select appropriate units, strategies, and tools to solve problems involving perimeter.<br><br>***Data Analysis:*** Addition, subtraction, multiplication, and division of whole numbers come into play as students construct and analyze frequency tables, bar graphs, picture graphs, and line plots and use them to solve problems.<br><br>***Number and Operations:*** Building on their work in grade 2, students extend their understanding of place value to numbers up to 10,000 in various contexts. Students also apply this understanding to the task of representing numbers in different equivalent forms (e.g., expanded notation). They develop their understanding of numbers by building their facility with mental computation (addition and subtraction in special cases, such as 2,500 + 6,000 and 9,000 − 5,000), by using computational estimation, and by performing paper-and-pencil computations. |

*Source:* Reprinted with permission from *Curriculum Focal Points for Prekindergarten Through Grade 8 Mathematics:* A Quest for Coherence, Copyright by the National Council of Mathematics of Teachers, Inc.

conceptual understanding of basic number and numeration concepts such as counting, or recognizing how many objects are present in a set, and how a number may be used to represent that set of objects" (p. 7). In this regard, a child must figure out what a number means and how to relate that number to the real world. By doing so the child develops meaning with regard to figures as symbols and what they mean in relation to counting or a set of objects. A student with number sense can take a quantity and develop a one-to-one relationship to objects. For example, a child would be able to pick out five pieces of candy to give to his or her four friends and keep one piece of candy for him- or herself. A child who does not have number sense would not be able to make that relationship. Teachers need to work on number sense for all children in the elementary grades, as number sense changes as a child matures.

**Computational Skills.** Computational competence remains important for two valid reasons: (a) It is valuable for determining correct answers in problem-solving tasks and (b) it helps a person determine the reasonableness of responses in everyday situations (Cawley, Miller, & Carr, 1989). In arithmetic computation students must possess certain skills to learn new facts and operations or must develop them quickly to progress in mathematical learning. A list of computational competencies is provided in Table 9-6 and a discussion of them follows.

***Precomputational Skills.*** Although teachers generally think of addition as the first step in arithmetic, a student must demonstrate certain readiness or precomputation skills to be able to handle the process successfully. Initially, students learn to count without meaning (by rote); next they learn to count with meaning, that is, with numerals associated with sets of objects; and finally, students learn to recognize different numerals and to write them.

During the same period students must learn to distinguish among quantities, shapes, and sizes of different common objects. Also at this time, students learn to differentiate among numbers as well as letters. Other concepts that teachers need to foster at the precomputational level include big/little, long/short, few/many, more/less, and round/square.

One of the most important precomputational skills that students need to acquire is a knowledge of one-to-one correspondence, the idea that every one thing seen can be matched to one other thing that may or may not be seen. Teaching one-to-one correspondence begins by having a pupil match similar objects; later this task can be made more difficult by shifting the dimensions of the objects the pupil is to match. For example, a pupil may first be required to match a red token with a red token; later the teacher requires the pupil to match a token with a token, ignoring color or size.

Learning to write numerals from 1 through 9 is the activity that bridges the gap between precomputation and computation. The writing of numerals should be coordinated with the learning of manuscript handwriting (see Chapter 8), but it is not totally dependent on mastery of handwriting.

***Addition.*** In most math programs, the skill area of addition forms the base of the arithmetic operational ladder. Many specific addition-related skills are used in other operations such as multiplication and arithmetic reasoning. Students who manifest deficits in basic addition skills are likely to have trouble in all other areas of computation as well.

Cawley et al. (1989) suggest that it is possible to teach the four basic operations in different sequences and that the strict requirement that addition and subtraction must precede multiplication and division may be misguided. The important point that they stress is that students should be taught to understand what the different operations mean rather than to remember a precise sequence of steps to obtain an answer.

Initial instruction in addition focuses on the concrete representations of the arithmetic reality being taught. Traditional techniques have included the use of felt boards and pocket charts. Other easy materials to manipulate are counters and Cuisenaire roads, which can be used directly for counting. The abacus—the ancient Egyptian counter containing different-colored beads—is also a useful device for teaching addition.

As teachers move from the concrete, students may still need some visual help with computations. This help can be secured through the use of number lines. A short number line with numbers stopping at 10 should be used first. Later, as pupils progress to numbers past 10, a longer number line can be used.

**Beginning Number Line**

0—1—2—3—4—5—6—7—8—9—10

**Advanced Number Line**

0—1—2—3—4—5—6—7—8—9—10—11—12—13—14—15

These number lines can be taped to pupils' desks or made of heavy cardboard and kept inside the desks. For younger children, number lines on the floor can be used to illustrate counting through movement. Familiarity with number lines will be useful later as pupils move into subtraction.

Throughout arithmetic instruction, teachers should be careful to emphasize only one new concept at a time and should continue to teach this concept until students reach a predetermined mastery level. Continued instruction does not mean that students must learn arithmetic facts through boring repetition; short, intensive practice using a variety of ways to

**TABLE 9–6** Computational competencies

| |
|---|
| **Precomputational Skills** |
| 1. Can discriminate among quantities, shapes, and sizes |
| 2. Understands one-to-one correspondence |
| 3. Can name symbols for numbers |
| 4. Can name symbols in order from 1 to 10 |
| 5. Can recognize numerals from 0 through 9 |
| 6. Can write numerals from 0 through 9 |
| **Addition** |
| 1. Can make combinations using at least two numbers from 1 to 10 |
| 2. Can add at least two numbers less than 10 to yield a sum greater than 10 |
| 3. Can count sequentially past 30 |
| 4. Understands place value and understands concept of zero |
| 5. Can add two-place numbers to two-place numbers without carrying |
| 6. Can count sequentially to 100 |
| 7. Can add sets of numbers using the process of carrying |
| 8. Can count sequentially past 200 |
| 9. Can add sets of numbers yielding a sum greater than 100 |
| 10. Can count sequentially past 1,000 |
| 11. Can add sets of numbers yielding a sum greater than 1,000 |
| 12. Can add numbers with decimals |
| 13. Can add fractional numbers |
| **Subtraction** |
| 1. Can subtract a one-place number from another one-place number to yield values between 0 and 9 |
| 2. Can subtract a one-place number from a two-place number less than 10 |
| 3. Can subtract a set of numbers from another set of numbers without borrowing |
| 4. Can subtract a set of numbers from another set of numbers using borrowing |
| 5. Can subtract numbers with decimals from each other |
| 6. Can subtract fractions from each other |
| **Multiplication** |
| 1. Can multiply a one-place number by a one-place number |
| 2. Can multiply a two-place number by a one-place number |
| 3. Can multiply a three- (or more) place number by a one-place number |
| 4. Can multiply a two-place number by a two-place number |
| 5. Can multiply a three- (or more) place number by a two- (or more) place number |
| 6. Can multiply a decimal by a whole number |
| 7. Can multiply a fraction by a fraction |
| **Division** |
| 1. Can divide a one-place number by a one-place number |
| 2. Can divide a two-place number by a one-place number |
| 3. Can divide a three- (or more) place number by a one-place number |
| 4. Can divide with numbers containing decimals |
| 5. Can divide with numbers containing fractions |

teach the same concept should be used to promote overlearning.

As students learn more and more about one-to-one correspondence and can recognize numbers from 1 to 9, they should be given opportunities to make additive combinations using at least two numbers. While pupils master initial combinations, they will still rely on the concrete, but a gradual transition should be made to pictorial representations of the processes. The last step in this sequence is for students to be able to understand the process of addition and to represent this process exclusively with symbols and signs. Encouraging students to verbalize what they are doing rather than just having them respond to worksheets enhance the achievement of this last stage.

***Subtraction.*** Most of the methods and procedures used for teaching addition can be used for subtraction instruction. Again, initial instruction starts in a concrete manner with gradual introduction of abstractions or number symbols.

The act of borrowing from one place to the next may be one of the most difficult parts of the subtraction process to grasp. Many students fail to understand why one cannot switch the 1 and 3 around when subtracting 23 from 41. It makes sense because we teach students that they can add in either direction (commutative property). Behind this confusion is a fundamental lack of understanding of place value. Getting pupils to perceive that the position a number occupies indicates something more about a number than just its name can be accomplished in several different ways. Initially, students need to see that regrouping numbers permits the lesser number to be subtracted from the greater number. For example, in subtracting 4 from 23, regrouping 23 into 2 tens (20) and 3 ones (3) and then changing this arrangement to 1 ten and 13 ones makes it easy to subtract 4 from 13 and then add that number to the 10 not used, to get an answer of 19. Cawley et al. (1989) recommend the use of expanded notation to help students understand this process (e.g., 23 = 20 + 3). Students must understand that the 2 in 20 really stands for 2 tens. Another way to help students understand borrowing is to show the relationship of carrying in addition to borrowing in subtraction, using examples similar to the following.

| 22 | 13 | 33 | 26 | 60 | 44 |
|---|---|---|---|---|---|
| −9 | −9 | −7 | +7 | −16 | +16 |
| 13 | 22 | 26 | 33 | 44 | 60 |

The first problem in each set shows the operation of borrowing, whereas the second problem shows the opposite operation of carrying. Once pupils understand the relationship, they can check their work by reversing the original operation.

***Multiplication and Division.*** As typically taught in schools, both multiplication and division demand a great deal of rote memory and neither process may frequently be used by some persons with disabilities after they leave the formal learning environment. Yet with the potential benefits of these skills for independent functioning and with the emphasis and importance placed on mainstreaming, teachers must consider teaching multiplication and division if students are to integrate successfully. Every attempt should be made to use practical examples to make multiplication and division relevant and to try varied ways of teaching the same content to reduce boredom. In addition, constantly requiring the student to verbalize various problem-solving operations enhances generalization and transfer of skills.

The importance of teaching students how to reason and problem solve cannot be overemphasized, yet traditional teaching of multiplication and division relies heavily on memorizing multiplication tables. Students may be taught to learn computational skills in such a rote fashion that this process itself interferes with understanding and learning problem-solving skills, or these students may learn rote computational skills but fail to learn how these skills are applied in practical situations, making the instructional time and effort expended impossible to justify.

Because rote learning may be circumvented by teaching children how to use a calculator, this will be the option of choice for many students. Teachers should use teaching time to explain and clarify what multiplication and division processes are and to give examples of how the processes may be applied to their everyday lives.

Multiplication can be thought of as a faster, more efficient way to add, and most students prefer a more facile method once they learn it; this is also an argument for the use of calculators. There are other similarities between multiplication and addition; carrying from one place to another in multiplication is much the same as in addition. Also, the principle of reversibility (commutative property) applies to both; that is, the same answer results, regardless of the positions of particular numbers in the original combination.

Instruction in multiplication must also focus initially on concrete examples involving sets. Later, the concrete examples can lead to practical examples that may vary in abstractness. When students come to multiplication, they may have a fairly good grasp of addition and subtraction facts. If so, they should be encouraged to begin checking answers to multiplication problems. This self-checking can be done in the same way that other arithmetic work is done, or students can be shown how to use a calculator for checking.

Division requires many of the skills and manipulations learned in multiplication. Teachers must provide clear and systematic instruction in this area. When beginning instruction in division, it is a good idea to require students to check all answers by multiplying the divisor by the quotient. For example, if the pupil divides 21 by 7 and gets the answer 3, the 7 should then be multiplied by the 3 to determine whether the product is actually 21. This process helps students develop a greater understanding of the relationship between multiplication and division.

**Time.** One procedure to begin teaching about time is an opening activity of the school day that requires a child to affix some symbol on a calendar showing the days of the week. Concepts of the days of the week and the months of the year are often presented when describing certain events during a particular time period, such as Monday being the first school day of the week or Christmas coming in the last month of the year.

As an option, if math is taught every day using small groups, it may be advantageous to begin each session with a quick, clear, precise presentation of the days of the week, months, and year. This is an example of a concept that is easy to present but may be exceedingly difficult for students to understand.

Learning to tell time on a clock is a difficult task for many children, and this difficulty may be compounded for students with learning problems. A prerequisite to telling time is an understanding of time itself. Concepts of today, tomorrow, yesterday, next week, and soon are basic to understanding time. Next, students need to understand that certain things happen at certain times, like lunch, recess, cleanup, and dismissal. The schedule of events aids in teaching time. An extension of posting a daily schedule is to write in the approximate (if possible, exact) times that specific activities occur. Later, the teacher can use a clock face to show the different times that these familiar activities happen. Teachers should keep in mind that the entire process of teaching temporal measurement must be evaluated in light of digital watches and clocks, which clearly alter the skills students need to be taught.

**Money.** Monetary skills are among the most important life skills that students will need later in their careers. Most of the critically important math skills that we use as adults involve monetary concepts and activity. As a result, effective instruction in this area provides a good preparation for the demands of adulthood.

Children usually enter school with some knowledge about money. A real-life interest in this concept develops over time. Students use money to buy lunch and go to school-sponsored activities. Teachers can easily take advantage of these activities to help pupils gain a more precise knowledge of money. A unit on different coins up to a dollar can be coordinated with instruction in addition and subtraction skills during the primary years.

One of the best ways to teach coin recognition and change making is to use real coins to make simulated purchases of various items; for example, a student may use two quarters to purchase a 30-cent candy bar and must then determine how much change should be received. With this approach the teacher does not have to worry about transfer of learning from play money to real money. Using real coins has the further advantage of providing concrete items for students to manipulate.

## Problem-Solving Skills

The mastery of computation skills or the compensatory use of calculators provides students with the tools to solve problems but does not teach (them the process of how to solve daily mathematics problems. Problem solving, therefore, has been targeted as one of the major areas of professional interest. Unquestionably, many regular educators are devoting much attention to this important skill area, and special educators need to attend to this issue as well.

Perhaps one reason why the skill of problem solving is so important yet so difficult to teach is that it requires many complex skills. As Cawley et al. (1988) state, problem solving involves a complex set of activities and

> Some of these components are the following: (1) the metacognitive acts of knowing that there is a problem, that planning and monitoring are required to solve the problem, and that evaluation and critique of the responses are necessary; (2) the cognitive acts of thinking, reasoning, and the search for procedures that will produce one or more desired responses; and (3) the appropriate use of skills to obtain the desired response. (p. 165)

To further complicate the problem-solving process. Moses (1983) indicates that there are three major barriers to solving word problems: interest and motivation; deficiencies in basic skills, including areas such as reading; and lack of facility in cognitive skill areas. All three factors can be significant obstacles for students with special learning needs and must be taken into account when assessing and planning instruction. Additionally, students with learning problems, as well as students from bilingual or different cultural backgrounds, may experience language and vocabulary problems that compound their inability to understand a word problem. These students may not have the background experiences that would help them relate to particular situations in a word problem and cannot rely on past experiences to help them compute the word problem. To teach problem solving, teachers must help students (a) make appropriate decisions, (b) understand the vocabulary being used, (c) use information, (d) identify sequences or patterns in the problem, and (e) develop strategies that allow them to work through a solution (Bley & Thornton, 2001).

Fuchs and Fuchs (2002) compared the performance of students with math difficulties to students with math difficulties in addition to reading difficulties on a hierarchy of problem-solving and real-world math problems. Their results indicated that large deficits existed for both groups of students. In the area of arithmetic story problems, the differences between the two groups were similar. However, as the complexity of the problems progressed, the differences were larger in that the students with math difficulties and reading difficulties performed at a lower level than the students with math difficulties only. The Fuchs' study adds to the growing literature that indicates that students with learning disabilities or reading difficulties will face more challenges as the complexity of the problem-solving and real-world problems increase.

**Make Decisions.** The process of decision making is complex and requires that students demonstrate several skills. These skills include (a) using abstract **reasoning;** (b) understanding and expressing words in a meaningful way; (c) drawing on previously learned concepts and skills; (d) distinguishing among different concepts, skills, operations, and situations; and (e) choosing the appropriate computation skills to solve a problem in any given situation. For example, one important decision students must make when solving a problem is to determine the type of problem that is to be solved. Cawley et al. (1989) discuss three different types of problem formats that students must learn to identify:

- traditional word problems comprised of a number of sentences followed by a question (word problem format)
- information that is presented in some graphic way—tables, figures, graphs (display format)
- a narrative passage that contains quantitative information

All three of these formats can be used to generate problem-solving activities. In fact, the display and story formats more closely resemble the way students will encounter problem solving that requires math applications in their everyday lives.

**Understand Vocabulary.** Bley and Thornton (2001) stress the need to teach the accurate use of words. Many students with learning problems may not know the meaning of a word just from reading it in context. They may have difficulties recognizing that a word should be associated with a symbol or that it might have multiple meanings (e.g., the word *and* is often associated with the operation of addition or the & symbol).

**Use Information.** Students also need to learn how to use information within a word problem. This skill involves the use of receptive and expressive language skills as well as understanding the vocabulary being used. In many cases, students with learning problems will have difficulties expressing ideas or associating the words within the word problem with the appropriate meaning. They are unable to determine what information is necessary and what information is irrelevant to the problem. The skills of understanding vocabulary and using information within a word problem are closely tied. The following examples will further explain the importance of teaching these skills.

Although understanding arithmetic terms and the language of problem situations may seem quite simple, students who do not understand the terms nor concepts embedded in the text are lost at the outset. Remediation of this problem depends on first determining exactly which terms and concepts are not understood and devising strategies to teach them. Often, students may have a reasonable grasp of language they encounter in their daily lives but are confused when problem situations do not use language exactly like their own. Essentially, they lose the ability to decipher the clues to solve the problem. The following problems illustrate this:

> **Word problem 1.** Elwood has 55 cents. He uses 15 cents to buy milk and 30 cents to buy a candy bar. How much money does Elwood have now?
>
> **Word problem 2.** Linda Sue bought a comic book for 75 cents. After reading it, she sold it for 40 cents, which she put with the 28 cents she already had. How much money did Linda Sue have originally? How much money does Linda Sue have now?

Even though students may be able to read and understand the words in these two problems, neither gives obvious directions about the operations that will produce a solution.

With problems of this type, the teacher's job is to help students understand what information is given and what needs to be done to solve the problem. In the first problem the significant words are *has, uses,* and *to buy*. *Has* tells the amount Elwood starts with, which is the amount to be added to or taken away from. *Uses* and *to buy* indicate that money is spent; therefore, subtraction should solve the problem. Teachers should have students ascertain the meanings of the crucial words specifically within the context of the particular problem.

The second example poses a somewhat more complex dilemma. In this problem one must determine not only how much money Linda Sue presently has but how much she started with; it is in effect two problems. In problems like this one, pupils must first find as many significant words as possible and then attempt to determine how these words contribute to answering the question at hand. Teachers should formulate and ask questions about the problem, causing students to verbalize possible solutions. Then pupils can ask their own questions, which may not be as precise as the teachers' but which will lead to a solution if teachers encourage the verbal interchange. Once pupils have gone through several of these verbal exchanges, they are in a position to form a tentative solution. Teachers should employ strategies to cause students to talk through or verbally explain their solutions. The simplest way is to continue the interchange just mentioned; another way is to have students write short explanations about the whole process or use drawings or diagrams.

**Identify Sequences and Patterns.** In word problems, students must recognize the sequences and patterns within a problem. Sequencing in mathematics often refers to the operations that must be used and their correct order (Bley & Thornton, 1995). Many problems require that students engage in more than one operation, and the sequence of those operations is crucial to solving the problem (e.g., first subtract or add, then multiply). Similarly, patterning is a skill that requires students to identify which of the four operations to apply in a given problem. Often, students can recognize that one word problem has similarities to other word problems that were solved correctly. Recognizing the similarities can help students perform the computations necessary in new problems. Unfortunately, many students with learning problems have difficulties recognizing sequences and patterns so they may be unable to find similarities to previous problems and experiences. Gaining these skills can accelerate the problem-solving processes.

**Develop Strategies.** Several strategies have been developed to help students experience more success when learning to solve problems. Bley and Thornton (1995) suggest that teachers begin by teaching certain prerequisite skills. These skills include (a) rounding off numbers (e.g., $7.85 can be rounded to $8.00 for easier use), (b) choosing efficient methods for calculating (e.g., use of a calculator), (c) predicting what the answer might be, (d) using the language of estimation (e.g., *about, nearly, almost, close to*), and (e) estimating what the answer will be. Each of these skills allows students to approximate an answer. The correct answer in these cases may not be as important as the procedure used or as important as arriving at an answer that is an estimate of the exact answer.

Another effective strategy with older students uses a sequence of tasks to be performed each time a word problem format is encountered:

1. Read (or listen) carefully.
2. Write a few words about the kind of answer needed (e.g., kilometers per hour).
3. Look for significant words and eliminate irrelevant information.
4. Highlight the numbers that are important.
5. Draw a diagram or sketch when appropriate. This graphic does not have to be a work of art but should depict what the problem is describing.
6. Decide on the necessary calculations, and identify a math sentence for this situation.
7. Perform the calculations.
8. Evaluate the answer to determine its reasonableness.
9. Write the answer with the appropriate units.

Although this strategy is straightforward, each step requires considerable instruction.

Students with language or vocabulary problems may wish to use the strategy of retelling the problem in their own words. A teacher can check for understanding through this method. If for some reason students cannot paraphrase or use their own words, teachers may wish to read the word problem aloud. Using different variations of the problem, ask the students to choose the correct one (Bley & Thornton, 2001).

Bley and Thornton (2001) also provide some teacher tips for teaching problem solving to children. These authors recommend that teachers make problem solving more attractive to students by using interesting problems that are within the students' experiences. Also, encourage students to give an estimate of the answer rather than an exact answer. Additionally, provide visual props or use concrete objects such as drawings or diagrams as the problem is read orally to the students. Another tip is to foster creative thinking about problem solving by letting students think of different ways to solve a problem—often there is more than one way to solve an open-ended problem. These authors also recommend that students be given opportunities to recognize and identify relevant and irrelevant information within a word problem. The identification of the necessary information is often the key to continuing the procedure of problem solving.

Some students whose reading skills limit their ability to comprehend word problems encounter great difficulty dealing with the linguistic demands of math materials. For these students Cawley (1984) recommends using reading materials that the student can handle and infusing mathematical features into these passages. From this adapted material, word problems can be developed using language that the student understands. An example of this idea is provided in Figure 9–6.

**Hot Math.** The National Center on Accelerating Student Learning (CASL) promotes success in the areas of reading, writing, and mathematics for children grades K–3. Among the scientists in this center. Fuchs and Fuchs (2002–2003) have developed a problem-solving program for students (with and without disabilities) called *Hot Math*. This problem-solving program integrates two well-researched procedures to promote mathematical problem solving: explicit instruction about transfer and self-regulation strategies. Through the use of explicit instruction, the teacher shows students how to solve a problem. An explanation of why the solution method was selected, why it makes sense, and why it works is then given to the students. The program authors promote the use of (a) posters so students can refer back to the procedures and (b) choral responding to promote classroomwide engagement with the children.

**FIGURE 9–6** Adapted reading passage

*Passage 1*

Catching Fish

A big black bear is fishing in the lake. He is standing near the shore where the lake is not deep. The bear is smacking his lips. He is thinking how the fish will taste when he eats them.

The bear is catching more fish than he can eat. When he is full of fish, he will leave the rest on the shore. A fox or a mink will come and eat them.

*Passage 2*

Catching Fish

Two black bears are fishing in the lake. One bear is standing near the shore. This bear has already caught 5 fish. The other bear is sitting in the water, holding on to the 6 fish that she has caught.

Each bear is thinking about catching some more fish. Each bear is also thinking about eating the fish. After each bear caught 2 more fish, they went home.

*Source:* From *Developmental Teaching of Mathematics for the Learning Disabled* (pp. 83–84), by J. F. Cawley (Ed.), 1984, Austin, TX: PRO-ED. Copyright 1984 by PRO-ED, Inc. Reprinted with permission.

*Hot Math* has 16 lessons (four units), with each unit lasting approximately 3 weeks. During that time, instruction includes skill acquisition and transfer of knowledge to relevant word problems. During this transfer piece, the teacher is required to teach four types of "problem features" in a word problem. Each feature can change a problem without altering its structure or solution. This aspect of the program can direct students toward thinking of the "ways problems can change." Additionally, the program includes skill acquisition or what the problem is asking and how to solve the problem. Practice and cumulative reviews are incorporated into the program as well as goal setting (the self-regulation piece) to promote motivation among students. The CASL research related to this program suggests that students in general and special education benefit, with small-group instruction showing the greatest gains.

## Math Through Children's Literature

In the early 1990s the idea of integrating math and literature was met with enthusiasm by proponents of the integrated curricula and the whole language approach (Bradden, Hall, & Taylor, 1993). Since that time teachers have been using children's books that facilitate the learning of math concepts as well as math skills. For example, by integrating math and literature, word problems can use familiar stories to allow students to address the mathematical functions rather than struggle with unfamiliar vocabulary. Table 9-7 outlines a few books that can facilitate math concepts and math skills if appropriate discussion and activities accompany the reading of the book. Although teachers can use children's books as independent or alternative systems of teaching math, some math curricula companies are now incorporating short stories that illustrate the math concept being presented in the unit lesson; two such companies are Mimosa Publications and Silver Burdett & Ginn. The complex process of integrated lessons should be based on district curriculum requirements. The stories that are used should contain elements of a story and be approved to use in an integrated curriculum program (Sharp & Hoiberg, 2005).

**Reflective Question 9–3: *What role does mathematical language play in the learning of concepts and computations?***

## Mathematics Instruction for Students in Middle School

Mathematics instruction for older children (11–13 years of age), in grades 6–8, is an extension and expansion of arithmetic and mathematical computations learned in elementary years. Unfortunately, for students with learning problems, mathematics becomes even more difficult if basic facts and skills have not been acquired. This section of the chapter will introduce the NCTM Curriculum Focus for middle school students (grades 6–8) and how teachers can plan to teach mathematics to older children who continue to struggle with mathematics.

**NCTM Curriculum Focus.** Recommendations from the NCTM *Curriculum Focal Points for Mathematics* (2006) include sixth through eighth grade level mathematics instruction. These focal points are designed to help teachers focus on specific goals in the areas of (a) number and operations (this includes fluency with multiplication and division of fractions and decimals as well as connecting ratio and rate to multiplication and division), (b) algebra, (c) geometry and measurement. Table 9-8 provides an example of Curriculum Focal

**TABLE 9–7** Examples of math through children's literature books

| *Book Title* | *Math Concept* | *Author* | *Publisher/Date* |
|---|---|---|---|
| *The Shape Race in Outer Space* | Shapes | Calvin Irons | Mimosa 1998 |
| *Baker Bill* | Telling time, money, and fractions | Calvin Irons | Mimosa 1998 |
| *A Week Away* | Days of the week, time | Calvin Irons | Mimosa 1998 |
| *The Icky Sticky Trap* | Subtraction | Calvin Irons | Mimosa 1998 |
| *Clarence the Clock* | Telling time | Calvin Irons | Mimosa 1998 |
| *The Crocodile Coat* | Measuring | Calvin Irons | Mimosa 1998 |
| *Fishy Scales* | Weighing | Calvin Irons | Mimosa 1998 |
| *The 500 Hats of Bartholomew Cubbins* | Counting | Dr. Seuss | Vanguard Press 1965 |
| *26 Letters and 99 Cents* | Counting | Tana Hoban | Mulberry Paperback Books 1995 |
| *One Hundred Hungry Ants* | Multiplication concepts | Elinor Pinczes | Houghton Mifflin 1993 |
| *What Is Cooking, Jenny Archer?* | Time, estimating, money, word problems | Ellen Conford | Little, Brown & Co. 1989 |

**TABLE 9–8** Curriculum focal points and connections for grade 7

The set of three curriculum focal points and related connections for mathematics in grade 7 follow. These topics are the recommended content emphases for this grade level. It is essential that these focal points be addressed in contexts that promote problem solving, reasoning, communication, making connections, and designing and analyzing representations.

| *Grade 7 Curriculum Focal Points* | *Connections to the Focal Points* |
|---|---|
| ***Number and Operations and Algebra and Geometry:* Developing an understanding of and applying proportionality, including similarity**<br>Students extend their work with ratios to develop an understanding of proportionality that they apply to solve single and multistep problems in numerous contexts. They use ratio and proportionality to solve a wide variety of percent problems, including problems involving discounts, interest, taxes, tips, and percent increase or decrease. They also solve problems about similar objects (including figures) by using scale factors that relate corresponding lengths of the objects or by using the fact that relationships of lengths within an object are preserved in similar objects. Students graph proportional relationships and identify the unit rate as the slope of the related line. They distinguish proportional relationships ($y/x = k$, or $y = kx$) from other relationships, including inverse proportionality ($xy = k$, or $y = k/x$). | ***Measurement* and *Geometry:*** Students connect their work on proportionality with their work on area and volume by investigating similar objects. They understand that if a scale factor describes how corresponding lengths in two similar objects are related, then the square of the scale factor describes how corresponding areas are related, and the cube of the scale factor describes how corresponding volumes are related. Students apply their work on proportionality to measurement in different contexts, including converting among different units of measurement to solve problems involving rates such as motion at a constant speed. They also apply proportionality when they work with the circumference, radius, and diameter of a circle; when they find the area of a sector of a circle; and when they make scale drawings. |
| ***Measurement and Geometry and Algebra:* Developing an understanding of and using formulas to determine surface areas and volumes of three-dimensional shapes**<br>By decomposing two- and three-dimensional shapes into smaller, component shapes, students find surface areas and develop and justify formulas for the surface areas and volumes of prisms and cylinders. As students decompose prisms and cylinders by slicing them, they develop and understand formulas for their volumes (*Volume* = *Area of base* × *Height*). They apply these formulas in problem solving to determine volumes of prisms and cylinders. Students see that the formula for the area of a circle is plausible by decomposing a circle into a number of wedges and rearranging them into a shape that approximates a parallelogram. They select appropriate two- and three-dimensional shapes to model real-world situations and solve a variety of problems (including multistep problems) involving surface areas, areas and circumferences of circles, and volumes of prisms and cylinders. | ***Number and Operations:*** In grade 4, students used equivalent fractions to determine the decimal representations of fractions that they could represent with terminating decimals. Students now use division to express any fraction as a decimal, including fractions that they must represent with infinite decimals. They find this method useful when working with proportions, especially those involving percents. Students connect their work with dividing fractions to solving equations of the form $ax = b$, where $a$ and $b$ are fractions. Students continue to develop their understanding of multiplication and division and the structure of numbers by determining if a counting number greater than 1 is a prime, and if it is not, by factoring it into a product of primes.<br><br>***Data Analysis:*** Students use proportions to make estimates relating to a population on the basis of a sample. They apply percentages to make and interpret histograms and circle graphs. |
| ***Number and Operations and Algebra:* Developing an understanding of operations on all rational numbers and solving linear equations**<br>Students extend understandings of addition, subtraction, multiplication, and division, together with their properties, to all rational numbers, including negative integers. By applying properties of arithmetic and considering negative numbers in everyday contexts (e.g., situations of owing money or measuring elevations above and below sea level), students explain why the rules for adding, subtracting, multiplying, and dividing with negative numbers make sense. They use the arithmetic of rational numbers as they formulate and solve linear equations in one variable and use these equations to solve problems. Students make strategic choices of procedures to solve linear equations in one variable and implement them efficiently, understanding that when they use the properties of equality to express an equation in a new way, solutions that they obtain for the new equation also solve the original equation. | ***Probability:*** Students understand that when all outcomes of an experiment are equally likely, the theoretical probability of an event is the fraction of outcomes in which the event occurs. Students use theoretical probability and proportions to make approximate predictions. |

*Source:* Reprinted with permission from *Curriculum Focal Points for Prekindergarten Through Grade 8 Mathematics: A Quest for Coherence,* copyright by the National Council of Mathematics of Teachers, Inc.

Points and connections that are presented by the NCTM for the middle school level.

**Big Ideas.** During the middle school years, mathematics instruction becomes more intensive for students with disabilities. As a result, teachers find that students with disabilities show a larger gap between performance and grade level. The need to become more fluent in their arithmetic operations is more apparent, and the mathematical application to the real world becomes more demanding. Additionally, special educators must be "highly qualified" to teach mathematics to students in their own classes or team with a mathematics instructor to make the necessary modifications for students who have diverse needs and disabilities. To address all these needs current researchers in curriculum development (e.g., Coyne et al., 2007; Lenz & Deshler, 2004) have suggested educational tools that should be promoted to facilitate student learning. One such educational tool is the notion of "**big ideas.**" Big ideas are regarded as the fundamental knowledge or root meanings in the content area of concern. If teachers can identify what fundamental knowledge is needed to master a concept or mathematical equation, then the teacher can focus on these important items and not other content areas that are confusing to the learner (Harris, Carnine, Silbert, & Dixon, 2007).

Harris and his colleagues (2007) talk about mathematical big ideas as not being "complex, nor difficult to understand at face value. The difficulty comes in knowing when they apply and how their application changes over time" (p. 142). How a teacher integrates these big ideas so the student can gain knowledge is of utmost importance. Harris presents an example of how four operations (addition, subtraction, multiplication, and division) are based on a few basic big ideas. These big ideas include: place value, expanded notation, commutative property, associative property, distributive property, equivalence, and rate of composition/decomposition. Table 9–9 demonstrates these big ideas.

**Planning a Mathematics Course.** Other educational tools that help teachers deliver mathematic concepts to middle and secondary students are the Course Organizer and Unit Organizer/Concept Map (Lenz & Deshler, 2004; Lenz et al., 1998; 1994). These tools are evidence-based practices used to enhance student understanding of big pictures. They work to organize their thinking with regard to what they are learning in their mathematics class.

***Course Organizer.*** Preparing to teach mathematics to middle school students will require some organization and planning so that the direct instruction and mathematics strategies can be delivered in a deliberate manner. Lenz and Deshler (2004) have produced evidence-based methods to help teachers organize entire courses and develop big ideas for their content classes. One such method is the designing of instruction through course planning. To do so, these researchers suggest that course planning will help teachers think about what is the most important information/concepts to be learned. By organizing an entire year, teachers will be able to gather the ideas needed to initiate at the beginning of the year as well as maintaining them through out the year. With this in place, the content delivered at the end of the year will focus on pulling all the information together in an integrated manner.

While developing a course plan in mathematics, teachers can address overall purposes for the course according to key concepts (big ideas) and determine the scope and sequence of individual units as well as lessons. This, in turn, can help in determining the amount of time to devote to each unit and consider the learning strategies, accommodations, or modifications that will be needed for student success. Lenz and Deshler consider the following guidelines as they relate to organizing a course for mathematics instruction:

1. Identify what the course is about and what the important big ideas are.
   a. The identification of big ideas may be obtained through the writing of no more than 10 course questions that are open-ended and address the important concepts of the mathematical content.
   b. Develop a mathematical picture or map that will show the major units the students will cover in their mathematics class. This picture/map will include the mathematic standards and benchmarks required for students to perform on standard-based tests.
2. To develop the course organizer, Lenz and Deshler suggest that the teacher consult the course textbook, a copy of the NCTM Standards, other textbooks that will help outline big ideas, and a syllabus for the course (if one is available).

Once a teacher has developed the big ideas for the entire year, he or she can develop those ideas into a particular format or graphic organizer. This format includes (a) the title of the course, (b) what the course is about, (c) course questions, (d) course standards, and

**TABLE 9–9** Big ideas in operations

| *Big Idea* | *Example* |
|---|---|
| *Place value:* The "place" a number holds in a sequence of numbers gives information about that number. | In the number 265, the 2 at the beginning of the number is a hundreds number. We know that the placement of the 2 tells us that there are two units of 100, or two 100s, in that number. Similarly, the location of the 6 tells us that there are 6 units of 10 in the number. |
| *Expanded notation:* The reduction of a number to its constituent units. | The number 213 is composed of two 100s, one 10, and three 1s, which can be represented in an equation as $100 + 100 + 10 + 1 + 1 + 1 = 213$ or conversely as $200 + 10 + 3 = 213$. |
| *Commutative property:* The order in which numbers are placed in the equation can be changed without affecting the outcome. | Addition and multiplication are commutative:<br>In addition, $3 + 4 = 7$ and $4 + 3 = 7$<br>In multiplication, $4 \times 5 = 20$ and $5 \times 4 = 20$. |
| $a + b = b + a$ | Subtraction and division are not commutative:<br>In subtraction, $5 - 3 = 2$ and $3 - 5 = -2$<br>In division, $6 \div 3 = 2$ and $3 \div 6 = 0.5$ |
| *Associative property:* The groupings in which numbers are placed in the equation can be changed without affecting the outcome. | Addition and multiplication are associative:<br>In addition, $1 (2 + 4) + 5 = 11$ and $2 + (4 + 5) = 11$<br>In multiplication, $(3 \times 2) \times 5 = 30$ and $3 \times (2 \times 5) = 30$. |
| $(a + b) + c = a + (b + c)$ | Subtraction and division are not associative:<br>In subtraction. $(15 - 3) - 5 = 7$ and $15 - (3 - 5) = 13$<br>In division, $(32 \div 8) \div 2 = 2$ and $32 \div (8 \div 2) = 8$. |
| *Distributive property:* Numbers in an equation involving multiple operations can be distributed. | |
| $a \times (b \div c) = (a \times b) + (a \times c)$ | $5 \times (3 \div 2) = (5 \times 3) + (5 \times 2)$ |
| You can also distribute numbers in an equation that includes division and subtraction or addition. | |
| $(a + b) \div c = (a \div c) + (b \div c)$ | $(8 + 4) \div 2 = (8 + 2) + (4 \div 2)$ |
| *Equivalence:* The quantity to the left of the equal sign (=) is the same as the quantity to the right. | $32 + 15 = 47$<br>$16 + 16 + 15 = 47$<br>$8 + 8 + 8 + 8 + (5 \times 3) = 20 + 20 + 7$<br>*Note:* Many students interpret the equal sign as an operation (e.g., "when I see the equal sign I add, subtract, etc.") rather than as a relationship (e.g., "when I see the equal sign I know that the quantity on one side must be the same as the other side"). |
| *Rate of composition/decomposition* (Ma, 1999): A form of number sense. The rate of composition (or decomposition) of sets of numbers in our base 10 system is simply 10. | When you have accumulated 10 ones you have one 10. When you have accumulated 10 tens you have one 100 and so on. This concept is sometimes referred to as *unitizing,* that is, creating a tens unit from 10 ones. Similarly, when you remove a 1 from a 10 you have 9 ones, that is you have decomposed the 10. |

*Source:* Coyne, M. E., Kame'enui, E . J., and Carnine, D. W., *Effective Teaching Strategies That Accommodate Diverse Learners,* 3rd Edition, © 2007, pp. 143–144. Reprinted by permission of Pearson Education, Inc., Upper Saddle River, NJ.

(e) course progress guide (which can include graphs or other evaluation procedures). Examples of these graphic organizers can be seen in Figures 9–7a and 9–7b. The course organizers are examples of the planning done for a sixth-grade mathematics class and outline what students will use as essential questions and how each unit of the course relates to NCTM standards and benchmarks.

**Concept Maps.** Once the course organizer has been constructed, the teacher should develop a concept map, such as the one introduced by Lenz and Deshler

(2004). The concept map further organizes the teacher's thoughts and can be used (in a modified student version) to teach students what they will be learning and how each concept connects with each unit they are studying. The concept map can include what information will be covered every week, what each unit will entail, key questions for the big ideas, and vocabulary or culminating activities. The teacher concept map in Figure 9–8 outlines what will be covered in the mathematic units that will refer to learning about numbers (or rational numbers). The teacher can then help students construct a student concept map so they will know what they will be learning and how each concept is interrelated. These maps help teachers and students organize the information to be learned and provide a structure for understanding the connections that need to be made when moving from one big idea to another.

**Teaching Learning Strategies.** A fourth education tool that may be used in mathematics instruction is the teaching of strategies. By introducing this tool, students begin to think in mathematical terms and they will begin to organize their thoughts into logical steps or strategies (Harris et al., 2007). These strategies are designed so that the student can acquire a meaningful application of the information. To accomplish this outcome, the teacher must explicitly instruct the strategy so the students can apply it to a variety of mathematical situations.

Research regarding strategy development indicates that a common problem pertains to the development of strategies that are too broad or too narrow in scope. In either case, the strategies may not help students apply the knowledge needed to navigate through the mathematical problems. Once a viable strategy is developed, teachers should explicitly instruct each strategy until students know each step, how to apply the steps, and how the strategy relates to acquiring the knowledge to be gained from its implementation (Tournaki, 2003). With the instruction of an effective strategy, students are more likely to utilize the strategy over various mathematical problems and achieve understanding of what concepts are being applied.

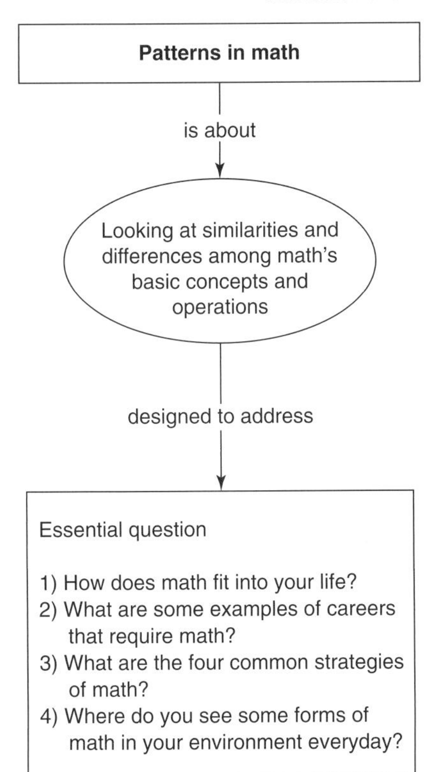


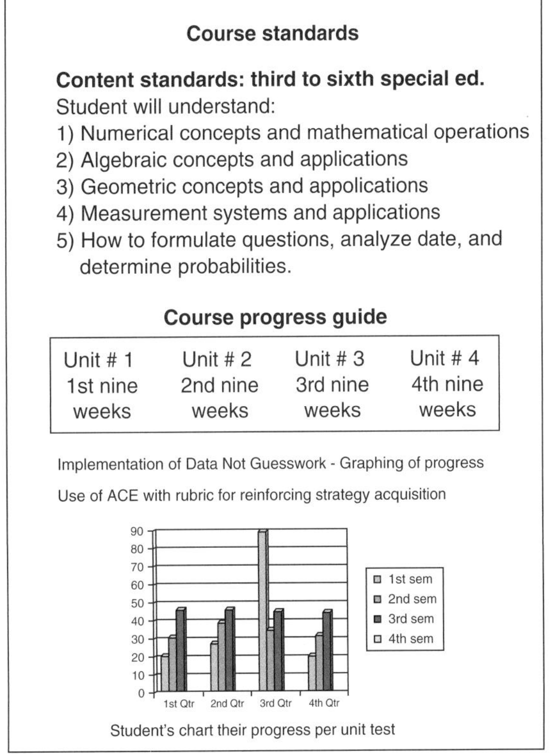


**FIGURE 9–7** Teacher course organizer for sixth-grade mathematics course

Donated by Ursula Nakai from Ernie Pyle Middle School

(continued)

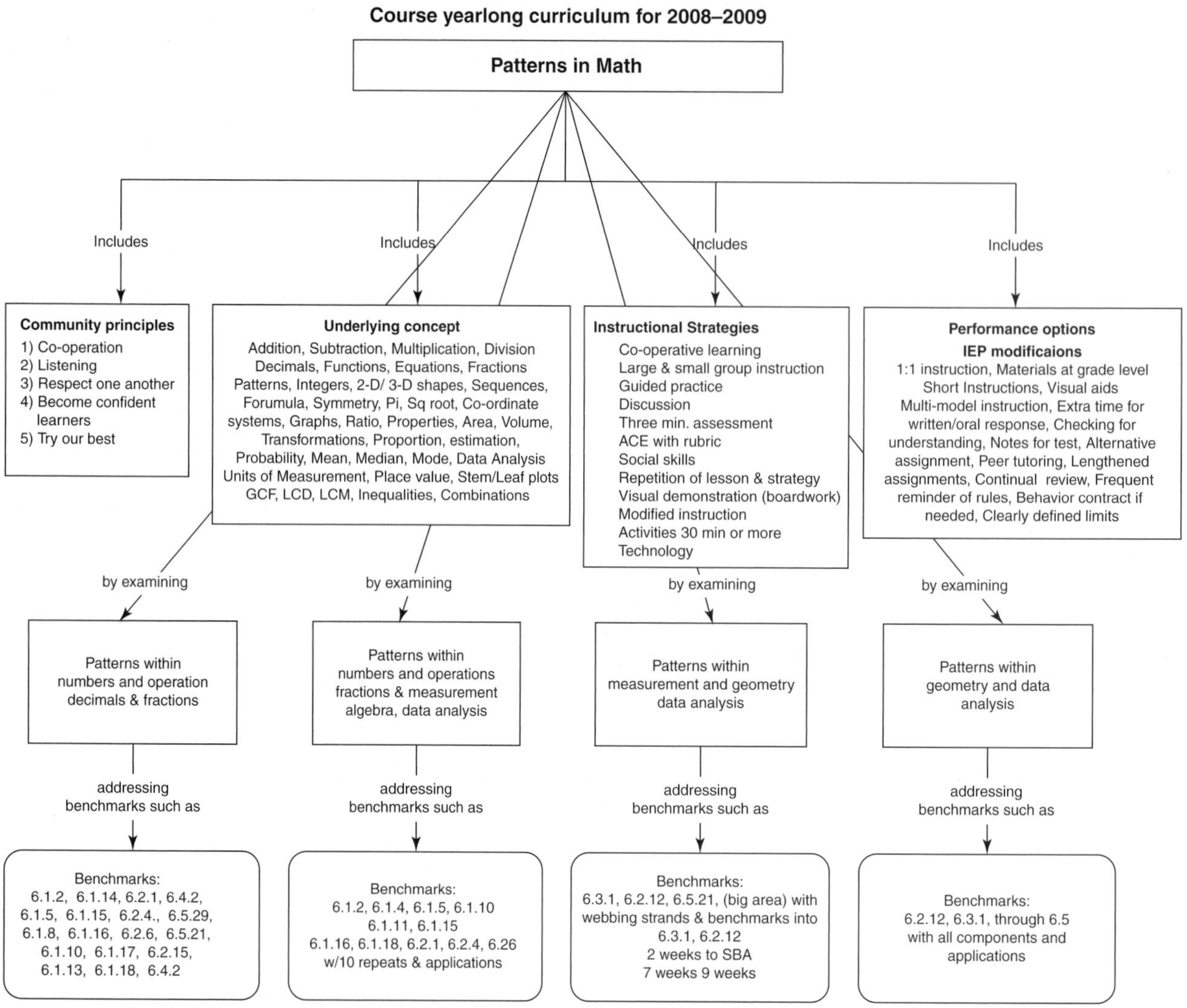

**Course yearlong curriculum for 2008–2009**

**Patterns in Math**

Includes

**Community principles**
1) Co-operation
2) Listening
3) Respect one another
4) Become confident learners
5) Try our best

Includes

**Underlying concept**
Addition, Subtraction, Multiplication, Division
Decimals, Functions, Equations, Fractions
Patterns, Integers, 2-D/ 3-D shapes, Sequences,
Forumula, Symmetry, Pi, Sq root, Co-ordinate
systems, Graphs, Ratio, Properties, Area, Volume,
Transformations, Proportion, estimation,
Probability, Mean, Median, Mode, Data Analysis
Units of Measurement, Place value, Stem/Leaf plots
GCF, LCD, LCM, Inequalities, Combinations

Includes

**Instructional Strategies**
Co-operative learning
Large & small group instruction
Guided practice
Discussion
Three min. assessment
ACE with rubric
Social skills
Repetition of lesson & strategy
Visual demonstration (boardwork)
Modified instruction
Activities 30 min or more
Technology

Includes

**Performance options**
**IEP modificaions**
1:1 instruction, Materials at grade level
Short Instructions, Visual aids
Multi-model instruction, Extra time for written/oral response, Checking for understanding, Notes for test, Alternative assignment, Peer tutoring, Lengthened assignments, Continual review, Frequent reminder of rules, Behavior contract if needed, Clearly defined limits

by examining

Patterns within numbers and operation decimals & fractions

addressing benchmarks such as

Benchmarks:
6.1.2, 6.1.14, 6.2.1, 6.4.2,
6.1.5, 6.1.15, 6.2.4., 6.5.29,
6.1.8, 6.1.16, 6.2.6, 6.5.21,
6.1.10, 6.1.17, 6.2.15,
6.1.13, 6.1.18, 6.4.2

by examining

Patterns within numbers and operations fractions & measurement algebra, data analysis

addressing benchmarks such as

Benchmarks:
6.1.2, 6.1.4, 6.1.5, 6.1.10
6.1.11, 6.1.15
6.1.16, 6.1.18, 6.2.1, 6.2.4, 6.26
w/10 repeats & applications

by examining

Patterns within measurement and geometry data analysis

addressing benchmarks such as

Benchmarks:
6.3.1, 6.2.12, 6.5.21, (big area) with webbing strands & benchmarks into
6.3.1, 6.2.12
2 weeks to SBA
7 weeks 9 weeks

by examining

Patterns within geometry and data analysis

addressing benchmarks such as

Benchmarks:
6.2.12, 6.3.1, through 6.5
with all components and applications

**FIGURE 9–7** (continued)

Examples of strategies can be seen in the nearby Teacher Tip.

## Developing Math Scaffolding

Another educational tool that has gained support is the practice of scaffolding. According to Harris and his colleagues (2007), "scaffolding is a means by which students receive support in various forms along the path to full understanding and doing the rest successfully. Along the way, teachers would remove more bits of the scaffolding, but in no instance would they abruptly remove all the scaffolding" (p. 155). One way of thinking about scaffolding is through task analysis. If a teacher is able to devise a detailed analysis of a strategy, the student can learn the strategy steps through instruction and practice. Once the student seems to understand each step of the strategy, a fading program would be implemented. For example, if a strategy has four steps, the last step might be removed when the student is able to work the entire problem. If the student can work the problem with the fourth step missing, the teacher would systematically remove the third step. The student would have the scaffolding of the first two steps, but would be required to complete the problem. If this is accomplished, the second step might be removed. This would continue until the teacher has an indication as to how much scaffolding a student needs to complete the problems. Harris and his colleagues (2007) give an example of the steps for a scaffolded strategy that finds the volume of a cone that is 5 inches tall with a radius of 1.6 inches.

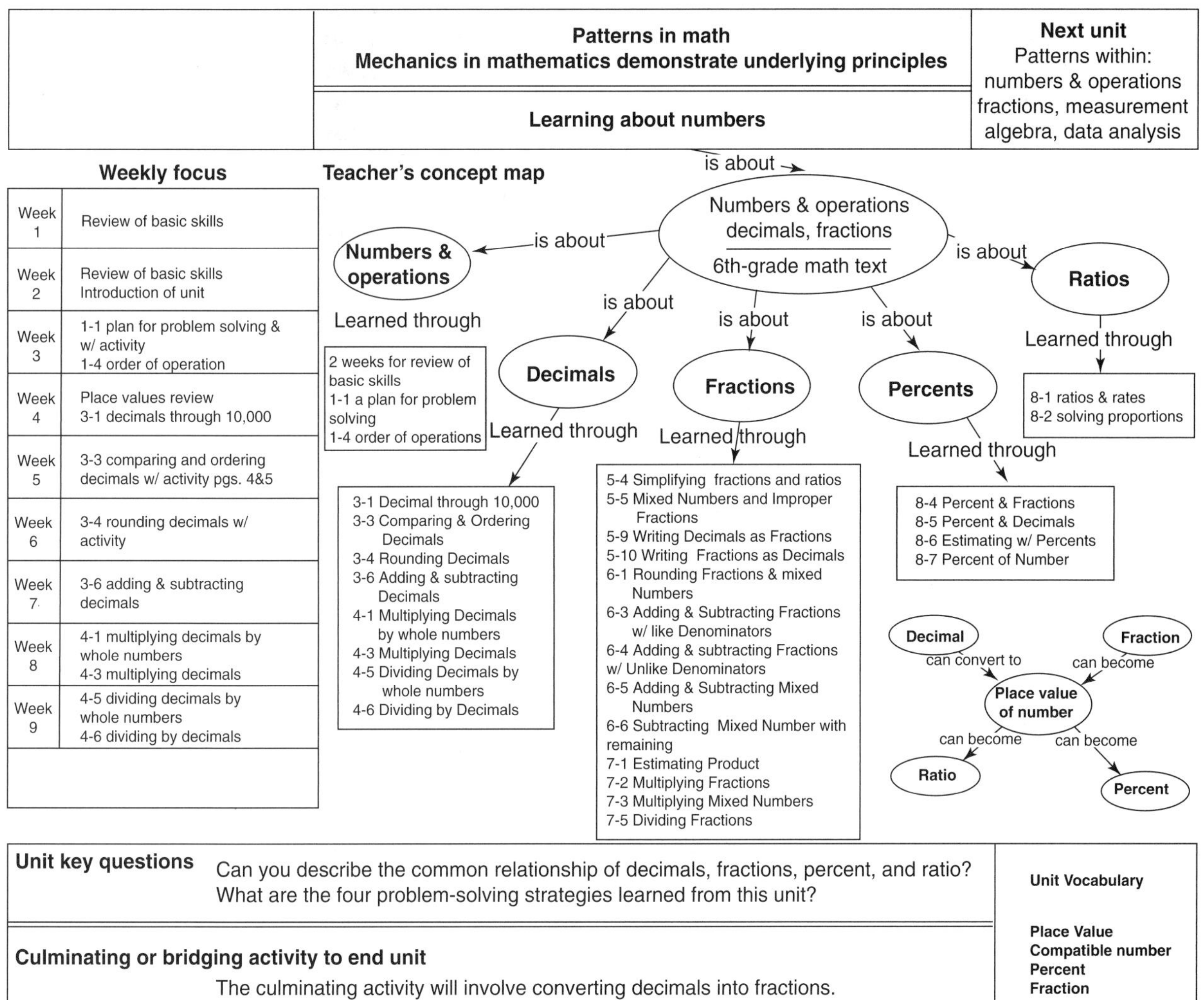


**FIGURE 9–8** Unit concept map for sixth-grade mathematics teacher

Donated by Ursula Nakai from Ernie Pyle Middle School

1. "Write the formula for the volume of the figure."

   Students write: B × 1/3 × h

2. "Calculate the area of the base for that figure."

   Students write: $3.14\ (1.6)^2 = 8.04$

3. "Calculate the volume."

   Students write: 8.04 × 1/3 × 5 = 13.4

4. "Write the complete answer with the appropriate unit."

   Students write: 13.4 cubic inches (p. 155)

After reviewing this scaffolded strategy, a teacher might decide that more steps or scaffolding are needed to meet the student's needs. If so, the teacher would continue to provide a scaffold throughout the strategy. Feedback would be given to the students as they work the problem and the scaffolding would be taken off, bit by bit, as the students are able to handle the steps without help. Thus, one important part of scaffolding is to develop a task analysis that is appropriate for the student's level of skill.

## Mathematics Programs for Middle School Students with Disabilities

Two remedial programs will be highlighted in this section. One mathematics program is Corrective Mathematics and is a direct instructions approach for students in need of skills involving basic operations. The second program is a recent program that combines

## Solving Word Problems

Mercer and Mercer (2005) explain that problem solving word problems are usually set in a social context, with the task of determining what information is being given and what information is lacking. Based on this information, the student will then figure out what operation is needed to solve the problem. Because many students with mathematics problems also have reading problems, teachers need to help students read the problem for information as well as determine what to do with the information gleaned. To do so, teachers can use two instructional tools or strategies.

The first strategy involves determining the classification of the operation needed in a word problem. The following is an example of categories for addition and subtraction word problems. In each category, a student must determine if (a) the result is unknown, (b) a change in the element set is unknown, or (c) the start of the element set is unknown.

*Join elements or add them to a given set* (e.g., money)

For example, a word problem with an Unknown Start might read like this: When Jim got his paycheck, he noticed he had received a $25 raise in pay. His paycheck was now $150. How much was Jim's paycheck before the raise?

*Separate elements or remove/subtract them from a given set* (e.g., money)

An example of a word problem with an Unknown Change in the element set might read like this: Jim receives a paycheck of $150. After he pays his cell phone bill, he has $125 left over. How much money was his cell phone bill?

*Part-Part-Whole represents comparisons between two disjoint sets*

An example of a word problem with an Unknown Result with two sets might read like this: Jim has $125 dollars. He finds $5 of dimes in his bedroom drawer. How much money does he have now?

*Compare*

In a comparison example, the word problem might read like this: Jim receives a $150 paycheck. His friend John has a $135 paycheck. How much more money does Jim have than John?

A second strategy that can be used when learning to solve word problems is a **mnemonic device.** In this strategy, a letter represents an action to be taken. The combination of letters represents a word that helps the student remember what steps are needed to solve the story problem successfully. Mercer and Mercer offer the following mnemonic device:

**R** *Read* the problem correctly

**I** *Identify* the relevant information

**D** *Determine* the operations and unit for expressing the answer

**E** *Enter* the correct numbers and calculate and check the answer

explicit instruction, problem solving and student groups constructing strategies to solve problems, and discussion or "debriefing." Transitional Mathematics goes beyond the basic operations and includes algebra and geometry for students with disabilities.

**Corrective Mathematics.** **Corrective Mathematics** (Engelmann & Carnine, 1981) is a remedial program developed for use with students in grade 3 through a postsecondary level. Its primary focus is on four basic operations, referred to as modules. Each module contains certain strands: facts, computation operations, and story problems. The addition module also has a strand on reading and writing numbers. The program was developed for students who have not mastered addition. Students do need certain preskills to use this program, although advanced reading skills are not required; poor readers can be placed in this program.

Corrective Mathematics is a systematic sequence of skill development following the direct instruction paradigm. Each module contains a presentation book answer keys, and a student book. Each module also includes a placement test, a preskill test, and a series of mastery tests. Using a teacher-directed approach, each presentation book provides specific instructional information for each of the many lessons. Each task within the lesson has a script telling exactly what the teacher should say and do as well as what the students should say and do. Each daily lesson involves some type of teacher-directed activity; most lessons also require some independent student work.

One feature of the program is the built-in point system by which students can accumulate points for successful performance with workbooks, in groups, in game situations, or on the mastery tests. Systems for awarding and monitoring points are programmed into the materials. A common theme in the Corrective Mathematics program is the concept of teaching to criterion. The idea is that at the completion of any exercise, each student should be able to perform a given task without error.

**Transitional Mathematics.** Transitional Mathematics (Sopris West, 2004) is a promising new program that was developed to address the needs of students who are at risk for special education services due to mathematics difficulties and students with learning disabilities. Woodard and Stroh use the title of Transitional Mathematics to communicate the program goal of transitioning "students from struggling with foundational math skills to thinking algebraically." This experimentally based program (Woodward & Brown, 2006) has been researched with students with disabilities in grades four through eight. As a basis for the program, these researchers explain that many of the current reform-based programs are limited in two ways:

- Instruction is often too highly embedded in problem-solving activities that require significant reading comprehension abilities.
- There is not enough distributed practice on concepts once they have been introduced. Reform programs simply move too quickly from one topic to the next. (p. 2)

To counter these limitations, the goal of Transitional Mathematics is to find a balance for students by presenting three levels of instruction. The first level is entitled *Number Sense* and is designed to transition students from the use of whole numbers and arithmetical operations to varied topics common to the middle school curriculum. The second level initiates a *Rational Number* series as well as geometry and data analysis. Finally, the third level is utilized to introduce pre-algebra topics (i.e., negative numbers, exponents, properties, and simple algebraic equations).

The instructional methods of this program involve three distinct components. Most lessons begin with a *warm-up* activity that reviews previously learned material or emphasizes prerequisite skills needed for the current lesson. The warm-up activity is brief and should only last about 5 minutes. The primary component of the instruction is called *guided practice*. As part of a direct instructional approach, the component is designed to explicitly teach the new concepts or procedures and model how to perform the computational method. Once the students understand the new concepts/procedures, a period of student practice with feedback occurs. A final, yet important instructional component is the *application or problem-solving* portion of the lesson. During this period, students can work alone, in pairs, or in teams to try to solve application problems. The purpose of this period is to teach students to work for a sustained time and get them to a point where they are comfortable talking about the problem they are trying to solve. Throughout this period, the teacher participates in a discussion with students (in groups or individually) checking for understanding, ensuring that multiple solutions can be obtained, and introducing explicit problem-solving strategies (e.g., making a table, working backward, etc.). The importance of this last procedure is underscored as it provides opportunities to get students to talk about mathematics, develop verbal skills involving mathematics, and transfer their knowledge to other problems or areas of their life.

Perhaps the most obvious feature of this program is the user-friendly textbooks that were developed for students. The pages of the textbooks have less information on each page when compared to general education textbooks. The examples are easy to follow and are sequential in nature. Separate student workbooks are designed to emphasize each lesson in the textbook and a homework book is provided for the students. In the research sited by Woodward and his colleagues, student attitudinal surveys regarding their experience with the program and the mathematics instruction seems to be more positive when compared to students receiving another method of instructional delivery. Figure 9–9 provides an example of lessons presented in the Number Sense level of the program.

## MATHEMATICS INSTRUCTION FOR STUDENTS AT THE SECONDARY LEVEL

Mathematics instruction for students with disabilities in secondary schools can be the most challenging of all school levels. A 9- to 10-year history of mathematics successes and failures come into the classroom at this

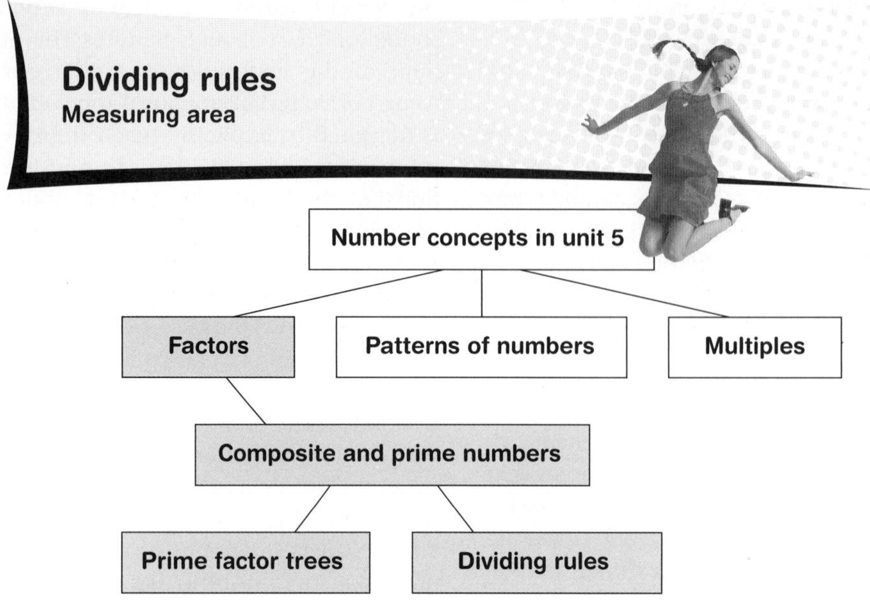


Dividing rules

Most of the numbers that you have factored so far are small numbers. You have been able to use your math facts to figure out the factors for these numbers. But what should you do when you have to factor a big number? You could guess at the factors, but that could take a while, and it would be frustrating.

One way to approach these numbers is to look at them closely and use strategies called dividing rules for factoring them. You already know some of these rules. We'll use examples to review them.

The dividing rules for the numbers 2, 10, 5, 3, and 6 are described on the following pages.

**Dividing rules for 2**

| Rule | Examples | | | | | |
|---|---|---|---|---|---|---|
| **Divide by 2** | 8 | 12 | 66 | 302 | 1,000 | 3,954 |

These are all even numbers. They end in 2, 4, 6, 8, or 0, so we can divide by 2.

**FIGURE 9–9** Sample page from student transitional mathematics textbook—number sense

*Source:* Sopris West. (2004). *Transitional mathematics program.* Longmont, CO: Author.

point. How these students are instructed now is crucial to their success in later years. The following section presents some suggested considerations that may impact mathematics learning for secondary students.

**Curriculum Considerations.** As students with disabilities enter into the higher grades of their secondary education, many instructional decisions must be made to prepare them to succeed according to their academic and real-world needs. For example, teachers may ask themselves whether they should prepare students to (a) access to the general education curriculum; (b) pass minimum competency exams; (c) attend general education classes with a strong tutorial component; (d) attend remedial or compensatory math classes; and/or (e) meet the demands of everyday living in the adult world. How these decisions are made vary from one school and school district to another. However, teachers must continue to develop or select mathematics curriculum according to the needs and demands of their students. To assist in this area, Miller (1997) suggests that teachers consider the characteristics and needs of the students they service. To do so, Miller suggests that teachers consider the setting demands, student characteristics, and curricular decisions involved in organizing the content of the mathematics instruction. For example, Miller notes that one school setting demand is the "grade-level textbook." In relation to this demand, students with mathematics difficulties exhibit the characteristics of poor reading skills (especially for reading problem-solving tasks), poor understanding of graphs and symbols, and poor use of technical language. In response to these setting demands of the classroom textbook and characteristics, Miller suggests that teachers instruct the students in strategies for reading math texts and use supplemental materials as well as practice in reading graphs. Table 9-10 illustrates the setting demands related to mathematics in school and out of school. Of special note, Miller (1996) states that "teachers have to consider and monitor students' attributes continually. Teachers must realize that even the best math curricula may have to be modified to meet the needs of certain students."

**Options to Enhance Attitude.** The NCTM has long recognized that a learner's attitude can profoundly impact success in mathematics. These teachers recognize that mathematics anxiety is no myth and that many students experience a high degree of stress due to the many years of failure or unpleasant experiences related the their instruction in mathematics. Poor attitudes, insecurity, learned helplessness, and no motivation are all descriptors of students who may need attention to their affective deficits and their mathematics performance. To address these deficits and anxieties, teachers may consider the following options designed to enhance learning and address attitudinal challenges.

***Goal Setting.*** Goal-setting procedures have been a primary component of self-determination curriculum (see Chapter 13) that teaches students to act on and promote their own learning. This procedure teaches students to embed a self-motivating component into their learning. In 1989, Fuchs, Bahr, and Rieth found that secondary students who engaged in goal setting in mathematical computation performed better than students who were assigned goals or did not have performance

**TABLE 9–10** Curricular decisions to merge setting demands and student characterists

| *Setting Demands* | *Student Characteristics* | *Curricular Decisions* |
|---|---|---|
| *In School* | | |
| Grade level textbooks | Poor reading skills; lack understanding of graphs, symbols, technical language | Teach strategies for reading math texts; use supplemental materials; practice reading graphs |
| Acquire basic skills<br>Pass competency tests | Deficits in basic facts; poor test-takers; test and math anxiety | Provide extensive practice in basic skills; reteach unmastered skills; provide test-taking strategies and anxiety-reducing techniques |
| Retain previous math learning | Memory deficits | Include daily review; conduct daily timings on basic skills; teach mnemonic devices |
| Demonstrate problem-solving ability | Passive learners; lack strategies; production deficiencies; difficulty deciding what information is important and what is extraneous | Teach strategies for attacking and solving word problems; provide relevant, functional practice |
| *Out-of-School* | | |
| Independent living | Lack basic math skills; history of math failures | Teach basic living skills; emphasize functional math; use real-life simulations |
| Employment | Lack basic math skills | Teach basic skills; provide work setting requirements as rationale for learning |
| Postsecondary and college programs | Poor test-takers; lack prerequisite match skills | Teach test-taking strategies; teach to mastery; teach college preparatory content |

*Source:* Miller, S. P. (1997). Perspectives on Mathematics Instruction. In D. D. Deshler, E. S. Ellis, and B. K. Lenz (Eds.). *Teaching Adolescents with Learning Disabilities: Strategies and Methods* (2nd Ed). Denver, CO: Love Publishing Co. (p. 329). Reprinted with permission.

goals. Additionally, Miller (1997) suggests that engaging students in setting goals for their future and connecting their mathematics instruction to these goals may be another motivational component in the student's learning of their mathematics content. Instructing students on how to develop long-term and short-term goals may provide an educational tool that is of immediate and future value for all involved.

**Peer Tutors.** The use of tutors to enhance instruction has been well documented. Miller et al. (1998) emphasize this enhancement when they review recent studies that look at the use of tutors for math instruction. The use of tutors proved to be beneficial in enhancing the learning of math through the use of counting-on procedures, rote memorization, oral and written drills, and practice using flashcards. Additionally, the use of corrective feedback by the tutors seemed to be an important component in the tutoring of students with learning disabilities.

**Positive Classroom Climate.** Modeling enthusiasm, giving positive feedback, promoting positive expectations, using specific praise, making learning fun, and reducing math anxiety may be considered techniques that promote a positive classroom climate when teaching mathematics (Miller, 1997). For the most part, these are all teacher-related variables that can be implemented into the classroom on a regular and consistent basis. In all cases, these variables require clear and positive communication skills. Additionally, the teacher's attitude or belief that the students can be successful is paramount for the climate to radiate a community of enthusiastic learners. To enhance these communication skills, Lerner (1993) suggests several strategies to facilitate the reduction of mathematics anxiety in the classroom. These strategies include (a) using competition carefully, (b) providing clear directions on assignments, (c) allowing students time to complete their math assignments, and (d) reducing the pressure involved in test taking.

**Evidence-Based Instructional Practices.** Maccini and Gagnon (2000, 2006) outlined the instructional practices most used by general and special education practices in mathematics. These authors suggest that the following evidence-based as well as recommended practices be incorporated in mathematics instruction for students who are struggling with the acquisition and generalization mathematics:

- individualized instruction by the teacher
- additional practice of skills
- reduced classwork problems
- extended time on assignments
- peer or cross-age tutoring
- problems read to students
- cue cards of strategy steps
- use of concrete objects
- individualized attention by class aide
- calculators
- graphic organizers
- mnemonics

Based on their national survey of teachers, Manccini and Gagnon found the above practices widely used by both special and general education teachers. However, the survey also indicated that many general and special education teachers reported that they were uncomfortable instructing students with disabilities in secondary mathematics due to the few mathematics method courses in their university preparatory degree programs. Special education teachers also reported few mathematics courses in general in their preparatory programs. Manccini and Gagnon recommend more collaboration between mathematics teachers of general and special education as well as more mathematics courses taken in degree programs.

**Life Skills Mathematics.** With all students (K–12), mathematics-related life skills need to be a major part of the curriculum. Even college-bound students benefit from life skills instruction if they are to successfully adjust as adults. In particular, however, those students who continue to struggle in their secondary mathematics courses are in great need of real-life related mathematics skills. If they have been unsuccessful in their academic mathematics courses, curriculum decisions must be made to provide them with life skills needed to be productive citizens (see Chapter 15). These students must acquire mathematics skills that will have practical value in their postsecondary lives. For most of these students, their secondary mathematics courses will be the last opportunity in their secondary education to learn these skills.

The major demands with which most adults will have to deal can be categorized into six adult domains: employment/further education, home and family, leisure pursuits, physical and emotional health, community participation, and personal responsibility and interpersonal relationships. These ideas and their curricular importance are discussed at length in Chapter 15;

the mathematical implications for these areas are addressed here.

Much of the everyday math that an individual needs involves various types of measurement. Some math life skills have already been presented in the section on measurement; however, a comprehensive listing of math skills used regularly by most adults is provided in Table 9-11. Math programs should be based on the current and future math needs of students as a function of their probable life situations.

Such planning will include coverage of some math skills that do not have an everyday feel to them. However, the life skills in Table 9-11 are important regardless of the subsequent environments in which students find themselves.

For secondary students, topics covering financial matters such as paychecks, checking and savings accounts, and home budgets are important items to cover, as will be discussed later in the chapter. One of the easiest and most effective ways to deal with these topics on the high

**TABLE 9–11** Mathematics skills typically encountered in adulthood

| | *Applied Skills* | | | | | |
|---|---|---|---|---|---|---|
| *Life Demand* | *Money* | *Time* | *Capacity/Volume* | *Length* | *Weight/Mass* | *Temperature* |
| **Employment** | | | | | | |
| transportation pay: | x | x | | x | | |
| -wages | x | x | | | | |
| -deductions | x | | | | | |
| -taxes | x | | | | | |
| -retirement | x | x | | | | |
| -investment savings | x | x | | | | |
| hours worked | | x | | | | |
| overtime | x | x | | | | |
| breaks/lunch | x | x | | | | |
| **Further Education** | | | | | | |
| budgeting | x | x | | | | |
| costs | x | | | | | |
| financing | x | | | | | |
| time management: | | x | | | | |
| -requisite course hours | | | | | | |
| -scheduling | | x | | | | |
| -extracurricular | | x | | | | |
| **Home/Family** | | | | | | |
| budgeting bills: | x | x | | | | |
| -payment options | x | x | | | | |
| -day-to-day costs | x | | | | | |
| -long-term purchases | x | | | | | |
| locating a home: | | | | | | |
| -rental or purchase | x | x | x | x | | |
| -moving | x | x | x | | x | |
| -insurance | x | x | | | | |
| -contracts | x | x | | | | |
| -affordability | x | | | | | |
| -utilities | x | x | | | | |
| mortgage | x | x | | | | |
| home repair/maintenance | x | x | x | x | x | x |
| financial management: | x | | | | | |
| -checking/savings account | | | | | | |
| -credit cards | x | x | | | | |
| -insurance | x | x | | | | |
| -taxes | x | x | | | | |
| -investment | x | x | | | | |

*(continued)*

**TABLE 9–11** (continued)

| Life Demand | Applied Skills: Money | Time | Capacity/Volume | Length | Weight/Mass | Temperature |
|---|---|---|---|---|---|---|
| automobile: | | | | | | |
| -payments | x | x | | | | |
| -maintenance | x | x | x | x | x | x |
| -repair | x | | | | | |
| -fuel costs | x | | x | | | |
| cooking | x | x | x | x | x | x |
| yard maintenance | x | x | x | x | x | x |
| home remodeling | x | x | x | x | x | x |
| decorating | x | x | x | x | x | x |
| shopping: | x | x | x | | x | |
| -comparing prices | x | x | x | | | x |
| laundry | | | | | | |
| **Leisure Pursuits** | | | | | | |
| travel | x | x | | x | x | x |
| subscription costs | x | x | | | | |
| reading newspaper | x | x | x | x | x | x |
| equipment costs: | | | | | | |
| -rental or purchase | x | x | | | | |
| sports activities | x | x | | x | x | x |
| entertainment | x | x | | x | | x |
| hobbies | x | x | x | x | x | x |
| **Personal Responsibility and Relationships** | | | | | | |
| dating | x | x | | | | |
| scheduling | | x | | | | |
| anniversaries/birthdays/etc. | x | x | | | | |
| correspondence | x | x | x | | x | |
| gifts | x | x | | | | |
| **Health** | | | | | | |
| physical development | | | | | | |
| -weight | | | | | x | |
| -height | | | | x | | |
| -caloric intake | | | | x | | |
| -nutrition | x | x | | | x | |
| physical fitness program | x | x | | x | x | |
| doctor's visits | x | x | | x | x | x |
| medications | x | x | | | | |
| medically related procedures (e.g., blood pressure) | | x | x | | | x |
| **Community Involvement** | | | | | | |
| scheduling | | x | | x | | |
| voting | | x | | x | | |
| public transportation | | x | x | | x | |
| menu use | | x | x | | | |
| financial transactions: | | | | | | |
| -phone usage | x | x | | | | |
| -using specific community services | x | x | | x | | |
| -emergency services | x | x | | x | | x |

*Source:* Adapted from "Preparing Students with Learning Disabilities for the Real-Life Math Demands of Adulthood: A Life Skills Orientation to Mathematics Instruction," by J. R. Patton, M. E. Cronin, D. Bassett, and A. Koppel, 1997, *Journal of Learning Disabilities, 30,* pp. 180–181. Copyright 1997 by PRO-ED, Inc. Adapted with permission.

school level is to print paychecks on ditto sheets and issue these checks to students at the end of the week. By explaining various types of withholding, students are forewarned that deductions are made from paychecks and they will actually receive less money than expected (i.e., take-home pay). Students can use numerous commercial materials in the exercise, but classroom instruction based on students' actual experiences with paychecks and yearly taxes is the most effective teaching technique. Students need to become familiar with various time schedules, reimbursements, deductions, taxes, and the corresponding calculations involved with each.

Home budgeting can be taught with reproductions of bills and statements for utilities, rent, food, and clothes. Basic bookkeeping skills can also be taught at this time. During the process students should be maintaining home records and filing receipts. Banking skills should also be taught directly. Students should learn how to deposit and withdraw money, write checks, and maintain a savings account, using both traditional methods and modern, electronic methods. It may be advisable to expose students to the variety of financial software now available as well.

An alternative to workbooks or a simulated unit of money is a currency-based token economy in the classroom. Although token economies are usually developed to provide external motivation for students or to control disruptive behavior, a currency-based economy can also be used effectively to teach children many economic concepts. It can enhance the teaching of counting, change making, and the relative value of money; and it provides an environment that promotes decision making regarding the safekeeping of money, buying power, and investments. In school-based vocational training programs, students can be paid for coming to class on time, punching in and out, getting to work quickly without delay, and doing accurate work (correct number of questions answered, as in piecework).

As students become accustomed to the currency system, a bank can be developed to introduce checking and savings accounts as well as other investment vehicles. Even more advanced is the development of a credit-card system. Also, students can set up their own proprietorships and sell things they make. If students do set up their own business, it might be interesting and educational to provide instruction in sales tax, sales skills, and advertising.

***Relevance of Life Skills.*** Those who have encountered much frustration with the acquisition of the skills they will need as adults must first find skills relevant to their present as well as their future needs. This is particularly true of older students, who feel the greatest cumulative effect of frustration and lack of interest. Students may feel that what they are learning is not applicable to real-life experiences.

Teaching students math-related life skills stimulates conceptual knowledge and improves student motivation, participation, and generalization (Maccini & Gagnon, 2000; Mercer, Jordan, & Miller, 1994). These skills can be addressed in any type of placement, whether it is a special class or general education class. The instructional options range from the development of life skills course work to integrating these topics into existing curricula. Life skills instruction is discussed in detail in Chapter 15.

A useful way of making math more interesting to more students is to provide examples of how math can be used in everyday life. Teachers may create materials to provide students with activities that require them to apply the math skills they have learned to fascinating real-life situations. The most important feature of this type of activity is that it can stimulate the development of other ideas that are relevant to the local area in which students live.

**Reflective Question 9–5:** ***What instructional practices are you most comfortable using when teaching mathematics skills to struggling learners?***

## TECHNOLOGY IN THE CLASSROOM

Mercer and Mercer (2005) present an argument for using technology to teach content areas such as mathematics to students with special needs. They state that teachers need "to examine the instructional possibilities of new technologies for educating students with learning problems" (p. 68) to enhance their learning experience. In today's world, children are introduced to tech-nology at a very early age. They are not afraid to explore new ways of playing with technology. Incorporating this familiar and engaging aspect of their lives is desirable for students who might be apprehensive to engage in mathematic problems with paper and pencil. When we think of technology and mathematics instruction, we generally think of the calculator as the technological tool of choice. Although true, Mercer and Mercer present several more options including the calculator:

- Calculator—use for arithmetic, algebraic, and trigonometric functions
- Computer-Assisted Instruction (CAI)/Integrated Learning Systems (ILS)—use for drill and practice skills

**TECHNOLOGY *Tips***

Teachers now have access to numerous websites to enhance the teaching of math in their classrooms. Of particular interest are the following websites.

- AskERIC Lesson Plans: Enigmas. This website was developed by the Educational Resources Information Center (ERIC) of the National Library of Education. The website can be found at the following link: *http://ericir.syr.edu/virtual/lessons/Interdisciplinary/INT0017.html.* The goal is to teach about mysterious elements of literature, math, science, and technology.
- Education in Science, Technology, Engineering, and Math (ESTEEM). You can reach this website at the following link: *http://www.sandia.gov/ESTEEM/home.html.* This website presents the Education of Science, Technology, Energy, Engineering, and Math (ESTEEM) program of the U.S. Department of Education. It includes information for teachers and students from middle school to college.
- Knowledge Adventure. This website is a collection of websites for children. It offers access to games and activities in the areas of art, early language, entertainment, math, reading, science, study skills, and typing, for all ages. A teacher can link up to this website by typing in *http://www.knowledgeadventure.com/home/*
- KidsClick. This website features a collection of links to online resources for children. The site was initiated under a federal Library Service and Technology Act (LSTA) grant. It contains links to many categories including math. A teacher can link up to this website by typing in *http://sunsite.berkeley.edu/kidsclick%21/*

- Distance Education—use for secondary students needing course work or additional help
- Laser Videodiscs—use as an interactive device with print and still or moving images; disc players are required
- Microcomputer-Based Labs (MBLs)—use to integrate mathematics with science projects
- Presentation Software—use with overhead projectors to present mathematic problems and rehearse verbal expression of mathematics as well as the use of graphs

Reflective Question 9–6: ***How can computers and calculators be integrated as part of the daily mathematics instruction?***

## MAKING IT WORK

Mathematics instruction requires attention to all of the components of the effective instruction model depicted in earlier chapters. Selected aspects of effective instruction practice as they apply to mathematics instruction contribute to making your mathematics instruction work in your class.

**Scheduling.** Of the various precursors to teaching, an important consideration is the organization of the math period. One way to schedule the class period includes the following components: review of previously covered material; teacher-directed instruction of new content when acquisition-stage learning occurs; a time for independent practice, typically during seatwork; and allocated time for assigning homework. Managing these components is complicated by the nature of the students in the class (i.e., the skill level of students) and the number of math groups that exist.

Many teachers have found a daily timed test (about 2 or 3 minutes long) to be effective for collecting curriculum-based data on students' performance as well as for management purposes. Students tend to get on task quickly when they know that they have only limited time to perform the tasks required.

**Student Motivation.** Many students find math uninteresting and lose any desire to pursue it later in their school careers. The subject can be taught so that it becomes a fun time of the school day. Teachers should attempt to make math instruction engaging by incorporating intriguing activities and topics in their lessons. Math games and brain teasers are some of the ways this can be done; relating mathematics to other academic areas can also be effective.

**Demonstration/Guided Practice/Independent Practice Paradigm.** Of particular importance among the teaching behaviors is ensuring that every student receives some teacher-directed instruction as part of the demonstration/guided practice/independent practice routine. Students with mild learning problems are not apt to acquire basic skills from workbooks or worksheets alone; they need to be taught these skills directly. Acquired skills can then be improved through practice. Unfortunately, some commercially available math materials do not provide enough practice, and few offer suggestions for presenting teacher-aided practice.

**Clear Communication.** Students get very confused when material is presented to them in disorganized and unclear ways. Teachers must take time to be sure that their verbal explanations are precise and meaningful to the students with whom they are working. Instructional attention needs to be given to the language of instruction, the types of examples used to explain a topic, and the manner in which instruction is delivered. In the absence of this attention, students will be confused and fail to understand the concepts being presented, which may result in them losing motivation to remain engaged in the lesson.

**Informational Feedback.** Foremost among follow-up activities is the need to give students feedback. For students who do not enjoy or see the relevance of mathematics, external systems may be required to provide motivational feedback. Such systems must be implemented consistently and fairly. All students require informational feedback on their performance, particularly if their responses are incorrect. Informational feedback implies that teachers solicit student explanations (i.e., verbalizations) about how they arrived at their answers. This evaluation will often result in reteaching some concepts if students fail to understand them. All too often student work is evaluated in terms of product rather than process. In other words, the only feedback students may receive is the number of items that are incorrect or correct.

## SUMMARY

The purposes of this chapter were to acquaint the reader with three aspects of mathematical instruction: background, assessment, and instruction. The field of mathematics and mathematics instruction is wide and quite diverse. To equip a teacher in this area would require mathematics methods courses that address the learning and teaching of mathematics to students with diverse needs in much more depth. Perhaps the most important message, however, is that teachers approach mathematics instruction with a professional obligation to assess student abilities, monitor their progress, choose evidence-based practices that best fits their needs, and engage their students in every aspect of their learning.

## ACTIVITIES

### ELEMENTARY LEVEL

#### Precomputational

1. To develop the ability to count from 1 to 10, have pupils play rhyming games such as "Buckle My Shoe."
2. Make different cutouts of three basic shapes (circles, triangles, rectangles); have pupils identify each shape. After pupils can identify each different shape, have them compare the sizes of the different shapes to determine which is larger, smaller, and so on.
3. Pupils can learn the concepts of "more" and "less" by comparing groups of objects. Start with one object in one group and two or more objects in another group. Have the pupil identify which group has more and which has less. This activity could also be used to teach sameness.
4. Draw a line of objects, such as apples; have a pupil put an *X* on the number of objects designated by the numeral at the beginning of the line.
5. Have pupils match strings to kites, sails to boats, or stems to flowers to help develop an understanding of one-to-one correspondence.
6. Make up ditto sheets with similar but different-sized figures (e.g., animals, toys, buildings) in each of several boxes. Have pupils cross out the largest and/or smallest figure in each box.
7. Using a felt board or pocket chart, have pupils match a set of objects with a numeral. For example, they might match two apples with the numeral 2.
8. Using a felt board or pocket chart, have pupils match a number word with a set of objects. Next, have pupils match a numeral and a number word with a set of objects.
9. Group objects in sets from 1 to 10; place several numerals next to each set and instruct pupils to circle the correct numeral.
10. Instruction in writing numerals from 1 through 9 should be started when a pupil is learning to write in manuscript. Have pupils trace the numerals to be learned, make the numerals by connecting dots, and finally write the numerals independently.
11. Have students complete dot-to-dot puzzles of simple designs (e.g., circle, square, triangle) and then of more complicated pictures (e.g., boats, animals, cars).

12. Cut numerals from old calendars and paste each on cardboard. Ask pupils to arrange the numbers in proper sequence without using the calendar page (Crescimbeni, 1965).
13. Request students to count silently the number of times you bounce a ball or buzz a buzzer. Challenge a pupil to state the correct number; if correct, ask that student to take your role.
14. Make seasonal puzzles with number as cues (e.g., jack-o-lanterns with different numbers of teeth, turkeys with different number of tail feathers, Christmas trees with different numbers of decorations). The student must count the items, find the puzzle piece with the corresponding numeral, and fit the pieces together.

### Computational

1. Have students make combinations of less than 10 by first counting real or pictured objects and then writing the correct number.
2. To ensure understanding of addition (or any other operation), introduce the concept of the missing element. This can be done in a way that is similar to the following example:

   $1 + 4 =$ ____ $1 +$ ____ $= 5$ ____ $-4 = 5$

3. An abacus is a good, concrete way to introduce students to the idea of place value. Show pupils when they get to 10 beads in the same row on the combinations and then write the number indicated on the abacus.
4. Have students play counting games in which the counting changes direction every time a bell rings.
5. Strengthen concepts of "before" and "after" by having pupils find the missing number in a series.
6. Help students learn to carry by covering all but the number column they are working with in a given problem.
7. Start work with fractional numbers by having students actually manipulate the fractional part to see that all parts are equal.
8. As students manipulate equal fractional parts, give them a chance to label them; for instance, if there are four parts, then each part should be labeled one fourth or ¼.
9. As students learn to count and write numerals, encourage them to make their own number line using tape or some other material.
10. Beginning instruction in subtraction should focus on actually taking away concrete objects, then crossing out pictures of objects, and finally working with pure abstraction.
11. Help students perceive the relationship of addition and subtraction by having them first add two sets of numbers and then subtract the two numbers from the derived sum.
12. Because multiplication involves grouping of sets, show students an arrangement like the following, requesting that they make several similar sets.
13. Make a ditto sheet with objects in sets like those in Activity 12. Have pupils write how many objects are in each set. Then instruct pupils to write the same statements, using only numbers.
14. To show the relationship between addition and multiplication, have students first add the same number several times and then multiply that number by the number of times it was added.

   $$\underline{3 + 3 + 3 + 3 = 15} \qquad \underline{3 \times 5 = 15}$$
   $$6 + 6 + 6 = 18 \qquad 6 \times 3 = 18$$

15. Concepts of "more" and "less" can be further developed by using multiplication facts. Require pupils to underline which is more or less.

| *more* | *less* |
|---|---|
| 2 threes or 5 | 3 fives or 18 |
| 3 twos or 7 | 4 twos or 10 |

16. A pupil with a short attention span can sometimes do as much work as another pupil if arithmetic work is broken into smaller segments. To achieve this goal, cut a worksheet into small parts (e.g., rows of problems) or make up arithmetic problems on three-by-five cards that the pupil picks up each time a problem is completed.
17. After students learn basic division facts, have them show how a given number is divided into several equal parts.

| | |
|---|---|
| 6 = ____ twos | 6 = ____ threes |
| 12 = ____ sixes | 12 = ____ threes |
| 12 = ____ twos | 12 = ____ fours |

## MIDDLE AND SECONDARY LEVEL

1. Make a math center using index cards with basic computational skills of addition, subtraction, multiplication, or division on each card. Arrange the cards according to sequential skills (i.e., basic addition facts, carrying, and so on). Students can

check their own recording sheets to show individual growth. Commercially prepared activity cards, such as Contemporary Math Facts Activity Cards (Prentice Hall Learning Systems), cover all math areas.

2. Many recently developed electronic games can be used to teach or reinforce math skills. Students also can check their work with them.
3. Simple calculators can be used to check work. In addition, these devices can be used for motivation; a student who finishes work on time or ahead of time can check it with the calculator.
4. More metric-related activities are needed to help students with disabilities understand the different systems of measurement. To show the difference in liquid measurement, empty a liquid from a container with a known measure to a container showing the metric equivalent.
5. Using pictures of various items that can be bought in restaurants, direct students to make up menus and choose what they will eat. Have them write the name of the food and its price, and then add the prices to determine the total bill. As a bonus, figure out what the tip would be.
6. Give students practice reducing fractions to the lowest terms by making fraction cookies. Reduce all the fractions in the recipe and follow the directions as given.

   **Ingredients:**

   a. $\frac{4}{2}$ cup of sugar
   b. $\frac{2}{4}$ cup of milk
   c. $\frac{3}{3}$ stick of margarine
   d. $\frac{4}{8}$ cup cocoa
   e. Bring ingredients to a boil in a saucepan. Cool slightly.
   f. Add $\frac{2}{2}$ cup peanut butter and $2\frac{2}{4}$ cup oatmeal.
   g. Drop on waxed paper.
   h. Makes $1\frac{4}{4}$ dozen cookies.

7. Let two students roll dice to practice addition facts. The object of the game is to be the first player to score 100 points from the totals on the dice rolled. The players take turns rolling the dice; each may continue to roll as long as neither die shows a 1 but may stop voluntarily at any point. When either die does show a 1, the player gives up the turn and loses all points earned during that turn. If a 1 is rolled on both dice, the player gives up the turn, loses all points, and starts again at zero (Mercer, 1979).
8. Have each student draw a place-value chart. Draw a card from a deck of 10 with a digit (0 to 9) written on each. Direct students to record that digit in any column they wish. Continue drawing until five cards have been drawn. The student with the largest number wins. Require the winner to read the winning number correctly. Modify as appropriate.
9. Cut a piece of tagboard into a circle as large as the center of a car tire. Tape the tagboard into the center of a tire. Write these directions on the circle: (a) measure the radius of the circle, (b) tell the diameter of the circle, (c) find the circumference of the circle. Use different types of tires and other circular items to vary this activity.
10. Real Life Math, Living on a Paycheck, is a math-based consumer education simulation program. Students move out of their parents' homes to Willow, U.S.A., the city where they get their first jobs and their first apartments. Students hunt for and choose apartments. They sign leases, pay security deposits, start paying rent, and move in. They buy starter furniture and basic household needs. Students who think they will have trouble affording an apartment on their own choose roommates and begin making joint decisions.
11. After filling out applications and being interviewed, students get a job. They receive paychecks based on actual school attendance. For 70 simulated days, they budget their money to:

    - rent and furnish their apartments
    - buy cars and gas fill-ups
    - pay bills
    - buy groceries
    - pay for leisure activities
    - buy clothes
    - pay for medical care

    The 70 simulated days can translate to either a one- or two-semester course activity. Choosing possible shortcuts, limiting elaboration, keeping all students working together, and doing activities in groups as needed to stay on track will allow the program to be completed in one semester.

CHAPTER

# 10

# *Science and Social Studies*

Science and social studies are two of the big four subject areas along with language arts and math. During the elementary grades, these subjects introduce students to critical content and concepts on which more advanced courses in these areas are based. Furthermore, these subject areas develop sets of skills (e.g., inquiry skills in science and analytical skills in social studies) that will be tapped in later coursework as well as in life outside of school.

More students with special needs are experiencing these subjects areas at higher rates than ever before for two major reasons. First, IDEA mandates that students with disabilities must be provided with access to the general education curriculum. Second, each year more students with disabilities are spending more time in inclusive settings.

Students are typically curious about their surroundings and about the people and things inhabiting them. As a result, they have a natural interest in seeking information about their environment and the events occurring within it. Teachers should take advantage of this curiosity by exposing students to science and social studies topics that capitalize on their interests and backgrounds. This subject area is rich with topics and issues that provide wonderful opportunities for active student involvement and ways to relate knowledge and skills to students' everyday lives.

In the past, science and social studies have often had a low priority in the educational curriculum for students with mild learning difficulties (Patton, Polloway, & Cronin, 1987, 1994). However, as students with mild learning problems engage the general education curriculum, as required by IDEA, consideration of these academic areas becomes critically important in order to provide appropriate instruction. As pointed out earlier in the book, these two subjects are key areas for which states have developed content and performance standards and on which many students with mild learning problems will be tested.

In considering why science and social studies have been underemphasized in the past, Price, Ness, and Stitt (1982) suggest that the overwhelming thrust in many programs for students with mild disabilities was on the development and remediation of basic skills. Without question, most students with mild learning problems were referred on the basis of difficulties in reading, written language, or math. Referrals were not made because a student had particular trouble in understanding a science or social studies concept.

In addition, personnel-preparation programs neglected these areas; few special education training programs required or even offered coursework in which topics were dedicated to how to teach science and social studies to students with special learning needs. Patton et al. (1994) found that a significant number of special education teachers reported that they had received no training of any type (i.e., preservice or inservice) in these areas. Not surprisingly, most special education personnel feel unprepared and uncomfortable teaching these subjects. However, many of them are assigned to teach in these areas, especially at the secondary level, and often find themselves teaching credit-generating science and social studies courses to students in diploma-track programs. The requirement of students being taught by "highly qualified" teachers, as espoused by the No Child Left Behind Act, has initiated measures to address this issue, especially for special education teachers at the secondary level.

The typical general education classroom contains students with a range of diverse needs. General educators who teach science and social studies often feel unprepared to work with special learners. Many general education teachers are faced with significant challenges in meeting the needs of students with learning and behavior problems in science and social studies, given the nature of the presenting problems that this group of students brings to the classroom, as discussed in the next section.

How to accommodate the needs of students with learning-related difficulties, especially in terms of science and social studies, is still not adequately covered in the preservice programs of many general education teachers. Method courses in science and social studies that general education teachers take at the preservice level allot very little time to the concept of universal design for learning (UDL), as discussed in Chapter 1, or the acquisition of skills to be able to accommodate the diverse needs of students. Textbooks typically dedicate some coverage to the topic of students with disabilities; however, explicit "what to do" information is meager.

Courses specifically designed for general educators that cover accommodative techniques typically do not go into enough detail to ensure that general education teachers become competent to address diverse learning needs. A few books, written to help general educators address the needs of special learners, do exist that actually provide specific information on teaching science and social studies (e.g., Lenz & Schumaker, 1999; Mastropieri & Scruggs, 2007). Unfortunately, more coverage is needed to adequately prepare general education teachers to deal with these students in inclusive settings.

Instructional suggestions for working with students with diverse learning needs have not usually been effectively conveyed to general education personnel on an inservice basis either. For this reason, special education personnel who work collaboratively and cooperatively with general educators need to be able to assist them in this task. To do so, however, means that special education personnel need to know the content and the methods for teaching science.

Another rationale for the importance of students with diverse learning needs receiving sound instruction in science and social studies is worth noting. Science along with social studies should be recognized as foundation subjects that have major life skill implications (Patton, 1995). As a result, these subjects must be taught to all students, sometimes utilizing different emphases depending on the current and future needs of the students. The functional implications of these subjects will be discussed in Chapter 14. There are many reasons for doing so, including the following important benefits of quality science programs.

- Firsthand experiences particularly help students become familiar with their surroundings (Jacobson & Bergman, 1991).
- Basic skills can be applied in meaningful contexts (Cronin, Patton, & Wood, 2007).
- A rich experiential background can be developed to establish "knowledge frameworks into which students can integrate new ideas, relationships, and details" (Jenkins, Stein, & Osborn, 1981, p. 37).
- Students have the opportunity to develop higher-thinking skills and problem-solving strategies (Carnine, 1992; Woodward & Noell, 1992).
- Certain topics covered in science and social studies are essential for dealing successfully with the demands of adulthood and are useful for lifelong interests (Cronin et al., 2007).

## PRESENTING CHALLENGES FOR STUDENTS WITH SPECIAL NEEDS IN SCIENCE AND SOCIAL STUDIES

In addition to the limitations imposed when teachers are not prepared appropriately to address the diverse and often challenging needs of students with learning-related problems, a number of other factors contribute to the challenge of providing appropriate instruction in science and social studies. Some of these factors include:

- specific characteristics that interfere with learning such as problems with attention or lack of appropriate interpersonal skills
- specific physical or sensory limitations that require specific accommodations
- scheduling issues that pull students out of these classes so that they may receive additional remedial attention
- the nature of the curricular materials that are used in the class
- the skill demands associated with activity-oriented lessons that teachers require, and assume, students possess

The last two factors will be explored further in this section of the chapter. Far too often students are unable to read the textbooks or participate appropriately in class discussions and activities. The results are minimum learning and increased undesirable behaviors. Attention to these issues, especially prior to actual instruction, is critical.

## Problems with Curricular Materials

As mentioned previously, few materials are designed with the idea of accommodating students' learning differences right from the start (Heron & Jorgensen, 1994)—the underlying concept of UDL. Given the heavy reliance on the use of textbooks (Jarrett, 1999)—with nearly 85% of public schools using a textbook approach to teaching science (Brownell & Thomas, 1998)—and the demanding features of these books, it is no surprise that many students have difficulties with these materials. Moreover, much of the accompanying tasks that students are required to use as in-class activities or as homework (e.g., worksheets to complete) present a similar set of challenges for students.

Lenz and Schumaker (1999) identified 12 design characteristics that are major determinants of how useful materials are for students with diverse learning needs. These design qualities are presented in Table 10–1 along with a brief explanation of what each feature

**TABLE 10–1** Design problems in curriculum materials and possible solutions

| *Design Problem* | *Short-Term Design Adaptation* | *Long-Term Instructional Goal* |
|---|---|---|
| 1. *Abstractness.* The content appears too conceptual, hypothetical, and impractical. | Provide students with more concrete examples, analogies, interpretations, or experiences. | Teach students how to seek more examples, explanations, and interpretations through questioning and research. |
| 2. *Organization.* The organization is not clear or is poorly structured. | Make the organization explicit for students by creating graphic organizers and reading guides and inserting cues that focus attention. | Teach students how to survey materials and identify text organization, read to confirm organization of ideas, and reorganize information for personal understanding and use. |
| 3. *Relevance.* The information does not appear to have any relationship to students or their lives. | Make the connections between the information and students lives explicit by building rationales and tying information to student experiences. | Teach students to ask appropriate questions about relevance, search for personal connections, and explore ways to make content relevant when given material that appears irrelevant to their lives. |
| 4. *Interest.* The information or presentation of the information is boring. | Present information and assignments in ways that build on students' attention spans, participation, strengths, and interests. | Teach students self-management strategies for controlling attention in boring situations and how to lake advantage of options and choices provided in assignments to make work more interesting. |
| 5. *Skills.* The information is written at a level that assumes and requires skills beyond those possessed by students. | Present information in ways that use the skills students have. | Provide intensive instruction in basic skills required for basic literacy to middle school students who are unprepared for secondary-school content. |
| 6. *Strategies.* The information is presented in ways that assume that students know how to approach tasks effectively and efficiently in strategic ways. | Provide instruction in learning strategies to students who do not know how to approach and complete tasks. | Cue and guide students in how to approach and complete learning and performance tasks by leading them through complex tasks. |
| 7. *Background.* Understanding information usually requires critical background knowledge, but students often lack the experiences and concepts (or cannot make connections to personal background experiences) to make new information meaningful. | Present information in ways that provide background experiences or make background linkages clear. | Teach students how to become consumers of information from a variety of information sources and how to ask questions of these sources to gain background knowledge and insights. |

(*continued*)

**TABLE 10–1** (continued)

| Design Problem | Short-Term Design Adaptation | Long-Term Instructional Goal |
|---|---|---|
| 8. *Complexity.* The information or associated tasks have many parts or layers. | Break down the information or tasks and present them explicitly and in different ways so that students can learn and perform. | Teach students how to "chunk" tasks, represent complex information graphically, ask clarifying questions, and work collaboratively in teams to attack complex tasks. |
| 9. *Quantity.* There is a lot of difficult or complex information that is crucial to remember. | Present the information in ways that facilitate remembering. | Teach strategies for chunking, organizing, and remembering information. |
| 10. *Activities.* The instructional activities and sequences provided do not lead to understanding or mastery. | Provide students with scaffolded learning experiences that include additional or alternative instructional activities, activity sequences, or practice experiences to ensure mastery at each level of learning before instruction continues. | Teach students to independently check and redo work, review information, seek help, ask clarifying questions, and inform others when they need more or different types of instruction before instruction in more content begins. |
| 11. *Outcomes.* The information does not cue students how to think about or study information to meet intended outcomes. | Inform students about expectations for their learning and performance. | Teach students how to identify expectations and goals embedded in materials or to create and adjust goals based on previous experiences with similar materials. |
| 12. *Responses.* The material does not provide options for students to demonstrate competence in different ways. | Provide opportunities to students to demonstrate what they know in different ways. | Teach students how they can best demonstrate competence, identify and advantage of performance options and choices when they are offered, and request appropriate adaptations of tests and competency evaluations. |

*Source:* From *Adapting Language Arts, Social Studies, and Science Materials for the Inclusive Classroom* by B. K. Lenz and J. B. Schumaker, 1999, pp. 12–13, Copyright 1999 by the Council for Exceptional Children. Adapted with permission.

means. In examining this list, teachers can identify potential problems and make necessary adaptations. Certain features highlighted in Table 10–1 warrant more attention:

- **Abstractness:** Much of science and social studies involves the understanding of concepts. For many students with diverse learning needs, being able to grasp complex concepts is not easy. This is particularly the case for students with mild intellectual disabilities.
- **Skills:** A range of skills is expected from students in these subject areas. The ability to skim or scan textual passages is essential to complete assignments and to study for tests. The ability to organize information gleaned from reading textual material is essential.
- **Strategies:** To effectively master the content of these subject areas the appropriate and efficient use of various strategies is required. For instance, in classes where the memorization of facts that are embedded in the textual material is demanded for success on quizzes or tests, certain strategic behaviors are needed. Many students do not possess these strategies.
- **Background:** Without question, those students who come to science and social studies with rich experiential backgrounds are at greater advantage in mastering what is presented, read, discussed, and tested. One of the most challenging aspects of these subject areas is the overwhelming amount of new vocabulary that is introduced. Mastropieri and Scruggs (1992), in their evaluation of textbooks, identified an amazing number of new vocabulary words introduced (750 in one series and 1,831 in another). For many students, this becomes a daunting reality that consumes their energy and takes away from mastering and integrating the meanings of science content (Cawley, Foley, & Miller, 2003).
- **Quantity:** Looking at almost any secondary level social studies textbook is a humbling experience.

The amount of information that is presented in a chapter is massive. The amount of detail that must be assimilated, and related to more general themes, borders on overwhelming for the best of students. The fact that many students with diverse learning needs become frustrated easily when trying to operate in this type of inclusive setting is not hard to understand.

### Problems with Skill Demands

The previous section already touched on the skills that are needed to handle science and social studies instruction, especially at the upper elementary grades and secondary level. Atwood and Oldham (1985) highlight the three major presenting problems of students who have learning-related problems when placed in activity-oriented general education settings: (a) deficiencies in language (i.e., reading, listening, writing, speaking); (b) difficulty with new concepts and vocabulary; and (c) inappropriate behaviors.

One of most critical problems that students with special needs have is their inability to engage the topics that are being discussed or presented in class. Heron and Jorgensen's (1994) description of James's problems with the unit on the Civil War illustrates a common situation.

> James is a gregarious ninth grader who is labeled learning disabled in both language and reading. . . .
>
> Last semester, James participated in an interdisciplinary unit on the Civil War. Students read *The Killer Angels*, a novel by Michael Shaara about Gettysburg; watched Ken Burns's *Civil War* documentary; and read from their history textbook. The students raised money for a class trip to Gettysburg, and their final assignment was a research paper. James floundered despite the activity-based focus of the classroom. The novel was too long and had difficult vocabulary. The textbook had some pictures, but the reading level was well above his ability.
>
> The trip to Gettysburg was a high point. James was deeply stirred by the number of casualties and chose to research the battle of Gettysburg. He began gathering sources; the encyclopedia was useful, but most of the other books in the high school library were at a high reading level. . . .
>
> He completed a traditional outline and went to the writing lab for help with his paper. The writing specialist realized that James knew something about Gettysburg but had not mastered the information in his notes and had difficulty expressing his ideas verbally. James only had time to complete one draft. The paper was two pages long, with stodgy sentences, and three references. (p. 56)

James's story illustrates that many students with special needs, when in inclusive settings, are faced with a host of demands for which they are not well-equipped to handle. James's situation underscores the reality that the skill requirements for which minimum levels of competence are needed cut across instructional activities.

Munk, Bruckert, Call, Stoehrmann, and Radandt (1998) describe another perspective on the problem of low rates of responding demonstrated by students with special needs in science classes. They note that students with special needs may display the following:

- poor performance in discussions requiring recall of vocabulary or simple facts (e.g., failure to recall layers of earth)
- low rates of active academic responding during extended reading assignments, whole-class lecture, or group activity-based lessons (e.g., not asking questions, waiting for peers to respond to questions or tasks; p. 74)

The important point to consider from the examples provided above is that the interaction between the demands of science and social studies and the skill levels of students with diverse learning needs will often create significant challenges for general education and special education teachers. Knowing what to expect in the way of presenting problems is a critical first step in addressing the needs of students either proactively through a "frontloaded" philosophy of dealing with diversity from the start that emphasizes proactive attention to projected needs (Heron & Jorgensen, 1994) or through a more "accommodative" philosophy where solutions are found for the issues as they arise.

**Reflective Question 10–1:** ***Why do the subject areas of science and social studies present unique challenges for students with special needs? How must teachers conceptualize the task of teaching these subjects to students who have difficulties in related areas such as reading or writing?***

## TEACHING SCIENCE TO LEARNERS WITH SPECIAL NEEDS

Science is very much a part of everyone's daily life. It includes topics that can have a major impact on our personal, family, workplace, and community needs and, as Sunal and Sunal (2003) stress: "It is the right of all citizens to be scientifically literate, since literacy affects the quality of life of every person" (p. 262). As a result, science should be made meaningful to students in a long-term sense as well as relevant to their current needs. It is essential to interest students of both genders with special needs in science early on and to maintain this interest over their school careers. And now IDEA essentially requires it.

Of all the subject areas taught, science may be one of the most fascinating as well as one of the most feared by many teachers. The following example, although it involves a student with unusually advanced language skills, illustrates both points.

> I was invited to go on a "reef walk" with a class of gifted third and fourth graders. It is very educational to do such a thing with this type of youngster. While we were wading in some shallow water, we came upon a familiar marine organism called a "feather duster." Being cognizant of being with a group of young students but forgetting that they were students with vocabularies which were well advanced of their nongifted age peers, I was about ready to say something like "Look how that thing hangs on the rock." Before I could get my highly descriptive statement out, Eddie, one of the students who always amazes us with his comments, offered the following: "Notice how securely anchored the organism is to the stationary coral." All I could say was "Yes, I do." (Blackbourn, Patton, & Trainor, 2004, p. 213)

How exciting to be out on a reef actually seeing, touching, and experiencing nature; but how threatening to realize that a student may know more about something than you do or that someone may ask you a question for which you do not have an immediate answer. Many teachers who do not have extensive science training express reservations about teaching anything connected with science. Nevertheless, by using effective instructional techniques as outlined in Chapter 1 and discussed in Chapter 3, by refusing to feel intimidated by the subject itself, and by recognizing the intriguing aspects of this subject area, teachers can provide dynamic and socially valid science programs.

Teachers need to acquire a comfort level with the subject of science. This includes a recognition that no one will ever know every science fact or even be able to recall instantaneously information that was formerly in one's memory. The teacher's role can be thought of as that of a travel guide who leads students on a wonderful journey.

## Science Education for Students with Special Needs

Teaching science can be exciting and rewarding. Few subject areas are as inherently interesting to teach, actively involve students as much, and can be made as relevant to students of diverse backgrounds. Interestingly, a teacher's attitude may be the most critical variable. Enthusiasm on the teacher's part can lead to excitement in students as well as to higher academic achievement and lower rates of off-task behavior (Brigham, Scruggs, & Mastropieri, 1992). However, not every student will share this enthusiasm. Even though many students are stimulated when presented with an engaging science program, others are not and may require other engagement strategies.

Science instruction must be designed for all students, not just those who will be future scientists (Jackson, Jackson, & Monroe, 1983). Patton et al. (1994) found in their study of special education teachers that substantial numbers of students were not receiving any science instruction and that those who were did not have much time allocated to this subject area each week. This trend has changed recently for two primary reasons: (1) a greater number of students with learning-related problems are in inclusive settings for a greater part of their instructional day—including science classes; and (2) the mandate in IDEA 1997 that students with disabilities must have access to the general curriculum that is provided to students without disabilities.

Before examining the general approaches to and specific strategies for teaching science, some basic guidelines and suggestions are warranted. Although offered in the early 1970s, Boekel and Steele's (1972) general guidelines about science still apply today. They suggest that science is discovering, solving problems, broadening curiosity, nurturing interests, and finding answers to questions. They warn that science is not hit-or-miss lessons, pure memorization, or just substantive knowledge. Rossman (1985) suggests that science is a way of whetting the appetites of students and that we should make every student a "scientist." Gurganus, Janas, and Schmitt (1995), in summarizing the trends in reform movements in science education, note the following four common elements: less is more—spend more time on fewer topics; more curricular integration; learning that results from constructing knowledge based on exploration and later concept development; and use of assessment techniques that are tied more closely to instruction.

As discussed in the previous section, students who are having difficulty learning will present specific challenges when we attempt to teach them science. Rakes and Choate (1990) have identified a number of science-related skills that students need in order to understand the many facets of science instruction. These skills have been organized according to three major dimensions: *information acquisition skills* (observation, listening, reading, study skills, directed experimentation); *information-processing skills* (organization, analysis, measurement, classification); and *integration skills* (synthesis, hypothesis, independent experimentation, generalization, evaluation). Most of these skills relate closely with the **inquiry skills** discussed later in the chapter that are part of the scientific process.

Teachers must be cognizant of the skill demands of science, particularly in the area of information acquisition, in light of the skill levels of students with special needs. In addition, as pointed out previously, familiarity with the content covered in this subject area along with awareness of features of instructional materials used with students are necessary to teach this subject to students with a range of learning-related needs.

Certain competencies are desirable in special education teachers who work with students with special needs in the area of science. The following list is not exhaustive; however, it can serve as a preliminary checklist. Although most of the items on this list should be evident in the teaching practices of general education teachers who teach science, some of the entries will require further attention.

- knowledge of basic content in the area of science
- awareness of state content and performance standards for a particular grade level or levels
- ability to follow a preestablished curriculum or to develop one
- knowledge of various approaches to and materials for teaching science to students with special learning needs
- ability to adapt materials and techniques to accommodate the individual needs of special learners
- knowledge of skills needed to plan and carry out science investigations
- understanding of certain laboratory (hands-on) skills
- familiarity with science-related resources (print, Internet, community)
- ability to apply relevant science education research to the educational programs of special populations
- ability to relate science topics and concepts to real, everyday situations and adult outcomes
- ability to work cooperatively with other teachers in delivery of science to students with special needs

## Content of Science Instruction

Different sources yield different goals for science education. In summarizing the findings of a major research effort that examined science education, Yager (1989) offers the following four goal clusters for science education:

- science for meeting personal needs
- science for resolving societal problems
- science for career awareness
- science for preparation for further study (p. 151)

Though all of these goal clusters may be appropriate for students with special needs, some of these goals are likely to be more important than others for certain students.

On an instructional level, three major objectives are woven throughout science education: the acquisition of relevant content and knowledge, the development of various inquiry-related skills, and the nurturing of a scientific attitude. Many of us have experienced science instruction that focused largely on content acquisition with little opportunity for hands-on activities. In recent years more emphasis has been given to the importance of skill acquisition and activity-oriented instruction, and attention is being directed toward the attitudinal/affective domain associated with science topics. All these objectives are important, and none should be emphasized to the detriment of the others.

Although no generally accepted curricular sequence in science education exists and some (e.g., Rossman, 1985) would suggest that science is every place we cast our attention, science includes the subjects depicted in Figure 10–1. These subject areas can be organized into three general areas: *life science* (the study of living things including biology, zoology, botany, ecology); *physical science* (the study of nonliving things including chemistry

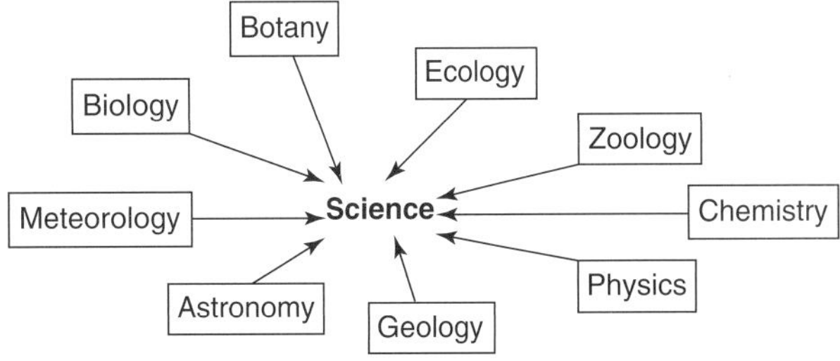


**FIGURE 10–1** Subject areas in science

*Source:* Spinelli, Cathleen G., *Classroom Assessment for Students in Special and General Education*, 2nd Edition, © 2006, p. 402. Reprinted by permission of Pearson Education, Inc., Upper Saddle River, NJ.

and physics); and *earth science* (the study of such topics as astronomy, meteorology, and geology).

In extracting the key initiatives set forth in the National Science Education Standards document (National Research Council, 1996) and the Project 2061 benchmarks (AAAS, 1993), Sandall (2003) identified the following common recommendations:

- Scientific literacy is for all students.
- Science is active, hands-on learning and in-depth study of fewer topics.
- Science should emphasize critical thinking, problem solving, and developing mathematics and science as a way of thinking and reasoning.
- Science should emphasize integration and interdisciplinary activities.
- Science should emphasize application of science, mathematics, and technology to real-life situations. (p. 18)

Gurganus et al. (1995) suggest that a set of common themes or concepts exists that can serve as a guide for what should be covered in science education. Cawley (1994) indicates that "the use of themes is both a provocative and potentially powerful curriculum organizer" (p. 70). A vast number of topics could be incorporated into a science curriculum, but given the trend to cover fewer topics while spending more time on each, one must select topics to the exclusion of others. It is possible to address major concepts by selecting appropriate related units of study. Figure 10–2 provides a list of key science concepts along with suggested activities for studying them.

**FIGURE 10–2** Concepts of science

| Concepts | Examples |
|---|---|
| Systems | Life in an aquarium, home heating systems |
| Models | Map of community, model of human heart |
| Scale | Inflation of a balloon, amount of moisture held by air |
| Change | Seasons of the year, growth of a seedling |
| Stability | Properties of sugar dissolved in water, phases of the moon |
| Diversity | Elements of an ecosystem, fingerprints |
| Structure/Function | Types of teeth, operation of a solar collector |
| Matter | Mixing liquids, dissolving solids into liquids |
| Energy | Effect of sunlight, heat produced through friction |

*Source:* From "Science Instruction: What Special Education Teachers Need to Know and What Roles They Need to Play," by S. Gurganus, M. Jonas, and L. Schmitt, *Teaching Exceptional Children, 27*(4), 1995, 7–9. Copyright 1995 by the Council for Exceptional Children. Reprinted with permission.

**Elementary Level.** The importance of quality science programs at the elementary level is generally recognized because this level of science instruction provides the foundation in skills, knowledge, and attitudes for further science study that supports a sound science education program. Cawley et al. (2003) identify four curricular models that can be found at the elementary level: spiral curriculum, intensified curriculum, integrated curriculum, and theme-based curriculum. Each of these is described in more detail in Table 10–2.

Most elementary programs follow a spiral curriculum orientation. In this curricular structure, as noted in Table 10–2, the curriculum is driven by the textbook series that has been adopted. For example, a topic like plants will be introduced at an early grade level and covered a number of times in subsequent grades in more conceptually complex ways. Figure 10–3 outlines the way an elementary science curriculum might look.

**Secondary Level.** The nature of science programs for students with special needs at the secondary level will depend the program orientation these students are following. If students are in a general education curriculum, they will take courses such as life science/biology, physical science, chemistry, physics, or earth and space science. If students are in a curriculum that affords access to the general education curriculum but is not provided in an inclusive setting, materials and procedures may not differ significantly from those used in the general education setting; however, different textbooks might be used and different activities might be utilized. If students are in an alternative curriculum, they may be exposed to functional science content that is completely related to life skills and/or vocational applications. This orientation will be discussed further in the chapter on functional academics.

## Approaches to Teaching Science

For many years, elementary science programs consisted primarily of a basic textbook and very few hands-on activities. As a result, many students did not find science engaging and did choose careers related to it.

**TABLE 10–2** Curricular models in science

| Curricular Model | Features |
|---|---|
| Spiral Curriculum | • dominant model of science education at the elementary level (K–5)<br>• textbook driven<br>• 15 topics covered each year<br>• topics are repeated each year<br>• scope of content is fixed<br>• textbooks allocate approximately the same number of pages to each topic<br>• same types of activities for each topic at each grade level<br>• limited opportunity to truly engage concepts and apply skills |
| Intensified Curriculum | • "less is more" orientation<br>• more in-depth coverage of topics along with a more activity-oriented, hands-on format<br>• allows for adaptations that might be needed |
| Integrated Curriculum | • combines two or more main topics<br>• uses the main content of these areas as the basis of the curriculum<br>• lack of comprehensiveness is possible |
| Theme-Based Curriculum | • nature of curriculum based on a particular broao-based theme (e.g., change)<br>• other concepts and skill development are woven into these themes<br>• opportunity to connect what is being taught to prior topics that were covered is possible |

*Source:* Adapted from "Science and Students with Mild Disability: Principles of Universal Design," by J. F. Cawley, T. E. Foley, and J. Miller, 2003. *Intervention in School and Clinic, 38,* 160–171. Copyright 2003 by PRO-ED, Inc. Reprinted with permission.

**FIGURE 10–3** Delta science modules II for elementary students

| | Life | Earth | Physical |
|---|---|---|---|
| K–1 | From Seed to Plant<br>Observing an Aquarium | Finding the Moon<br>Sunshine and Shadows | Investigating Water Properties |
| Grades 2–3 | Using Your Senses<br>Butterflies and Moths<br>Classroom Plants<br>Plant and Animal Populations | Amazing Air<br>Weather Watching<br>Soil Science | Force and Motion<br>Length<br>Sink or Float?<br>States of Matter |
| Grades 3–5 | Animal Behavior<br>Dinosaur Classification<br>Food Chains and Webs<br>Insect Life<br>Plant and Animal Life Cycle<br>Small Things and Microscopes | Earth Movements<br>Solar System<br>Water Cycle<br>Weather Instruments | Electrical Circuits<br>Looking at Liquids<br>Magnets<br>Measuring<br>Powders and Odors<br>Sound |
| Grades 5–6 | Fungi—Small Wonders<br>Pollution<br>Pond Life<br>You and Your Body | Erosion<br>Oceans<br>Rocks and Minerals<br>Solar Energy<br>Weather Forecasting | Flight and Rock<br>Color and Light<br>Electromagnetic<br>Lenses and Mirrors<br>Simple Machines |
| Grades 6–8 | DNA—From Genes to Protein<br>Plants in Our World | Astronomy<br>Earth, Moon, and Sun<br>Earth Processes | Chemical Interaction<br>Electrical Conduction<br>Newton's Toy |
| | | **Interdisciplinary**<br>Famous Scientists<br>If Shipwrecks Could Talk | |

Fortunately, changes have occurred to the way science is taught; unfortunately, these changes are not yet evident in a significant number of settings.

A number of descriptors can be used to capture the essence of science instruction that exists in classrooms in schools today. Saul and Newman (1986) conceptualize the various orientations to teaching science in a fascinating way. Their categorization, as well as the advantages and disadvantages of each approach, is presented in Table 10-3. For special education teachers working in inclusive settings, the information provided in the table can provide a strategy for anticipating some of the issues that will arise for students who are in these settings.

The remainder of this section will discuss approaches to providing science instruction from the perspective of how content is typically presented. The major approaches covered include commercial programs (textbooks, hands-on programs, and special programs designed for students with special needs), customized programs that usually are developed locally, and Internet-based programs that are emerging. Mastropieri and Scruggs (1994a) and their colleagues (Scruggs, Mastropieri, Bakken, & Brigham, 1993) have conducted a substantial amount of research on the first two approaches.

**Textbook Approach.** This traditional approach continues to be used frequently, especially at the upper elementary and secondary levels (Brownell & Thomas, 1998; Mastropieri & Scruggs, 1994a). Yager (1989), in referring to general education science programs, remarked that "textbooks are in use over 90% of the time by 90% of the science teachers" (p. 148). The reality for most students is that they are introduced to science by means of the textbook and continue to be exposed to this type of material as the primary "vehicle of instruction throughout their science education" (Memory & Uhlhorn, 1991, p. 64).

In their study of science education in special education settings, Patton et al. (1994) found that nearly 60% of the special education teachers who taught science used a general education textbook in some fashion. This figure is only 60% primarily because many students in special education simply cannot use a regular textbook.

Teachers can use commercially published textbooks in various ways. For most, a textbook is the primary vehicle of the science program, with students regularly reading and consulting it. A class discussion or lecture format usually accompanies this type of approach, which emphasizes a verbal mode of presenting information (Scruggs & Mastropieri, 1993). Another

**TABLE 10–3** Advantages and disadvantages of various science orientations

| *Orientation* | *Advantages* | *Disadvantages* |
|---|---|---|
| Gee-Whiz Science | Is engaging<br>Provides an entry point to more in-depth science | Gives only isolated bits of information<br>Should not be the only format for teaching science |
| Learn-the-Facts Science | Gives students information with which to work<br>Allows students to formulate questions and initiate investigations<br>Minimizes the need to look up information | Can lead to the presentation of meaningless and useless pieces of information |
| Theoretical Science | Provides students with frameworks for organizing and categorizing: what they encounter<br>Is not only for the brighter students | Can be a turn-off for students if this is the only way science is taught<br>May exceed the conceptual levels of some students |
| Hands-on Science | Is activity/experiment-oriented<br>Provides students with experience working with the materials of science<br>Calls for exploration<br>Promotes the idea that science can be done by everyone<br>Is fun | Is more difficult to provided—many materials may be needed<br>May not dispel naive misconceptions<br>Requires different type of teaching behavior |
| Eclectic Science | Combines elements of all previous orientations | Can lead to gaps in students' programs |

feature is regular quizzes and tests. Most textbook series also now include activities for students to perform and an assortment of laboratory materials to assist them in doing so.

Textbooks can also be used in a supplementary way, as part of a program that utilizes additional sources of science information and activities. In certain science programs, textbooks are used only as occasional reference materials, as in the theme-based *Science for All Children* program (Cawley, Miller, Sentman, & Bennett, 1993).

Textbook use has both advantages and disadvantages. Textbooks can serve as excellent teacher resources, can be of great assistance to the beginning teacher, can help organize a science program, are durable, and should be aligned with state content standards. On the other hand, they require complex literacy and study skills competence, are often abstract, typically have readability levels above the reading levels of students, may be the only source of science information, become outdated, and may not be in concert with the curricular needs or goals of some students.

Student inability to read grade level materials looms as the most significant barrier to using science texts with special populations. However, as Armbruster and Anderson (1988) note, problems with textbooks can also arise because of three other factors: *structure* (arrangement of ideas), *coherence* (smoothness in the way ideas stick together), and *audience appropriateness* (suitability to reader's level of knowledge and skills). Teachers do not have the time to regularly rewrite textual material to meet the needs of their students, nor should they do so. However, if the textbook approach is used, certain textbook series are worth considering because of the nature of the reading demands and their hands-on orientation.

Another problem related to reading ability is the need for certain reading skills for effective comprehension of information. Carnine et al. (2004) highlight some characteristics of content-area materials that can be problematic for students with restricted reading abilities:

- **Vocabulary:** It is usually more difficult than that used in narrative material.
- **Content:** Often the information presented is not familiar to students and can cause conceptual problems.
- **Style and organization:** There may be extensive use of headings/subheadings. Writing is very succinct and matter-of-fact.
- **Special features:** Graphics and illustrations play an important part in presentation of information.

Suggestions for addressing these potential problems are provided later in this chapter.

**Hands-On/Activity-Based Approach.** Hands-on approaches to science stress the use of process/inquiry skills more than the accumulation of substantive information. They underscore doing and discovery. These programs include those associated with the first wave of science curriculum reform in the 1960s and 1970s, as well as newer programs developed in more recent years.

Over 30 years ago, Boekel and Steele (1972) believed that many aspects of these approaches could be used with students with disabilities. Scruggs et al. (1993) found that students with learning disabilities who were exposed to activity-oriented science experiences performed better on follow-up unit testing than those students who used a textbook approach. Atwood and Oldham (1985) found that this type of curricular orientation worked well for students with special needs who were placed into general education settings.

Cawley et al. (2003) point out some of the many attractions of hands-on approaches to teaching science. They suggest that these approaches

- provide the teacher with an opportunity to make on-the-spot adjustments,
- allow students to raise and answer questions using different sources,
- enhance conceptualizations through the use of alternative representations,
- offer the teacher an opportunity to pace the lessons according to the rates of student learning, and
- present an opportunity for students to demonstrate selected principles at high levels of generalization. (p. 162)

Often hands-on approaches are linked with **inquiry-based science instruction.** Jarrett (1999) describes three types of inquiry-based teaching: structured inquiry, guided inquiry, and student-directed inquiry. These inquiry options are described more fully in Table 10–4. For many students with special needs, a more structured-oriented approach may be the most desirable option.

For the most part, hands-on and inquiry-based approaches require teachers to be facilitators of learning rather than distributors of information or fonts of knowledge. Not every teacher is comfortable with these curricula because of this facilitating role, but Kyle, Bonnstetter, McClosky, and Fults (1985) found that students tend to prefer this type of science program to more traditional approaches.

**TABLE 10–4** Types of inquiry-based teaching

| *Types of Teaching* | *Features* |
|---|---|
| Structured Inquiry | • hands-on activities<br>• inquiry skills utilized<br>• precise directives from the teacher<br>• allows for a closer monitoring of progress and implementation of special tactics when needed |
| Guided Inquiry | • students have some control related to the process (e.g., deciding which procedures to use)<br>• teacher still plays a key role (e.g., may decide the questions that need to be answered or the materials to be used) |
| Student-Directed Inquiry | • students are largely in control of key decisions (i.e., students generate their own questions and decide the procedures that will be used in the investigation)<br>• teacher may choose the overall topic |

*Source:* Adapted from *Mathematics and Science Instruction for Students with Learning Disabilities: It's Just Good Teaching*, by D Jarrett, 1999, Portland. OR: Northwest Regional Educational Laboratory.

To help teachers who are reticent to try activity-based or hands-on experiences with their students, Salend (1998) suggests several guidelines for success. The first guideline involves the use of a structured learning cycle when introducing activity-oriented lessons. This instructional cycle involves a sequence of learning phases: (a) engagement, (b) exploration, (c) development, and (d) extension (Guillaume, Yopp, & Yopp, 1996). The engagement phase is designed so that real-life activities or problems are used to motivate the students to want to learn the content area and to assess prior knowledge of the topic. The exploration phase involves the development of hypotheses. Students generate ideas and ask questions concerning the real-life problem. Once these ideas and questions are formulated, the students explore and manipulate the contents and equipment of the problem to predict how the problem might be addressed. The third phase of teaching is the development phase. In this phase students gather information and make conclusions. The resources the students use to gather information are usually multimedia sources as well as qualified professionals. The final phase involves the extension phase of the students learning by applying their acquired knowledge to new or similar situations.

Another guideline that Salend (1998) provides emphasizes the use of real-life situations. For example, the instructional cycle can be applied to summer jobs. A teacher might engage the students with the content of establishing the job of cutting lawns for the summer. To do so, he brings in several broken lawn mowers; the students can explore the mowers, develop skills to fix them, and finally extend their knowledge to fixing other machines or appliances.

A final guideline promoted by Salend (1998) concerns the organization of instruction around Carnine's (1995) concept of "big ideas." These refer to "important concepts or principle that help students organize, connect, and apply material so that they see a meaningful relationship between the material and their own lives" (Salend, 1998, p. 70).

Regardless of the guidelines and programs that can be used with learners with disabilities, attention to classroom and behavior management is essential because the instructional situations encourage more movement and less overt structure. Furthermore, hands-on activities may involve the use of equipment and materials that can be dangerous if used improperly. Some students require more instructional structure and direction than is inherent in many activity-oriented programs. For instance, it may be useful to prepare data collection sheets ahead of time to help students. Students may also require teacher-directed, explicit instruction to understand certain vocabulary concepts and facts.

A variety of commercial programs that accentuate a hands-on approach to teaching science are available. These programs are worth considering for use with students who have learning-related disabilities because they emphasize relevance to students, fewer topics covered, active engagement in the activities, integration of science with other subject areas, and better balance of content and process. Table 10–5 lists some of these programs and provides descriptive information about them.

**Specially Designed Programs.** Although not plentiful, instructional programs developed specifically with special populations in mind are available. One of the first comprehensive efforts to develop curricula for students in special education was the publication

**TEACHER *Tips*** **Secondary Level**

McCleery and Tindal (1998) published a study that looked at three different teaching approaches when teaching science to middle school children who are at risk and with learning disabilities in inclusive settings. The experimental conditions included a pull-away group and a Period A group with a comparison group (Period B). The pull-away group received both direct instruction and administration of the outcome measure from a trained teacher. These children were taught concepts, explicit rule-based instruction, and hands-on activities. Period A received hands-on constructivistic instruction from a science teacher but had the final lab and outcome measure administered by the trained teacher who emphasized the concepts within the explicit rule basis. The third group, the comparison group, received only the constructivistic hands-on instruction (no concepts or explicit rules were presented). The results of this experiment showed that the pull-away and Period A group performed at higher levels than the comparison group. The study was quite revealing in terms of the importance of science instruction for all children. The authors recommended the following:

> Although hands-on instruction may be important in framing conundrums and engaging students in the process of scientific inquiry, it cannot replace instruction. Even the use of single lesson lab (provided to period A students) was helpful in improving performance, indicating that instruction in the scientific method should include at least some degree of structured teaching. This structure should be framed on concepts taught with explicit rules. To achieve this kind of literacy, science instruction must move beyond minimally introducing facts or simply exposing students to hands-on activities in a constructivist manner. Rather, direct, systematic instruction must focus on the conceptual knowledge and introduce guided rule-based activities. The planning and implementation of a curriculum must remain clearly connected, as the pull-away intervention demonstrated. Students need to make connections when learning. Furthermore, all students need thoughtful instruction, including those with learning disabilities and a risk for failure. With instruction that is conceptually focused and explicit, it may be possible to compensate for the language and background knowledge deficits these students often possess, (pp. 16–17)

*Source:* From "Teaching the Scientific Method to At-Risk Students and Students with Learning Disabilities Through Concept Anchoring and Explicit Instruction," by J. A. McCleery and G. A. Tindal, 1999. *Remedial and Special Education, 20,* 1, pp. 7–18.

**TABLE 10–5** Hands-on science programs

| *Science Program* | *Source* | *Features* |
|---|---|---|
| Delta Science Modules | Delta Education | • allows schools to develop their own scope and sequence by selecting modules that relate to local situation<br>• modules designed for 3–5 week duration<br>• emphasizes the application of scientific concepts and higher-order thinking<br>• integrates science-technology issues whenever possible<br>• hands-on |
| Full Option Science System | *Encyclopedia Britannica* | • 27 modules designed for grades K–6<br>• four themes scientific reasoning, physical science, earth science, life science |
| Science and Technology for Children | National Science Resource Center Smithsonian institute | • thematic-based program<br>• activities-oriented<br>• intensive teacher in-service component |

of the *Me Now, Me and My Environment*, and *Me in the Future* programs. Developed by the Biological Sciences Curriculum Study (BSCS), these programs were originally designed for students with varying levels of intellectual disabilities. The programs were multicomponent kits for conducting science activities. Arguably their most attractive feature was that they did not require reading, thus avoiding this major barrier for some students. Moreover, the curricula focused on topics that were relevant to students. Another feature was that the teacher manuals provided precise directions for carrying out the activities.

Four other specially designed programs are discussed here.

- ***Science Activities for the Visually Impaired* (SAVI)/*Science Enrichment for Learners with Physical Handicaps* (SELPH):** SAVI/SELPH is a major adaptation of selected topics from the Science Curriculum Improvement Study (SCIS) program. SAVI was the original program and it focused on providing hands-on science to students who had vision problems. The program was later modified for use with other populations.
- ***Science for All Children* (SAC):** SAC (Cawley et al., 1993) is a theme-based elementary-level program that includes a multiple-option curriculum that is characterized by the design feature referred to as the interactive unit (IU). The four interrelated themes are: systems, change, structure, and relationship. According to the authors, the four most essential features of SAC are:
  - All teachers have all the materials for all the grades.
  - There are multiple means of representation, expression, and engagement.
  - There are no significant demands for proficiency in reading and writing.
  - There is an unlimited number of material formats and supplemental activities that can be incorporated into the program. (p. 164)
- ***Applications in Biology/Chemistry* (ABC):** ABC (Prescott, Rinard, Cockerill, & Baker, 1996) is a secondary-level program that targets students who are performing in the middle 50% in academic areas. It is very much real-life oriented and achieves this goal by linking science topics to a student's personal world.
- ***You, Me, and Others:*** This K–6 program designed for students with intellectual disabilities was developed by the BSCS (Biological Sciences Curriculum Study) and is distributed through the March of Dimes Foundation (Carin, Bass, & Contant, 2005). Its focus is in the area of biology generally and genetics specifically. The curriculum includes three units: variety (grades K–2), change (grades 3–4), and the chain of life (grades 5–6).

**Integrated Curriculum.** Interdisciplinary themes are good ways to develop big ideas—the concept discussed earlier in this section. For example, science, music, art, literature, and social science can be integrated under a common theme that will (a) motivate students, (b) provide opportunities to teach high-level content, and (c) relate content to real life (Savage & Armstrong, 1996). The major objective of this type of programming is to integrate science and other subject and skill areas. Although this programming model has been used effectively with gifted students (e.g., Nakashima & Patton, 1989), it can also be used with students with special learning needs.

This curricular option focuses on working other subjects and skills areas into science. One example of how this can be done involves an integrated science unit of study, as depicted in Table 10–6. This unit on marine biology utilizes many different activities from other areas. Science serves as the backdrop, but much of the school day is devoted to the integration of other subject and skills areas into ongoing science-themed instruction.

The relationship of mathematics to science may be apparent, as exemplified by the availability of commercial materials that link these two areas: AIMS (Activities for Integrating Math and Science), GEMS (Great Expectations in Math and Science), and TIMS (Teaching Integrated Mathematics and Science). However, other areas relate well too. Many science topics involve art-related activities or can be followed up by art activities. For example, in a unit entitled "Life of Beans and Peas" (from the Elementary Science Study materials), students typically keep regular drawings of plant development. They also might use unsprouted beans in a decorative art project.

In an ongoing unit entitled "Appliance Science," students might take apart and analyze telephones donated by the phone company. Students enjoy opening up phones and observing the amazing number of simple machines inside. They also might be excited to make creative art projects using the variety of disassembled materials from inside the phones.

In addition, language arts can be worked into science very easily. In the integrated study of marine biology, depicted in Table 10–6, students might be asked to produce various types of creative writing products (e.g., cinquains, haikus, acrostic poems, limericks), or they might give oral and written reports as an ongoing part of the program. Figure 10–4 is an example of a cinquain that was developed within a unit on insects. Science eventually engages most students in some type of research endeavor, which typically requires reading, vocabulary development, note taking, and outlining.

Many career and life skill topics can be worked into science lessons, as will be discussed in Chapter 14. For instance, in a unit entitled "Clay Boats," a number of careers (e.g., merchant marine, stevedore) and hobbies (e.g., sailing, fishing) are easily linked to the theme of

**TABLE 10–6** Integrated programming: marine biology

| *Disciplines* | | | | |
|---|---|---|---|---|
| ***Reading*** | ***Research*** | ***Written Expression*** | ***Oral Expression*** | ***Spelling*** |
| Research to gain/locate information on individual marine animals<br>Teacher-made handouts specific to area of study: narratives poetry<br>In-class story (story combining "It was a hot summer day . . .")<br>Class poetry book | Brainstorming questions of interest<br>Classifying questions into five categories<br>Outlining<br>Note taking<br>Drafts<br>Table of contents<br>Referencing (APA style)<br>Intro/body/conclusion<br>About the author | Whale short story<br>Note taking<br>Outlining<br>Research paper drafts editing<br>Poetry traditional cinquain, limerick, acrostic | Magic Circle (daily group counseling)<br>Group discussions<br>Brainstorming<br>Oral reading of stories/poetry<br>Oral presentations (public speaking skills)<br>Responses to teacher inquires<br>Oral sharing of observations | Functional spelling<br>Dictionary/thesaurus skills<br>New vocabulary |

| *Disciplines* | | | | |
|---|---|---|---|---|
| ***Math Application*** | ***Science*** | ***Social Studies/Issues*** | ***Visual Arts, Music, Performing Arts*** | ***Computer Skills*** |
| Averaging hermit crab race times<br>Graphing shell preferences of hermit crabs<br>Animal measurement<br>Counting of syllables/words for poetry<br>Problem solving | Inquiry skills<br>Observation of hermit crabs<br>Comparisons<br>Classifications of species<br>Hypothesizing<br>Collecting/recording data<br>Description<br>Inferencing<br>Experimenting<br>Dissection<br>Research<br>Database entries<br>Fieldwork | Careers related to marine biology<br>Endangered species | Rap song<br>Individual lyrics<br>Class song<br>Rhythm<br>Performance<br>Seaweed pressing<br>Fish printing<br>Rubber stamp art<br>Illustration/diagrams to accompany poetry/research project/short stories<br>Marine animal world/picture art<br>Cross section of shoreline and ocean<br>True coloration of student-selected Hawaiian reef fish | Word processing<br>Marine organism database information sheet (10 categories)<br>Printout of database Information on marine animals<br>Graphics (cross section of shoreline and ocean)<br>Word processing and graphics for title page of research paper |

the lesson and can be explored. The science program *Me in the Future* was designed specifically to capitalize on this relationship between science and careers.

Science is an ideal subject for integration with other subject areas. Integrated programming is a powerful teaching strategy that engages students in many different ways (Kataoka & Lock, 1995). The possibilities are exciting. Some schools have fashioned entire basic skills programs around the themes of science and social studies. With reasonable effort science can be incorporated into all curricular areas.

**Customized Approaches.** Many special education teachers who teach science in self-contained settings have developed their own curricula. With this approach, the content of the program needs careful consideration. Concern must be given to making sure that what is taught relates to the general curriculum for compliance reasons and aligns with state content and performance standards. Some students will benefit immensely from exposure to a decidedly functional science program based on life skills needed in adulthood.

Regardless of the specific content, however, a **customized program** must be sequenced appropriately with regard to concept development and teaching strategies (Price et al., 1982). Teachers interested in designing their own curricula should first consult other resources. One such resource is the scope and sequence chart of a commercial program.

**Web-Based Programs.** Entire science curricula are now available online, and some school systems have decided to deliver their entire science curriculum this way.

### Teaching Science to Diverse Students with Disabilities

In addition to the challenges of teaching science to children with disabilities, a special challenge involves teaching science to such children who also come from culturally and linguistically different backgrounds. Although some studies have been devoted to the teaching of science to diverse learners, more are needed. Raborn and colleagues (Raborn, 1988; Raborn & Daniel, 1999) indicate that these children learn best when science lessons include inquiry-based and hands-on activities that provide high-context and meaningful opportunities. These types of lessons promote the reciprocal interactions necessary for second-language acquisition with Spanish–English bilingual students with disabilities.

Reflective Question 10–2: ***Although science instruction is most often delivered via a textbook-based approach, the available research suggests that students with special needs will learn more effectively through programs that are adapted to emphasize more use of hands-on approaches as well as programs that focus on big ideas and concepts. Consider a specific topic or unit in science: how would your instructional strategies vary based on the general type of approach being used?***

## TEACHING SOCIAL STUDIES TO LEARNERS WITH SPECIAL NEEDS

Increased attention is being paid to the adult outcomes of learners with special needs. As a result, preparing them to be contributing, competent citizens and active participants in their communities has become a major goal of education. Perhaps as much as any other subject area, the functional aspects of the subject area of social studies become obvious. At its very core is citizenship education. Moreover, this content area promotes informational skills and value development that contribute substantially to an understanding of human diversity, societal complexity, and general world knowledge.

Although we are learning more about how best to teach social studies to students with special needs, historically we knew very little (Passe & Beattie, 1994). Of all the subject areas to which students with special needs are exposed, social studies had been studied and written about the least. For example, more attention had been paid to science than to its companion subject area, social studies; special issues of different journals (*Remedial and Special Education, Intervention in School and Clinic, Teaching Exceptional Children*) have been dedicated to science instruction and students with mild disabilities. Less attention had been dedicated to social studies and learners with special needs, although increased attention is now recently being directed to this important area (McCoy, 2005). For example, the *Journal of Learning Disabilities* featured a recent special series on teaching history (Gersten & Okolo, 2007).

### Nature of Social Studies Education for Students with Special Needs

The specific goals of social studies are not generally agreed upon but can be extracted from professional organizations and councils, state standards, competency requirements, and professional literature. Goals

**DIVERSITY IN THE CLASSROOM *Tips***

**Scott Gullett** is a teacher, researcher, and a UNM doctoral candidate in gifted education. His work in gifted education and special education includes teaching and consulting with Native Americans and Pueblo communities in Arizona and New Mexico.

Teaching science to Native American students with special needs is a vital issue for educators, parents, and most of all students. There has been concern in recent years among multicultural and Native American communities that many such students have been misidentified for learning or emotional disorders because of their linguistic and cultural issues (Artiles, et al., 2002). In addition, teenage students from Native American communities are often exposed to higher rates of drug and alcohol abuse than non-Native communities, which can result in additional educational and emotional barriers (USDHS, 1999).

Other difficulties lie in different cultural perceptions of education. Native American tribes traditionally taught their own children through a tribal culture that involved the entire tribe, as opposed to the Western tradition of sending students to formal schools (Prucha, 2000). That change, which was brought about through decades of modernization and government intervention, has resulted in the additional educational problems of isolation and misunderstanding.

Some Native American communities have tried solutions that involve creating science standards that apply to their culture, and allow for research and investigation (Southern Pueblos Agency, 2005). The benchmarks are similar to traditional science benchmarks, and incorporate Native American cultural needs. The standards include calls for a specific understanding of:

> - The technological design process and how it applied in the development of various tools and technologies employed by early American Indians, such as salmon spearing platforms, and road and building construction technologies
> - The technological design through an examination of the building materials used in traditional American Indian housing
> - The ability to articulate examples of the scientific inquiry necessary to develop and improve technologies employed by early American Indians, such as tempered pottery, corn agriculture, and arched roof structures.
> - The principle of changes of properties in materials applied in the daily activities of early Indians, such as evidenced in the preparation of wood splints for basketry, the production of glue from the hooves of a deer, and the preparation of natural dyes.
> - Concepts of nature's diversity, codependency and the intricate balance between natural forces and how they are reflected in traditional Indian philosophies and symbols, such as the Medicine Wheel.
> - Immune system factors which led to the devastating effects of European-based diseases on American Indians.
> - The environmental degradation that may be occurring in (Native American) communities and/or on reservation lands.
> - American Indian past and contemporary contribution to science and technology (agriculture and pharmacology). (p. 3)

Native American leaders say that keeping their culture alive through education, life skills training, and an emphasis on tribal values creates survival skills and prepares students for the workplace (LaFromboise, 1996).

have also been predicated on the pervading philosophy of the times.

Prior to the late 1970s, the "new social studies" movement was prevalent, espousing inquiry-oriented techniques and including disciplines beyond history, geography, and civics (Birchell & Taylor, 1986). This orientation was replaced in the late 1970s and early 1980s by a "back-to-basics" movement that emphasized five primary areas: reading skill development; American history and heritage; geography (including map and globe skills); American government; and tradition, values, attitudes, and beliefs (Birchell & Taylor, 1986). A new orientation arose in response to the criticism of social studies programs that emerged during the 1980s. McGowan and Guzzetti (1991) summarize the spirit of these reforms:

> Reformers advance a "kinder, gentler" social studies, founded on a content framework largely drawn from history and geography, but enhanced with teaching strategies encouraging student engagement, subject matter integration, global awareness, social participation, and the formation/application of significant ideas. (p. 16)

In 1992, the Board of Directors of the National Council for the Social Studies (NCSS) adopted the following definition of social studies:

> Social studies is the integrated study of the social sciences and humanities to promote civic competence. Within the school program, social studies provides coordinated, systematic study drawing upon such disciplines as anthropology, archaeology, economics, geography, history, law, philosophy, political science,

psychology, religion, and sociology, as well as appropriate content from the humanities, mathematics, and natural sciences. The primary purpose of social studies is to help young people develop the ability to make informed and reasoned decisions for the public good as citizens of a culturally diverse, democratic society in an interdependent world.

The NCSS (1994) has also issued curriculum standards for social studies, which include 10 thematic strands that should pervade every level of schooling. The strands are interrelated and draw from all the disciplines associated with this area. The 10 organizational themes for social studies are listed and described in Table 10–7.

Regarding whether these themes apply to students with special needs, if we want these students to be well-adjusted, contributing members of society, then indeed they do. Moreover, students with special needs must have access to these themes, as required by IDEA. However, program planning must also be guided by a realistic appraisal of student values and abilities, as well as current and future needs—the functional overlay that is always needed.

A significant number of learners with disabilities were not receiving social studies instruction when they were in special education settings for most of their instructional day. In a study of special education classes for students with mild and moderate learning problems, Patton et al. (1987) found that no social studies instruction was occurring in almost one third of the classes where it should be taught. What could not

**TABLE 10–7** Ten organizational themes for social students

| *Themes* | *Theme Descriptions* |
|---|---|
| 1. Culture | Students will learn the common characteristics and significant differences among the world's cultural groups. The content related to this theme comes primarily from the social science field of anthropology. |
| 2. Time, Continuity, and Change | Students will learn how to reconstruct the past and develop a historical perspective to interpret the present. The content related to this theme comes primarily from the social science field of history. |
| 3. People, Places, and Environments | Students will learn to understand the significance of place and develop a geographic perspective to interpret current social conditions. The content related to this theme comes primarily from the social science field of geography. |
| 4. Individual Development and Identity | Students will learn how culture, social groups, and institutions shape personal identity. The content related to this theme comes primarily from the social science field of psychology. |
| 5. Individuals, Groups, and Institutions | Students will learn how institutions such as schools, churches, families, and government influence people's lives. The content related to this theme comes primarily from the social science field of sociology. |
| 6. Power, Authority, and Governance | Students will learn how forms of government distribute power and authority. The content related to this theme comes primarily from the social science field of political science. |
| 7. Production, Distribution, and Consumption | Students will learn that resources are limited and that people must make decisions on what things will be produced, how those things will be distributed, and the rate at which they will be consumed. The content related to this theme comes primarily from the social science field of economics. |
| 8. Science, Technology, and Society | Students will learn that new technology changes the way people live. The content related to this theme comes from several social sciences fields. |
| 9. Global Connections | Students will learn about the global connections among the world's societies. The content related to this theme comes from social science fields. |
| 10. Civic Ideals and Practices | Students will learn the importance of civic participation in a democratic society. The content related to this theme comes primarily from political science. |

*Source:* Zarillo, James, *Teaching Elementary Social Studies: Principles and Applications*, 2nd Edition, © 2004, p. 13. Reprinted by permission of Pearson Education, Inc., Upper Saddle River, NJ.

be determined was the appropriateness of the social studies programs that were offered. Things are different now, as many more students are in general education social studies classes and thus an increased focus on how to teach them has developed (see De La Paz, morelles, & Winston, 2007).

Social studies is a subject area that contains many complex topics, issues, and concepts. For instance, the concept of "community" is abstract, requiring certain cognitive and conceptual skills. The subject also favors students with rich experiential backgrounds, who find many topics more meaningful as a result of their varied experiences. In addition, most social studies classes demand proficiency in a variety of areas, particularly reading, writing, oral expression, interactive/group skills, study skills, and research-related skills (e.g., Internet and library skills). L. J. Smith and Smith (1990) suggest that students need a significant set of "social studies skills," including the following:

- *Acquiring information:* reading, study skills, information search, technical skills (e.g., Internet skills)
- *Organizing and using information:* classifying, interpreting, analyzing, summarizing, synthesizing, evaluating, decision making
- *Participating socially:* personal skills, group interaction, social and political skills (i.e., related to group dynamics) (p. 5)

Another concern related to social studies instruction is the training background of special education teachers, many of whom feel unprepared to teach social studies. Patton et al. (1987) found that 43% of the special education teachers they surveyed had no training in how to teach this subject. Many secondary-level special education teachers, in particular, are unfamiliar with curriculum, instructional practices, and appropriate materials in this area. This has become a particularly problematic issue with the NCLB provision that all teachers must be "highly qualified."

The reality is that an increasing number of students with special needs is being taught in inclusive settings. Even though, as McCoy (2005) notes, "the role of the special education teacher is to be the instructional

## DIVERSITY IN THE CLASSROOM *Tips*

**Lynnette Oshima** is an associate professor in the social studies education program at the University of New Mexico. Her academic interests are centered on curriculum and instruction—especially with regard to equity and accessibility in education through content, pedagogy, and audience.

Social studies content that is taught must be useful to the learner. For example, why is the civil rights movement an important topic in American History? How can students find a study of Rosa Parks and the bus boycott meaningful? These questions ask for understanding that goes beyond the level of factual knowledge. Responding to racism is personal and not just academic. Lessons and units on diversity and inequity need to help students develop empathy for others (e.g., multiple perspectives) as well as provide opportunities to "practice" what can be done (e.g., take action) individually or collectively to address the problem.

Teachers need to have knowledge of content and pedagogy that is both broad and deep. All topics have complexity and require scholarly study. Was 1492 the discovery of the Americas or the unprovoked invasion of North America by white Europeans? Did you know that Charles Perrault's *Cinderella* story could only have happened after 1492 because the pumpkin was imported from the Western Hemisphere? This was also true of the beans used in the story of *Jack and the Beanstalk*. In fact, the biological exchange that occurred after contact between the two hemispheres had lasting effects today. Corn first grown by Native Americans, is an essential food source for Egypt and other countries in the world.

Teaching strategies have to be systemic to be effective. That is, they need to be based on themes or principles that transcend a particular topic. For example, young adult and children's books are popular "tools" or resources for students across the disciplines. A fifth-grade teacher used three different children's books to teach about Columbus. One emphasized the traditional story of the difficulties Columbus faced in his first voyage; the second described people who were already here; and the third fictionalized the arrival of Columbus from a native perspective. The question the teacher posed was not which book did students prefer but asked them instead to think about how language was used by each author to tell a different story of the same event. This is a challenging question that could be used at any grade level, though its value would be lost if students did not learn how to think about the content first. Debriefing readings should incorporate the purpose for social studies. In this lesson, students learn not only that there are different interpretations of the same event, but also that authors can control the meaning of what they write by the way they use language to tell their story. Engaging students through content and pedagogy is key to teaching social studies to diverse learners in our pluralistic society.

strategist, not the content specialist" (p. 3), teachers will need to be able to accommodate their needs in the context of the demands of the general social studies classes. As a result, special education teachers will need to possess at least a working knowledge of content and clearly will need to possess skills in being able to provide assistance in modifying curricular materials and designing effective cognition strategies that will work within the instructional practices used in these classes (De La Paz et al., 2007).

Nonetheless, teachers need not be intimidated by this subject area and must realize that obstacles identified can be overcome. Much like science, social studies can be an extremely fascinating subject area to teach. And perhaps most importantly, social studies can be made meaningful and relevant to students with special learning-related needs. To do so, illustrating causal networks of topics and actions can be a productive approach (Espin, Cevasco, Van den Broeck, Baker, & Gerster, 2007).

## Content of Social Studies Instruction

The scope and sequence of any social studies program for special education students is likely to depend on where the student receives such instruction. For the most part, students with mild learning problems are taught in general education classes, where they have the best access to the general curriculum. A program that parallels the general education curriculum is indicated for some students who remain in special education settings and for whom the topics covered in the general education program are appropriate. Others, especially students at the secondary level who will not go on to postsecondary education, can benefit from a program that covers the key elements of the general education curriculum but emphasizes a more functional orientation that will be useful to them in adjusting to adulthood.

The subject areas that are represented by the umbrella term of *social studies* include the 12 areas depicted in Figure 10–4. The K–12 curricular sequence in social studies has been fairly standard in classrooms across the nation. The common grade level themes are reflected in Table 10–8, which reveals two major patterns: a focus in grades K–6 on expanding environments (movement from family/neighborhood to world perspective), followed by recurrent attention (grades 7–9 and 10–12) on contracting environments. Other subjects such as economics may be options that are available to students.

This sequence represents social studies curricula in general, even though not all states, and as a result, commercially available textbook series, adhere to this

**TABLE 10–8** Typical social studies themes by grade level

| *Grade Level* | *Theme* |
|---|---|
| K | Self, school, community, home |
| 1 | Families |
| 2 | Neighborhoods |
| 3 | Communities |
| 4 | State history, geographic regions |
| 5 | U.S. history |
| 6 | World cultures, Western Hemisphere |
| 7 | World geography or history |
| 8 | American history |
| 9 | Civics or world cultures |
| 10 | World history |
| 11 | American history |
| 12 | American government |

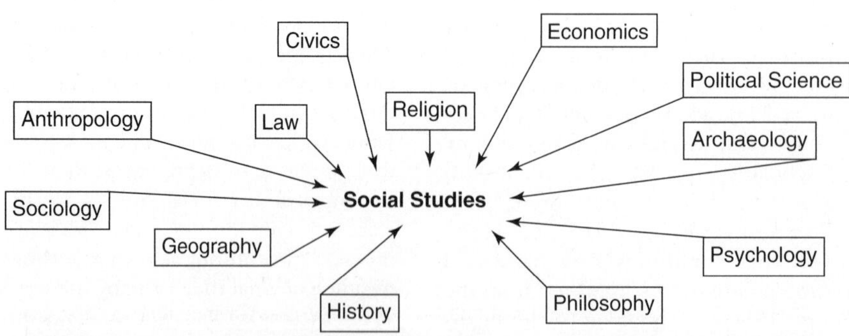


**FIGURE 10–4** Subject areas in social studies

*Source:* Spinelli, Catherine G., *Classroom Assessment for Students in Special and General Education*, 2nd Edition, © 2006, p. 408. Reprinted by Permission of Pearson Education, Inc., Upper Saddle River, NJ.

sequence. The themes designed to guide social studies curriculum are to be woven into the sequence depicted in Table 10-7. The scope of the social studies curriculum at the high school level may vary considerably from one state to another; however, courses such as U.S. history and world history are typically required for graduation. In addition, particular states commonly require that students take units pertaining to their own state histories and cultures (e.g., fourth and seventh graders in Texas take a course on Texas history).

## Approaches to Teaching Social Studies

What should be taught and how it should be taught have always been debatable topics. Yet certain emphases or orientations have been observed at various times, as noted. Of the various ways to cover social studies content, the most frequently used techniques in general education setting remain the textbook, lecture, and discussion format. This was the case in the 1970s (Turner, 1976) and remained so during the 1980s and in to the 1990s (Hayes, 1988; Steinbrink & Jones, 1991; Woodward, Elliott, & Nagel, 1986), and remains the case today.

The major approaches discussed in this section fall into three major categories: textbook/lecture/discussion (i.e., traditional content) approach, inquiry approach, and balanced approach. These approaches are based on Brophy's (1990) categorical distinctions, which resulted from his study of social studies instruction. Each of them is discussed here and summarized in Table 10-9.

**Textbook/Lecture/Discussion Approach.** This approach is characterized by an emphasis on textbooks, lectures, and discussion as the primary mechanisms for organizing the course and disseminating information. Teachers familiar with textbook series in social studies know that the most significant problem is readability or, more specifically, students' inability to manage the textual material and ultimately to comprehend the material. Woodward and Noell (1992) note the complexity of the problem: "Important topics in social studies texts, for example, are discussed insufficiently, references arc ambiguous, too many concepts are presented in too short a space, and a considerable amount of background knowledge is simply assumed" (p. 40).

Shepherd and Ragan (1982) corroborate the problems associated with textbooks, suggesting that elementary social studies textbooks may have the most challenging readability levels of any textual material at a particular grade level. This fact remains problematic for at least two reasons. First, many students with special needs are not effective readers and have a difficult time comprehending grade level materials. Second, as implied by Woodward and Noell (1992), readability is compounded by a number of other dimensions that impede the comprehension of material. These factors need to be considered in the selection of any material—textbook, supplement reading, other printed material, or web-based textual material.

Kinder, Bursuck, and Epstein (1992) underscored the problems with the textbooks used in social studies in their evaluation of 10 eighth-grade history textbooks. They found that the readability of all the textbooks was 1 or more years above the grade level. They also found important differences in certain organizational dimensions of the textbooks that have an effect on a student's ability to use them successfully.

Most major publishers have developed a social studies series, and some of the series accommodate individual differences better than others. Teachers should examine these series closely, looking for certain features in the student materials (e.g., controlled reading levels, organizational elements, language demands, conceptual levels) and in the teacher materials (e.g., guidelines for adapting instruction, additional activity-oriented ideas for covering the topic, supplemental materials). These factors can make a big difference in increasing the ability of reading-challenged students to use these materials. Further, teachers shall consider texts that emphasize, for example in history, the relationship between events and actives and how they are made explicit (Harriss, Carus, & Gersten, 2007).

**Inquiry Approach.** This approach, also referred to as a process approach, puts a premium on skills used in solving problems or addressing issues. Although attractive in many ways, this approach requires that students possess certain abilities and prerequisite skills such as the social studies skills previously noted. Many general education social studies teachers find that they must explicitly teach some of these "social studies skills" and provide organizational supports for many students in their classes. Teachers also need specific skills, and for this reason many find the approach unattractive (Jarolimek, 1981).

A completely inquiry-oriented approach for teaching social studies to learners with special needs must be used with caution. As in science, the use of process approaches with students with special needs is not prohibited, but a certain amount of structured instruction (i.e., structured inquiry; see Jarrett, 1999) that helps students make connections across topics

**TABLE 10–9** A summary of instructional approaches in social studies

| *Approach* | *Positive Features* | *Negative Features* | *Components* |
|---|---|---|---|
| Textbook/Lecture/ Discussion | Has been simplified in series (Birchell & Taylor, 1986)<br>Includes good aesthetic features (e.g., illustrations)<br>Includes good resource/reference materials<br>Introduces content-related terms (Armstrong, 1984)<br>Lessens teacher's workload (i.e., preparation time) | Presents readability problems<br>Introduces language complexity<br>Develops too many concepts too quickly<br>Lacks sufficient organizational aids (e.g., headings and subheadings; Adams, Carnine, & Gersten, 1982)<br>Makes understanding difficult because of superficial and disconnected coverage of topics (Woodword, Elliott, & Nagel, 1986)<br>Does not adequately accommodate special learners in teacher's guides<br>Is typically used only in combination with discussion | Teacher's guide<br>Student text<br>Student workbook<br>Supplemental materials (e.g., filmstrips) |
| Inquiry | Emphasizes organizational problem-solving skills<br>Is student-centered<br>Capitalizes on student curiosity and interest | Requires organizational and problem-solving skills<br>Demands self-directed behavior (i.e., independent learning)<br>Requires the use of outside materials that may not be readable and/or available (e.g., in Braille or on tape)<br>Requires special skills of the teacher | Trade books<br>Reference materials<br>Library work<br>Field work<br>Media<br>Resource persons<br>Student reports (oral or written)<br>Microcomputers |
| Balanced | Focuses on students' and teacher<br>Is relevant to students' interests and experiences<br>Uses local context<br>Can be student-generated<br>Should be activity-oriented<br>Can include a combination of instructional practices<br>Can integrate curricular areas | Typically requires considerable teacher effort<br>May be conceptually confusing<br>Can result in too narrow a focus | Texts<br>Trade books<br>Media role-playing<br>Simulations<br>Group work<br>Microcomputers |

and concepts (Kinder & Bursuck, 1993) is recommended, and often necessary. Thus, it is important first to assess whether students can effectively use inquiry skills and then to present a schema of substantive information via a systematic teaching paradigm.

Curtis and Shaver (1980) report that an inquiry-oriented social studies program that focuses primarily on the study of contemporary problems relevant to students can be employed effectively with special students. Such a program can be very interesting and meaningful to students because it deals with local community issues and helps develop decision-making skills using topics to which students can relate. These authors also stress that high expectations should be maintained as these special students "can engage in more sophisticated studies than those described in many social studies curriculum guides" (p. 307). Learners with special needs are too infrequently afforded opportunities to experience innovative, dynamic programs. Such programs should be considered, but their effectiveness should be evaluated.

**Balanced Approaches.** Many teachers have developed social studies programs that combine features of the textbook/lecture/discussion approach with inquiry- or issue-oriented elements. For example, a program might use a textbook but also regularly include inquiry-oriented activities. The type of class that James was in—the student in the scenario described at the beginning of the chapter—is a good example of a balanced program.

Many of these "balanced" programs are developed at a local level. They can be engaging, relevant, and appropriate for special learners. However, teachers should consult available resources for assistance in developing such curricula. It may be important that the customized curriculum not deviate too much from the general education curriculum and the state standards in terms of content even though methodology and selected topics may be very different.

**Reflective Question 10–3:** ***What are the key principles that should be considered when designing social studies programs for classrooms that include students with special needs? What types of classroom adaptations will be likely to have the most positive impact on learning?***

## ASSESSMENT IN SCIENCE AND SOCIAL STUDIES

Four key reasons exist for collecting information on students in most academic areas: monitor progress, make instructional decisions, evaluate student achievement, and evaluate program effectiveness (National Council of Teachers of Mathematics, 1995). For the purposes of this chapter, we will focus mainly on the first two reasons.

A number of techniques are available for collecting information on students' knowledge and skills in science and social studies. The major ways of measuring performance include standardized testing, curriculum-based measurement, performance measures, rubrics, and various student-centered assessment techniques.

The traditional use of weekly quizzes and regularly scheduled tests is still prevalent in many secondary-level science and social studies classes. This longstanding process is organized in the following way: students read the textbook, listen to in-class presentations, participate in discussions, and then are evaluated via a closed-book quiz or test. Though this scenario might be common, other ways of assessing students exist and should be considered.

Due to the emphasis on standards and accountability, standardized, norm-referenced group achievement tests are given to students throughout the United States as part of the system to determine annual yearly progress (AYP). Students are usually assessed via high-stakes tests in science and social studies at specific grade levels, depending on the state in which a student resides.

Curriculum-based measures are generally teacher-made, nonstandardized tests that relate closely to the actual curriculum to which students are being exposed. This type of assessment is extremely useful as it allows for a monitoring of student progress in the specific lessons being presented. Examples of curriculum-based measures in science can be found in Idol (2007).

If an activity-oriented science program is used, some type of performance-based measure is extremely useful for assessing how well students have mastered what has been taught and what they were expected to do. In subjects like science and social studies, where projects and other types of hands-on activities are used, this type of assessment is a good fit for evaluating student performance. According to Stepanek and Jarrett (1997), performance assessments "typically focus on the process of solving problems or completing complex tasks. The emphasis is on what students can do, not just what they know" (p. 11).

Similar to behavioral checklists is the rubric assessment (Finson & Ormsbee, 1998). A rubric assessment refers to the use of specific guidelines to help navigate the grading of the student's work. A teacher may use **analytic rubrics** that outline specific criteria to determine the level of a student's performance. This type of rubric is objective in nature. A more subjective assessment is the **holistic rubric,** which implies that a teacher assesses and rates the overall quality of the student's work (e.g., as superior, acceptable, inadequate, or unacceptable). Either rubric system can be used for the assessment of a science and social studies project/performance.

Salend (1998) has identified some additional ways in which students can be involved in the assessment process. Each of those assessment strategies are discussed below:

- **Portfolios:** Portfolio assessment is one of the most popular techniques used in schools. Portfolio assessment implies the accumulation of student products to reflect their performance. This increasingly implemented method is attractive for use with students with special needs because it deemphasizes the need for optimal demonstration of competence in a standardized format. Instead, it allows students to show their best work that has been generated over time. Table 10–10 provides examples of the types of entries that could be included in science and social studies portfolios.

**TABLE 10–10** Suggested items for science and social studies portfolios

| Portfolio Entries |
|---|
| • Notes from science or history fair project |
| • History journal entries including self-evaluation |
| • Design of travel brochure, packet, or itinerary of trip |
| • Research assigned related to a specific topic |
| • Report on a historical or contemporary character or event |
| • Concept web illustrating a topic search |
| • Construction of a relief map |
| • Photograph of a geographic relief map |
| • Videotape of a famous battle representation |
| • Timelines of historic or current events |
| • Artistic construction illustrating a social studies topic |
| • Audio tape of a dramatic historic speech or debate |
| • Diagrams, charts, and graphs of scientific experiment |
| • Crucial questions related to political event |
| • Letter to the editor related to community planning controversy |
| • Journal entries about working on an environmental project |
| • Written interview of a political candidate |
| • Photograph collection of community current events |
| • Laser disc presentation of a research project |
| • Selected science or social studies homework assignments |
| • Laboratory reports |
| • Summaries of performance-based assessments |
| • Videotapes of student completing laboratory experiments |
| • Teacher observations and anecdotal records |
| • Conference records (student-teacher-parent) |
| • Current events with students commentary and analysis |
| • Field trip reports |
| • Interest inventories |
| • Scientific investigations |
| • Proposals for experiments or research |
| • Project reports, summaries, or videos |
| • Computer disks of research material |
| • File notes on the student's contribution to group work |

*Source:* Spinelli, Cathleen G., *Classroom Assessment for Students in Special and General Education*, 2nd Edition, © 2006, p. 420. Reprinted by permission of Pearson Education, Inc., Upper Saddle River, NJ.

- **Journals and learning logs:** Science, in particular when hands-on activities are implemented, provides a great opportunity for students to maintain records of the activities in which they have been involved. This is often accomplished through the use of journals or learning logs. For some students with special needs, some structure and explicit instruction may be needed at first so that they get the idea of what is expected.
- **Think-alouds:** According to Spinelli (2006), the think-aloud technique asks the student to verbally explain the processes he or she used in solving a problem or performing an activity. The teacher may have to spend some time showing students how this technique works.
- **Self-evaluation questionnaires:** This type of questionnaire allows students to evaluate their own performance as well as other aspects of the science or social studies activities in which they have participated.
- **Interviews:** Interviews are useful not only to determine what a student has learned but also to determine interest and attitudes. If there is sufficient time to do this, teachers are encouraged to gather information through conversations with students as an adjunct to other techniques.

Reflective Question 10–4: ***Identify and discuss the options available for informal assessment in science and social studies. What types of information can be obtained from each of these assessment strategies?***

## INSTRUCTIONAL TECHNIQUES IN SCIENCE AND SOCIAL STUDIES

Like other subject areas, science and social studies require sound instructional practices that maximize the probability that learning will occur. The components of effective instruction introduced in Chapter 1 and discussed more thoroughly in Chapter 3 apply to these subject areas. In addition, certain instructional-related topics that are unique to these subject areas are also noteworthy.

### General Instructional Considerations

Some instructional practices apply to both science and social studies. These practices are discussed in the following sections.

**Universal Design for Learning.** As discussed in Chapter 1 and referred to earlier in this chapter, the philosophy of designing curriculum, materials/equipment, and instruction in such a way that all students with diverse needs can be included appropriately is strongly recommended.

**Classroom Management and Organization.** Teachers must be able to control their classrooms. This objective can be achieved by establishing rules and procedures for specific tasks and appropriate functioning, as mentioned earlier. This requirement is especially important for science activities of a hands-on nature that use potentially dangerous materials or for community-based social studies lessons.

In science, we recommend establishing systematic procedures for distributing and collecting materials before, during, and after an activity or class period. One method is to designate part of the room as the science area and to conduct most science instruction in this area. Within this area or wherever science instruction occurs, tables should be used as much as possible. Scheduling time at the end of class to clean up and organize all of the materials used is essential.

**Effective Instructional Strategies.** Mastropieri and Scruggs (2002) emphasize that good instructional techniques benefit all students in the general education classroom. A number of variables are particularly important to address when teaching students with special needs in inclusive settings. Mastropieri and Scruggs (1994b) refer to these as the SCREAM variables: Structure, Clarity, Redundancy, Enthusiasm, Appropriate pace, and Maximized engagement. For instance, as Mastropieri and Scruggs (2007) suggest, students may have to be explicitly taught charting and graphing strategies.

**Reading Rates.** The point has been made that most programs in science and social studies require students to be competent readers. However, certain types of reading skills—ones that are often overlooked in terms of their importance—may need to be taught or refined. These skills involve the ability to *skim* (reading to get a general sense of the material) and to *scan* (reading to find a particular piece of information). Both of these skills are used frequently in these content areas.

**Study Skills.** The importance of study skills is evidenced by the fact that we have devoted an entire chapter to the topic (see Chapter 12). The point that needs to made here is that when it is determined that a student has problems with certain study skills, these skills will need to be taught explicitly to students. Instruction should be based on present levels of educational performance that are established through valid assessment and related to goals that should be included in the student's IEP.

**Cooperative Learning.** Cooperative learning arrangements have been found useful for increasing achievement, student involvement, and motivation (Manning & Lucking, 1991) and recommended for students with special needs (Carin, Bass, & Contant 2005). Science and social studies can utilize activities that are ideal for creating opportunities for students to work together cooperatively. Sunal and Sunal (2003) note that "when students work together to achieve a science objective, the potential or positive interactions within the group is enhanced" (p. 264). Most of the various cooperative learning methods (e.g., jigsaw, teams-games-tournaments) can be used to develop effective instruction.

**Alternative Products.** Science and social studies provide a great opportunity to consider a wide range of authentic products that students can generate in lieu of some of the more traditional requirements (quizzes, tests). With digital technology readily available in schools, more options are now available in terms of innovative, alternative products that students can pursue to demonstrate skill and knowledge acquisition. Table 10–11 provides a list of some of the options that one might consider. In social studies, two ideas that have been discussed in the literature are the use of plays (Zigo, 1999) and cartoons (Grskovic, 2002).

**Field Experiences.** Field experiences (i.e., field trips) for many teachers conjure up unpleasant memories (e.g., kids too hyped up, gift shops, etc.). However, appropriate use of this type of learning activity can enrich the world knowledge of many students with limited experiential backgrounds. Field experiences involve planning and preparation; instructional objectives should be identified, students should be told what to look for, and follow-up discussions should be scheduled. However, these trips need not involve colossal effort. For instance, a trip to the produce section of a grocery store can easily introduce a number of science topics to pursue, and a trip to a local cemetery can lead to a fascinating discussion of history and local culture.

**Some "To Do's."** We thought a few general recommendations would be helpful. Some of these suggestions come from Saul and Newman (1986).

- Be flexible in terms of curriculum and instructional technique.

**TABLE 10–11** Product ideas

| | |
|---|---|
| Advertisement | Museum |
| Annotated bibliography | Musical composition |
| Board game | Oral report or speech |
| Book | Overhead transparency |
| Chart or graph | Pamphlet or brochure |
| Collage | Panel discussion |
| Collection | Paper folding |
| Comic strip | Photo album |
| Computer program | Photo essay |
| Crossword puzzle | Play or skit |
| Dance | Poem |
| Demonstration | Portfolio of artwork |
| Diary | Poster or bumper sticker |
| Dictionary or glossary | Puppet show |
| Diorama | Radio show |
| Display | Recipe |
| Experiment | Sample specimens |
| Film | Scavenger hunt |
| Illustrated story | Scrapbook |
| Invention | Sculpture |
| Guest speaker | Slide show |
| Jigsaw puzzle | Song (original) |
| Letter | Tape recording |
| Magazine or newspaper | Terrarium |
| Map with key | Timeline |
| Mini-center | Travelogue |
| Mobile | TV program |
| Model | Video |
| Mural | Written paper |

*Source:* From "Product Development for Gifted Students," by K. R. Stephens, 1996, *Gifted Child Today Magazine, 19*(16), p. 19. Copyright 1996 by Prufrock Press. Reprinted with permission.

- Have fun teaching science and social studies—enthusiasm has positive effects on students.
- Build on students' questions and interests.
- Model scientific or social study related interest.
- Strive to show students "big picture" ideas that apply across different topics.
- Encourage socially responsible science and community involvement.

## Specific Instructional Practices for Science

**Inquiry Skills.** One of the goals of science instruction is skill development. Many different abilities can be addressed, including organizational, basic academic, and social/behavioral skills. Other specific inquiry-oriented skills are the heart and soul of science instruction. These skills are not only extremely useful in science but also beneficial in other areas of school and life as well. These skills include the following (as adapted from Cain & Evans, 1984, pp. 8–9):

- observation: using the senses to find out about subjects and events
- measurement: making quantitative observations
- classification: grouping things according to similarities or differences
- communication: using the written and spoken word, drawings, diagrams, or tables to transmit information and ideas to others
- data collection, organization, and graphing: making quantitative data sensible, primarily through graphic techniques
- inference: explaining an observation or set of observations
- prediction: making forecasts of future events or conditions, based on observations or inferences
- data interpretation: finding patterns among sets of data that lead to the construction of inferences, predictions, or hypotheses
- formulation of hypotheses: making educated guesses based on evidence that can be tested
- experimentation: investigating, manipulating, and testing to determine a result

These inquiry skills can and should be included regularly in science activities. Most activities require some of these skills; however, the goal is to get students to use as many of them as often as possible. An example of each inquiry skill can be demonstrated from one of the subtopics from the marine biology unit of study introduced earlier in the chapter. Students worked regularly with hermit crabs on a variety of activities and in so doing they used all of the inquiry skills, as highlighted in Table 10–12.

**Elements of a Science Lesson.** Effective teaching practice incorporates variety and explicit instruction of material. Some science lessons might be devoted to discussing a topic of current interest, using educational media, reading science materials, listening to a guest speaker, going on a field trip, or carrying out activities in the classroom. However, all science lessons should be planned to accommodate individual differences (i.e., UDL) and follow an organizational schema that provides a certain structure that is helpful to teachers and to students.

**TEACHER Tips** — **Elementary Level**

## Reinventing the Classroom

Combining entrepreneurial skills with academic and social survival skills is a great way to teach students about real life while also motivating them to do well in school. In classrooms like Ronni Cohen's in Wilmington, Delaware, students invent, produce, and market their own products.

With each entrepreneurial project, students are required to keep an inventor's portfolio, in which they write a design abstract and log their thoughts, progress, difficulties, research, and amount of time spent thinking about and working on their projects. A brainstorming session is used to come up with a name for the product, which often uses word play and unusual lettering. Students must design their invention on paper; list the land, labor, and capital requirements needed to produce it; and calculate the cost involved. Students then conduct a market survey, graph a supply schedule, and determine the market clearing price. They create an advertising campaign and when they are done, the students, their peers, and the teacher evaluate each product based on a demonstration.

A project called "Pastamania, required students to invent something that would help people eat spaghetti more neatly. The demonstrations included "Leyla's Loony Linguini Looper," and the "Super Slicer Spaghetti Sweeper," and "Splngetti." Final products were required to be demonstrated by a student bystander, who had to figure out how to use the instrument by following the inventor's written instructions.

*Source:* Garrison (1994).

**TABLE 10–12** Examples of inquiry skills

| *Inquiry Skill* | *Hermit Crab Activity* |
|---|---|
| Observation | Identification of body parts |
| Measurement | Timing of crab races |
| Classification | Species identification |
| Communication | Description of habitat poetry |
| Data collection, organization, and graphing | Shells preferred by crabs |
| Inference | How crab attaches to inside of shell |
| Prediction | Location/movement of crabs as a function of time of day and tides |
| Data interpretation | Conclusions derived from information collected (e.g., species data) |
| Hypothesis generation | Generation of ideas about how often crabs change shells based on growth patterns |
| Experimentation | How crabs will react to changes in their habitats |

The actual format of the instructional period depends to a great degree on the nature of the lesson. For most lessons, the class session can be organized into five major components: introduction, attention getting and motivation, data gathering, data processing, and closure (Cain & Evans, 1990).

- **Introduction:** The first component of a lesson should be an introduction to the day and an update on what was done previously. The primary purpose of this part of the lesson is administrative and management related. The teacher's goal should be to get the students settled, prepared, and focused. If done properly, it will serve as a nice transition to the beginning phase of the actual science lesson.
- **Attention-Getting and Motivating Techniques:** Attention-getting and motivating techniques attempt to engage students in the lesson. They set the tone for the day's activities and should make clear to students what they are to do. The key is to activate student interest, get students to ask questions, and initiate discussion.
- **Data-Gathering Techniques:** This stage typically involves hands-on activities. For many special learners some explicit instruction and supports may be needed. In an inquiry-based program, structured inquiry or guided inquiry is useful (Jarrett, 1999).

However, the emphasis is on students working individually or cooperatively in small groups and performing tasks related to the topic under study. Students should record their observations and collect data in logs or journals. Logs, which work best if they are in binders, can be enhanced by using pre-punched teacher-produced materials that help structure the assignment. Students should make entries in their logs regularly, and the logs should not be graded for handwriting, spelling, or syntactic correctness.

- **Data-Processing Techniques:** This part of the lesson asks students to try to make sense of the data they have collected or the activity they have performed. They must organize the data so as to explain the results. Data can be analyzed individually or pooled and examined on a classwide basis. This part of the lesson is an excellent time for discussion of observations, trends, and outcomes. Students can now begin to draw conclusions, make predictions, and suggest additional activities and experimentation.
- **Closure:** Allocating time to close out the lesson is important to ensure that students understand what they have been doing. This is a good time to review the day's activities, evaluate performance, emphasize major conclusions, and relate the lesson to the real world. This time might also be used to lead into the next day's activity or other future lessons. From a classroom management perspective, it is also important to use this time to clean up by having the students take responsibility for assisting in making sure the classroom is organized.

**Safety.** Safety is a primary concern. Teachers should anticipate and prepare for potential problems. All planned science activities should be performed ahead of time, and equipment should be checked to ensure that it is in proper working condition. Students' eyes should be protected, fire extinguishers should be readily available, and safety instructions should be demonstrated and practiced regularly. Dangerous or potentially dangerous materials should be secured and off-limits signs posted to protect students from injury and the teacher from liability. It is also advisable to consult the safety guidelines of the school district.

**Equipment and Materials.** To be able to perform hands-on activities, it is essential that the appropriate equipment and materials are available when students perform an assigned activity. Furthermore, special education teachers who are working cooperatively with general education science teachers need to anticipate potential problems that might arise when using certain equipment/materials, thus necessitating various accommodations.

**Animals in the Classroom.** Careful consideration should also be given to animals in the classroom. Teachers should be aware of the responsibilities that come with this idea (e.g., daily care, humane treatment, costs, care during vacations, safety). It also should be noted that some students may be allergic to animals.

## Specific Instructional Practices in Social Studies

**Innovative In-Class Ideas.** Teaching social studies can involve many different instructional practices. Within the classroom setting, teachers can employ discussions, demonstrations, and learning centers. The efficient use of media and the Internet is another way of making content interesting and instructionally relevant. A substantial number of videotapes and digitized media are available for instructional use. (However, note the potential issues associated with media raised by the case study of James earlier in the chapter.) Another approach is to immerse students in a culture. For example, if the topic under consideration is a particular foreign country and its culture, then students might be introduced to its food, dress, music, and any other identifiable characteristics.

It is also well worth the effort to obtain materials such as maps, globes, charts, diagrams, and graphs. In addition, teachers should keep up to date on the multimedia software and the wealth of online resources that are available for instructional use.

**Outside-Class Ideas.** Outside the classroom, field trips to museums, historical sites, and community locations can be engaging. The local neighborhood can serve as a plentiful and primary source of information (see Table 10–13). Another outside resource is people from the community who can augment and embellish most social studies programs.

**Integration with Other Curricular Areas.** Social studies, like science, relates easily to other subject and skill areas. Instruction can therefore be designed to promote context acquisition with other skills such as listening and reading (Williams et al., 2007).

**TABLE 10–13** Select chapters from *My Backyard History Book*

| *Section Title* | *Description of Activities* |
|---|---|
| Whathisname | Students analyze their family names—what it means and from where it came |
| Getting a line on your past | Students examine their own personal family timeline |
| A birthday time capsule | Students assemble a time capsule on every birthday—then they "secure" it at their house somewhere |
| A family map | Using a large map, students track the movement (i.e., cities of residence) of their family members |
| Families come in all shapes and sizes | Students develop a kinship chart—showing their nuclear and extended family |
| Eating your way through history | Students ask their elders about old, family-shared recipes |
| Hand-me-down history | Students and their families work together to assemble all sorts of items related to their family's past, and present, assembling these items in some type of collection |
| History that talks | Students record their elders talking about various topics—pictures are used as story starters |
| Thingamajig | Students try to identify pieces of equipment that were part of everyday life many years ago |
| History in the yellow pages | If "thingamajigs" are not available in one's immediate home or that of relatives, students can consult the yellow pages, locate antique shops, and then explore the items in these stores |
| History at the cemetery | Students go to a local cemetery and look for all sorts of things—information about their ancestors, interesting quotes, sayings, and pictures engraved on various headstones, and related historical events that are associated with certain dates |
| At the corner of Yolo and Poonkinney | Students investigate the origins and meaning of street names |
| What's that doing there? | Students look for old structures that still remain in their communities |

*Source:* Allison, L., Burns, M., & Weitzman, D. (1975). *My Backyard History Book.* Boston: Little, Brown Young Readers.

One successful example involves a unit on ecology. The unit starts off with the old Marvin Gaye song "Mercy, Mercy, Me . . . the Ecology." It then explores topics such as government regulation and historical examples of the effect of pollution on the environment.

Music is a great way to demonstrate how other subject areas can be worked into social studies lessons. Much popular music can be easily integrated for this purpose. For instance, such songs as Madonna's "Papa, Don't Preach," the Pretenders' "My City Was Gone," and Billy Joel's "We Didn't Start the Fire" all address issues worthy of discussion within a social studies class.

Another method for integrating social studies with other areas is the use of a literature-based approach to instruction (McGowan & Guzzetti, 1991). In this system the primary mechanism for covering social studies topics is through trade books. An example of such a resource is the book *Literature-Based Social Studies: Children's Books and Activities to Enrich the K-5 Curriculum* (Laughlin & Kardaleff, 1991). Many publishers now incorporate literature within elementary-level basal programs.

Reflective Question 10–5: ***What are the strategies and classroom accommodations and modifications that can be developed and used across these two content areas?***

## TECHNOLOGY IN THE CLASSROOM

Technology is used extensively in education. The growing amount of innovative media and online resources offers intriguing interactive possibilities for engaging science and social studies topics. The possibilities of using the Internet for instructional purposes are almost endless. It is now possible to find websites that address any topic, thus providing a way to enrich ongoing instruction. It should also be noted that computer technology has distinct advantages for use with special populations.

### Science Applications

Some examples of intriguing computer use in science are offered here.

- Simulations: This type of software can substitute for certain dangerous situations (e.g., chemistry experiments) or can provide wonderful interactive experiences for students.
- Databases: Different types of databases are available. Some commercially produced software contains already established databases on topics such as animals; teachers can also create customized databases for their own needs.

- Probeware: Hardware devices (probes) and software that can be used to analyze information that is collected are now available that can be used as laboratory tools. Instruments that connect to the microcomputer can measure light intensity, voltage, temperature of liquids, and time. The measurements can be displayed on the monitor and recorded for future reference.
- Content enrichment: Male (2003) suggests that a rich array of software is available that can enhance the topics that are being covered in class. Some suggestions for the area of science are provided in Table 10–14.
- Utility software:
  - Presentation: It is hard to find a school where students are not required to develop presentations on various topics using presentation software. Much instruction is also presented via this style.
  - Graphing/charting: Data that is collected can easily be graphed for visual analysis using software such as Excel or other programs that are specifically designed for this purpose.

**TABLE 10–14** Software for content enrichment

| | |
|---|---|
| **Science Software** | |
| Sammy's Science House | Edmark |
| Thinkin' Science ZAP! virtual labs | " |
| The Great Ocean Rescue | Tom Snyder Productions |
| The Great Solar System Rescue | " |
| Rainforest Researchers | " |
| Science Seekers | " |
| Voyage of the Mimi | Sunburst |
| **Social Studies Software** | |
| Carmen Sandiego series | The Learning Company |
| Where in the USA? | |
| Where in the World? | |
| Carmen Sandiego Jr. Detective | |
| Oregon Trail | |
| Amazon Trail | |
| TimeLiner | Tom Snyder |
| Decisions, Decisions | " |
| Neighborhood Map Machine | " |
| Map Maker's Toolkit | |

*Source:* From Male, Mary, *Technology for Inclusion: Meeting the Special Needs of All Students*, 4/e. Published by Allyn & Bacon, Boston, MA. Copyright © 2003 by Pearson Education. Reprinted by permission of the publisher.

## Social Studies Applications

Computers are well suited for use in social studies. One of the most exciting uses of microcomputers in this subject area is with CD-ROM and interactive videos. Some of the ways computers can be used in social studies include:

- Content enrichment: Much media exists now that can be used to supplement what is being taught in social studies classes. Some software that has been designed to show simulations and creating maps/timelines are particularly useful (some examples can be found in Table 10–14).
- Utility applications:
  - word processing/desktop publishing: school newspapers, reports
  - databases: data on community demographics, information on legislators, CD-ROM encyclopedias
  - spreadsheets: economic trends, census data
  - graphing/charting: demographic information
  - communications: electronic field trips, online databases, e-mail

In addition to microcomputer applications, electronic references can be of great benefit to teachers of social science. For example, Partin (1998) offers teachers a valuable resource in his *Online Social Studies Resources: 1000 of the Most Valuable Social Studies Web Sites, Electronic Mailing Lists and Newsgroups*. In this book, Partin introduces the teacher to the Internet as an educational resource. He offers resources in the areas of general social studies, American history, world history, consumer economics, sociology, psychology, geography, American government, and current events.

> Reflective Question 10–6: ***With the limitations in equipment and materials that many teachers face in providing quality instruction in science and social studies, what technological interventions can be effective in enhancing the curriculum?***

# INSTRUCTIONAL PRACTICES

## Adaptive Practices for Inclusive Settings

As noted throughout this chapter, most published science and social studies materials used in general education settings are not designed for the diverse learning needs of certain students and must be changed to be effective. Special education teachers must develop the ability to adapt materials and instruction proficiently and expeditiously for students to be successful in inclusive environments. In general, the fewer adaptations required, the better, and modifications (i.e., changes to the content) should not change the concept being addressed.

An assortment of content enhancement techniques is available to teachers to use in science and social studies. As noted by Bulgren (2004), content enhancement tactics include practices such as graphic organizers, study guides, charts, outlines, visual-spatial displays, and mnemonics. These techniques have been found to improve student performance.

Lenz and Schumaker (1999) point out that two types of adaptations exist: content adaptations (i.e., changing the nature or the amount of information to be learned) and format adaptations (i.e., changing the way in which information is presented to students). Content adaptations must be done in light of the federal requirement that students with disabilities must have access to the general curriculum. The more likely type of adaptation for those students who are following the general curriculum involves format adaptations. Lenz and Schumaker subdivide format adaptations into three categories: altering existing materials, mediating existing materials, and selecting alternative materials.

A number of techniques can be implemented that will enhance the probability that students with special needs will learn science and social studies content. Table 10-15 provides many recommendations for accommodating student needs as a function of the typical types of demands and activities encountered in the science or social studies classroom across grade levels. Selected content enhancement ideas contained in Table 10-15 are discussed in further detail in this section as a function of level of schooling.

## Elementary Level Focus

**Textual Material.** Strategies for enhancing textbook use are outlined by Munk et al, (1998). Munk suggests that teachers (a) prioritize materials to reduce the amount and complexity of the text, (b) preteach vocabulary words prior to reading the assignments so that decoding and comprehension may be enhanced, and (c) paraphrase passages or have students retell what they have read after each paragraph or page. Teachers may want to supplement the reading of content with audiotaped texts. Although the audiotapes may not offer many benefits, they may increase comprehension of the content (Ellis, 1996).

Because textbooks are used so widely in science and social studies education, certain techniques may be needed to help students with special needs deal with these materials. Lovitt and Horton (1991) do not recommend that teachers rewrite or tape textbooks. They do recommend a number of techniques for adapting textbook material, some of which are discussed here:

- Advanced organizers: written material or oral discussion related to textual material to be read
- Study guides: selected important information from the textual material, usually in the form of questions or statements that help guide students' understanding of the material
- Vocabulary drills: timed activities in which students relate terms to their appropriate definitions
- Graphic organizers: graphic representations of key information (e.g., vocabulary or content), including visual-spatial illustrations.

**Vocabulary Issues.** The reality that many students have trouble mastering the rather large amount of new and often complex vocabulary that is presented in science and social studies warrants attention. Teachers must take time to identify the words and concepts that students do not know prior to actual class coverage. In some instances, this vocabulary will need to be taught explicitly, and students need to be provided opportunities to gain mastery (e.g., vocabulary drills).

**Procedural Issues.** Both science and social studies require students to follow sets of procedures. For example, all hands-on science involves a sequence of activities that students have to follow. Some students have great difficulty in remembering and/or following a sequence of steps. Teachers may need to take extra time to ensure that the directions are understood and may need to provide supplemental prompts (e.g., visual aids) to help students follow the directions that have been given.

**Organizational Needs.** Students far too often have difficulties in organizing not only their personal possessions but also the way they study. These students can benefit greatly from being provided assistance in this area. For instance, when assigned a project to do, they may need help in organizing their ideas and planning how to achieve the goal of a completed product. Often graphic aids can assist greatly with this task. Hoover and Patton (2006) offer a number of examples of this type of supplemental support.

**TABLE 10–15** Adaptation techniques

| *Instructional Practice* | *Area of Concern* | *Suggestion* |
|---|---|---|
| Textual Materials | Readability | • Use other content-area books that cover the same material—lower readability<br>• Have the text put on tape (e.g., Recordings for the Blind and Dyslexic)<br>• Use supplemental reading materials that can be read for access to content<br>• Use peer-directed grouping |
| | Vocabulary | • Introduce new words and terminology prior to students encountering this material<br>• Use teacher-generated glossaries<br>• Incorporate various word acquisition practices (e.g., card games, etc.) |
| | Comprehension | • Preview textual material with students (e.g., identify key terms, concepts)<br>• Discuss all pictures, figures, tables, and graphs<br>• Use advanced organizers<br>• Use reading guides<br>• Use semantic maps and other graphic organizers<br>• Ensure that students have competencies in skimming and scanning<br>• Help students learn how to go through the text more than once for different purposes<br>• Discuss what was read |
| Class Lectures | Attention | • Teach self-monitoring techniques<br>• Use self-monitoring aids (e.g., checklists)<br>• Make sure that lectures are not too long or complex (i.e., break up into briefer segments)<br>• Infuse lectures with discussion and other engaging activities |
| | Comprehension | • Provide students with advanced notes, PowerPoint slides, various types of graphic organizers, or general outlines of what is to be covered<br>• Introduce new terminology before lecturing<br>• Discuss all graphics that are presented in class |
| | Note taking | • Teach note-taking skills<br>• Provide teacher-prepared notes/outlines that conain missing information that must be filled in during the lecture |
| Instructional Materials | Procedural issues | • Ensure that students know how to use the materials and equipment.<br>• Develop criteria or qualifications for using certain equipment (e.g., utility knives) |
| | Conceptual difficulties | • Teach map and globe skills<br>• Preview and discuss all vocabulary and concepts that might be problematic |
| Projects | Following directions | • Clearly presented instructions and verify understanding—always provide directions in written format |
| | Self-direction | • Monitor progress<br>• Set up intermediate deadlines<br>• Use cooperative group projects if individual work is not possible |
| | Content development | • Require outlines from students soon after giving the assignment<br>• Allow variant formats for a final product—capitalizing on student strengths and interests<br>• Have students submit drafts of their work prior to the final product |
| Media | Vocabulary<br>Comprehension | • Introduce and discuss new vocabulary and terminology prior to viewing<br>• Allocate time to discuss background information and context prior to viewing<br>• Use various graphic aids when viewing<br>• Discuss key points after viewing |
| Web-Based Activities | Procedural issues | • Make sure that students know how to access the sites and information you prescribe<br>• Choose websites that are well designed and easy to navigate<br>• Teach students to use bookmarks and ways to organize their bookmarks so that they can retrieve important information |
| | Comprehension | • Provide graphic aids to assist students in acquiring the appropriate information |

## Secondary Level Focus

**Textual Material.** As students move through school, the challenges of handling textual material only increase in terms of difficulty. As mentioned previously, some of the textbooks used in these subject areas are the most complex in terms of readability. Several suggestions for dealing with this challenge are presented in Table 10-15; however, some examples of content enhancement at the secondary level are provided below.

- Advanced organizers: written material or oral discussion related to textual material to be read
- Study guides: selected important information from the textual material, usually in the form of

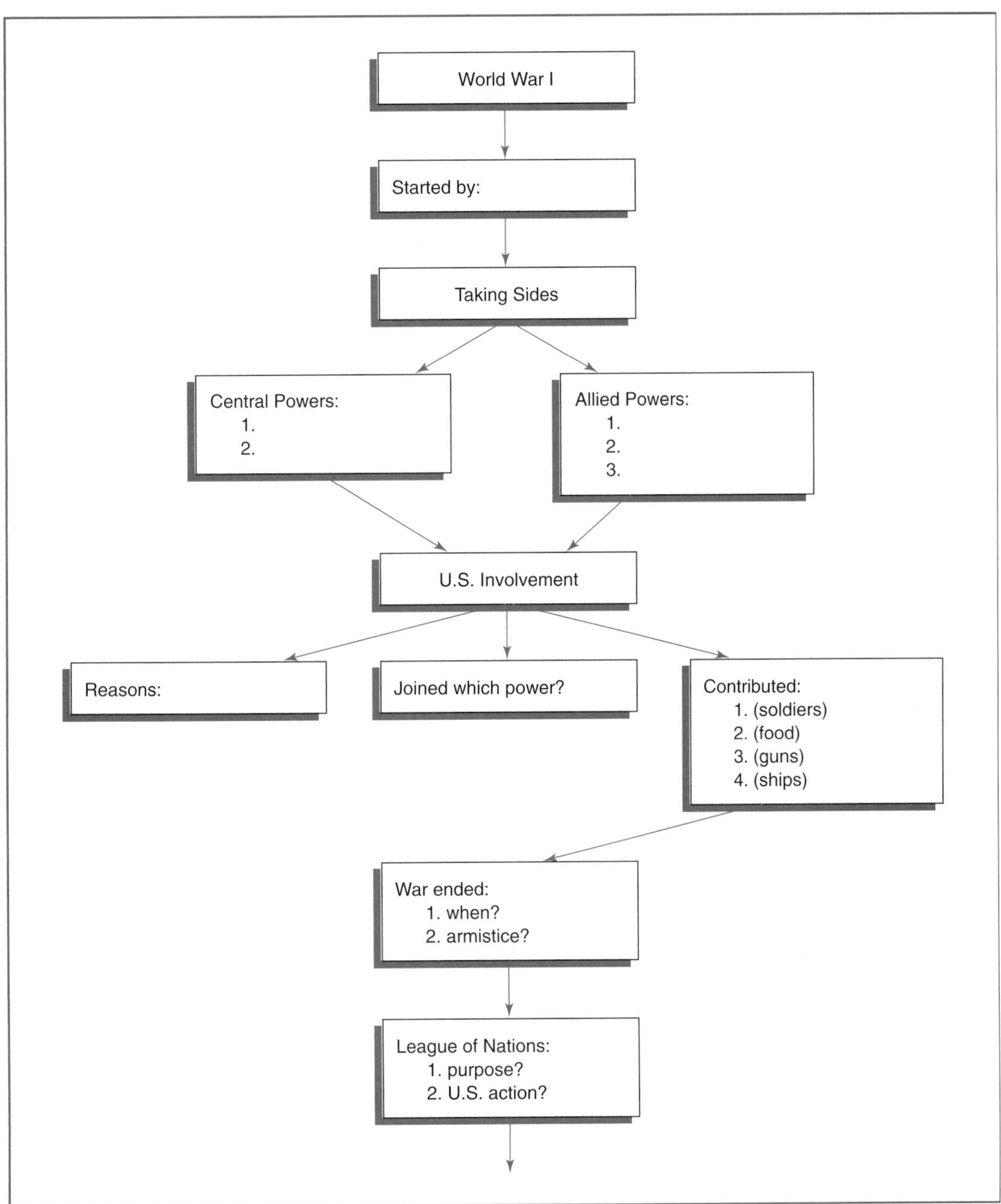


**FIGURE 10–5** Graphic organizer for World War I

questions or statements that help guide students' understanding of the material
- Vocabulary drills: timed activities in which students relate terms to their appropriate definitions
- Graphic organizers: graphic representations of key information (e.g., vocabulary or content), including visual-spatial illustrations. Figure 10–5 is a social studies example on "World War I."

The benefit of graphic organizers and other content enhancement strategies have been demonstrated in a series of recent studies on the teaching of history (e.g., Bulgren, Deshler, & Lenz, 2007; Williams, Nubla-Kung, Pollini, Stafford, Garcia, & Snyder, 2007).

**Lecture/Oral Presentation of Information and Discussion.** One of the presenting problems that some students with special needs bring to inclusive classroom settings is their inability to engage the information being presented by their teacher or the discussions that are part of science and social studies classes. Aside from the ideas provided in Table 10–5 on how to deal with this issue, some effective techniques involve ideas as simple as where students sit in class and the dynamics of lessons where lecturing and discussion are common.

**Mnemonic Strategies.** Mnemonic strategies are useful for helping students deal with vocabulary, terminology, and other label tasks that are associated with science and social studies instruction. Mastropieri and Scruggs (1995) describe mnemonic strategies as the "pairing of unfamiliar, new terminology with acoustically similar, familiar words (keywords) and associating the keyword with the definition" (pp. 11–12). Figure 10–6 provides a science example of this technique for remembering the meaning of deciduous and evergreen trees.

**Adapting Laboratory-Related Materials.** Many elements of an activity-oriented general education program may need to be adapted. Science materials at the secondary level, even if they include hands-on activities through laboratory experiences, often require some reading and the understanding of more complex vocabulary and advanced concepts. Sasaki and Serna (1995) demonstrate how a middle school science program developed for general education, the *Foundational Approach to Science Teaching I* (FAST I) (Pottenger & Young, 1992), could be adapted for use with students with disabilities. Through the use of techniques such as notebooks, direct vocabulary development, and thorough introduction to laboratory procedures, students were able to perform successfully in these general education materials.

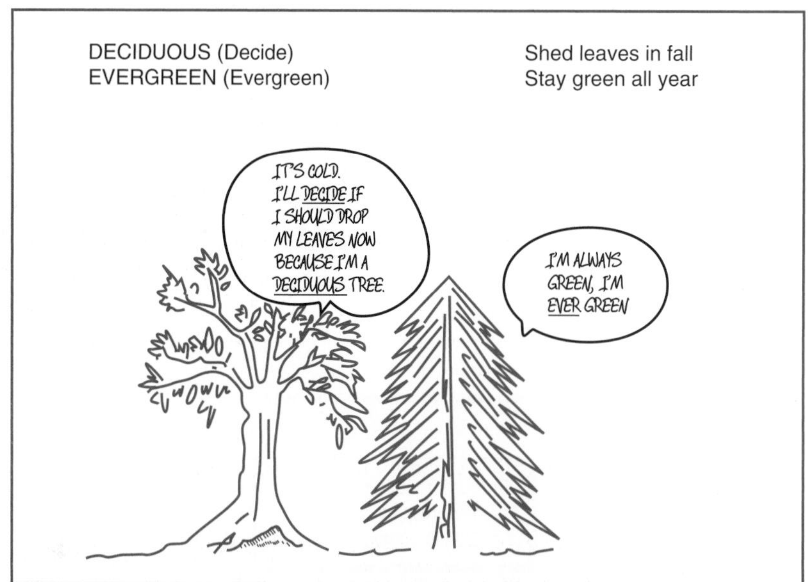


**FIGURE 10–6** Mnemonic illustration of deciduous and evergreen trees

*Source:* From "Reconstructive Elaboration: Strategies for Adapting Content Area Information," by M. A. Mastropieri and T. E. Scruggs, 1989. *Academic Therapy, 24*(4), p. 394. Copyright 1989 by PRO-ED, Inc. Reprinted with permission.

## SUMMARY

This chapter provides strategies for teaching science and social studies, two critical content areas. With the trend toward increased inclusion of students with special needs in general education classrooms, teachers are increasingly being asked to provide appropriate instruction, consistent with state standards, in science and social studies. The chapter provides an overview of the nature of science and social studies instruction, including attention to the specific challenges associated with teaching these subjects as well as general approaches for instruction. Information is also provided on strategies for assessment, specific instructional practices that can be used in both content areas, recommended classroom adaptations, and recommendations for the use of technology to enhance instruction.

## ACTIVITIES

### SCIENCE ACTIVITIES

1. Study anatomy by examining parts of a chicken. This is an easy animal to get, and it lends itself well to study because students are familiar with it.
2. Have pupils collect plant seeds or small plants: ask them to describe what they see when the seeds are planted or the plants are small. Have them make periodic written observations to demonstrate that plants do change. Have them place the plants under different conditions—no water, no sun, too much water—and observe the results.
3. So that pupils can better understand weather changes, have them keep weather charts that record temperature on different days, rain or snow accumulation, and other data students may want to collect. Questions to ask are, "Does it rain when the sun shines?" "What happens to water when you freeze it?" "What does snow look like close up?"
4. Science in the home provides a wealth of opportunities for a science unit: What makes an iron work? What causes cakes to rise? What causes bread to mildew?
5. Depending on students' ages and the area in which the school is located, take students to farms where food is grown and/or animals are raised. Older pupils or pupils who live in farming regions can actually grow food products or raise farm animals.
6. Build small models of simple machines, such as a pulley, wheel and axle, wedge, screw, and inclined plane. Use a spring scale to measure the amount of energy saved by using the machines to move and raise books or other heavy objects.
7. A study of different types of plants and flowers can be aided by keeping a log of the plants for the project. The log can be most effective if the plants are sketched or pressed. (To press, put the plant in a catalog with heavy objects on top and leave it for approximately 4 to 6 days.)

### SOCIAL STUDIES ACTIVITIES

1. Obtain pictures of different people in the community, show one picture, and have students discuss what that person does, how the person is important to the community, and what would happen if this person did not do the job. Students need to be aware of sources of help in the community. Examples can include police officers, postal workers, doctors, and rescue squads.
2. To develop awareness of societal values, discuss the Declaration of Independence and the Bill of Rights of the Constitution. List specific values, rights, and responsibilities on the chalkboard. Discuss applications to the school setting.
3. Grandparents are an often-overlooked treasure of information. A great way to investigate history is to ask them about past events. Students might also request autobiographical information from them.
4. For additional work on map skills, have students make maps of their neighborhoods. If cameras are available, have students take pictures of various significant sites.
5. Develop a unit on tools. Other subject-area content can be easily incorporated into it (e.g., science, career education). Have students study the tools used by workers in different vocations today and in times past.
6. Another neighborhood-based activity to assist students in refining their map and directional skills is a walk rally—similar in format to a road rally. Give students directions (e.g., written prompts, pictures) that they must use to follow a preplanned course. They are to answer questions along the way and ultimately reach a designated destination.
7. To assist students with map work and learning the location and capitals of the 50 states, enlarge a map to fit on a bulletin board. Then make cards that have a state's name on one side and the

capital on the other, within an outline of the shape of the state. Have students match the outline of the state on the map with the name on the card and then identify the capital. They can check themselves.

8. To help students remember the great amount of information found in a social studies curriculum, mnemonic strategies are great aids. For example, if memorizing the capitals of the 50 states, sayings like the following can help: Charles Ton lives west of his friend, the Rich Man (Charleston, West Virginia, and Richmond, Virginia).
9. Study cards can help special needs learners prepare for exams. On one side of an index card print the important event, name, or place covered in the chapter. On the back make a mark of any sort to use as a key. On another card print information that explains, defines, or identifies the word printed on the first card. Place the same symbol on the back of this second card. Students can then study at school or at home by reading the study cards and matching them. The cards are self-checking, provide instant reinforcement, and let students work on information in small, manageable pieces.
10. Combine practice of written expression and reference skills by having your class make a travel brochure for a state or region of study. Have students use library sources to gather interesting information about a specific area, tourist attraction, or culture found within this region. Then have them prepare a paragraph that highlights the facts and sparks interest in visiting that spot. They can also find pictures that add meaning to their writing. Both pictures and paragraphs can be cut, pasted, and copied to make a brochure for all to read.
11. Have students conduct opinion polls on several topics. This exercise requires students to use various data-gathering and interpretative skills.
12. Have students use graphing skills as often as possible. Activities requiring graphing can be found in almost any area; for example, students can graph the number of brothers and sisters they have.

CHAPTER

# 11

# Creative Arts: Visual Arts, Music, Dance, and Drama

Glenn H. Buck

The creative arts are an essential part of the human experience. Their expression and appreciation has been, and remains, universal (Pascale, 1993; Rodale, 2003). We see evidence of this universality across cultures and historical periods (M. D. Cohen & Hoot, 1997). Even in everyday life the creative arts can be observed, such as when a child draws on a sidewalk or when a group of adolescents sing and dance while listening to the radio. Clearly, the creative arts help children to discover their inner selves while making connections with their world (Wells, 2005).

Despite their universality, the degree to which the creative arts have been incorporated into public schools has been inconsistent, often changing in response to political and economic forces prevalent at the time. "The arts give voices to divergent intelligences and point out markers for different pathways to success. But for many the arts are viewed as an accessory to core curricular areas and, as such, are nice to have, but fundamentally unnecessary" (Gerrish, 2000, p. 35).

For students with disabilities, the situation is even more tenuous (Dugger-Wadsworth & Rieck, 2003). In fact, students with disabilities are less likely than their nondisabled peers to belong to school or community arts groups (Reis, Schader, & Milne, 2003). For many, leisure time is spent on passive activities such as viewing television rather than participation in community-based creative arts activities (Salend, 1994; Wilkening, 1993). Unfortunately, for many students with disabilities, the potential benefits that can be derived from participation in the creative arts are not realized.

This chapter introduces basic guidelines for incorporating a variety of creative arts activities into the educational programs of students with disabilities. Both general and specific teaching techniques are presented. However, even though this book focuses on teaching methods for students with high-incidence disabilities, art-based instructional strategies effective for both mild and severe levels of disabilities have been included in this chapter. This broad approach is based on several factors. First, special educators in today's special education classes may work with students from a wide range of severity levels, no matter how they were trained or how the classroom is defined (e.g., resource room). Therefore, teachers who have a variety of instructional techniques are better prepared to meet the challenges of teaching in diverse classrooms. Second, many teaching ideas for the low-incidence population can be adapted for students with high-incidence disabilities. And third, because many special educators are collaborating with general education and arts-specific teachers (e.g., choral directors), they need to be somewhat familiar with teaching strategies in the creative arts. A basic knowledge of the arts helps special educators to be more effective teachers and collaborators; this chapter can serve as a reference for them.

## RATIONALE FOR CREATIVE ARTS INSTRUCTION

Whereas all students can benefit from involvement of the creative arts, students with disabilities benefit most of all. Some of these benefits include improved cognition, literacy and basic language skills, verbal and nonverbal communication skills, peer acceptance, self-expression, self-discipline, self-awareness, self-esteem, mutual respect, trust, and decision-making skills (Cohen & Hoot, 1997; de la Cruz, Lian, & Morreau 1998; Whitehurst & Howells, 2006). The creative arts also stimulate intellectual curiosity, develop motor skills, reduce levels of physical and emotional stress, and foster appreciation for cultural heritage and human diversity. Even in an evolving climate of high-stakes accountability and standards-based curricula, the creative arts still offer a powerful and effective means by which to teach students with disabilities. When combined with standards-based, academic subject areas, the creative arts can provide novel and enjoyable means of learning new information (Reis, Schader, Milne, & Stephens, 2003).

For persons with disabilities especially, involvement in the creative arts can lead to the development of certain leisure-related skills, such as those related to self-expression, communication, and social behavior, which are learned as a consequence of such participation. Acquisition of such skills (a) allows persons greater freedom in making choices about how to utilize free time, (b) allows persons to access more complex leisure and recreation activities, and (c) reduces the dependency on others for lifelong leisure participation (Buck & Gregoire, 1996; Hawkins, 1994; S. L. Smith, 2001).

Schools can play an important role in helping students with disabilities to gain benefits from the creative arts. Formal groups (e.g., band) and planned classroom arts activities offer opportunities for students to develop artistic skills as well as experience the enjoyment that comes with involvement in the arts. Students benefit from the arts especially when they engage in arts activities with their nondisabled peers. Unfortunately, however, creative arts opportunities in many schools are presented in ways that often reduce their effectiveness for students with disabilities (Henley, 1990). Some of these problems include:

- Arts-related teachers often lack information about the needs of students with special needs, because these teachers tend to work in isolation and have few opportunities to collaborate. As a result, creative arts teachers may perceive the inclusion of students with disabilities less than favorably. According to Sideridis and Chandler (1996), such attitudinal problems are more pronounced for certain disability types (e.g., music teachers are apt to perceive the inclusion of students with emotional and behavioral challenges less favorably than students with other types of disabilities, and physical education teachers are more likely to hold similar perceptions for the inclusion of students with orthopedic impairments). Increased opportunities for disability-related professional development in this area can promote better inclusive experiences for all students.
- Creative arts teachers tend to rely on traditional instructional practices (e.g., large-group instruction with minimal efforts toward individualization) that are not always effective with students with disabilities (Pfeuffer-Guay, 1993a). Again, increased efforts to sensitize and educate all teachers about effective instructional methods for students with disabilities can lead to more favorable outcomes.
- Special and general educators often incorporate the arts into their curricula in a random and haphazard manner (Carter, 1993). Often, creative arts activities are provided infrequently or they are planned as time fillers rather than as valuable learning experiences. When creative arts activities are provided in an unconnected manner, teachers inadvertently reinforce the idea that art is less important than other subjects. Such an idea is misplaced because the benefits of creative arts activities, especially when they occur across a variety of settings, are numerous. If the benefits of education in the creative arts are to be realized, teachers must provide arts activities in a broader and more holistic manner.
- The current decline in arts opportunities across school districts reduces the opportunities for involvement in the arts for all students. This situation has resulted from overall reductions in financial support for creative arts programs (Wells, 2005). Ironically, expensive special education programs often deplete the resources needed to maintain arts programs that would benefit the students with disabilities.

Taken together or separately, these factors may in part explain the negative attitudes some art and music teachers hold toward the inclusion of students with disabilities in their classes (Pfeuffer-Guay, 1993a; Sideridis & Chandler, 1996). Given that the creative arts are often the first areas within which students with disabilities are mainstreamed (because they require less reading and fewer other academic-related skills) this potential negativity on the part of arts teachers presents a disconcerting paradox.

Fortunately, some of the problems inherent in the education of students with disabilities in the creative arts can be resolved by effective collaboration. Special educators can assist creative arts educators by providing knowledge of the learning and behavioral characteristics of students with disabilities (Oi, 1988; Pfeuffer-Guay, 1993a). In turn, creative arts educators can provide special and general educators with knowledge about creative activities, procedures, and materials that can be used in both segregated and inclusive classroom activities. Through such collaboration, arts teachers become more positive toward and knowledgeable about working with students with disabilities, and special and general educators become more skilled at integrating creative arts activities into their classes.

**Reflective Question 11–1:** ***What knowledge and skills should be included in professional development activities that are targeted to helping arts teachers better deal with student diversity?***

## GENERAL INSTRUCTIONAL GUIDELINES

Teachers should consider several guidelines when planning and implementing creative arts activities. Though they are effective for all students, these guidelines are especially relevant to students with disabilities. Creative arts should be:

- **Integrated:** Creative arts activities should be integrated throughout the curriculum, not just added on as isolated activities used to fill up time. Pfeuffer-Guay (1993b) observed a special education teacher who turned a measuring and cake baking unit into a celebration of Van Gogh's birthday; another teacher led students to create box sculptures that represented first-aid kits during a unit on safety. Likewise, Frye-Mason and Miko (2002) describe the Critter Dance, an activity that (depending on the age) incorporates music, creative movement, science, geography, and social studies. These examples point to the idea that the creative arts do not have to occur in an isolated time period but can be used in a variety of contexts.

When arts activities are incorporated in an integrated fashion, students learn the skills and attitudes necessary for lifelong participation in the creative arts. For students with disabilities, who typically have difficulty generalizing skills, integration of the arts throughout the curriculum promotes transfer of learned behaviors and attitudes across multiple settings.

- **Student-centered:** Creative arts activities should be based on students' interests, preferences, and abilities. Teachers who include students in the planning of creative arts activities increase student motivation. Once planned, students should be encouraged to engage in arts activities as independently as possible (Wells, 2005). Students develop independence when given choices and when they are allowed to express preferences. According to Harlan (1993), "creativity flourishes where individuals have choices . . . a variety of art materials and open-ended activities allow participants to take initiative and to express their preferences" (p. 1).

- **Age-appropriate:** Any creative arts activity should be planned with consideration of the students' chronological and developmental age. Secondary teachers who require their students to sing nursery school songs continue the image of the older student with disabilities as being childlike. Likewise, elementary-level students are rarely successful when they are required to create intricate art products that require them to follow complex directions.

For young children, creative arts activities should focus on self-expression, exploration, and experimentation. Students should be able to play with colors, shapes, three-dimensional objects, textured materials, sound, sound-producing toys, and unstructured movement. In drama, children should have opportunities to engage in make-believe, role-playing, simple storytelling, puppetry, and pantomime.

As students get older, activities should gradually change to the development of skills and attitudes that will result in lifelong participation in the arts. Learning the history of great artists, musicians, and theatrical personalities, as well as learning how to recognize styles and characteristics of an art form, leads to appreciation. By focusing on the technical skills related to the production of artistic products and the social behaviors and attitudes necessary for participation in an organized community arts group, students increase their potential for access, participation, and enjoyment in arts opportunities throughout life.

Creative arts should also be process-oriented. No matter what the chronological age, teachers should never lose sight of the fact that the act of creating is often more exciting and fun than completing a product. For example, for young children, watching colors mix together is often much more exciting than finishing a picture. This simple, vicarious type of learning is a necessary developmental step that should be allowed because it serves as a basis for more complex creativity. Unfortunately, too many teachers have an unrelenting desire to see young children make something—any product that approximates what the teacher rather than the child had in mind. This push to make young children product-oriented frequently results in children feeling inadequate (a feeling often expressed in the phrase "I don't know how to make that"). Often, children end up avoiding arts activities because of frustration and a belief that they cannot draw, paint, sing, dance, or act as well as they should. How many adults avoid singing in public because they were told at a young age they couldn't carry a tune?

This criticism of teacher-directed, product-oriented activities is not to be interpreted as a call for their elimination. Children who spend all their efforts in "free-form" creativity activities may never learn the basic skills needed for more complex creative endeavors. As a result, they may never have the opportunity to achieve satisfaction from a product well done. Any future artist, musician, dancer, or actor must learn fundamental skills. However, teachers should balance activities with both high and low structure. Given the current **standards-based** educational environment, teachers should try to relate their arts activities to one or more academic standards (while still respecting the need to focus on process over product). For example, students can still create with clay while learning the concepts of smooth, angular, and think. Likewise, Arkenberg (2005) described a collaborative project between a textile museum and a math program. Students were able to learn about symmetry and asymmetry, their manipulation (translocation, reflection, and rotation), and a number of other geometric definitions via the study and application of textile design.

Many standards-based skills and concepts can be taught via the arts in fun, creative ways such as the following:

- **Multisensory:** Students with disabilities often retain new information for longer periods of time when lessons include opportunities to learn information by using a variety of senses. Lessons that incorporate music, art, movement, and drama (separately or in combination) allow students to acquire and practice new skills and concepts in multiple ways. Students who are learning about Native Americans, for example, will remember information about the culture if they have opportunities to experience the culture through song, art, dance, and drama.
- **Multidimensionally taught:** Students tend to learn when they have opportunities to learn from each other and when they become actively engaged in the learning process. One of the criticisms of traditional arts programs has been the overemphasis on teacher-directed instruction (Platt & Janeczko, 1991). Though students with disabilities benefit from task-analyzed arts activities that are taught via a direct instruction model, creativity is reduced when these approaches are the sole form of instruction. This shortcoming has been documented in current literature, and arts educators are now recommending the use of a variety of teaching methods for students with disabilities. Advocates are calling for more extensive use of the cooperative learning and peer tutoring models (e.g., Wells, 2005). Other recommendations for enriching arts activities include teaching students to access arts opportunities on the Internet and using field trips, guest speakers, video recordings, and other nontraditional approaches.
- **Set in a creative environment:** Teachers should make their classrooms places where creativity is allowed to flourish. One of the best ways for teachers to accomplish such a goal is for them to model creative behaviors themselves and to show sincere interest in the creative arts. Specifically, teachers can incorporate the arts throughout their curriculum, display art in their classrooms, and report about concerts, art exhibits, and dance and theatrical performances attended. During arts activities, teachers can provide nonfrustrating and age-appropriate materials, reinforce students' efforts as well as their products, and remain nonjudgmental, helping students take pride in their creativity.
- **Supplemented by technology:** new developments in instructional technology hold great promise for enhancing the academic as well as creative abilities of students with disabilities. According to Wehmeyer et al. (2002), the manner in which students' progress can be measured does not need to be limited to paper and pencil writing activities. Rather, students can demonstrate progress in the curriculum via artwork, photography, drama, music, animation, and video products.

**Reflective Question 11–2:** ***To what degree can teachers incorporate process-oriented (versus product-oriented) arts activities when they work in a standards-based instructional environment?***

## INSTRUCTION IN THE VISUAL ARTS

Painting, drawing, sculpting, collage, and photography represent the most common types of visual art forms found in most schools. Students experience these art forms in formal art classes and when their classroom teachers incorporate art activities into lessons. Modification and activity ideas related to these five visual arts are addressed in this chapter. However, teachers should investigate the use of other arts and crafts activities that often are enjoyed, particularly by secondary students.

Some of these include jewelry making, gem crafts, metalworking, woodworking, plastic crafts, silk screening, leather crafts, papier-mâché, weaving, shell crafts, and ceramics. Books on these topics are available in most libraries and bookstores.

Table 11-1 includes an observation checklist of skills related to the visual arts. Teachers may find this checklist useful when they incorporate this art form into their programs, or by special educators as they collaborate with general educators. Depending on the goals targeted for an individual student, this list can be modified and some of the skills rewritten as objectives and included in the student's IEP, or in the general educator's lesson plans.

## Adaptations

Across all settings, students with disabilities frequently need material and instructional adaptations in order for them to participate fully in the creative process. In deciding which adaptations are appropriate, teachers should focus on individual abilities and preferences. A sample list of prerequisite skills that often are required when participating in visual arts activities is presented in Table 11-2. Although deficits in any of these skill areas certainly do not preclude participation, such deficits often necessitate certain adaptations (listed in the following section).

**General Adaptations.** Although students with cognitive and behavioral difficulties constitute a highly heterogeneous population, several **adaptations** can be made to improve their ability to participate in art activities. The following suggestions have been adapted from Pascale (1993), Pfeuffer-Guay (1993a), and Wells (2005).

1. Reduce the number of materials (in order to reduce the number of decisions students have to make).
2. Break down complex procedures into small sequential steps (task analysis).
3. Provide hand-over-hand assistance (when needed).
4. Make directions simple and direct.
5. Provide activities that involve cutting and gluing for students who work too quickly.

**Adaptations for Students with Physical Limitations.** Students who have difficulty with reaching, grasping, or keeping hands steady can benefit from art activities that require them to manipulate materials. With adaptations, students with physical limitations strengthen fine and gross motor skills and improve overall range of motion (i.e., the extent to which a person can move various parts of the body). Specific adaptations for students with physical limitations (as adapted in part from Ensign,

**TABLE 11–1** Visual arts skill checklist

**Observation**

1. Student communicates feelings evoked while observing a work of art.
2. Student identifies details and characteristics in a work of art (e.g., colors, shapes, objects, themes).
3. Student defines the concept "art gallery."
4. Student behaves appropriately while visiting an art gallery.

**Participation**

5. Student prepares the work area before initiating an art activity.
6. Student begins working without prompting.
7. Student manipulates materials.
8. Student completes an art activity.
9. Student displays his or her artwork.
10. Student cleans up the work area.

**Appreciation**

11. Student critiques his or her artwork, or the work of others.
12. Student participates in discussions about art.
13. Student reports about a public arts event that she or he attended.

**TABLE 11–2** Prerequisite skills for participation in visual arts activities

1. Student is able to hold and manipulate an art tool (e.g., brush).
2. Student is able to distinguish colors and shapes.
3. Student is able to distinguish same and different concepts.
4. Student is able to hold and manipulate pieces of materials of various sizes.
5. Student is able to communicate preferences.

1992, 1994; Pfeuffer-Guay, 1993b; Platt & Janeczko, 1991) include:

1. Use large-handled brushes, attach Hoyle pencil grippers (see Chapter 10) to brushes, or attach brushes to hands using Velcro straps. Allow students to hold brush by teeth or toes.
2. Use large, chunky crayons or oaktag.
3. Melt crayons and let them cool. The resulting mass is easier for students with manual dexterity problems to grasp.
4. Give hand-over-hand assistance if needed.
5. Attach a turntable to top of work table so that students with restricted reach are better able to access materials.
6. Secure paper to the desk for drawing and painting. Paper can be secured with tape (or magnets if working on a metal surface).
7. Attach a small easel to the top of the work table.
8. Raise or lower the height of the table depending on wheelchair size.
9. It may be easier for some students to work on the floor, with an angled wedge provided to support the arm. (Consult with physical or occupational therapist.)
10. Use less frustrating materials (e.g., use yarn instead of string, sponges instead of brushes, cardboard or thick paper instead of construction paper).
11. Provide adaptive scissors.
12. Place fingerpaints on a cookie sheet or in a baking pan.

## Teaching Tips for Visual Arts

**Painting.** Free-form painting is one of the most common art activities used in the classroom. Painting helps students practice combinations of gross and fine motor movements and extend range of motion, as well as allows them to experiment with color. Teachers should provide ample opportunities for students to paint with a variety of colors, textures, and painting tools (e.g., brushes, fingers, wooden blocks, string). Some recommendations for the use of painting in the classroom include:

1. Students can paint while listening to different styles of music. Encourage the students to discuss feelings evoked by the music.
2. Have students paint by a variety of means—painting with fingers, feet, paintbrushes, sponges, or blocks. Students often enjoy placing paint on paper and blowing on the paint through a straw to create interesting designs.
3. Write students' names or other letters of the alphabet in very large letters (36 inches tall) on large paper (can be obtained from newspaper printers). Have students fill in the letters with tempera paints.
4. Let students work together to create a large mural. Murals are large pictures that are made on walls or on large pieces of paper attached to a wall. Murals can have a particular theme (e.g., children around the world), although this is not necessary.
5. Painting large pieces of uncooked macaroni is a good activity for students with physical dexterity problems. (Use watercolor or tempera paint.) When the macaroni is dry, have children string it into a necklace. (Use kite string or shoelaces.)
6. Have students help design and produce backdrops for school plays and musical productions.
7. Young children can be introduced to color theory (primary and secondary colors) via a storybook called *The Color Tree*, by Minnerly (2005).

**Free-Form/Object/Figure Drawing.** Drawing not only is good for creative expression, but also is believed to be a good foundation during early childhood for later writing skill development (Sidelnick & Svoboda, 2000). Teachers should encourage drawing for all students because it helps them develop manual dexterity and attention, thereby helping to develop handwriting skills. Drawing also allows children to observe details in the world (e.g., shape, size, proportion, perspective) and it allows them to represent the world in two-dimensional form (Spencer, 1992). For **free-form drawing** especially, the process of creating a picture expands a student's imagination and provides an excellent forum to promote social interaction with peers (as students discuss each other's pictures). Some recommendations for the use of drawing in the classroom include:

1. Encourage students to draw pictures of real or imagined objects. Students can be given actual objects to use as models. It is especially important to let students with visual difficulties manipulate the objects before drawing. Also, some evidence suggests that students tend to draw with more detail when they work on large paper (Spencer, 1992).
2. Have students draw pictures using a variety of writing and drawing tools, such as rules, compasses, stencils, protractors, and so on.
3. Some computer software is designed to allow students to make drawings electronically.
4. Teach students simple elements of perspective (e.g., objects that are far away are drawn smaller than closer objects).
5. Provide activities in which students copy simple pictures. Although copying certainly would not be considered to be a highly creative activity, it does have value in helping students develop the mechanical skills necessary for more complex creative work. When copying activities are used, teachers should keep them simple by limiting the number of details in the prompts.
6. Draw part of a picture for the student, based on a particular theme or topic. Let the student finish the drawing. A series of creative workbooks based on this idea is available through the Owl Book Company. The workbooks are known as the Anti-Coloring Books and are available in most school-supply stores.

**Sculpting.** Sculpting (i.e., creating three-dimensional objects) can be an effective means for developing students' fine and gross motor skills and for developing a sense of size, shape, and proportion. A variety of materials can be used in the sculpting process, some of which include clay, play dough, mud, sand, plaster, cardboard, and Styrofoam. Some recommendations for the use of sculpting in the classroom include:

1. Give students ample opportunities to explore with different sculpting materials. Often, students enjoy repetitive movement patterns, such as rolling, pushing, pounding, and chopping. These basic movements should be encouraged because they form the basis for later, more complex, work.
2. For representational sculptures, move from simple to more complex projects. For instance, it is better for students to start with sculpting representations of mountains and valleys in a sandbox rather than sculpting representations of people. However, students' individual preferences should be allowed to influence the process and product.
3. Have students create sculptures from objects and materials found in the immediate environment. For example, a leather glove can be positioned upside down, filled with water (provided it doesn't leak), and suspended in a freezer by string and clothespins. Once the water has frozen, students can quickly cut the glove from the ice. Through this type of activity, students learn the idea of casting. Follow-up information about art forms that use this type of process (e.g., ceramics) can be incorporated into the lesson.
4. Students can design an outside sculpture garden.
5. Have students mold numbers or letters (such as the letters in their names) from clay or play dough. Let them dry and then have students paint them with watercolors or tempera paint.
6. Teach mathematical concepts such as fractions, addition, and subtraction by requiring children to count clay balls and tear clay into more than one part.
7. For students prone to eating clay, teachers can use homemade, nontoxic play dough. The recipe is as follows:

> Add 1 package unsweetened Kool-Aid mix to 2 cups of water in a pan; add 2 cups flour, 2 teaspoons cream of tartar, 11/4–2 cups of salt, and 2 tablespoons oil to the pan. Cook over medium heat for 5–10 minutes, stirring constantly. Play dough is done when color deepens and it comes together in a ball. Let cool and cover tightly to store.

**Collage.** Collage (French, meaning "to paste") is an effective medium for self-expression. Just about any material can be used in the making of a collage (Pascale, 1993; see Table 11-3). Collage making requires students to select, cut, and manipulate various-sized materials and to make decisions about their placements on the paper. Collages can be personalized by including pictures of students or by including pictures cut from

TEACHER *Tips* Secondary Level

## Integrating Sculpture into Content-Area Units

Innovative teachers are always creating new ways to link core subject areas with the arts. Khilnani and Culhane (1995) describe a unit that used sculpture in a unit on habitats. The teacher and an artist worked with a class of 13-year-olds with learning disabilities. Their final products included individually sculpted habitats and a class mural depicting forests, mountains, and deserts. Instructional strategies included:

- brainstorming discussions to generate ideas and words (used later in writing assignments)
- instruction from an artist in the technical aspects of the project
- step-by-step procedures for construction of their habitats from the ground up

Concepts in language arts (descriptive words), science (characteristics of plants and animals), math (fractions), social studies (land forms), social skills (following directions), and art (mixing colors) were all part of the habitat unit.

When using art activities as part of thematic units, be creative. Your evaluation process can include individual portfolios, a group celebration, individual presentations, or a group video that records everyone's contributions. Students will enjoy the hands-on nature of the assignments and may learn more from the activities than they would from more traditional pencil-and-paper tasks.

*Source*: From "Linking Sculpture to Core Subjects," by S. Khilnani and D. Culhane, 1995, *Teaching Exceptional Children, 27*(4), 68–70.

**TABLE 11–3** Sample materials used in collage

| | |
|---|---|
| Tinsel | Cut-up balloons |
| Wallpaper samples | Yarn |
| Gift wrap | Cotton balls |
| Doilies | Sandpaper |
| Foil | Corrugated paper |
| Newspaper | String |
| Cellophane | Tape |
| Sheet plastic | Glue |
| Ribbon | Glue cups |
| Assorted contact paper | Stick |
| Magazines | Scissors |
| Brass fasteners | Paper plates |
| Napkins | Material scraps |
| Scrap paper | Sawdust |

*Source:* From *Multi-Arts Resource Guide*, by L. Pascale, 1993, Boston: Very Special Arts Massachusetts. (ERIC Reproduction Service No. ED 370 330)

magazines that represent students' interests. However, not all collages need to be thematic; often, students enjoy creating a collage without any theme. Instead, they may focus on color, shape, or size of materials (Pascale, 1993). Some recommendations for the use of collage in the classroom include:

1. Limit the amount of material that is available for students to use in making the collage, depending on the abilities and learning style of students.
2. Cut up the collage and make a mobile.
3. Students can make a collage by cutting pictures from magazines that reflect their interests, hobbies, or future career and life desires.
4. Take a walk or have a scavenger hunt to collect flowers, leaves, nuts, and seeds. Have students glue these to a sheet of paper to make a picture or put them in between sheets of waxed paper, iron the sheets together (low setting), and make a placemat. Coordinate this with a discussion about changing seasons (fall or spring). Talk about things found in the woods or coordinate with a unit on ecology.
5. Obtain scrap wallpaper from paint stores. Let students develop appreciation for shape by making wallpaper collages.

**Photography.** Photography can be an effective instructional medium for all students. Given a camera's ability to capture reality, students are able to record events and things of interest to them that have real-life relevance. Students not only learn to use a camera, but also learn to make decisions about what to photograph. Students may wish to photograph objects of beauty or situations that represent social injustices. Also, the introduction of digital cameras and camcorders has opened a new arena for creativity. Students can now manipulate images (in terms of color and shading) to create alternative representations of objects and settings. Some specific recommendations for using photography in the classroom include:

1. Students can digitally manipulate images taken on a digital camera. Ask the students to re-create an image that expresses a feeling, such as somber (i.e., the students make the image dark). Students can then link a poem (one that is self-written or commercial) to the image.
2. Remove color from a digital image (i.e., turn it into a black-and-white image). Ask students to express how the image is different.
3. Have students take photos of each other engaged in activities they enjoy (e.g., sports, music) and make a mobile or collage of the photos.
4. Students can take photos of an outside object at different times throughout the school year. Place the photos side-by-side and have the students discuss or write about how the scenery changes according to the seasons.
5. Have students take pictures of classroom, school, or community events and activities. Later, students can give PowerPoint presentations in other classrooms (good for developing some public speaking skills).
6. Assist students in developing their own "photography portfolios" that include photos they have taken. Have an open house where students get to show off their portfolios to visitors.
7. Hold a class photo exhibit and invite school administrators, teachers, and other students. Provide background music and refreshments.

**Reflective Question 11–3:** ***In what types of environments can art activities occur beyond the classroom?***

## DIVERSITY IN THE CLASSROOM *Tips*

**Linney Wix** is an artist and associate professor at the University of New Mexico. She is studying the life of Friedl Dicker-Brandeis (1898–1944) who taught art to the children of political refugees and to Jewish children who were not allowed in schools beginning in 1938.

Maintaining consistency in time, place, and materials for arts activities helps create the "container" for creative work. The container, which is both physical and psychological, differs from that for academic activities because the goals for each type of activity are different. While many academic activities call for a single correct answer, arts activities have an open-endedness to them that supports students in observing, finding, and making choices in regard to working at their own aesthetic. For example, a child might think.

- Hmm, do I want the red to flow across the page, or do I like it better when I paint it around the edges? How is red different/the same when it flows or edges?
- Do I like the dissonant sound of these notes played together, or do I want a more consonant harmony? What do I like about the dissonance or the consonance?
- I'd rather crawl on the floor than stand and twirl in dance class. I've tried both (and more) and I like moving down low. What's it like to move low to the ground?
- I know the teacher assigned me the part in the play of the quiet child because I'm kind of quiet. But I wanted to play the rowdy kid. I don't know what being rowdy is like.

Offering children opportunities to make choices in working in/toward their own personal aesthetic supports them in observing, making judgments, and unfolding imagination. It supports them in being close to and understanding their own experiences.

Working in the arts is a healthy thing—it involves engagement with self and others as well as with materials, be they paints and clay, a keyboard or a triangle, the body, costumes and props. Thus, while teaching about relationship with self and other, the arts invite engagement with various processes and products. The multiple relationships potentially enrich children's lives and contribute to self-knowledge. Maintaining consistency in time, space, and materials contributes to balancing the chaos and order inherent in arts processes by supporting children in knowing what to expect and when and where to expect it.

I believe in the power of materials in children's art making and trust children choosing from an array of possibilities. In visual art, I hope you'll offer a minimum of three mediums and a variety of paper sizes. In music, make available various instruments; encourage children to try out different instruments, including their voices. Offer lots of hats and scarves for movement and drama. Set out materials and invite children to choose. Watch what they choose. In the long run, trying out different colors, sounds, movements, and parts supports children in experiencing who they are and who they might be in their worlds.

Several final things: Cleaning up provides natural emotional and physical closure to an activity; have children participate. Remember that even though you may integrate arts experiences throughout your teaching, the arts are content areas in themselves and need their own time and space. Have fun!

## INSTRUCTION IN MUSIC

Attention to the relationship between music and human behavior has a long history. Through the centuries, poets, writers, and philosophers have written about the power of music to evoke images, emotions, abilities, and belief systems (Marshall & Tomcala, 1981). Today, music is very much a part of everyday life. Think about how many times music enters our lives each day and how it affects us. Music has frequent applications ranging from simple sounds for improving the environment to complex, integrated, artistic works forming the core of life's important ceremonies.

Music plays an important role in the curriculum of most schools. Although students with disabilities have access to musical opportunities, it should be remembered that for all students, the extent to which they participate in music activities and the types of music activities that are provided are relative to school type. Elementary students often receive instruction in a general music class where they are introduced to the basic elements and history of music, group singing, and musical instruments. In middle school, students often continue in general music class; however, the content becomes more sophisticated. Students are expected to have a basic understanding of musical notation, harmony and theory, and music history. Many schools introduce basic keyboarding skills at this time. In middle school, students also are provided opportunities to participate in an organized music ensemble such as a choir, band, or orchestra. At the secondary level, however, it is unusual for students to receive general music classes. At this level, music involvement is typically focused on the organized ensembles (with admittance often contingent upon a tryout and continued participation dependent on the maintenance of a certain level of competence) (Buck & Gregoire, 1996).

Students with disabilities should participate in general music classes with peers who are not disabled (Shields, 2001). Depending on level of interest, they should also be given the opportunity to participate in music ensembles. Such participation may require that adaptations be made. For example, a student with manual dexterity problems may be able to play a bass drum more easily than a snare drum (which requires a high degree of hand and finger movements). Likewise, the arrangement of choir sections on risers may need to be changed before a concert (e.g., the tenors placed on the bottom row risers), so that a student with cerebral palsy will not have to stand in a location separate from his or her section because of accessibility problems.

In whatever context music participation occurs, teachers should take into account the variability among student abilities, interests, and preferences. To assist teachers in the identification of these musical abilities, a checklist is presented in Table 11–4. Teachers can use this checklist, or a modified version, to identify students' level of performance and thereby derive sample objectives and ideas for instruction. Also, depending on the involvement of the music teacher or the goals for a given student, some of the objectives can be written into the IEP. The checklist is divided into six areas. The items under each area are sequenced from easiest to most complex. The teacher circles the item that best represents the present level of performance for a student. The IEP objective is the item directly below the circled item, because the lower item is the next skill in sequence. Classroom teachers may need the assistance of the school music teacher in the assessment of these skills.

### Adaptations

Instructional adaptations are often necessary in order for students with disabilities to have successful musical experiences. The following is a list of adaptations that may prove useful.

**General Adaptations.** Cognitive and behavioral disabilities certainly do not reduce a person's interest and motivation to participate in musical activities. Adaptations include:

1. Use more demonstration and practice when learning new musical concepts.
2. Teach new songs at a slower tempo.
3. Use songs with repetitive melodies or phrases.
4. Use songs in combination with movement.
5. Keep songs age appropriate (in terms of lyrics and melodies).

**Adaptations for Students with Physical Limitations.** Playing a musical instrument is an effective means of increasing a student's manual dexterity, large-muscle strength, coordination, and range of motion. With practice, students with physical limitations benefit from playing musical instruments (i.e., rhythm instruments used in

**TABLE 11–4** Musical abilities checklist

**Participation**

1. Student becomes agitated and prefers to leave room/area during music activities.
2. Student prefers to stay in room/area during music activities.
3. Student sits on the sidelines and watches the group during music activities.
4. Student sits on the sidelines but participates by singing, clapping, and so on.
5. Student sits with the group, but does not participate.
6. Student sits with group and participates with adult prompting.
7. Student sits with group and actively participates without adult prompting.
8. Student will lead group in music activities when invited (e.g., leading the group in singing).

**Melodic Abilities**

9. Student appears agitated while others are singing.
10. Student makes no sound while others are singing.
11. Student tries to sing while others are singing, but sounds are unintelligible.
12. Student sings while others are singing, but pitches do not relate to group pitches.
13. Student sings while others are singing, and pitches approximate group pitches.
14. Student sings on pitch.
15. Student sings a familiar melody without assistance.
16. Student creates and sings a new melody.
17. Student expresses desire to sing in formal singing ensemble (i.e., choir).
18. Student expresses a desire to sing in front of class (solo or in a small group).

**Rhythm**

19. Student attempts to clap, move, or play a rhythm instrument while listening to music.
20. Student consistently claps, moves, or plays a rhythm instrument while listening to music, without prompting.
21. Student matches beat of teacher (by clapping, moving, or playing a rhythm instrument).
22. Student matches the beat while listening to a song (by clapping, moving, or playing a rhythm instrument).
23. Student maintains a steady beat for a brief period of time (0–20 seconds).
24. Student maintains a steady beat for prolonged period of time (more than 20 seconds).

**Basic Music Theory**

25. Student identifies dynamics of music (i.e., loud, soft) while listening to music, singing, or playing an instrument.
26. Student identifies tempo of music (i.e., fast, slow) while listening to music, singing, or playing an instrument.
27. Student identifies differences in pitch (i.e., same, different, high, low) while listening to music.
28. Student recognizes familiar melodic phrases or rhythmic pattern that reoccur in a song.
29. Student reads basic musical notation.

**Music Appreciation**

30. Student sings or asks for a favorite song.
31. Student identifies one or more traditional musical instruments.
32. Student identifies different musical genres (e.g., classical, jazz).
33. Student identifies well-known composers within musical genres.
34. Student demonstrates knowledge of how music is produced (in terms of acoustics).
35. Student demonstrates knowledge of how music is recorded.
36. Student attends community music events.

circle time activities, and traditional band instruments). Specific adaptations include:

1. Alter the position of a musical instrument. For example, a guitar can be positioned flat on a student's lap or on a table if the student finds holding the instrument in the traditional manner too difficult. Instruments also can be secured to a lap or table using straps.
2. Use electronic keyboards rather than traditional pianos in the classroom because their height can be adjusted (often necessary for students who use wheelchairs) and because the keys of an electronic keyboard are much easier to press down than traditional keys on a piano, making them easier to use.
3. For students with respiratory limitations, playing a recorder (i.e., a simple wind instrument that is available from most music stores) is much easier than playing a flute; very little breath is required to produce sound on a recorder.
4. Songs can be shortened for students with endurance problems.
5. Use peer tutors to help hold instruments.

## Teaching Tips for Music

**Singing.** Almost everyone loves to sing. Singing can be used for the expression of emotions, a reward, free time, socialization, or as a means of celebrating an important event. Teachers should incorporate singing in a variety of contexts. Some suggestions include:

1. Personalize songs by inserting a child's name into the song.
2. Make up new words to old melodies. Words about holidays and other special events can replace words in traditional melodies (Hildebrandt, 1998).
3. Sing songs at a slower tempo (i.e., speed). One of the problems with many of the commercial music recordings for children is that they have songs that are recorded at too fast a speed. For students with speech and language difficulties, fast tempos often lead to frustration (i.e., students get frustrated because they cannot sing all of the words). Teachers need to consciously slow their tempos while singing. Slowing down, however, is not easy. It feels unnatural and it is too easy to speed up without realization. Some teachers put a yellow sign on the wall that says slow down as a memory prompt.
4. Use singing as part of a reward contingency included in a student's behavior management plan. For instance, take the song, "The Ballad of Davy Crockett." Switch the name Davy Crockett with the student's name. Sing the song to the child when he or she has met the criteria for a good behavior day.
5. Shy students can also be motivated to get in front of groups of people with the "air band" strategy. Air band is a method of entertainment in which a small group of people pretend to perform in a rock-and-roll band. They dress and behave like real rocks stars while they lip-synch (pretend they are singing) to recordings.
6. For students with learning disabilities and an elementary reading level, reinforcing reading skills (e.g., sight-word vocabulary and speed) using the popular music video disk machine (known as karaoke) can be effective (Brick & Wagner, 1993). Students sing words to a song displayed on a video monitor while a musical accompaniment is played in the background.
7. Many popular children's songs can be related to a theme connected with social studies. For example, as children are learning about our country, they could also learn the song "This Land Is Your Land"; or when studying transportation, they could learn such songs as "City of New Orleans."
8. All adolescents like to feel that they are an integral part of the school society. One way of increasing the sociability of students with disabilities is to teach them school-related songs, such as the alma mater or school fight song. These same songs can provide many pleasurable moments for students on bus trips, hiking experiences, and camping expeditions.
9. For students who are nonverbal, songs can be "sung" via an electronic device known as the VOCA (single switch).
10. Students with disabilities may benefit from visual representations of the objects sung about in songs. According to Hagedorn (2003), many commercial products are available that provide symbols with songs (e.g., *Songs to Communicate*, by Rhinehart and Brodin-Lennon).

**Playing Musical Instruments.** Involving students in the production of music is a very motivating and beneficial activity. Simple musical instruments can be purchased or made and used in a variety of ways.

Figure 11-1 shows examples of easy-to-make instruments. Specific activity ideas include:

1. Have students tap on a drum the number of syllables that are heard in a particular word.
2. Have students listen for rhythms that occur in the natural world, such as the ticking of a clock or the rhythm of someone skipping on a sidewalk. Discuss the importance of rhythm in our lives.
3. Play rhythm games in which students must imitate rhythms or move when a certain rhythm is heard.
4. A variety of software programs have been developed recently to provide specific instruction in rhythm—consult with your school's music teacher or a local music store.

**Active Listening.** Students should learn how to listen attentively to music. Specifically, they should learn to focus on certain elements of style, such as volume, rhythm, melody, and texture, and they should learn how to express their reactions to music. Time should be set aside for students to listen to a variety of musical

**FIGURE 11–1** Easy-to-make musical instruments

styles and to discuss personal reactions to the music. Specific activities could include:

1. Take students on a walk through a variety of environments (e.g., forests, urban areas). Have them record all the sounds they hear. Make comparisons between the sounds in terms of the way the sounds make them feel.
2. Play a game in which short sound segments are played on a tape recorder, and have the students guess what each sound is. For instance, play the sound of water dripping and ask the students to identify the sound. Follow up this activity with playing commercially made environmental recordings (such as recordings of the rain forest, whales, etc.).
3. Have students watch different types of movies and note the type of music that is played during the movie. Discuss how the music affects the mood of a scene. Teachers can also black out the monitor while the movie is playing, so students can hear the dialogue and the music but cannot see the picture. Discuss whether the music has the same effect on mood when you cannot see what's going on.
4. Have students listen to the recording of the classical masterpiece "The Moldau," by Smetana. This programmatic musical work represents through sound the progress of a river that flows through Eastern Europe. The river starts out as a trickle and grows steadily. The music parallels this progression by its increasing complexity. Other well-known programmatic classical works include "Symphonie Fantastique" by Berlioz, "Romeo and Juliet" by Tchaikovsky, and "Danse Macabre" by Saint-Saens.
5. Take the students to a public concert. Some local music groups will present concerts in schools.
6. Invite local musicians to come in and present information about their musical activities, their musical instruments, and their lives as musicians.
7. Expose students to various types of ethnic music, especially when studying different cultures in social studies. The Smithsonian Institute includes several interactive multicultural music listening programs on its website.

**Background Music.** Background music is everywhere—in shopping centers, on elevators, and in classrooms. Although not everyone likes background music, a survey conducted in Florida (Buck, 1993) found that a sizable proportion (37%) of general and special education teachers who responded to the survey played background music in their classrooms. Reported purposes of playing music included creating an enjoyable environment, calming their students (and themselves), increasing student creativity, teaching relaxation techniques, providing novelty, promoting higher-level thinking, and/or improving students' academic performance. Background music was played during independent seatwork, free time, art, and creative writing activities. Several teachers also reported using background music as a cue for students at transition times (they paired specific songs with cleanup time). Interestingly, the most frequently used styles of music were classical and easy listening, although some teachers used various esoteric music styles such as Native American flute music and Scottish bagpipe music.

**Musart.** *Musart* is a term that refers to the combining of music and visual arts into a single multisensory experience (Nowak, 1981). Lessons are developed on particular concepts or themes, and art activities are implemented while music is being produced or listened to. The following is an example of a musart activity: Given the theme "sweet and sour," students are assigned a variety of art activities, such as painting yellow lemons with real lemon halves on green paper cut into the shape of trees. While the students paint, the teacher leads them in a modified version of the popular 1960s song "Lemon Tree." Modified lyrics:

> Lemon tree very pretty,
> And the lemon smells so sweet,
> But the juice of the lemon,
> Tastes so sour when we eat.
> Take lemon in your hand,
> Put a lemon on the tree,
> Yellow lemons grow so pretty,
> Won't you count them now for me?
> *(words modified by Nowak, 1981)*

Other similar activities that relate to the theme follow this musart activity (such as cooking with lemons or reading a story about a "sweet" grandmother). The focus of this approach is on the bombardment of the senses while concepts are simultaneously reinforced in a continuous fashion.

**Reflective Question 11–4:** ***How can music enhance the classroom and environment and complement the instruction taking place across the curriculum?***

## INSTRUCTION IN DANCE AND CREATIVE MOVEMENT

Moving to music is one of the most basic characteristics exhibited by humans. Whether we are tapping our feet, clapping our hands, or moving our entire bodies, the power of music to elicit physical response is remarkable. The benefits of dance and creative movement for all people are numerous and include such outcomes as improved physical coordination, emotional well-being, social interactions, and identification with one's cultural background or the cultural backgrounds of others (Bond & Deans, 1997).

Unfortunately, in most schools, dance and creative movement activities are restricted to physical education classes or weekend social events (i.e., school dances). In classrooms, dance and movement activities typically are limited to lower grades and narrowly defined movements (e.g., marching). For older students, dance opportunities often are accessed only through expensive, private lessons. This limited attention to dance and creative movement in schools is unfortunate given the number of benefits that can be derived from their inclusion in the curriculum. For students with disabilities, especially, benefits from this art form can lead to leisure-related skills and interests that last a lifetime.

Dance and creative movement activities can be incorporated easily into the curriculum. For instance, students can choreograph a simple dance that reflects the events in a story or the mood of a poem. Students also can learn about other cultures through exposure to a variety of dances taught by people living in the community who represent diverse cultural backgrounds. Movement activities also can facilitate the acquisition of academic content when, for example, students move in letter or number patterns.

In whatever context dance and creative movement activities occur, movements should be shaped and controlled in a structured environment (Cook, Klein, & Tessier, 2004). Young children in groups can get hurt when movements are without purpose. Teachers who are untrained in dance and movement may want to consult a local dance instructor. Dance instructors can be an excellent source of information on basic dance steps and how to adapt the steps to a diverse population of students.

Movement activities should also take into account students' gross motor, vision, and hearing abilities; ability to concentrate; and understanding of basic vocabulary (e.g., up, down, under-over, jump, stop, start, together, fast, slow). Teachers often will need to consult with a student's physical or occupational therapist, speech therapist, physician, family, and other teachers in order to gather information about abilities and limitations, as well as interests and preferences. This information is important because a student's ability to move, see, hear, attend, and understand concepts will significantly influence the level of participation. The more impairment present in any of these areas, the greater the level of instructional adaptations that need to be made. Table 11-5 includes an observation checklist of skills related to dance and movement that can be used by teachers incorporating this art form into their

**TEACHER *Tips*** **Elementary Level**

### Using Poetry and Movement with Children

Want to increase students' appreciation of poetry and also allow them to release excess tension? You can do both at the same time with a movement poetry program. Boswell and Mentzer (1995) describe a teaching style, lesson plan format, and program that combines creative movement and the presentation of poetry. The movement poetry program lessons include three phases: warm-up, movement to poems, and closure. Using an interesting poem with a sequence of action words can motivate students to listen to and read poetry; foster peer interactions; and provide a healthy, productive way to release pent-up energy. Consider the fun that students could have with a poem like this one suggested by Boswell and Mentzer:

**"Jump or Jiggle"** by Evelyn Beyer

Frogs jump
Caterpillars hump
Worms wiggle
Bugs jiggle
Rabbits hop
Horses clop
Snakes slide
Seagulls glide
Mice creep
Deer leap
Puppies bounce
Kittens pounce
Lions stalk
But—
I walk!

*Source:* From "Integrating Poetry and Movement for Children with Learning and/or Behavioral Disabilities," by F. F. Boswell and M. Mentzer, 1995, *Intervention in School and Clinic, 31*, 108–113.

**TABLE 11–5** Observation checklist for dance and creative movement

1. Student shows interest in dance and creative movement activities (watches others while movement activities are occurring).
2. Student engages in dance and creative movement activities without prompting.
3. Student follows directions for initiating a movement activity (e.g., lines up, gathers materials such as streamers).
4. Student follows directions during movement activities (e.g., responds to words like *start, stop, jump, crawl, freeze*).
5. Student demonstrates required movements during activities (e.g., marching, skipping, turning, stepping, bending, leaning, twisting).
6. Student behaves appropriately during activities (e.g., does not touch others when not supposed to, does not leave activity area).
7. Student finishes activity when directed.
8. Student is able to create new movements during spontaneous dance activities.

programs. Depending on the goals targeted for an individual student, some of these skills can be rewritten as objectives and included in the student's IEP.

## Adaptations

Most instructional adaptations in dance are focused on modifying the environment and complexity of the movements. The following is a listing of adaptation ideas in these two areas.

**Environmental Adaptations.** Environmental adaptations in dance are primarily concerned with space. Teachers will need to consider modifying the movement area when assisting students who are not able to deal with confined areas, who may be unable to control aggressive behaviors, who use wheelchairs, or who may have vision difficulties. The following ideas are suggested:

1. Provide an area that is large and free of obstacles.
2. Make the movement area boundaries clearly known to students.
3. Be especially careful when students in wheelchairs are on a stage. Accidents can happen when wheelchairs get too close to the edge.
4. Place large cardboard cylinders (accessible from a cloth store) upright on the floor and give directions to the students that they are only to move around their own cylinders. The cylinders are reference points from which students are able to define their own space. This is especially good for students who have tendencies to wander or to invade the space of their peers. For students with visual difficulties, the cylinders may have to be painted a highly visible color to improve visibility.

**Procedural Adaptations.** Because of the physical and cognitive limitations of many students with disabilities, modifications will need to be made in terms of simplifying the directions, procedures, and physical requirements demanded in the activities. Specifically:

1. Teachers should focus on basic dance steps rather than complicated choreographed movements that require a lot of imitation. Basic steps should be modeled for students, with plenty of opportunities for practice. Steps can include stepping, jumping, turning, bending, leaping, crawling, skipping, hopping, and sliding.
2. Use warm-up activities, such as stretching, "Simon Says," or "Follow the Leader" (Broughton, 1986).
3. Teachers should adapt movement vocabulary and directions (Kaufmann, 2002). Teachers can teach simple commands, directionality words, and form concepts by modeling. Command words can include *start, begin, move, go, slower, faster, stop, freeze, follow the leader, no touching,* and *help a friend.* Directionality words can include *above, below, forward, backward, under, over, beside,* and *inside*. Form concepts can include *together, apart, separate, divide, split, connect,* and *circle*.
4. Alternative movements can be required for students with severe physical limitations, such as requiring a student to wave the fingers instead of the entire arm. In such cases, students can be asked which movements they prefer to use in activities.
5. When dancing, use popular music that has a strong, steady, and distinctive beat. The tempo (i.e., speed) of the music should be appropriate to the abilities of the students.

## Teaching Tips for Dance

**Dance.** Dance can be used either during structured group activities or during free time. Students can create dances individually or in cooperative groups, or they can learn dances taught by students in other classes or by adults from the community. Dance can be used to commemorate an important current or historical event, to learn about another culture, or simply as an enjoyable means of self-expression or social interaction. Activities can include:

1. Students should be provided opportunities to attend school and community dance performances and to learn about the profession of dance. Students can learn how dance has changed throughout history and how each culture has developed a unique form of dance.
2. For younger children, play a modified version of "Simon Says." During circle time students are directed to do a series of behaviors, such as put your hands over your head, under your chin, above your eyes, beside your ears. These movements can be done while listening to music, with the movements timed with the music's tempo.
3. Have students create a dance that represents different seasons. For example, during spring, students can create a dance that represents the growth of flowers and trees, the melting of snow, or the migration of birds.
4. Develop wheelchair dances. Students who are in wheelchairs hold onto one side of a hula hoop and an adult or peer holds onto the other side. While music is playing, the adult or peer guides the student in a wheelchair around the dance area (Morris, 1991). Certain movements can be incorporated for expressiveness.
5. Incorporate manual signing into dances.
6. Integrate poetry and movement (Boswell & Mentzer, 1995; Gabbei & Clemmens, 2005).
7. Learn simple dances of other cultures. Invite a community member from a different culture to the class to demonstrate and teach ethnic dances.

**Reflective Question 11–5:** ***Dance is almost universally enjoyed by students of school-age. How can dance and creative movement be used differentially to enhance the curriculum of elementary-, middle, and/or secondary-level students?***

## INSTRUCTION IN CREATIVE DRAMATICS

The abilities that allow us to imagine, pretend, improvise, act, entertain, and create and communicate stories are uniquely human characteristics. These abilities begin to develop early in life. Very young children often are observed in play activities where they pretend to be a teacher, a parent, or an animal. Such spontaneous play activities are a child's attempt to mimic and interpret reality, a process that stands as the basis of what we consider **creative drama.** Through creative play, children practice expressing the emotions and activities that are necessary for functioning within the world. This process is the same for all children, regardless of disability.

As we become older, imaginative and pretend activities become more elaborate and formalized. In schools, children are engaged in reading and interpreting literature, acting in classroom or school plays, and sometimes being members of a drama club. As adults, unless we become involved in a community theater group, participation in drama is usually limited to passive observation (i.e., attending theater events).

Whether we are young or old, actively or passively engaged in dramatic activities, creative drama allows us to think imaginatively, to define and redefine our realities, to experience the diversity of emotions, and to interact with the human community. Through drama we learn about our own and other cultures. For students with learning disabilities, drama can serve to remediate difficulties in oral language and social skills (de la Cruz et al., 1998).

There are several forms of drama that can be incorporated in educational settings. The ones addressed in this chapter include spontaneous improvisation, puppetry, pantomime, storytelling, role-playing, and more advanced acting. Table 11–6 includes an observation checklist of skills related to creative drama that can be used by teachers incorporating this art form into their programs. Depending on the goals targeted for an individual student, this list can be modified and some of the skills can be rewritten as objectives and included in the student's IEP.

### Adaptations

When developing creative drama activities, teachers should be conscious of the abilities and limitations manifested by the participating students with disabilities. The following is a listing of adaptation ideas that may be pertinent:

1. Teachers should take a greater role as leaders and participants in the planned activities. This is especially true in early childhood, when children with disabilities tend to not engage in imaginative play for prolonged periods of time. For example, in the play kitchen area, while other children are playing

**TABLE 11–6** Observation checklist for creative drama

1. Student shows interest in play activities (watches others during dramatic play activities).
2. Student engages in dramatic play activities, alone or with others (picks up and engages with toys for prolonged periods of time).
3. Student engages in group creative drama activities (i.e., role-playing, puppets) without prompting.
4. Student follows directions for initiating a drama activity (e.g., lines up, gets in correct position).
5. Student follows directions during drama activities (e.g., responds to words like *start, stop, look toward*).
6. Student behaves appropriately during drama activities (e.g., delivers spoken lines, shows expression, does not touch others when not supposed to, does not leave activity area).
7. Student finishes activities when directed.
8. Student is able to create ideas for new dramatic activities.

tea party, children with disabilities tend to walk to the area, pick up a toy cup, bang the cup on the table, and leave the area within a very short time. Although these children may learn more sophisticated play behaviors incidentally by watching their nondisabled peers, teachers can speed up the learning process by creating and leading play situations that encourage higher levels of thinking and attending. Some of the ways facilitation can occur include:

- cuing the child in the play area through a series of tasks (such as telling the child to pick up and pour tea [imaginary] from the tea kettle)
- providing prompts that facilitate imagination (such as handing children cut-up pieces of construction paper that serve as tickets when children pretend that they are taking a train trip)
- modeling imaginative thinking by using pantomime during play time (such as pretending to cut an imaginary person's hair)

2. When role-playing, teachers should begin with simple activities that are nonthreatening, comfortable, and familiar to the students. For instance, having older students with disabilities act out all the complex behaviors required in a job interview may be less effective than having them practice a few job-interviewing behaviors (such as shaking hands and making eye contact).
3. Teachers should engage students in individual, one-to-one activities (e.g., puppets, one-to-one storytelling) before moving on to small-group and large-group activities.
4. Teachers can use group responding methods instead of one-person responses during creative drama activities with shy students. For instance, instead of calling on each individual student to tell the group what's in his or her imaginary box, ask all of them to respond at the same time. Listen for the shy student's response, call attention to the student's response, and positively reinforce it.
5. Many students enjoy making up and telling a story or reciting one from memory, rather than always reading a story. Teachers can serve as models when they create stories or tell well-known folk tales during group sessions. Students can provide the parameters for the teacher's story, such as when and where the story takes place.
6. Teachers can provide props for dramatic activities. Many students enjoy dressing up when playing certain characters.

## Teaching Tips for Creative Dramatics

**Spontaneous Improvisation.** Teachers can provide opportunities for students to act out certain themes or scenarios. For instance, students learning about transportation safety can act out a scenario about the importance of buckling seatbelts. Depending on the students' abilities, the scene can be done without preparation (spontaneous improvisation) or planned ahead of time. Teachers and students can set certain parameters for the scene (such as determining the number and type of characters). Similarly, teachers can give students the beginning of a scenario and then ask the students to finish the scene. For example, the teacher can say, "Mrs. Bear is having an awful night. She is not able to fall asleep." Following this, the teacher asks students why they think Mrs. Bear is not able to sleep. Students decide on one specific reason and then act out the scene. Other ideas for encouraging spontaneous improvisation include:

1. Placing a large, gutted-out television in the play area can be a great motivator for young children to engage in solitary or group improvisation.

2. Putting out a box of various adult clothing will invariably lead children to put on the clothing and act out certain parts.
3. Giving students a real microphone and telling them to develop a show in which some of them are comedians and others are singers or dancers can be very motivating.
4. Have students practice verbal exchanges in pairs or small groups to replicate real or imagined human encounters. Students or teacher can set parameters for exchanges.

**Puppetry.** "Puppetry can be a highly effective teaching tool because the imaginary personality of the puppet enables the puppeteer to establish deep, psychological relationships with children and adults in a relatively short period of time. Puppetry can help students see the other's point of view, reach students' hearts, increase humor in lessons, and involve students in lessons" (Levy, 2002, p. 48). Some teachers also use puppets to convey academic information, develop vocabulary, and increase the frequency and quality of verbal communication.

Whatever their purpose, puppets do not have to be the expensive commercial type. Puppets can be made by drawing faces on a hand, a paper bag, or a sock (Pascale, 1993). Ensign (1992) recommends making puppets by recycling stuffed animals, opening their seams, removing the stuffing, and sewing a child's tube socks inside them. Some activities that can be done with puppets include:

1. Use puppets that represent people of diverse cultural backgrounds, but do not perpetuate inaccurate stereotypes.
2. Teach students academic concepts by having puppets complete academic problems correctly and incorrectly. For example, students can tell the puppets how to do two-digit math problems correctly.
3. Have students resolve conflicts with puppets. Students talk to each other through their puppets.
4. Set out several puppets during free play time.

**Pantomime.** Pantomime (also referred to as mime) is one of the most underused educational methods in schools. It rarely appears in the educational literature and it is infrequently observed in classrooms. This lack of attention is unfortunate because pantomime can be an effective means of increasing imagination, social behavior, and conceptual development. Teachers who pantomime life-related activities (such as reading an imaginary newspaper) serve as models to students who often are delayed in their level of imaginative thinking and interpersonal behaviors. When combined with children's literature (i.e., children pantomime a story), motivation and comprehension improve (Gabbei & Clemmens, 2005).

Pantomime can be used effectively in structured group activities. During group activities, teachers can ask students to guess what is being pantomimed. Concepts such as hygiene, social manners, and career activities can be conveyed through pantomimes. Students often sit spellbound as the teacher pantomimes some of the following:

- waking up in the morning (getting dressed, washing hands and face, brushing teeth, combing hair, eating breakfast, leaving for school)
- reading a book
- cutting someone's hair
- playing a piano
- running (in the Special Olympics)
- building a house

Teachers also can have students pantomime certain activities. Especially for students with dysarthria, pantomiming eating ice cream (with exaggerated tongue movements), eating spaghetti (with exaggerated sucking movements of the lips), and blowing on hot coffee can be therapeutic. Providing opportunities for students to pantomime various life roles or vocations (e.g., waiter, astronaut, parent, police officer, or mail carrier) is also beneficial.

Elliot (2002) uses a prepantomime phase. Lasting about a week, the teacher and the students do a number of activities involving observation, concentration games, and sensory recall. For instance, objects may be placed in boxes and the children must study the object that they remove from the box. A writing activity follows. Later in the week, the students must perform a pantomime character. The students create a situation in which two characters are in some type of conflict. The unit's final project is a solo pantomime performed to instrumental music.

**Storytelling.** Stories have been told and retold throughout human history. Often, students love hearing stories as much as they like stories being read to them. The act of telling stories and the act of listening to stories are very basic to human nature. Unfortunately, the advent of modern technology has made storytelling a much more passive and visual process than it was in the past.

Infusing storytelling into classrooms can have several benefits. Craig, Hull, and Haggart (2001) point out that "storytelling is a great way to bridge apparent cultural divides by encouraging many interpretations of the core story the teacher is telling. Storytelling helps children connect prior knowledge and experience with the larger world of text. It promotes reading comprehension in ways that build the capacity of all children to academically succeed" (p. 46). Additionally, storytelling improves academic skills by enhancing children's observation abilities, creativity, and problem-solving and decision-making skills. Storytelling also introduces children to the symbols and traditions that characterize their cultural backgrounds (Turner & Oaks, 1997).

Teachers can encourage storytelling both by serving as a model and by providing opportunities for students to engage in the activity themselves. Stories can be either created spontaneously or memorized in advance, and they can be used with students of all ages.

Spontaneous stories are easy to develop when teachers relate subject matter to students' interests. Knowing that Jason has an interest in UFOs can lead to a story about three aliens who descended in a space craft and taught villagers how to improve their environment by recycling and saving endangered species. Likewise, knowing that Sara has an interest in dolphins can lead to a story about a young girl who befriends a dolphin. Students can follow up these types of stories by gathering information about the topics, writing the stories down on paper, and creating related stories. Often, students enjoy hearing their own names interjected into the story.

Memorized stories are often good to use when teachers do not feel confident creating their own spontaneous stories. Reading a favorite book repeatedly often results in the teacher's memorizing the story. Often students enjoy just sitting and listening to the story, rather than looking at the pictures in the book.

For teachers who use storytelling in their classrooms, the following ideas are suggested:

1. Some students need to be taught the difference between fact and fantasy. At the end of the story or activity, some children need to be told that they are back in reality. For students with disabilities, this recommendation may be especially relevant.
2. Exaggerate events, characters, and behaviors in stories. A big, old, near-sighted owl who lost his spectacles in the stream is certainly more interesting than just a wise, old owl. Likewise, a little girl who makes many friends because she is kind and generous (something she learned from her grandmother, who lives in a one-room apartment) is more interesting than a little girl who makes a lot of friends because she is nice.
3. Do not perpetuate traditional and inaccurate stereotypes in stories. Not all doctors are men nor are all teachers women.
4. Storytelling and gossiping are clearly not the same thing and students should be taught the difference. We do not make up stories about familiar friends and family. Also, we do not tell stories about people we know that are true and that might hurt their feelings if they knew we told them.
5. Use exaggerated inflections, different dialects, and words or phrases (Yes! Si! Oui!) in different languages when telling stories. Encourage students to do the same when they tell stories.
6. Have students work in small groups to shape and highlight the sounds of interesting poems with vocal inflection, coloring, and orchestration. Have them generalize these behaviors to their own spontaneous storytelling.
7. Use mime so that students can act out stories.
8. Sound effects can make a story come alive. Giving students instruments like finger cymbals and egg shakers (both available from music stores) can give students the ability to make the sound of rain (for example) when a peer is reading a story. Teachers can introduce the concept of sound effects by walking the students through the school and nearby environment and recording the sounds that are heard. Then, students are asked to replicate the sounds in the environment by finding materials and devising ways in which to manipulate the materials to create sound.
9. See Craig et al. (2001) for additional ideas.

**Reflective Question 11–6:** ***To what degree can teachers incorporate these creative approaches to drama if they don't perceive themselves to be creative?***

## SOURCES OF TEACHING IDEAS

Teachers often express the concern that they feel untrained in the creative arts. As a result, they tend to have a limited repertoire of activities and those activities that they do use tend to get used repeatedly. Fortunately, there are many sources of information from which to collect a variety of creative arts teaching ideas. One of the most comprehensive sources of teaching ideas is the Very Special Arts program. This is a national organization that provides (a) ongoing support for the training of teachers in the creative arts, and (b) opportunities for students with disabilities to participate in a variety of creative arts activities (frequently in the form of an annual festival). Teachers should contact their state departments of education to see if any districts in their state participate in the Very Special Arts program. Sometimes, state groups publish a teachers' guide that includes numerous teaching ideas across all the creative arts areas. A guide by the Very Special Arts in Massachusetts can be accessed on microfiche (see Pascale, 1993). Teachers can also gain a number of ideas from attending a local, state, or national Very Special Arts festival. If an organization does not exist in a local district, teachers may want to write to the national office and request information about how to form a group.

Teachers can gain movement and dance activity ideas from local dance instructors. Basic movements can be demonstrated and taught to students. Teachers can ask dance instructors for catalogs from which they can purchase cassette tapes of music that is appropriate for dance activities.

## TECHNOLOGY IN THE CLASSROOM

Recent advances in technology are providing new ways in which students can present their artwork. Scanners, CD burners, digital cameras, and camcorders are some of the new types of equipment that can make learning come alive.

Web-based learning activities are also available in most schools. One effective way to engage students in this technology is by the use of virtual museums. Across all of the visual arts, teachers can make use of virtual museums (e.g., Metropolitan Museum website and ibiblio.org). According to Roland (2005), Internet-based learning activities allow students to "explore, gather information, think critically, and construct their own understandings of the curriculum topic at hand" (p. 28). Web-based assignments can be a springboard for students' creativity, as well as allowing them to compare and contrast, and critique artwork. For example, students can compare and contrast artworks from different cultures, time periods, or style periods. They can create their own artwork based on certain attributes of works found in the virtual museums.

> **Reflective Question 11–7:** ***The opportunities for using technology applications in the arts are too expansive to describe within this chapter. What specific examples for technology applications can you suggest to enhance instruction in the visual arts, music, dance and creative movement, and drama?***

## MAKING IT WORK

Special education teachers can be proactive in the use of the creative arts across all areas of the curriculum. In fact, any teacher can infuse arts activities during the instructional planning process by asking the following questions:

1. What is the purpose/objective of this lesson?
2. What concepts and skills are to be taught during this lesson?
3. Is there enough time available to include one or more creative arts activities?
4. If so, are there ways in which I can teach the concepts and skills with the addition of creative arts activities?
5. If I don't have ideas related to specific arts activities that can be used to teach these concepts and skills, are there arts teachers and other professionals with whom I can consult?
6. Are there websites and other sources of information from which I can gain additional ideas as to how to use the creative arts in my lessons?

Lessons that include a blend of creative arts and teacher-centered, direct instruction can be highly effective for students with disabilities. Students benefit when teachers think outside of the box and create lessons that capitalize on students' natural inclinations and desires to create and express themselves. For the arts to be effectively infused into the curriculum, however, teachers must do the following:

1. Keep focused on the standards of learning (most school arts activities must be developed with the

standards in mind) and be able to justify how and why such activities are beneficial.

2. Remember that ability in the arts is highly personal; one students' area of strength may be another student's area of weakness. Making comparisons among students' art products and being overly critical are usually counterproductive.
3. Convey a sense of enjoyment when engaged in creative arts activities. Teachers are role models and their excitement about participation in the arts is often instrumental in helping students to develop a similar attitude.
4. Remember that interest and participation in the arts can be a lifelong endeavor. Teachers who encourage students, especially those with disabilities, to seek out and join community-sponsored arts activities help them to develop that lifelong interest.

## SUMMARY

This chapter presents information that will assist educators to include the creative arts (i.e., visual arts, music, dance, and drama) into educational settings. Following a discussion that outlines the rationale for including the arts in special education, general instructional guidelines (relevant across all creative arts areas) are outlined. Next, specific areas of the creative arts are presented, with each of these sections including (a) a short description of the arts area, (b) specific strategies for adapting instruction in the arts area for persons with disabilities, and (c) curriculum activities. The chapter ends with suggestions for locating additional sources of teaching ideas related to the creative arts.

PART THREE

# Critical Skills

CHAPTER 12
*Study Skills*

CHAPTER 13
*Social Competence and Self-Determination Skills*

CHAPTER 14
*Functional Academics and Career Development*

CHAPTER 15
*Transitions Across the School Years*

CHAPTER

# 12

# Study Skills

*John J. Hoover*

Study skills are essential for all students at all grade levels. Although the appropriate use of study skills is particularly essential at the upper elementary, middle, and secondary levels, acquisition of study skills should begin early in the educational career. Hoover and Patton (2007) emphasize the need for integrated study skills programs throughout one's schooling and as lifelong skills. Schumm and Post (1997) wrote that effective use of study skills facilitates personal learning.

Current literature suggests the need for increased study skills development in students with learning problems (Bos & Vaughn, 2006; Cohen & Spenciner, 2005; Coman & Heavers, 2001; Hoover, 2000). Wolfolk (2000) stresses that teachers need to provide opportunities for students to use study skills and that some students with learning problems often do not possess adequate study skills. Unfortunately, adolescent students with learning disabilities generally have not been taught study skills during elementary education, and as secondary students they often lack sufficient skills to meet their various educational demands. Deficiencies are often found in the listening, note-taking, test-taking, time-management, and organizational abilities of secondary students with disabilities. Hoover (2004) and Brown (2004) discuss students' lack of self-management abilities. Deficient test-taking skills in students with high-incidence disabilities are noted by Hoover and Rabideau (1995) and Mercer and Mercer (2000). Thus, evidence continues to suggest the need for an increased emphasis on effective study skills for students with special learning needs at both the elementary and secondary levels of education.

## STUDY SKILLS RESEARCH

Much of the need to acquire and use study skills in learning is intuitive based on their connections to various educational tasks. For example:

- Knowing how to take tests contributes to better test taking
- Effective note taking facilitates greater understating of lecture content
- Efficient use of time contributes to more effectively completing tasks
- Ability to accurately interpret graphic aids is necessary to effectively use picture clues
- Self-management facilitates efficiency in task completion

These and other examples strongly imply the necessity for developing study skills, beginning in early elementary school, and continuing into and beyond secondary education. In support, various researchers and experts in the field of study skills have documented research results or other evidence highlighting the significance of study skills development and usage. For example, Good and Brophy (1992) noted that educators must build the use of study strategies into daily instruction. Devine (1987) and Lerner (2000) wrote that listening abilities can be strengthened through direct teaching. Ekwall and Shanker (2003) indicated that note taking becomes easier for students once outlining skills have been mastered. Hoover and Trujillo-Hinsch (1999) found that students with limited English proficiency lack positive self-perceptions concerning overall test preparation and benefit from instruction in how to better prepare for tests. In addition, Brown (2004) documented that strengthening self-management skills facilitates greater student responsibility for own learning. Also, Bos and Vaughn (2006) reported that research indicates that lectures in the secondary levels are infrequently preceded by advance organizers needed to facilitate effective and attentive listening. As suggested in the above research, sufficient evidence exists to support the development and implementation of an ongoing study skills program for students with special needs.

Study skills include those competencies associated with acquiring, recording, organizing, synthesizing, remembering, and using information and ideas. Such skills assist students in confronting the educational tasks associated with the learning process. Students with learning problems often lack strategies for organizing and remembering information (Day & Elkins, 1994). Thus, study skills facilitate mastery of a number of learning components, which are illustrated and defined in the following list:

- **acquisition:** the crucial first step involved in learning; the first experiences encountered by learners
- **recording:** any activity in the classroom that requires the learner to record responses, answers, or ideas, including both written and verbal forms of communication
- **location:** seeking and finding information
- **organization:** arranging and managing learning activities effectively
- **synthesis:** integrating elements or parts to form a whole, creating something that was not clearly evident prior to synthesis
- **memorization:** remembering learned material; storing and recalling or retrieving information

For a more detailed discussion the reader is referred to Hoover and Patton (2007).

> **Reflective Question 12–1:** ***Given the fact that study skills instruction is often part of a school's "hidden curriculum" and given that students with special needs often have difficulty in independent learning tasks, what specific skills would you anticipate would be problematic for these students?***

## TYPES OF STUDY SKILLS

Various study skills exist, including reading at different rates, listening, note taking/outlining, report writing, making oral presentations, using graphic aids, test taking, using the library, using reference materials, managing time, organizational skills, and managing behavior. Table 12-1 briefly identifies the importance of each of these skills. These skills are discussed in the following sections.

### Reading at Different Rates

The ability to use different reading rates is an important study skill (Harris & Sipay, 1990) that is most evident as students progress through the grades. Teachers at the elementary and secondary levels must often teach their students how to develop **reading rate** skills. Kiewra and DuBois (1998) stressed the importance of reading with purpose and reading rates vary to meet different purposes. Although various terms are

**TABLE 12–1** Study skills for effective and efficient learning

| *Study Skill* | *Significance for Learning* |
|---|---|
| Reading rate | Reading rates should vary with type and length of reading assignments. |
| Listening | Listening skills are necessary to complete most educational tasks or requirements. |
| Note taking and outlining | Effective note-taking/outlining skills allow students to document key points or topics for future study. |
| Report writing | Report writing is a widely used method of documenting information and expressing ideas. |
| Oral presentations | Oral presentations provide students an alternative method to express themselves and report information. |
| Graphic aids | Graphic aids may visually depict complex or cumbersome material in a meaningful format. |
| Test taking | Effective test-taking abilities help to ensure more accurate assessment of student abilities. |
| Library usage | Library usage skills facilitate easy access to much information. |
| Reference materials usage | Independent learning may be greatly improved through effective use of reference materials and dictionaries. |
| Time management | Time management assists in reducing the number of unfinished assignments and facilitates more effective use of time. |
| Self-management | Self-management assists students to assume responsibility for their own behaviors. |
| Organizational skills | Effective organizational skills assist learners to more effectively complete multiple tasks. |

*Source:* From *Study Skills for Students with Learning Problems: A Teacher's Guide*, 2e (p. 3), by J. J. Hoover and J. R. Patton, 2007, Austin, TX: PRO-ED. Reprinted with permission.

used to describe the different rates, reading rates include skimming, scanning, rapid reading, normal reading, and careful, or study-type, reading.

Skimming refers to a fast-paced reading rate used to grasp the general idea of material. As students quickly skim materials, they may deliberately skip over different sections. Scanning is also a fast-paced reading rate, used to identify specific items or pieces of information. Students might scan material to search for a name or a telephone number. Rapid reading is used to review familiar material or grasp main ideas. In rapid reading, some details may be identified, especially if the reader needs the information only temporarily.

Normal rate is used when students must identify details or relationships, solve a problem, or find answers to specific questions. Careful or study-type reading is a slow rate used to master details, retain or evaluate information, follow directions, or perform other similar tasks (Harris & Sipay, 1990).

The nature of the material being read helps to determine the need for varied reading rates; different activities also require different reading rates. In many reading situations two or more rates must be employed. For example, a student may scan several pages to locate a name and then use normal or study-type reading to learn the details surrounding that name. Varied reading rates, when used appropriately, can be highly effective and important study skills for students with learning problems.

## Listening

Listening also is involved in many different activities. Gearheart, Weishahn, and Gearheart (1995) estimate that listening-related activities comprise approximately 66% of a student's school day. Similarly, much instruction in elementary and secondary school relies heavily on the listening abilities of students. Listening includes both hearing and comprehending a spoken message. As was noted earlier in this text, listening involves the ability to receive information, apply meaning, and provide evidence of understanding what was heard. **Effective listening** is required in formal presentations, conversations, exposure to auditory environmental stimuli, and attending to various audio and audiovisual materials (Gearheart et al., 1995). Lerner (2000) suggests that listening skills can be improved through teaching and practice. Since students spend more time listening than in other types of learning (i.e., reading, writing; Bos & Vaughn, 2006), teachers must ensure that classroom conditions facilitate effective listening.

## Taking Notes/Outlining

**Taking notes or outlining** requires students to document major ideas and relevant topics for later use to classify and organize information. Note taking is a skill that requires students to determine the most essential information on the topic and record that content (Marzano, Pickering, & Pollock, 2001). Outlining is necessary to structure notes into main and subheadings for effective study (Coman & Heavers, 2001). Note taking becomes less difficult once outlining skills have been acquired (Ekwall & Shanker, 2003). Furthermore, study skills associated with reading, listening, thinking, and using vocabulary may improve significantly as students develop effective note-taking abilities. These involve summarizing ideas and organizing information into a useful format for future use. Instruction in this study skill area is particularly appropriate for students with learning problems as they often experience difficulties with organizing and recording information. With sufficient practice and systematic instruction, these students are capable of acquiring note-taking/outlining skills, even though they tend to exhibit some difficulty in the process.

## Writing Reports

**Report writing** involves the various skills necessary to organize and present ideas on paper in a meaningful and appropriate way. Included are topic selection, note taking, organization of ideas, outlining, spelling and punctuation, and sentence structure. Because students with learning problems often have writing problems (Welch & Jensen, 1990), teachers must provide direction in each area associated with written reports to ensure satisfactory growth and progress. Bos and Vaughn (2006) noted that students with special needs require more time devoted to writing than typically spent in classrooms.

## Making Oral Presentations

Many skills necessary for report writing are also important in oral presentations of various types—interviews, debates, group discussions, and individual or group presentations. Caution should be used to ensure that oral presentations occur in a nonthreatening environment to minimize student anxiety. Oral presentation tasks should be clearly defined and students need preparation time, guidance, and structure in planning their oral presentations. On occasion, oral reports can be an effective supplement to or substitute for written assignments.

## Using Graphic Aids

**Graphic aids**—materials such as charts, graphs, maps, models, pictures, or photographs—can be an effective tool to facilitate learning. Graphic aids may (a) assist students in more easily comprehending complex material; (b) facilitate the presentation of large amounts of information into small, more manageable pieces; and (c) assist students in ascertaining similarities within and differences among cultural, geographic, and economic situations. Thus, numerous important concepts or events can be addressed through visual materials. Students with disabilities can benefit from graphic aids if they are taught what to look for and attend to while reading and interpreting visual material.

## Taking Tests

Students in any grade are frequently subjected to various forms of assessment and evaluation. Even though tests are one of the primary means of assessing students in school, many students do not possess sufficient test-taking skills (Good & Brophy, 1995). Test-taking skills are those abilities necessary to (a) prepare and study for tests, (b) take tests, and (c) review completed and graded test results. They are important to ensure that tests accurately measure students' knowledge rather than their poor test-taking abilities. Test-taking skills include reading and following directions, thinking through questions prior to recording responses, and proofreading and checking answers. Students who lack these abilities can learn them through instruction and practice (Good & Brophy, 1995).

## Using the Library

Library activities are periodically required of students at every grade level. Library use requires skills in locating library materials, including using computerized systems; locating films, filmstrips, resource guides, and curriculum materials; and understanding the general layout and organization of the library. Knowledge of the role of the media specialist is also important. Although library use becomes especially important at the secondary level of education, it should be taught gradually and systematically through a student's schooling.

## Using Reference Materials

Other study skills become important when students locate materials within the classroom or school library. Students must be knowledgeable about the uses and functions of dictionaries and various other reference materials and must be familiar with various aspects of their design. They must be able to use a table of contents and an index; to alphabetize and use chapter headings; and to understand how content is arranged in dictionaries, encyclopedias, and other reference books. Use of encyclopedias and reference materials on computerized CD-ROM discs and on the World Wide Web is also a necessary reference material study skill. Students with disabilities are capable of acquiring these skills if they receive guided instruction and practice (Lerner, 2000).

## Managing Time

**Time management** involves using time effectively to complete daily assignments and carry out responsibilities. It includes allocating time and organizing the environment to study, complete projects, and balance various aspects of individual schedules effectively. Deshler et al. (2001) emphasize that some students with special needs lack awareness of time. Lewis and Doorlag (1998) indicate that some students have difficulty with the organization and management of time, which may lead to incorrect or unfinished assignments. As students enter secondary school and workloads increase, effective time management becomes increasingly important. Teachers of learners with disabilities must structure learning situations to encourage students to manage their time responsibly throughout elementary and secondary schooling.

## Developing Self-Management Skills

Another important tool necessary for learning is the ability to manage one's own behavior, especially during independent work time. Inappropriate behavior can seriously interfere with task completion. Students learn to assume responsibility for their own behavior only when educational programs emphasize self-management and behavior control (Brown, 2004). Self-management assists students to mediate their own behaviors (Swicegood, 1994) and resolve social problems (Bos & Vaughn, 2006). In addition, self-monitoring is effective in increasing time on task and reducing time required to complete tasks. Self-monitoring also reduces the demands on teachers for data collection (Lewis & Doorlag, 1998). In addition, the very act of self-recording or monitoring a behavior often results in desirable changes in that behavior (McCarl, Svobodny, & Beare, 1991). Several programs concerned

**TEACHER *Tips*** **Elementary Level**

## Self-Management Techniques

Instruction of study skills can and should begin at the elementary level. Integrating study skills development into the curriculum at the elementary level enhances the probability that students with special needs will be able to handle the demands of inclusive settings. One of the study skills discussed in this chapter is self-management. This skill is considered a study skill because of the importance that self-regulatory behaviors can play in a student's academic success.

Various techniques that assist students in managing their own behaviors can be very helpful. An example of such a technique is a weekly checklist to which a student can refer to make sure that certain behaviors are performed (see Lovitt, 2000). These behaviors would be generated based on the needs of the student. The student places a check in the box when the behavior has been performed. The form could be tailored to use for each class or for an entire school day.

*Source: Preventing School Failure* (2nd ed.), by T. C. Lovitt, 2000, Austin; TX: PRO-ED. Reprinted by permission.

with self-control and self-management currently exist (Brown, 2004; Workman & Katz, 1995); the reader is referred also to Chapter 2 for more comprehensive coverage of this topic.

### Using Organizational Skills

Increased demands placed on students requires them to better organize and manage their learning. Organizational skills assist learners to arrange information so it is easier to remember (Bos & Vaughn, 2006). Today, learners are expected to complete more work within shorter time frames and achieve higher standards. Keeping organizational charts or guides will help students with the organization and maintenance of daily or weekly tasks (Cohen & Spenciner, 2005). The ability to effectively organize and manage classroom learning is essential to meet the pressures and expectations found in today's classrooms.

### Early Development of Study Skills

Although the use of study skills is most reflected in upper elementary and secondary education literature and books, many students will experience difficulty with study skills at the time they are most needed unless a basic study skills foundation is laid in early elementary school. In addition, it is misguided to believe that only students in upper elementary and secondary education are capable of learning study skills. Further, educators should not ignore the fact that students in lower elementary grades are required to engage in the identical activities as students in upper elementary and secondary schooling. For example, students in lower elementary grades:

- complete tests
- do homework
- write reports
- must listen to the teacher instruct
- use a library
- locate and use reference materials
- manage and organize time
- manage own behaviors

These are just a few of the tasks that students in lower elementary grades engage in on a regular, daily basis. Study skills are "tools" that any learner may use to complete tasks and assignments. Although some of the structured study strategies discussed in this chapter may be too complex for students in the lower elementary grades, appropriate modifications of these can easily be made to facilitate the development of a sound study skills base in the lower grades. Table 12-2 provides examples of early development of study skills to build a solid foundation for later use. Teachers should use these types of activities on a regular basis to best help students in the lower grades to develop a solid foundation for study skills from which to build upon as they move into the upper elementary and secondary grades.

Reflective Question 12–2: ***As you consider your own educational career in elementary and secondary education, which, if any, of the study skills discussed in this section were explicitly taught as part of your educational program?***

**TEACHER Tips** Secondary Level

## Lifelong Use of Study Skills

Study skills are lifelong skills. We use most of them frequently in our everyday lives. For this reason, a strong case can be made for ensuring that these skills are taught to students with special needs. The following list provides examples of how study skills are part of our lives.

| Study Skill | School Examples | Life Skills Applications |
|---|---|---|
| Reading rate | Reviewing an assigned reading for a test | Reviewing an automobile insurance policy |
| | Looking for an explanation of a concept discussed in class | Reading the newspaper |
| Listening | Understanding instructions about a field trip | Understanding how a newly purchased appliance works |
| | Attending to morning announcements | Comprehending a radio traffic report |
| Graphic aids | Setting up the equipment of a chemistry experiment based on a diagram | Understanding the weather map in the newspaper |
| | Locating the most densely populated regions of the world on a map | Deciphering the store map in a mall |
| Library usage | Using picture files | Obtaining travel resources (books, videos) |
| | Searching a computerized catalog | Viewing current periodicals |
| Reference materials | Accessing CD-ROM encyclopedias | Using the yellow pages to locate a repair service |
| | Using a thesaurus to write a paper | Ordering from a mail-order catalog |
| Test taking | Developing tactics for retrieving information for a closed-book test | Preparing for a driver's license renewal test |
| | Comparing notes with textbook content | Participating in television self-tests |
| Note taking and outlining | Capturing information given by a teacher on how to dissect a frog | Writing directions to a party |
| | Framing the structure of a paper | Planning a summer vacation |
| Report writing | Developing a book report | Completing the personal goals section on a job application |
| | Completing a science project on a specific marine organism | Writing a complaint letter |
| Oral presentations | Delivering a personal opinion on a current issue for a social studies class | Describing car problems to a mechanic |
| | Describing the results of a lab experiment | Asking a supervisor for time off from work |
| Time management | Allocating a set time for homework | Maintaining a daily "to do" list |
| | Organizing a file system for writing a paper | Avoiding overscheduling of activities |
| Self-management | Assuring that homework is signed by parents | Regulating a daily exercise program |
| | Rewarding oneself for controlling temper | Evaluating the quality of a home repair |
| Organization | Managing multiple tasks | Keeping organized records for tax purposes |
| | Organizing one's locker | Balancing work and leisure time |

*Source:* From *Study Skills for Students with Learning Problems: A Teacher's Guide*, 2e, (p. 30), by J. J. Hoover and J. R. Patton, 2007, Austin, TX: PRO-ED. Reprinted with permission.

**TABLE 12–2** Developing the foundation for study skills in early elementary grades

| *Study Skills* | *Early Development Considerations* |
|---|---|
| Reading rate | Rates of reading relate specifically to reading purposes. As students begin to read or are read to, help them to listen or read for different purposes (pleasure, identifying main character, etc.) |
| Listening | List and post *Good Listener Skills* in the classroom. Be certain to include and discuss the difference between **hearing** something and **understanding** what is heard. Periodically stop verbal discussions or instruction and ask students to state what is being talked about and how it relates to the topic at hand. |
| Note taking/outlining | Critical to effective note taking/outlining is the ability to recognize and record essential information in an organized manner. In early elementary school, use of semantic webs or graphic organizers helps students providing a foundation for more complex note-taking/outlining tasks in the future. |
| Report writing | Written reports provide students opportunities to discuss, evaluate, or explore a topic in writing. A variety of tasks help students in early elementary grades to begin to develop these skills, including use of the cloze procedures, sentence completion activities, or language experience tasks. |
| Oral presentations | An underlying skill needed to successfully give oral presentations is the ability to speak in front of others to formally share ideas or information. A variety of tasks in early elementary school facilitate initial development of this study skill, including reporting orally about lessons learned on a fieldtrip, experiences during summer vacation, or briefly sharing a talent or hobby. |
| Graphic aids | Studying pictures is one of the first ways children learn about different topics (e.g., items in a forest) as well as to support written text (i.e., picture clues). Activities that combine pictures with simple text help students in early grades to develop an appreciation for use of graphic material, not only in reading but also in making oral presentations as discussed above. |
| Test taking | Students in any grade are subjected to some form of testing in the classroom. Early support for test-taking skills in the early elementary grades should include the development and posting of three graphic aids: (1) how to study for a test, (2) how to take at test, (3) reviewing a graded test. Each poster should depict (in written and/or graphic form) two or three main items associated with each of the three poster topics so all students in the class understand the items. These should be reviewed regularly. |
| Library usage | Most, although not all, students have some experience with the elementary school's school library. The foundation for library usage can easily be strengthened in early elementary school through simple tasks that require students to use the library to locate a book, resource, map, or other library material. These types of activities should be encouraged to begin early the process of using a library effectively. |
| Reference materials | As discussed above, teachers should provide students in early elementary school with tasks that require locating and using simple reference materials, including using the World Wide Web. Providing activities that requires use of dictionaries and encyclopedias written for lower elementary grades assists in building a solid foundation for more complex uses of reference materials in later grades. |
| Time management | Effective use of time becomes more important as learners experience increased workloads and responsibilities. However, simple, yet effective time-management skills can be acquired in lower elementary grades. Examples include development of brief daily schedules with associated times, posting and periodically reviewing a time-management poster with two or three easy-to-understand tips, posting the daily tasks along with beginning and ending times, or providing students with two tasks that must be complete within a specified time. |
| Self-management | "Behaving" or keeping one's behavior under control is an expectation of all students beginning with the first day they enter a formal school setting. A most effective strategy for helping early elementary students with self-management is through the use of self-monitoring techniques. This method is easily adapted to meet younger student needs and helps learners become more aware of their own behaviors. |
| Organizational skills | Similar to time management, organizing one's learning becomes more important as workloads and responsibilities increase. Helping students develop and use a simple organization chart documenting daily tasks helps younger students begin the process of developing effective organizational skills. |

*Source:* Adapted from *Study Skills for Students with Learning Problems: A Teacher's Guide*, 2e, (pp. 28–29), by J. J. Hoover and J. R. Patton, 2007, Austin, TX: PRO-ED. Reprinted with permission.

## ASSESSMENT OF STUDY SKILLS

Numerous instruments exist for assessing study skills; they include norm-referenced, criterion-referenced, and standardized devices as well as informal and teacher-made checklists. Table 12–3 identifies a variety of such devices. The appropriate use of the various types of instruments is discussed here; selected devices are presented to familiarize the reader with existing instruments, not to provide evaluative judgments. The reader should consult each instrument's manual or cited references for additional information and evaluative reviews. Table 12–4 summarizes additional information about selected norm- and criterion-referenced instruments. It is based on information provided by Harris and Sipay (1990), McLoughlin and Lewis (2000), and Salvia and Ysseldyke (2003).

**TABLE 12–3** Study skills assessment instruments

**Norm-Referenced General Achievement Tests**

California Achievement Tests (CTB/McGraw-Hill)

Comprehensive Test of Basic Skills (CTB/McGraw-Hill)

Iowa Silent Reading Tests (Harcourt Brace Jovanovich)

Iowa Tests of Basic Skills (Riverside)

SRA Achievement Series—Reading (Science Research Associates)

**Criterion-Referenced Instruments**

Analysis of Skills: Reading (Scholastic Testing Service)

BRIGANCE Diagnostic Inventories (Curriculum Associates)

Diagnosis: An Instructional Aid: Reading (Science Research Associates)

Fountain Valley Reading Skills Tests (Zweig Associates)

Individual Pupil Monitoring System—Reading (Riverside)

System for Objective-Based Assessment—Reading (Science Research Associates)

System FORE (Foreworks Publications)

**Standardized Study Skill Instruments**

Study Habits Checklist (Science Research Associates)

Study Skills Counseling Evaluation (Western Psychological Services)

**Observational-Based Study Skill Devices**

Study Skills Inventory (SSI) (Hoover and Patton, in press)

Study-Reading Skills Checklist (Rodgers, 1984)

Checklist of the Writing Process (Kemp, 1987)

Analytic Scoring Sheet for Writing (Bratcher, 1994)

### Norm-Referenced Instruments

Although norm-referenced general achievement tests are used in most schools, these measures tend to produce a low estimate of students' performance (McLoughlin & Lewis, 2000). In addition, this type of test may pose particular problems to students with disabilities because such instruments are often timed and require students to record their own answers.

**Norm-referenced tests** attempt to separate student results into a distribution of scores (Salvia & Ysseldyke, 2003). Such tests assume that students have sufficient independent work habits to monitor their own time and behavior and to sustain attention to the various tasks presented by the tests (McLoughlin & Lewis, 2000). Furthermore, these tests frequently include only a small number of items to assess study skills and thus may not adequately assess student abilities. Nonetheless, group tests are often appropriate as screening devices to identify students who require additional assistance (Salvia & Ysseldyke, 2003). When study skill assessment does include use of group-administered, norm-referenced general achievements tests, results must be interpreted carefully.

### Criterion-Referenced Instruments

Salvia and Ysseldyke (2003) noted that **criterion-referenced tests** measure one's development of skills in terms of absolute levels of mastery. They suggest that criterion-referenced tests be used to assist classroom teachers in program planning. The criterion-referenced tests listed in Table 12–4 may assist in identifying specific study skills that students have or have not mastered.

### Standardized Devices

Standardized devices designed to specifically assess study skills also exist. The Study Habits Checklist is designed for students in grades 9 to 14 and assesses a variety of study skill areas, providing scores for 37 study skills and habits (Harris & Sipay, 1990). The Study Skills Counseling Evaluation is another instrument normed with secondary and postsecondary students. This instrument contains 50 items within several study skill areas, including study-time distribution, test taking, study conditions, and note taking (McLoughlin & Lewis, 2000).

**TABLE 12–4** Norm-referenced (NR) and criterion-referenced (CR) assessment devices

| *Test* | *Type* | *Subtest* | *Grade Level* |
|---|---|---|---|
| Analysis of Skills: Reading | CR | Study Skills | 1 to 8 |
| Brigance Diagnostic Inventories | CR | Reference Skills/Graphs and Maps | K to 12 |
| California Achievement Tests | NR | Reference Skills | 3.6 to 12.9 |
| Comprehensive Test of Basic Skills (CTBS) | NR | Reference Skills | 1 to 6 |
| Diagnosis: An Instructional Aid: Reading | CR | Study Skills | 1 to 6 |
| Fountain Valley Reading Skills Test | CR | Study Skills | 1 to 6, Secondary |
| Individual Pupil Monitoring System—Reading | CR | Discrimination/Study Skills | 1 to 6 |
| Iowa Silent Reading Tests | NR | Directed Reading | 6 to 14 |
| Iowa Tests of Basic Skills | NR | Reference Materials | 1.7 to 9 |
| System for Objective-Based Assessment—Reading | CR | Study Skills | K to 9 |
| System FORE | CR | Study Skills | K to 12 |

### Informal Devices

Several informal inventories and teacher-made checklists for assessing study skills also exist. Various study habits inventories assess skills including time management, note taking and outlining, use of graphic aids, reading rates, library use, reference material/dictionary use, and report writing. The reader is referred to Hoover and Patton (2007) for examples of informal study skills inventories and assessments. Despite the availability of these instruments, many teachers find themselves needing to develop their own informal checklists to assess study skills efficiently, as areas requiring further assistance are identified (McLoughlin & Lewis, 2000). Informal analysis of students' study skills may be the easiest aspect of diagnosis for helping students improve their learning abilities. Hoover and Patton (2007) identify several steps that should be followed in an informal assessment of study skills. These are summarized as follows:

1. Identify study skills necessary to complete various tasks.
2. Construct a teacher checklist to assess study skills.
3. Construct a student self-analysis scale similar to the teacher's checklist.
4. Develop and implement learning tasks that require students to employ needed study skills, and observe students engaged in those tasks.
5. Complete teacher and student checklists documenting student uses of the study skill; compare results.

If commercial study skills devices are inappropriate for a particular situation or student, teachers may want to develop an inventory like the one provided in Figure 12-1.

Reflective Question 12–3: ***How can instructional lessons be designed to assess the acquisition of study skills and the development of proficiency and maintenance over time?***

## TEACHING STUDY SKILLS

Study skills are best learned and used within the actual context of completing meaningful academic tasks (Hoover & Rabideau, 1995) and when used strategically increase class participation (Bos & Vaughn, 2006). This chapter presents numerous study skill strategies and teaching suggestions; however, these must be used within the overall classroom structure as well as within specific teaching practices. As with any area of education, the teaching and learning of study skills must be individualized to meet unique learning needs. Though the development and application of each study skill is specific to that study skill, a general process may be followed for learning and using study skills in the classroom to assist students in their development. One such process is presented next, followed by a discussion of two effective classroom practices for facilitating additional study skills use for students with learning problems.

### Steps to Teaching Study Skills

The classroom development and use of study skills should follow a circular process that begins with assessment and is refined through ongoing evaluation.

**FIGURE 12–1** Study skills inventory

Name:________________________________________

Date (pre):____________________ Date (post):____________________

Rating scale: 1 = not mastered; 2 = partial/mastered/needs improvement; 3 = mastered

| Study Skills | Pre | Post |
|---|---|---|
| Reading Rates<br>Scanning | | |
| Skimming | | |
| Normal rate | | |
| Rapid reading | | |
| Careful reading | | |
| Listening<br>Attends to listening tasks | | |
| Applies meaning to verbal messages | | |
| Filters out auditory distractions | | |
| Note Taking/Outlining<br>Appropriately uses headings | | |
| Takes brief and clear notes | | |
| Records important information | | |
| Uses for report writing | | |
| Uses during lectures | | |
| Test Taking<br>Organizes answers | | |
| Proofreads | | |
| Reads and understands directions | | |
| Identifies clue words | | |
| Properly records responses | | |
| Answers difficult questions last | | |
| Narrows possible correct answers | | |
| Corrects previous test-taking errors | | |
| Library Usage<br>Use of card catalog | | |
| Ability to locate materials | | |
| Organization of library | | |
| Role of media specialist | | |
| Reference/Dictionary Usage<br>Identifies components | | |
| Makes well-organized outlines | | |

| Study Skills | Pre | Post |
|---|---|---|
| Uses organized note card format | | |
| Report Writing<br>Organizes thoughts | | |
| Uses proper punctuation | | |
| Uses proper spelling | | |
| Uses proper grammar | | |
| Oral Presentations<br>Participates freely | | |
| Organizes presentation | | |
| Uses gestures | | |
| Speaks clearly | | |
| Use of Graphic Aids<br>Attends to relevant elements | | |
| Understands purposes | | |
| Incorporates in presentations | | |
| Develops own visuals | | |
| Uses guide words | | |
| Understands uses of each | | |
| Uses for written assignments | | |
| Identifies different reference materials | | |
| Time Management<br>Organizes daily activities | | |
| Completes tasks on time | | |
| Organizes weekly/monthly schedules | | |
| Understands time management | | |
| Reorganizes time when necessary | | |
| Prioritizes activities | | |
| Self-Management of Behavior<br>Monitors own behavior | | |
| Changes own behavior | | |
| Thinks before acting | | |
| Is responsible for own behavior | | |

*Source:* Adapted from *Teaching Study Skills to Students with Learning Problems,* 2nd ed. (pp. 50–53), by J. J. Hoover and J. R. Patton, 2007, Austin, TX: PRO-ED.

The four components are assessment, selection, implementation, and evaluation.

**Assessment.** The initial step in teaching study skills to learners is to assess particular need areas within the classroom to determine the study skills the student must acquire. During this assessment stage, specific study skill areas requiring some development or refinement are determined (e.g., time management, report writing, listening during lectures). This process is specific to individual learners as unique classroom needs often arise. The process for assessing needed study skills was discussed in a previous section in this chapter and the reader is referred to those procedures. The steps for informally assessing study skills is most appropriate in this process although general information may be obtained through standardized measures. Once the specific study skill areas requiring development have been determined through assessment the second step begins.

**Selection.** In this second step two major decisions must be made: (1) which study skill area(s) will be initially addressed, and (2) which methods or strategies will be selected to help the student learn the identified study skill(s). The selection of the study skill(s) to initially address should be determined based on classroom needs, immediate academic needs, and student motivation. Once the study skill to address has been selected, one or more methods or strategies for developing the skill must be determined. Numerous strategies for assisting students with the different study skills are presented in this chapter. Some of these are individual teaching strategies (e.g., follow a consistent form of note taking, ensure proper reading rates are used, reward effective use of time, review test-taking errors); others are fully developed student strategies that contain procedures where a specific process is outlined and followed (e.g., **SQ3R,** Guided Lecture Procedure [GLP], **COPS, TOWER, ReQuest**). In the selection step, the teacher and student must identify the study skill area to address (e.g., reading rate, time management) and then select teaching and student strategies that will assist the learner to develop and use the targeted study skill more successfully. Once this process has been completed, the third step begins.

**Implementation.** During the implementation step, the study skill teaching strategies and student strategies are reviewed and applied within actual classroom situations whenever the targeted study skill is needed. Teaching suggestions can easily be incorporated into various lessons and activities to help the student focus on the appropriate use of the study skill. The use of selected student strategies (e.g., ReQuest) requires some preparation and training on the part of the teacher. These student strategies (see Table 12-5) each contain specific steps to follow to be properly used in the classroom and learning situation. Initial development of these student strategies should include time for practicing and learning the steps. Most of these strategies contain a few simple steps through which students may easily progress. Once the learner is familiar with

**TABLE 12–5** Study skill strategies

| *Strategy* | *Task Areas* | *Process* | *Description* |
|---|---|---|---|
| CAN-DO | Acquiring Content | Create list of items to learn<br>Ask self if list is complete<br>Note details and main ideas<br>Describe components and their relationships<br>Overlearn main items followed by learning details | This strategy may assist with memorization of lists of items through rehearsal techniques. |
| COPS | Written Reports | Capitalization correct<br>Overall appearance<br>Punctuation correct<br>Spelling correct | This strategy provides a structure for proofreading written work prior to submitting it to the teacher. |
| DEFENDS | Written Expression | Decide on a specific position<br>Examine own reasons for this position<br>Figure order for main topic and details<br>Expose position in first sentence of written task<br>Note each reason and associated points<br>Drive home position in last sentence<br>Search for and correct any errors | This strategy assists learners to defend a particular position in a written assignment. |

*(continued)*

**TABLE 12–5** (continued)

| *Strategy* | *Task Areas* | *Process* | *Description* |
|---|---|---|---|
| FIST | Reading Comprehension | First sentence is read<br>Indicate a question based on material in first sentence<br>Search for answer to question<br>Tie question and answer together through paraphrasing | This questioning strategy assists students to actively pursue responses to questions related directly to material being read. |
| GLP | Note Taking | Guided<br>Lecture<br>Procedures | GLP provides students with a structure for taking notes during lectures. Group activity is involved to facilitate effective note taking. |
| PANORAMA | Reading | Preparatory Stage—identify purpose<br>Intermediate Stage—survey and read<br>Concluding Stage—memorize material | This strategy includes a three-stage process to assist with reading comprehension. |
| PARS | Reading | Preview<br>Ask questions<br>Read<br>Summarize | PARS is recommended for use with younger students and with those who have limited experiences with study strategies. |
| PENS | Sentence Writing | Pick a formula<br>Explore different words to fit into the formula<br>Note the words selected<br>Subject and verb selections follow | PENS is appropriate for developing basic sentence structure and assists students to write different types of sentences by following formulas for sentence construction. |
| PIRATES | Test Taking | Prepare to succeed<br>Inspect instructions carefully<br>Read entire question, remember memory strategies and reduce choices<br>Answer question or leave until later<br>Turn back to the abandoned items<br>Estimate unknown answers by avoiding absolutes and eliminating similar choices<br>Survey to ensure that all items have a response | PIRATES may assist learners to more carefully and successfully complete tests. |
| PQ4R | Reading | Preview<br>Question<br>Read<br>Reflect<br>Recite<br>Review | PQ4R may assist students to become more discriminating readers. |
| RARE | Reading | Review selection questions<br>Answer all questions known<br>Read the selection<br>Express answers to remaining questions | RARE emphasizes reading for a specific purpose while focusing on acquiring answers to selection questions initially not known. |
| REAP | Reading<br>Writing<br>Thinking | Read<br>Encode<br>Annotate<br>Ponder | REAP is a method that assists students to combine several skills to facilitate discussion about reading material. |

**TABLE 12–5** (continued)

| *Strategy* | *Task Areas* | *Process* | *Description* |
|---|---|---|---|
| ReQuest | Reading Questioning | Reciprocal questioning | Teacher and student ask each other questions about a selection. Student modeling of teacher questions and teacher feedback are emphasized as the learner explores the meaning of the reading material. |
| RIDER | Reading Comprehension | Read sentence<br>Image (form mental picture)<br>Describe how new image differs from previous sentence<br>Evaluate image to ensure that it contains all necessary elements<br>Repeat process with subsequent sentences | This visual imagery strategy cues the learner to form a mental image of what was previously learned from a sentence just read. |
| SCORER | Test Taking | Schedule time effectively<br>Identify clue words<br>Omit difficult items until end<br>Read carefully<br>Estimate answers requiring calculations<br>Review work and responses | This test-taking strategy provides a structure for completing various tests by assisting students to carefully and systematically complete test items. |
| SQRQCQ | Math Word Problems | Survey word problem<br>Identify question asked<br>Read more carefully<br>Question process required to solve problem<br>Compute the answer<br>Question self to ensure that the answer solves the problem | This strategy provides a systematic structure for identifying the question being asked in a math word problem, computing the response, and ensuring that the question in the problem was answered. |
| SQ3R | Reading | Survey<br>Question<br>Read<br>Recite<br>Review | SQ3R provides a systematic approach to improve reading comprehension. |
| TOWER | Written Reports | Think<br>Order ideas<br>Write<br>Edit<br>Rewrite | TOWER provides a structure for completing initial and final drafts of written reports. It may be used effectively with COPS. |
| TQLR | Listening | Tuning in<br>Questioning<br>Listening<br>Reviewing | This strategy assists with listening comprehension. Students generate questions and listen for specific statements related to these questions. |

*Source:* Adapted from *Study Skills for Students with Learning Problems: A Teacher's Guide*, 2nd ed. (pp. 132–136), press by J. J. Hoover and J. R. Patton, 2007, Austin, TX: PRO-ED. Reprinted with permission.

and has practiced the steps within the selected strategy, its use should be applied on a regular basis when needing the targeted study skill; for example, if COPS is selected it should be used regularly when completing written reports. The use of selected teaching suggestions and student study strategies should be continued for a specified amount of time (e.g., 2 school weeks; next five written reports) and the impact on the targeted study skill should be documented. For example, if COPS is used for five consecutive written reports, the students should document how their reports have improved in punctuation and capitalization. Once the targeted study skill has been determined and implementation of relevant teaching and student study strategies has begun, the final step occurs. For further information on these strategies and their sources, please consult Hoover and Patton (2007).

**Evaluation.** As discussed in the preceding step, the teacher should determine the specific amount of time that each strategy will be used. The evaluation of the effectiveness of the strategy used on the targeted study skill must also be determined. That is, how you will know if the strategy is working must be determined. Use of simple checklists or anecdotal logs will facilitate regular and easy documentation of the effectiveness of the strategy on the student's use of the targeted study skill (e.g., better written reports, more effective use of time, more organized lecture notes). As the study skill strategies are used by the learner, the effects on student use of the study skill will become apparent and should be documented. Use of the strategies should continue for the specified amount of time. Using the ongoing documentation as a guide, the use of the strategy to assist with the targeted study skill should be evaluated. If sufficient progress has been made, its use should continue. If not, other strategies should be tried following the procedures outlined in the second and third steps of the process.

In addition to the four-step process for teaching study skills, other popular and widely used classroom practices facilitate study skills development. Two of these are semantic webbing and cooperative learning. Both of these teaching practices facilitate the development, maintenance, and generalization of study skills while also assisting students with learning problems with various academic tasks. When used in conjunction with the preceding steps, varied experiences and opportunities are provided for students to develop and use the study skills discussed in this chapter.

## Semantic Webbing and Study Skills

Semantic webs (or maps) are frequently discussed as an effective teaching practice to assist with reading comprehension and related areas of learning (Harris & Sipay, 1990). Use of semantic webs provides students opportunity to collectively relate new and existing knowledge. **Semantic mapping** is also useful in assisting students to learn and apply study skills within actual classroom situations (Hoover & Rabideau, 1995). Semantic webbing or mapping is also discussed in Chapter 7; the reader should refer to this chapter or to Hoover and Patton (in press) for an overview of this teaching practice. As students use semantic webs they elaborate on what they know and graphically organize that knowledge. In addition, Marzano, Pickering, and Pollock (2001) wrote that a concrete visual representation of information (i.e., semantic web; graphic organizer), by its very nature, further develops that knowledge.

Through semantic webbing, students build on previous study skill knowledge and experiences, no matter how inexperienced they may be in using study skills (Hoover & Rabideau, 1995). Table 12-6 lists several of the most important study skills discussed in this chapter, along with several suggested semantic web topics for which subordinate ideas may be generated by the students.

Table 12-6 shows that many different semantic web topics and subtopics exist to help learners use their study skills. These may easily be adapted and expanded. Figure 12-2 provides an example of a completed semantic web for helping students learn how to take multiple-choice tests. In this example, the teacher identifies the main topic (test taking: multiple choice) and the subtopics (studying for the test, taking the test, reviewing completed test). The items surrounding subtopics are examples of student-generated ideas for using the study skill and applying the subtopics to their test taking. Once the web has been completed by an individual or a small group of students, all learners should receive copies of the semantic web and select one or two ideas from the web to begin to apply in their learning. After students complete a multiple-choice test, they should analyze why and in what ways the web ideas helped them and what they can do in the future to best study for, complete, and review multiple-choice tests. This test-taking example is only one of many that teachers can model and adapt as they use semantic mapping to help students use study skills in the classroom.

A second example of a semantic web and study skills is presented in Figure 12-3. In this example, the

**TABLE 12–6** Semantic web topics for major study skills

| *Study Skill* | *Semantic Web Topics* |
|---|---|
| Test Taking | Essay tests, multiple-choice tests, short-answer tests, *studying for tests, taking the test, reviewing the completed test* |
| Library Usage | Cataloging system, library organization, media specialist role |
| Reference Materials/ Dictionary Usage | Dictionary, encyclopedia, atlas, *material's purpose, finding information, guide words, table of contents, glossary* |
| Presenting Information | Written reports, oral presentations, visual presentations, *topic selection, organizing thoughts, proper grammar, punctuation using visuals, speaking mechanics* |
| Note Taking/Outlining | Formal papers, draft papers, research project, *organizing notes, sufficient details, headings and subheadings, organizational format, collecting ideas* |
| Time Management | Task identification, prioritizing tasks, recording task completion, daily, weekly, monthly |
| Listening | Formal lectures, small-group discussions, audiovisual presentations, *attending to message, clarifying speaker's ideas, applying meaning to message, remembering message* |
| Reading Rate | Fast-paced, slow-paced rates, *getting main idea, locating details, determining sequence of ideas, retaining information* |
| Self-Management of Behavior | Monitoring own behavior, assuming responsibility, changing own behavior |
| Organizational Skills | Complete larger amounts of work in shorter time frame, achieve higher proficiency due to increased organization |

*Note:* Main semantic web topics appear in roman type; suggested subtopics appear in italics.

*Source:* From "Teaching Study Skills Through Semantic Webs," by J. J. Hoover and D. K. Rabideau, 1995, *Intervention School and Clinic, 30,* p. 293. Copyright 1995 by PRO-ED, Inc. Reprinted with permission.

important study skill of note taking/outlining is presented. Procedures for the development are similar to those previously discussed for the test-taking web. Students may draw on this example to guide them in their documenting activities related to lectures or other oral presentations as well as printed material.

Students who have learning problems may require specific training or coaching to successfully complete semantic webs for study skills development. A critical follow-up in the use of semantic webs is to develop and use study skills in actual classroom situations. As students share their successes with their study skill webs, they will assist others to become more proficient in that study skill. Use of the various study strategies and teaching suggestions discussed in this chapter will help students apply the study skills they have identified through semantic webbing.

## Study Skills and Cooperative Learning

A classroom structure built on **cooperative learning** and its principles may also teach essential study skills. Marzano et al., (2001) wrote that "organizing students in cooperative learning groups has a powerful effect on learning" (p. 87). The use of cooperative learning on a regular basis in the classroom is a decision left to each individual teacher. However, should cooperative learning be used, study skills education should be an integral part of each student's academic and social growth. The following discussion provides a general overview of cooperative learning, along with consideration of ways to teach study skills through this method. Although researchers in this area have identified various ways of implementing cooperative learning, several common elements are frequently discussed. These include (Roy, 1990):

- positive interdependence
- individual accountability
- positive interactions
- interpersonal training
- group processing

Through cooperative learning, students learn that their individual goals are best achieved through shared work and cooperation with others. Each of the five

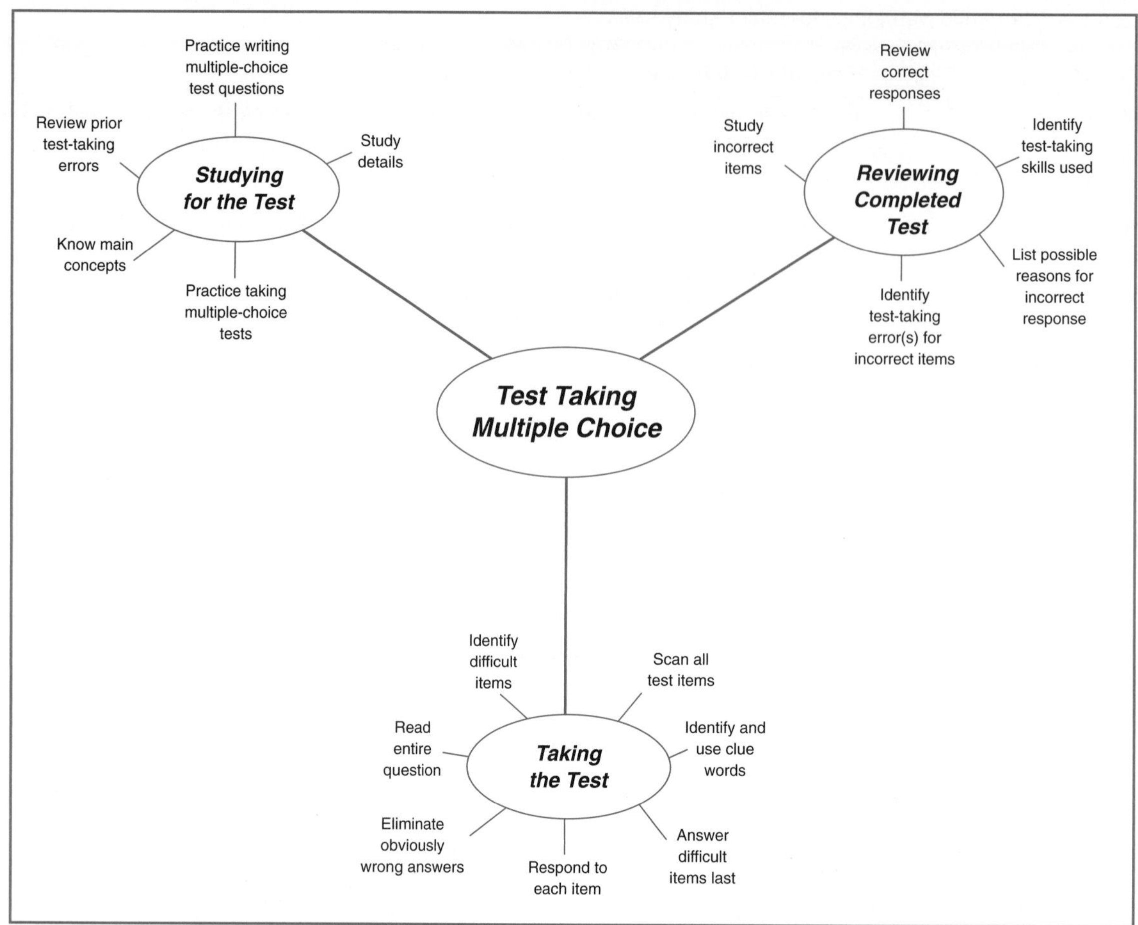


**FIGURE 12–2** Semantic web of the test-taking multiple-choice study skill

*Source:* From "Teaching Study Skills Through Semantic Webs," by J. J. Hoover and D. K. Rabideau, 1995, *Intervention in School and Clinic, 30*, p. 29. Copyright 1995 by PRO-ED, Inc. Reprinted with permission.

elements is briefly summarized (Johnson & Johnson, 1998; Roy, 1990):

- **Positive Interdependence:** refers to a shared sense of mutual goals and tasks. All members complete their assignments and draw on the knowledge and skills of other group members in their own learning.
- **Individual Accountability:** allows each student to individually acquire the knowledge and skills, and also requires individual demonstration of mastery while learning in a group situation.
- **Positive Interactions:** is the element that supports sharing ideas and assisting others in their learning. As students interact in meaningful ways, important individual and group learning occurs.
- **Interpersonal Training:** is necessary to prepare students, especially those unfamiliar with cooperative learning, to successfully and fully participate in the process. This is an important element in the strategy as the success of cooperative learning in the classroom depends on how well prepared students are to take on group work and group functioning.
- **Group Processing:** is the culminating task where the cooperative group members evaluate their own contributions to the task. Through this culminating task, group members discuss their contributions, identify ways to improve overall member interactions, and suggest recommendations for future efforts. Documented student or teacher observations of the group's functioning may facilitate the debriefing of the group by providing objective data for members to discuss.

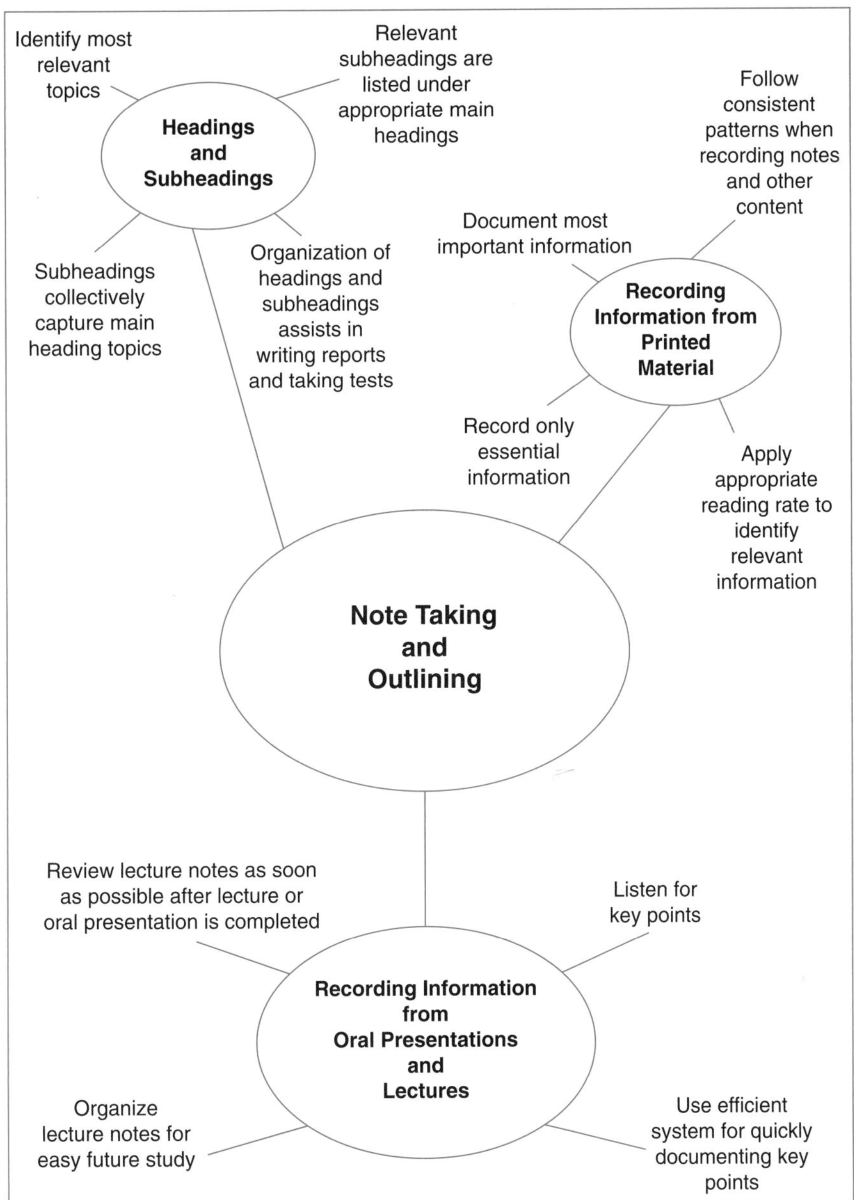


**FIGURE 12–3** Semantic web: Note taking/outlining

**Effective Use of Study Skills and Cooperative Learning.** As previously discussed, study skills were identified as competencies or support skills that learners use to more effectively and efficiently record, organize, synthesize, and evaluate tasks and skills. To best learn in school, regular and consistent use of study skills is necessary, especially in an era when increased workloads and expectations exist for all learners. In addition, as tasks become more complex, use of study skills becomes even more critical. Therefore, whether working cooperatively or independently, students must develop, maintain, and generalize the use of various study skills.

Within the parameters of cooperative learning, a direct relationship exists between effective use of study skills and the efficient implementation of cooperative learning. Table 12-7 provides examples of how study skill development and use are integral to cooperative learning structures. Illustrated are the five elements of cooperative learning along with suggested

**TABLE 12–7** Study skills development and cooperative learning

| *Cooperative Element* | *Study Skills Development* |
|---|---|
| Positive Interdependence | Effective study skills usage by each member affects in a positive way the actions and learning of all members within a cooperative learning group or pair. |
| Individual Accountability | As individuals within a group recognize their own study skill strengths and weaknesses, they are able to identify ways to best contribute to the group and ways the group may best assist them with their study skill development. Pre- and postassessment of study skill abilities will ensure that individual accountability is maintained. |
| Positive Interactions | Once individual strengths and weaknesses in the use of study skills have been identified, students are better prepared to help others with study skills they may already possess as well as learn from others. Exchanging study skill ideas and strategies that have been effective and that are relevant to completion of the cooperative learning task at hand will serve to strengthen the study skill abilities of group members. It will also provide a basis for constructive interactions and decision making required for effective cooperative learning to occur. |
| Interpersonal Training | A major goal of any comprehensive study skills program is to promote greater independence in learning. As teachers engage students in interpersonal training activities, study skills should be an integral part of this training. As students become proficient with skills such as time management, self-management of behavior, note taking, and library usage, they will be better prepared to engage in interpersonal interactions relative to a cooperative learning academic task. Interpersonal training will not be complete unless these and similar study skills are mastered. |
| Group Processing | As students engage in discussions and reflect on how well their group or pair functioned relative to specific tasks, the specific study skills used to facilitate completion of the task or learn the content should be addressed. |

*Source:* From *Study Skills for Students with Learning Problems: A Teacher's Guide*, 2e (p. 45), by J. J. Hoover and J. R. Patton, 2007, Austin, TX: PRO-ED. Reprinted with permission.

connections to students' use of study skills. The degree to which students use study skills effectively can affect the overall performance of other group members. This includes student development and use of study skills, group sharing of study strategies for effective use of study skills, or the reflection of study skills use by group members during the group processing stage. Conversely, the inefficient use of time, inappropriate behavioral self-management, inefficient library or reference materials usage, ineffective test-taking abilities, or inability to select and use appropriate reading rates can significantly interfere with the group's overall success. However, when used appropriately in cooperative groups, more effective group interactions and learning can occur.

> Reflective Question 12–4: ***After reviewing the table that lists multiple examples of specific study strategies, consider your individual teaching responsibilities and design a strategy that will promote independent skill development for students with special needs specific to that subject area. What components need to be built in to the strategy?***

## IMPLEMENTING A STUDY SKILLS PROGRAM

Study skills programs should introduce simple variations of study skills in lower elementary grades and gradually increase in complexity as students progress through the grades (Hoover & Patton, 2007). The age, ability, and individual needs of special learners must determine the extent of that complexity; however, early efforts may prove beneficial throughout the entire educational program. The following list outlines several guidelines for teachers to follow in developing and/or improving their study skills programs. These are adapted from Hoover and Patton (2007) and can be applied to all students; however, they are of particular significance for teachers of students who have special learning needs.

1. Introduce simple variations of the different study skills in the early grades.
2. Gradually increase to the more complex elements associated with each study skill as students progress through the grades.

3. Identify specific goals and objectives for a study skills program prior to program implementation.
4. Let students' individual strengths and weaknesses guide decision making concerning which study skills to emphasize at any particular time.
5. Know what motivates students to use different study skills and emphasize these motivations in program implementation.
6. Explain and demonstrate the proper use of each study skill.
7. Expect students to use different study skills appropriately through guided practice and planned learning experiences.
8. Provide continued opportunity for practicing study skill use to assist students in acquiring and maintaining mastery of the skills.
9. Facilitate the use of study skills in natural classroom settings and on a regular basis as the need arises in different subject areas and learning activities.
10. Assist students in generalizing acquired study skills through an emphasis on more complex use of the skills once initial mastery of the basic study skills has been achieved.

Students at any grade level, especially students with disabilities, require direct teacher guidance in study skill areas. In addition to the general guidelines just presented, teachers may find more specific instructional strategies useful in implementing a study skills program. Specific instructional strategies for improving targeted study skills are as follows.

## Reading Rates

1. Ensure that proper reading rates are used for different reading activities.
2. Establish clear purposes for each reading assignment.
3. Ensure that each student is familiar with each type of reading rate.
4. Provide opportunities for the appropriate use of each reading rate.

## Listening Skills

1. Reduce distractions and deal quickly with classroom disruptions.
2. Encourage each student to speak loudly enough so that all can hear.
3. Repeat and emphasize important items in the verbal message.
4. Summarize the verbal message at strategic points in the lecture.
5. Use visual materials to support oral presentations.

## Note Taking/Outlining

1. Encourage students to follow a consistent note-taking/outlining format.
2. Teach students to identify and focus on key topics and ideas.
3. Discuss with students the uses and advantages of making outlines and taking notes.
4. Model different note-taking/outlining formats for students.
5. Begin with simple note-taking/outlining activities, and gradually introduce more complex types of activities.

## Report Writing

1. Clarify the purpose for each writing assignment and assist students in organizing their ideas.
2. Begin writing activities with simple, less complex written assignments and gradually introduce more difficult types of written reports.
3. Insist that students use a dictionary and other reference materials when necessary and that they proofread their written work.
4. Work with students as they complete different stages of writing assignments.
5. Provide periodic review and encouragement to students as they complete writing reports.

## Oral Presentations

1. Allow sufficient time for students to prepare for oral presentations.
2. Conduct oral presentations in a nonthreatening environment to minimize peer criticism.
3. Provide different situations for oral presentations (e.g., with students seated or standing by their desks, standing in front of a small group, addressing the whole class).
4. Ensure that students know and understand the purposes for oral presentations.

## Use of Graphic Aids

1. Allow students to use graphic aids with, or as alternatives to, oral and written reports.
2. Ensure that students know why specific material is presented in graphic form.
3. Incorporate visual material into oral presentations.
4. Assist students in focusing on important aspects of graphic aids.
5. Provide sufficient time for students to read and interpret graphic aids presented during lectures.

## Test Taking

1. Discuss with students the purposes of tests and show them how to complete different types of tests.
2. Explain the different methods of study necessary to prepare for various types of tests (e.g., objective, essay).
3. Review test-taking errors with students.
4. Ensure that students know the time allotted for completion of each test.
5. Explore test-taking procedures with students to ensure that they are familiar with different types of test questions.

## Library Use

1. Review the uses and importance of a library, and familiarize students with the organizational layout of a library.
2. Structure assignments so that students must use a library to complete them.
3. Be sure that students know the purpose of using the library in any library activity.
4. Teach students to consult media specialists and other library personnel as necessary.

## Reference Materials Usage

1. Ensure that dictionaries are readily available to all students.
2. Structure various assignments to require students to use reference materials.
3. Be sure that each student possesses sufficient skills to successfully use general reference and dictionary materials when these are required.
4. Create situations that help students understand the uses of reference materials.
5. Familiarize students with the different components of general reference materials and dictionaries prior to requiring their use in assignments.

## Time Management

1. Reward effective use of time.
2. Structure classroom activities so that students are required to budget their own time periodically.
3. Praise on-task behaviors, especially during independent work times.
4. Ensure that students know the amount of time allotted for completion of each activity.
5. Provide sufficient time and opportunity for students to manage their own time and to complete assigned tasks.

## Self-Management of Behavior

1. Be sure that students know specific behavioral expectations.
2. Establish student self-management programs and monitor associated progress.
3. Assist students in setting realistic and attainable goals in a self-management program.
4. Be consistent in enforcing behavioral expectations of students.
5. Allow sufficient time for a self-management program to be implemented before the effects of the program are tested.

## Organizational Skills

1. Emphasize need and benefits of organizing one's own learning.
2. Provide students time and opportunity to monitor their own organizational skills.
3. Provide students with several daily assignments and instruct them to create a chart illustrating the order they will follow to complete the tasks.
4. Encourage students to share their organizational strategies with others, especially when cooperative learning is used in the classroom.

**Reflective Question 12–5:** ***What are the differences in terms of overall emphasis and specific skills taught for a study skills curriculum implemented with elementary v. secondary school students?***

## TECHNOLOGY IN THE CLASSROOM

Using computers and other technology to improve the personal productivity of students with disabilities has become popular. Word processors, speech recognition software, computer databases, Internet search engines, and electronic communication can help students with disabilities improve their efficiency and proficiency as learners.

Technology provides unique opportunities for students in the development and use of study skills. For example, learning how to use a database to keep lists of assignments may enable the student to transfer this skill to organizing information collected for a research paper at a later time. Use of computerized databases to locate references in local and regional libraries may also facilitate effective study in students. Additionally, CD-ROM encyclopedias, computer spell-check programs, grammar and sentence structure computer programs, and use of the Internet to locate materials and specific sources of information are all examples of how technology can facilitate study skill development in the areas of reference materials, time management, note taking, library use, and report writing. When developing an overall classroom study skills program, students' access to computers, the Internet, CD-ROM materials, and other technology should be identified and used to help learners use study skills as efficiently and effectively as possible. Use of the World Wide Web will prove beneficial to assist students in using research-related study skills (e.g., researching current events or locating resource materials).

Reflective Question 12–6: ***Select a specific content area and identify procedures that can be used to instruct students on how to take advantage of Internet resources in order to develop specific skills and content knowledge through independent study.***

## MAKING IT WORK

This chapter concludes with a general overview of six learning strategies that are appropriate for use with students who experience learning or behavior problems. Learning strategies are methods that help learners solve problems, achieve goals independently, and evaluate their own learning (Bos & Vaughn, 2006; Deshler, Ellis, & Lenz, 1996). Although related, study skills and learning strategies are different approaches to meeting similar learning needs. Bender (2002) described a primary difference between study skills and learning strategies as one emphasizing the cognitive aspects associated with learning (i.e., learning strategies), whereas the other (i.e., study skills) emphasizes the actual task itself (e.g., writing the report, taking the test, being organized). Although different in scope and/or purpose, when used collectively the study skills discussed in this chapter and the learning strategies presented below facilitate improved teaching and learning. The six learning strategies are not all-inclusive; rather, they represent additional types of study strategies effective in meeting academic and educational needs. Learning strategies emphasize learning how to learn and complement use of existing study skills known to the student. As such,

### TECHNOLOGY *Tips*

Teachers can now log on to different websites for ideas about how to enhance the study skills of their students. Of particular interest is the site put out by Educational Resources Information Center (ERIC) of the National Library of Education. Available at ERIC's site are lesson plans that outline the grade level of each lesson, objectives, materials needed, and procedures to implement the lessons. Examples and links that can be found on this website are as follows:

AskERIC Lesson Plans: Request Reciprocal Teaching. This site can be found at the following link: http:/ericir.syr.edu/Virtual/Lessons/Lang_arts/Reading/RDG0006.html. The goal of the lessons in "Request Reciprocal Teaching" is to improve students' questioning skills.

AskERIC Lesson Plans: Reinforcing Alphabet Names/Sounds. This site can be found at the following link: http:/ericir.syr.edu/Virtual/Lessons/Lang_arts/Reading/RDG0005.html. The goal of the lessons in "Reinforcing Alphabet Names/Sounds" is to reinforce skills for beginning readers.

AskERIC Lesson Plans: Our Day at School. This site can be found at the following link: http:/ericir.syr.edu/Virtual/Lessons/Lang_arts/Reading/RDG0033.html. The goal of the lessons in "Our Day at School" is to enhance students' reading and writing skills.

AskERIC Lesson Plans: Interviewing. This site can be found at the following link: http:/ericir.syr.edu/Virtual/Lessons/Lang_arts/Journalism/JNL0002.html. The goal of the lessons in "Interviewing" is to teach students about developing questioning skills and using the computer.

they are excellent ways in which teachers can make study skills instruction work more effectively.

### Active Processing

Active processing involves the use of self-talk or self-questioning in order to activate knowledge. Self-talk or verbalization supports student learning by allowing students to say to themselves what they have just learned or heard (Deshler, Ellis, & Lenz, 1996). This strategy also assists students to elaborate on a particular content area in order to complete a task. Skills such as summarizing, scanning, questioning, and predicting may be used. When using this strategy, teachers must make certain that students know that self-talk is appropriate and acceptable to help them define, evaluate, monitor, and complete a task.

### Analogy

Analogy allows an individual to recall previously acquired learning and knowledge and relate these to a new topic or experience. In addition, Marzano et al. (2001) wrote that "analogies help us see how seemingly dissimilar things are similar, increasing our understanding of new information" (p. 26). This strategy may use schema, metaphor, or cloze procedures as students learn new material. The effective use of analogy in the classroom requires that teachers help students to recall prior learning and then compare, contrast, substitute, or elaborate on that knowledge to learn and retain new information. Use of analogy also helps students increase their confidence in learning (Cottrell, 2001).

### Coping

Coping is a problem-solving learning strategy that enables students to confront issues and tasks systematically and objectively. A variety of problems may be addressed as the learner confronts issues, develops solutions, identifies necessary assistance, attempts solutions, persists with a task, and eventually generates successful resolution to the problem or learning task. Students with learning problems benefit from problem solving or coping tasks by helping them relate solutions to learning outcomes and social needs (Bos & Vaughn, 2006). Teachers should be sensitive to students' values and problem-solving preferences when assisting them to develop this learning strategy.

### Evaluation

Evaluation helps students to become aware of what is needed to successfully complete a task and monitor whether that task has been completed. Self-monitoring, reflection, prediction, generalization, and feedback skills are all used with this strategy. Independent work skills of students may improve through this strategy. Teachers should demonstrate to students how to check answers, monitor progress toward task completion, reflect on procedures and results of the completed task, and transfer skills to new tasks or situations. Self-evaluation is also important as this facilitates students' judgments of the quality of their work (Bos & Vaughn, 2006). Successful mastery of these and similar skills will facilitate effective use of the evaluation strategy.

### Organization

The strategy of organization emphasizes student abilities to group or cluster items, tasks, ideas, and skills. Classifying items includes knowing the rules that guide the groupings (e.g., color, function; Marzano et al., 2001). A variety of organizational patterns may exist for specific items or skills, and specific instructional situations may dictate the use of different organizations (e.g., broad versus narrow groupings). Students may initially experience problems with knowing what types of categories or clusters are acceptable or appropriate for different learning situations. Teachers should employ direct teaching to help learners explore possible ways to categorize and then evaluate effectiveness.

### Rehearsal

Rehearsal helps students to think about a task prior to beginning the task, while working at it, and upon its completion. Elements such as reviewing, reciting, and recalling different aspects related to an assignment are important in rehearsal. This strategy allows students to think through what they are doing as they proceed in task completion. This, in turn, minimizes problems and facilitates more effective use of time. Pausing, questioning, visualizing, and summarizing are important features of this strategy, and teachers should help students practice these as tasks are completed. Additionally, verbal rehearsal is particularly useful to access short-term memory (Hughes, 1996).

The six strategies just discussed will help students in their overall study skill development. In actual practice study skills and learning strategies are frequently used in combination. Table 12-8 illustrates examples of the integrated uses of study skills and learning strategies. As shown in the table, for each learning strategy several relevant study skills are identified along with potential interrelationships among each. In addition, Figure 12-4 through 12-6 provide teacher guides for identifying selected student learning strategy needs in the classroom. The items in each guide reflect important skills needed to successfully use the strategy and offer a quick way to begin student assessment in this area. Additional guides for teachers and for students using these learning structures in the classroom can be found in Hoover and Collier (2003).

**TABLE 12–8** Integrating study skills and learning strategies

| *Learning Strategy* | *Overview* | *Integrated Study Skills* |
|---|---|---|
| **Active Processing** | Use of self-talk/questioning to activate and recall prior knowledge | *Self-Management*—Managing self is necessary to successfully using self-questioning<br>*Test Taking*—Various test-taking strategies help students recall knowledge and skills<br>*Library Usage*—Effective use of library resources supports further development of activated knowledge |
| **Analogy** | Relating new knowledge with previously acquired knowledge/skills | *Note Taking/Outlining*—Skills that help learners integrate new/existing knowledge<br>*Reference Materials*—Reference materials provide access to new knowledge<br>*Reading Rates*—Various rates are used to acquire new knowledge building on existing skills |
| **Coping** | Use of problem-solving techniques in learning to address needs, issues | *Test Taking*—Test-taking strategies help students break down test items and problem solve to identify solutions to correct test-taking errors<br>*Organizational Skills*—Effective organizational skills are needed to help students cope with learning new skills/knowledge<br>*Time Management*—Effective time management helps students persevere and persist with learning setbacks |
| **Evaluation** | Use of self-monitoring to check work and reflect on solutions | *Self-Management*—Self-management facilitates effective evaluation of own learning<br>*Organizational Skills*—Students must work in an organized manner to best check and reflect on own learning<br>*Note Taking/Outlining*—Skills associated with taking notes and creating outlines help with documenting self-monitored progress |
| **Organization** | Unique ways that students organize learning and group concepts and skills | *Note Taking/Outlining*—These abilities contribute to better organized and grouped ideas, concepts, and skills<br>*Test Taking*—Test-taking abilities assist learners to organize and group acquired learning while preparing for tests<br>*Graphic Aids*—Graphic aids assist learners to better understand and group complex material |
| **Rehearsal** | Reflecting on tasks; thinking through issues prior to beginning assignment | *Listening*—Listening to others' views helps to better reflect on assignment prior to starting task<br>*Self-Management*—Skills provide a structure to help students reflect on own learning<br>*Organizational Skills*—Organizational skills help learners organize thoughts to think through steps necessary to complete tasks |

*Source:* Hoover, John J., Klingner, Jeanette K., Baca, Leonard M., and Patton, James M., *Methods for Teaching Culturally and Linguistically Diverse Exceptional Learners*, © 2008, Table 12–7. Reprinted by permission of Pearson Education, Inc., Upper Saddle River, NJ.

**FIGURE 12–4** Guide for identifying use of active processing

Name: ______________________ Date: ______________________

Classroom: ______________________ Completed by: ______________

**Instructions**: Place a check next to each item if it is exhibited by the student on a regular and consistent basis. Summarize the student use of active processing to complete the guide.

The student uses self-talk or self-questioning to . . .

_____ identify the task to be completed

_____ clarify how to go about completing a task

_____ check completed written work for accuracy of responses

_____ examine the appropriateness of the method or strategy used to complete a task

_____ reinforce his or her efforts related to the task

_____ clarify potential mistakes made while completing the task

_____ identify possible methods to prevent making similar mistakes

_____ evaluate his or her progress toward task completion if an alternative method is used

_____ verify that the task was completed

_____ congratulate self for successful completion

Summary Comments:

*Source:* From *Classroom Applications of Cognitive Learning Styles* (p. 91), by J. J. Hoover, 1991, Boulder, CO: Hamilton Publications. 

**FIGURE 12–5** Guide for identifying use of analogy

Name: ______________________ Date: ______________________

Classroom: ______________________ Completed by: ______________

**Instructions**: Place a check next to each item if it is exhibited by the student on a regular and consistent basis. Summarize the student use of analogy to complete the guide.

The student . . .

_____ identified items or situations previously experienced that are similar to a current task or topic of study

_____ compares similar characteristics of like items

_____ is able to identify differences between dissimilar items

_____ identifies similar uses for similar types of items

_____ applies knowledge from prior experiences to better understand a current situation or topic of study

_____ is able to substitute items or situations showing how they may be used or studied interchangeably

_____ is able to provide examples, based on own experiences, that are relevant to the study of current topics

_____ recognizes the fact that one effective way to study an unknown topic is to draw similarities to previous topics already learned

_____ elaborates on prior knowledge relative to new information

_____ recalls previously learned patterns of study and uses them to acquire new information

Summary Comments:

*Source:* From *Classroom Applications of Cognitive Learning Styles* (p. 94), by J. J. Hoover, 1991, Boulder, CO: Hamilton Publications. 

**FIGURE 12–6** Guide for identifying use of organization

Name: ______________________ Date: ______________________

Classroom: ______________________ Completed by: ______________

**Instructions**: Place a check next to each item if it is exhibited by the student on a regular and consistent basis. Summarize the student use of organization skills to complete the guide.

The student is able to . . .

_____ determine similarities and differences between situations

_____ identify various ways to sort and organize items, tasks, or situations

_____ cluster similar characteristics in a meaningful way in order to complete various tasks

_____ provide an accurate name or title for grouped items or tasks

_____ adjust the organization of the grouping of required tasks if the initial clustering does not facilitate successful completion of the tasks

_____ review the process used to group items or assignments and adjust in future groupings, if necessary

_____ group items of a topic or skill in a way that facilitates learning and remembering the items

_____ remember group names or titles as well as items within those titles

_____ continually search for additional meaningful ways to group topics or items to best learn new skills and retain information

Summary Comments:

*Source:* From *Classroom Applications of Cognitive Learning Styles* (p. 103), by J. J. Hoover, 1991, Boulder, CO: Hamilton Publications. Copyright 1991 by Hamilton Publications. Reprinted with permission.

## SUMMARY

This chapter emphasizes that study skills are essential for students across all grade levels. For students with disabilities, learning and using these skills is particularly problematic. Several study skills have been identified as critical to academic and postsecondary success, including differential reading rates, listening, note taking, report writing, presentations, test taking, and time management. A variety of approaches can be used to informally assess skills within this domain.

Study skills instructional programs can be designed to include a variety of elements. These include the use of semantic mapping, cooperative learning strategies, specific curricular components emphasizing individual study skills, and the use of learning strategies. Suggestions for early development of study skills, a model for study skills programs in classrooms, and the interrelated uses of study skills and learning strategies were discussed. Numerous teaching and student strategies were also presented throughout the chapter.

CHAPTER

# 13

# Social Competence and Self-Determination Skills

This chapter provides information for teachers wanting to establish a social and self-determination skills program for students exhibiting failure in the classroom and community. Several topics are addressed. First, the history of social and self-determination skills instruction and definitions of social competency, social skills, social problem-solving skills, and self-determination skills are briefly presented. Second, assessment procedures are reviewed. Third, the contents of social and self-determination skills programs for children and adolescents and the teaching procedures used to effectively teach these skills are described. Fourth, strategies that promote the generalization of social and self-determination skills across situations, persons, and environments are summarized. Fifth, sequenced procedures for establishing a social and self-determination skills program conclude the chapter.

## HISTORY AND DEFINITIONS

Although a complete history of social and self-determination skills teaching has not been written, the work of Wolpe (1958) is often singled out as the most influential antecedent to the development of these fields. Initially he emphasized the use of behavioral principles and techniques to ameliorate adult psychiatric patients' problems with interpersonal interaction. He and his colleagues introduced the idea of teaching assertive and self-advocacy behaviors to people who were experiencing such problems due to stressful life events.

Behavioral principles of shaping and chaining were soon applied to the teaching of many new behaviors (Bandura, 1977). Simultaneously, Argyle (1967; Argyle & Kendon, 1967) was developing a body of knowledge that attempted to explain appropriate social interactions between two or more individuals. Argyle noted that several skills were necessary. These skills included the ability to accurately (a) determine social goals (e.g., the need to make friends); (b) perceive, interpret, and act upon cues in the environment (e.g., determine which peers would be most receptive to becoming a friend, determine whether a peer would be an appropriate friend, and introduce oneself to the peer); and (c) understand and respond to the feedback given (e.g., interpret whether the peer positively responds to the initiation of friendship). Once these models were established, several researchers (Argyle, 1967; Bellack & Hersen, 1979; Liberman, King, DeRisi, & McCann, 1975) developed social skills teaching programs for various populations. The positive results achieved sparked the enthusiasm of professionals in special education.

As researchers worked to promote the success of children and adolescents, they realized that certain personal or self-determination skills were not being learned. In addition, many children with disabilities were not well accepted by peers without disabilities or by teachers (Bryan, 1983). Reports concerning adolescents with various disabling conditions indicated a rise in the number of students dropping out of school, having difficulties establishing relationships, and deciding on inappropriate life goals, and a decrease in those exhibiting independent behaviors and maintaining long-term jobs (e.g., Schumaker, Hazel, Sherman, & Sheldon-Wildgen, 1982; Serna & Lau-Smith, 1994–1995). Many self-determination skills were lacking, and students were not being taught to develop goals for themselves, collaborate with others to attain goals (e.g., seek out mentors), and solve problems that present barriers to goal attainment (Serna & Lau-Smith, 1994–1995).

To add to this growing body of research, investigators (e.g., Dyson, 2003) continue to gather data indicating that the social competence of children with learning disabilities and behavioral disorders is rated lower than peers or siblings. These researchers promote the idea that environmental and contextual variables play a large role in the social and self-determined behavior of these children and adolescents. Furthermore, Wong (2003) proposed that educators consider the need for a resilience and empowerment framework that promotes social and self-determined behavior if students are to succeed. It seems, therefore, that teachers have been (and will continue to be) given the responsibility of ameliorating behavioral problems as well as developing appropriate social interactions and personal competence skills (i.e., self-determination skills) among children and adolescents with special needs.

In response to this need, professionals in special education and psychology have not only developed several well-used and evidenced-based programs and procedures to teach social skills (Campbell & Siperstein, 1994; Hazel, Schumaker, Sherman, & Sheldon-Wildgen, 1981a; McGinnis, Goldstein, Sprafkin, & Gershaw, 1998), but also developed self-determination skills programs (Gibbons, 2002; Hoffman & Field, 1995; Martin & Huber-Marshall, 1995; Serna & Lau-Smith, 1995; Wehmeyer, 1995) for children and adolescents with disabilities. The following discussion introduces the concepts of social and personal competence by defining three dimensions: social skills, social problem-solving skills, and self-determination skills.

## Social and Personal Competence

Professionals define the constructs of **social and personal competence** as a person's overall ability to achieve his or her goals and desires in the personal and social aspects of life (Ford, 1985). Ford elaborates by identifying three components that interact to comprise social and personal competence: self-perception (i.e., an individual's ability to recognize and set goals for oneself), behavioral repertoire (i.e., a person's ability to effectively perform social skills, problem-solving skills, role-taking abilities, assertive skills, and language/communication skills), and effectiveness (i.e., a person's ability to determine whether set goals and desires are achieved).

Ford (1985) continues by outlining three additional factors that interact with the components of social and personal competence: (a) motivation, (b) development, and (c) environment. Motivation is a factor that interacts with social and personal competence in that an individual may have the desired skills (i.e., setting goals, behaving appropriately, and evaluating achievement) in his or her behavioral repertoire but may not be motivated to use these skills. Development, on the other hand, interacts with social and personal competence in that a person's age or developmental growth may influence the type of goals set and achieved by an individual. Finally, environment pertains to the culture, society, or family expectations that influence the social and personal behavior of an individual (e.g., some Native American populations do not believe in long-term goal setting). A competent person is able to move from one environment to another, recognizing the social rules of each setting and acting accordingly. The individual who consistently demonstrates the ability to shift from one environment to another and exhibit appropriate social behavior in each setting is considered a socially competent person. The person who demonstrates the ability to set and achieve goals, make appropriate decisions, and persist through difficult times by using problem-solving skills is considered a personally competent individual.

**Social Skills.** The definition of **social skills** reflects the knowledge that researchers have acquired concerning social behavior. For example, Schumaker and Hazel's (1984) behavioral definition of social skills included overt behaviors as skill components necessary in the interactions between two or more people and also cognitive functions (i.e., covert behavior). Overt behaviors include observable nonverbal behaviors (e.g., eye contact and facial expression) and verbal behavior (what words are used and how the person communicates a message). Covert behaviors consist of a person's ability to empathize with another person and discriminate social cues. The appropriate and fluent use of these behaviors is rewarded by the attainment of the person's goal.

The definition of social skills has also been broadened to eliminate the possibility that an individual would use specific social skills to manipulate, intimidate, or violate a person's rights. Phillips (1978), for example, defined a socially skilled person according to "the extent to which he or she can communicate with others in a manner that fulfills one's rights, requirements, satisfactions, or obligations to a reasonable degree without damaging the other person's similar rights, requirements, satisfactions, or obligations, and shares these rights, etc., with others in free and open exchange" (p. 13). This definition is quite encompassing in that it includes the reciprocal interactions of both individuals involved in the social exchange. Social skills should be proactive, prosocial, and reciprocal in nature. In this way the participants of the interaction share in a mutually rewarding experience.

**Social Problem Solving.** Bijou and Baer (1978) define problem solving as a sequence or an algorithm of behaviors. When we are able to identify this sequence or algorithm of behaviors, we are able to teach it to others. Because problem solving is a covert or cognitive behavior, much of its analysis must be done through language. **Social problem solving,** therefore, is the sequence of behaviors developed to ameliorate a particular social interaction problem. We are able to identify

**TEACHER *Tips*** **Elementary Level**

### Fostering Resiliency in Children

Teachers who wish to profile resilient children as socially competent or self-determined may look for their ability to problem solve, think critically, and take initiative. These children foresee a positive future for themselves as they set goals for themselves and are motivated to achieve in school and life situations.

Henderson and Milstein (2003) outline 12 protective factors or individual behaviors that facilitate resilient responses to life situations. They believe that these children:

1. Engage in service activities for others
2. Exhibit good decision-making, assertiveness, problem-solving, and self-management skills
3. Establish friendships and positive relationships
4. Show a sense of humor
5. Feel in control of themselves
6. Show independent thinking and behavior
7. Establish a positive view of personal future
8. Show flexibility in challenging situations
9. Can generalize learned information or skills to other situations
10. Appear to be motivated
11. Show "excellence" in some area (e.g., sports, music, etc.)
12. Exhibit confidence in interactions with others or in performance situations

*Source:* From N. Henderson and M. M. Milstein, *Resiliency in Schools: Making It Happen for Students and Educators*, Copyright, 2003 by Corwin Press. Reprinted by permission of Corwin Press.

the social problem-solving process through the analysis of a person's language about a particular social event.

Several researchers propose an algorithm for teaching social problem solving (Kazdin, 2001; Shure, 1997, 1999). These authors outline five components to be used in a social problem-solving algorithm: (a) problem orientation, (b) problem definition and formulation, (c) generation of solutions, (d) decision making, and (e) implementation of plan and evaluation and verification of the outcome. This algorithm may include other covert behaviors that influence the effectiveness of the problem solving. These additional covert behaviors include empathy, moral judgment, the ability to process nonverbal cues, and the ability to make inferences.

**Self-Determination Skills.** The area of **self-determination** skills for students with disabilities is relatively new. When federally funded projects were initiated between 1990 and 1993, self-determination was researched, skills were identified, and curricula were developed for adolescents with disabilities and for those who are at risk for failure in their communities and schools. The definition of self-determination is continually evolving as the research in this area continues to develop. All of the definitions in the current literature, however, are similar in considering that goal-setting skills, self-regulation skills, decision-making skills, problem-solving skills, social skills, and self-evaluation skills are among the behaviors needed to identify a self-determined person (e.g., Palmer & Wehmeyer, 2003). For the purposes of this chapter, the following definition is offered:

> Self-determination refers to an individual's awareness of personal strengths and weaknesses, the ability to set goals and make choices, to be assertive at appropriate times, and to interact with others in a socially competent manner. A self-determined person is able to make independent decisions based on his or her ability to use resources, which includes collaborating and networking with others. The outcome for a self-determined person is the ability to realize his or her own potential, to become a productive member of a community, and to obtain his or her goals without infringing on the rights, responsibilities, and goals of others. (Serna & Lau-Smith, 1995, p. 144)

Individuals who are self-determined also exhibit the skill of persistence through problem solving. In meeting one's goals, everyone is faced with barriers or problems. To succeed in accomplishing these goals, the ability to overcome barriers is needed. Usually, this is done through continuous use of the skill of problem solving. With all of this in mind, the individual pursues his or her goals through ethical and appropriate strategies.

**Expanding the Social/Self-Determination Skills Model.** In the early 1990s, Mayer, DiPaolo, and Salovey introduced the term *emotional intelligence*, which refers to a student's ability to recognize emotions and their meaning as they relate to other people or situations. Eventually, Goleman (1998) took the vague constructs of emotional recognition, management, motivating oneself, and handling relationships and included the more teachable skills of self-awareness, self-regulation, motivation (e.g., goal setting), empathy, and social skills. The specification of these skills give educators more realistic and data-based programs from which to draw and closely aligned with evidenced-based social skills and self-determination skills programs.

Growing out of the emotional intelligence movement are the terms *emotional literacy* (Joseph & Strain, 2003) and *social-emotional learning* (Elksnin & Elksnin, 2006). These two expansions continue to promote the social and self-determination skills of self-awareness, self-regulation, communication, problem solving, decision making, and collaboration (Cohen, 2001). Additionally, Elias (2004) emphasizes the need for goal-setting skills as well as developing lasting relationships (a bit vague). Although the terms and theories may differ in these recent additions to the literature, the skills for teaching social/self-determination skills remain the same.

Reflective Question 13–1: ***What has 50 years of social skills research taught us?***

## ASSESSMENT

The previous discussion concerning the definitions of social competence, social skills, social problem solving, and self-determination skills is important because it directly relates to the assessment of child and adolescent behaviors. The construct of social competence, for instance, introduces global behaviors as well as several dimensions of social behaviors. The assessment instruments for social competence, therefore, are usually global in nature, addressing many behaviors that contribute to a student's total behavior in school and community environments. The instruments designed for the assessment of social skills and social problem solving, however, are more specific in nature. They identify specific nonverbal and verbal behaviors that are required to complete a successful social interaction with another person. The assessment measures for self-determined behaviors are still developing and are in the initial stages of validation on a large population of students.

In the following discussion, each assessment category is discussed by presenting brief descriptions of the assessment instruments, how the instruments are implemented, and the advantages and disadvantages of using each assessment category. Particular attention is given to the assessment of specific social, problem-solving, and self-determination skills. These assessments are most accessible to teachers and most relevant in establishing social skills and self-determination programs for students in any type of classroom environment.

### Assessment of Social Competence

There are many assessment instruments related to social competence. These instruments usually collect global information and are particularly useful when screening a student for a certain program. Assessment measures under this category are sociometric ratings, ratings by teachers and other adults, and self-report measures.

**Sociometric Ratings.** Sociometric ratings are assessment instruments that typically have an adult or peer evaluate the student according to some designated dimension (e.g., best friend, most popular). The most common procedures used with children and adolescents are (a) nominations by peers with regard to who is liked or disliked and (b) peer ratings of each student in the classroom (usually on a Likert-type scale) according to how much the student is liked. For example, a teacher may gather information from peer ratings by giving students a list of their peers (or by displaying snapshots of peers) and asking them to identify their best friend or with whom they would most like to play or work. Scores taken from peer nominations and peer rating scales are compiled to determine the student(s) who are most liked or most disliked.

One advantage of using sociometric measures is that they generally exhibit reliability and validity in predicting the student who is at risk for behavior problems. A disadvantage or limitation of the sociometric procedures is that they often do not provide teachers with information concerning specific behaviors that must be taught or ameliorated. At most, the teachers know that a student receiving votes in the "dislike" category is in need of an intervention.

**Ratings by Teachers.** Several standardized adaptive behavior and social skills rating scales have been developed as screening instruments for identifying children and adolescents at risk for behavior problems. Some of the most common and well-validated scales are presented in Table 13-1.

Implementation of the scales may be demonstrated by the Social Skills Rating System developed by Gresham and Elliott (1990). This adaptive scale not only identifies students at risk for behavior problems but also provides teachers with information concerning specific social

**TABLE 13–1** Adaptive behavior scales commonly used

| *Assessment Skills* | *Authors* | *Publisher* |
|---|---|---|
| AAMR Adaptive Behavior Scale—2nd edition | Lambert, Nihira, & Leland, 2005 | American Association on Mental Retardation/PRO-ED |
| Quay-Peterson Behavior Problem Checklist | Quay & Peterson, 1983 | Children's Research Center |
| The Social Skills Rating System | Gresham & Elliott, 1990 | American Guidance Service |
| Vineland Adaptive Behavior Scales—2nd edition | Sparrow, Balla, & Cicchetti, 2004 | American Guidance Services |

skill deficits. Gresham and Elliott developed an assessment tool for elementary and secondary students. Parents, teachers, and students are asked to rate a student's behavior on the following dimensions: (a) cooperation (e.g., helping others, sharing), (b) assertion (e.g., asking for information), (c) responsibility (e.g., ability to communicate about property and work), (d) empathy (e.g., behaviors showing concern or respect), and (e) self-control (e.g., behaviors that emerge during conflict situations). Ratings are based on the memory of parents, teachers, and students with regard to the frequency (i.e., never, sometimes, very often) that a specific behavior occurs. Additionally, a second assessment requires the teachers, parents, and students to rate the importance of each behavior. Gresham and Elliott report high validity and reliability scores for the parent and teacher scales but note that the reliability and validity scores for the student scales are less impressive.

Perhaps the most valuable aspect of the Social Skills Rating System is that the authors provide several examples that illustrate how to use the results of the assessment to target specific social skills and develop an intervention program for a student. Teachers should remember, however, that the assessment relies on the memory of the rater and does not indicate the exact frequency with which the behaviors occur (i.e., we don't know what "sometimes" means). Finally, unless several raters fill out the assessment on each child, the teacher cannot be sure if the problem behaviors are due to social deficits or motivation problems within the classroom environment.

## Assessment of Specific Social, Problem-Solving, and Self-Determination Skills

Adaptive behavior scales and other rating scales have received criticism regarding their reliance on the memory of the rater or subjective interpretations. Because of this dissatisfaction, researchers developed direct observation assessment procedures that require a student to respond to specific instructions or stimuli and then allow observers to rate the performance of the student in that particular situation. These assessments are usually related to specific social skills and can help the teacher or tester identify specific nonverbal and verbal behavioral component deficits of a particular skill. For example, a teacher can assess a student's nonverbal skills of eye contact, facing a person, posture, and facial expression while a student is trying to ask for help. Similarly, a teacher can assess the verbal components (e.g., verbal statements as well as voice tone, interrupting) a student exhibits while trying to ask for help. This direct observation assessment procedure provides information concerning the student's performance of the specific skill components (e.g., eye contact) of a particular social skill and in a specific situation. Additionally, the observation can determine whether the social skill is absent due to skill deficits or lack of motivation to use the social skill. Teachers wanting to pursue this form of assessment may want to initiate the following procedures when developing an assessment instrument for their particular classroom of students (see Table 13–2).

**Step 1: Task Analyze the Social Skill.** Once the teacher identifies a problem area (e.g., student is unable to attend to and follow the teacher's instructions), the teacher can develop a social skill that meets the needs of the student (e.g., following instructions skill). The teacher should consider the nonverbal and verbal components of the social skill. In most social skills four nonverbal behaviors can be identified: facing the person, eye contact, facial expression (e.g., serious or smiling), and posture (e.g., straight or relaxed). The paraverbal behaviors of voice tone (e.g., pleasant or serious) and volume are also considered during the

**TABLE 13–2** Procedures used to establish direct observation assessments of specific social skills

**Steps**

1. Task analyze the social skill.
2. Develop definitions for each behavioral component of the skill.
3. Implement a rating scale to assess the defined behavioral components.
4. Secure a reliability observer.
5. Generate real-life situations that require the student to use the targeted social skills.
6. Plan for individual test sessions.

observation of the social skill. The teacher can then task analyze the verbal components of the "following instructions" skill. For example, after the student listens to the instruction, he or she may need to clarify the instructions and then say that she or he will follow the instructions. The task analysis will require a step-by-step sequence of behaviors that must be executed while following instructions. Table 13–3 exhibits a task analysis of one example of a skill. Notice how the verbal components of the skill are labeled and followed by a verbal example. This analysis is important when working with students exhibiting verbal expression problems.

**Step 2: Develop Definitions for Each Behavioral Component of the Skill.** This step requires that the teacher develop a definition of each behavioral component of the skill. For instance, the nonverbal behavioral component of "face the person" may be defined as "the student's shoulders are positioned parallel to the person giving the instruction, with face and eyes directed toward the person." An approximation of this nonverbal behavioral component may be defined as the "student's shoulders are positioned at a 45-degree angle away from the person giving the instructions, but the face and eyes are still directed toward the person." A definition that describes an inappropriate use of this behavioral component may state that the "student turns the whole body away from the person giving the instructions."

**Step 3: Implement a Rating Scale to Assess the Defined Behavioral Components.** Although there are a variety of rating scales to be adopted, one of the most efficient scales is the one advocated by Hazel et al. (1981b). These authors use a 2, 1, 0 rating scale for each behavioral component of a skill. For example, the score of 2 is recorded when the student is performing the behavioral component exactly as defined. A score of 1 is recorded when the student approximates the defined behavior (see Step 2). A score of 0 is recorded if the student exhibits the behavioral component inappropriately or does not perform the behavior at all. When the rating scale is applied to the definition of each behavioral component of a skill, the teacher can determine what behavioral components need intervention. Additionally, the teacher can secure a mean score for the student's performance of the skill in a particular situation.

**TABLE 13–3** Task analysis of the "following instructions" skill

**Skill Sheet**

Following Instructions

1. Face the person.
2. Maintain eye contact.
3. Keep a neutral facial expression.
4. Use a normal tone of voice.
5. Keep a straight posture.
6. Listen closely to the instruction so that you will know what to do and remember to give feedback with head nods and by saying "mm-hmm" and yeah."
7. Acknowledge the instruction, "*OK.*"
8. Ask for more information if you don't understand the instruction. "*But I don't understand. . . .*"
9. Say that you will follow the instruction. "*I'll do it . . .* "
10. Follow the instruction.
11. Throughout, give polite, pleasant responses.
12. Do not argue with the person about the instruction: follow it and talk to the person later about problems.

*Source:* From *ASSET: A Social Skills Program for Adolescents* (p. 113), by J. S. Hazel, J. B. Schumaker, J. A. Sherman, and J. B. Sheldon-Wildgen, 1981, Champaign, IL: Research Press. Copyright 1981 by the authors. Reprinted with permission.

**Step 4: Secure a Reliability Observer.** In this step, the teacher is required to seek out another individual who can observe the student's performance and reliably score the behaviors according to the definition criteria developed in Step 3 of these procedures. The teacher should instruct the observer by explaining the definitions of the behavioral components in each skill and demonstrating the desired behaviors. The teacher and observer should practice the scoring procedures by independently observing a student performing a skill (e.g., following instructions) and then comparing their scores. When the teacher's and observer's scores agree on 80% or more of the behavioral components, the teacher can feel confident that the scoring of the behavioral components (according to the stated definitions) is accurate.

**Step 5: Generate Real-Life Situations That Require the Student to Use the Targeted Social Skills.** After the definitions, scoring, and reliability observer are secure, the teacher generates several situations that require the student to use the targeted skills. These situations are used during role-play test sessions (i.e., the teacher and student act out the situation so that the student's performance can be evaluated). The situations should be based on real-life incidences that occur in many different settings (home, school, community). For example, a situation that is common to most children and adolescents takes place at home when the parent asks the youth to take out the trash. The situation may read as follows: "You are in the kitchen when your mother asks you to take out the trash. I'll be your mother and let's act out the situation. '__________, would you take the garbage out to the trash bin?'" This particular situation is used during a role-play test session that assesses the student's performance for the "following instructions" skill.

**Step 6: Plan for Individual Test Sessions.** The final step in developing a skill-specific assessment procedure is to plan individual test sessions for each student. There are three methods of collecting the assessment information. First, the teacher can wait for naturally occurring interactions to take place in the classroom and then score the behavior. Although this is the most preferable method to use, it can be problematic if there are few opportunities for the behavior to occur or if the behavior does not occur at all. A second method, the use of confederates, can also be employed if the teacher desires to obtain information in the natural setting. With this method, the teacher must secure the cooperation of other peers or teachers to set up situations so that the student can respond to the peer's (or teacher's) initiations. This method is advantageous if the peers are cooperative; do not prompt the student to use certain behaviors, and do not tell the student that they were asked to participate in this endeavor.

A third method of assessing a student's social skill behavior is during a simulated role-play situation. Using this method, the teacher should begin a test session by securing a private room for the student, teacher, and reliability observer. Once the teacher has eliminated as many distractions and interruptions as possible, the student is told that he or she will be role-playing (acting out) several situations with the teacher. Because preteaching assessments do not require the student to act in accordance with the targeted social skill, the student is instructed to be himself or herself and respond as normally as possible. The teacher then reads the situation (developed in Step 5) to the student, making sure that the student understands the scenario before beginning. Once the student understands the situation, the role-play interaction begins. During the interaction the teacher must not prompt the student and must observe the student's behavior carefully (in addition to acting out the role designated in the situation). After this brief role-play interaction (it should not last more than 2 or 3 minutes), the teacher and reliability observer should score each nonverbal and verbal behavior of the social skill according to the designated definitions rating scale (Steps 2 and 3). This procedure continues until all the targeted social skills are assessed.

Regardless of the test method used, the teacher can assess the student's behavior on specific social skills. Multiple assessments (at least three), using different situations and different methods, should be gathered to obtain an overall performance score. With this information, a student's mean scores (or cluster of scores) can be graphed or recorded so that pretest and after-teaching scores can be compared.

## Assessment of Self-Determination Skills

Assessment tools for self-determination skills reflect the work of researchers who developed self-determination skills curricula (e.g., Hoffman & Field, 1995; Martin & Huber-Marshall, 1995; Serna & Lau-Smith, 1995). The following description outlines criterion-referenced and curriculum-based assessment tools, as well as behavioral observation checklists, designed for each of five self-determination curricula described later in this chapter.

**Assessment Tools for the Steps to Self-Determination Curriculum.** Hoffman and Field (1995) describe two assessment tools that were developed to accompany their curriculum. The first tool, the Self-Determination Observation Checklist (SDOC), is a teacher-administered behavioral observation checklist that identifies 38 behaviors that are correlated with self-determination skills found in the classroom. The second assessment tool is called the Self-Determination Knowledge Scale (SDKS). This tool is a 30-item structured response test designed to assess students' cognitive knowledge of different self-determination skills.

**Assessment Tools for the Learning with PURPOSE Curriculum.** Three assessment tools were developed to complement the Learning with PURPOSE Curriculum (Serna & Lau-Smith, 1995). The first assessment involves a behavioral checklist for each self-determination skill covered in the seven-domain curriculum. Each component of each skill is rated on a three-point rating system to determine if the student was able to demonstrate the skill component as described, approximated the skill component, or did not exhibit the skill component. The second assessment form is a teacher and parent general report in which the individual is required to rate the student's skill competency on a seven-point Likert scale for each of the seven skill areas. Complementing the teacher and parent report is a student self-report measure in which the student rates himself or herself according to perceived skill proficiency in each of the skill areas. The third assessment tool is a 75-item report filled out by the teacher, parent, and student. Each individual is required to rate the student's skill according to proficiency in the skill, the frequency of the skill being used, and the importance of the skill.

**Assessment Tool for the ChoiceMaker Curriculum.** A criterion-referenced tool was developed by Martin and Huber-Marshall (1995) to be used in conjunction with their curriculum that emphasizes self-determination skills to be used during individualized education program (IEP) meetings. The teacher is required to rate the student's self-determination skills and whether opportunities to use the skills occur in the school settings.

**A Final Note on Assessment.** As with all assessment instruments, we must be aware of cultural differences that children might be exhibiting when they interact with others. The way teachers perceive these interactions may affect their ratings of children's behaviors.

In response to this bias, teachers might find that they must create a positive culture in their own classroom. This culture is created with all the students working together to develop verbal and nonverbal social behaviors that are acceptable in the classroom culture. In this way behaviors may be predictable in a safe, social environment.

> Reflective Question 13–2: ***During the direct observation of a social skill (through a role-play situation), how can the teacher determine if the student does not have the skill in his or her repertoire or if he or she has the skill, but is not motivated to use the skill?***

## SOCIAL SKILLS AND SELF-DETERMINATION SKILLS: CURRICULA AND INSTRUCTION

### Social Skills Curricula

Several commercially produced social skills curricula are available to teachers of students with special needs. Many of these social skills programs have been developed by experts in child and adolescent behavior disorders (e.g., Hazel et al., 1981a; McGinnis et al., 1998) and have been field-tested to ensure their adaptability to the classroom environment. Perhaps the most notable of these available social skills programs for children in the elementary grades are Skillstreaming the Elementary Child (McGinnis et al., 1998) and the ACCEPTS Program (Walker et al., 1983). Two popular social skills programs for adolescents with special needs are Skillstreaming the Adolescent (Goldstein, Sprafkin, Gershaw, & Klein, 1998) and the ASSET Program (Hazel et al., 1981a). The authors of these programs have developed adaptable curricula that are recommended for the use of teachers in their classrooms. Whether teachers decide to use any one of these programs depends on their preferences, the adaptability of the program to the students' needs, and the teachers' familiarity with social skills instruction.

The following discussion will briefly describe each of the social skills curricula mentioned with regard to the assessment procedures recommended, skill content, instructional material, and instructions to the teacher. (Table 13–4 summarizes this discussion.)

**Skillstreaming the Elementary Student.** *Skillstreaming the Elementary School Child: A Guide for Teaching Prosocial Skills* (McGinnis et al., 1998) is one of the most popular social skills programs for students in the elementary grades. This program is designed to provide the teacher with different assessment options from direct observation to sociometric ratings. Particular emphasis is placed on teacher frequency ratings of the students' skill performances. The authors recommend

**TABLE 13–4** Social skills curricula

| *Social Curricula* | *Assessment Procedures* | *Skill Content* | *Instructional Materials* | *Instruction to Teacher* |
|---|---|---|---|---|
| 1. Skillstreaming the Elementary School Child (McGinnis et al., 1998) | Student skill checklist<br>Teachers skill checklist<br>Group chart | Classroom survival<br>Friendship making<br>Dealing with feelings<br>Alternatives to aggression<br>Dealing with stress | Samples of homework reports<br>Contingency contracts<br>Self-monitoring<br>Home journals | Beginning a group<br>Constructing a structured learning group<br>Suggestions<br>Managing behavior problems |
| 2. ACCEPTS Program (Walker et al., 1983) | Teacher questionnaire<br>Screening checklist<br>Observation forms<br>Placement test<br>Recess rating form<br>Behavior rating form | Classroom skills<br>Basic instructions<br>Getting along<br>Making friends<br>Coping skills | Videotapes | Direct instruction<br>Teaching scripts for each skill<br>Behavior management procedures |
| 3. Skillstreaming the Adolescent (Goldstein et al., 1998) | Skill checklist<br>Group chart<br>Master record | Beginning skills<br>Advanced skills<br>Dealing with feelings<br>Alternatives to aggression<br>Dealing with stress<br>Planning skills | Videotapes | Structured learning procedures<br>Selection and grouping<br>Managing behavior problems |
| 4. The ASSET Program: A Social Skills Program for Adolescents (Hazel et al., 1981a) | Criterion checklist<br>Pre- and posttraining checklist<br>Parent questionnaire<br>Parent satisfaction<br>Participant satisfaction | Giving positive feedback<br>Giving negative feedback<br>Accepting negative feedback<br>Negotiation<br>Following instruction<br>Problem solving<br>Resisting peer pressure<br>Converstion | Skill sheets<br>Videotapes<br>Home notes<br>Sample parent letter<br>Sample telephone conversation with parent | Starting a group<br>Basic teaching steps<br>Group leader steps<br>Conducting group meetings<br>Group rules and behavior problems<br>Maintaining skills<br>Quick-reference guide |
| 5. Social Storytelling Curriculum (Serna, Nielsen, & Forness, 2006) | Direct observation | Listening and following instructions<br>Problem solving<br>Self-management of behavior sharing | Story book<br>Coloring book<br>Songs | Instructor's manual for each skill area |

this assessment when deciding on the social skills to be targeted for teaching. The social skills presented in this program are divided into five groups: (a) surviving-in-the-classroom skills, (b) friendship-making skills, (c) dealing with feelings, (d) using alternatives to aggression, and (e) dealing with stress. The skills are task analyzed so that each skill has up to six general steps outlined for the student. The teaching of each step in the social skill, though, must be extended by teachers through modeling, discussion, and prompting. Finally, a social learning approach/direct instructional procedure is outlined for teachers to use when teaching the social skill. A set of transcripts, used as examples of instruction, are provided for teachers.

**ACCEPTS Program.** The *Walker Social Skills Curriculum: The ACCEPTS Program* (Walker et al., 1983) was developed to promote teacher–student and peer-to-peer interaction skills. The program includes a placement test, direct instructional procedures for teachers, guidelines for teaching, scripts for teaching the social skills, and activities that enhance the skill learning. A behavior management procedure and a videotape are also available with the program. Five social skill areas are emphasized in this program: (a) classroom skills (e.g., listening, following rules), (b) basic interaction skills (e.g., eye contact, starting, taking turns), (c) getting along skills (e.g., sharing, assisting others), (d) making friends skills (e.g., smiling, complimenting), and (e) coping skills (e.g., when to say "no").

**Skillstreaming the Adolescent.** *Skillstreaming the Adolescent: A Structured Learning Approach to Teaching Prosocial Skills* (Goldstein et al., 1998) initially presents the teacher with a rating scale for evaluating the social behavior of their students. Like the teacher rating scales described in the assessment section of this chapter, the authors list the target skill (e.g., saying "thank you"), give an example of the skill (e.g., "Does the student let others know that he or she is grateful for favors, etc.?"), and then provide a frequency rating scale of 1 to 5 (i.e., a rating of 1 would indicate "never" and a rating of 5 would indicate "always"). The assessment of these 50 skills allows the teacher to target the most deficient skills in the student's repertoire.

Once the deficient skills have been targeted, the authors present the 50 skills categorized under six groups: (a) beginning social skills (e.g., listening, starting a conversation, question asking), (b) advanced social skills (e.g., asking for help, joining in, following instructions), (c) skills for dealing with feelings (e.g., knowing your feelings, dealing with fear), (d) skill alternatives to aggression (e.g., asking permission, sharing something, negotiating), (e) skills for dealing with stress (e.g., making a complaint, dealing with embarrassment, responding to persuasion), and (f) planning skills (e.g., deciding on something to do; setting a goal; making a decision). Each skill is then task analyzed into three- to four-step directions for the student. The authors then instruct the teacher by providing transcripts of social skills instruction groups. These transcripts provide examples of the direct instructional procedures and how to prompt a student to use each step of the targeted skill. A videotape instructing teachers how to conduct a social skills group is available separately.

**ASSET Program.** The *ASSET Program: A Social Skills Program for Adolescents* (Hazel et al., 1981a) consists of a leader's guide manual and skill sheets that are used during the skill-teaching sessions.

Research associated with this social skills program reveals that the investigators socially validated the eight skills presented in the curriculum. Teachers, court officers, and professionals working with adolescents identified eight skills they thought were the most beneficial for adolescents to learn and be successful in the academic, home, and community environments (Hazel et al., 1981b). These skills include giving positive feedback, giving negative feedback, accepting negative feedback, resisting peer pressure, problem solving, negotiation, following instructions, and conversation. The program is designed so that a teacher will teach all eight skills to students.

An attractive feature of this program is the skill sheets that are provided for the teacher and students. Each skill sheet involves a step-by-step task analysis of each skill. The task analysis is divided into nonverbal, verbal, and some covert skill components (e.g., listening). Each verbal step of the skill is accompanied by a verbal example of what an adolescent might say in a certain situation. This feature is advantageous for those students who require verbal prompts and possess limited English/verbal skills. The skill sheets are also adaptable to all grade levels by modifying the number of skill steps and the difficulty of the language used. The final section of the leader's guide includes sociometric measures for teachers, parents, and students. Instructional videotapes are also available separately but are not necessary to conduct an effective social skills program.

## Social and Self-Determination Curricula for Young Children

The majority of the social and self-determination curricula have been developed for adolescents with disabilities. Ultimately, however, skill building in this area should begin as early as possible (Forness, Serna, Kavale, & Nielsen, in press). If children are taught following-instruction, self-evaluation, self-advocacy, self-regulation, problem-solving, and decision-making skills at an early age, numerous social and mental health issues that plague young children can be prevented (Serna, Forness, & Nielsen, 1998).

One attempt to develop and field-test a curriculum for young children is the Social Storytelling Curriculum (Serna, Nielsen, & Forness, 2006). After socially validating four social and self-determination skills for young children (i.e., following instructions, sharing, self-regulations, and problem solving) a curriculum based on storytelling was initiated. This storytelling process involves the orchestration of carefully developed animal stories with direct instructional procedures embedded throughout the introduction, plot, and resolution of the story (see Figure 13–1 for an example of a storyline that introduces the skills of "saying hello" and

**FIGURE 13–1** Teaching social and self-determination skills through stories: An example of a story that teaches how to say hello and give compliments

**The Ballad of Sammy the Scorpion**
**By Dwayne Norris**

Larry the Lizard came loping along.
Shuffling his shoes and singing a song.

When looking around at the dry desert land
His eyes did spy a scorpion named Sam.

"Hola, partner," the lizard exclaimed.
"They call me Larry. What is your name?"

The scorpion lashed his stinger at Larry; how rude!
Larry jumped back and said, "What's wrong with you, dude?"

"I didn't mean to offend you," said Sammy so slow.
"I was only trying to tell you 'Hello.'"

"That's an odd way to greet someone, Sir Scorpion.
It's easy to see why you don't have many friends.
But, if you will listen, I'll try to explain
How to tell someone you like them without causing pain."

"Would you, oh could you?" the scorpion asked.
"Certainly, there's very few steps to the task...
When you meet a new person who you really dig,
Square your shoulders with them, don't dance a jig."
That lets them know that you care what they say.
Now keep eye contact with them and don't turn away.
Smile when you're talking and you'll be surprised
How a glow of warm friendship will fill your friend's eyes.

"Now, when you're facing the person, eyes meet and teeth flashed,
Remember to keep a posture that says you're relaxed.
And don't be afraid to point out things that you like
About your friend's tail or stinger or bike."

"Wow, that's so cool. I never thought about that.
I will have to try some of this positive feedback."

Just then Pete the Prairie Dog appeared from the ground
Burrowing, out of his prairie dog mound.

He said: "What's up? What are you guys doing?"
And Sammy remembered that he shouldn't sting.

A new friend, rather, he turned clockwise,
Squared his shoulders with Pete and looked at his eyes.
He smiled at the rodent with a body most calm.
He said: "Hello! I like your buckteeth and how you tunnel along."
The Lizard was happy, singing "Way to go, Sam."
And Sammy and Pete became very good friends.

*Source:* Reprinted with the author's permission.

"giving compliments"). The teacher begins by (a) introducing the animal in the story (e.g., "What is a porcupine?"), (b) reading the story, (c) talking about each section of the story that emphasizes a directional step, (d) modeling the skill steps introduced in the story, and (e) requiring each child to practice the steps.

Once the children learn the self-determination/social skill in the story-time portion of the day, a learning center is available for the children to practice their newly acquired skill. The practice is monitored by the teacher and feedback is given to each child. Generalization of the skill is prompted and reinforced at other learning centers and during outside play time.

Preliminary observations indicate that very young children can learn these social/self-determination skills through a story format. Longitudinal studies, however, are required to establish the maintenance and long-term effects of this type of teaching for young children.

## Self-Determination Curricula

The Office of Special Education and Rehabilitative Service initiated a series of grants to fund demonstration projects in self-determination. Approximately 26 demonstration models were funded between 1990 and 1993. The charge given to these researchers was to investigate and develop self-determination programs that taught youth to become more independent and future oriented. Of these projects, five socially validated programs are outlined below.

**Steps to Self-Determination Curriculum.** The Steps to Self-Determination program (Field & Hoffman, 1992), consists of six steps to independence and self-determination. These steps include (a) knowing yourself, (b) valuing yourself, (c) planning, (d) acting, (e) experiencing outcomes, and (f) learning. Each of these steps is divided into 16 class sessions where the students are taught specific skills of self-evaluation, goal setting and planning, risk taking, decision making, independent performance, and adjustment. The program is designed to be implemented in a one-semester period and involves the parents and community members as support people during the program. Figure 13–2 represents this curriculum model.

**Learning with PURPOSE.** Learning with PURPOSE (Serna & Lau-Smith, 1995) is a curriculum developed for use by teachers who work in inclusive settings with students who (a) have mild to moderate disabilities, (b) are at risk for failure in their school and community, and (c) are in the general education classroom. The teaching model of the curriculum was piloted with students who were high, regular, and at-risk

TEACHER *Tips* — Secondary Level

### Fostering Self-Advocacy Skills: The LEAD Group

Pocock, Lambose, Karvonen, Test, Algozzine, Wood, and Martin (2002) emphasize the importance of developing programs that support the self-determination and self-advocacy skills of high school students with learning disabilities (LD). The authors highlight a high school program called The LEAD Group.

The LEAD Group was developed in response to concerns voiced by high school students with LD and their parents. These individuals reported that "some general education teachers were reluctant to provide accommodations and modifications" for classroom assignments. Additionally, the guidance counselor at the school was aware that some students with LD were having trouble coping with the challenges that their disability presented.

In response to the need the guidance counselor formed a support group to educate the students about their disability and instruct them in the area of self-advocacy skills. The components of the group (LEAD) include:

- Lessons in self-awareness and disability knowledge
- Meetings to support students with LD who are having trouble coping with their disability
- Presentations to community groups regarding learning disabilities and being a student

Presently LEAD consists of two cohorts: one cohort for ninth graders and another for advanced students. Both cohorts meet four days a week. Two days focus on educational activities. One day is devoted to meeting with mentors. Finally, a fourth day emphasizes support group work with the guidance counselor. All the students work on developing community presentations and participate in their execution.

*Source:* From "Successful Strategies for Promoting Self-Advocacy Among Students with LD: The LEAD Group," by A. Pocock, S. Lambros, M. Karvonen, D. W. Test, B. Algozzine, W. Wood, and J. E. Martin, 2002, *Intervention in School and Clinic, 37,* 209–216.

**FIGURE 13–2** Model for self-determination

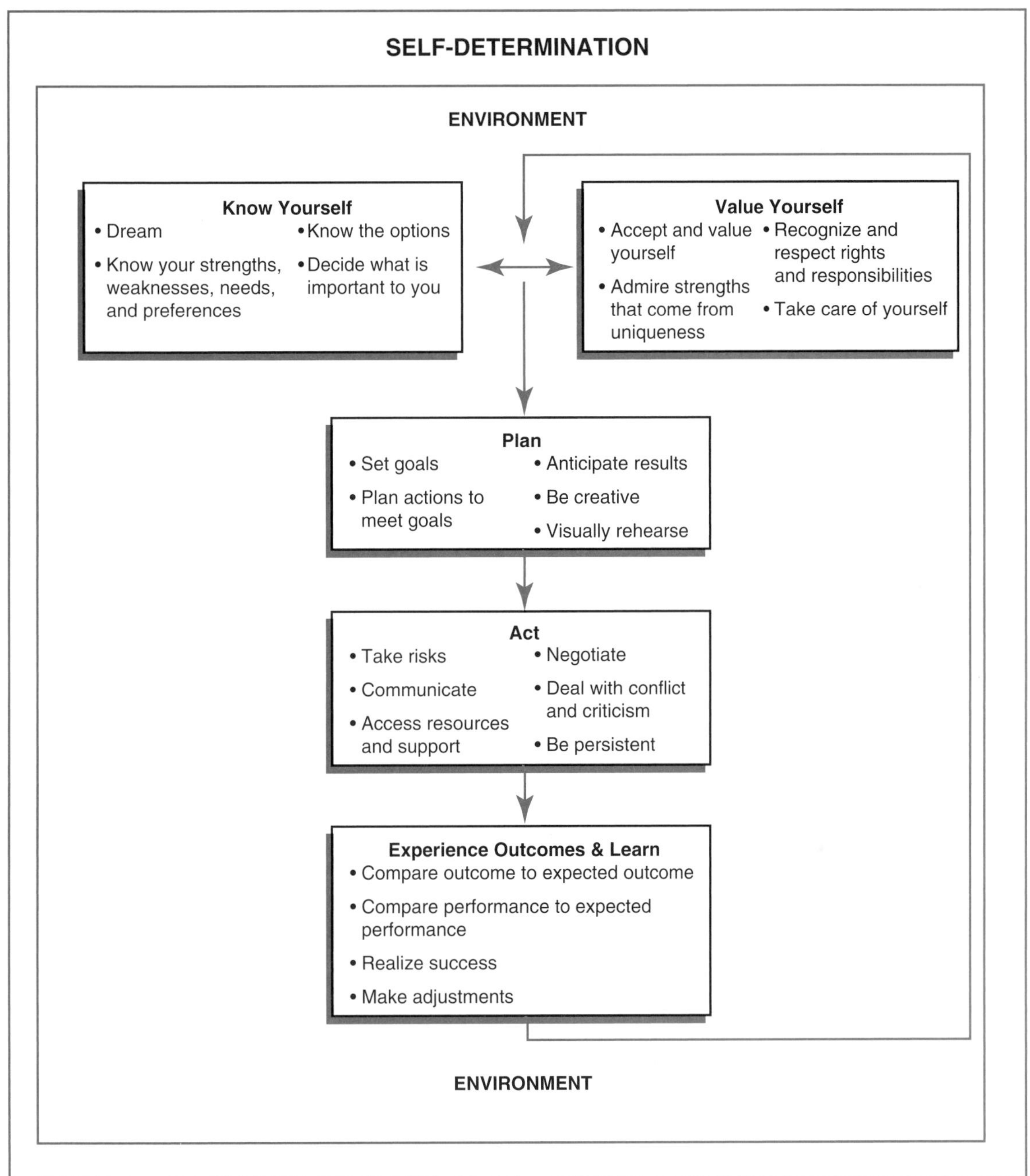


*Source:* From "Development of a Model for Self-Determination," by S. Field and A. Hoffman, 1994, *Career Development for Exceptional individuals, 17*, 145. Copyright 1994 CDEI. Reprinted with permission.

achievers as well as students receiving special education services. Based on this research, Figure 13–3 lists those skills that many high achievers exhibit as compared to students who are at risk for failure in the classroom and community and shows how the curriculum skills address these deficit areas.

The curriculum contains seven domain areas with a total of 34 skills and three guideline areas. The domain areas consist of (a) prerequisite social skills, (b) self-evaluation skills, (c) self-direction skills, (d) networking skills, (e) collaboration skills, (f) persistence and risk-taking skills, and (g) stress management. The program

| A Comparison of Successful and At-Risk Student Behaviors | | Identification of Self-Determination Skills Needed to Be Successful | | | | | | | | |
|---|---|---|---|---|---|---|---|---|---|---|
| | | Identified Self-Determination Skills | | | | | | | | |
| **In many cases, successful students:** | **In many cases, at-risk students exhibit:** | Social Skills | Self-Evaluation | Self-Direction | Informal and Formal Networking | Collaboration | Problem Solving & Decision Making | Stress Management | Family Program | |
| • Succeed in areas of academics, art, drama, and sports. | • Difficulties in school (e.g., work habits, coping, peer relations). | • | | • | | | | • | • | |
| • Exhibit survival skills in different situations. | • Functional skills only in their subculture (e.g., gangs). | • | | | | | | • | | |
| • Exhibit healthy communication and social skills. | • Communication and social skill problems. | • | | | | | | | • | |
| • Gain positive attention from others. | • Self-defeating behaviors to gain negative attention. | • | | | | | | | | |
| • Make statements of positive self-regard, indicating self-esteem. | • Behaviors that indicate self-esteem problems vary according to situation. | • | • | | | | | | | |
| • Use reflective/self-evaluation skills. | • No or few self-evaluation skills. | | • | | | | | | | |
| • Exhibit ability to delay gratification. | • Impulsive behavior—need immediate gratification. | • | | • | | | | | • | |
| • Maintain future orientation/ goals. | • No self-direction or goal-setting skills. | | | • | | | | | • | |
| • Acquire supportive and encouraging teachers, peers, and adults. | • No acquisition of teacher support or few collaboration and networking skills. | • | | | • | • | | | • | |
| • Seek help when needed. | • Asking for help skills, but not always. | • | | | • | • | | | | |
| • Exhibit locus of control through decision-making skills. | • Little or few decision-making skills. | | | | | | • | | | |
| • Overcome problem/barriers. | • Few problem-solving skills. | • | | | | | • | | | |
| • Learn to survive stress and use humor. | • Inappropriate stress-management skills (e.g., drugs). | | | | | | • | • | | |
| • Use negative situations to learn from and for future positive outcomes. | • Listless, nonproductive behavior due to their negative view of personal situation (e.g., depressed, hopeless). | | • | | • | • | • | | | |
| • Experience positive parent discipline and interactions. | • Behaviors that indicate fluctuating family environments. | • | | • | | | | | • | |

**FIGURE 13–3** Comparison of successful and at-risk student behaviors and ways the Learning with PURPOSE curriculum meets these students' needs

is designed to be used during a 5-year period (grades 8 through 12). For example, 8th-grade students could begin learning the skills of communication and assertiveness (social skills) as well as self-direction skills. By the time they are in the 12th grade, they should be learning the skills of collaboration and formal networking to prepare them for their transition into the community and workplace.

**TABLE 13–5** Self-determination concepts

| *Self-Awareness* | *Self-Advocacy* | *Self-Efficacy* | *Decision Making* | *Independent Performance* | *Self-Evaluation* | *Adjustment* |
|---|---|---|---|---|---|---|
| Identify needs | Assertively state wants and needs | Expect to obtain goals | Assess situation demands | Initiate tasks on time | Monitor task performance | Change goals |
| Identify interests | Assertively state rights | | Set goals | Complete tasks on time | Compare performance to standard | Change strategies |
| Identify and understand strengths | Determine needed supports | | Set standards | Use self-management strategies | Evaluate effectiveness of self-management strategies | Change standards |
| Identify and understand limitations | Pursue needed support | | Identify information to make decision | Perform tasks to standard | Determine if plan completed and goal met | Change plan |
| Identify own values | Obtain and evaluate needed support | | Consider past solutions for new situations | Follow through on own plan | | Change support |
| | Conduct own affairs | | Generate new, creative solutions | | | Persistently adjust |
| | | | Consider options | | | Use environmental feedback to aid adjustment |
| | | | Choose best option | | | |
| | | | Develop plan | | | |

*Source:* From "ChoiceMaker: A Comprehensive Self-Determiantion Transition Program," by J. E. Martin and L. H. Marshall, 1995, *Intervention in School and Clinic, 30*, p. 149. Copyright 1995 by PRO-ED, Inc. Reprinted with permission.

**ChoiceMakers.** ChoiceMakers (Martin & Huber-Marshall, 1995) is a curriculum that specifically focuses on the leadership of students during their IEP meetings. This curriculum contains three basic sections: (a) choosing goals, (b) expressing goals, and (c) taking action. Within these three sections, seven concepts are taught in the form of skills areas. These areas include (a) self-awareness, (b) self-advocacy, (c) self-efficacy, (d) decision making, (e) independent performance, (f) self-evaluation, and (g) adjustment. All skills taught in the curriculum address transition areas and student attainment during their high school years. The goal is to plan and prepare students for a successful transition into the working world and the community outside of school. Table 13–5 outlines the curriculum concepts and their associated skills.

**Life-Centered Career Education Curriculum.** This well-established curriculum was originally developed by Brolin (1993, 2004) for youth with developmental disabilities. As part of the federally funded self-determination projects, Wehmeyer (1995) adapted and field-tested the curriculum to promote self-determination skills for adolescents with disabilities. The curriculum includes 350 lesson plans for students who are 12 to 18 years of age. Self-determination lessons are intended to be used sequentially beginning with lesson 10 (goal setting), yet all lessons enhance the learning of independence among adolescents.

**Classroom Competency-Building Program.** Abery, Rudrud, Arndt, and Eggeben (1995) developed a 10-module curriculum that includes the following skill areas: (a) self-awareness, (b) self-esteem, (c) perceptions of personal control, (d) personal values, (e) goal setting, (f) assertive communication, (g) choice making, (h) self-regulation, (i) problem solving, and (j) personal advocacy. The curriculum is designed for students with mild to moderate developmental disabilities and is, for the most part, experiential in nature to encourage active learning among the students. A parent program also was incorporated along with this curriculum. Table 13–6 illustrates the curriculum skill modules.

**TABLE 13–6** Classroom competency-building modules

| Classroom Competency-Building Modules |
| --- |
| **Self-awareness:** The purpose of this module is for students to gain an understanding of who they are as individuals. |
| **Self-esteem:** This module provides students with the opportunity to examine their own esteem and identify ways to maintain positive self-esteem. |
| **Enhancing perceptions of personal controls:** This module is designed to help students identify areas in their lives in which they would like to have more control and develop strategies for gaining increased control. |
| **Values:** The purpose of this module is to help students identify sources of values in the community, values their families identify as important, and values they hold for themselves. |
| **Goal setting:** This module assists students in understanding short- and long-term goals and provides practice in identifying and setting goals. |
| **Assertive communication:** The purpose of this module is for students to understand and practice verbal and nonverbal communication and listening skills. Students role-play situations with passive, aggressive, and assertive communication styles. |
| **Choice making:** This module facilitates student acquisition of the steps necessary for choice making: recognizing opportunities for choice, generating alternatives, evaluating alternatives, and selecting an alternative. |
| **Realizing your vision:** The purpose of this module is to provide students with information to assist them in being able to regulate their own behavior in order to reach a goal. |
| **Problem solving:** This module facilitates student understanding of the steps in solving problems and an opportunity to discuss previous experiences with solving problems. |
| **Personal advocacy:** The purpose of this module is to promote discussion about rights, responsibilities, and ways to be a self-advocate. Guest speakers from local advocacy organizations are part of the module. |

*Source:* From "Evaluating a Multicomponent Program for Enhancing the Self-Determination of Youth with Disabilities," by B. Abery, L. Rudrud, K. Arndt, L. Schauben, and A. Eggebeen, 1995, *Intervention in School and Clinic, 30*, p. 174. Copyright 1995 by PRO-ED, Inc. Reprinted with permission.

## Direct Instruction of Social and Self-Determination Skills

The teaching process typically employed in social skills instruction is structured learning or direct instruction. This behavioral approach to teaching consists of modeling, role-playing, corrective feedback, and planning for generalization (Goldstein et al., 1998). Historically, the most celebrated structured learning model is a teaching interaction procedure perfected by Phillips, Phillips, Fixsen, and Wolf (1974). This procedure requires the teacher to engage in specific steps that can be used with an individual and in a group situation. The steps include the following: (a) begin with a positive statement about the student, (b) define the social skill to be learned, (c) give a rationale regarding the importance of the skill, (d) give an example of when the skill could be used, (e) introduce and explain each nonverbal and verbal component of the targeted social skill, (f) model how the skill should be used, (g) rehearse the social skill with the student using real-life situations, (h) provide corrective feedback regarding the student's performance, (i) practice the social skill until the student is able to perform it exactly as described, and (j) plan when the skill could be used (see Table 13–7 for a detailed breakdown of the teaching behaviors adapted from Phillips et al., 1974, and Hazel et al., 1981a).

Besides being an effective instructional procedure, the teaching interaction procedure provides additional advantages because it (a) follows a structured format for teachers and students, (b) minimizes emotional reactions from teacher and students, (c) encourages incidental teaching, and (d) encourages preventive teaching. The key to successful implementation of the teaching interaction is to involve the student in the teaching procedure. For example, before defining the targeted social skill, the teacher should ask the students if they know what the skill means. Likewise, asking the students to provide rationales for why the skill is important to learn allows the student to think of how the skill can be integrated into everyday social interactions. By personalizing the social skill, the teacher may find that students are more willing to use the skill.

## Generalization of Skills

As social, problem-solving, and self-determination skills instruction has assumed increasing importance in the promotion of competent behaviors, the effectiveness of direct instructional procedures is well noted in the literature. Yet the success of acquiring these skills in

**TABLE 13–7** Teaching interaction

**Nonverbal Behavior**

1. Face the student.
2. Maintain eye contact.
3. Maintain a neutral or pleasant facial expression.

**Paraverbal Behavior**

4. Maintain a neutral tone of voice.
5. Speak at a moderate volume.

**Verbal Teaching Behavior**

6. Begin with a compliment related to the student's efforts and achievements.
7. Introduce the social skill and define what the social skill means.
8. Give a rationale for learning the skill and for using the skill with others.
9. Share an experience when you used the social skill or could have used the social skill.
10. Specify each behavior (e.g., nonverbal and verbal behavior) to be considered when exhibiting the skill.
11. Demonstrate or model the use of the skill.
12. Have the student rehearse the social skill. (Observe the student's behavior.)
13. Provide positive corrective feedback. State what the student did correctly. Provide suggestions for improvement. Demonstrate the corrective suggestions.
14. Practice the social skill with the student. (Make sure you do not prompt.)
15. Continue to provide corrective feedback to practice until the student masters (100%) the social skill in a novel situation.
16. Plan, with the student, when and where to use the social skill.

*Note:* Make sure the student participates throughout the lesson. To do so, ask questions and let the student share ideas and thoughts. Always praise the student for participating and rehearsing the social skill.

the instructional setting is only half the journey toward fluency of skills and eventual social and personal competence. Skill generalization is the other key factor in promoting social and personal competence.

Haring and Liberty (1990) define the generalization of social or self-determination skills as the use of acquired skills (a) with people other than the social or self-determination skills instructor, (b) across environments other than the instructional settings, and (c) applied to situations other than those experienced during instruction of the social or self-determination skill.

In the past, the generalization of any skill was thought to be a phenomenon that just happened (Stokes & Baer, 1977). Teachers were accustomed to the idea that once a skill was taught, a student could naturally perform the skill when needed. Generalization, though, was quickly recognized as the performance of acquired skills through the use of procedures specific to the skill (Stokes & Baer, 1977).

Acknowledging the problems with generalization of social and self-determination skills, researchers are currently investigating the use of different generalization strategies. A majority of these strategies are the outcome of the work by Stokes and Baer (1977). In their classic article, the authors outline a technology of generalization that can be used to facilitate the use of any acquired skill with different people, in different settings, and in varied situations. The following discussion outlines strategies that are based on the work of Stokes and Baer and provides examples of the identified strategies.

## Generalization Strategies and Examples

Stokes and Baer (1977) identify nine strategies that can be used to facilitate generalization of skills. The nine strategies will be presented under four categories: (a) antecedent strategies, (b) setting strategies, (c) consequent strategies, and (d) other strategies (Haring & Liberty, 1990). When available, examples of the strategies will be taken from investigations concerning the generalization of social skills for students who exhibit mild to moderate disabilities.

**Antecedent Strategies.** Haring and Liberty (1990) suggest that two generalization strategies can be categorized as antecedent strategies, or strategies introduced during the teaching of the social skill. By using antecedent strategies during instruction of the social skill, teachers are incorporating environmental factors that may prompt or maintain the use of the social skill outside the teaching setting.The use of antecedent strategies may accomplish the goal of acquisition and generalization through one intervention.The first antecedent strategy, program common stimuli, uses a predominant factor or a salient stimulus that is common to both the instructional setting and a generalization setting. A teacher, therefore, should consider what stimuli are present in both settings and then employ the salient stimulus (or stimuli) during the instruction of the social skill. A very obvious salient stimulus is exemplified by classroom peers. Using peers (especially peers from general education classes) to participate in the teaching, learning, or monitoring of social skills can facilitate the use of social skills.The second antecedent strategy used to facilitate generalization is sufficient exemplars.This strategy incorporates the teaching of several examples using the same direct teaching procedures, so generalization of social skills to new settings and new situations and responses can occur.An example of teaching sufficient exemplars can be seen in the study by Hazel et al. (1981b).These authors taught sufficient exemplars during the rehearsal portion of their teaching interaction.A new situation was used each time a student rehearsed the social skill.This continued until the student rehearsed the skill to 100% criteria in a novel role-playing situation. The outcome was generalization to hypothetical situations presented during posttesting of the social skills.

**Setting Strategies.** The second category of generalization strategies involves a strategy intervention that is implemented whenever the social skills behavior is desired.This strategy, sequential modification, is a tactic of planning a social skills program in every condition (i.e., across people, setting, or situation) in which generalization is desired. For example, a teacher might develop a program of study in social skills instruction whereby the teaching was provided in one classroom and the generalization of the acquired skills was assessed in different desired settings (other classrooms, cafeteria, and playground). If the generalization of the skills did not occur in the different settings, the teacher must teach the social skills, sequentially, in each setting until generalization occurs over all the desired settings.

**Consequence Strategies.** Haring and Liberty (1990) propose that a third category of generalization strategies deals with the reinforcement of social skill behaviors in the natural setting (outside the instructional setting). The reinforcement or punishment (i.e., consequences) of the social skill directly relates to the continued use of the social skill and, therefore, directly relates to the generalization of the behavior. The authors target three generalization strategies (Stokes & Baer, 1977) under this category: (a) introduce to natural maintaining contingencies, (b) use indiscriminable contingencies, and (c) train to generalize.

The first generalization strategy under the category of consequences is introduce to natural maintaining contingencies.This strategy deals with the use of people (or outcomes) who may reinforce the student for appropriate use of the social skill in the natural environment.Teaching the social skill to fluency can facilitate this strategy as well as make sure that the student experiences reinforcement for social skill performances. Although empirically based studies demonstrating the effectiveness of this strategy are not found in the social skills literature, teachers employ this strategy throughout the school year when they inform teachers and parents that a student has learned a particular skill and should be praised for the use of the skill in their classrooms or at home.

The use of reinforcement is highly desirable when one wishes to maintain a skill in any environment.The use of intermittent reinforcement can maintain a behavior for long periods of time (Kazdin, 2001).The use of indiscriminable contingencies, therefore, becomes another generalization strategy under the category of consequent strategies.This strategy is recognized when a student is unable to determine when reinforcement is going to occur for a desired behavior. Not knowing when reinforcement will occur makes students more likely to engage in the behavior in hope that a positive outcome will emerge.

The last strategy under the category of consequent strategies is the train-to-generalize strategy. This strategy can be described as a systematic use of instruction to facilitate generalization. A teacher can tell the student about generalization, model the generalized use of the social skill, and ask the student to use the skill.

**Other Strategies.** Haring and Liberty (1990) created a fourth "catch-all" category of other strategies.The strategies under this category are: (a) train loosely, (b) mediate generalization, and (c) train and hope.The strategy of train loosely is described as teaching social skills during every appropriate opportunity during the school day. This means that a teacher may elect to teach social skills using the context of the presenting classroom or school environment. By doing so, the teacher can enhance the possibility that students will begin to use their social skills in a variety of settings, with other people, and in different situations. This strategy has not been investigated through experimental procedures but can be demonstrated when teachers and parents use every opportunity to teach social skills to a student (e.g., parents often teach their children to say "please" and "thank you" at every available opportunity).

The second strategy in this category is the mediate generalization strategy. Using this generalization strategy, a teacher will instruct a student in the use of covert or overt behaviors that will facilitate remembering how and when to use a social skill. Most exemplified in the literature on social skill generalization for adolescents is the self-monitoring or self-control procedures. Self-monitoring procedures are taught to students so that they can remember to use the learned social skills in settings outside the teaching environment (e.g., Kiburtz, Miller, & Morrow, 1984).

Finally, Haring and Liberty (1990) (based on Stokes & Baer, 1977) identify the "train and hope" practice that is employed by many researchers and teachers alike. Actually, train and hope signifies the nonexistence of any generalization strategy. Providing social skills instruction, therefore, and then "hoping" the skills will occur across different settings, people, or situations exemplifies this aspect of generalization. Train and hope strategies are not recommended as they rarely produce generalization effects.

**Reflective Question 13–3:** ***What criteria would you use to select a social or self-determination curriculum for students in your classroom?***

## USING TECHNOLOGY IN YOUR SOCIAL OR SELF-DETERMINATION SKILLS PROGRAM

The use of technology in the field of social and self-determination skills is a new frontier. Although the programs and information are growing, we do not have a substantial amount of data to support the use of technology in the area of social skills. Most of the information we have encountered has focused on students' use of the Internet and its potential usefulness as a learning tool for children. The use of computer technology is an important form of learning, teaching, and communicating.

Critics of the Internet cite the perils of technology. Wallace (1999) reported a study that indicated 43% of school dropouts were staying up all night using the Internet. A common observation is the sense of isolation from so much use of the Internet. People blame excessive use of the Internet as reasons for the breakup of their marriages, and students state that their computer is their best friend (Eykyn, 1999). Clearly, there is controversy over technology as it relates to social interactions and social skills.

Because technology has the potential to isolate children and impede their face-to-face social interactions with others, teachers must carefully plan the use of technology. The following discussion will begin with the use of simple technological interventions and proceed with more sophisticated uses of technology with social and self-determination skills.

Teachers might start out using simple tools such as cell phones, digital cameras, and video cameras. By employing cell phones in the classroom, teachers might show students proper etiquette when using this technology. A discussion of cell phone rules and when to use the cell phone is important. How to talk to authority figures (e.g., employers) over the phone can be useful as well as how to leave a message that is meaningful to friends and authority figures.

Another useful classroom tool is the digital camera or a video camera. Teachers can use these tools to capture interactions between individuals and give appropriate feedback on the social behavior. Videotaping role-play situations and discussing the interactions can have great learning potential as well as being useful for the generalization of the skills.

Skouge, Kelly, O'Brien, and Thomas (2003) reported on the use of video cameras by students to create video stories about themselves. The student (and parents) can produce a self-advocacy film by initiating a story about his or her life and how others can help him or her reach the goals they have developed. Video stories can be used to promote "visualization" and self-modeling to create plays or stories to explore alternative futures and act out dreams. In this way, students are developing social and self-determination skills as well as learning how to communicate their goals and action plans to others.

Currently, many education-oriented publishing companies (e.g., Attainment Company) are marketing social skills program on computer disks. For the most part, these programs offer knowledge-based information about social situations and interactions. Students are able to view the programs on CDs (and sometimes videotapes). Some programs have workbooks as a companion to the program. Unfortunately, there are limited data to substantiate whether children benefit from these programs. One recommendation is that teachers use these programs as an initial introduction to the

## TECHNOLOGY *Tip*

Some researchers (e.g., Muscott & Gifford, 1994) have promoted the use of virtual reality applications for teaching skills to students who have social interaction problems with others. According to Muscott and Gifford, the technology of virtual reality is the interface between computers and humans in that it is an interactive, three-dimensional (3-D), multisensory experience. The virtual reality experience can be sophisticated enough that the immersion experience convinces the learner that he or she is actually in the simulation. During a successful virtual reality simulation, the learner can try out the social skill just acquired. In this way, the learner can see how effectively his or her performance of the skill was executed. This practice can be very helpful in learning to handle emotional or volatile situations. The learner can practice the skills without being in the actual situation.

At this point, virtual reality hardware and software are still expensive and limited. These barriers can make the use of these programs prohibitive. Nonetheless, the technology holds potential for enhancing social and self-determination programs.

skills. Role-playing and practice must follow in order that students demonstrate knowledge *and* performance of the skill.

**Reflective Question 13–4:** ***How can technology facilitate the generalization of acquired social skills?***

## ESTABLISHING A SOCIAL OR SELF-DETERMINATION SKILLS PROGRAM

Once a teacher decides that a social or self-determination skills program should be made part of the school curricula, preparation for implementing the program must begin. To do so, the teacher should follow the presented sequence of events: (a) identify students through observation and assessment, (b) develop students' social skills profiles, (c) consider the grouping of the students, (d) prepare for program implementation, (e) implement social skills teaching procedures, (f) evaluate student performances after each skill is taught, and (g) program for generalization of the learned social skills to the natural environment.

### Identify Students

The first step in establishing a social or self-determination skills program is to identify the students who are exhibiting interpersonal and personal problems in or outside the classroom environment. This may be done by observing student behaviors during classroom activities, using standardized adaptive behavior scales, and surveying significant other people (i.e., other teachers, parents, and peers) concerning the students' social behaviors. Once the teacher has gathered this first- and secondhand information, an analysis of the data may reveal that specific social skills are needed. At this point, the teacher will broaden the scope of information by isolating a set of specific social or self-determination skills and assessing the student's performance of each skill during simulated situations. From this information, the teacher can identify whether (a) skill components (e.g., recognizing that a skill should be used, nonverbal behaviors, verbal behaviors) of each skill are present in the student's repertoire and if (b) students are choosing not to use social skills that are in their repertoire (motivation problem). From this analysis, a final set of social or self-determination skills can be targeted for the overall needs of the students.

### Develop Student Profiles

After the teacher compiles a set of targeted skills for each student, a skills profile may be developed. The profile will illustrate the competency level of each skill and indicate which skills need to be taught. When a profile is constructed for each student, the teacher may wish to identify a group of social skills that seem to be common across all the students.

### Group Your Students

If a teacher plans to implement a social or self-determination skills program with a select number of students (rather than the entire class), it is wise to identify several aspects of the group's composition (Goldstein et al., 1998). An important consideration may be grouping students who are friends and would enjoy learning the social skills together. Although this may work well for the students, a teacher also must consider if a group of this composition would exhibit unmanageable behaviors; if

## DIVERSITY IN THE CLASSROOM *Tips*

**Cathy Kea** is a professor of special education at North Carolina State University. Her current research focuses on preparing teachers to design and deliver culturally responsive instruction in the classroom.

Social competence is a critical life skill needed by all students. Social skills correlate positively with school success and must be taught formally and informally throughout the curriculum. Students with and without disabilities or cultural differences who misperceive the social situation and choose the wrong option may find themselves rejected by peers, continuously being the recipients of harsh discipline consequences, or isolated from peers, family, and authority figures because of undesirable behaviors. All too often the behaviors of children from diverse populations are misunderstood and devalued, and a level of disconnectedness occurs in the teaching and learning process.

- **Building relationships is a must.** Know the value orientation standards for achievement, social taboos, relational patterns, communication styles, and motivational systems of diverse learners. Be personally inviting and create a family-type learning community in the classroom. Acknowledge how different cultural groups sanction behavior, celebrate accomplishments, and use rules of decorum and deference. Even when it's necessary to reject specific behaviors, respect, relate, and communicate acceptance of students. Manage classrooms with firm, consistent, and loving control. Employ culturally responsive discipline (culturally contextualized competence, caring, connectedness, and community).
- **Accommodating culture is essential to learning.** Social skills instruction is an integral part of the daily curriculum and should be taught explicitly as an academic content subject weekly/daily. Analyze the curriculum for cultural and linguistic and student relevance. Use cooperative learning and peer and cross-age tutoring strategies as a means to encourage and reinforce skill development and positive communal peer interactions. Organize learning as a social event rather than a competitive or individual endeavor. Create socially just and caring learning communities in the classroom, in which students' and teachers' voices, experiences, and perspectives are recognized and respected. Identify and affirm students' individual and cultural strengths. Children need to be continuously affirmed in their cultural connections.
- **Empower diverse parents in the teaching and learning process.** Create a welcoming environment for diverse parents by building relationships and providing information and resources to parents on an ongoing basis. All parents want their children to succeed; some need additional support. Identify family management techniques for discipline and problem solving. Verify preferred modes of communication and maintain frequent contacts through home notes and or a home resource notebook. Incorporate cultural values in the behavior intervention plan and develop a home–school contract or behavior management plan collaboratively with family members. Adapt interventions to the learning and lifestyles of the family.

Culturally responsive instruction and curricula can help prevent behavior problems, but classrooms and teachers must be personally and physically inviting. Students learn best when they are actively engaged and are co-constructors in the teaching and learning process. Relationships must be built with diverse learners and their families, and behavior interventions should use a strength-based approach rather than a punitive one. Diverse learners in need of social skill instruction can develop social competence if taught and affirmed in a caring, connected, culturally relevant learning school community.

so, a different grouping may be considered. Most often, authors of social skills curricula (e.g., Goldstein et al., 1998) suggest that teachers compose a group that is heterogeneous (males and females) in nature. Also, a group of students with varying intelligence is beneficial because students needing help can be paired with a peer who already knows the skill. The two students can work together in a tutor–tutee relationship.

Finally, a teacher may wish to consider the size of the skills instruction group. Although an entire class (15 or more) can engage in the skills program, teachers might find the behavioral rehearsal of the skills (role-playing) difficult to manage. This monitoring is especially crucial when establishing mastery performance criteria. On the other hand, more student participants can add to the diversity of the shared problems so that everyone can learn that other students have similar or worse problems. Sharing these experiences, coupled with learning how to deal with situations through the use of social and self-determination skills, may facilitate the generalization of the social skills among peers.

### Prepare for Program Implementation

Once the assessment and student groupings are established, preparation for the social skills teaching must take place. This preparation includes deciding when and where the teaching will take place (e.g., three times a week), making sure the teaching procedures are well understood (refer to the skill teaching section of this chapter), and explaining the program to the students (e.g., describing the social skills that will be learned, explaining the benefits of learning the social skills, enlisting their cooperation, and creating enthusiasm for learning the social skills).

### Implement the Program

The direct instructional procedures outlined in this chapter and in social and self-determination skills curricula have been experimentally evaluated to be some of the most effective methods for teaching skills to children and adolescents. In addition to these procedures, though, Hazel et al. (1981a) stress that teachers must exhibit other teaching behaviors. These behaviors include (a) controlling off-task behavior, (b) using students' names, (c) programming for student participation throughout the teaching process, (d) teaching at a lively pace to avoid boredom, (e) using praise continuously, (f) exhibiting enthusiasm during the teaching of social skills, (g) using humor whenever possible, (h) being sincere and interested in the successful acquisition and mastery of the social skills, (i) displaying a pleasant manner, and (j) being empathetic with the students.

Another aspect of teaching social skills that is not usually emphasized is teaching to mastery. Teachers should make sure that the students have learned the components of each social skill (e.g., use a learning strategy or memorize the skill for long-term retention) without hesitation and can then exhibit the skill at a 100% mastery in a novel role-playing situation during the social skills teaching sessions.

### Evaluate Student Performances

Once the students have reached a 100% mastery level in the social skill teaching setting, the teacher should evaluate the students' performances in the test setting or in the natural environment. Assessments that take place in the test setting allow the teacher to evaluate the student's individual performance on novel, simulated situations in a setting outside the teaching environment. Assessing the students' social skill performances in the natural environment may involve using confederate peers or teachers or arranging the environment so that the teacher can observe whether a student recognizes the need for the social skill and then engages in that particular social or self-determination skill. In either case, teachers are assessing some aspect of skill generalization and should use the information to program for further teaching of the social skill or to progress to the teaching of a new skill.

### Program for Generalization

Once the teacher determines that the students have acquired the targeted social skills, an analysis of whether the social skills are generalizing to the natural environment must be made. If students are not using their newly acquired skills, teachers should plan for and employ the generalization strategies (discussed earlier). Additionally, classroom activities may be planned so that students have opportunities to use their learned social and self-determination skills and teachers have opportunities to reinforce the students' use of their social and self-determination skills. The following Activities section provides activities that may facilitate the generalization of specific social and self-determination skills to the natural environment.

> Reflective Question 13–5: ***How can you enlist the cooperation, motivation, and enthusiasm of your students so that participation in a social skills program will be optimal?***

## MAKING IT WORK

Teaching social and self-determination skills within the classroom or in the community may prove to present challenges when students do not meet the expectations of the program. The following suggestions are taken from years of implementing social and self-determination skills programs as well as instructing teachers how to develop programs of their own.

### Schedule Regular Times for Instruction

With the many demands that teachers and students must adhere to, the idea of finding time to include one more thing is daunting. Nonetheless, if social and self-determination skills are to be learned, teachers will want to have a regular time to teach these skills. For example, these instructional times can be regular classes designated for teaching social skills, 20 minutes during each day of a particular class period, every Friday afternoon, or during some integrated curriculum series. The time or form will vary according to the particular teacher. The important idea here is that the instruction is regular and focused.

## Perfect the Skill of Modeling

As part of the direct instructional model, the teacher is to demonstrate or model how the skills should be used. Usually, a role-play situation is delineated and the teacher models how the skill is to be performed. It is during this time that teachers should give a flawless performance of the skill. The rationale behind this suggestion is that the students will perform the skill exactly how it was demonstrated. Therefore, if the teacher leaves out one or two skill steps during the modeling of the skill, the students are likely to leave out those same skill steps. Students usually perform what they see—even if the skill is not modeled correctly. So practice modeling the skill to perfection so students will follow suit.

## Develop Many Realistic Role-Play Situations Ahead of Time

A final step in the direct instructional model is the practice of the skill by the students. Usually, students do this via role-play situations. In order that students practice novel role-play situations (so they don't practice the same situation over and over again), teachers should generate many realistic situations for students to practice the skills. The situations can range from easy to difficult and cover an array of people, events, and opportunities. By employing these varied situations, teachers are using the "multiple exemplar" strategy that can promote generalization of the skill.

## Ensure the Development of Fluency in Three Areas

Students must develop some degree of fluency if the execution of a skill is to be successful. Three areas have been identified as needing fluency in order to be successful in the execution of a skill. First, students must be able to recognize when a specific skill should be used. Many times, students learn 5 to 8 skills and become confused when to use each skill in different situations. Often they try to use the wrong skill to accommodate a particular situation because they do not recognize the characteristics of the situation and how to match it with the specific learned skills. Teachers can build fluency in this area by playing games that require a student to recognize which skill should be used. For example, call out a situation (e.g., your friends are trying to get you to cheat on a test) and see if they can come up with the correct skill to use (i.e., resisting peer pressure).

A second area of fluency is the knowledge of the skill and skill steps. When teaching the skill steps to the students, develop some strategy that students can used to remember all the skill steps of the skill. Some devices that have been used are memorization strategies or mnemonic strategies that facilitates the learning of the skill steps. If students know all the skill steps, their speech will flow from one step to the next when interacting with others. In this way, the student will not hesitate and will seem more confident in executing the skill.

A final area of fluency is the performance of the skill. Plan that the students try to meet a goal of 100% accuracy when performing a skill. If a student can reach a 100% accuracy rate during the acquisition stage of learning the skill, that same student will probably maintain the skill at 80% over time. This maintenance score will ensure that the student is performing the skill at a fairly fluent level and can be successful in his or her interactions with others.

## Plan for Generalization of the Skills

Of course, the primary goal of teaching social and self-determination skills is to have students be able to use the skills outside of the instructional situation. Planning to use generalization strategies can only help ensure the success of the students. Employ other people to mentor students outside the classroom so their social and self-determination skills can be perfected. Plan with students so they know that they have tools to use on their behalf. Provide opportunities for the skill to be used in safe situations so feedback can be given and student performances will improve.

## SUMMARY

In a society where emotional problems, verbal and physical aggression, and failure among youth are becoming the most predominant problems within schools, the importance of social competence and self-determination skills must not be underestimated. Teachers who exhibit the skills to teach these behaviors are equally important. It is necessary, therefore, to make deliberate efforts to train future teachers in the area of social and self-determination skills. Through concerted efforts, teachers and parents may foster independent behaviors and appropriate interactions that contribute to successful individuals.

The purpose of this chapter is to provide information to teachers wanting to establish a social and self-determination skills program for students exhibiting failure in the classroom and community. A history of the area of social skills is presented, with a rationale for teaching social competency skills (social skills and social problem-solving skills) to students. With knowledge of this history and rationales, the reader is then introduced to assessment procedures and program content in social and self-determination skills. This discussion includes examples of different social skills programs as well as new and innovative self-determination skills programs. The chapter then addresses the instruction of these skills and how to promote generalization of social and self-determination skills. Of utmost importance is the presentation of activities that teachers can use when facilitating the use of social or self-determination skills in their classrooms. It is not the intent, however, for these activities to be confused with instruction in these skills. For students to gain the benefits of these skills, the following components must be initiated: (a) structured learning, (b) guided practice, (c) individual practice, and (d) planned generalization of the skills.

## ACTIVITIES

### ELEMENTRY LEVEL

1. Institute a regular "Friday Shakes" activity in which students line up at the door before Friday dismissal and the teacher shakes the hand of each student and gives him or her some personalized compliment or praise (Kataoka, personal correspondence, 1990).
2. As students learn appropriate behaviors and social skills in the classroom, they should start identifying these behaviors in other students. Place a box with a slot in a prominent location and label it the "Praise Box" (or whatever creative title is desired). As you and the students (stress student participation) observe someone doing acts of kindness, consideration, encouragement, and learning social skills in and out of the classroom, have them write a note (or write a note yourself) telling of the appropriate activity, noting the time, the place, and the name of the person doing the behavior. At the end of the day or week, open the box and give all praise notes to the named students. Be sure that each student gets at least one "praise" note per time (Hayden, 1980).
3. In class, during a specified time, have each student find and say one thing he or she likes about two classmates.
4. Develop specific routines to welcome new students to the classroom. During class meetings, ask the students, "What things would you want to know if you were new in this school?" Make a list of informational facts about the school so that the students can answer any questions a new student might have.
5. Assign "buddies" to new students in your classroom. The buddy is responsible for introducing the new student to peers and other teachers as well as for asking the new student to participate in different social situations (e.g., eat lunch together, play games, sit together at school assemblies).

### MIDDLE LEVEL

1. Develop a specific skill for welcoming visitors to the classroom. Each week, assign a student to greet visitors, ask them to sit down, and perform any other task that may make the visitors more comfortable in the classroom.
2. Read a story involving a particular social interaction problem or issue. Through a class discussion, let the students identify the problem, list possible solutions and the outcomes of each solution, and decide which solution would be most beneficial to all involved.
3. Instead of just playing team sports, have students work together to decide the best offensive and defensive strategies to use during a game. The position of each team member can be discussed and agreed upon by the team as a whole instead of being assigned by the coach.
4. During the morning class meeting, have students talk about personal or interpersonal problems around school and the community. Conduct a problem-solving session where peers provide possible solutions to the problems. Then, as a class, decide on the best solution for all involved and how the solution will be implemented. Role-play the implementation of the solution, as it often requires the use of many social skills. Always follow up to see if the implemented solution worked.
5. Each time a group of students seems to be disagreeing, have them resolve the conflict by each "giving and taking" a little through the skill of negotiation. Make sure you foster a "win-win" situation.

## SECONDARY LEVEL

1. Teach students the skill of negotiation. Each week, select a student to be the peer mediator who will facilitate a conflict resolution when it occurs between two or more persons. Make sure the peer mediator is well liked and respected among the peers.
2. Have students develop goals that relate to their learned social skills. For example, one goal may be this: "I will use my skill of problem solving three times this week." Have students monitor their achievements with goal accomplishment sheets and graphs.
3. Have each student think of a social skill upon which he or she would like to improve, and write this goal on a card (e.g., "I will use my Accepting Criticism skill with Mr. K__________________"). The students check off each time they used or did not use the skill on the card (which is filed in a box in the classroom) every day for 2 weeks. At the end of 1 week and at the end of 2 weeks, have the students discuss their progress and any changes they recognize.
4. Arrange for professionals from the community to come visit your class. People involved in real estate, dentists, telephone operators, and so forth can provide information that students can seek out. As a follow-up, have the professional agree to mentor a student at the work cite for one day. The student can list the professional behavior, social skills, and self-determination skills that are expected and required at the professionals' work situation.
5. Keep a problem box in your classroom. Students may write down problems and put them in the box. Once a week, take time to discuss the problems in a group. Have students generate solutions to the problems and discuss the possible outcomes to each problem. Emphasize that problem solving is a way to persist toward a certain goal or to overcome a barrier.

CHAPTER

# 14

# Functional Academics and Career Development

Whatever goal of education one claims or espouses to, ultimately we want our children and those of others to be able to function in the ever-changing society in which we live. We want them to be productive and contributing citizens. All the skill and content-related topics that have been covered in the book up to this point contribute in various ways to this goal.

Functioning effectively at home, in postsecondary education, in the workplace, or in community settings requires many varied skills. Unfortunately, most students are directly taught very few of the requisite skills needed to deal with the demands of adulthood that we all face on a daily basis. The assumptions that students automatically adjust to community living after exiting formal schooling and that they will demonstrate proficiency with a wide range of everyday challenges are erroneous, as the evidence from the many follow-up studies has shown.

The intent of this chapter is to explore a variety of topics that relate to dealing successfully with the many demands of adulthood that await all students who are moving into a new lifestyle when high school ends. The first section of the chapter discusses the importance of teaching functional topics to all students. The second section establishes a framework for conceptualizing and operationalizing the specific demands of adulthood. The third section discusses the functional implications of the four key subject areas (language arts, math, science, social studies) around which curricula are designed. The next section provides an overview of career development and vocational preparation that is essential for students. The fifth section of the chapter covers formal and informal ways to assess functional competence. The last major section focuses on making it work and includes a number of critical topics related to teaching real-life content in schools today with an emphasis on how to integrate real-life topics into the general education curriculum and how to align this content with state content and performance standards.

## FUNCTIONAL SKILLS AND KNOWLEDGE

This section provides some basic information about functional knowledge and skills. A discussion of terminology is followed by some examples of what is meant by this concept.

### Terminology Defined

The term *functional* is used in different ways and its meaning is very much determined by context. A wide range of terms has been used to convey the concept of functional skills. Table 14-1 lists some of the most frequently used terms to describe those skills that are needed to "function" in everyday life. Cronin, Patton, and Wood (2007) explain this point.

> At times, the meaning associated with the terms is interchangeable; however, at other times, differences in meaning are apparent. For instance, the term *applied academics* suggests skills that are clearly different from self-care skills of toileting and grooming that are associated with *daily living skills*. (p. 2)

Functionality, as stated above, is also determined by context. It is safe to say that the term *functional* typically refers to practical types of everyday living skills. However, certain higher-order skills involving complex math calculations have "functionality" in an engineering application. Nevertheless, the term, as used in this chapter will follow the more common application to everyday living situations.

This chapter will cover three major functional topics: functional academics, other selected real-life skills, and occupational/vocational preparation. Each of these is defined below.

- **Functional academics:** the real-world application of core academic content and related skills that are meaningful and relevant to an individual's

**TABLE 14–1** Terminology used to describe functional skills

| | |
|---|---|
| Activities of daily living | Functional curriculum |
| Applied academics | Functional literacy |
| Career education | Functional skills |
| Daily living skills | Independent living skills |
| Everyday intelligence (practical & social intelligence) | Life skills |
| Functional academics | Real-life skills |
| | Survival skills |

life now and in the future. (Table 14-2 lists some examples of functional academic content.)

- **Real-life skills:** specific competencies (i.e., knowledge, skills, application) of local and cultural relevance needed to perform everyday activities across a variety of settings.
- **Occupational/vocational preparation:** a variety of developmentally related events and activities needed to prepare an individual for the world of work immediately after high school or after pursuing further education or additional training.

**TABLE 14–2** Examples of functional academic activities

| *Academic Content Area* | *Examples of Functional Activities* |
|---|---|
| Reading | Read a newspaper article |
| | Read a recipe |
| | Read the signs on restroom doors |
| | Read instructions for video game |
| | Read a job application |
| | Read a course schedule of classes for college |
| Expressive Writing | Write a thank-you note |
| | Dictate a personal story |
| | Write a biography for college entrance application |
| Math | Add sales tax to purchase order |
| | Use calculator to add grocery item totals |
| | Compare prices at a local video store |
| | Calculate income tax return |
| | Compute square footage for a carpentry task |
| Science | Calculate boiling point of candy recipe |
| | Use medication chart |
| | Plant and harvest vegetable garden |
| | Identify weather to select appropriate clothing |
| Science (Health) | Brush teeth and practice proper oral hygiene |
| | Plan balanced meals |
| | Identify and purchase items for class first aid kit |
| | Identify health services in the community |
| | Label sexual feelings and attitudes |
| Social Studies | Register to vote |
| | Identify cultural holidays and customs |
| | Identify headlines in newspapers |
| | Determine bus route in the community |

*Source:* Adapted from *Functional Curriculum for Elementary, Middle, and Secondary Age Students with Special Needs*, 2nd ed., by P. Wehman, and V. Kregel, 2004. Copyright 2004 by PRO-ED, Inc. Adapted with permission.

The term *functional curriculum* must be distinguished from the terms presented above, as it is used frequently in the field of special education. This term refers to a specifically designed scope and sequence of content coverage (i.e., curriculum) that is completely focused on functional topics. Clark (1994) defined functional curriculum as "a way of delivering instructional content that focuses on the concepts and skills needed by all students with disabilities in the areas of personal-social, daily living, and occupational adjustment" (p. 37). Valletutti, Bender, and Baglin (2007) simply state "that life is the curriculum" (p. 1).

### Relationship of Functional Topics to Traditional Scholastic Areas

Understanding the relationship of knowledge and skills associated with the general education curriculum to functional topics is very important. The merging of scholastic instruction and instruction on functional topics provides a likely solution to the balance between addressing content and performance standards and meeting the functional needs of students. Figure 14–1 provides secondary-level examples of how the integration of these concepts into students' programs can take place. Activities emphasizing functional application of scholastic skills can, and should, be developed at the elementary level as well [see Cronin, Patton, & Wood (2007) for elementary examples].

> Reflective Question 14–1: ***In your own words, how would you define functionality in terms of curriculum? How can this concept relate to the specific subject areas that commonly constitute the standard curriculum?***

## DEMANDS OF ADULTHOOD

Young adults with special needs face an array of challenges when they move from high school to community living. The identification of critical functional skills needed in adulthood should be based on the behaviors that will be demanded of those individuals in the specific community settings in which they will live, learn, and work. The identification of the major demands of life after high school provides the foundation for local school systems to address the need to ensure competency across a range of everyday living areas.

A number of taxonomies exist depicting the **demands of adulthood** (see Cronin, Patton, & Wood, 2007, p. 16). One viable source on which to base the organization of functionally oriented curricula is the transition planning literature. Additional sources of information include various curricular materials.

Two curricular sources that provide a framework for understanding the demands of everyday adult life and that are highlighted in this chapter include Cronin, Patton, and Wood's (2007) Major Life Demands model and Brolin's (2004) Life-Centered Career Education (LCCE) model. Table 14–3 provides an overview of these two models. As can be seen, the Major Life Demands model is organized according to 6 adult domains and 23 subdomains. These subdomains are further subdivided into 146 major life demands. The LCCE model includes 3 major domains and 22 competencies that are further subdivided into 97 subcompetencies.

The list of subcompetencies used by Brolin (2004), the list of major life demands developed by Cronin and colleagues (2007), and the functional competencies that can be found in other sources tend to correlate with one another. One resource is not necessarily any better than another; they all represent reasonable efforts to help practitioners develop meaningful programs for students.

Once the major life demand areas are recognized, specific life skills associated with these areas can be identified. This is an important level of activity because it addresses local needs and personal relevance.

> Reflective Question 14–2: ***How does a consideration of the demands of adulthood allow teachers to develop a "top down" curricular focus?***

## FUNCTIONAL ACADEMICS

Functional academics refers to the real-world application of content and skills that are associated with the core subjects areas. Traditionally, functional academics have been restricted to three areas: reading, writing, and math. We have expanded the view of functional academics to include the other core subject areas of science and social studies. Furthermore, we are collapsing functional reading and writing under the category of functional language arts.

A key distinction needs to be made in regard to the areas included under the term *functional academics*. Functional reading and functional writing really refer to skill areas, whereas functional math, science, and social studies refer to knowledge acquisition and skill performance, as depicted in Figure 14–2. What this means is that functional reading and writing are essential tool skills that are not content specific; they are used in a

**FIGURE 14–1** Secondary matrix: Relationship of scholastic skills to functional topics

| | *Employment/ Education* | *Home and Family* | *Leisure Pursuits* | *Community Involvement* | *Emotional/ Physical Health* | *Personal Responsibility and Relationships* |
|---|---|---|---|---|---|---|
| ***Reading*** | Read classified ads for jobs. | Interpret bills. | Locate and understand movie information in a newspaper. | Follow directions on tax forms. | Comprehend directions on medication. | Read letters from friends. |
| ***Writing*** | Write a letter of application for a job. | Write checks. | Write for information on a city to visit. | Fill in a voter registration form. | Fill in your medical history on forms. | Send thank-you notes. |
| ***Listening*** | Understand oral directions of a procedure change. | Comprehend oral directions for making dinner. | Listen to a weather forecast to plan outdoor activity. | Understand campaign ads. | Attend lectures on stress. | Take turns in a conversation. |
| ***Speaking*** | Ask your boss for a raise. | Discuss morning routines with your family. | Inquire about tickets for a concert. | State your opinion at a school board meeting. | Describe symptoms to a doctor. | Give feedback to a friend about the purchase of a CD or DVD. |
| ***Math Applications*** | Understand the difference between net and gross pay. | Compute the cost of doing laundry in a laundromat versus at home. | Calculate the cost of a dinner out versus eating at home. | Obtain information for a building permit. | Use a thermometer. | Plan the costs of a date. |
| ***Problem Solving*** | Settle a dispute with a coworker. | Decide how much to budget for rent. | Role-play appropriate behaviors for various plates. | Know what to do if you are the victim of fraud. | Select a donor. | Decide how to ask someone for a date. |
| ***Survival Skills*** | Use a prepared career planning packet. | List emergency phone numbers. | Use a shopping center directory. | Mark a calendar for important dates (e.g., recycling, garbage collection). | Use a system to remember to take vitamins. | Develop a system to remember birthdays. |
| ***Personal/ Social*** | Apply appropriate interview skills. | Help a child with homework. | Know the rules of a neighborhood pool. | Locate self-improvement classes. | Get a yearly physical exam. | Discuss how to negotiate a price at a flea market. |

*Source:* From *Life Skills Instruction* by M. E. Cronin, J. R. Patton, and S. J. Woods, 2007. Copyright 2007 by PRO-ED, Inc. Reprinted with permission.

variety of ways and across many different settings. For instance, the reading as an academic area does not have content; the content comes from other areas such as literature, science, or social studies. Functional math, science, and social studies are content-laden and, as a result, a significant amount of information (facts, concepts) is considered part of the discipline. There is no question that, in addition to the knowledge that is imparted in these subjects, certain specific skills are typically developed in these subject areas as well (e.g., inquiry skills in science, problem-solving skills in math, research skills in social studies).

**TABLE 14–3** Models of adult functioning

| *Model* | *Adult Domain/Curriculum Area* | *Subdomains/Competency Areas* |
|---|---|---|
| Major Life Demands (Cronin, Patton, & Wood 2007) | Employment/education | General job skills<br>General education/training considerations<br>Employment setting<br>Career refinement and reevaluation |
| | Home and family | Home management<br>Financial management<br>Family life<br>Childrearing |
| | Leisure pursuits | Indoor activities<br>Outdoor activities<br>Community/neighborhood activities<br>Travel<br>Entertainment |
| | Community involvement | Citizenship<br>Community awareness<br>Services/resources |
| | Physical/emotional health | Physical health<br>Emotional health |
| | Personal responsibility and relationships | Personal confidence/understanding<br>Goal setting<br>Self-improvement<br>Relationships<br>Personal expression |
| Life-Centered Career Education (Brolin, 2004) | Daily living skills | Managing personal finances<br>Selecting and managing a household<br>Caring for personal needs<br>Raising children and meeting marriage responsibilities<br>Buying, preparing, and consuming food<br>Buying and caring for clothing<br>Exhibiting responsible citizenship<br>Utilizing recreational facilities and engaging in leisure<br>Getting around the community |
| | Personal-social skills | Achieving self-awareness<br>Acquiring self-confidence<br>Achieving socially responsible behavior<br>Maintaining good interpersonal skills<br>Achieving independence<br>Making adequate decisions<br>Communicating with others |
| | Occupational guidance and preparation | Knowing and exploring occupational possibilities<br>Selecting and planning occupational choices<br>Exhibiting appropriate work habits and behavior<br>Seeking, securing, and maintaining employment<br>Exhibiting sufficient physical-manual skills<br>Obtaining specific occupational skills |

*Source:* Adapted from *Infusing Real-Life Topics into Existing Curricula at the Elementary, Middle, and High School Levels: Recommended Procedures and Instructional Examples*, by J. R. Patton, M. E. Cronin, and S. Wood, 1999, Austin, TX: PRO-ED.

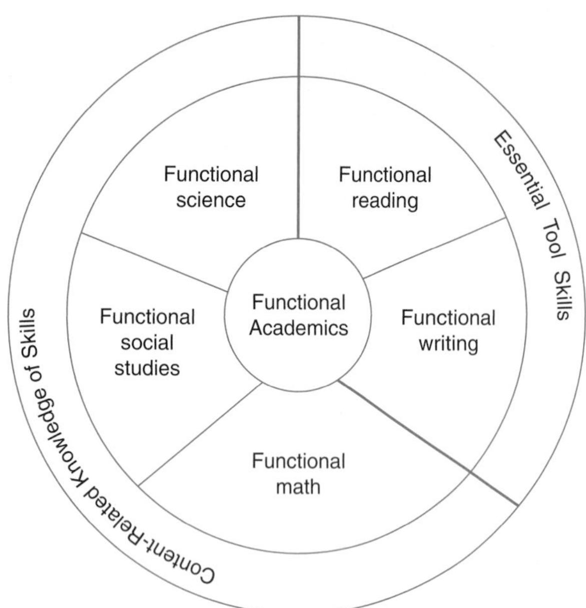


**FIGURE 14–2** Functional academics components and areas of emphasis

The general education curriculum is composed of four major subject areas for which content and performance standards have been created and on which students are tested regularly throughout their school careers. As indicated at the beginning of this section and to remain in line with the organization of the general education curriculum, we have conceptualized functional academics in the following way:

- **Functional language arts:** includes functional reading and functional writing
- **Functional math:** focuses on math content in the areas of money management and other measurement applications (volumetric, linear, temporal, temperature, weight)
- **Functional science:** focuses on science content as it relates to life (especially health), physical, and environmental science in the everyday world
- **Functional social studies:** focuses on social studies content that relates to community involvement and citizenship

Specific real-life applications for all these areas are listed in Tables 14–4 to 14–8 and discussed in the following sections. Although the tables are comprehensive, they will not include every possible situation where functional competence is needed. We have organized each of the tables into five major life areas: everyday living, school, community, work, and leisure.

## Functional Language Arts (Reading and Writing)

The subject area of language arts, at the elementary level, is dedicated to the development of critical tool skills in reading and writing that will be needed in school, at home, in the community, and in the workplace. As students move to the secondary level, critical reading and writing skills are emphasized. This subject area requires students to be able to read a variety of different types of narrative and expository material.

The functional application of language arts includes a number of areas that individuals encounter everyday. An extensive list of areas in which reading is needed in the real world is provided in Table 14–4.

In addition to developing competence in comprehending a vast array of textual material, as highlighted in Table 14–4, students must also achieve mastery of other types of reading skills. For instance, the ability to scan and skim textual material has high functional value in higher education as well as in daily life. These reading skills as well as other reading skills were discussed in Chapter 12. Hoover and Patton (2007) provide more detailed coverage on what these skills are and how to teach them.

Although not as extensive and arguably not as devastating if one has problems in this area, the need to be able to write in everyday life occurs in many different ways, as suggested in Table 14–5. Unless one chooses a career in which large amounts of writing are required, most of the functional applications involve short writing tasks. Frequently writing tasks are coupled with the need to read materials as well (e.g., completing an application). For those who pursue further education after high school, writing demands will often be encountered.

## Functional Math

The idea of teaching functional math has been around for a long time. It has been a major component of many life skills programs over the years. One of the first comprehensive resources written for teachers to use with learners with special needs was a book entitled *Functional Mathematics for the Mentally Retarded* (Peterson, 1972).

Public schools typically offered a course called "consumer mathematics" or "practical mathematics" until recently, as part of the general education curriculum. The No Child Left Behind Act and other aspects of educational reform has shifted the curricular landscape, resulting in different requirements, such as algebra.

**TABLE 14–4** Functional reading: Real-life applications

| *Functional Setting* | *Specific Skills* |
|---|---|
| | ***Individual can read:*** |
| Everyday living | • personal information (name, address, phone number)<br>• important documents:<br>  • contracts (e.g., leases)<br>  • policies (e.g., insurance)<br>  • warranty information<br>  • terms of agreement (e.g., purchase of software)<br>• tax-related documents<br>• mail:<br>  • personal mail<br>  • bills<br>  • advertisements<br>• manuals:<br>  • appliances<br>  • equipment<br>  • car/truck<br>  • technology<br>  • driver's license material<br>• various print materials:<br>  • catalogs<br>  • telephone book<br>• directions:<br>  • recipes<br>  • food preparation<br>  • taking medicine<br>  • laundry recommendations<br>  • assembling materials<br>• documents from service providers (e.g., plumber, vet)<br>• shopping-related material:<br>  • receipts for items purchased<br>  • return policy information<br>• warning labels<br>• applications (e.g., credit cards)<br>• charts and tables |
| School | • course schedules<br>• syllabi<br>• textual material:<br>  • textbooks<br>  • required readings<br>  • printed class materials (e.g., handouts)<br>• in-class material:<br>  • exam materials<br>  • slides shown in class<br>  • material written on board<br>• Internet material:<br>  • searches<br>  • websites<br>• menus—cafeteria<br>• material posted on bulletin boards<br>• policies, rules, regulations of the school, dorm |
| Community | • functional signage:<br>  • restrooms designations (men, women)<br>  • warnings (e.g., "danger") |

(*continued*)

**TABLE 14–4** (continued)

| *Functional Setting* | *Specific Skills* |
|---|---|
| | ***Individual can read:*** |
| | • directives (e.g., "keep off the grass")<br>• informational (e.g., "men working")<br>• descriptive signage:<br>  • road/street<br>  • business names<br>  • advertisements/billboards<br>  • notices, announcements, directives<br>  • posters<br>• procedural signage:<br>  • directions on how to use (e.g., gas pump)<br>  • directions on where to go<br>• menus in restaurants<br>• shopping-related material:<br>  • hours of operation information<br>  • unit price data<br>• schedules (e.g., bus)<br>• maps/other visual materials:<br>  • directory of businesses (e.g., at a mall)<br>  • room location in a building (e.g., courthouse)<br>  • park<br>  • campus |
| Workplace | • applications<br>• policy manuals<br>• notices, memos (print or electronic)<br>• job-related manuals<br>• reports and other documents<br>• Internet material:<br>  • searches<br>  • websites |
| Leisure | • newspaper(s):<br>  • front page<br>  • local/state news<br>  • weather information<br>  • sports<br>  • business section<br>  • everyday section<br>  • classified ads<br>  • special advertisements<br>• local entertainment periodicals<br>• magazines<br>• expository/narrative material:<br>  • books—fiction<br>  • books—nonfiction<br>  • short stories<br>  • poetry<br>• comic books<br>• directions to boardgames, card activities, etc.<br>• travel brochures |

**TABLE 14–5** Functional writing: Real-life applications

| *Functional Setting* | *Specific Skills* | |
|---|---|---|
| | *Individual can write:* | *Individual can complete:* |
| Everyday Living | • personal information (name, address, phone number)<br>• letters:<br>  • personal<br>  • business<br>  • action (e.g., complaint)<br>• notes:<br>  • to others<br>  • on behalf of others (e.g., notes to school for children)<br>• phone messages<br>• information from other sources (e.g., telephone book)<br>• greeting cards (e.g., birthday) | • bills<br>• legal documents:<br>  • leases<br>  • contracts<br>• tax forms<br>• order forms<br>• product registration forms (print or Internet) |
| School | • in-class products:<br>  • activities that are part of the class session<br>  • assignments/information given in class<br>• course requirements:<br>  • papers<br>  • reports<br>  • other projects involving writing<br>• exams/quizzes:<br>  • essay<br>  • short-answer<br>• notes from:<br>  • in-class lectures/presentations<br>  • PowerPoint slides/board<br>  • assigned readings<br>  • material from researching a topic (e.g., searchers)<br>• messages to fellow students, instructor, or others (print or e-mail) | • course registration materials<br>• school-related forms:<br>  • housing<br>  • health services |
| Community | • directions for locating a street address | • bank deposit/withdrawal/transfer slip<br>• surveys |
| Workplace | • memos/e-mail messages<br>• reports | • job application<br>• job-related forms (e.g., W-4)<br>• grievance form<br>• quality control materials |
| Leisure | • personal journal/diary<br>• e-mails, text messages, instant messages with friends<br>• creative writing products | • puzzles involving writing (e.g., crossword) |

As a result, courses such as consumer math or practical math have been dropped from the curriculum in many school districts. This is too bad because no other course that was part of the general education curriculum had more "functional" value than this one for students. The usual content of practical math courses included units on topics such as (Staudacher & Turner, 1990):

- On Your Own (budgeting)
- Earning a Paycheck
- Banking and Saving (using a checking accounts)
- Selecting Housing
- Buying and Preparing Food
- Buying Personal Items
- Owning a Vehicle
- Cash or Credit
- Recreation, Travel, and Entertainment

Everyday life is full of situations where math knowledge and skills are needed. What might be surprising is that a great deal of the math that we use on a daily basis involves estimation and approximations—not precise math. For instance, most of us estimate how long it will take to get to work or we have a general idea of how much money is in our checking account. Table 14-6 organizes the functional areas where some degree of math competence is needed to deal successfully with the everyday demands of adulthood.

## Functional Science

As noted earlier, functional science is not a concept that has been used often. However, the implication that certain topics in science have functional utility is no

**TABLE 14–6** Functional math: Real-life applications

<table>
<tr><th>Functional Setting</th><th>Specific Skills</th></tr>
<tr><td></td><td>Individual can use math skills in the following areas:</td></tr>
<tr><td>Everyday Living</td><td>
Money management:
<ul>
<li>budgeting income and expenses</li>
<li>banking-related services:
<ul>
<li>checking and savings accounts</li>
<li>online banking</li>
<li>credit card use:
<ul><li>APR</li><li>credit limits</li><li>payment cycles</li></ul></li>
<li>monitor investments</li>
<li>retirement planning</li>
<li>credit rating status</li>
</ul></li>
<li>paying bills:
<ul><li>due dates</li><li>payment options</li><li>late fees, penalties</li></ul></li>
<li>insurance:
<ul><li>life</li><li>disability</li><li>home/rental</li><li>long-term care</li></ul></li>
<li>paying fines/penalties</li>
<li>paying taxes</li>
<li>making and receiving change</li>
</ul>
Living arrangements:
<ul>
<li>locating a place to live</li>
<li>comparison shopping</li>
<li>costs and affordability:
<ul><li>rent or mortgage</li><li>initial closing costs</li><li>ongoing fees</li><li>taxes</li><li>insurance</li><li>moving costs</li><li>utilities</li></ul></li>
</ul>
Home management:
<ul>
<li>food preparation:
<ul>
<li>scheduling meals throughout week</li>
<li>measuring amounts for recipes</li>
<li>cooking times</li>
<li>appliances/equipment usage around the home:
<ul><li>phone</li><li>clocks (digital and analog)</li><li>timer (for cooking)</li><li>microwave</li><li>stove/oven/crock pot</li><li>washer/dryer</li><li>thermostat</li></ul></li>
</ul></li>
<li>home repair and maintenance:
<ul>
<li>seasonal needs</li>
<li>repair and upgrades:
<ul><li>linear measurement</li></ul></li>
<li>yard maintenance</li>
<li>contrast for services</li>
</ul></li>
</ul>
Automobile/truck:
<ul>
<li>comparison shopping</li>
<li>costs and affordability:
<ul><li>price</li><li>insurance</li><li>maintenance costs</li><li>fuel costs</li><li>depreciation</li></ul></li>
<li>payment options</li>
<li>scheduling:
<ul><li>routine maintenance</li><li>repairs</li></ul></li>
</ul>
Heath-related:
<ul>
<li>health management:
<ul><li>caloric intake</li><li>nutritional content of food</li><li>exercise schedule</li><li>measure weight of self and others</li></ul></li>
<li>budgeting medical/dental costs:
<ul><li>regular check-ups</li><li>treating problems</li></ul></li>
<li>illness identification and treatment:
<ul><li>taking temperature</li><li>monitoring of conditions (e.g., blood pressure, sugar levels, weight)</li></ul></li>
</ul>
</td></tr>
<tr><td>School</td><td>
<ul>
<li>budgeting:
<ul><li>finances</li><li>meal account</li></ul></li>
<li>purchasing, school-related materials (books, equipment)</li>
<li>time management:
<ul>
<li>hours needed to graduate</li>
<li>scheduling of courses</li>
<li>scheduling of time for:
<ul><li>study, test preparation, projects</li><li>extracurricular activities</li><li>work responsibilities</li></ul></li>
</ul></li>
</ul>
</td></tr>
</table>

**TABLE 14–6** (continued)

| *Functional Setting* | *Specific Skills* |
|---|---|
| | ***Individual can use math skills in the following areas:*** |
| | • meetings<br>• rest and relaxation |
| Community | • paying for various transportation services<br>• shopping/purchasing:<br>  • personal items<br>  • groceries<br>  • services (e.g., cell phone)<br>  • commodities (e.g., gas)<br>• banking services:<br>  • ATM<br>  • walk-in services<br>  • drive-through services<br>• restaurants:<br>  • menu use<br>  • payment<br>  • tipping<br>• using specific devices:<br>  • vending machines<br>  • stamp machines |
| Workplace | • pay/salary:<br>  • wages/income<br>  • deductions (taxes, social security, retirement, insurance)<br>  • commission<br>• hours worked (including overtime)<br>• benefits (number of personal/sick days, vacation)<br>• scheduled holidays<br>• time management (quotas, deadlines)<br>• specific math skills related to a particular job (e.g., truck driver—miles driven, amount of gas used, etc.)<br>• dues |
| Leisure | • home entertainment (costs—purchase/rental, math needed to use):<br>  • TV<br>  • VCR, DVD player, Tivo<br>  • electronic devices<br>• games/sports:<br>  • keeping score<br>• membership fees—clubs, organizations<br>• subscription costs (newspaper, magazines, online services)<br>• hobbies:<br>  • measurement skills<br>  • costs of equipment, supplies, etc.<br>• entertainment costs<br>• vacation/travel:<br>  • scheduling<br>  • budgeting<br>• playing the lottery |

different than making the same claim in math. Nonetheless, the term *functional science* may be alien to many professionals.

The idea of considering the functional linkage of science facts, concepts, and skills to everyday lives of people is straightforward. Many topics covered in life, physical, and environmental science have real-world applications, as documented in Table 14-7.

Functional science extends beyond basic, simple science knowledge and skills competence; it also involves being scientifically literate. This notion is embodied in the idea that "Scientifically literate people are able to use thought processes and the scientific knowledge they have acquired to think about and make sense of many ideas, claims, and events they encounter in their everyday lives" (American Association for the Advancement of Science, 1993, in Sunal and Sunal, 2003).

Science is one of easiest subjects to relate to one's everyday world, as it is all around us. Aside from the benefit of having access to functional content that students need to know, another key reason exists for linking science topics covered in textbooks and in class to real-world situations to which students can relate: Doing so increases the chance that they will retain what is being presented.

## Functional Social Studies

If the term *functional science* seemed strange at first, then *functional social studies* is likely to really seem odd. However, like science and math, the subject area of social studies includes many topics that have relevance to everyday life. One could argue, using the same rationale as was used in functional science, that every student should leave school being literate in a range of functional social studies topics, as identified in Table 14-8.

One area that is discussed in social studies and has important functional value is the topic of transportation. Although a discussion on transportation in a world geography course may be more on the economic relevance of transportation, a functional application of this topic is warranted. Table 14-8 includes this topic in the "community" setting section and lists various forms of transportation. Wehman and Targett (2004) show how this topic could be expanded to include other forms of mobility (see Table 14-9).

The curricular material, *Finding Wheels: A Curriculum for Nondrivers with Visual Impairments for Gaining Control of Transportation Needs* (Corn & Rosenblum, 2000), provides a number of instructional

**TABLE 14–7** Functional science: Real-life applications

| *Functional Setting* | *Specific Knowledge* | *Specific Skills* |
|---|---|---|
| Everyday Living Health: | *Maintenance:* | |
| | • healthy lifestyle | • identifying and maintaining healthy diet<br>• exercising regularly |
| | • personal care and hygiene | • dressing appropriately for situation<br>• maintaining good self-care skills |
| | *Prevention of problems:* | |
| | • food tolerance | • avoiding certain foods |
| | *Treatment:* | |
| | • first aid/emergency procedures<br>• illness identification and treatment | • taking care of minor cuts, bites, allergic reactions<br>• recognizing when someone is sick<br>• using appropriate treatment for the illness<br>• knowing when to consult professional help (doctor, ER, etc.) |
| Physical/Environmental: | • tool identification<br>• home maintenance and repair | • using tools appropriately<br>• performing simple home repairs (e.g., toilet repair, screen door)<br>• performing seasonal home maintenance<br>• fertilizing lawn |
| | • safety at home: | |
| | • fire<br>• electricity<br>• poisonous materials<br>• bathroom | • implementing a home evacuation plan<br>• safeguarding outlets<br>• keeping dangerous material in protected location<br>• safeguarding bathrooms |
| School Health: | • unsafe conditions<br>• possible activities:<br>• tattoo/piercing | • avoiding situation where one's health is in jeopardy<br>• getting safe procedure |
| Community Health: | • safety concerns:<br>• playgrounds<br>• bicycles<br>• skateboards<br>• animals | |
| Physical/Environmental: | • weather-related:<br>• severe storm: | |
| | • lightening<br>• flooding<br>• hurricanes | • taking protective action<br>• avoiding low water crossings |
| | • brush fire<br>• drought | • implementing an evacuation plan<br>• protecting one's house<br>• implementing a mandated/volunteer watering schedule |
| Workplace Health: | • protection from contagious conditions<br>• safe behaviors | • implementing protective measures (e.g., hand washing)<br>• following work safety procedures<br>• wearing protective gear as directed<br>• lifting heavy items appropriately |
| Physical/Environmental: | • office machinery maintenance and repair<br>• hazardous materials | • making simple repairs (e.g., jammed copy machine)<br>• avoiding dangerous areas<br>• initiating emergency procedures |
| | • operation of machinery, equipment, tools | • using machines, equipment, and tools as directed in the operation guidelines |
| Leisure Health: | • preventing illness when traveling | • keeping hydrated<br>• washing hands regularly |
| | • sports-related injuries:<br>• prevention | • stretching before activity |
| | • treatment | • wrapping ankles, using braces |

**TABLE 14–7** (continued)

| Functional Setting | Specific Knowledge | Specific Skills |
|---|---|---|
| Physically/Environmental: | • hobbies (select examples): | |
| | • gardening | • choosing plants<br>• using nutrients |
| | • astronomy | • using telescope |
| | • hiking | • selecting equipment<br>• protecting environment |
| | • bicycling | • repairing flat tire |

**TABLE 14–8** Functional social studies: Real-life applications

| Functional Setting | Specific Knowledge | Specific Skills |
|---|---|---|
| Everyday Living | • contributing citizen: | |
| | • awareness of current events | • keeping up with local news and issues |
| | • personal legal information: | |
| | • rights | |
| | • procedural safeguards | • explaining and reacting to Miranda warning<br>• filing a small claims complaint |
| | • home ownership: | |
| | • deed restrictions | |
| | • tax liability | |
| | • personal liabilities | • consulting with key individuals who provide insurance |
| | • personal grooming: | |
| | • dresses stylishly | |
| | • maintains good appearance | |
| School | • legal rights as a student: | |
| | • confidentiality | |
| | • harassment | |
| | • protections | • filing a grievance |
| | • participation in various groups and organizations | • taking action to join |
| | • participation in student governance | • running for office or voting for candidates |
| | • advocate for issues of concern to students | • attending rallies, meetings, presentations |
| Community | • citizen responsibilities/choices: | |
| | • voting | • registering<br>• participating in elections |
| | • jury duty | • responding to call for jury duty |
| | • neighborhood activities (e.g., crime watch) | |
| | • volunteer opportunities | |
| | • awareness of local community | • using map skills to identify locations in the community |
| | • governmental services: | • locating and contacting appropriate office |
| | • health | |
| | • social | |
| | • housing | |
| | • employment | |
| | • community services: | • locating, contacting, going to appropriate service |
| | • transportation: | • acquiring bus pass |
| | • bus | • contacting airlines |
| | • taxi | • purchasing tickets |
| | • train | • navigating an airport |
| | • plane | • distinguishing different types of mail service |
| | • post office | |
| | • recreation | |

*(continued)*

**TABLE 14–8** (continued)

| Functional Setting | Specific Knowledge | Specific Skills |
|---|---|---|
| | • retail businesses:<br>  • department store<br>  • specialty store<br>  • drug store<br>  • grocery store<br>  • convenience store/gas<br>• specialized service:<br>  • lawn<br>  • cleaning<br>  • repair<br>  • maintenance<br>• professional services | |
| Workplace | • legal rights as an employee:<br>  • discrimination<br>  • harassment<br>  • protections/safeguards | • filing a grievance |
| | • participation in a union | • joining and maintaining membership |
| Leisure | • vacation planning | • contacting travel agent<br>• making reservations |
| | • city, public, state, national parks | • locating and finding transportation |
| | • local hiking/biking trails | • locating and finding transportation |
| | • free, public entertainment:<br>  • cultural events<br>  • outdoor concerts | • scheduling, planning, arranging transportation |
| | • local entertainment venues:<br>  • sporting events<br>  • nightclubs | • scheduling, planning, arranging transportation |
| | • visual and performing arts:<br>  • theater<br>  • concerts<br>  • museums | • scheduling, planning, arranging transportation |

ideas for teaching students how to address their transportation needs. Although the curriculum was designed for students with visual challenges, much of the content of the curriculum works for any students who must find ways to get from point A to point B.

> Reflective Question 14–3: ***While curriculum is most often governed by state standards, what are specific examples of functional academic skills that are important to teach in order to complement the core curriculum in language arts, math, science, and social studies?***

## OCCUPATIONAL AND VOCATIONAL PREPARATION

This section addresses four important topics related to the occupational preparation of students for life after high school. The section discusses the concept of career development, the need to develop a positive work attitude, the need to ensure that students have an understanding of the occupational vocabulary that they will encounter in the work world, and the array of vocational options that may be available at the secondary level.

### Career Development

The concept of career development is akin to the idea of instruction in functional areas. It was used often in the early 1970s but never caught on in the field of education, as it should have. Career development suggests that individuals should be presented with information that is related to a variety of situations (i.e., careers) associated with community living. The term *career* can be misleading because it is often viewed solely from an occupational perspective. However, the broader notion of career includes various adult roles (e.g., in the home and community).

**TABLE 14–9** Functional examples related to modes of transportation

| *Mode of Transportation* | *Possible Instructional Ideas* |
|---|---|
| Operating a motor vehicle | Following driving rules<br>Reading road signs<br>Practicing driving skills<br>Reading maps<br>Using roadside emergency services |
| Using specialized transportation services | Selecting a service provider<br>Getting documents to access services<br>Purchasing a ticket<br>Scheduling a ride<br>Solving service problems |
| Riding public transportation (bus, subway, train, or taxi) | Reading a schedule<br>Locating the stop<br>Riding<br>Problem solving |
| Walking | Reading street signs<br>Following written directions<br>Using a map<br>Crossing streets |

*Source:* Adapted from *Functional Curriculum for Elementary, Middle, and Secondary Age Students with Special Needs,* 2nd ed., by P. Wehman and J. Kregel, 2004. Copyright 2004 by PRO-ED, Inc. Adapted with permission.

Career development should be viewed as a lifelong process that begins at the preschool level and continues past retirement. This view has been espoused by the Division on Career Development and Transition (DCDT) of the Council for Exceptional Children. The view of the DCDT is reflected in the following principles (Clark, Carlson, Fisher, Cook, & D'Alonzo, 1991):

- Education for career development and transition is for individuals with disabilities at all ages.
- Career development is a process that begins at birth and continues throughout life.
- Early career development is essential for making satisfactory choices later.
- Significant gaps or periods of neglect in any area of basic human development affect career development and the transition from one stage of life to another.
- Career development is responsive to intervention and programming when the programming involves direct instruction for individual needs.
- Guided by these principles, schools and adult services should strive to provide mechanisms for facilitating lifelong career development.

The first career development activities are likely to begin during the elementary years, although they may begin at the preschool level. The typical stages include career awareness, career exploration, career preparation, and job placement (see Figure 14–3). In his classic work in this area, Clark (1979) suggested some objectives that should be included in an elementary-level career education program that still hold today:

- Provide instruction and guidance for developing positive habits, attitudes, and values toward work and daily living.
- Provide instruction and guidance for establishing and maintaining positive human relationships at home, at school, and at work.
- Provide instruction and guidance for developing awareness of occupational alternatives.
- Provide instruction for an orientation to the realities of the world of work, as a producer and as a consumer.
- Provide instruction for acquiring actual job. (p. 13)

Because of the close relationship of career education to transition planning, we suggest that additional goals be added to Clark's list to highlight other roles that become important as individuals enter young adulthood:

- Explore the variety of leisure activities, including hobbies and recreational activities.

**FIGURE 14–3** Stages of career development during the school years

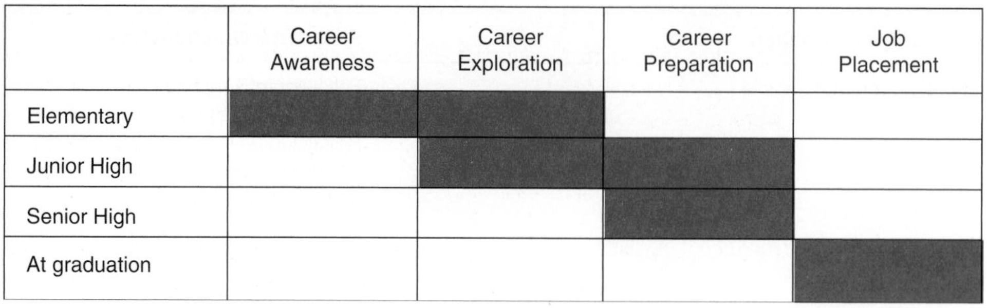

| | Career Awareness | Career Exploration | Career Preparation | Job Placement |
|---|---|---|---|---|
| Elementary | ■ | ■ | | |
| Junior High | | ■ | ■ | |
| Senior High | | | ■ | |
| At graduation | | | | ■ |

*Source:* Wehman, P., & Targett, P. S. (2004). "Principles of Curriculum Design: Road to Transition from School to Adulthood." In P. Wehman & J. Kregel (Eds.), *Functional Curriculum for Elementary, Middle, and Secondary Age Students with Special Needs* (2nd ed., p. 9). Austin: PRO-ED.

- Discuss what is expected of and required from a contributing member of the community.
- Examine the responsibilities of maintaining a house or an apartment, assuming both an owner's and a renter's perspective.

Efforts must be made to provide teachers with appropriate information, resources, and techniques for teaching about careers. Accentuating the importance of career education, demonstrating its educational and personal relevance, and providing ways for incorporating it into the existing curriculum will assist in its successful implementation. Two examples of excellent resources that are now available online are: O*NET Online (http://online.onetcenter.org/) and the Occupational Outlook Handbook (http://www.bls.gov/oco/home.htm). Both of these resources provide detailed information about occupations.

An activity that is recommended for upper elementary or middle school students is maintaining a portfolio that includes information related to occupations. Students should be engaged in activities that lead to acquiring information that will answer some of the following questions: What occupations interest me? Who works in these occupations? What is the lifestyle of the workers? Whom do they work with? Where are their jobs? How do the workers accomplish their jobs? What type of education and training is necessary? What is the typical salary for this job? Activities such as these expose students to the different roles of different workers and also aid students in clarifying alternatives for future study and consideration. A resource that can be used to ascertain this information is the *Informal Assessments for Transition: Employment and Career Planning* (Synatschk, Clark, Patton, & Copeland, 2007). This book contains 62 informal instruments that cover four areas: interests and preferences, abilities and skills, career exploration, and job searching and securing.

As the need for specific occupational preparation becomes more urgent, other program goals arise. These include:

- Enhance the occupational awareness and aspirations of students through career counseling.
- Conduct an assessment of each student's occupational interests and aptitudes.
- Integrate the assessment findings into the individualized educational program.
- Provide students with community-based training opportunities.
- Ensure the development of entry-level job skills.
- Provide job placement for and work supports to students as needed.

Most individuals with special needs will usually obtain a job or continue their education and training and begin to assume their roles in the community and/or within their families. However, changes often occur in jobs (e.g., layoffs, promotions) and in families (e.g., offspring, divorce), requiring a reeducation process for many people. As a result, some of the early phases just described may have to be repeated at a later point in life.

## Developing a Positive Work Attitude

U.S. culture is result-oriented. Good or bad, many of the results that are usually accorded positive treatment in our society are work related (i.e., those who hold a job are held in higher esteem than those who do not hold a job). The individual with a results- or work-oriented attitude is in a better position to obtain a job than the individual who is negative or naïve about work, so it is clear that education should assist students in developing strong positive work personalities with habits and attitudes that will ultimately lead them to become what they are interested in and capable of becoming.

During the preschool stage, youngsters observe the daily living and working habits of those around them. Their observations, as well as interactions with older persons in their environment, begin to yield the perceptions of life that will ultimately cause these individuals to develop a particular type of work personality. The family has a tremendous influence on the child. Families who are consistent in meeting family members' needs or who are work-oriented tend to produce persons who behave in the same fashion. Families who are not consistent in meeting family members' needs or who are not work-oriented tend to produce young adults who exhibit these latter types of behaviors. Certainly, there are exceptions to this generalization, but it depicts the tremendous importance of the family to the preschool child.

During the elementary school stage, students form a clearer, more precise perception of the world and their immediate surroundings. As students engage in academic and nonacademic endeavors, teachers need to be aware of the importance of their developing behaviors that will lead to positive work habits and positive work personalities—for example, starting a task on time, cooperating with others, being neat, or cleaning up and putting things away. As children get older and can accept more responsibilities, they should be given more important jobs in school. Students should also be given tasks that require them to express their ideas and understanding about different occupations. For example, students might be asked to write a composition or tell a story about a certain job, such as being a plumber, or students might role-play the actions of different persons, such as a park ranger, magician, or travel agent.

The secondary school period is a crucial stage in the life of the potential worker. Most adolescents with learning-related problems require a comprehensive curriculum (see Chapter 3) that is responsive to their current needs and consistent with their transitional needs across the life span. Some facet of their secondary programming should include attention to the development of occupational knowledge and the acquisition of some specific vocational skill.

## Developing a Usable Occupational Vocabulary

To be proficient in the job-seeking process (school, vocational rehabilitation, vocational training) or the world of work, individuals must understand the vocabulary that is associated with these settings. Research has identified and validated the most important occupational terms with which individuals need to be familiar. Figure 14–4 provides a list of the 52 most frequently used occupational vocabulary terms. In an effort to

**FIGURE 14–4** Essential occupational vocabulary

| | | | |
|---|---|---|---|
| ability | eligible | job description | responsibility |
| accommodation | employment | layoff | safety |
| apply | experience | merchandise | satisfactory |
| benefits | fired | occupation | schedule |
| break | first aid | on time | shift |
| breakage | full time | overtime | signature |
| checklist | harassment | part time | skill |
| competent | hazardous | paycheck | supervisor |
| cooperation | hire | policy | transportation |
| deduction | hours | preferences | union |
| department | income | promotion | vacation |
| dependable | interests | qualification | wages |
| directions | interview | raise | warning |

*Source:* From *Understanding Occupational Vocabulary* (p. 4), by S. Fisher, G. Clark, and J. Patton, 2004, Austin, TX: PRO-ED.

address this important area of knowledge and skill development, Fisher, Clark, and Patton (2004) have developed an occupational vocabulary development curricular material, entitled *Understanding Occupational Vocabulary,* that provides direct instruction along with card-deck activities to increase a person's oral proficiency in this important area.

**Reflective Question 14–4:** ***Consider the students who often receive special education services in the secondary school. For which students not bound for higher education are occupational and vocational preparation emphases particularly critical?***

## Vocational Training Options

A number of school-based options for vocational training may be available in a school system. The various alternatives are graphically depicted in Figure 14-5. Many students with special needs must receive some form of vocational experience and skill development prior to exiting from formal schooling. This is critical because many of these students will not access such training at a later time.

Unfortunately, many students with special needs leave school without any vocational skills, often because they are in academically oriented programs that do not allow time for vocational training. Also not all of the vocational options highlighted in Figure 14-5 are available to students with special needs.

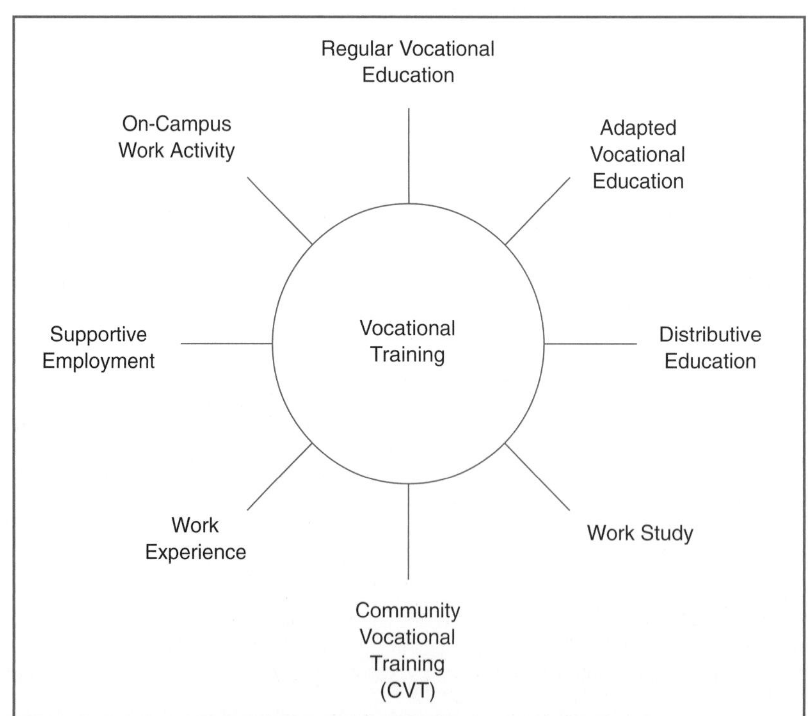


**FIGURE 14–5** School-based vocational training

# ASSESSING FUNCTIONAL COMPETENCE

To adequately address the functional needs of students with special needs, teachers need to use appropriate functional assessments for the following four reasons. First, they must determine a student's present levels of functioning in key functional areas so that appropriate planning can be developed. Second, teachers must monitor the progress of their students as instruction is provided. Third, teachers, particularly as a student approaches age 16, must engage in the process of identifying the transition needs of students and plan for their postschool life. This planning must, according to IDEA, be based on a student's preferences and interests. Fourth, as a result of the 2004 reauthorization of IDEA, students must be provided with a summary of their functional performance and academic achievement prior to their exit from high school. The very intent of this mandate involves assembling all pertinent information of a functional nature.

To accomplish the goals stated above, teachers have a variety of instruments and techniques from which to choose. Some are formal (i.e., commercially available) instruments and may be standardized or nonstandardized. Other techniques are informal in nature and may include observation, recollection methods (interviews, checklists, rating scales), curriculum-based assessment, and performance-based procedures. Both types of assessments will be discussed.

## Formal Instruments

Four types of formal measures provide information about functional competence: adaptive behavior instruments, life skills/functional skills instruments, transition instruments, and occupational measures. Table 14–10 is a list of representative instruments from each of these four areas. For detailed information on these instruments, readers are encouraged to consult professional resources on assessment (e.g., Cohen & Spenciner, 2003; McLoughlin & Lewis, 2005; Overton, 2006; Taylor, 2006).

**Adaptive Behavior.** As Cronin, Patton, and Wood (2007) note, "more than any other measure used in schools—excluding specific transition instruments—adaptive behavior measures provide the most extensive set of information about real-world functioning" (p. 30). These measures examine the following areas: self-care/daily living skills, home living skills, social behavior, communication skills, leisure skills, community use skills, health/safety skills, functional academic skills, self-direction, and work-related skills.

One way to conceptualize adaptive behavior is the ability to cope with the demands of everyday life.

**TABLE 14–10** Formal instruments for assessing functional competence

| *Type of Assessment* | *Specific Instruments* |
|---|---|
| Adaptive behavior | • AAMR Adaptive Behavior Scale—Residential and Community—Second Edition<br>• AAMR Adaptive Behavior Scale—School—Second Edition<br>• Adaptive Behavior Assessment System—Second Edition<br>• Adaptive Behavior Evaluation Scale—H–R<br>• Adaptive Behavior Inventory<br>• Inventory for Client and Agency Planning<br>• Scales of Independent Behavior–R<br>• Vineland Adaptive Behavior Scales–II |
| Life skills instruments | • Kauffman Functional Academic Skills Test (K-FAST)<br>• Life Centered Career Education Knowledge Battery<br>• Life Centered Career Education Performance Battery<br>• Life Skills Inventory (LSI)<br>• Quality of Student Life Questionnaire<br>• Street Skills Survival Questionnaire (SSSQ) |
| Transition instruments | • Enderle-Severson Transition Rating Scale—J–443Revised<br>• Enderle-Severson Transition Rating Scale–III<br>• Transition Behavior Scales—Second Edition<br>• Transition Skills Inventory<br>• Transition Planning Inventory—Updated Version |
| Occupational measures | • Ashland Interest Assessment<br>• Career Assessment Inventory<br>• Career Directions Inventory<br>• Career Maturity Inventory<br>• Harrington-O' Shea Career Decision-Making System–R<br>• Interest Determination Exploration and Assessment System<br>• Minnesota Importance Questionnaire<br>• Occupational Aptitude Survey and Interest Schedule–3<br>• Reading-Free Vocational Interest Inventory–2<br>• Self-Directed Search<br>• Your Employment Selection |

Assessment focuses on the measurement of typical behavior over time—the fact that an individual was able to perform the behavior on some occasion does not matter. Consideration of age and cultural context is an essential caution when conducting this type of assessment.

Most adaptive behavior measures listed in Table 14–10 use a structured-interview format whereby information is obtained through the reports of others about the performance of the student being assessed. For the most part, adaptive behavior measures do not use direct observation to generate data; the information is obtained indirectly through interviews with persons who have observed and are familiar with the individual.

**Life Skills Instruments.** Certain instruments measure only functional areas primarily by directly assessing whether the person has the knowledge or can perform a particular skill or set of skills related to a functional area. In other words, life skill measures "typically involve the student in some observable activity—answering questions (knowledge-related) or performing activities (skill-related)" (Cronin et al., 2007, p. 30). Some of the more frequently used measures are listed in Table 14–10.

**Transition Instruments.** The topic of transition is covered in detail in the next chapter and attention is given to assessment in that chapter. As Cronin and colleagues (2007) point out, "Transition instruments, while related in some ways to adaptive behavior and life skills measures, focus on the perceived competence levels of students. Most instruments seek the perspective of different parties—student, family, and school personnel. The main intent of these types of instruments is ultimately to guide programming and contribute to transition planning" (p. 30).

**Occupational Measures.** Many instruments have been developed for a variety of purposes related to career interests, job preparation, and employment. In this section, we have focused only on the area of occupational/career interests. In our opinion, students must be provided with opportunities to become aware of and explore various occupational options that are potentially available to students. Generally, formal assessment in this area is conducted by guidance and counseling staff or by vocational assessment personnel. However, we feel it is important for teachers to be aware of the instruments highlighted in Table 14–10.

### Informal Instruments

Information about the functional competence and career interests of students can be obtained through informal measures. These techniques can be used to compliment, supplement, or replace the data generated through formal techniques. The key variable is that, whatever the technique that is selected, it should be appropriate and effective for the purpose of the assessment. Table 14–11 provides a comprehensive list of informal procedures along with examples of the type of probes that might be used with a given procedure.

One of the most useful techniques for assessing functional competence is **performance assessment.** Wolfe and Kubina (2004) describe performance assessment as "concerned with how a student applies knowledge" (p. 122) as opposed to whether he or she knows something or not. In this type of assessment the individual must "produce or perform a response" (Wolfe & Kubina, 2004, p. 122). **Authentic assessment** is a form of performance assessment that requires the individual to produce or perform certain behaviors in the natural context where they should be performed. For example, to determine whether a student can use a microwave oven, the assessment would occur in the kitchen and the person would have to perform the appropriate sequence of behaviors to cook an item in this device.

Ultimately, the method of assessing functional competence will be predicated on the following variables: the purpose of the assessment (i.e., the information that is needed), the amount of time available for performing the assessment (e.g., performance assessment takes much more time than a recollective technique), the availability of certain instruments, and the comfort level (i.e., the competence level) of the personnel doing the assessment with a specific instrument or technique.

## MAKING IT WORK: TEACHING REAL-LIFE CONTENT

This section focuses on the instructional dimensions of teaching functional topics. Seven topics are addressed and include considering various curricular issues related to teaching functional skills, developing real-life coursework, integrating real-life topics into existing content, aligning functional topics to standards, using assistive technology to enhance functional competence, implementing effective instructional strategies, and knowing about curricular materials that have a functional base.

**TABLE 14–11** Informal assessment instruments or procedures, with sample items

| *Instrument/Procedure* | *Sample Items/Information* |
|---|---|
| Learning styles inventories | How do you learn a list of words for a test?<br>Do you like studying with a partner? |
| Observational learning styles assessments | Student always goes to a quiet place to read.<br>Student remembers things she sees. |
| Curriculum-based assessments (course specific) | Name the three branches of the federal government.<br>What are two examples of toxic waste in your home? |
| Observational reports | J. C. complained of a headache twice today.<br>M. N. needs help with grooming.<br>O. P. makes no eye contact with girls. |
| Structured situational assessments | M. C. has been absent 10 days in 6 weeks.<br>P. M. has been on time for work all month.<br>J. P. completed every task assigned today. |
| Environmental assessments of students' situational placements or future placement options | M. C. is expected to prepare evening meals for five people every evening at home.<br>N. L. will be expected, in algebra class, to compute probability problems.<br>J. S. will be working in a work setting that is extremely high pressure and fast paced. |
| Person-centered planning or futures planning procedures | What is your dream in life?<br>What is your greatest fear of the future?<br>Who are your best supports? |
| Structured interviews with students | What do you like to do with your free time?<br>What are three occupations that interest you at this time? |
| Structured interviews with parents/guardians | What would you like to see M. C. doing after she leaves school next year?<br>Where and with whom would you like P. M. to live when he leaves home? |
| Adaptive, behavioral, or functional skills assessments | Does P. M. manage his own money?<br>Does M. C. use the bus to get to work?<br>Does G. G. purchase her own clothes? |
| Social histories | M. C. has shown a consistent pattern of relating well to male authority figures.<br>Since P. M.'s family moved and he went to live with his grandmother, he has run away from home six times. |
| Rating scales (employability, independent living, personal–social skills, etc.) | M. C. follows directions without prompts.<br>P. M. relates well to co-workers.<br>L. P. cleans room and makes bed regularly. |
| Applied technology/vocational education prerequisite skills assessments | Can________perform metric linear measurements?<br>Can_______demonstrate safety procedures on a drill press, band saw, and jointer? |
| Self-determination checklists (Yes or No) | I can describe why I am in a special education program.<br>I can explain my disability to a teacher/peer/employer/supervisor. |

*Source:* From "Transition Planning Assessment for Secondary-Level Students with Learning Disabilities," by G. M. Clark, 1996, *Journal of Learning Disabilities, 28*(1), pp. 79–92. Copyright 1996 by PRO-ED, Inc. Reprinted with permission.

## Curricular Considerations

As emphasized throughout this chapter, a great need exists to expose and to teach students with special needs a comprehensive set of functional skills within a framework of providing these students with access to the general education curriculum.The need to make the general education curriculum more relevant to students has been underscored for years by secondary-level teachers (e.g., Halpern & Benz, 1987).

Once a comprehensive list of functional skills has been identified at a local level, the next important task is to organize these topics so that they can be presented to students in their programs. Instruction of functional academics and career education involve different things for different students. For example,

**TEACHER *Tips*** **Elementary Level**

As has been mentioned throughout this book, the precursors of many adult-referenced competencies can be taught at the elementary level. The following examples show how various transition planning domains [i.e., those used in the Transition Planning Inventory (Clark & Patton, 1997)] can be addressed at the elementary level. The examples provided are most appropriate for upper elementary levels.

**Employment**

Assign students to keep a journal for a week, writing about their interests, hobbies, strengths, and preferred lifestyles. Have them incorporate these into the "perfect job" for themselves.

**Further Education/Training**

Explain to the student what vocational/technical school is and what kinds of occupations are served in these schools. Also, introduce resources to access a vocational/technical school.

**Daily Living**

Set up a mock store in the classroom with fake checkbooks, cash, and different things to buy. The students can practice making change and balancing checkbooks.

**Leisure Activities**

Ask the students to discuss their favorite "hangouts," and explain why they like them.

**Community Participation**

Have the class as a whole take part in a community volunteer program. For example the class could "adopt" a stretch of road near the school that they could keep clean by picking up trash. Time can be provided weekly, or every few weeks, for students to work on it.

**Health**

Have each student tell the class what he or she does when feeling bad in order to cheer up. The students can make a book with these ideas for reference.

**Self-Determination**

Assign the students to write about things in their lives about which they would like to make decisions, or about decisions that they have already made. This can be done in journal or as a separate writing assignment.

**Communication**

Have the students keep a daily journal.

**Interpersonal Relationships**

Have students write descriptions of both positive and negative qualities that their best friends possess.

students for whom higher education is a possibility should have access to academically oriented programs in general education that is balanced with exposure to other important adult outcome areas. Other students, for whom high school may be the termination of formal schooling, are likely to be in different courses of study.

The challenge for school administrators, curriculum development specialists, and teachers is how to cover important life skills topics within existing curricular structures. Figure 14-6 depicts a continuum of options for teaching functional skills. The reality of schools today is that more students with special needs are receiving their education in inclusive settings. Given this scenario, along with the IDEA mandate of access to the general education curriculum, the options at the right of the figure are the more likely avenues for covering functional topics.

## Real-Life Coursework

Three of the options depicted in Figure 14-6 involve teaching functional topics through the development of *life skills coursework.* The intent of this option is to offer coursework that is adult-referenced. The coursework could be either noncredit or credit; however, most often it will be the former. Moreover, this type of coursework is likely to be implemented in non-diploma-track programs that exist in most schools.

An example of a credit-generating life skills course is a course entitled "Science for Living" that was developed using the "major life demands" model that was introduced in an earlier section of the chapter (Helmke, Harekost, Patton, & Polloway, 1994). The major life demands chosen as the framework for the course are listed in Table 14-12. Even though this course was

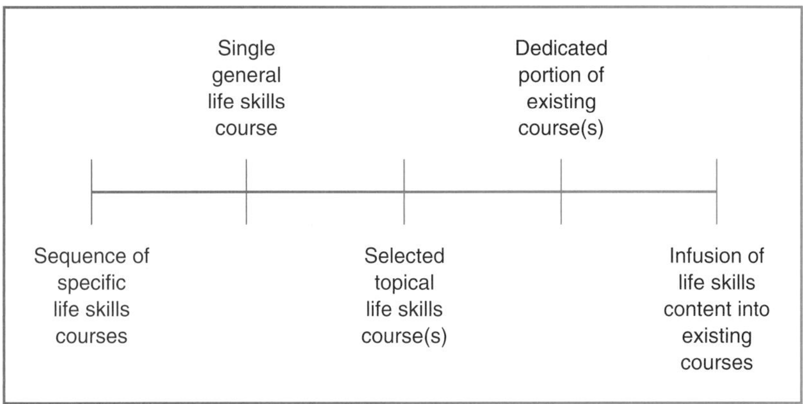


**FIGURE 14–6** Options for organizing life skills content for formal instruction

**TABLE 14–12** Major life demands for "Science for Living" course

| | |
|---|---|
| • Planning nutrition and diet | • Seeking a healthy lifestyle |
| • Administering simple first aid | • Recognizing the physical changes of aging |
| • Exercising | • Recognizing family genetic features |
| • Using medicine | • Recognizing health risks |
| • Knowing basic anatomy | • Understanding sexuality |
| • Knowing and identifying illness (adult, childhood, communicable) | • Dealing with depression |
| • Seeking regular physical and dental checkups | • Managing stress |
| • Using proper dental hygiene and dental care | • Managing life changes |
| • Decision making about substance use and abuse | • Dealing with anxiety |
| • Knowing appropriate dress for the weather | • Dealing with the separation or death of a family member |
| • Knowing how the body fights disease | • Dealing with relationships |
| • Preventing illness and mishaps | • Seeking personal counseling |
| • Recognizing signs of health problems | • Recognizing signs of emotional problems |
| • Dealing with emergencies | • Exploring career options |

*Source:* From "Life Skills Programming. Development of a High School Science Course," by L. M. Helmke et al., *Teaching Exceptional Children, 26*(2), 1994, p. 53. Copyright 1994 by the Council for Exceptional Children. Reprinted with permission.

developed prior to the No Child Left Behind Act and the educational reforms that resulted from this law, this course would likely aligned well with performance and content standards. For more detailed coverage of life skill course development, see Cronin et al (2007).

## Integrating Real-Life Topics into Existing Content

The more realistic option for covering functional topics involves the *integration of life skills topics* into the predetermined content of existing coursework. This approach is important and has received acceptance because it can be used in settings in which many students with special needs receive their education (i.e., general education classrooms or special education settings in which general education content is taught) and is inherently consistent with access to the general curriculum. Two variations of the integration technique exist: augmentation and infusion.

**Augmentation.** Augmentation implies extending the coverage of what is being taught as part of the explicit curriculum into more meaningful, functional areas. This can be accomplished by dedicating a portion of a course to "applied" topics (e.g., one session every

People also exchanged mandarin oranges happily. The oranges are symbols of happiness and prosperity. Yang loved the New Year's celebration. It was her favorite holiday because it was a very happy time, and there was lots of merrymaking and good food.

After breakfast, Yang and her family started on their visits. Everywhere, happy people greeted them. Everyone said "Kong Hee Fatt Choy." That means "We wish you prosperity."

**FIGURE 14–7** Infusion guide: Text example

*Source:* From *Reading Milestones: An Alternative Reading Program*, Level 6, Orange Reader 9 (2nd ed., p. 36), by S. P. Quigley, C. M. King, P. L. McAnally, and S. Rose, 1991, Austin, TX: PRO-ED. Copyright 1991 by PRO-ED Inc. Reprinted with permission.

week or two). For instance, in a math course, a teacher might dedicate instructional time to addressing topics such as "the economics of dating" or the real-life skills associated with maintaining an apartment.

**Infusion.** In the infusion method, the objective is to infuse into the existing content real-life topics that are related to a topic being covered in the natural progression of a class. This approach can be either spontaneous (i.e., capitalizing on teachable moments) or planned (i.e., careful examination of course content to identify "infusion points").

A more detailed discussion of infusion procedures along with examples of how to do infusion are provided by Patton, Cronin, and Wood (1999). One of the examples from this resource is shown in Figure 14–7 and Table 14–13. In this third-grade example, one can see in the infusion guide (Table 14–13) how certain infusion points found on the textbook page of the cultural event (Figure 14–7) could be used to generate discussion about some real-life topics. One cautionary note is that this approach is not meant to suggest that every opportunity to infuse real-life topics into the curriculum should be capitalized upon. A teacher does not typically have that much time to devote to such activities.

Special education teachers who are working in collaborative roles with general education teachers can use their knowledge of major life demands and functional skills to enhance their contributions to the collaborative effort by making instruction more relevant for all students in the class. Most general education teachers will greatly appreciate the benefits of such contributions.

## Aligning Real-Life Content to Content and Performance Standards

Teachers can easily apply skills associated with reading, speaking, listening, writing, computing, and problem solving to the context of adult situations (i.e., functional academics) and relate these functional topics to content and performance standards (Patton & Trainor, 2003). Wolfe and Kubina (2004) illustrate how an assortment of functional competencies relate to general education social studies objectives that are linked to content and performance standards (refer to Table 14–14).

## Instructional Considerations

The importance of applying various academic skills to and demonstrating social competence in real-life situations cannot be overemphasized. The intent of teaching life skills is to prepare individuals to use foundational, basic tool skills in ways that will make their lives more productive and meaningful, leading to some sense of personal fulfillment.

When teaching functional topics, it is crucial to recognize the difference between two seemingly similar terms: *meaningful* and *relevant*. These terms are also used interchangeably but they have different meanings. Patton et al. (1999) distinguish the terms in the following way:

> - *Meaningful*—implies that a given topic has some degree of impact on one's life, perhaps in some future sense or context.
> - *Relevance*—implies that content is not only meaningful but also timely in that it has impact on one's life now. (p. 5)

Teaching content that is relevant is far easier than teaching content that is meaningful.

An instructional technique that teachers should adopt as a way of regularly self-assessing the importance of what they are teaching, and really what students are learning, is the set of "So What?" questions. The questions can be incorporated into almost any lesson that is being taught. Their value is that they get the students to apply what they have learned. The questions are:

- So who else might use this _____?
- So what kinds of job, activities, etc., might use this _____?
- So when might you use this _____?

**TABLE 14–13** Infusion guide

| *Content Referent* | *Possible Life Skills Topics* | *Adult Domain* |
|---|---|---|
| Celebration | • List family celebrations other than the typical holidays. | Home and Family |
| Celebration | • Identify some neighborhood celebrations that occur throughout the year. | Leisure Pursuits |
| Symbols | • Identify symbols you see every day in your community (e.g., traffic signs, parking for drivers who are disabled, hospital signs, railroad signs, deer crossing). | Community Involvement |
| New Year's | • Name some New Year's resolutions that people make to improve their health. | Physical/Emotional Health |

**TABLE 14–14** Alignment of functional areas with general education content

| **Social Studies** | |
|---|---|
| Identify and participate in discussions about local, national, and world current event topics from newspapers, television, and current periodicals. | Use newspapers to identify current event topics.<br>Discuss current event issues with regular education peers.<br>Watch news and discuss events with parent, peers, and teacher.<br>Read and recall current event articles from periodicals (e.g., *Newsweek*).<br>Participate in current event games. |
| Use a map to plan a trip, calculating number of miles for the trip, identifying restaurants and hotels, and estimating the total cost for the trip. | Choose a rental car from a local dealership. Call or visit dealerships and compare prices, miles per gallon, safety features, and available options.<br>Determine items needed for trip such as location, planned activities, and season of the year and write a detailed packing list.<br>Plan route using map, including miles, cities, routes to follow, time required for trip, and when to stop for gas.<br>Call travel agencies (e.g., AAA) for literature on hotels, restaurants, leisure activities, and local tourist attractions.<br>Estimate costs of trip. |

*Source:* From *Functional Curriculum for Elementary, Middle, and Secondary Age Students with Special Needs,* 2nd ed., by P. Wehman and J. Kregel, 2004. Copyright 2004 by PRO-ED, Inc. Reprinted with permission.

**TECHNOLOGY *Tips***

The selection of appropriate assistive technologies for young adults with special needs requires careful consideration of four interrelated factors (Raskind, 1998): the individual, the specific tasks that need to be performed, the specific technology to be used, and the nature of the context in which the technology is to be used. Key issues associated with each of these factors are listed below.

- *Individual:* Consideration of strengths and weaknesses in relation to various skill areas to enable the identification of areas of difficulty and areas on which to capitalize.
- *Technology:* Consideration of certain factors: technology's effectiveness in accomplishing its primary compensatory purpose, reliability/dependability of the technology over time, compatibility with other technologies, ease of learning and use, technical support, and cost.
- *Task:* Observation of the person's use of a technology to compensate for a specific difficulty; some factors to consider are: effectiveness of the technology, ease and extent of use, individual's interest and comfort level, degree to which the technology taps a person's strengths, and general psychological and behavioral response.
- *Context:* Consideration of the use of a specific technology across differing settings in which a person functions with attention to practical and social appropriateness.

*Source:* From "Literacy for Adults with Learning Disabilities Through Assistive Technology," by M. H. Raskind 1998, in A. Vogel and S. Reder (Eds.), *Learning: Learning Disabilities, Literacy, and Adult Education* (pp. 253–268). Baltimore, Paul H. Brookes Publishing.

- So where might you use this _____?
- So how could you use this _____ in a job, with your friends, etc.?
- So why is this important?

The questions may have to be adapted somewhat depending on the topic(s) being discussed. The intent of asking these questions relates to the suggestion that Kregal (2004) makes about considering the conditions under which a functional behavior may occur.

## Assistive Technology

Some students will benefit from the support that comes with the use of various types of assistive technology. Assistive technology devices and services are mandated by IDEA to assist a student obtaining an appropriate education. Another perspective on the use of assistive technology is to consider its use in helping a student deal with the functional demands of everyday living outside of school.

**TABLE 14–15** Assistive technology contributions to functional competence

| *Functional Academic Area* | *Assistive Tech Idea* |
|---|---|
| Functional Reading | • text-to-speech features of software (eg., Word)<br>• Reading pen that reads words aloud and provides definitions of words<br>• books on CD (e.g., Recordings for the Blind and Dyslexic)<br>• book holders |
| Functional Writing | • voice recognition software<br>• small, portable voice recorder/tape player to record notes instead of having to write them<br>• various input devices for keying in information<br>• specially designed writing instruments<br>• spell-checker as part of word processing software<br>• outlining and concept mapping software |
| Functional Math | • portable, pocket calculators<br>• specialized calculators<br>• personal finance software<br>• prepaid tag—express lane of toll roads |
| Functional Science | • thermoscan device for taking temperature<br>• weekly pill boxes<br>• weather alert radios<br>• insulin level monitors |
| Functional Social Studies | • GPS navigation systems for getting around in the community<br>• responding to jury duty online<br>• making reservations online |

**TABLE 14–16** Curricular and instructional materials in the life skills area

| *Type of Resource* | *Title* | *Publisher* | *Feature(s)* |
|---|---|---|---|
| Comprehensive Curricula | • Life-Centered Career Education (LCCE) | Council for Exceptional Children | • 3 major areas: Daily Living Skills, Personal-Social Skills, Occupational Guidance & Preparation |
| | • The Transitions Curriculum | Stanfield House | • 3 modules: Get a Plan, Get a Job, Get a Life |
| | • Daily Experiences and Activities of Living (DEAL) | PRO-ED | • 6 areas: Working, Consumer Buying, Information Sources, Nutrition & Health, Housing, Transportation |
| | • The Syracuse Community–Referenced Curriculam | | • 3 major domains: Community Living; Functional Paul Brooks Academic Communication, and Motor Skills |
| Activity Resources | • Life Skills Activities for Special Children | Center for Applied Research in Educ. | • 145 ready-to-use activities |
| | • Life Skills Activities for Secondary Students with Special Needs | Center for Applied Research in Educ. | • 190 ready-to-use activities |
| | • Finding Wheels | PRO-ED | • Transportation/mobility |
| | • Language for Living Series | PRO-ED | • Manuals on Practical Time, Out in the World, The Newspaper |
| Professional Resources | • Functional Curriculum for Elementary, Meddle, and Secondary Age Students with Special Needs (2nd ed.) | PRO-ED | • Includes ideas for self-determination, activities of daily living, community living, social skills, transportation, work, home living, money management |

Often, in the context of dealing successfully with the demands of the real world, simple, low-tech supports can make a big difference in the lives of individuals with learning-related challenges. Table 14–15 provides a few examples of how low-tech solutions can supplement attempts to develop competence in the functional academic areas described earlier in the chapter.

## Curricular Materials

To teach functional content, teachers should have access to curricular materials and resources in all of the areas of interest. Cronin et al. (2007) dedicate over 60 pages of their book to a listing of materials that can be used to teach real-life topics. This list focuses mainly on instructional materials that can be used directly with students.

Table 14–16 provides a list of selected resources that teachers should find helpful for teaching functional topics. The table includes the type of resource, the title of the special product, the name of the publisher, and a brief description of the features of the material.

The major features that should characterize innovative instruction of functional topics for most students with learning-related problems include the following: adult-referenced, comprehensive, relevant to students, empirically and socially valid (i.e., appropriate to one's specific situation), flexible, community-based when possible, and sensitive to cultural and family values.

> **Reflective Question 14–5:** ***What are the specific strategies that can be used to integrate real-life topics in to the existing curriculum? How can these efforts be made consistent with attention to content and performance standards?***

## SUMMARY

This chapter presented a host of topics that were related to teaching functional topics to students with learning-related problems. The chapter began by introducing and defining what is meant by functional. Next, the identification of the demands of adulthood occurred. This was followed by the topic of functional academics. An expansive conceptualization of functional academics was used in the chapter to include areas such as functional science and functional social studies. The chapter then covered the important topic of career development and vocational preparation. This discussion was followed by coverage of how to assess functional competence using formal and informal techniques. The last major section of the chapter presented ideas on how to cover functional topics and how to teach these topics.

CHAPTER

# 15

# Transitions Across the School Years

James R. Patton

Audrey Trainor

Gary M. Clark

This final chapter of the book focuses on the articulation that should exist throughout the schooling process that assists a student and his or her family with the key transitions that will occur during school and ultimately with the realities of life beyond high school. Although the chapter provides closure to the many topics covered in previous chapters, it is more than just final thoughts.

This chapter addresses four major sections. First, it explores the important school-related transitions that students with special needs are likely to encounter and provides tactics for preparing for them. Second, the chapter examines a number of transitions that may occur during the early childhood years, leading to the important transition to formal schooling. Third, the chapter discusses the critical transitions from the elementary level to middle school. This transition is often overlooked. Fourth, the chapter explores the basic issues related to the transition from school to life in the community. This section focuses on the specific elements of the transition planning process, as mandated by IDEA, for students who are exiting school.

## TRANSITIONS ALONG AND ACROSS THE SCHOOL YEARS

We all experience many transitions in our lives. Some of the transitions that students might encounter in their lives are depicted in Figure 15-1. Although the focus of this chapter is on those transitions that occur during school years, it is worthwhile to think about transitions as a lifelong reality (see Price & Patton, 2003), as dramatic transitions will occur in life as well.

### Key Elements of Successful Transitions

Certain important elements are associated with increasing the chances of any transition being successful (Bruder & Chandler, 1996; Patton & Dunn, 1998). The three key elements identified by Patton and Dunn include:

- Systematic and comprehensive planning (assessment and individual planning)
- Implementation of a plan of action
- Coordination/cooperation/communication/collaboration

*Systematic and comprehensive planning* involves two major activities: needs assessment and individual planning. The assessment phase should address two separate but related elements: (1) the evaluation of the demands and requirements of the setting(s) to which the person is likely to go next, and (2) the evaluation of the individual's competence (i.e., knowledge and skill levels) associated with handling these impending demands. In assessing a student's competence, attention should be directed to both areas of strength and areas of need. Individual planning is the formal or informal process of formulating an action plan to address areas of concern. The plan could be a document that is mandated by law, such as an IEP, or something much less formal; however, developing some type of plan of action is needed.

The *action phase* refers to the follow-through on the planning that was previously done. Wonderfully executed needs assessment and the resulting comprehensive planning are meaningless if the plans are not carried out in an efficient, effective, and timely way. Some of the action items that are part of the plan may be simple activities that are achieved in a relatively short time; others, however, may be more elaborate and require a larger investment of time and effort.

*Coordination, cooperation, communication, and collaboration* refers to the various relationships and ongoing efforts between the sending environment (preschool, elementary school, high school) and any number of receiving settings. Ideally, representatives from specific receiving settings would participate actively in the individual planning phase; however, regular participation of these individuals is often not possible. As a result, some level of cooperation and communication must exist between sending agencies and receiving agencies.

If transition planning, regardless of the transition of interest, is not conducted at all, is conducted in some minimal fashion, or is conducted ineffectively, several problems are likely to arise. They may include the following:

- Interruption of important services
- Termination of needed services through oversight or lack of information
- Inadequate preparation of the student in the sending environment
- Inadequate preparation of the receiving environment

## Vertical and Horizontal Transitions

As mentioned, throughout life we all experience many different transitions. Some (e.g., beginning kindergarten, moving from elementary to secondary school) are predictable or normative and most people experience them. These types of transitions have also been referred to as *developmental* or *age-based* (Wolery, 1989) and *chronological* (Lazzari, 1991). In this chapter they are referred to as **vertical transitions.**

Other transitions (e.g., frequent changes in living situations, recovery from a major illness or accident) are nonnormative—more individual-specific and not as predictable. Some people experience them, others will not. Wolery (1989) describes these as *nondevelopmental* in nature and Lazzari (1991) as *ongoing*. These types of transition are referred to as **horizontal transitions** in this chapter.

The school years include many of these normative and nonnormative transitions. As mentioned, most vertical transitions are common to all students, whereas many of the horizontal transitions are person-specific and are relevant to certain students. The horizontal transitions highlighted in Figure 15-1 represent only some of many different changes that can occur. This chapter will focus in some detail on three important vertical transitions that occur during the school years and to which attention is either warranted or mandated. Of all of the transitions depicted in Figure 15-1

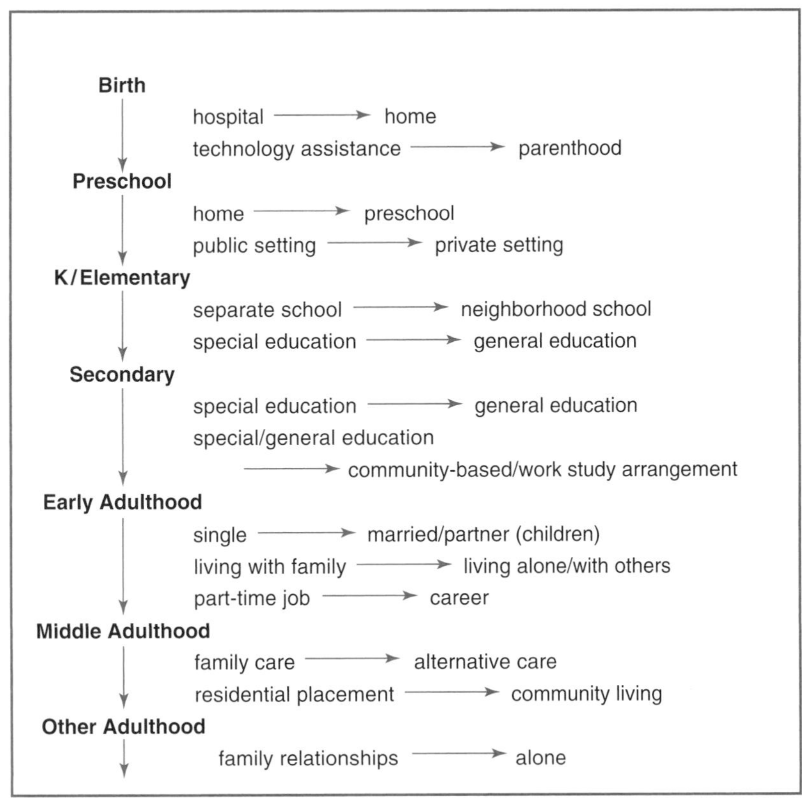


**FIGURE 15–1** Vertical and selected horizontal transitions

*Source:* From *Transition from School to Young Adulthood for Students with Special Needs: Basic Concepts and Recommended Practices*, by J. R. Patton and C. Dunn, 1996, Unpublished manuscript. Copyright 1996 by J. R. Patton. Adapted with permission.

and other horizontal transitions that could be added to this figure, only two of them require attention by law. IDEA mandates that transition activities occur for the following situations: (1) young children who are moving from early intervention services (i.e., birth to 3 years of age—Part C of IDEA) to a range of options at the preschool level, and (2) students who are 16 years of age and who are preparing to move from high school to life in the community. Many other important transitions may be encountered; however, only these two require transition planning.

For infants and toddlers who qualify and are served through early intervention programs, the transition from early intervention programs to any number of possible preschool settings (e.g., early childhood special education, private day care) is extraordinarily important and is a key component of the individualized family service plan (IFSP).

The other mandated transition that has received considerable attention in recent years is from school to living in the community as a young adult. This transition should be a focal point of the special education process for students who have reached the age of 16. As the major school-level transition, a major section of this chapter has been devoted to it. It is obvious, though, that there is a gap between age 3 transition planning and age 16 transition planning. We strongly believe that that gap should not exist and encourage elementary teachers K–5 or K–6 to consider transition knowledge and skill needs of their students.

Reflective Question 15–1: ***How do the concepts of vertical and horizontal transitions impact on the educational programming that should be provided to students with special needs across their school careers?***

## EARLY CHILDHOOD TRANSITIONS AND ENTRY INTO PUBLIC SCHOOLS

Children with disabilities under the age of 5 may receive services under two parts of the Individuals with Disabilities Education Improvement Act of 2004 (IDEA, 2004). Through a formula based on census counts and poverty levels, states and local school systems receive federal resources to provide special education and related services to pre-school-age children with disabilities under Part B, Section 619 of the IDEA. Part C of the Act provides federal resources to designated state agencies to provide initial services to infants and toddlers with disabilities. Through Part C, states receive funds to plan, develop, and implement services, supports, and information systems for children with disabilities, birth to age 3, and their families.

Although educators focusing on secondary students' transition from school to adult living like to think they "invented" the notion of transition planning and transition services, early childhood educators began thinking about this at about the same time in the mid-1980s. Both groups of educators had different outcomes in mind for their groups, but much of the conceptual base was the same. Repetto and Correa (1996) pointed out the common features of the delivery of transition services for both early and secondary levels. For example, in comparing definitions applied to both age-level groups, the following commonalities are seen: curriculum, location of services, futures planning, multi-agency collaboration, and family and student focus.

### Federal Perspective of Early Childhood Transition Services

Congress established its first initiatives for providing early intervention services in 1986 in recognition of an urgent and substantial need to meet the needs of children and families in dealing with disabilities, reduce educational costs later on in special education, minimize the likelihood of institutionalization and maximize independent living, and enhance the capacities of families to meet their children's needs (NECTAC, 2005). P.L. 99-457, a reauthorization of the Education for All Handicapped Children Act, encouraged states to develop early interventions for infants and toddlers, birth to age 3, and extended a free and appropriate education (FAPE) to children 3 to 5 years of age, and required, for the first time, individualized transition planning with each family as part of its individualized family service plan (IFSP) (Rosenkoetter, Whaley, Hains, & Pierce, 2001).

In 1991, the reauthorization of IDEA (P.L. 102-119) expanded the individualized planning of transitions as families moved from their 0–3 (infant/toddler) early intervention services. The law required, with parental consent, that early intervention programs convene a meeting with the family and the child's potential school district *at least 90 days* before the child's third birthday to plan the transition process of moving from an infant-toddler program to an early childhood education program. The new law also required systemic efforts to improve transitions by requiring states to include specific early childhood policies in their state plans when applying for federal funds, interagency planning, and a state Interagency Coordinating Council. The intent of the changes in 1991 was to promote a "seamless system" of services from birth to age 6 and to prevent gaps in services (Rosenkoetter, 1992).

Federal policy memorandums in the early 1990s clarified some aspects of the 1991 requirements but new language in the IDEA Amendments of 1997 responded to concerns in the field by requiring that schools send representatives to the pre-age-3 transition planning meeting and also required transition planning for children from early intervention programs who do not meet eligibility for services under special education (Rosenkoetter et al., 2001). The latter provision was to align Part C programs under 1997 with parallel actions with Head Start's performance standards, which directed Head Start grantees to conduct transition planning for children and families entering and leaving Head Start and Early Head Start programs (ACF, 1996).

Part C of the Individuals with Disabilities Education Improvement Act (IDEA, 2004) continued the requirements for early intervention and other services for infants and toddlers with disabilities and their families (from birth through age 3). These early interventions and other services are provided in accordance with an individualized family service plan (IFSP). This plan is the equivalent of the individualized education program (IEP) required under Part B of the IDEA and is developed in consultation between families of infants and toddlers and the appropriate state agency providing Part C services.

The consultation process is based on a multidisciplinary assessment and evaluation of a child's strengths and needs and involves the identification of a child's present levels of development and performance, establishes goals for future development and performance, and outlines how the child will receive early intervention and other services, including a description of the appropriate transition services for the infant or toddler (Rosenkoetter et al., 2001). The transition services plan must include "specific steps to be taken to support the transitions of both toddlers with disabilities and at-risk children who are not eligible for special education services to preschool or other appropriate services (IDEA, 2004, §635 (9)(C)). Unlike the IEP, the IFSP explicitly integrates the needs of the family with those of the child and presents a comprehensive plan that enables the family to meet its goals.

## Conceptual Perspective of Early Childhood and Elementary School Transition Services

Kagan (1992) and Patton and Dunn (1998) used the terms *vertical* and *horizontal* transitions, as introduced in the previous section. Instruction at home, school, and in the community relates to both vertical and horizontal transitions in that children move vertically through age and service system experiences and horizontally make adjustments within each of the vertical transitions.

From a conceptual viewpoint, the notion of transitions from one age or developmental level to another is another way of thinking about young children's growth and development. Professionals in this field have long used developmental norms for physical, cognitive, and motor development to establish performance expectations and even intervention procedures. It is not difficult for adolescent transition professionals to communicate to early childhood teachers that the concepts and language about vertical transitions across age or developmental levels is very similar to early childhood professionals' terminology about child and human development. The best way to see the congruence between the conceptual models of transition advocates (Sitlington & Clark, 2005) and early childhood education professionals (Howard, Williams, Port, & Lepper, 2001) is to look at the basic components of each group's primary knowledge and skill domains. Each is listed in Table 15-1.

Even the concept of "horizontal" transitions that Patton and Dunn (1998) described for all age levels relates to traditional early childhood and elementary school developmental view that children have to make changes and adjustments to new situations and environments while at a particular age or development level (dealing with divorce, loss of a parent, moving to another community, moving into an inclusive preschool education program, etc.). To be sure, the primary emphasis in secondary school transition planning and programming is adult outcomes, but acquiring the knowledge and skills adults need in performing their roles as citizens, community participants, workers, friends, and family members begins immediately after birth and continues throughout life.

## Early Childhood and Elementary School Transition-Related Knowledge and Skill Domains

Transition knowledge and skill domains refer to those skills or performance areas that are important for successfully coping with life demands across developmental

**TABLE 15–1** Comparison of conceptual models of transition

| *Transition Knowledge/Skill Domains* | *Early Childhood Knowledge/Skill Domains* |
|---|---|
| Communication/academic performance<br>Further education and training | Language development/symbol recognition |
| Self-determination | Self-help skills/independence/problem solving |
| Independent/interdependent living | Self-help/independence/collaboration |
| Interpersonal relationships | Socialization |
| Integrated community participation | Adaptability/routines and order |
| Health and fitness | Motor development/hygiene |
| Leisure and recreation | Play/creativity/motor skills |
| Employment | Following directions, on-task behavior, role-playing, task completion, motor coordination |

levels, as introduced in Chapter 14. That is, at every stage of life, from birth to death, there are demands or expectations of people that require certain kinds and amounts of knowledge or skill to adjust successfully to that stage of life. The best way to see how the transition and knowledge and skill domains relate to early childhood instruction and interventions is to take each of them and describe in more detail the nature of the domain and give age-appropriate examples for instruction.

**Communication and Academic Performance.** Communication skills refer to receptive and expressive skills. Receptive skills for infants and toddlers and preschool-age children include recognition of auditory and visual cues that have meaning, such as facial expressions, laughs, tone of voice, alarm signals, auditory and visual understanding of basic vocabulary words or signs. Expressive skills include first attempts at speaking or signing, demonstrating nonverbal cues (gestures, facial expressions, and body language), then developing beginning vocabularies. A major goal for preschool programs would be that the children match or exceed a normal pattern of language development and have a functional use of their family's language system by the age of 5. If this functional outcome is achieved, the children have enough vocabulary to express their needs and understand most of the language that is directed specifically toward them. Those with average to above-average cognitive abilities will also have mastered the basic rules of grammar and syntax for oral expression and some will have started learning to read, write their own names, and copy letters and numbers.

**Further Education or Training.** The knowledge and skills needed for further education and training are those that build on communication skills and academic learning outcomes. The early intervention programs for children in poverty or at risk for not doing well in school have made it easier to justify the need to start early with children so that the academic instruction that begins in kindergarten is not new content and new learning. Part of the role of early childhood education is to help children be prepared for the move from preschool programs to kindergarten programs. This transition is often a transition of children from a nurturing but not necessarily intellectually challenging environment to an environment that will be more intellectually challenging but not necessarily as nurturing.

The new elementary school environments, beginning with kindergarten, for former preschool children may also have other transition issues requiring planning and preparation besides academic instruction. The buildings may be much larger, the school populations much larger, and the diversity of students much more expanded. For the first time, children may be introduced to busing, eating in a large cafeteria, playground fighting and bullying at a new level, and hundreds of older children with a variety of behaviors and attitudes. Will the new kindergarten children be able to make decisions about personal safety, ask for assistance when needed, and find the school resources that might be needed (e.g., office, telephone, library, school nurse's office)? These are transition knowledge and skills examples that are important not only for the children's age levels and horizontal adjustments, but also for the transitions ahead in the elementary grades, middle school, high school, and beyond.

**Self-determination.** Field and Hoffman (1994) placed knowing oneself and valuing oneself at the earliest stage of self-determination development. The earlier children can learn about their strengths and differences from others, the easier it is to start the process of personal growth and development of self-confidence and self-esteem. The earlier children can learn to attribute success on a task to planning, skill, and effort, the easier it is for them to see the connection between effort and success rather than attribute success to luck, favoritism, one's ethnicity, or income level. Making choices is new learning for some children and important in self-determination development. Setting goals is also important learning as children need to learn group goal setting and individual goal setting. Even young children can be guided into problem-solving skill learning with skillful questions and good modeling from the parent or teacher: "We want to do _____. What do we need? How can we do this? What will happen if _____?"

**Independent/Interdependent Daily Living Skills.** For young children, another term for independent behavior related to basic life skills in self-care and home living is *adaptive behavior*—dressing, eating, bathing, taking care of personal belongings, performing simple chores, and the like. There are numerous daily living tasks that present themselves and require some knowledge or skills. These occur at home, at school, and in the community. Here is where early childhood and elementary teachers and parents need to work together to anticipate the tasks that a child should be doing now or in the very near future, and then provide the training for the child. Examples of these skills are calling 911 for emergencies, using toys and tools safely, knowing how to respond to strangers when alone, toileting, brushing teeth, pouring liquids, using candles and matches properly, and responding to strange animals.

Interdependence skills are those that acknowledge that some tasks require assistance or support. Children need to learn early when to ask for help, how to ask for help, how to inform the helper about the task or problem and what help is needed, how to show appreciation for assistance and support, and to know the difference between help and support (encouragement, listening, empowerment, etc.). Children learn many of these skills at home as well as in inclusive settings at school and in the community, but not without some forethought and deliberate attention to them.

**Interpersonal Relationships.** Hanson et al. (2001) reported that families frequently cited their children's need for appropriate role models for behavior, speech, and social skills. Interpersonal relationship skills, or socialization skills, are the building blocks for human interactions in the family, at school, and in the community. At the earliest possible stage, children need to learn how to share, understand roles in groups, respect others, follow the rules of a classroom or game, make friends, listen to others, show friendship and affection appropriately, relate to adults, meet and greet strangers, and know the difference between appropriate and inappropriate behavior. Inclusive learning environments in the elementary school provide a variety of opportunities for children to learn appropriate interpersonal relationships.

**Integrated Community Participation.** Children with disabilities that are identified before preschool age may have severe problems related to mobility, communication, sensory acuity, cognition, and/or behavior. Going out into the community may be a challenge for the family for a number of reasons. A child might be well integrated into the primary or extended family. However, unless the family makes real effort to get the child into integrated situations in the community, including a community program or preschool, this area will be left largely to a public elementary school. If for no other reason, inclusive education settings are important for children like this. Within integrated programs, there can be a number of activities for children that get them into the community for additional experiences. As much of this as possible during the preschool and elementary years is important for future community integration opportunities.

**Health and Fitness.** Children cannot learn if they are hungry, sleepy, sick, or upset. Physical and mental health are important parts of every individual's life, regardless of age. Schools frequently have to take on some of the roles of parents in infant-toddler programs and preschool programs by providing nourishing food and time for naps, administering medications, and monitoring physical situations. They also observe children's emotional well-being, watching for fears, depression, inappropriate affect, excessive aggressive behavior, persistent emotional outbursts, and signs of abuse. In addition, early childhood programs see the need to provide play equipment and activities that help children develop motor skills and coordination, strength, and stamina. All of these are important for lifelong learning and functioning in the home and in the community as they make the transitions from preschool to elementary to secondary programs and adult living.

**Leisure and Recreation.** As a learning strategy for young children, play has been valued for cognitive, motor, and social learning for many years (Howard et al., 2001). In the development of leisure and recreational skills, play is a natural way to develop game skills, such as learning rules; taking turns; learning how to pretend and play roles; learning music, movement, and dancing skills; assuming leadership skills; and learning how to handle competition, winning, and losing. Children at very young ages are learning to play with computers, iPods, MP3s, Gameboys, and the like, as well as manipulative toys such as Duplos, Legos, and Bionicles. Quiet leisure activities of picture books, music, storybooks (audio and print), and children's videos are also common and viewed as positive learning activities for the present and the future. In elementary school many opportunities present themselves for growth in leisure and recreation skills through school activities and related community organizations.

**Employment.** Self-help skills are the foundation for employability skills. Learning to listen or watch for learning a task, following directions, making choices, asking for help when needed, knowing when a task is completed or not, knowing when a mistake or error has been made in the task, knowing when to ask for additional materials or tools, and the like are examples of childhood development tasks that are important in future learning outcomes. Role-playing of adult roles with costumes or uniforms that are associated with adult workers is a traditional play activity that fosters career development visualization and begins the process of saying, "I want to be a _____ when I get big."

## Early Childhood Transition-Related Services

Knowledge and skill domains are important for learning, but equally important is the planning and attention given to movement of young children through their first service systems. In early childhood, a child with disabilities makes several major transitions. If a child is identified as an infant or toddler and is placed in an infant/toddler center-based program, the first major transition may be from home to a center environment for part of a day without the mother or primary caregiver. If the first system is a preschool, the first major transition is from home to a preschool program. It is possible that a decision is made to move a child from a segregated preschool program to an inclusive preschool program, or vise versa, and either of these options has its own set of transition adjustments (Hanson et al., 2001). Thus, some children might make two or three major transitions in moving into and through service systems by age 5. The type of planning and practices that are employed can affect the success of transitions and the satisfaction with the transition process by all concerned (Bruder & Chandler, 1993).

**Home to Infant/Toddler Center-Based Preschool.** Although there is disagreement in the early childhood field as to the value of center-based services and IDEA requires a more family-centered or natural environments orientation to services for infants and toddlers (Campbell & Halbert, 2002), some young children will be making the home to center-based transitions. This is frequently more difficult for parents and family than it is for the children, and the transition process focuses much more on parent–center communication and collaboration than child-focused procedures (Bricker, 2001).

**Infant/Toddler Services to Preschool.** Many practices and principles have been identified that promote a more successful and satisfying transition from an infant/toddler program to a preschool program. Factors such as community contexts (e.g., cultural, ethnic, population size), collaboration (interagency agreements, policies, etc.), communication, family concerns, and continuity (follow-up) have been identified as important principles to guide transition practices (Malveaux, Welker, & Norlin, 2003). Communication between preschool providers and parents of children with disabilities who are leaving infant/toddler programs is especially critical (Hadden & Fowler, 1997). It is at this stage that the first legal requirement for transition planning occurs. Serious consideration of the least restrictive environments, instructional needs, and supports from related services personnel begin officially at this stage.

**Preschool to Kindergarten.** Moving into kindergarten is the next major transition and is a much more challenging adjustment, according to some professionals and parents (Chandler, 1993; Meier & Schafran, 1999; Pianta & Kraft-Sayre, 1999). This challenging transition was noted early on after the federal initiatives for establishing preschool programs for children with disabilities. Instruction in transition skills for making the move to kindergarten became recommended practice with "survival skills" curricula appearing in the literature (Rule, Fiechtl, & Innocenti, 1990). Rule et al. stated, "One rationale for teaching survival skills to preschoolers with handicaps is that they will encounter different learning conditions when they graduate into kindergarten or first grade" (p. 79). This same statement could be made for high school to postsecondary education settings, underscoring again the conceptual similarities in planning for life transitions.

Teachers often find it more helpful to have a set of specific skills in mind when starting to think more specifically about transition planning from infant/toddler programs to preschool, from preschool to kindergarten, and, finally, from elementary school to middle or junior high school. Table 15-2 below provides some of these specific skill examples generated by Chandler (1993) for preparing children to make a successful transition from preschool to kindergarten and the elementary school.

Table 15-3 proposes some sample strategies for integrating transition knowledge and skills into grades K-5 through activities. The number and variety of such strategies is limited only by the commitment and creativity of elementary school teachers planning instructional activities.

Regardless of the type or location of early intervention services, there is strong support for a "seamless system" of services for birth through kindergarten (Bruns & Fowler, 2001; Campbell & Halbert, 2002). Transitions are more likely to be successful when children are taught survival skills for entering new environments through group and individual instructional interventions. Children are also more likely to succeed in transitions when there is a clear policy on interagency

**TABLE 15–2** Transition skills related to successful transition from preschool to kindergarten

**Social Behaviors and Classroom Conduct**

- Understands role as part of group
- Respects others and their property
- Interacts and defends self without aggression
- Plays cooperatively; shares toys and materials
- Expresses emotions and affections appropriately
- Takes turn: participates appropriately in games
- Is willing to try something new
- Follows class rules and routines
- Lines up and waits appropriately
- Imitates peer actions
- Sits appropriately
- Plays independently

**Communication Behaviors**

- Follows two- to three-part directions
- Initiates and maintains peer interactions
- Modifies behavior when given verbal feedback
- Asks peers or teachers for information or assistance
- Recalls and follows directions for tasks previously described
- Follows group instructions
- Relates ideas and experiences
- Answers questions
- Communicates own needs and wants

**Task-Related Behaviors**

- Finds materials needed for tasks
- Does not disrupt peers during activities
- Complies quickly with teacher instructions
- Generalizes skills across tasks and situations
- Follows task directions in small or large group
- Replaces materials and cleans up work space
- Monitors own behavior; knows when a task is done
- Begins and completes work at appropriate time without extra teacher attention
- Makes choices
- Stays in own space
- Follows routine in transition
- Uses a variety of materials
- Seeks attention appropriately
- Attends to teacher in a large group

**Self-Help Behaviors**

- Recognizes when a problem exists
- Locates and cares for personal belongings
- Avoids dangers and responds to warning words
- Takes outer clothing off and puts it on in a reasonable amount of time
- Tries strategies to solve problems
- Feeds self independently
- Cares for own toileting needs

*Source:* From "Steps in Preparing for Transition: Preschool to Kindergarton," by L. K. Chandler, 1993, *Teaching Exceptional Children, 25*, p. 48, Copyright 1993 by Council for Exceptional Children. Reprinted with permission.

**TABLE 15–3** Transition skills related to successful transition from elementary school to middle school

**Social Behaviors**
- Gets along with siblings, peers, and adults
- Initiates conversation with students one does not know
- Handles teasing and bullying
- Shows appropriate behavior for a variety of events and settings in public
- Uses appropriate humor
- Respects cultural or ethnic differences
- Respects rights and property of others

**Communication Behaviors**
- Demonstrates listening skills
- Demonstrates skills in speaking orally in front of peers
- Understands common nonverbal cues
- Knows when and how to report a problem
- Knows when to keep silent
- Uses appropriate language at school
- Knows how and when to ask for help
- Uses appropriate telephone communication
- Accepts and gives praise/compliments

**Task-Related Behaviors**
- Makes choices about clothes, study times, and personal activities
- Follows through on goals
- Completes tasks with highest quality possible
- Organizes school work assignments
- Demonstrates punctuality
- Uses basic skills in using computers
- Shows personal responsibility
- Follows written/oral directions

**Independent Behaviors**
- Chooses appropriate clothing for the weather or the occasion
- Uses good judgment in choice of food
- Takes initiative to solve problems
- Uses good judgment in choice of friends and leisure activities
- Takes responsibility for personal hygiene and basic health practice
- Volunteers to help others

collaborations, specific guidelines for sending and receiving programs for planning and implementing children's movement from program to program, and a commitment to include parents in the process. Still, it is more than just a seamless system among interagency organizations. Mangione and Speth (1998) identified "families as partners" as the number one element in determining continuity of transition for early childhood. Involving families as partners in this process is the key to the entire process. Figure 15–2 is an example of a document that provides an agreement between parents and preschool staff to facilitate the transition of a student from preschool to kindergarten. Agreements such as this, even though they are not required under IDEA, make partnerships more likely to succeed.

The guiding principle of starting early in transition education and the transition services delivery process is one that professionals at the early childhood, elementary, and secondary education levels can agree. An early start that is effective can set the stage for a positive K–5 education.

Reflective Question 15–2: ***What are the respective roles that educators and parents should play in effecting a successful transition from preschool to elementary school? What collaborative efforts will facilitate this process?***

## TRANSITION FROM ELEMENTARY TO SECONDARY EDUCATION

One of the most neglected developmental transitions during the school years for all students is from elementary school to the secondary level. Although middle schools typically have an orientation for fifth-grade students and their parents, these events are not sufficient to make this transition as seamless as possible. Unique challenges exist as a student moves from elementary to middle school (Robinson, Braxdale, & Colson, 1985) and from middle to a ninth-grade center or high school setting (Wells, 1996). Moreover, the time when a student leaves the elementary setting and moves on to middle school is a time of many critical changes. This time period is one of major biological change in the students.

### Key Differences Between Elementary and Middle School

The nature of the school experience and the school structure changes. For many students, the way education is delivered also changes. For students with special needs, the experience is like being an English-speaking traveler in a non-English-speaking country. Given the

**FIGURE 15–2** Parent transition plan

## PARENT TRANSITION PLAN

Child: Missy

The following plan states the steps that the parents (and/or guardian) of the above named child and the staff of the Preschool Transition Project (PTP) will take, at the beginning of the 2004/05 school year to ensure an orderly transition to the school district for the child.

Recommended Placement: Regular Kindergarten

Neighborhood School: Seven Oaks Elementary

In completing this plan, please write out the step to be taken, who will be responsible for the step, and by what date the step will be accomplished.

| Step | Person Responsible | Target Date | Date Accomplished |
|---|---|---|---|
| 1. Missy is recommended for enrollment in regular kindergarten at Seven Oaks Elementary. Parents will contact the principal to discuss Missy's physical status and capabilities. | Parents | May 30, 2005 | |
| 2. Send records to school principal, district special education office, and provide the parents with copies of preschool reports for their file. | B. Fiechti, teacher | June 2, 2005 | |
| 3. Provide kindergarten teacher with preschool teacher's report, stressing Missy's skills and possible adaptations for the environment. | B. Fiechti, teacher | June 9, 2005 | |
| 4. Monitor Missy's progress throughout the year; inform kindergarten teacher whenever physical status changes. | Parents | 2004-05 school year | |
| 5. Contact psychologist if advice needed or problems occur. | | 2004-05 school year | |

This plan has been read and agreed to by the following parties. A signature on this plan imparts permission for the person responsible to contact other significant persons (e.g., teachers, principals) necessary to complete the step. These contacts are only to include information relevant to completing the objective of the step.

| Persons | Title | Date |
|---|---|---|
| | | |
| | | |
| | | |

*Source:* From "It's Time to Get Ready for School," by B. Fiechtl et al., 1989, *Teaching Exceptional Children, 21*(2), p. 54. Copyright 1988 by The Council for Exceptional Children. Reprinted with permission.

significant differences that exist between elementary and secondary schooling, it is extremely important that systematic transition planning occur, especially for those who will be in inclusive settings.

Certain features of the secondary school setting make it particularly alien to the new arrivals. Some of the most obvious features include a larger student population, more teachers to deal with each day, heavy curricular emphasis on content areas, increased amounts of homework, need for more self-regulated behavior, different in-school procedures (e.g., use of lockers, physical education), and different type of class scheduling.

### Specific Demands at the Secondary Level

In addition to the obvious distinctions just noted, major demands are placed on students that affect their academic success and social acceptance.

Robinson et al. (1985) introduce three areas that are crucial to school success: academic demands, self-management/study skills demands, and social/adaptive demands. Based on Robinson and colleagues' original conceptualization, we have adapted these areas into a slightly different organizational system that includes five areas. Each of these areas is briefly described as follows:

- **Academic demands:** Behaviors/competencies that relate to the application of basic skills to the demands of the classroom setting. These skills include reading, listening, speaking, and writing and, when successfully used, result in successful performance as evidenced by being able to complete assignments/activities and receiving passing grades (at a minimum). This area does not include mastery of content.
- **Content demands:** Behaviors/competencies that relate to knowledge and skill acquisition in specific subject areas.
- **Academic support skills demands:** Behaviors/competencies associated with the acquisition, recording, remembering, and use of information. The majority of these skills are typically associated with study skills and include skills such as organizational skills, note-taking skills, the ability to use reference materials, and test taking.
- **Social/adaptive demands:** Behaviors/competencies that lead to acceptance by peers, balanced by compliance with school-based and classroom-based rules and procedures. As Robinson et al. point out, this latter point is particularly problematic for some students, as explicit and implicit classroom-specific rules and procedures vary from one teacher to another and are often difficult for students with special needs to recognize.
- **Nonacademic demands:** Behaviors/competencies that do not relate directly to scholastic success but are required to be successful at the middle school level. Some examples of demands in these areas are using a locker, changing clothes/showering for physical education class, and bringing appropriate materials (books, notebooks, calculators) to specific classes. This dimension also taps the "informal" demand of participating in an assortment of extracurricular activities that become available at the middle school level.

## Enhancing the Transition from Elementary School to Middle School

Like all other transitions, the successful movement from the sending school to the receiving school depends on (a) the identification of the skills required in the receiving environment, and (b) the assessment of student competence vis-à-vis these demands. As McKenzie and Houck (1993) point out, this must be accomplished before students arrive at the secondary level by maximizing communication and implementing pretransition programs (i.e., the essence of coordination/cooperation/communication/collaboration). Robinson et al. (1985) went as far as recommending that a transition curriculum be implemented prior to moving to middle school.

Carter, Clark, Cusing, and Kennedy (2005) recommend that students, their families, and school-based personnel incorporate strategies into the planning process for moving from elementary to middle school. Although their suggestions were developed with students with significant disabilities as the focal group, their recommendations have merit for other students with milder challenges and align with the themes offered in this chapter. Incorporating many of the strategies proffered by Carter and colleagues (2005), we recommend the following actions.

**Start Planning Early.** The message embedded in this discussion is that the demands of the secondary level must be recognized and the requisite competencies must be addressed at the elementary level, especially during the fourth and fifth grades. Thoughtful consideration must be given to this transition much sooner that the waning weeks of fifth grade.

**Assess the Transition Needs of Students.** Based on the demands that will be required of students at the middle school, especially as they relate to inclusive settings, it is imperative that a comprehensive assessment of the competence levels of students in the four areas discussed above occur. To assist with this process, we have developed an informal measure, entitled Middle School Transition Inventory (MSTI). This instrument, shown in Figure 15-3, includes items that are rated by both the student (when appropriate) and his/her teacher(s). The intent of the instrument is to identify areas of strength as well as areas that will become barriers to success at the middle school level. Ideally, the instrument should be implemented at the end of

**FIGURE 15–3** Middle school transition inventory

| *Secondary Demands* | *Specific Areas of Focus* | *Level of Proficiency* | | | |
|---|---|---|---|---|---|
| | | *Not Proficient* | *Partially Proficient* | *Proficient* | *Highly Proficient* |
| **Academic Skill Demands** | • Reading rate—flexibility in using different types of reading skills such as reading for meaning, skimming, and scanning | 0 | 1 | 2 | 3 |
| | • Listening skills—primarily for lecture-type classes; following directions | 0 | 1 | 2 | 3 |
| | • Writing skills—to complete in-class assignments, homework, report writing, and other course requirements that involve writing | 0 | 1 | 2 | 3 |
| | • Speaking skills—for oral presentations in class, communication with classmates/ teacher, negotiation, persuasion | 0 | 1 | 2 | 3 |
| **Content/Performance Demands** | • Adequate knowledge base in foundational content areas: | | | | |
| | • language arts | 0 | 1 | 2 | 3 |
| | • math | 0 | 1 | 2 | 3 |
| | • science | 0 | 1 | 2 | 3 |
| | • social studies | 0 | 1 | 2 | 3 |
| | • Adequate levels of skill competence in performing certain activities related to foundational content areas (e.g., lab skills, manipulating materials) | 0 | 1 | 2 | 3 |
| **Academic Support Demands** | • Technological competence | 0 | 1 | 2 | 3 |
| | • Homework skills (school and home) | 0 | 1 | 2 | 3 |
| | • Research skills (papers, projects) | 0 | 1 | 2 | 3 |
| | • Note taking/outlining/paraphrasing | 0 | 1 | 2 | 3 |
| | • Use of graphic aids | 0 | 1 | 2 | 3 |
| | • Test preparation/test taking | 0 | 1 | 2 | 3 |
| | • Library usage | 0 | 1 | 2 | 3 |
| | • Use of reference materials—print and online | 0 | 1 | 2 | 3 |
| | • Organizational strategies | 0 | 1 | 2 | 3 |
| | • Scheduling and time management | 0 | 1 | 2 | 3 |
| | • Self-management (e.g., goal setting) | 0 | 1 | 2 | 3 |
| **Social/Personal/Adaptive Demands** | • Interpersonal skills: | | | | |
| | • Collaborative competence (i.e., ability to learn with peers) | 0 | 1 | 2 | 3 |
| | • Cooperating with others in group situations | 0 | 1 | 2 | 3 |
| | • Perspective taking (i.e., ability to appreciate others' points of view) | 0 | 1 | 2 | 3 |
| | • Negotiation (e.g., ability to resolve different points of view) | 0 | 1 | 2 | 3 |
| | • Making and maintaining friendships | 0 | 1 | 2 | 3 |
| | • Initiating conversation | 0 | 1 | 2 | 3 |

(*continued*)

**FIGURE 15–3** (continued)

| | | | | | |
|---|---|---|---|---|---|
| | • Getting along with classmates | 0 | 1 | 2 | 3 |
| | • Respecting the rights of others | 0 | 1 | 2 | 3 |
| | • Personal skills: | | | | |
| | • Having self-advocacy skills | 0 | 1 | 2 | 3 |
| | • Being aware of one's strengths and weaknesses (e.g., academic, social, behavioral) | 0 | 1 | 2 | 3 |
| | • Accepting feedback/criticism | 0 | 1 | 2 | 3 |
| | • Accepting praise/compliments | 0 | 1 | 2 | 3 |
| | • Managing stress | 0 | 1 | 2 | 3 |
| | • Handling failure/rejection/ disappointments | 0 | 1 | 2 | 3 |
| | • Managing anger | 0 | 1 | 2 | 3 |
| | • Disagreeing appropriately | 0 | 1 | 2 | 3 |
| | • Giving critical feedback | 0 | 1 | 2 | 3 |
| | • Giving praise/compliments | 0 | 1 | 2 | 3 |
| | • Being aware of and understanding classmates' behavior | 0 | 1 | 2 | 3 |
| | • Expressing appreciation | 0 | 1 | 2 | 3 |
| | • Encouraging classmates | 0 | 1 | 2 | 3 |
| | • Classroom survival skills: | | | | |
| | • Following classroom rules and procedures | 0 | 1 | 2 | 3 |
| | • Respecting authority | 0 | 1 | 2 | 3 |
| | • Obtaining teacher attention appropriately | 0 | 1 | 2 | 3 |
| | • Seeking assistance appropriately | 0 | 1 | 2 | 3 |
| **Nonacademic Demands** | • Logical demands: | | | | |
| | • Locker usage | 0 | 1 | 2 | 3 |
| | • Lunch | 0 | 1 | 2 | 3 |
| | • Managing daily class schedule | 0 | 1 | 2 | 3 |
| | • Movement from classroom to classroom | 0 | 1 | 2 | 3 |
| | • Transportation (e.g., bus identification) | 0 | 1 | 2 | 3 |
| | • Personal safety (i.e., how to take protective measures to ensure safety) | 0 | 1 | 2 | 3 |
| | • Readiness for extracurricular opportunities: | | | | |
| | • Clubs and organizations | 0 | 1 | 2 | 3 |
| | • Sports | 0 | 1 | 2 | 3 |
| | • Social events | 0 | 1 | 2 | 3 |

fourth grade or the beginning of fifth grade so that instruction can be provided and/or supports can be established to address the areas of need. Ratings are based on levels of proficiency (not proficient, partially proficient, highly proficient)—terminology that is associated with the language of No Child Left Behind.

A comprehensive needs assessment should result in identifying areas where the student is proficient as well areas where intervention is needed. As Carter et al. (2005) mention, information on which instructional strategies were effective and which needed to be adapted at the elementary level should also be noted and shared with the school staff at the middle school level.

**Collaborate and Communicate Across Schools.** This recommendation is a major element of successful transitions, no matter when they occur. Far too often, special education teachers at the elementary level are not aware of many aspects of what happens at the secondary level. Ongoing communication must be established, at a minimum, and meaningful collaboration should be developed, as much as possible, between personnel at both the sending school (elementary school) and the receiving school (middle school). This can be accomplished by having regular contact with each other or by developing systems whereby information is shared. One idea would be to customize the Middle School Transition Inventory by having middle school teachers review it and make suggestions for adding, deleting, or changing items. Elementary teachers could recommend ways to address these areas via instruction and supports.

**Prepare Students Early.** As can be gleaned from examining the entries listed in the inventory provided in Figure 15-3, many of these topics will require skill development in areas that teachers do not typically cover at the elementary level as part of the explicit curriculum (Hoover & Patton, 2005). The key message, however, is that these areas, when students are identified as being not proficient or partially proficient, will require innovative ways in terms of time and technique to address them within the context of all of the other existing demands to cover content. Many of the ideas presented in Chapter 12 on study skills will be extremely helpful to this end.

**Encourage and Support Family Involvement.** The increasing rigor of schooling that comes with moving to the middle school level has great implications on families. The more families can be made aware of the challenges that their child and they will encounter the more likely that some issues can be avoided and others can be minimized.

Home-school collaboration was discussed in Chapter 2 and necessitates that systems be established early in the school year and their vitality be maintained throughout the year. The major problem that arises at the secondary level is that no one teacher is responsible for communicating with parents. At this level, a team, made up of teachers in the four focal subjects of language arts, math, science, and social studies, is typically the primary group with whom families will need to have contact. Complicating matters is the need to communicate with teachers of other classes being taken (e.g., foreign language, technology, band/choir/theater).

One area in particular that will become a predictable area of problem at some time is homework. Students become frustrated not only with the amount of homework assigned but also with making sure that they know what homework they are to do. Families recoil from these same factors. Assignment books may be helpful, assuming the student can use it successfully. Systems (e.g., class websites) can be helpful if they are maintained appropriately and parents have access to them; the former often does not happen and the latter sometimes is not possible.

**Develop Peer Support Programs.** One of the greatest concerns that parents have about their son or daughter moving to middle school will be related to their social development and opportunities. The middle school years is a time when friendships and interpersonal relationships become paramount issues in the lives of middle school students.

Giving this area of potential concern some attention prior to the transition to middle school is warranted. One technique that can be considered is the use of pre-identified peers who become ongoing supports for students with special needs. The actual ways these peers can be utilized can vary; however, the main objective is to make the social war zone of middle school more tolerable for students.

**Foster Independence.** One of the most important points made by Carter et al. (2005) is that middle school teachers often assume that students are able to display a certain degree of independent behavior associated with academic performance and demonstrate behavior that is in line with established expectations. Many students with special needs do not display consistent patterns of independent behavior and therefore attention to this area is very important.

The concept of self-management, as discussed in both Chapters 12 and 13, relates to this issue. Students need to be taught how to be more in control of their school lives, as they will be expected to do so and the support systems that might have been in place at the elementary level are not likely to be as evident at this level.

Upon examination of all of the elements that contribute to the seamless transition from elementary to middle school and the array of demands that are needed to be successful at this level, it is amazing that so little attention is devoted to this critical transition. To help organize the information provided in this section, a checklist for planning for this transition is provided in Figure 15-4. The checklist is an adaptation on a timeline developed by Carter and colleagues (2005). Following their structure, the checklist is organized along four time frames: during the final years of elementary school, during the months prior to entering middle school, during the first few weeks of middle school, and throughout middle school. The checklist can contribute to establishing a framework for thinking through this process and making sure that essential activities are accomplished. It, too, can be the impetus for establishing ongoing collaborative efforts between elementary and secondary personnel.

> **Reflective Question 15–3:** ***Using a top-down approach to transition for students with special needs, what are the responsibilities of elementary school teachers in preparing their students for a successful transition to secondary education?***

**FIGURE 15–4** Checklist for transition to middle school

**During the final year of elementary school:**

— Administer some type of needs assessment such as the Middle School Transition Inventory
— Address areas identified through the needs assessment through instruction
— Identify supports and services that will be needed when the student gets to middle school
— Determine concerns that the student might have in regard to going to middle school
— Determine concerns of parents/guardians regarding the middle school experience
— Ensure that student demonstrates self-management/self-advocacy skills, especially if the student will be in general education classes
— Connect parents/guardians with other parents who have had children attend middle school

**During the months prior to entering middle school:**

— Visit the middle school on more than one occasion and at different times of day, especially at the beginning and end of the school day
— Check out the website of the middle school to get a feel for what is going on
— Identify key individuals at the middle school who can be contacted for information and guidance
— Request meeting that includes student, parents/guardians, current school personnel (elementary level), and future school personnel (middle school) to increase the probability of a seemless transition to middle school
— Become acquainted with course offerings, extracurricular options, and other features of the middle school experience
— Attend ALL orientation events (typically there will be only one) that are provided to students and their families who will be moving from the elementary level to the middle school level
— Provide opportunities for students to practice using lockers, moving quickly from one class to another, getting from and to transportation

**During the first few weeks of middle school:**

— Identify/locate a peer or peers who can act as supports for the students across all areas of need
— Assess how well the student is handling the routines/procedures of middle school
— Modify routines/procedures that have become problems for the student (e.g., tardiness to getting to classes on time)
— Assess how well the student is handling the academic demands of middle school
— Assess how well the student is handling the social aspects of middle school
— Encourage students to get involved in extracurricular activities

**Throughout middle school:**

— Monitor areas of problem as identified prior to going to middle school as well as any problems that arose after arrival
— Monitor student's academic and social/behavioral performance on an ongoing basis
— Continue to assess any concerns that parents/guardians might have
— Create opportunities for families to talk with each other about a wide range of issues and concerns that arise
— Begin to prepare for the next transition: moving from middle school to high school

## TRANSITION FROM SCHOOL TO COMMUNITY

Although earlier parts of this chapter draw attention to the importance of transition planning during various stages of a child's life, the transition from high school to adulthood is most often the subject of policy, research, and practice. In fact the concept of transition planning was first developed in the 1980s in response to the difficulty adolescents with disabilities sometimes experienced after leaving high school. At that time, family members, teachers, researchers, and policy makers focused on how to help youth with disabilities find employment. Members of this community came to realize, however, that finding fulfilling and gainful employment was only one component of adult life (Halpern, 1985).

Research and practice in the area of transition planning quickly expanded to include the much broader concept of community involvement. This expanded focus included independent living skills and social networks of people with disabilities, in addition to employment. Now, a wide range of transition planning domains are commonly identified as areas in need of attention: employment, postsecondary education, daily living skills, leisure activities, community participation, health care, self-determination, communication, and interpersonal relationships (Clark & Patton, 2006).

Originally mandated by the Individuals with Disabilities Education Act (IDEA) of 1990, transition services were defined as "a coordinated set of activities for a student, designed within an outcome-oriented process, which promotes movement from school to post-school activities including postsecondary education, vocational training, integrated employment, continuing adult education, adult service, independent living, or community participation" (cited in Williams & O'Leary, 2001). Most recently, this law was reauthorized as the Individuals with Disabilities Education Improvement Act of 2004. The latest reauthorization of IDEA (2004) includes the following mandated components of transition:

- Transition services, defined as "a coordinated set of activities for a student, designed within a results-oriented process"
- A transition plan, updated annually and in effect when the student reaches 16 years of age
- Measurable postsecondary goals, based on transition assessment results in education, employment, and independent living skills
- Services needed to attain postsecondary goals (this would include courses of study)
- Documentation that the student is informed of his or her rights as an adult no later than one year before age of legal adulthood (according to state law)

Despite the addition of transition services to special education programs, postsecondary outcomes for youth with disabilities continue to generate concern. One important measurement of postsecondary success is obtaining a high school diploma. This remains a challenge for adolescents with disabilities. The overall dropout rate for youth served under the IDEA is 29%, with only 57% of students in special education receiving a regular diploma and 11% receiving an alternative credential (U.S. General Accounting Office, 2003). See Figure 15-5 for details regarding disability type and high school diploma obtainment. Of course, educational attainment is relevant to other indicators of postsecondary success such as employment.

In 2000, the National Longitudinal Transition Study (NLTS), a 10-year study that follows youth with disabilities throughout their transition into young adulthood, began (SRI International, 2004). The results of this ongoing study provide a detailed picture of experiences across multiple transition domains including education, employment, and community involvement, to name only a few. Data also provide information about transition experiences across groups of youth by disability category, race/ethnicity, age, and gender. Although the first National Longitudinal Study (NLTS1), based on data gathered between 1985 and 1993, documented gaps in both types of employment (full and part time) and wages earned between transition-aged youth with disabilities and youth without disabilities, NLTS2 has provided evidence that employment and wage gaps are narrowing for youth with disabilities when compared to their age-peers without disabilities (Wagner, Newman, Cameto, & Levine, 2005). About 55% of youth with disabilities in NLTS1 gained paid work experiences after high school, whereas nearly 71% of youth with disabilities in NLTS2 had done so. Further, youth with disabilities in the second study were more likely to earn more than the federal minimum wage; however, this gain is mitigated by the fact that youth from NLTS2 were actually *less* likely to be employed full time (Wagner et al., 2005). Also, as with the NLTS1, gaps in employment and wages between these two groups may increase as youth age because youth with disabilities are less likely to obtain the benefits that are

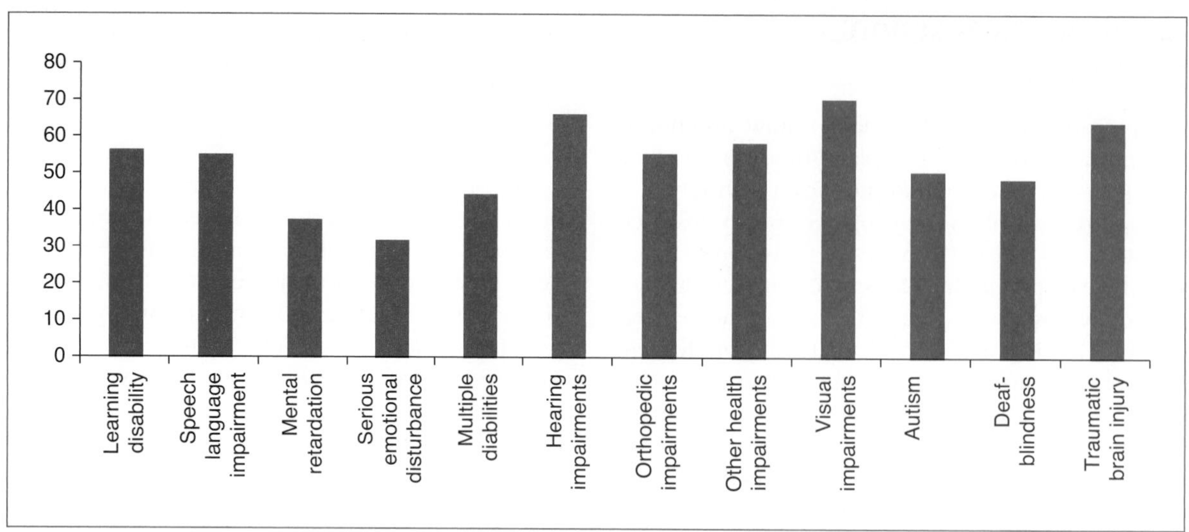


**FIGURE 15–5** Rate of high school diploma attainment in 2001–2002 for youth with disabilities across disability categories

*Source:* U.S. Department of Education (2006). Twenty-sixth annual report to congress on IDEA. Washington, DC: Author.

associated with college degrees (Blackorby & Wagner, 1996). Figure 15-6 details the types of jobs youth with disabilities are currently likely to hold compared to youth with disabilities from NLTS1.

Although the transition provisions in the IDEA 2004 provide specific information regarding the age of the child and the types of documents that must be in place to meet the letter of the law (policy compliance), they do little to describe the range of transition services that best meet the spirit of the law (alignment with preferred practices). In other words, what do effective transition services for adolescents with disabilities *actually* look like? Key elements of the postsecondary transition process are depicted in Figure 15-7. This model conveys the importance of a broad range of planning activities that requires collaboration among home, school, and adult agencies, occurring simultaneously with the purpose of increasing a student's ability to respond with knowledge, skills, and experience to the demands of adulthood.

In practice, postsecondary transition services vary widely from state to state, district to district, and even school to school (Destafano, Heck, Hasazi, & Furney, 1999). Some elements of transition planning may vary according to the needs and strengths associated with specific disabilities. For example, transition-related needs of young adults with high-incidence disabilities such as learning disabilities may differ from the needs of young adults with low-incidence disabilities such as students who are deaf/blind. Yet, several decades of practicing and researching transition services have resulted in a wide range of recommended transition practices. Three key, recommended practices are individualization of transition components, active student and family involvement, and interagency collaboration.

## Individualized Transition Components

An individualized transition plan is one part of a student's individualized education program (IEP) (Wehman, 2002). The transition document itself, however, may be a part of the IEP or a separate document altogether (Patton, 2004). The plan must be a formal, written plan that includes specific learning objectives relative to the transition goals of the student. Although recommended practices in transition suggest that domains other than education and employment should be addressed in individual transition plans, a review of existing transition plans revealed that other domains such as health care and transportation are far less likely to be addressed (Everson, Zhang, & Guillory, 2001).

Because transition is results-based, the document itself must contain a statement of expected outcomes in each postschool domain that the plan addresses. For example, in the domain of postsecondary education, is the expected outcome to attend college? If so, will the individual attend a community college, junior college, four-year university, or some other learning institution? Clearly, the learning objectives addressed in each major domain of the transition plan, as well as the plan to access the general education curriculum, must address

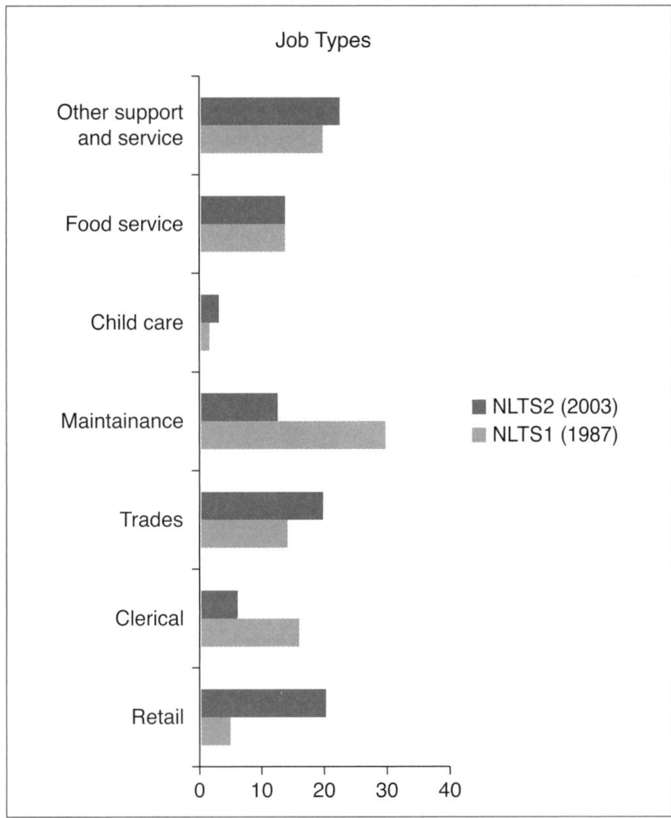


**FIGURE 15–6** Types of jobs held by young adults with disabilities after high school

*Source:* Wagner, M., Newman, L., Cameto, R., Garza, N., & Levine, P. (2005). *After High School: A First Look at the Postschool Experiences of Youth with Disabilities* (p. 4). Menlo Park, CA: SRI International.

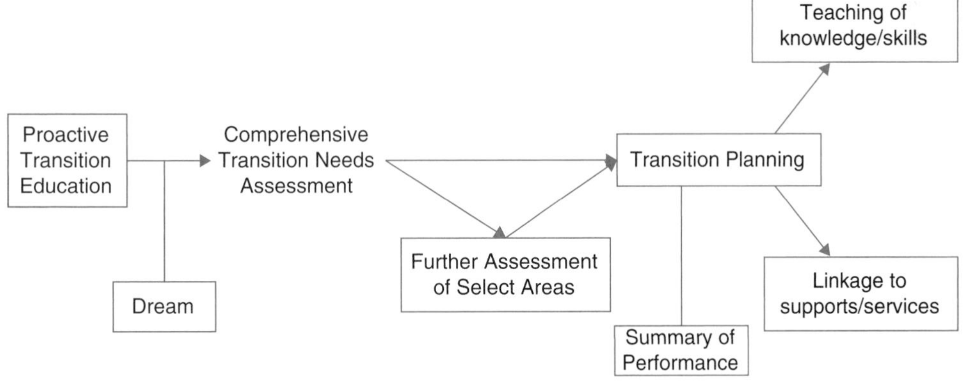


**FIGURE 15–7** The transition planning process

*Source:* Patton, J. R. (2007). *Transition Assessment and Planning: Evolution of a Concept and Actual Practice.* Unpublished manuscript. Austin, TX.

the expected outcome in that domain (Wehmeyer, 2002). This is important so that the educational goals in the IEP align with the long-term goals (or expected outcomes) stated in the transition component.

For example, if a student states that he wants to attend a four-year university, his IEP must contain learning objectives that contribute to making this goal become a reality. In this example, objectives would include necessary academic skills to prepare the student for a university setting (addressing strengths and needs in study skills, as well as core academic subjects such as reading and language arts). Furthermore, in this example, access to the general curriculum and state-wide assessments, whether stated in the IEP or in the transition component, must align with the goal of attending university. Although transition components may vary from one locale to the next, information essential to any transition component includes:

- employment
- postsecondary education
- daily living
- community involvement
- self-determination

A necessary activity in developing effective transition components based on individualized postschool goals is to collect data regarding the present level of functioning, as well as ongoing assessments of needs and strengths (Sitlington & Clark, 2006). For example, subject-specific, criterion-referenced tests provide a snapshot of students' academic abilities, and norm-referenced tests can be used to assess career aptitudes or establish college entrance criteria. Other assessments, both formal and informal, are specific to transition-related competencies, and may include career, vocational, functional, and ecological assessments (Sitlington, Neubert, & Leconte, 1997). These can include formal assessment tools (e.g., pen and paper tests), or informal observations and interviews of students and important adults (e.g., a supervisor at a part-time job setting). In addition to aptitude and ability, transition-related assessments are used to pinpoint students' preferences. Identifying students' preferences is an important step in individualizing the transition component. Table 15–4 lists examples of both formal and informal transition-related assessment activities.

Individualization is an essential element of any comprehensive transition component, yet this practice has not been implemented with widespread success. Many studies that have included reviews of transition components of IEPs have revealed that individualization was not occurring. At times, this lack of individualization resulted from the use of disability-based expected outcomes rather than the preferences of the student (Grigal, Test, Beattie, & Wood, 1997). More frequently, however, has been the documentation of a lack of student involvement in developing transition plans (Williams & O'Leary, 2001). One way to increase the individualization, and therefore the usefulness, of transition components is to increase the participation of the individual in the plan's creation.

## Active Student and Family Involvement

Increasing the active involvement of students with disabilities in the development and implementation of their transition component has the potential to increase the individualized nature of the document. In addition, incorporating students' perspectives (as required by the IDEA of 2004) fosters a sense of student ownership, increasing the active involvement of students in the implementation of plans that reflect

**TABLE 15–4** Formal and informal transition assessments

| | |
|---|---|
| **Formal Transition Assessments** | |
| Life Skills Inventory (Brigance, 1995) | Measurement assesses youth's life skill knowledge in a variety of transition-related domains (e.g., money and financial management, self-concept, personal safety) |
| The Social and Prevocational Information Battery—Revised (Halpern, Irvin, & Munkres, 1986) | Measurement assesses youth's skills in transition-related areas (e.g., communication, family living) |
| **Informal Transition Assessments** | |
| Work samples | An observation of youth in a natural setting (e.g., youth is at a computer performing a data-entry task) to determine level of interest and skill level |
| Interest inventories | A questionnaire that assesses youth's interest in particular activities related to a specific transition domain (e.g., recreation or employment) |
| Transition Planning Inventory (Clark & Patton, 2006) | A 46-item informal inventory that assesses youth's preferences, strengths, and needs in multiple transition domains (e.g., employment, education, health, self-determination) |

their goals for the future (Bassett & Lehmann, 2002). When planning and providing services related to postsecondary transition, incorporating the preferences of students with disabilities makes sense.

Adolescents must actively participate in transition planning and instructional activities so that teachers, family members, and personnel from outside agencies (for example, a job coach) understand adolescents' short- and long-term goals and are able to facilitate goal attainment. Although adolescents with and without disabilities may display a wide variety of preferences and maturity levels when invited to participate in formal meetings with adults, preliminary research shows that skills such as self-advocacy, goal setting, and problem solving can be taught (Powers, Turner, Westwood, Matuszewski, & Phillips, 2001).

**Self-Determination.** To capitalize on this active involvement, teachers and other adults must consistently promote student self-determination skills (see Chapter 13), as well as listen to the decisions young adults with disabilities make about their own lives and support them while they work to make their dreams become realities. Self-determination is a complex concept and has been defined in numerous ways (Field, Hoffman, & Spezia, 1998). Generally, the term refers to the attitudes and skills necessary to make choices, decisions, and goals, as well as take action to realize these goals. An underlying assumption is that self-determination includes causal agency, or the ability to act independently (Wehmeyer, 1994).

During the 1990s, research efforts focused on the development of transition curricula (for examples, see Table 15-5) that increased student self-determination during the transition planning process (Malian & Nevin, 2002). Research regarding the efficacy of these curricula has helped establish a correlation between self-determination and positive transition experiences from adolescence to adulthood. For example, use of the *Steps to Self-Determination* curriculum increased student competencies in decision making, goal setting, and self-assessment (Hoffman & Field, 1995). The use of another model, *ChoiceMaker*, resulted in an increase in student self-determination during the transition planning process (Martin & Huber-Marshall, 1995).

Some studies have found that teachers value active student participation in transition planning (Mason, McGahee-Kovac, Johnson, & Stillerman, 2002), but others have found adult service providers to be reluctant to share in decision-making processes with young adults with disabilities (Lehmann, Deniston, Tobin, & Howard, 1996). Increasing the active roles of students requires opportunity for practice, material and time resources for training, and professional collaboration (Lehmann, Bassett, Sands, Spencer, & Gliner, 1999).

**Parent Participation.** Student engagement in the transition planning process is important, but the involvement of other family members is also an essential element in transition planning. In fact, parent participation throughout all special education processes is mandated by the IDEA (2004). Additionally, parents and siblings, and in many cases extended family members, play important roles as advocates, role models, and supporters, to name just a few. When educators and other school personnel invite family members to actively participate in transition planning, the end result is a meaningful, individualized plan that addresses postsecondary transition goals that are specific to the person with a disability (Hanley-Maxwell, Pogoloff, & Whitney-Thomas, 1998).

Positive collaboration between families and schools during the transition process can, and does, occur. Families have expressed that professionals who listen carefully to their needs while arranging connections between them and community resources are highly valued (deFur, Todd-Allen, & Getzel, 2001). The creation of a trusting relationship between home and school, as well as effective communication and logistics that favor parents' schedule constraints, have the potential to facilitate parent

**TABLE 15–5** Selected self-determination programs that address transition-related skills and knowledge

Field, S., & Hoffman, A. (1996). *Steps to self-determination.* Austin, TX: PRO-ED.

Martin, J. E., & Huber Marshall, L. (1994). *ChoiceMaker self-determination transition assessment and curriculum.* Colorado Springs: University of Colorado at Colorado Springs, Center for Educational Research.

Brolin, D. (1993). *Life-centered career education: A competency-based approach.* Reston, VA: Council for Exceptional Children.

Wehmeyer, M. (1995). *Whose future is it anyway?* Arlington, TX: The ARC National Headquarters.

involvement (Salembier & Furney, 1997). Barriers to the active involvement of family members have also been identified in research. Some concerns family members have shared about the successful transition of their children with disabilities include a sense that partnerships between school and home were limited (Schuster, Timmons, & Molony, 2003) and that family-identified transition needs and goals are not consistently represented on transition plans (Thompson, Fulk, & Piercy, 2000).

**Cultural Reciprocity.** One consideration when involving both students and their family members in transition-related planning and implementation is cultural reciprocity. As the U.S. student population becomes more racially/ethnically diverse, America's teaching force must learn to respond to this diversity in ways that engage members of culturally and linguistically diverse subpopulations. Cause for concern about the efficacy of transition planning and instruction and diverse groups of young adults stem from evidence

### DIVERSITY IN THE CLASSROOM *Tips*

**Ginger Blalock**, Ph.D., is an emeritus professor at the University of New Mexico and principal investigator on three New Mexico state-funded grants. Considerations listed below are taken from these grants regarding transition, self-determination skills, and evaluation of a long-term community of practice model in transition.

Educators (general and special education teachers, administrators, transition specialists, related services staff) and families (as their critical transition partners) need to consider several diversity-related factors when helping youth chart their paths for the future.

1. When implementing future-focused planning and new curricula related to preparing for the future (such as self-determination or life skills curricula), asking families for permission to implement new curricula is essential. During that process, families should be introduced to the curriculum (its purposes and procedures) and asked if they wish to provide suggestions or guidelines for using the curriculum in culturally appropriate ways. Their guidance may make the difference in the new intervention's success, since more collectivist-oriented cultures and communities may have varied perspectives on the place of personal goal-setting in one's development.
2. Based on the guidance above, in concert with guidance from community educational leaders, modify self-determination and other instruction to incorporate as many family/community/cultural elements as feasible. Record and monitor those changes and their impact, in order to examine the effect of such instructional changes.
3. From a district perspective, all evidence points to the importance of starting early with student involvement in the IEP planning and with family discussions of long-range planning. As soon as children enter the system, they can play a role in discussing their annual and long-term plans. Self-determination instruction may be essential as a structure to prepare students for such activity, but the cautions in paragraph 1 above apply.
4. Identify all school system guidelines that relate to career development and transition programming to align as closely as possible with imperatives that affect ALL students. Use these in discussions with colleagues, families, and students as a way to avoid duplication of efforts and as a structure for making culturally/linguistically appropriate changes.
5. Use parents and parent advocates (e.g., home/school liaisons common in very diverse communities) to help families understand the importance of transition planning for all students, particularly for those with special needs. These support staff can also help inform families regarding their roles in the transition process.
6. In advance of implementing new training or procedures, hold informational meetings after school in community centers, churches or synagogues, tribal chapter houses, or other appropriate locations your students' families frequent. With the help of cultural or language "interpreters" and local community leaders, share information on transition planning procedures and importance, transition resources, family roles/rights/responsibilities, and student self-determination.
7. Help initiate a community (local or regional) transition team as a vehicle to ensure cultural/linguistic representation affecting transition programming.
8. Inform youth and families far in advance (no later than eighth grade) of all the building-block steps that should occur each year for successful transitions to adult life.
9. Low-income youth will need *paid* internships or work-study placements in order to participate and often are extremely productive workers due to economic need.
10. Youth in rural and remote districts will have the fewest opportunities for work-based learning as well as linkages to adult services. Teaching these youth how to establish and run student-led enterprises will be a critical option. In some communities, tribal enterprises and family-run businesses will be essential options for work-based learning.

illustrating that youth of color, English language learners, and youth of all races/ethnicities from low socioeconomic backgrounds all face challenges to successful postsecondary transition in employment and postsecondary education. Outcomes for many adolescents in these groups are noticeably less positive than outcomes for adolescents without disabilities, as well as European American adolescents with disabilities. For example, results from NLTS2 revealed that, despite gains in employment African American and Latino youth with disabilities between NLTS1 (1987) and NLTS2 (2003), gaps in employment outcomes among European Americans, African Americans, and Latinos with disabilities after high school commencement or completion continue to be a problem. Table 15-6 depicts differences in earnings among groups based on ethnicity and socioeconomic background, comparing data sets from NLTS1 (1987) and NLTS2 (2003).

In addition to differential measurements of outcomes such as employment rates and enrollment in colleges and universities, surveys of diverse groups of parents indicate that collaborative experiences with schools have the potential to be negative experiences in which the cultural identity of families has been disregarded (Geenen, Powers, Lopez-Vasques, & Bersani, 2003).

Understanding the values and beliefs embedded in special education and transition is one of the first steps in becoming culturally responsive (Kalyanpur & Harry, 1999). For example, the concept of transition itself is built upon ideals of independence and equity, which means that the preferred practices in transition planning and implementation support increasing students' abilities to become self-determining, as well as obtaining the same opportunities as their peers without disabilities. These values and beliefs, however, may be

**TABLE 15–6** Changes in wages of youth with disabilities across groups by socioeconomic status and ethnicity

| | *Income* | | | *Race/Ethnicity* | | |
|---|---|---|---|---|---|---|
| | ***Lowest*** | ***Medium*** | ***Highest*** | ***White*** | ***African American*** | ***Hispanic*** |
| Percentage earning: | | | | | | |
| Less than minimum wage | | | | | | |
| Wave 1 | 48.8 | 45.8 | 34.3 | 39.0 | 51.7 | 69.1 |
| | (11.1) | (11.5) | (8.4) | (6.2) | (18.5) | (16.9) |
| Wave 2 | 12.2 | 5.1 | 7.7 | 6.1 | 13.9 | 8.4 |
| | (5.7) | (4.4) | (4.5) | (2.8) | (8.8) | (8.6) |
| Percentage-point change | –36.6** | –40.7*** | –26.6** | –32.9*** | –37.8 | –60.7** |
| More than $7.00 per hour | | | | | | |
| Wave 1 | 13.5 | 15.3 | 20.9 | 18.1 | 5.8 | 7.0 |
| | (7.0) | (8.3) | (7.2) | (4.9) | (8.7) | (0.3) |
| Wave 2 | 32.3 | 29.9 | 49.1 | 45.8 | 31.0 | 24.6 |
| | (8.2) | (9.2) | (8.4) | (5.9) | (11.8) | (13.3) |
| Percentage-point change | +18.8 | +14.6 | +28.2* | +27.7*** | +25.2 | +17.6 |
| Average hourly wage per week | | | | | | |
| Wave 1 | $6.20 | $5.60 | $6.30 | $6.00 | $6.30 | $5.70 |
| | ($.80) | ($.60) | ($.40) | ($1.30) | ($1.00) | ($1.00) |
| Wave 2 | $6.90 | $7.10 | $7.50 | $7.60 | $6.50 | $6.60 |
| | ($.40) | ($.50) | ($.50) | ($.30) | ($.60) | ($.80) |
| Dollar amount change | +$.70 | +$1.50 | +$1.20 | +$1.60*** | +$.20 | +$.90 |

*Note*: Statistically significant difference in a two-tailed test at the following levels: *$p < .05$; **$p < .01$; ***$p < .001$.

Standard errors are in parentheses.

*Source:* Wagner, M., Newman, L., Cameto, R., Garza, N., & Levine, P. (2005). *After high school: A first look at the postschool experiences of youth with disabilities.* Menlo Park, CA: SRI International.

interpreted differently by people, in part based on their cultural identities (deFur & Williams, 2002). Although racial/ethnic identities are an important contributing factor to our cultural identities, socioeconomic status, as well as disability status, and many other characteristics contribute to our identities as individuals and as members of groups.

Additional surveys of parents' perspectives on transition provide evidence that the type of disability also influences parents' expectations for transition planning and instruction (Grigal & Neubert, 2004). For example, these researchers found that parents of children with low-incidence disabilities (e.g., traumatic brain injury) placed more emphasis on the importance of transition activities that address life skills than parents of children with high-incidence disabilities (e.g., learning disabilities). On the other hand, both groups of parents stated their intention for their children to attend postsecondary education.

Student and family involvement are also important to successful postsecondary transition because their active engagement in transition activities will better prepare them for interagency collaboration as they access service providers as adults. If parents are involved in planning meetings along with representatives of adult agencies, acquaintances are made and information about services is shared prior to exiting high school.

## Interagency Collaboration

Whereas educational and related services are guaranteed to youth with disabilities in the public schools, adult agencies provide services based on eligibility rather than entitlement (Cozzens, Dowdy, & Smith, 1999). This means that postsecondary transition involves a shifting of shared responsibility, and that an adult with a disability, and in some cases with the assistance of his or her family members, must learn to disclose disability status, access adult agencies, and participate in eligibility determination activities.

The IDEA of 1997 required that connections between the school-aged student with disabilities and appropriate adult agencies be explicitly addressed in transition components of IEPs: "a statement of the interagency responsibilities or any need linkages" will be in place by age 16 (Section 614, vii, II). Although the 2004 reauthorization of this legislation did not include this specification, such collaboration is a necessary component of successful transition, as emphasized at the beginning of this chapter. Linking services to schools for the purpose of transition planning necessitates interagency collaboration (Agran, Cain, & Cavin, 2002).

Some examples of adult agencies are:

- Social Security Administration
- Federal employment programs (e.g., Ticket to Work)
- Vocational rehabilitation agencies
- State/local/private service providers for people with cognitive disabilities or mental health needs
- Postsecondary educational institutions
- Disability advocacy groups

Connecting youth with disabilities to programs and agencies they will need to access once they have exited high school is one way to increase the potential for postsecondary success in a variety of transition domains, including employment, education, and community participation. These connections, like all other aspects of transition planning, must be individualized. Some young adults with disabilities may need to establish connections to independent living facilities such as group homes, whereas others may need to contact offices for student services at colleges and universities to determine available academic supports.

Key to establishing these relationships is to formalize the connection within the transition component, including inviting adult agency representatives to transition planning meetings as well as incorporating related short-term goals that establish contact between the student and the agency representative. For a student who has an interest in pursuing a career in photography, for example, linking her to adult service providers might involve arranging a visit to the local community college where she would meet with a student services provider/counselor to determine how the college could accommodate her needs. In addition, subsequent visits could be arranged where she could meet other students with similar interests, perhaps sit in on a class, and/or participate in a tour of the photography facilities. The point here is to establish a multiyear, outcomes-based goal (e.g., pursue an associate's degree in photography) and develop short-term goals that both align with the long-term goal and create connections to adult agencies.

Although linking students to adult services providers is a recommended practice, Agran et al. (2002) surveyed rehabilitation counselors and teachers and found that counselors were rarely invited to transition planning meetings, and that a lack of collaboration between adult vocational rehabilitation agencies and schools characterized the process. A lack of connections to other adult services such as social security administrators and representatives from work incentive programs have also been documented (Schuster et al., 2003; Thompson et al., 2000). Weak or nonexistent connections to adult service providers may also serve as additional barriers for culturally and linguistically diverse families. Geenen et al. (2003) found that language barriers and unfamiliarity with adult agencies contributed to diverse family members' decisions to *not* pursue services for their young adult children with disabilities.

### Other Issues in Postsecondary Transition

The preceding discussion has not exhaustively addressed postsecondary transition issues. The transition needs of youth in special education are being addressed in both general and special education, by transition specialists within special education, and by researchers who specialize in studying how adolescents with disabilities move from high school to the demands of adult living. Additionally, parents and families engage children with disabilities in transition-related issues in an ongoing manner.

Considering the breadth of transition within the field of special education, many important discussions are beyond the scope of this chapter. Additional issues concern access and accountability during the transition process, including access to the general curriculum (Wehmeyer, 2002) and graduation requirements and high-stakes assessment outcomes (Johnson, Stodden, Emanuel, Lueking, & Mack, 2002). Each of these issues intersects with the aforementioned foci in this field.

Students with disabilities, and their family members, are key players in making decisions about courses and participation in assessments, for example. Additionally, questions about linguistic and cultural diversity must be addressed in problem-solving efforts around access and accountability. Last, each of these issues must be considered in the context of the individual, with a particular focus on related strengths, needs, and preferences.

Reflective Question 15–4: ***What are the key considerations that serve as a foundation for the successful development and implementation of individual transition programs?***

## SUMMARY

This chapter covered a number of topics related to transition, as this process applies to students with special needs. The first part of the chapter introduced the notion of vertical and horizontal transitions. It also highlighted the critical components that contribute to successful transitions. The next three sections of the chapter focused on three key transitions that students with special needs face during their school careers: transition into school, transition from elementary school to middle school, and transition from high school to young adulthood. Important points that must be recognized and understood in regard to each of these transitions were discussed.

# References


A long way to go. (1995, November/December). *Teacher Magazine*, 17.

A4esl.org. (2006). *Self-study idiom quizzes*. Retrieved August 18, 2006, from http://a4esl.org/q/h/idioms.html

Abbott, M., Walton, C., & Greenwood, C. R. (2002). Phonemic awareness in kindergarten and first grade. *Teaching Exceptional Children, 34*, 20–26.

Abery, B., Rudrud, L., Arndt, L., Schauben, L., & Eggebeen, A. (1995). Evaluating a multicomponent program for enhancing the self-determination of youth with disabilities. *Intervention in School and Clinic, 30*, 170–179.

Abrams, B. J., & Segal, A. (1998). How to prevent aggressive behavior. *Teaching Exceptional Children, 30*(4), 10–15.

Abruscato, J., & Hassard, J. (1978). *The earthpeople activity book: People, places, pleasures and other delights*. Santa Monica, CA: Goodyear.

Academe Today. (1998, May 21). How technology changes the way we read and write. *Academic Today Daily Report*.

Ackerman, P. T., Holloway, C. A., Youngdahl, P. L., & Dykman, R. A. (2001). The double-deficit theory of reading disability does not fit all. *Learning Disabilities Research and Practice, 16*, 152–160.

Adams, A., Carnine, D., & Gersten, R. (1982). Instructional strategies for studying content area texts in the intermediate grades. *Reading Research Quarterly, 18*, 27–55.

Adger, C. T. (1993). No talking is no good: Student voices in academic discourse. *LD Forum, 18*(2), 26–28.

Administration for Children and Families. (1996). *Head Start Program Performance Standards* (45-CFR 1304). Washington, DC: Department of Health and Human Services.

Administration for Children, Youth, and Families, Head Start Bureau. Bricker, D. (2001). A natural environment: A useful construct? *Infants and Young Children, 13*(4), 21–31.

Agran, M., Cain, H. M., & Cavin, M. D. (2002). Enhancing the involvement of rehabilitation counselors in the transition process. *Career Development for Exceptional Individuals, 25*, 141–155.

Al Otaiba, S., & Rivera, M. O. (2006). Individualized guided oral reading fluency instruction for students with emotional and behavioral disorders. *Intervention in School and Clinic*, 41, 144–149.

Alberto, P. A., & Troutman, A. C. (2003). *Applied behavior analysis for teachers* (6th ed). Upper Saddle River, NJ: Merrill/Prentice Hall.

Alberto, P. A., & Troutman, A. C. (2006). *Applied behavior analysis for teachers* (7th ed.). Upper Saddle River, NJ: Merrill/Prentice Hall.

Alexander, J. E. (1988). *Teaching reading*. Glenview, IL: Scott Foresman/Little, Brown.

Algozzine, B., & Ysseldyke, J. (1994). *Simple ways to make teaching math more fun* (Elementary school edition). Longmont, CO: Sopris West.

Algozzine, B., & Ysseldyke, J. (1995). *Tactics for improving parenting skills*. Longmont, CO: Sopris West.

Allen, J. (1999). *Words, words, words: Teaching vocabulary in grades 4–12*. Portland, ME: Stenhouse.

Allen, R. V., & Halvorsen, G. C. (1961). *The language experience approach to reading instruction*. Boston: Ginn.

Alley, G., & Deshler, D. (1979). *Teaching the learning disabled adolescent: Strategies and methods*. Denver, CO: Love.

Alliance for Excellent Education. (2005). *Reading Next: A vision for action and research in middle and high school literacy*. Retrieved March 11, 2005, from http://www.all4ed.org/publications/ReadingNext/AppendixA.html

Alliance for Technology Access. (2006). *Assistive technology in K–12 schools*. Retrieved August 9, 2006, from http://www.ataccess.org/resources/atk12/default.html

Allison, L., Burns, M., & Weitzman, D. (1975). *My backyard history book*. Boston: Little, Brown Young Readers.

Allor, J. H. (2002). The relationships of phonemic awareness and rapid naming to reading development. *Learning Disability Quarterly, 25*, 47–57.

Alston, J., & Taylor, J. (1987). *Handwriting: Theory, research, and practice*. New York: Nichols.

Amdor N. (2006). *Lesson plan: Assistive technology in the writing process*. Retrieved August 17, 2006, from http://www.intime.uni.edu/lessons/001.ahs/default.htm

American Association on Mental Retardation. (1994). AAMR Board approves policy on facilitated communication. *AAMR News & Notes, 7*(5), 2.

American Speech-Language-Hearing Association. (1982). Definitions: Communicative disorders and variations. *ASHA, 24*, 949–950.

American Speech-Language-Hearing Association. (1983). Position paper: Social dialects. *ASHA, 25*, 23–24.

American Speech-Language-Hearing Association. (1991a). Augmentative and alternative communication. *ASHA, 33*(Suppl. 5), 8.

American Speech-Language-Hearing Association. (1991b). A model for collaborative service delivery for students with language-learning disorders in the public schools. *ASHA, 33*(Suppl. 5), 44–50.

American Speech-Language-Hearing Association. (2003a). Technical report: American English dialects. *ASHA Supplement 23*, in press. Retrieved June 5, 2003, from http://professional.asha.org/resources/deskrefs/loader.cfm?url=/commonspot/security/getfile.cfm&PageID=21330

American Speech-Language-Hearing Association. (2003b). *How does your child hear and talk?* Retrieved June 5, 2003, from http://www.asha.org/speech/development/child_hear_talk.cfm

American Speech-Language-Hearing Association. (2003c). *Language and literacy development*. Retrieved June 5, 2003, from http://www.asha.org/speech/development/lang_lit.cfm

American Speech-Language-Hearing Association. (2003d). *Communication facts: Incidence and prevalence of communication disorders and hearing loss in children—2002 edition*. Retrieved May 15, 2003, from http://professional.asha.org/resources/factsheets/children.cfm

American Speech-Language-Hearing Association. (2003e). *Late bloomer or language problem?* Retrieved June 5, 2003, from http://www.asha.org/speech/disabilities/Late-Blooming-or-Language-Problem.cfm

American Speech-Language-Hearing Association. (2003f). *Language-based learning disabilities*. Retrieved June 5, 2003, from http://www.asha.org/speech/disabilities/Language-Based-Learning-Disabilities.cfm

American Speech-Language-Hearing Association. (2003g). *Introduction to augmentative and alternate communication*. Retrieved June 5, 2003, from http://www.asha.org/speech/disabilities/disabilities.cfm

Archer, A., & Gleason, M. (1989). *Skills for school success*. North Billerica, MA: Curriculum Associates.

Archer, A., & Gleason, M. (1995). Skills for school success. In P. T. Cegelka & W. H. Berdine (Eds.), *Effective instruction for students with learning difficulties* (pp. 227–263). Boston: Allyn & Bacon.

Area Education Agency 7, Cedar Rapids, IA. (2003). *Development of play*. Retrieved June 23, 2003, from http://specialed.aea7.k12.ia.us/childfind/playdevel.html

Argyle, M. (1967). *The psychology of interpersonal behavior*. London: Penguin.

Argyle, M., & Kendon, A. (1967). The experimental analysis of social performance. In L. Berkowitz (Ed.), *Advances in social psychology*. New York: Academic Press.

Arkenberg, R. (2005). Symmetry and pattern. *School Arts, 105*, 59.

Armbruster, B. B., & Anderson, T. H. (1988). On selecting considerate content area textbooks. *Remedial and Special Education, 9*, 47–52.

Armstrong, D. G. (1984). Helping youngsters grapple with textbook terminology. *The Social Studies, 75*, 216–219.

Artiles, A. J., & Ortiz, A. (Eds.). (2003). *English language learners with special needs: Identification, placement and instruction*. Washington, DC: Center for Applied Linguistics.

Asher, S. R., & Hymel, S. (1981). Children's social competence in peer relations: Sociometric and behavioral assessment. In J. D. Wine & M. D. Smye (Eds.), *Social competence*. New York: Guilford Press.

Ashlock, R. B. (2006). *Error patterns in computation: Using error patterns to improve instruction*. Upper Saddle River, NJ: Merrill/Prentice Hall.

Assistive technology policy and practice: What is the right thing to do? What is the responsible thing to do? What is required and must be done? A conversation with Dr. Diane Golden. (January, 1999). *Special Education Technology and Practice*. Whitefish Bay, WI: Knowledge by Design, Inc.

Association for Supervision and Curriculum Development. (1997, Spring). Teaching young writers. *Curriculum Update*.

Association for Supervision and Curriculum Development. (1999). Speaking and listening: The first basic skills. *Education Update, 41*, 6–7.

Atwood, R. K., & Oldham, B. R. (1985). Teachers' perceptions of mainstreaming in an inquiry-oriented elementary science program. *Science Education, 69*, 619–624.

August, D., & Shanahan, T. (Eds.). (2006). *Developing literacy in second-language learners: Report of the national literacy panel on language-minority children and youth*. Mahwah, NJ: Lawrence Erlbaum.

Austin, T. (1994). *Changing the view: Student-led parent conferences*. Portsmouth, NH: Heinemann.

Axelrod, S., Hall, R. V., & Tams, A. (1979). Comparison of two common classroom seating arrangements. *Academic Therapy, 15*, 29–36.

Bae, J. T., & Clark, G. (2005). Incorporate diversity awareness in the classroom: What teachers can do. *Intervention in School at Clinic, 41*, 49–51.

Bailey, E. J. (1975). *Academic activities for adolescents with learning disabilities*. Evergreen, CO: Learning Pathways.

Baker, C., & Gulley, B. (2004). The impact of the No Child Left Behind Act. In S. Burkhardt, F. Obiakur, & A. Rotatori (Eds.), *Current perspectives or learning disabilities* (pp. 235–250). Amsterdam: Elsevier.

Baker, M. (1981). *Focus on life science*. Columbus, OH: Merrill.

Baker, S., Gersten, R., & Scanlon, D. (2002). Procedural facilitators and cognitive strategies: Tools for unraveling the mysteries of comprehension and the writing process, and for providing meaningful access to the general curriculum. *Learning Disabilities Research and Practice, 17*, 65–77.

Ball, D. W. (1978). *ESS/Special education teacher's guide*. St. Louis: Webster/McGraw-Hill.

Ballew, H. (1973). *Teaching children mathematics.* Columbus, OH: Merrill.

Bandura, A. (1977). Self-efficiency: Toward a unifying theory of behavior change. *Psychological Review, 84,* 191–215.

Bankson, N. (1990). *Bankson language test* (2nd ed.). Austin, TX: PRO-ED.

Barclay, K. D. (1990). Constructing meaning: An integrated approach to teaching reading. *Intervention, 26,* 84–91.

Baroni, D. (1987). Have primary children draw to expand vocabulary. *The Reading Teacher, 40,* 819–820.

Barrera, I., Corso, R., & Macpherson, D. (2003). *Skilled dialogue: Strategies for responding to cultural diversity in early childhood.* Baltimore, MD: Paul H. Brookes.

Barrera, I., & Kramer, L. (1997). From monologues to skilled dialogues: Teaching the process of crafting culturally competent early childhood environments. In P. J. Winton, J. A. McCollum, & C. Catlett (Eds.), *Reforming personnel preparation in early intervention: Issues, models, and practical strategies* (pp. 217–251). Baltimore, MD: Paul H. Brooks.

Barrish, H. H., Saunders, M., & Wolf, M. M. (1969). Good behavior game: Effects of individual contingencies for group consequences on disruptive behavior in a classroom. *Journal of Applied Behavior Analysis, 2,* 119–124.

Bartel, N. R. (1990). Problems in mathematics achievement. In D. D. Hammill & N. R. Bartel (Eds.), *Teaching children with learning and behavior problems* (5th ed., pp. 289–343). Boston: Allyn & Bacon.

Barton, L. E., Brulle, A. R., & Repp, A. C. (1983). Aversive techniques and the doctrine of least restrictive alternative. *Exceptional Education Quarterly, 3*(4), 1–8.

Bassett, D. S. (n.d.). *Content area reading teaching packet.* Unpublished guide. Anchorage, AK: University of Alaska.

Bassett, D. S., & Lehmann, J. (2002). *Student-focused conferencing and planning.* Austin, TX: PRO-ED.

Bateman, B. D. (1971). *The essentials of teaching.* Sioux Falls, SD: Dimensions.

Bateman, B. D. (1982). Legal and ethical dilemmas of special educators. *Exceptional Education Quarterly, 2*(4), 57–67.

Bateman, B. D., & Linden, M. A. (1998). *Better IEPs: How to develop legally correct and educationally useful programs* (3rd ed.). Reston, VA: Council for Exceptional Children.

Bates, E. (1976). *Language in context.* New York: Academic Press.

Bates, E., Thal, D., & MacWhinney, B. (1991). A functionalist approach to language and its implications for assessment and intervention. In T. M. Gallagher (Ed.), *Pragmatics of language: Clinical practice issues.* San Diego, CA: Singular.

Baumback, D., & Bird, M. (1999). The seven habits of highly effective technology-using educators. *Special Education Technology Practice, 1*(2), 12–14.

Bauwens, J., & Hourcade, J. (1995). *Cooperative teaching.* Austin, TX: PRO-ED.

Bauwens, J., & Korinek, L. (1993). IEPs for cooperative teaching: Developing legal and useful documents. *Intervention in School and Clinic, 28,* 303–306.

Bean, T. W., Valerio, P. C., & Senior, H. M. (1999). Intertextuality and the e-mail discussion of a multicultural novel in secondary American literature. In T. Shanahan & F. V. Rodriguez-Brown (Eds.), *National Reading Conference Yearbook* (p. 48). Chicago: National Reading Conference, Inc.

Beatty, L. S., Gardner, E. G., Madden, R., & Karlsen, B. (1985). *Stanford Diagnostic Mathematics Test* (3rd ed.). San Antonio, TX: Psychological.

Beck, I. L., McKeown, M. G., & Kucan, L. (2002). *Bringing words to life: Robust vocabulary instruction.* New York: Guilford Press.

Beck, J., Broers, J., Hogue, E., Shipstead, J., & Knowlton, E. (1994). Strategies for functional community-based instruction and inclusion for children with mental retardation. *Teaching Exceptional Children, 26,* 44–48.

Becker, W. C., & Carnine, D. W. (1980). Direct instruction. In B. B. Lahey & A. E. Kazdin (Eds.), *Advances in clinical child psychology* (Vol. 3, pp. 429–473). New York: Plenum Press.

Becker, W. C., & Carnine, D. W. (1981). Direct instruction: A behavior theory model for comprehensive educational intervention with the disadvantaged. In S. W. Bijou & R. Ruiz (Eds.), *Behavior modification: Contributions to education* (pp. 145–210). Hillsdale, NJ: Erlbaum.

Becker, W. C., Engelmann, S., & Thomas, D. R. (1971). *Teaching: A course in applied psychology.* Chicago: Science Research Associates.

Beirne-Smith, M., & Riley, T. (2004). Spelling assessment and instruction. In E. A. Polloway, L. Miller, & T. E. C. Smith (Eds.), *Language instruction for students with disabilities* (pp. 395–430). Denver, CO: Love Publishing.

Beirne-Smith, M., & Thompson, B. (1992). Spelling instruction. In E. A. Polloway & T. E. C. Smith (Eds.), *Language instruction for students with disabilities* (pp. 347–376). Denver, CO: Love.

Bellack, A. S., & Hersen, M. (1979). *Research and practice in social skills.* New York: Plenum Press.

Bellack, A. S., & Hersen, M. (1997). *Research and practice in social skills* (2nd ed.). New York: Plenum Press.

Bender, W. N. (2002). *Differentiated instruction for students with learning disabilities.* Thousand Oaks, CA: Corwin Press.

Bender, W. N. (2005). *Differentiating math instruction: Strategies that work for K–8 classrooms.* Thousand Oaks, CA: Corwin Press.

Bereiter, C., & Engelmann, S. (1966). *Teaching disadvantaged children in the preschool.* Upper Saddle River, NJ: Prentice Hall.

Berger, J. (2005, June 5). Striving in America, and the spelling bee. *New York Times,* p. 5, section 4.

Bergeron, B. (1990). What does the term whole language mean? Constructing a definition from the literature. *Journal of Reading Behavior, 22,* 301–330.

Bergland, B., & Hiffbauer, D. (1996). New opportunities for students with traumatic brain injuries. *Teaching Exceptional Children, 28*, 54–56.

Berliner, D. C. (1988). The half-full glass: A review of research on teaching. In E. L. Meyen, G. A. Vergason, & R. J. Whelan (Eds.), *Effective instructional strategies for exceptional children* (pp. 7–31). Denver, CO: Love.

Berninger, V., Abbott, R., Rugan, L., Reed, E., Abbott, J., Brooks, A., Vaughn, K., & Graham, S. (1998). Teaching spelling to children with learning disabilities: The mind's ear and eye beats the computer or pencil. *Learning Disability Quarterly, 21*, 106–122.

Bernstein, D. K., & Tiegerman, E. (1993). *Language and communication disorders in children* (3rd ed.). Upper Saddle River, NJ: Merrill/Prentice Hall.

Bernstein, D. K., & Tiegerman-Farber, E. (1997). *Language and communication disorders in children* (4th ed.). Boston: Allyn & Bacon.

Bertin, P., & Perlman, E. (2000). After your students write: What's next? *Teaching Exceptional Children, 20*, 4–9.

Bhat, P., Rapport, M. J. K., & Griffin, C. C. (2000). A legal perspective on the use of specific reading methods for students with learning disabilities. *Learning Disability Quarterly, 23*, 283–297.

Bickel, W. E., & Bickel, D. D. (1986). Effective schools, classrooms, and instruction: Implications for special education. *Exceptional Children, 52*, 489–500.

Bigge, J. L., & Stump, C. S. (1999). *Curriculum, assessment, and instruction for students with disabilities*. Belmont, CA: Wadsworth.

Bijou, S. W., & Baer, D. M. (1978). *Behavior analysis of child development*. Upper Saddle River, NJ: Prentice Hall.

Bijou, S. W., Birnbrauer, J. S., Kidder, J. D., & Tague, C. (1966). Programmed approach to retarded children. *Psychological Record, 16*, 505–522.

Birchell, G. R., & Taylor, B. L. (1986). Is the elementary social studies curriculum headed back-to-basics? *The Social Studies, 77*, 80–82.

Bishop, K., & Jubala, K. (1994). By June, given shared experiences, integrated classes, and equal opportunities, Jaime will have a friend. *Teaching Exceptional Children, 27*, 36–40.

Blachowicz, C., & Ogle, D. (2001). *Reading comprehension: Strategies for independent learners*. New York: Guilford Press.

Blackburn, J. M. (1989). Acquisition and generalization of social skills in elementary-aged children with learning disabilities. *Journal of Learning Disabilities, 22*, 28–34.

Blackburn, J., Patton, J. R., & Trainor, A. (2003). *Exceptional individuals in focus* (7th ed.). Upper Saddle River: NJ: Merrill/Prentice Hall.

Blackorby, J., & Wagner, M. (1996). Longitudinal postschool outcomes of youth with disabilities: Findings from the National Longitudinal Transition Study. *Exceptional Children, 62*, 399–413.

Blagden, C. M. (1991, April). *Whole language: The natural way to improve language skills*. Paper presented at the Council for Exceptional Children Conference, Atlanta, GA.

Blalock, G. (1991). Paraprofessionals: Critical team members in our special education programs. *Intervention in School and Clinic, 26*, 200–214.

Blalock, G., Bassett, D., & Donisthorpe, L. (1989). *Team strategies for serving special needs students in vocational programs*. Unpublished manuscript, University of New Mexico.

Blalock, G., Mahoney, B., & Dalia, J. (1992). *Albuquerque Public Schools job coach training manual*. Albuquerque, NM: A P. S. Transition Services Project.

Blalock, G., Rivera, D., Anderson, K., & Kottler, B. (1992). A school district/university partnership in paraprofessional training. *LD Forum, 17*(13), 29–36.

Blalock, V. E. (1984). *Factors influencing the effectiveness of paraprofessionals with disabled populations*. Unpublished doctoral dissertation, University of Texas at Austin.

Blandy, D. (1993). Community-based lifelong learning in art for adults with mental retardation: A rationale, conceptual foundation, and supportive environment. *Studies in Art Education, 34*, 167–175.

Bley, N. S., & Thornton, C. A. (1995). *Teaching mathematics to students with learning disabilities* (3rd ed.). Austin, TX: PRO-ED.

Bley, N. S., & Thornton, C. A. (2001). *Teaching mathematics to students with learning disabilities* (4th ed.). Austin, TX: PRO-ED.

Bloom, L., & Lahey, M. (1978). *Language development and language disorders*. New York: Wiley.

Blough, G., & Schwartz, J. (1974). *Teaching elementary science*. New York: Holt, Rinehart & Winston.

Boehm, A. E. (1986). *Boehm Test of Basic Concepts—Preschool*. San Antonia, TX: Psychological.

Boekel, N., & Steele, J. M. (1972). Science education for the exceptional child. *Focus on Exceptional Children, 4*(4), 1–15.

Bogojavlensky, A. R., Grossman, D. R., Topham, C. S., & Meyer, S. M., III. (1977). *The great learning book*. Menlo Park, CA: Addison-Wesley.

Bolster, L. C., et al. (1978). *Mathematics around us: Skills and applications*. Glenview, IL: Scott Foresman.

Bond, K., & Deans, J. (1997). Eagles, reptiles, and beyond: A co-creative journey in dance. *Childhood Education, 73*, 366–371.

Bos, C. S., & Vaughn, S. (1998). *Strategies for teaching students with learning and behavior problems* (4th ed.). Boston: Allyn & Bacon.

Bos, C.S., & Vaughn, S. (2006). *Strategies for teaching students with learning and behavior problems* (6th ed.). Boston: Pearson.

Boswell, F. F., & Mentzer, M. (1995). Integrating poetry and movement for children with learning and/or behavioral disabilities. *Intervention in School and Clinic, 31,* 108–113.

Bott, D.A. (1988). Mathematics. In J. Wood (Ed.), *Mainstreaming: A practical guide for teachers.* Columbus, OH: Merrill.

Bottge, B.A., & Yehle, A. (1999). Making standards-based instruction meaningful for all. *Journal for Vocational Special Needs Education, 22*(1), 23–32.

Bowen, J., Hawkins, M., & King, C. (1997). *Square pegs: Building success in school and life through MI.* Tucson, AZ: Zephyr Press.

Bowers, L., Barrett, M., Huisingh, R., Orman, J., & LoGiudice, C. (1994). *Test of Problem Solving-Revised-Elementary.* East Moline, IL: LinguiSystems.

Bracken, B.A. (1984). *Bracken basic concept scale.* Columbus, OH: Merrill.

Bradden, K. L., Hall, N. J., & Taylor, D. (1993). *Math through children's literature: Making the NCTM standards come alive.* Englewood, CO: Teacher Ideas Press.

Brahier, D. J. (2005). *Teaching secondary and middle school mathematics.* Boston, MA: Allyn & Bacon/Pearson.

Brand, S. (1989). Learning through meaning. *Academic Therapy, 24,* 305–314.

Bray, J., & Wiig, E. H. (1987). *The "Let's Talk" Inventory for Children.* Upper Saddle River, NJ: Merrill/Prentice Hall.

Brice, R. G. (2004). Connecting oral and written language through applied writing strategies. *Intervention in School and Clinic, 40,* 38–47.

Brick, J., & Wagner, M. (1993). Using karoake in the classroom. *Music Educators Journal, 77*(7), 44–46.

Bricker, D. D. (1986). *Early intervention for at-risk and handicapped infants, toddlers, and preschool children.* Palo Alto, CA: VORT.

Bricker, D. D., & Cripe, J. J. W. (1993). *An activity-based approach to early intervention.* Baltimore, MD: Paul H. Brookes.

Brigance, A. H. (1983). *Brigance Diagnostic Inventory of Basic Skills.* Billerica, MA: Curriculum Associates.

Brigance, A. H. (1985). *Brigance Life Skills Inventory.* North Billerica, MA: Curriculum Associates.

Brigance, A. H. (1990). *Brigance Diagnostic Inventory of Essential Skills.* Billerica, MA: Curriculum Associates.

Briggs, J. (1988). The role of metacognition in enhancing learning. *Australian Journal of Education, 32,* 127–138.

Brigham, F. J., Scruggs, T. E., & Mastropieri, M. A. (1992). Teacher enthusiasm in learning disabilities classrooms: Effects on learning and behavior. *Learning Disabilities Research and Practice, 7,* 68–73.

Brinton, B., Fujiki, M., & Sonnenberg, E. (1988). Responses to requests for clarification by linguistically normal and language-impaired children in conversation. *Journal of Speech and Hearing Research, 53,* 383–391.

Brizzi, E. (1982). *Developing a partnership: A resource guide for working with paraprofessionals.* Downey, CA: Los Angeles County Superintendent of Schools.

Brolin, D. (1993). *Life-centered career education: A competency-based approach* (4th ed.). Reston, VA: Council for Exceptional Children.

Brolin, D. E. (1982). Life-centered career education for exceptional children. *Focus on Exceptional Children, 14*(7), 1–15.

Brolin, D. E. (1986). *Life-centered career education: A competency-based approach* (4th. ed.). Reston, VA: Council for Exceptional Children.

Brolin, D. E. (1989). *Life-centered career education: A competency-based approach* (Rev. ed.). Reston, VA: Council for Exceptional Children.

Brolin, D. E. (1997). *Life-centered career education: A competency-based approach* (5th ed.). Reston, VA: Council for Exceptional Children.

Brolin, D. E., & Kokaska, C. (1984). *Career education for handicapped children and youth.* Columbus, OH: Merrill.

Brophy, J. (1979). Teacher behavior and its effects. *Journal of Teacher Education, 71,* 733–750.

Brophy, J. (1990). Teaching social studies for understanding and higher-order application. *The Elementary School Journal, 90,* 351–417.

Browder, D. M., Wood, W. M., Test, D. W., Karvonen, M., & Algozzine, B. (2001). Reviewing resources on self-determination: A map for teachers. *Remedial and Special Education, 22,* 233–244.

Brown, A. L., & Palinscar, A. (1982). Inducing strategic learning from texts by means of informed, self-control training. *Topics in Learning and Learning Disabilities, 2*(1), 1–17.

Brown, L. (2004). Evaluating and managing classroom behavior. In D. D. Hammill & N. R. Bartel (Eds.), *Teaching students with learning and behavior problems* (7th ed.). Austin, TX: PRO-ED.

Brown, V. L., Cronin, M., & McEntire, E. *TOMA-2: Test of mathematical abilities.* Bloomington, MN: Pearson Assessment.

Brown, V. L., & McEntire, E. (1984). *Test of mathematical abilities.* Austin, TX: PRO-ED.

Bruder, M. B., & Chandler, L. K. (1993). Transition: DEC recommended practices. In *DEC recommended practices: Indicators of quality in programs for infants and young children with special needs and their families* (pp. 96–106). Arlington, VA: Author. ED370265

Bruder, M. B., & Chandler, L. (1996). Transition. In S. L. Odom & M. E. McLean (Eds.), *Early intervention/early childhood special education: Recommended practices* (pp. 287–307). Austin, TX: PRO-ED.

Brueckner, L. J., & Bond, G. L. (1967). Diagnosis and treatment of learning difficulties. In E. C. Frierson & W. B. Barbe (Eds.), *Educating children with learning disabilities.* New York: Appleton-Century-Crofts.

Bruner, J. (1975). The ontogenesis of speech acts. *Journal of Child Language, 2,* 1–19.

Bruner, J., Goodnow, J. J., & Austin, G. A. (1977). *A study of thinking.* New York: Science Editions.

Bruns, D. A., & Fowler, S. A. (2001). *Transition is more than a change in services: The need for a multicultural perspective*. Champaign, IL: Early Childhood Research Institute on Culturally and Linguistically Appropriate Services, University of Illinois at Urbana-Champaign.

Bryan, T. (1983, October). *The hidden curriculum: Social and communication skills*. Paper presented at Lynchburg College, Lynchburg, VA.

Bryan, T., & Bryan, J. H. (1978). Social interactions of learning-disabled children. *Learning Disability Quarterly, 1*, 33–38.

Bryan, T., Donahue, M., & Pearl, R. (1981). Learning-disabled children's peer interactions during a small-group problem-solving task. *Learning Disability Quarterly, 4*, 13–22.

Bryan, T., & Pflaum, S. (1978). Social interactions of learning-disabled children: A linguistic, social, and cognitive analysis. *Learning Disability Quarterly, 1*, 70–79.

Bryan, T., Wheeler, R., Felcan, J., & Henek, T. (1976). "Come on, Dummy"; An observational study of children's communications. *Journal of Learning Disabilities, 9*, 53–61.

Bryant, D. P., Engelhand, J., & Reetz, L. (2002). Secondary students with learning disabilities in reading: Developing word identification skills. *CLD Infosheets*. Retrieved November 3, 2002, from http://www.cldinternational.org/c/@aH47Gt6iaSFzg/Pages/wordID.html

Bryant, D. P., Ugel, N., Thompson, S., & Hamff, A. (1999). Instructional strategies for content-area reading instruction. *Intervention in School and Clinic, 34*, 293–302.

Bryant, D. P., Vaughn, S., Linan-Thompson, S., Ugel, N., Hamff, A., & Hougen, M. (2000). Reading outcomes for students with and without reading disabilities in general education middle-school content area classes. *Learning Disability Quarterly, 23*, 238–252.

Buck, G. H. (1993). Teachers' use of background music in general and special education classrooms. *Dissertation Abstracts International, 55*, 07A.

Buck, G. H., & Gregoire, M. A. (1996). Teaching music-related leisure skills to secondary students with disabilities. *Teaching Exceptional Children, 29*(1), 44–47.

Buck, G.H., & Gregoire, M.A. (1996). Teaching recreation and leisure skills to students with disabilities through music. *Teaching Exceptional Children, 29*, 44–47.

Buck, G. H., Polloway, E.A., & Mortorff-Robb, S. (1995). Alternative certification programs: Implications for special education. *Teacher Education and Special Education, 18*, 39–48.

Bulgren, J., Deshler, D., & Lenz, K. (2007). Engaging adolescents with LD in higher order thinking about history concepts using integrated content enhancement routines. *Journal of Learning Disabilities, 40*, 97–192.

Bulgren, J. A., Schumaker, J. B., & Deshler, D. D. (1988). Effectiveness of a concept teaching routine in enhancing the performance of LD students in secondary-level mainstream classes. *Learning Disability Quarterly, 11*(1), 3–17.

Bunce, B. H. (1997). Children with culturally diverse backgrounds. In L. McCormick, D. E. Loeb, & R. L. Schiefelbusch (Eds.), *Supporting children with communication disorders in inclusive settings: School-based language intervention* (pp. 467–506). Boston: Allyn & Bacon.

Burkhardt, S., Obiakor, F., & Rotatori, A. (Eds.). (2004). *Advances in special education: Current perspectives on learning disabilities*. San Diego, CA: Elsevier.

Burns, J. (1988). *Spelling mnemonics*. Unpublished manuscript. Lynchburg College, Lynchburg, VA.

Burrill, G., Allison, J., Breaux, G., Kastberg, S., Leatham, K., & Sanchez, W. (2002). *Handheld graphing technology in secondary mathematics: Research findings and implications for classroom practice*. Dallas, TX: Texas Instruments.

Butera, G., Klein, H., McMullen, L., & Wilson, B. (1998). A state-wide study of FAPE in school discipline policies. *The Journal of Special Education, 32*, 108–114.

Butler, D. L., Elaschuk, C. L., & Poole, S. (2000). Promoting strategic writing by postsecondary students with learning disabilities: A report of three case studies. *Learning Disability Quarterly, 23*, 196–213.

Butzow, C. M., & Butzow, J. W. (1989). *Science through children's literature: An integrated approach*. Englewood, CO: Libraries Unlimited.

Cain, S. E., & Evans, J. M. (1984). *Sciencing: An involvement approach to elementary science methods* (2nd ed.). Columbus, OH: Merrill.

Cain, S. E., & Evans, J. M. (1990). *Sciencing: An involvement approach to elementary science methods* (3rd ed.). Upper Saddle River, NJ: Prentice Hall.

Callahan, K., Rademacher, J. A., & Hildreth, B. L. (1998). The effect of parent participation in strategies to improve the homework performance of students who are at risk. *Remedial and Special Education, 19*(3), 131–141.

Calvert, M. B., & Murray, S. L. (1985). Environmental communication profile: An assessment procedure. In C. S. Simon (Ed.), *Communication skills and classroom success: Assessment of language learning-disabled students* (pp. 135–165). Austin, TX: PRO-ED.

Campbell, P H., & Halbert, J. (2002). Between research and practice: Provider perspectives on early intervention. *Topics in Early Childhood Special Education, 22*, 213–226.

Canfield, J., & Wells, H. C. (1994). *100 ways to enhance self-concept in the classroom* (2nd ed.). Boston: Allyn & Bacon.

Carden-Smith, L., & Fowler, S. A. (1983). An assessment of student and teacher behavior in treatment and mainstreamed classes for preschool and kindergarten. *Analysis and Intervention in Developmental Disabilities, 3*, 35–57.

Carnine, D. (1983). Direct instruction: In search of instructional solutions for educational problems. In *Interdisciplinary voices in learning disabilities and remedial education* (pp. 1–60). Austin, TX: PRO-ED.

Carnine, D. (1992). Introduction. In D. Carnine & E. J. Kame'enui (Eds.), *Higher-order thinking: Designing curriculum for mainstreamed students* (pp. 1–22). Austin, TX: PRO-ED.

Carnine, D. W., Silbert, J., & Kame'enui, E. (1990). *Direct instruction reading* (2nd ed.). Upper Saddle River, NJ: Prentice Hall.

Carnine, D. W., Silbert, J., Kame'enui, E. J., & Tarver, S. (2004). *Direct instruction reading* (4th ed.). Upper Saddle River, NJ: Merrill/Prentice Hall.

Carrow-Woolfolk, E. (1974). *Carrow Elicited Language Inventory*. Allen, TX: DLM Teaching Resources.

Carrow-Woolfolk, E. (1985). *Test for Auditory Comprehension of Language—Revised*. Allen, TX: DLM Teaching Resources.

Carter, S. (1993). The forgotten entity in art education. *Art Education, 46*(5), 52–57.

Cartledge, G., & Milburn, J. F. (1986). *Teaching skills to children: Innovative approaches* (2nd ed.). New York: Pergamon Press.

Cartledge, G., & Milburn, J. F. (1995). *Teaching skills to children: Innovative approaches* (3rd ed.). New York: Pergamon Press.

Caskey, H. J. (1970). Guidelines for teaching comprehension. *The Reading Teacher, 23*, 649–654.

CAST. (2006). *Digital content in the classroom: Understanding plot and vocabulary (grades 9 and 10) Lesson 2: UDL approach*. Retrieved, August 30, 2006, from http://www.cast.org/teachingeverystudent/toolkits/tk_modellesson.cfm?tk_id=41&tkl_id=101&disp=uldapproach

Castellani, J., & Jeffs, T. (2001). Emerging reading and writing strategies using technology. *Teaching Exceptional Children, 33*, 60–67.

Cates, D. L., McGill, H., Brian, L., Wilder, A., & Androes, T. (1990, April 23–27). *Severely and profoundly handicapped students in the regular classroom: It is happening now*. Paper presented at the 68th Annual Convention of the Council for Exceptional Children, Toronto, Canada.

Catlett, C., & Winton, P. (2000). *Selected early childhood/early intervention training manual* (9th ed.). Chapel Hill, NC: Systems Change in Personnel Preparation Project's Resource Guide.

Catts, H. W. (1997). The early identification of language-based reading disabilities. *Language, Speech, and Hearing Services in Schools, 28*, 86–89.

Catts, H. W., Gilliespie, M., Leonard, L. B., Kail, R. V., & Miller, C. A. (2002). The role of speed of processing, rapid naming, and phonological awareness in reading achievement. *Journal of Learning Disabilities, 35*, 509–524.

Cawley, J. F. (Ed.). (1984). *Developmental teaching of mathematics for the learning disabled*. Austin, TX: PRO-ED.

Cawley, J. F. (1994). Science for students with disabilities. *Remedial and Special Education, 15*, 67–71.

Cawley, J. F. (2002). Mathematics interventions and students with high-incidence disabilities. *Remedial and Special Education, 23*, 2–6.

Cawley, J. F., Baker-Kroczynski, S., & Urban, A. (1992). Seeking excellence in mathematics education for students with mild disabilities. *Teaching Exceptional Children, 24*, 40–43.

Cawley, J. F., Fitzmaurice, A. M., Shaw, R. A., Kahn, H., & Bates, H. (1979a). Mathematics and learning disabled youth: The upper grade levels. *Learning Disability Quarterly, 1*, 37–52.

Cawley, J. F., Fitzmaurice, A. M., Shaw, R. A., Kahn, H., & Bates, H. (1979b). Math word problems: Suggestions for LD students. *Learning Disability Quarterly, 2*, 25–41.

Cawley, J. F., Fitzmaurice-Hayes, A. M., & Shaw, R. A. (1988). *Mathematics for the mildly handicapped: A guide to curriculum and instruction*. Boston: Allyn & Bacon.

Cawley, J. F., Goodstein, H. A., Fitzmaurice, A. M., Lepore A., Sedlak, R., & Althaus, V. (1976). *Project MATH*. Tulsa, OK: Educational Development.

Cawley, J. F., Miller, D., & Carr, S. (1989). Arithmetic. In G. A. Robinson, J. R. Patton, E. A. Polloway, & L. R. Sargent (Eds.), *Best practices in mental retardation* (pp. 67–86). Reston, VA: Division on Mental Retardation, Council for Exceptional Children.

Cawley, J. F., Miller, J., Sentman, J. R., & Bennett, S. (1993). *Science for all (SAC)*. Buffalo: State University of New York at Buffalo.

Cazden, C. B. (1988). *Classroom discourse: The language of teaching and learning*. Portsmouth, NH: Heinemann.

Cazden, C. B. (2001). *Classroom discourse: The language of teaching and learning* (2nd ed.). New York: Heinemann.

CEC Today. (1995). Research shows phonological awareness key to reading success. *CEC Today, 2*(4), 1, 9, 15.

Center for Applied Special Technology. (2006). *Research and development in universal design for learning*. Retrieved August 30, 2006, from http://www.hcrel.org/sdrs/areas/issues/mehtods/technlgy/te800.htm

Center for the Future of Teaching and Learning. (1996). Thirty years of NICHD research: What we now know about how children learn to read. *Effective School Practices, 15*(3), 33–46.

Chalfant, J. C., & Pysh, M. V. (1989). Teacher assistance teams: Five descriptive studies on 96 teams. *Remedial and Special Education, 10*(6), 49–58.

Chalk, J. C., Hagan-Burke, S., & Burke, M. D. (2005). The effects of self-regulated strategy development on the writing process for high school students with learning disabilities. *Learning Disability Quarterly*, 28, 75–87.

Chamberlain, S. P. (2006). An interview with Don Deshler: Perspectives on teaching students with learning disabilities. *Intervention in School and Clinic, 41,* 302–306.

Chandler, L. K. (1992). Promoting young children's social competence as a strategy for transition to mainstreamed kindergarten program. In S. L. Odom, S. R. McConnell, & M.A. McEvoy (Eds.), *Social competence of young children with disabilities* (pp. 245–276). Baltimore: Paul H. Brookes.

Chandler, L. K. (1993). Steps in preparing for transition: Preschool to kindergarten. *Teaching Exceptional Children, 25,* 52–55.

Chaney, A. L., & Burk, T. L. (1998). *Teaching oral communication in grades K–8*. Boston: Allyn & Bacon.

Chard, D. J., & Dickson, S. V. (1999). *Phonological awareness: Assessment and instructional guidelines*. Retrieved August 18, 2006, from http://www.ldonline.org/article/6254

Chiang, B., & Ford, M. (1990). Whole language alternatives for students with learning disabilities. *Learning Disabilities Forum, 16,* 31–33.

Christenson, S. L., Ysseldyke, J. E., & Thurlow, M. L. (1989). Critical instructional factors for students with mild handicaps: An integrative review. *Remedial and Special Education, 10*(5), 21–31.

Clark, D. J. (1985). *The IMPACT project: Project report*. Clayton, Victoria, Australia: Monash Centre for Mathematics Education.

Clark, D. J. (1987). The interactive monitoring of children's learning of mathematics. *For the Learning of Mathematics, 7*(1), 2–6.

Clark, D., Stephens, M., & Waywood, A. (1992). Communication and the learning of mathematics. In T.A. Romberg (Ed.), *Mathematics assessment and evaluation: Imperatives for mathematics education* (pp. 184–212). Albany: State University of New York Press.

Clark, G. M. (1979). *Career education for the handicapped child in the elementary classroom*. Denver, CO: Love.

Clark, G. M. (1996). Transition planning assessment for secondary-level students with learning disabilities. *Journal of Learning Disabilities, 29,* 79–92.

Clark, G. M., Carlson, B. C., Fisher, S., Cook, I. D., & D'Alonzo, B. J. (1991). *Career development for students with disabilities in elementary schools: A position statement of the Division on Career Development*. Reston, VA: Division on Career Development, Council for Exceptional Children.

Clark, G. M., Field, S., Patton, J. R., Brolin, D., & Sitlington, P. (1994). Life skills instruction: A necessary component for all students with disabilities. *CDEI, 17,* 125–134.

Clark, G. M., & Kolstoe, O. P. (1990). *Career development and transition of education for adolescents with disabilities*. Boston: Allyn & Bacon.

Clark, G. M., & Patton, J. R. (2006). *Transition Planning Inventory*: Updated version. Austin, TX: PRO-ED.

Cochran, P. S., & Bull, G. L. (1993). Computers and individuals with speech and language disorders. In J. D. Lindsey (Ed.), *Computers and exceptional individuals* (2nd ed., pp. 143–158). Austin, TX: PRO-ED.

Cohen, H., & Staley, F. (1982). Integrating with science: One way to bring science back into the elementary day. *School Science and Mathematics, 82,* 565–572.

Cohen, J. (2001). *Caring classrooms/intelligent schools: The social emotional education of young children*. New York: Teachers College Press.

Cohen, L., & Spenciner, L. J. (2005). *Teaching students with mild and moderate disabilities: Research-based practices*. Columbus, OH: Pearson.

Cohen, M. D., & Hoot, J. L. (1997). Educating through the arts: An introduction. *Childhood Education, 73,* 338–340.

Cohen, R. (1983). Self-generated questions as an aid to reading comprehension. *The Reading Teacher, 36,* 770–775.

Cohen, S., & deBettencourt, L. (1983). Teaching children to be independent learners: A step-by-step strategy. *Focus on Exceptional Children, 16*(3), 1–12.

Cohen, S. B., Perkins, V. L., & Newmark, S. (1985). Written feedback strategies used by special education teachers. *Teacher Education and Special Education, 8,* 183–187.

Cohen, S. B., & Plaskon, S. P. (1980). *Language arts for the mildly handicapped*. Columbus, OH: Merrill.

Cohen, S. B., Safran, J., & Polloway, E.A. (1980). Minimum competency testing and its implications for retarded students. *Education and Training for the Mentally Retarded, 15,* 250–255.

Coiro, J. (2003). Reading comprehension on the Internet: Expanding our understanding of reading comprehension to encompass new literacies. *The Reading Teacher, 56,* 458–464.

Cole, M., & Cole, J. (1980). *Effective intervention with the language impaired*. Rockville, MD: Aspen Systems.

Coleman, J. (1978). Using name anagrams. *Teaching Exceptional Children, 11,* 41–42.

Collier, C., & Hoover, J. J. (1987). *Cognitive learning strategies for minority handicapped students*. Boulder, CO: Hamilton Publications.

Coman, M., & Heavers, K. (2001). *How to improve your study skills*. New York: Glenco McGraw-Hill.

Combs, W. E. (1975). Sentence combining practice aids reading comprehension. *Journal of Reading, 21,* 18–24.

Comenius English Center. (2003). *Idioms*. Retrieved June 5, 2003, from http://www.comenius.com/idioms/index.tpl?ltr=d&idiom=idiom59

Connolly, A. (2007). *KeyMath-Revised: A diagnostic inventory of essential mathematics*. Bloomington, MN: Pearson Assessment.

Connolly, A. J. (1988). *Keymath Revised: A Diagnostic Inventory of Essential Mathematics*. Circle Pines, MN: American Guidance Service.

Conn-Powers, M. C., Ross-Allen, J., & Holburn, S. (1990). Transition of young children into the elementary education mainstream. *Topics in Early Childhood Special Education, 9*(4), 92–105.

Cook, L., & Friend, M. (1995). Co-teaching: Guidelines for creating effective practices. *Focus on Exceptional Children, 28*(3), 1–16.

Cook, R. E., Klein, M. D., & Tessier, A. (2004). *Adapting early childhood curricula for children in inclusive settings* (6th ed.). Columbus, OH: Merrill Pearson.

Cooke, N. L., Heron, T. E., & Heward, W. L. (1983). *Peer tutoring: Implementing classwide programs in the primary grades*. Columbus, OH: Special Press.

Cotton, P. (1991). A flowing start to handwriting. *Times Educational Supplement*, 3906, 9.

Cottrell, S. (2001). *Teaching study skills and supporting learning*. New York: Palgrave Macmillan.

Council of Chief State School Officers. (1986). *Disabled students beyond school: A review of the issues*. A position paper and recommendations for action. Washington, DC: Author.

Coyne, M. D., Kame'enui, E. J., & Carnine, D. W. (2007). *Effective teaching strategies that accommodate diverse learners* (3rd ed.). Upper Saddle River, NJ: Merrill/Prentice Hall.

Coyne, M. D., Kame'enui, E. J., & Simmons, D. C. (2001). Prevention and intervention in beginning reading: Two complex systems. *Learning Disabilities Research and Practice, 16*, 62–73.

Coyne, M. D., Zipoli, R. P., Jr., & Ruby, M. F. (2006). Beginning reading instruction for students at risk for reading disabilities: What, how, when. *Intervention in School and Clinic, 41*, 161–168.

Cozzens, G., Dowdy, C., & Smith, T. E. C. (1999). *Adult agencies: Linkages for adolescents in transition*. Austin, TX: PRO-ED.

Crago, M., & Cole, E. (1991). Using ethnography to bring children's communicative and cultural worlds into focus. In T. M. Gallagher (Ed.), *Pragmatics of language: Clinical practice issues* (pp. 99–132). San Diego, CA: Singular.

Craig, H., & Evans, J. (1989). Turn exchange characteristics of SLIO children's simultaneous and non-simultaneous speech. *Journal of Speech and Hearing Disorders, 54*, 334–347.

Craig, S., Hull, K., & Haggart, A. G. (2001). Storytelling. *Teaching Exceptional Children, 33*(5), 46–51.

Crescimbeni, J. (1965). *Arithmetic enrichment activities for elementary school children*. West Nyack, NY: Parker.

Crisculo, N. P. (1985). Creative approaches to teaching reading through art. *Art Education, 38*(6), 13–16.

Critchlow, D. (1996). *Dos amigos verbal language scale*. Novato, CA: Academic Therapy Publications.

Cronin, M. E. (1988). Adult performance outcomes/life skills. In G. Robinson, J. R. Patton, E. A. Polloway, & L. R. Sargent (Eds.), *Best practices in mental disabilities* (Vol. 2). Des Moines: Iowa Department of Education, Bureau of Special Education.

Cronin, M. E., & Gerber, P. J. (1982). Preparing the learning-disabled adolescent for adulthood. *Topics in Learning and Learning Disabilities, 2*(3), 55–68.

Cronin, M. E., & Patton, J. R. (2007). *Life skills for students with special needs: A practical guide for developing real-life programs* (2nd ed.). Austin, TX: PRO-ED.

Cronin, M. E., Patton, J. R., & Polloway, E. A. (1991). *Preparing for adult outcomes: A model for developing a life skills curriculum*. Unpublished manuscript, University of New Orleans, LA.

Cronin, M. E., Patton, J. R., & Wood, S. (2004). *Life skills instruction for all students with special needs: A practical guide for integrating real-life content into the curriculum* (2nd ed.). Austin, TX: PRO-ED.

Curtis, C. K., & Shaver, J. P. (1980). Slow learners and the study of contemporary problems. *Social Education, 44*, 302–309.

Cyber Smart. (2003). *Smart keyword searching*. Retrieved May 16, 2007, from http://www.cybersmartcurriculum.org/lesson_plans/68_17.asp

Czarnecki, E., Rosko, D., & Fine, E. (1998). How to call up notetaking skills. *Teaching Exceptional Children, 30*, 14–19.

D'Zurilla, T. J., & Goldfried, M. R. (1971). Problem solving and behavior modification. *Journal of Abnormal Psychology, 78*, 107–126.

D'Zurilla, T. J., & Nezu, A. (1980). A study of the generalization of alternatives: Process in social problem solving skills. *Cognitive Therapy and Research, 4*, 67–72.

Dale, F. J. (1993). Computers and gifted/talented individuals. In J. D. Lindsey (Ed.), *Computers and exceptional individuals* (2nd ed., pp. 201–223). Austin, TX: PRO-ED.

Damico, J. S., & Oller, J. W. (1985). *Spotting language problems: Pragmatic criteria for language screening*. San Diego, CA: Los Amigos Research Associates.

Damico, J. S., Smith, M., & Augustine, L. E. (1995). Multicultural populations and language disorders (pp. 272–299). In M. D. Smith & J. S. Damico (Eds.), *Childhood language disorders*. New York: Thieme Medical Publishers.

Damico, J. S., Smith, M., & Augustine, L. L. (1996). Multicultural populations and childhood language disorders. In M. Smith & J. S. Damico (Eds.), *Childhood language disorders*, (pp. 272–299). New York: Thieme Medical Publishers.

Daniels, J. L., & Wiederholt, J. L. (1986). Preparing problem learners for independent living. In D. D. Hammill & N. R. Bartel (Eds.), *Teaching students with learning and behavior problems* (4th ed., pp. 294–345). Austin, TX: PRO-ED.

Davies, J. M., & Ball, D. W. (1978). Utilization of the elementary science study with mentally retarded students. *Journal of Research in Science Teaching, 15*, 281–286.

Day, V. P., & Elkins, L. K. (1994). Promoting strategic learning. *Intervention in School and Clinic, 30*, 262–270.

de la Cruz, R. E., Lian, M. J., & Morreau, L. E. (1998). The effects of creative drama on social and oral language skills of children with learning disabilities. *Youth Theater Journal, 12*, 89–95.

deFur, S., & Williams, B. T. (2002). Cultural considerations in the transition process and standards-based education. In C. A. Kochhar-Bryant & D. S. Bassett (Eds.), *Aligning transition and standards-based education: Issues and strategies* (pp. 105–123). Arlington, VA: Council for Exceptional Children.

deFur, S. H., Todd-Allen, M., & Getzel, E.E. (2001). Parent participation in the transition planning process. *Career Development for Exceptional Individuals, 24*, 19–35.

de la Paz, S. (1997). Strategy instruction in planning: Teaching students with learning and writing disabilities to compose persuasive and expository essays. *Learning Disability Quarterly, 20*, 227–248.

de la Paz, S. (1999). Self-regulated strategy instruction in regular education settings: Improving outcomes for students with and without learning disabilities. *Learning Disabilities Research and Practice, 14*, 92–106.

de la Paz, S., Morales, P., & Winston, P. (2007). Source interpretations: Teaching students with and without LD to read and write historically. *Journal of Learning Disabilities, 40*, 97–192

de Lin, G., DuBois, B., & McIntosh, M. E. (1986). Reading aloud to students in secondary history classes. *The Social Studies, 77*, 256–259.

Deeney, T., Wolf, M., & O'Rourke, A. G. (2001). "I like to take my own sweet time": Case study of a child with naming-speed deficits and reading disabilities. *Journal of Special Education, 35*, 145–155.

Demchak, M.A., & Koury, M. (1990). Differential reinforcement of leisure activities: An observation form for supervisors. *Teaching Exceptional Children, 22*(2), 14–17.

Denton, C. A., Foorman, B. R., & Mathes, P. G. (2003). Perspective: Schools that "beat the odds." R*emedial and Special Education, 24*, 258–261.

Deshler, D. D. (2005). Adolescents with learning disabilities: Unique challenges and reasons for hope. *Learning Disability Quarterly, 28*, 122–124.

Deshler, D. D., Ellis, E. S., & Lenz, B. K. (1996). *Teaching adolescents with learning disabilities: Strategies and methods*. Denver, CO: Love Publishing.

Deshler, D. D., & Schumaker, J. B. (1986). Learning strategies: An instructional alternative for low-achieving adolescents. *Exceptional Children, 52*, 583–590.

Deshler, D. D., & Schumaker, J. B. (1988). An instructional model for teaching students how to learn. In J. L. Graden, J. E. Zins, & M. J. Curtis (Eds.), *Alternative educational delivery systems: Enhancing instructional options for all students*. Washington, DC: National Association of School Psychologists.

Destefano, L., Heck, D., Hasazi, S., & Furney, K. (1999). Enhancing the implementation of the transition requirements of IDEA: A report on the policy forum on transition. *Career Development for Exceptional Individuals, 22*, 85–100.

Dietz, M. J. (Ed.). (1997). *School, family, and community: Techniques and models for successful collaboration*. Gaithersburg, MD: Aspen.

DiGangi, S. A., Maag, J. W., & Rutherford, R. B., Jr. (1991). Self-graphing of on-task behavior: Enhancing the reactive effects of self-monitoring on on-task behavior and academic performance. *Learning Disability Quarterly, 14*, 221–230.

Dodge, K. A., & Murphy, R. (1984). The assessment of social competence in adolescents. In P. Karoly & J. J. Steffen (Eds.), *Adolescent behavior disorders: Foundations and contemporary concerns*. Lexington, MA: Lexington Books.

Donahue, M. (1994). Differences in classroom discourse of students with learning disabilities. In D. Ripich & N. Creaghead (Eds.), *School discourse problems*. (2nd ed.). San Diego, CA: Singular.

Donahue, M., Pearl, R., & Bryan, T. (1982). Learning-disabled children's syntactic proficiency on a communicative task. *Journal of Speech and Hearing Disorders, 47*, 22–28.

Donahue, M. L. (1984). Learning disabled children's conversational competence: An attempt to activate the inactive listener. *Applied Psycholinguistics, 5*, 21–35.

Donaldson, R., & Christiansen, J. (1990). Consultation and collaboration: A decision-making model. *Teaching Exceptional Children, 23*, 22–25.

Dougherty, E. H., & Dougherty, A. (1977). The daily report card: A simplified and flexible package for classroom behavior management. *Psychology in the Schools, 14*, 191–195.

Dowdy, C., Patton, J. R., Smith, T. E. C., & Polloway, E.A. (1998). *Attention deficit disorder*. Austin, TX: PRO-ED.

Downey, M.T. (1980). Pictures as teaching aids: Using the pictures in history textbooks. *Social Education, 44*, 93–99.

Doyle, W. (1986). Classroom organization and management. In M. C. Wittrock (Ed.), *Handbook of research on teaching* (3rd ed., pp. 392–431). New York: Macmillan.

Dreikurs, R., Grunwald, B. B., & Pepper, F. C. (1982). *Maintaining sanity in the classroom: Classroom management techniques* (2nd ed.). Philadelphia: Harper & Row.

Duchan, J. G. (1982). The elephant is soft and mushy: Problems in assessing children's language. In N. Lass, L. McReynolds, J. Northern, & D. Yoder (Eds.), *Speech, language and hearing: Pathologies of speech and language*. Philadelphia: Saunders.

Dudley-Marling, C. (1985). The pragmatic skills of learning-disabled children: A review. *Journal of Learning Disabilities, 18*, 193–262.

Duerksen, G. L. (1981). Music for exceptional students. *Focus on Exceptional Children, 14*(4), 1–11.

Dugger-Wadsworth, D. E., & Rieck, W.A. (2003). *Performing and visual arts in special education*. Paper presented at the Annual Council for Exceptional Children conference, Seattle, WA.

Dumas, E. (1971). *Math activities for child involvement*. Boston: Allyn & Bacon.

Duncan, J. R., Schofer, R. C., & Veberle, J. (1982). *Comprehensive system of personnel development: Inservice considerations*. Columbia: University of Missouri, Department of Special Education.

Dunlap, L. K., Dunlap, G., Koegel, L. K., & Koegel, R. L. (1991). Using self-monitoring to increase independence. *Teaching Exceptional Children, 23*(3), 17–22.

Dunn, L. M., & Dunn, L. M. (1997). *Peabody Picture Vocabulary Test—Third Edition*. Circle Pines, MN: American Guidance Service.

Durkin, D. (1978–1979). What classroom observations reveal about reading comprehension instruction. *Reading Research Quarterly, 14*, 481–533.

Dyson, L. L. (2003). Children with learning disabilities within the family context: A comparison with siblings in global self-concept, academic self-perception, and social competence. *Learning Disabilities Research and Practice, 18*, 1–9.

Edelen-Smith, P. J. (2003). *How now brown cow: Phoneme awareness activities for collaborative classrooms*. Retrieved June 13, 2003, from http://www.ldonline.org/ld_indepth/teaching_techniques/cld_hownow.html

Edgar, E. (1988). Employment as an outcome for mildly handicapped students: Current status and future directions. *Focus on Exceptional Children, 21*(1), 1–8.

Edgar, E., & Polloway, E. A. (1994). Education for adolescents with disabilities: Curriculum and placement issues. *Journal of Special Education, 27*, 438–452.

Education Podcast Network. (2007). *The Education Podcast Network*. Retrieved March 26, 2007, from http://www.epnweb.org/

Education Update. (1999, June). *Speaking and listening: The first basic skills*. Alexandria, VA: Association for Supervision and Curriculum.

Ehman, L. H., & Glenn, A. D. (1991). Interactive technology in social studies. In J. P. Shaver (Ed.), *Handbook of research on social studies teaching and learning* (pp. 513–522). Upper Saddle River, NJ: Merrill/Prentice Hall.

Ehren, B. J. (1994). New directions for meeting the academic needs of adolescents with language learning disabilities. In G. P. Wallach & K. G. Butler (Eds.), *Language learning disabilities in school-age children and adolescents* (pp. 393–417). Upper Saddle River, NJ: Merrill/Prentice Hall.

Eisner, E. W. (1985). *The educational imagination*. New York: Macmillan.

Ekwall, E. E., & Shanker, J. L. (1985). *Teaching reading in the elementary school* (2nd ed.). Columbus, OH: Merrill.

Ekwall, E. E., & Shanker, J. L. (1993). *Locating and correcting reading difficulties* (6th ed.). Upper Saddle River, NJ: Merrill/Prentice Hall.

Ekwall, E. E., & Shanker, J. L. (2003). *Teaching reading in the elementary school*. Upper Saddle River, NJ: Merrill/Prentice Hall.

Elias, M. (1995, September 19). Can do ways give hope to young pessimists. *USA Today*, p. 6D.

Elias, M. J. (2004). The connection between social-emotional learning and learning disabilities: Implications for intervention. *Learning Disability Quarterly, 27*, 53–63.

Elium, M. D., & McCarver, R. B. (1980). *Group vs. individual training on a self-help skill with the profoundly retarded*. (ERIC Document Reproduction Service No. ED 223 060)

Elksnin, C. K., & Elksnin, N. (2006). *Teaching social-emotional skills at school and home*. Denver, CO: Love Publishing.

Elliot, I. (2002). Puppetry, pantomime, and clowning around. *Teaching PreK–8, 32*(6), 44–47.

Elliott, D., & McKenney, M. (1998). Four inclusion models that work. *Teaching Exceptional Children, 30*(4), 54–58.

Ellis, E. (1992). *LINCS: A starter strategy for vocabulary learning*. Lawrence, KS: Edge Enterprises.

Ellis, E. S. (1996). Reading strategy instruction. In D. D. Deshler, E. S. Ellis, & B. K. Lenz (Eds.), *Teaching adolescents with learning disabilities: Strategies and methods* (2nd ed., pp. 63–121). Denver, CO: Love.

Ellis, E. S., Deshler, D. D., Lenz, B. K., Schumaker, J. B., & Clark, F. L. (1991). An instructional model for teaching learning strategies. *Focus on Exceptional Children, 23*(6), 1–24.

Ellis, E. S., Deshler, D. D., & Lenz, B. K. (Eds.). (1996). *Teaching adolescents with learning disabilities: Strategies and methods* (2nd ed). Denver, CO: Love Publishing.

Ellis, E. S., & Rock, M. L. (2002). Strategic solutions to promoting incremental change. *Exceptionality, 10*, 223–247.

Ellis, E. S., & Sabornie, E. J. (1986). *Teaching learning strategies to learning-disabled students in post-secondary settings*. Unpublished manuscript, University of South Carolina, Columbia.

Embry, D. D., & Flannery, D. J. (1994). *Peacebuilders—reducing youth violence: A working application of cognitive-social-imitative competence research*. Tucson, AZ: Heartsprings.

Emmer, E. T., Evertson, C. M., Sanford, J. P., Clements, B. S., & Worsham, M. E. (1984). *Classroom management for secondary teachers*. Upper Saddle River, NJ: Prentice Hall.

Engelmann, S. (1999). *Corrective reading program*. Chicago: Science Research Associates.

Engelmann, S. (2003). *Reading mastery program*. Chicago: Science Research Associates.

Engelmann, S., & Bruner, E. (1974, 1975, 1988). *DISTAR reading*. Chicago: Science Research Associates.

Engelmann, S., & Carnine, D. (1981). *Corrective mathematics*. Chicago: Science Research Associates.

Englehard, J. B. (1991). Yes, Virginia, whole language includes reading, decoding and spelling. *VCLD Newsletter, 3*(1), 3–5.

Englert, C. S. (1983). Measuring special education teacher effectiveness. *Exceptional Children, 50*, 247–254.

Englert, C. S., Mariage, T. V., Garmon, M. A., & Tarrant, K. L. (1998). Accelerating reading progress in early literacy project classrooms: Three exploratory studies. *Remedial and Special Education, 19*, 142–159, 180.

Englert, C. S., Tarrant, K. L., & Mariage, T. V. (1992). Defining and redefining instructional practice in special education: Perspectives on good teaching. *Teacher Education and Special Education, 15*, 62–86.

Englert, C. S., Wu, X., & Zhao, Y. (2005). Cognitive tools for writing: Scaffolding the performance of students through technology. *Learning Disabilities Research and Practice, 20*, 184–198.

Ensign, A. (1994). *Art is for everyone*. Lansing, MI: PAM Assistance Centre. (ERIC Document Reproduction Service No. ED 346 082)

Ensign, A. S. (1992). *Low-tech solutions: A place to begin*. Lansing, MI: PAM Assistance Centre. (ERIC Document Reproduction Service No. ED 342 183)

Epstein, J. L. (1995). School/family/community partnerships: Caring for the children we share. *Phi Delta Kappan, 76*, 701–712.

Epstein, M. H., & Cullinan, D. (1983). Academic performance of behaviorally disordered and learning-disabled pupils. *Journal of Special Education, 17*, 303–308.

Epstein, M. H., Polloway, E. A., Foley, R. M., & Patton, J. R. (1993). Homework: A comparison of teachers, and parents, perceptions of the problems experienced by students identified as having behavioral disorders, learning disabilities, and no disabilities. *Remedial and Special Education, 14*(5), 40–50.

Epstein, M. H., Polloway, E. A., & Patton, J. R., & Foley, R. (1989). Mild retardation: Student characteristics and services. *Education and Training in Mental Retardation, 24*, 7–16.

ERIC/OSEP. (1997). School-wide behavioral management systems: A promising practice for safer schools. *Research Connections in Special Education, 1*(1), 1–5.

Esler, W. K., Midgett, J., & Bird, R. C. (1977). Elementary science materials and the exceptional child. *Science Education, 61*, 181–184.

Espin, C., Cevasco, J., Broke, P., Baker, S., & Gersten, R. (2007). History as narrative: The nature and quality of historical understanding for students with LD. *Journal of Learning Disabilities, 40*, 97–192.

Essa, E. (2003). *A practical guide to solving preschool behavior problems*. Clifton, NY: Delmar Learning.

Eurich, G. (1996). Modeling respect in the classroom. *Intervention in School and Clinic, 31*, 119–120.

Evans, R. W. (1989). The future of issue-centered education. *The Social Studies, 80*, 176–177.

Evans, S. S., Evans, W. H., & Mercer, C. D. (1986). *Assessment for instruction*. Boston: Allyn & Bacon.

Everson, J. M., Zhang, D., & Guillory, J. D. (2001). A statewide investigation of individualized transition plans in Louisiana. *Career Development for Exceptional Individuals, 24*, 37–49.

Evertson, C. M., Emmer, E. T., Clements, B. S., Sanford, J. P., & Worsham, M. E. (1984). *Classroom management for elementary teachers*. Upper Saddle River, NJ: Prentice Hall.

Eykyn, G. (1999). *Internet behavior and addiction*. Retrieved May 16, 2007, from http://www.victoriapoint.com/marriages.htm

Eylon, B. S., & Linn, M. C. (1988). Learning and instruction: An examination of four research perspectives in science education. *Review of Educational Research, 58*, 251–301.

Fad, K., & Riddle, M. (1995). *Inclusion notes for busy teachers*. Longmont, CO: Sopris West.

Fad, K. M., & Gilliam, J. E. (1996). *Putting it all together for student success*. Longmont, CO: Sopris West.

Fad, K. S., & Ryser, G. R. (1993). Social/behavioral variables related to success in general education. *Remedial and Special Education, 14*(1), 25–35.

Family Education Network. (2003). *Metaphor unit poems*. Retrieved June 12, 2003, from http://www.teachervision.com/lesson-plans/lesson-5454.html

Family Village. (2006). *Family Village school: Assistive technology for students with disabilities*. Retrieved August 9, 2006, from http://www.familyvillage.wisc.edu/education/at.html

Felton, R. G., & Allen, R. F. (1990). Using visual materials as historical sources. *The Social Studies, 81*, 84–87.

Fenson, L., Dale, P., Reznick, S., Thal, D., Bates, E., Hartung, J., Pethick, S., & Reilly, J. (1993). *The MacArthur Communicative Development Inventories*. San Diego, CA: Singular.

Ferguson, D. L. (1994). Magic for teacher work groups: Tricks for colleague communication. *Teaching Exceptional Children, 27*, 42–47.

Fernald, G. M. (1943). *Remedial techniques in basic school subjects*. New York: McGraw-Hill.

Ferster, C. B., Culbertson, S., & Boren, M. C. P. (1975). *Behavior principles* (2nd ed.). Upper Saddle River, NJ: Prentice Hall.

Fey, M. (1986). *Language intervention with young children*. San Diego, CA: College-Hill Press.

Fey, M., Warr-Leeper, G., Webber, S., & Disher, L. (1988). Repairing children's repairs: Evaluation and facilitation of children's clarification requests and responses. *Topics in Language Disorders, 8*, 63–64.

Fiechtl, B., Rule, S., & Innocenti, M. S. (1989). It's time to get ready for school. *Teaching Exceptional Children, 21*(2), 63–65.

Fiedler, J. F., & Knight, R. R. (1986). Congruence between assessed needs and IEP goals of identified behaviorally disabled students. *Behavioral Disorders, 12*, 22–27.

Field, S., & Hoffman, A. (1992). *Steps to self determination* (field-test version). Detroit: Wayne State University, College of Education, Developmental Disabilities Institute.

Field, S., & Hoffman, A. (1994). Development of a model for self-determination. *Career Development for Exceptional Individuals, 17,* 159–169.

Field, S., Hoffman, A., & Spezia, S. (1998). *Self-determination strategies for adolescents in transition.* Austin, TX: PRO-ED.

Fink, W. T., & Sandall, S. R. (1980). A comparison of one-to-one and small group instructional strategies with developmentally disabled preschoolers. *Mental Retardation, 18,* 73–84.

Finson, K. D., & Ormsbee, C. K. (1998). Rubrics and their use in inclusive science. *Intervention in School and Clinic, 34,* 79–88.

Fitzgerald, J. (1951). *The teaching of spelling.* Milwaukee: Bruce.

Fleck, R. M. (1995). Easing into elementary school. *Principal, 74,* 25–27.

Fletcher, J. M., Foorman, B. R., Francis, D. J., & Schatschneider, C. (1998, June). Prevention of reading failure. *The Virginia Branch (of the Orton Society) Newsletter,* 3–5.

Fletcher, T. V., Bos, C. S., & Johnson, L. M. (1999). Accommodating English language learners with language and learning disabilities in bilingual education classes. *Learning Disabilities Research and Practice, 14,* 80–91.

Florida Tech Net. (2003). *GED 2002 teacher's handbook of lesson plans: Homonyms.* Retrieved June 12, 2002, from http://www.floridatechnet.org/ged/LessonPlans/LanguageArtsWriting/LanguageArtsLesson28.pdf

Florida Tech Net. (2003). *GED 2002 Teacher's handbook of lesson plans: Antonyms and Synonyms.* Retrieved June 12, 2003 from http://www.floridatechnet.org/ged/LessonPlans/LanguageArtsWriting/LanguageArtsLesson3.pdf

Fogarty, R. (1995). *Designs for cooperative interactions.* Palatine, IL: Skylight.

Foorman, B. R., & Torgesen, J. (2001). Critical elements of classroom and small-group instruction promote reading success in all children. *Learning Disabilities Research and Practice, 16,* 203–212.

Ford, M. E. (1985). The concept of competence: Themes and variations. In H. A. Marlow & R. B. Weinberg (Eds.), *Competence development: Theory and practice in special populations* (pp. 3–38). Springfield, IL: Charles C. Thomas.

Forest, M., & Lusthaus, E. (1989). Promoting educational equality for all students: Circles and maps. In S. Stainback, W. Stainback, & M. Forest (Eds.), *Educating all students in the mainstream of regular education* (pp. 43–58). Baltimore: Paul H. Brookes.

Forness, S. R., Serna, L. A., Kavale, K. A., & Nielsen, E. (in press). Mental health and Head Start: Teaching adaptive skills. *Education and Treatment of Children.*

42explore. (2005). *The topic: Figurative language.* Retrieved March 26, 2007, from http://42explore.com/figlang.htm

Fowler, G. L., & Davis, M. (1986). The story frame approach: A tool for improving reading comprehension for EMR children. *Teaching Exceptional Children, 17,* 296–298.

Freeman, S. (1992). *Literature notes for "Alexander and the terrible, horrible, no good, very bad day."* Torrence, CA: Frank Schaffer.

Freides, D., & Messina, C. A. (1986). Memory improvement via motor encoding in learning disabled children. *Journal of Learning Disabilities, 19,* 113–115.

Friebel, A. C., & Gingrich, C. K. (1972). *Math applications kit.* Chicago: Science Research Associates.

Friedman, R. (2003). *How media shapes perception.* Retrieved June 11, 2003, from http://www.thirteen.org/edonline/lessons/media/

Friend, M., & Cook, L. (2003). *Interactions: Collaboration skills for school professionals* (4th ed.). New York: Longman.

Fritz, M. T. (1990). A comparison of social interactions using friendship awareness activity. *Education and Training in Mental Retardation, 25,* 352–359.

Frye-Mason, J., & Miko, P. (2002). Critter dance. *Journal of Physical Education, Recreation, & Dance, 73*(3), 49–53.

Fuchs, D., Fernstrom, P., Scott, S., Fuchs, L., & Vandermeer, L. (1994). Classroom ecological inventory: A process for mainstreaming. *Teaching Exceptional Children, 26*(3), 11–15.

Fuchs, D., & Fuchs, L. (2005). Peer-assisted learning strategies: Promoting word recognition, fluency, and reading comprehension in young children. *Journal of Special Education, 39,* 34–44.

Fuchs, D., & Fuchs, L. S. (1987). *Mainstream assistance teams to accommodate difficult-to-teach students in general education.* Nashville, TN: George Peabody College for Teachers. (ERIC Document Reproduction Service No. ED 292 277)

Fuchs, D., Fuchs, L. S., & Burish, P. (2000). Peer-assisted learning strategies: An evidence-based practice to promote reading achievement. *Learning Disabilities Research and Practice, 15,* 85–91.

Fuchs, D., Fuchs, L. S., Mathes, P. G., & Martinez, E. A. (2002). Preliminary evidence on the social standing of students with learning disabilities in PALS and NO-PALS classrooms. *Learning Disabilities Research and Practice, 17,* 205–215.

Fuchs, D., Fuchs, L. S., Thompson, A., Svenson, E., Yen, L., Al Otaiba, S., et al. (2001). Peer-assisted learning strategies in reading: Extensions for kindergarten, first grade, and high school. *Remedial and Special Education, 22,* 15–21.

Fuchs, L., Deno, S., & Mirkin, P. (1984). The effects of frequent curriculum-based measurement and evaluation on pedagogy, student achievement, and student awareness of learning. *American Educational Research Journal, 21,* 449–460.

Fuchs, L., Fuchs, D., Hamlett, C., & Hasselbring, T. (1987). Using computers with curriculum-based monitoring: Effects on teacher efficiency and satisfaction. *Journal of Special Education Technology, 8*(4), 14–27.

Fuchs, L. S., Bahr, C. M., & Rieth, H. J. (1989). Effects of goal structures and performance contingencies on the math performance of adolescents with learning disabilities. *Journal of Learning Disabilities, 22*, 554–560.

Fuchs, L. S., & Deno, S. L. (1994). Must instructionally useful performance assessment be based in the curriculum? *Exceptional Children, 61*, 15–24.

Fuchs, L. S., & Fuchs, D. (1987). Effects of systematic formative evaluation: A meta-analysis. *Exceptional Children, 53*, 199–208.

Fuchs, L. S., & Fuchs, D. (2001). Helping teachers formulate sound test accommodation decisions for students with learning disabilities. *Learning Disabilities Research & Practice, 16*, 174–181.

Fuchs, L. S., & Fuchs, D. (2002). Mathematical problem solving profiles of students with mathematical disabilities with and without comorbid reading disabilities. *Journal of Learning Disabilities, 35*(6), 563–573.

Fuchs, L.S., & Fuchs, D. (2002–2003). Hot Math: Promoting mathematical problem solving among children with disabilities. *National Center on Accelerating Students Learning (CASL) News*. Nashville, TN: Vanderbilt University.

Garard, J. E., & Weinstock, G. (1981). *Language Proficiency Test*. Novato, CA: Academic Therapy Publications.

Garcia, E. E. (1988). Attributes of effective school for language minority students. *Education and Urban Society, 20*, 387–398.

Garcia, G. E. (1994). Ethnography and classroom communication: Taking an "emic" perspective. In K. G. Butler (Ed.), *Best practices I: The classroom as an assessment arena* (pp. 3–15). Gaithersburg, MD: Aspen.

Garcia, S. B., & Malkin, D. H. (1997). Toward defining programs and services for culturally and linguistically diverse learners in special education. In K. L. Friberg (Ed.), *Education exceptional children* (9th ed., pp. 113–119). Guilford, CT: Dushkin/McGraw-Hill.

Gardner, E. F., Rudman, H. C., Karlsen, B., & Merwin, J. C. (1982). *Stanford Achievement Test*. San Antonio, TX: Psychological.

Gardner, M. (2000). *Expressive One-Word Picture Vocabulary Test—2000 Edition*. Novato, CA: Academic Therapy Publications.

Garosshen, C. (2003). *Homonyms*. Retrieved June 12, 2003, from http://www.askeric.org/cgibin/printlessons.cgi/Virtual/Lessons/Language_Arts/Reading/RDG0015.html

Garrison, B. (1994). Ronni Cohen reinvents the classroom. *University of Delaware Messenger, 3*(3), 12.

Gartland, D. (1994). Content area reading: Lessons from the specialists. *LD Forum, 19*(3), 19–22.

Gast, D. L., & Nelson, C. M. (1977). Legal and ethical considerations for the use of timeout procedures in special education settings. *Journal of Special Education, 11*, 457–467.

Gearheart, B. R., Weishahn, M. W., & Gearheart, D. (1995). *The exceptional student in the regular classroom* (4th ed.). Upper Saddle River, NJ: Merrill/Prentice Hall.

Gebhard, J. G. (1996). *Teaching English as a foreign or second language*. Ann Arbor: University of Michigan Press.

Geenen, S., Powers, L. E., Lopez-Vasquez A., Bersani, H. (2003). Understanding and promoting the transition of minority adolescents. *Career Development for Exceptional Individuals, 26*, 27–46.

Geller, E. S. (1994a). The human element in integrated environmental management. In J. Cairns, T. V. Crawford, & H. Salwasser (Eds.), *Implementing integrated environmental management* (pp. 5–26). Blacksburg: Virginia Tech.

Geller, E. S. (1994b). Ten principles for achieving a total safety culture. *Professional Safety, 39*(9), 18–24.

Gentry, J. R. (2000). A retrospective on invented spelling and a look forward. *Reading Teacher, 54*, 318–333.

George, N. L., & Lewis, T. J. (1991). EASE: Exit assistance for special educators—Helping students make the transition. *Teaching Exceptional Children, 23*(2), 34–39.

Georgia Department of Education. (2007). *Teacher resource center*. Retrieved March 26, 2007, from http://www.glc.k12.ga.us/trc/

Gerber, A. (1993). *Language-related learning disabilities: Their nature and treatment*. Baltimore, MD: Paul H. Brookes.

Gerber, M. M. (1985). The Department of Education's sixth annual report to Congress on PL 94-142: Is Congress getting the full story? *Exceptional Children, 51*, 209–224.

Gerber, M. M. (1988). Cognitive-behavioral training in the curriculum: Time, slow learners, and basic skills. In E. L. Meyer, G. A. Vergason, & R. J. Whelan (Eds.), *Effective instructional strategies for exceptional children* (pp. 45–64). Denver, CO: Love.

Gerlach, K. (2001). *Let's team up! A checklist for paraeducators, teachers, and principals*. Washington, DC: National Education Association.

Gerrish, M. (2000). Digital artistry: Technology infused projects created in the art room. *Multimedia Schools, 7*(5), 34–39.

Gersten, R., Baker, S. K., & Moses, S. U. (1998). *Teaching English-language learners with learning difficulties*. Reston, VA: Council for Exceptional Children.

Gersten, R., & Dimino, J. (2001). The realities of translating research into classroom practice. *Learning Disabilities Research and Practice, 16*, 120–130.

Gersten, R., & Okolo, C. (2007). Teaching history—in all its splendid messiness—to students with LD: Cotemporary research. *Journal of Learning Disabilities* 40, 97–192.

Giangreco, M. F., Broer, S. M., & Edelman, S. W. (2001). *A guide to schoolwide planning for paraeducator supports*. Burlington: University of Vermont, Center on Disability and Community Inclusion.

Giangreco, M. F., Cloninger, C. J., & Iverson, V. S. (1993). I've counted Jon: Transformational experiences of teacher educating students with disabilities. *Exceptional Children, 59*, 359–372.

Giangreco, M. F., & Doyle, M. B. (2002). Students with disabilities and paraprofessional supports: Benefits, balance, and band-aids. *Focus on Exceptional Children, 34*(7), 1–12.

Gibb, G. S., & Dyches, T. T. (2000). *Guide to writing quality individualized education programs: What's best for students with disabilities?* Boston: Allyn & Bacon.

Gibbons, M. (2002). *Self-directed learning handbook: Challenging adolescent students to excel*. San Francisco: Jossey-Bass.

Gillam, R. B., & Bedore, L. M. (2000). Communication across the lifespan. In R. B. Gillam, T. P. Marquardt, & F. N. Martin (Eds.), *Communication sciences and disorders: From science to clinical practice* (pp. 25–61). San Diego: Singular.

Gillam, R. B., & Pearson, N. A. (2004). *The test of narrative language*. Austin, TX: PRO-ED.

Gillies, R. M., & Ashman, A. F. (2000). The effects of cooperative learning on students with learning difficulties in the lower elementary school. *The Journal of Special Education, 34*, 19–27.

Gillingham, A., & Stillman, B. (1960). *Remedial teaching for children with specific disability in reading, spelling, and penmanship*. Cambridge, MA: Educators Publishing Service.

Gillon, G. (2004). *Phonological awareness: From research to practice*. New York: Guildford Press.

Ginsburg, H. P., & Mathews, S. C. (1984). *Diagnostic Test of Arithmetic Strategies*. Austin, TX: PRO-ED.

Goddard, Y. L., & Heron, T. E. (1998). Please, teacher, help me learn to spell better. *Teaching Exceptional Children, 30*, 38–43.

Goetz, L., Lee, M., Johnston, S., & Gaylord-Ross, R. (1991). Employment of persons with dual sensory impairments: Strategies for inclusion. *Journal of the Association for Persons with Severe Handicaps, 16*, 131–139.

Golden, D. (1999). Assistive technology policy and practice: What is the right thing to do? What is the reasonable thing to do? What is required and must be done? *Special Education Technology Practice, 1*(1), 12–14.

Goldstein, A. P., Sprafkin, R. P., Gershaw, N. J., & Klein, P. (1998). *Skillstreaming the adolescent: A structured learning approach to teaching prosocial skills*. Champaign, IL: Research Press.

Goldsworthy, C. (1982). *Multilevel Informal Language Inventory*. Columbus, OH: Merrill.

Goleman, D. (1998). *Working with emotional intelligence*. New York: Bateman Books.

Good, T. L., & Brophy, J. E. (1995). *Contemporary educational psychology*. Reading, MA: Addison-Wesley.

Goodman, K. (1991). Whole language: What makes it whole? In B. M. Power & R. Hubbard (Eds.), *Literacy in process* (pp. 88–95). Portsmouth, NH: Heinemann.

Gordon, J. M., Vaughn, S., & Schumm, J. S. (1993). Spelling interventions: A review of literature and implications for instruction with students with learning disabilities. *Learning Disabilities Research and Practice, 8*, 175–181.

Graden, J., Thurlow, M. L., & Ysseldyke, J. E. (1982). *Academic engaged time and its relationship to learning: A review of the literature* (Monograph No. 17). Minneapolis: University of Minnesota, Institute for Research on Learning Disabilities.

Graham, S. (1992). Helping students with LD progress as writers. *Intervention in School and Clinic, 27*, 134–144.

Graham, S. (1999). Handwriting and spelling instruction for students with learning disabilities: A review. *Learning Disability Quarterly, 22*, 78–98.

Graham, S. (2000). Should the natural learning approach replace traditional spelling instruction? *Journal of Educational Psychology*, 92, 235–247.

Graham, S., Berninger, V., Abbott, R., Abbott, S., & Whitaker, D. (1997). The role of mechanics in composing of elementary school students: A new methodological approach. *Journal of Educational Psychology, 89*, 170–182.

Graham, S., & Harris, K.R. (2005). Improving the writing performance of young struggling writers: Theoretical and programmatic research from the Center on Accelerating Student Learning. *Journal of Special Education, 39*, 19–33.

Graham, S., Harris, K. R., & Fink, B. (2000). Is handwriting causally related to learning to write? Treatment of handwriting problems in beginning writers. *Journal of Educational Psychology, 92*, 620–633.

Graham, S., Harris, K. R., & Larsen, L. (2001). Prevention and intervention of writing difficulties for students with learning disabilities. *Learning Disabilities Research and Practice, 16*, 74–84.

Graham, S., Harris, K. R., & Loynachin, C. (1994). The spelling for writing list. *Journal of Learning Disabilities, 27*, 210–214.

Graham, S., Harris, K., & Sawyer, R. (1987). Composition instruction with learning-disabled students. *Focus on Exceptional Children, 20*(4), 1–11.

Graham, S., & Johnson, L. A. (1989). Teaching reading to learning-disabled students: A review of research supported procedures. *Focus on Exceptional Children, 21*, 1–12.

Graham, S., & Miller, L. (1979). Spelling research and practice: A unified approach. *Focus on Exceptional Children, 12*(2), 1–16.

Graham, S., & Miller, L. (1980). Handwriting research and practice: A unified approach. *Focus on Exceptional Children, 13*(2), 1–16.

Graham, S., & Voth, V. P. (1990). Spelling instruction: Making modifications for students with learning disabilities. *Academic Therapy, 25*, 447–457.

Grant, R. (1993). Strategic training for using text headings to improve students, processing of content. *Journal of Reading, 36*, 482–488.

Graves, D. H. (1985). All children can write. *Learning Disabilities Focus, 1*(1), 36–43.

Graves, D. H. (1994). *A fresh new look at writing*. Portsmouth, NH: Heineman.

Green, R. L. (1994). Speech time is all the time. *Teaching Exceptional Children, 27*(1), 60-61.

Greene, G. (1994). Research into practice: The magic of mnemonics. *LD Forum, 19*(3), 34-37.

Greene, J. F. (1998). Another chance. Help for older students with limited literacy. *American Federation of Teachers*, 74-79.

Greenland, R., & Polloway, E. A. (1995). Handwriting and students with disabilities: Overcoming first impressions. (ERIC Document Reproduction Service No. ED 378 754)

Gregg, N., & Mather, N. (2002). School is fun at recess: Informal analyses of written language for students with learning disabilities. *Journal of Learning Disabilities, 35*, 7-22.

Gregory, G. P. (1979). Using the newspaper in the mainstreamed classroom. *Social Education, 43*, 140-143.

Gregory, R. P., Hackney, C., & Gregory, N. M. (1982). Corrective reading programme: An evaluation. *British Journal of Educational Psychology, 52*, 33-50.

Gresham, F. M., & Elliott, S. N. (1990). *Social skills rating system*. Circle Pines, MN: American Guidance Service.

Grigal, M., & Neubert, D. A. (2004). Parents' in-school values and post-school expectations for transition-aged youth with disabilities. *Career Development for Exceptional Individuals, 27*, 65-85.

Grigal, M., Test, D. W., Beattie, J., & Wood, W. (1997). An evaluation of transition components of individualized education programs. *Exceptional Children, 63*, 357-372.

Grossen, B. (n.d.). The research base for corrective reading SRA—University of Oregon. Retrieved May 16, 2007, from https://www.sraonline.com/di_home_research.html?PHPSESSID=784bb902f57458c78e92c9bae162569f

Grossen, B., & Carnine, D. (1993). Phonics instruction: Comparing research and practice. *Teaching Exceptional Children, 25*(2), 22-25.

Guillaume, A. M., Yopp, R. H., & Yopp, H. K. (1996). Accessible science. *The Journal of Educational Issues of Language Minority Students, 17*, 67-85.

Gurganus, S., Janas, M., & Schmitt, L. (1995). Science instruction: What special education teachers need to know and what roles they need to play. *Teaching Exceptional Children, 27*(4), 7-9.

Guttman, M. (1995, October 29). Doctors and parents are focusing on whether popular drugs "unquestionably helpful to some children" are overprescribed. *USA WEEKEND*.

Haberman, M., & Post, L. (1998). Teachers for multicultural schools: The power of selection. *Theory into Practice, 37*, 96-104.

Hackney, C. (1993). *Handwriting: A way to tell expression*. Columbus, OH: Zaner-Bloser.

Hadden, S., & Fowler, S. A. (2000). Intergency agreements: A proactive tool for improving the transition from early intervention to preschool special education services. *Young Exceptional Children, 3*(4), 2-7.

Hadden, S., & Fowler, S. A. (1997). Preschool: A new beginning for children and parents. *Teaching Exceptional Children, 30*(1), 36-39.

Hagedorn, V. S. (2003). Communicating with inclusion students. *General Music Today, 16*(2), 37-42.

Hagood, B. F. (1997). Reading and writing with help from story grammar. *Teaching Exceptional Children, 29*(4), 10-14.

Haight, S. L. (2003). Raising questions about questions: Benefits of using a content enhancement routine. Retrieved June 7, 2006, from http://www.ku-crl.org/archives/cer/questions.shtml

Haines, A. H. (1992). Strategies for preparing preschool children with special needs for the kindergarten mainstream. *Journal of Early Intervention, 16*, 320-333.

Hallahan, D. P., Kauffman, J. M., & Lloyd, J. W. (1985). *Introduction to learning disabilities* (2nd ed.). Upper Saddle River, NJ: Prentice Hall.

Hallahan, D. P., Lloyd, J. W., & Stoller, L. (1982). *Improving attention with self-monitoring: A manual for teachers*. Charlottesville: University of Virginia Learning Disabilities Research Institute.

Hallenbeck, M. J. (2002). Taking charge: Adolescents with learning disabilities assume responsibility for their own writing. *Learning Disabilities Quarterly, 25*(4), 227-246.

Halpern, A. S. (1985). Transition: A look at the foundation. *Exceptional Children, 51*, 479-486.

Halpern, A. S. (1993). Quality of life as a conceptual framework for evaluating transition outcomes. *Exceptional Children, 59*, 486-498.

Halpern, A. S., Irvin, L., & Munkres, J. (1986). *Social and Prevocational Information Battery—Revised*. Monterey, CA: CTB/McGraw-Hill.

Hamilton, C., Miller, A., & Wood, P. (1987). Group books. *Teaching Exceptional Children, 19*(3), 46-47.

Hammill, D., & Bryant, B. (1999). *The Detroit Tests of Learning Aptitude—Primary 4*. Austin, TX: PRO-ED.

Hammill, D., Mather, N., & Roberts, R. (2001). *The Illinois Test of Psycholinguistic Abilities—3*. Austin, TX: PRO-ED.

Hammill, D. D. (1986). Correcting handwriting deficiencies. In D. D. Hammill & N. E. Bartel (Eds.), *Teaching children with learning and behavior problems* (4th ed., pp. 154-177). Boston: Allyn & Bacon.

Hammill, D. D. (1987). Assessing students in the schools. In D. D. Hammill (Ed.), *Assessing the abilities and instructional needs of students*. (pp. 5-37). Austin, TX: PRO-ED.

Hammill, D. D. (2004). What we know about correlates of reading. *Exceptional Children, 70*, 453-468.

Hammill, D. D., & Bartel, N. R. (1982). *Teaching children with learning and behavior problems* (3rd ed.). Boston: Allyn & Bacon.

Hammill, D. D., Brown, V. L., Larsen, S. C., & Wiederholt, J. L. (1994). *Test of Adolescent Language—3*. Austin, TX: PRO-ED.

Hammill, D. D., & Larsen, S. C. (1996). *The Test of Written Language—3 (TOWL-3)*. Austin, TX: PRO-ED.

Hammill, D. D., Mather, N., Allen, E. A., & Roberts, R. (2002). Using semantics, grammar, phonology, and rapid naming tasks to predict word identification. *Journal of Learning Disabilities, 35*, 121–136.

Hammill, D. D., & Newcomer, P. L. (1991). *Test of Language development—2: Intermediate*. Austin, TX: PRO-ED.

Hamre-Nietupski, S., McDonald, J., & Nietupski, J. (1992). Integrating elementary students with multiple disabilities: Challenges and solutions. *Teaching Exceptional Children, 24*(3), 6–11.

Handleman, J. S., & Harris, S. L. (1983). A comparison of one-to-one versus couplet instruction with autistic children. *Behavioral Disorders, 9*, 22–26.

Hanley-Maxwell, C., Pogoloff, S. M., Whitney-Thomas, J. (1998). Families: The heart of transition. In F. Rusch & J. Chadsey (Eds.), *Beyond High School: Transition from school to work* (pp. 234–264). Belmont, CA: Wadsworth.

Hansen, M. J., & Lynch, E. W. (1995). *Early intervention: Implementing child and family services for infants and toddlers who are at risk or disabled*. Austin, TX: PRO-ED.

Hanson, M. J., Horn, E., Sandall, S., Beckman, P., Morgan, M., Marquart, J., Barnwell, D., & Chou, H. Y. (2001). After preschool inclusion: Children's educational pathways over the early school years. *Exceptional Children, 68*, 65–83.

Harden, L. (1987). Reading to remember. *The Reading Teacher, 40*(6), 580–581.

Hardman, M. L., & Drew, C. J. (2005). *Human exceptionality: Society, school, and family* (8th ed.). Boston: Allyn & Bacon.

Haring, N., & Liberty, K. A. (1990). Matching strategies with performance in facilitating generalization. *Focus on Exceptional Children, 22*(8), 1–16.

Harlan, J. E. (1993). *Yes we can: Overcoming obstacles to creativity*. Paper presented at the annual meeting of the American Association on Mental Retardation, Washington, DC. (ERIC Document Reproduction Service No. Ed 360 761)

Harn, W. E., Bradshaw, M. L., & Ogletree, B. (1999). The speech-language pathologist in the schools: Changing roles. *Intervention in School and Clinic, 34*, 163–169.

Harniss, M., Caros, J., & Gersten, R. (2007). Impact of the design of U.S. history textbooks on content acquisition and academic engagement of special education students: An experimental investigation. *Journal of Learning Disabilities, 40*, 97–192.

Harris Middle School. (2003). *A simile and metaphor sample lesson plan for teaching similes and metaphors*. Retrieved June 12, 2003, from http://volweb.utk.edu/Schools/bedford/harrisms/2poe.htm

Harris, A. J., & Sipay, E. R. (1990). *How to increase reading ability*. New York: Longman.

Harris, K. R., & Graham, S. (1992). *Helping young writers master the craft: Strategy instruction and self-regulation in the writing process*. Cambridge, MA: Brookline Books.

Harris, K. R., Graham, S., Reid, R., McElroy, K., & Hamby, R. S. (1994). Self-monitoring of attention versus self-monitoring of performance: Replication and cross-task comparison studies. *Learning Disability Quarterly, 17*, 121–139.

Harris, M.K., Carnine, D.W., Silbert, J., Dixon, R. C. (2007). Effective strategies for teaching mathematics. In M.D. Coyne, E. J. Kame'enui, & D. W. Carnine (Eds), *Effective teaching strategies that accommodate diverse learners* (3rd ed.). Upper Saddle River, NJ: Merrill/Prentice Hall.

Harris, R. E., Marchand-Martella, N., & Martella, R. C. (2000). Effects of a peer-delivered corrective reading program. *Journal of Behavioral Education, 10*, 21–36.

Hart, B., & Risley, T. R. (1975). Incidental teaching of language in preschool. *Journal of Applied Behavioral Analysis, 8*, 411–420.

Harter, S. (1982). The perceived competence scale for children. *Child Development, 52*, 87–97.

Haughton, E. (1974). Myriad counter: Or beads that aren't for worrying. *Teaching Exceptional Children, 7*, 203–209.

Hawaii Transition Project. (1987). Transition resources. Honolulu: University of Hawaii, Department of Special Education.

Hawkins, B. (1994). Leisure as an adaptive skill area. *AAMR News and Notes, 7*(1), 5–6.

Hayden, T. (1980). *One child*. New York: Avon Books.

Hayes, D. (1988). Toward students learning through the social studies text. *The Social Studies, 79*, 266–270.

Haynes, W. O., Moral, M. J., & Pindzola, R. H. (1990). *Communication disorders in the classroom*. Dubuque, IA: Kendall/Hunt.

Hazel, J. S., Schumaker, J. B., Sherman, J. A., & Sheldon-Wildgen, J. B. (1981a). *ASSET: A social skills program for adolescents*. Champaign, IL: Research Press.

Hazel, J. S., Schumaker, J. B., Sherman, J. A., & Sheldon-Wildgen, J. B. (1981b). Group social skills: A program for court-adjudicated probationary youth. *Criminal Justice and Behavior, 9*, 35–52.

Heacox, D. (2002). *Differentiating instruction in the regular classroom: How to reach and teach all learners, grades 3–12*. Minneapolis, MN: Free Spirit Publishing.

Hedeen, D. L., & Ayres, B. J. (2002). "You want me to teach *him* to read?" Fulfilling the intent of IDEA. *Journal of Disability Policy Studies, 13*, 180–189.

Hedrick, D., Prather, E., Tobin, A. (1995). *Sequenced Inventory of Communication Development—Revised*. Austin, TX: PRO-ED.

Heilman, A., Blair, T., & Rupley, W. (1981). *Principles and practices of teaching reading*. Columbus, OH: Merrill.

Heimlich, J. E., & Pittelman, S. D. (1986). *Semantic mapping: Classroom applications*. Newark, DE: International Reading Association.

Heller, H. W., Spooner, F., Anderson, D., & Mimms, A. (1988). Homework: A review of special education practices in the southwest. *Teacher Education and Special Education, 11*, 43–51.

Helmke, L., Havekost, D. M., Patton, J. R., & Polloway, E. A. (1994). Life skills programming: Development of a high school science course. *Teaching Exceptional Children, 26*(2), 49–53.

Henderson, N., & Milstein, M. M. (2003). *Resiliency in schools: Making it happen for students and educators*. Thousand Oaks, CA: Corwin Press.

Henley, D. R. (1990). Adapting art education for exceptional children. *School Arts, 90*(4), 18–20.

Heron, T. (1978). Punishment: A review of the literature with implications for the teacher of mainstreamed children. *Journal of Special Education, 12*, 243–252.

Heron, T. E. (1987). Response cost. In J. O. Cooper, T. E. Heron, & W. E. Heward (Eds.), *Applied behavior analysis* (pp. 454–464). Upper Saddle River, NJ: Merrill/Prentice Hall.

Heron, T. E., & Harris, K. C. (1982). *The educational consultant: Helping professionals, parents, and mainstreamed students*. Boston: Allyn & Bacon.

Hess, L. J., & Fairchild, J. L. (1988). Model, analyse, practise (MAP): A language therapy model for learning-disabled adolescents. *Child Language Teaching and Therapy, 4*, 325–338.

Heukerott, P. B. (1987). "Little books" for content areas vocabulary. *The Reading Teacher, 40*, 489.

Heward, W. L. (2003a). *Exceptional children: An introductory survey of special education* (7th ed.). Upper Saddle River, NJ: Merrill/Prentice Hall.

Heward, W. L. (2003b). Ten faulty notions about teaching and learning that hinder the effectiveness of special education. *The Journal of Special Education, 36*, 186–205.

Higgins, E. L., & Raskind, M. H. (2000, Winter). Speaking to read: The effects of continuous versus discrete speech recognition systems on the reading and spelling of children with learning disabilities. *Journal of Special Education Technology eJournal, 15*(1), Retrieved May 16, 2007, http://jset.univ.edu/15.IT/tissuemenue.html

Hildebrandt, C. (1998). Creativity in music and early childhood. *Young Children, 53*(6), 68–74.

Hitchcock, C., Meyer, A., Rose, D., & Jackson, R. (2002, Nov./Dec.). Providing new access to the general curriculum: Universal design for teaching. *Teaching Exceptional Children, 35*, 8–17.

Hoffman, A., & Field, S. (1995). Promoting self-determination through effective curriculum development. *Intervention in School and Clinic, 30*, 134–142.

Hofmeister, A., & Thorkildsen, R. (1993). Interactive videodisc and exceptional individuals. In J. D. Lindsey (Ed.), *Computers and exceptional individuals* (2nd ed., pp. 87–107). Austin, TX: PRO-ED.

Hogan, K. M. (2000). Educational reform in Texas. In A. A. Glatthorn, & J. Fontana (Eds.), *Coping with standards, tests, and accountability: Voices from the classroom* (pp. 51–62). Washington, DC: National Education Association.

Homme, L. (1969). *How to use contingency contracting in the classroom*. Champaign, IL: Research Press.

Hoover, J. J. (1989). Implementing a study skills program in the classroom. *Academic Therapy, 24*, 471–476.

Hoover, J. J. (1990a). Curriculum adaptations: A five-step process for classroom implementation. *Academic Therapy, 25*, 407–416.

Hoover, J. J. (1990b). *Using study skills and learning strategies in the classroom: A teacher's handbook*. Boulder, CO: Hamilton.

Hoover, J. J. (1991). *Classroom applications of cognitive learning styles*. Boulder, CO: Hamilton.

Hoover, J. J. (2000). *Assessment of English language learners* [CD-ROM]. Boulder: BUENO Center, University of Colorado.

Hoover, J. J., & Collier, C. (1992). Sociocultural considerations in teaching study strategies. *Intervention in School and Clinic, 27*, 228–232.

Hoover, J. J., & Collier, C. (2001). *Learning styles* [CD-ROM]. Boulder: BUENO Center, University of Colorado.

Hoover, J. J., Klingner, J. K., Baca, L. M., & Patton, J. (in press). *Methods for teaching culturally and linguistically diverse exceptional learners*. Columbus, OH: Merrill.

Hoover, J. J., & Patton, J. R. (2004a). *Curriculum adaptations for students with learning and behavior problems: Principals and practices* (3rd ed.). Austin, TX: PRO-ED.

Hoover, J. J., & Patton, J. R. (2004b). *Teaching students with learning problems to use study skills: A teacher's guide* (2nd ed.). Austin, TX: PRO-ED.

Hoover, J. J., & Patton, J. R. (2004c). Differentiating standards-based education for students with diverse needs. *Remedial and Special Education, 25*, 74–78.

Hoover, J. J., & Patton J. R. (2005). *Curriculum adaptations for students with learning and behavioral problems: Differentiating instruction to meet diverse needs* (3rd ed.). Austin, TX: PRO-ED.

Hoover, J. J., & Patton, J. R. (2007). *Teaching study skills to students with learning problems: A teacher's guide to meeting diverse needs* (2nd ed.). Austin, TX: PRO-ED.

Hoover J. J. & Patton J. R. (in press). Role of special education in a multi-tiered instructional system. *Intervention in School and Clinic*.

Hoover, J. J., Patton, J. R., Hresko, W., & Hammill, D. (in press). *Prereferral assessment inventories*. Austin, TX: PRO-ED.

Hoover, J. J., & Rabideau, D. K. (1995). Teaching study skills through semantic webs. *Intervention in School and Clinic, 30*, 292–296.

Hoover, J. J., & Trujillo-Hinsch, J. (1999). *Test taking skills of English language learners*. Final Research Grant Report, OBEMLA. Boulder, CO: BUENO Center, University of Colorado.

Horn, E. (1954). *Teaching spelling*. Washington, DC: American Educational Research Association.

Hoskins, B. (1994). Language and literacy: Participating in the conversation. In K. G. Butler (Ed.), *Best practices II:*

*The classroom as an intervention context* (pp. 201–217). Gaithersburg, MD:Aspen.

Houck, C., & McKenzie, R. G. (1985). *ASSIST:Aides serving students:An individual system of training*. Bowling Green:Western Kentucky University College of Education.

Hourcade, J. J., & Bauwens, J. (2003). *Cooperative teaching: Rebuilding and sharing the schoolhouse* (2nd ed.). Austin, TX: PRO-ED.

Howard, V. F., Williams, B. F., Port, P. D., & Lepper, C. (2001). *Very young children with special needs:A formative approach for the twenty-first century* (2nd ed.). Upper Saddle River, NJ: Merril/Prentice Hall.

Howe, E., Joseph, A., & Victor, E. (1971). *A source book for elementary science*. New York: Harcourt Brace Jovanovich.

Howell, K. W., Kaplan, J. S., & O'Connell, C. Y. (1979). *Evaluating exceptional children:A task analysis approach*. Upper Saddle River, NJ: Merrill/Prentice Hall.

Howell, K. W., & Morehead, M. K. (1987). *Curriculum-based evaluation in special and remedial education*. Columbus, OH: Merrill.

Howell, K. W., Rueda, R., & Rutherford, R. B. (1983). A procedure for teaching self-recording to moderately retarded students. *Psychology in the Schools, 20*, 202–209.

Hresko, W. (1996). *Test of Early Written Language—2*. Austin, TX: PRO-ED.

Hresko, W., Reid, K., & Hammill, D. (1999). *Test of Early Language Development—3rd Edition*. Austin, TX: PRO-ED.

Hresko, W. P., Reid, D. K., & Hammill, D. D. (1982). *Prueba del Desarrollo Inicial del Lenguaje*. Austin, TX: PRO-ED.

Hresko, W. P., Reid, D. K., & Hammill, D. D. (1991). *Test of Early Language Development*. Austin, TX: PRO-ED.

Hughes, C. A. (1996). Memory and test taking strategies. In D. D. Deshler, E. S. Ellis, & B. K. Lenz (Eds.), *Teaching adolescents with learning disabilities: Strategies and methods* (2nd ed., pp. 209–266). Denver, CO: Love.

Hughes, C. A., Ruhl, K. L., & Misra, A. (1989). Self-management with behaviorally disordered students in school settings: A promise unfulfilled? *Behavioral Disorders, 14*, 250–262.

Hulit, L. M., & Howard, M. R. (1997). *Born to talk:An Introduction to speech and language development* (2nd ed.). Boston, MA:Allyn & Bacon.

Hunt, K. W. (1965). *Grammatical structures written at three grade levels*. Research Report No. 3. Champaign, IL: National Council of Teachers of English.

Hunt, P. (1995, Summer). *Collaboration:What does it take? What's working:Transition in Minnesota* (p. 1). Minneapolis: University of Minnesota Institute on Community Integration.

Hurst, J. B. (1986). A skills-in-living perspective rather than trivial pursuit. *The Social Studies, 77*(2), 69–73.

Hymes, D. (1971). Competence and performance in linguistic theory. In R. Huxley & E. Ingram (Eds.), *Language acquisition: Models and methods* (pp. 3–24). New York: Academic Press.

Idiom Connection. (2003). *The idiom connection*. Retrieved June 12, 2003, from http://www.geocities.com/Athens/Aegean/6720/

Idol, L. (1989). The resource/consulting teacher: An integrated model of service delivery. *Remedial and Special Education, 10*(6), 41–48.

Idol, L. (1993). *Special educator's consultation handbook* (2nd ed.). Austin, TX: PRO-ED.

Idol, L. (1997). *Reading success:A specialized literacy program for learners with challenging reading needs*. Austin, TX: PRO-ED.

Idol, L. (2002). *Creating collaborative and inclusive schools*. Austin TX: PRO-ED.

Idol, L. (2004). *Creating collaborative and inclusive schools*. Austin: PRO-ED.

Idol, L., Nevin, A., & Paolucci-Whitcomb, P. (1986). *Models of curriculum-based assessment*. Austin, TX: PRO-ED.

Idol, L., Nevin, A., & Paolucci-Whitcomb, P. (1994). *Collaborative consultation* (2nd ed.). Austin, TX: PRO-ED.

Idol, L., & West, J. F. (1991). Educational collaboration: A catalyst for effective schooling. *Intervention in School and Clinic, 27*, 70–78.

Idol, L., & West, J. F. (1992). *Effective instruction of difficult-to-teach students:An in-service and preservice professional development program for classroom, remedial, and special education teachers*. Austin, TX: PRO-ED.

Illinois State Board of Education. (2003). *English language arts performance descriptors*. Retrieved June 9, 2003, from http://www.isbe.state.il.us/ils/default.htm

Individuals with Disabilities Education Act Amendments of 1991, 20 U.S.C.§1400–1485.

Individuals with Disabilities Education Act Amendments of 1997, 20 U.S.C.§140.

*Individuals with Disabilities Education Improvement Act of 2004*, HB 1350.

International Reading Association. (2006). *The role of phonics in reading instruction*. Retrieved August 9, 2006, from http://www.reading.org/resources/issues/positions_phonics.html

Internet TESL Journal. (2003a). *Self-study homonym quizzes*. Retrieved June 12, 2003, from http://a4esl.org/q/h/homonyms.html

Internet TESL Journal. (2003b). *Self-study idiom quizzes*. Retrieved June 12, 2003, from http://a4esl.org/q/h/idioms.html

Isaacson, S. (2004). Instruction that helps students meet state standards in writing. *Exceptionality, 12*, 39–54.

Isaacson, S. L. (1987). Effective instruction in written language. *Focus on Exceptional Children, 19*(6), 1–12.

Isaacson, S. L. (1989). Role of secretary vs. author in resolving the conflict in writing instruction. *Learning Disability Quarterly, 12*, 200–217.

Israel, L. (1984). Word knowledge and word retrieval: Phonological and semantic strategies. In G. Wallace &

K. Butler (Eds.), *Language learning disabilities in school-age children* (pp. 230–250). Baltimore, MD: Williams & Wilkins.

Jackson, N. F., Jackson, D. A., & Monroe, C. (1983). *Program guide: Getting along with others*. Champaign, IL: Research Press.

Jacobson, W. J., & Bergman, A. B. (1991). *Science for children: A book for teachers* (3rd ed.). Upper Saddle River, NJ: Prentice Hall.

James, S., & Pedrazzini, L. (1975). *Simple lattice approach to mathematics*. Upper Saddle River, NJ: Prentice Hall Learning Systems.

Jamison, P. J., & Shevitz, L. A. (1985). RATE: A reason to read. *Teaching Exceptional Children, 18*(1), 46–50.

Jarolimek, J. (1981). The social studies: An overview. In H. D. Mehlinger & O. I. Davis (Eds.), *The social studies: Eightieth yearbook of the National Society for the Study of Education* (pp. 3–18). Chicago: University of Chicago Press.

Jastak, S. R., & Wilkinson, G. S. (1984). *The Wide Range Achievement Test—Revised*. Wilmington, DE: Jastak Associates.

Jayanthi, M., Bursuck, W., Epstein, M. H., & Polloway, E. A. (1997). Strategies for successful homework. *Teaching Exceptional Children, 30*(1), 4–7.

Jayanthi, M., Bursuck, W., Havekost, D. M., Epstein, M. H., & Polloway, E. A. (1994). School district testing policies and students with disabilities: A national survey. *School Psychology Review, 23*, 694–703.

Jayanthi, M., Nelson, J. S., Sawyer, V., Bursuck, W., & Epstein, M. H. (1994). *Homework communication problems among parents, general education and special education teachers: An exploratory study*. Unpublished manuscript.

Jeffs, T., Morrison F., Messenheimer T., Rizz G., & Banister, S. (2003). *A retrospective analysis of techological advancements in special education*. Retrieved April 10, 2004, from http://www.haworthpress.com/store/products.asp?sku=J)25

Jenkins, J. R., Leigh, J., & Patton, J. (1996). *State certification standards for teachers of students with learning disabilities: An update*. Manuscript submitted for publication.

Jenkins, J. R., Stein, M. L., & Osborn, J. R. (1981). What next after decoding? Instruction and research in reading comprehension. *Exceptional Education Quarterly, 2*(1), 27–39.

Jitendra, A. K., Edwards, L. L., Choutka, C. M., & Treadway, P. S. (2002). A collaborative approach to planning in the content areas for students with learning disabilities: Accessing the general curriculum. *Learning Disabilities Research and Practice, 17*, 252–267.

Jitendra, A. K., & Hoppes, M. K., Xin, Y. P. (2000). Enhancing main idea comprehension for students with learning problems: The role of a summarization strategy and self-monitoring instruction. *Journal of Special Education, 34*, 127–139.

Johnson, D. A., & Rising, G. R. (1972). *Guidelines for teaching mathematics*. Belmont, CA: Wadsworth.

Johnson, D. W., & Johnson, R. T. (1989a). Cooperative learning in mathematics education. In P. R. Trafton & A. P. Shulte (Eds.), *New directions for elementary school mathematics* (1989 yearbook, pp. 234–245). Reston, VA: National Council of Teachers of Mathematics.

Johnson, D. W., & Johnson, R. T. (1989b). Using cooperative learning in math. In N. Davidson (Ed.), *Cooperative learning in mathematics* (pp. 103–125). Menlo Park, CA: Addison-Wesley.

Johnson, D. W., & Johnson, R. T. (1990). What is cooperative learning? In M. Brubacher, R. Payne, & K. Rickett (Eds.), *Perspectives on small group learning* (pp. 5–30). Oakville, Ontario, Canada: Rubicon.

Johnson, D. W., & Johnson, R. T. (1998). *Learning together and alone: Cooperative, competitive, and individualistic learning* (2nd ed.). Boston: Allyn & Bacon.

Johnson, D. W., Johnson, R. T., & Holubec, E. J. (1994). *The new circles of learning*. Alexandria, VA: Association for Supervision and Curriculum Development.

Johnson, D. R., Stodden, R. A., Emanuel, E. J., Lueking, R., & Mack, M. (2002). Current challenges facing secondary education and transition services: What research tells us. *Exceptional Children, 68*, 519-531.

Johnston, E. B., & Johnston, A. V. (1990). *Communication Abilities Diagnostic Test*. Chicago: Riverside.

Johnston, J. R. (1983). Discussion: Part I: What is language intervention? The role of theory. In J. Miller, D. E. Yoder, & R. Schiefelbusch (Eds.), *Contemporary issues in language intervention*. Rockville, MD: ASHA.

Johnston, R. C. (1994). Policy details who paddles students and with what. *Education Week, 14*(11), 5.

Jones, B. F., Palincsar, A. S., Ogle, D. S., & Carr, E. G. (1987). *Strategic teaching and learning: Cognitive instruction in the content areas*. Washington, DC: Association of Supervision and Curriculum Development.

Jones, C. J. (2001). Teacher-friendly curriculum-based assessment in spelling. *Teaching Exceptional Children, 34*, 32–38.

Jones, M. M., & Carlier, L. L. (1995). Creating inclusionary opportunities for learners with multiple disabilities: A team-teaching approach. *Teaching Exceptional Children, 27*(3), 23–27.

Jones, R. M., & Steinbrink, J. E. (1991). Home teams: Cooperative learning in elementary science. *School Science and Mathematics, 91*, 139–143.

Jones, T. S. (2005). Incorporate diversity into your classroom. *Intervention in School and Clinic, 41*, 9–12.

Joseph, G. E., & Strain, P. S. (2003). Enhancing emotional vocabulary in young children. *Young Exceptional Children, 6*(4), 18–26.

Joseph, L. M., & Seery, M. E. (2004). Where is the phonics? A review of the literature on the use of phonetic analysis with students with mental retardation. *Remedial and Special Education, 24*, 88–94.

Kagan, S. (1990). A structural approach to cooperative learning. *Educational Leadership, 47*(4), 12–15.

Kagan, S. (1992). *Cooperative learning resources for teachers* (7th ed.). San Juan Capistrano, CA: Resources for Teachers.

Kagan, S. L. (1992). The strategic importance of linkages and the transition between early childhood programs and early elementary school. In *Sticking together: Strengthening linkages and the transition between early childhood education and early elementary school* (summary of a National Policy Forum). Washington, DC: U.S. Department of Education.

Kalyanpur, M., & Harry, B. (1999). *Culture in special education: Building reciprocal family-professional relationships*. Baltimore, MD: P. H. Brookes Pub.

Kangas, K. A., & Lloyd, L. L. (1998). Augmentative and alternative communication. In G. H. Shames, E. Wiig, & W. A. Secord (Eds.), *Human communication disorders* (5th ed., pp. 510–551). Boston: Allyn & Bacon.

Kataoka, J. C., & Lock, R. (1995). Whales and hermit crabs: Integrated programming and science. *Teaching Exceptional Children, 27*(4), 17–21.

Katims, D. S. (2000). Literacy instruction for people with mental retardation: Historical highlights and contemporary analysis. *Education and Training in Mental Retardation and Developmental Disabilities, 35*, 3–15.

Katims, D. S. (2001). Literacy assessment of students with mental retardation: An exploratory investigation. *Education and Training in Mental Retardation, 36*, 363–372.

Kauffman, J. M. (1989). The regular education initiative as Reagan-Bush education policy: A trickle-down theory of education of the hard-to-teach. *The Journal of Special Education, 23*, 256–278.

Kauffman, J. M. (2002). *Education reform: Bright people sometimes say stupid things about education*. Lanham, MD: Scarecrow Press.

Kauffman, J. M., & Hallahan, D. P. (1995). *The illusion of full inclusion*. Austin, TX: PRO-ED.

Kauffman, J. M., & Payne, J. S. (1975). *Mental retardation: Introduction and personal perspectives*. Columbus, OH: Merrill.

Kauffman, J. M., Pullen, P. L., & Akers, E. (1988). Classroom management: Teacher-child-peer relationships. In E. L. Meyen, G. A. Vergason, & R. J. Whelan (Eds.), *Effective instructional strategies for exceptional children* (pp. 32–44). Denver, CO: Love.

Kaufman, A. S., & Kaufman, N. L. (1985). *Kaufman Test of Educational Achievement*. Circle Pines, MN: American Guidance Service.

Kaufmann, K. A. (2002). Adaptation techniques for modeling diversity in the dance class (teaching tips). *Journal of Physical Education, Recreation, and Dance, 73*(7), 16–20.

Kavale, K. A., & Forness, S. R. (1987). The far side of heterogeneity: A critical analysis of empirical subtyping research in learning disabilities. *Journal of Learning Disabilities, 20*, 374–382.

Kayser, H. (1995). Intervention with children from linguistically and culturally diverse backgrounds. In M. E. Fey, J. Windsor, & S. F. Warren (Eds.), *Language intervention preschool through the elementary years*. Baltimore: Paul H. Brookes.

Kazdin, A. E. (2001). *Behavior modification in applied settings* (6th ed.). Belmont, CA: Wadsworth/Thomson Learning.

Kazdin, A. E., & Bootzin, R. R. (1972). The token economy: An evaluative review. *Journal of Applied Behavior Analysis, 5*, 343–372.

Kazdin, A. E., & Erickson, L. M. (1975). Developing responsiveness to instructions in severely and profoundly retarded residents. *Journal of Behavior Therapy and Experimental Psychiatry, 6*, 17–21.

Kelley, S., Serna, L. A., & Noonan, M. J. (1992). *Preparing elementary students for the mainstream: A study of the generalization of social skills across environments*. Unpublished manuscript.

Kellough, R.D. (2005). *Your first year if teaching: Guidelines for success*. Upper Saddle River, NJ: Merrill/Prentice Hall.

Kelly, E. J. (1979). *Elementary school social studies instruction: A basic approach*. Denver, CO: Love.

Kelner, L. B. (1993). *Creative classroom: A guide for using creative drama in the classroom, PreK–6*. Portsmouth, NH: Heinemann.

Kerr, M. M., & Nelson, C. M. (2006). *Strategies for addressing behavior problems in the classroom*. Upper Saddle River, NJ: Pearson Prentice Hall.

Kerr, M. M., Nelson, C. M., & Lambert, D. L. (1987). *Helping adolescents with learning and behavior problems*. Columbus, OH: Merrill.

Khilnani, S., & Culhane, D. (1995). Linking sculpture to core subjects. *Teaching Exceptional Children, 27*(4), 68–70.

Kiburtz, C. S., Miller, S. R., & Morrow, L. W. (1984). Structured learning using self-monitoring to promote maintenance and generalization of social skills across settings for a behaviorally disordered adolescent. *Behavior Disorders, 4*, 47–55.

Kiewra, K. A., & DuBois, N.E. (1998). *Learning to learn*. Boston: Allyn & Bacon.

Kim, A., Vaughn, S., & Wanzek, J. (2004). Graphic organizers and their effects on the reading comprehension of students with LD: A synthesis of research. *Journal of Learning Disabilities, 37*, 105–118.

Kinder, D., & Bursuck, W. (1992). The search for a unified social studies curriculum: Does history really repeat itself? In D. Carnine & E. J. Kame'enui (Eds.), *Higher order thinking: Designing curriculum for mainstreamed students* (pp. 23–37). Austin, TX: PRO-ED.

Kinder, D., & Bursuck, W. (1993). History strategy instruction: Problem-solution-effect analysis, time-line, and vocabulary instruction. *Exceptional Children, 59*, 324–335.

Kinder, D., Bursuck, W., & Epstein, M. (1992). An evaluation of history textbooks. *Journal of Special Education, 25*, 472–491.

King, E. W. (1980). *Teaching ethnic awareness: Methods and materials for the elementary school*. Santa Monica, CA: Goodyear.

Kirk, S., Kirk, W., & Minskoff, E. (1986). *Phonic remedial reading lessons*. Novato, CA: Academic Therapy.

Kirk, S. A., & Johnson, G. O. (1951). *Educating the retarded child*. Cambridge, MA: Houghton Mifflin.

Kirk, S. A., Kliebhan, J. M., & Lerner, J. (1978). *Teaching reading to slow and disabled learners*. Boston: Houghton Mifflin.

Kirk, S. A., & Monroe, M. (1940). *Teaching reading to slow-learning children*. Boston: Houghton Mifflin.

Klien, D. (2003). A brief history of American K-12 mathematics education in the 20th century. In J. M. Royer (Ed.), *Mathematical cognition* (pp. 175–225). Greenwich, CT: Information Age Publishing.

Kline, H. B, Moses, N. (1990). *Intervention planning for children with communication disorders*. Boston: Allyn & Bacon.

Klingner, J. K., Vaughn, S., Arguelles, M. E., Hughes, M. T., & Leftwich, S. A. (2004). Collaborative strategic reading: "Real-world" lessons from classroom teachers. *Remedial and Special Education, 25*, 291–302.

Knackendoffel, E. A., Robinson, S. M., Deshler, D. D., & Schumaker, J. B. (1992). *Collaborative problem solving: A step-by-step guide to creating educational solutions*. Lawrence, KS: Edge Enterprises.

Knapczyk, D. (1991). Effects of modeling in promoting generalization of student question asking and question answering. *Learning Disabilities Research and Practice, 6*, 75–82.

Knoff, H. M., & Batsche, G. M. (2006). Project ACHIEVE: Analyzing a school reform process for at-risk and underachieving students. *School Psychology Review, 24*, 579–603.

Knowles, M. (1990). *The adult learner: A neglected species* (4th ed.). Houston, TX: Gulf.

Kochhar, C. A., & West, L. L. (1996). *Handbook for successful inclusion*. Gaithersburg, MD: Aspen.

Kohn, A. (1993). *Punished by rewards: The trouble with gold stars, incentive plans, A's, praise, and other bribes*. Boston: Houghton Mifflin.

Kolstoe, O. P. (1976). *Teaching educable mentally retarded children* (2nd ed.). New York: Holt, Rinehart & Winston.

Kolstoe, O. P., & Frey, R. M. (1965). *A high school work-study program for mentally subnormal students*. Carbondale: Southern Illinois University Press.

Kotting, D. (1987). Round robin vocabulary. *The Reading Teacher, 40*, 711–712.

Kounin, J. (1970). *Discipline and group management in classrooms*. New York: Holt, Rinehart & Winston.

Kovarsky, D. (1992). Ethnography and language assessment: Toward the contextualized description and interpretation of communicative behavior. *Best Practices in School Speech-Language Pathology, 2*, 115–122.

Kroger, S.D., & Kouche, B. (2006). Using peer-assisted learning strategies to increase response to intervention in inclusive middle math setting. *Teaching Exceptional Children, 38*, 6–13

Kroegel, M. (1999). *Making the grade: A case study of assessment and grading practices in an elementary inclusive classroom*. Unpublished doctoral dissertation, Virginia Tech.

Krueger, K., & Fox, H. (1984). *Techniques for teacher-aide communication*. Paper presented at in-service training workshop, Albuquerque Public Schools Special Education Department, Albuquerque, New Mexico.

KU-CRL. (2006a). *Routines for increasing student performance*. Retrieved June 7, 2006, from http://www.ku-crl.org/sim/ceroutines.html

KU-CRL. (2006b). *What is content enhancement teaching routine*? Retrieved June 7, 2006, from http://www.ku-crl.org/sim/ceroutines.html

Kyle, W. C. (1984). Curriculum development projects of the 1960s. In D. Holdzkom & P. B. Lutz (Eds.), *Research within reach: Science education* (pp. 3–24). Washington, DC: National Science Teachers Association.

Kyle, W. C., Bonnstetter, R. J., McClosky, S., & Fults, B. A. (1985). Science through discovery: Students love it. *Science and Children, 23*(2), 39–41.

LaFromboise, T. D. (1996). *American Indian life skills development curriculum*, Madison: University of Wisconsin Press.

Lahey, M. (1988). *Language disorders and language development*. New York: Macmillan.

Lake, J. C. (1987). Calling all letters. *The Reading Teacher, 40*, 815.

Lambert, N., Nihira, K., & Leland, H. (1993). *AAMR Adaptive Behavior Scale—School*. Austin, TX: PRO-ED.

Lambert, N., Nihira, K., & Leland, H. (2005). *AAMR Adaptive Behavior Scale—School* (2nd ed.). Austin, TX: PRO-ED.

Landers, M. F. (1984). Helping the LD child with homework: Ten tips. *Academic Therapy, 20*, 209–215.

Langerock, N. L. (2000). A passion for action research. *Teaching Exceptional Children, 33*(2), 26–34.

Langone, J. (1990). *Teaching students with mild and moderate learning problems*. Boston: Allyn & Bacon.

Langone, J. (1998). Managing inclusive instructional settings: Technology, cooperative planning, and team-based organization. *Focus on Exceptional Children, 30*(8), 1–15.

Larsen, S., Hammill, D., & Moats, L. (1999). *Test of Written Spelling (TWS-4)*. Austin, TX: PRO-ED.

Larsen, S. C., & Hammill, D. D. (1989). *Test of Legible Handwriting*. Austin, TX: PRO-ED.

Larson, V. L., & McKinley, N. (1995). *Language disorders in older students: Preadolescents and adolescents*. Eau Claire, WI: Thinking Publications.

Larson, V. L., & McKinley, N. L. (1987). *Communication assessment and intervention strategies for adolescents*. Eau Claire, WI: Thinking Publications.

Lasky, E., & Cox, L. (1983). Auditory processing and language interactions: Evaluation and intervention strategies. In E. Lasky & J. Katz (Eds.), *Central auditory processing disorders: Problems of speech, language, and learning* (pp. 243–268). Austin, TX: PRO-ED.

Lasley, T. J., & Walker, R. (1986). Time on-task: How teachers can use class time more effectively. *National Association of Secondary School Principals Bulletin, 70*, 59–64.

Laughlin, M. K., & Kardaleff, P. P. (1991). *Literature-based social studies: Children's books and activities to enrich the K–5 curriculum*. Phoenix, AZ: Oryx Press.

Lawton, M. (1999). Co-teaching: Are two heads better than one in an inclusion classroom? *Harvard Education Letter, 15*(2), 1–4.

Lazzari, A. M. (1991). *The transition sourcebook: A practical guide for early intervention programs*. Tucson, AZ: Communication Skill Builders.

LD Online. (2003a). *Teaching organization, active listening/reading, and study skills*. Retrieved June 13, 2003, from http://www.ldonline.org/ld_indepth/teaching_techniques/strategies.htmlorganization

LD Online. (2003b). *Technology*. Retrieved June 13, 2003, from http://www.ldonline.org/ld_indepth/technology/technology.htmlclassroom_applications

LD Online. (2003c). *LD Online tech guide*. Retrieved June 13, 2003, from http://www.ldonline.org/ld_indepth/technology/techguide.html

Learning Disabilities Association. (1999a). *Fact sheet: Spoken language problems*. Retrieved May 17, 2007, from http://www.ldanatl.org/factsheet/Spoken.html

Learning Disabilities Association. (1999b). *Speech & language milestone chart*. Retrieved May 17, 2007, from http://www.ldonline.org_indepth/speech-language/lda-milestones.html

Leavell, A., & Ioannides, A. (1993). Using character development to improve story writing. *Teaching Exceptional Children, 25*(4), 41–45.

Lehmann, J. P., Bassett, D. S., Sands, D. J., Spencer, K., & Gliner, J. A. (1999). Research translated into practices for increasing student involvement in transition related activities. *Career Development for Exceptional Individuals, 22*, 3–19.

Lehmann, J. P., Deniston, T. L., Tobin, R., & Howard, D. (1996). Sharing the journey: An individual and integrated systems approach to self-determination. *Career Development for Exceptional Individuals, 19*, 1–14.

Leitner, R. K., & Bishop, K. (Eds.). (1989). *Competency-based training for job coaches: A self-guided study course for trainers in supported employment*. San Francisco: University of San Francisco, California Supported Employment Training Project.

Lenz, B. K. (2006). Creating school-wide conditions for high-quality learning strategy classroom instruction. *Intervention in School and Clinic, 41*, 261–266.

Lenz, B. K., Deshler, D. D., with Kissam, B. R. (2004). *Teaching content to all: Evidence-based inclusive practices in middle and secondary schools*. Boston: Pearson Education, Inc./Allyn & Bacon.

Lenz, K., & Schumaker, J. (1999). *Adapting language arts, social studies, and science materials for the inclusive classroom*. Alexandria, VA: The Council for Exceptional Children.

Lerner, J. W. (1996). *Learning disabilities: Theories, diagnosis, and teaching strategies*. Boston: Houghton Mifflin.

Lesson Planz.com. (2003). *Poetry*. Retrieved June 11, 2003, from http://209.61.147.16/Lesson_Plans/Language_Arts/Grades_6-8/Poetry/index.shtml

Lettau, J. H. (1975). *3-R math readiness*. Upper Saddle River, NJ: Prentice Hall Learning Systems.

Leverentz, F., & Garman, D. (1987). What was that you said? *Instructor, 96*, 66–77.

Levy, M. B. (2002). Some uses of puppetry in Jewish education. *Journal of Jewish Education, 68*(3), 48–57.

Lewis, R. B., & Doorlag, D. H. (1999). *Teaching special students in general education classrooms* (6th ed.). Upper Saddle River, NJ: Merrill/Prentice Hall.

Lewkowicz, N. (2002, Winter). On the question of teaching decoding skills to older students. *VBIDA Newsletter*, 9–10.

Liaupisn, C. J., Scott, T. M., & Nelson, C. M. (2004). *Functional behavioral assessment: An interactive training & module*. Longmont, CO: Sopris West.

Liberman, R. P., King, L. W., DeRisi, W. J., & McCann, M. (1975). Personal effectiveness: *Guiding people to assert themselves and improve their social skills*. Champaign, IL: Research Press.

Lindamood, C., & Lindamood, P. (2004). *Auditory conceptualization tests* (3rd ed.). Austin, TX: PRO-ED.

Lindsey, J. D. (2000). *Technology end exceptional individuals*. Austin: PRO-ED.

Lindsley, O. R. (1964). Direct measurement and prosthesis of retarded behavior. *Journal of Education, 147*, 62–81.

Link to Learn. (2003). *Archetypes and symbols*. Retrieved June 12, 2003, from http://205.146.39.13/success/lessons/Lesson5/HLAb2_L.htm

Lloyd, J. W., Forness, S. R., & Kavale, K. A. (1998). Some methods are more effective than others. *Intervention in School and Clinic, 33*, 195–200.

Lloyd, J. W., & Hallahan, D. P. (2005). Going forward: How the field of learning disabilities has and will contribute to education. *Learning Disability Quarterly, 28*, 133–136.

Lloyd, J. W., Landrum, T., & Hallahan, D. P. (1991). Self-monitoring applications for classroom intervention. In G. Stoner, M. R. Shinn, & H. M. Walker, (Eds.), *Interventions for achievement and behavior problems* (pp. 201–213). Washington, DC: National Association of School Psychologists.

Loeb, D. F. (1997). Diagnostic and descriptive assessment. In L. McCormick, D. F. Loeb, & R. L. Schiefelbusch (Eds.), *Supporting children with communication disorders in inclusive settings: School-based language intervention* (pp. 179–222). Boston: Allyn & Bacon.

Logging in. (1994, November 16). *Education Week, 14*(11), 2.

Lorenz, L., & Yockell, E. (1979). Using the neurological impress method with learning-disabled readers. *Journal of Learning Disabilities, 12*, 67–69.

Lovano-Kerr, J., & Savage, S. L. (1976). Survey of art programs and art experiences for the mentally retarded in Indiana. *Education and Training of the Mentally Retarded, 11*, 200–211.

Loveless, T., & Diperna, P. (2002). *How well are American students learning: Focus on math achievement*. Washington, DC: Brookings Institution Press.

Lovitt, T. C. (1975). Applied behavior analysis and learning disabilities: Part 2. *Journal of Learning Disabilities, 8*, 504–518.

Luckasson, R., Borthwick-Duffy, S., Buntinx, W. H. E., Coulter, D. L., Craig, E. M., Reeve, A., et al. (2002). *Mental retardation: Definition, classification, and systems of supports* (10th ed.). Washington, DC: American Association on Mental Retardation.

Luckasson, R., Coulter, D., Polloway, E. A., Reiss, S., Schalow, R. Snell, M., Spitalnick, S., & Stark, J. (1992). *Mental retardation: Definition, classification, and systems of support* (9th ed.). Washington, DC: American Association on Mental Retardation.

Lynch, E. W., & Hanson, M. J. (1997). *Developing cross-cultural competence: A guide for working with children and their families* (2nd ed.). Baltimore, MD: Brookes.

Lyon, G. R. (1995, May). *Research in learning disabilities supported by the National Institute of Child Health Human Development*. Presentation to Subcommittee on Disability Policy, Committee on Labor Human Resources, United States Senate. Unpublished manuscript.

MacArthur, C. A., Graham, D., & Skarvold, J. (1986). *Learning-disabled students, composing with three methods: Handwriting, dictation, and word processing* (Research report #109). College Park: University of Maryland, Institute for the Study of Exceptional Children and Youth.

Maccini, P., & Gagnon, J. C. (2000). Best practices for teaching mathematics to secondary students with special needs. *Focus on Exceptional Children, 32*(5), 1–16.

Maccini, P., & Gagnon, J.C. (2006). Mathematics instructional practices and assessment accommodations by secondary special and general educators. *Exceptional Children, 72*, 217–235.

Maccini, P., Gagnon, J. C., & Hughes, C. A. (2002). Technology-based practices for secondary students with learning disabilities. *Learning Disability Quarterly, 25*, 247–261.

Macciomei, N. R. (1995). Loss and grief awareness: A class book project. *Teaching Exceptional Children, 28*(2), 72–73.

Machart, N. C. (1987). Creating an opportunity for student-teacher reading conferences. *The Reading Teacher, 40*, 488–489.

MacMillan, D. L., Forness, S., & Trumbull, J. (1973). The role of punishment in the classroom. *Exceptional Children, 40*, 85–96.

Maguire, J. (1985). *Creative storytelling: Choosing, inventing, and sharing tales for children*. New York: McGraw-Hill.

Maheady, L., Harper, G. F., & Mallette, B. (2001). Peer-mediated instruction and interventions and students with mild disabilities. *Remedial and Special Education, 22*, 4–14.

Maki, H. S., Vauras, M. M. S., & Vainio, S. (2002). Reflective spelling strategies for elementary school students with severe writing difficulties: A case study. *Learning Disability Quarterly, 25*, 189–207.

Malderez, A., & Bodoczky, C. (1999). *Mentor courses: A resource book for trainer-trainers*. Cambridge, UK: University Press.

Male, M. (1991). Cooperative learning and computers: Maximizing instructional power with minimal equipment. *ConnSENSL Bulletin, 8*(1), 12–13.

Malian, I., & Nevin, A. (2002). A review of self-determination literature: Implications for practitioners. *Remedial and Special Education, 23, 68–74*.

Malveaux, J. A., Welker, P. L., & Norlin, J. W. (2003). *Transitioning from Part C to Part B: Practical guidelines and legal issues*. Horsham, PA: LRP Publications.

Mandlebaum, L. H., Lightbourne, L., & VandenBrock, J. (1994). Teaching with literature. *Intervention in School and Clinic, 29*, 134–150.

Mandlebaum, L. H., & Wilson, R. (1989). Teaching listening skills in the special education classroom. *Academic Therapy, 24*(4), 449–459.

Mangione, P. L., & Speth, T. (1998). The transition to elementary school: A framework for creating early childhood continuity through home, school, and community partnerships. *The Elementary School Journal, 98*, 381–398.

Mann, P., Suiter, P., & McClung, R. (1979). *Handbook in diagnostic-prescriptive teaching*. Boston: Allyn & Bacon.

Manning, M. L. (1986). Responding to renewed emphasis on handwriting. *The Clearing House, 59*, 211–213.

Manning, M. L., & Lucking, R. (1991). The what, why, and how of cooperative learning. *The Social Studies, 80*, 173–175.

Mannix, D. (1987). *Oral language activities for special children*. West Nyack, NY: The Center for Applied Research in Education.

Marchand-Martella, N. E., Slocum, T. A., & Martella, R. C. (2004). *Introduction to direct instruction*. New York: Allyn & Bacon.

Marchison, M. L., & Alber, S. R. (2001). The write way: Tips for teaching the writing process to resistant writers. *Intervention in School and Clinic, 36*, 154–162.

Markwardt, F. C. (1989). *Peabody Individual Achievement Test—Revised*. Circle Pines, MN: American Guidance Service.

Markwardt, Jr., F. C. (1998). *Peabody Individual Achievement Test—Revised/Normative Update*. Circle Pines, MN: American Guidance Service.

Maroney, S. A., & Searcy, S. (1996). Real teachers don't plan that way. *Exceptionality, 6*, 197–200.

Marshall, O. W., & Tomcala, M. J. (1981, August). *Effects of different genres of music on stress levels*. Paper presented at the 89th annual meeting of the American Psychological Association, Los Angeles, CA. (ERIC Document Reproduction Service No. ED 255 883)

Marston, D., Deno, S. L., Kim, D., Diment, K., & Rogers, D. (1995). Comparison of reading intervention approaches for students with mild disabilities. *Exceptional Children, 62*, 20–37.

Martin, B. (1983). *Brown bear, brown bear, what do you see?* New York: Scholastic.

Martin, E. W. (1986). Some thoughts on transition: A current appraisal. In L. G. Perlman & G. F. Austin (Eds.), *The transition to work and independence for youth with disabilities* (pp. 107–117). Alexandria, VA: National Rehabilitation Association.

Martin, G., & Pear, J. (2006). *Behavior modification: What it is and how to do it*. Upper Saddle River, NJ: Prentice Hall/Pearson.

Martin, J. E., & Huber-Marshall L. (1995). ChoiceMaker: A comprehensive self-determination transition program. *Intervention in School and Clinic, 30*, 147–156.

Marzano, R. J. (2003). *What works in schools: Translating research into action*. Alexandria, VA: Association for Supervision and Curriculum Development.

Marzano, R. J., & Marzano, J. S. (2006). *Classroom management that works*. Alexandria, VA: Association for Supervision and Curriculum Development.

Marzano, R. J., Pickering, D. J., & Pollock, J. E. (2001). *Classroom instruction that works: Research-based strategies for increasing student achievement*. Alexandria, VA: Association for Supervision and Curriculum Development.

Mason, C. Y., McGahee-Kovac, M., Johnson, L., & Stillerman, S. (2002). Implementing student-led IEPs: Student participation and student teacher reactions. *Career Development for Exceptional Individuals, 25*, 171–192.

Massialas, B. G. (1989). The inevitability of issue-centered discourse in the classroom. *The Social Studies, 80*, 173–175.

Masters, L. F., & Mori, A. A. (1986). *Teaching secondary students with mild learning and behavior problems*. Rockville, MD: Aspen.

Masters, L. F., Mori, B. A., & Mori, A. A. (1999). *Teaching secondary students with mild learning and behavior problems* (3rd ed.). Austin, TX: PRO-ED.

Mastropieri, M. A., & Scruggs, T. E. (1989). Reconstructive elaborations: Strategies for adapting content area information. *Academic Therapy, 24*, 394–397.

Mastropieri, M. A., & Scruggs, T. E. (1994a). *Effective instruction for special education* (2nd ed.). Austin, TX: PRO-ED.

Mastropieri, M. A., & Scruggs, T. E. (1994b). Text-based vs hands-on science curriculum: Implications for students with disabilities. *Remedial and Special Education, 15*, 72–85.

Mastropieri, M. A., & Scruggs, T. E. (1995). Teaching science to students with disabilities in general education settings. *Teaching Exceptional Children, 27*(4), 10–13.

Mastropieri, M. A., & Scruggs, T. E. (1997). Best practices in promoting reading comprehension in students with learning disabilities. *Remedial and Special Education, 18*, 197–213.

Mather, N. (1992). Whole language reading instruction for students with learning disabilities: Caught in the cross fire. *Learning Disabilities Research and Practice, 7*, 87–95.

Mathes, P. G., & Torgesen, J. K. (1998). All children can learn to read: Critical care for the prevention of reading failure. *Peabody Journal of Education, 73*, 317–340.

Matson, J. L., DiLorenzo, T. M., & Esveldt-Dawson, K. (1981). Independence training as a method of enhancing self-help skills acquisition of the mentally retarded. *Behavior Research and Therapy, 19*, 399–405.

Mattox, G. L. (2005). Adolescent students with disabilities and learning strategies. *Lynchburg College Online Journal of Special Education, 1*, 1–20.

Mayer, J. E., DiPaolo, M. T., & Salovey, P. (1990). Perceiving affective content in ambiguous visual stimuli: A component of emotional intelligence. *Journal of Personality Assessment, 54*, 772–781.

McBride, J. W., & Forgnone, C. (1985). Emphasis of instruction provided LD, EH, and EMR students in categorical and cross-categorical programming. *Journal of Research and Development in Education, 18*(4), 50–54.

McCarl, J. J., Svobodny, L., & Beare, P. L. (1991). Self-recording in a classroom for students with mild to moderate mental handicaps: Effects on productivity and on-task behavior. *Education and Training in Mental Retardation, 26*, 79–88.

McClure, A. A. (1985). Predictable books: Another way to teach reading to learning disabled children. *Teaching Exceptional Children 17*, 267–273.

McCombs, B. L., & Miller, L. (2007). *Learner-centered classroom practices and assessments: Maximizing student motivation, learning, and achievement*. Thousand Oaks, CA: Corwin Press.

McConnell, K., Patton, J. R., & Polloway, E. A. (2006). *Behavioral intervention planning* (3rd ed.). Austin, TX: PRO-ED.

McConnell, K., Ryser, G., & Patton, J. R. (2002a). *Practical ideas that really work for students with disruptive, defiant, or difficult behaviors: Preschool through grade 4*. Austin, TX: PRO-ED.

McConnell, K., Ryser, G., & Patton, J. R. (2002b). *Practical ideas that really work for students with disruptive, defiant, or difficult behaviors: Grade 5 through grade 12*. Austin, TX: PRO-ED.

McConnell, M. E., Hilvitz, P. B., & Cox, C. J. (1998). Functional assessment: A systematic process for assessment and intervention in general and special education classrooms. *Intervention in School and Clinic, 34*, 10–20.

McCord, J., & Haynes, W. (1988). Discourse errors in students with learning disabilities and their normally achieving peers: Molar versus molecular views. *Journal of Learning Disabilities, 21*, 237–243.

McCormick, L. (1997a). Ecological assessment and planning. In L. McCormick, D. F. Loeb, & R. L. Schiefelbusch (Eds.), *Supporting children with communication disorders in inclusive settings: School-based language intervention* (pp. 223–256). Boston: Allyn & Bacon.

McCormick, L. (1997b). Language intervention and support. In L. McCormick, D. F. Loeb, & R. L. Schiefelbusch (Eds.), *Supporting children with communication disorders in inclusive settings: School-based language intervention* (pp. 257–306). Boston: Allyn & Bacon.

McCormick, L., & Kawate, J. (1982). Kindergarten survival skills: New directions for preschool special education. *Education and Training of the Mentally Retarded, 17*, 247–252.

McCray, A. D., Vaughn, S., & Neal, L. V. I. (2001). Not all students learn to read by third grade: Middle school students speak out about their reading disabilities. *The Journal of Special Education, 35*(1), 17–30.

McEvoy, M. A., Shores, R. E., Wehby, J. H., Johnson, S. M., & Fox, J. J. (1990). Special education teachers, implementation of procedures to promote social interactions among children in integrated settings. *Education and Training in Mental Retardation, 25*(3), 267–275.

McFall, R. M., & Dodge, K. A. (1982). Self-management and interpersonal skills learning. In P. Karoly & F. H. Kanfer (Eds.), *Self-management and behavior change: From theory to practice*. New York: Pergamon Press.

McGinnis, E., Goldstein, A. P., Sprafkin, R. P., & Gershaw, N. J. (1998). *Skillstreaming the elementary school child: A guide for teaching prosocial skills* (2nd ed.). Champaign, IL: Research Press.

McGowan, T., & Guzzetti, B. (1991). Promoting social studies understanding through literature-based instruction. *The Social Studies, 82*, 16–21.

McGuire, J., & Shaws, S. (2006). Universal design and its application in educational environments. *Remedial and Special Education, 27*, 166–175.

McKay, B., & Sullivan, J. (1990, April 23–27). *Effective collaboration: The student assistance team model*. Paper presented at the 68th Annual Convention of the Council for Exceptional Children, Toronto, Canada. (ERIC Document Reproduction Service No. ED 322 695)

McKenzie, R. G., & Houck, C. S. (1993). Across the great divide: Transition from elementary to secondary settings for students with mild disabilities. *Teaching Exceptional Children, 25*(2), 16–20.

McKeown, M. G., & Beck, I. L. (1988). Learning vocabulary, different ways for different goals. *Remedial and Special Education 9*, 16–23.

McLaughlin, T. F., Krappman, V. E., & Welsh, J. M. (1985). The effects of self-recording for on-task behavior of behaviorally disordered special education students. *Remedial and Special Education, 6*(4), 42–45.

McLaughlin, T. F., & Skinner, C. H. (1996). Improving academic performance through self-management: Cover, copy and compare. *Intervention in School and Clinic, 32*, 113–118.

McLoughlin, J. A., & Lewis, R. B. (2000). *Assessing special students: Strategies and procedures* (5th ed.). Upper Saddle River, NJ: Merrill/Prentice Hall.

McMaster, K. N., & Fuchs, D. (2002). Effects of cooperative learning on the academic achievement of students with learning disabilities: An update of Tateyama-Sniezek's review. *Learning Disabilities Research and Practice, 17*, 107–117.

McNaughton, D., Hughes, C. A., & Clark, K. (1994). Spelling instruction for students with learning disabilities: Implications for research and practice. *Learning Disability Quarterly, 17*, 169–185.

McNeil, M. (1994). Creating powerful partnerships through partner learning. In J. S. Thousand, R. A. Villa, & A. I. Nevin (Eds.), *Creativity and collaborative learning: A practical guide to empowering students and teachers* (pp. 243–259). Baltimore: Paul H. Brookes.

McNinch, G. H. (1981). A method for teaching sight words to disabled readers. *The Reading Teacher, 34*, 269–272.

McNutt, G., & Mandlebaum, L. H. (1980). General assessment competencies for special education teachers. *Exceptional Education Quarterly, 1*(3), 21–29.

McTighe, J., & Lyman, F. G., Jr. (1988). Cueing thinking in the classroom: The promise of theory-embedded tools. *Educational Leadership, 47*(7), 18–24.

Mecham, M. (1989). *Utah Test of Language Development—3*. Salt Lake City, UT: Communication Research Associates.

Medina, V. (1982). *Issues regarding the use of interpreters and translators in a school setting*. (ERIC Document Reproduction Services No. ED 329 454)

Meehan, K. A., & Hodell, S. (1986). Measuring the impact of vocational assessment activities upon program decisions. *Career Development for Exceptional Individuals, 9*, 106–112.

Meichenbaum, D. (1983). Teaching thinking: A cognitive-behavioral approach. In *Interdisciplinary voices in learning disabilities and remedial education* (pp. 127–155). Austin, TX: PRO-ED.

Meier, D., & Schafran, A. (1999). Strengthening the preschool-to-kindergarten transition: A community collaborates. *Young Children, 54*(3), 40–46.

Mellard, D. F., & Lancaster, P. E. (2003). Incorporating adult community services in students' transition planning. *Remedial and Special Education, 24*, 359–368.

Memory, D. M., & McGowan, T. M. (1985). Using multilevel textbooks in social studies classes. *The Social Studies, 76*, 174–179.

Memory, D. M., & Uhlhorn, K. W. (1991). Multiple textbooks at different readability levels in the science classroom. *School Science and Mathematics, 91*, 64–72.

Mercer, C. D. (1979). *Students with learning disabilities*. Columbus, OH: Merrill.

Mercer, C. D., Campbell, K. U., Miller, M. D., Mercer, K. D., & Lane, H. B. (2000). Effects of a reading fluency intervention for middle schoolers with specific learning disabilities. *Learning Disabilities Research and Practice, 15*, 179–189.

Mercer, C. D., Jordan, L., & Miller, S. P. (1994). Implications of constructivism for teaching math to students with moderate to mild disabilities. *Journal of Special Education, 28*, 290–306.

Mercer, C. D. & Mercer, A. R. (2005). *Teaching students with learning problems*. Upper Saddle River, NJ: Merrill/ Prentice Hall.

Merriam-Webster.com. (2003). Retrieved June 19, 2003, from http://www.merriam-webster.com/cgi-bin/dictionary

Merritt, D. D., & Culatta, B. (1998). *Language intervention in the classroom*. San Diego: Singular.

Meyen, E. L., Vergason, G. A., & Whelan, R. J. (Eds.). (1983). *Promising practices for exceptional children: Curriculum implications*. Denver, CO: Love.

Meyer, L. A. (1984). Long-term academic effects of the direct instruction project Follow-Through. *The Elementary School Journal, 84*, 380–394.

Michael, A. (1989). *The transition from language theory to therapy: Test of two instructional methods*. Unpublished doctoral dissertation. Vanderbilt University. Nashville, TN.

Miles, D. D., & Forcht, J. P. (1995). Mathematics strategies for secondary students with learning disabilities or mathematics deficiencies: A cognitive approach. *Intervention in School and Clinic, 31*, 91–96.

Miller, J. C. (2003). *It's raining cats and dogs*. Retrieved June 12, 2003, from http://www.education-world.com/a_tsl/archives/00-1/lesson0001.shtml

Miller, J. F., & Yoder, D. E. (1984). *Miller-Yoder Language Comprehension Test*. Baltimore MD: University Park Press.

Miller, L. (1999a). *Bird and his ring*. Austin, TX: Neon Rose Productions.

Miller, L. (1999b). *Two friends*. Austin, TX: Neon Rose Productions.

Miller, L., Gillam, R. B., & Peña, E. C. (2001). *Dynamic assessment and intervention: Improving children's narrative skills*. Austin, TX: PRO-ED.

Miller, L., & Hoffman, L. (2002). *Linking IEPs to state learning standards: A step-by-step guide*. Austin, TX. PRO-ED.

Miller, L., & Newbill, C. (2006). *Section 504 in the classroom: How to design an implement accommodation plans* (2nd ed.). Austin, TX: PRO-ED.

Miller, S. P. (1997). Perspectives on Mathematics Instruction. In D. D. Deshler, E. S. Ellis, & B. K. Lenz (Eds.), *Teaching adolescence with learning disabilities* (pp. 313–367). Denver; Love Publishing.

Miller, S. P., Butler, F. M., & Lee, K. (1998). Validated practices for teaching mathematics to students with learning disabilities: A review of literature. *Focus on Exceptional Children, 30*, 1–16.

Mira, M. P., Tucker, B. F., & Tyler, J. S. (1992). *Traumatic brain injury in children and adolecents: A sourcebook for teachers and other school personnel*. Austin, TX: PRO-ED.

Mle, M. (2004). *Technology for inclusion: Meeting the special needs of all students*. Boston: Allyn & Bacon.

Mlyniec, V. (2001). Handwriting help. *Parents, 76*, 169–170.

Modolfsky, P. B. (1983). Teaching students to determine the central story problem: A practical application of schema theory. *The Reading Teacher, 36*, 740–745.

Montague, M., & Graves, A. (1993). Improving students, story writing. *Teaching Exceptional Children, 25*(4), 36–40.

Montague, M., & Leavell, A. G. (1994). Improving the narrative writing of students with learning disabilities. *Remedial and Special Education, 15*, 21–33.

Montague, M., & Warger, C. (1997). Helping students with attention deficit hyperactivity disorder succeed in the classroom. *Focus on Exceptional Children, 30*(4), 1–16.

Moody, S. W., Vaughn, S., R., Hughes M. Y., & Fischer, M. (2000). Reading instruction in the resource room: Set up for failure. *Exceptional Children, 16*, 305–316.

Moore, J. E., & Camilli, T. (1991). *Exploring science through literature*. Monterey, CA: Evan-Moor.

Moore, V. (2003). *High school students with learning disabilities' perceptions of their educational placements: The move towards full inclusion*. Unpublished doctoral dissertation. Albuquerque: University of New Mexico.

Moos, R. (1976). *The human context: Environmental determinants of behavior*. New York: Wiley.

Moran, M. R. (1983). Analytical evaluation of formal written language skills as a diagnostic procedure. *Diagnostique, 8*, 17–31.

Morgan, D. L., & Guilford, A. M. (1984). *Adolescent Language Screening Test*. Austin, TX: PRO-ED.

Morgan, K. B. (1995). Creative phonics: A meaning-oriented reading program. *Intervention in School and Clinic, 30*, 287–291.

Morgan, M., & Moni, K. B. (2005). Use phonics activities to motivate learners with difficulties. *Intervention in School and Clinic, 41*, 42–45.

Morocco, C., & Neuman, S. (1987). *Teachers, children, and the magical writing machine*. Newton, MA: Education Development Center.

Morris, L. (1991). *Creative movement activities for students with disabilities*. Paper presented at the annual Florida Council of Exceptional Children conference, Daytona, FL.

Moses, B. (1983). Individual differences in problem solving. *Arithmetic Teacher, 30*(4), 10–14.

Moyer, S. B. (1982). Repeated reading. *Journal of Learning Disabilities, 15*, 619–624.

Mullins, J., Joseph, F., Turner, C., Zawadski, R., & Saltzman, L. (1972). A handwriting model for children with learning disabilities. *Journal of Learning Disabilities, 5*, 306–311.

Munk, D. D., Bruckert, J., Call, D.T., Stoehrmann, T., & Radant, E. (1998). Strategies for enhancing the performance of students with LD in inclusive science classes. *Intervention in School and Clinic, 34*, 73–78.

Munk, D. D., & Bursuck, W. D. (2001). Preliminary findings on personalized grading plans for middle school students with learning disabilities. *Exceptional Children, 67*, 211–234.

Munk, D. D., & Bursuck, W. D. (2004). Personalized grading plans: A systematic approach to making the grades of included students more accurate and meaningful. *Focus on Exceptional Children, 36*, 1–11.

Munson, S. M. (1987). Regular education teacher modifications for mainstreamed mildly handicapped students. *Journal of Special Education, 20*, 489–502.

Murawski, W., & Swanson, H. L. (2001). A meta-analysis of co-teaching research: Where are the data? *Remedial and Special Education, 22*, 258–267.

Murray, F. B. (1994). Why understanding the theoretical basis of cooperative learning enhances teaching success. In J. S. Thousand, R. A. Villa, & A. I. Nevin (Eds.), *Creativity and collaborative learning: A practical guide to empowering students and teachers* (pp. 3–11). Baltimore: Paul H. Brookes.

Muscott, H. S., & Gifford, T. (1994). Virtual reality applications for teaching social skills to students with emotional and behavioral disorders. Paper included in the 1994 Virtual Reality Conference. Retrieved May 17, 2007, from http://www.csun.edu/cod/conf/1994/proceedings/Tssts~1.htm

Myers, P. I. (1987). *Assessing the oral language development and intervention needs of students*. Austin, TX: PRO-ED.

Nagy, W. E. (1998). *Teaching vocabulary to improve reading comprehension*. Newark, DE: International Reading Association.

Nakashima, J. C., & Patton, J. R. (1989). An integrated approach to teaching exceptional learners. *Science and Children, 27*, 48–50.

National Assessment of Educational Progress (NAEP). (2003). Washington, DC: NAEP publisher.

National Center for Education Statistics. (2005). *The nation's report card: Mathematics* 2003. Washington, DC: Institute of Education Sciences, U.S. Department of Education.

National Commission on Excellence in Education. (1983). *A nation at risk*. Washington, DC: U.S. Department of Education.

National Communication Association. (2003). *The speaking, listening, and media literacy standards and competency statements for K-12 education*. Retrieved May 15, 2003, from http://www.natcom.org/Instruction/K-12/standards.pdf

National Communication Association. (2006). K–12 resources: Definitions of speaking, listening, and media literacy for elementary-school children. Retrieved August 8, 2006, from http://www.natcom.org/nca/Template2.asp?bid=269

National Council for the Social Studies. (1994). *Curriculum standards for social studies: Expectations of excellence*. Washington, DC: Author.

National Council of Supervisors of Mathematics. (1977). Position paper on basic mathematical skills. *The Arithmetic Teacher, 25*, 19–22.

National Council of Teachers of Mathematics. (1980). *An agenda for action: Recommendations for school mathematics of the 1980s*. Reston, VA: Author.

National Council of Teachers of Mathematics. (1989). *Curriculum and evaluation standards for school mathematics*. Reston, VA: Author.

National Council of Teachers of Mathematics. (1991). *Professional standards for teaching mathematics*. Reston, VA: Author.

National Council of Teachers of Mathematics. (2000). *Principles and standards for school mathematics*. Reston, VA: Author.

National Council of Teachers of Mathematics. (2006). *Curriculum focal points for prekindergarten through grade 8 mathematics: A quest for coherence*. Reston, VA: National Council of Mathematics of Teachers.

National Information Center for Children and Youth with Disabilities. (2003, January). *General information about speech and language disorders (Facts Sheet No. 11)*. Retrieved May 14, 2003, from http://www.nichcy.org/pubs/factshe/fs11txt.htm

National Reading Panel. (2000). *Report of the National Reading Panel: Teaching children to read*. Washington, DC: National Institute of Child Health and Human Development.

National Research Council. (1996). *National science education standards*. Washington, DC: National Academy Press.

National Science Board. (1998). *Science and engineering indicators-2000*. Arlington, VA: National Science Foundation.

NECTAC. (2005). Early intervention program for infants and toddlers with disabilities: Overview to the Part C Program under IDEA. Retrieved March 6, 2005, from http://www.nectac.org/partc/partc.asp/

Neel, R. S., Meadows, N., Levine, P., & Edgar, E. B. (1988). What happens after special education: A statewide follow-up study of secondary students who have behavioral disorders. *Behavioral Disorders, 13*, 209–216.

Nelson, C. M., & Rutherford, R. B. (1983). Time-out revisited: Guidelines for its use in special education. *Exceptional Education Quarterly, 3*(4), 56–67.

Nelson, J. R., Benner, G. J., & Gonzalez, J. (2005). An investigation of the effects of a prereading intervention on the early literacy skills of children at risk of emotional disturbance and reading problems. *Journal of Emotional and Behavioral Disorders, 13*, 3–12.

Nelson, J. R., Crabtree, M., Marchand-Martella, N., & Martella, R. (1998). Teaching good behavior in the whole school. *Teaching Exceptional Children, 30*(4), 4–9.

Nelson, J. R., Smith, D. J., Young, R. K., & Dodd, J. M. (1991). A review of self-management outcome research conducted with students who exhibit behavioral disorders. *Behavioral Disorders, 16*, 169–179.

Nelson, J. S., Epstein, M. H. Bursuck, W. D., Jayanthi, M., & Sawyer, V. (1998). The preferences of middle school student for homework adaptations made by general education teachers. *Learning Disabilities Research & Practice, 13*, 109–117.

Nelson, J. S., Jayanthi, M., Epstein, M. H., & Bursuck, W. D. (2000). Students preferences for adaptations in classroom testing. *Remedial and Special Education, 21*, 41–52.

Nelson, N. W. (1989). Curriculum-based language assessment and intervention. *Language Speech, and Hearing Services in School, 20*, 170–183.

Nelson, N. W. (1993). *Childhood language disorders in context: Infancy through adolescence*. Upper Saddle River, NJ: Merrill/Prentice Hall.

Nelson, N. W. (1998). *Childhood language disorders in context: Infancy through adolescence*. Boston: Allyn & Bacon.

Nelson, R. O., Lipinski, D. P., & Boykin, R. A. (1978). The effects of self-recorders, training and the obtrusiveness of the self-recording device on the accuracy and reactivity of self-monitoring. *Behavior Therapy, 9*, 200–208.

Nestvold, R. (2002). *A brief introduction to point of view: Narratology 101*. Retrieved June 10, 2003, from http://www.ruthnestvold.com/narratology.htm

Neville, D. D., & Hoffman, R. R. (1981). The effect of personalized stories on the cloze comprehension of seventh grade retarded readers. *Journal of Reading, 24*, 475–478.

Nevin, A., Thousand, J., Paolucci-Whitcomb, P., & Villa, R. (1990). Collaborative consultation: Empowering public school personnel to provide heterogeneous schooling for all or, Who rang that bell? *Journal of Educational and Psychological Consultation, 1*, 41–67.

Newbill, C., & Miller, L. (2006). *Section 504: What is it and how do I use it?* Online course in preparation. Austin, TX: PRO-ED.

Newcomer, P., & Barenbaum, E. (2003). *Test of Phonological Awareness Skills*. Austin, TX: PRO-ED.

Newcomer, P., & Hammill, D. (1997b). *Test of Language Development—3 Primary*. Austin, TX: PRO-ED.

Newcomer, P. L. (2001). *Diagnostic Achievement Battery—3*. Austin, TX: PRO-ED.

Newcomer, P. L., & Hammill, D. D. (1997a). *Test of Language Development-Intermediate*. Austin, TX: PRO-ED.

Nezu, A., & D'Zurilla, T. J. (1981). Effects of problem definition and formulation of decision making in the social problem-solving process. *Behavior Therapy, 12*, 100–106.

Nibbelink, W. H., & Witzenberg, H. G. (1981). A comparison of two methods for teaching younger children to tell time. *School Science and Mathematics, 81*, 429–435.

Nickell, P., & Kennedy, M. (1987). How to do it: Global perspectives through children's games. *Social Education, 51*(3), 1–8.

Nihira, K., Foster, R., Shellhaas, M., & Leland, H. (1974). *AAMD adaptive behavior scale manual*. Washington, DC: American Association of Mental Deficiency.

Nolan, K., & Polloway, E. A. (1993). *The use of reconstructive elaborations: Applications in science instruction*. (ERIC Document Reproduction Service No. ED 350 770)

Nolet, V., & Tindal, G. (1993). Special education in content area classes: Development of a model and practical procedures. *Remedial and Special Education, 14*(1), 36–48.

Norris, J., & Hoffman, P. (1993). *Whole language intervention for school-aged children*. San Diego, CA: Singular.

North Central Regional Education Laboratory. (2000). *Critical issue: Addressing literacy needs in culturally and linguistically diverse classrooms*. Retrieved August 15, 2006, from http://www.ncrel.org/sdrs/areas/ issues/content/cntareas/reading/li400.htm

North Central Regional Education Laboratory. (2006). *Critical issue: Using technology to improve student achievement*. Retrieved August 30, 2006, from http://www.ncrel.org/sdrs/areas/issues/methods/technlgy/te800.htm.

Norton, D. E. (1985). *The effective teaching of language arts* (2nd ed.). Columbus, OH: Merrill.

Notari-Syverson, A., & Losardo, A. (1996). Curriculum-based assessment. In K. Cole, P. Dale, & D. Thal (Eds.), *Advances in assessment of communication and language*. Baltimore, MD: Paul H. Brookes.

Nowacek, E. J. (1991). Cooperative learning. *VCLD Journal, 2*(1), 3–4.

Nowak, F. (1981). *Musart*. Paper presented at the Utica Department of Education, Seminar in Resource Teaching, Utica, NY.

O'Leary, K. D., & Drabman, R. (1971). Token reinforcement programs in the classrooms: A review. *Psychological Bulletin, 75*, 379–398.

O'Neil, B. (1994). The invention of the school discipline lists: A concocted story of myths about public education passed down. *The School Administrator, 51*(11), 8–11.

O'Neil, J. (1994, June). Rewriting the book on literature. *Curriculum Update, 5*.

O'Shea, D. J., O'Shea, L. J., Algozzine, R., & Hammitte, D. J. (2001). *Families and teachers of individuals with disabilities: Collaborative orientations and responsive practices*. Boston: Allyn & Bacon.

O'Shea, D. J., Williams, A. L., & Sattler, R. O. (1999). Collaboration across special education and general education: Preservice teachers, views. *Journal of Teacher Education, 50*(2), 147–157.

Oak Ridge Associated Universities. (1978). *Solar energy*. Oak Ridge, TN: U.S. Department of Energy.

Oberlin, L. (1982). How to teach children to hate mathematics. *School Science and Mathematics, 82*, 261.

Ochoa, A. S., & Shuster, S. K. (1980). *Social studies in the mainstreamed classroom, K–6*. Boulder, CO: Social Science Education Consortium.

Oi, A. K. (1988). *Art and special education*. Unpublished master's paper, University of Hawaii.

Okolo, C. M. (1993). Computers and individuals with mild disabilities. In J. D. Lindsey (Ed.), *Computers and exceptional individuals* (2nd ed., pp. 111–114). Austin, TX: PRO-ED.

Oliver, P. R. (1983). Effects of teaching different tasks in group versus individual training formats with severely handicapped individuals. *Journal of the Association for Persons with Severe Handicaps, 8*, 79–91.

Oliver, P. R., & Scott, T. L. (1981). Group versus individual training in establishing generalization of language skills with severely handicapped individuals. *Mental Retardation, 19*, 285–289.

Olson, L. (1995, February 8). Student's best writing needs work, study shows. *Education Week, 5*.

Online Writing Lab (OWL). (2003). *Writing across the curriculum and writing in the disciplines*. Retrieved June 11, 2003, from http://owl.english.purdue.edu/handouts/wac/index.html

Orelove, F. P. (1982). Acquisition of incidental learning in moderately and severely handicapped adults. *Education and Training of the Mentally Retarded, 17*, 131–136.

Organization for economics co-operation and development. (2001). *Knowledge and skills for life: First results from the COECD program for international student assessment (PISA) 2000*. Paris: OECD.

Orton, J. L. (1964). *A guide to teaching phonics*. Winston-Salem, NC: Orton Reading Center.

Osborn, R., Curlin, L., & Hill, G. (1979). Revision of the NCSS social studies curriculum guidelines. *Social Education, 43*, 261–273.

Overton, S. (2005). *Collaborating with families: A case study approach*. Upper Saddle River, NJ: Merrill/Prentice Hall.

Owens, R. E. (1995). *Language disorders* (2nd ed.). Boston: Allyn & Bacon.

Owens, R. E. (1999). *Language disorders* (3rd ed.). Boston: Allyn & Bacon.

Owens, R. E. (2004). *Language disorders: A functional approach to assessment and intervention* (4th ed.). Boston: Allyn & Bacon.

Palincsar, A. S. (1986). Metacognitive strategy instruction. *Exceptional Children, 53*, 118–124.

Palinscar, A. S., & Brown, A. L. (1984). Reciprocal teaching of comprehension—Fostering and monitoring activities. *Cognition and Instruction, 1*, 117–175.

Palincsar, A. S., Brown, A., & Campione, A. (1994). Models and practices of dynamic assessment. In G. P. Wallach & K. G. Butler (Eds.), *Language learning disabilities in school-age children and adolescents*. New York: Merrill/Macmillan.

Palmer, S., & Wehmeyer, M. (2003). *Promoting self-determination in early education. Remedial and special education* (pp. 115–126).

Parish, P. (1992). *Amelia Bedelia*. Dallas: Harpercollins Juvenile Books.

Partin, R. L. (1998). *The Prentice Hall directory of online social studies resources: 1000 of the most valuable social studies web sites, electronic mailing lists and newsgroups*. Paramus, NJ: Prentice Hall.

Pascale, L. (1993). *Multi-arts resource guide*. Boston: Very Special Arts Massachusetts. (ERIC Document Reproduction Service No. ED 370 330)

Passe, J., & Beattie, J. (1994). Social studies instruction for students with mild disabilities: A progress report. *Remedial and Special Education, 15*, 227–233.

Patton, J. R. (1988). Science. In G. Robinson, J. R. Patton, E. A. Polloway, & L. R. Sargent (Eds.), *Best practices in mental disabilities* (vol. 2, pp. 325–349). Des Moines: Iowa Department of Education, Bureau of Special Education.

Patton, J. R. (1993). Individualization for science and social studies. In J. Wood (Ed.), *Mainstreaming: A practical approach for teachers* (2nd ed., pp. 366–413). Upper Saddle River, NJ: Merrill/Prentice Hall.

Patton, J. R. (1994). Practical recommendations for using homework with students with learning disabilities. *Journal of Learning Disabilities, 27*, 570–578.

Patton, J. R. (1995). Teaching science to students with special needs. *Teaching Exceptional Children, 27*(4), 4–6.

Patton, J. R. (2004). Transition issues: Process, practices, and perspectives. In A. McCray Sorrells, H. Prehm, & P. Sindelar (Eds.), *Critical issues in special education: Access, diversity, and accountability* (pp. 180–204). Boston: Allyn & Bacon.

Patton, J. R., Blackbourn, J. M., & Fad, K. (1996). *Exceptional individuals in focus* (2nd ed.). Upper Saddle River, NJ: Merrill/Prentice Hall.

Patton, J. R., & Browder, P. (1988). Transitions into the future. In B. Ludlow, R. Luckasson, & A. Turnbull (Eds.), *Transitions to adult life for persons with mental retardation: Principles and practices* (pp. 293–311). Baltimore: Paul H. Brookes.

Patton, J. R., Cronin, J. F., Bassett, D. S., & Koppel, A. E. (1997). A life skills approach to mathematics instruction: Preparing students with learning disabilities for real life math demands of adulthood. *Journal of Learning Disabilities, 30*, 178–187.

Patton, J. R., Cronin, M. E., & Wood, S. (1999). *Infusing real-life topics into existing curricula at the elementary, middle, and high school levels: Recommended procedures and instructional examples*. Austin, TX: PRO-ED.

Patton, J. R., & Dunn, C. (1998). *Transition from school to young adulthood: Basic concepts and recommended practices*. Austin, TX: PRO-ED.

Patton, J. R., Polloway, E. A., & Cronin, M. E. (1986). *Science education for students with mild disabilities: A status report*. (ERIC Document Reproduction Service No. ED 370 329)

Patton, J. R., Polloway, E. A., Smith, T. E. C., Clark, G., Edgar, E., & Lee, S. (1996). Individuals with mild retardation: Postsecondary outcomes and implications for educational policy. *Education and Training in Mental Retardation and Developmental Disabilities, 31*, 75–85.

Patton, J. R., & Trainor, A. (2002). Using applied academics to enhance curricular reform in secondary education. In C. A. Kochhar-Bryant & D. S. Bassett (Eds.), *Aligning transition and standards-based education: Issues and strategies*. Arlington, VA: Council for Exceptional Children.

Patton, J. R., & Trainor, A. (2003). Using applied academics to enhance curricular reform in secondary education. In C. Kochhar-Bryant & D.S. Bassett (Eds.), *Aligning transition and standards-based education: Issues and strategies* (pp. 55–75). Arlington, VA: CEC.

Paul, R. (1995). *Language disorders from infancy through adolescence*. St. Louis, MO: Mosby.

Paul, R. (2001). *Language disorders from infancy through adolescence: Assessment and intervention* (2nd ed.). St. Louis, MO: Mosby.

Paulson, F. L., Paulson, P. R., & Mayer, C. A. (1991). What makes a portfolio a portfolio? *Educational Leadership, 48*(5), 60–63.

Pearson, V. L. (1987). Vocabulary building: Old word retirement. *Teaching Exceptional Children, 19*(2), 77.

Peck, C. A. (1989). Assessment of social communicative competence: Evaluating environments. *Seminars in Speech and Language, 10*, 1–15.

Pemberton, J.B., Rademacher, J.A., Tyler-Wood, T., & Careijo, M.V. (2006). Aligning assessment with state curricular standards. *Intervention in School and Clinics, 41*, 283–289.

Peña, E., & Bedore, L. (2008). Child language disorders in bilingual contexts. In R. Schwartz (Ed.), *Handbook of child language disorders* (pp. 310–332). New York: Psychology Press.

Peña, E., Summers, C., & Resendiz, M. (2007). Assessment and intervention of children from diverse cultural and linguistic backgrounds. In A. Kamhi, K. Apel, & J. Masterson (Eds.), *Clinical decision making in developmental language disorders.* Baltimore: Brookes.

Peterson, D. L. (1972). *Functional mathematics for the mentally retarded*. Columbus, OH: Merrill.

Peter-Walters, S. (1999–2000). Accessible website design. In K.L. Freiberg (Ed.), *Educating exceptional children* (pp. 176–180). Gillford, CT: Dushkin/McGraw-Hill.

Pfeuffer-Guay, D. M. (1993a). Cross-site analysis of teaching practices: Visual art education with students experiencing disabilities. *Studies in Art Education, 34*, 222–232.

Pfeuffer-Guay, D. M. (1993b). Normalization in art with extra challenged students: A problem-solving framework. *Art Education, 46*(1), 58–63.

Phelps-Terasaki, D., & Phelps, T. (1980). *Teaching written expression: The Phelps sentence guide program*. Novato, CA: Academic Therapy.

Phelps-Terasaki, D., & Phelps-Gunn, T. (1992). *Test of Pragmatic Language*. Austin, TX: PRO-ED.

Phelps-Terasaki, D., & Phelps-Gunn, T. (1998). *Teaching competence in written language: A systematic program for developing writing skills*. Austin, TX: PRO-ED.

Phillips, E. L. (1978). *The social skills basis of psychopathology: Alternative to abnormal psychology and psychiatry*. New York: Grune & Stratton.

Phillips, E. L. (1985). Social skills: History and prospect. In L. L'Abate & M. A. Milan (Eds.), *Handbook of social skills: Training and research*. New York: Wiley.

Phillips, E. L., Phillips, E. A., Fixsen, D. L., & Wolf, M. M. (1974). *The teaching-family handbook*. Lawrence, KS: Beach Center on Families and Disability.

Pianta, R. C., & Kraft-Syre, M. (2003). *Successful kindergarten transition: Your guide to connecting children, families and schools*. Baltimore: Paul H. Brookes.

Pickett, A. L. (1989). *A training program to prepare teachers to supervise and work more effectively with paraprofessional personnel*. New York: City University of New York, National Resource Center for Paraprofessionals.

Pickett, A. L., Faison, K., & Formanek, J. (1993). *A core curriculum and training program to prepare paraeducators to work in inclusive classrooms serving school age students with disabilities*. New York: City University of New York.

Pickett, A. L., & Gerlach, K. (Eds.). (1997). *Supervising paraeducators in school settings*. Austin, TX: PRO-ED.

Pickett, A. L., Gerlach, K., Morgan, R., Likins, M., & Wallace, T. (2007). *Paraeducators in schools: Strengthening the educational team*. Austin: PRO-ED.

Platt, J. M., & Janeczko, D. (1991). Adapting art instruction for students with disabilities. *Teaching Exceptional Children, 24*(1), 10–12.

Pocock, A., Lambose S., Karvonen M., Test, D.W., Alogizine, B., Wood., Martin, J. E. (2002). Successful strategies for promoting self-advocacy among students with LD: The LEAD Group. *Intervention in School and Clinic, 37*, 209–216.

Polloway, C. H., & Polloway, E. A. (1978). Expanding reading skills through syllabication. *Academic Therapy, 13*, 455–462.

Polloway, E.A. (2002). The profession of learning disabilities: Progress and promises. *Learning Disabilities Quarterly, 25*, 103–112.

Polloway, E.A., Bursuck, W., Jayanthi, M., Epstein, M., & Nelson, J. (1996). Treatment acceptability: Determining appropriate interventions within inclusive classrooms. *Intervention in School and Clinic, 31*, 133–144.

Polloway, E.A., Bursuck, W. D., & Epstein, M. H. (2001). Homework for students with learning disabilities: The challenge of home-school communication. *Reading and Writing Quarterly, 17*, 181–187.

Polloway, E.A., Epstein, M. H., & Bursuck, W. D. (2003). Testing adaptations in the general education classroom: Challenges and directions. *Reading and Writing Quarterly, 19*, 1–4.

Polloway, E.A., Epstein, M. H., Bursuck, W., Roderique, T., McConeghey, J., & Jayanthi, M. (1993). A national survey of classroom grading policies. *Remedial and Special Education, 15*, 162–170.

Polloway, E.A., Epstein, M. H., Bursuck, W. D., Jayanthi, M., & Cumblad, C. (1994). Homework practices of general educational teachers. *Journal of Learning Disabilities, 27*, 500–509.

Polloway, E.A., Miller, L., & Smith, T. E. C. (2004). *Language instruction for students with disabilities* (3rd ed.). Denver, CO: Love.

Polloway, E.A., Patton, J. R., & Cohen, S. B. (1983). Written language for mildly handicapped students. In E. L. Meyen, G.A. Vergason, & R. J. Whelan (Eds.), *Promising practices for exceptional children: Curriculum implications* (pp. 285–320). Denver, CO: Love.

Polloway, E.A., Patton, J. R., Smith, J. D., & Roderique, T.W. (1992). Issues in program design for elementary students with mild retardation: Emphasis on curriculum development. *Education and Training in Mental Retardation, 26*, 142–150.

Polloway, E.A., & Polloway, C. H. (1979). Auctions: Vitalizing the token economy. *Journal for Special Educators, 15*, 121–123.

Polloway, E.A., & Polloway, C. H. (1981). Survival words for disabled readers. *Academic Therapy, 16*, 443–448.

Polloway, E.A., Smith, J. P., Patton, J. R., & Smith, T. E. C. (1996). Historic changes in mental retardation and developmental disabilities. *Education and Training in Mental Retardation and Developmental Disabilities, 31*, 3–12.

Polloway, E.A., & Smith, T. E. C. (1999). *Language instruction for students with disabilities* (2nd ed., rev.). Denver, CO: Love Publishing.

Poteet, J., Choate, J. S., & Stewart, S. C. (1993). Performance assessment and special education: Practices and prospects. *Focus on Exceptional Children, 26*(1), 1–20.

Pottenger, F. M., & Young, D. B. (1992). *Foundational approaches in science teaching (FAST I Program)*. Honolulu: Curriculum Research and Development Group, University of Hawaii. (ERIC Document Reproduction Service No. ED 365 549)

Potter, M. L., & Wamre, H. M. (1990). Curriculum-based measurement and developmental reading models: Opportunities for cross-validation. *Exceptional Children, 57*, 16–23.

Potter, S. (1978). Social studies for students with reading difficulties. *The Social Studies, 69*, 56–64.

Prater, M.A., Joy, R., Chilman, B., Temple, J., & Miller, S. R. (1991). Self-monitoring of on-task behavior by adolescents with learning disabilities. *Learning Disability Quarterly, 14*, 164–177.

Premack, D. (1959). Toward empirical behavior laws: I. Positive reinforcement. *Psychological Review, 66*, 219–233.

Prescott, G.A., Balow, I. H., Hogan, T. P., & Farr, R. (1984). *Metropolitan Achievement Tests*. San Antonio, TX: Psychological.

President's Commission on Excellence in Special Education. (2002). *A new era: Revitalizing special education for children and their families*. Washington, DC: Department of Education.

Pressley, M., & Rankin, J. (1994). More about whole language methods of reading instruction for students at risk for early reading failure. *Learning Disabilities Research and Practice, 9*, 157–168.

Pressley, M., Rankin J., & Yokoi, L. (1996). A survey of instructional practices of primary teachers nominated as effective in promoting literacy. *The Elementary School Journal, 96*, 363–384.

Pressley, M., Roehrig, A., Bogner, K., Raphael, L. M., & Dolezal, S. (2002). Balanced literacy instruction. *Focus on Exceptional Children, 34*(5), 1–14.

Price, L., & Patton, J. R. (2003). A new world order: Connecting adult developmental theory to learning disabilities. *Remedial and Special Education, 24*, 328–338.

Price, M., Ness, J., & Stitt, M. (1982). Beyond the three R's: Science and social studies instruction for the mildly handicapped. In T. L. Miller & E. E. Davis (Eds.), *The mildly handicapped student* (pp. 367–370). New York: Grune & Stratton.

Prucha, F. P. (Ed.). (2000). *Documents of the United States Indian policy* (3rd ed.). Lincoln: University of Nebraska Press.

Prutting, C.A., & Kirchner, D. M. (1987). A clinical appraisal of the pragmatic aspects of language. *Journal of Speech and Hearing Disorders, 52*, 105–119.

Purdue University. (2003). *Online writing lab (OWL)*. Retrieved June 11, 2003, from http://owl.english.purdue.edu/

Quay, H. C., & Peterson, D. R. (1967). *Manual for the behavior problem checklist*. Champaign: University of Illinois, Children's Research Center.

Raborn, D.T. (1988). *The effects of language of instruction and review-preview-review on science achievement for bilingual Hispanic handicapped students*. Unpublished dissertation, University of New Mexico.

Raborn, D.T., & Daniel, M. J. (1999). Oobleck: A scientific encounter of the special education kind. *Teaching Exceptional Children, 31*(6), 32–40.

Rakes, T.A., & Choate, J. S. (1990). *Science and health: Detecting and correcting special needs*. Boston: Allyn & Bacon.

RAND Reading Study Group. (2002). *Reading for understanding: Toward a R&D program in reading comprehension. A report prepared for the Office of Educational Research and Improvement (OERI)*.

Ranieri, L., Ford, A., Vincent, L., & Brown, L. (1984). 1:1 versus 1:3 instruction of severely multihandicapped students. *Remedial and Special Education, 5*(5), 23–28.

Rankin-Erickson, J., & Pressley, M. (2000). A survey of instructional practices of special education teachers nominated as effective teachers of literacy. *Learning Disabilities Research and Practice, 15*, 206–225.

Reed, V.A. (1986). *An introduction to children with language disorders*. New York: Macmillan.

Reed, V.A. (1994). *An introduction to children with language disorders* (2nd ed.). Upper Saddle River, NJ: Merrill/Prentice Hall.

Reeve, R. E. (1990). ADHD: Facts and fallacies. *Intervention in School and Clinic, 26*, 71–78.

Reeves, C. K. (1989). Designing a mainstreamed environment. In J. W. Wood (Ed.), *Mainstreaming: A practical approach for teachers*. Columbus, OH: Merrill.

Reid, D. K., Baker, G., Lasell, C., & Easton, S. (1993). Teaching reading comprehension to special needs learners: What matters? *Intervention in School and Clinic, 28*, 198–215.

Reid, D. K., & Kuykendall, M. (1996). In D. K. Reid, W. P. Hresko, & H. L. Swanson (Eds.), *Cognitive approaches to learning disabilities* (3rd ed.). Austin, TX: PRO-ED.

Reid, R., Schmidt, T., Harris, K., & Graham, S. (1997). Cognitive strategy instruction: Developing self-regulated learners. *Reclaiming Children and Youth, 6*, 97–102.

Reis, S. M., Schader, R., & Milne, H. (2003). Music and minds: Using a talent development approach for young adults with William Syndrome. *Exceptional Children, 69*, 293–313.

Reisman, F. K., & Kauffman, S. H. (1980). *Teaching mathematics to children with special needs*. Columbus, OH: Merrill.

Rekate, A. C. (2003). *I have a metaphor*. Retrieved June 11, 2003, from http://www.thirteen.org/edonline/lessons/mlk/index.html

Repetto, J. B., & Correa, V. I. (1996). Expanding views on transition. *Exceptional Children, 62*, 551–563.

Repp, A. C. (1983). *Teaching the mentally retarded*. Upper Saddle River, NJ: Prentice Hall.

Repp, A. C., Felce, D., & Barton, L. E. (1991). The effects of initial interval size on the efficacy of DRO schedules of reinforcement. *Exceptional Children, 57*, 417–424.

Results with corrective reading. (2003). *McGraw-Hill Education, Council of Chief State School Officers & Association for Supervision and Curriculum Development.*

Reynolds, K. E. (1978). Science space. *California Science Teachers Journal, 8*(4), 8–9.

Rice, M. L., Sell, M.A., & Hadley, P.A. (1990). The social interactive coding system (SICS): An on-line clinically relevant descriptive tool. *Language, Speech, and Hearing Services in Schools, 21*, 2–14.

Richard, G. J., & Hanner, M.A. (1985). *Language Processing Test*. East Moline, IL: LinguiSystem.

Richardson, J., Harris, A., & Sparks, O. (1979). *Life science*. Morristown, NJ: Silver Burdett.

Rights, M. (1981). *Beastly neighbors: All about wild things in the city, or why earwigs make good mothers*. Boston: Little, Brown.

Rincover, A., & Koegel, R. L. (1977). Classroom treatment of autistic children: II. Individualized instruction in a group. *Journal of Abnormal Child Psychology, 5*, 113–126.

Rizzo, R. (2003). *What are idioms?*. Retrieved June 12, 2003, from http://k-6educators.about.com/library/lp/bllpla46c.htm

Robinson, S. M., Braxdale, C.T., & Colson, S. E. (1985). Preparing dysfunctional learners to enter junior high school: A transition curriculum. *Focus on Exceptional Children, 18*(4), 1–10.

Rodale, A. (2003). Education: The human touch. *Prevention, 55*(10), 180.

Roe, B. D., Stoodt, B. D., & Burns, P. C. (1995). *Secondary school reading instruction: The content areas* (5th ed.). Boston: Houghton Mifflin.

Roff, J. E. (1972). The academic and social competence of school children vulnerable to schizophrenia and other behavior pathologies. *Journal of Abnormal Psychology, 80*, 225–243.

Rohena, E. I., Jitendra, A. K., & Browder, D. M. (2002). Comparison of the effects of Spanish and English constant time delay instruction on sight word reading by Hispanic learners with mental retardation. *Journal of Special Education, 36*, 169–184.

Rojewski, J. W., Pollard, R. R., & Meers, G. D. (1990). Grading mainstreamed special needs students: Determining practices and attitudes of secondary vocational educators using a qualitative approach. *Remedial and Special Education, 12*(1), 7–28.

Roman, H.T. (2003). The 8 skills you need to succeed. *Today's Engineer*. Retrieved August 8, 2006, from http://www.todaysengineer.org/careerfocus/oct01te/oct01features/skills.html

Rooney, K. (1998). *Independent strategies for effective study*. Richmond, VA: Educational Enterprises.

Rooney, K., Polloway, E.A., & Hallahan, D. P. (1985). The use of self-monitoring procedures with low-IQ learning disabled students. *Journal of Learning Disabilities, 18*, 384–390.

Rose, T. L. (1988). Current disciplinary practices with handicapped students: Suspensions and expulsions. *Exceptional Children, 55*, 230–239.

Rose, T. L. (1989). Corporal punishment with mildly handicapped students: Five years later. *Remedial and Special Education, 10*(4), 43–51.

Roseberry-McKibbon, C. (2003). *Serving the children from the culture of poverty. ASHA Leader online*. Retrieved May 19, 2003, from http://professional.asha.org/news/011106_5.cfm

Roseberry-McKibbon, C., & Brice, A. (2003). *Acquiring a second language: What's normal and what's not.* Retrieved June 5, 2003, from http://www.asha.org/speech/development/easl.cfm

Rosenkoetter, S. E. (1992). Guidelines from recent legislation to structure transition planning. *Infants and Young Children, 5*(1), 21–27.

Rosenkoetter, S. E., Whaley, K. T., Hains, & Pierce, L. (2001). The evolution of transition policy for young children with special needs and their families: Past, present, and future. *Topics in Early Childhood Special Education, 21*(1), 3–15.

Rosenshine, B., & Stevens, R. (1986). Teaching functions. In M. C. Wittrock (Ed.), *Handbook of research on teaching* (3rd ed., pp. 376–391). Columbus, OH: Merrill.

Rossman, M. (1985). Why kids fail to learn science and what to do about it. *Learning, 12*, 77–80.

Rotter, K. (2006). Creating instructional material for all pupils. *Intervention in School and Clinic, 41,* 281.

Roy, P. A. (1990). *Cooperative learning: Students learn together*. Richfield, MN: Patricia Roy.

Rubin, D. L. (1994). Divergence and convergence between oral and written communication. In K. G. Butler (Ed.), *Best practices I: The classroom as an assessment arena* (pp. 56–73). Gaithersburg, MD: Aspen.

Rucker, G., & Dilley, C. (1981). *Health mathematics*. Lexington, MA: Allyn & Bacon.

Rucker, W. E., Dilley, C., & Lowry, D. W. (1987). *Heath mathematics: Teacher's edition*. Lexington, MA: D.C. Heath.

Ruder, K., Bunce, B., & Ruder, C. (1984). Language intervention in a preschool classroom setting. In L. McCormick & R. Schiefelbusch (Eds.), *Early language intervention* (pp. 267–298). Upper Saddle River, NJ: Merrill/Prentice Hall.

Ruef, M. B., Higgins, C., Glaeser, B. J. C., & Patrode, M. (1998). Positive behavioral support: Strategies for teachers. *Intervention in School and Clinic, 34*, 21–32.

Rule, S., Fiechtl, B. J., & Innocenti, M. S. (1990). Preparation for transition to mainstreamed post-preschool environments: Development of a survival skills curriculum. *Topics in Early Childhood Special Education, 9*(4), 78–90.

Runge, A., Walker, J., & Shea, T. (1975). A passport to positive parent-teacher communications. *Teaching Exceptional Children, 7*(3), 91–92.

Saint-Exupéry, A. (1968). *The little prince*. New York: Harcourt Young Classics.

Salembier, G., & Furney, K. S. (1997). Facilitating participation: Parents' perceptions of their involvement in the IEP/transition planning process. *Career Development for Exceptional Individuals, 20*, 29–42.

Salend, S. J. (1998). *Effective mainstreaming: Creating inclusive classrooms* (3rd ed.). Upper Saddle River, NJ: Merrill/Prentice Hall.

Salend, S. J. (2005). *Creating inclusive classrooms: Effective and reflective practices* (5th ed.). Upper Saddle River, NJ: Merrill.

Salvia, H., & Ysseldyke, J. E. (1998). *Assessment in special and remedial education*. Boston: Houghton Mifflin.

Salvia, H., & Ysseldyke, J.E. (2003). *Assessment in special and remedial education*. Boston: Houghton Mifflin.

Salvia, J., & Hughes, C. (1990). *Curriculum-based assessment: Testing what is taught*. Upper Saddle River, NJ: Merrill/Prentice Hall.

Sample, K. J. (2005). Promoting fluency in adolescents with reading difficulties. *Intervention in School and Clinic, 40,* 243–246.

Samuels, S. J. (1979). The method of repeated readings. *The Reading Teacher, 32*, 403–408.

Sanders, J. (2003a). *The college slang page*. Retrieved June 12, 2003, from http://www.intranet.csupomona.edu/~jasanders/slang/

Sanders, J. (2003a). *The college slang page*. Retrieved August 18, 2006, from http://www.intranet.csupomono.edu/~jasanders/slang.html

Sanders, J. (2003b). *Way cool FAQs about college slang*. Retrieved June 12, 2003, from http://www.intranet.csupomona.edu/~jasanders/slang/FAQs.html

Sanders, J. (2003b). *Way cool FAQs about college slang*. Retrieved August 18, 2006, from http://www.intranet.csupomona.edu/~jasanders/slang/FAQs.html

Sanger, D., Maag, J. W., & Shapera, N. R. (1994). Language problems among students with emotional and behavioral disorders. *Intervention in School and Clinic, 30*, 103–105.

Sarathy, P. (2003). *"Together we succeed": Building a better system for transitioning preschoolers with disabilities*. Horsham, PA: LRP Publications.

Sasaki, J., & Serna, L.A. (1995). FAST science: Teaching science to adolescents with mild disabilities. *Teaching Exceptional Children, 27*(4), 14–16.

Sass, E. J. (2003). *Language arts lesson plans and resources*. Retrieved June 12, 1993, from http://www.cloudnet.com/~edrbsass/edeng.htm. synonyms

Saul, W., & Newman, A. R. (1986). *Science fare: An illustrated guide and catalog of toys, books, and activities for kids*. New York: Harper & Row.

Savage, J. F, & Mooney, J. F. (1979). *Teaching reading to children with special needs*. Boston: Allyn & Bacon.

Savage, T. V., & Armstrong, D. G. (1996). *Effective teaching in elementary social studies* (3rd ed.). Upper Saddle River, NJ: Merrill/Prentice Hall.

Scarmadalia, M., & Bereiter, C. (1986). Research on written composition. In M. C. Wittrock (Ed.), *Handbook of research on teaching* (3rd ed., pp. 778–803). Columbus, OH: Merrill.

Schatschneider, C., Carson, C. D., Francis, D. J., Foorman, B. R., & Fletcher, J. M. (2002). Relationship of rapid automatized naming and phonological awareness in early reading development: Implications for the double-deficit hypothesis. *Journal of Learning Disabilities, 35*, 245–256.

Schewel, R. H. (1989). Semantic mapping: A study skills strategy. *Academic Therapy, 24*, 439–447.

Schewel, R. H., & Waddell, J. G. (1986). Metacognitive skills: Practical strategies. *Academic Therapy, 22*, 19–25.

Schilit, J., & Caldwell, M. L. (1980). A word list of essential career/vocational words for mentally retarded students. *Education and Training of the Mentally Retarded, 15*, 113–117.

Schloss, P., Alper, S., & Jayne, D. (1994). Self-determination for persons with disabilities: Choice, risk, and dignity. *Exceptional Children, 60*, 215–225.

Schmidt, W., Houang, R., & Cogan, L. (Summer, 2002). A coherent curriculum: The case for mathematics. *American Educator*, 1–17.

Schminke, C., & Dumas, E. (1981). *Math activities for child involvement*. Boston: Allyn & Bacon.

Schneider, D. O., & Brown, M. J. (1980). Helping students study and comprehend their social studies textbooks. *Social Education, 44*, 105–112.

Schniedewind, N., & Salend, S. (1987). Cooperative learning works. *Teaching Exceptional Children, 19*, 22–25.

Schoeller, K. (1995, Summer). Coordinating success: PACER's Project Youth. *What's working: Transition in Minnesota*. Minneapolis: State of Minnesota.

Schoenbrodt, L., Kumin, L., & Sloan, J. M. (1997). Learning disabilities existing concomitantly with communication disorders. *Journal of Learning Disabilities, 30*, 261–281.

Scholastic, Inc. (2003). *Building language for literacy*. Retrieved May 23, 2003, from http://teacher.scholastic.com/products/bll/correl.htm

Schrumpf, F. (1994). The role of students in resolving conflicts in schools. In J. S. Thousand, R. A. Villa, & A. I. Nevin (Eds.), *Creativity and collaborative learning: A practical guide to empowering students and teachers* (pp. 275–291). Baltimore: Paul H. Brookes.

Schubert, W. H. (1993). Curriculum reform. In G. Cawelti (Ed.), *ASCD 1993 yearbook: Challenges and achievements of American education* (pp. 80–115). Alexandria, VA: Association for Supervision and Curriculum Development.

Schulz, E. (1994, October 5). Beyond behaviorism. *Education Week, 14*(5), 19–21, 24.

Schulz, J. B., Carpenter, C. D., & Turnbull, A. P. (1991). *Mainstreaming exceptional students: A guide for classroom teachers* (3rd ed.). Boston: Allyn & Bacon.

Schumaker, J. B., Deshler, D. D., & Denton, P. (1984). *The learning strategies curriculum: The paraphrasing strategy*. Lawrence: University of Kansas.

Schumaker, J. B., Deshler, D. D., Nolan, S., Clark, F. L., Alley, G. R., & Warner, M. M. (1981). *Error monitoring: A learning strategy for improving academic performance of LD adolescents* (Research Report No. 32). Lawrence: University of Kansas, Institute for Research on Learning Disabilities.

Schumaker, J. B., Deshler, D. D., Woodruff, S. K., Hock, M. F., Bulgren, J. A., & Lenz, B. K. (2006). Reading strategy interventions: Can literacy outcomes be enhanced for at risk adolescents? *Exceptional Children, 38*(3), 64–68.

Schumaker, J. B., & Hazel, J. S. (1984). Social skill assessment and training for the learning disabled: Who's on first and what's on second? Part I. *Journal of Learning Disabilities, 17*, 422–430.

Schumaker, J. B., Hazel, J. S., & Pederson, C. S. (1989). *Social skills for daily living*. Circle Pines, MN: American Guidance Service.

Schumaker, J. B., Hazel, J. S., Sherman, J. A., & Sheldon-Wildgen, J. B. (1982). Social skill performances of learning disabled, non-learning disabled, and delinquent adolescents. *Learning Disability Quarterly, 5*, 358–397.

Schumaker, J. B., Pederson, C. S., Hazel, J. S., & Meyen, E. L. (1983). Social skills curricula for mildly handicapped adolescents: A review. *Focus on Exceptional Children, 4*, 1–16.

Schumm, J. S., Moody, S. W., & Vaughn, S. (2000). Grouping for reading instruction: Does one size fit all? *Journal of Learning Disabilities, 33*, 477–488.

Schumm, J. S., & Post, S. A. (1997). *Executive learning: Successful strategies for college reading and studying*. Columbus, OH: Prentice Hall.

Schumm, J. S., & Strickler, K. (1991). Guidelines for adapting content area textbooks: Keeping teachers and students content. *Intervention, 27*, 79–84.

Schuster, E. (2002). *Sentence mastery, level A*. New York: Phoenix Learning Resources.

Schuster, E. H. (2005). No, Virginia, diagramming will not improve students' writing. *Education Week, 24*(29), 34.

Schuster, J. L., Timmons, J. C., & Moloney, M. (2003). Barriers to successful transition for young adults who receive SSI and their families. *Career Development for Exceptional Individuals, 26*, 47–66.

Scientific Research Institute International. (2004). *National longitudinal transition study—2*. Retrieved December 3, 2004, from http://www.nlts2.org/nlts2faq.html

Scott, B. J., & Vitale, M. R. (2003). Teaching the writing process to students with LD. *Intervention in School and Clinic, 38*, 220–224.

Scott, C. (1999). Learning to write. In H. Catts & A. Kamhi. (Eds.), *Language and reading disabilities* (pp. 224–258). Boston: Allyn & Bacon.

Scruggs, T. E., Mastropieri, M. A. (1993). Current approaches to science education: Implications for mainstream instruction to students with disabilities. *Remedial and Special Education, 14*, 15–24.

Scruggs, T. E., Mastropieri, M. A., Bakken, J. P., & Brigham, F. J. (1993). Reading vs. doing: The relative effectiveness of textbook-based and inquiry-oriented approaches to science education. *Journal of Special Education, 27*, 1–15.

Scruggs, T. E., Mastropieri, M. A., & Wolfe, S. (1994–1995). Scientific reasoning of students with mild retardation: Investigating preconceptions and conceptional changes. *Exceptionality, 5*, 223–244.

Searcy, S., & Maroney, S. A. (1996). Lesson planning practices of special education teachers. *Exceptionality, 6*, 175–185.

Secondary School Educators homepage. (2001). Retrieved May 17, 2007, from http://7-12educators.about.com/cs/rubrics/

Secord, W., & Wiig, E. (1993). *Test of Language Competence—Expanded*. San Antonio, TX: Psychological.

Sedlak, R. A., & Fitzmaurice, A. M. (1981). Teaching arithmetic. In J. M. Kauffman & D. P. Hallahan (Eds.), *Handbook of special education* (pp. 475–490). Upper Saddle River, NJ: Prentice Hall.

Semel, E. M., Wiig, E. H., & Secord, W. (1987). *Clinical Evaluation of Language Fundamentals—Revised*. San Antonio, TX: Psychological.

Semel, E. M., Wiig, E. H., & Secord, W. (1998). *Clinical Evaluation of Language Fundamentals—Preschool*. San Antonio, TX: Psychological.

Sendak, M. (1962). *Chicken soup with rice*. New York: Harper & Row.

Serna, L., Nielsen, E., & Forness, S. (2006). *Social lessons with stories and songs*. Champaign, IL: Research Press.

Serna, L. A., Forness, S. R., & Nielsen, M. E. (1998). Intervention versus affirmation: Proposed solutions to the problem of disproportionate minority representation in special education. *Journal of Special Education, 32*, 48–51.

Serna, L. A., & Lau-Smith, J. A. (1994–1995). *Learning with PURPOSE: Instruction manuals for teaching self-determination skills to students who are at risk for failure*. Unpublished manuals, Honolulu: University of Hawaii.

Serna, L. A., & Lau-Smith, J. A. (1995). Learning with PURPOSE: Self-determination skills for students who are at risk for school and community failure. *Intervention in School and Clinic, 30*(3), 142–146.

Serna, L. A., Nielsen, M. E., & Forness, S. R. (1997). Systematic early detection and self-determination approach for mental health intervention Head Start. Grant funded by Department of Health and Administration for Children and Families. *CDFA*: 93.600.

Serna, L. A., Nielsen, M. E., Lambros, K., & Forness, S. R. (in press). The use of self-determination curriculum to impact the behavior of young children with behavior problems. *Behavior Disorders*.

Shames, G. J., Wiig, E., & Secord, W. A. (1998). *Human communication disorders: An introduction* (5th ed.). Boston: Allyn & Bacon.

Shanahan, T. (2003). Research-based reading instruction: Myths about the National Reading Panel report. *The Reading Teacher, 56*, 646–655.

Shanahan, T., & Beck, I. (2006). *Effective literacy teaching for English-language learners*. Mahwah, NJ: Lawrence Erlbaum.

Shannon, T., & Polloway, E. A. (1993). Promoting error monitoring in middle school students with learning disabilities. *Intervention in School and Clinic, 28*, 160–164.

Sharp, J. M., & Hoiberg, K. B. (2005). *Learning and teaching K–8 mathematics*. New York: Allyn & Bacon.

Shaywitz, S., & Shaywitz, B. (1997). *The science of reading: Implications for children and adults with learning disabilities*. 13th Annual Learning Disorders Conference, Harvard Graduate School of Education.

Shea, T. M., & Bauer, A. M. (1987). *Teaching children and youth with behavior disorders*. Upper Saddle River, NJ: Prentice Hall.

Shelbyville Middle School. (2003). *Lesson plan for puns*. Retrieved June 13, 2003, from http://volweb.utk.edu/Schools/bedford/harrisms/5lesson.htm

Shepherd, G. D., & Ragan, W. B. (1982). *Modern elementary curriculum* (6th ed.). New York: Holt, Rinehart & Winston.

Shields, C. (2001). Music education and mentoring as intervention for at-risk urban adolescents: Their self-perceptions, opinions, and attitudes. *Journal of Research in Music Education, 49*, 273–287.

Shields, J. D., Green, R., Cooper, B. A. B., & Ditton, P. (1995). The impact of adults, communication clarity versus communication deviance on adolescents with learning disabilities. *Journal of Learning Disabilities, 28*, 372–384.

Shore, K. (1986). *The special education handbook*. New York: Teachers College Press.

Shulman, B. (1986). *Test of Pragmatic Skills—Revised*. Tucson, AZ: Communication Skill.

Shure, M. B. (1997). Interpersonal cognitive problem solving: Primary prevention of early high-risk behaviors in the preschool and primary years. In G. W. Albee & T. P. Gulotta (Eds.), *Primary prevention works*. Thousand Oaks, CA: Sage.

Shure, M. B. (1999). Preventing violence the problem-solving way. *Juvenile Justice Bulletin*, April, 1–11. Washington, DC: Publication of the U.S. Department of Justice, Office of Juvenile Justice and Delinquency Prevention.

Shymansky, J. A. (1989). About ESS, SCIS, and SAPA. *Science and Children*, 33–35.

Sidelnick, M. A., & Svoboda, M. L. (2000). The bridge between drawing and writing: Hannah's story. *The Reading Teacher, 54*, 174.

Sideridis, G. D., & Chandler, J. P. (1996). Comparison of attitudes of teachers of physical and musical education toward inclusion of children with disabilities. *Psychological Reports, 78*, 768–771.

Silbert, J., Carnine, D., & Stein, M. (1990). *Direct instruction mathematics* (2nd ed.). Upper Saddle River, NJ: Merrill/Prentice Hall.

Simmons, D. C., Gunn, B., Smith, S. B., & Kame'enui, E. J. (1994). Phonological awareness: Applications of instructional design. *LD Forum, 19*(2), 7–10.

Simon, C. (1998). When big kids don't learn: Contextual modifications and intervention strategies for age 8–18 at-risk students. *Clinical Linguistics and Phonetics, 12*, 249–280.

Simon, C. S. (1979). *Communicative competence: A functional-pragmatic approach to language therapy*. Tempe, AZ: Communi-Cog Publications.

Simon, C. S. (1985a). Functional flexibility: Developing communicative competence in speaker and listener roles. In C. S. Simon (Ed.), *Communication skills and classroom success* (pp. 135–178). San Diego, CA: College-Hill Press.

Simon, C. S. (1985b). The language-learning disabled student: Description and therapy implications. In C. S. Simon (Ed.), *Communication skills and classroom success* (pp. 1–56). San Diego, CA: College-Hill Press.

Simon, C. S. (1987a). *Classroom communication screening procedures for early adolescents*. Tempe, AZ: Communi-Cog Publications.

Simon, C. S. (1987b). Out of the broom closet and into the classroom: The emerging SLP. *Journal of Childhood Communication Disorders, 11*, 41–66.

Simpson, R. (1998). Behavior modification for children and adolescents with exceptionalities. *Intervention in School and Clinic, 33*, 219–226.

Sink, D. M. (1975). Teach-write/Write-teach. *Elementary English, 52*, 175–177.

Sitlington, P. L., & Clark, G. M. (2006). *Transition education and services for students with disabilities* (4th ed.). Boston: Allyn & Bacon.

Sitlington, P. L., Clark, G. M., & Kolstoe, O. P. (2000). *Transition education and services for adolescents with disabilities* (3rd ed.). Boston: Allyn & Bacon.

Sitlington, P. L., Neubert, D. A., & Leconte, P. J. (1997). Transition assessment: The position of the division on career development and transition. *Career Development for Exceptional Individuals, 20*, 69–79.

Skinner, B. F. (1971). *Beyond freedom and dignity*. New York: Knopf.

Skouge, J. R., Kelly, M., O'Brien, R., & Thomas, K. (2003). *Creating futures: Video empowerment for self-determination*. Paper included in the 2003 Virtual Reality Conference. Retrieved May 16, 2007, from http://www.csun.edu/cod/conf/2003/proceedings/Tssts~1.htm

Slavin, R. E. (1989). Student team learning in mathematics. In N. Davidson (Ed.), *Cooperative learning in mathematics: A handbook for teachers* (pp. 69–102). Menlo Park, CA: Addison-Wesley.

Slavin, R. E., Madden, N. A., Dolan, L. J., & Wasik, B. A. (1996). *Every child, every school: Success for all*. Newbury Park, CA: Corwin.

Slavin, R. E., Madden, N. A., Dolan, L. J., Wasik, B. A., Ross, S. M., Smith, L. J., & Dianda, M. (1996). Success for all: A summary of research. *Journal of Education for Students Placed at Risk, 1*, 41–76.

Smedley, T., & Higgins, K. (2005). Virtual technology: Bringing the word into the special education classroom. *Intervention in School and Clinic, 41*, 114–120.

Smith, C. L. (1986). *Classroom survival skills: Requisites to mainstreaming*. Unpublished master's thesis, University of Hawaii at Manoa, Honolulu.

Smith, F. (1979). *Reading without nonsense*. New York: Teachers College Press.

Smith, F. (1988). *Understanding reading: A psycholinguistic analysis of reading and learning to read* (4th ed.). New York: Holt, Rinehart & Winston.

Smith, G. J., Edelen-Smith, P. J., & Stodden, R. A. (1995). How to avoid the seven pitfalls of systematic planning: A school and community plan for transition. *Teaching Exceptional Children, 27*, 42–47.

Smith, G. P. (1998). *Common sense about uncommon knowledge: The knowledge bases for diversity*. Washington, DC: American Association of Colleges for Teacher Education (AACTE) Publications.

Smith, J. (2003). *Horrid homonyms*. Retrieved June 12, 2003, from http://askeric.org/cgibin/printlessons.cgi/Virtual/Lessons/Language_Arts/Writing/WCP0016.html

Smith, J. D., Polloway, E. A., & West, K. G. (1979). Corporal punishment and its implications for exceptional children. *Exceptional Children, 45*, 264–268.

Smith, J. E., & Payne, J. S. (1980). *Teaching exceptional adolescents*. Columbus, OH: Merrill.

Smith, L. J., & Smith, D. L. (1990). *Social studies: Detecting and correcting special needs*. Boston: Allyn & Bacon.

Smith, S. B., Simmons, D. C., & Kame'enui, E. J. (2003). *Phonological awareness: Curricular and instructional implications for diverse learners*. National Center to Improve the Tools of Educators, funded by the U.S. Office of Special Education Programs. Retrieved May 29, 2003, from http://idea.uoregon.edu/~ncite/documents/techrep/tech22.html

Smith, S. W. (1990a). Comparison of IEPs of students with behavioral disorders and learning disabilities. *Journal of Special Education, 24*, 85–99.

Smith, S. W. (1990b). Individualized education programs (IEPs) in special education: From intent to acquiescence. *Exceptional Children, 57*, 6–14.

Smith, T. E. C. (2001). Section 504, the ADA, and public schools: What educators need to know. *Remedial and Special Education, 22*, 335–382.

Smith, T. E. C., & Patton, J. R. (2000). *Section 504 and public schools*. Austin, TX: PRO-ED.

Smith, T. E. C., Polloway, E. A., & Beirne-Smith, M. (1995). *Written language instruction for students with disabilities*. Denver, CO: Love.

Smith, T. E. C., & Polloway, E. A., Patton, J. R., & Dowdy, C. A. (2004). *Teaching students with special needs in inclusive settings* (4th ed.). Boston: Allyn & Bacon.

Smith, T. E. C., Price, B. J., & Marsh, G. E. (1986). *Mildly handicapped children and adults*. St. Paul, MN: West.

Smith, W. D. (1978). Minimal competencies: A position paper. *The Arithmetic Teacher, 26*(3), 25–26.

Smull, M. W. (1994). Moving toward a system of support. *AAMR News & Notes, 7*(5), 3–5.

Snow, C., Midkiff-Borunda, S., Small, A., & Proctor, A. (1984). Therapy as social interaction: Analyzing the contexts for language remediation. *Topics in Language Disorders, 7*(2), 32–44.

Soderlund, J., Bursuck, B., Polloway, E. A., & Foley, R.A. (1995). A comparison of the homework problems of secondary school students with behavior disorders and nondisabled peers. *Journal of Emotional and Behavioral Disorders, 3*, 150–155.

Sopris West. (2004). *Transitional mathematics program*. Longmont, CO: Author.

Sosniak, L. A., & Ethington, C. A. (1994). When teaching problem solving proceeds successfully in U.S. eighth-grade classrooms. In I. Westbury, C. A. Ethington, L. A. Sosniak, & D. P. Baker (Eds.), *In search of more effective mathematics education* (pp. 33–60). Norwood, NJ: Ablex.

Southern Pueblos Agency. (2002). *Science checklist, building exceptional schools for tomorrow*. BEST Council: Albuquerque, NM. Retrieved July 15, 2006, from compact disc.

Spalding implementation of research findings from the report of the National Reading Panel. (2000). Phoenix, AZ: Spalding Education International.

Sparrow, S. S., Balla, D. A., & Cicchetti, D. V. (2005). *Vineland Adaptive Behavior Scales* (2nd ed.). Circle Pines, MN: American Guidance Service.

Speech Communication Association. (1996). *Speaking, listening, and medial literacy standards for K through 12 education*. Annandale, VA: Clark Publishing.

Spekman, J. J. (1981). Dyadic verbal communication abilities of learning disabled and normally achieving fourth- and fifth-grade boys. *Learning Disability Quarterly, 4*, 139–151.

Spencer, I. (1992). *Recent approaches to art instruction in special education: A review of the literature*. (ERIC Document Reproduction Service No. ED 349 724)

Sperling, R. A. (2006). Assessing reading materials for students who are learning disabled. *Intervention in School and Clinic, 41*, 138-143.

Spinelli, C. G. (2005). *Classroom assessment for students in special and general education* (2nd ed.). Upper Saddle River, NJ: Merrill/Prentice Hall.

Spivack, G., & Shure, M. B. (1974). *Social adjustment of young children: A cognitive approach to solving real-life problems*. San Francisco: Jossey-Bass.

Spivack, G., Spotts, J., & Haines, P. (1966). *Devereux adolescent behavior rating scale*. Devon, PA: Devereux Foundation.

Sprague, J. R., & Golly, A. (2004). *Best behavior: Building positive behavior supports in schools*. Longmont, CO: Sopris West.

Sprague, J. R., Sugai, G., & Walker, W. (1998). Antisocial behavior in schools. In T. S. Watson & F. M. Gresham (Eds.), *Handbook of child behavior therapy*. (pp. 451–474). New York: Plenum Press.

Sprague, J. R., & Walker, H.M. (2005). *Safe and healthy schools: Practical prevention strategies*. New York: Guilford Press.

Springate, K. W., & Stegelin, D. A. (1999). *Building school and community partnerships through parent involvement*. Upper Saddle River, NJ: Merrill/Prentice Hall.

Squires, D. A., Huitt, W. G., & Segars, J. K. (1983). *Effective schools and classrooms: A research-based perspective*. Alexandria, VA: Association for Supervision and Curriculum Development.

Staats, A. W. (1971). *Child learning, intelligence, and personality*. New York: Harper & Row.

Staats, A. W. (1975). *Social behaviorism*. Homewood, IL: Dorsey Press.

Stainback, W. C., Payne, J. S., Stainback, S. B., & Payne, R. A. (1973). *Establishing a token economy in the classroom*. Columbus, OH: Merrill.

Stanovich, K. E. (1986). Matthew effects in reading: Some consequences of individual differences in the acquisition of literacy. *Reading Research Quarterly, 21*(4), 360–406.

Stanovich, K. E., & Stanovich, P. J. (1995). How research might inform the debate about early reading acquisition. *Journal of Research in Reading, 18*, 87–105.

Stebbins, L. B., St. Pierre, R. G., Proper, E. C., Anderson, R. B., & Cerva, T. R. (1977). *Education as experimentation: A planned variation model* (Vol. 4A). Cambridge, MA: Abt Associates.

Steele, K. (2003). *Ideas for teaching writing*. Retrieved June 11, 2003, from http://www.kimskorner4teachertalk.com/writing/menu.html

Stein, M., Kinder, D., Silbert, J., & Carnine, D. W. (2006). *Designing effective mathematics instruction: A direct instruction approach*. Upper Saddle River, NJ: Merrill/Prentice Hall.

Steinbrink, J. E., & Jones, R. M. (1991). Focused test review items: Improving textbook-test alignment in social studies. *The Social Studies, 82*, 72–76.

Stephens, T. M. (1970). *Directive teaching of children with learning and behavioral problems*. Columbus, OH: Merrill.

Sternberg, L., & Sedlak, R. (1978). Mathematical programming for problem adolescents. In D. Sabatino & A. Mauser (Eds.), *Intervention strategies for specialized secondary education*. Boston: Allyn & Bacon.

Stevens, D. D., & Englert, C. S. (1993). Making writing strategies work. *Teaching Exceptional Children, 26*(1), 34–39.

Stevens, R., & Rosenshine, B. (1981). Advances in research on teaching. *Exceptional Education Quarterly, 2,* 1–9.

Stodden, R. A. (1998). School-to-work transition: Overview of disability legislation. In F. R. Rusch & J. G. Chadsey (Eds.), *Beyond high school: Transition from school to work.* Belmont, CA: Wadsworth.

Stokes, T. F., & Baer, D. M. (1977). An implicit technology of generalization. *Journal of Applied Behavior Analysis, 10,* 349–367.

Stone, C. A. (1998). The metaphor of scaffolding: Its utility for the field of learning disabilities. *Journal of Learning Disabilities, 31,* 344–364.

Strichart, S. S., Iannuzzi, P., & Mangrum, C. (1998). *Teaching study skills and strategies to students with learning disabilities, attention deficit disorders, or special needs.* Upper Saddle River, NJ: Prentice Hall.

Strong, W. (1973). *Sentence combining: A composing book.* New York: Random House.

Strong, W. (1983). *Sentence combining: A composing book* (2nd ed.). New York: Random House.

Sugai, G., & Horner, R. (1994). Including students with severe behavior problems in general education settings: Assumptions, challenges, and solutions. *Oregon Conference Monograph, 6,* 102–120.

Sund, R., Tillery, B., & Trowbridge, L. (1970). *Elementary science discovery lessons: The earth sciences.* Boston: Allyn & Bacon.

Swanson, H. L. (1999). Reading research for students with disabilities: A meta-analysis of reading outcomes. *Journal of Learning Disabilities, 32,* 504–532.

Swanson, H. L., & Deshler, D. D. (2003). Instructing adolescents with disabilities: Converting a meta-analysis to practice. *Journal of Learning Disabilities, 36,* 124–135.

Swanson, P. N., & de la Paz, S. (1998). Teaching effective comprehension strategies to students with learning and reading disabilities. *Intervention in School and Clinic, 33,* 209–218.

Talbott, E., Lloyd, J. W., & Tankersley, M. (1994). Effects of reading comprehension interventions for students with learning disabilities. *Learning Disability Quarterly, 17,* 223–232.

Tamura, E. H., & Harstad, J. R. (1987). Freewriting in the social studies classroom. *Social Education, 51,* 256–259.

Taylor, F., Artuso, A. A., Hewett, E. M., Johnson, A., Kramer, G., & Clark, K. (1972). *Individualized reading instruction: Games and activities.* Denver, CO: Love.

Taylor-Green, S., Brown, D., Nelson, L., Longton, J., Gassman, T., Cohen, J., Swartz, J., Horner, R. H., Sugai, G., & Hall, S. (1997). School-wide behavioral support: Starting the year off right. *Journal of Behavioral Education, 7,* 99–112.

Teacher Net.com. (2003). *Synonyms and antonyms.* Retrieved June 12, 2003, from http://www.teachnet.com/lesson/langarts/terminology/synandant.html

Teacher's Desk.com. (2003). *Hinky pinky.* Retrieved June 12, 2003, from http://www.teachersdesk.org/vocabhink.html

Teacher's Planet. (2003). *Teacher's guide to phonological awareness.* Retrieved June 12, 2003, from http://teachersplanet.com/subjects/pa.shtml

Terwilliger, J. S. (1999). *Test for Auditory Comprehension of Language—3rd Edition.* Chicago: Riverside.

Teters, P., Gabel, D., & Geary, P. (1984). Elementary teachers, perspectives on improving science education. *Science and Children, 22*(3), 41–43.

Texas Reading Initiative. (2000). *Comprehension instruction.* Austin: Texas Education Agency.

*The Spalding method catalog.* (2002). Phoenix, AZ: Spalding Education International.

Therrien, W. J., Gormley, S., & Kubina, R. M. (2006). Boosting fluency and comprehension to improve reading achievement. *Teaching Exceptional Children, 38*(3), 22–26.

Therrien, W. J., & Kubina, Jr., R. M. (2006). Developing reading fluency with repeated reading. *Intervention in School and Clinic, 41,* 156–160.

Thistle, L. (1987). Make a story come alive: Dramatize. *Arts and Activities, 101*(5), 24–28.

Thomas, P. J., & Carmack, F. F. (1997). Speech: Language: The foundation of learning. In J. S. Choate (Ed.), *Successful inclusive teaching* (2nd ed., pp. 148–153). Boston: Allyn & Bacon.

Thompson, J. R., Fulk, B. M., & Piercy, S. W. (2000). Do individualized transition plans match the postschool projections of students with learning disabilities and their parents? *Career Development for Exceptional Individuals, 23,* 3–725.

Thompson, K. L., & Taymans, J. M. (1994). Development of a reading strategies program: Bridging the gaps among decoding, literature, and thinking skills. *Intervention in School and Clinic, 30,* 17–27.

Thomsen, K. (2002). *Building resilient students: Integrating resiliency into what you already know and do.* Thousand Oaks, CA: Corwin Press.

Thorkildsen, R., Fodor-Davis, J., & Morgan, D. (1989). Evaluation of a videodisc training program. *Journal of Special Education Technology, 10*(2), 86–97.

Thorne, M. T. (1978). Payment for reading: The use of the corrective reading scheme with junior maladjusted boys. *Remedial Education, 13*(2), 87–90.

Thorp, E. K. (1997). Increasing opportunities for partnership with culturally and linguistically diverse families. *Intervention in School and Clinic, 32,* 261–269.

Thurber, D. N. (1987). *D'Nealian handwriting* (rev. ed.). Glenview, IL: Scott Foresman.

Thurlow, M. L. (2000). Standards-based reform and students with disabilities: Reflections on a decade of change. *Focus on Exceptional Children, 33*(3), 1–16.

Tikunoff, W. J. (1982). *An emerging description of successful bilingual instruction: An executive summary of Part I of SBIF descriptive study*. Washington, DC: National Institute of Education.

Tikunoff, W. J. (1987). Mediation of instruction to obtain equality of effectiveness. In S. H. Fradd & W. J. Tikunoff (Eds.), *Bilingual education and bilingual special education: A guide for administrators,* Austin, TX: PRO-ED.

Tilly, D. (2006). Response to intervention. *The Special Edge*. Rohnert Park, CA: Sonoma State University.

Tindal, G.A., & Marston, D. B. (1990). *Classroom-based assessment: Evaluating instructional outcomes*. Upper Saddle River, NJ: Merrill/Prentice Hall.

Tindall, S. K. (1985). *Adaptation of a basic math text for special learners*. Unpublished master's paper, University of Hawaii.

Tolerance.org. (2006). *Harry Potter: Upper grades activity*. Retrieved August 18, 2006, from http://www.tolerance .org/teach/activities/jsp?ar=622

Tompkins, G. E. (2002). Struggling readers are struggling writers, too. *Reading and Writing Quarterly, 18,* 175–193.

Tompkins, G.E. (2005). *Language arts patterns of practice*. (6th ed.). Columbus: Merrill/Prentice Hall.

Tompkins, G.E. (2006). *Literacy for the 21st century a balanced approach* (4th ed.). Columbus: Merrill/ Prentice Hall.

Torgesen, J. K. (1982). The learning-disabled child as an inactive learner: Educational implications. *Topics in Learning and Learning Disabilities, 2*(1), 45–51.

Torgesen, J. K. (2000). Individual differences in response to early interventions in reading: The lingering problem of treatment resisters. *Learning Disabilities Research and Practice, 15*, 55–64.

Torgesen, J. K., & Bryant, B. R. (2004). *Test of Phonological Awareness* (2nd ed). Austin, TX: PRO-ED.

Torgesen, J. K., & Mathes, P. G. (2000). *A basic guide to understanding, assessing, and teaching phonological awareness*. Austin, TX: PRO-ED.

Tournaki, N. (2003). The differential effects of teaching addition through strategy instruction versus drill and practice to students with and without learning disabilities. *Journal of learning Disabilities, 36,* 559–458.

Trainor, A.A., & Patton, J. R. (in press). Culturally responsive transition planning and instruction from early childhood to postsecondary life. In J. Hoover, J. Klingner, L. Baca, & J. Patton (Eds.), *Methods for teaching culturally and linguistically diverse exceptional learners*. Upper Saddle River, NJ: Merrill/Prentice Hall.

Troia, G. (2004). Phonological awareness. *Current Practice Alerts*, 10, 1–4.

Troia, G.A., & Graham, S. (2002). The effectiveness of a highly explicit, teacher-directed strategy instruction routine: Changing the writing performance of students with learning disabilities. *Journal of Learning Disabilities, 35*, 290–305.

Troia, G.A. (2002). Teaching writing strategies to children with disabilities: Setting generalization as the goal. *Exceptionality*, 10, 249–269.

Troia, G.A. (2005). The writing instructional research we have, the writing instruction research we need. *LARC Symposium on Literacy Achievement.*

Truch, S. (1998). *Phonological processing, reading and the Lindamood Phoneme Sequencing Program: A review of related research*. Austin, TX: PRO-ED.

Tucker, J. (1985). Curriculum-based assessment: An introduction. *Exceptional Children, 52*, 199–204.

Turla, P.A., & Hawkins, K. L. (1983). *Time management made easy*. New York: Dutton.

Turnbull, A. P., & Turnbull, H. R. III. (1997). *Families, professionals, and exceptionality: A special partnership* (3rd ed.). Upper Saddle River, NJ: Merrill/Prentice Hall.

Turnbull, A. P., Turnbull, R., Erwin, E., & Soodak, L. (2005). *Families, professionals, and exceptionality: Positive outcomes through partnerships and trust*. (5th ed.). Upper Saddle River, NJ: Merrill/Prentice Hall.

Turnbull, A. P., Turnbull, R., Shank, M., & Smith, S. J. (2004). *Exceptional lives: Special education in today's schools* (4th ed.). Upper Saddle River, NJ: Merrill/Prentice Hall.

Turnbull, H.R., Turnbull, A.P., Shank, S., Smith S., & Lead, D. (2002). *Exceptional lives: Special education in today's schools* (3rd ed.). Upper Saddle, NJ: Merrill.

Turnbull, H. R. III., & Stowe, M. J. (2001). Classification, social contracts, obligations, civil rights, and the Supreme Court: *Sutton v. United Air Lines*. *Remedial and Special Education, 22*, 374-382.

Turner, T. N. (1976). Making the social studies textbook a more effective tool for less able readers. *Social Education, 40*, 38–41.

Turner, T. N., & Oaks, T. (1997). Stories on the spot: Introducing students to impromptu storytelling. *Childhood Education, 73*, 154–157.

Tyler, J. S., & Mira, M. P. (1999). *Traumatic brain injury in children and adolescents: A sourcebook for teachers and other school personnel* (2nd ed.). Austin, TX: PRO-ED.

U.S. Census Bureau. (1997). *Computer use in the United States*. Washington, DC: Author. Retrieved May 18, 2007, from http://www.census.gov/prod99/pubs/p20-522.pdf

U.S. Congress. (1991). National Literacy Act of 1991, PL No. 102-73, Fed. Reg. §10, 65 Stat. 2463–2489.

U.S. Department of Health and Human Services. (1999). *Trends in Indian health*, Washington DC: Office of Planning, Evaluation, and Legislation: Indian Health Service.

United States Department of Education. (1986). *The reading report card*. Washington, DC: Author.

United States Department of Education. (2002). *Twenty-fourth annual report to Congress on the Implementation of the Individuals with Disabilities Education Act*. Washington DC: Author.

U.S. General Accounting Office. (2003). Federal actions can assist states in improving postsecondary outcomes of youth. Washington, DC: GAO.

United States National Research Center for TIMSS. (1996, September). *A splintered vision: An investigation of U.S. science and mathematics education*. Dordrect, The Netherlands: Kluwer.

Unrau, N. (2004). *Content area reading and writing: Fostering literacies in middle and high school cultures*. New Jersey: Pearson.

Vail, P. L. (1999). *Reading comprehension: Students' needs and teacher tools*. Rosemont, NJ: Modern Learning Press.

Valeri, M., & McKelvey, J. (1985). *Wiggle your waggles away: A movement handbook for preschool teachers*. Hyattsville, MD: Krieg-Taylor Lithograph.

Vallecorsa, A. L., & deBettencourt, L. U. (1992). Teaching composition skills to learning-disabled adolescents using a process-oriented strategy. *Journal of Developmental and Physical Disabilities, 4*, 277–296.

Vasa, S. F., Steckelberg, A. L., & Sundermeier, C. A. (1989). *Supervision strategies for special educators in working with instructional professionals*. (ERIC Document Reproduction Service No. ED 312 830)

Vaughn, S. (2003, December). *How many tiers are needed for response to intervention to achieve acceptable prevention outcomes?* Paper presented at the National Research Center on Learning Disabilities Responsiveness-to-Intervention Symposium, Kansas City, MO.

Vaughn, S., Bos, C. S., & Schumm, J. S. (2003). *Teaching exceptional, diverse, and at-risk students in the general education classroom* (3rd ed.). Boston: Allyn & Bacon.

Vaughn, S., Bos, C.S., & Schumm, J. (2006). *Teaching exceptional, diverse, and at-risk students in the general education classroom* (4th ed.). Boston: Allyn & Bacon.

Vaughn, S., & Edmonds, M. (2006). Reading comprehension for older students. *Intervention in School and Clinic*, 41, 131–137.

Vaughn, S., Gersten, R., & Chard, D. J. (2000). The underlying message in LD intervention research: Findings from research syntheses. *Exceptional Children, 67*, 99–114.

Vaughn, S., Hughes, M.T., Moody, S.W., & Elbaum, B. (2001). Instructional grouping for reading for students with LD: Implications for practice. *Intervention in School and Clinic, 36*, 131–137.

Vaughn, S., Levy, S., Coleman, M., & Bos, C. S. (2002). Reading instruction for students with LD and EBD: A synthesis of observation studies. *Journal of Special Education, 36*, 2–13.

Vaughn, S., Moody, S. W., & Schumm, J. S. (1998). Broken promises: Reading instruction in the resource room. *Exceptional Children, 64*, 211–225.

Vaughn, S. & Schumm, J. S. (1997). Are they getting it? How to monitor student understanding in inclusive classrooms. *Intervention in School and Clinic, 32*, 168–172.

Vergason, G.A. (1983). Curriculum content. In E. L. Meyen, G. A. Vergason, & R. J. Whelan (Eds.), *Promising practices for exceptional children: Curriculum implications*. Denver, CO: Love.

Viadero, D. (1995, March). Who's minding the books? *Teacher Magazine, 19*.

Viadero, D. (1999). Make or break. *Education Week, 18*(34), 158–172.

Villa, R.A., Thousand, J. S., Nevin, A. I., & Malgeri, C. (1996). Instilling collaboration for inclusive schooling as a way of doing business in public schools. *Remedial and Special Education, 17*(3), 169–181.

Vinograd-Bausell, C. R., Bausell, R. B., Proctor, W., & Chandler, B. (1986). Impact of unsupervised parent tutors on word recognition skills. *Journal of Special Education, 20*, 83–90.

Voltz, D. L. (1998). Associate editor's exchange: Cultural diversity and special education teacher preparation: Critical issues confronting the field. *Teacher Education and Special Education, 21*, 63–70.

Voltz, D. L., Brazil, N., & Ford, A. (2001). What matters most in inclusive education: A practical guide for moving forward. *Intervention in School and Clinic, 37*(1), 23–30.

Vygotsky, L. S. (1962). *Thought and language*. Cambridge, MA: MIT Press.

Wade, N. (2003). In click languages, an echo of the tongues of the ancients. *New York Times*, March 18. Retrieved May 19, 2003, from http://www.nytimes.com/2003/03/18/science/social/18CLIC.html?ex=1053489600en=8a5efde1a2581390ei=5070

Wagener, E. H. (1977). Drama: Key to history for the visually impaired child. *Education of the Visually Handicapped, 9*, 45–47.

Wagner, M., Newman, L., Cameto, R., Garza, N., & Levine, P. (2005). *After high school: A first look at the postschool experiences of youth with disabilities* (p. 4). Menlo Park, CA: SRI International.

Wagner, M., Newman, L., D'Amico, R., Jay, E. D., Butler-Nalin, P., Marder, C., & Cox, R. (1991). *Youth with disabilities: How are they doing?* The first comprehensive report from the National Longitudinal Transition Study of special education students. Menlo Park, CA: SRI International.

Walberg, H. J. (1986). What works in a nation still at risk. *Educational Leadership, 44*(1), 7–10.

Walker, B., Shippen, M.E., Alberto, P., Houchins, D.E., & Cihak, D.F. (2005). Using the expressive writing program to improve writing skills of high school students with learning disabilities. *Learning Disabilities Research and Practice*, 20, 175–183.

Walker, H. M. (1983). Applications of response cost in school settings: Outcomes, issues, and recommendations. *Exceptional Education Quarterly, 3*(4), 47–55.

Walker, H.M., Kavanaugh, K., Steller, B., Golly, A., Serverson, H. M., & Feil, E. G. (1997). First step to success: An early intervention approach for preventing school antisocial behavior. *Journal of Emotional and Behavioral Disorders*, 6, 163–172.

Walker, H. M., McConnell, S., Holmes, D., Todis, B., Walker, J., & Golden, N. (1983). *The Walker social skills curriculum: The ACCEPTS program*. Austin, TX: PRO-ED.

Walker, H.M., & Severson, H.H. (1992). *Systematic screening for behavior disorders*. Longmont, CO: Sopris West.

Wallace, A. (1999). *The psychology of the Internet*. New York: Cambridge University Press.

Wallace, G., Cohen, S. B., & Polloway, E.A. (1987). *Language arts: Teaching exceptional students*. Austin, TX: PRO-ED.

Wallace, G., & Hammill, D. D. (1994). *Comprehensive Receptive and Expressive Vocabulary Test*. Austin, TX: PRO-ED.

Wallace, G., & Kauffman, J. M. (1986). *Teaching children with learning and behavior problems* (2nd ed.). Columbus, OH: Merrill.

Wallace, G., Larsen, S. C., & Elksnin, L. (1992). *Educational assessment of learning problems: Testing for teaching*. Boston: Allyn & Bacon.

Wallace, G., & McLoughlin, J.A. (1988). *Learning disabilities: Concepts and characteristics* (3rd ed.). Columbus, OH: Merrill.

Wallace, T. (2007). The importance of paraeducator preparation and ongoing development. In A. L. Pickett, K. Gerlach, R. Morgan, M. Likisn, & T. Wallace (Eds.), *Paraeducators in schools: Strengthening the educational team* (pp. 115–137). Austin, TX: PRO-ED.

Wallach, G. (1994). Magic buries Celtics: Looking for broader interpretations of language learning and literacy. In K. G. Butler (Ed.), *Best practices II: The classroom as an intervention context* (pp. 137–154). Gaithersburg, MD: Aspen.

Wallach, G. P., & Miller, L. (1988). *Language intervention and academic success*. Boston: College-Hill/Little, Brown.

Wanzek, J., Dickson, S., Bursuck, W. D., & White, J. M. (2000). Teaching phonological awareness to students at risk for reading failure: An analysis of four instructional programs. *Learning Disabilities Research and Practice, 15*(4), 226–239.

Waterman, B. B. (1994). Assessing children for the presence of disability. *NICHY News Digest, 4*, 277–296.

Web English Teacher. (2003). *6 trait and 6+1 trait writing*. Retrieved June 11, 2003, from http://www.webenglishteacher.com/6traits.html

Webber, J. (1997). Responsible inclusion: Key components for success. In P. Zionts (Ed.), *Effective inclusion of students with behavioral and learning problem*. Austin, TX: PRO-ED.

Webber, J., & Scheuerman, B. (1991). Managing problem behavior: Accentuate the positive—eliminate the negative. *Teaching Exceptional Children, 24*, 13–19.

Wehman, P. (1995). *Individual transition plans: The teacher's curriculum guide for helping youth with special needs*. Austin, TX: PRO-ED.

Wehman, P. (2002). *Individual transition plans*. Austin, TX: PRO-ED.

Wehman, P., & Kregel, J. (2004). *Functional curriculum for elementary, middle, and secondary age students with special needs* (2nd ed.). Austin, TX: PRO-ED.

Wehman, P., Renzaglia, A., & Bates, P. (1985). *Functional living skills for moderately and severely handicapped individuals*. Austin, TX: PRO-ED.

Wehman, P., & Targett, P. S. (2004). Principles of curriculum design: Road to transition from middle school to adulthood. In P. Wehman & J. Kregel (Eds.), *Functional curriculum for elementary, middle, and secondary age students with special needs* (2nd ed., p. 9). Austin, TX: PRO-ED.

Wehmeyer, M. (1992). Self-determination as an educational outcome. *Impact, 6*(4), 16–17, 26.

Wehmeyer, M. (2006). Universal design for learning, access to general education curriculum, and students with mental retardation. *Exceptionality, 14*, 225-236.

Wehmeyer, M. L. (1994). Perceptions of self-determination and psychological empowerment of adolescents with mental retardation. *Education & Training in Mental Retardation & Developmental Disabilities, 29*, 9–21.

Wehmeyer, M. L. (1995). A career education approach: Self-determination for youth with mild cognitive disabilities. *Intervention in School and Clinic, 30*(3), 157–163.

Wehmeyer, M. L. (2002). *Teaching students with mental retardation: Providing access to the general curriculum*. Baltimore: Paul H. Brookes.

Wehmeyer, M. L., Lance, G. D., & Bashinski, S. (2002). Promoting access to the general curriculum for students with mental retardation: A multi-level model. *Education and Training in Mental Retardation and Developmental Disabilities, 37*, 223–234.

Wehmeyer, M. L., Lattin, D. L., Lapp-Rincker, G., & Agran, M. (in press). Access to the general curriculum of middle school students with mental retardation. *Remedial and Special Education*.

Wehmeyer, M. L., Morningstar, M., & Husted, D. (1999). Family involvement in transition planning and implementation. Austin, TX: PRO-ED.

Weintraub, N., & Graham, S. (1998). Writing legibly and quickly: A study of children's ability to adjust their handwriting to meet common classroom demands. *Learning Disabilities Research and Practice, 13*, 146–152.

Weisenfeld, R. B. (1986). The IEPs of Down syndrome children: A content analysis. *Education and Training of the Mentally Retarded, 21*, 211-219.

Weiss, M. P., & Lloyd, J. W. (2002). Congruence between roles and actions of secondary special educators in co-taught and special education settings. *The Journal of Special Education, 36*, 58–68.

Weitzman, D. (1975). *My backyard history book*. Boston: Little, Brown.

Welch, M., & Jensen, J. B. (1990). Write, P.L.E.A.S.E.: A video-assisted strategic intervention to improve written expression of inefficient learners. *Remedial and Special Education, 12*(1), 37–47.

Welch, M., & Link, D. P. (1991). The instructional priority system: A method for assessing the educational environment. *Intervention in School and Clinic, 27*, 91–96.

Wells, C. (1996). *Literacies lost: When students move from progressive middle school to a traditional high school*. New York: Teachers College Press.

Wells, W. (2005). Art and music for special education. *School Arts, 105*(4), 15–17.

Welsch, R.G. (2006). Increase oral reading fluency. *Intervention in School and Clinic*, 41, 180–183.

Wepman, J. M. (1973). *Auditory Discrimination Test*. Palm Springs, CA: Language Research Associates.

Wesson, C., King, R., & Deno, S. (1984). Facilitating the efficiency of ongoing curriculum-based measurement. *Teacher Education and Special Education, 9*, 166–172.

Wesson, C., Otis-Wilborn, A., Hasbrouck, J., & Tindal, G. (1989). Linking assessment, curriculum, and instruction of oral and written language. *Focus on Exceptional Children, 22*, 1-12.

West, G. K. (1986). *Parenting without guilt*. Springfield, IL: Charles C. Thomas.

West, G. K. (1994, November 10). Discipline that works: Part one. *The News and Daily Advance* (pp. 13–14).

West, G. K., & Polloway, E.A. (1996). Murphy's laws of higher education. *PsychoIllogical Bulletin, 4*, 17–18.

West, J. F., Idol, L., & Cannon, G. (1989). *Collaboration in the schools: An inservice or preservice curriculum for teachers, support staff, and administrators*. Austin, TX: PRO-ED.

Westby, C. (1991). *Steps to developing and achieving language-based curriculum in the classsroom*. Rockville, MD: American Speech-Language-Hearing Association.

Westby, C. E., & Costlow, L. (1994). Implementing whole language in a special education class. In K. G. Butler (Ed.), *Best practices II: The classroom as an intervention context* (pp. 39–54). Gaithersburg, MD: Aspen.

Westling, D. L., Ferrell, K., & Swenson, K. (1982). Intra-classroom comparison of two arrangements for teaching profoundly mentally retarded children. *American Journal of Mental Deficiency, 86*, 601–608.

Whitehurst, T., & Howells, A. (2006). When something is different people fear it: Children perceptions of arts-based inclusion project. *Support for Learning*, 21(2), 40–45.

Wiebe, J. H. (1993). The software domain. In J. D. Lindsey (Ed.), *Computers and exceptional individuals* (2nd ed., pp. 45–64). Austin, TX: PRO-ED.

Wiederholt, J. L., & Bryant, B. R. (2001). *Gray Oral Reading Tests—IV*. Austin, TX: PRO-ED.

Wiederholt, J. L., Hammill, D. D., & Brown, V. L. (1983). *The resource teacher: A guide to effective practices* (2nd ed.). Austin, TX: PRO-ED.

Wiederholt, J. L., & McNutt, G. (1979). Assessment and instructional planning: A conceptual framework. In D. Cullinan & M. H. Epstein (Eds.), *Special education for adolescents: Issues and perspectives* (pp. 63–87). Columbus, OH: Merrill.

Wiig, E. H. (1982). *The "Let's Talk" Inventory for Adolescents*. Columbus, OH: Merrill.

Wiig, E. H. (1990). *Wiig Criterion-Referenced Inventory of Language*. San Antonio, TX: Psychological.

Wiig, E. H., & Secord, W. (1992). *Test of Word Knowledge*. San Antonio, TX: Psychological.

Wiig., E. H., & Secord, W. W. (1989). *Test of Language Competence–Expanded Edition*. San Antonio, TX: Psychological.

Wiig, E. H., & Semel, E. (1984). *Language assessment and intervention for the learning disabled* (2nd ed.). Columbus, OH: Merrill.

Wilkening, P. (1993). *Recreation and leisure time as part of the transition program for individuals with disabilities*. (Technical Assistance Packet #4). Gainesville: University of Florida, Project Retain/Florida Network.

Wilkinson, G. S., & Robertson, C.J. (2006). *Wide Range Achievement Test—III*. Wilmington, DE: Wide Range.

Will, M. (1984). *OSERS programming for the transition of youth with disabilities: Bridges from school to working life*. Washington, DC: Office of Special Education and Rehabilitative Services.

William, J., Nubla-Kung, A., Pollini, S., Stafford, B., Garcia, A., & Snyder, A. (2007). Teaching cause-effect text structures through social studies content to at-risk second graders. *Journal of Learning Disabilities, 40*, 97–192.

Williams, J. M., & O'Leary, E. (2001). What we've learned and where we go from here. *Career Development for Exceptional Individuals, 24*(1), 51–69.

Williams, R. M., & Rooney, K. J. (1986). *A handbook of cognitive behavior modification procedures for teachers*. Charlottesville: University of Virginia Institute for Research on Learning Disabilities.

Willis, S. (1995, May). Making integrated curriculum a reality. *Education Updated 37*(4), 4.

Wilson, C. R. (1983). Teaching reading comprehension by connecting the known to the new. *The Reading Teacher, 36*, 382–390.

Wilson, M. (1992). Measuring levels of mathematical understanding. In T. A. Romberg (Ed.), *Mathematics assessment and evaluation: Imperatives for mathematics education* (pp. 213–241). Albany: State University of New York Press.

Winzer, M.A., & Mazurek, L. (1998). *Special education in multicultural contexts*. Upper Saddle River, NJ: Merrill/Prentice Hall.

Wisconsin Department of Public Instruction. (1989). *Strategic learning in the content areas*. Madison: Wisconsin Department of Public Instruction.

Wolery, M. (1989). Transitions in early childhood special education: Issues and procedures. *Focus on Exceptional Children, 22*(2), 1–16.

Wolf, M., & Bowers, P. G. (2000). Naming-speed deficits in developmental reading disabilities: An introduction to the special series on the double-deficit hypothesis. *Journal of Learning Disabilities, 33*, 322–324.

Wolf, M., Bowers, P. G., & Biddle, K. (2000). Naming-speed processes, timing, and reading: A conceptual review. *Journal of Learning Disabilities, 33*, 387–407.

Wolfolk, A. E. (2000). *Educational psychology*. Upper Saddle River, NJ: Prentice Hall.

Wolford, P. L., Heward, W. L., & Alber, S. R. (2001). Teaching middle school students with learning disabilities to recruit peer assistance during cooperative learning group activities. *Learning Disabilities Research and Practice, 16*, 161–173.

Wolpe, J. (1958). *Psychotherapy by reciprocal inhibition*. Palo Alto, CA: Stanford University Press.

Wong, B. Y. L. (1982). Understanding learning-disabled students' reading problems: Contributions from cognitive psychology. *Topics in Learning and Learning Disabilities, 1*(4), 43–50.

Wong, B. Y. L. (2003). General and specific issues for researchers' consideration in applying the risk and resilience framework to the social domain of learning disabilities. *Learning Disabilities Research and Practice, 18*(2), 68–76.

Wong, K. L. H., Kauffman, J. M., & Lloyd, J. W. (1991). Choices for integration: Selecting teachers for mainstreamed students with emotional or behavioral disorders. *Intervention in School and Clinic, 27*, 108–115.

Wood, J. W. (1992). *Adapting instruction for mainstreamed and at-risk students* (2nd ed.). Upper Saddle River, NJ: Merrill/Prentice Hall.

Wood, J. W. (1993). *Mainstreaming: A practical approach for teachers* (2nd ed.). Upper Saddle River, NJ: Merrill/Prentice Hall.

Wood, J. W., & Miederhoff, J. W. (1989). Bridging the gap. *Teaching Exceptional Children, 21*(2), 66–68.

Wood, R. W., Webster, L., Gullickson, A., & Walker, J. (1987). Comparing handwriting legibility with three teaching methods for sex and grade differences. *Reading Improvement, 24*, 24–30.

Woodcock, R. W. (1991). *Woodcock Language Proficiency Battery—Revised*. Chicago: Riverside Publishing.

Woodcock, R. W. (1998). *Woodcock Reading Mastery Tests—Revised—Normative Update. (WRMT-R/NU)*. Circle Pines, MN: American Guidance Service.

Woodcock, R. W., & Muñoz-Sandoval, A. (1991). *Woodcock Language Proficiency Battery*. Itasca, IL: Riverside.

Woodward, A., Elliott, D. L., & Nagel, K. C. (1986). Beyond textbooks in elementary social studies. *Social Education, 50*, 50–53.

Woodward, J., & Brown, C. (2006). Meeting the curricular needs of academically low-achieving students in middle grad mathematics. *Journal of Special Education, 40*, 151–159.

Woodward, J., & Noell, J. (1992). Science instruction at the secondary level: Implications for students with learning disabilities. In D. Carnine & E. J. Kame'enui (Eds.), *Higher-order thinking: Designing curriculum for mainstreamed students* (pp. 39–58). Austin, TX: PRO-ED.

Workman, E. A., & Katz, A. M. (1995). *Teaching behavioral self-control to students*. Austin, TX: PRO-ED.

Worrall, R. S. (1990). Detecting health fraud in the field of learning disabilities. *Journal of Learning Disabilities, 23*, 207–212.

Yager, R. E. (1989). A rationale for using personal relevance as a science curriculum focus in schools. *School Science and Mathematics, 89*, 144–156.

York, J., Doyle, M. B., & Kronberg, R. (1992). A curriculum development process for inclusive classrooms. *Focus on Exceptional Children, 25*(4), 1–16.

Young, K. R., West, R. P., Li, L., & Peterson, L. (1997). Teaching self-management skills to students with learning and behavior problems. *Reclaiming Children and Youth, 6*, 90–96.

Ysseldyke, J. E., & Christenson, S. L. (1986). *The Instructional Environment Scale*. Austin, TX: PRO-ED.

Ysseldyke, J. E., & Christenson, S. L. (1987). Evaluating students, instructional environments. *Remedial and Special Education, 8*(3), 17–24.

Zachman, L., Huisingh, R., Barrett, M., Orman, J., & Bragden, C. (1989). *The Word Test—Adolescent*. East Moline, IL: LinguiSystems.

Zarillo, J. J. (2004). *Teaching elementary social studies: Principles and applications* (2nd ed.). Upper Saddle River, NJ: Merrill/Prentice Hall.

Zentall, S. (1983). Learning environments: A review of physical and temporal factors. *Exceptional Education Quarterly, 4*, 90–109.

Zhang, D. (2001). Self-determination and inclusion: Are students with mild mental retardation more self-determined in regular classrooms? *Education and Training in Mental Retardation and Developmental Disabilities, 36*, 357–362.

Zigmond, N. (1990). Rethinking secondary school programs for students with learning disabilities. *Focus on Exceptional Children, 23*(1), 1–12.

Zigmond, N., & Magiera, K. (2001, Autumn). A focus on co-teaching. *Current Practice Alerts, 6*, 1–4.

Zimmerman, I., Steiner, V., & Pond, R. (1992). *Preschool Language Scale—3*. San Antonio, TX: Psychological.

Zurkowski, J. K., Kelly, P. S., & Griswold, D. E. (1998). Discipline and IDEA 1997: Instituting a new balance. *Intervention in School and Clinic, 34*, 3–9.

# Name Index

# Subject Index